THE WORLD'S HISTORY

Combined Volume

THE WORLD'S HISTORY

Combined Volume

HOWARD SPODEK

Prentice Hall, Upper Saddle River, NJ 07458

Published 2001 by Prentice Hall, Inc.
A Division of Pearson Education
Upper Saddle River, New Jersey 07458

10 9 8 7 6 5 4 3

ISBN 0-13-028257-X (hardcover)

This book was designed and produced by
CALMANN & KING LTD., London
www.calmann-king.com

Editorial work by Damian Thompson, Melanie White, Nell Webb, and Gerald Lombardi
Supplementary editorial work by Robert Shore, Lydia Darbyshire, Callie Kendall, Andrew Heritage, Laura Szumanski, and Delia Gaze (glossary)
Design by Ian Hunt Design
Maps by Ailsa Heritage and Andrea Fairbrass
Artworks by Dave Kemp
Picture research by Peter Kent and Callie Kendall
Printed and bound by R.R. Donnelley & Sons Co., USA

Cover picture: Benin Plaque. Brass. Sixteenth to seventeenth century C.E. Hiller Burger/Peabody Museum, Harvard University. © Pres. and Fellows of Harvard College. All rights reserved.

Title-page picture: Arab trader, illustration from the *Maqamat* of al-Hariri, twelfth century. Bibliothèque Nationale, Arabe 5847 fol 94v.

BRIEF CONTENTS

CONTENTS

PART 1

Human Origins and Human Cultures

5 million B.C.E.–10,000 B.C.E.

BUILDING AN INTERPRETIVE FRAMEWORK: WHAT DO WE KNOW AND HOW DO WE KNOW IT?

1 THE DRY BONES SPEAK   4

5 million B.C.E.–10,000 B.C.E

WHAT IS PALEOANTHROPOLOGY AND
WHY IS IT IMPORTANT?

PART 2

SettlingDown

10,000 B.C.E.–1000 C.E.

THE FIRST CITIES AND WHY THEY MATTER: DIGS, TEXTS, AND INTERPRETATIONS

2 FROM VILLAGE COMMUNITY TO CITY STATE 38

10,000 B.C.E.–750 B.C.E.

WHAT ARE CITIES AND WHY ARE THEY IMPORTANT?

3 RIVER VALLEY CIVILIZATIONS 62

7000 B.C.E.–750 B.C.E.

THE RISE OF CITIES AND STATES ALONG THE NILE AND INDUS

4 A POLYCENTRIC WORLD 86

1700 B.C.E.–1000 C.E.

CITIES AND STATES IN EAST ASIA, THE AMERICAS, AND WEST AFRICA

PART 3

Empire and Imperialism

2300 B.C.E.–1100 C.E.

WHAT ARE EMPIRES AND WHY ARE THEY IMPORTANT?

5 DAWN OF THE EMPIRES   120

2300 B.C.E.–300 B.C.E.

EMPIRE-BUILDING IN NORTH AFRICA, WEST ASIA, AND THE MEDITERRANEAN

8 INDIAN EMPIRES 231

1500 B.C.E.–1100 C.E.

CULTURAL COHESION
IN A DIVIDED SUBCONTINENT

PART 4

The Rise of World Religions

600 B.C.E.–1500 C.E.

NOT BY BREAD ALONE: HOW DO HISTORIANS UNDERSTAND RELIGION IN WORLD HISTORY?

9 HINDUISM AND BUDDHISM 257

300 B.C.E.–1200 C.E.

THE SACRED SUBCONTINENT: THE SPREAD
OF RELIGION IN INDIA AND BEYOND

PART 5

World Trade

1100–1776 C.E.

CHANNELS OF COMMUNICATION: THE EXCHANGE OF COMMODITIES, DISEASES, AND CULTURE

PART 6

Migration: Free People and Slaves

1300–1750

"BE FRUITFUL AND MULTIPLY, FILL UP THE EARTH AND SUBDUE IT": DEMOGRAPHIC CHANGES IN A NEW GLOBAL ECUMENE

PART 7
Social Change

WESTERN REVOLUTIONS AND THEIR EXPORT

PART 8

Exploding Technologies

1914–2000

CONTESTED VISIONS OF A NEW INTERNATIONAL ORDER

MAPS

TIMECHARTS

REVIEWERS OF THE TEXT

First Edition Reviewers

J. Lee Annis, Jr., Montgomery College; Samuel Brunk, University of Nebraska at Lincoln; Nancy S. Crump, Wayne State College; David L. Ferch, Sierra College; William Jones, Mt. San Antonio College; David L. Longfellow, Baylor University; Mark Mcleod, University of Delaware; Eleanor W. McCluskey, Broward Community College; Joseph Mitchell and Oliver B. Pollock, University of Nebraska at Omaha; John Powell, Penn State University at Erie; David K. Robinson, Northeast Missouri State University; Charles R. Sullivan, University of Dallas.

Second Edition Reviewers

Ewa Bacon, Lewis University; Wood Bouldin, Villanova University; Michael Doran, University of Central Florida; Evelyn Hu-DeHart, University of Colorado at Boulder; James Lindsay, Colorado State University; Frank Nobiletti, San Diego State University; Sandra Norman, Florida Atlantic University; Phyllis Pobst, Arkansas State University; John Powell, Penn State University at Erie; Reniqu Yu, Purchase College, State University of New York.

QUOTED EXTRACTS: ACKNOWLEDGMENTS

For permission to reprint copyright material the publishers gratefully acknowledge the following:

AMS Press Inc.: *The Gandhi Reader, No. 1*, ed. Homer Jack (Grove Press, 1956), by permission of AMS Press Inc.

American Historical Association: "Imperialism and History: A Century of Theory, from Marx to Postcolonialism" by Patrick Wolfe from *American Historical Review* (Volume CII, No. 2, April 1997).

Bantam Doubleday Dell Publishing Group Inc.: *Bhagavad-Gita*, trans. Barbara Stoler Miller, © 1986 Barbara Stoler Miller; *My Mission in Life* by Eva Peron, trans. Ethel Cherry (Doubleday, 1952), both by permission of the publisher.

Blackwell Publishers: *The Information Age: Economy, Society and Culture* by Manuel Castells (Oxford: Blackwell, 1997, 1999), by permission of the publisher.

Dennis Brutus: "Their Behaviour" from *The Heritage of African Poetry*, ed. Isidore Okpewho (Longman, 1985), by permission of the author.

Cambridge University Press: *The New English Bible*, © Oxford University Press and Cambridge University Press 1961, 1970, reprinted by permission; *Cross Cultural Trade in World History* by Philip Curtin (1984).

John Pepper Clark: "Agbor Dancer" from *The Heritage of African Poetry*, ed. Isidore Okpewho (Longman, 1985).

Columbia University Press: *Poems of Love and War*, trans. A.K. Ramanujan, © 1985 by Columbia University Press; *Introduction to Contemporary Civilization in the West*, © 1954 by Columbia University Press; *Sources of Chinese Tradition* by William Theodore de Bary, © 1960 by Columbia University Press; *The Autobiography of Yukichi Fukuzawa*, © 1966 by Columbia University Press; *Sources of Indian Tradition* by William Theodore de Bary © 1988 by Columbia University Press, all by permission of the publisher.

Duke University Press: "Towards an Analogy of City Images" by A.K. Ramanujan from *Urban India: Society, Space and Image*, © 1970, Duke University Program in Comparative Studies on Southern Asia, reprinted by permission of the publisher.

Farrar, Straus & Giroux Inc.: *Night* by Elie Wiesel (Bantam Books, 1962), by permission of Farrar, Straus & Giroux Inc.

Grove/Atlantic Inc.: *The Wretched of the Earth* by Frantz Fanon (Penguin Twentieth Century Classics, 1990), by permission of Grove/Atlantic.

Harcourt, Brace & Company: *A Brief History of Chinese and Japanese Civilizations*, ed. Conrad Schirokauer; *The City in History* by Lewis Mumford; "How Should We Live" by Wislawa Szymborska from *View With a Grain of Sand* (Harcourt Brace, 1995), by permission of the publisher.

HarperCollins Publishers: *A Forest of Kings: The Untold Story of the Ancient Maya* by Linda Schele and David Freidel (New York: William Morrow, 1990), by permission of HarperCollins Publishers, Inc.

The Harvill Press: *The Gulag Archipelago. 3 Volumes*, trans. T. Whitney and H. Willetts (Harvill Press, 1974–78).

Heinemann Publishers Oxford: *God's Bits of Wood* by Sembene Ousmane, trans. Francis Price (Heinemann, 1970), reprinted by permission of Heinemann Educational Publishers, a division of Reed Educational & Professional Publishing Ltd; "Moroccan Woman's Poem" from *Third World Lives of Struggle*, eds. Hazel Johnson and Henry Bernstein (Heinemann Educational Books, 1982).

Houghton Mifflin Company: *The Human Record : Sources of Global History*, eds. A. Andrea and J. Overfield (1990, 1994).

Macmillan Ltd: *Don Quixote of La Mancha* by Miguel de Cervantes, trans. Walter Starkie (New American Library, 1957), by permission of Macmillan Ltd.

Monthly Review Press: "Woman the Gatherer: Male Bias in Anthropology" by Sally Linton from *Women in Cross-Cultural Perspective: A Preliminary Sourcebook*, ed. Sue-Ellen Jacobs (University of Illinois, 1971).

John Murray (Publishers) Ltd: *An Arab Philosophy of History*, trans. Charles Issawi (1950), by permission of the publisher.

Jawaharlal Nehru Memorial Fund: *The Discovery of India* by Jawaharlal Nehru (Asia Publishing House, 1960), by permission of Jawaharlal Nehru Memorial Fund on behalf of Mrs. Sonia Gandhi.

Oxford University Press, Inc.: *The Republic* by Plato, trans. Francis MacDonald Cornford; *Historical Records*, trans. Raymond Dawson.

Oxford University Press (India): *Asoka and the Decline of the Mauryas* by Romila Thapar, by permission of the publisher.

Oxford University Press Ltd: "Prayer to Masks" and "Relentlessly She Drives Me" by Léopold Sédar Senghor from *Selected Poems*, trans. John Reed and Clive Wake, © Oxford University Press 1964, by permission of the publisher.

Penguin UK: *The Travels* by Marco Polo, trans. Ronald Latham; *The Epic of Gilgamesh*, trans. N.K. Sandars; *The Koran*, trans. N.J. Dawood; *History of the Peloponnesian War*, trans. Rex Warner; *Speaking of Siva*, trans. A.K. Ramanujan.

Penguin USA: "The Doll's House" by Henrik Ibsen, trans. Rolf Fjelde from *Literature of the Western World, Volume II*, eds. Brian Wilke and James Hurt (Macmillan, 1984), by permission of Penguin USA.

Princeton University Press: *Ancient Near Eastern Texts Relating to the Old Testament*, ed. James Pritchard (1969); *Medieval Cities* by Henri Pirenne (1925).

Random House, Inc.: *The Prince* by N. Machiavelli (Modern Library, 1950); *The Odyssey* by Homer, trans. Robert Fitzgerald.

Paul E. Sigmund: *The Ideologies of the Developing World*, ed. Paul E. Sigmund (Praeger, 1972), by permission of the editor.

Simon & Schuster, Inc.: "The Second Coming" from *The Collected Works of W.B. Yeats, Volume I: The Poems*, revised and edited by Richard J. Finneran, © 1924 by Macmillan Publishing Company, renewed 1952 by Bertha Georgie Yeats, by permission of the publisher; *The Aeneid of Virgil*, trans. Rolfe Humphries, © 1951 by Charles Scribner's Sons, by permission of Scribner; *Popul Vuh*, trans. Dennis Tedlock, by permission of Pocket Books; *The Wonder that was India* by A.L. Basham (Grove/Atlantic Press, 1954); *Chinese Civilization: A Sourcebook*, ed. Patricia Ebrey (1993).

Stanford University Press: *The Pattern of the Chinese Past* by Mark Elvin.

University of California Press: *Canto General*, by Pablo Neruda, trans./ed. Jack Schmitt, © 1991 Fundacion Pablo Neruda, Regents of the University of California; *Japan, Inc.: Introduction to Japanese Economics (The Comic Book)* by Shotaro Ishinomori, © 1988 The Regents of the University of California; *Unesco, General History of Africa, Volume 1, Methodology and African Prehistory*, ed./trans. J. Ki-Zerbo, © 1993 The Regents of the University of California, all reprinted by permission of the publisher.

The University of Chicago Press: *The Iliad of Homer*, trans. R. Lattimore (1951); *Africa and the Disciplines*, eds. Robert Bates, V. Mudimbe, and Jean O'Barr (1993), both by permission of the publisher.

The University of Wisconsin Press: *The Atlantic Slave Trade* by Philip Curtin (1969), by permission of the publisher.

Verso: *Rigoberta Menchu: An Indian Woman in Guatemala* by Rigoberta Menchu, trans. Elisabeth Burgos Debray (1984), by permission of the publisher.

Yale University Press: *The Moral Economy of the Peasant* by James Scott (1976), by permission of the publisher; poems from *Shang Civilization* by Kwang-chi Chang, trans. Arthur Waley.

Zondervan Publishing House: *Holy Bible: New Revised Standard Version* (1989).

Every effort has been made to obtain permission from all copyright holders, but in some cases this has not proved possible. The publishers therefore wish to thank all authors or copyright holders who are included without acknowledgment. Prentice Hall Inc./Calmann & King apologizes for any errors or omissions in the above list and would be grateful to be notified of any corrections that should be incorporated in the next edition.

PICTURE CREDITS

T=top; B=bottom; R=right; L=left

Introduction I–10 and I–11 Novosti (London)

Chapter 1 1 ESA European Space Operations Center, Darmstadt, Germany; 2, 20 Natural History Museum, London; 7 Cambridge University Library (by permission of the Syndics of) (DAR 140.4); 11B ©National Geographic Society; 15 Science Photo Library/John Reader; 30B Jean Vertut, Issy-les-Moulineaux; 32T Yan, Toulouse; 33 J. Clottes, Ministère de la Culture et de la Communication-Direction du Patrimoine-sous Direction de l'Archeologie

Chapter 2 37 South American Pictures; 42 Howard Spodek; 43T Ancient Art and Architecture Collection; 46 AKG London/Erich Lessing; 47T Photo: Günter Schörlitz, Fotozentrum der Universität; 47B, 53 ©The British Museum; 48, 50B Hirmer Verlag, München; 56, 59 RMN

Chapter 3 64 A.F. Kersting, London; 66, 67T, 69, 71T ©The British Museum; 67B Ancient Art and Architecture Collection; 68, 74 Hirmer Verlag, München; 72 RMN; 79 Scala, Florence; 83, 84 James Blair

Chapter 4 92 Academia Sinica, Taipei; 93 Institute of Archeology, Beijing; 97 Werner Forman Archive; 99, 110, 111 South American Pictures; 103 ©The British Museum; 104 University of Pennsylvania Museum; 114T Howard Spodek; 114B Bridgeman Art Library/Heini Schneebeli

Chapter 5 119, 132 Zefa Pictures; 124 Scala, Florence; 125, 127T, 147 ©The British Museum; 127B Robert Harding Picture Library; 133 Giraudon; 136L RMN; 136R American School of Classical Studies at Athens; 137 BPK, Berlin; 144, 145 Alison Frantz, Princeton, N.J.; 152–153 ©Fotografica Foglia, Naples; 156 Alinari, Florence

Chapter 6 162, 168, 181 Alinari, Florence; 166 Leonard von Matt; 167 A.F. Kersting, London; 170 Spectrum, London; 171, 174 Scala, Florence; 180 Fototeca Unione, Rome; 182T Werner Forman Archive; 182B ©The British Museum; 186 ©Hunting Aerofilms; 192 G.E. Kidder-Smith

PICTURE CREDITS **xxiii**

SUPPLEMENTARY INSTRUCTIONAL MATERIALS

The World's History comes with an extensive package of supplementary print and multimedia materials for both instructors and students.

FOR THE INSTRUCTOR

- The *Instructor's Manual* includes chapter outlines, overviews, key concepts, discussion questions, and suggestions for useful audiovisual resources.
- *Prentice Hall Custom Test* is a commercial-quality computerized test management program for Windows and Macintosh environments. The program allows instructors to select items from the test item file to create tests. It also allows online testing.
- The *Transparency Package* provides instructors with full color transparency acetates of all the maps, charts, and graphs in the text for use in the classroom.

FOR THE STUDENT

- The *Study Guide* (Volumes I and II) provides chapter overviews, objectives, practice tests, essay questions, and map exercises to help reinforce the chapter content.
- The *Documents Set* (Volumes I and II) is a collection of additional primary and secondary source documents organized by chapter. Questions accompanying the documents can be used for discussion or as writing assignments.
- The *Map Workbook* is a collection of map exercises to help students review basic geographical knowledge.
- The *Hammond Historical Atlas of the World* is a collection of maps illustrating the most significant periods and events in the history of civilization. This atlas is available at a discounted price to students when packaged with *The World's History*.
- *World History: An Atlas and Study Guide* is a four-color map workbook that includes over 100 maps with exercises, activities, and questions that help students learn both geography and history. It is available at a discounted price to students when packaged with *The World's History*.
- *Reading Critically About History* is a brief guide to reading effectively that provides students with helpful strategies for reading a history textbook. It is available free to students when packaged with *The World's History*.

- *Understanding and Answering Essay Questions* suggests helpful analytical tools for understanding different types of essay questions, and provides precise guidelines for preparing well-crafted essay answers. It is available free to students when packaged with *The World's History*.
- *Themes of the Times* is a newspaper supplement prepared jointly by Prentice Hall and *The New York Times*, the premier news publication. Issued twice a year, it contains recent articles pertinent to historical study. These articles connect the classroom to the world. For information about a reduced rate subscription to *The New York Times*, call toll-free: 1-800-631-1222.

MEDIA RESOURCES

- *History on the Internet* is a brief guide to navigating the Internet and World Wide Web and using the *Companion Website*™ accompanying *The World's History*. It also includes an introduction to critical thinking skills for effectively evaluating sources found on the World Wide Web, a list of useful sites related to history, and a guide to documenting online sources. This guide is free to students when packaged with *The World's History*.
- The *Companion Website*™ (www.prenhall.com/spodek) works in tandem with the text and features objectives, study questions, web links to related resources on the World Wide Web, document exercises, interactive map activities, message boards and a chat feature, all organized according to the chapters in the text.
- *Powerpoint Images CDROM* for use in Windows or Macintosh environments includes the maps, charts, and graphs in the text on disk for use with Microsoft Powerpoint™, allowing instructors to integrate the graphics into lectures.

For those instructors interested in *online course management and distance learning*, Prentice Hall is pleased to offer a number of options with *The World's History*, including WEBCT and Blackboard online course material to support the text online. For more information, please contact your local Prentice Hall representative.

To my children, Susie, Josh, and Sarah,
who are always in my thoughts;
and to my wife Lisa,
who has made this work possible

PREFACE

WHY HISTORY?

The professional historian and the student of an introductory course often seem to pass each other on different tracks. For the professional, nothing is more fascinating than history. For the student, particularly one in a compulsory course, the whole enterprise often seems a bore. This introductory text is designed to help that student understand and share the fascination of the historian. It will also remind professors of their original attraction to history, before they began the specialization that has almost certainly marked their later careers. Furthermore, it encourages student and professor to explore together the history of the world and the significance of this study.

Professional historians love their field for many reasons. History offers perspective and guidance in forming a personal view of human development. It teaches the necessity of seeing many sides of issues. It explores the complexity and interrelationship of events and makes possible the search for patterns and meaning in human life.

Historians also love to debate. They love the challenge of demonstrating that their interpretations of the pattern and significance of events are the most accurate and the most satisfying in their fit between the available data and theory. Historians also love the detective work of their profession, whether it is researching through old archives, uncovering and using new sources of information, or reinterpreting long-ignored sources. In recent years historians have turned, for example, to oral history, old church records, files of photographs, cave paintings, individual census records, and reinterpretations of mythology.

Historical records are not simply lists of events, however. They are the means by which historians develop their interpretations of those events. Because interpretations differ, there is no single historical record, but various narrations of events each told from a different perspective. Therefore the study of history is intimately linked to the study of *values*.

To construct their interpretations, historians examine the values—the motives, wishes, desires, visions—of people of the past. In interpreting those values, historians must confront and engage their own values, comparing and contrasting these values with those of people in the past. For example, they ask how various people viewed slavery in the slave-holding societies of the past. In the back of their minds they compare and contrast those older values with values held by various people today and especially with their own personal values. They ask: How and why have values changed or remained the same through the passage of time? Why, and in what way, do my values compare and contrast with values of the past? By learning to pose such questions, students will be better equipped to discover and create their own place in the continuing movement of human history. This text, therefore, consistently addresses three fundamental questions: What do we know? How do we know it? What difference does it make? It emphasizes **historiography**, the process of creating historical records. Students will see that these records are neither gospel truth nor fabricated fiction, but a first step in understanding and interpreting the past. They will learn how historians frame questions for study and how the questions that are asked determine the answers that are found. They will learn to frame their own, new questions about both the past and the present.

Professional historians consider history to be the king of disciplines. Synthesizing the concepts of fellow social scientists in economics, politics, **anthropology**, sociology, and geography, historians create a more integrated and comprehensive interpretation of the past. Joining with their colleagues in the humanities, historians delight in hearing and telling exciting stories that recall heroes and villains, the low born and the high, the wisdom and the folly of days gone by. This fusion of all the social sciences and humanities gives the study of history its range, depth, significance, and pleasure. Training in historical thinking provides an excellent introduction to understanding change and continuity in our own day as well as in the past.

WHY WORLD HISTORY?

Why specifically world history? Why should we teach and study world history, and what should be the content of such a course?

First, world history is a good place to begin for it is a new field for professor and student alike. Neither its content nor its pedagogy is yet fixed. Many of the existing textbooks on the market still have their origins in the study of western Europe, with segments added to cover the rest of the world. World history as the study of the inter-relationships of all regions of the world, seen from the many perspectives of the different peoples of the earth, is still virgin territory.

Second, for citizens of multicultural, multiethnic nations such as the United States, Canada, South Africa, and India, and for those of the many other countries such as the United Kingdom and Australia which are moving in that direction, a world history course offers the opportunity to gain an appreciation of the national and cultural origins of all their diverse citizens. In this way, the study of world history may help to strengthen the bonds of national citizenship.

Third, as the entire world becomes a single unit for interaction, it becomes an increasingly appropriate subject for historical study. The noted historian E.H. Carr explained that history "is an unending dialogue between the present and the past." The new reality of global interaction in communication, business, politics, religion, culture, and ecology has helped to generate the new academic subject of world history.

THE ORIGINS AND DEVELOPMENT OF THIS TEXT

The inspiration for this text was a ground-breaking four-year program in the School District of Philadelphia, 1988–92. Teachers in the District asked for instruction in world history so that they could better teach their ninth-grade course and, indeed, rewrite its curriculum. In the program established to meet their request, some thirty college professors met with about one hundred Philadelphia teachers. I was the academic coordinator, teaching several of the formal courses offered and responsible for staffing the others. From the courses we designed for teachers came the basic framework for the current text. There is no better, more interactive, more critical, yet more helpful audience for new teaching materials than students who are themselves teachers. Together we learned a great deal about the study and teaching of world history at high school, college, and graduate levels.*

Following this schools-based project, twenty college professors from twelve different colleges and universities and twenty high school teachers from fifteen different schools in the Philadelphia metropolitan region were awarded a substantial grant from the National Endowment for the Humanities to pursue further methods of teaching world history—content and pedagogy—at the college level in ways that would best prepare future teachers. I served as project director. Participation in this two-year collaborative project helped me further to refine the content and the method of the current text.†

Finally, in conjunction with these major projects, I began in 1990 to offer a year-long course in world history at Temple University, Philadelphia. The structure of that course is the structure of this text.

As each chapter was completed, I included it in the reading materials of the course. So the text has had five years of field testing.

ORGANIZATION AND APPROACH

The text, like the year-long course, links *chronology*, *themes*, and *geography* in eight units, or parts of study. The parts move progressively along a time line from the emergence of early humans to the present day. Each part emphasizes a single theme—for example, urbanization or religion or trade—and students learn to use all eight themes to analyze historical events and to develop a grasp of the chronology of human development. Geographically, each part covers the entire globe, although specific topics place greater emphasis on specific regions.

IMPORTANT SPECIAL FEATURES

To provide the students with direct experience of the historian's craft the text includes:

- Primary sources to illuminate the experiences of an age and place directly. Their analysis is an essential part of the study of history.
- Historians' later interpretations to provide perspective on how historical records were produced and fought over. The analysis of these secondary sources is an essential part of the study of historiography.
- Sidebars to provide more detailed discussions of particular issues beyond the narrative. Such supplements appear in every chapter.
- Extensive, clear, and informative charts and maps to represent information graphically and geographically.
- A wide range of illustrations, many in color, to supplement the written word. Some of the illustrations are grouped into "Spotlights" to illuminate specific issues. These include, for example, at the earliest, a Spotlight on the reconstruction of Neanderthals, which explores the ways in which Neanderthals have been represented through time, to, at the latest, a portfolio of the murals of Diego Rivera, indicating how an individual artist interprets and represents the history of his people through his painting.

Collectively, these materials provide a rich, comprehensive, and challenging introduction to the study of world history and the methods and key interpretations of its historians.

REVISIONS IN THE SECOND EDITION

The second edition brings many additions and revisions. Some of the new materials reflect increases in knowledge in the last three years: new material on *Ardipithecus ramidus*, reported in Chapter 1; the oldest known alphabetic writing, a Semitic script discovered in Egypt from 1900 B.C.E., noted in Chapter 2; 9000-year old, still-playable flutes from China, and significant new excavations on the Niger River at Jenne Jeno, reported and discussed in Chapter 4. Others analyze recent events such as the precipitous decline and partial rebound of the economies of several Asian countries; nuclear weapons tests in India and Pakistan; the influence of drug traffic in Latin America; the election of President Mohammed Khatami in Iran and the resignation of President Boris Yeltsin in Russia.

The new materials also respond in part to the author's experience in teaching the text, suggestions made by friends and colleagues, and evaluations gathered by the publisher from professors selected from across the United States. Thus, the discussion of the Roman Empire has been restructured for greater clarity; the coverage of medieval, early modern, and twentieth-century Europe has been expanded; and the history of science has been augmented. The introduction to the twentieth century has been enhanced with new materials on the cold war, decolonization, economic globalization, the internet, the human genome project, and the international drug trade. Greater attention has been given to America's role in the world including its continuing struggles with issues of civil rights at home and abroad.

Chapters now conclude with explicit explorations of the consequences and significance of their subject matter. Comparisons of the institutions of different areas of the world, fundamental to the structure of each part of the text, are now drawn explicitly throughout the book. Several of the "Spotlight" artwork features of the first edition have been replaced by new ones, as have many of the illustrations and several of the maps. Each chapter now includes a "Profile" biography illuminating the significance of an important person from its era. These include emperors and an empress dowager, historians, a film maker, a popular singer, an explorer, religious leaders, a family of archaeologists, warriors, democratically elected political politicians, and some whose careers defy simple categorization. Timecharts in each chapter have been revised and redesigned to improve accessibility and usefulness, and new "Connection" boxes link material between chapters and enhance the chronological framework of the book.

All these changes do not, however, change the essential structure of the text, with its emphasis on chronology, theme, and geography; its integration of text, primary and secondary source materials, maps, and artwork; and its emphasis on the fundamental questions of "What Do We Know?", "How Do We Know It?", and "What Difference Does it Make?"

---

* Carol Parsinnen and Howard Spodek, " 'We're Making History': Philadelphia Educators Tackle a National Issue," *The History Teacher* XXV, No. 3 (May 1992), 321–38.
† Howard Spodek, *et al.*, "World History: Preparing Teachers through High School–College Collaboration, The Philadelphia Story, 1993–1995," *The History Teacher* XXIX, No. 1 (November 1995), 1–41.

ACKNOWLEDGMENTS

After several years of work, at last comes the opportunity to thank publicly the many people who have made this book possible through their encouragement, careful reading of early drafts, comments, and general support. The idea for this text took form in the course of work with many superb teachers in a world history workshop in the School District of Philadelphia. The administrators of that program—Carol Parssinen and Ellen Wylie of the Philadelphia Alliance for Teaching Humanities in the Schools and Jim Culbertson and Joe Jacovino from the School District—set the framework for that program which led to writing this text. I thank them and the many participants who helped make our studies so fruitful. Three of the participants later joined me at Temple University, Philadelphia, in teaching future teachers of history, and I thank Patricia Jiggetts Jones, Gloria Mitchell-Barnes, and Karen Kreider for helping me plan the content and pedagogy of an introductory world history course. Sue Rosenthal reminded me to encourage students to find their own place in history and thus inspired the afterword of this book.

As I prepared a new introductory course in world history at Temple University, I was granted a semester's study leave for which I thank the Temple University Faculty Senate. Throughout this project I received the constant support of Dean Carolyn Adams and department chairs Jim Hilty and Morris Vogel.

Many colleagues have read or discussed parts of this text in manuscript and have made helpful suggestions. Within Temple University's history department these include Barbara Day-Hickman,

Ruth Karras, Tim Mixter, Dieu Nguyen, Arthur Schmidt, Teshale Tibebu, and Kathy Walker. Vasiliki Limberis of our religion department and Len Greenfield from anthropology helped with issues outside the immediate discipline. In addition I thank Michael Adas, Al Andrea, Joan Arno, Terry Burke, Tim Burke, Lee Cassanelli, Richard Eaton, Narayani Gupta, Chris Jones, Maghan Keita, Dina Rizk Khoury, Lynn Lees, Alan Mann, David O'Connor, Greg Possehl, Jerry Ruderman, and Gail Vander Heide. Jim Krippner-Martinez' help with Latin America was critical, as was the assistance of Susannah Ruth Spodek on Japan. I trust that all these colleagues and friends will find in the finished book evidence of their contributions, and that they will forgive me for not following their advice even more carefully.

I first used most of the text materials in this book with my students at Temple University. They provided the first indications of what worked well in teaching world history and should be kept in the final product, and what did not and should be scrapped. I thank them both for their patience and for the many suggestions they made.

I owe a great debt to the editors and staff at Calmann & King, London, who saw this book through from its inception to its conclusion. They seemed to know just when to encourage, to support, to understand, and to demand. Rosemary Bradley (now with Prentice Hall) commissioned the book; Melanie White edited and guided the book from beginning to end; Damian Thompson prepared the layout and design and helped select, gather, and caption the illustrations which drive the written text forward; Lee Ripley Greenfield had overall executive charge of the project in its last four years.

The most profound and personal thanks come last. My father and mother, may their memories be a blessing, always encouraged and supported my studies. My father, though a man of business rather than of the academy, always enjoyed historical discussions. Mother, of course, prepared, and presided over, the dinner table at which these discussions took place, often adding her own comments as well.

When I began writing this book, my two older children, Susie and Josh, were already in college. Sarah, the youngest, was still in high school. All three were always in my mind as I wrote. They were my first audience as I asked myself: What should students know about world history? They were usually the first readers of early drafts of each chapter, and their comments were perceptive and helpful. Most gratifying of all: Susie, who spent four years living and working in Japan, graciously provided early drafts of materials on Japan; Sarah, who spent two years with the Peace Corps in Morocco, helped me through issues in the Arab and Berber worlds; and Josh, training as a physicist, reminded me to give proper attention to the importance of science in history. To them I dedicate the first volume of this work.

I met Lisa Hixenbaugh about a year into the writing of this book, and we were married just a few months before its completion. She has enriched and enhanced my life. Graciously and without complaint she gave up time that we might have spent together so that the writing could be completed. She endured interminable monologues on the status of the project. Her support and encouragement helped make the entire task feasible.

ACKNOWLEDGMENTS FOR THE SECOND EDITION

One of the great joys of completing the revisions for a second edition is the opportunity to thank friends and colleagues who helped: Laura Szumanski, Ph.D. candidate in history at Temple University, who drafted several of the biographical "Profiles" with her characteristic fine style and in record time; Jayant Joshi who urged me not to omit Abraham Lincoln and the many struggles for freedom in America, for they belong to the history of the world; Father Jose Heredero who increased the accuracy of coverage and interpretation on Christianity; students in the class of Gail Zlotowitz at Yeshivat Rambam who kept me alert to orthodox Jewish religious sensitivities; the anonymous evaluators of the first edition; sales representatives at Prentice Hall who advised me periodically on the strengths and weaknesses of the text from the viewpoint of the faculty who chose to use it—or not; Nell Webb, whose contributions at Calmann & King added to the enduring support of Melanie White and Damian Thompson; Gerald Lombardi for deft editing.

During the six months of revision, friends and family tolerated my absences from normal socializing; I missed them even more! Students and colleagues tolerated my fragmented attention. My wife put up with even less time together than usual, and more monologues. And special thanks to her parents, Sandra and Al Hixenbaugh, who spent the last couple of days before Lisa and I left for India in 1997 helping to pack up our house, freeing me to sit at the word processor typing the last pages of the first edition in a scene that none of us has forgotten!

HOWARD SPODEK
March 2000

INTRODUCTION

"History will be kind to me, for I intend to write it."

WINSTON CHURCHILL

THE WORLD THROUGH HISTORIANS' EYES

hat's history!" In common usage this phrase diminishes an event as belonging only to the past, implying that it is no longer important and has no further consequence. For the historian, however, history is just the opposite. History records those events that are of greatest importance, of most lasting significance, and of most enduring consequence. History is the assortment of records that humans create, preserve, fight over, revise, and transmit from one generation to the next. It contains the deepest understandings of how we got to where we are now; the struggles fought, won, and lost; the choices made and not made; the roads taken and not taken. We study history to know who we are, who we might have become, and who we might yet become.

HISTORIOGRAPHY

History is not a single, dry record of names, dates, and places. Nor is it a record that somehow, magically, came into being by itself. Historical records are the products of many human choices. From all the events that have occurred, historians choose those they believe worth remembering for inclusion in their accounts and leave out those that seem less relevant. Historians differ, however, in their assessment of the significance of events. They debate which events are most significant and which are less so, which should be included in the records and which may be left out. Differences in historians' assessments lead to the writing and preservation of different histories. These differences are important because they represent different understandings of who we have become, and how, and of who we may become, and how. The debates and discussions of historians in forming and arguing about these assessments form part of the historiographical record. **Historiography** is the study of the making of historical records, of the work historians do and how they do it.

Even when historians are in agreement as to which events are most significant, they may differ in evaluating why the events are significant. One historian's interpretation of events may be diametrically opposed to another's. For example, virtually all historians agree that part of the significance of World War II lay in its new policies and technologies of destruction: nuclear weapons in battle and genocide behind the lines.

In terms of interpretation, pessimists might stress the continuing menace of these legacies of terror, while optimists might argue that the very violence of the war and the Holocaust triggered a search for limits on nuclear arms and greater tolerance for minorities. With each success in nuclear arms limitation and in toleration, the optimists seem more persuasive; with each spread of nuclear weapons and each outbreak of genocide, the pessimists seem to win.

The study of history is thus an interpretation of significance as well as an investigation of facts. The significance of events is determined by their consequences. Sometimes we do not know what the consequences are; or the consequences may not have run their course; or we may differ in our assessments of the consequences. This play between past events and their current consequences is what historian E.H. Carr had in mind in his famous description of history as "an unending dialogue between the present and the past" (Carr, p. 30).

After historians ask the factual questions of Who, Where, When, What, Why, and How, they reach the "So what?" questions. These affect fundamentally the historians' discussion about what to include in their accounts and what to leave out. In world history, where the subject matter is everything that humans have ever done, this problem of selection is fundamental. The problem of interpretation comes with it. These "So what?" questions depend finally on individual interpretation, on the personal values of the historian. Readers, in turn, will evaluate the historians' argument partly by its consistency with the available data, partly by the values implicit or explicit in it, and partly by comparing the author's values with their own. The study of history thus becomes a dialogue between the values of the historian and the values of the student of history. As you read this text, for example, you should become aware of the values held by the author and of your own values as reader.

As historians present their differing interpretations, each tries to mount the most persuasive arguments, marshaling **primary source** materials, that is, materials from contemporary participants in the events; **secondary sources**, that is, later comments on the consequences of the events; and appeals to the sensibilities of the reader. In turn, the reader will be asking: Does the historians' interpretation sound reasonable? Do people really act as the historian suggests they do? Do the motivations suggested by the historian sound reasonable or is some

other interpretation more consistent with the primary and secondary sources and with human motivation? When historians differ in their interpretations of events, readers must judge which argument is more persuasive.

HISTORY AND IDENTITY

History is among the most passionate and bitterly contentious of disciplines because most people and groups locate a large part of their identity in their history. Americans may take pride in their nationality, for example, for having created a representative, constitutional democracy that has endured for over 200 years (see Part 7). Yet they may be saddened, shamed, or perhaps incensed by the existence of 250 years of slavery followed by inequalities in race relations continuing to the present (see Part 6). Christians may take pride in two thousand years of missions of compassion toward the poor and downtrodden, yet they may be saddened, shamed, or even incensed by an almost equally long record of religious warfare and persecution of those whose beliefs differed from their own (see Part 4).

As various ethnic, religious, class, and gender groups represent themselves in public political life, they seek not only to understand the history that has made them what they are, but also to attempt to persuade others to understand that history in the same way. Feminist historians, for example, find in their reading of history that **patriarchy**, a system of male-created and male-dominated institutions, has subordinated women. To the extent that they weave a persuasive argument from available data and their interpretation of it, or discover new data and create new interpretations, they win over others to their position.

Meanwhile, other historians may present women's position in the world more as a product of biological differentiation than of human decisions. Some may not even agree that women have been subordinated to men, but argue that both genders have shared in a great deal of suffering (and joy) throughout history (see Parts 1 and 7). The historical debates over the origins and evolution of gender relationships evoke strong emotions because people's self-image, the image of their group, and the perceptions others hold of them are all at stake. And the stakes are high. As historian Gerda Lerner writes in *The Creation of Patriarchy*: "Women's history is indispensable and essential to the emancipation of women" (p. 3)

CONTROL OF HISTORICAL RECORDS

From earliest times, control over the historical records and their interpretation has been fundamental to political rule. The first emperor of China, Qin Shihuang (r. 221–207 B.C.E.), the man who built the concept of a united China that has lasted until today, "discarded the ways of the former kings and burned the writings of the hundred schools in order to make the people ignorant" (deBary, p. 167). So wrote Qia I (201–169 B.C.E.), poet and statesman of the succeeding Han dynasty. Shihuang wished that only his interpretation of China's past, and his place in it, be preserved. Later intellectuals condemned his actions—but the lost records were irretrievable (see Part 3).

Colonial governments seeking to control subject peoples sometimes attempt to interpret their histories by explaining that the conquered people were so backward that they benefited from the conquest.

Later historians may be less kind to the colonizers. Some 1900 years ago the historian Tacitus wrote bitterly of the ancient Romans in their conquest of England: "Robbery, butchery, rapine, the liars call Empire; they create a desolation and call it peace" (*Agricola*, 30).

In our own century, the many nations that have won their freedom from colonialism echo similar resentments against their foreign rulers and set out to revise the historical record in keeping with their newly won political freedom. Jawaharlal Nehru, the first prime minister of independent India (1947–64), wrote in 1944 from the cell in which he had been imprisoned for his leadership of his country's independence movement:

> British accounts of India's history, more especially of what is called the British period, are bitterly resented. History is almost always written by the victors and conquerors and gives their viewpoint; or, at any rate, the victors' version is given prominence and holds the field. (Nehru, p. 289)

Lenin addressing troops in Sverdlov Square, Moscow, May 5, 1920. The leaders of the Russian Communist revolution crudely refashioned the historical record to suit the wishes of the winners. After Lenin's death in 1924, his second-in-command Leon Trotsky (pictured sitting on the podium in the left-hand picture) lost to Josef Stalin the bitter power struggle that ensued. Not only was Trotsky banished from the Soviet Union, but so was his appearance in the official archives (see doctored picture on right).

Philip Curtin, historian of Africa and of slavery, elaborates an equally critical view of European colonial accounts of Africa's history:

> African history was seriously neglected until the 1950s. . . . The colonial period in Africa left an intellectual legacy to be overcome, just as it had in other parts of the world. . . . The colonial imprint on historical knowledge emerged in the nineteenth and early twentieth centuries as a false perspective, a Eurocentric view of world history created at a time of European domination . . . Even where Europeans never ruled, European knowledge was often accepted as *modern* knowledge, including aspects of the Eurocentric historiography. (Curtin, p. 54)

Instead, Curtin continues, a proper historiography must:

> show the African past from an African point of view. . . . For Africans, to know about the past of their own societies is a form of self-knowledge crucial to a sense of identity in a diverse and rapidly changing world. A recovery of African history has been an important part of African development over recent decades. (p. 54)

Even without colonialism, thugs sometimes gain control of national histories. George Orwell's satirical novel *Animal Farm* (published in 1945) presented an allegory in which pigs come to rule a farm. Among their many acts of domination, the pigs seize control of the historical records of the farm animals' failed experiment in equality and impose their own official interpretation, which justifies their own rule. The rewriting of history and suppression of alternative records by the Communist

Party of the former Soviet Union between 1917 and 1989 reveals the bitter truth underlying Orwell's satire (see Part 8).

Although the American experience is much different, in the United States, too, records have been suppressed. Scholars are still trying to use the Freedom of Information Act to pry open sealed diplomatic archives. (Most official archives everywhere have twenty-, thirty-, or forty-year rules governing the waiting period before certain sensitive records are opened to the public. These rules, which are designed to protect living people and contemporary policies from excessive scrutiny, are the rule everywhere.)

Religious and ethnic groups, too, may seek to control historical records. The Roman Catholic Church in 1542 established an Index of Prohibited Books to ban writings it considered heretical. (The Spanish Inquisition, ironically, stored away many records that later scholars used to recreate its history and the history of those it persecuted.) More recently, despite all the evidence of the Holocaust, the murder of 6 million Jews by the Nazi government of Germany during World War II, a few people have claimed that the murders never took place. They deny the existence of such racial and religious hatred, and its consequences, and ignore deep-seated problems in the relationships between majority and minority populations.

HISTORICAL REVISION

Interpretations of events may become highly contested and revised even after several centuries have passed. The significance of the voyages of Columbus was once celebrated uncritically in the United States in tribute both to "the Admiral of the Ocean Sea" himself and to the courage and enterprise of the European explorers and early settlers who brought their civilizations to the Americas. In South America, however, where Native American Indians are more numerous and people of European ancestry often form a smaller proportion of the population, the celebrations have been far more ambivalent, muted, and meditative.

In 1992, on the 500th anniversary of Columbus' first voyage to the Americas, altogether new and more sobering elements entered the commemoration ceremonies, even in the United States. The negative consequences of Columbus' voyages, previously ignored, were now recalled and emphasized: the death of up to 90 percent of the Native American Indian population in the century after the arrival of Europeans; the Atlantic slave trade, initiated by trade in Indian slaves; and the exploitation of the natural resources of a continent until then little touched by humans. The ecological consequences, which are only now beginning to receive more attention, were not all negative, however. They included the fruitful exchange of natural products between the hemispheres. Horses, wheat, and sheep were introduced to the Americas; potatoes, tomatoes, and corn to Afro-Eurasia. Unfortunately, the spread of syphilis was one of the consequences of the exchange; scholars disagree on who transmitted this disease to whom (see Part 5).

WORLD HISTORY VS. WESTERN HISTORY

Because the study of history is so intimately tied to our sense of identity, as individuals, groups, and citizens of the world, the field is emotionally and bitterly contested. For this reason, the place of world history in the American college curriculum has itself been contested. The contest has been primarily between the advocates of European/Western history and those favoring a global view. Advocates of Western history wish to educate a student to know the central political, cultural, and religious institutions of the Western world, which are the basis of the political life of the United States and the roots of the cultural and religious heritage of most of its citizens. Advocates of world history recognize the validity and importance of these claims, but advance countervailing positions:

- Increasingly dense networks of transportation and communication have brought the world, for many purposes, into a single unit. The growth and consolidation of that global unit deserve its own historical study.

- America is increasingly drawn into a world far wider than Europe alone, with the nations and peoples of the Pacific Rim and of Latin America becoming particularly prominent partners.

- The population of America, always at least 15 percent non-European in ancestry, especially African–American, is now adding large new immigrant streams from Latin America and Asia, increasing the need for knowledge of these

Indians giving Hernán Cortés a headband, from Diego Duran's *Historia de las Indias*, 1547. Bent on conquest and plunder, the bearded Spaniard Cortés arrived on the Atlantic coast of Mexico in 1519. His forces sacked the ancient city of Tenochtitlán, decimated the Aztec people and imprisoned their chief, Montezuma, before proclaiming the Aztec Empire "New Spain." By stark contrast, this bland Spanish watercolor shows local tribesmen respectfully paying homage to the invader as if he were a god; in ignoring the brutality exercised in the colonization of South America, the artist is, in effect, "rewriting" history. (*Biblioteca National, Madrid*)

many cultures and their histories if there is to be a rich, balanced understanding of all the peoples of the United States.

The fierce debate between the advocates of Western history and those favoring world history is thus, in part, a contest for an understanding of the nature of America's population, culture, and place in the world as it has been and may become.

The current text is addressed primarily to American students, and many of its references are to American experience, but as global immigration increases the ethnic diversity of most countries of the world, the same need to understand world history in order to understand national history will increase everywhere.

TOOLS

The study of history requires many tools, and this text includes most of the principal ones:

- The core of historical study is a direct encounter with primary materials, usually documents, but including other artifacts—for example, letters,

diaries, newspaper accounts, photographs, and artwork. Every chapter includes representative primary materials.

- Visual images, a strong feature of this book, complement the text, offering non-verbal "texts" of the time.

- "Spotlight" spreads contain brief essays, linked to the main text, that treat pictures as a springboard for discussion.

- Maps place events in space and in geographical relationship to one another.

- Chronological timecharts situate events in time and sequence.

- Brief charts supply summaries as well as contextual information on topics such as religion, science, and trade.

- Biographical sketches of outstanding individuals, and of average ones, provide personal insights and points of identification.

- Various, often conflicting, interpretations demonstrate the existence of multiple perspectives. They help students to challenge their own values and develop their own interpretive criteria.

CHRONOLOGY AND THEME

History is a study of change over time and also of continuities in the face of change. In this text we mark eight turning points in human history, setting each as the focus of a single unit, or part. The choices may seem arbitrary, but they do capture fundamental transformations. They also demonstrate how a historian argues for the significance of one turning point over another. Each turning point is marked by the rise to prominence of a new theme in human history and a new focus in the narrative. For example, we move from an emphasis on early human cultures in Part 1 to agricultural and urban "revolutions" in Part 2, to the establishment of the first empires in Part 3. Within each chronological/thematic part, we stress a single disciplinary or interdisciplinary approach—for example, anthropology in early human cultures, urban studies in the rise of early cities, and political science in the establishment of empires.

We highlight a specific discipline in each chronological part for teaching purposes, in order to demonstrate the usefulness of each discipline in illuminating historical change. We recognize, however, that all the disciplinary approaches and the realities to which they refer, are relevant in each time period. Our method allows readers to understand how various disciplines, alone and together, help us understand the varied aspects of historical narratives.

The eight turning points by which we mark world history and the specific themes and disciplines we pair with them are:

1 The emergence of the first humans and human culture, 4,500,000 B.C.E. to 10,000 B.C.E. Focus on *anthropology* and *historiography*.

2 The emergence of the first cities and urban civilization following the agricultural revolution, 10,000 B.C.E. to 400 C.E. Focus on *interdisciplinary urban studies*.

3 The emergence of early empires, from Sargon of Assyria and Alexander of Macedon through China, Rome, and India, and the trade routes that linked them, 2000 B.C.E. to 200 C.E. Focus on *politics*.

4 The rise and spread of world religions, focusing on Islam, 622–1500 C.E.; reviewing the historical background of Judaism and Christianity and their contemporary systems; and comparing the Asia-centered religions of Hinduism, Buddhism, and the ethical system of Confucianism. Focus on *religion*.

5 World trading systems, 1000–1776, with the linkage of eastern and western hemispheres as the fulcrum, about 1500. By the end of this period, capitalism was defined as a new economic system. Focus on *economics*.

6 Migrations, free and slave, 1000–1750. Focus on *demography*.

7 Revolutions, political and industrial, beginning in Europe and spreading globally, 1750–1914. Focus on *social changes*, especially *changes in family and gender roles*.

8 Technological change and its human control, 1914 to the present. Focus on *the human uses of technological systems*.

COMPARATIVE HISTORY AND HYPOTHESIS TESTING

Because each part is built on comparisons among different regions and civilizations of the world, the reader will become accustomed to posing hypotheses based on general principles, and then testing them against comparative data from around the world. This method of playing back and forth between general theory and specific case study, testing whether the general theory and the specific data fit each other, is at the heart of the social sciences. For example, in Part 2 we will explore the general characteristics of cities, and then check if the generalizations hold up through case studies of various cities around the world. In Part 3, we will seek general theories of the rise and fall of early empires based on comparisons among China, Rome, and India. In Part 4 we will search for commonalities among religious belief systems through a survey of several major religions.

FOCUS

Continuity versus Change in History

Feminist historian Judith Bennett argues that between 1300 and 1700, women's economic and social position did not change much. She also maintains that women's history in Europe is the study of unchanging economic subordination to men at least from 1300 to the present:

In the study of women's work . . . we should take as our central question not transformation . . . but instead continuity. We should ask: why has women's work retained such dismal characteristics over so many centuries? . . . We should ask: why wages for "women's work" remained consistently lower than wages paid for work associated with men? We should ask, in short: why has women's work stood still in the midst of considerable economic change? . . . I think that this emphasis on continuity demands an attention to the mechanisms and operations of patriarchy in the history of women. (p. 164)

Pieter de Hoogh, *A Woman and Her Maid, c.* **1650.** In this Dutch domestic scene, the high walls of the courtyard and the formal business attire of the paterfamilias as he returns home can be read as emphasizing the separation between the male world of public commerce and the female world of private domesticity. (*National Gallery, London*)

FRAMING QUESTIONS FOR MULTIPLE PERSPECTIVES

The text highlights the importance of multiple perspectives in studying and interpreting history. The answers we get—the narrative histories we write—are based on the questions we ask. Each part suggests a variety of questions that can be asked about the historical event being studied, and a variety of interpretations that can emerge in the process of answering them. Often there is more than one "correct" way of understanding change over time and its significance. Different questions will trigger very different research and very different answers. For example, in Part 5 we ask about the stages and processes by which Western commercial power began to surpass that of Asia. This question presupposes the fact that at earlier times Asian power had been superior and asks why it declined and why European power advanced. In Part 7 we ask how the industrial revolution affected and changed relationships between men and women; this question will yield different research and a different narrative from questions about, for example, women's contributions to industrialization, which is a useful question, but a different one.

FINDING ONE'S PLACE IN HISTORY

We want readers to understand world history not as a burden to learn and to live with, but as a legacy within which to find their own place. This text shows people throughout history reckoning with the alternatives available and making choices among them. Their examples should provide some solace, courage, and guidance to readers now making their own choices. History has always been seen as both bondage to the past and liberation from it. We write so that students should understand both potentials, and seek a path of freedom.

BIBLIOGRAPHY

Bennett, Judith M. "Medieval Women, Modern Women: Across the Great Divide," in David Aers, ed., *Culture and History, 1350–1600: Essays on English Communities, Identities, and Writing* (New York: Harvester Wheatsheaf, 1992), 147–75.

Carr, E.H. *What Is History?* (Harmondsworth, Middlesex: Penguin Books, 1964).

Curtin, Philip D. "Recent Trends in African Historiography and Their Contribution to History in General," in Joseph Ki-Zerbo, ed., *General History of Africa*, Vol. I: *Methodology and African Pre-History* (Berkeley: University of California Press, 1981), 54–71.

deBary, William Theodore, *et al.*, comps. *Sources of Chinese Tradition* (New York: Columbia University Press, 1960).

Lerner, Gerda. *The Creation of Patriarchy* (New York: Oxford University Press, 1986).

Nehru, Jawaharlal. *The Discovery of India* (Delhi: Oxford University Press, 1989).

Orwell, George. *Animal Farm* (New York: Harcourt, Brace, 1946).

Tacitus, Cornelius. *Tacitus' Agricola, Germany, and Dialogue on Orators*, trans. Herbert W. Benario (Norman: University of Oklahoma Press, 1991).

Tosh, John. *The Pursuit of History: Aims, Methods, and New Directions in the Study of Modern History*, 2nd ed. (London: Longman, 1991).

THE WORLD'S HISTORY

Volume I: To 1500

PART 1

Human Origins and Human Cultures

5 million B.C.E.–10,000 B.C.E.

BUILDING AN INTERPRETIVE FRAMEWORK: WHAT DO WE KNOW AND HOW DO WE KNOW IT?

Historians ask some very big questions. Often, of course, the stereotype of the historian searching in dusty archives for concrete, exact bits of data is correct. Detail and accuracy are important. However, profound questions of fundamental importance inspire the historian's rigorous research. In this chapter we address some of the biggest questions of all: Where did humans come from? How did our collective life on earth begin? How are we similar to other living species, and how are we unique?

Many historians would consider such questions to be **pre-history**, for no written records exist to answer them. We choose, however, to include pre-history as part of our search, for we historians are eclectic in our methods; we begin with questions about the past and our relationship to it, and then choose whatever methods help us find answers. In this chapter we find that until the mid-nineteenth century, the answers to our questions about human origins were provided by myths, often religious narratives. Then a re-evaluation of religious and mythical traditions invited a search for new answers and, at about the same time, new techniques of archaeology developed to provide them.

Neanderthal family. A reconstructed scene outside Gorham's Cave, Gibraltar.

What does it mean to be human? This profound question turns most historians and pre-historians to the study of human creativity. Humans are what humans do. We travel and migrate, both out of sheer inquisitiveness as well as to find safe and productive homes. As we shall see, by about 15,000 B.C.E., humans had traveled, mostly over land, and established themselves on all the continents of the earth except Antarctica. We also create and invent tools. Our account will begin with the simplest stone tools dating back millions of years and continue up to the invention of pottery and of sedentary farming some 10,000 years ago. Finally, to be human is to express our feelings and ideas in art, music, dance, ritual, and literature. In this chapter we examine early evidence of this creativity in the forms of sculptures and cave paintings from 20,000 years ago.

1 THE DRY BONES SPEAK

5 million B.C.E.—10,000 B.C.E.

". . . whilst this planet has gone cycling on according to the fixed laws of gravity, from so simple a beginning endless forms most beautiful and most wonderful have been, and are being, evolved."

CHARLES DARWIN

WHAT IS PALEOANTHROPOLOGY AND WHY IS IT IMPORTANT?

HUMAN ORIGINS IN MYTH AND HISTORY

Where did we come from? How did humans come to inhabit the earth? For more than a century, we have sought the answer to these questions in the earth, in the records of the fossils discovered and interpreted by archaeologists and paleoanthropologists (students of the earliest humans). But before the diggers came with their interpretations, we had myths of human origins, stories based on popular beliefs and passed from generation to generation as folk wisdom. To those who believe them, myths of human origins give meaning to human existence. They tell not only *how* humans came to inhabit the earth, they also suggest *why*. Some of these myths, especially those that have been incorporated into religious texts like the Bible, still inspire the imaginations and govern the behavior of hundreds of millions of people around the world.

"Myth and history are close kin inasmuch as both explain how things got to be the way they are by telling some sort of history" (p. 7). So William McNeill opened his presidential address to the American Historical Association in 1985. We usually call "myth" a story we believe untrue, or at least not supported by known facts, yet, McNeill continues, myths have great significance and consequences:

> What a particular group of persons understands, believes, and acts upon, even if quite absurd to outsiders, may nonetheless cement social relations and allow the members of the group to act together and accomplish feats otherwise impossible. . . . What a group of people knows and believes about the past channels expectations and affects the decisions on which their lives, their fortunes, and their sacred honor all depend. (p. 22)

EARLY HUMANS AND THEIR ANCESTORS

DATE B.C.E.	PERIOD	HOMINID EVOLUTION	MATERIAL CULTURE
5 million	• PLIOCENE	• Fragments found in northern Kenya; possibly *Australopithecus*	
3.75 million	• PLEISTOCENE	• *Australopithecus* genus, inc. Lucy (east and southern Africa) • *Homo habilis* (eastern and southern Africa) • *Homo erectus* (Africa) • *Homo erectus* thought to have moved from Africa into Eurasia	• Tools • Stone artifacts • Use of fire
500,000		• *Homo sapiens* (archaic form) • Remains of Peking man (*Sinanthropus*) found at Zhoukoudian	
130,000–80,000		• *Homo sapiens* (Africa and western Asia)	• Stone artifacts
100,000–33,000		• Neanderthals (Europe and western Asia)	
40,000	• AURIGNACIAN		• Tools include long blades • First passage from Siberia to Alaska
30,000	• GRAVETTIAN	• Human remains of the Upper Paleolithic type, *Homo sapiens sapiens* (25,000) found in China	• Venus figures (25,000–12,000)
20,000	• SOLUTREAN		• Chauvet cave, France (18,000)
17,000	• MAGDALENIAN		• Lascaux cave paintings (*c.* 15,000) • Altamira cave paintings (*c.* 13,550)

EARLY MYTHS

Akkad

What, then, have been some of the more powerful and widely accepted myths of the origin of human life? One of the earliest known myths is the *Enuma Elish* epic of the people of Akkad in Mesopotamia, discovered in King Ashurbanipal's library at Nineveh, 669–626 B.C.E., but probably dating back to almost 2000 B.C.E. The goddess Tiamat and her consort Kingu revolt against the existing gods of Mesopotamia. These gods call on Marduk, a young, strong god, who defends the old order by defeating, killing, and dismembering the rebellious deities.

According to the *Enuma Elish*, the victorious gods created humans out of the blood of the defeated and slain leader of the rebels. The humans were to devote themselves to the service of the victors. In the context of the violent city-states of Mesopotamia at the time the epic was written down, this myth gave meaning and direction to human life and affirmed the authority of the powerful priestly class.

India

India, vast and diverse, has many different myths of the origin of humans. Two of the most widespread and powerful illustrate two principal dimensions of the thought and practice of Hindu religious traditions (see Chapter 9). The ancient epic *Rigveda*, which dates from about 1000 B.C.E., emphasizes the mystical, unknowable qualities of life and its origins:

> Who verily knows and who can here declare it,
> whence it was born and whence comes this creation?
>
> The Gods are later than this world's production.
> Who knows then whence it first came into being?
>
> He, the first origin of this creation, whether he
> formed it all or did not form it, whose eye controls
> this world in highest heaven, he verily knows it …
> or perhaps he knows not.

In contrast to this reverent but puzzled view of creation, another of the most famous hymns of the *Rigveda*, the Purusha-sakta, describes the creation of the world by the gods' sacrifice and dismemberment of a giant man, Purusha:

> His mouth became the Brahmin; his arms were
> made into the Warrior, his thighs the People, and
> from his feet the Servants were born.
>
> The moon was born from his mind; from his eye
> the sun was born. Indra and Agni came from his
> mouth, and from his vital breath the Wind was born.
> (Ch. 10; v. 129)

In this account, humans are part of nature, subject to the laws of the universe, but they are not born equal among themselves. They are created with different qualities, in different castes. This myth of creation supports the hierarchical organization of India's historic caste system (see pp. 263–4).

West Asia

Perhaps the most widely known creation myth is told in the book of Genesis in the Hebrew Bible. Beginning from nothing, in five days God created heaven and earth; created light and separated it from darkness; created water and separated it from dry land; and created flora, birds, and fishes, and the sun, moon, and stars. God began the sixth day by creating larger land animals and reptiles, and then humans "in his own image."

Genesis assigns humans a unique and privileged place as the final crown and master of creation. Humans are specially created in God's own image, with dominion over all other living creatures. When the creation of humans and the charge to them are complete, God proclaims the whole process and product of creation as "good." Here humans hold an exalted position within, but also above, the rest of creation.

Vishnu represented as the whole world, Indian painting from Jaipur, nineteenth century. In the Hindu trinity Brahma is the creator of the world, Vishnu is its preserver, and Shiva its destroyer. The earth and all living beings—Brahma's creation—are often referred to as figments in the dream of Vishnu. He is the energy underlying all forms of life (see picture, p. 268). (*Victoria & Albert Museum, London*)

THE FUNCTION OF CREATION MYTHS

For thousands of years various creation myths have presented people with explanations of their place in the world, their relationship to the gods, to the rest of creation, and to one another. The narratives have similarities, but also sharp differences. Some portray humans as the exalted crown of creation, others as reconfigured parasites; some depict humans as partners with the gods, others as their servants; some suggest the equality of all humans, others stress a variety of caste, race, and gender hierarchies. To some degree, surely, people transmitted the myths as quaint tales told for enjoyment only, but the myths were also seen as providing guidance on how people should understand and live their lives.

Until the late eighteenth century, the myths were the only accounts we had of the origins of humans. No other explanations seemed necessary. In any case, no one expected to find actual physical evidence for the processes by which humans came to be.

EVOLUTIONARY EXPLANATIONS OF HUMAN ORIGINS

By the mid-1700s some philosophers and natural scientists in Europe challenged the Bible's story of individual, special creation of each life form. They saw so many similarities among different species that they could not believe that each had been created separately. But they could not demonstrate the processes through which these similarities and differences had developed. They saw some creatures changing forms even during their life cycle, like the metamorphosis of the caterpillar into the moth, or the tadpole into the frog, but they could not establish the processes by which one species metamorphosed into another. They knew the processes of breeding by which farmers encouraged the development of particular strains in their farm animals and plants, but they lacked the conception of a time frame of millions of years that would allow for the natural evolution of a new species from an existing one.

Challenging the biblical account required a new method of inquiry, a new system for organizing knowledge. In the mid-eighteenth century

these new forms began to emerge (see Chapter 15). In this new intellectual environment, Denis Diderot (1713–84), compiler of the first modern encyclopedia, suggested that as animals experience new needs in their environment they produce new organs to adapt and transmit them to their descendants. The physician Erasmus Darwin published a similar argument in 1794. Jean-Baptiste de Lamarck, a student of natural history, published additional similar views in 1809 after he classified the collections of plants and animals in the Paris Museum of Natural History. We now know that these men were on the right track, but that they had missed a key point.

Finally, Erasmus' grandson, Charles Darwin (1809–82), and Alfred Russel Wallace (1823–1913), separately, formulated the modern theory of the biological evolution of species. With the earlier theorists, they also saw the mounting evidence of biological similarities among related species, they understood that these similar species were, in fact, related to one another, not separate creations, and they allowed a time frame adequate for major

"That Troubles Our Monkey Again," cartoon of Charles Darwin from *Fun*, November 16, 1872. As scientists and theologians struggled to come to terms with the implications of evolutionary theory, popular reaction was often hostile and derisive. In this cartoon from a contemporary British weekly, Darwin is caricatured as an ape checking the pulse of a woman—or, as the cartoonist ironically refers to her, a "female descendant of marine ascidian" (a tiny invertebrate).

transformation of species to take place. They then pushed on to demonstrate the method by which small differences within a species were transmitted from generation to generation, increasing the differentiation until new forms were produced.

Both Darwin and Wallace reached their conclusions as a result of extensive travel overseas. Darwin carried out his observations on a scientific voyage around the world in 1831–6 aboard the British warship *Beagle*, and especially during his stay in the Galapagos Islands off the equatorial west coast of South America. Wallace traveled for many years in the islands of southeast Asia. In 1855 he published a paper "On the Habits of the Orang-Utan of Borneo," suggesting a common ancestor for primates and man. In 1858 Wallace and Darwin published a joint paper on the basic concepts of evolution. In 1859 Darwin published his findings and conclusions in *On the Origin of Species by Means of Natural Selection*, a book that forever altered humankind's conception of itself.

Darwin explained that the pressure for each organism to compete, survive, and reproduce created a kind of natural selection. The population of each species increased until its ecological niche was filled to capacity. In the face of this population pressure, the species that were better adapted to the niche survived; the rest were crowded out and tended toward extinction. Small differences always appeared within a species: some members were taller, some shorter; some brighter colored, others less radiant; some with more flexible hands and feet, others less manipulable. Those members with differences that aided survival in any given ecological setting tended to live on and to transmit their differences to their descendants. Others died out. A kind of breeding process was taking place within nature. Darwin called this process "natural selection" or "survival of the fittest."

Darwin's argument challenged two prevailing mythological views of creation, especially the biblical views. First, the process of natural selection had no goal beyond survival and reproduction. Unlike many existing creation myths, especially biblical myths, evolutionary theory postulated no **teleology**, no ethical or moral goals and purposes of life. Second, the theory of natural selection described the evolution of ever more "fit" organisms, better adapted to their ecological environment, evolving from existing ones. The special, separate creation of each species was not necessary.

To support his argument, Darwin compared natural selection to the selection process practiced by humans in breeding animals. Farmers know that specific traits among their animals can be exaggerated through breeding. Horses, for example, can be bred either for speed or for power by selecting those horses in which the desired trait appears. In nature the act of selection occurs spontaneously, if more slowly, as plants and animals that have traits more appropriate to an environment survive and reproduce while others do not.

In the isolated Galapagos Islands, Darwin found various kinds of finches, all of which were similar to each other except in their beaks. He rejected the idea that each kind of finch had been separately created. Rather, there must have been an ancestor common to them all throughout the islands. Because each island offered slightly different food sources, different beaks were better suited to each separate island. The different ecological niches on each separate island to which the birds had immigrated had evoked slightly different evolutionary development. So from a single, common ancestor, new species evolved over time, on the different islands.

For Darwin, the process of natural selection of more complex, better adapted forms also explained the evolution of humans from simpler, less well-adapted organisms. Perhaps this was "the Creator's" method. Darwin concluded *On the Origin of Species*:

> Thus, from the war of nature, from famine and death, the most exalted object which we are capable of conceiving, namely, the production of the higher animals, directly follows. There is grandeur in this view of life, with its several powers, having been originally breathed *by the Creator* [my italics] into a few forms or into one; and that, whilst this planet has gone cycling on according to the fixed law of gravity, from so simple a beginning endless forms most beautiful and most wonderful have been, and are being, evolved. (*On the Origin of Species*, reproduced in Appleman, ed., *Darwin*, p. 131)

Note, however, that the words "by the Creator" did not appear in the first edition. Darwin added them later, perhaps in response to criticisms raised by more conventional Christian religious thinkers.

Within a decade, Darwin's work, and the parallel work of Alfred Russel Wallace, had won over the scientific community. In 1871, Darwin published *The Descent of Man*, which extended his argument to the evolution of humans, concluding explicitly that "man is descended from some lowly organized form" (Appleman, ed., p. 208).

The search now began for evidence of the "missing link" between humans and apes, for some creature, alive or dead, that stood at an intermediate point in the evolutionary process. In this search archaeology flourished, and the adjunct field of paleoanthropology, which explores the nature of early humans in their environment, was born. We shall now investigate the findings, and disputes, of these disciplines.

THE EVOLUTIONARY RECORD: HOW DO WE KNOW?

THE ARCHAEOLOGICAL RECORD

We begin the discussion of the archaeological search for the missing link with an account of the major discoveries in the order they were uncovered, addressing the question "How do we know?" At the conclusion, in the chart on page 18 and the representation of skulls on page 19 we see how the pieces of the puzzle fit together in a chronology of evolutions representing "What we know."

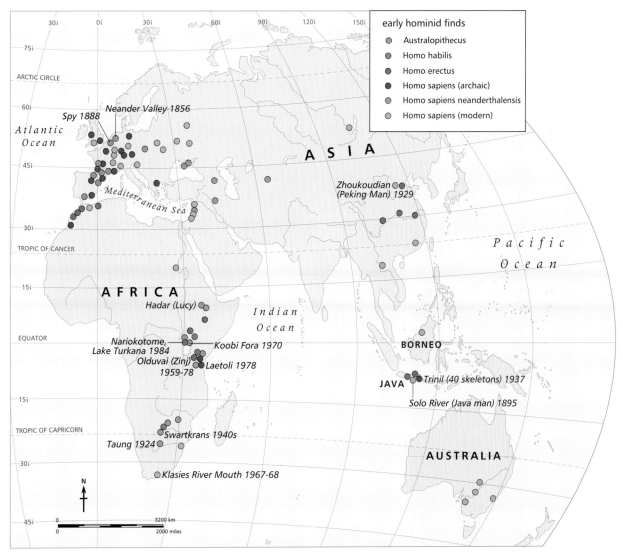

Human ancestors Fossil remains of the earliest direct human ancestors, *Australopithecus* and *Homo habilis*, dating from 1 million to 5 million years ago, have been found only in tropical Africa. The unique soil and climatic conditions there have preserved the fossils. *Homo erectus* remains, from 1.5 million years ago, are the earliest to be found outside Africa. They, along with *Homo sapiens*, have been found throughout Eurasia.

SPOTLIGHT
Reconstructing Neanderthals

Marcellin Boule, a paleoanthropologist at the French National Museum of Natural History, published his (mis)understanding of the anatomy of the Neanderthals between 1911 and 1913. Boule

Figure 1 Diorama of "bovine" Neanderthals.

described the Neanderthal as walking like an ape, with a spine that had no curves, and hunchbacked, with its head pushed forward on top of its spine. He believed that the Neanderthal's long, low skull allowed little space for the segments of the brain that carry higher intelligence. Boule wrote of the "brutish appearance of this muscular and clumsy body, and of the heavy-jawed skull that declares the predominance of a purely vegetative or bestial kind over the functions of the mind" (cited in Time-Life, *The Neanderthals*, p. 19). Later paleoanthropologists found numerous errors in Boule's reading of the fossil record, but for many years his interpretation, and others similar to it, carried great weight. Museum representations carried the erroneous message to the general public. Consider, for example, **figure 1** from a diorama displayed for decades by the world-famous Field Museum of Natural History in Chicago.

How much freedom does an anthropologist, or an artist, have in reconstructing images of the Neanderthals from skeletal

remains? In representing Neanderthals as clumsy and unintelligent, Boule was misreading the fossil bones. Then, his imagination carried him further as he reconstructed the soft tissue that does not survive as fossils: the hair, flesh, and cartilage. **Figure 2** represents

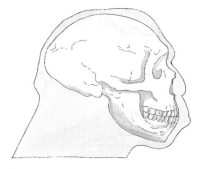

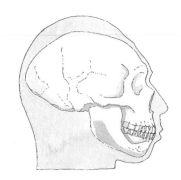

Figure 2 Alternate reconstructions from Neanderthal skull.

two different reconstructions of a Neanderthal man based on a single skull found in La Chapelle-aux-Saints, France, the same skull from which Boule reconstructed his images. The lower diagram is much more human looking, the one on the top far more ape-like. Both are justifiable interpretations based on the evidence available.

Moving beyond the individual skeleton in isolation, teams of experts from disciplines such as biology, geology, and climatology cooperate to reconstruct the natural setting of human and hominid development. As Neanderthal skeletons have been found from northern Europe to Africa, from Gibraltar to Iran, these natural settings vary greatly. In **figure 3**, the Natural History Museum in London represents Neanderthals living in a nuclear family, based on remains discovered at various caves at Gibraltar. Many Neanderthals also lived in larger bands of up to twenty to thirty individuals.

Scholarship on Neanderthals takes new turns with new research technologies. Researchers at the University of Illinois at Chicago, for example, have applied computer technology for reconstructing faces from the skeletal remains of unidentified children to creating images of Neanderthal faces with greater accuracy than ever before. In **figure 4,** Paul Neumann prepares to graft images of living humans on to Neanderthal skulls, bringing new life to the "dead" past.

Figure 3 Reconstructed scene of Neanderthal family outside Gorham's Cave, Gibraltar.

BIBLIOGRAPHY
Bahn, Paul G. ed. *Archaeology* (Cambridge; Cambridge University Press, 1996).

Constable, George and the Editors of Time-Life Books. *The Neanderthals* (New York: Time-Life Books, 1973).

Figure 4 Computer manipulation of Neanderthal facial profiles.

Neanderthals

In August 1856, workers quarrying for limestone in a cave in the Neander Valley near Düsseldorf, Germany, found a thick skullcap with a sloping forehead and several skeletal bones of limbs. Some speculated that it was a deformed human. Others thought it was a soldier lost in a previous war. Other, similar, skeletal remains had been found, but without any clearer understanding of their meaning.

In 1863, Thomas Henry Huxley (1829–95), a leading advocate of Darwin's theory of evolution, argued that the skull was part of a primitive human being who stood between non-human primates and *Homo sapiens*, our own species. He claimed that it was the "missing link." Against those who thought in terms of biblical time spans,

Huxley argued that "Evolution will extend by long epochs the most liberal estimate that has yet been made of the Antiquity of Man" (cited in Fagan, *Journey*, p. 10). In 1864, the English anthropologist William King gave a name to the find that signified this intermediate position: *Homo neanderthalensis*. When similar bones and skulls were discovered in Belgium in 1888, scholars began to see that Neanderthal man, far from being a single random accident, was part of a distinct species. Research on Neanderthals continues even now (see Spotlight, pp. 10–11), and in October 1999 palaeoanthropologists Alban Defleur of the University of the Mediterranean at Marseilles, France, and Tim White from the University of California at Berkeley reported in an article in the journal *Science* that at least some Neanderthals were cannibals. The evidence comes from a cave in southern France. A total of seventy-eight bones from at least two adults, two teenagers, and two children of about seven show that the flesh from all parts of the bodies was carefully removed. Bones were smashed with rocks to get at the inside marrow and skulls were broken open. The Neanderthal bones and the bones of deer were tossed together into a heap and show similar marks from the same stone tools. As Defleur notes, "If we conclude that the animal remains are the leftovers from a meal, we are obliged to expand that conclusion to include humans." On the other hand, there are many other examples of Neanderthals burying their dead carefully, suggesting that their cultural behavior differed from group to group.

LANDMARKS IN EARLY LIFE

Years ago (millions)	Geological period	Life form
2500	Archaean	earliest living things
590	Cambrian	first fossils
505	Ordovician	first fish
438	Silurian	first land plants
408	Devonian	first amphibians
360	Carboniferous	first reptiles
286	Permian	reptiles expanded
248	Triassic	first mammals and dinosaurs
213	Jurassic	first birds
144	Cretaceous	heyday of dinosaurs
65	Cretaceous	mammals flourished; dinosaurs extinct
25	Tertiary	first hominoid (ancestor of apes and humans)
5	Tertiary	first hominid (human ancestor)
0.01	Quaternary	modern humans appeared

Homo erectus

In 1891, Eugène Dubois (1858–1940), a surgeon in the Dutch army in Java, Indonesia, inspired by the earlier findings of Alfred Russel Wallace, was exploring for fossils. Employing the labor of convicts in Dutch prisons, along the bank of the Solo River, he discovered a cranium with a brain capacity of 900 cubic centimeters (compared to the modern human average of 1400 cc), a molar, and a femur. Dubois claimed to have discovered "pithecanthropus," ape-man. This find, widely referred to as Java Man, was the first early hominid discovered outside Europe. (Hominids are the human family, from our earliest ancestors and relatives emerging as the human line branched off from apes, up to and including ourselves at present.) Dubois' Java Man forced scholars to consider the theories of the evolution of humans more seriously and to understand the process in a global context.

In 1929, in the vast Zhoukoudian cave 30 miles (48 kilometers) from Beijing, the Chinese archaeologist Bei Qen-Xung and his colleagues discovered a skullcap of *Homo erectus* from about 500,000 years B.P. (Before the Present, a time frame used by archaeologists). In the next few years, in this fossil-rich cave, they discovered fourteen more fossil skulls and the remains of some forty individuals, whom they dated from 600,000 to 200,000 years ago. The cave seems to have been the home of a band of hunters living in a forested, grassy, riverine area, and eating plants as well as animals such as bison and deer. With a brain capacity ranging from 775 to 1300 cubic centimeters and a height up to 5 feet 6 inches (1.7 meters), anatomically Peking (Beijing) Man was almost identical to Java Man.

Beginning in 1937, G.H.R. van Koenigswald, who had followed Dubois' discoveries by returning to Java, excavated a nearly complete skull of *Homo erectus*. This led directly to the discovery of some forty individuals who had lived in Java in 900,000–100,000 B.P. These forty skeletons represent one-third of all the *Homo erectus* skeletons uncovered to this day in the entire world. Another third were in the Zhoukoudian cave. The most complete skeleton we have of *Homo erectus* was discovered, however, in 1984 on the shores of Lake Turkana, Kenya, by Richard Leakey.

Australopithecus africanus

In 1924, in South Africa, a student of professor of medicine Raymond Dart, at the University of Witwatersrand, called to his attention some fossils in a quarry near Taung. After investigation, Dart proclaimed the Taung skull to be *Australopithecus africanus*, "southern apelike creature of Africa," a 2-million-year-old ancestor of humans. Setting out to substantiate Dart's claims, another medical doctor in South Africa, Robert Broom, searched for more fossils. In 1938, he discovered and named *Paranthropus robustus*, or "robust creature parallel to man." Continuing his searches, in the 1940s, in Swartkrans, South Africa, Broom discovered yet another species, which turned out to be *Homo erectus*, the same as had been discovered in China and Java.

Between 1945 and 1955, Dart and his colleagues began to discover bone tools among the hominid fossils. Dart claimed that he had found the first known hominid culture, dating back 3 million years. Dart also claimed that these hominids had discovered and used fire, a hypothesis based on brown coloration on the bones. Later evaluation suggested that the coloration had come from the dark mineral manganese of the ground in which they lay, but evidence of the use of fire from 1 million years ago, the earliest known control of fire, was subsequently found at Swartkrans. Although some of their claims concerning human control of fire and creation of tools were exaggerated, Dart and his colleagues were extending their concerns beyond the archaeology of the individual hominid skeletons themselves to paleoanthropology, the study of the entire environment in which these hominids had lived. They included in their ecological analyses the animals whose fossils they discovered by the hundreds.

Homo habilis

In the 1930s, Louis Leakey (1903–72) was also excavating in Africa. His most important excavations, however, which were carried out with his wife Mary (1913–96), came between 1959 and 1978 in the Olduvai Gorge, where the Great Rift Valley cuts through northern Tanzania (see Profile, p.14). The Great Rift Valley runs from the Jordan River valley and the Dead Sea southward through the Red Sea through Ethiopia, Kenya, Tanzania, and Mozambique. The Rift is a fossil-hunter's delight. From at least 7 million years ago until perhaps 100,000 years ago, it was a fertile, populated region; it is geologically still shifting and, therefore, has covered and uncovered its deposits over time. Rivers that run through the Rift Valley further the process of uncovering the fossils, and it is volcanic, generating lava and ash that preserve the fossils caught within it and provide the material for relatively accurate dating.

At Olduvai in 1959, the Leakeys discovered *Zinjanthropus boisei*, soon nicknamed Zinj. At first they thought, and hoped, that Zinj might be an early specimen of *Homo*, but its skull was too small, its teeth too large, its arms too long, and its face too much like an ape's. Zinj, who was 1,750,000 years old, was an *Australopithecus*, a hominid closer to apes than to modern humans.

Continued excavations at Olduvai turned up skull fragments of creatures with brain capacities of 650 cubic centimeters, between the 400–500 cc of australopithecines and the 1400 cc of modern

Louis and Mary Leakey

ARCHAEOLOGISTS

With his brilliant finds in the Olduvai Gorge in East Africa, and his tireless efforts at publicizing them, Louis Leakey (1903–72) took paleoanthropology to the public and revolutionized how we think about early humans and their evolution. Before him, most scientists had believed that the earliest human evolution had taken place in Asia; he demonstrated that Africa was the most likely location. His most important finds included the first Proconsul skull complete with face, an early link between monkey and ape; *Zinjanthropus boisei*, a member of the *Australopithecus* genus, at the time the only ape fossil known; and *Homo habilis*, "handy person," who had lived at about the same time as Zinj, demonstrating that *Homo* and *Australopithecus* had lived side by side about 2 million years ago.

Born in Kenya to missionary parents, Louis grew up among the Kikuyu, and was initiated as a member of the tribe. He was most comfortable in the Kikuyu language and published a three-volume anthropological study entitled *Southern Kikuyu*. He had a brilliant academic career at Cambridge University in England, although he suffered rugby injuries that afflicted him with headaches and epilepsy for the rest of his life. The legendary energy that inspired his field work, and the academic fund-raising to support it, also led him to seek the limelight and to exaggerate the significance of many of his discoveries. He was scorned as well as praised by his colleages. Throughout his adult life, he also turned his charismatic charms to attracting young women, another part of his legend. He left his first wife, Frida, just after she delivered their second child, to live with and later marry Mary Douglas Nicol (1913–96). The scandal devastated not only his parents but also his professors and colleagues, putting his early academic career at risk.

Mary, however, was perhaps the perfect academic colleague for the young man. Her father, Erskine Nicol, brought his family from London to southern France where the cave paintings at Dordogne inspired Mary's interest in prehistory and where she began to draw prehistoric artifacts. When they met, Leakey hired her to illustrate his book *Adam's Ancestors*. Soon he invited her to Olduvai Gorge. On site, it was actually Mary who found the skull of the 16-million-year-old Proconsul africanus and the skull of Zinj. Then she painstakingly reconstructed both of these finds from hundreds of fragments. Within the profession, Louis was described as "flamboyant," Mary as meticulous and "scientific." Their son Richard, himself a distinguished archaeologist, talked about the mesh of their styles: "Her commitment to detail and perfection made my father's career. He would not have been famous without her. She was much more organized and structured and much more of a technician. He was much more excitable, a magician." The difference in styles, combined with Louis' attraction to many younger women, finally led to their estrangement, both personal and professional. After Louis' death, Mary's talents became even more clear when she discovered perhaps the most famous of all the Leakey discoveries, the 3.5-million-year-old hominid footprints at Laetoli (see picture opposite). Mary retired from active excavation in 1984 and died in Nairobi in 1996.

Louis and Mary Leakey examining the palate of the Zinj skull, 1959.

humans, and the Leakeys named them *Homo habilis*, "handy person," because of the stone tools they made and used in scavenging, hunting, and butchering food. The Leakeys' discoveries at Olduvai furthered the search for the ancestors of modern humans in several directions: they pushed back the date of the earliest known representative of the genus *Homo* to 1.5–2 million years ago; they indicated the extent of the tool-using capacity of these early *Homo* representatives; and they reconstructed the ecology of the region 2.5–1.5 million years ago, placing *Homo habilis* within it as hunter and scavenger. Along with the earlier discoveries of Dart and Broom, they identified Africa as the home of the earliest hominids and the earliest representatives of the genus *Homo*.

In the 1970s, Richard Leakey (1944–), the son of Louis and Mary, was excavating at Koobi Fora on the east side of Lake Turkana in Kenya, and he discovered additional bones of the species *Homo habilis*. The finds confirmed the size of its brain at about 650 cc; its opposable thumb, which allowed it to grip objects powerfully and manipulate them precisely, and thus to make tools; and its upright, bipedal (two-legged) walk, evident from the form of its thigh and leg bones.

Australopithecus afarensis

In 1974, at Hadar, Ethiopia, near the Awash River, Donald Johanson (1943–) discovered "Lucy," the first known representative of *Australopithecus afarensis*, named for the local Afar people. (Lucy herself was named for the popular Beatles song "Lucy in the Sky with Diamonds.") This important discovery pushed back the date of the earliest known hominid to about 3.2 million years B.P. Lucy's overall height was between 3 feet 6 inches and 4 feet (91–120 centimeters). Her weight was an estimated 60 pounds (27 kilograms). The archaeologists were able to uncover about 40 percent of her total skeleton. In later excavations at Hadar, numerous additional skeletons were found, including the first complete skull of an *Australopithecus afarensis*, discovered by Johanson in 1992.

The cranial capacity of Lucy and her fellow *Australopithecus afarensis* was only 400 cubic centimeters, too small for her to be a *Homo*. Her pelvis was too small to allow the birth of offspring with a larger skull, but the form of that pelvis, and the fit of her knee joints, characterized Lucy as a two-legged hominid. Lucy had walked upright. She was a kind of bipedal ape, and, in her

Hominid footprints, Laetoli, Northern Tanzania. These footprints in ash at Laetoli confirmed that hominids were walking upright 3.5 million years ago. The tracks suggest that *Australopithecus afarensis* had a slower, more rolling gait than modern man, although the prints reveal well-defined feet. Mary Leakey (pictured), who discovered the prints, saw in them a slight sideward turn, a hesitation in direction, which she interpreted as the first evidence of human doubt.

bipedalism, an ancestor of modern humans. Further evidence of the bipedalism of these apelike creatures came from Laetoli, Tanzania, where, in 1978, Mary Leakey discovered the footprints of two *Australopithecus afarensis* walking side by side. In volcanic ash, she found seventy footprints walking a distance of 80 feet (24 meters). The ash provided material for dating the prints; they were 3.5 million years old.

Ardipithecus ramidus

In 1994, seventeen fossils of a new genus, *Ardipithecus ramidus*, "ground ape," were discovered at Aramis in the bed of the Awash River not far from the Lucy find. They were analyzed by an international team of Tim White from the University of California at Berkeley, Gen Suwa from the University of Tokyo, and Berhane Asfaw from the Paleoanthropology laboratory of the Ethiopian Ministry of Culture and Sports Affairs. Ten of the fossils were teeth, two were from the cranium, the remainder were bones from the left arm. Later, the team recovered about 80

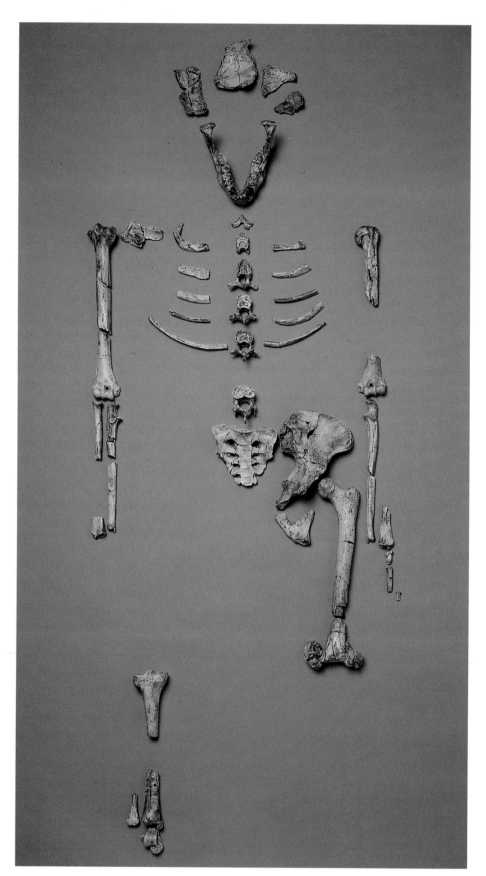

"Lucy" skeleton, *Australopithecus afarensis*, found at Hadar, Ethiopia. "Lucy" is thought to have lived about 3.2 million years ago and was at the time of her discovery in 1974 the earliest known hominid ancestor of modern man. She had humanlike hands and could walk upright; however, there is no evidence that she made or used tools, and her sturdy, curved arms are still consistent with tree-climbing. Until the discovery of Ardipithecus in 1994, Lucy was the most complete hominid skeleton from the period before 2 million years ago. (*Natural History Museum, London*)

percent of an *Ardipithecus ramidus* skeleton. It dated to 4.4 million years, pushing back the date of the earliest ape-like hominid by a half million years.

Because evolution is a process of change over time, there is no more discussion of *the* missing link between apes and humans, but *Ardipithecus ramidus* was *a* missing link in the evolutionary process.

> They [the fossils] represent the remains of a species that lies so close to the divergence between the lineages leading to the African apes and modern humans that its attribution to the human line is metaphorically—and literally—by the skin of its teeth. . . . The metaphor of a "missing link" has often been misused, but it is a suitable epithet for the hominid from Aramis. (Wood, pp. 280–1)

Homo sapiens

The earliest known anatomically modern *Homo sapiens* (Human, wise) fossil was discovered in 1967–8 by the anatomist Ronald Singer and the archaeologist John Wymer in caves at the Klasies River Mouth on the coast of South Africa. These fossil remains of the oldest known example of the species *Homo sapiens* date to 75,000 to 115,000 B.P. They include lower and upper jaws, skull fragments, teeth, and bones of limbs. With them were found thousands of stone quartzite tools, an abundance of bones from numerous land mammals, and the remains of hundreds of thousands of shellfish, suggesting a diet rich in meat and seafood. The Klasies River Mouth discovery raised most provocatively the question of where the first *Homo sapiens* emerged and how they spread.

Before turning to these questions relating to modern humans, let us summarize our current knowledge of the process of hominid evolution.

PUTTING IT ALL TOGETHER

A SUMMARY OF HOMINID EVOLUTION: WHAT DO WE KNOW?

Our account so far has emphasized How We Know. It has examined some of the major archaeological excavations that have shaped our current understanding of hominid evolution. Now we put those various discoveries into a framework that shows their relationship to one another. We begin to see how each discovery is a building block in our structure of understanding. The chart on page 18 represents that structure. Harvard biologist Stephen Jay Gould has called it the "luxuriant bush" of hominid evolution for we no longer see evolution as a straight-line process moving from apes to humans, but rather as a process resulting in many different species. The arrangement of skulls on page 19 is another representation of the chronology of evolution.

AFRICAN ORIGIN

Almost all paleoanthropologists and archaeologists believe that *Homo erectus* appeared first in Africa and spread from there to Asia and, perhaps, to Europe between 1 and 2 million years ago. But then the scholars split into two camps: the "multi-regionalists" argue that *Homo erectus* evolved into *Homo sapiens* in each region of migration; the "out-of-Africa" camp argues that *Homo erectus* evolved into *Homo sapiens* only in Africa and that about 100,000 years ago the new humans emigrated to the rest of the world in another wave of emigration from Africa. The former thesis is often called the candelabra theory, since it sees the evolutionary branches beginning far back in history in many different locations; the other is often designated the "Noah's Ark" theory, since it proposes a much more recent common ancestry in Africa (see diagram, p. 20).

The two groups of scholars therefore disagree on the origin of racial differentiation among humans. All agree that the varieties of racial development are responses to different ecological niches. If the evolution to *Homo sapiens* began in several different locations based on the *Homo erectus* species already having lived there for up to 2 million years, racial differentiation is very old. If all modern *Homo sapiens* share a common origin until just 100,000 years ago and began to differentiate by race only after emigrating from Africa to new locations, these differences are much more recent. At present, the "out-of-Africa" camp are in the majority. They point out that it is common for just one branch of any particular species to evolve into another and ultimately to displace all the other branches. Indeed, that process is more common than the mutual evolution of all the branches. They therefore tend to minimize the significance of race as a relatively recent, and only "skin-deep," difference among the peoples of the earth.

THE DOMINANT CURRENT VIEW OF THE EVOLUTIONARY PROCESS

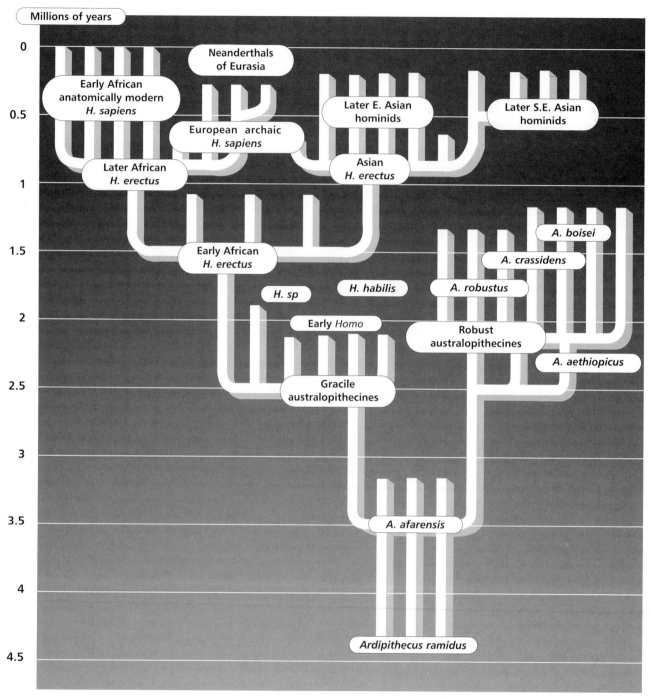

Popular thought usually imagines a straight-line development from apes to humans, but anthropologists speak of a human "bush," a variety of interacting and inter-breeding species that finally produced *Homo sapiens*. Most anthropological models see *Ardipithecus ramidus* and *Australopithecus afarensis* as the first steps in the branching-apart of humans from apes about 5 million years ago. One line of further evolution led toward modern *Homo sapiens*. All the other hominid forms, those in our own line and those in other lines, subsequently became extinct. The model above suggests that the final stages of evolution took place in Europe and Asia as well as Africa, thereby siding with the Candelabra thesis (see p. 20).

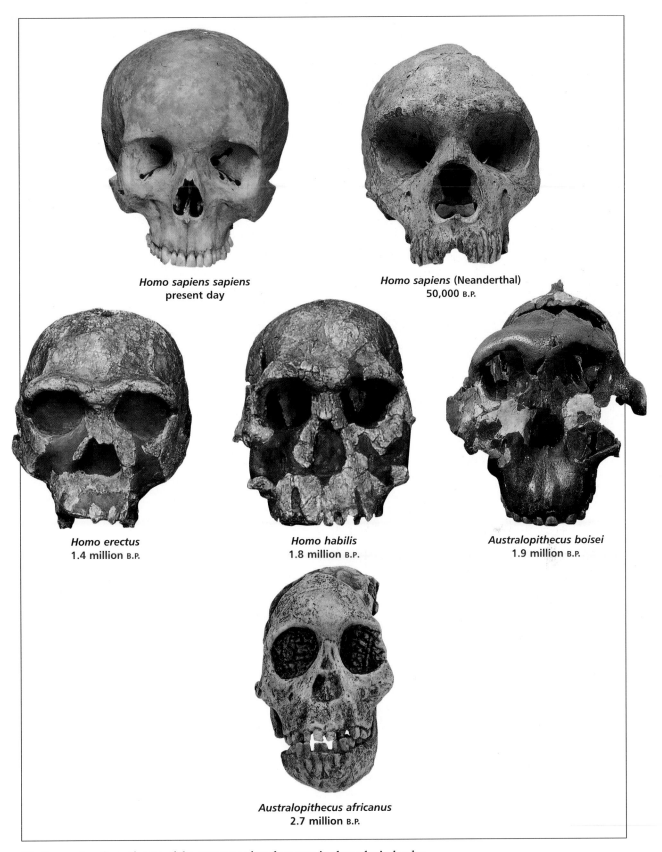

Homo sapiens sapiens
present day

Homo sapiens (Neanderthal)
50,000 B.P.

Homo erectus
1.4 million B.P.

Homo habilis
1.8 million B.P.

Australopithecus boisei
1.9 million B.P.

Australopithecus africanus
2.7 million B.P.

Skull reconstructions of some of the ancestors of modern man in chronological order.

CANDELABRA
No migration, no replacement

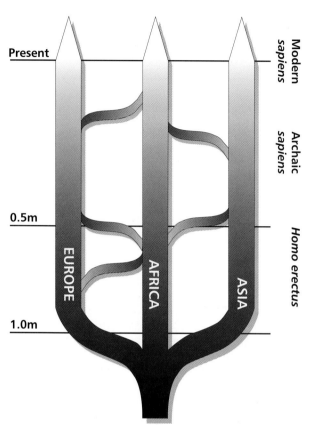

Present

Modern sapiens

Archaic sapiens

0.5m

Homo erectus

1.0m

EUROPE   AFRICA   ASIA

The candelabra, or multiregional, model suggests that *Homo erectus* emigrated from Africa throughout Europe and Asia and developed into *Homo sapiens* separately in all three regions. Some interbreeding did take place.

NOAH'S ARK
Migration, replacement

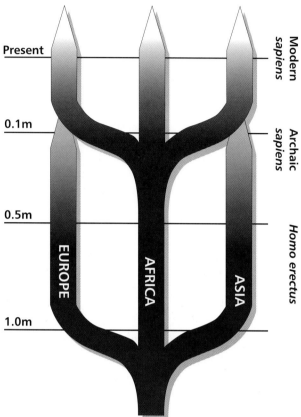

Present

Modern sapiens

0.1m

Archaic sapiens

0.5m

Homo erectus

1.0m

EUROPE   AFRICA   ASIA

The Noah's Ark model suggests that *Homo erectus* did emigrate from Africa, but then died out everywhere else. The evolution to *Homo sapiens* took place only among those that remained in Africa—who later emigrated to Europe and Asia.

READING THE GENETIC RECORD

In the search for the time and place of the origins of *Homo sapiens*, a different kind of discovery, based on genetics rather than fossils, on laboratory research rather than field excavations, emerged about thirty years ago. At the University of California at Berkeley and at Emory University in Atlanta, scientists began to study the DNA record of human and animal genes. DNA is each cell's chemical code of instructions for building proteins. The DNA research reveals the degrees of similarity and difference among the creatures studied.

Differences and similarities in the proteins and DNA of animals (including humans) living today suggest the date up to which they might have shared common ancestors before separating into different streams of evolution. In 1970, for example, biochemists Vincent Sarich and Allan Wilson first analyzed the protein albumin and the DNA of apes and humans and found that, genetically, modern humans are 97 percent the same as chimpanzees and 96 percent the same as gorillas. They argue that chimpanzees, gorillas, and humans must have shared common ancestors until about 5 million years ago when evolutionary separation must have occurred. This genetic dating matches and reinforces the fossil record.

Both Wilson and Emory scientist Douglas Wallace, extending the method further, have used mitochondrial DNA (genetic material found outside the cell nucleus) to hypothesize that *Homo sapiens* emerged solely from Africa around 100,000 years ago. This confirmation of the "out-of-Africa" theory is, however, controversial—and debate continues to rage. The journal *Nature* frequently carries the reports.

CULTURAL CHANGE AND BIOLOGICAL CHANGE

In addition to the physiological changes favored by natural selection, hominids began actively to shape their environment through cultural activities. *Homo habilis* sculpted stone tools of increasing sophistication. They apparently hunted, scavenged, and gathered in groups and shared their booty. Increasing facility in tool-making would mark all future stages of the evolution of the genus *Homo*.

As the *Homo* brain continued to develop and get bigger, it became impossible for the genus *Homo* to give birth through a relatively narrow birth canal to a child with a fully formed brain in a fully formed cranium. The brain capacity of the young must continue to develop for some time after birth. (The brain of a newborn human weighs about 14 ounces (400 grams), doubles to 35 ounces (990 grams) in about one year, and reaches 45 ounces (1.27 kilograms), adult size, only by about age six or seven.) Within the genus *Homo*, therefore, parents must devote significant time to nurturing and teaching their young children. In addition, in female *Homo sapiens* the oestrus cycle, the alternating period of fertility and infertility, occurs each month rather than seasonally, allowing them to bear children more frequently than other primates. Increased childbearing further increases the time and energy devoted to nurturing the young. Because of the increased attention to nurturing, cultural life could flourish.

Homo sapiens, like *Homo erectus* before them, migrated and spread over the entire earth, except the polar regions. Unlike their predecessors, however, they developed forms of symbolic expression, apparently spiritual and cultural in nature, including burial rituals and artwork that is sometimes stunningly beautiful and creative. These cultural forms suggest that about 35,000 years ago the human brain, but not the rest of human anatomy, went through some further evolutionary development. *Homo sapiens* (wise human) evolved into *Homo sapiens sapiens* (wise, wise human).

KEY STAGES IN HUMAN DEVELOPMENT

4.5 m B.C.E.	First appearance of bipedalism.
2 m B.C.E.	Change in structure of forelimbs—bipedalism is perfected. Gradual expansion and reorganization of the brain. Hunting, scavenging, and gathering cultures stimulate production of stone tools.
500,000 B.C.E.	Rapid brain growth.
200,000 B.C.E.	First forms of *Homo sapiens*. Early speech development. Fire now in use.
40,000 B.C.E.	Interglacial period. Existence of modern humans, with fully developed brain and speech. Tools constructed from component parts.
c. 25,000 B.C.E.	Cave art and portable art in Europe. Human migration begins from Asia into America.
10,000 B.C.E.	Invention of bow and arrows. Domestication of reindeer and dog (N. Eurasia). Settled food production.
8000–4000 B.C.E.	Increase of human population by 1500 percent. Domestication of sheep and goats (Near East). Earliest pottery (Japan). Farming spreads to W. Europe. Rice cultivation starts in Asia.
3000 B.C.E.	Writing, metals.

KEY QUESTIONS REMAINING

The study of early hominids and their evolution into *Homo sapiens sapiens* is filled with questions. Every new excavation and laboratory method of analysis presents new data but often raises questions as well. Sometimes a new discovery can be easily assimilated into existing models: *Ardipithecus ramidus*, for example, had a place ready for it in the evolutionary charts. "The presence of a hominid much like it had been predicted" (Wood, p. 281). Sometimes, however, discoveries are unexpected and create new problems. The analysis of mtDNA, at first viewed as a breakthrough in our understanding of an "African Eve," later posed challenges of method, interpretation, and reliability that remain unresolved.

At present, archaeologists and paleoanthropologists are asking these major questions:

FOCUS
Gender Issues and Cultural Evolution

In 1971 anthropologist Sally Slocum, writing under the pseudonym of Sally Linton, published one of the first feminist critiques of the current understanding of the evolution of hominids. Slocum was responding to a conference and set of papers published from it in 1968 entitled *Man the Hunter*. One of the papers, by Sherwood Washburn and C. Lancaster, asserted: "The biology, psychology, and customs that separate us from the apes—all these we owe to the hunters of time past." This argument, Slocum replied, put excessive emphasis on aggressive behavior, the tools and organized planning required for hunting, the importance of fresh meat in the hominid diet, and male activities generally.

In "Woman the Gatherer: Male Bias in Anthropology," Slocum asserts that gathering was more important than hunting:

> We know that gathering was important long before much animal protein was added to the diet, and continued to be important. Bones, sticks, and hand-axes could be used for digging up tubers or roots, or to pulverize tough vegetable matter for easier eating. If, however, instead of thinking in terms of tools and weapons, we think in terms of *cultural inventions*, a new aspect is presented. I suggest that two of the *earliest and most important* cultural inventions were containers to hold the products of gathering, and some sort of sling or net to carry babies. (p. 46)

Further, she argues, the skills of raising and nurturing young children, usually women's tasks, evoked more innovation and perhaps more development of the brain than did hunting:

> I suggest that longer periods of infant dependency, more difficult births, and longer gestation periods also demanded more skills in social organization and communication—creating selective pressure for increased brain size without looking to hunting as an explanation. The need to organize for feeding after weaning, learning to handle the more complex social–emotional bonds that were developing, the new skills and cultural inventions surrounding more extensive gathering—all would demand larger brains. Too much attention has been given to the skills required by hunting, and too little to the skills required for gathering and the raising of dependent young. The techniques required for efficient gathering include location and identification of plant varieties, seasonal and geographical knowledge, containers for carrying the food, and tools for its preparation. (pp. 46–7)

Slocum concluded that she could reach her new interpretations only after confronting assumptions of male dominance. As she puts it, "The basis of any discipline is not the answers it gets, but the questions it asks."

1 Did *Homo sapiens* evolve in a more or less straight line, family tree development from *Ardipithecus ramidus* and *Australopithecus afarensis* through *Homo habilis* and *Homo erectus*, or was there a "bush" of clades, related species, and subspecies at every level? Was the development through that "bush" different from evolution supported by the majority of paleoanthropologists?

2 In what ecological environment did the australopithecines live? *Australopithecus afarensis*, according to Johanson and the Leakeys, seemed to inhabit a savanna region in which bipedalism was an advantage in crossing open land quickly and efficiently. Paleoecological studies surrounding *Ardipithecus ramidus*, however, suggest a wooded habitat.

3 What were the group living conditions of australopithecines and of the genus *Homo*? Were they monogamous, as some researchers have claimed? Did they live in groups, and if so, of what size? Clearly they came together to hunt, scavenge, and share the preparation and eating of food, but did they also live more permanently at home bases?

4 To what extent did early members of the genus *Homo* hunt and to what extent did they forage and scavenge? Apparently they did both, hunting small game and scavenging the remains of big game left over from the kills of predatory animals. Further studies of regional ecology and of fossils of human prey will reveal more about the diet of our early ancestors and their method of food procurement.

5 Fire was first used and then controlled by *Homo erectus*, perhaps 1 million years ago, as discovered in the Swartkrans cave in South Africa, more certainly in China 500,000 years ago. Fire gave warmth, light, protection from predators, a means of cooking food, a hearth around which a feeling of community could develop, and thus the capacity of turning a cave into a home. Can we know more about when and how this mastery occurred?

6 Why did each of the evolutionary lines die out, the various *Australopithecus robustus* and *boisei* species of 1–2 million years ago, the later hominids of east and southeast Asia, and the "archaic" *Homo* species of approximately 100,000 years ago, such as *Homo sapiens neanderthalensis*?

7 When did the genus *Homo* become capable of speech? What is the relationship between the biological evolution of *Homo* and the mastery of new cultural skills, such as control of fire, group planning, tool-making, speech, and the use of symbols? To what extent do biological changes enable cultural change? Conversely, to what extent do cultural advances enable species to survive biologically, perpetuating themselves and their offspring?

8 What was the division of labor between males and females in the various hominid species? Were males more likely to hunt and scavenge abroad, and females more likely to raise children and gather food near to home? (see Focus opposite). What was the significance of the large difference in size between males and females among the australopithecines?

THE THEORY OF SCIENTIFIC REVOLUTION

We have given a lengthy introduction on the emergence of the first humans. Many historians would choose to move more quickly toward the present, although, of course, in covering 4.5 million years in one chapter we *are* moving swiftly! Some historians would be more comfortable covering "historic" times and places—that is, working with written records—but we have chosen to elaborate this account not only for its intrinsic interest but also because it helps demonstrate most clearly our concern with "how we know" as well as with "what we know," a concern that continues throughout this text.

Paleoanthropologists maintain a lively debate about each of their findings and interpretations. They not only present their views but situate them within the ongoing debates in their field. This admirable procedure should inform all historical research and presentation, showing the historical record as an ongoing search and argument. Existing data may be reevaluated; new data may be added; interpretations may be revised; new questions may arise. The historical record is never complete.

Amendments to the historical record, however, are usually minor additions to, or revisions of, a pattern already well known. Thomas Kuhn, in his pathbreaking study of the history of science, *The Structure of Scientific Revolutions*, wrote of his own field that

> normal science . . . is a highly cumulative enterprise, eminently successful in its aim, the steady extension of the scope and precision of scientific knowledge. Normal science does not aim at novelties of fact or theory and, when successful, finds none. (Kuhn, p. 52)

The history of the evolution of hominids, for example, usually follows this pattern of "normal science." Thus when *Ardipithecus ramidus* was discovered in 1994, paleoanthropologists were not surprised. "There was . . . enough 'morphological space' between the hypothetical common ancestor of African apes and hominids, on the one hand, and *A. afarensis* on the other, to predict that a hominid, as yet undiscovered, would occupy it" (Wood in *Nature*, p. 281). This was normal science filling in an existing model, or paradigm, with new detail.

Sometimes, however, new discoveries challenge existing paradigms. At first the new discoveries are discounted as exceptions to the rule. But when the anomalies increase, scientists seek new explanatory paradigms. Darwin's breakthrough followed this second pattern of scientific revolution. His discoveries on the voyage of the *Beagle* and his subsequent analyses of his findings challenged the existing concepts of creation that were based on biblical narratives. Darwin provided a radically different scientific explanation of the mechanisms of evolution that displaced the biblical paradigm. Both Darwin's scientific analysis and Genesis' mythological narrative, however, postulate the creation of an entire cosmos and world, replete with flora and fauna, before humans achieve their place in the universe and begin to name the other species.

Major revisions of the historical record often follow a similar trajectory. A general pattern of explanation is followed until new research raises new questions and new theoretical paradigms provide more fitting explanations for all the available data and information. Throughout this text we shall continue to see changes in historical explanation over time. A "paradigm shift" may occur not only as a result of the discovery of new data, or of new interpretations better fitting the available data, but also in response to new questions being raised that may not have been asked before. The historical record, like the scientific record on evolution, is always subject to reevaluation.

HUMANS CREATE CULTURE

The first appearance of *Homo sapiens* in the archaeological record dates to about 120,000 years ago in South Africa at the Klasies River Mouth excavation, although the DNA record suggests that their first appearance might have been as early as 250,000 B.C.E. Since that time the species

Two Aurignacian implements, France, Mesolithic era (*c.* 30,000 B.C.E.). Stone Age cultures first appeared in western Europe in 33,000 B.C.E. and underwent constant changes in technology—implying a gradual evolution in human behavior. By the Aurignacian era, flint-end scrapers (right) were employed in processing skins, woodworking, and carving artifacts like this bone spearpoint (left). (*Natural History Museum, London*)

Homo sapiens has not changed anatomically. The skeletons unearthed at the Klasies River Mouth are no different from our own. About 100,000–50,000 years B.C.E., however, a new creativity appeared in the cultural and social life of *Homo sapiens*, perhaps the result of a modification in the internal structure of the brain. The people who lived before this development are called "archaic" *Homo sapiens*; those with the new cultural capabilities are considered a new subspecies, *Homo sapiens sapiens* (Human wise, wise). They are us.

The remainder of this chapter presents seven creative behaviors that mark the arrival of *Homo sapiens sapiens*. First, we persisted. We are the lone survivor from among all the hominids of the last 5 million years. Second, we continued to spread to all parts of the globe in waves of migration that had begun even earlier. Third, we built small, temporary settlements to serve as base camps for hunting and gathering. Fourth, we continued to craft more sophisticated tools from stone. The steady improvements in tool technology give this period its archaeological names. The entire period is called the old stone age, **Paleolithic**, and exhibits slow progression from the Lower Paleolithic, older old stone age, the remains of which are found lower in the ground, ending about 150,000 B.C.E., to the newer old stone age or Upper Paleolithic, which continued to about 10,000 B.C.E. (The Mesolithic and Neolithic, middle and new stone ages, 8000–6000 B.C.E. and 6000 B.C.E. to about 3000 B.C.E., respectively, will be explored in Chapter 2.) Fifth, by about 25,000 B.C.E., on cave walls and in stone, we began to paint and sculpt magnificent works of art and symbolism. Sixth, we elaborated more sophisticated use of language. Seventh, by 10,000–15,000 B.C.E., we began to domesticate plants and animals, introducing the art and science of agriculture.

HOW DID WE SURVIVE?
HOW DO WE KNOW?

From about 120,000 B.C.E., when we first appear in the archaeological record, until about 35,000 B.C.E., anatomically modern *Homo sapiens sapiens* seems to have coexisted alongside archaic *Homo sapiens* in several sites. The best studied are caves in the area of Mount Carmel near Haifa, Israel. First excavated in 1929 by Dorothy Garrod of Cambridge University, these caves have revealed skeletons and tools of both Neanderthals and modern humans. The fossils from the Tabun, Amud, and Kebara caves seem to be Neanderthals; those from Skhul and Qafzeh appear more modern.

DATING ARCHAEOLOGICAL FINDS

Continuous improvements in dating techniques have changed our understanding of the relationships among the *Homo* residents who inhabited these caves. The most common technique, since its discovery in 1949, is **radiocarbon dating**, sometimes called the carbon 14 (C14) method. Living organisms contain the same percentage of atoms of radioactive carbon as the atmosphere in which they live. When they die, the radiocarbon atoms disintegrate at a steady, known rate. By measuring the amount of radiocarbon remaining in a fossil skeleton, scientists can calculate backward to the date of death. Because the total amount of radiocarbon in any organism is small, little is left after 40,000 years, and the method does not work at all beyond 70,000 years. Until 1987, paleoanthropologists using carbon 14 dating believed that Neanderthals dated to approximately 60,000–50,000 years B.C.E., and *Homo sapiens sapiens* to 50,000–45,000.

After 1987, the method of **thermoluminescence** was applied to burned flints discovered in the caves. Radioactivity occurring in nature releases electrons in flint and clay, but they can finally escape only when the substance is heated. When the flints were first burned by the people of the caves, the electrons freed up to that time were released. Reheating the flints in the laboratory today releases the electrons stored up since the first burning. Scientists calculate the date of the first burning by measuring the light of those electrons. This technique works not only for burnt flint from 50,000–300,000 years of age, but also for burnt clay, enabling scientists to date pottery from the last 10,000 years.

The measurement of age through thermoluminescence gave new and astounding dates to the skeletons in the caves. The oldest Neanderthal, from Tabun, dated to 120,000–100,000 B.C.E.; the two *Homo sapiens sapiens* at Qafzeh and Skhul were almost equally old, at 92,000 B.C.E.; the two Neanderthal specimens at Kebara and Amud dated to 60,000–50,000 B.C.E. One can only conclude, therefore, that Neanderthals and modern humans had coexisted in the area of modern Israel for tens of thousands of years. Moreover, they had shared similar types of tools. The simpler, smaller Mousterian stone tools (named for the village of Le Moustier in southwestern France where they have been most clearly documented) of the Neanderthals were used alongside the thinner, longer, more precisely crafted Aurignacian tools (named for another hunter-gatherer site in southern France) of the moderns.

How, then, did modern *Homo sapiens sapiens* eventually displace all other hominids? Three principal interpretations, in various combinations, have been suggested. The first is that modern humans defeated all the other hominids through aggression, warfare, and murder. This theory suggests a violent streak in the earliest humans. The second theory suggests that processes of mating and reproduction among the species bred the new human. This suggests that our immediate ancestors made love not war, and that we contain a Neanderthal heritage. Finally, it has been proposed that modern humans successfully filled up the ecological niche available, outcompeting archaic *Homo sapiens* for the available resources. According to this final theory, modern humans did not directly confront the archaic forms but displaced them—in a sense, we ate them out of house and home.

GLOBAL MIGRATION

Homo sapiens sapiens appeared in Africa not later than 120,000 B.C.E., evolving from *Homo erectus*. Within 30,000 years the species began to appear throughout Europe and Asia. Harvard anthropologist Clive Gamble asserts that it was not

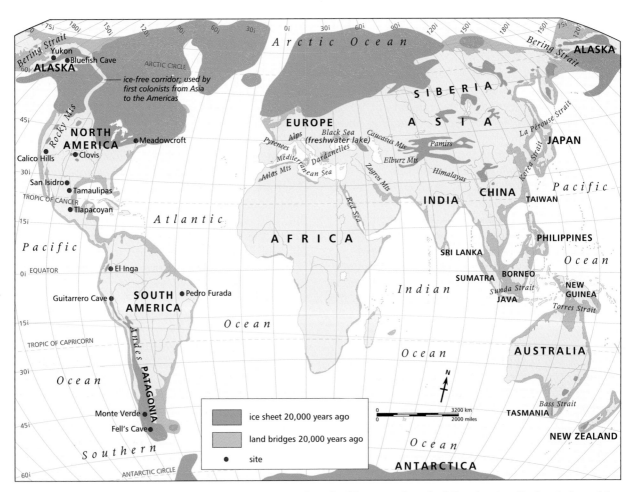

Early humans in the Ice Age By 20,000 B.C.E., when ice covered much of Europe and much of Canada, virtually the whole world (except Polynesia) had been colonized. Early humans were able to spread north because water frozen into ice sheets reduced sea levels so much that land bridges appeared, linking most major areas. The cold was intense, and the migrants' survival depended on their ability to stitch together animal hides into primitive clothing, control fire, and hunt large mammals.

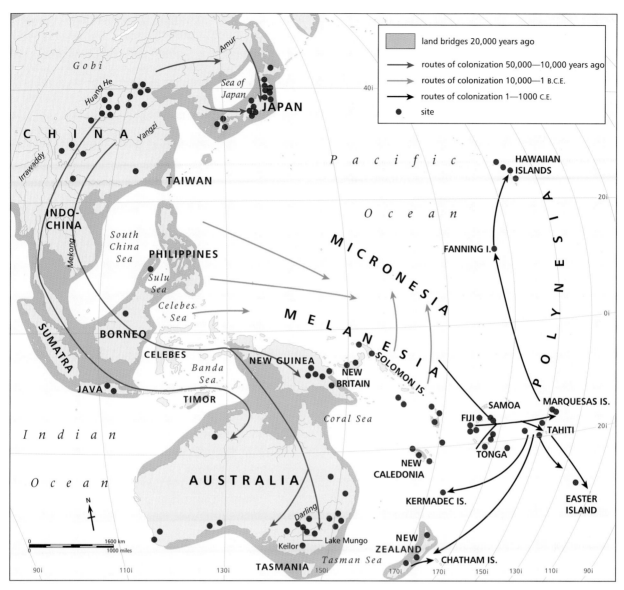

The colonization of the Pacific The land bridges of the last Ice Age enabled early humans to spread south from China to Java and Borneo. There some knowledge of navigation was required to cross the Banda Sea to New Guinea and Australia. The most spectacular voyages were undertaken by the Polynesians, who journeyed hundreds and thousands of miles by canoe into the uncharted Pacific waters.

simply a part of human nature to migrate around the globe. Rather, each migration was purposeful and specific. From earliest prehistory, people weighed their choices and opportunities, and chose appropriate actions. Global migration was the ultimate outcome.

Brian Fagan's analysis of the "Saharan pump" provides an example of such migration. Up to about 90,000 B.C.E., when the earth was in a warm, wet stage, the Sahara region was fertile and attractive to human settlement, and people and animals from southern Africa migrated there. But

then began an "ice age," one of the periods of global cooling that have affected the earth's climate over millions of years. When the ice age of about 90,000 B.C.E. began, much of the earth's water was frozen. The Sahara dried up, turning the land to desert, and people and animals emigrated. Some may have turned back to southern Africa; some may have journeyed toward the North African coast (a few archaeologists believe that they may have crossed the Straits of Gibraltar into western Europe); still others may have followed the Nile valley corridor into western Asia. So began what Fagan calls *The Journey from Eden*, the first step in a global process of migration.

To reach the most distant areas, such as Australia, the islands of the Pacific, and the Americas, took tens of thousands of years. These migrations required changes in climate as well as in the skills of *Homo sapiens sapiens*. The successive ice ages of 90,000–10,000 years ago froze much of the water of the seas, reducing sea levels, extending the coasts of the continents, and creating land bridges linking modern China with Japan, southeast Asia with the Philippines and Indonesia, and Siberia with Alaska. As long as the ice ages continued and the waters of seas and oceans were in frozen retreat, people could migrate across land passages. There were exceptions. The Pacific islands known as Polynesia were not connected by land bridges to anywhere. This helps explain why they were peopled so much later in history than most other regions. Only in 1000 B.C.E. was Polynesia colonized by native New Guineans, performing extraordinary feats of navigation in simple canoes.

INCREASED POPULATION AND NEW SETTLEMENTS

Gradually, as human population expanded, so, too, did the number of human groups and the closeness or "density" of their relationships to one another. Such increasing density and population pressure became a staple of human history. Some groups chose to stand and fight for their territory, others reached accommodation with newcomers, and yet others emigrated, either by choice or by force, following losses in battle. These patterns, too, have repeated themselves for tens of thousands of years, and today there are some 20 million refugees in the world.

How large were these groups? They had to include enough members to provide security in defense and cooperation in work, yet be small enough to resolve the interpersonal frictions that threatened the cohesion of the group and the safety of its members. Calculated from the experience of modern hunter-gatherers, such as the Khoisan of the African Kalahari Desert, and theoretical mathematical models of group process, a five-family group of twenty-five persons seems the ideal balance. Mating and marriage rules

might well have required, as they often do today, choosing a mate from outside the immediate band. For such an **exogamous** marriage pattern to function, "a tribe would require at least 475 people to provide an adequate mating pool or a mating network of nineteen twenty-five-member bands, a theoretical figure reasonably close to the real life 500" found in modern hunter-gatherer societies, concludes anthropologist John Pfeiffer in *The Creative Explosion* (p. 192).

How much territory did such bands require to support themselves? Anthropologist H. Martin Wobst calculated that an individual using the technology of Upper Paleolithic times (150,000 –10,000 B.C.E.) would have required 77 square miles (200 square kilometers) of relatively unproductive land or 7–8 square miles (20 square kilometers) of fertile land to meet survival needs. At such densities, the area of the United States (excluding Alaska and Hawaii) might have supported a maximum of 600,000 people; the entire world, 10 million at most, although actual populations were less. Bands began to stake out their own territories, and to mark out boundaries.

> There is increasing evidence that Upper Paleolithic groups may have occupied certain key locations on a more stable, semi-permanent basis, which would almost inevitably act as a further incentive to the definition of more sharply defined social territories, and to a more formalized pattern of reciprocal relationships between the occupants of adjacent territories. (Mellars, p. 356)

The groups began to establish small settlements. The Neanderthals had occupied upland sites, but the later Cro-Magnon *Homo sapiens sapiens* (named for the region in France where this subspecies was originally discovered) moved down into the more valuable valleys and riverbeds. About half of their sites are within 1100 yards (1000 meters) of a river, and all of them are near fords or shallows. These sites not only allow for easy crossing, but they are also at the points of animal crossings and therefore good for hunting.

Tools took on regional patterns both in processes of manufacture and in styles of aesthetic appearance. These local patterns marked off each group from its neighbors. Mellars argues that this regional, tribal differentiation, marking the production of increasingly sophisticated tools, suggests also the development of "relatively complex, structured language" (Mellars, p. 359) (see p. 34).

CHANGES IN THE TOOLKIT

STONE TOOLS

Even as the pace of exploration, migration, and trade increased, the clearest changes in human development appeared in our stone toolkits. From about 2.5 million years ago until about 150,000 years ago, the dominant technology of *Homo erectus* had been Acheulian hand-held axes and cleavers made of stone (named for St. Acheul

THE EARLIEST TOOL KITS

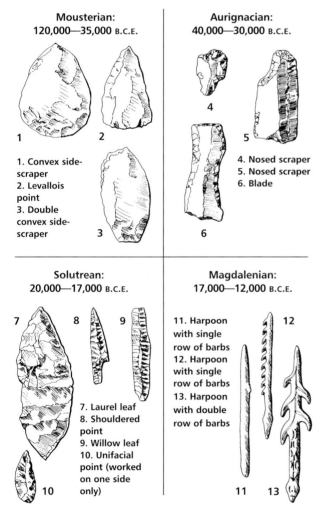

Mousterian:
120,000—35,000 B.C.E.

1
2
3

1. Convex side-scraper
2. Levallois point
3. Double convex side-scraper

Aurignacian:
40,000—30,000 B.C.E.

4
5
6

4. Nosed scraper
5. Nosed scraper
6. Blade

Solutrean:
20,000—17,000 B.C.E.

7 8 9
10

7. Laurel leaf
8. Shouldered point
9. Willow leaf
10. Unifacial point (worked on one side only)

Magdalenian:
17,000—12,000 B.C.E.

11. Harpoon with single row of barbs
12. Harpoon with single row of barbs
13. Harpoon with double row of barbs

11 12 13

Many of the earliest human tools were crafted from stone and show increasing sophistication. The "tool kits" shown here are named for the four different locations in which they were found. At first, humans simply chipped away at stone until edges and points were exposed. Later they began to carve the stone to meet more specific needs. The development took 100,000 years.

in northern France, but actually developed first in Africa and only later throughout Europe and Asia).

About 250,000 B.C.E. the European sites, and some elsewhere, reveal a more sophisticated technique, the Levallois (named for a suburb in Paris where the first examples were discovered). This Levallois technique produced more precise tools, including side scrapers and backed knives, fashioned by more consistent patterns of preparing flakes from the stone, and a more standardized final shape and size. This technique marked the emergence of archaic *Homo sapiens*.

The technology of *Homo sapiens sapiens* developed much more rapidly. By about 40,000 B.C.E., Aurignacian tools were being produced in or near a cave near the present-day village of Aurignac in the Pyrenees. This technology included narrow blades of stone as well as tools crafted from bone, ivory, and antler. Gravettian styles followed, about 30,000 to about 20,000 B.C.E; then came Solutrean styles, 20,000–17,000 B.C.E., which included the production of the first known needles; Magdalenian, about 17,000–12,000 B.C.E., which included barbed harpoons carved from antlers; and finally Azilian, 12,000–8000 B.C.E. Each location and time period had its own aesthetic style, and each produced an increasing variety of tools. Tool patterns began to differ increasingly from one region to another, suggesting the formation of new communities among small hunter-gatherer bands, and a greater sense of separation and distinction between groups.

Not all tools were directly related to food production, nor even to work. Flutes from as early as 35,000 B.C.E., made from the bones of birds, reindeer, and bears, suggest that creating and performing instrumental music had already become part of the human repertoire. Aesthetics and play already had their roles.

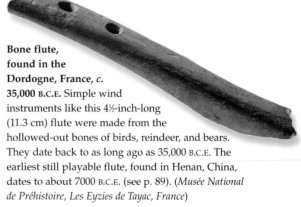

Bone flute, found in the Dordogne, France, *c.* 35,000 B.C.E. Simple wind instruments like this 4½-inch-long (11.3 cm) flute were made from the hollowed-out bones of birds, reindeer, and bears. They date back to as long ago as 35,000 B.C.E. The earliest still playable flute, found in Henan, China, dates to about 7000 B.C.E. (see p. 89). (*Musée National de Préhistoire, Les Eyzies de Tayac, France*)

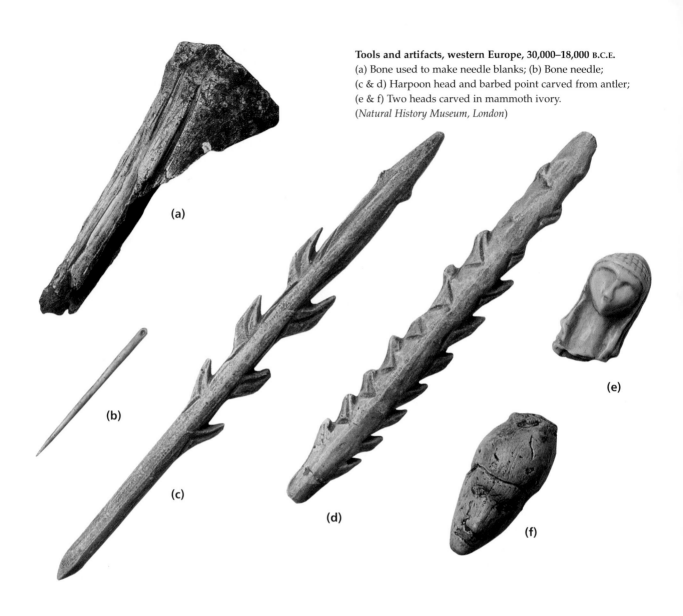

Tools and artifacts, western Europe, 30,000–18,000 B.C.E.
(a) Bone used to make needle blanks; (b) Bone needle;
(c & d) Harpoon head and barbed point carved from antler;
(e & f) Two heads carved in mammoth ivory.
(*Natural History Museum, London*)

(a)

(b)

(c)

(d)

(e)

(f)

Spearthrower, Montastruc, France, 12,000
B.C.E. More than 14,000 years ago, beauty played
an integral part in purely functional objects.
Spearthrowers allowed hunters to propel their missiles
with a surer aim and added leverage, as is symbolized by
the streamlined and powerful figure of this leaping horse. Did
the shape of the bone suggest the animal, or did the artist
search for a bone to match his (or her) preconceived idea?

CAVE ART
AND PORTABLE ART

Finds of artwork from before 35,000 B.C.E., such as
beads, pendants, and incised animal bones, are rare
and disputed. Cave paintings and the statuettes
came later, and they appeared in numerous sites
around the world. At Kundusi, Tanzania, Mary
Leakey discovered stylized ocher paintings of
human beings dating back perhaps 25,000 years.
On the southern coast of Australia, in the
Koonalda Cave, a flint mine at least 20,000
years old, a crisscross of abstract
finger patterns was engraved
into the soft limestone. In

eastern Australia at about the same time, people were stenciling images of a hand and a pipe and stem onto the walls of Kenniff Cave. And at Kakadu, in northern Australia, a series of rock paintings begin about 20,000 B.C.E. Local peoples continued to paint new ones almost to the present.

In Europe, the artwork begins with some figurines and some wall painting as early as 30,000 B.C.E. and climaxes about 17,000–12,000 B.C.E. More than 200 decorated caves and more than 10,000 decorated objects (portable art) have been discovered in Europe, 85 percent of them in southern France and northern Spain. Many of the tools from the Magdalenian period, as noted above, were fashioned to be beautiful as well as practical. Many of the figurines include delicately carved features, such as the face and hair on the figurine from about 22,000 B.C.E. discovered at Brassempouy, France, and only about 1½ inches (4 centimeters) high (see picture (e), opposite). Many others pay scant attention to face and personal features, but accentuate and exaggerate sexual organs and buttocks, such as the 25,000-year-old figurine discovered at Dolní Vestonice, Moravia. On some cave walls, people have created bas reliefs, shallow sculptures still attached to the rock, of similarly exaggerated female forms. The portable art represents a desire to create and enjoy beautiful objects. The exaggerated forms of the female, "Venus" objects that appear throughout Europe and on into northwestern Asia suggest also a desire for human fertility.

FOCUS
Women's Tools, Women's Work

Not all tools have survived. Those made from natural fibers have, of course, disintegrated, which precludes exploring the preparation of food and clothing. A fascinating book by Elizabeth Wayland Barber, *Women's Work: The First 20,000 Years: Women, Cloth, and Society in Early Times*, explains why these functions usually belonged to women. Barber cites an article by anthropologist Judith Brown that argues that most societies have decided, overtly or tacitly, that women's work must be compatible with the demands of child care. Women can and do undertake all kinds of work, but the only work on which the community relies on a regular basis is work compatible with child care, including pregnancy, breast feeding, and child watching.

> Such activities have the following characteristics: they do not require rapt concentration and are relatively dull and repetitive; they are easily interruptable and easily resumed once interrupted; they do not place the child in potential danger; and they do not require the participant to range very far from home. (Brown, cited in Barber, pp. 29–30)

What tasks fit this description? Spinning, weaving, sewing, and food preparation. "Food and clothing: These are what societies worldwide have come to see as the core of women's work (although other tasks may be added to the load, depending upon the circumstances of the particular society)" (Barber, p. 30). For historians of the stone age, the problem of presenting this aspect of the human record is in finding evidence, because food substances and textiles decay with hardly a trace.

What can we speculate about the first clothing? Some "Venus" figures (see p. 32) had sculpted on them skirts made of twisted strings suspended from a hip band. The sculpture itself indicates that woven strings of fiber rather than a single piece of leather were worn. Speculating on the use of these early string skirts, Barber notes that they would not have provided much warmth or protection, and she suggests that they were symbolic of the sexually attractive see-through adornments that women must have worn to attract men or to invoke spirits to increase their fertility. The further representation of loosely woven, transparent, short skirts on later sculptures supports these theories. Combining artifacts from the past and examples from the present, historians begin to reconstruct a whole area of technological development, most likely in the hands of women, that had been overlooked through the focus on stone tools.

The first of the cave art was rediscovered only in 1868, although the 14,000-year-old art of this cave, at Altamira near Santander, Spain, was not recognized as prehistoric until 1902. By now, 200 caves decorated with artworks have been discovered in Europe, most of them in the river valleys of southwest France and the adjacent Pyrenees and the Cantabrian Mountains of northern Spain. The latest discoveries, stunning in the variety of animal life depicted and the artistry employed, have been the Cosquer Cave in 1991 and the Chauvet Cave in December 1994. The painters used natural pigments like ocher that produced reds, browns, and yellows, and manganese oxides that made black and violet. Blues and greens have not been found. Human figures are rare in the European caves, the usual representations being of large animals, such as bison, deer, wild oxen, and horses. Occasionally there are mammoths, lions, and even fish. Fantasy figures, such as unicorns, also appear. At caves such as Le Tuc d'Audoubert, France, sculptures of clay bison have been found. In many caves, human hands have been stenciled onto cave walls by projecting pigment around the hands. No one knows how the pigments were applied, but the most common guess is that they were chewed and then either spat directly or blown through a pipe onto the walls.

Some of the cave art was abstract, some representational, some painted, some in relief, but it was not continued past the Magdalenian age, about 12,000 B.C.E, when the traditions and their meanings were abandoned. Many of the techniques of the cave paintings, such as perspective and the feeling of movement, did not reappear in Western art until the Renaissance, about 1400 C.E. (see p. 404). When the cave art was rediscovered in the nineteenth century, its antiquity was not understood. Ever since its rediscovery, however, people have wondered about its function and meaning.

The first interpretation to gain widespread acceptance argued that the paintings represented a kind of magic designed to bring good fortune to the hunters of the animals represented on the cave walls. The seemingly abstract geometrical patterns, argued the Abbé Henri Breuil, represented hunting equipment such as traps, snares, and

Clay bison, from Tuc d'Audoubert, Ariège, France, after 15,000 B.C.E. Most cave art owes its survival to the very particular atmospheric conditions formed in the limestone caves in which they were sealed thousands of years ago. Only a very small number of sculptures have survived. The one reproduced here—in high relief—shows a female being pursued by a male bison.

weapons. The mural paintings of animals may represent a hope for their fertility so that the hunters might find abundant prey. Other interpretations of the functions of the cave art followed. Margaret Conkey, author of *Art and Design in the Old Stone Age*, argued that the caves were meeting grounds to which neighboring bands of people returned each year to arrange marriages and to cement political and social alliances. The different styles of paintings in each cave represent the artistic production of many different groups.

The art is often located not at the mouth of the cave, where it would have been on daily view of the campsites, but deep in the inner recesses. Why were so many images—about one-third of the total—painted so deep in the caves? It has been suggested that they were not just decorative, but

"Venus" figurine, found at Dolní Vestonice, Moravia, c. 23,000 B.C.E. Several hundred early female figures have been recovered, but no male figures. This seems to support the thesis that these statuettes were created, not so much as representations of ideal feminine beauty, but as fertility charms—notice how the breasts, buttocks, and thighs are emphasized to the exclusion of any individualizing facial traits.

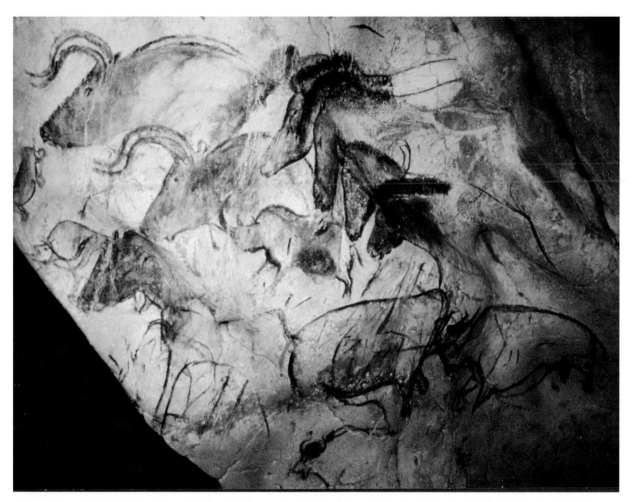

Chauvet Cave, Rhône-Alpes region, France, 18,000 B.C.E. On Christmas Day 1994, a team of archaeologists led by Jean-Marie Chauvet discovered a cave 1640 feet (500 m) deep in the Ardèche River Canyon. The cave's 300-plus Paleolithic wall paintings of horses, buffalo, and lions are the earliest examples anywhere in the world.

were links to ancient spirits, which were remembered and invoked in the dark depths of the cave. David Lewis-Williams, a South African archaeologist trying to puzzle through the origins of the cave art not only in western Europe but also in Namibia, southern Africa, where cave art goes back more than 25,000 years, observed the shamanistic rituals of the San people of the Kalahari desert. Shamans self-induce trances through the use of drugs, breathing exercises, singing, dancing, and rhythmic clapping. They enter into trance states of increasing intensity in which they "see" first geometric patterns, then images from nature, and finally creatures not found in nature at all. Sometimes they see these various images as projections on the wall. Lewis-Williams suggests that the Upper Paleolithic cave paintings represent such shamanistic hallucinations or visions from trance states.

The cave art and the portable art of 25,000–10,000 B.C.E. begin the known record of human aesthetic creation. For the first time we have examples of what humans felt to be beautiful and therefore worth creating and preserving. From this time onward, the desire to create and appreciate beauty is part of the human story. The cave creations also give us insight into their creators' search for meaning and purpose in life. Our art gives outward expression to our understanding of and our deepest feelings about our place in the world. In our art we express our fears and our hopes for ourselves, our loved ones, our communities, our world. Through our art we attempt to connect with larger forces in the world and to communicate with one another. By studying the form and meaning of art, historians attempt to understand the external aesthetics and the inner world of the people who produced it.

LANGUAGE AND COMMUNICATION

Language is an intangible innovation, invisible in the archaeological record. It must be inferred from more solid evidence: global migration, fixed settlement sites, new tools and new materials, regional differences in production, trade across long distances, social hierarchies often marked by personal adornment and ritual burials, and the creation of art and instrumental music. Lewis Binford concludes:

> If you ask "what makes this possible," you'd say intelligence, yes. But more important is language, and, specifically, symboling, which makes abstraction possible. I don't see any medium through which such a rapid change could occur other than a fundamentally good, biologically based communication system. (cited in Lewin, p. 163)

Exactly when the system of spoken language emerged is much debated, especially because we can only infer the answer from circumstantial evidence. The craniums of archaic *Homo sapiens*, such as Neanderthals, were as large as, or even larger than our own, and they seem to have indentations indicating the presence of areas in the brain that influence speech capacity. Archaic *Homo sapiens* probably possessed a larynx that had descended sufficiently low in the throat to produce the sounds of modern human language.

The dispute enters here. Some anthropologists believe that with this biological equipment, humans began slowly to develop modern language and speech through cultural evolution. Others, notably linguist Noam Chomsky, believe that a change took place within the organization of the brain that gave humans a new capacity for language. Chomsky draws his conclusion from analyzing similarities in the "deep structure" of languages around the world. These universal similarities suggest that the rules of syntax of human language are embedded in the brain. Chomsky argues that just as humans are born to walk so they are born to talk. Just as bipedalism is not a learned cultural capacity, but has evolved biologically, in the same way talking is not culturally learned but has biologically evolved. The use of individual languages is, of course, culturally specific.

Modern language provided the ability to communicate with others on an individual basis. It also allowed for increasingly elaborate social structures and greater complexity in human relationships. It facilitated deliberation over ethical principles of conduct for guiding and regulating those relationships. Moreover, it allowed for increasingly sophisticated internal thought and reflection. We could become more introspective as well as more communicative with others. The sophisticated psychological and social relationships that make us human became possible only with the development of language.

AGRICULTURE: FROM HUNTER-GATHERER TO FARMER

Some hunter-gatherers began to stay for longer periods at their temporary campsites. They noted the patterns of growth of the grains they gathered and the migration habits of the animals they hunted. They began to experiment in planting some of the seeds of the largest, most nutritious cereals in the Middle East and Europe; maize in the Americas; root crops in southeast Asia. In addition to pursuing animals as prey, men may have tried to restrict their movements to particular locations, or to have built their own campsites at points frequented by the animals, adjusting human movements to those of the animals. They learned to domesticate dogs, and domesticated dogs may have accompanied the first Americans on their travels across Beringia. In the Middle East the sheep was the first species to be domesticated, perhaps 10,000 years ago.

By 15,000–10,000 B.C.E., humans had the biological and cultural capacity to farm and raise animals. But first they had to want to do so. Otherwise why give up hunting and gathering? Why settle down? Perhaps the transformation took place at sites of especially valuable and accessible natural resources, such as the fishing sites of the Jomon people of Japan, or the quarries of obsidian stone, used for making sharp cutting tools, around Çatal Hüyük in modern Turkey. A permanent source of food to eat or materials to trade might have outweighed the desire to shift with the seasons and travel with the herds.

Perhaps rising population pressures left humans no alternative. The press of neighbors restricted scope for travel. On limited land, hunter-gatherers found that planting their own crops and domesticating their own animals could provide them with more food than hunting and gathering. Despite the risks of weather and of plant and animal diseases that left agricultural settlements vulnerable, some groups began to settle. Ten thousand years ago, almost all humans lived by hunting and gathering. Two thousand years ago, most were farmers or herders. Moreover, in the midst of this transformation, which created the first agricultural villages, cities, too, grew up as the central administrative, economic, and religious centers of their regions. A new era was beginning. It is the subject of the next chapter and Part 2.

BIBLIOGRAPHY

Barber, Elizabeth Wayland. *Women's Work: The First 20,000 Years: Women, Cloth, and Society in Early Times* (New York: W.W. Norton & Co., 1994).

Brown, Judith. "Note on the Division of Labor by Sex," *American Anthropologist* LXXII (1970), 1075–6.

Chauvet, Jean-Marie, Eliette Brunel Deschamps, and Christian Hillaire. *Dawn of Art: The Chauvet Cave, the Oldest Known Paintings in the World* (New York: Abrams, 1996).

Clottes, Jean and Jean Courtin. *The Cave Beneath the Sea: Paleolithic Images at Cosquer* (New York: Abrams, 1996).

Conkey, Margaret W. *Art and Design in the Old Stone Age* (San Francisco: Freeman, 1982).

Darwin, Charles. *The Origin of Species by Means of Natural Selection or the Preservation of Favored Races in the Struggle for Life*, reprinted from the Sixth Edition, ed. Edmund B. Wilson (New York: Macmillan Company, 1927).

Darwin, Charles. *The Works of Charles Darwin*, ed. Paul H. Barrett and R.B. Freeman, Vol. XV *On the Origin of Species* 1859 (New York: New York University Press, 1988).

Darwin, Charles. *Darwin*, ed. Philip Appleman (New York: W.W. Norton and Co., 2nd ed., 1979).

Defleur, Alban, Tim White *et al.* "Neanderthal Cannibalism at Moula-Guercy, Ardèche, France," *Science* (October 1, 1999), 286:128–131.

Fagan, Brian M. *The Journey from Eden* (London: Thames and Hudson, 1990).

Fagan, Brian M. *People of the Earth* (New York: HarperCollins Foresman and Co., 8th ed., 1995).

Fedigan, Linda. "The Changing Role of Women in Models of Human Evolution," *Annual Review of Anthropology* XV (1986), 22–66.

Gamble, Clive. *Timewalkers: The Prehistory of Global Colonization* (Harvard University Press, 1994).

Gould, Stephen Jay. *Ever Since Darwin: Reflections in Natural History* (New York: Norton & Company, 1977).

Holm, Jean, with John Bowker, eds. *Myth and History* (London: Pinter Publishers, 1994).

Johanson, Donald, Lenora Johanson, and Blake Edgar. *Ancestors: In Search of Human Origins* (New York: Villard Books, 1994).

Leakey, Richard and Roger Lewin. *Origins Reconsidered* (New York: Doubleday, 1992).

Lee, Richard B. and Irven DeVore, eds. *Man the Hunter* (New York: Aldine, 1968).

Lewin, Roger. *The Origin of Modern Humans* (New York: Scientific American Library, 1993).

Linton, Sally (pseud. for Sally Slocum). "Woman the Gatherer: Male Bias in Anthropology," in Sue-Ellen Jacobs, ed. *Women in Perspective: A Guide for Cross-Cultural Studies* (Urbana: University of Illinois Press, 1971).

McNeill, William H. *Mythistory and Other Essays* (Chicago: University of Chicago Press, 1986).

Mellars, Paul and Chris Stringer, eds. *The Human Revolution: Behavioural and Biological Perspectives on the Origins of Modern Humans* (Princeton: Princeton University Press, 1989).

Morell, Virginia. *Ancestral Passions: The Leakey Family and the Quest for Humankind's Beginnings* (New York: Simon & Schuster, 1995).

The New English Bible (New York: Oxford University Press, 1976).

Past Worlds: The (London) Times Atlas of Archaeology (London: Times Books Ltd., 1988).

Pfeiffer, John. *The Creative Explosion* (Ithaca: Cornell University Press, 1982).

Scott, Joan W. "Gender: A Useful Category of Historical Analysis," *American Historical Review* XCI (1986), 1053–76.

White, Tim D., Berhane Asfaw, and Gen Suwa. "Ardipithecus ramidus, A Root Species for Australopithecus," in F. Facchini ed. *The First Humans and Their Cultural Manifestations* (Forli, Italy: A.B.A.C.O., 1996), 15–23.

Wood, Bernard. "The Oldest Hominid Yet," *Nature* Vol. 371 (Sept. 22, 1994), 280–81.

2 *Settling Down*

THE FIRST CITIES AND WHY THEY MATTER: DIGS, TEXTS, AND INTERPRETATIONS

The establishment of urban settlements marked a new era in many parts of the world. Although the physical existence of the new cities, with their thousands of inhabitants, is the most obvious transformation, many equally significant, though less tangible changes, accompanied it. Cities were nodes in the regional networks of exchange of goods and culture, and they encouraged the production of sophisticated arts, the specialization of labor, and the elaboration of a social hierarchy. Most significantly, however, cities signaled the emergence of a state organization. The new state, hand-in-glove with the new city, provided leadership, organization, control of official armed power, an inegalitarian stratification of population, and power over the people, sometimes with their consent, sometimes without. In all these functions, the ancient city reminds us of our own.

Unlike modern cities, however, almost all early cities were relatively small. The largest contained perhaps 100,000 people in 8 square miles (20 square kilometers); most had only a few thousand inhabitants. Until the industrial revolution in the late nineteenth century, a few thousand people concentrated in 100 acres (40 hectares) might have constituted a city, for cities held only a tiny percentage of the total population of any region. Most of the world's population were farmers or hunter-gatherers when the first cities were invented. The multiplication of cities and urban residents that we see today took place only after the industrial revolution created new urban factories, transportation hubs, and mass labor

Teotihuacán, Mexico. The Pyramid of the Moon (foreground) is linked to the Pyramid of the Sun by the Avenue of the Dead.

forces. Moreover, many of the early cities, although small, were centers of independent city-states; most cities today are single points in much larger national and even international networks.

Finally, the earliest cities emerged in each of seven regions around the world. They developed as cosmo-magical shrines. Paul Wheatley traced this concern for the supernatural in the Chinese city especially, but it is a phenomenon we will see from Mesopotamia to the Nile, from the Indus to the Niger, and perhaps most of all in the Valley of Mexico and in the high Andes Mountains. Many of the early cities were dedicated to gods and were built on existing shrine centers. As the cities grew, the shrines grew with them, providing a more profound meaning to the lives of their inhabitants by linking their mundane existence to transcendent and powerful supernatural forces.

2 FROM VILLAGE COMMUNITY TO CITY STATE

10,000 B.C.E.—750 B.C.E.

"Man is by nature a zoon politikon, *a creature of the city-state."*

ARISTOTLE

WHAT ARE CITIES AND WHY ARE THEY IMPORTANT?

FOOD FIRST: THE AGRICULTURAL VILLAGE

Until about 12,000 years ago humans hunted and gathered their food, following the migrations of animals and the seasonal cycles of the crops. They established temporary base camps for their activities, and caves served them for homes and meeting-places, but they had not established permanent settlements. They had begun to domesticate some animals, especially the dog and the sheep, but they had not yet begun the systematic practice of agriculture. Then, about 10,000 B.C.E., people began to settle down, constructing the first agricultural villages. Why did they do it? Is food production through agriculture easier than hunting and gathering? Surprisingly the answer seems to be "no." Research by Cohen and Reed suggests that, with the technology available at that time, adult farmers had to work an equivalent of 1000–1300 hours a year for their food, while hunter-gatherers needed only 800–1000 hours. Moreover, agricultural work was more difficult.

Why did they change? An appealing, although unproved, answer is that increasing population pressure, perhaps accompanied by worsening climatic conditions, forced people to take on the more productive methods of agriculture. Scientists estimate that even in a lush tropical environment, 0.4 square miles (1 square kilometer) of land could support only nine persons through hunting and gathering; under organized, sedentary agricultural techniques, the same area could support 200–400 people. In the less fertile sub-tropical and temperate climates into which the expanding populations were moving at the end of the last ice age, after about 13,000 B.C.E., hunting and gathering were even less productive. To survive, sedentary agriculture was a necessity. The myth of Shen Nung, the Chinese inventor of agriculture and its wooden tools (and of poetry), captures the transformation:

> The people of old ate the meat of animals and birds. But in the time of Shen Nung, there were so many people that there were no longer enough animals and birds to supply their needs. So it was that Shen Nung

EARLY WEST ASIA

DATE	POLITICAL	RELIGION AND CULTURE	SOCIAL DEVELOPMENT
4500 B.C.E.	● Ubaid people in Mesopotamia		
3500 B.C.E.	● Sumerians (3300–2350)	● Cuneiform writing ● Sumerian pantheon ● Ziggurats built	● Urbanization in Mesopotamia
3000 B.C.E.	● Hereditary kings emerge		● Mycenaean traders in Aegean ● Invention of the wheel ● Bronze casting ● Sumerian city–states (2800–1850)
2500 B.C.E.	● Ur, First Dynasty (2500–2350) ● Akkadian kingdoms (2350–2150); Sargon of Akkad (2334–2279) ● 3rd Dynasty of Ur (c. 2113–1991)	● Akkadian language used in Sumer ● *Epic of Gilgamesh* (c. 2113–1991)	
2000 B.C.E.	● Semitic rulers gain control of Mesopotamia ● 1st dynasty of Babylon (c. 1894–1595) ● Hammurabi (1792–1750) ● Hittites in Asia Minor		
1500 B.C.E.	● Hittite Empire (c. 1460–1200)	● "Golden age" of Ugarit	● Code of Law
1000 B.C.E.	● Assyrian Empire (900–612)	● Hebrew Scriptures recorded	
750 B.C.E.	● Sargon II (d. 705) ● Sennacherib (c. 705–681) ● Ashurbanipal (d. 626) ● Fall of Nineveh (imperial capital) (612) ● Nebuchadnezzar (605–562)	● *Gilgamesh* (complete version) ● Homer (*fl*. 8th century) ● Hesiod (*fl*. 700)	
600 B.C.E.	● Neo–Babylonian Empire	● Library at Nineveh	
500 B.C.E.	● Persian Empire in control of Mesopotamia		

taught the people how to cultivate the earth. (Bairoch, p. 6)

In addition to increasing agricultural productivity, villages facilitated an increase in creativity of all kinds. It may have taken longer to raise food than to hunt and gather it, but the sedentary farmers did not stop work when they had secured their food supply. In their villages they went on to produce textiles, pottery, metallurgy, architecture, tools, and objects of great beauty, especially in sculpture and painting. Did the agriculturists work comparatively harder than the hunter-gatherers simply to survive under greater population pressure, or because they craved the added rewards of their extra labor, or both? We can never know for sure, but the agricultural village opened new possibilities for economic, social, political, and artistic creativity—while closing others. It changed forever humanity's concepts of life's necessities and potentials.

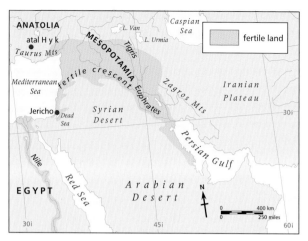

The Fertile Crescent The Tigris and Euphrates rivers gave life to the first known agricultural villages, about 10,000 years ago, and the first known cities in human history, about 5000 years ago. Fertile land extended to the Mediterranean and some contact apparently continued on to the Nile Valley. Its parameters were defined to the north and east by mountains and semi-arid plateaus and to the south by arid regions receiving less than 10 inches (250 mm) of rainfall per year.

Basic Crops and Livestock

The first agricultural villages that archaeologists have discovered date to about 10,000 B.C.E. They are located in the "fertile crescent," which curves from the Persian Gulf and the Zagros Mountains in the east and south, on the border of today's Iraq and Iran, northwest into Anatolia, present-day Turkey, and then turns south and west through present-day Syria, Lebanon, and Israel on the Mediterranean Sea. Here, wild grasses, the ancestors of modern wheat and barley, provided the basic grains, first for gathering, and later for cultivation. By 8000 B.C.E. the Natufians, named for their valley in northern Israel, and the peoples immediately to the south, in the Jordan River valley near Jericho, were growing fully domesticated cereals. Peas and lentils and other pulses and legumes followed. The peoples of the fertile crescent hunted gazelles and goats. Later, they domesticated the goat and the sheep. In Turkey they added pigs; around the Mediterranean, cattle.

In other parts of the world, agriculture and animal domestication focused on other varieties. In the western hemisphere, these included maize, especially in Mesoamerica, and root crops such as manioc and sweet potatoes in South America. Amerindians domesticated the llama, the guinea pig, and the turkey. Domesticated dogs probably accompanied their migrant masters across the

Bering Straits about 15,000 years ago. Perhaps the process of domestication was then repeated with the dogs found in the Americas.

In southeast Asia and in tropical Africa, wild roots and tubers, including yams, were the staple crops. In the Vindhya Mountain areas of central India, rice was among the first crops to be cultivated, about 5000 B.C.E. Anthropologists are uncertain when rice was first cultivated, rather than just being harvested from the wild, in southeast and east Asia, but a date similar to India's seems likely. From earliest times, as today, China's agriculture seems to have favored rice in the south and millets in the north. Some crops, including cotton and gourds, were brought under cultivation in many locations around the globe.

Our knowledge of early agriculture continues to grow as the archaeological record is expanded and revised. European sedentary agriculture, for example, which was once thought to have been borrowed from the Near East, may have been a local response to changing climate conditions.

Neolithic Tools, Products, and Trade

The era in which villages took form is usually called **Neolithic**, or New Stone Age, named for its tools rather than its crops. In the fertile crescent, where the process first began, this corresponds to about 8000–4000 B.C.E. For cutting, grinding, chopping, scraping, piercing, and digging, village artisans fashioned new tools from stone. Archaeological digs from Neolithic villages abound with blades, knives, sickles, adzes, arrows, daggers, spears, fish hooks and harpoons, mortars and pestles, and rudimentary plows and hoes.

As villages expanded their economic base these stone tools were often valued as items of trade. Obsidian—a kind of volcanic glass—was traded from Anatolia and is found in hundreds of digs from central Turkey to Syria and the Jordan valley. Among other items of trade, recognized by their appearance in digs a long distance away from their point of origin, are seashells, jade, turquoise, and ceramics.

Although ceramics occasionally appear among non-sedentary populations, the weight and fragility of clay make pottery essentially a creation of the more established Neolithic village. As a vessel for storage, pottery further reflected the sedentary character of the new village life. The fine designs and colors decorating its pottery became the most distinctive identifying mark of the Neolithic

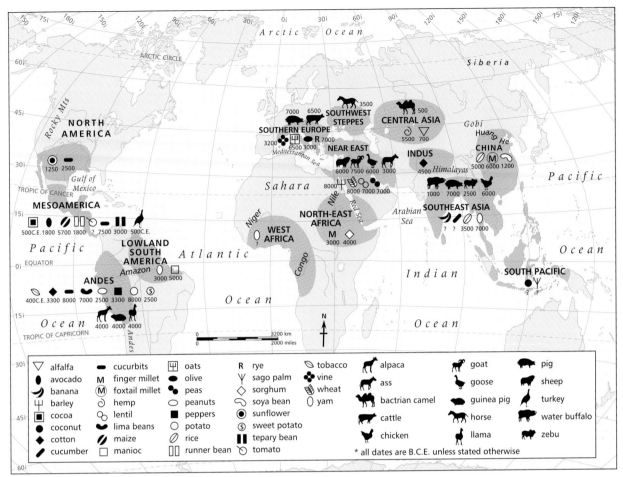

The origins of agriculture and domestic animals. The development of agriculture and the domestication of animals took place independently in different parts of the world, but the Near East, Mesoamerica, southeast Asia, and China were among the first and most significant regions. Cereal grasses such as wheat, barley, rice, and maize, and tubers such as potatoes, yams, and cassava, became staple crops in the major centers. This cultivation of plants was complemented by the domestication of wild animals, beginning with dogs, cattle, goats, sheep, pigs, and, in the western hemisphere, llamas.

village, and archaeologists often designate eras, locations, and groups of people by descriptions of their pottery—the "grayware," the "red glazed," or the "cord-marked," for example. Simple pottery is easy to make and accessible to anyone, but specialized craftspeople developed ceramics into a medium of artistic creativity. Fine ceramic jewelry, statuary, and figurines attained great beauty and were frequently used in religious rituals.

Historical change, however, does not proceed in a uniform, straight line. Historians must be alert not only to general patterns, but also to exceptions. Some villages did form on an economic base of hunting-and-gathering. In southern Japan, for example a non-agricultural village society appeared among the Jomon people along with some of the earliest and most beautiful of pottery. Jomon pottery, which is marked by distinctive cord lines,

dates back to 10,500 B.C.E. and spread from the southern island of Kyushu, northward through Honshu, reaching Hokkaido by 6500 B.C.E. The Jomon villagers supported themselves from fishing, hunting deer and wild boar, and gathering and storing nuts. They created stone tools and lived in caves and in pit-houses in settled villages with central, communal buildings. Yet the Japanese did not develop agricultural cultivation for another several thousand years.

THE FIRST CITIES

The first cities were constructed on the economic base of sedentary village agricultural communities. In excavating these earliest cities around the globe, archaeologists ask which city forms were invented

SPOTLIGHT
Ban Po, China
INTERPRETING AN EARLY NEOLITHIC VILLAGE

While digging the foundation for a factory ten miles (16 kilometers) west of X'ian, China, in 1953 workers uncovered one of the world's oldest and best-preserved Neolithic villages dating back to 6000 B.C.E. Archaeological investigation revealed that the residents cultivated millet and domesticated pigs and dogs. They practiced slash-and-burn (swidden) agriculture; pollen samples show distinct alternating periods of cultivation and fallow.

The Ban Po Excavation, preserved today under an enormous hangar-like structure, provides insights not only into the life of the villagers, but also into the interpretive frameworks of the modern archaeologists and government officials responsible for the site. **Figure 1** presents a model of the original village displayed on-site. It represents Ban Po's three housing styles: square, round, and an oblong split-level, with part underground and part above. Underground pits used for storage are visible throughout the village. A moat surrounds the entire settlement.

A large square building dominates the village center. What function did it serve? In many regions such a structure might have housed a political or religious official. Here, the official posting on the excavation identifies the central structure as "a place for the Ban Po inhabitants to discuss public affairs." This emphasis on shared community planning is consistent with understandings of many early villagers, before the establishment of states. It is also consistent with the ideology of the current Chinese communist government: Before the creation of states, village communities were egalitarian and self-governing.

Figure 2 represents one of the three forms of housing. Its perimeter is identified by the holes in the ground, still recognizable today, that were made by the wooden posts supporting the walls. Building materials were all natural to the area, from the plaster of the floor

Figure 1 Model reconstruction of Ban Po.

Figure 3 Burial urn from Ban Po, 4500 B.C.E.

Farming in China Evidence of the earliest established agriculture in east Asia is found in the arid but fertile regions of north central China, along the central reaches of the Huang He (Yellow River). Villages such as Ban Po grew up on the floodplain, rich in alluvial and loess deposits, where drought-resistant plants such as millet could be cultivated.

and walls to the straw of the thatched roof and the brushwood covering the external walls.

Burial urns, **figure 3**, held the remains of children who died young. Seventy-six such burial urns have been discovered within the residential area. Adults were buried in a public graveyard to the north of the village, adjacent to a pottery production center with six kilns. Some 250 graves were excavated there. It is unclear why children and adults were buried separately. Ban Po villages stored their grain in some 200 pits that were dug throughout the village. An interpretive sign on-site explains "This reflects *public ownership* in the clan community" (my emphasis). Could the scattering of the storage pits suggest instead *private ownership*, in which each family had its own nearby pit? How deeply does the official ideology of a nation affect its interpretation of archaeological remains? How deeply does each reader's value system affect his or her interpretation?

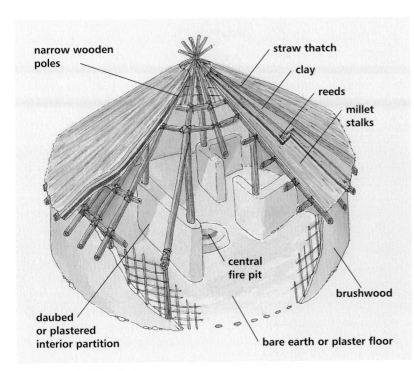

Figure 2 Typical Ban Po dwelling.

THE EARLIEST URBAN SETTLEMENTS

3500 B.C.E.	Rise of Sumer, southern Mesopotamia.
3100	Emergence of Egyptian state; new capital at Memphis.
2500	Development of Mohenjo-Daro, urban civilization on the Indus plain.
2500	City-states in northern Mesopotamia and the Levant, dominated by palace complexes.
1800	Urban growth after Shang dynasty established in northeast China.
1200	Formative period in Mesoamerica, marked by first shrine centers, especially the Olmec.
c. **400** B.C.E.	City states in Mesoamerica and South America.
400 C.E.	Urbanization of Jenne-Jeno, Nigeria, sub-Saharan Africa.

indigenously, by their own inhabitants, and which were borrowed from earlier examples or, perhaps, imposed from outside on local rural populations. Technically, the question is one of **innovation** versus **diffusion**. Thus far, most experts agree that innovative primary urbanization, not borrowed or imposed from outside, took place in seven places: five river valleys in the eastern hemisphere—Mesopotamia, the Nile, the Indus, the Huang He, and the Niger—and, in the western hemisphere, along the Gulf of Mexico and in the interior valleys of Mexico, and in the Andes Mountains. The birth of primary urbanization took place in these seven locations at very different times, with Mesopotamia the oldest at about 3300 B.C.E. and the Niger the most recent at about 400 C.E.

THE MEANING OF CITIES

Cities transform human life. The physical form of the early cities tells the story vividly. Even today we can trace on the surface of the earth the 5500-year-old designs of the first cities and the irrigation systems that supported them. Remnants of walls and fragments of monuments of these first cities still rise from their sites. From under the surface archaeologists salvage artifacts: bricks; pottery; tools of wood, bone, stone, and metal; jewelry; and skeletons of citizens and slaves. The technology of the early cities included new means of transportation; we find the remains of wheeled vehicles and of sailboats. The earliest city dwellers advanced their skills in metallurgy, and products of their craftsmanship in copper, tin, and their alloys abound in the archaeological excavations. In recognition of these technological break-throughs we often call the era of the first cities the "bronze age."

But cities are more than bricks and mortar, metal and artifacts. They require institutions for their larger scale of organization and administration. As society and economy became more complex, new class hierarchies emerged. Professional administrators, skilled artisans, long-distance traders, local merchants, and priests and kings enriched the diversity and sophistication of the growing cities. External relations with other cities required skilled negotiations, and a diplomatic corps emerged. Armies mobilized for defense and attack. In short, with the growth of the city the early state was also born, with its specialized organization, centralized rule, and powerful armies.

To keep track of business transactions and administrative orders, the proclamations of rulers and the rituals of priests, the legends of gods and the histories of the city, new methods of record keeping were developed. At first these were tokens, pictures, seals, personalized markings, and, in the Andes, *quipu*, knots made in special lengths of string (see picture, p. 379). By about 3300 B.C.E., in Sumer, which is geographically equivalent to today's southern Iraq, the world's first system of writing had evolved, one of the most revolutionary inventions in human history. The prestigious occupation of scribe was born, and schoolteachers soon followed. (College professors took much longer.)

From earliest times, city dwellers and analysts understood and commented on the significance of the first urban revolution. Today, we have more reason than ever to value and to evaluate its 5000-year-old heritage, for in modern times we are living through two new urban revolutions. By 1800 the industrial revolution opened a new era of urban development that re-invented the cities of western Europe and North America (see Chapter 16). In the twentieth century peasants streamed by

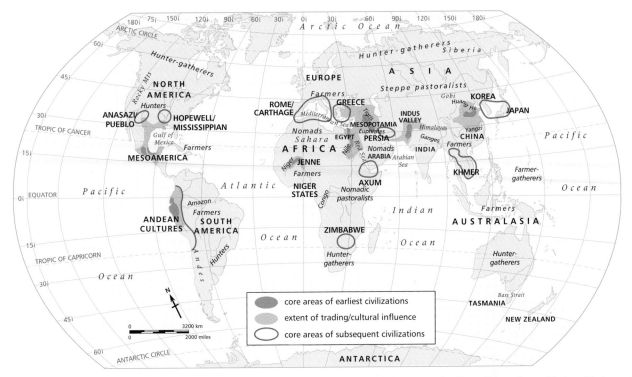

The spread of civilizations The first civilizations developed where unique local climatic and soil conditions, favorable to settled agriculture, occurred, mostly in major river basins. With the development of an agricultural surplus came the growth of urban centers, trade, and population. Secondary civilizations tended to develop in regions adjacent to these heartlands, or along trade routes between them.

the millions and tens of millions from rural villages to mammoth cities, creating massive, unprecedented urban environments around the globe (see Part 6). So we search humanity's earliest experiences with cities not only to understand our ancestors but also to understand ourselves.

SUMER

SUMER: WHAT DO WE KNOW?

The Birth of the City

The Sumerians pioneered the world's first urban revolution in Mesopotamia. They migrated into southern Mesopotamia about 3500 B.C.E., perhaps from around the Caspian Sea, but no one knows for sure. Archaeological excavations of pottery show the earlier presence in Mesopotamia of the Ubaid peoples, beginning about 4500 B.C.E. The use of Semitic word forms and names by the Sumerians suggest that Semites, too, had preceded them in the area. But for a millennium, from 3300

B.C.E. until 2350 B.C.E., the Sumerians lived in warring city-states and dominated the region. In 2350 B.C.E., Sargon, the Semitic ruler of Akkad, just to the north, conquered Mesopotamia and ruled it as a consolidated empire.

After some 200 years under Akkadian rule, the Mesopotamian city-states regained independence and resumed their inter-urban warfare until about 1750 B.C.E., when Hammurabi of Babylon dealt them a final defeat and the Sumerian peoples began to vanish from history. The cities they had built—Kish, Uruk, Ur, Nippur, Lagash, Umma, and dozens of smaller ones—died out, having fought each other to exhaustion. Mesopotamia was conquered successively by Hittites, Assyrians, Babylonians once again, Achaeminid Persians, and Greeks under Alexander the Great. The Sumerian cultural legacy lived on, however, absorbed into the literature, philosophy, religion, law, and new patterns of urbanization of their conquerors.

Size

What are the characteristics of the urban revolution in Mesopotamia? How do its cities differ from the earlier villages? The most obvious feature is that urban scale in physical size, population, and territorial control is much greater. The Neolithic village housed a few dozens or a few hundreds of residents on a few acres. Jericho, the oldest known sedentary agricultural village, was founded about 8500 B.C.E. and grew to about 10 acres (4 hectares) by 7000 B.C.E. It was surrounded by a stone wall 10 feet (3 meters) thick, capped at one point by a stone tower 30 feet (9 meters) high. The largest Neolithic site in the Near East, Çatal Hüyük in Anatolia, grew by 5500 B.C.E. to occupy slightly more than 30 acres (12 hectares). It became a town. By comparison, the first cities of Mesopotamia were ten times larger, accommodating about 5000 people.

Stone tower and wall, Jericho, c. 8000 B.C.E. Before Sumer, a Neolithic community based at Jericho in the Jordan valley, Palestine, was the first to develop cereals of a fully domesticated type. In 8000 B.C.E these farmers, keen to secure their settlement in the arid environment, constructed a stone perimeter wall 10 feet (3 m) thick that was strengthened at one point by a circular stone tower over 30 feet (9 m) high. This wall is one of the earliest such defenses known.

Over time, the larger ones reached populations of 35,000–40,000 and covered more than 1000 acres, 1½ square miles (3.88 square kilometers). The major cities were walled and the ramparts of Uruk (modern Warka, biblical Erech), the city of the king-god-hero Gilgamesh, stretched to a circumference of 6 miles (9.7 kilometers), engirdling a population of 50,000 by 2700 B.C.E. By 2500 B.C.E. Sumer held 500,000 people, four-fifths of them in its cities and villages! Urbanism in Sumer became a way of life.

Control of the Countryside

To support these growing urban populations, the range of control of the Sumerian cities over the surrounding countryside, and its agricultural and raw material resources, continued to expand. The Russian scholar I.M. Diakanoff estimated that the total sway of Lagash, one of the major cities, extended over 1200 square miles (3100 square kilometers). The king, priests, and private citizens controlled the fields of this area (cited in Kramer, *The Sumerians*, p. 76).

Civic Loyalty

Networks of irrigation canals supported agriculture in this arid region and expanded Sumerian control over the land and its productivity. Irrigation permitted settlement to extend southward to central Mesopotamia, where the first cities would later emerge about 3300 B.C.E. The construction and maintenance of the canals required larger gangs of workers than the work teams that were based on family and clan alone. Loyalties that had been limited to blood relatives now extended beyond kinship to civic identity. In organizing these public works projects, a sense of citizenship, based on a shared space rather than on blood kinship, was born. As Numa Fustel de Coulanges, writing about a similar phenomenon in pre-Classical Greece, pointed out, the concept of legal identity and loyalty based on geography is the real beginning of city life.

Leadership and the State

Organizing the canal systems required more powerful leaders than villages had known. At first, this leadership appears to have been exercised by councils of aristocratic elders, who worked closely with religious leaders of the temple-

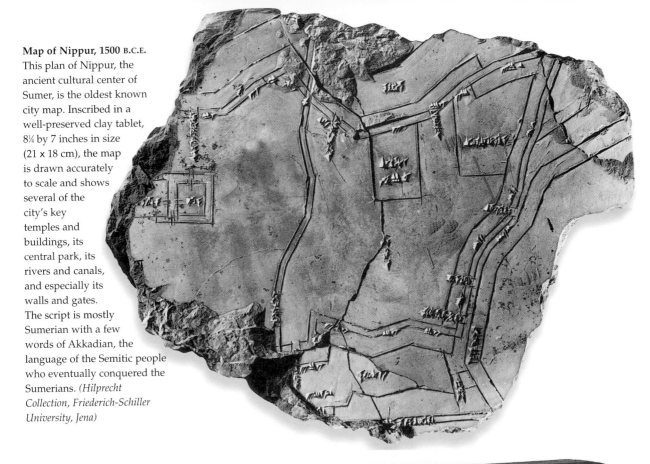

Map of Nippur, 1500 B.C.E.
This plan of Nippur, the ancient cultural center of Sumer, is the oldest known city map. Inscribed in a well-preserved clay tablet, 8¼ by 7 inches in size (21 x 18 cm), the map is drawn accurately to scale and shows several of the city's key temples and buildings, its central park, its rivers and canals, and especially its walls and gates. The script is mostly Sumerian with a few words of Akkadian, the language of the Semitic people who eventually conquered the Sumerians. *(Hilprecht Collection, Friederich-Schiller University, Jena)*

Standard of Ur, from Iraq. Sumerian, Early Dynastic II. *c.* 2800–2400 B.C.E. In Sumer the city-state was created as strong kings came to rule over walled cities and the surrounding countryside. This banqueting scene, found in a tomb in the royal cemetery at Ur, shows the court drinking to the health of the king. The boxlike "standard" is thought to have rested on top of a long pole during festive processions. *(British Museum, London)*

ziggurats. In times of crisis, especially during warfare with other cities, the council appointed a temporary single leader, but after about 2800 B.C.E., these men began to assume the position of hereditary kings and to rule in conjunction with temple priests. Political power and organization were both centralized and sanctified. Thus was the state born and consolidated.

Religion: The Priesthood and the Cosmo-magical City

Considerable power rested with the priests of the many deities of Sumer. In contrast to modern patterns, in which the countryside is often considered more religious than the secular city, the authority of the ancient temple community gave the religious establishment enormous prestige and power in the city, and urban ritual practice was more

FOCUS
The City as Ceremonial Center

The geographer Paul Wheatley summarized a great deal of his own research and that of many other scholars in stressing the religious and ceremonial significance of the ancient city, a significance not so apparent in our own cities of today:

Whenever, in any of the seven regions of primary urban generation we trace back the characteristic urban form to its beginnings we arrive not at a settlement that is dominated by commercial relations, a primordial market, or at one that is focused on a citadel, an archetypal fortress, but rather at a ceremonial complex. . . . The

predominantly religious focus to the schedule of social activities associated with them leaves no room to doubt that we are dealing primarily with centers of ritual and ceremonial. Naturally this does not imply that the ceremonial centers did not exercise secular functions as well, but rather that these were subsumed into an all-pervading religious context. . . . Above all, they embodied the aspirations of brittle, pyramidal societies in which, typically, a sacerdotal [priestly] elite, controlling a corps of officials and perhaps a praetorian [elite] guard, ruled over a broad understratum of peasantry.
(Wheatley, pp. 225–6)

Ziggurat at Ur, Iraq, 2300 B.C.E. For the plain-dwelling Sumerians, mountains represented the mysterious sources of the waters that brought vegetation to the valleys. It is not surprising, then, that the buildings they conceived for sacred rituals—ziggurats, a form of stepped pyramids—were made in the form of holy mountains.

fully elaborated than was the rural counterpart (see Focus, opposite).

To consolidate their temporal and supernatural influences, the priests built in the cities great temples, called **ziggurats**, a form of stepped fortress. (Ziggurats are probably the model for the Bible's Tower of Babel, which was depicted as a threat to the God Jehovah.) The ziggurats dominated the fields that the priests controlled and farmed, rented out, or turned over to their servants and favorites. As their power increased, the priests built the ziggurats taller and more massive. From within these vast temple complexes, they controlled huge retinues, including artisans and administrators, and retained gangs of field workers to farm the temple's estates. Temples employed and fed multitudes. The chief temple in the city of Lagash, for example, provided daily food and drink (ale) to some 1200 people by about 3000 B.C.E. The leading temples became virtual cities within cities.

Rituals, especially those of the priests and kings, suggest further the significance of religious thought in the minds of Sumerians. On New Year's day the king of Ur proceeded to the top of the city's major ziggurat where he was symbolically married to the goddess of fertility, Inanna. The entire population witnessed this affirmation of his divinity. Royal burials also asserted the divinity and authority of the king. Sir Leonard Wooley described the death pit adjacent to the royal burial place in Ur, which he excavated in the 1920s:

> Six men servants carrying knives or axes lay near the entrance lined up against the wall; in front of them stood a great copper basin, and by it were the bodies of four women harpists, one with her hands still on the strings of her instrument. Over the rest of the pit's area there lay in ordered rows the bodies of sixty four ladies of the court. All of them wore some sort of ceremonial dress . . . Clearly these people were not wretched slaves killed as oxen might be killed, but persons held in honor, wearing their robes of office, and coming, one hopes, voluntarily to a rite which would in their belief be but a passing from one world to another, from the service of a god on earth to that of the same god in another place. (pp. 70–72)

The royal graves required specialized artisans. While most common people were buried in small brick vaults in basement chambers of their own houses, and some were interred in cemeteries out-

side the city walls, the royal tombs were elegant. Their arches, vaults, and domes, suggesting new levels of architectural skill, were built of brick and stone, and many of the funeral objects interred with the dead were of gold and silver. As in other ancient civilizations we shall encounter in later chapters, some of the royal dead were accompanied by attendants who were sacrificed for the purpose and were buried nearby. They, too, were adorned with jewelry of gold and silver.

Occupational Specialization and Class Structure

The priests and the political-military rulers were only the most powerful of the new classes of specialists that emerged in the complex, large cities. Managers, surveyors, artisans, astronomers, brewers, warriors, traders, and scribes—all in addition to the farmers working their own fields and those of the temples and landowners—gave the cities a far more sophisticated hierarchical class structure than villages possessed.

Arts and Invention

Creativity flourished. Artisans crafted works of art in terra cotta, copper, clay, and colors surpassing village standards in their beauty and technical skill. Cylinder seals (small cylinders of stone engraved with designs for stamping clay tablets and sealing jars) became a common form of practical art in Sumer and spread as far as Anatolia and Greece. Astronomers established an accurate calendar based on lunar months that enabled them to predict the onset of seasons and to prepare properly for each year's planting and harvesting. Musicians created, designed, and played the lyre and composed and chanted songs, often dedicated to gods. Designers and architects, supervising armies of workers, built the canals of the countryside and the monuments of the cities.

Sumerians apparently invented the first wheels, the potter's wheel for ceramics and wagon wheels for transportation. They dramatically improved the plow, harnessing it for oxen. Metallurgists, smelting their new alloy of copper and tin, ushered in the bronze age, and from the new metal fashioned tips for the plow as well as "tools such as hoes, axes, chisels, knives, and saws; arms such as lance points and arrowheads, swords, daggers, and harpoons; vessels and containers; nails, pins, rings, and mirrors" (Kramer, *The Sumerians*, p. 103).

Trade and Markets; Wheeled Cart and Sailboat

Traders carried merchandise by land, river, and sea, in the world's first wheeled carts and sailboats, as well as by donkey caravan. Rich in agricultural commodities and artisan production but poor in raw materials, Sumerians traded with the inhabitants of hilly areas to the north for wood, stone, and metal. They sailed into the Persian Gulf to find copper and tin and then continued along the Arabian Sea coast as far east as the Indus valley for ivory and ceramics. They traveled east overland through the passes of the Zagros Mountains to bring back carnelian beads from Elam. Shells from the Mediterranean coast that have been found in Sumer indicate trade westward, probably overland, as well.

In the city marketplace, merchants sold locally produced foodstuffs, including vegetables, onions, lentils and beans, more than fifty varieties of fish taken from the Tigris and Euphrates rivers, milk, cheese, butter, yoghurt, dates, meat—mostly mutton—and ale. In vats in their homes, women, especially, brewed up to 40 percent of the barley and wheat harvest into ale for home use and for sale. For taste, effect, and storage purposes the Sumerians preferred ale to grain. (Hops had not yet been introduced to enable the processing of ale into beer.)

Monumental Architecture and Adornment

For the Sumerians, the size and elegance of their cities and monuments were a source of great pride. The earliest introduction to Gilgamesh, hero of the greatest surviving Sumerian epic, proclaims his excellence as city builder:

Soundbox of royal harp, from the tomb of Queen Puabi at Ur. Sumerian, *c.* 2600 B.C.E. Many sumptuous artworks were discovered buried in the royal cemetery at Ur in the tombs of Sumerian kings and queens. Though the meaning is often obscure, the motifs and poses used in the decorations are often also found in west Asian and Egyptian art of about the same period, suggesting the possibility of cultural transmission. (*University Museum, Philadelphia*)

Engraved cylinder seal (left) and impression (right). Seals were first used as signatures before the invention of writing. The cylinders produce continuous patterns that are repetitive, but the figures themselves are remarkably naturalistic.

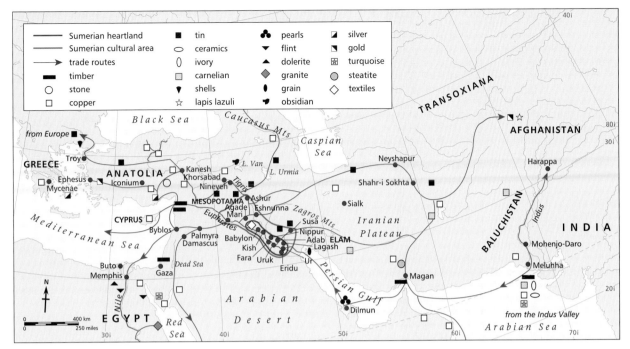

Mesopotamian trade The Sumerian trading network, revealed by the wide range of valuable and exotic materials used by Mesopotamian craftsmen, was both extensive and sophisticated, drawing on resources often well over 2000 miles distant. Egyptian tomb paintings show Semitic merchants with donkey caravans, while some of the earliest writing is found on Sumerian clay tablets recording commercial transactions.

In Uruk he built walls, a great rampart, and the temple of blessed Eanna for the god of the firmament Anu, and for Ishtar the goddess of love. Look at it still today: the outer wall where the cornice runs, it shines with the brilliance of copper; and the inner wall, it has no equal. Touch the threshold, it is ancient. Approach Eanna the dwelling of Ishtar, our lady of love and war, the like of which no latter-day king, no man alive can equal. Climb upon the wall of Uruk; walk along it, I say; regard the foundation terrace and examine the masonry: is it not burnt brick and good? The seven sages laid the foundations. (*The Epic of Gilgamesh*, p.61)

Gilgamesh is discussed more fully on page 54.

Art work adorned the city, especially the temple precincts. Sculptures, murals, mosaics, and especially stone **bas reliefs** provided not only beauty and elegance, but represented pictorially key scenes in the history of the cities and their rulers.

Thus, from king and priest through professionals, artisans, craftsmen, farmers, and laborers, specialization and division of labor and a hierarchical class structure marked the city's social and economic life as far more complex than that of the smaller, simpler village.

Writing and Literature

The Sumerians invented writing, thereby altering human history. Although some of the earliest town dwellers in other parts of the world—the settlers of the Niger valley of West Africa, the Olmec and Teotihuacanos of Mesoamerica, and the Chavin and Inca of the Andes Mountains of South America—achieved urban forms without writing, most of the earliest cities did invent some system of recording. As in Sumer, these systems moved "from token to tablet"—that is, from a simple recording of business transactions and registration of ownership through designated tokens, often marked with individual notations, through picture writing, to **ideograms**, and finally to phonetic, alphabetical writing.

As we shall see in Chapters 3 to 5, not all civilizations followed this sequence. In China, for example, the first writing seems to have been symbolic inscriptions on oracle bones, and they seem to have represented an attempt to divine the future. Chinese as a written language has only recently been transliterated into a phonetic alphabet; its basic script is still ideographic. The Chavin and Inca developed a form of recording transactions and chronology through knots made

Pictographic c. 3000 B.C.E.										
Early cuneiform representation c. 2400 B.C.E.										
Late Assyrian c. 650 B.C.E.										
Sumerian phonetic equivalent and meaning	k / eat	mušen / bird	sag / head	gu⁴ / ox	še / barley	ud / day	šu / hand	ku⁶ / fish	a / water	b / cow

Writing was invented in west Asia in the fourth millennium B.C.E. and developed from the need to keep a record of business transactions. From the wedge-shaped marks formed by a hollow-shaped reed, or stylus, cuneiform script evolved gradually. In this pictographic script, stylized drawings are used to represent words; each pictograph stands for a syllable, and abstract concepts are conveyed by using concrete notions that are close in meaning (e.g. "open mouth" for "eat"). See Spotlight, pp. 66–7.

in strings called *quipu* (see picture, p. 379), but they did not develop an independent system of writing. Nor did the people of the Niger valley.

Writing facilitated communication, commerce, administration, religious ritual, and, later, the recording and transmission of literature. It enabled society to enlarge to a scale never seen before. It encouraged a self-consciousness and historical analysis previously unknown. It created a "knowledge industry," transmitted through systems of formal education and headed by scribes. Samuel Noah Kramer, the great expositor of ancient Sumerian texts, pointed out: "as early as 3000 B.C., some scribes were already thinking in terms of teaching and learning.... by the middle of the third millennium B.C., there must have been a number of schools throughout Sumer where writing was taught formally." In a sense this textbook had its origins in Sumer some 5000 years ago.

Writing not only enriched the lives of the Sumerians, it has enabled our own historical study to recapture crucial information about their society. The discovery of that writing, and its deciphering, is barely a century old.

SUMER:
HOW DO WE KNOW?

The Sumerians wrote no historical interpretive accounts of their accomplishments, but at least five kinds of written materials help us to reconstruct their past. King lists give us not only the names and dates of many of the principal kings of the major cities but also some chronology of their continuing warfare. Royal correspondence with officials illuminates relations with neighbors. Epics transmit Sumerian values and their sense of the heroic, while lamentations recount the continuing devastation wrought by their inter-city religious warfare. Finally, legal codes suggest the principles and hierarchies of their everyday life.

Despite their accomplishments, the Sumerians and their literature were lost to history for at least 2000 years. Indeed, even the history of their Semitic neighbors in the region was little known except through tangential references in the Bible. The locations of even the greatest of the historic sites passed from memory until they were recovered in the late nineteenth century.

Early modern investigations of the lost civilizations of Mesopotamia and its literature were driven by interest in biblical history. In the twelfth century, Rabbi Benjamin of Tudela, who was visiting Mosul (in northern Iraq), correctly identified the nearby ruins of ancient Nineveh, but his find was not published until the sixteenth century. The identification of Babylon had to wait until 1616. During the seventeenth and eighteenth centuries, travelers through Mesopotamia continued to identify ruins in Mesopotamia with biblical sites. They also began, unsystematically, to send stones and tablets with inscriptions back to Europe. In 1811, James Rich, a resident for the British East India Company in Baghdad, began to examine and map the ruins of Babylon and even to excavate

He-Goat and Flowering Tree. Offering stand for fertility god. Sumerian, from Ur, *c.* **2500** B.C.E. This offering stand was created with a magical as well as a functional purpose in mind, being intended to work as a fertility charm too. The goat, an ancient symbol of male sexuality, is shown rearing up against a flowering tree, emblem of nature's fecundity. (*British Museum, London*)

parts of it. He sketched and investigated the mounds of ancient Nineveh. He collected tablets, bricks, boundary stones, and cylinders, which began the nucleus of the Mesopotamian antiquities collection of the British Museum, London. But no one could decipher their cuneiform script (see Spotlight, pp. 66–7).

The Sumerians had invented cuneiform writing, using reed styluses to make wedge-like forms (*cuneus* means wedge in Latin), part pictographic, part alphabetic, on clay tablets. Later conquerors had adapted this script for writing Akkadian, Assyrian, and Babylonian. The conquest of Alexander the Great in the fourth century B.C.E., however, helped to introduce the more functional Aramaic alphabet and cuneiform died out. The last known cuneiform text had been written in 75 C.E.

In the 1830s and 1840s, near Kermanshah, Persia, H.C. Rawlinson, a British army officer, began to copy the inscriptions from a cliff at Behistun. The stone was 300 feet (90 meters) above

SOURCE
The Epic of Gilgamesh

Much of what we know about the ancient Sumerian imagination and world vision comes from its greatest literary work, a series of tales about the hero Gilgamesh that were woven together into *The Epic of Gilgamesh*. Its most complete version comes from various shorter stories found in the library at Nineveh from about 750 B.C.E., but earlier fragments in the Sumerian excavations corroborate the antiquity of the core legends going back to the time Gilgamesh ruled Uruk, about 2600 B.C.E.

Gilgamesh introduces the first hero in written literature:

> I will proclaim to the world the deeds of Gilgamesh. This was the man to whom all things were known; this was the king who knew the countries of the world. He was wise, he saw mysteries and knew secret things. . . . When the gods created Gilgamesh they gave him a perfect body. Shamash the glorious sun endowed him with beauty, Adad the god of the storm endowed him with courage, the great gods made his beauty perfect, surpassing all others, terrifying like a great wild bull. Two-thirds they made him god and one-third man.

The first depiction of the hero as a city builder, as noted above:

> In Uruk he built walls, a great rampart, and the temple of blessed Eanna for the god of the firmament Anu, and for Ishtar the goddess of love.

The first male bonding, forged through a test of physical strength in an epic wrestling match:

> They broke the doorposts and the walls shook, they snorted like bulls locked together. They shattered the doorposts and the walls shook. Gilgamesh bent his knee with his foot planted on the ground and with a turn Enkidu was thrown. Then immediately his fury died. [Enkidu praises Gilgamesh's strength.] So Enkidu and Gilgamesh embraced and their friendship was sealed.

Enkidu had been created by Aruru, the goddess of Uruk, who had also created Gilgamesh. He lived in the forest. *Gilgamesh* highlights the suggestive myth of Enkidu's seduction by an urban harlot, who then lures him from the wilderness to the pleasures of the city as well as to his wrestling match with Gilgamesh:

> . . . the harlot and the trapper sat facing one another and waited for the game to come . . . on the third day the herds came; they came down to drink and Enkidu was with them. . . . The trapper spoke to her: "There he is. Now, woman, make your breasts bare, have no shame, do not delay but welcome his love. Let him see you naked, let him possess your body. When he comes near

uncover yourself and lie with him; teach him, the savage man, your woman's art, for when he murmurs love to you the wild beasts that shared his life in the hills will reject him." She was not afraid to take him, she made herself naked and welcomed his eagerness; as he lay on her murmuring love she taught him the woman's art.

For six days and seven nights they lay together, for Enkidu had forgotten his home in the hills; but when he was satisfied he went back to the wild beasts. Then, when the gazelle saw him, they fled. Enkidu would have followed, but his body was bound as though with a cord, his knees gave way when he started to run, his swiftness was gone. And now the wild creatures had all fled away; Enkidu was grown weak, for wisdom was in him, and the thoughts of a man were in his heart. So he returned and sat down at the woman's feet, and listened intently to what she said. "You are wise, Enkidu, and now you have become like a god. Why do you want to run wild with the beasts in the hills? Come with me. I will take you to the strong-walled Uruk, to the blessed temple of Ishtar and of Anu, of love and of heaven: there Gilgamesh lives, who is very strong, and like a wild bull he lords it over men." When she had spoken Enkidu was pleased; he longed for a comrade, for one who would understand his heart. "Come, woman, and take me to that holy temple, to the house of Anu and of Ishtar, and to the place where Gilgamesh lords it over the people. I will challenge him boldly . . ."

The epic unveils a driving ambition for fame and glory, both for himself and for his city, as Gilgamesh courageously chooses to enter the strongholds of Humbaba, guardian of the forest, and, with Enkidu, to fight him.

I will go to the country where the cedar is cut. I will set up my name where the names of famous men are written; and where no man's name is written I will raise a monument to the gods . . . I, Gilgamesh, go to see that creature of whom such things are spoken, the rumour of whose name fills the world. I will conquer him in his cedar wood and show the strength of the sons of Uruk, all the world shall know of it.

The importance of metallurgy and metals, especially for weapons, is revealed:

He went to the forge and said, "I will give orders to the armourers: they shall cast us our weapons while we watch them." So they gave orders to the armourers and the craftsmen sat down in conference. They went into the groves of the plain and cut willow and box-wood; they cast for them axes of nine score pounds, and great swords they cast with blades of six score pounds each one, with pommels and hilts of thirty pounds. They cast for Gilgamesh the axe "Might of Heroes" and the bow of Anshan; and Gilgamesh was armed and Enkidu; and the weight of the arms they carried was thirty score pounds.

The victory of Gilgamesh and Enkidu over Humbaba parallels the massive assault by urbanites on the natural resources of the world, turning the products of nature into objects of trade and commerce, and using them to build cities.

Now the mountains were moved and all the hills, for the guardian of the forest was killed. They attacked the cedars, the seven splendours of Humbaba were extinguished. So they pressed on into the forest . . . and while Gilgamesh felled the first of the trees of the forest Enkidu cleared their roots as far as the banks of Euphrates.

Lower Mesopotamia has no stone, wood, or metal. To get these raw materials, Sumerians had to send parties over long distances to quarry, cut, and dig; to trade; and to conquer. The mixed responses of the gods to the murder of Humbaba suggest the deep ambivalence of the Sumerians to their own increasing power:

[Gilgamesh and Enkidu] set [the corpse of] Humbaba before the gods, before Enlil; they kissed the ground and dropped the shroud and set the head before him. When he saw the head of Humbaba, Enlil raged at them, "Why did you do this thing? From henceforth may the fire be on your faces, may it eat the bread that you eat, may it drink where you drink."

SOURCE
The Code of Hammurabi

Hammurabi legislated in the name of the gods for the benefit of his people:

Anum and Enlil named me
    to promote the welfare of the people,
    me, Hammurabi, the devout god-fearing prince,
    to cause justice to prevail in the land,
    to destroy the wicked and the evil,
    that the strong might not oppress the weak
    . . . that justice might be dealt the
    orphan and the widow.

The legislation was wide ranging and included:
• Laws governing slavery, including a prohibition on concealing a fugitive slave.
• Laws for maintaining the irrigation canals, and penalizing a landlord who allows his dikes to break causing damage to his neighbor's crop.
• Numerous laws governing marriage, bride price, dowry, adultery, and incest. Although women do own the dowries given them, their rights of ownership are limited. Marriage is presented in large part as a commercial transaction, in which the groom's family pays a bride-price to the bride's father while the bride's father gives her a dowry. Childlessness is grounds for divorce but the husband must return his wife's dowry. Behavioral restraints in marriage are unequal: if the husband "has been going out and disparaging her greatly," the wife may leave, taking her dowry; if the wife is "a gadabout, thus neglecting her house (and) humiliating her husband," he may have her drowned.
• Laws of adoption that recognize the parental rights of the adoptive parents over those of the biological parents.

If a seignior has destroyed the eye of a member of the aristocracy, they shall destroy his eye.

If he has broken another seignior's bone, they shall break his bone.

If he has destroyed the eye of a commoner or broken the bone of a commoner, he shall pay one mina of silver.

If he has destroyed the eye of a seignior's slave or broken the bone of a seignior's slave, he shall pay one half his value.

• Laws specifying payments to physicians as well as punishments for medical malpractice. Both vary in accord with the class of the patient.
• Laws of consumer protection for house buyers, boat renters, contractors for services. In one case, a brutal punishment for faulty workmanship indicates that common people, too, were viewed as commodities:

"If [the collapse of a building] has caused the death of a son of the owner of the house, they shall put the son of that builder to death."

• Laws fixing payments for services, rental rates, and daily wages for various occupational categories, suggesting powerful state control of the economy.

Stele of Hammurabi, from Susa, Iran, *c.* 1760 B.C.E. Hammurabi, the great king of Babylon, is the first known ruler to have created a detailed legal code. On this commemorative stone slab, he is shown receiving the Babylonian laws from the sun-god Shamash (compare Moses receiving the Torah from God, p. 299). The laws themselves are inscribed below on the stele. (*Louvre, Paris*)

the ground, and Rawlinson had a scaffolding constructed so that he could reach it, sometimes hanging suspended from a rope. Rawlinson and other scholars found that the three scripts represented different, but related languages. Two were in Old Persian—one in an alphabetic script, the other in cuneiform—and the third was in a cuneiform version of Elamite. Now the key to deciphering cuneiform, and thus rediscovering Sumerian, was at hand.

In the 1840s, extensive archaeological digs in Mesopotamia uncovered thousands of tablets and fragments, especially at Khorsabad in the palace of Sargon II (r. 721–705 B.C.E.), ruler of Assyria in the eighth century B.C.E., and at Nineveh, in the library of King Ashurbanipal, his great-grandson (r. 669–626 B.C.E.). Beginning in 1877, excavations of Sumerian sites began, first at Lagash, then at Nippur, where 30,000 tablets and fragments were excavated, most in Sumerian. Later excavations were carried on at Fara, Adab, Kish, Warka (the modern Arabic name for the city called Uruk by the ancient Sumerians, and Erech in the Hebrew Bible), Ur, and Eridu. Through texts and digs the Sumerians—their economy, belief systems, and culture—were resurrected.

Most of the texts deal with practical, everyday business transactions and administration. One contains the first known recipe for the ale that Sumerians enjoyed so much. Others recorded the world's first written literature.

Gilgamesh (see Source, pp. 54–5) presents a world of many gods before whom humans are passive and frightened subjects. Gilgamesh, however, defers neither to human nor to god. Devastated by the death of his closest friend Enkidu, he sets off to the underworld in search of eternal life. Along the way he encounters the Sumerian prototype of Noah. Utnapishtim tells him of a flood that destroyed all human life except his family. They had been saved by a god who counseled him to build a boat. In the bleak underworld of the dead, Gilgamesh obtains a plant that will give eternal youth, but on his return voyage a snake rises from the water and snatches it from him. Gilgamesh recognizes a fundamental truth: "Misery comes at last to the healthy man, the end of life is sorrow" (p. 93) and "There is no permanence" (p. 106). Resigned to death, Gilgamesh returns to Uruk. Finally, he dies at a ripe old age, honored and mourned by his fellow citizens.

A second form of written document that marks the evolution to a more complex society is the legal code. Archaeologists discovered at Ur fragments of a legal code that dates to the twenty-first century B.C.E., and legal systems must have already existed even before this. Legal systems remained crucial for all Mesopotamian urban societies. The post-Sumerian code of the Babylonian King Hammurabi (see Source opposite), formulated about 1750 B.C.E. (but rediscovered to the modern world only in 1901–02), seems to have been built on the earlier concepts.

EARLY URBANIZATION: SOME MODERN CRITIQUES

Politically, each of the major cities of Sumer was also a state, ruling over the contiguous agricultural areas and often in conflict with neighboring city-states. The bas relief pictorial records of the city-states often depict royal armies, military expeditions, conquests, and a general appreciation, even an exaltation, of warfare. The armies included the personal palace guards of the king, professional soldiers, and additional forces conscripted in times of war. The fighting seems to have been frequent, and the main combatants were the largest of the city-states: Kish, Uruk, Ur, and, later, Lagash and Umma. Battles were fought hand-to-hand and also from donkey-drawn chariots.

The warfare was especially destructive because the kings and soldiers believed themselves to be upholding the honor not only of their cities but also of their gods. A Hymn to the Ekur, "Mountain House," the famous temple of the god Enlil in the city of Nippur, fixes the link between the city, its chief temple, and its principal god:

> The great house, it is a mountain great,
> The house of Enlil, it is a mountain great,
> The house of Ninlil, it is a mountain great,
> (Pritchard, p. 582)

When cities are sacred, conflicts between them mean holy war, fights to the finish.

The "Lamentation over the Destruction of Ur," which was addressed to Ningal, goddess of the Ekushnugal Temple, describes that city's utter destruction after the Elamites sacked it, exiled its ruler, and destroyed the temple, about 1950 B.C.E.:

After your city had been destroyed, how now can
you exist!
After your house had been destroyed, how has your
heart led you on!
Your city has become a strange city; how now can
you exist!
Your house has become a house of tears, how has
your heart led you on!
Your city which has been made into ruins—you are
no longer its mistress!
Your righteous house which has been given over to
the pickax—you no longer inhabit it,
Your people have been led to slaughter—you are no
longer their queen . . .

(Kramer, *The Sumerians*, p. 142)

Lewis Mumford, one of the most respected modern commentators on the history of cities, regarded this early union of power, religion, and continuous warfare as a permanent curse of urban life:

Once the city came into existence, with its collective
increase in power in every department . . . mass
extermination and mass destruction came to prevail.
. . . war, even when it is disguised by seemingly
hardheaded economic demands, uniformly turns
into a religious performance; nothing less than a
wholesale ritual sacrifice. (p. 42)

The socialist philosopher Karl Marx further blamed the first cities for establishing two fundamental antagonisms in human society—the conflict between city and countryside and class conflict. In *Capital* he wrote: "The foundation of every division of labor that is well developed, and brought about by a change in commodities, is the separation between town and country. It may be said that the whole economic history of the society is summed up in the movement of this antithesis." In *The German Ideology*, he wrote: "Here first became manifest the division of the population into two great classes, which is directly based on the division of labor and on the instruments of production."

The first Sumerian cities did, indeed, foster division of labor into occupational categories, but the hierarchies seem to have been more differentiated than Marx suggests. We have noted the roles of kings, priests, landowners, architects, scribes, long-distance traders, local merchants, artisans, cooks, farmers, soldiers, laborers—the whole panoply of occupational categories absent in villages but forming the backbone of a sophisticated urban economy and society. Priests and kings did hold great wealth and power, and much control of the means of production, but it is not clear that they formed an exclusive category of "haves" versus "have nots." The spectrum seems to have been more varied, including a substantial group of middle classes. But there is, nevertheless, much evidence of the enormous power of the aristocracy. The death pits of kings and their servants suggest that the Sumerians may have acquiesced in enormous royal and priestly power.

At the bottom of the hierarchy were slaves. People entered slavery in four ways: some were captured in battle; some were sentenced to slavery as punishment for crimes; some sold themselves (or their family members) into slavery to cope with poverty and debt; and some were born into slavery. We have no record of the number or proportion of slaves in the general population of Sumer and its cities. The law codes' extensive regulations of slaves and slavery suggest, however, their widespread existence.

Finally, the transformation of society from a rural, egalitarian, kin base to an urban, hierarchical, territorial, and class base may have provided the entering wedge for the subordination of women. Some women in Sumer had great power. Several seem to have held independent high administrative posts in major temples controlling large land holdings. Some like Shagshag, wife of King Uruinimgina (also known as Urukagina), *c.* 2300 B.C.E., held similar powers in the name of their husband. Lady Pu-abi (*c.* 2500 B.C.E.) was discovered in death-pit 800, adorned with gold and buried with several other bodies, presumably servants, suggesting a woman of high rank, perhaps a queen. Women in Sumer generally had certain basic rights, including the rights to hold property, engage in business, and serve as legal witness. Nevertheless, argues the feminist historian Gerda Lerner, women, even queens, were often only pawns in the power struggles of men. Before the evolution of city-states, with their warfare and hierarchical class structures, Lerner argues, the status of women and men had been more equal.

Lerner enlists the historical record to demonstrate that inequalities between men and women are not products of unchanging and unchangeable biological differences, but rather cultural patterns emerging at specific times, created by humans, that can be altered to restore a previous equality. She cites the anthropologist Rayna Rapp:

The stele of vultures. This limestone tablet, or stele, depicts in bas relief Lagash's victory over Umma, in about 2450 B.C.E. Some 3600 of the enemy were slaughtered by King Eannatum of Lagash and his soldiers, who are seen here marching into battle. (*Louvre, Paris*)

In pre-state societies, total social production was organized through kinship. As states gradually arose, kinship structures got stripped and transformed to underwrite the existence and legitimacy of more powerful politicized domains. In this process . . . women were subordinated with (and in relation to) kinship. (Lerner, p. 55)

Patriarchy and gender hierarchy, Lerner and Rapp both argue, were not natural to human society; they were introduced for the first time in human history in the cities of Sumer. Our own historical era, they imply, should reject them.

The evidence from both pre-state societies and early Sumer concerning gender relations is fragmentary, and many eminent scholars suggest that Lerner's interpretations go beyond the available data. However, the new questions addressed by contemporary feminist historians to the ancient data will continue to motivate new research into neglected aspects of the past.

MYTHISTORY

The modern critiques of Mumford, Marx, and Lerner remind us how seriously the past, and our preconceptions—or myths—about it, have influenced our thinking. They urge us to rethink in order to redirect our future from repeating some terrible mistake of the distant urban past: making warfare into a religious obligation, isolating city from countryside, establishing oppressive class distinctions, and institutionalizing patriarchal suppression of women.

Underlying these warnings, however, is yet another myth. The pre-urban agricultural village, it is widely believed, was more egalitarian, less warlike, more integrated into nature. We do not know if this was so. Pre-urban villagers produced no written records, and their artifactual remains are thin, inconclusive, and subject to widely divergent interpretation. Scholars draw many of their conclusions concerning pre-urban life from observing isolated groups in today's world, such as the !Kung people of the African Kalahari desert of a generation ago. But here, too, both observations and interpretations differ.

We do know, however, that early cities facilitated accomplishments that people then and now considered vitally important: increases in human population (a questionable asset under today's conditions, but not then); economic growth; effective organization for common tasks; creative breakthroughs in technology, art, and, perhaps most significantly, in writing and literature; the inauguration of a rule of law (see Source, p. 56); and the formation of a non-kin-based community with a sense of purpose and humanity.

They did not always succeed. In addition to the critiques cited above, the city-states could not work out a system of government and regulation that would enable them to live in peace. Both powerful and vulnerable, oscillating between psalms of victory and lamentations of defeat, they seemed to fall into one of two painful alternatives: inter-state warfare or conquest by imperial rulers. Their shortcomings cost them dearly. As long as each political entity was a law unto itself, as were the city-states of Sumer, and of classical Greece, and of pre-Han China, and of India during much of its history, and of medieval Europe, war was the likely result. This problem of warfare among competitive states persists to our own day, although the scale has escalated from the city-state to the independent nation-state.

SUMER: KEY EVENTS AND PEOPLE

c. 3300 (B.C.E.)	Sumerians invent writing.
c. 3000 (B.C.E.)	Sumerians become dominant power in southern Mesopotamia.
c. 2800–2340	Sumerian city-states: early dynastic period sees spread of Mesopotamian culture to the north.
c. 2350	Sargon captures Sumer and establishes Semitic dynasty at Akkad, the new capital.
c. 2125–2027	Third dynasty of Ur.
c. 1900	Ammorites at Babylon.
1792–1750	Reign of Hammurabi; Babylon is the new capital of Mesopotamia.
c. 1600	Invasion by Hittites and Kassites, destroying Hammurabi's dynasty.

The evolution of the large, complex city implies the evolution of a state capable of organizing and administering it. In aristocratic and monarchical Sumer, much depended on the disposition of the king. Even Gilgamesh, who ended his royal career devoted to, and honored by, his people, had begun differently. In Gilgamesh's youth, "the men of Uruk muttered in their houses":

> his arrogance has no bounds by day or night. No son is left with his father, for Gilgamesh takes them all, even the children . . . his lust leaves no virgin to her lover, neither the warrior's daughter nor the wife of the noble.

They realized that it should have been different— "The king should be a shepherd to his people"— but they apparently had to submit. The only recourse they saw was muttering in their houses and praying to their gods.

This question of the proper organization of the state became the key question of urbanization since the time of Gilgamesh and the Sumerian city-states. Two thousand years afterward—and two thousand years before our own day—in the city-states of ancient Greece, Aristotle summed up the issue:

> When several villages are united in a single complete community, large enough to be nearly or quite self-sufficing, the state comes into existence, originating in the bare needs of life, and continuing in existence for the sake of a good life . . . man is by nature a political animal [*zoon politikon*, a creature of the polis or city-state] . . . the association of living beings who have this sense makes a family and a state . . . justice is the bond of men in states, for the administration of justice, which is the determination of what is just, is the principle of order in political society.

From the time of Sumer, the political questions, the questions of how to organize and administer the **polis** or city-state to achieve a good life, have been central to the process of urbanization. In Sumer the answers depended on the edicts of the king and the priests. In the next two chapters, we shall see how these questions and answers evolved in other primary cities and city-states around the world.

CONNECTION: *The reign of Sargon I and Mesopotamia's first empires, pp. 123–4*

BIBLIOGRAPHY

Aristotle. *Basic Works*, trans. and ed. Richard McKeon. (New York: Random House, 1941).

Bairoch, Paul. *Cities and Economic Development: From the Dawn of History to the Present*, trans. Christopher Braider. (Chicago: University of Chicago Press, 1988).

Cohen, Mark. *The Food Crisis in Prehistory* (New Haven: Yale University Press, 1977).

Fagan, Brian M. *People of the Earth: An Introduction to World Prehistory* (New York: HarperCollins, 8th ed., 1995).

Gilgamesh, The Epic of, trans. and ed. N.K. Sandars. (Harmondsworth, Middlesex: Penguin Books, 1972).

Kramer, Samuel Noah. *History Begins at Sumer* (New York: Doubleday and Co., Inc., 1959).

Kramer, Samuel Noah. *The Sumerians: Their History, Culture, and Character* (Chicago: University of Chicago Press, 1963).

Lerner, Gerda. *The Creation of Patriarchy* (New York: Oxford University Press, 1986).

Marx, Karl. *Capital: A Critique of Political Economy*, trans. Ben Fowkes (New York: Vintage Books, 1977).

Marx, Karl and Friedrich Engels. *The German Ideology* (New York: International Publishers, 1939).

Moore, Andrew M.T. "The Development of Neolithic Societies in the Near East," *Advances in World Archaeology*. Vol. 4., ed. Fred Wendorf and Angela E. Close (Orlando: Academic Press, Inc., 1985).

Mumford, Lewis. *The City in History* (New York: Harcourt, Brace and World, Inc., 1961).

Oppenheim, A. Leo. *Ancient Mesopotamia. Portrait of a Dead Civilization* (Chicago: University of Chicago Press, 1964).

Past Worlds: The Times Atlas of Archaeology (Maplewood, NJ: Hammond Inc., 1988).

Postgate, Nicholas. *The First Empires* (Oxford: Elsevier Phaidon, 1977).

Pritchard, James B., ed. *Ancient Near Eastern Texts Relating to the Old Testament* (Princeton: Princeton University Press, 3rd ed. with supplement, 1969).

Redman, Charles L. *The Rise of Civilization: From Early Farmers to Urban Society in the Ancient Near East* (San Francisco: W.H. Freeman and Co., 1978).

Sjoberg, Gideon. "The Origin and Evolution of Cities," *Scientific American*. (September 1965), 19–27.

Wheatley, Paul. *The Pivot of the Four Quarters* (Chicago: Aldine Publishing Company, 1971).

Wooley, C. Leonard. *Excavations at Ur* (London: Ernest Benn, Ltd., 1954).

3 RIVER VALLEY CIVILIZATIONS

7000 B.C.E.—750 B.C.E.

"[Cities exhibit] marked individuality, so strong, so full of 'character' from the beginning that they have many of the attributes of human personalities."

LEWIS MUMFORD

THE RISE OF CITIES AND STATES ALONG THE NILE AND INDUS

Two urban civilizations flanked Mesopotamia: the Nile valley to the southwest and the Indus valley to the southeast. Scholarly opinion is divided as to whether these two city systems learned to build cities and states from the Mesopotamian example or invented them independently. Whatever the truth, peoples of these three river valleys created separate and distinct patterns of urbanization and political life.

In the Tigris–Euphrates valley, development of the physical city and the institutional state went hand-in-hand. In the Nile valley, the creation of the Egyptian state had greater significance than the growth of individual cities. In the Indus valley we have extensive archaeological information on the cities, but know next to nothing about the formation of the state. Until scholars learn to decipher the script and language of the Indus civilization, our knowledge of their institutional development will remain limited.

EGYPT: THE GIFT OF THE NILE

The pyramids and Sphinx at Giza near modern Cairo in the north of Egypt, the temples at Karnak and Thebes in the south, and the pharaohs' tombs nearby in the Valley of the Kings proclaim the wealth, skills, and organizational capacity of ancient Egypt. Despite these monumental structures, we know less about Egypt's ancient cities than about those of Mesopotamia, for the Nile, the ribbon of water that is Egypt's life, has washed away many ancient structures and eroded their foundations. On the other hand, we know much more about the Egyptian state, and for ancient Egypt, the written record provides more information than the physical artifacts.

EARLIEST EGYPT: HOW DO WE KNOW?

During its 5000 years of recorded history, Egypt was conquered and ruled by several civilizations. Rule by indigenous dynasties

ANCIENT EGYPT

DATE	POLITICAL	RELIGION AND CULTURE	SOCIAL DEVELOPMENT
3500 B.C.E.		● Hieroglyphics in use	● Villages in Nile valley
3000 B.C.E.	● Archaic Period (c. 3000–2700)	● Ruler of Egypt becoming godlike	● First use of stone in building
2500 B.C.E.	● Old Kingdom (c. 2700–2200)	● Step pyramid at Saqqara ● Pyramids at Giza, including Great Pyramid (of Khufu)	● Irrigation programs along Nile
2000 B.C.E.	● First Intermediate Period (c. 2200–2050) ● Middle Kingdom (c. 2050–1750) Second Intermediate Period (c. 1750–1550)	● Golden age of art and craftwork (1991–1786)	● Social order upset; few monuments built (2181–1991) ● Country divided into principalities (1786–1567)
1500 B.C.E.	● New Kingdom (c. 1550–1050)	● Akhenaten (d.1335) rejected pantheon for worship of Aten ● Temple complexes at Karnak/Luxor	● Began with colonial expansion; ended with divided rule
1000 B.C.E.	● Third Intermediate Period (c. 1050–650); three Libyan dynasties (from 945) give way to a Nubian one (from 751)	● Book of the Dead (c. 1000)	● Revival of prosperity and restoration of cults
650 B.C.E.	● Late Period (650–332)		● Completion of Nile–Red Sea canal
500 B.C.E.	● Alexander the Great founds Alexandria (332)		
100 B.C.E.		● Rosetta Stone	
30 B.C.E.	● Romans conquer Egypt		

began about 3100 B.C.E. and continued with few exceptions for 2600 years. For the next 2500 years, foreign rulers dominated Egypt: Persia conquered in 525 B.C.E., followed by Alexander the Great in 332 B.C.E., and Rome in 30 B.C.E. As the Roman Empire divided in 395 C.E. (see p. 188), Egypt came under the rule of Byzantine Christians until they, in turn, were conquered by Arabs in 641 C.E. Islam then gradually became the dominant religious culture, and remained so even after Europeans came to dominate Egypt in the late nineteenth century. Egypt has undergone so many transformations over such a long time that its earliest indigenous roots are hard to uncover. Even the language of ancient Egypt has been lost; today Arabic is Egypt's main language. Many cities in Egypt carry several names, imposed by successive conquerors. For example, the city called Nekhen by the Egyptians was renamed Hierakonpolis by the Greeks.

The modern attempt to reconstruct the past of ancient Egypt began with Napoleon's invasion in 1798. His military expedition failed to establish French rule in Egypt, but the historical and linguistic research it encouraged led to the recovery of much of Egypt's past. In 1799 an officer in Napoleon's engineering corps discovered a large stone near the western, or Rosetta, mouth of the Nile. The Rosetta Stone (see p. 67) carried an inscription from the year 196 B.C.E. by the Greek ruler of Egypt in three languages: the most ancient Egyptian script, hieroglyphics; demotic Egyptian, a simplified script based on the hieroglyphs; and Greek. By comparing the ancient Egyptian forms with the Greek, which he knew, Jean François Champollion le Jeune began to decipher the hieroglyphs, as well as their simplifications into later scripts. In 1822 he published the results of his work. Modern Egyptology was born.

Writing began early in Egypt, almost simultaneously with ancient Mesopotamia, about 3500–3000 B.C.E. Egyptians may have learned the concept of writing from Mesopotamia, but in place of cuneiform, they developed their own hieroglyphic script (see Spotlight, pp. 66–7). In fact some scholars believe that the invention of writing in Egypt was completely independent of the Mesopotamian invention, and possibly preceded it. Scribes, an important and highly regarded occupational group in ancient Egypt, later invented two shorthand transcriptions of hieroglyphs—first, hieratic script, later, the even more abbreviated form, demotic script. They wrote on stone tablets, like the Rosetta Stone; on limestone flakes; on pottery; and on papyrus, a durable paper-parchment, made by laying crossways the inner piths of the stalk of papyrus plants and pressing them until they formed into sheets.

As in Mesopotamia, some of the earliest Egyptian writing is notation for business and administration. Over the millennia it grew into a rich literature, including chronological lists of kings, religious inscriptions, spells to protect the dead (see Source, p. 75), autobiographies (see Source, p. 76), stories, wisdom texts of moral instruction, love poems, hymns to gods, prayers, and mathematical, astronomical, and medical texts. From this literature, scholars have reconstructed a substantial picture of the history of Egypt. But for the earliest 500 to 1000 years, until about 2400 B.C.E., the written records are thin. They do, however, provide a list of *nomes*, or administrative districts, suggesting the structure of the Egyptian state as early as 2900 B.C.E. They also provide lists of the earliest kings of Egypt.

King lists written on stone about 2400 B.C.E., and on papyrus about 1200 B.C.E., combined with lists compiled by the Greek historian Manetho in the third century B.C.E., give the names of the entire sequence of kings from Zekhen and Narmer,

The Great Sphinx and the Pyramid of Khefren, Giza. The greatest of all the pyramids, the burial tombs of the pharaohs, are at Giza, near modern Cairo, and date to around 2600–2500 B.C.E. The face of the sphinx—a mythological creature with a lion's body and a human head—is thought to be a likeness of King Khafre, who ruled Egypt some time after 2600 B.C.E.

about 3100 B.C.E, all the way through the Persian conquest in 525 B.C.E. and Alexander the Great's victory in 332 B.C.E. After that event we know the basic chronology of Egypt's political history from many sources.

Archaeological excavations, primarily for monumental objects, began in 1858, although tomb robbing and the theft of ancient artifacts had been continuous from earliest times. The annual expeditions of British Egyptologist W.M. Flinders Petrie, beginning in 1880, introduced more scientific archaeological studies of Egypt and of Nubia, immediately to the south. By about 1900 scholars had identified the basic outlines of Egypt's history from, perhaps, 3600 B.C.E. to their own time.

EARLIEST EGYPT: WHAT DO WE KNOW?

By 12,000 B.C.E., residents of Nubia and Upper Egypt were using stones to grind local wild grasses into food, and by 8000 B.C.E., flour was prepared from their seeds. By 6000 B.C.E. the first traces appear of the cultivation of wheat and barley, grasses and cereals, and of the domestication of sheep and goats. To the west, the Sahara was becoming drier and some of its inhabitants may have moved to the Nile valley bringing with them more advanced methods of cultivation. Between 4000 and 3000 B.C.E. the bronze age began in Egypt as the new metal was used in tools and weapons. Population increased, as did the size of villages, and by 3300 B.C.E. the first walled towns appeared in the upper Nile, at Nagada and Hierakonpolis. Tombs for their rulers and elites were built nearby.

King lists, records of the *nomes* of Upper Egypt, and inscriptions and designs on pottery suggest strongly that Egyptian national life and history began with the unification of the kingdom about the year 3000 B.C.E. A single king, perhaps Narmer, succeeded in bringing all Egypt under his rule. The king was becoming a god, responsible for maintaining *ma'at*, justice and order, throughout the kingdom. The increase in monumental tombs and funerary objects suggests an increasing hierarchy and an uneven distribution of wealth, two common characteristics of state building. A more or less unified artistic style in both pottery and architecture after that time mirrors the unification of Egyptian politics.

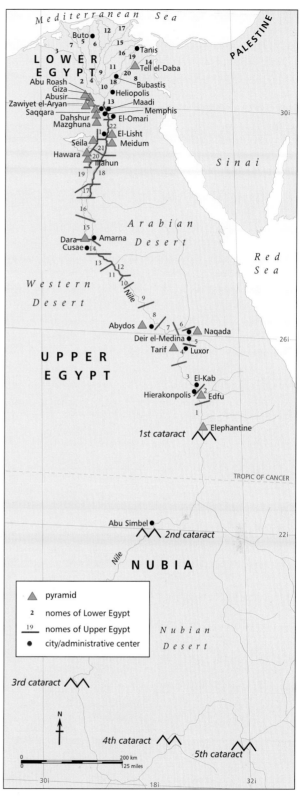

Land of the Nile Stretching over 1000 miles along the Nile River, ancient Egyptian civilization depended on a strong government. The kingdom was divided into Lower and Upper Egypt, and further subdivided into *nomes* (tax districts).

SPOTLIGHT *Writing*

INVENTING IT, DECIPHERING IT

The contents of commercial packages, the names of their owners, lists of all kinds—these were the subject matter of the world's first writing, invented in Sumer about 3300 B.C.E. The earliest Sumerian scribes employed styluses made of bone or of hollow reed stems to incise **pictograms,** picture representations of the objects of their writing, onto clay tablets. By 3000 B.C.E. they were representing the key features of the pictures in wedge-shaped signs that we call **cuneiform**, (*cuneus* means wedge in Latin). Some cuneiform signs represent whole words, but others represent individual phonetic sounds based on the words. **Figure 1**, a clay tablet from about 3000 B.C.E., represents the transitional period, combining some picture representation with some cuneiform. Read from right to left, it lists various rations to be distributed over a five-day period, including the name and location of the recipient.

As the cuneiform became more sophisticated, so too did the subject matter, and by about 2400 B.C.E. Sumerian writing began to transmit stories, proclaim political and military victories, sing the poetry of lovers, praise the glories of gods, and lament the fall of cities. Written literature had begun. Many later peoples in the region, Elamites, Babylonians, Assyrians, and Akkadians, adopted cuneiform to write their own languages. Tens of thousands of Sumerian clay tablets have been excavated and transferred to research institutions around the world.

How did scholars learn to read the cuneiform? At Behistun, twenty miles from Kermanshah, Iran, a huge rock inscribed with 414 lines in Old Persian and 263 in Elamite came to the attention of British army officers in the mid-nineteenth century. The two inscriptions were translations of one another, enabling linguists who could already read the Persian to decipher the cuneiform script.

A similar process of decipherment yielded the secrets of the ancient Egyptian **hieroglyphs** (Greek for "sacred carvings"). The earliest of these pictographs

Figure 1 Clay tablet with cuneiform, Jemdet Nasr, Iraq, 3000 B.C.E.

Figure 2 The "Rosetta Stone," ancient Egyptian, 196 C.E. (*British Museum, London*)

date to about 3300 B.C.E., the concept probably deriving from Sumer although the forms of the writing are different. A stone inscription in three scripts—hieroglyphic, a later Egyptian shorthand called demotic, and Greek— was discovered at Rosetta in the Nile Delta by an officer in the French army in 1799. This "Rosetta stone" (**figure 2**) enabled scholars to decipher the hieroglyphs by comparing them with the Greek that they did know. Coincidentally, the earliest hieroglyphs had also been written on stone, but after about 2600 B.C.E. Egyptian scribes usually wrote on papyrus, "paper" produced from pressing a weave of flattened reeds together. The dry desert air of the Nile valley preserved multitudes of these papyrus manuscripts.

Climaxing a century and a half of research, scholars in the 1980s scored new breakthroughs in the decipherment of the hieroglyphic writing of the Central American Maya peoples, which dates back as far as 100 B.C.E. The "Madrid Codex" (**figure 3**), named for the city where it is now stored and dating to 800–1200 C.E., is one of the four books remaining from the Maya. Written on beaten-bark paper, folded like an accordion, it is read from left to right to the bottom of the page, then turned over for the next page. Its hieroglyphs and pictures, developed independently of any contact with the eastern hemisphere, provide an almanac of calendrical, astronomical, religious, ritual, and sacrificial information. The 1980s scholarship has also deciphered the accounts of the wars and conquests of the Maya kings, adding a new dimension to our understanding of their life and culture.

The oldest known alphabetic writing, a Semitic script with influences dating to about 1900 B.C.E., was discovered on limestone in the Egyptian desert near Thebes in 1999. The *New York Times* described this alphabetic writing as "an invention by workaday people that simplified and democratized writing, freeing it from the hands of official scribes. [It] was revolutionary in a sense comparable to the invention of the printing press much later" (November 14, 1999, p. A–1).

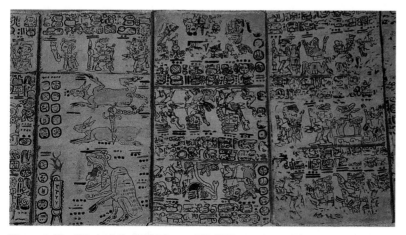

Figure 3 The "Madrid Codex," Mayan, 800–1200 C.E.

The Palette of King Narmer, *c.* **3200 B.C.E.** This slate palette, used for ritual purposes, shows the power of King Narmer, who had just united Upper and Lower Egypt. In the top register, Narmer (left) inspects the bodies of dead enemies (right); at the bottom, the strength of the pharaoh is symbolized by the bull shown destroying the walls of a city. (*Egyptian Museum, Cairo*)

By 2700 B.C.E. Egypt exhibited the cultural complexity associated with early civilizations, including a national religious ideology and the centralized control of political administration and even of artistic productivity. Nevertheless, thousands of small, largely self-sufficient communities seem to have persisted within a largely decentralized economy for the local production and consumption of food and basic commodities.

In ancient Egyptian records the creation of a centralized kingdom was more valued than the construction of individual cities. Unlike Mesopotamia, Egypt has almost no existing record of independent city-states. The Nile River, the passage of time, overbuilding, and re-cycling have exacted their toll:

Few pharaonic towns have survived in anything like their original form. Some have disappeared beneath the rising alluvium, others have been destroyed by the overbuilding of later generations, while those which remained reasonably intact have suffered severely from the depredations of the peasantry looking for *sebakh* (a fertilizer made from sediment) among the ruins. (Walters, cited in Cotterell, p. 38)

Written records for the earliest years do not provide much help:

The Early Dynastic period is calculated as having lasted for nearly 500 years [3100–2613 B.C.E.], but the almost total absence of written evidence makes it a dark age for historians, illuminated only infrequently. (Walters, cited in Cotterell, p. 23)

The Cities

We do have some information, however. Flinders Petrie, who established the foundations of modern, systematic archaeology in Egypt about a century ago, argued that by 3600 B.C.E. a string of villages lined the Nile River, at intervals of every 20 miles (30 kilometers) or so. The village economies were based on cereal agriculture, and they were linked by trade along the river, although, since they mostly produced the same basic foodstuffs, these villages traded only a little among themselves. They give little evidence of social stratification. These settlements characterized the "Nagada I" period (*c.* 3500 B.C.E.).

Among the villages, however, somewhat larger market towns must have grown up. Geographers have developed "central place theory" to describe the growth of villages into towns, and it suggests that where ecological factors are approximately equal, as they would have been along the Nile, equally spaced, small settlements will grow up. Then, because the functions of administration, business, and transportation require some centralization, some of the villages will begin to house those functions. These selected villages, spaced strategically at larger intervals in the landscape, will grow into larger settlements, and perhaps even into full-fledged cities.

In early dynastic Egypt, the siting of the administrative headquarters of the *nomes*, regional administrative units, would have given just such a boost to the towns in which they were located. Some settlements also hosted additional functions, including irrigation control and religious observance. Urban consolidation marks the beginning of "Nagada II" culture (*c.* 3300 B.C.E.). The development of Hierakonpolis along the Nile in Upper Egypt illustrates the process.

Excavations under a team led by Michael Hoffman in about 1980 found that the population of Hierakonpolis grew from a few hundred in 3800 B.C.E. to 10,500 by 3500 B.C.E. At least two cemeteries served the city, one for common people, another for the wealthier traders and more powerful administrators. What precipitated the population growth, occupational specialization, and social hierarchy? Hoffman argues that the ecological balance between desert and grassland collapsed, perhaps because of droughts that occurred periodically along the Nile, or perhaps because of overgrazing. Local leaders introduced and implemented irrigation systems that saved agriculture and even enriched it. These changes enhanced the economy of the region and created the subsequent growth and change. Indeed, Hierakonpolis seems to have been the capital from which Pharaoh Narmer, the mythical Menes, unified Egypt.

Political/administrative leaders continued to create irrigation systems along the Nile. Anthropologist Karl Butzer has noted the introduction of irrigation programs in Old Kingdom Egypt, *c.* 2700–2200 B.C.E., the development of the Fayyum Lake region and the transfer of population to it during the Middle Kingdom, *c.* 2050–1750 B.C.E.; and the development of "shaduf" irrigation during the New Kingdom, *c.* 1550–1050 B.C.E. Egypt, the gift of the Nile, had different, and much less frequent problems with its water supply than did Mesopotamia, but here, too, the control of water resources influenced the formation of cities and the state.

Hierakonpolis housed a palace, a temple, and prominent tombs. Perhaps the city flourished because its temple community and worship became especially attractive to

surrounding villages. The combination of irrigation, administration, and worship built the city.

Earlier archaeological reports seemed to suggest that after unification under a single pharaoh, Egyptian cities were not usually walled. The central government may have taken action against the kind of inter-city warfare that characterized Mesopotamia, rendering defensive walls unnecessary. Also, although invasions occurred from time to time and required defensive precautions, the desert to the east and west of the Nile valley provided an adequate natural shield. More recent excavations, however, question this view of open cities. The walls of some cities have been uncovered, and archaeologists are beginning to suspect that other walls may have been removed and the materials used for other purposes. Robert Wenke, Professor of Anthropology at the University of Washington, endorses this revised view:

> Most of the major Old Kingdom Upper Egyptian settlements seem to have been walled complexes of tightly packed mudbrick houses. . . . Few of the Old Kingdom sites in the Delta seem to have been enclosed in walls, but it is entirely possible that these Old Kingdom Delta settlements in fact had walls that have long since been destroyed by the action of *sebakhiin*—farmers who dig out old occupations and use the sediments for fertilizing and raising agricultural fields. (Wenke, p. 312)

Excavations at El-Kab, across the Nile from Hierankopolis, revealed a city enclosed in a wall, 1600 feet square, dating to 1788–1580 B.C.E. This wall, in turn, seems to have

Figurine of bone and ivory, "Nagada I" period, *c.* 4000–3600 B.C.E. Egypt's rise to a mighty empire had modest roots: a string of loosely affiliated villages lining the Nile. This attractive figurine, whose eyes are inlaid with lapis lazuli, was unearthed from a tomb of this early, predynastic age. (*British Museum, London*)

PROFILE
Akhenaten
AND HIS CITY AKHETATEN

Modern excavations at Amarna on the east bank of the Nile unearthed the ruins of an ancient Egyptian capital that owed its entire existence to the idiosyncratic vision of one ruler—King Amenhotep IV, better known as Akhenaten.

Within a few years of coming to the throne, King Amenhotep IV (r. 1353–35 B.C.E.) challenged the order of ancient Egypt by adopting a new monotheistic religion. Instead of worshiping a whole pantheon of gods, he offered his devotion to a single deity—Aten, god of the solar disk (or sun). Amenhotep appointed himself mediator between his people and the god and abandoned his official dynastic name in favor of Akhenaten ("he who serves Aten"). The name of Ammon, principal god of the old religion, was swiftly erased from inscriptions throughout Egypt, as were the words "all gods" in certain texts.

To bolster the new order and escape the power of the hostile priesthood, Akhenaten moved his capital 200 miles (300 kilometers) north from the established center of Thebes to an untouched site in the desert. The city that he built was named Akhetaten ("horizon of Aten"; present-day Amarna) and it was here that Akhenaten, the Great Royal Wife Queen Nefertiti, and their six daughters practiced the new religion. The eccentricity of Akhetaten's ruler was reflected in the city's architecture, sculpture, and wall painting. Solid statements of eternity gave way to a freedom of expression that emphasized the here-and-now. Aten was worshiped in an open temple that ushered in the sun's rays rather than in the dark, austere sanctuary usually designated for worship. Residential buildings included spacious villas with large gardens and pools to house wealthy officials. In artistic expression, solemnity gave way to an unprecedented liveliness and invention. Curious depictions of Akhenaten's drooping jaw and misshapen body capture his individuality, marking a departure from the highly stylized representations of previous pharaohs. (Perhaps they were sculpted by his opponents who took pleasure in representing his deformities.)

In the late nineteenth century, over 300 clay cuneiform tablets were discovered by Egyptian farmers in the ruins of Akhetaten. These tablets, known as the Amarna Letters, formed part of an archive of royal correspondence between Asian princes and the courts of Amenhotep III and Akhenaten. It appears that Akhenaten ignored repeated pleas for assistance from countries facing foreign invasion. Moreover, his isolated position, both geographically and intellectually, threatened the stability of Egypt's empire. When he died, Akhenaten's successors abandoned Akhetaten and later razed it to the ground. The capital returned to Thebes where the old religious and political order could resume.

Sandstone statue of Akhenaten, Amarna period. (*Egyptian Museum, Cairo*)

Wooden model of a sailing boat from Meir, Egypt, *c.* 2000 B.C.E. The presence of a mummy on board this Twelfth-dynasty model boat indicates that it was intended as a funerary artifact, used to symbolize the journey of the dead into the afterlife. We can glean important details about early Egyptian vessels—from the large central sail to the figures on deck, representing the pilot, the owner, and sailors working the halyards. (*British Museum, London*)

intersected a more primitive town, of circular or oval shape surrounded by a double wall.

Largest of all the Nile towns, presumably, were the political capitals—first in the north at Memphis, later in the south at Thebes, occasionally at other locations. Most of the spectacular temples and monuments at Thebes today, for example, date only to the eighteenth and nineteenth dynasties, 1550–1196 B.C.E. Archaeologists cannot excavate below these monuments to reach older urban levels, and the residential buildings of that older city are probably below the current water table. They are irrecoverable.

The best known capital city archaeologically is Akhetaten (sometimes referred to as Amarna, the name of the village at the site today), which was built by the Pharaoh Akhenaten (r. 1353–35; see Profile opposite), as the capital of his own religious philosophy, the worship of the sun, Aten, as the only god (except for the pharaoh himself). Akhetaten, however, is unrepresentative of other Egyptian cities. It was built comparatively late, as a capital, and was in use during only one reign. Subsequent pharaohs so hated Akhenaten's religion that they dismantled the city and used its building materials on other sites.

Other types of cities completed the urban network. Trade cities, especially in the Nile delta, linked Egypt internally and to the outside world. As early as 3650 B.C.E.,

the city of Buto in the Nile delta near the Mediterranean, served as the port of landing for shipping from the Levant and Mesopotamia. At El-Omari, further south in the delta, many imports of goods from the Mediterranean coast have been found. Goods off-loaded in these ports must have

Limestone statuette, Egypt, late second millennium. This New Kingdom statuette shows a woman molding clay on a *tournette*, a simple precursor to the modern potter's wheel, which appeared in Egypt and the Indus valley as early as the fourth millennium B.C.E. (*Flinders-Petrie Collection, London*)

been trans-shipped in smaller boats or carried by donkey caravan to Maadi, near Memphis. Maadi was the trade link between the delta and Upper Egypt.

Finally, there were the burial sites. Lewis Mumford, the great architect/planner/historian of the city, and Paul Wheatley, the geographer/anthropologist, maintained that shrine locations preceded cities. Egypt may be their best example. At least from the first dynasty, 2920 B.C.E., large cemeteries with rich burial goods have been found throughout the Nile valley and delta. Kings and members of the court were buried at Abydos in southern Egypt in tombs of modest size but excellent craftsmanship (see Focus below). A group of high officials was buried in the north, near Saqqara, in mudbrick tombs, and their funerary goods included copper objects and stone vessels. At the beginning of the second dynasty, 2770 B.C.E., the royal necropolis, the city of tombs,

FOCUS

The Legend of Isis, Osiris, and Horus

The legend of Isis, Osiris, and their son Horus triumphing over disorder and evil represents in mythic terms the importance of the unification of Egypt. Osiris represented order (ma'at) and virtue; his brother, Seth, disorder and evil. Seth tricked Osiris into lying down inside a box and then set the box on the Nile. Isis, Osiris' wife and sister, found the box and brought Osiris back home. Seth, however, seized the body and cut it into fourteen pieces. Once again Isis found the body and brought it back to Egypt. From the dead body, she conceived a son, Horus. Horus defeated Seth in battle and gave Osiris new life, this time as king and principal god of the underworld.

Horus became a patron god of the pharaohs. He was the first Egyptian god worshiped nationally. In painting and sculpture he is often depicted in the form of a falcon, either representing the king, perched on his head or shoulder, or atop the double crown, which symbolized the unity of Upper and Lower Egypt. The pharaohs believed that if they lived proper, ordered lives they would be united with Osiris after they died.

In some representations Horus and Seth are seen in reconciliation, binding Egypt into a single state. Seth represents southern areas around Nagada and Thebes; Horus, less specifically, represents the north.

Stele from the tomb of Djet (the "Serpent King"), Abydos, c. 3000 B.C.E. Horus, in the form of a falcon, is pictured above a serpent representing Djet, the "Serpent King," and the façade of a palace (*pharaoh* literally meant "great house" or "palace"). (*Louvre, Paris*)

was sited at Saqqara itself. Adjacent to the burial sites were the towns of the workers. Several of these workers' towns have been excavated, most notably Deir el Medina, near the Valley of the Queens, opposite Thebes, although it dates to a later period.

The State and its Architecture

Who first unified the upper and lower Nile into the single kingdom of Egypt? Most king lists mention Menes, but some name Narmer. Some scholars believe that these were two different names for the same person. The event took place about 3100 B.C.E., but tombs of kings excavated at Abydos predate this by about 200 years. Perhaps these were kings of local regions, or perhaps unification was actually accomplished under a "pre-dynastic" king before Menes. Or unification may have been a long process and "Menes" simply symbolizes the whole process. As noted, scholarly knowledge of this early period up to the fourth dynasty, which begins the Old Kingdom, c. 2700–2200 B.C.E., is especially fragmentary.

In the third dynasty, 2649–2575, King Djoser had a *mastaba* built to hold his remains at death. This forerunner of the pyramids shows an astonishing royal control over labor, finances, and architectural and building techniques. The administrative organization and economic productivity of government continued to increase, until, by the end of this dynasty, Egypt had extended its control of the Nile valley as far south as the first cataract (river rapids), its classical southern frontier. At the same time, Egypt's artistic genius continued to develop in the sculpture of its tombs and the sophistication of its script.

Within a half century, architects realized the beauty of filling in the steps of the *mastaba* to create the simple triangular form of the true pyramid. Kings of the fourth dynasty, 2575–2465, supervised the construction of the greatest pyramids in history. The 450 foot (137 meter) high pyramids of Khufu (Cheops; r. 2551–2528) and of Khefren (r. 2520–2494), and the smaller pyramid of Menkaure (r. 2490–2472), all arranged in a cluster with the Sphinx, proclaim aspiration to immortality, creative vision, and organizational power. The sculpture, reliefs, paintings, and inscriptions in the pyramids and in the many tombs of court officials and other powerful men of the time express the highest artistic achievements of the era. Tombs of queens and officials are situated in

GODS OF THE EGYPTIANS

Belief in one god (Aten, represented by the sun) was promoted during the reign of Akhenaten (r. 1353–1335), when the capital of Egypt was moved from Thebes to Amarna. At other times, the Egyptians worshiped a pantheon, whose main gods and goddesses are listed below:

Amon-Re	The universal god, depicted as ram-headed
Anubis	Jackal-headed god of funerals, son of Nephthus and Osiris. He supervised the weighing of souls at judgment
Hathor	The goddess of love, represented either as a woman with a cow's horns or as a cow with a solar disk
Horus	The falcon-headed god of light
Isis	Goddess of magic and fertility; sister and wife of Osiris; as mother of Horus, she was mother goddess of all Egypt
Nephthus	Sister of Isis, this funerary goddess befriended dead mortals at judgment
Osiris	Ruler of the underworld and chief judge of the dead, Osiris is normally depicted mummified or as a bearded man wearing the crown of Upper Egypt and with a flail and crook in his hands
Ptah	Magician and patron of the arts and crafts, Ptah later became judge of the dead. Normally represented as a mummy or holding an ankh (looped cross)
Seth	The god of evil and the murderer of Osiris
Thoth	The supreme scribe, depicted either with the head of an ibis or as a dog-headed baboon

Step pyramid of King Djoser, Saqqara, Egypt, *c.* **2700** B.C.E. This step pyramid, forerunner to the ancient architectural masterpieces at Giza (see picture, p. 64), developed from the *mastaba*, a low rectangular benchlike structure that covered a grave. The purpose of this early pyramid, effectively a 200-foot-high (61 m) ziggurat without a temple on top, was to mark and protect the underground tomb chamber 90 feet (27 m) below.

Cutaway of Great Pyramid of Khufu, Giza. The rectangular plan and stepped form of Djoser's pyramid were gradually modified to become the colossal, smooth-faced monuments with which we are familiar. This pyramid is some 450 feet (137 m) high on a square base occupying 13 acres and was built using forced labor.

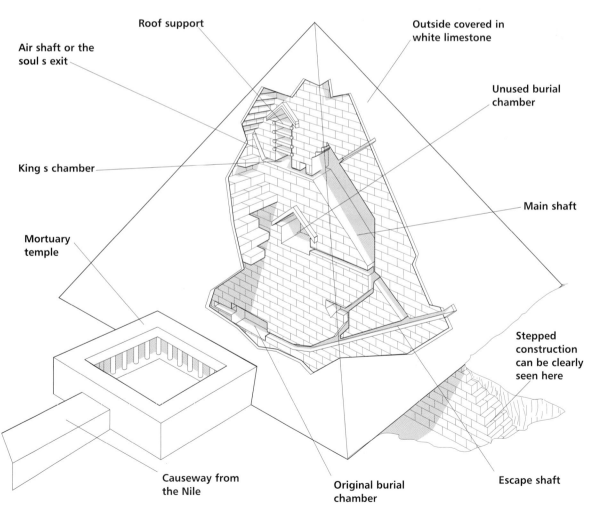

Roof support

Outside covered in white limestone

Air shaft or the soul s exit

Unused burial chamber

King s chamber

Main shaft

Mortuary temple

Stepped construction can be clearly seen here

Causeway from the Nile

Original burial chamber

Escape shaft

proximity to the kings' pyramids to reflect their power and rank. (Tomb robbing was, however, so common that we have no idea how long any of them lay undisturbed in their tombs.)

Following Menkaure, whose pyramid was already smaller than those of Khufu and Khefren, the building of such enormous monuments dimin-ished, which may reflect a lessening of Egyptian power generally.

Egyptian trading, raiding, and mining initiat-ives began to extend southward into Nubia, above the first cataract of the Nile. These expeditions were protected and consolidated through the construction of the Buhen fortress at the second

The Egyptian Book of the Dead and the "Negative Confession"

Many ancient Egypt texts concern the attempt to secure eternal happiness after death. A selection from these mortuary texts has been collected by modern scholars and titled *The Book of the Dead*. A segment of these texts presents the "negative confession" of a deceased person in the court of judgment of the dead protesting his innocence of evil and crime:

I have not committed evil against men.
I have not mistreated cattle.
I have not committed sin in the place of truth.
I have not tried to learn that which is not meant for mortals.
I have not blasphemed a god.
I have not done violence to a poor man.
I have not done that which the gods abominate.
I have not defamed a slave to his superiors.
I have not made anyone sick.
I have not made anyone weep.
I have not killed.
I have given no order to a killer.
I have not caused anyone suffering.
I have not cut down on the food or income in the temples.
I have not damaged the bread of the gods.
I have not taken the loaves of the blessed dead.
I have not had sexual relations with a boy.
I have not defiled myself.
I have neither increased or diminished the grain measure.
I have not diminished the measure of land.
I have not falsified the land records.

I have not added to the weight of the balance.
I have not weakened the plummet of the scales.
I have not taken milk from the mouths of children.
I have not driven cattle away from their pasturage.
I have not snared the birds of the gods.
I have not caught fish in their marshes.
I have not held up the water in its season.
I have not built a dam against running water.
I have not quenched a fire at its proper time.
I have not neglected the appointed times and their meat-offerings.
I have not driven away the cattle of the god's property.
I have not stopped a god on his procession.
I am pure: I am pure: I am pure: I am pure. . . .

Behold me—I have come to you without sin, without guilt, without evil, without a witness against me, without one against whom I have taken action. I live on truth, and I eat of truth. I have done that which men said and that with which gods are content. I have satisfied a god with that which he desires. I have given bread to the hungry, water to the thirsty, clothing to the naked, and a ferry-boat to him who was marooned. I have provided divine offerings for the gods and mortuary offerings for the dead. So rescue me, you; protect me, you.

(Pritchard, pp. 34–6)

SOURCE
The Autobiography of Si-nuhe and the Glorification of Court and Capital

Si-nuhe, a high-ranking official and royal attendant, fled from the Egyptian court when a new king came to the throne. Apparently he feared that his loyalty to the new ruler was suspect and his safety endangered. A skilled warrior and administrator, even in self-imposed exile he earned high positions in several Asian kingdoms. In Si-nuhe's old age, however, the king of Egypt and his family invited him back to the court so that he could spend his last years "at home" in comfort and be buried with appropriate rites.

This personal tale of reconciliation is almost certainly based on reality. Its glorification of Egypt over other countries, of the city over the countryside, and especially of the royal capital and the royal court represented the beliefs of the Egyptian elite. This account of the career and the moral personality of a court official, and of the excellence of the reigning pharaoh, is an outstanding example of the autobiographies inscribed in ancient Egyptian tombs.

Si-nuhe's story became one of the most popular classics of Egyptian literature, and manuscripts that include it began to appear about 1800 B.C.E. and continued to about 1000 B.C.E. One modern scholar refers to it as "the crown jewel of Middle Egyptian literature" (Lichtheim, I, 11).

Si-nuhe returned to the capital, then in the city of Lisht, near the Faiyum Lake.

So I went forth from the midst of the inner chambers, with the royal children giving me their hands. Thereafter we went to the Great Double Door. I was put into the house of a royal son, in which were splendid things. A cool room was in it, and images of the horizon. Costly things of the Treasury were in it. Clothing of royal linen, myrrh, and prime oil of the king and of the nobles whom he loves were in every room. Every butler was busy at his duties. Years were made to pass away from my body. I was plucked, and my hair was combed. A load of dirt was given to the desert, and my clothes to the Sand-Crossers. I was clad in fine linen and anointed with prime oil. I slept on a bed. I gave up the sand to them who are in it, and wood oil to him who is anointed with it. I was given a house which had a garden, which had been in the possession of a courtier. Many craftsmen built it, and all its woodwork was newly restored. Meals were brought to me from the palace three or four times a day, apart from that which the royal children gave, without ceasing a moment.

There was constructed for me a pyramid-tomb of stone in the midst of the pyramid-tombs. The stone-masons who hew a pyramid-tomb took over its ground-area. The outline-draftsmen designed in it; the chief sculptors carved in it; and the overseers of works who are in the necropolis made it their concern. Its necessary materials were made from all the outfittings which are placed at a tomb-shaft. Mortuary priests were given to me. There was made for me a necropolis garden, with fields in it formerly extending as far as the town, like that which is done for a chief courtier. My statue was overlaid with gold, and its skirt was of fine gold. It was his majesty who had it made. There is no poor man for whom like has been done. (Pritchard, pp. 18–22)

cataract, probably at about the time of the building of the great pyramids. That fortress, too, seems to have declined after about 2400 B.C.E., although trading and raiding expeditions continued.

The ninety-four-year-long reign of Pepy II (r. 2246–2152 B.C.E.) brought the Old Kingdom almost to its end. Perhaps this pharaoh continued to rule beyond his capabilities. The later years of his reign have not produced historical records, and they may, indeed, be mythical. Several kings succeeded Pepy, but their reigns were short, and none seems to have exercised national control. As central authority weakened, provincial officials in each *nome*, called nomarchs, asserted their powers. They collected and kept the taxes, and their private armies ruled locally. Based on the size and records of cemeteries, the death rates seem to have increased at this time. Famine was prevalent. Apparently the Nile did not reach optimal flood heights for agriculture, and weak rulers could not create adequate irrigation works to make up for it.

From State to Empire

In 2134 B.C.E. the Old Kingdom fell. At first, several nomarchs held independent local power. Then two separate centers began to stand out in the contest for power: Herakleopolis to the north and Thebes in the south. Finally, about 2040 B.C.E., King Mentuhotpe of Thebes defeated his rivals in the north and re-united the kingdom, initiating the Middle Kingdom, *c.* 2050–1750 B.C.E. The Middle Kingdom saw the state develop more organization and power than ever before. It administered Egypt efficiently and spread its power into Nubia and into the Middle East more aggressively than before, as Egypt began to rule over more distant, foreign peoples. It became an **empire**. That story is told in Part 3, in Chapter 5. At the same time, both the fine arts and literature flourished.

The Middle Kingdom was overthrown by foreign invaders. They were called "Hyksos" or "ruler of foreign lands," and little is known of their origins or their rule. When Egyptian kings expelled the Hyksos about 1550 B.C.E., Egypt began its New Kingdom. The New Kingdom, perhaps the most powerful in Egypt's ancient history, was probably the strongest in terms of internal control and external conquest. It, too, became an empire and lasted until about 1050.

CONNECTION: *Egypt and empire, pp. 125–30*

THE INDUS VALLEY CIVILIZATION AND ITS MYSTERIES

The civilization of the Indus valley was rediscovered only in the 1920s. Archaeologists have now identified over 1000 settlement sites of this civilization distributed over more than 400,000 square miles (1 million square kilometers), making it the most widespread civilization of its time. Archaeologists have pushed back the origins of settlement history in the region to 7000 B.C.E., fixed the apex of its material and cultural creativity at about 2500–2000 B.C.E., and identified its forward connections as far as the Ganges civilization, which developed into urban form in 700 B.C.E. The three largest cities of the Indus valley—Harappa (for which the civilization is often named), Mohenjo-Daro, and Kalibangan—may have housed 35,000–40,000 inhabitants each. It is not known which of the three, if any, served as the capital.

We see the urban formations in the excavations, but we do not know if the Harappan civilization developed urban institutions for governance, trade, religion, or worship, much less the quality of any such institutions. While Egypt had a state but, perhaps, few cities, Harappa had cities but no clearly delineated state. Indeed, some scholars argue that the Indus valley did not create state structures at all. Until the Harappan language is deciphered, its civilization will remain mysterious: How was it organized? Why did it disperse? How did it move eastward? In what ways did it enrich its successor, the Aryan civilization of the Ganges River valley?

THE INDUS VALLEY: HOW DO WE KNOW?

In 1856 Britain ruled India. Builders of the section of the East Indian Railway connecting Lahore and Karachi found hundreds of thousands of old fire-baked bricks in the semi-desert area and used them to lay the road bed. Among the old bricks, workers discovered steatite stone seals marked with artistic designs. They gave some of the seals to Major General Alexander Cunningham, a British officer who was visiting in the area. In 1861, Cunningham retired from the army and was appointed first Surveyor General of the

THE INDUS VALLEY

DATE	POLITICAL	CULTURE AND RELIGION	SOCIAL DEVELOPMENT
7000 B.C.E.			• Traces of settlements; trade with Mesopotamia
3000 B.C.E.			• Cotton cultivated
2500 B.C.E.	• Height of Harappan civilization in northern India (2500–2000)		• Cities of Harappa and Mohenjo–Jaro
2000 B.C.E.	• Collapse of Harappan civilization (2000–1900)	• Evidence of decline in standards of architecture	
1500 B.C.E.	• Immigration of Aryans into India (c. 1250)		
1000 B.C.E.	• Aryan immigrants reach west Ganges valley (c. 1000) and build first cities (c. 750)		• Iron tools used to clear Ganges valley for agriculture (c. 1000)

Archaeological Survey of Northern India. He alerted archaeologists to the Indus find, but formal, systematic excavations did not begin until 1920, under John Marshall, Director General of Archaeology in India. Marshall commissioned Daya Ram Sahni to survey a huge mound that rose above the desert floor where the seals had been found. Sahni's excavations soon revealed a 4500-year-old city, Harappa. Two years later, R.D. Banerji, an Indian officer of the Survey, recognized and began to excavate a twin site 200 miles (500 kilometers) to the southwest, later named Mohenjo-Daro, "Hill of the Dead." The two cities had many urban design and architectural features in common. Both were about 3 miles (5 kilometers) in circumference, large enough to hold populations of 40,000.

With these two excavations, an urban civilization that had been lost for thousands of years was uncovered. Before these excavations, scholars had believed that the civilization of India had begun in the Ganges valley with the arrival of Aryan invaders from Persia or central Asia about 1250 B.C.E. and the construction of their first cities about 700 B.C.E. The discovery of the Harappan cities pushed the origin of Indian civilization back an additional 1500 years and located it in an entirely different ecological zone.

The revelations multiplied. In the late 1930s, Ernest Mackay discovered and excavated Chanhu-Daro, a smaller town of the Harappan civilization. At the same time, Sir Aurel Stein, known for his archaeological discoveries in Persia and Mesopotamia, found further Harappan settlements in Baluchistan, Sind, and Rajputana. As Director of the Archaeological Survey, Mortimer Wheeler continued the excavations in both Mohenjo-Daro and Harappa in the late 1940s and early 1950s. In the early 1950s, extensive excavations began in Gujarat, especially at Lothal near Cambay. Although these sites were more recent than the Indus valley excavations, they were similar in design and architecture. Their discovery extended the time-frame of the Indus civilization forward by several centuries and its geographical frame southeastward by hundreds of miles.

Excavating in these relatively recent and peripheral sites, archaeologists like Gregory Possehl of the University of Pennsylvania Museum, and Jim Shaffer of Case Western Reserve University, have explored the relationship of the Indus civilization to that of the Ganges a thousand years later. Unlike John Marshall, who felt that the two civilizations were discontinuous and that the Aryan invaders had thoroughly destroyed the earlier Harappan civilization, both Possehl and Shaffer argued that Harappan civilization had not been destroyed, but had become de-urbanized and more rural. The cities may have come to an end, but Harappan culture and influence persisted. They could be found in the agricultural practices and religious symbolism of the Aryans.

As the end date of Harappan civilization was pushed forward, so its origin was pushed backward. In the 1980s an archaeological team from France, working under Jean-François Jarrige, and with the cooperation of the Department of Arch-aeology of Pakistan, excavated the settlement of Mehrgarh in the foothills of the Bolan Pass, but still on the Indus valley side. The Mehrgarh site has yielded early settlement artifacts going back to 7000 B.C.E. and, with ever-increasing sophistication, coming forward to 2500–2000 B.C.E. Jarrige explained:

> One and one-half millennia before the emergence of the Indus civilization, large settlements with elaborate architectural features and a vast network of communication already existed in the greater Indus valley. (p. 29)

Harappa, with its antecedents going back to Mehrgarh, Jarrige asserted, was not a derivative of Mesopotamia but had grown up indigenously. It is conceivable that the later civilizations of both Mesopotamia and the Indus had a common ancestor in the settlements of the hills and mountains between them.

Excavation of the two largest cities has now reached severe limits. The city of Harappa was van-dalized for thousands of years before, as well as during, the railroad construc-tion, and few artifacts remain to be discovered. Mohenjo-Daro sits on a high water table, and any deep-er excavation threatens to flood the site. It is impossible to dig down to the foundation level of the city.

Further exploration of Mohenjo-Daro's surface, however, continues to yield fascinating results. An expedition from the University of Aachen, Germany, began its survey of the surface of Mohenjo-Daro in 1979. Michael Janson and his team discovered an outlying segment of Mohenjo-Daro about a mile away from the known city.

Limestone bust from Mohenjo-Daro, *c.* **2300–1750 B.C.E.** This half-figure with horizontal slits for eyes, flat thick lips, and fringes of beard is thought to have represented a priest or shaman because of the way the robe is hung over its left shoulder. Despite its monumental appearance, the figure is only 7 inches (17.8 cm) high. (*National Museum of Pakistan, Karachi*)

Was it part of an industrial area or a residential suburb? It is impossible to determine. The discovery, however, identifies Mohenjo-Daro as a larger city than Harappa. Perhaps it was the capital city of the civilization.

Written records, the key that re-opened the civilizations of ancient Mesopotamia and Egypt, are lacking in the Indus valley. The only written materials so far discovered are seal inscriptions that give only limited information, and thus far, even they have not been interpreted satisfactorily. Scholars such as Akso Pranpola seem to have identified some specific names and dates on the seals, but other academics dispute these interpretations.

Without written records our understanding of Indus civilization is limited. Artifactual remains give a good representation of the physical cities and settlements, but not of their institutions. Moreover, while we can make educated guesses about the function and meaning of the remaining artifacts and physical structures from our own perspective, we do not have the words of the Harappans themselves to explain their own understanding of their civilization.

THE INDUS VALLEY: WHAT DO WE KNOW?

Archaeological evidence to date reveals an urban civilization with its roots beginning as early as 7000 B.C.E. in simple settlements like Mehrgarh in the foothills of the Bolan Pass. Over the millennia, people moved down into the plains and river valley. At first, they may have moved into the forested river valley only in the colder months, herding their flocks of sheep and cattle, including the humped zebu, back to the hills for the summer. Over time they may have decided to farm the river-watered alluvial lands of the valley. They began to trade by boat along the Indus and even down the Indus into the Arabian Sea and, further, into the Persian Gulf and up the Tigris and Euphrates into Mesopotamia. Goods from the Indus have been found in Mesopotamia and vice versa (see map, p. 51).

By about 2500 B.C.E., a thriving civilization reached its apex, maintaining it for about 500 years. One thousand sites of the Indus civilization have been located. Each of the two largest settlements, Harappa and Mohenjo-Daro, has a core area of about 3 miles (5 kilometers) in circumference, while Mohenjo-Daro also had a suburb—residential or industrial—about a mile away. Both cities accommodated about 40,000 people.

Both cities share similar features of design. To the north is a citadel, or raised area; to the south is a lower town. In Mohenjo-Daro, the citadel is built on an architectural platform about 45 feet (14 meters) above the plain, and it measures 1400 feet (430 meters) by 450 feet (140 meters). On the summit was a bath 8 feet (2.4 meters) deep and 23 feet (7 meters) by 29 feet (8.8 meters) in area. Numerous cubicles—perhaps small, individual baths—flanked it. Adjacent to the large bath was a huge open space, identified as a granary, where food was stored safe from possible flood. Other spaces may have been used for public meetings. Fortified walls mark the southeast corner, and it appears that the entire citadel was walled.

In the nearby lower city were private residences. The lower city was layed out in a gridiron, with the main streets about 45 feet (14 meters) wide. Almost every house had its own well, bathing space, and toilet, consisting of a brick seat over a drainage area. Brick-lined drains flushed by water carried liquid and solid waste to sumps, where it would be collected and carted away, probably to fertilize the nearby fields. The town plan was orderly and regular. Even the prefabricated, fire-baked bricks were uniform in size and shape. A uniform system of weights and measures was also employed throughout.

The regularity of plan and construction suggest a government with great organizational and bureaucratic capacity, but no truly monumental architecture clearly marks the presence of a palace or temple, and there is little sign of social stratification in the plan or buildings. Those burials that have been discovered are regular, with the heads pointing to the north, and with some grave goods, such as pots of food and water, small amounts of jewelry, simple mirrors, and some cosmetics. These were not the extravagant burials of Egypt or even of Mesopotamia.

Interpretations of these artifacts stress the apparent classlessness of the society, its equality, efficiency, and public conveniences. Some interpreters view these qualities negatively, equating them with oppressively rigid governments and drab lives. Archaeologist Walter Fairservis argues that the cities changed little over long periods of time and, unlike the cities of Mesopotamia and the Nile, "lacked dynamism." With no contemporary literature to guide us, interpretation of what is found is in the eyes, and the value system, of the beholder.

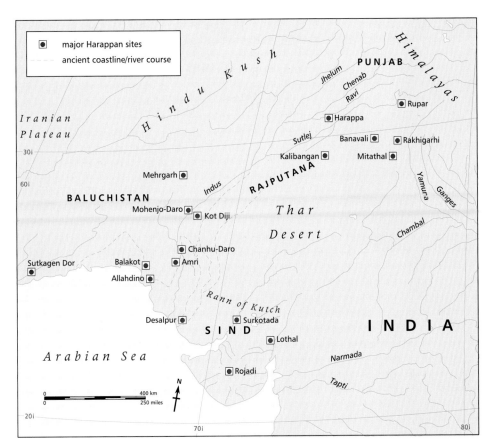

Cities of the Indus

Confined to the north and west by mountains, and to the east by desert, the Indus valley had, by 2500 B.C.E., developed a sophisticated urban culture based on individual walled cities, sharing common patterns of urban design. In terms of geographical extent this civilization was the largest in the world in its time.

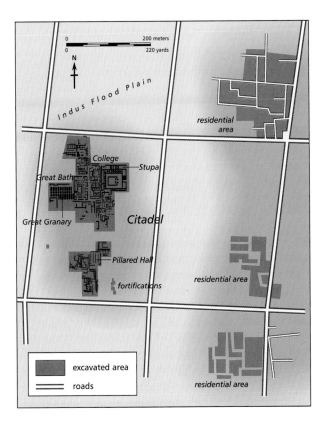

We also do not know if this uniform, planned civilization had a single capital city, or several regional capitals, or no centralized political system at all. Was it like Egypt before unification or after unification? Was it like Mesopotamia, with numerous city-states all participating in a single general culture? All three suggestions have been made.

Crafts in the Indus included pottery making, dyeing, metal working in bronze, and bead making. Bead materials included jade from the Himalayas, lapis lazuli from Afghanistan, turquoise from Persia, amethyst from Mewar in India, and steatite, which was found locally. Small sculptures in stone, terra cotta, and bronze presumably represent members of the society, and guesses as to the identity of some include a priestly or

Planned Cities With an area of 150 acres, and about 40,000 inhabitants, Mohenjo-Daro was a thriving Indus city. Excavations reveal a raised citadel area, containing ceremonial and administrative buildings, and a residential quarter centered on boulevards about 45 feet (14 m) wide, with grid-patterned streets, an underground sewerage and drainage system, and a range of brick-built dwellings.

Limestone dancing figure from Harappa, *c.* 2300–1750 B.C.E.
This dancing figure displays a grasp of three-dimensional movement and vitality rare in the arts until much later periods. Human sculptures in contemporary Mesopotamia and Egypt are by contrast symbols of pure power, either immutable ideals of divinity or semidivine kingship. Indeed, this Harappan accomplishment is so extraordinary that some scholars have cast doubt on its early date. (*National Museum of India, New Delhi*)

EARLY SCIENCE AND TECHNOLOGY (7000–1000 B.C.E.

7000–6000	Pottery made in Middle East
c. 5500	Copper, gold, and silver worked in Mesopotamia and Egypt
c. 4000–3500	In Asia and Africa, potter's wheel and kiln invented; mud bricks used; spindle developed for spinning; basket-making begins
c. 3500–3000	Plow and cart invented; bronze cast and cuneiform writing developed in Sumer
3100	Reed boats in Egypt and Assyria; appearance of hieroglyphs in Egypt
3000	Cotton cultivated in the Indus valley
c. 2500	Wooden boats used in Egypt; ink and papyrus writing material used
2050	First glass in Mesopotamia
1790	Mathematics and medicine practiced in Babylon
1740	War chariots introduced from Persia to Mesopotamia (and later Egypt)
1370	Alphabetic script used in western Syria
1000	Industrial use of iron in Egypt and Mesopotamia

governmental official, a dancing girl, and a mother goddess. Dice and small sculptures of bullock carts were probably used as toys and games.

The first known use of cotton as a fiber for weaving textiles occurred in the Indus valley, introducing one of India's and the world's most enduring and important crops and crafts.

By about 2000 B.C.E. the architecture of the Indus civilization began to decline. New buildings and repairs to existing structures lacked attention to quality and detail. Residents began to leave the

The citadel of Mohenjo-Daro, *c.* **2300 B.C.E. and later**. The citadel at Mohenjo-Daro, a massive, mud-filled embankment that rises 43 feet (13 m) above the lower city, was discovered by archaeologist Daya Ram Sahni while investigating the second-century C.E. Buddhist stupa (burial mound) that can be seen in the distance. The citadel's summit houses the remains of several impressive structures, of which the most prominent is the so-called Great Bath (foreground).

towns along the Indus and to relocate northeastward into the Punjab, to towns like Kalibangan, and southeastward, to towns like Lothal in Gujarat. Meanwhile, newcomers—squatters—seem to have moved into the old cities. Again a variety of arguments suggests the reasons for the decline in the cities and the geographical redistribution of their populations. Perhaps the river changed course or became erratic; perhaps the soil became too saline; perhaps the forests were cut down and topsoil eroded.

An older opinion—that the Indus civilization was destroyed by the invasion of Aryan peoples from somewhere northwest of India—is now less widely held. It rested on Harappan archaeological evidence and Aryan literature. Several sets of skeletal remains in Mohenjo-Daro indicate violent deaths, while Aryan religious texts suggest that the invaders burned and destroyed existing settlements. The *Rigveda*, one of the earliest and most important of these texts, tells of the destructive power of the god Indra:

> With all-outstripping chariot-wheel, O Indra, thou
> far-famed, hast overthrown the twice ten kings of
> men
>
> With sixty thousand nine and ninety followers . . .
> Thou goest on from fight to fight intrepidly,
> destroying castle after castle here with strength.
>
> (i, 53)
>
> . . . in kindled fire he burnt up all their weapons,
> And made him rich with kine and carts and horses.
>
> (ii, 15)

The Aryan god of fire, Agni, is still more fearsome:

> Through fear of you the dark people went away, not
> giving battle, leaving behind their possessions,
> when, O Vaisvanara, burning brightly for Puru, and
> destroying the cities, you did shine. (7.5.3)

Newer archaeological evidence, however, suggests that the decline, de-urbanization, and dispersal of the Indus civilization seem to have preceded the

Aryan invasion. Further evidence suggests that the Aryans may not have swept into the region in a single all-conquering expedition, but in a series of smaller waves. The arrival of the Aryans may have only completed the Harappan decay.

LEGACIES OF THE INDUS

Interchange between the resident Harappans and the invading Aryans produced new, hybrid cultural forms that we know primarily from the Aryan records. Ironically, these records are almost entirely literary and artistic. Reversing the Harappan pattern, the early Aryans have left a treasure of literature, but virtually no architectural or design artifacts.

Four legacies of Harappa stand out. First, the Aryan invaders were a nomadic group, who must have adopted at least some of the arts of settlement and civilization from the already settled residents. Second, as newcomers to the ecological zones of India, the Aryans must also have learned methods of farming and animal husbandry from the Harappans. Later, however, as they swept eastward into the Ganges valley, they confronted a new ecology based on rice cultivation and the use of iron. Here Harappan skills were useless. Third, a three-headed figure frequently appearing in Harappan

**Steatite seal of seated "yogi,"
Mohenjo-Daro,** *c.* 2300–1700 B.C.E.
This famous seal is important for several reasons, chief among them being that it may show the first representation in Indian history of a deity in human form. Sir John Marshall suggested that it appears to delineate a prototype for the later Hindu god Shiva. (*National Museum of Pakistan, Karachi*)

seals resembles later representations of the Aryan god Shiva. Perhaps an earlier Harappan god may have been adopted and adapted by the Aryans.

Finally, the Aryan caste system, which ranks people at birth according to occupation, color, and ritual purity, and prescribes the people with whom they may enter into social intercourse and marry, may reflect the need of the Aryans to regulate relationships between themselves and the Harappans. To claim and maintain their own supremacy, the Aryans may have elaborated the social structures of the caste system and relegated the native inhabitants to permanent low status within it.

The Aryan groups grew increasingly skilled and powerful as they moved east. The first known archaeological evidence of their urban structures dates to about 700 B.C.E. and is found in the Ganges valley. We will read more about it when we analyze the first Indian empire, in Chapter 8.

CONNECTION: *Settlement in South Asia after 1500 B.C.E.,* pp. 232–5

BIBLIOGRAPHY

Aldred, Cyril. *The Egyptians* (New York: Thames and Hudson, 1986).

Allchin, Bridget and Raymond. *The Birth of Indian Civilization: India and Pakistan before 500 B.C.* (Baltimore, MD: Penguin Books, 1968).

Baines, John and Jaromir Malek. *Atlas of Ancient Egypt* (New York: Facts on File Publications, 1980).

Cotterell, Arthur, ed. *The Penguin Encyclopedia of Ancient Civilizations* (London: Penguin Books, 1980).

Fagan, Brian. *People of the Earth: An Introduction to World Prehistory* (New York: HarperCollins, 8th ed., 1995).

Fairservis, Walter. *The Roots of Ancient India* (Chicago: University of Chicago Press, 2nd ed., 1975).

Hassan, Fekri A. "The Predynastic of Egypt," *Journal of World Prehistory* II, No. 2 (June 1988), 135–85.

Janson, Michael R.N. "Mohenjo-daro: Type Site of the Earliest Urbanization Process in South Asia," Spodek and Srinivasan, 35–51.

Jarrige, Jean-François. "The Early Architectural Traditions of Greater Indus as Seen from Mehrgarh, Baluchistan," Spodek and Srinivasan, 25–33.

Kemp, Barry J. *Ancient Egypt: Anatomy of a Civilization* (London: Routledge, 1989).

Lichtheim, Miriam. *Ancient Egyptian Literature: A Book of Readings* (Berkeley: University of California Press, 3 vols., 1973).

Mumford, Lewis. *The City in History* (New York: Harcourt Brace, and World, 1961).

Noble Wilford, John. "Egypt Carvings Set Earlier Date for Alphabet," *New York Times* (November 14, 1999), A–1, 16.

Past Worlds: The (London) Times Atlas of Archaeology (Maplewood, NJ: Hammond, Inc., 1988).

Piggott, Stuart. *Prehistoric India* (Baltimore, MD: Penguin Books, 1952).

Possehl, Gregory L., ed. *Ancient Cities of the Indus* (New Delhi: Vikas Publishing, 1979).

—— ed. *Harappan Civilization: A Recent Perspective* (New Delhi: Oxford University Press and IBH Publishing, 2nd ed., 1993).

Pritchard, James B., ed. *Ancient Near Eastern Texts Relating to the Old Testament* (Princeton: Princeton University Press, 3rd ed. 1969).

Shaffer, Jim G. "Reurbanization: The Eastern Punjab and Beyond," Spodek and Srinivasan, 53–67.

Spodek, Howard and Doris Meth Srinivasan, eds. *Urban Form and Meaning in South Asia: The Shaping of Cities from Prehistoric to Precolonial Times* (Washington: National Gallery of Art, 1993).

Time-Life Books. *Time Frame 3000–1500: The Age of God-Kings* (Alexandria, VA: Time-Life Books, 1987).

—— *Time Frame 1500–600 BC: Barbarian Tides* (Alexandria, VA: Time-Life Books, 1987).

Wenke, Robert J. "The Evolution of Early Egyptian Civilization: Issues and Evidence," *Journal of World Prehistory* V, No. 1 (September 1991), 279–329.

Wheatley, Paul. *Pivot of the Four Quarters* (Chicago: Aldine Publishing Company, 1971).

Wheeler, Mortimer. *Civilizations of the Indus Valley and Beyond* (London: Thames and Hudson, 1966).

CHAPTER

4 A POLYCENTRIC WORLD

1700 B.C.E–1000 C.E

"Only by accepting a major role for ideology as a direct source of power can one understand the institutions of these civilizations, their history, and the elaborate cultural concepts that sustained them."

ARTHUR DEMARE

CITIES AND STATES IN EAST ASIA, THE AMERICAS, AND WEST AFRICA

This chapter completes the survey of the seven areas of primary urbanization. It covers the four areas which developed primary urbanization somewhat more recently: Yellow River valley of China; two regions of the western hemisphere—Mesoamerica and the South American Pacific coastal plain with the adjacent Andes Mountains that tower above it; and the Niger River valley of West Africa. The first cities in these regions date from as early as 1700 B.C.E. in China to as late as 400 C.E. in the Niger valley. They include cities that were not in major river valleys as well as some that were. They all show evidence of state formation, but they include settlements that did not have written languages and records, and therefore require us to base our understanding entirely on the archaeological record and to stretch our definition of urbanization.

CHINA: THE XIA, SHANG, AND ZHOU DYNASTIES

Chinese historical texts tell of three early dynasties—the Xia, the Shang, and the Zhou—that ruled over large regions of China. In its time, each ruled over the most powerful single kingdom among the embattled states of northern China. All were based primarily around the Huang He (Yellow River) valley in north China. State formation may have begun under the Xia, *c.* 2205–1766 B.C.E., although records are too sparse to recreate its cities and institutions. The archaeological record on urbanization under the Shang, *c.* 1766–1122 B.C.E., is far more revealing and reliable. The Zhou, *c.* 1100–256 B.C.E., consolidated both city and state, and left extensive archaeological remains and written records. None of the

86   SETTLING DOWN (10,000 B.C.E.–1000 C.E.)

EARLY CHINA

DATE	POLITICAL	RELIGION AND CULTURE	SOCIAL DEVELOPMENT
8000 B.C.E.		● Neolithic decorated pottery	● Simple Neolithic society established
5000 B.C.E.	● Yangshao culture in China (5000–2700)	● Marks on Yangshao pottery possibly writing	● Penal code; defensive structures round villages
3500 B.C.E.	● Longshan late Neolithic culture	● Delicate Longshan ceramics	● Farming, with domesticated animals
2000 B.C.E.	● Xia dynasty (2205–1766) ● Shang dynasty (1766–1122)	● The "sage kings" in China known from legend; first known use of writing in this area ● City of Zhengzhou (c. 1700) ● Under Shang, bronze vases found in ceremonial burials	● Agricultural progress ● Cities (by 1700) under control of Shang kings
1100 B.C.E.	● Zhou dynasty (1100–256)	● Poetry extant from Zhou period	● Under Zhou, iron, money, and written laws in use
500 B.C.E.	● Warring States period (481–222)	● Confucius (d. 479) ● Great Wall of China begun (214) to keep out Xiongnu	● Crossbow invented (c. 350)
100 B.C.E.		● Sima Qian (d. 85)	

three dynasties succeeded in annexing all its enemies and building a single unified empire. That process would come later.

The traditional chronological dating suggests that the states succeeded one another, but recent evidence indicates that there may, in fact, have been considerable overlap. For centuries, they may have coexisted in neighboring regions, with first one, then another, having comparatively greater power and prestige. One of the leading archaeologists of China today, K.C. Chang, describes

> the political interrelationship of Hsia [Xia], Shang, and Chou [Zhou], as three parallel, or at least overlapping, polities. . . . Hsia, Shang, and Chou were subcultures of a common—ancient Chinese—culture, but more particularly they were political groups in opposition to one another. (*Shang Civilization*, p. 348)

By the time of the Shang Dynasty, if not already in the Xia, cities had been founded in north China as centers of administration and ritual. State formation was well under way, and cities served as capitals and administrative centers. The entire dynastic state was ruled through its urban network. Capitals were frequently shifted, suggesting that new rulers wanted to make their mark through new construction, or that confrontations with neighboring, enemy states required strategic redeployments for improving offensive or defensive positions. The regional cities and their administrations were frequently entrusted to blood relatives of the king. It appears that rulers performed productive economic functions for their subjects, especially in water control. In exchange the lineages on top lived lives of considerable wealth while those on the lower levels had little as sharp class differences emerged in the early dynastic states. The cemeteries of different classes were geographically segregated into different neighborhoods within the city and its suburbs, and were of different quality.

Like primary cities in other parts of the world, the Chinese cities were also, as we shall see, cosmo-magical centers (see Focus pp. 92–3), with the kings presiding over rituals as well as administration and warfare. Indeed, the warfare was necessary to supply the human and animal sacrifices that were central to the rituals.

EARLIEST TIMES: HOW DO WE KNOW?

Texts

Texts ascribed to the Chinese teacher Confucius (551–479 B.C.E.) refer to the Xia and Shang dynasties but give little detail. Confucius lamented "the insufficiency of their records and wise men" (Chang, p. 2).

Later, Sima Qian (Ssu-ma Ch'ien; *c.* 145–85 B.C.E.), court historian of the Han dynasty, wrote the first of China's official historical annals. Sima, who had access to many texts that have not survived to today, devoted a chapter to the Shang royal house beginning with its legendary founder Xie, who located his capital in a town called Shang, now believed to have been in eastern Henan. Successive rulers moved this capital eight times. Xie's fourteenth successor, Tang, established the hereditary dynasty of Shang. Once in power, the Shang dynasty established a series of successive capital cities, all of which are in north China. Seven are recorded. Sima's sources of information were limited, however, and his chapter mostly outlined the genealogy of the rulers, recounted moralistic tales of their rule, and briefly noted their capital cities.

Oracle Bones

A new source of information came to light in the 1890s and early 1900s. Numerous oracle bones—some apparently hidden away for many years, others recently uncovered—appeared in antique markets in China. Over the decades, more than 100,000 were discovered. These bones of birds, animals, and especially the shells of turtles, had been inscribed with markings and writings for use in predicting the future. Inscribed and marked lightly, they were placed in a fire and tapped lightly with a rod until they began to crack. The cracks were then "read" by specialists in predicting the future. A poem from the later Zhou dynasty noted the use of oracle bones in deciding the location of a new city:

> The plain of Chou was very fertile,
> Its celery and sowthistle sweet as rice-cakes.
> "Here we will make a start; here take counsel,
> Here notch our [turtle]."
> It says, "Stop," it says, "Halt.
> Build houses here."
>
> (Chang, *Shang Civilization*, pp. 31–2)

Inscribed oracle bone, China. Shang Kings communicated with their ancestors through both sacrificial rituals and divination. Diviners would pose questions—about health, harvest, or politics—by applying a red-hot poker to animal bones or turtle shells and then analyze the resulting heat-induced cracks. (*East Asian Library, Columbia University*)

Some of the oracle bone inscriptions confirmed the names and approximate dates of the Shang rulers whom Sima Qian had listed. The location of the bones and the content of their inscriptions encouraged archaeologists to search further in the north central Chinese plains, near the point where the Yellow River flows out of the mountains. They concentrated on Anyang.

Archaeology

Archaeology was in fashion in China in the 1920s. Peking man had been discovered at Zhoukoudian (see p. 13) and, in the process, a new generation of Chinese archaeologists had received on-the-job training. Meanwhile, the new "doubting antiquity" school of Chinese historiography began to question the dating and to challenge the authenticity of many ancient Chinese historical events. In response, the newly established National Research Institute of History and Philology dispatched the young archaeologist Dong Zobin to explore the Anyang region. Dong recommended excavating for oracle bones. These excavations, mostly under the direction of Li Ji, uncovered not only bones but also sites from the Shang dynasty. These led to the discovery of artifacts from earlier eras as well. Ancient texts, bronzes, oracle bones, and excavations reinforced one another in recounting parts of ancient China's urbanization and state formation. Civil war in China, beginning in 1927, and war with Japan, beginning in 1937, interrupted excavations until 1950, but since then, continuous archaeological research has yielded new understandings.

EARLIEST TIMES: WHAT DO WE KNOW?

The Earliest Villages

Thousands of years before the Xia dynasty, as early as the eighth millennium B.C.E., Neolithic pottery decorations marked the transition from hunting and gathering into the culture of farming and village life. This Yangshao culture, first excavated in 1921, was named for the location in which it was first discovered in western Henan province. Excavations continue in Henan and in late 1999 archaeologists in China and at the Brookhaven National Laboratory in the United States reported uncovering a set of tiny flutes carved some 9000 years ago from the wing bones of a large bird. Three thousand years older than the next known playable instruments, from Sumer, one of them is still playable. (The "Neanderthal" flutes discovered in southern France [see picture, p. 29] are no longer playable.) The sounds of this flute playing a Chinese folk song are available at the Brookhaven web site, http://www.bnl.gov/bnl.web/flutes.html.

The Yangshao lasted to c. 2700 B.C.E. Farmers of this era grew millet, wheat, and rice, and domesticated pigs, dogs, goats, and perhaps horses. They lived mostly in river valleys, and the villages were often surrounded with earthen walls for

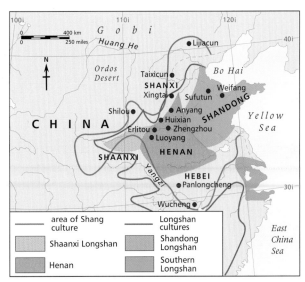

Shang China Centered where the Huang He (Yellow River) enters its floodplain from the mountains of northeast China, the Longshan farming communities of about 2500 B.C.E benefited from rich alluvial soils and extensive metal ore deposits. By 1800 B.C.E. a powerful, highly organized, urban, metal-working culture, the Shang, had developed.

defense. Ban Po, discussed in the Spotlight on pages 42–3, is the best excavated village of the Yangshao culture.

Slightly later and slightly to the northeast, a more sophisticated Neolithic culture, the Longshan, grew up. The people of the Longshan made their pottery on wheels, whereas the Yangshao had coiled or molded their pots by hand. The Longshan people domesticated sheep and cattle, which were not seen in Yangshao sites. Longshan graves were dug under their own homes, while the Yangshao had buried their dead in graveyards far from their villages. Sometimes Longshan funeral urns were cemented into foundation walls, suggesting ancestor worship.

Several hundred miles to the east, somewhat further down the Yellow River in Shandong, and one or two centuries later, yet another branch of Longshan culture developed, with yet another distinct type of pottery, often distinctively reddish-brown and gray in color, quite different from the black of the Longshan of Henan. Although the high points of Yangshao and the western and eastern Longshan cultures appeared at successively later times, they overlapped each other to a considerable extent.

The Henan Longshan culture was characterized in later historical accounts as harsh, having "a penal code internally and armed forces externally"

5000 (B.C.E.)	Rice cultivation, basketry, weaving, use of wooden tools, primitive writing
3000	Domestication of sheep, cattle, water buffalo
2000	Human grave sacrifices
1900	Metal working, class system, domestication of horse
1200	Chariots in warfare

(cited in Chang, p. 339). Excavations reveal the burials of victims of killing, some decapitated and showing signs of struggle, suggesting warfare between villages. The defensive walls of pounded earth that encircle some of the villages support this hypothesis, as does the presence of bronze knives.

Historical Evidence of the Xia Dynasty

At Erlitou, east of Luoyang, in western Henan, a culture was discovered in precisely the areas described by ancient texts as the site of the legendary Xia dynasty. The pottery at Erlitou seemed intermediate in style and quality between the earlier Longshan and the later Shang. Although the link is not certain, many archaeologists took Erlitou to be representative of the Xia dynasty.

The Xia, like the later Shang and Zhou, seems to have been ruled by specific internal clans, each with its own king. As the historian Mark Elvin puts it, kingship and kinship were interrelated. As head of both his biological clan and his geographical realm, the king performed rituals, divinations, and sacrifices; waged war; constructed irrigation and flood control works; and administered his government. The king mediated between the world of the spirits and the world of humans. He was thought to be descended from the god of the spirits who controlled human health, wealth, agriculture, and warfare. The king's assertion of his right to perform sacrifice in any particular place was, in effect, his assertion of his right to rule over that place. Rights over ritual implied rights over land and people (Blunden and Elvin, p. 73).

Even before the Xia dynasty, control over water had been vital. The first settlements had avoided the immediate flood plain of the Yellow River, one of the most hazardous in the world. Its bed filled with the silt from the mountains, the Yellow River has jumped its course twenty-six times in recorded history, wreaking untold devastation. As early as the Longshan culture, people built great levees and canals for flood control, drainage, and irrigation. Chinese legend credits the first success in taming the Yellow River to one of the culture heroes of ancient history, Yu the Great of the twenty-third century B.C.E. The legend reflects the reality of a royal house's gaining power in part through its ability to organize great gangs of laborers to construct a system of water control.

The Xia dynasty went further with human organization. It assembled armies, built cities, carved jade, cast and worked bronze into both weapons and ritual vessels, created the pictograms that would evolve into Chinese script, and may have designed China's first calendar.

Similarities among the Three Dynasties

All three of these earliest dynasties, the Xia, Shang, and Zhou, built walled towns. Indeed, in written Chinese the same character, *cheng*, represents both city and city wall. At times these towns were loosely connected to one another, forming a network of rule and trade. At other times, when a single powerful king headed the dynasty, a single capital city predominated. Archaeologists see many similarities among the towns and the political structures of all three dynasties. In the absence of earlier written records, they cite literary evidence from later dynasties as evidence for patterns in the earlier dynasties. For example, in arguing for the supremacy of royal rule during the Shang Dynasty, K.C. Chang takes his supporting proof from "Pei shan," a poem of the Zhou dynasty:

> Everywhere under Heaven
> Is no land that is not the king's
> To the borders of all those lands
> None but is the king's slave.
>
> (trans. Arthur Waley; cited in Chang, *Shang Civilization*, p. 158)

Another well-known poem from the western Zhou rulers uses blunt imagery to suggest royal oppression and a parasitic relationship between ruler and ruled. Chang suggests that it may also be applied to Shang and Xia times:

Big rat, big rat,
Do not gobble our millet.
Three years we have slaved for you,
Yet you take no notice of us.
At last we are going to leave you
And go to that happy land;
Happy land, happy land,
Where we shall have our place.

(trans. Arthur Waley; cited in Chang,
Shang Civilization, p. 238)

CITY AND STATE UNDER THE SHANG

"The Shang state can be characterized, simply, as the network of such towns that was under the Shang king's direct control" (Chang, p. 210). The king ruled from his capital city. Regional cities were apportioned to his designated represent-atives, who were usually blood relatives. These

Shang dynasty bronze wine vessel, fourteenth to eleventh century B.C.E. The thousands of Shang bronze vessels that survive today continue to astonish us with their technical mastery and elegance. They testify to the elite's willingness to devote huge quantities of a precious resource to ritual purposes. During times of war, such bronzes were often melted down to produce weapons but once peace resumed, they were recast into ritual objects. *(Historical Museum, Beijing)*

relatives were granted title to land, shares in the harvests, and rights to build and control the regional capital cities. In exchange, they represented and served the king and his interests in the provinces.

Territorially, the Shang dynasty was always based in northern and central Henan and southwestern Shandong. At its most powerful it extended as far south as Wucheng, south of the Yangzi River; east to the Pacific, incorporating the Shandong Peninsula; north into Hebei and southern Manchuria; and west through Shanxi into the mountains of Shaanxi. At its greatest extent it may have controlled 40,000 square miles (100,000 square kilometers). On the fringes, Shang territories were interspersed with those of other rulers, and warfare between them was apparently frequent.

The capital was shifted often, but always remained within the core area of Shang urbanization. One of the earliest capitals was located at Luoyang; later, and for many decades, it was at Zhengzhou; and, finally, *c.* 1384 B.C.E., at Anyang. Luoyang has been difficult to excavate because it lies directly under a modern city. Zhengzhou, however, has been excavated extensively. Founded *c.* 1700 B.C.E., its core covered about 1¼ square miles (3 square kilometers), enclosed by a wall 4½ miles (7 kilometers) long and, in places, still surviving to a height of 30 feet (9 meters).

Inside the walled area lived the royal family, the nobility, and their retainers. Outside this palace/ ritual center was a network of residential areas; workshops making bone, pottery, and bronze artifacts; and cemeteries. The class divisions written into this spatial pattern were reinforced by the geography of the suburbs: to the north were the dwellings and graves of the wealthy and powerful, marked by ritual bronze vessels and sacrificial victims; to the south were the dwellings of the commoners and their burial places in trash pits. Occupations tended to be inherited within specific family units (compare the caste system of India discussed in Chapters 8 and 9). Many *zu*, or lineage groups, corresponded to occupational groups. K.C. Chang argues that the emblems of the Shang family lineages also suggest their occupations.

Anyang, the Last Shang Capital

The final, most powerful, and most elaborate capital of the Shang dynasty was at Anyang. Shang texts report that the nineteenth king, Pan Gieng,

FOCUS

The Cosmo-Magical City

In his classic and convincing Pivot of the Four Quarters, Paul Wheatley argues that ancient Chinese cities, like most ancient cities, began as ritual centers. He calls these cities "cosmo-magical." Archaeological and textual records support this interpretation for China. Consider, for example, this Zhou poem illustrating the siting of a royal capital. The process begins with reading the oracle shell of a tortoise to determine its location and ends with sacrifices to mark the completion of construction:

> Of old Tan-fu the duke
> At coming of day galloped his horses,
> Going west along the river bank
> Till he came to the foot of Mount Ch'i.
> Where with the lady Chiang
> He came to look for a home.
>
> The plain of Chou was very fertile,
> Its celery and sowthistle sweet as rice-cakes.
> "Here we will make a start; here take counsel,
> Here notch our tortoise."
> It says, "Stop," it says, "Halt.
> Build houses here."
>
> So he halted, so he stopped,
> And left and right
> He drew the boundaries of big plots and little,

> He opened up the ground, he counted the acres
> From west to east;
> Everywhere he took his task in hand.
>
> Then he summoned his Master of Works,
> Then he summoned his Master of Lands
> And made them build houses
> Dead straight was the plumb-line,
> The planks were lashed to hold the earth;
> They made the Hall of Ancestors, very venerable.
>
> They tilted in the earth with a rattling,
> They pounded it with a dull thud,
> They beat the walls with a loud clang,
> They pared and chiselled them with a faint *p'ing*, *p'ing*;
> The hundred cubits all rose;
> The drummers could not hold out.
>
> They raised the outer gate;
> The outer gate soared high.
> They raised the inner gate;
> The inner gate was very strong.
> They raised the great earth-mound,
> Whence excursions of war might start.

The rituals seem to have conferred worldly benefits. Potential enemies fled. The poem continues:

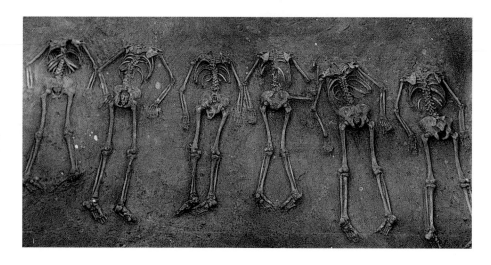

Headless skeletons of human sacrificial victims, tomb 1001, Anyang, China. The royal tombs discovered at Anyang testify to the wealth and power of the Shang rulers. Numerous servants and prisoners-of-war gave their lives willingly or unwillingly to accompany their masters to the grave. The heads of the decapitated figures shown here were located elsewhere in the tomb.

And in the time that followed they did not abate their sacrifices
Did not let fall their high renown;
The oak forests were laid low,
Roads were opened up.
The K'un tribes scampered away;
Oh, how they panted!

(trans. Arthur Waley; cited in Chang, *Shang Civilization*, pp. 159–60)

Oracle records recognize more than twenty titles of officials grouped into three categories: ministers, generals, and archivists,

> but the most important categories of officials insofar as our available data are concerned are the diviners . . . and the inquirers. . . . Jao Tsung-yi enumerated the activities of as many as 117 diviners and inquirers in the oracle records. Ch'en Meng-chia counted 120. (Chang, p. 192)

Besides the diviners, a cadre of priests performed religious rituals, including human sacrifices.

Military force was needed to sustain these rituals, by providing the prisoners-of-war to be sacrificed when rituals demanded. Oracle records speak of Shang military campaigns of 3000, 5000, and even 13,000 troops. As many as 30,000 prisoners-of-war were claimed in one large battle, and 300 prisoners were sacrificed in a ritual of ancestor worship. Archaeological finds show that 600 humans were sacrificed at the completion of a single house; 164 for a single tomb.

Burial pit, unearthed at Liulihe, Hebei province, Western Zhou period. Evidence for the centrality of ritual in ancient Chinese culture can be found in this tomb, which contains the remains of horses and chariots. These important instruments of rule would have been regarded as valuable offerings to the gods and were thus buried along with their owner.

moved his capital to Yin and that the dynasty remained there until its fall 273 years later. Archaeologists identify that site as Anyang. This capital was the center of a network of sites stretching about 200 miles (320 kilometers) from northwest to southeast. The core area around Anyang is difficult to excavate fruitfully. The city burned to the ground, and farmers have been plowing the area, and robbers pillaging it, for 3000 years. Remains of royal graves and of buildings that appear to be royal palaces hint at the greatness of the ancient city, but they do not yield many secrets.

The Shang dynasty fell to the Zhou around 1122 B.C.E., but it did not disappear, just as the Xia had

not disappeared when it had fallen to the Shang *c.* 1766 B.C.E. Instead, in defeat, these kingdoms continued to exist, albeit with diminished territories and powers. Until the Qin dynasty unified China in 221 B.C.E., the defeat of a dynasty did not mean that it completely disappeared. Rather, it became one of the many smaller kingdoms competing for power in continuous warfare in north China.

CONNECTION: *China and empire, 200 B.C.E.–910 C.E.*, pp. 195–230

THE WESTERN HEMISPHERE: MESOAMERICA AND SOUTH AMERICA

The first cities of the Americas share several characteristics with those of east Asia. They began as cosmo-magical shrine centers, linked by **shaman** priest-rulers to otherworldly realms. They developed into city-states with important functions in rule and trade as well as in religion, and some even incorporated whole empires under their sway. Specific individual cities, most notably Teotihuacán, had enormous cultural influence over other settlements that were spread across great distances.

There were also great differences between the hemispheres. Geographically, the cities of the western hemisphere were built at water's edge, usually near lakes or small rivers, but not on major

THE EARLY AMERICAS

DATE	POLITICAL	RELIGION AND CULTURE	SOCIAL DEVELOPMENT
6000 B.C.E		● Stone tools in Mexico (6700)	
5000 B.C.E			● Plants (including maize) cultivated in Mesoamerica
3000 B.C.E			● Villages established in Mesoamerica; gourds and beans grown
2500 B.C.E	● Maya culture originated	● Pottery from Mesoamerica (2300)	
1500 B.C.E	● Olmecs, Gulf of Mexico (1500 B.C.E.–400 B.C.E.) ● Zapotecs, S. Mexico (1400 B.C.E –900 C.E.)	● Olmec center of San Lorenzo; pottery, mirrors, ceramics	
1000 B.C.E	● Chavin, N. Peru (c. 900–200 B.C.E) ● Tiwanaku, Bolivia (c. 800 B.C.E–1200 B.C.E.)		
200 B.C.E	● First Teotihuacán buildings, Valley of Mexico ● Moche, N. coast of Peru (200 B.C.E.–600 C.E.)		
100 B.C.E	● Nazca, Peru (1–600 C.E.)		
500 C.E	● Maya culture (S. Mexico, Guatemala, Belize) at peak (325–900) ● Teotihuacán culture at peak (450–600) ● Huari, Peru (c. 650–800)		● Teotihuacán population 100,000 ● First fully developed towns in the Mississippi valley (c. 700)
1000 C.E	● Toltecs (900–1170) ● Chimu, N.W. Peruvian coast (c. 1000–1470)		
1200 C.E	● Aztecs (c. 1100–1521) ● Inca, Andean S. America (c. 1200–1535)	● Aztec pictographs and hieroglyphs ● Aztec gold, jade, and turquoise jewels, textiles, and sculptures	● Aztec tribute empire over over surrounding lands from capital of Cuzco

river systems. Technologically, the people of the Americas did not use metals in their tools. In fact, they hardly used metal at all except for ornaments, jewelry, and artwork. They used neither wheels nor draft animals in transportation. Llamas served as pack animals for small loads, but otherwise goods were carried by hand, dragged, or shipped by canoe. Construction and transportation were thus far more labor intensive than in most of Afro-Eurasia. Finally, except for the Maya, the cities of the Americas did not create writing systems. Some, like the Zapotecs and Toltecs, used limited hieroglyphic symbols and calendar formats, but these did not develop into full, written languages. In Afro-Eurasia, only in the Niger River area did settlements grow into cities without developing writing systems.

In many respects, the cities of the western hemisphere had one foot in the stone age. The archaeologist Richard MacNeish has underlined the comparatively slow evolution of urban society in the western hemisphere. Stone tools ground by hand first appeared in central Mexico about 6700 B.C.E.; the domestication of plants began about 5000 B.C.E.; villages were established about 3000 B.C.E.; pottery appeared about 2300 B.C.E.; and population suddenly increased in about 500 B.C.E. These processes were much slower than in the river-valley civilizations of Eurasia.

ORIGINS: MIGRATION AND AGRICULTURE

Humans arrived in the western hemisphere from across the Beringia land bridge (connecting Alaska and Siberia) between 15,000 and 40,000 years ago and then spread throughout both North and South America (see map, p. 26). By 5000 B.C.E., they were cultivating maize, at least in small quantities, as well as gathering wild crops and hunting animals. By around 3000 B.C.E. they also grew beans and gourds.

Working with botanists, Richard MacNeish documented the beginnings of domestication of maize in the valley of Tehuacan, 200 miles (320 kilometers) southeast of Mexico City. He traced the development from wild corn cobs about 5000 B.C.E. to an early variety of modern corn 5000 years later. In subsequent excavations in Peru, MacNeish found that the cultivation of maize began there by 4000 B.C.E., perhaps introduced from Mesoamerica. In both regions, at about the same time, the other two staples of the American diet, beans and

squashes, also appear. Further, in the Andes mountains, potatoes and root crops were also grown. The valley of Mexico and the high Andes of Peru thus became incubators of much of the civilization of the Americas from an early date. Agricultural innovation, urbanization, and the foundation of empires originated in these regions and spread outward.

MESOAMERICAN URBANIZATION

By 2000 B.C.E., the agricultural foundations for an urban civilization were in place in Mesoamerica. Farmers throughout present-day Mexico and central America were cultivating maize, gourds, beans, and other food crops. In addition to farming dry fields, their methods included "slash-and-burn," which kept them moving from place to place in search of new land; "pot irrigation," dipping pots into wells and simply pouring the water onto the fields; canal irrigation; and, in low-lying swamplands, the creation of *chinampas*, raised fields or so-called "hanging gardens." Chinampas were created by piling up the mud and the natural vegetation of the swamps into grids of raised land crisscrossed by natural irrigation channels. When the Spanish arrived in 1519, they estimated that the chinampas could feed four persons per acre; more recent archaeological estimates of their productivity suggest eight.

Olmec Civilization along the Gulf Coast

On the basis of these agricultural systems, localized permanent settlements that centered on religious shrines and were led by local chiefs began to emerge. Trade and shared cultural and ceremonial practices gave a common character to specific geographical regions within Mesoamerica. Along the Gulf coast of Mexico, the earliest of these civilizations, the Olmec, took shape from about 1200 B.C.E.

The Olmec built raised platforms, settlements, and shrines above the low-lying woodlands. The first that we know of was built at San Lorenzo about 1150 B.C.E. Labor brigades constructed *chinampas*, and the population of the settlement may have reached 2500. Olmec artwork—representations of animals and mythological creatures in sculpture and bas relief—suggests a shared religious and "cosmo-magical" basis to the society. About 900 B.C.E. the San Lorenzo site was

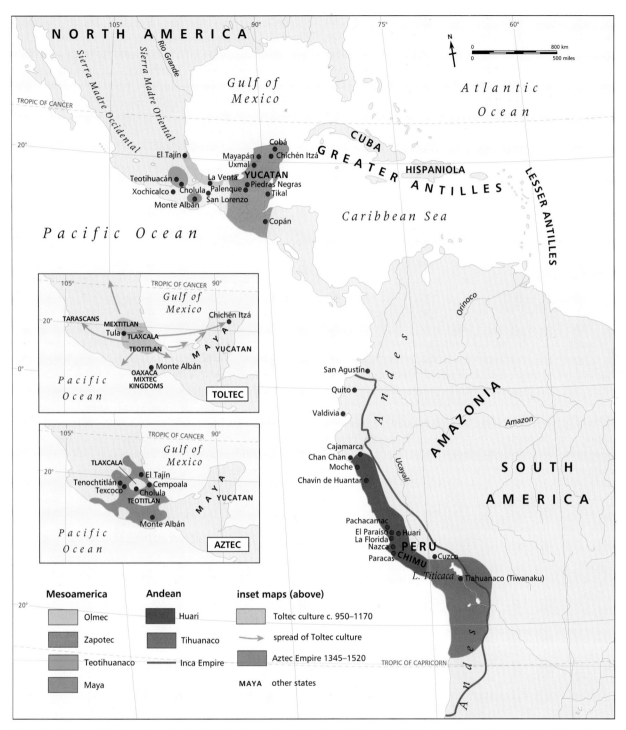

Classic cultures of the Americas Sophisticated urban cultures developed in two tropical regions of the Americas: humid southern Mexico and the more temperate valleys of the central Andes. Both regions witnessed a succession of distinctive cultural and political centers. The Maya civilization of the Yucatán emerged, by 250 C.E., as the outstanding power in Mesoamerica, while the Huari empire of the Andes prefigured that of the Inca. In South America, urban civilizations appeared both near sea level along the Pacific coast and in the Andes Mountains, at altitudes from 6,500 to 12,000 feet (2000 to 3700 meters).

Colossal head from San Lorenzo, Veracruz, Mexico, before 400 B.C.E. Weighing around ten tons, this massive sculpted head is one of nine that were found at San Lorenzo. Made from basalt and carved with stone tools, the heads originally stood in rows on the site and are most probably portraits of Olmec rulers. All display the same full, resolute lips and broad, flat noses. Similar sculptures were also found at La Venta. (*Museo Regional de Veracruz, Jalapa, Mexico*)

Zapotec Civilization in the Oaxaca Valley

Olmec products—pottery, ritual objects, mirrors, and ceramics—appeared in the highlands around modern Oaxaca as early as 1150 B.C.E., along with natural products, such as obsidian and seashells from around the Gulf of Mexico. At first, therefore, scholars believed that the Zapotec culture of the Oaxaca valley was an offshoot of the Olmec. More recent finds in the village of San Jose Mogote, dating to 1400–1150 B.C.E., demonstrate, however, that the Zapotecs had begun settlements no later than the Olmecs. The imported products reflected trading between the two groups.

Zapotec civilization peaked on the slopes of Monte Albán. By 400 B.C.E. ceremonial and public buildings dotted the summits of the hills. The settlement grew over the centuries, reaching its peak in the centuries after 200 C.E., when up to 50,000 people lived there. The settlement was not entirely concentrated into a single city, but extended over 15 square miles (39 square kilometres), with some 2000 terraces built into the hills, each with a house or two and its own water supply. Temples, pyramids, tombs, and an array of religious images suggest the importance of cosmo-magical symbolism among the Zapotecs, too. Monte Albán peaked in population and creativity about 700 C.E. and then declined.

Teotihuacán in the Valley of Mexico

Meanwhile, in the valley of Mexico, another civilization was coalescing, dominating the lands near it, and finally creating a substantial empire. At its core, about 40 miles (65 kilometers) to the northeast of present day Mexico City, stood Teotihuacán, one of the great cities of the ancient world. René Millon, an archaeologist at the University of Rochester who supervised an immense project mapping all the thousands of structures in the city, wrote of "how radically different Teotihuacán was from all other settlements of its time in Middle America. It was here that the New World's urban revolution exploded into being" (Millon, p. 83). At its peak, about 550 C.E., Teotihuacán accommodated about 100,000 inhabitants on some 8 square miles (20 square kilometres). Teotihuacán civilization had no system of writing so, again, our knowledge is limited to the excavation and interpretation of physical artifacts.

The city sat astride the major communication line between the valley of Mexico and the passes

destroyed, its artwork defaced. No one today knows why.

About one hundred years later, some 100 miles (160 kilometers) to the northeast and closer to the Gulf, Olmec peoples at La Venta built a small island in the middle of a swamp, and constructed on it an earth mound, half again as large as a football field and 100 feet (30 meters) high. Buildings atop the mound were probably used as temples. Monumental stone sculptures, including some of the giant stone heads typical of Olmec art, also mark the space. Some of them probably served also as altars. The stone building materials were transported here from at least 60 miles (97 kilometers) away, the jade from much further. La Venta flourished for four centuries until about 400 B.C.E. it, too, was destroyed and its monuments defaced. Again, no one today knows why.

eastward to the Gulf of Mexico. Life in the city was a gift of the low-lying lake system of the valley of Mexico, especially of nearby Lake Texcoco. The lakes provided irrigation waters for the fields of the Teotihuacán valley and salt, fish, and waterfowl. Basalt, limestone, and chert stone for building and clay for pottery were readily available in the valley, but other raw materials were imported, notably obsidian for tools and weapons from Pachuca and Otumba in the surrounding mountains. Marine shells and copal (a tree resin used as incense) were

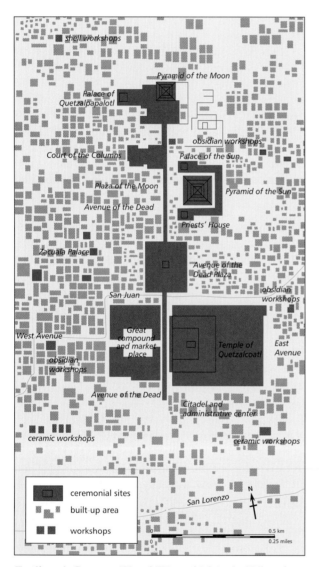

Teotihuacán Between 400 and 750 C.E., high in the Valley of Mexico, Teotihuacán was the dominant power in Mesoamerica. Covering over 7.5 square miles, with a population of 100,000, the city was laid out on a regular grid plan connecting the elements of a massive ceremonial complex. The residents thrived on agriculture, craftwork, and trade in ceramics and locally quarried obsidian.

imported from the Gulf region, and feathers of the quetzal bird came from the Mayan regions of the southeast. Trading outposts of Teotihuacán appeared 700 miles (1100 kilometers) south in Maya areas, and Teotihuacán ceramics have been found as far south as Tikal (see the discussion of Maya civilization on page 100). More than 400 workshops in the city produced pottery, obsidian manufactures, ornaments fashioned from seashells, and art and jewelry from jade and onyx.

A huge pyramid, at its base as broad as the great pyramid of Khufu in Egypt, though only half as high, dominated the Teotihuacán cityscape. The pyramid sits above a natural cave that early inhabitants enlarged into a clover-leaf-shaped chamber. The combination of natural cave and pyramid suggests that local people may have believed that this cave was the "navel of the universe." As Mircea Eliade, the historian of religions, has demonstrated, the belief that all human life, or at least the lives of the local people, had emerged upward onto earth from a "navel," a single specific geographical point, was widely held in many civilizations of the ancient world. (The Garden of Eden story is a later variant of this belief.) Two additional massive shrines—the adjacent, smaller Pyramid of the Moon, and a central temple dedicated to the god Quetzalcoatl— enhance the religious dimensions of the city. Throughout its lifetime, and indeed even afterward until the Spanish conquest, Teotihuacán attracted multitudes of pilgrims from as far away as Guatemala.

The first buildings of Teotihuacán appeared about 200 B.C.E. One hundred years later, there were still only about 600 inhabitants. By 150 C.E., however, the population had grown to 20,000 and the area to 5 square miles (13 square kilometers). At about this time the Pyramids of the Sun and the Moon were constructed. Then the population multiplied as the city exploded with religious, trade, artisanal, and administrative functions and personnel.

The city was laid out on a monumental, geometric grid that centered on the 150 feet (45 meter) wide Avenue of the Dead, the north–south axis of the city. More than seventy-five temples line this road, including the Pyramid of the Sun. The Pyramid of the Moon demarcated its northern terminal. The regularity of the city plan suggests a powerful government and, indeed, a large administrative headquarters, the Ciudadela, dominates the southeastern terminus of the

Avenue. The placement of the central Temple of Quetzalcoatl within the Ciudadela implies a close relationship between religion and administration.

At its peak, about 500–650 C.E., Teotihuacán exercised a powerful imperial force over its immediate surrounding area and exerted spiritual, religious, cultural, economic, and military influence for hundreds of miles, especially to the south, into Maya areas. In 650, however, the city was deliberately burned down. Teotihuacán began to decline in significance. By 750 its power was broken, its population scattered to smaller towns and rural areas. Several reasons have been suggested: the region may have become increasingly arid, incapable of supporting so large a population; increasing density of population, augmented by government programs for moving rural populations into the city, might have led to conflict and revolt from within; neighboring city-states, pressured by the increasing militarization in Teotihuacán, may have attacked the city. These are, however, only educated guesses. In the absence of written records, no one knows for sure.

Cities interact with one another in networks of exchange, so advances or declines in one usually echo in the others. Teotihuacán and Monte Albán both declined simultaneously about 750 C.E., but smaller, nonurban centers kept the political, cultural, and religious legacies of Teotihuacán alive in the region. (Compare this with the experience of western Europe after the decline of Rome, discussed in Chapter 6.) Three subsequent civilizations—the Toltec, the Aztec, and the Maya—absorbed and perpetuated its influence.

Toltec Civilization in the Valley of Mexico

When the Toltecs arrived in the valley of Mexico from the north and came to dominate the region from a new capital at Tula, about 900 C.E., they apparently ruled on Teotihuacán foundations and built their chief ceremonial center in honor of

Teotihuacán, Mexico, with the Pyramid of the Moon (foreground) linked to the Pyramid of the Sun by the Avenue of the Dead.
By 200 B.C.E. in the valley of Mexico, the combined effects of intensified trading, growing religious activity, and huge surpluses of food led to the founding of this major city, which for centuries enjoyed religious, political, and economic dominance in the region. Teotihuacán reached an enormous size (8 square miles; 2072 hectares) and population (100,000) before eventually being deliberately, and mysteriously, burned down in 650 C.E.

Quetzalcoatl. Their rule, however, was shortlived. About 1170 C.E. still newer immigrants destroyed the Toltec temples and government.

Aztec Civilization in the Valley of Mexico

After Tula fell, the Aztecs entered the valley. They established settlements on the southeastern shores of Lake Texcoco and built Tenochtitlán as their capital only 40 miles (65 kilometers) from the earlier site of Teotihuacán. As the Aztecs built their large, militaristic empire, the population of Tenochtitlán grew to 200,000. Militarism and the demand of their gods for human sacrifice led the Aztecs into a constant quest for captives to sacrifice and, therefore, into constant warfare with their neighbors. When the Spanish conquistadores arrived in 1519, the neighboring peoples helped them overthrow the Aztecs and their empire. The Spanish then razed Tenochtitlán to the ground and established their own capital, Mexico City, atop its ruins (see Chapter 12).

Teotihuacán's third legacy was to the Maya.

Maya Civilization:
How Do We Know?

The Maya live today in the Yucatán peninsula of Mexico, in Guatemala, and in Belize. For centuries the connection between their current, often impoverished, existence and the glories of their civilization in the third through the tenth centuries C.E. had been lost. Then, in 1839–41, a New York lawyer, John Lloyd Stephens, and a Scottish artist, Frederick Catherwood, discovered the remnants of the cities of Copán and Palenque in the rainforests of Mesoamerica, and Uxmal and Chichén Itzá in the Yucatán. Stephens and Catherwood wrote and painted what they saw and made rubbings of the designs they found on Maya **stelae,** stone marker tablets. They brought to Europe and the United States information about this civilization that had long been lost to the outside world and demonstrated the lost link between the modern Maya and the earlier, destroyed cities of Mesoamerica. Their book, *Incidents of Travels in Central America, Chiapas, and Yucatan*, published in 1841, opened the modern academic study of the Maya. This was almost exactly the same time as H.C. Rawlinson and others were rediscovering the great archaeological sites of Mesopotamia and deciphering its language.

Stelae and other inscriptions revealed the Maya language, but no one could read it. Even the Maya themselves, prevented by the Spanish from keeping their language alive (see Chapter 13), had forgotten the script. Scholars could read parts of the elaborate and sophisticated Maya calendar system, but they could not discern whether the events recorded were historical, mythical, or some combination of the two. In the 1950s and 1960s, at Harvard University, Tatiana Proskouriakoff began to demonstrate that the Maya stelae recorded the reigns and victories of real kings who had ruled real states. Adding to Proskouriakoff's interpretation of the glyphs, the Russian scholar Yuri Knorozov demonstrated, against fierce opposition, that the Maya script included representations of phonetic sound as well as of full words. In the 1970s a new generation of linguistic scholars began to decode the syntactical structure of the writing. They learned to distinguish which signs represented nouns and which verbs, and where they fell in the structure of the narrative. They were well on their way to discovering Maya history.

The archaeologists Linda Schele and David Freidel finally mastered the hieroglyphs and scripts of the people of the city of Palenque. They found records of their copious warfare, the exact lineage of the Palenque kings, and the picture of a tree used to symbolize the king—the Maya represented their royal families as forests of trees and forests of kings. Schele and Freidel found a record of constant warfare among the local shaman kings and their profoundly religious local city-states. The wars were fought in search of captives to serve as slaves and as human sacrifices to the demanding gods (see Profile, pp. 106–7).

The Maya calendar recorded three related chronologies: dates and events in cosmic time periods of thousands of years; historic events in the lives of specific rulers and their states; and the yearly cycle of agricultural activity. Maya rituals were permeated by the sense of living at once in the world of here-and-now and in a spiritual realm connected with other worlds and gods (see Source opposite). Their kings were **shamans**, bridges between the two worlds (see picture, p. 103).

The Maya shared a single, general culture and two closely related languages, one from the southern, lowland region, another from the northern highlands.

Although fiercely competitive, the Maya, like the ancient Greek city-states, presented a unified ethnic

SOURCE
The Popul Vuh

The *Popul Vuh* is the most complete existing collection of creation myths to survive the Spanish conquistadores. Originally written in Maya hieroglyphs, it was transcribed into Latin in the sixteenth century and then translated into Spanish by a Dominican priest in the eighteenth century. The selection cited here is reminiscent of the biblical story of the tree in the garden of Eden whose fruits were forbidden. But the tale in *Popul Vuh* has even more significant differences. The tree, a calabash, is forbidden because the skull of a god, named One Hunahpu, was placed in a fork in it. As a young woman reached out to take the fruit of the tree, the skull spat out saliva on her, making her pregnant and thus preserving the god's lineage among humans.

And this is when a maiden heard of it, the daughter of a lord. Blood Gatherer is the name of her father, and Blood Woman is the name of the maiden.

And when he heard the account of the fruit of the tree, her father retold it. And she was amazed at the account:

"I'm not acquainted with that tree they talk about. 'Its fruit is truly sweet!' they say." "I hear," she said.

Next she went all alone and arrived where the tree stood. It stood at the Place of Ball Game Sacrifice:

"What? Well! What's the fruit of this tree? Shouldn't this tree bear something sweet? They shouldn't die, they shouldn't be wasted. Should I pick one?" said the maiden.

And then the bone spoke; it was here in the fork of the tree:

"Why do you want a mere bone, a round thing in the branches of a tree?" said the head of One Hunahpu when it spoke to the maiden. "You don't want it," she was told.

"I do want it," said the maiden.

"Very well. Stretch out your right hand here, so I can see it," said the bone.

"Yes," said the maiden. She stretched out her right hand, up there in front of the bone.

And then the bone spat out its saliva, which landed squarely in the hand of the maiden.

And then she looked in her hand, she inspected it right away, but the bone's saliva wasn't in her hand.

"It is just a sign I have given you, my saliva, my spittle. This, my head, has nothing on it—just the bone, nothing of meat. It's just the same with the head of a great lord: it's just the flesh that makes his face look good. And when he dies, people get frightened by his bones. After that, his son is like his saliva, his spittle, in his being, whether it be the son of a lord or the son of a craftsman, an orator. The father does not disappear, but goes on being fulfilled. Neither dimmed nor destroyed is the face of a lord, a warrior, craftsman, orator. Rather, he will leave his daughters and sons. So it is that I have done likewise through you. Now go up there on the face of the earth; you will not die. Keep the word. So be it," said the head of One and Seven Hunahpu—they were of one mind when they did it.

This was the word Hurricane, Newborn Thunderbolt, Raw Thunderbolt had given them. In the same way, by the time the maiden returned to her home, she had been given many instructions. Right away something was generated in her belly, from the saliva alone, and this was the generation of Hunahpu and Xbalanque.

And when the maiden got home and six months had passed, she was found out by her father. Blood Gatherer is the name of her father.

FOCUS
Agricultural Towns of North America

Agricultural settlements took root in many locations in continental North America in the first few hundred years C.E. Several grew into small towns, reaching their maximum size about 1000–1400 C.E., and some scholars see the signs of early urbanization. Nevertheless, these towns are not included among the seven sites of primary urbanization because few of them reached a population size that might be considered urban; nor do they demonstrate clearly a non-agricultural base to their economies. They may also be derivative of earlier settlements to the south. For example, those in the southwestern United States, like the Hohokam, Mogollon, and Anasazi peoples, show evidence in their art work and building patterns of influences from Mexico and even South America.

The first fully developed towns in the Mississippi valley appeared about 700 C.E. Their inhabitants built temple mounds and left evidence of elaborate, ritual funerals, suggesting a hierarchical social and political organization. The largest of the temple mound towns, Cahokia, occupied land along the Mississippi, across the river and a few miles east of present-day Saint Louis. Cahokia held a population of 10,000 in the city and 38,000 in the region in the twelfth and thirteenth centuries. Around the town were sited some 100 mounds that served as burial tombs or as platforms for homes of the elite. The mounds resemble those of Mexican cities and suggest interchange between the two regions. Archaeologist Brian Fagan concludes, "There is every reason to believe that Cahokia was planned and controlled by a powerful central authority and that there were many craft specialists" (Fagan, p. 336). Cahokia, like almost all the towns of North America, was in decline, or even deserted, before the arrival of European invaders after 1500 for reasons that are not entirely clear. Archaeologists continue active research in the towns of North America, their cultures, and their links to one another and to other regions.

Earthen jar in the form of a human face, Fortune Mound, Arkansas, Mississippian, 1000–1700 C.E. French explorers, who reached the towns of the Mississippi valley in the sixteenth century, discovered a ranked matrilineal society, headed by a chief and divided into four well-defined classes. This effigy vessel may represent either a dead ancestor or a trophy head taken in war. The arrival of Europeans, who brought contagious diseases with them, triggered the gradual decline of early urban centers in North America. (*Peabody Museum, Cambridge, Mass.*)

identity to outsiders—especially those who spoke other languages (Schele and Freidel, p. 51).

The number of kingdoms ruled by kings grew from perhaps a dozen in the first century B.C. to as many as sixty at the height of the lowland civilization in the eighth century.

Maya Civilization: What Do We Know?

The Maya built on Olmec and Teotihuacano foundations as well as on their own practices. Arriving in the Yucatán and central America, they began to construct ceremonial centers by 2000 B.C.E. Between 300 B.C.E. and 300 C.E., they expanded their centers to plazas surrounded by stone pyramids and crowned with temples and palaces. The classic phase, 300–600 C.E., followed with full-fledged cities and monumental architecture, temples, extensive sacrifices, and elaborate burials, and the Olmec and Teotihuacán cultural influences are evident. Maya culture flourished in the southern lowlands, and major construction took place at Palenque, Piedras Negras, Copán, Coba, and elsewhere.

Tikal, in today's Guatemala, is one of the largest, most elaborate, and most completely excavated of these cities. In its center, Tikal holds five temple

A blood-letting rite, limestone lintel from Yaxchilán, Mexico (Maya), *c.* 725 C.E. The king, Lord Shield Jaguar, in his role of shaman, brandishes a flaming torch to illuminate the drama about to unfold. His principal wife, Lady Xoc, kneeling, pulls through her tongue thorn-lined rope that falls into a woven basket holding blood-soaked strips of paper cloth. These will be burned and thereby transmitted to the gods. Few works of art made by the Maya capture so completely the link between their political and religious ideas in an appropriately sacramental style. (Having deciphered the hieroglyphics of the Mayan calendar, scholars know that this event took place on October 28, 709 C.E.) (*British Museum, London*)

pyramids, up to 200 feet (60 meters) high and built from 300 to 800 C.E. (One appeared so massive, powerful, and exotic that film-maker George Lucas used it as a setting for *Star Wars*.) As the first modern archaeologists hacked away the tropical rainforest and uncovered this temple core, they concluded that Tikal was a spiritual and religious center. Later they uncovered housing and water cisterns that accommodated up to 50,000 people outside the temple precincts. This find led them to change their assessment of Tikal. Instead of viewing it as a purely religious shrine, they began to see it as a large city of considerable regional political and economic significance as well. Still later, as the hieroglyphic script was deciphered, the extent of expansionism, warfare, and human sacrifice was also uncovered. At the height of its powers, Tikal's authority covered almost 1000 square miles (2500 square kilometers) containing 360,000 people. Most Maya states held only 30,000–50,000 subjects.

By 900 C.E., the great classical period of the Maya in the southern lowlands ended. No one knows why. The most frequent hypotheses include: excessive population pressure on natural resources, especially agriculture; climatic changes beyond the

Temple I at Tikal, Guatemala (Mayan), before 800 C.E. At its height the city-state of Tikal covered almost 1000 square miles (2500 square km) and was home to 360,000 inhabitants. Its symbols of authority were centralized in its monumental shrines. This unusually steep stepped pyramid—230 feet (70 m) high—would have been the backdrop for self-inflicted blood-letting and the sacrifice of prisoners of war as offerings to the gods.

CIVILIZATIONS FLOURISHING IN CENTRAL AMERICA BEFORE COLUMBUS

Olmec   *c.* 1500–400 B.C.E. Gulf of Mexico. First complex society in region, with centralized authority. Known for carvings of giant stone heads and jade animals.

Maya   *c.* 2000 B.C.E.–900 C.E. S. Mexico, Guatemala, Belize. Most enduring of the Middle American civilizations, the Mayans had by 325 C.E. become superb astronomers who built stepped pyramids, smelted metal tools, and developed hieroglyphs.

Zapotec   *c.* 1400 B.C.E.–900 C.E. S. Mexico. Built ceremonial center of Monte Albán and peaked as a civilization around 300 C.E.

Teotihuacán   *c.* 300 B.C.E.–750 C.E. Valley of Mexico. Major trading and cultural center. At its peak populated by 100,000 inhabitants in an area (8 square miles) larger than Rome. Contains huge Pyramid of the Sun, Mexico's largest pre-Columbian edifice.

Toltec   *c.* 900–1170 C.E. Central Mexico. Toltecs ruled much of the country from Tula (northeast of Mexico City), where symbols of blood and war predominate, and the similar city of Chichén Itzá in Yucatán.

Aztec   *c.* 1100–1521 C.E. Central Mexico. Sophisticated culture run by priestly aristocracy that built capital of Tenochtitlán. Known for their architecture, textiles, and a complex sacred calendar, the Aztecs were conquered by the Spanish in 1519–21.

ability of the Maya to adjust to; excessive warfare that wore out the people and destroyed their states. No one knows for sure.

No one knows, either, why at the time of the Maya decline in the lowlands, new Maya cities and states grew up in the northern highlands of the Yucatán peninsula, notably at Uxmal and Chichén Itzá. These cities, in turn, declined by 1200, and the last Maya capital, Mayapán, was constructed between 1263 and 1283. It adapted many of the cultural monuments of Chichén Itzá, but grew only to some 10,000 to 20,000 inhabitants. Mayapán seemed militaristic, beleaguered, and possessed of tough sensibilities as evidenced by wholesale human sacrifices. The city was later destroyed in civil wars in the mid-1400s.

By the time the Spanish conquistadores reached Mesoamerica in 1517, only a few small Maya towns remained. The period of Maya power and splendor had ended. The Toltecs, too, had fallen by then. The Aztecs had become the reigning power, and they were destroyed by the Spanish.

URBANIZATION IN SOUTH AMERICA

South America had few established trade links with Mesoamerica, but the two regions share many similarities. Both regions constructed religious shrine centers that seem to have dominated their general cultural foundations by about 1500 B.C.E.; they developed small city-states that defined local cultural variations from about 300–200 B.C.E.; created proto-empires throughout significant regions about 500–600 C.E.; and generated large, urban empires—the Aztecs in the valley of Mexico, the Inca in the Andes—that were destroyed by the Spanish. Both developed trading relationships between their coastal regions and their mountainous inland cores. But the contrast between coast and inland mountains is far more striking in South America. The Pacific coast of Ecuador, Peru, and Chile is a desert in most places. The prevailing winds come not from the Pacific, but from the Amazon basin to the east. The Andes Mountains thus have little rainfall from the Pacific Ocean to trap on their western slopes, but they do intercept the precipitation from the Atlantic, making the eastern slopes fertile while leaving the west coast dry. The most spectacular urban civilizations of South America took root in the 10,000 foot (3000 meter) high plains and passes of the Andes rather than in the arid Pacific coast

PROFILE
Great-Jaguar-Paw
MAYAN KING OF TIKAL

By deciphering, translating, and interpreting the stelae at Tikal, Linda Schele and David Freidel recreate an heroic moment of military victory in the life of the king Great-Jaguar-Paw and in the history of his kingdom. Their interpretation is based primarily on the stela illustrated here and on comparison with later stelae representing the same event:

> Despite the fact that he was such an important king, we know relatively little about Great-Jaguar-Paw's life outside of the spectacular campaign he waged against Uaxactun. His reign must have been long, but the dates we have on him come only from his last three years. On one of these historical dates, October 21, A.D. 376, we see Great-Jaguar-Paw ending the seventeenth katun [a ritual cycle of twenty years]. . . .This fragmentary monument shows him only from the waist down, but he is dressed in the same regalia as his royal

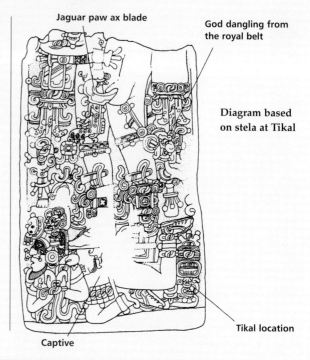

Jaguar paw ax blade

God dangling from the royal belt

Diagram based on stela at Tikal

Tikal location

Captive

below. The contrast with the river-basin civilizations of Afro-Eurasia could not be more vivid.

Coastal Settlements and Networks

The Pacific coast is not, however, uninhabitable. It yields abundant quantities of fish, seaweed, and salt. Even today these ocean products are traded to the mountain cities in exchange for their food crops. In some areas the cultivation of cotton is also possible, and coastal Peru rivals the Indus valley as the home of the first production of cotton textiles, about 4500 B.C.E. The quality of the textiles and the colorful designs dyed into the cotton show up most clearly in the burial cloths of semi-mummified bodies in the Paracas peninsula near Pisco, Peru.

In addition, although climatically a desert, the coast does have some small mountain-fed rivers running through it. People who could organize labor brigades to channel the rivers for irrigation created ceremonial centers along the coast,

beginning perhaps by 2000 B.C.E. The oldest of these shrine centers, and the one closest to the Pacific, is El Paraiso, near modern Lima, at the mouth of the Chillon River. Built in a typically U-shaped complex of buildings, El Paraiso appears to have been constructed by people from many separate villages and kin groups. Few lived at El Paraiso, but apparently the shrine served them all, and many used the location as a burial place.

The largest of the shrine centers is Sechin Alto, a 130 foot (40 meter) high mound, 1000 feet (300 meters) by 800 feet (270 meters), on which was built a U-shaped ceremonial complex surrounded by houses and platforms. The oldest building dates to 1300 B.C.E. It continued to expand until 400 B.C.E.

The Moche In the Moche valley of coastal northern Peru, settlements of up to 2000 separate structures had grown up by 200 B.C.E. From about 200 B.C.E. to 600 C.E., in this and neighboring valleys, the Moche state established itself. The Moche created irrigation

ancestors, with the god Chac-Xib-Chac dangling from his belt. His ankle cuffs display the sign of day on one leg and night on the other. . . . He holds an executioner's ax, its flint blade knapped into the image of a jaguar paw. In this guise of warrior and giver of sacrifices, he stands atop a captive he has taken in battle. The unfortunate victim, a bearded noble still wearing part of the regalia that marks his noble station, struggles under the victor's feet, his wrists bound together in front of his chest. He will die to sanctify the katun ending at Tikal.

Warfare was not new to the Maya. Raiding for captives from one kingdom to another had been going on for centuries, for allusions to decapitation are present in even the earliest architectural decorations celebrating kingship. The hunt for sacrificial gifts to give to the gods and the testing of personal prowess in battle was part of the accepted social order and captive sacrifice was something expected of nobles and kings in the performance of their ritual duties. Just as the gods were sustained by the bloodletting ceremonies of the kings, so they were nourished as well by the blood of noble captives. Sacrificial victims like these had been buried as

offerings in building terminations and dedications from late Preclassic times on, and possibly even earlier. . . .

The war waged by Great-Jaguar-Paw of Tikal against Uaxactun, however, was not the traditional hand-to-hand combat of proud nobles striving for personal glory and for captives to give to the gods. This was war on an entirely different scale, played by rules never before heard of and for stakes far higher than the reputations or lives of individuals. In this new warfare of death and conquest, the winner would gain the kingdom of the loser. Tikal won the prize on January 16, A.D. 378. . . .

The subjugation of Uaxactun by Great-Jaguar-Paw and Smoking Fog [his commander-in-chief], which precipitated this new kind of war and rituals, survives in the inscriptional record almost entirely in the retrospective histories carved by later rulers at Tikal. The fact that these rulers kept commemorating this event shows both its historical importance and its propaganda value for the descendants of these conquerors. (Schele and Freidel, pp. 144–8)

systems, spectacular monuments, and important tombs. In the late 1980s, at nearby Sipan, Peruvian archaeologist Walter Alva discovered three royal tombs that demonstrate the social and political stratification of the society. Each tomb housed a lord, sometimes made of gold, and surrounded by servants, who had been buried with him. Paintings and ceramic designs within the tombs show the sacrifice of prisoners-of-war (see Spotlight, pp. 108–9). The Moche built provincial centers in nearby river valleys from which they apparently ruled, traded, and introduced irrigation systems.

The Chimu By about 600 C.E. the Moche left the region, for reasons not entirely clear, and were succeeded by the Chimu kingdom that controlled twelve coastal river valleys. The Chimu built irrigation and water storage facilities, trade networks, and a powerful state that stretched some 1000 miles (1600 kilometers) along the Peruvian coast. Their monumental capital, Chan Chan, built

near the earlier Moche, was surrounded by a 35 foot (11 meters) high mud wall, and it covered nearly 4 square miles (12 square kilometers), with palaces, temples, administrative offices, and housing for the common people. Chan Chan contained ten royal compounds. Apparently each king in turn built his own center, ruled from it during his life, and was buried in it after his death.

In each area they dominated, the Chimu built subsidiary administrative centers that formed a network reaching as far south as modern Lima. The Chimu empire reigned until it was conquered by the Inca in 1470. Ironically, thanks to the Inca transportation and communication network, Chimu artwork influenced western South America even more after the Inca conquest than it had before.

Urbanization in the Andes Mountains

The Chavin Despite these coastal settlements and networks, most scholars believe that the core areas

SPOTLIGHT
The Royal Tombs at Sipan

"The richest treasure ever excavated archaeologically in the Western hemisphere," proclaimed archaeologist Walter Alva when he discovered the Moche Royal Tombs at Sipan, a village on the Pacific coast of Peru.

The Moche kingdom had flourished from about the first to the sixth century C.E., but it appeared that the best of its art, especially the art of precious metals, had been looted by centuries of grave robbers. In late 1986, however, police nabbed a group of robbers who had just uncovered some new treasures. They informed Walter Alva of the nearby Museo Nacional Bruning de Lambayeque and he began digging professionally, unearthing materials that dated from the first to the third century C.E. Hollow beads, many of them fashioned from gold "into a wondrous variety of shapes and sizes," were the first discoveries. A banner, 19.5 inches (48.5 centimeters) high **(figure 1)**, covered in sheets of gilded copper, had perhaps been carried in royal processions. Personal adornments included an ear ornament **(figure 2)**, 9.4 centimeters (4.2 inches) in diameter, representing a warrior fashioned from hammered gold and clad in a tunic of turquoise. Alva's team named him "The Lord of Sipan."

The central burial figure in the first tomb was "the skeleton of a man wrapped in a cotton shroud . . . . In his left hand and mouth were lumps of copper. He wore a gilded copper helmet, and resting on his right forearm was a round copper shield" (Alva and Donnan, p. 55). Red textiles, now decomposed, must have been his burial shroud. Several skeletons of humans and animals accompanied his. A second tomb held skeletons of an adult male,

Figure 1 Banner, cleaned and reconstructed (tomb 1).

Figure 2 Warrior ear ornament, cleaned and reconstructed (tomb 1).

in tomb two a Bird Priest; in the third tomb a Warrior Priest of an earlier era. The dismembered bones suggested that the sacrifices and dismemberment of victims had been performed nearby. Moche drawings also depict a "Decapitator," a supernatural figure resembling a spider, for "Spiders capture their prey, tie them with ropes of web, and later extract their vital fluids – just as Moche warriors [did]" (p. 139). Collectively, the treasures of "one of the most remarkable civilizations of the ancient world" (p. 227) had been resurrected from the royal tombs at Sipan.

Figure 3 Spider bead, cleaned and reconstructed (tomb 3).

two twenty-year-old females, a teenage male, an eight to ten-year-old child, llamas, a dog, and a snake. A third tomb, from a somewhat earlier period, yielded a single adult male buried with a teenage girl, a llama, ornaments, ceramics, two elaborately carved spear throwers, a gold scepter, burial masks, and necklaces of gold beads, some in the shape of spiders **(figure 3)**, 8.3 centimeters (4.1 inches) in diameter. They named this male "The Old Lord of Sipan." Nearby, the archaeologists found decomposed rooms containing ceramic vessels, miniature ornaments, and the dismembered bones of humans and llamas.

The discoveries were breathtaking, but what did they mean? In the Fowler Museum of the University of California, Los Angeles, Christopher Donnan had charge of some 125,000 photographs of Moche objects in museums and collections around the world. They provided context. Many Moche fine line drawings illustrate various priests engaged in warfare and performing human sacrifices. Sipan confirmed these realities: in tomb one a Warrior Priest;

Mummy wrapped in textiles, Pisco, Paracas Peninsula, Peru, c. 500 B.C.E. The weaving artistry of the Pacific Coast Indians was virtually unrivaled among prehistoric cultures. Cotton and wool materials have survived remarkably well in the dry coastal environment, especially in huge underground cemeteries where the dead were wrapped in fabric burial shrouds.

1200–200 B.C.E. The civilization is named for its best known and largest ceremonial center at Chavin de Huantar, which flourished in central Peru from about 900 to about 200 B.C.E. Chavin temples include a pantheon of gods preserved in paintings

CIVILIZATIONS OF SOUTH AMERICA

Chavin	*c.* 1200–200 B.C.E. N. Peru. Farming society, comprising different regional groups, whose main town may have been a pilgrimage site.
Moche	200 B.C.E.–600 C.E. N. coast of Peru. Modeled ceramics of animals in a realistic style. Religious and political life focused on the Huaca de la Luna (artificial platform) and Huaca del Sol (stepped pyramid).
Nazca	?1–600 C.E. Peru. Known principally for its series of enormous figures drawn with lines of pebbles. Best seen from the air, the largest (a hummingbird) is 900 feet (275 m) long.
Tiwanaku	*c.* 200 C.E.–1200 C.E. Bolivia. Named for the ancient city, near Lake Titicaca, that was occupied by a series of five different cultures, then abandoned.
Huari	*c.* 650–800 C.E. Peru. Empire whose style of architecture and artifacts, similar to Tiwanaku's, was dispersed throughout the region.
Chimu	*c.* 700–1470 C.E. Northwest Peruvian coast. Large urban civilization (capital: Chan Chan) responsible for fine gold work, record-keeping, and aqueducts. Conquered by the Aztecs.
Inca	*c.* 1200–1535 C.E. Andean South America. Last and largest pre-Columbian civilization (capital: Cuzco) that was destroyed by Spanish conquistadores in the 1530s.

of South American urbanization were in the Andes, the 20,000 foot (6000 meter) high mountain chain that parallels the Pacific coast for the entire length of South America. From earliest times to today, there has been considerable "vertical trade," linking coastal lowlands with high mountain areas in an exchange of the different products of their different ecologies. With the trade came networks of cultural, religious, and political communication, and some archaeologists have argued that the civilization of the Andes Mountains was developed from "maritime foundations" (Moseley).

The first known civilization of the Andes, the Chavin, flourished for about a millennium,

and carvings, including jaguar-like humans with serpents for hair, eagles, caymans, and many mixed figures, part human, part animal, reminiscent of similar figures in China. Like El Paraiso and the coastal shrines, Chavin seems to have been built by the joint efforts of many nearby kin and village groups. At its height, it held only 2000 inhabitants, but its culture and its gods inspired common religious forms in the vicinity, and carried them throughout the high Andes.

Tiwanaku, Huari, and Nazca Some 600 miles (1000 kilometers) to the south, south of Lake Titicaca, on today's border between Peru and Bolivia, at an elevation of 12,000 feet (3700 meters), lay the largest open, flat plain available for agriculture in the Andes. By 200 C.E., Tiwanaku (Tihuanaco) at the southern end of the lake, near the modern La Paz, became the capital of the region. Its rulers irrigated their high plains, *altiplano*, region to support perhaps 20,000 people and to create a ritual center of monumental structures and religious and spiritual practices that suffused the Andes and the coast. When Tiwanaku collapsed, for reasons now lost to history, successor states in the region, notably at Huari and Nazca, kept alive many of their administrative and religious practices.

The Inca These five states—Chimu, Chavin, Tiwanaku, Huari, and Nazca—established found-ations on which the Inca built their powerful but shortlived empire, which stretched for 2000 miles (3200 kilometers) from north to south and as far as 200 miles (320 kilometers) inland, during the years 1476–1534. The Inca adapted many of the gods and religious symbols, artwork, ceramics, and textiles of these earlier states. They built a new capital, Cuzco, at 10,000 feet (3000 meters), and connected it to all the mountain and coastal regions of their empire by an astonishing 25,000 mile (40,000 kilometer) system of roads, with tunnels, causeways, suspension bridges, travel lodges, and storage places. The roads were sometimes broad and paved, but often narrow and unpaved, especially because the Inca had no wheeled vehicles. Enforced, *mit'a* labor was exacted from local populations for the construction.

In 1438, Cusi Yupanqui was crowned "Inca," or king-emperor, after he won a victory over a neighboring tribe, and forged his quarreling peoples into a conquering nation. Thereafter, the whole nation was called Inca. Cusi Yupanqui established an hereditary monarchy, and his descendants built a great empire from his early conquests. They employed the *mit'a* system of enforced labor, demanding unpaid labor for part of each year from all adults in the empire for public construction. The Inca did not develop writing, but they did create an abacus-like system of numerical recording through the use of knots tied on strings. These *quipu* held the administrative records of the empire (see picture, p. 379).

Nazca lines, San Jose pampa, Peru desert, *c.* **500** C.E. Another of the successor states of Tiwanaku, the Nazca, created great patterns of lines drawn with pebbles on the desert surface. The designs, like this 900-foot-long (275 m) hummingbird figure, are visible only from the air, and their function and meaning are as elusive as the culture that fashioned them.

In each conquered region, the Inca established administrative centers, from which tax collectors gathered two-thirds of the crops and the manufactured products, like beer and textiles, half of it for the state, half for the gods and their priests. They established state workshops to produce official and consumer goods, and they seem to have encouraged significant standard-ization of production, for Inca arts and crafts show little variation over time and place. Inca religion apparently encouraged different gods and worship for different people. The sun god was the chief deity, and the emperor was considered his descendant; the nobility worshiped the military god Viracocha; while the common people continued to worship their own indigenous spirits, along with the newer sun god. The organization and the study of empire, however, take us to Part 3.

WEST AFRICA: THE NIGER RIVER VALLEY

Until 1977, all the cities in sub-Saharan Africa that were known to archaeologists had developed along patterns introduced from outside the region. Meroe and Kush on the upper Nile had adapted urban patterns from Egypt; Aksum in modern Ethiopia had followed examples of urbanization from both the Nile valley and from the trading powers of the Indian Ocean, including the Roman Empire; port cities along the East African coast, such as Malindi, Kilwa, and Sofala, had been founded by traders from across the Indian Ocean; the walled stone enclosures, called **zimbabwes**, built in the region of

modern Zimbabwe and Mozambique to house local royal rulers, had been initiated through contact with Swahili traders from the coast (see p. 381).

In west Africa, the first known cities, such as Timbuktu, Jenne, and Mopti along the Niger River, and Ife and Igbo Ukwu deeper south in the Yoruba lands near the tropical forests, had been built as centers of exchange. They were thought to be responses to the arrival of Muslim traders from north Africa who crossed the Sahara southward after the seventh century C.E. Archaeologists believed that Africans, like Europeans, had learned of city building from outsiders.

WEST AFRICA BEFORE URBANIZATION

The most important developments of pre-urban west Africa were iron smelting, apparently initiated by contact with north Africa; the development of new artistic traditions, especially by the Nok peoples; and the spread of agricultural civilization by the Bantu people. Iron smelting entered the archaeological record in west Africa suddenly about 500 B.C.E. In most places the technology jumped from stone to iron directly, with only a few examples of copper-work in between. Most archaeologists interpret this technological jump to indicate that iron working was introduced from outside, probably from the Phoenician colonies along the north African coast, and they find evid-ence for this idea in the rock art of the Sahara desert. Along the routes crossing the desert, rock engravings and paintings dating from between 1200 B.C.E. and 400 B.C.E. depict two-wheeled chariots that suggest trans-Saharan traffic.

THE EARLY AFRICAS			
DATE	POLITICAL	RELIGION AND CULTURE	SOCIAL DEVELOPMENT
500 B.C.E.		● Nok terra cotta sculptures	● Iron smelting ● Bantu adopting settled agricultural lives
250 B.C.E.	● Jenne–jeno founded	● Copper and semi–precious stone ornaments from Niger	
500 C.E.	● Ancient Ghana recorded by Arab visitors		● Cities in Niger valley (400)
1000 C.E.	● Foundation of Benin (c. 1000)		
1200 C.E.	● Ghana falls; Kingdom of Mali founded		

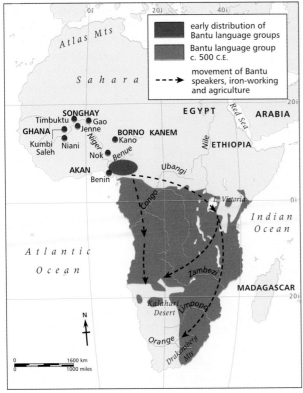

The spread of Bantu About 1500 B.C.E. an extraordinary cultural migration began to transform sub-Saharan Africa. From their homeland near the Niger delta, groups of Bantu-speaking farmers began to move east and south, spreading cattle domestication, crop cultivation, and iron-working. By about 500 C.E. southern Africa had been reached, the original hunter-gatherers having been marginalized to remote regions such as the Kalahari Desert.

In northern Nigeria, the Nok peoples were producing terra cotta sculptures, especially of human heads, from about 500 B.C.E. Living in settlements along the Niger, near its confluence with the Benue in modern Nigeria, the Nok also built iron-smelting furnaces, dating to 500–450 B.C.E.

Meanwhile, also in the lower Niger, some Bantu peoples were giving up nomadic pastoralism for settled agriculture, although many remained nomadic for a long time. They began great migrations southward and eastward over thousands of miles, introducing their languages, their knowledge of iron production, and their experience with settled agriculture. In one thousand years, 500 B.C.E. to 500 C.E., the Bantu carried their languages, their new, settled way of life, and their metallurgical skills almost to the southern tip of Africa.

JENNE-JENO: HOW DO WE KNOW?

Neither the Nok nor the Bantu built cities. Other people of the Niger River, however, did. In excavations that began in 1977 and continue today, Susan and Roderick McIntosh, archaeologists at Rice University in Houston, Texas, uncovered Jenne-jeno, "Ancient Jenne," the first known indigenous city in sub-Saharan Africa. The Jenne-jeno settlement began about 250 B.C.E. as a small group of round mud huts. Its herding and fishing inhabitants were already using iron implements, and the village grew to urban size by 400 C.E., reaching its peak of settlement by about 900 C.E.

The physical form of the city was different from that of the other six centers we have studied. A central inhabited area of some 80 acres (32 hectares) was surrounded by a city wall 10 feet (3 meters) wide and 13 feet (4 meters) high with a perimeter of 1¼ miles (2 kilometers). Near this central area were some forty smaller, but still substantial additional settlements. They extended to a radius of 2½ miles (4 kilometers). "Conservative estimates of between 7,000 and 13,000 persons for Jenne-jeno and between 15,000 and 27,000 for that site plus the 25 satellites within a one-kilometer radius just begin to tell the true story of mid-to-late first millennium population density"

Head from Jemaa, Nigeria, c. 400 B.C.E. The Nok were a nonliterate farming people that occupied the Jos Plateau in northern Nigeria during the first millennium B.C.E. Their distinctive sculptures—of elephants, snakes, monkeys, people, and even a giant tick—are all boldly modeled and skillfully fired in terra cotta. This powerful lifesize head would probably have formed part of a full-length statue. (*National Museum, Lagos, Nigeria*)

Pirogues, Niger River. For hundreds and even thousands of years fleets of graceful pirogues, like these photographed near Jenne, have carried the cargoes of the 2600 mile long Niger River valley — gold, ivory, textiles, grains, fish, and slaves — as well as the goods imported from the Sahara and beyond — salt, ceramics, glass, and copper — to waiting customers and merchants.

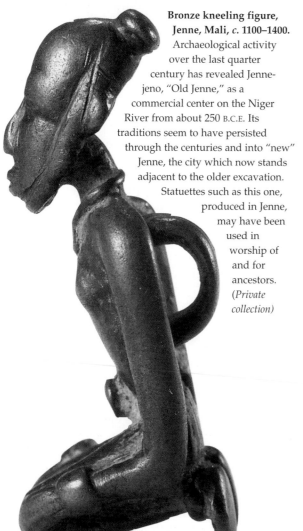

Bronze kneeling figure, Jenne, Mali, c. 1100–1400. Archaeological activity over the last quarter century has revealed Jenne-jeno, "Old Jenne," as a commercial center on the Niger River from about 250 B.C.E. Its traditions seem to have persisted through the centuries and into "new" Jenne, the city which now stands adjacent to the older excavation. Statuettes such as this one, produced in Jenne, may have been used in worship of and for ancestors. (*Private collection*)

(R. McIntosh, p. 200). By the year 1000, the settled area may have included 50,000 persons.

Excavations through numerous levels revealed that the people of Jenne-jeno ate fish from the river, rice from their fields, and beef from their herds. They probably drank the cows' milk as well. At least some wore jewelry and ornaments of imported copper and semi-precious stones. Dozens of burial urns, each up to 3 feet (1 meter) high, yielded human skeletons arranged in fetal position. The urns date from 300 to 1400 C.E., and their burial inside and adjacent to the houses suggests a reverence for ancestors. Statuettes in a kneeling position set into walls and under floors further suggest the probability of ancestor worship.

This part of the religious and cultural heritage of Jenne-jeno seems to have endured. The McIntoshes believe that these statuettes were the forerunners of similar sculptures used in Jenne as late as 1900 in sacrifices and prayers to and for ancestors. Although not built primarily as a shrine center, Jenne-jeno included religious functions as an important part of its activities, as its modern counterpart does today. The McIntoshes also found similarities between the arrangement of the huts of Jenne-jeno 1000 years ago and the grouping of family huts today. In ancient times as in modern, they argue, the husband-father lived in one large central hut while one of his wives occupied each of the surrounding huts.

Jenne-jeno must have engaged in trade because even in 250 B.C.E. its inhabitants were using iron and stone that had to be brought from at least 30 miles (48 kilometers) away. Sandstone for their

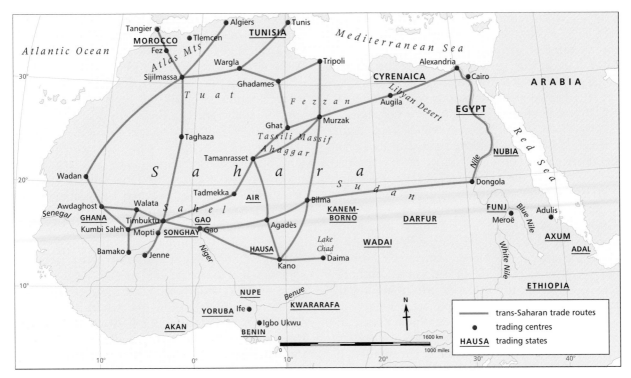

Trade across the Sahara Ivory, gold, hardwoods, and slaves were the magnets which drew trading caravans south across the arid Saharan wastes, often following routes established before the desert had formed. These routes linked the classical cultures of the Mediterranean and southwest Asia with an array of rich trading states strung along the Sahel/Sudan axis.

grinding stones had to have been imported from at least 60 miles (97 kilometers) away, while copper and salt came from hundreds of miles away. The McIntoshes discovered one gold earring, dating to about 750 C.E. The nearest site of gold mining was 500 miles (800 kilometers) away. Perhaps the people of Jenne-jeno traded the fish of the Niger and the rice of their fields for these imports. Some Jenne-jenoites may have become professional merchants.

Innovation in architectural concepts may also have come to Jenne from external contacts. By about 900 C.E. some rectangular houses began to appear among the circular ones, perhaps introduced through contact with northern peoples.

Outside contacts increased with the introduction of camel transportation across the Sahara about 300 C.E. and with the Muslim Arab conquest of north Africa about 700 C.E. (see p. 347). Especially after 1200 C.E., Muslim traders crossing the Sahara linked the savanna and forest lands of the south to the cities of the Mediterranean coast. Most scholars have argued that these external contacts and trade possibilities encouraged the growing importance of new cities like Timbuktu, Jenne, Niani, Gao, Kano, and, further south, Benin. The McIntoshes suggest an opposite perspective: These cities pre-date the

northern connections, and, indeed, their prosperity and control of the trade routes and the gold further to the south encouraged the northerners to dispatch their camel caravans across the Sahara.

By 1100, the settlements peripheral to Jenne-jeno began to lose population. Some of their inhabitants apparently moved to the central settlement. In another century the rural population also began to decline. By 1400, Jenne-jeno and its satellites were no more. Why? Roderick McIntosh cites several possible, but not certain, causes: "growing warfare and slave raiding…, changes to family structure and land rights…, migrations…, and … new forms of social stratification" (R. McIntosh, p. 203).

STATE FORMATION?

Could the settlements of the Middle Niger at Jenne-jeno be an example of early urbanism without a strong centralized government? Without a state? The McIntoshes certainly think so. They suggest that the population at Jenne-jeno lived in neighboring clusters that were functionally interdependent rather than in a single urban center with a prominent core marked by large scale, monumental architecture as was found in most of the other centers of primary urbanization. They see this settlement pattern as "a precocious, indigenous, and highly individual form of urbanism" (R. McIntosh, p. 203). They suggest that Jenne-jeno rose on the basis of trade and expanded into geographically neighboring, interactive settlements, but without a hierarchical social structure, without "overt signs of chiefly power" (S. McIntosh, p. 396), without a government. In contrast to primary urbanization in all the other regions of the world we have examined, Jenne-jeno may have experienced relative equality and cooperation among its citizens rather than competition, dominance, and coercion.

On the other hand, a comparative assessment might suggest that Jenne had developed only to about the stage of the Olmec settlements, and had not yet created the kind of centralized authority that emerged clearly and powerfully among the later Maya. Had Jenne-jeno persisted longer and grown larger, perhaps centralization and stratification would have developed. Indeed the presence of a central settlement surrounded by smaller adjacent settlements suggests that some hierarchy was already emerging. Did Jenne-jeno represent an alternative kind of urbanization, as the McIntoshes argue, or was it a settlement that was on its way to full-scale conventional urbanization? These are the kinds of questions of comparison that archaeologists—and historians—love to debate.

CONNECTION: Later cities and states in sub-Saharan Africa, pp. 347–8

THE FIRST CITIES: WHAT DIFFERENCE DOES IT MAKE?

With the creation of cities, humanity entered into many new forms of living. The first of these cities, in the river valleys of Mesopotamia and the Nile almost 5500 years ago, introduced not only new scale and density in human settlement patterns but also new technology in the metallurgy of copper, tin, and bronze; monumental scale in architecture; and specialization and hierarchy in social, political, and economic life. These cities flourished also as nodes in networks for the exchange of goods and ideas. The invention of writing in these cities not only gave new life to cultural creativity, but also provided new means of record keeping for the

bureaucrat, businessperson, and scholar. These new cities allowed and demanded complex and hierarchical government to keep them functioning. Although we sometimes see cities today as homes of secularism and heterogeneity, these early cities were "cosmo-magical" in their dedication to specific gods and in their physical and ritual organization. Differences in climate and culture separate Egyptian from Mesopotamian urbanization, but they also shared many similarities. We know somewhat less about Egyptian urbanization because the Nile itself washed away many of its foundations, but more recent archaeology has uncovered Egyptian as well as Sumerian city walls and residential structures.

Sumer and Egypt provide what scholars sometimes refer to as a "master narrative," a conventional, widely accepted view of historical transformation, suggesting that historical process at other times and places will follow similar patterns. Each of our subsequent case studies has reinforced some dimensions of the "master narrative" while challenging others.

• Indus valley urbanization suggested that a generally consistent civilization could extend over an immense geographical space, over thousands of years. A few of its cities stood out as capitals, but even after they were evacuated other cities of the far-flung network kept the civilization alive. Moreover, Indus agricultural practices were adopted and adapted by invaders who transplanted some of them from the Indus valley to the Ganges valley.

• Early Chinese urbanization, represented in the historical record through oracle bones and through the geometrical design of city plans, placed added emphasis on the cosmo-magical dimension of cities, although the rulers did not neglect to mobilize large and powerful armed forces.

• In the Americas, cities like Teotihuacán and the later cities of the Maya demonstrated again the importance of monumental, religious architecture, although each additional excavation reveals the extent of both long-distance trade and of everyday, mundane activities as well. Urbanization in the Andes mountains indicates that not all early cities needed river beds. Urban rulers could construct fabulous networks for trade, communication, and troop movement at forbidding altitudes. From their capital cities they could launch empires. They could also administer cities, and even empires, without having invented writing.

• In the Niger River valley of West Africa, the single urban settlement that has been excavated challenges the "master narrative," suggesting that cities may develop through the inter-relationship of adjacent smaller settlements without the need for hierarchy, centralization, government structure, and written language. The data presented thus far may be, however, subject to different interpretations. Perhaps the central mound in Jenne-jeno does, in fact, represent some hierarchical structure. Or perhaps it is a collection of contiguous villages rather than an urban center. The interpretation depends in part on how far the definition of a city and its functions may be—and ought to be—stretched. Continuing excavation and interpretation will help decide the degree to which the "master narrative" concerning early urbanization will hold up, and to what degree new ideas of the role of urbanization in human history are yet be formulated.

BIBLIOGRAPHY

Alva, Walter and Christopher Donnan. *The Royal Tombs of Sipan* (Los Angeles: Fowler Museum of Cultural History, University of California, Los Angeles, 1993).

Blunden, Caroline and Mark Elvin. *Cultural Atlas of China* (New Haven: Facts on File, 1983).

Chang, Kwang-chih. *The Archaeology of Ancient China* (New Haven: Yale University Press, 3rd ed., 1977).

Chang, Kwang-chih. *Shang Civilization* (New Haven: Yale University Press, 1980).

Coe, Michael, Dean Snow, and Elizabeth Benson. *Atlas of Ancient America* (New York: Facts on File, 1986).

Connah, Graham. *African Civilizations* (Cambridge: Cambridge University Press, 1987).

Cotterell, Arthur, ed., *The Penguin Encyclopedia of Ancient Civilizations* (London: Penguin Books, 1980).

Curtin, Philip, Steven Feierman, Leonard Thompson, and Jan Vansina. *African History from Earliest Times to Independence* (New York: Longman, 2nd ed., 1995).

deBary, William Theodore, *et al.*, comp., *Sources of Chinese Tradition* (New York: Columbia University Press, 1998).

Demarest, Arthur and Geoffrey Conrad, eds, *Ideology and Pre-Columbian Civilizations* (Santa Fe, NM: School of American Research Press, 1992).

Eliade, Mircea. *The Sacred and the Profane* (New York: Harper and Row, 1959).

Fagan, Brian. *People of the Earth: An Introduction to World Prehistory* (New York: HarperCollins, 8th ed., 1995).

Keightly, David N., ed. *The Origins of Chinese Civilization* (Berkeley: University of California Press, 1983).

MacNeish, Richard S. "The Origins of New World Civilization," *Scientific American* (November 1964). Reprinted in *Scientific American, Cities: Their Origin, Growth, and Human Impact* (San Francisco: W.H. Freeman and Company, 1973), 63–71.

McIntosh, Susan and Roderick McIntosh. "Finding West Africa's Oldest City," *National Geographic* CLXII No. 3 (September 1982), 396–418.

McIntosh, Roderick James. *The Peoples of the Middle Niger: the Island of Gold* (Oxford: Blackwell, 1998).

McIntosh, Susan Keech, ed. *Excavations at Jenné-Jeno, Hambarketolo, and Kaniana (Inland Niger Delta, Mali), the 1981 Season* (Berkeley: University of California Press, 1995).

Millon, René. "Teotihuacan," *Scientific American* (June 1967). Reprinted in *Scientific American, Cities: Their Origin, Growth, and Human Impact*, 82–91.

Moseley, Michael E. *The Maritime Foundations of Andean Civilization* (Menlo Park, CA: Cummings, 1975).

Murray, Jocelyn, ed. *Cultural Atlas of Africa* (New York: Facts on File, 1982).

Schele, Linda and David Freidel. *A Forest of Kings: The Untold Story of the Ancient Maya* (New York: William Morrow, 1990).

Scientific American, ed. *Cities: Their Origin, Growth, and Human Impact* (San Francisco: W.H. Freeman and Company, 1973).

Time-Life Books. *Time Frame 3000–1500 BC: The Age of God-Kings* (Alexandria, VA: Time-Life Books, 1987).

—— *Time Frame 1500–600 BC: Barbarian Tides* (Alexandria, VA: Time-Life Books, 1987).

—— *Time Frame AD 200–600: Empires Besieged* (Alexandria, VA: Time-Life Books, 1988).

Times (London). *Past Worlds* (Maplewood, NJ: Hammond Inc., 1988).

Zhang, Juzhong, *et al.* "Oldest Playable Instruments Found at Jiahu Early Neolithic Site in China," *Nature*, Vol. 40 (September 23, 1999), 366–68.

Empire and Imperialism

WHAT ARE EMPIRES AND WHY ARE THEY IMPORTANT?

The first empires grew up in the areas of the first civilizations we studied in Part 2—that is, Mesopotamia, the Nile valley, and the Yellow River valley. The Akkadian Empire of Sargon, about 2350 B.C.E., is the first for which we have documentary evidence, and it was followed in the same Mesopotamian region by the Babylonians and, later, by the Assyrians. In their successions we see a pattern that will become familiar in this part: the building of a large, powerful military force in the hands of a strong ruler, followed by a decline, a challenge by an outsider, the overthrow of the old empire, and the rise of a new one.

Chapter 5 begins with Akkad as the earliest example of empire building. Egypt provides the second example, and then we turn to the Persian Empire. In Persia's struggle against Greece in the fifth century B.C.E., we see a fundamental clash between monarchy and democracy, and between empire and city-state. A confederation of small, local city-states stopped the conquering force of the world's most powerful empire. Ultimately, however, in the subsequent dissolution of the Greek system into civil war and the succession of Alexander the Great, we see one of the great ironies of history. Those cities that had earlier prided themselves on their independence and their victory over the largest empire of the time, lost their independence and became integrated into Alexander's empire.

Chapter 6 will explore in greater depth the empire of Rome, while Chapter 7 examines those of China and, briefly, its daughter civilization in Japan. Chapter 8 explores India and

Hall of the Hundred Columns, Persepolis, Iran, 550–330 B.C.E. The remains of these audience halls still inspire a sense of imperial grandeur.

touches on southeast Asia. These three systems controlled vast areas, had enormous impact on tens of millions of people, and have continued to make their influence felt to our own time. They represent turning points in the history of most of humankind.

Rome, China, and India were so successful that their ideologies of empire—their explanations of why they should rule—prevailed for centuries. Indeed, the Roman Empire endured for almost a thousand years, from about 500 B.C.E. to almost 500 C.E., and if we include the Eastern Empire, based in Constantinople, Rome's duration is some 2000 years. Moreover, Rome inspired an imperial image that was expressed throughout later Europe in the so-called Holy Roman Empire. The Chinese Empire, founded in 221 B.C.E., lasted more or less continuously until 1911 C.E., and some would argue that it persists even today in new, Communist garb. The first emperor to rule almost all of the Indian subcontinent, Ashok (Aśoka) Maurya (r. 273–232 B.C.E.), is still commemorated today on every rupee currency note printed in India. Throughout these chapters, we also consider the trade routes that kept these three great empires in communication with each other.

CHAPTER

5 DAWN OF THE EMPIRES

2300 B.C.E.–300 B.C.E.

"Our opinion of the gods and our knowledge of men lead us to conclude that it is a general and necessary law of nature to rule whatever one can."

THUCYDIDES

"To the size of states there is a limit."

ARISTOTLE

EMPIRE-BUILDING IN NORTH AFRICA, WEST ASIA, AND THE MEDITERRANEAN

THE MEANING OF EMPIRE

New York proudly calls itself the Empire State; Daimler Chrysler advertises its Chrysler Imperial luxury automobile; until recently, Britain maintained the "Imperial Gallon" as a measure of volume. Yet today the word "imperialism" has a generally negative connotation. The demise within the past generation of many empires, most recently that of the Soviet Union, has met with general approval around the world. Why does the concept of empire evoke such conflicting attitudes? What is an empire?

Empires grow from the conquest of one people by another—in fact, a definition of empire is the extension of political rule by one people over other, different peoples. Empires have been as natural in human history as the desire of people for power and control over other people and their resources, and they have been as frequent as

the ability of rulers to build military organizations capable of attaining those goals.

The word "empire" stirs in most of us conflicting images and feelings. We think of the monumental structures of palaces and the ruling establishments of the emperor and the leadership core. In our imaginations we see majestic buildings, adorned with the finest artworks. The emperor and the imperial administrators, we imagine, wear the finest clothes, eat the choicest foods, enjoy the most select luxuries, and support and command the most powerful technologies. Often they encourage great creativity in the arts and in learning. Sometimes, however, we see them using their power over others in acts of cruelty, arrogance, irresponsibility, and decadence.

We see, too, vast marketplaces and, perhaps, ports and dockyards processing goods from the far corners of the empire, since one of the purposes of empire building is to bring natural riches to the imperial power. Leading into the capital city, connecting it with the remotest areas of empire, are lines of communication and transportation, sea lanes, and, most important of all, roads. Specific examples stand out. Notable are the grand canals linking the rich agricultural lands of south China to the capital in the north and dating back as early as the Sui dynasty, in the seventh century C.E. Similarly, the phrase "All roads lead to Rome," the capital of an equally powerful empire, may have been an exaggeration, but its central idea was correct. Empires bring exotic goods and diverse peoples together under a common ruler. People of different languages, religions, ethnic origins, and cultural and technological levels are brought under a single, centralized rule.

ANCIENT GREECE AND ITS NEIGHBORS

DATE	POLITICAL	RELIGION AND CULTURE	SOCIAL DEVELOPMENT
600 B.C.E.	• Cyaxares of Media (r. 625–585) • Age of Greek tyrants (657–570)	• Zoroaster (630–553)	• City–states in Greece
550 B.C.E.	• Cyrus II (559–530); defeat of Medes, Lydia, Babylon • Peisistratus (d. 527) controlled Athens • Cambyses II (530–522) conquered Egypt	• Pasargadae and Susa developed	• Nile–Red Sea canal
500 B.C.E.	• Darius I (522–486); Persian Empire extended to Indus River; war against Greek city states • Ionian revolt (499) • Battle of Marathon (490) • Xerxes I (486–465) • War between Athens and Sparta: 1st Peloponnesian War (461–451)	• Pythagoras (d. c. 500) • Piraeus established as port of Athens • Persepolis built	• Athens at the height of its power. Acropolis built (c. 460); architecture, city-state democracy, political philosophy flourish
450 B.C.E.	• Pericles (d. 429) and Delian League • 2nd Peloponnesian War (431–404) and end of Athenian power	• Persian script written down • "Golden Age" of Athens • Aeschylus (d. 456) • Herodotus (d. c. 420) • Sophocles (d. 406) • Euripides (d. 406) • Thucydides (d. c. 401)	• Persian Empire: regional laws codified; roads built; centralized administration; irrigation systems extended
400 B.C.E.		• Socrates (d. 399)	
350 B.C.E.	• Philip II (359–336) and Alexander the Great (336–323) extend Macedonian Empire • Athens and Thebes defeated (338), ending Greek independence • Alexander conquers Asia Minor (334) and Egypt (332), and reaches Indus (326)	• Aristophanes (d. c. 388) • Plato (d. 347) • Aristotle (d. 322) • Demosthenes (d. 322) • Alexandria (Egypt) founded (331) • Persepolis burned (331)	• Spread of Hellenistic culture
300 B.C.E.	• Ptolemies in Egypt • Seleucids in Asia		

Vast systems of administration are needed to hold the imperial structure together. In order to organize and maintain communication and exchange among all parts of the empire, a system of administration must be established. The administrators and rulers must also regulate the fate of conquered peoples in accordance with the needs of the empire. Some are granted full citizenship, most of the remainder receive fewer rights and privileges, while those at the bottom, especially war captives, might be enslaved. A few—those who proved particularly dangerous or costly to the imperial rulers—might be executed, with a warning to potential rebels.

The administration must ensure either that different kinds of monies from various parts of the empire are consolidated into a single system of coinage or that means of exchanging them are readily available. It must communicate across the many languages of the empire, and it may adopt and impose a single administrative language so that the writ of empire is universally understood. It must establish a legal system with at least some degree of uniformity. Indeed, the administration must provide sufficient uniformity in language, currency, weights, measures, and legal systems to enable it to function as a single political structure. Perhaps the most significant administrative task of all is the collection of taxes from its subjects and tribute from those it conquers. Such revenues represent the continuing financial profits to the rulers.

Twentieth-century scholars emphasize two forms of imperial rule: **hegemony** and **dominance**. For the imperial power, hegemony is to be preferred, for this is rule that the subjects accept willingly. They may admire the empire's power or justice; they may benefit from the stability and peace it imposes, from the technological improvements it introduces, from the more extensive networks it develops and opens to their trade and profit, from the cultural sophistication it exhibits and shares with them, or from the opportunities for new kinds of advancement that membership in the empire may offer. If imperial membership is perceived to have such benefits, the subject peoples may welcome it peacefully, even eagerly. They may accept the ideology of the imperial power and its explanation for the legitimacy and benefit of its foreign rule. In short, hegemony can be defined as foreign rule that governs with the substantial consent of the governed.

Should the imperial ideology not be acceptable, however, rulers will impose their government through dominance, the exercise of sheer power. In these circumstances, military force, and the threat to exercise it, are central to the empire's existence, so the state expends vast sums on recruiting, training, and equipping its armies. The troops mobilize across the vast spaces of empire, using the same roads that carry the imperial commerce. The military is often supplemented by offensive and defensive architecture; perhaps the most famous example is the Great Wall of China, built about 220 B.C.E. to keep the Mongols and the Huns (Xiongnu) from invading China. Imperial rulers may try to win the allegiance of conquered peoples by conferring benefits—legal, economic, social, educational, and political—but ultimately, the final recourse is coercion.

No wonder we feel ambivalent about great empires. They control enormous resources and may use them to create productive, beautiful, inspiring civilizations, but the benefits of empire are not shared evenly. We are often appalled at the subjection of conquered peoples. The glory of empire rests on the control of the many by the few; slaves and war captives are among those who pay the heaviest price. So, while we may be awed by the glory and majesty of empire, we may also be inspired by the anti-imperial revolts of conquered peoples eager for self-rule.

Resistance to imperial rule is as normal as empires themselves. Rulers of empires usually dominate because they are able to mobilize more power than the peoples they control. Often, intentionally or unintentionally, the secrets of their power spread among the conquered, thereby enriching their lives. The subject populations learn from the technology introduced by their conquerors, whether it is the use of weapons, materials, military formations, agricultural methods, administrative organizations, or techniques of production. Empires that begin by using their superiority to rule, eventually produce change among the peoples they conquer. Subject peoples, who may originally have felt some gratitude toward their imperial benefactors, may later grow resentful, restive, and finally rebellious. Goths, for example, no longer wished to be subordinate to Romans, nor Mongols to Chinese, as we shall see in Chapters 6 and 7. Empires are not static. They rise and they fall. Ironically, the imperial masters are often forced to trade places with those they had subjugated.

The causes of the decline and fall of empires include:

- Failure of leadership—the inability of the empire to produce or select rulers capable of maintaining the imperial structures;

- Overextension of the administration—the inability of the imperial rulers to sustain the costs of a far-flung empire while coping simultaneously with critical domestic problems;

- Collapse of the economy—the overextension of empire to territories so remote or so difficult to subdue and to govern that costs outrun benefits;

- Doubts over the ideology—the end of belief in the justice or benefit of empire, which may occur either when cynical colonizers abandon the colonial enterprise, or when frustrated colonized peoples revolt, or both;

- Military defeat of the empire by the combined forces of external enemies and of colonized people in revolt.

THE EARLIEST EMPIRES

MESOPOTAMIA AND THE FERTILE CRESCENT

Mesopotamia's earliest power centers were independent city-states that could not reach political accommodation among themselves. They fought constantly for land, irrigation rights, and prestige, as we can see from the scenes of warfare that fill the bas relief artwork from third-millennium Sumer. From this artwork and from cuneiform records, archaeologists have reconstructed two main antagonists, the cities of Lagash and Umma, which, with their allied forces, dominated the warfare of the time. Victory by either one, however, or by any of the city-states over any of the others, was frequently avenged in the next generation.

Geographically, the city-states of Mesopotamia were also vulnerable to immigrant groups crossing their territory and challenging their powers. About 2350 B.C.E., Sargon (r. c. 2334–2279 B.C.E.), leading an immigrant group of Semitic peoples from the Arabian peninsula, entered Sumer. The new

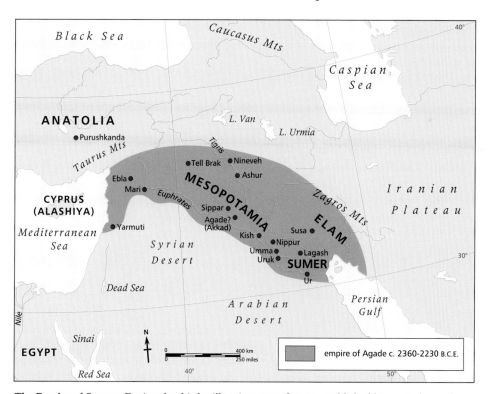

The Empire of Sargon During the third millennium B.C.E. Sargon established his control over the city-states of southern Mesopotamia, creating the world's first empire. Building a capital at Agade, he founded the Akkadian dynasty, which for a century ruled the Fertile Crescent, from the Persian Gulf to the Mediterranean Sea.

Bronze head of an Akkadian ruler (Sargon I?), *c.* **2250 B.C.E.**
Exuding royal self-confidence, this near-lifesized bronze
head probably depicts Sargon I, founder of the Akkadian
dynasty. For over half a century, Sargon dominated one city-
state after another until he had conquered most of
Mesopotamia. After his death, his successors worshiped him
as a god.

arrivals settled in and around northern Sumer and
called their land Akkad. Sargon led the Akkadians
to victories over the leading cities of Sumer, over
the Elamites to the east, over northern Mesopotamia, and over a swath of land connecting
Mesopotamia to the Mediterranean. He founded
the Akkadian capital at Agade, a city whose exact
location is now unknown.

Historical records are skimpy, but those that do
exist correspond to our assessment of the key
characteristics of empire. First, the Akkadians
conquered widely. Administrative tablets of the
Akkad dynasty have been found as far away as
Susa, several hundred miles to the east in Persia,
suggesting a far-flung governmental administration. Second, after razing the walls of the major
cities of Ur, Lagash, and Umma, Sargon displaced
the traditional local civilian hierarchies with his
own administrators, designated the "sons of
Akkad." Third, the Akkadian language was used in
administrative documents in Sumer. Fourth,

measurements throughout the empire were
standardized: "The measures of length, area, dry
and liquid capacity, and probably also weight were
integrated into a single logical system which
remained the standard for a thousand years and
more" (Postgate, p. 41). Finally, Sargon imposed his
own imagery and ideology of empire. Documents
were dated from the founding of the Akkadian
kingdom, legal oaths were taken in the name of
the Akkadian king, and Sargon installed his own
daughter as high-priestess of the moon-god
Nanna at Ur.

Sargon's empire lasted for about a century, and
was followed by other outsiders, the Gutians, and
then by a revival of internal Sumerian power under
Ur-Nammu. Culturally, Sumer was so advanced
that it influenced even its conquerors, the Akkadians, the Gutians, and later arrivals. The Akkadian
language, however, did supplant Sumerian by
about 2000 B.C.E.

Politically, Sumer's system of independent city-
states did not endure. The next conquerors were
again Semitic nomads, the Amorites, who founded
a new dynasty at Babylon about 1900 B.C.E. They,
too, were absorbed culturally by Sumer. Their sixth
ruler, Hammurabi, is most famous for his law codes
(see p. 56), but he was also a skilled military leader
who defeated the Sumerian city-states and created
the Babylonian Empire which stretched from the
Persian Gulf to Syria and endured for 250 years,
until its defeat about 1500 B.C.E. by the Hittites.

For a thousand years rival empires in the
region—Hittites, Assyrians, Mitannis, and Babylonians—competed for power. The Israelites under
their kings, David and Solomon, *c.* 1000–922 B.C.E.,
also had a period of expansion within the region, as
did the Phoenician trading cities along the coast.
The Egyptians entered actively into local warfare
for some centuries, 1600–1200 B.C.E., and were
always a force in the political balance of the region.

The city-state organizational structure of Mesopotamia, and its geographical openness, had left
the region very vulnerable. As the city-states fought
destructively among themselves, they were repeatedly attacked by, and absorbed into, powerful
empires. Some of these empires were based outside
the region, others grew up, or transplanted themselves, within the region. The Mesopotamians had
to expend their resources on military technology
and organization as their local units of government
faced increasing challenges from ever-greater
powers that sought to consolidate them into ever-
larger empires.

EGYPT AND INTERNATIONAL CONQUEST

Egypt's background to empire was very different from Mesopotamia's. First, the region was protected from outside invasion by the deserts to the west and east, and by cataracts (steep rapids) on the Nile River toward the south. Second, from very early times Egypt was governed as a unified state.

Statues and pictures usually depict Egyptian pharaohs wearing crowns. Until about 3000 B.C.E., the most important of these was a tall white crown with a vulture symbolizing dominance over the upper Nile valley of southern Egypt. Later pharaohs often wore an additional crown, a squat red one with a cobra, to symbolize their conquest of Lower Egypt, the northern lands of the Nile delta. From about 3000 B.C.E., when the legendary god-king Menes united Upper and Lower Egypt, until about 2134 B.C.E. the kingdom remained united. The subsequent breakup of Egypt into warring segments, especially the division between the delta and the upper Nile valley, suggests that through the centuries the original split may never have been completely healed. On the other hand, as Egyptologist John Baines of Oxford University suggests, the kingdom may have been forged from many geographical parts. Scholars need to be alert to the evidence and not be swayed by presuppositions:

> The idea of two Predynastic kingdoms may be a projection of the pervasive dualism of Egyptian ideology, not a record of a true historical situation. More probably there was a gradual unification of a previously uncentralized society. (*Baines and Malek*, p. 31)

Geography encouraged Egyptian unity. With vast deserts separating the Nile valley from the outside world to the east and west, and cataracts on the

Five-string painted wooden harp, tomb of Ani, Thebes, *c.* 1200 B.C.E. This harp from the Nineteenth Dynasty, inlaid with ivory, terminates in a head wearing the royal double crown, a symbol of the conquest and unification of Upper and Lower Egypt. (*British Museum, London*)

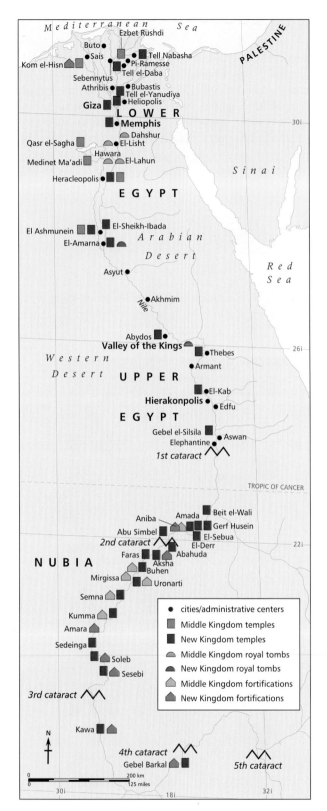

Middle and New Kingdom Egypt By 2040 B.C.E. the unification of Egypt into a centralized, militaristic state was under way. Its hierarchic society focused on the priesthood and the dynastic succession of semi-god rulers, the Pharaohs. The consolidation of power was reflected in the size and scale of royal building projects, including fortifications, new cities, temples, and grandiose tombs, and by conquests in Nubia.

Map legend:

- • cities/administrative centers
- ■ Middle Kingdom temples
- ■ New Kingdom temples
- ◠ Middle Kingdom royal tombs
- ◠ New Kingdom royal tombs
- ▲ Middle Kingdom fortifications
- ▲ New Kingdom fortifications

Nile making southward sailing difficult, Egypt tended naturally to become a single administrative unit incorporating the entire Nile valley from the first cataract northward to the Mediterranean Sea. Situating the capital city at Memphis (near today's Cairo), where the Nile River disgorged into the delta, centralized and unified the government. The centrality of the pharaohs' palaces and the awesome ceremonial pyramids nearby further proclaimed national unity.

The kingdoms sometimes did fracture, as in the period c. 2200–2000 B.C.E., when north and south split apart. But from 3000 B.C.E. to the present, Egypt has usually remained a single political unit. So we think of it as a kingdom with a single government ruling a single civilization rather than as an empire of one people ruling over others.

This unity was forged from the diversity of peoples who came to inhabit Egypt. Semites from the desert to the east, Phoenicians from the sea coast, Blacks from Nubia and the heart of Africa, and Europeans from across the Mediterranean immigrated and amalgamated into a common national stock, which intermarried and recognized each other without apparent reference to race or ethnicity. Martin Bernal's *Black Athena* discusses this mixture of peoples in linguistic and cultural terms. Paintings of ancient Egyptians show them sometimes pale in color, sometimes black, very often red.

Egyptian forces did not always stay within their own borders, however. During the Middle Kingdom, c. 2000–1750 B.C.E., Egyptians moved into Nubia, the territory stretching southward some 900 miles (1400 kilometers) from just above the first cataract in the Nile, at present-day Aswan in Egypt, to present-day Khartoum, capital of the Sudan. At first, the move was only into lower Nubia. During the New Kingdom, c. 1550–1050 B.C.E., however, Egypt conquered the heartland of central Nubia, the core of the sophisticated, independent state and a source of gold, minerals, wood, and recruits for Egypt's army and police.

Separated from Egypt by the cataracts of the Nile, Nubia's black, African people represented just

Relief from the temple of Beit el-Wali (detail), Lower Nubia, c. 2000–1850 B.C.E. The rich variety of produce here presented to Ramses II after his conquest of Lower Nubia—bags of gold, incense, tusks, ebony logs, ostrich eggs, bows, shields, fans, and wild animals—seems to mirror the ethnic diversity on display. Pale-, brown-, and black-skinned peoples coexisted in Egypt and Nubia. (*British Museum, London*)

one of the strands that made up the cosmopolitan mix of people in Egypt, and historical records indicate continuing political and military rivalry between the two kingdoms. Egypt's conquest of Nubia was an imperial expansion. Nubia later expelled the Egyptian conquerors and even marched northward to capture Egypt itself. For half a century, 712–657 B.C.E., Nubia ruled over an empire of its own, which included all of Egypt. Thereafter Nubia remained strong, with its capital

first at Napata and later at Meroe, while Egypt fell into decline.

Egypt also pursued imperial ventures along the trade routes into the Levant, occupying Syria and Palestine at the height of the New Kingdom, 1530–1200 B.C.E. Here, frequent conflict with the powerful Hittites culminated in perhaps the first major battle in history, fought at Qadesh, Syria, in 1285 B.C.E. Although the Egyptian pharaoh Ramses II claimed a crushing victory, the Hittites continued to

Royal pyramids and adjacent iron slag heaps at Meroe, Sudan, c. 600 B.C.E. The rulers of Meroe and Egypt shared many artistic traditions, but often gave them a distinctive local interpretation, as can be seen in the forms of their pyramids and palaces.

5: DAWN OF THE EMPIRES (2300 B.C.E.–300 B.C.E.)   127

maintain a hold along the eastern Mediterranean. Thutmosis I (r. 1504–1492 B.C.E) not only extended Egypt's control southward to the fourth cataract of the Nile, but also northwest as far as the Euphrates River, creating Egypt's greatest historical empire. The small states of Syria and Palestine managed to remain self-governing, but Egypt stationed army units and administrative officials in the region and collected taxes. Here in western Asia, Egypt seemed more interested in access to raw materials than in governance.

Egypt's imperial control over remote and div-erse peoples met resistance from local powers within the Fertile Crescent. The Hittites, the Babylonians, and, especially, the Mitannis mounted frequent revolts. They developed a new weapons system: two-wheeled, horse-drawn chariots carrying archers in bronze armor, shooting bronze-tipped arrows. Egypt's military technology lagged, and Egyptian control was ended by about 1200 B.C.E., although its political and economic influence in the region continued for centuries.

Suffering defeats in the Levant and Nubia, Egypt was pushed back within its river and desert

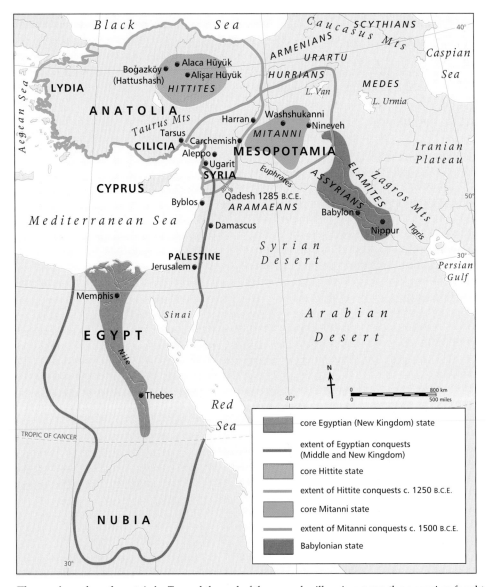

The empires of southwest Asia Toward the end of the second millennium B.C.E. three empires fought for control of the Fertile Crescent. Egyptians, Mitannians of northern Mesopotamia, and Hittites of Anatolia came into direct conflict. Building on strong political control over their core regions, each dispatched powerful armies with the most up-to-date weapons to seize more territory from the others.

niche as a powerful and independent nation-state—the world's oldest and most deeply rooted—but no longer an empire. Indeed, Egypt itself came under attack and even occupation. In 671 B.C.E., while Nubians ruled southern Egypt, Assyrians conquered and occupied the north.

THE ASSYRIANS

Assyrians, descendants of the Akkadians, had thrice emerged triumphant from the continuous warfare in Mesopotamia among the Hittites, the Mitannians, the Babylonians, and themselves. In the twentieth century B.C.E. they had gained their independence, and some prosperity through the trade of their private businessmen. Then, subjugated by the Mitannians, they regained their independence in the thirteenth century to lose it again to the Arameans about 1000 B.C.E. Around 900 B.C.E. a Neo-Assyrian (New Assyrian) kingdom began a series of conquests, sweeping westward to the Mediterranean coast, northward to Syria and Palestine, and southeastward into Babylon. Infantry provided the Assyrian main force, while archers riding in chariots led the attacks, and battering rams and siege towers assaulted fixed positions.

More than most ancient empires, the Assyrians controlled conquered peoples through policies of forced migration. They deported some nations into exile from their homelands, including ten of the tribes of Israel who were subsequently "lost," that is they lost their sense of ethnic and religious identity and presumably ceased their opposition to the Assyrians, just as the conquerors had hoped. In other regions, the Assyrians imported their own people to settle among the defeated peoples and keep them under control.

Only the last of the Neo-Assyrian kings, Ashurbanipal (669–626 B.C.E.), is known to have been literate, and he constructed a great library in his capital at Nineveh. 20,000 tablets are still preserved from that library, including the earliest complete version of *The Epic of Gilgamesh* (see pp. 54–5).

King Esarhaddon conquered Egypt in 671 B.C.E., making Assyria the greatest power of its day. His successors held the entire province, driving the Nubians from the southern regions and suppressing rebellions. Assyria finally withdrew from Egypt, defeated not primarily by the Egyptians, but by internal dynastic struggles, and by the combined forces of Babylonians, Arameans, the Medes of Iran, and Scythian invaders who attacked Assyria's Mesopotamian heartland. The Assyrian capital, Nineveh, fell in 612 B.C.E.

EGYPT UNDER OCCUPATION

Egypt had become one of the contestants in the many wars for control over the eastern Mediterranean and, like many of the other powers, Egypt employed Greek mercenary soldiers. Trade and cultural exchange also increased between Egypt and Greece, and many of the historical

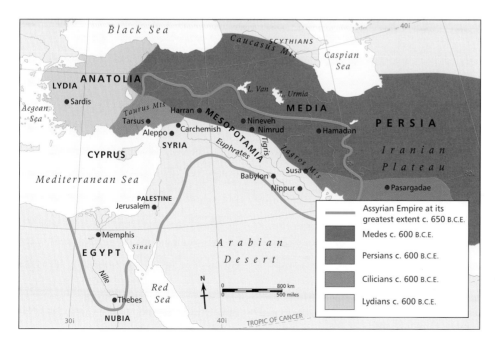

Assyria and its rivals The shifting political map of southwest Asia was dominated between 850 and 650 B.C.E. by the powerful and martial Assyrians, who even occupied Egypt. Anatolia was fragmented into smaller states. To the north a powerful federation of Median tribes was a growing threat. In 614, in alliance with the Babylonians, they crushed Assyria.

records of this time and region derive from the work of Greek historians.

Egypt continued to fall into the empires of others. It was conquered by the Persians in 525 B.C.E. Two centuries later, in 332 B.C.E., Alexander the Great captured Egypt from Persia, and in 30 B.C.E., Egypt passed to the next great Mediterranean empire, that of Rome. Some of these conquests are noted in later sections of this part.

PERSIA

Medes and Persians began to appear in the region east of Mesopotamia about 1300 B.C.E., bringing with them the use of iron. By the mid-ninth century B.C.E., written cuneiform records confirm the archaeological evidence of their arrival. At first the Medes were more numerous and powerful, but later the Persians came to predominate. Both groups were **Indo-Europeans**—that is, in language and cultural heritage they were related to some of the same major groups who came to inhabit Europe and northern India. Cyaxares of Media (r. 625–585 B.C.E.) established an army; conquered the Scyth-

ians, another immigrant group in the region; sealed an alliance with the Babylonians by marrying his granddaughter to the son of their ruler; and, together with them, captured Nineveh, the capital of Assyria. Assyria was destroyed as a major military force. A new **balance of power** among the Egyptians, Medes, Babylonians, and Lydians resulted in western Asia.

The balance was broken, however, when Cyrus II, the Great, of Persia (r. *c.* 559–530 B.C.E.) defeated the other three kingdoms and incorporated them into his own empire. He conquered, first, the Medes in 550; then, in 546, the Lydians with their king, the fabulously wealthy Croesus; and finally, in 539, the Babylonians. Under Cyrus, the Achaeminids (named in honor of their legendary ancestor Achaemenes) dominated the entire region from Persia to the Mediterranean. Cyrus died in 529 B.C.E., defending this empire against attacks from the east.

His eldest son, Cambyses II (r. 530–522 B.C.E.), expanded Cyrus' conquests. Crossing the Sinai Desert, he captured Memphis, the capital of Egypt, and carried its pharaoh back to Susa in captivity, thus completing the conquest of all of the major powers that had influenced the Middle East.

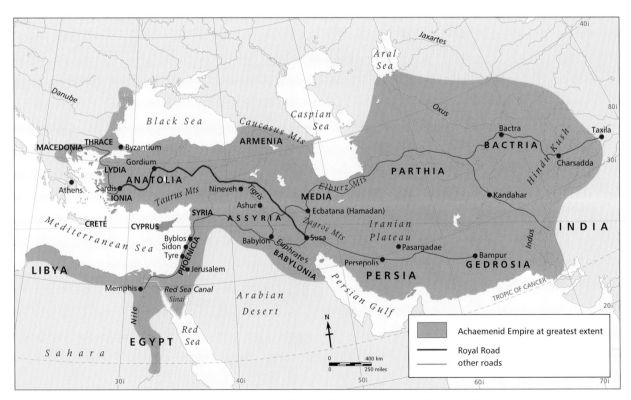

Achaemenid Persia The Medes and the Persians were united under Cyrus the Great in 550 B.C.E. to form the Achaemenid or Persian Empire. Cyrus and his successors, notably Darius and Xerxes, extended the empire to the Indus in the east and to Egypt and Libya in the west, and twice invaded Greece.

Egypt frequently revolted and large garrisons were required to keep it under control, so the Achaeminids under Darius I (r. 522–486 B.C.E.) completed a canal across the desert, connecting the Nile River and the Red Sea. This early "Suez Canal," first envisioned by the Egyptians as a trade route, became a troop supply line for Persian control over Egypt.

Darius also extended the Persian empire more deeply into the Indian subcontinent, as far as the Indus River. The Achaeminids now controlled some of the most valuable trade routes in Asia; the **satrapy**, or colony, of "India" submitted one-third of the annual cash receipts of the Achaeminids, and Indian troops served in the Achaeminid armies. From this time forward, Indian- and Persian-based powers would regularly confront one another across the borders of what is today Afghanistan and Pakistan. Meanwhile, in the west, Darius expanded onto the fringes of Europe, capturing Thrace and Macedonia, and bringing the Persian Empire to its greatest extent.

Attempts to move further were stymied. The Scythians to the north and west fought a kind of guerrilla warfare that the massed forces of the Persians could not overcome. To the south and west, Darius' armies of invasion into Greece were defeated at Marathon in 490 B.C.E. Under Darius' eldest son, Xerxes I (r. 486–465 B.C.E.), wars continued between the Persian Empire and the Greek city-states. The Greeks were hard pressed and lost many important battles, and in 480 B.C.E. Xerxes' troops captured and burned the Acropolis at Athens. But overall, the Greeks held off the invading Persians until 465 B.C.E., when Xerxes was assassinated. Thereafter the Persians lost the will and the power to fight. Persia continued to intervene in the politics of the Greek city-states, contributing financial aid to its allies among them but no longer dispatching military forces. A confederation of small, democratic, Greek city-states had managed to repulse the mighty Persian Empire. *The Persian Wars*, written by Herodotus in the late fifth century B.C.E. and presenting the story from a Greek perspective, is the first great book of secular history still preserved (see Source, p. 141).

IMPERIAL POLICIES

The Persian imperial form of rule and administration changed in the three generations from Cyrus II its chief architect, through his son and successor Cambyses II, to Darius I, its most

powerful emperor. The differences among the three emperors became especially clear in their policies for achieving a balance between the power of the central government and the desire of local, conquered peoples for some degree of autonomy. Under Cyrus and Darius, Persia respected local customs and institutions even as the empire expanded. Cambyses was more dictatorial, and met an early end.

Cyrus II

When Cyrus (r. *c.* 559–530 B.C.E.) conquered the Medes, he allowed their king to escape with his life. He administered his newly acquired lands through the existing Median bureaucracy and army, allowing Median officials to keep their positions, though under Persian control. When Cyrus conquered Lydia, he spared Croesus and even enlisted his advice as a consultant. In conquered Ionian cities he retained local rulers who were willing to work under Persian direction. On defeating Babylon, his most powerful rival, Cyrus chose to rule in the name of the Babylonian god Marduk and to worship daily in his temple, thus maintaining the support of the priests. He continued to employ local bureaucrats and to protect and secure the trade routes that brought wealth to the empire and secured the loyalty of the merchant classes.

Perhaps most strikingly, Cyrus allowed the peoples that Babylonia had captured and deported to return to their homes. For example, he permitted the Jewish community of exiles in Babylon to return home to Judaea and to rebuild their temple in Jerusalem. He also returned to them the gold and silver that had been taken from the temple. The 40,000 exiles who returned over 1000 miles (1600 kilometers) to Judaea hailed Cyrus as their political savior and kept their renewed state loyal to the Persian Empire.

Cambyses II

Unlike his father, Cambyses (r. 530–522 B.C.E.) seems to have lost sight of the need for restraint in both the expansion and the administration of his empire. His conquest of Egypt and his use of Egyptians in his own administration of that land followed Cyrus' model, but then he overextended his reach. His attempted campaign against the Phoenician city of Carthage in distant north Africa failed when Phoenician sailors in his own navy refused to fight. An army sent south from Egypt to Nubia, attempting to capture its fabled gold supplies, failed to reach its destination and retreated from the desert in tatters. Cambyses may not have been emotionally stable, and it was rumored that he kicked to death his pregnant wife/sister. When he died, as he was returning to Persia to put down an insurrection, it was further rumored that he had committed suicide. His seven-year rule had been costly to Persia.

Darius I

Darius (r. 522–486 B.C.E.), a general in the Persian army and prince of the Achaeminid dynasty, succeeded to the throne by murdering the previous incumbent Bardiya (r. 522) and ruled for thirty-five years. He was more deliberate, more balanced, and more capable as an administrator than Cambyses, and he became much richer as emperor than either of his predecessors. Like Cyrus, he used local administrators to staff local governments. He sought to create smaller, more efficient units of government by increasing the number of administrative units, or **satrapies,** even faster than he expanded the empire. Some of the regional administrators, or satraps, were local elites; some were Persian. In each satrapy, loyalty to the empire was assured by the presence of Persian army units, which reported directly back to the king, and by a secretary, who monitored the actions of the satrap and also reported back to Persia.

Darius commissioned the design of the first written Persian script. He established the tradition that royal inscriptions were to be trilingual—in Persian, Babylonian, and Elamite. In the midst of the multitude of languages used across the empire, these were to be the official written languages of administration. The most widely spoken public language was Aramaic, however, and this language of the common people throughout much of the eastern Mediterranean greatly influenced the development of formal Persian.

Legal codes varied among the satrapies to reflect local usage, and the Persian rulers frequently codified and recorded these laws. Tax codes were rationalized. The size and productivity of agricultural fields were measured, evaluated, and recorded, with their tax rate fixed at about 20 percent. In each satrapy the various taxes—on industry, mining, ports, water, commerce, and sales—were gathered by a Persian collector. Most of the revenues were

Lion killing a bull, bas relief, Persepolis, Iran, 550–330 B.C.E. The great palace complex of Persepolis, encompassing many smaller palaces within it, was designed as the central symbol of Darius' empire. Construction began in 518 B.C.E. and took some seventy years to complete. Scenes such as this bas relief of a lion killing a bull seem to emerge from Achaeminid mythology, which read the signs of the zodiac, Leo following Taurus, as representing the end of the old year and the coming of the new.

Homage rendered to Darius, bas relief, Persepolis, Iran, 550–330 B.C.E. On New Year's Day, ambassadors of each of Persia's twenty and more satrapies presented themselves to the emperor in his audience hall at Persepolis. Darius, bejeweled and arrayed in royal robes of purple and gold, received them.

remitted to Persia, but some were retained locally for administrative and development expenses.

Darius built, maintained, and guarded an imperial system of roads, the most famous of which was a 1700-mile (2735-kilometer) royal road, stretching from his capital at Susa to Sardis across Anatolia (but not quite reaching the Mediterranean). Along these roads he established a series of inns for travelers and a royal courier service with stations at about every 15 miles (24 kilometers). He completed the construction of the Nile–Red Sea canal, which the Egytians had abandoned.

To increase agricultural production, Darius renewed the irrigation systems of Mesopotamia, and encouraged the introduction of new crops from one part of the empire to another. He standardized the gold coinage of the empire, and permitted only his own imperial mints to strike the official coinage, the gold daric, in his name. Agriculture and commerce flourished, and not only for the benefit of the wealthy. Goods for everyday use—leather sandals, cheap cloth, iron implements and utensils, and pottery—were produced in increasing quantities.

Substantial sums of the enormous wealth of the flourishing empire went to the construction of four capital cities. Cyrus had built up Pasargadae and its great gardens as a retreat and capital. He had also begun to rebuild Susa, the old Elamite capital, which continued to serve as the principal administrative center under the Persians. Darius added here an impressive palace for himself. In the summer, Susa was too hot, so Darius moved the court to Ecbatana, the former capital of the Medes, in the northern hills. But as his most sumptuous and lavish capital, and the one in the most Persian style, Darius built Persepolis.

EMPERORS OF PERSIA

The heart of the Persian Empire came together from two separate kingdoms: the original homeland of the Persians, known as Fars or Parsa (now in southwest Iran); and Media (now in northwest Iran). When Cyrus the Great conquered his Median overlord in the sixth century B.C.E., the two realms were united. Persians and Medes in any case shared ethnic origins—they were both Aryans, the word from which Persia gets its modern name, Iran.

Cyrus II, the Great	559–530 (B.C.E.)
Cambyses II	530–522
Bardiya	522
Darius I	522–486
Xerxes I	486–465
Ataxerxes I	465–424
Xerxes II	424–423
Sogdianus	424–423
Darius II	423–404
Ataxerxes II	404–359
Ataxerxes III	359–338
Arses	338–336
Darius III	336–330

In accordance with the political theory that had evolved in imperial Persia, the emperor legally possessed all the property of the realm as well as the power of life and death over his subjects. Darius had not, however, elected to become a god. He was probably a follower of the religion of the teacher Zarathustra, or Zoroaster as the Greeks called him, believing in one god of goodness and light, represented by fire and engaged in continuing warfare with the forces of evil, darkness, and falsehood. Moreover, like his predecessor Cyrus, Darius had not tried to impose his religious beliefs on the peoples he conquered. He tried to soften the imposition of imperial administration and tax collection by maintaining local traditions and by enlisting local elites to serve in his administration. Like Cyrus, Darius managed to balance imperial majesty with local autonomy.

GREEK CITY-STATES: REALITY AND IMAGE

As Darius expanded his empire into western Anatolia (present-day Turkey) and began to conquer the Greek city-states of that region, he encountered a different form of political organization to that of the Persian imperial structure. The Greek city-state, or **polis**, was an intentionally small, locally organized government based on a single central city with enough surrounding land to support its agricultural needs. Most of the city-states had populations of a few thousand, with only the very largest of them exceeding 40,000 people.

Geography and topography played a large part in limiting the size of the Greek city-state. In and around the Greek peninsula, mountains, rivers, and seas had kept the units of settlement rather small and isolated. When a region could no longer support an expanding population, it hived off colonies to new locations. Most of the Greek city-states in Anatolia seem to have originated as colonial settlements of older cities on the Greek mainland, part of an array of Greek city-states that spread throughout the Mediterranean coast, extending as far west as present-day Marseille in France and Catalonia in Spain. Although separate and usually independent politically, the city-states were united culturally by the use of the Greek language, a mythistory centered on the *Iliad* and *Odyssey* of the poet Homer (see Source below), and such

SOURCE
Homer and the Value System of Early Greece

The historical folk tales from which Homer (8th century B.C.E.) wove his two great epic poems, the *Iliad* and the *Odyssey*, had probably circulated orally since the 12th century B.C.E. This was the time of the Trojan War, the fulcrum on which both epics turn. The *Iliad* tells of this war, which, Homer writes, was launched by a coalition of Greek city-states against the Trojans in response to the seduction of Helen, the wife of the king of Sparta, by Paris, the son of the king of Troy. Just as the war begins in a personal vendetta, so, too, individual feuds during the war break out among the Greeks themselves, for personal more than for political reasons. The bitter personal quarrel between Agamemnon, brother of the king of Sparta and himself king of Mycenae, and Achilles, the mightiest of the Greek warriors, cripples the effectiveness of the Greek coalition and dominates the storyline of the *Iliad*. The *Odyssey* tells the still more personal post-war story of Odysseus' ten-year struggle to reach his home in Ithaca and of his ultimate reunion with his wife and son in that kingdom.

Although many literary critics believe that "Homer" was really more than one author, most today believe that just one person wrote, or dictated, the epics. The stories on which Homer bases his poetic accounts were probably well known among the Greeks of his time. Homer's lasting reputation and fame rest on his skill in crafting these stories into coherent narratives told in poetry of great power. Further, by focusing on personal stories within the national epics, Homer created images of human excellence (*arete* in ancient Greek) at levels of heroism which inspire readers to this day. He writes with equal power of excellence in war and in love.

Bravery in warfare is a cardinal virtue, and, in the *Iliad*, Homer portrays Hektor, the mightiest of the Trojans, praying that his son might inherit his own strength in battle, and even surpass it. The child's mother would apparently share this vision of her son as warrior:

> Zeus, and you other immortals, grant that this boy, who is my son,
> may be as I am, pre-eminent among the Trojans, great in strength, as am I, and rule strongly over Ilion;
> and some day let them say of him: "He is better by far than his father",
> as he comes in from the fighting; and let him kill his enemy
> and bring home the blooded spoils, and delight the heart of his mother.
>
> (*Iliad*, VI:476–481)

Praising excellence in warfare and combat, Homer portrays Odysseus, Telemachus, and their followers in the *Odyssey* as fierce raptors swooping down upon their prey:

> After them the attackers wheeled, as terrible as falcons
> from eyries in the mountains veering over and diving down
> with talons wide unsheathed on flights of birds, who cower down the sky in chutes and bursts along the valley—
> but the pouncing falcons grip their prey, no frantic wing avails,
> and farmers love to watch those beaked hunters. So these now fell upon the suitors in that hall, turning, turning to strike and strike again, while torn men moaned at death, and blood ran smoking
> over the whole floor.
>
> (XXII:310–319)

Homer sang equally vividly, and far more sweetly and poignantly, of excellence in love. As the *Odyssey* moves toward its conclusion, hero and heroine, Odysseus and Penelope, make love after a wartime separation of twenty years:

> Now from his breast into his eyes the ache
> of longing mounted, and he wept at last,
> his dear wife, clear and faithful, in his arms,
> longed for as the sunwarmed earth is longed for by a swimmer
> spent in rough water where his ship went down under Poseidon's blows, gale winds and tons of sea.
> Few men can keep alive through a big surf
> to crawl, clotted with brine, on kindly beaches
> in joy, in joy, knowing the abyss behind:
> and so she too rejoiced, her gaze upon her husband,
> her white arms round him pressed as though forever.
> . . . .
> (XXIII:234–244)

> So they came
> into that bed so steadfast, loved of old,
> opening glad arms to one another,
> Telemachus by now had hushed the dancing,
> hushed the women. In the darkened hall
> he and the cowherd and the swineherd slept.
> The royal pair mingled in love again
> and afterward lay revelling in stories:
> hers of the siege her beauty stood at home
> from arrogant suitors, crowding on her sight,
> and how they fed their courtship on his cattle,
> oxen and fat sheep, and drank up rivers
> of wine out of the vats.
> Odysseus told
> of what hard blows he had dealt out to others
> and of what blows he had taken—all that story.
> She could not close her eyes till all was told.
>
> (*Odyssey* XXIII:298–313)

War and love, the bloody heroism of the battlefield and the warm intimacy of family life—Homer addressed both in imagery which has inspired readers, and listeners, to this day.

SPOTLIGHT
Everyday Life in Ancient Greece

Much of the literature and art of ancient and classical Greece represented a search for personal excellence and aesthetic perfection: Homer's epic heroes, Plato's ideal forms, Aristotle's celestial spheres, the architecture and sculpture of the Acropolis in Athens. But some observers regarded the search for artistic perfection as financially wasteful and politically misguided. Opponents criticized Pericles for endangering the defense of

Figure 1 Terra cotta statuette of man with plow and oxen, Boeotia, sixth century B.C.E. (*Louvre, Paris*)

Athens through wasteful extravagance in gussying up the city "like a harlot with precious stones, statues, and temples costing a world of money" (Plutarch, p. 191). And while Athens' public architecture remains a model of beauty until today, private housing in the city was quite dingy.

An alternative aesthetics devoted to representing everyday life appeared, although it left no formal artistic canon. In the late sixth century, in Boeotia, bordering Athens to the west, small terra cotta figurines representing people at work in

quite ordinary jobs were produced in large numbers, frequently to be placed in tombs. These included barbers cutting hair, porters carrying baskets, and, in **figure 1** here, one of the most common tasks of all, a farmer behind his plow guiding two oxen through the fields. A statuette of an equally common daily activity is represented in

Figure 2 Terra cotta figurine of woman kneading dough, Tanagra, Boeotia, fifth century B.C.E. (*American School of Classical Studies, Athens*)

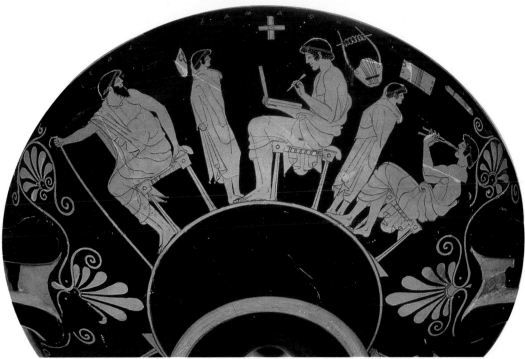

figure 2, a woman kneading dough in a stone basin. This terra cotta dates to the fifth century, contemporary with classical Athens. **Figures 3** and **4**, painted on a single red-figure cup, also of the fifth century, depict four

scenes from the education of a young man—learning to play the lyre and the flute, and learning to read and write, all under the watchful eye of a pedagogue. These vase paintings, in their subject matter and their style,

represent a mid-point between everyday activities (for the upper classes) and classical forms.

Figure 3 and 4 Two halves of a red-figure cup by the sculptor Douris, fifth century B.C.E. (*Staatliche Museen, Berlin*)

Minoans and Myceneans: The Earliest City-States of the Aegean

How Do We Know?

Until the 1870s scholars of classical Greece believed that the Greek city-states had begun their slow evolution about the ninth century B.C.E. after hundreds of years of political and military turmoil. Naturally they knew of Homer's great epic poems of the Trojan War, the *Iliad* and the *Odyssey* (see Source, pp. 134–5), in which the king of Mycenae led the Greek city-states in war against Troy around 1400 B.C.E., but they understood these tales of earlier times to be myths without foundation in fact.

Then, in the 1870s, Heinrich Schliemann, a classicist and amateur archaeologist, discovered evidence of the existence of city-kingdoms at both Troy and Mycenae, dating to about 1600 to 1450 B.C.E., while in 1900 Arthur Evans discovered a massive palace complex at Knossos, north-central Crete, that confirmed the possible reality of the mythical king Minos. Thus archaeologists discovered two ancient kingdoms, with trade links, confirming popular folk legends and locating some of the roots of Greek civilization a thousand years further back in time.

What Do We Know?

Immigrants began to settle Crete about 6000 B.C.E. By 3000 B.C.E., they had built villages, and by 2000 B.C.E. at Knossos they erected the first and largest of at least four major palace complexes on the island. The palaces combined three functions: elaborately furnished royal residences, religious and ritual centers, and headquarters for administering the Cretan economy. The craftspeople of Crete produced bronze tools, gems, and extraordinarily fine pottery, eggshell-thin vessels which they exported throughout the eastern Mediterranean. As an island kingdom located at the crossroads of multiple trade routes, Crete excelled in commerce.

Pictographic writing existed from at least 2000 B.C.E. and about 1700 B.C.E. syllabic writing was introduced. Known as Linear A, this script has not yet been deciphered. About 1450 B.C.E., some, now unknown, disaster led to the destruction of three of the major palaces. (For a time scholars believed that eruptions of the volcano Thera might have caused the destruction, but deep-sea excavations show that the eruption was too early, *c.* 1625 B.C.E., and too far distant to have caused such devastation.) Crete seems to have become more deeply enmeshed in the affairs of Mycenae at this time. A new script, called Linear B, was created for transcribing Greek, suggesting that this had now become the language of Crete. In 1370 B.C.E. the palace at Knossos was also destroyed, and Crete came under the sway of Mycenae. Finally the glories of Knossos were lost, preserved for thousands of years only in legend.

Homer portrays Mycenaeans as brave and heroic

festivals as the Olympic games, held every four years after 776 B.C.E.

Some of the Greek cities in Anatolia had earlier fallen under the kingdom of Lydia. These and more were now captured by Darius' empire. Although Persian rule rested rather lightly, and the Greek city-states of Anatolia were permitted to retain their own form of local government as long as they paid their taxes to Persia, some of them revolted and called on the Greek cities of the peninsula to aid the resistance. Athens, joined by Eretria, tried, half-heartedly and unsuccessfully, to assist its overseas

relatives with ships and soldiers. According to Herodotus, Darius

> asked who the Athenians were and, being
> informed, called for his bow, and placing an arrow
> on the string, shot upward into the sky, saying
> as he let fly the shaft, "Grant me, Zeus, to revenge
> myself on the Athenians!" After this speech, he
> bade one of his servants every day, when his dinner
> was spread, three times repeat these words to him,
> "Master, remember the Athenians."
>
> (*The Persian Wars*, V:105)

warriors as well as active sailors and traders. They carried on extensive trade and cultural exchange with Crete, including sharing the use of Linear B script. After 1450, when several of Crete's important towns were destroyed, Mycenae came to dominate the relationship. Mycenae was home to several small kingdoms, each with its own palace or citadel and accompanying cemetery of beehive-shaped tombs. The greatest of the cities was Mycenae itself, the administrative center of the entire region, surrounded by a colossal wall up to 25 feet (7 meters) thick and entered through a massive gate topped with huge stone lions looking down on all who entered and left. The site is rich in the evidence of warfare: weapons, armor, paintings of warriors, and, at the seashore a few miles distant, ships of war. Some of the kings, at least, were quite wealthy: one was buried with 11 pounds (5 kilograms) of gold, and the funeral "mask of Agamemnon" was a work of consummate craftsmanship in gold. Scholars have been unable to discover the reason for the fall of Mycenaean civilization; perhaps it was invaded, perhaps it imploded in internal warfare. By the end of the twelfth century B.C.E., all the palaces and towns of Mycenae were destroyed or abandoned.

The archaeological excavations of Schliemann and others who followed him, however, demonstrated that for some five hundred years in Mycenae, and for a thousand in Crete, local, brilliant, urban civilizations had flourished. Their fall ushered in the Greek "Dark Ages," a period of general upheaval throughout much of the eastern Mediterranean. The Greeks even lost their knowledge of how to write. Apparently additional waves of nomadic immigrants entered Greece from the north. By about 850 B.C.E. the peoples of Greece began to emerge from an age of darkness and once again to settle, to build towns, to trade overseas, to receive new waves of immigrants that increased their population, and to restore their written culture.

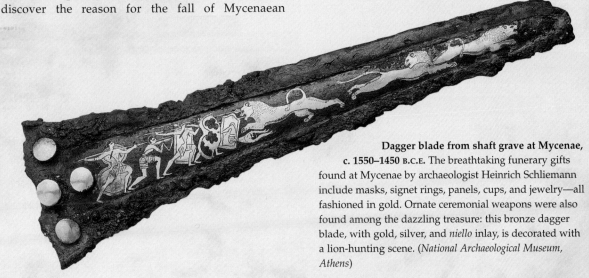

Dagger blade from shaft grave at Mycenae, c. 1550–1450 B.C.E. The breathtaking funerary gifts found at Mycenae by archaeologist Heinrich Schliemann include masks, signet rings, panels, cups, and jewelry—all fashioned in gold. Ornate ceremonial weapons were also found among the dazzling treasure: this bronze dagger blade, with gold, silver, and *niello* inlay, is decorated with a lion-hunting scene. (*National Archaeological Museum, Athens*)

By the turn of the fifth century B.C.E. the cultural, geo-political, and military struggle between the Greek city-states and the Persian Empire had begun. In 512 and again in 492, Persia under Darius had crossed the Hellespont into Europe, and invaded and taken parts of Thrace. In 490, Darius dispatched a naval expedition directly across the Aegean in order to punish Athens for its part in the revolt in Anatolia.

War with the Persians tested the Greeks' fundamental mode of political organization. Persia was a huge, centrally governed empire; each Greek city-state was individually independent, although many had joined into regional confederations and leagues for mutual assistance and trade. Persia was headed by a single emperor who set policies for the entire empire; each individual Greek city-state, for the most part, was governed by an assembly of all its adult, free, male citizens. These assemblies passed laws, judged criminal and civil cases, provided for administration and implementation of legislation, and arranged for military defense as the need arose. The Greek city-states were moving toward democracy; they understood their legal systems to be their own creation and responsibility, neither ordained by the gods nor imposed by a powerful external emperor.

Moreover, the city assemblies had organized themselves by **deme,** or neighborhood. Political identity was thus based on geographical residence in the city, not on heredity and kinship, nor on class and wealth. This new concept of civic identity allowed the city to welcome new residents and the ideas they brought with them, regardless of their place of origin. It allowed people of different ethnic origins, even of enemy ethnic stocks, to enter the city, although they were not eligible for full citizenship. The human interaction in the small Greek city-state nurtured the intellect of its citizens. Life in the *polis* meant constant participation in a kind of ongoing public seminar. As Socrates (*c.* 470–399 B.C.E.), the leading philosopher of fifth-century Athens, said: "I'm a lover of learning, and trees and open country won't teach me anything, whereas men in the town do" (Plato, *Phaedrus*, 230:d).

How could the tiny Greek city-states hold off Darius' imperial armies and keep their incipient democracies alive? First, they had the enormous advantage of being close to home, with a good knowledge of local geography and conditions. Second, the largest among them, especially Athens and Sparta, chose to cooperate in defense against a common enemy. When the Persian fleet of 600 ships landed 20,000 Persian soldiers at Marathon in 490 B.C.E., a force of some 10,000 Greek **hoplite** soldiers (see picture below), mostly Athenian, confronted them. The hoplite forces were solid phalanxes of soldiers arrayed in tight lines, the right arm and shield of one man pressed against the left shoulder of the other, in row on row, so that if a soldier in the front row fell, one from the next line took his place. (In these hoplite formations, each individual soldier is crucial to the welfare of all. Many analysts have seen in this egalitarian military formation the rationale for Athenian political democracy.)

The discipline of the Athenians, plus their strategy of letting their center fall back and then outflanking and surrounding the ensuing Persian charges, defeated their enemy. At the Battle of Marathon in 490 B.C.E. Persia lost 6400 men, Athens 192. The remaining Persians reboarded their ships, however, and sailed for Athens and a second round of fighting. The Athenian general at Marathon, Miltiades, sent his fastest runner, Pheidippides, racing back to Athens to tell of the victory at Marathon to strengthen the resolve of the Athenians at home and to hasten their preparations for battle. Pheidippides delivered the message, and died of exhaustion on the spot. (The marathon race of today is named for his 26-mile/41.8-kilometer run.) Darius planned to attack Greece again, then, but rebellion in Egypt and a struggle for succession within his own family diverted his attention until his death in 486 B.C.E. He was succeeded by his son Xerxes (r. 486–465 B.C.E.), who mounted a renewed attack on the Greek mainland

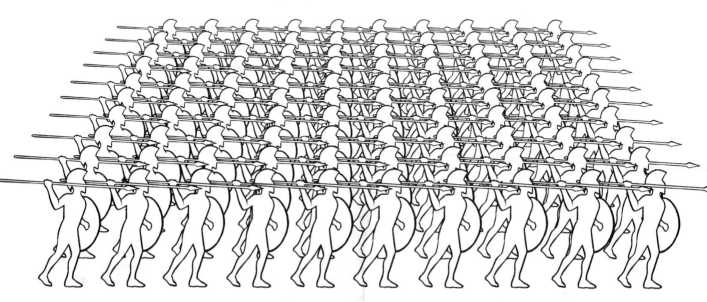

Formation of Greek hoplites. The soldiers of the Greek armies, called hoplites, fought in especially tight formations, row upon row of soldiers pressed closely together, so that they were completely dependent on one another and upon the entire formation. Some historians argue that this interdependency encouraged them to seek a democratic voice in formulating Greek political policies.

Greek trireme. The Greeks developed triremes (with three banks of oars) as warships and had them specially strengthened so that they could ram other ships. The triremes were slower and less maneuverable than the Persian ships. To compensate, the Greeks put soldiers aboard and, at Salamis, relied mostly on hand-to-hand combat.

SOURCE
Herodotus Describes Darius' Preparations for War Against Greece

Herodotus (c. 485–420 B.C.E.), the "father of history," took the whole known world as his subject matter, although his reports on lands distant from the Mediterranean, such as India, are more myths and legends than accurate accounts. *The Persian Wars*, his greatest work, portrays the great war of 499–479 B.C.E. as a moral as well as a military conflict between two continents, two polities, and two ideologies. For Herodotus the Greeks represent Europe, the city-state, and democracy, the land, the form of government, and the values to which he is committed; the Persians represent Asia, empire, and despotism, the enemy. Herodotus seeks explanations for the war in chains of events rooted deeply in the past as well as in the personalities of contemporary leaders making immediate decisions. Herodotus believed that the gods abhorred human arrogance, so his depiction of Darius' furious preparation for retaliation against the Greeks prepares the reader for the irony of Darius' death before he could mount his invasion.

Now when tidings of the battle that had been fought at Marathon reached the ears of King Darius, the son of Hystaspes, his anger against the Athenians, which had been already roused by their attack upon Sardis, waxed still fiercer, and he became more than ever eager to lead an army against Greece. Instantly he sent off messengers to make proclamation through the several states, that fresh levies were to be raised, and these at an increased rate; while ships, horses, provisions, and transports were likewise to be furnished. So the men published his commands; and now all Asia was in commotion for three years, while everywhere, as Greece was to be attacked, the best and bravest were enrolled for service and had to make their preparations accordingly. (*The Persian Wars*, VII:1)

THE GREAT PELOPONNESIAN WAR

435 (B.C.E.)	Civil war at Epidamnus
432	Sparta declares war on Athens
431	Peloponnesian invasion of Athens
421	Peace of Nicias
415–413	Athenian invasion of Sicily
405	Battle of Aegospotami
404	Athens surrenders

by land and sea in 480 B.C.E. Xerxes himself marched southward from Macedonia to Thessaly, in the direction of Athens and the Peloponnese. Courageous resistance by the Spartan general Leonidas and his troops at Thermopylae cost the lives of all the defenders, but won time for the Athenians to evacuate their city and regroup their forces. Xerxes continued to push onward to Athens, capturing, burning, and plundering the city and its Acropolis, but the Athenian warriors had withdrawn to the nearby port of Piraeus and the Bay of Salamis. A force of some 1000 Persian ships was bearing down on the same location. Fortunately for the Athenians, the city had devoted the silver of its mines at Laurion to constructing a fleet of 200 triremes, named for the three levels in which its approximately 170 rowers were arranged, and to fortifying Piraeus. When the opposing fleets engaged, between the island of Salamis and the mainland of Attica, the Athenians bottled up the more massive Persian fleet in the Salamis Channel. The Greeks lost 40 ships; the Persians lost 200. Xerxes sailed for home, and Persia never again attacked Greece by sea.

The Persians did, however, continue to fight by land. In the next year, 479 B.C.E., in alliance with their subjects in Macedonia and some northern Greeks, they prepared an army of some 100,000 men at Plataea, on the edge of the plains opening southward to Athens and the Peloponnese. Sparta and Athens formed an alliance with some other

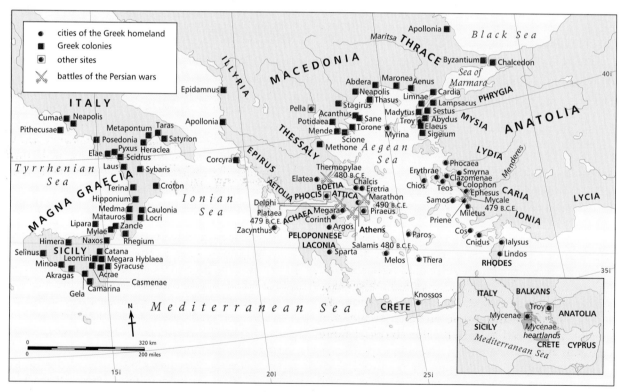

Classical Greece The hilly terrain and sea-boundaries of Greece discouraged the growth of large settlements, and Greek philosophers also stressed the importance of local community. When population grew too great the citizens encouraged their younger cohort to establish new city-states of their own. The resulting spread of settlements established Greek influence all the way from Sicily to Anatolia.

city-states to field an opposing army of about 40,000. Despite initial confusion in the ranks, the allied Spartan and Athenian forces destroyed the Persian armies and their camp, annihilated the elite guard, and killed Mardonius, the Persian general. At about the same time, the Greek fleet defeated the surviving Persian fleet at Mycale, on the Ionian coast of Anatolia.

In the face of these losses, and with weaker leadership at home, Persia left Europe, never to return in such force. (Still powerful, however, the Persians did continue to exert influence in Greek affairs from a distance, by subsidizing allies. Its later contributions to Sparta in the Peloponnesian War helped to fund its victory.) The small Greek city-states, led by arch-rivals Athens and Sparta, had shown an ability to combine in the face of a common enemy. They had demonstrated the virtues of small-scale, local units of society and the resilience of popular, democratic forms of government. Conversely, the Persians had exhibited one of the great flaws of empire: the tendency to overextend its powers.

ATHENS: FROM CITY-STATE TO MINI-EMPIRE

With the Persian threat removed, the Greek city-states turned at first to rebuilding their losses. The historical records that remain tell us most about Athens, the largest, most illustrious, and most provocative of the city-states.

Athenian Democracy: Historical Background and Historians

In the year 600 B.C.E., Solon (c. 630–c. 560 B.C.E.), who had risen to high office as a general and a poet, ended the monopoly over public office held by the Athenian hereditary aristocracy. He opened to all free men participation and voting in the decision-making public assembly, although only those meeting certain income levels could be elected to high public office. The Council of Four Hundred, which Solon also created, represented the interests of the wealthy and noble factions, while the assembly balanced them with the voices of more common men.

Perhaps more importantly, Solon cancelled all public and private debts, and abolished the practice of enslaving people to pay off their debts. Solon's reforms crumbled when he left office, and decades of struggle between rich and poor and between men of different hereditary clans ensued until

about 550 B.C.E. when Peisistratus seized control of the government. Peisistratus (d. 527 B.C.E.) fostered economic growth through loans to small farmers; export promotion programs; road construction; and public works, including major building programs for the beautification of Athens and its Acropolis. On Peisistratus' death, the city-state again fell into disarray and even civil war. In 510 B.C.E., at the invitation of a faction of Athens' noblemen, the king of Sparta, already Athens' greatest rival, invaded Athens, besieged the Acropolis, and deposed the descendants of Peisistratus.

Through all the warfare and strife, the ideals of Solon survived. A new ruler, Cleisthenes (c. 570–c. 500 B.C.E.), came to power and dramatically reorganized the city and its surrounding countryside. He did away with the aristocratic family centers of power by registering each Athenian as a citizen according to his geographical residence, or *deme*, in the city. Similarly, he reorganized the electoral districts of Attica, the region around Athens, into ten electoral units, creating new political identities and allegiances. The assembly resumed meeting about every ten days, and all male citizens were expected to participate; 6000 were necessary for a quorum. Above the assembly, and setting its agenda, was a Council of Five Hundred, even more open than Solon's Council of Four Hundred had been, since members were selected from each *deme* for one-year terms by lottery, and members were not allowed to serve for more than two terms. When Darius' Persian Empire challenged Athens, and the Greek city-states generally, the contrast between the combatants was stark: city-state versus empire; local administration versus imperial power; evolving, decentralized democracy versus established, centralized imperial control.

Following the victory over the Persians in the fifth century B.C.E., Athens was at the height of its power and prestige under the military and civic leadership of Pericles (c. 495–429 B.C.E.). Historians began to reflect on its origins, accomplishments, and the challenges it had faced. Indeed, the modern profession of history as a systematic attempt to understand the influence of past experience on the present began in Athens. Two of the most outstanding historians of the fifth century B.C.E. have given us the history of the city and its relationships with its neighbors. Herodotus (d. *c.* 420 B.C.E.) wrote *The Persian Wars*, and in the narrative recaptured a general, but anecdotal, history of the whole eastern Mediterranean and eastward as far as Persia and India. Thucydides (d.

c. 401 B.C.E.), far more systematically and carefully, recounted the subsequent *History of the Peloponnesian War*, and the events surrounding those three decades of anarchy and warfare among the city-states of Greece. Collectively, native historians narrated the evolution of Athens from city-state to mini-empire.

Architecture, Design, the Arts, Philosophy, and Drama

Greek victory, led by Athens, triggered immense pride in the city-state, its democratic philosophy (see Source pp. 148–9), and its artistic creativity. The physical design of the city itself tells much of its origins, functions, and ideals, as R.E. Wycherley's *How the Greeks Built Cities* points out. Athens rose from a plain, and with each level upward its functions and the architecture became more exalted. At the bottom were the houses of commoners, built simply from local materials of stone and mud, with little concern for architectural merit. Further up the hill was the **agora**, or civic and market center, with clusters of buildings for trade in goods, ideas, and political decision-making. These public buildings were more elegant, designed for greater comfort and show. Nearby were gymnasia for exercise and competition. In the splendor of the *agora* Athenians demonstrated the value they placed on public life and on physical prowess and discipline. Further to the side, built into the side of the hill, was an amphitheater where plays were regularly performed, often representing in dramatic form scenes from Greek mythological history and suggesting their significance in understanding the moral issues of the day. At the

Parthenon, Athens, 447–432 B.C.E. The Parthenon on the Athenian Acropolis was a temple dedicated to the goddess Athena, the city's patron-deity. It was built at the instigation of Pericles as a symbol of Athens' growing importance and represents, in architectural terms, the summit of classical Greek achievement.

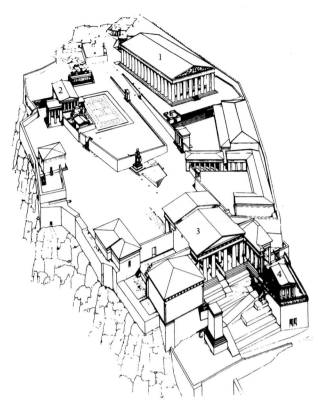

Plan of Acropolis. The construction of the Acropolis (Greek for "high city") beginning in *c.* 460 B.C.E. under the leadership of Pericles, signified the beginning of a Golden Age for Athens. The plan above indicates some of its most celebrated buildings—the Parthenon (1), the Erectheum (2), the Propylaea (3), and the Temple of Athena Nike (4).

philosophy explored the working of the city-state itself and the relationship of the individual to it. Plato's own teacher, the philosopher Socrates (*c.* 470–399 B.C.E.), had argued for the supremacy of the city-state over the individual. The citizen had obligations to the state for all the benefits he

A marble, second-century-C.E. copy of the statue of Athena Parthenos, dedicated in 438 B.C. Phidias' 40-foot (12 m) Athena, the divine guardian of the city, dominated the central chamber of the Parthenon on the Acropolis. This miniature Roman copy of the destroyed statue hardly suggests the glittering magnificence of the enormous gold-and-ivory original, a powerful symbol of the might of the goddess and her city, Athens. (*Acropolis Museum, Athens*)

top of the hill, on the Acropolis ("city on high"), surrounded by a wall, were the chief temples of the city, especially the shrine of the goddess Athena, the divine guardian of the city.

During the war years, the Persians had destroyed and burned much of Athens. When victory was secure, the Athenians not only rebuilt and improved their city, they now crowned its Acropolis with stunning new architecture and art. Architects and urban designers Ictimus and Callicrates planned the new Acropolis and built the Parthenon while the sculptor Phidias carved the friezes on the Parthenon and created a 40-foot (12-meter) high statue of Athena, the city's patron goddess, to reside within it.

Philosophers such as Socrates and Plato introduced questions, methods of analysis and of teaching, and examinations of the purpose of life, which continue to command attention for their range and depth. Plato's prize student, Aristotle (384–322 B.C.E.), later wrote that man is a *zoon politikon*, a "political animal," a creature of the city-state, and many of the key works in Greek history, drama, and

received from it, but had no rights to claim against the power of the state.

For Socrates the Athenian state was father and mother; he derived his sense of self and purpose from the education the state gave him and from his continual debates with fellow citizens both in public and private. He opposed and satirized the sophist philosophers who earned their salaries by training future statesmen how to argue any side of any question without necessarily staking any personal commitment. Through his incessant questions, he taught *his* students to be thoughtful but critical about the truths of others and about their own truths, and, after having reached their own conclusions, to live their own truths fully even if it meant their death, as it did for Socrates himself.

Plato, Socrates' leading pupil and the founder of the Academy, which endured for centuries as Athens' leading school of philosophy, chose the state as his subject in his search for justice. Early in one of his greatest works, *The Republic*, he proposes, in the name of Socrates:

> There is a justice of one man, we say, and, I suppose, also of an entire city? . . . Is not the city larger than the man? . . . Then, perhaps, there would be more justice in the larger object, and more easy to apprehend. If it please you, then, let us first look for its quality in states, and then only examine it also in the individual, looking for the likeness of the greater in the form of the less.
>
> (*The Republic*, II:368:e.)

The ideal state, according to Plato, would be administered by a philosopher-king who by virtue of innate good character and intensive training would know and do what was best for all citizens in the state.

Aristotle, Plato's greatest pupil, addressed an astonishing array of subjects: logic, physics, astronomy, metaphysics, religion, rhetoric, literary criticism, and natural science; but he, too, devoted some of his most important writing to ethics and politics. His analysis of the principal forms of constitutional government in his *Politics* remains a useful introduction to the field even today. Aristotle later was engaged as a tutor to Alexander the Great of Macedon, although how much influence he had over the future world-conqueror is a matter for conjecture.

In the theaters of Athens, drama was born and flourished. The pursuit of justice, morality, and equity was a core theme. Athenian playwrights invented the dramatic forms of tragedy and comedy, and their most important plays all include themes related to the evolution of their city and its institutions. Aeschylus' (524?–456 B.C.E.) *Oresteia* trilogy follows three generations of murders within the royal family of Atreus, as one act of revenge provokes the next, until finally, in a trial at Athens, Athena, patron goddess of the city, acquits Orestes, suggesting that divinely ordained vengeance will be replaced by human justice and the cycle of murder will be ended. *Oedipus Rex* of Sophocles (496–406 B.C.E.), perhaps the most famous single play of ancient Athens, centers on the family tragedy of Oedipus' murder of his own father, the King of Thebes, and his subsequent marriage to his own mother. (Oedipus did not know that the man he killed was his father and that he had married his own mother. Oedipus had been abandoned as an infant and raised by shepherds.) The play opens with the people of Thebes gathered round King Oedipus, before his tragedy is revealed, crying out for his help in arresting a plague that is afflicting the city. Oedipus' own moral corruption has brought the plague on the city, although that is revealed only later. Sophocles' *Antigone* confronts the conflict in loyalty to family versus loyalty to the city-state, as Antigone chooses to bury her brother Polynices despite the royal decree to leave his corpse unattended as an enemy of the state. Euripides (480–406 B.C.E.) saw more clearly Athens' move toward imperialism, and criticized it in *The Trojan Women*. Aristophanes' (450?–385? B.C.E.) hilarious, sexually explicit comedy, *Lysistrata*, portrays the women of Athens and Sparta agreeing to go on strike sexually until their men stop fighting the Peloponnesian wars. So long as the men make war the women will not make love! The best of the Athenian dramatists addressed directly the political and social issues that confronted their city.

THE LIMITS OF CITY-STATE DEMOCRACY

HOW DO WE KNOW?

WHAT DO WE KNOW?

The very art and literature through which citizens praise their city-states contain within themselves the core of a critique against the legacy of the city-state. Socrates' justification of the state demonstrates that even in the most democratic Greek city-state, government could exact respect and service from the citizen, but the citizen had few rights vis-à-vis the state. The citizen had the right, and indeed the obligation, to participate in the activities of the state and to serve the state, but not to have the state serve him.

For women, even the right of participation was absent. Participatory democracy was reserved for men. *The Reign of the Phallus: Sexual Politics in Ancient Athens* by art historian Eva Keuls rages against Athens as both cruelly misogynist and aggressively militaristic, and suggests that these two characteristics were interrelated. Classical Athens, Keuls argues, was a **phallocracy**,

a society dominated by men who sequester their wives and daughters, denigrate the female role in reproduction, erect monuments to the male genitalia, have sex with the sons of their peers, sponsor public whorehouses, create a mythology of rape, and engage in rampant saber-rattling. (p. 1)

Psykter (wine cooler) painted by Douris with cavorting satyrs, 500–490 B.C.E. Feminist historian Eva Keuls argues that, contrary to the cradle-of-civilization clichés, Athenian society was excessively warlike and women-hating. She finds much of her evidence on Greek vases of the type used in male drinking parties. (*British Museum, London*)

SOURCE
Two Views of Athenian Democracy

PERICLES' FUNERAL ORATION

As political and military leader of Athens, 460–429 B.C.E., Pericles delivered this eulogy at a mass-funeral of troops who had died of plague in the early years of the Peloponnesian War. As reported by Thucydides, it is one of the great proclamations of the civic, aesthetic, moral, and personal virtues of the Athenian city-state:

Our system of government does not copy the institutions of our neighbors. It is more the case of our being a model to others, than of our imitating anyone else. Our constitution is called a democracy because power is in the hands not of a minority but of the whole people. When it is a question of settling private disputes, everyone is equal before the law; when it is a question of putting one person before another in positions of public responsibility, what counts is not membership of a particular class, but the actual ability which the man possesses. No one, so long

as he has it in him to be of service to the state, is kept in political obscurity because of poverty. . . .

We [obey] those whom we put in positions of authority, and we obey the laws themselves, especially those which are for the protection of the oppressed, and those unwritten laws which it is an acknowledged shame to break. . . .

When our work is over, we are in a position to enjoy all kinds of recreation for our spirits . . . all the good things from all over the world flow in to us, so that to us it seems just as natural to enjoy foreign goods as our own local products. . . .

Our love of what is beautiful does not lead to extravagance; our love of the things of the mind does not make us soft. We regard wealth as something to be properly used, rather than as something to boast about. As for poverty, no one need be ashamed to admit it: the real shame is in not taking practical measures to escape from it. Here each individual is interested not only in his own affairs but in the affairs of the state as well: even those who are mostly occupied with their

Keuls finds most of her evidence in the painting on Greek vases, specifically of a type used in male drinking parties, but she asserts that additional support for her claims is widespread and easily accessible. She then asks, and answers, the historiographical question: Why have we not heard more of these phallocratic elements previously?

The story of phallic rule at the root of Western civilization has been suppressed as a result of the near-monopoly that men have held in the field of Classics, by neglect of rich pictorial evidence, by prudery and censorship, and by a misguided desire to protect an idealized image of Athens. (p. 1)

Plato (*c.* 429–347 B.C.E.) recognized the prejudices against women in his society. When he suggested in his visionary *Republic* that women should be treated equally with men in their access to the highest professional and civic responsibilities, and in the education needed to achieve them, he knew

that his ideas were revolutionary for Athens in his time and that they would be greeted with derision. Plato himself believed that men were generally more talented than women, but he argues here that both should be offered equal access to political opportunity. On the issue of gender equality, he seemed to remain consistent with his general philosophy: the state should encourage each citizen to reach his or her educational potential, and should direct the most talented into governmental affairs.

There is no occupation concerned with the management of social affairs which belongs either to women or to men, as such. Natural gifts are to be found here and there in both creatures alike; and every occupation is open to both, so far as their natures are concerned, though woman is for all purposes the weaker. . . . Women of this type must be selected to share the life and duties of Guardians with men of the same type, since they are competent

own business are extremely well informed on general politics—this is a peculiarity of ours: we do not say that a man who takes no interest in politics is a man who minds his own business; we say that he has no business here at all. We Athenians, in our own persons, take our decisions on policy or submit them to proper discussions: for we do not think that there is an incompatibility between words and deeds; the worst thing is to rush into action before the consequences have been properly debated. . . .

I declare that our city is an education to Greece, and I declare that in my opinion each single one of our citizens, in all the manifold aspects of life, is able to show himself the rightful lord and owner of his own person, and do this, moreover, with exceptional grace and exceptional versatility. (Book II:37–41; pp. 145–8)

SOCRATES ON THE RIGHTS OF THE STATE OVER THE INDIVIDUAL

Condemned to death on trumped-up charges of corrupting the political morals of youth and blaspheming against the gods of Athens, Socrates is offered the opportunity to escape and live out his life in another city-state. He refuses. He notes that the state has acted through formal legal process and has the right to execute him. He, in turn, has the obligation to accept the sentence. In Plato's *Crito*, Socrates explains his rationale.

Are you too wise to see that your country is worthier, more to be revered, more sacred, and held in higher honor both by the gods and by all men of understanding, than your father and your mother and all your other ancestors; and that you ought to reverence it, and to submit to it, and to approach it more humbly when it is angry with you than you would approach your father; and either to do whatever it tells you to do or to persuade it to excuse you; and to obey in silence if it orders you to endure flogging or imprisonment, or if it sends you to battle to be wounded or to die? That is just. You must not give way, nor retreat, nor desert your station. In war, and in the court of justice, and everywhere, you must do whatever your state and your country tell you to do, or you must persuade them that their commands are unjust. But it is impious to use violence against your father or your mother; and much more impious to use violence against your country. (Plato, *Crito* XII:51:b)

and of a like nature, and the same natures must be allowed the same pursuits. . . . Now, for the purpose of producing a woman fit to be a Guardian, we shall not have one education for men and another for women, precisely because the nature to be taken in hand is the same. . . . If we are to set women to the same tasks as men, we must teach them the same things. They must have the same two branches of training for mind and body and also be taught the art of war, and they must receive the same treatment. . . .

Now that we have started on this subject, we must not be frightened of the many witticisms that might be aimed at such a revolution, not only in the matter of bodily exercise but in the training of women's minds, and not least when it comes to their bearing arms and riding on horseback. (*Republic*, V:452–6; pp. 149–54)

Aristotle confirmed Plato's apprehensions, but not his optimism nor his sense of potential equality.

Aristotle wrote of women: "The temperance of a man and of a woman, or the courage and justice of a man and of a woman, are not, as Socrates maintained, the same; the courage of a man is shown in commanding, of a woman in obeying" (*Politics*, I:13; 20–25; p. 1144). Aristotle quotes with approval the general view that "Silence is a woman's glory" (I:13; 30; p. 1145). In practice, Athens followed Aristotelian rather than Platonic views on the role of women in public life.

Even among males, only the sons of native-born Athenian mothers and fathers were eligible for citizenship. Slaves captured in war, and even allies, could not gain citizenship. The Roman emperor Claudius reflected, "What proved fatal to Sparta and Athens, for all their military strength, was their segregation of conquered subjects as aliens" (Tacitus, p. 237). When Classical Athens reached its maximum population, 250,000, only about one adult Athenian in six qualified for citizenship. These limits on Athenian democracy increased domestic social strains.

ATHENS BECOMES AN IMPERIAL POWER

Most ironically, the city-state of Athens, having led the Greek city-states in the struggle against the Persian Empire, subsequently set out to construct an empire of its own. Following major victories in the Persian wars, Athens assembled its principal allies into the Delian League, with its council and treasury situated in Delos. At first, membership was voluntary, but soon Athens forbade withdrawal. Thucydides reports the consequences:

> Naxos left the league [c. 470 B.C.E.] and the Athenians made war on the place. After a siege Naxos was forced back to allegiance. This was the first case when the original constitution of the League was broken and an allied city lost its independence, and the process was continued in the cases of the other allies as various circumstances arose. The chief reasons for these revolts were failures to produce the right amount of tribute or the right number of ships, and sometimes a refusal to produce any ships at all. For the Athenians insisted on obligations being exactly met, and made themselves unpopular by bringing the severest pressure to bear on allies who were not used to making sacrifices and did not want to make them. In other ways, too, the Athenians as rulers were no longer popular as they used to be. (I:98; p. 93)

In 454 B.C.E. Pericles moved the treasury of the Delian League to Athens and appropriated its funds in order to create at Athens a spectacular center of power and authority, particularly by building the Parthenon and expanding the fleet. Then:

> the Athenians began to encroach upon Sparta's allies. It was at this point that Sparta felt the position to be no longer tolerable and decided by starting this present war to employ all her energies in attacking and, if possible, destroying the power of Athens. (I:118; p. 103)

In 432 B.C.E. Sparta declared war. The struggle was for power, not for higher ideals. Thucydides, historian of the conflict, portrays Athens setting forth its claims increasingly bluntly in statements of **realpolitik** (power politics). He reports the Athenian ultimatum bullying the people of the island of Melos and calling on them to submit to Athenian authority:

> Our opinion of the gods and our knowledge of men lead us to conclude that it is a general and necessary law of nature to rule whatever one can. (V:105; p. 404)

Melos nevertheless chose to resist. When the Athenians finally conquered the Melians, they "put to death all the men of military age whom they took, and sold the women and children as slaves" (V:116; p. 408).

By 404 Sparta, supported by Persian funding, defeated Athens and captured the city. Both sides were exhausted. Nevertheless, warfare soon resumed among the Greeks with Thebes and Corinth now entering the lists as major contenders. The balance of power among city-states had no further stability. Each major city-state sought advantage over the others and the stronger continued to force the weaker into subordinate alliances. Greece fell into the intermittent warfare of its city-states.

THE EMPIRE OF ALEXANDER THE GREAT

To the north of the major Greek city-states lay the rougher, less urbanized Macedonia, a borderland between Greece and the Slavic regions to the north and east. The principal language and culture of Macedonia were Greek, but other languages and less cultivated manners were also present. Here in 359 B.C.E., in the Macedonian capital of Pella, Philip II (r. 359–336 B.C.E.) persuaded the Macedonian army to declare him king, in succession to his brother, who had died in warfare.

After consolidating his power in Macedonia, Philip declared two goals. The first of these was to unify and bring peace to Greece; the second, to liberate the Greek city-states in Asia Minor from Persian control. Skillful as a diplomat and careful to introduce economic improvements in the lands he conquered, Philip nevertheless realized that his army was the real key to achieving his goals. He built up its phalanxes, armed the soldiers with spears up to 15 feet (4.6 meters) long, and augmented the foot soldiers with powerful and swift cavalry. Philip led the troops himself, suffering numerous, serious wounds in battle.

Between 354 and 339 Philip conquered the Balkans from the Danube to the Aegean coast and from the Adriatic to the Black Sea. To pacify and administer the area, he established new towns, which were populated by both Macedonians and local peoples. Similarly, he employed many local people in his administration. Within Greece proper his accomplishments were more mixed. He won some allies, like Thessaly; defeated the armies of several city-states; and mediated the end of a war between two coalitions of Greek city-states. He was honored with election as president of the Pythian Games at Delphi in 346, but his overtures for greater power in Greece were bitterly opposed by Athens and Thebes.

The orator Demosthenes (384–322 B.C.E.) delivered three "Philippics," public addresses calling Athens to battle against the Macedonian king and predicting the end of Athenian democracy if Philip defeated the city-state. In the face of this opposition, Philip declared war on Athens and its allies, defeating them at Chaeronea in 338 B.C.E. Philip now sought to create a self-governing league of Greek city-states, to accomplish his first goal, and to forge an alliance between Macedonia and the league to fight Persia, his second goal. But he was assassinated in 336. His twenty-year-old son, Alexander, continued his father's mission.

Like his father Philip and like the Persian emperors Cyrus II and Darius I, Alexander (356–323 B.C.E.) followed a policy of benevolent despotism much of the time. But, also like them, he implemented this policy only after his power had been amply demonstrated. Unfortunate Thebes provided an early site for this demonstration. Soon after assuming the throne, Alexander had marched north to the Danube River to suppress revolts in Thrace. Mistakenly informed that Alexander had been killed in battle, Thebes revolted against his local forces. Alexander quickly marched his troops back to Thebes, captured and sacked the rebel city, killed 6000 of its inhabitants, and sold into slavery 20,000 of those who survived.

In 334 Alexander was ready to cross into Asia, where his first major victory came at Granicus. From there he continued southward, forcing the Persians out of the Greek cities that lined the Ionian coast. To make sure that the Persians would not return, Alexander marched eastward through Anatolia with 35,000 Greek troops, routing the 300,000-man army of the Persian Emperor Darius III at Issus in 333 B.C.E., and forcing Darius himself into flight.

Alexander continued southward down the coast of the eastern Mediterranean. At Tyre, which held out in siege against him for seven months, he again demonstrated power and brutality, killing 7000 men and selling 30,000, mostly women and children, into slavery. Elsewhere, however,

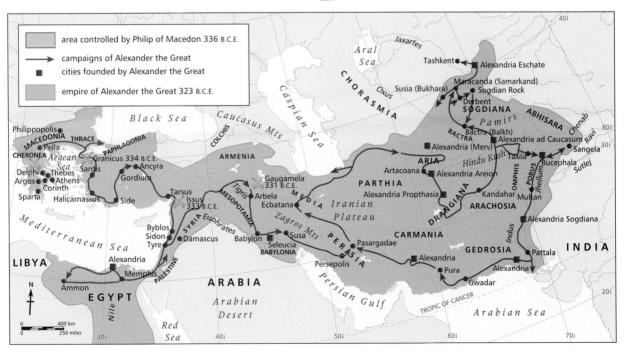

The Empire of Alexander In 338 the Greek city-states were defeated by Philip of Macedon. His son, Alexander, extended the imprint of Greek culture far beyond its Mediterranean homeland. In a series of whirlwind campaigns between 334 and 323 B.C.E., Alexander gained control of Syria and Egypt and then destroyed the might of Persia. He took his armies east to the Indus and north to central Asia, but died at age 33 in Babylon.

Alexander showed the velvet glove, respecting local religions, ruling through local hierarchies, and maintaining local tax rates. To drive Persia from the Mediterranean basin and to establish his own control, Alexander continued south and then west, conquering Egypt. He was welcomed as Egypt's liberator from Persian rule and treated as a god by the Egyptian priests of the god Amon, whose shrine he visited. At the western end of the Nile delta, Alexander laid the foundation of what would be for several centuries the most attractive and cultured city of the Mediterranean coast, Alexandria.

His appetite whetted, again a common experience with empire builders once they begin their careers, Alexander moved onward to conquests previously unplanned. He set out to conquer the Persian Empire and make it his own. He marched northeastward across the Fertile Crescent and through Mesopotamia. At Gaugamela in 331 B.C.E. he again faced the Persian emperor, Darius III, and again routed him. The historical capital cities of Babylon, Susa, Persepolis, and Pasargadae lay open to Alexander. He destroyed Persepolis, Darius' own capital, almost totally, then, having captured the heartland of the Persian Empire, he set off to conquer the eastern half as well, finally reaching and capturing the Indus River valley in the east, and Sogdiana, across the Oxus River, in the northeast. Although he had wanted to continue into India as far as the Ganges, his troops mutinied. They would go no farther. As he was returning from his new frontiers, Alexander contracted a fever and died in 323 B.C.E. in Babylon at the age of thirty-three. Several accounts report that he was poisoned. Some said that the instigator was his own former teacher Aristotle. In the battle for succession among his generals, Alexander's wife Roxane and their thirteen-year old son were murdered.

The empire Alexander created did not survive two generations. In the east, local rulers regained power in India and Afghanistan. In the west, the Greeks returned to their internal warfare, finally breaking up once more into individual city-states, kingdoms, and leagues. Macedonia remained a separate kingdom and meddled in Greek affairs. Two major kingdoms emerged: Egypt under the dynasty of Ptolemy, which ruled through a Greek and Macedonian elite until the Roman conquest; and the empire established by Seleucus I Nicator (d. 281 B.C.E.), who was governor of Babylon when the empire split apart, and who added to his own

domain Iran, Afghanistan, and Anatolia. But the Seleucid Empire, too, fragmented. Parthians reclaimed Persia in the east, and Anatolia divided into numerous local governments. By 200 B.C.E. the Seleucid Empire was limited primarily to the area around Syria.

THE LEGACY OF ALEXANDER: THE HELLENISTIC ECUMENE

What were the legacies of the empire Alexander built? He made the language and culture of Greece dominant among the ruling intellectual and commercial elites from the Mediterranean, east to India, Afghanistan, and the borders of Russia, and south as far as Egypt. A common dialect of Greek, known as Koine, spread as the language of educated people throughout the ancient western world. Waves of Greek administrators, businessmen, and soldiers followed Alexander's conquests and helped to transmit Greek culture. At the same time, their

The "Alexander Mosaic," first century B.C.E. mosaic copy from Pompeii (see Spotlight, pp. 170–1) of a painting by Philoxenos, c. 300 B.C.E. This mosaic portrays the Battle of Issus (333 B.C.E.) in terms of a personal duel between Alexander the Great and Darius, Emperor of Persia. Darius (right) is shown about to turn and flee in his chariot as the youthful Alexander (left), wild-haired and helmetless, charges toward him. (*Museo Archeologico Nazionale, Naples*)

expression of Hellenic culture was often infiltrated by local customs, especially the imperial ceremonial forms of Persia. The simplicity of the earlier Hellenic culture was transformed into the more complex, elaborate, and cosmopolitan Hellenistic culture of Alexander. One striking example of its spread and mix can be seen in some of the first representations of the Buddha in sculpture from the area of India/Pakistan after it was conquered by Alexander. These sculptures represent the Buddha wearing a toga (see Spotlight, p. 288).

To make travel and commerce, as well as conquest and administration, more feasible, Alexander built roads, canals, and whole new cities, including at least sixteen Alexandrias across the length and breadth of his conquests, using the gold and silver captured from Persia to finance

many of these constructions. The most famous and illustrious Alexandria was the metropolis in Egypt, which became the leading city of its day. Egyptian Alexandria housed palaces, administrative centers, theaters, stadia, the greatest library of Greek knowledge, containing 700,000 manuscripts, and the final resting place of Alexander himself.

At the eastern end of the empire, on the Oxus River in today's Uzbekistan, the Greeks constructed, on Persian foundations, Ai Khanoum, a small, well-defended city centered on a palace. Ai Khanoum was rediscovered and excavated only in the 1960s, and archaeologists believe it may prove to be Alexandria Oxiana, a lost city from the age of Alexander the Great.

Between Alexandria in Egypt and Ai Khanoum in central Asia were dozens of cities and small

PROFILE
Alexander the Great
HISTORICAL REINTERPRETATIONS

The twenty-year-old Alexander succeeded to the throne of Macedonia in 336 B.C.E. after the assassination of his father, Philip II. No stranger to warfare, Alexander had fought by his father's side just two years beforehand as he defeated Athens at the Battle of Chaeronea. Applauded by the army, Alexander succeeded to the throne without opposition and continued his father's career of conquest. Over the next twelve years, his disciplined army traversed some 22,000 miles (35,400 kilometers), conquering lands that stretched from Egypt in the west to the Indus River in the east. Alexander's empire was the largest ever known and in 324 B.C.E. he declared himself a god. A year later, at the age of thirty-three, Alexander died in Babylon from an illness induced by heavy drinking. On his deathbed he reputedly declared, "Let the job go to the strongest."

By the end of his life, however,

> there were few men, and *a fortiori* fewer women, who lamented Alexander's passing. In Greece and Asia alike, during his lifetime and for several centuries after his death, he was regarded as a tyrannous aggressor, a foreign autocrat who had imposed his will by violence alone. When the news of his death in Babylon reached Athens, it was the orator Demades who crystallized public reaction. "Alexander dead?" he exclaimed. "Impossible; the whole world would stink of his corpse."
> (Green, p. 477)

In these words historian Peter Green introduces a brief historiographical sketch of Alexander's reputation through the ages.

The earliest remaining accounts of Alexander's life date from the first century B.C.E., at least 200 years after his death, while the most reliable and fullest of the earliest biographies still extant, that written by Arrian Flavius Arrianus, dates to the second century C.E. For the most part, all historians work from these same basic records, but their assessments reflect the issues and conditions of their own day.

Arrian, who lived at the height of the Roman empire, and approved of it, praises Alexander for his conquests. Alexander was the prototype of Rome's own Caesars. Closer to our own times, in the late eighteenth and nineteenth centuries, during the democratic era of the American and French

towns, which served as seeds of Greek culture throughout the empire. The Alexandrian Empire and its successors built a Hellenistic **ecumene**—that is, a unified urban culture, encompassing vast lands and diverse peoples. Some of its cities, which had long, independent Greek heritages, retained strong elements of their pre-Alexandrian culture and even their autonomy. These were the cities of the Greek heartland, such as Athens, Sparta, Thebes, Corinth, and Delphi. Others were cities of empire, built later by Alexander and his successors either from the ground up or on existing but relatively minor urban bases. These cities served as new regional capitals, to administer the new empire, to extend its economy, and to broadcast its culture. Alexandria in Egypt and some fifteen other Alexandrias as well as Seleucia-on-the-Tigris were principal examples.

Alexander and his successors also administered their empire through the already existing indigenous urban framework, but added to it the principal institutions and monuments of Hellenistic culture: temples to Greek gods frequently located on a walled acropolis; theaters; an *agora*; civic buildings such as a *bouleuterion* (council chamber) and *prytaneion* (town hall); gymnasia; and stadia. Examples of this style of urban Hellenization in newly conquered lands included Susa, Damascus, Tyre, Kandahar, and Merv. Residents of these varied cities might feel themselves to be both citizens of the locality and participants in a semi-universal ecumene, although the balance of these

revolutions, and of the Greek War for Independence (see Chapter 15), historical opinion turned against Alexander. George Grote's *History of Greece* (1888) represented both Philip and Alexander as "brutalized adventurers simply out for power, wealth, and territorial expansion, both of them inflamed by the pure lust for conquest" (Green, p. 482).

On the other hand, Johann Gustav Droysen, an ardent advocate of a reunified, powerful Germany (see Chapter 17), saw Alexander as a model. Droysen's scholarly biography, *Alexander der Grosse* (1833), praised Alexander for introducing Greek culture into large parts of Asia. As their empire expanded in the nineteenth and early twentieth centuries many British scholars also adopted a favorable view of Alexander. William Tarn's two-volume biography saw his conquests as instrumental in spreading a social philosophy of the Brotherhood of Man, bringing together Greeks and Persians, the conquerers with the conquered. Even in our post-imperial day, Cambridge University scholar N.G.L. Hammond agrees, citing the essay by the biographer Plutarch (*c.* 46–126 C.E.):

He harnessed all resources to one and the same end, mixing as it were in a loving-cup the lives, manners, marriages and customs of men. He ordered them all to regard the inhabited earth as their fatherland and his armed forces as their stronghold and defense.

Nonetheless, Green remains critical, arguing that his own assessment is closest to that at the time of Alexander's death:

his all-absorbing obsession through a short but crowded life, was war and conquest. It is idle to palliate this central truth, to pretend that he dreamed. . . of wading through rivers of blood and violence to achieve the Brotherhood of Man by raping an entire continent. He spent his whole life, with legendary success, in the pursuit of personal glory, Achillean *kleos*; and until very recent times this was regarded as a wholly laudable aim. The empire he built collapsed the moment he was gone; he came as a conqueror and the work he wrought was destruction (p. 488).

Head of Alexander, from Pergamon, western Turkey, *c.* 200 B.C.E. (*Archaeological Museum, Istanbul*)

feelings might vary from city to city and from time to time. A sharp division intensified between urban high culture, now very much Hellenized throughout the empire, and the rural areas, which continued their traditional patterns of life without much change.

The empire allowed trade and culture to flow in all directions. Greek ships have been found as far west as the British Isles as well as in the Indian Ocean in the east. At Taxila, Ai Khanoum, Begram, and Merv, European, African, and Asian trade routes intersected. The Persians had begun to create an Asian–African–European ecumene, but Alexander carried the process further and deeper. Rome, already beginning to rise by the time of Alexander, would later extend a similar imperial mission throughout much of Europe to the west and north, although Rome would not control the east, as we shall see in Chapter 6.

EMPIRE-BUILDING:

WHAT DIFFERENCE DOES IT MAKE?

Mesopotamians, Egyptians, Persians, Greeks, and Macedonians launched their imperial ambitions from very different backgrounds. Mesopotamians and Greeks began as city-states, while Egyptians and Persians started as consolidated nations. Out of the fractious chaos of the Greek city-states

Macedon built its small state to imperial dimensions under a father and son who ruled as ambitious and skillful kings. Although our coverage was necessarily sketchy, we have seen that each empire erected a central capital; administered a government based in that center that could control the provinces; provided a uniform language, coinage, and legal system across the empire; constructed a road and communication network; articulated an ideology of empire that won the loyalty of many of its citizens and subjects; and created art and architecture to impress on friend and foe alike the power of the empire. Each assembled military forces to apply coercion where necessary.

A time finally came for each empire to rein in its ambitions and limit further expansion. Sometimes it reached the limit of its capacity to conquer and administer profitably; sometimes it was defeated in warfare; often it encountered a combination of both these humbling experiences.

The imperial armies of Alexander the Great refused to proceed to newer, more distant conquests beyond the Indus River. So he turned back toward home. Ironically, Alexander's school tutor had been the philosopher Aristotle, who had written: "To the size of states there is a limit" (*Politics*, VII:4; p. 1325). Aristotle's ideal political unit was the Greek city-state because it promoted the maximum personal participation in democratic government through intense social and political interaction among the citizens:

If the citizens of a state are to judge and to distribute offices according to merit, then they must know each other's characters; where they do not possess this

Dying Gaul, Roman copy in marble of a bronze original of c. 230–220 B.C.E. When Attalus I of Pergamum defeated an enemy force of Gauls, a series of statues showing dead or dying invaders was cast. This poignant example illustrates the many artistic developments in sculpture that epitomize Hellenistic Greece: a special emphasis on the portrayal of suffering and pain, dramatically conveyed through facial expression; a widening subject-matter (not merely male and female nudes); a twisting pose for the body; and a design that allows the composition to be viewed from all sides. (*Museo Capitolino, Rome*)

knowledge, both the election to offices and the decision of lawsuits will go wrong. When the population is very large they are manifestly settled at haphazard, which clearly ought not to be. (VII:4; p. 326)

In choosing to build an empire rather than a city-state, Alexander was neither the first nor the last student to disregard his teacher's advice. (Alexander wanted the Greek city-states to be self-governing, but he did not want other areas to have such powers.) Nor was Aristotle the first or last to weigh the relative merits of small, local democratic government units against those of large, centralized bureaucracies. Similar debates still go on in our own day. Debates over the usefulness, limits, and legitimacy of empire were also central to the political thought of ancient Rome, China, and India, the three huge empires that are the focus of Chapters 6, 7, and 8.

BIBLIOGRAPHY

Aristotle. *Basic Works*, ed and trans. Richard McKeon (New York: Random House, 1941).

Baines, John and Jaromir Malek. *Atlas of Ancient Egypt* (New York: Facts on File, 1980).

Bernal, Martin. *Black Athena: The Afroasiatic Roots of Classical Civilization* (New Brunswick, NJ: Rutgers University Press, 1987).

Green, Peter. *Alexander of Macedon* (Berkeley: University of California Press, 1991).

Hamilton, J.R. *Alexander the Great* (London: Hutchison University Library, 1973).

Hammond, Mason. *The City in the Ancient World* (Cambridge: Harvard University Press, 1972).

Hammond, N.G.L. *The Genius of Alexander the Great* (Chapel Hill: The University of North Carolina Press, 1997).

Herodotus. *The Persian Wars*, trans. George Rawlinson (New York: Modern Library, 1942).

Homer. *Iliad*, trans. Richmond Lattimore (Chicago: University of Chicago Press, 1951).

Homer. *Odyssey*, trans. Robert Fitzgerald (New York: Doubleday & Co., 1961).

Hornblower, Simon. *The Greek World 479–323 BC* (London: Methuen, 1983).

Keuls, Eva C. *The Reign of the Phallus: Sexual Politics in Ancient Athens* (New York: Harper and Row, 1985).

Levi, Peter. *Atlas of the Greek World* (New York: Facts on File Publications, 1982).

Mumford, Lewis. *The City in History* (New York: Harcourt, Brace and World, 1961).

O'Brien, John Maxwell. *Alexander the Great: The Invisible Enemy* (London: Routledge, 1992).

Past Worlds: The (London) Times Atlas of Archaeology (Maplewood, NJ: Hammond, Inc., 1988).

Plato. *Apology*, trans. F.J. Church (Indianapolis: Library of Liberal Arts, 1956).

—— *The Collected Dialogues of Plato*, ed. Edith Hamilton and Huntington Cairns (New York: Bollingen Foundation [distributed by Pantheon Books], 1961).

—— *The Republic of Plato*, trans. Francis MacDonald Cornford (New York: Oxford University Press, 1945).

Plutarch. *The Lives of the Noble Grecians and Romans*, trans. John Dryden, revised by Arthur Hugh Clough (New York: Modern Library, n.d.).

Postgate, J.N. *Early Mesopotamia* (London: Routledge, 1992).

Saggs, H.W.F. *The Might that Was Assyria* (London: Sidgwick & Jackson, 1984).

Sophocles. *Oedipus Rex and Oedipus at Collonus*, trans. Robert Fitzgerald in *The Oedipus Cycle* (San Diego: Harcourt Brace Jovanovich, 1969).

Tacitus. *The Annals of Imperial Rome*, trans. Michael Grant (Baltimore: Penguin Books, 1959).

Tarn, W.W. *Alexander the Great*. 2 Vols. (Cambridge: Cambridge University Press, 1948).

Thucydides. *History of the Peloponnesian War*, trans. Rex Warner (Harmondsworth: Penguin Books, 1972).

Time-Life Books. *Time Frame 3000–1500 BC: The Age of God-Kings* (Alexandria, VA: Time-Life Books, 1987).

—— *Time Frame 1500–600 BC: Barbarian Tides* (Alexandria, VA: Time-Life Books, 1987).

—— *Time Frame 600–400 BC: A Soaring Spirit* (Alexandria, VA: Time-Life Books, 1987).

—— *Time Frame 400 BC–AD 200: Empires Ascendant* (Alexandria, VA: Time-Life Books, 1987).

Wycherley, R.E. *How the Greeks Built Cities* (Garden City, NY: Anchor Books, 1969).

6 ROME AND THE BARBARIANS

750 B.C.E.–480 C.E.

". . . remember Romans, To rule the people under law, to establish the way of peace"

VIRGIL

"They create a desert and call it 'Peace.'"

TACITUS

FROM CONQUEST, COLONIZATION, AND ALLIANCE TO REVOLT, BANKRUPTCY, AND DISMEMBERMENT

THE EXTENT OF THE ROMAN EMPIRE

All roads, by land and sea, led to Rome. Situated on the Tiber River, not far from the sea and the river's intersection with Italy's north–south mountain chains, Rome served as a center of communication and trade for the Italian peninsula. To the sea that surrounds the peninsula, the Romans gave the name "Mediterranean," the middle of the earth, for the Mediterranean is surrounded by the three continents that were known to them: southern Europe, northern Africa, and western Asia. In time, Roman armies conquered and ruled an empire that radiated outward to encompass the Italian peninsula, the lands surrounding the Mediterranean, and many territories still more distant. They began to call the Mediterranean *Mare Nostrum* ("Our Sea").

At its greatest extent in the second century C.E., the Roman Empire sprawled over 2700 miles (4400 kilometers) east to west and 2500 miles (4000 kilometers) north to south, extending from Scotland to the Persian Gulf. It ruled between 70 and 100 million people of vastly diverse ethnic, racial, religious, and cultural roots. At its most powerful, between 27 B.C.E. and 180 C.E., Rome enforced the **Pax Romana**, the Roman peace, a reign of stability and relative tranquillity throughout all these vast regions.

FOUNDING THE REPUBLIC

The legendary date for the founding of the city of Rome is 753 B.C.E., and although this is probably not exact, it is approximately correct. For two and a half centuries the city was ruled by kings of neighboring Etruria, the land to Rome's north. The Romans learned much from these Etruscans about city building, art, religion, mythology, and even language. As Rome entered the Mediterranean trade networks of the Etruscans, merchants and craft workers immigrated to the city. The Etruscan king Servius Tullius (579–534 B.C.E.) reformed the military, creating the *Comitia centuriata*, a deliberative ruling council composed of representatives of the soldiers of Rome. This assembly of Roman citizens persisted for centuries after Etruscan rule had ended, reinforcing the connection between the armies of Rome and its government.

About 509 B.C.E., the wealthy, powerful, veteran citizens of Rome expelled the Etruscan kings. They declared Rome a **republic**, from the Latin **res publica**, public property, in contrast to its earlier status as the private property of the Etruscan kings. Although they overthrew the monarchy, the new oligarchs—the small, elite group of rulers—retained many other political institutions. Their armies remained the center of power. Because soldiers were expected to provide their own arms, only men with some wealth and property could command and rise in the ranks. They in turn were ordered by class, according to the quality and cost of the weapons they provided, and divided into military units called **centuries**, or groups of one hundred, as they had been under the Etruscans. The leaders of the centuries continued to meet together in assembly to elect magistrates and decide questions of peace and war.

THE ROMAN EMPIRE

DATE	POLITICAL	RELIGION AND CULTURE	SOCIAL DEVELOPMENT
500 B.C.E.	● Rome independent of Etruscan rule (509); republic founded		
450 B.C.E.	● Rome sacked by Gauls (390)		● Laws of Twelve Tables promulgated
350 B.C.E.	● Roman expansion into Italy south of Po (327–304)		
300 B.C.E.	● 1st Punic War (264–241)		● Earliest Roman coinage (280–75)
250 B.C.E.	● 2nd Punic War (218–201) ● Hannibal invaded Italy ● Roman conquest of Cisalpine Gaul (202–191)	● Stoicism – Zeno	
200 B.C.E.	● Rome annexed Spain (197) ● Conquest of Macedon (167)	● Polybius (200–118)	
150 B.C.E.	● 3rd Punic War (149–146) ● T. Gracchus tribune (133) ● G. Gracchus tribune (123 and 122) ● Gallia Narbonensis a Roman province	● Carthage destroyed ● Corinth destroyed	● Pax Romana led to widespread trade throughout Empire; roads built
100 B.C.E.	● Sulla conquers Greece ● Civil war in Rome (83–2) ● Conquest of Syria (66) ● 1st Triumvirate (60)		● Spartacus slave revolt (73–71)
50 B.C.E.	● Civil war (49) ● Caesar dictator (47–44) ● 2nd Triumvirate (43) ● Annexation of Egypt (30) ● Augustus Caesar (d. 14 C.E.)	● Cicero (d. 43) ● Virgil (d. 19) ● Augustus deified on his death ● Forum in Rome ● Livy (d. 17 C.E.)	

The magistrates, administrative and judicial officials, administered the Roman government. At the lowest level of **quaestor** they had limited financial authority. At the highest level, **consuls** held power that extended over all the lands Rome ruled. At each level, two officials were paired, so that they would have to consult with one another, and neither could seize excessive power. The power of the former kings, for example, was now shared between the two consuls in this new system of checks and balances. (In extraordinary emergencies, one man could be named as dictator for the limited term of six months.) As magistrates ended their one-year (renewable) term of office, they automatically entered the Senate of Rome, the highest legislative and consultative body of the government.

EXPANSION TO EMPIRE

The Conquest of Italy

The Roman Republic established alliances with other nearby city-states in Latium and began to challenge the Etruscans. In 405 B.C.E., the Romans besieged Veii, a principal city of the Etruscans only 12 miles (20 kilometers) from Rome, and captured it in 396 B.C.E. Although Rome itself was sacked by Celtic invaders (see p. 185) in 390 B.C.E., the setback was brief, and Rome's expansion continued. By 264 B.C.E., it controlled all of Italy south of the Po valley. In its expansion, Rome often offered its opponents a choice between alliance and conquest. Subsequently it bestowed various levels of

THE ROMAN EMPIRE

DATE	POLITICAL	RELIGION AND CULTURE	SOCIAL DEVELOPMENT
25 C.E.	• Christianity reaches Rome • Invasion of Britain (43)		
50 C.E.	• Trajan (98–117)	• Seneca (d. 65) • Destruction of Temple in Jerusalem (70) • Pompeii and Herculaneum buried by eruption of Vesuvius (79)	• Jewish revolt (66–73) • Roman women gain new rights
100 C.E.	• Dacia conquered by Trajan • Hadrian (117–38)	• Tacitus (d. 120) • Trajan's column and forum (112–113) • Pantheon in Rome • Hadrian's Wall	
150 C.E.	• Marcus Aurelius (161–180)	• Apuleius (d. c. 170) • Galen (d. 199)	
200 C.E.	• Caracalla (212–217) • Decius (249–51)	• Baths of Caracalla	• Roman citizenship for all males
250 C.E.	• Gallienus (253–268)	• Persecution of Christians	
300 C.E.	• Constantine (r. 306–337)	• Edict of Milan (313) • Constantinople inaugurated (330)	
350 C.E.		• St. Augustine (354–430) • End of state support for paganism (394)	
400 C.E.	• Sack of Rome (410)		
450 C.E.	• End of Roman Empire in West (476)		
550 C.E.			• Justinian codifies Roman law

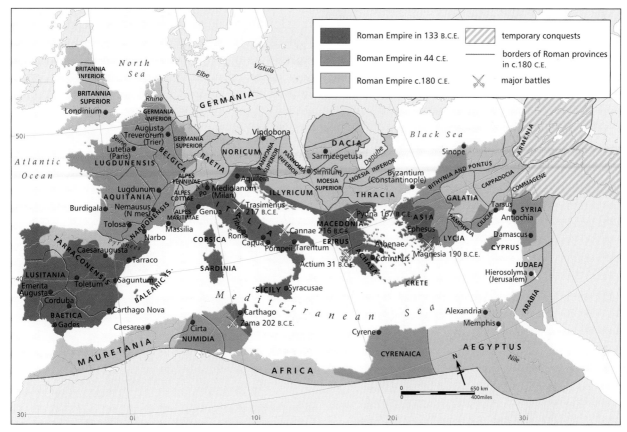

The Roman Empire Rome built its empire on military expansion, first within Italy by overthrowing its neighbors, then across the Mediterranean by defeating the Carthaginians, then northwest to Gaul and Britain and north to the Danube. Rome offered many benefits to the peoples it conquered, but finally its power rested in its armies.

Roman citizenship throughout Italy to induce its residents to support Rome and join its armies.

Roman armies, and a new navy designed to dominate the Mediterranean, continued to expand Roman rule. In the next 140 years Rome conquered Carthage, its arch-rival across the Mediterranean in north Africa; Cisalpine Gaul, the Celtic region of Italy between the Alps and the Po River; Macedonia and the city-states of Greece; most of Spain; and southern France (Gaul). Of these wars, the most bitter and the most decisive, were the three Punic Wars against Carthage, in 264–241, 218–201, and 149–146 B.C.E.

The Conquest of Carthage and the Western Mediterranean

Carthage, only 130 miles (210 kilometers) across the narrow waist of the Mediterranean from Italy, had developed as a trade outpost of Phoenician seafarers. Just as Rome had dominated Italy, the Carthaginians had dominated the north central coast of

Africa and the western Mediterranean. One of their trade networks had focused on the mineral wealth of Spain, especially its silver mines, and to protect that route, Carthage had developed ports and cities in Sicily and Sardinia. It controlled trade outposts even on the Italian mainland in Etruria. Carthage (in Latin Punicum—that is, "of the Phoenicians") and Rome were set on a collision course.

The fighting opened in Sicily in 264 B.C.E. By 241 B.C.E. when the first Punic War ended, Rome was victorious both on land and at sea. Four years later, Rome took advantage of a mutiny among Carthaginian troops in Sardinia to occupy both Sardinia and Corsica. In 227 B.C.E., it annexed them. For the first time, Rome had provinces outside the Italian peninsula. Carthage, however, rebuilt its forces, especially in Spain. When the Spanish city of Saguntum asked for Roman help, the Romans intervened and threatened Carthage's Spanish colonies. The brilliant, twenty-seven-year-old Carthaginan commander Hannibal (247–183 B.C.E.) defeated Rome's troops in 219 B.C.E., and the second

Punic War had begun. It continued for almost twenty years.

Hannibal unexpectedly took the offensive by land, marching tens of thousands of troops and thirty-seven elephants 1000 miles (1600 kilometers) along the French coast, over the Alps, into the Po valley and toward Rome. In two months he overran most of north Italy and destroyed the armies sent against him. But Hannibal could not break the power of Rome. Most of Rome's allies remained loyal and Rome raised new armies. Those cities that went over to Hannibal, like Capua, Syracuse, and Tarentum, were recaptured. Hannibal did annihilate a Roman army at Cannae in south Italy, but ultimately he was isolated there. Meanwhile, Rome won victories in Spain (211–206 B.C.E.), especially under the general Scipio Africanus. In 204 B.C.E.

Scipio invaded Africa. Hannibal returned to defend his homeland, but was defeated by Scipio at the Battle of Zama (202 B.C.E.) 75 miles (120 kilometers) southwest of Carthage. The war was over. Carthage became a dependency of Rome. In the Third Punic War (149–146 B.C.E.), Rome utterly destroyed Carthage (see Focus opposite).

Expansion into Spain and France

With the Carthaginian threat ended, Rome conquered the Gauls in Italy north of the Po and south of the Alps, 202–191 B.C.E., and annexed the territory. It annexed Spain in 197 B.C.E., but treated that province so harshly that constant revolts simmered until Rome finally crushed them in 133 B.C.E. In southern Gaul (France), Rome's ally Massilia

Capitoline Wolf, *c.* **500 B.C.E.** According to legend, Rome was founded by Romulus and Remus, twin sons of Mars, at the spot where they were rescued from the River Tiber and suckled by a she-wolf. The group of she-wolf with twins was adopted as the symbol of Rome, although the children in this particular statue were added almost two thousand years later, in the Renaissance. (*Museo Capitolino, Rome*)

"New Wisdom"–Rome's Policy of Brute Force

When, in 148 B.C.E., the Greek city-state of Corinth and its allies flouted Roman wishes, and even attacked Roman envoys, Rome razed Corinth to the ground, sold all its surviving inhabitants into slavery, and carried its artistic works to Rome. Similar brutality met Carthage's attempts to defend itself against Rome's treacherous African ally King Masinissa of Numidia. Disregarding Carthage's claims that its land was being encroached upon, Rome sided with its ally, provoked the third Punic War (149–146 B.C.E.), conquered Carthage, sold its survivors into slavery, and sowed salt into the soil so that it would never again flourish. As they had done in Macedonia and Greece, the Romans annexed their conquests, incorporating all of Carthage into the Roman province of Africa. Rome had become mistress of the Mediterranean, which the Romans began to call *Mare Nostrum*, "Our Sea."

Named the "New Wisdom," Rome's brutal use of military power served as a warning to potential foes. Roman generals were not pressed to win quick, brilliant victories, but to defeat the enemy through patient, deliberate preparation, and decisive force. Ideally, the enemy would be so awed by Roman forces that it would never dare oppose them. Indeed, the next addition to Rome's holdings came by inheritance when, in 133 B.C.E., the king of Pergamum in Asia Minor bequeathed his kingdom to Rome at his death.

(Marseille) asked for help against Gallic tribes and by 121 B.C.E. Rome had annexed most of southern France (modern Provence).

The Conquest of the Greeks: The Eastern Mediterranean

In the eastern Mediterranean, the Romans encountered Macedonians and Greeks, the proud heirs of Alexander the Great who still ruled the lands that he had conquered and Hellenized. Rome's first battle on Greek soil came in 200 B.C.E., and it began the complete restructuring of political power in the eastern Mediterranean. At the death of Alexander the Great in 323 B.C.E. his empire had divided into three regional kingdoms. In 203–202 B.C.E. two of these kingdoms, Macedonia and Syria, where the Seleucid dynasty ruled, combined to threaten the third, Egypt, where the Ptolemaic family ruled. Neighboring Greek city-states encouraged Rome to use these divisions to establish its own balance of power in the region. Rome accepted the invitation, warning Macedonia not to interfere in Greek affairs. Philip V of Macedon rejected this warning, but was defeated. In victory, the Romans declared the Greek city-states of the eastern Mediterranean "free," granting them nominal independence, but, in fact, placing them under Roman control.

Rome had similarly warned Antiochus III, the Great, of Syria to stay out of Europe and Egypt. When Antiochus ignored the warning, he was crushed, pushed back to Syria, and forced to pay a huge indemnity.

In the next generation, Philip V's son Perseus (r. 179–168 B.C.E.) was defeated decisively at Pydna in 168 B.C.E. ending the Macedonian monarchy. Also in 168 B.C.E. Rome again protected Egypt from the Seleucids, asserting its own control of the eastern Mediterranean. Rome was now the dominant power throughout the Mediterranean.

The Conquest of Northwestern Europe

During the entire period of the Roman Empire, numerous ethnic and tribal groups were on the move throughout Europe, especially northern Europe. These included a variety of Germanic groups—Ostrogoths, Visigoths, Franks, Vandals, and Lombards—as well as Celts and Huns. By the third century B.C.E. some of the German groups were settling into village life and beginning to establish small tribal states in central and northern

Europe, but as more groups continued to push in from Central Asia, including the ferocious Huns, northern and central Europe remained in constant flux. Tribes migrated, fought each other, and constantly pressed on the Roman frontiers. Dealing with all these Barbarian groups was one of Rome's greatest challenges.

Northern Gaul (modern France) seemed stably divided among various Gallic and Celtic peoples until the Helvetii, Celts driven out of Switzerland, began to invade. In response, Julius Caesar (100–44 B.C.E.), the Roman commander in north Italy and southern Gaul, moved with his army into central and northern Gaul. Caesar's *Gallic Wars* tells of his conquests in 58–52 B.C.E. By the time his campaigns ended in 49 B.C.E., all Gaul belonged to Rome.

Completing the Conquests: The Empire at its Zenith

In the east, the general Pompey (106–48 B.C.E.) added Syria and most of Asia Minor to the empire in 66 B.C.E. In 63 B.C.E. he captured Jerusalem, the capital of Judaea, although he allowed a Jewish king to rule as a client-monarch. Pompey favored such indirect rule through local potentates throughout the east, where sophisticated governmental structures had existed for centuries. He also founded some forty cities as centers of Roman political influence.

The richest state in the east, Egypt, remained quasi-independent. As he fought in the civil war after the assassination of Julius Caesar in 44 B.C.E.,

PROFILE
Augustus Caesar
EMPEROR

Julius Caesar (c. 100–44 B.C.E.) seized control of the Senate of Rome and became dictator in 47 b.c.e., but three years later he was assassinated. His adopted son and heir was his grandnephew Octavian, who took the new name of Gaius [son of] Julius Caesar. By 30 B.C.E., he had defeated his rivals and enemies—Brutus, Mark Anthony, Cleopatra—to become master of a re-unified Roman world. A grateful Senate heaped him with honors, including in 27 B.C.E. the title "Augustus," meaning "sacred" or "venerable." His achievements were immense and after his death, the Romans made Augustus a god.

Under one name or another, Augustus ruled Rome for fifty-six years until his death in 14 B.C.E. He fought wars that stabilized the borders of the empire while ensuring peace and facilitating trade, commerce, and economic growth throughout the Mediterranean. He restructured imperial administration into a form that lasted for almost two centuries. He inaugurated public projects that beautified Rome and kept its workers employed. He pacified the Roman masses and won over the aristocracy. He patronized the arts and literature, which flourished in Rome's Golden Age. He built new roads and cities throughout the length and breadth of the empire.

Augustus instituted conservative policies affecting religion and family life. He introduced incentives for producing children and enforced laws against adultery. He believed in the authority of men over women and forced his daughter Julia into three devastatingly unhappy marriages. In the face of the general religious skepticism and indifference of the Roman upper classes, Augustus rebuilt temples and encouraged the worship of ancestral gods.

Our primary sources on Augustus' life are limited, and almost all of his own autobiography has been lost. Therefore, the "Res Gestae Divi Augusti," or account of the accomplishments of Augustus, has become a crucial text. Written for the people of Rome by Augustus himself shortly before he died and inscribed on several temples throughout the empire, it records the emperor's own statement of how he wanted to be remembered. Its thirty-five paragraphs fall into three sections: the offices and honors bestowed on him; his personal donations for public purposes; and his accomplishments in war and peace:

the Roman general Mark Antony (*c.* 82–30 B.C.E.) established his headquarters in Egypt. Antony betrayed Rome by sharing local rule with Cleopatra, queen of Egypt (r. 51–30 B.C.E.). Octavian (63 B.C.E.–14 C.E.), Julius Caesar's adopted son and designated heir, defeated Antony and Cleopatra at the Battle of Actium in 31 B.C.E., formally annexed Egypt, and won the title of Emperor Augustus Caesar (see Profile below).

As the empire continued to expand through military conquests, Rome's generals demanded, and were granted, increasing powers until, with Augustus, they supplanted republican, civilian government with an administration headed by the commander-in-chief. Before we analyze the significance of this political transformation, however, let us complete our account of the continuing geographical expansion of the empire.

Augustus annexed Switzerland, Austria, and Bavaria in 16–15 B.C.E. and established Rome's historical frontier in central Europe at the Danube River. After an attempt to conquer central Germany failed in 9 C.E., the Rhine became the normal border in the northeast.

England and Wales were conquered in the 40s C.E. and became the Roman province of Britain. Some 2000 miles (3200 kilometres) to the east, the Emperor Trajan (r. 98–117 C.E.) conquered Dacia, modern Romania, and briefly annexed Armenia and Parthia (Mesopotamia).

Trajan's successor, Hadrian (117–138 C.E.), consolidated Roman gains. He permanently withdrew

1. At the age of nineteen, on my own initiative and at my own expense, I raised an army by means of which I liberated the Republic. . . . the people elected me consul and a triumvir for the settlement of the commonwealth . . . .
3. I waged many wars throughout the whole world by land and by sea, ... and when victorious I spared all citizens who sought pardon. . . . About 500,000 Roman citizens were under military oath to me.
15. To the Roman plebs I paid 300 sesterces apiece in accordance with the will of my father [Julius Caesar]; and in my fifth consulship [29 B.C.E.] I gave each 400 sesterces in my own name out of the spoil of war, reaching never less than 250,000 persons . . . . In the eighteenth year of my tribunician power and my twelfth consulship [29 B.C.E.] I gave out of the spoils of war 1,000 sesterces apiece to my soldiers settled in colonies . . . . received by about 120,000 persons. . . . In my thirteenth consulship [2 B.C.E.] I gave sixty denar-ii apiece to those of the plebs who at that time were receiving public grain. . . . a little more than 200,000 persons.

19. I built. . . the senate house and. . . the temple of Apollo. . . .
22. I gave a gladiatorial show three times in my own name, and five times in the names of my sons or grandsons; at these shows about 10,000 fought. . . . Twenty-six times I provided for the people . . . hunting spectacles of African wild beasts in the circus or in the Forum or in the amphitheaters. . . .
23. I turned over to their masters for punishment nearly 30,000 slaves who had run away from their owners and taken up arms against the state.
28. I established colonies of soldiers in Africa, Sicily, Macedonia, in both Spanish provinces, in Achaea, Asia, Syria, Narbonese Gaul, and Pisidia. Italy, moreover, has twenty-eight colonies established by me which grew large and prosperous in my lifetime. . . .
31. Royal embassies from India, never previously seen before any Roman general, were often sent to me. . . .
(Lewis and Reinhold, Vol. I, pp. 561-572)

Augustus of Prima Porta, **early 1st century** C.E. (*Musei Vaticani, Rome*)

the Roman forces from Mesopotamia back to the Euphrates and he built a wall west to east across the narrow neck of England in the northern part of Britain. Twenty-five years later, his successor, Antoninus Pius, built another wall some 50 miles (80 kilometers) further north. The limits of the Roman Empire had been reached.

IMPERIAL ROME: HOW DO WE KNOW?

Multiple Perspectives

Thus far we have studied the expansion of Rome from city-state to imperial power. On pages 172–94 we will analyze the institutions of the empire, its decline and fall, and its significance. Here we pause to examine the sources of information on which this history is based.

The earliest years of Rome's history are shrouded in legends. The most famous of these sets the founding of the city in 753 B.C.E. From that time Rome was ruled by Etruscan kings from the neighboring northern area of Etruria until they were expelled in 509 B.C.E. and a self-governing republic was established in Rome, its government elected by the citizens. The city was sacked by invading Celts in 390 B.C.E., and most of the records preserved until that time were lost. The only surviving traces are segments incorporated into accounts recorded by historians following the invasion. Most of what has been preserved are lists of rulers, at first the kings but later the chief elected officials: consuls, **praetors**, and **tribunes**.

During the later republic historians began consciously to write the history of the city. The most famous of the early historians was Polybius (*c.* 200–*c.* 118 B.C.E.), a Greek brought to Rome as a political captive. Polybius narrated the overwhelming event of his own time, Rome's conquest of an empire through its victories over Carthage, Macedonia, and Spain:

> There can surely be no one so petty or so apathetic in his outlook that he has no desire to discover by what means and under what system of government the Romans succeeded in less than fifty-three years [220–167 B.C.E.] in bringing under their rule almost the whole of the inhabited world, an achievement which is without parallel in human history. (*The Histories* I:1; p. 443, cited in Finley)

Column of Trajan, Rome. Dedicated 113 C.E. The Romans built tall commemorative columns in order to celebrate the power and military might of the empire. The Column of Trajan is covered by a continuous strip of carving that tells the story of the Emperor Trajan's victories over the barbarian tribes along the Danube.

The Roman aqueduct at Segovia, Spain, early first or second century C.E. Unlike the Greeks, the Romans are remembered less for their art than for their great engineering feats. The need to improve the water supply to Roman settlements increased along with urban population growth. The popularity of the public bathing houses heightened the demand even more. The Romans developed a massive network of aqueducts to channel water into cities across uneven terrain.

Livy (59 B.C.E.–17 C.E.) praised the glories of Rome's later expansion to imperial dimensions, but he decried the class conflict between Rome's aristocrats and its common people that was ripping apart Rome's self-governing, elected, republican form of government.

Tacitus (*c*. 55–120 C.E.) continued the story to the height of imperial power. He praised the heroism of the Roman conquerors, but he also understood the anguish and bitterness of the conquered peoples. In *Agricola*, Tacitus attributes to the Celtic chieftain Calgacus one of the most devastating critiques of imperialism ever articulated. In Tacitus' account, Calgacus condemns

the Romans, whose tyranny cannot be escaped by any act of reasonable submission. These brigands of the world have exhausted the land by their rapacity,

Arch of Trajan, Benevento, 114–117 C.E. Triumphal arches are another peculiarly Roman means of celebrating the power of the ruler and his empire. This particular arch, dedicated to Trajan, stands at the point where the road to Brindisi, a port on the east coast, branches off the Appian Way, the first major road in the Romans' strategic network.

so they now ransack the sea. When their enemy is rich, they lust after wealth; when the enemy is poor, they lust after power. Neither East nor West has satisfied their hunger. They are unique among humanity insofar as they equally covet the rich and the poor. Robbery, butchery, and rapine they call "Empire." They create a desert and call it "Peace."

(I:129, cited in Andrea and Overfield)

Other historians also illuminated the empire from its fringes rather than from its center, and they, too, were often critical of the effects of empire on its subjects. For Jewish historians, such as Philo of Alexandria (*c.* 13 B.C.E.–*c.* 45 C.E.) and Josephus (*c.* 37–*c.* 100 C.E.), as for Christian theologians, such as Tertullian (*c.* 155–*c.* 225 C.E.) and Augustine, bishop of Hippo in north Africa (354–430 C.E.), the Roman Empire was not the central concern, but it was an inescapable presence. They had to take account of Rome in their own teaching, writing, and actions (see p. 321), and although they were not prepared to praise the empire, they counseled accommodation rather than direct military opposition. They wrote of coping with Rome's power from their own marginal positions.

As the empire began to decay, more mainstream historians became critical. Dio Cassius (*c.* 150–*c.* 235 C.E.) nostalgically recalled the rule of Augustus as Rome's golden age and lamented the empire's subsequent decline "from a monarchy of gold to one of iron and rust."

In addition to these formal histories, leading men of the empire often left important documents that shed light on their times. The great orator and political leader Cicero (106–43 B.C.E.) left dozens of letters, fifty-seven public speeches, and extensive writings on public affairs. Julius Caesar's account of the *Gallic Wars* describes his military organization and strategy, the Roman virtues that characterized his troops, and the land and the peoples against which he fought. In part, this was a propaganda piece, preparing the path for Caesar's assertion of personal power in Rome.

Rome has also bequeathed rich material artifacts. Much of the infrastructure of the empire—its roads, aqueducts, stadiums, public baths, forums, temples, triumphal arches—as well as substantial parts of many of the military camps and cities it constructed still stand. Roman coinage and statuary are everywhere. The cities of Pompeii (see Spotlight, pp. 170-1) and Herculaneum, comprising a total population of about 20,000, were buried in dust and cinders in the volcanic eruption of Mount Vesuvius in 79 C.E., giving, when they began to be uncovered in the eighteenth century, an unparalleled view of the city's structure and furnishings. Off-shore, archaeologists have uncovered sunken ships in the Italian Mediterranean that shed light on Roman trade missions and their cargoes. They have also been able to reconstruct *latifundia*, rural estates that were controlled by rich owners who bought up family farms and ran them as plantations.

Archaeological digs also uncover the history of the many Gothic, Celtic, and other groups of migrating peoples who lived on the fringes of the empire, later settled within its territories, and finally established their own states on those lands as the empire was dismembered. Their settlements, burial grounds, tools, and artwork yield significant information about their lives,

ROMAN EMPERORS

Augustus (27 B.C.E.–14 C.E.)

Julio-Claudian dynasty	Tiberius (14–37)
	Caligula (37–41)
	Claudius (41–54)
	Nero (54–68)
Flavian dynasty	Vespasian (69–79)
	Titus (79–81)
	Domitian (81–96)
Age of the Antonines	Nerva (96–98)
	Trajan (98–117)
	Hadrian (117–138)
	Antoninus Pius (138–161)
	Marcus Aurelius (161–180)
	Commodus (180–193)
Severan dynasty	Septimius Severus (193–211)
	Caracalla (212–217)
	Elagabalus (218–222)
	Severus Alexander (222–235)
The late empire	Philip the Arabian (244–249)
	Decius (249–251)
	Gallus (251–253)
	Valerian (253–260)
	Gallienus (253–268)
	Claudius (268–270)
	Aurelian (270–275)
	Tacitus (275–276)
	Florian (276)
	Probus (276–282)
	Carus (282–283)
	Numerianus (283–284) and Carinus (283–285)
	Diocletian (284–305)

SPOTLIGHT *Pompeii*

A ROMAN TOWN

The volcano Vesuvius erupted on August 24, 79 C.E., burying the town of Pompeii, and its smaller neighbor Herculaneum, under 13 feet (4 meters) of pumice stone, ash, and gravel. Some of the town's 10,000 inhabitants fled on the first day of the eruption, escaping with their lives. Those who did not were trapped in the next two days' rain of volcanic ash. The ash cooled and solidified around them, so archaeologists have been able to recover their forms by pouring concrete into the molds left where their bodies decayed. **Figure 2** indicates that dogs as well as human beings suffered.

Although covered over, the fate of Pompeii was known through the eyewitness account of Pliny the Younger:

They debated whether to stay indoors or take their chance in the open, for the buildings were now shaking with violent shocks, and seemed to be swaying to and fro as if they were torn from their foundations. Outside, on the other hand, there was the danger of falling pumice-stones, even though they were light and porous; however, after

Figure 1 Temple of Apollo, Pompeii, with Vesuvius in the background.

comparing the risks, they chose the latter.*

Archaeologists began to excavate Herculaneum in 1783, Pompeii in 1765. Preserved like time capsules, these cities revealed their urban design, buildings, furniture, and household objects. Pompeii was walled, with seven gates, and housed a forum, council chamber, offices of magistrates, temples dedicated to Apollo and Jupiter, market buildings, a stock exchange, law court, theater, auditoria, an amphitheater for gladiatorial contests and wild beast hunts, three Turkish-style baths, workshops, shops, brothels, and homes. **Figure 1** resurrects the Temple of Apollo and shows Vesuvius, still active to this day, in the background. Carbonized food, preserved and sealed in hot volcanic mud, suggests the everyday menus of the inhabitants. Walls, surviving to their full

Figure 3 The young Hercules wrestling with a snake, fresco, House of the Vettii, Pompeii.

Figure 2

Cast of the body of a watch dog, Pompeii.

height, have preserved vivid murals from the residences and businesses, the best of them since carried off to the National Museum in Naples. We have already seen, on pp. 152–3, one of the most valuable and beautiful of the Pompeii mosaics, depicting the victory of Alexander the Great over Darius at the Battle of Issus. Since this mosaic itself copies an earlier, lost painting from about 300 B.C.E. its preservation is especially fortunate.

The murals on the walls of many homes reflect both opulence and cultured taste. Those in the house of the Vettii **(figure 3)** present scenes from Greek mythology. Specific elements also allude to contemporary Roman interests and power; for example, the eagle at the top center position in the painting symbolizes the might of the Roman army.

* Cited in Paul G. Bahn, *The Cambridge Illustrated History of Archaeology*, p.59.

even though they had no writing systems until they learned from the Romans.

With such extensive artifacts complementing the rich documentary record, scholars can reconstruct the rise and fall of the Roman Empire and its relationships with neighboring peoples. As new topics are explored, such as the extent of slavery, the treatment of women, and the patron–client relationship, relatively abundant materials provide the raw materials to answer new questions.

THE INSTITUTIONS OF EMPIRE: FROM REPUBLICAN ROME TO IMPERIAL ROME

MILITARY POWER

From its beginning, Rome was a military state. According to one legend, its founders, Romulus and Remus, were sons of Mars, the god of war. An alternative legend, described in Virgil's *Aeneid*, which was written during the age of Augustus, depicted Rome as founded by Aeneas, one of the heroes of Troy.

Rome's armies were central to its life and it excelled in military organization and technology. Its professional armed legions proved superior even to the Greek phalanxes. Although it had never possessed a navy, Rome built one that conquered Carthage, the greatest seapower of the day. Coming against great walled towns in the east, it developed unprecedented machinery to besiege the walls, catapult firepower into them, and batter them down. Confronting groups of migrating Goths, it created new, mobile cavalry units to supplement its more conventional legions.

To be a free man was to serve as an officer in the army. Within Italy, captured city-states were required to supply not gold and taxes but men for the armies. At the time of Julius Caesar, the average Italian male served seven years in the army. Under Augustus, soldiering became more professional: men enlisted for between sixteen and twenty-five years. Conquered peoples outside of Italy also contributed troops to Rome's armies. The Barbarians who invaded the empire were often encouraged to settle in Roman territories and to enlist in Roman armies. A spiral of imperial expansion resulted. As Rome expanded, so did its armed forces; it then expanded further in part to capture the wealth to pay its larger armies; this expansion, in turn, enlarged its armies once more.

In the field, the soldiers built their support systems: strings of fortress watch-towers along all the borders, military camps, administrative towns, roads, and aqueducts. Roman engineering feats astonished the world in their day, and many of them remain to astonish us as well. Many of the walled military camps were kernels from which sprouted later towns and cities, one of Rome's most distinctive contributions. These urban outposts established Rome's military and administrative rule in the midst of rural, even nomadic, regions. In the reign of Augustus, these nodes were linked by 50,000 miles (80,000 kilometers) of first-class roads and 200,000 miles (320,000 kilometers) of lesser roads.

Rome's military leaders were at first constrained by the aristocratic senate and the general assembly of Rome. Later, the generals began giving the orders. General Gaius Marius campaigned to have himself elected consul in 107 B.C.E. He broke with the normal practice of recruiting only troops who owned property, and accepted soldiers who were indebted to him personally for their maintenance. Elected consul six times between 107 and 100 B.C.E., Marius restructured the armies into more efficient organizations. He arranged large allotments of land for veteran soldiers in north Africa, Gaul, Sicily, Greece, and Macedonia. The armies now depended for their welfare on him rather than on the state.

The generals began to compete among themselves for power, instigating civil war in Rome. To fight against Mithridates IV, king of Pontus, the Roman Senate called on a new general, Sulla. Marius, however, arranged to have the command transferred to himself. In response, Sulla rallied soldiers loyal to him and invaded Rome, initiating the first civil war. He declared Marius an outlaw and left with his troops for Greece, where he defeated Mithridates. Meanwhile Marius, joined by another general, Cinna, seized Rome and banned Sulla. Sulla returned with his army, invaded Italy and Rome, and had himself declared dictator, a position he held for two years, and then abdicated.

Twenty years later, in 60 B.C.E., two great generals, Julius Caesar and Pompey, and Crassus, a wealthy businessman who aspired to generalship, formed a "**triumvirate**" to rule. The three competed among themselves until Caesar won out. Caesar ruled as dictator from 47 until 44 B.C.E., when he was assassinated by rivals who felt he had usurped too much power. Caesar's successor, Augustus (63 B.C.E.–14 C.E.), was also a military hero who triumphed in civil wars. He, too, was part of a "triumvirate," until he defeated his rival Mark Antony, ending another civil war.

With Augustus Rome became an imperial monarchy, a government ruled by a single military commander, the imperator, or Emperor and his armies. For years generals had wanted this centralized power. Now, in gratitude, the Senate was willing to turn it over to Augustus. Augustus rejected the title of monarch, preferring to be called "princeps," or "first citizen." This gesture of humility fooled no one. With Augustus' reign, the imperial form of government begins even though the Senate and the consuls and other magistrates survived. From Augustus on, all real power in the Roman state lay in the hands of the Emperor.

As the size and wealth of the empire grew, many Romans felt that they had conquered the world but lost their souls. They spoke not of victory, but of loss. The historian Livy, writing at the height of the age of Augustus, lamented the end of innocence:

> with the gradual relaxation of discipline, morals first gave way, as it were, then sank lower and lower, and finally began the downward plunge which has brought us to the present time, when we can endure neither our vices nor the cure.
>
> (Lewis and Reinhold, Vol. I, p. 8)

Livy proclaimed the widely held myth of an older, golden age of simplicity which had been lost:

> No state was ever greater, none more righteous or richer in good examples, nor ever was where avarice and luxury came into the social order so late, or where humble means and thrift were so highly esteemed and so long held in honor. For true it is that the less men's wealth was, the less was their greed. Of late, riches have brought in avarice, and excessive pleasures the longing to carry wantonness and license to the point of personal ruin and universal destruction.
>
> (Lewis and Reinhold, Vol. I, p. 8)

This nostalgia for the past had two related, but different versions. One drew on examples from the days of simple, rustic equality before the advent of the Etruscan kings. It condemned the maltreatment of the plebeians and the slaves at the hands of the patricians that had begun under Etruscan rule and intensified under the Republic. The other regretted the later transfer of power from the Senate to the generals. It wished to recreate the days of the oligarchic, patrician republic.

CLASS AND CLASS CONFLICT

Class and class conflict, however, were a staple of Rome's history. The system of government under the early Republic had included only about 7 to 10 percent of the population: the wealthy, the powerful, and some with hereditary ties to Rome. The overwhelming majority, those without property or long-standing ties, and, of course, slaves and women, could not serve as officers in the military and were thus excluded from government. The two classes, patricians, (from the Latin "pater," father) and "plebeians," commoners without hereditary ties to the state, had become increasingly polarized under Etruscan rule, as the patricians forbade intermarriage with the plebeians and monopolized the magistracies, the Senate, and even the religious offices of the state. In response the plebeians had looked to the Etruscan king as their protector. The fall of the monarchy reduced the status of the plebeians still further.

The Struggle of the Orders, the conflict between patricians and plebeians, marked more than a half century—494 to 440 B.C.E.—of the early republic. The plebeians relied on their ultimate strengths: their bodies and their numbers. They were the foot soldiers of Rome, and their periodic boycotts of the patricians, by withdrawing to the Aventine Hill, threatened the city of Rome itself. In 451 B.C.E., in an attempt to resolve the conflict, a commission of ten patricians codified Rome's laws into Twelve Tables. The patricians were pleased with their apparent liberality, but the plebeians were horrified when they recognized the force of all the laws that were imposed upon them. Slowly, under pressure, the patricians yielded power, and the first plebeian consul was elected in 360 B.C.E. A series of measures to relieve debt was also passed, although indebtedness continued to be a problem throughout Roman history.

Patriarchs, Patrons, and Clients

Asymmetrical power relationships characterized all of Roman life under the Republic. The earliest enduring social structure in Rome was the patron–client relationship. Strong men acted as protectors of the weak; the weak, in turn, provided services for the strong as requested. The same relationship structured the family. The father of the family, the paterfamilias, had the right of life and death over his children as long as he lived. In reality, fathers were not tyrants, and in exercising the

FOCUS

Gender Relationships

According to Roman custom and practice, woman's role was subordinate to man's. Subject to her father throughout his life, a woman was, after his death, required to obey the advice of her husband or a legally appointed guardian in any kind of legal or business transactions. (In practice, if she had reached adulthood, she usually gained her independence at the death of her father, as did her brothers.) Marriages were arranged by the families of the bride and groom. Motherhood was considered the most significant rite of passage for women, and free-born women were exempted from having a guardian after giving birth to three children, freed women after four.

Women were respected if they lived chastely and more or less contentedly within these guidelines of family, motherhood, and domesticity. The feminine ideal was the faithful and loyal *univira*, the "one-man woman." A woman caught in adultery was banished from her home and might well be executed; men apprehended in adultery were not punished. Women found drinking wine could also be punished; again, men could not. These principles of behavior were, of course, fully applicable only to the upper classes. The masses of lower-class free women entered the working world outside the home, and slaves had little control over their lives. The prevalence of prostitution further indicated the

limited applicability of the Roman female ideal. The excavation of Pompeii has uncovered seven brothels.

At times even upper-class women escaped the constraints. The growth of urban life, especially in the capital at Rome in the first century B.C.E., offered new opportunities to a few upper-class Roman women to gain education and even to participate in public life, although sometimes behind the scenes. New marriage laws enabled them to live as equals of their husbands and gave them the right to divorce and to act without reference to a legal guardian. Women did not, however, have access to the professions or to public political office.

Augustus sought to restore the earlier family order. He made adultery a criminal offense, punishable by exile, confiscation of property, and even execution. Indeed, he exiled his own daughter and only child, Julia, for sexual profligacy. He encouraged marriage and childbearing and punished celibacy. These laws were widely disobeyed and opposed, but they reveal to us the link in Augustus' mind between a well-ordered family and a well-ordered empire, a link that was repeated in the official policies of many empires throughout history. (Compare China and India in Chapters 7 and 8, Britain in Chapter 16, Japan in Chapter 17, and Germany in Chapter 18.)

Mosaic of Neptune and Amphitrite (detail), Herculaneum, before 79 C.E. Art sometimes seems to contradict the legal evidence concerning gender relationships in the Roman Empire. The artist responsible for this mosaic of the sea-god Neptune and his wife Amphitrite has accorded the couple an apparent equality.

right to choose their children's occupations and spouses, and to control their economic possessions, they would normally try to consider their needs and desires. Nevertheless, fathers had the legal power to act as they wished: they continued to have control over their daughters' economic lives even after their marriages, for these rights did not pass to the husbands (see Focus, opposite). These rights were enshrined in the law of patria potestas, the right of the head of the household. Similar patron–client relationships later characterized imperial control over conquered provinces. They were the Roman way.

Imperial expansion exacerbated class conflicts within Rome. The benefits of the conquests went mostly to the rich, while the yeoman farmers, who supplied the troops, were often bankrupted by the wars. After serving in the army for years, they would return home to find that in their absence their wives and children had not been able to maintain the family farms and might even have sold them to owners of large estates, *latifundia*, and left for the city, impoverished.

Urban Splendor and Squalor

Class divisions were most glaring in the capital. The city of Rome itself grew seemingly without limit and without adequate planning. As it came to control Italy and then the Mediterranean, Rome's population multiplied, reaching 1 million by about the first century C.E. Some of the newcomers were wealthy and powerful, and they adorned the city, adding new examples of Greek architecture and urban design to the earlier Etruscan forms. They replaced wood, mud, and local volcanic rock with concrete and finer stone. Augustus himself boasted that he had found Rome a city of brick and left it one of marble. The poor also came streaming into the city, but from bankrupt family farms. For them, Rome was a nightmare. Lewis Mumford, the historian of urbanization, highlighted the contrast:

> The houses of the patricians, spacious, airy, sanitary, equipped with bathrooms and water closets, heated in winter by hypocausts, which carried hot air through chambers in the floors, were perhaps the most commodious and comfortable houses built for a temperate climate anywhere until the twentieth century; a triumph of domestic architecture. But the tenements of Rome easily take the prize for being the most crowded and insanitary buildings produced in Western Europe until the sixteenth

century. . . . Not only were these buildings unheated, unprovided with waste pipes or water closets, unadapted to cooking; not merely did they contain an undue number of airless rooms, indecently over-crowded: though poor in all the facilities that make for decent daily living, they were in addition so badly built and so high that they offered no means of safe exit from the frequent fires that occurred. And if their tenants escaped typhoid, typhus, fire, they might easily meet their death in the collapse of the whole structure. Such accidents were all too frequent.

These buildings and their people constituted the core of imperial Rome, and that core was rotten. As Rome grew and its system of exploitation turned more and more parasitic, the rot ate into ever larger masses of urban tissue. The main population of the city that boasted its world conquests lived in cramped, noisy, airless, foul-smelling, infected quarters, paying extortionate rents to merciless landlords, undergoing daily indignities and terrors that coarsened and brutalized them, and in turn demanded compensatory outlets. These outlets carried the brutalization even further, in a continuous carnival of sadism and death.
(pp. 220–21)

Attempts at Reform

Mumford refers to the "bread and circuses" that characterized Rome from the time of the reforming Gracchi brothers, Tiberius Sempronius (163–133 B.C.E.) and Gaius Sempronius (153–121 B.C.E.). As tribune of the people in 133 B.C.E., Tiberius proposed distributing some public lands among the poor, especially among poor soldiers. Opposed to this liberal proposal and fearing that Gracchus was attempting to gain too much political power for himself, a number of senators, supported by their clients, clubbed Tiberius and 300 of his supporters to death. This was the first political murder over a public policy issue in Rome in nearly 400 years. Despite the murder, the redistribution of public land did take place.

In 123 B.C.E., Gaius Gracchus was elected tribune. He extended his brother's plan for land redistribution by establishing colonies for the resettlement of some of the poor people of Rome, as well as for their commercial advancement, in the regions conquered in the Punic Wars, including Carthage itself. He also introduced subsidized grain sales to the poor people of Rome. Gaius' measure was later expanded into a dole of free bread for the poor people of Rome. Gaius argued that citizenship should be granted to all Latins and to the local civic officials in all other communities.

He was not equally sensitive to the problems of non-Italians, however, for his legislation exploited the provinces by enabling Roman knights to serve as "publicans" or tax farmers. These tax farmers struck an agreement with the state to turn over a fixed amount of net taxes while retaining the right to collect from their region as much as they were able and to keep the balance for themselves. Tax farming enabled the state to collect taxes without monitoring the process; it enabled the tax farmers to become wealthy; and it exploited the people

SOURCE

Romes's Code of Laws: Two Contrasting Perspectives

Rome's incipient international law has been described by modern historians from two very different perspectives. Michael Grant, Fellow of Trinity College, Cambridge, describes the written law in glowing terms as:

> one of the most potent and effective ideas that the Romans ever originated. . . . It demonstrated that a body of law could be established upon a foundation acceptable to the members of different peoples and races at any and every phase of social, economic, and political evolution; and so it brought the laws of the Romans nearer to universal applicability than any others that have ever been devised, and it uniquely displayed their genius for social organization. (Grant, pp. 104–5)

Nicholas Purcell, on the other hand, writing in the *Oxford History of the Classical World*, acknowledges the majesty of Roman law in theory, but emphasizes the perversion of the law in practical application.

> The law was not always sufficiently universal, and the underprivileged might well not reap its benefits. Jewish nationalist writers, for example, compare the hypocrisy of Rome to the ambiguous associations of the unclean pig: "Just as a pig lies down and sticks out its trotters as though to say 'I am clean' [because they are cloven], so the evil empire robs and oppresses while pretending to execute justice." (Boardman et al., p. 582)

Purcell cites Juvenal, the satirist, on the inability of law to curb the arbitrary violence of Roman soldiers:

> Your teeth are shattered? Face hectically inflamed, with great black welts? You know the doctor wasn't too optimistic about the eye that was left. But it's not a bit of good your running to the courts about it. If you've been beaten up by a soldier, better keep it to yourself. (Cited in Boardman et al., 575)

Legal theory and practice did not always coincide in ancient Rome (just as they do not always coincide today). The poor did not receive the same protection and benefits as the rich, soldiers abused their authority, and laws were not always applied consistently. Even Grant concedes the persistent class bias of Roman law:

> Roman law, despite all its concern for equity, had always favored the upper echelon of society, from which its own practitioners originated; and now, from the time of Trajan or Hadrian onwards, such preferential treatment became crystallized in legal forms. This greater explicitness was ominous, for . . . it confirmed the depressed status of the underprivileged and thus deepened the basic rift that in the following centuries would help bring the empire down. (Grant, p. 325)

Revolt and Suppression

Roman power reinforced Roman hegemony. Revolt often simmered in the conquered territories, especially among the most exploited. Augustus' own account of his actions noted: "I pacified the sea by suppressing piracy. In that struggle I turned over to their masters for punishment nearly 30,000 fugitive slaves who had taken up arms against the state" (Lewis and Reinhold, I: 569). Three great slave revolts wracked the empire, two of them before Augustus, one after: 70,000 slaves resorted to armed resistance in the Great Slave War in Sicily, 134–131 B.C.E.; a second revolt in Sicily, 104–100 B.C.E., broke out when it seemed that Germanic tribes would invade Italy and being taxed.

keep the imperial troops occupied in the north; the revolt among the gladiators led by Spartacus in 73–71 B.C.E. was eventually crushed, and 6000 slaves were crucified on the roads leading into Rome.

Revolts in the conquered provinces were also brutally crushed. When Rome believed that Corinth might be planning a revolt in 146 B.C.E., the city was razed to the ground. Jews revolted three times— 66–73 C.E., 115–117 C.E., and 132–135 C.E.—resulting in the destruction of Judaea as a Jewish state, the physical destruction of Jerusalem and its principal Temple, and the establishment of a Roman colony, Aelia Capitolina, on its site.

---

being taxed. Gaius auctioned off the collection of taxes in Asia. While this profited the elite and helped to secure their loyalty to him personally, it impoverished the residents of the Roman province of Asia. Many senators became increasingly hostile to Gaius Gracchus, and in 121 B.C.E. he too was assassinated along with his fellow tribune, Flaccus. Some 3000 of his supporters were executed.

The reforms of the Gracchi brothers seemed blocked, but in fact they set the framework for the end of the republic a century later. They challenged the power of the senate and exposed the problems of the poor and the war veterans, while their enemies employed violence, murder, and thuggery as tools for making public policy. Julius Caesar and Augustus Caesar, the two men most responsible for finally turning the republic into a militaristic empire headed by a single person, learned from the experiences of the Gracchi brothers to play on Rome's class divisions and to garner the support of the lower classes.

A new method of coping with class conflict was developing: "bread and circuses." Rome bribed the poor, many of them former soldiers from its conquering armies, with a dole of free bread. Up to 200,000 people a day were served. The dole encouraged them to while away their time in public religious festivities, races, the theater, and gladiatorial contests of great cruelty, which pitted man against

man and man against beast in spectacles witnessed by tens of thousands. Between them, the arenas of Rome, including Rome's largest race-track, and the Colosseum, parts of which exist even today, could accommodate one half of Rome's adult population. On days of gladiatorial contests, as many as 5000 animals, including elephants and water buffalo, were slaughtered. Hundreds of humans, too, were slain in a single day. The combination of spectacle and free food was offered to sedate the unemployed urban masses.

Augustus and his successors continued these policies designed to keep the plebeians quiet without actually solving the problems of unemployment and lack of dignity. Until its final collapse, the empire was threatened by unrest and revolt and one of the reasons for the popularity of Christianity in Rome was its message of compassion and salvation for the poor and downtrodden (Chapter 10).

EXTENDING CITIZENSHIP AND INTERNATIONAL LAW

Empires are ultimately sustained by military force, but successful empires must also win at least some degree of support from among the conquered peoples, some measure of hegemony. Rome won such support through several of its political, cultural, economic, and ideological policies. First, politically, it bestowed benefits on conquered peoples, especially the benefits of citizenship.

All free Roman males were citizens automatically; the rest of the men of Italy, however, were not. In 381 B.C.E., the town of Tusculum, some 15 miles (24 kilometers) from Rome and surrounded by Roman territory, seemed poised to oppose Rome. The Romans won the Tusculuns over, however, by offering incorporation into Rome and full citizenship. In 338 B.C.E. full citizenship was bestowed on four additional Latin cities; others received partial citizenship with no voting rights but with rights of property, contracts, and the right to marry Roman citizens. They were also freed of property taxes. Roman citizenship also protected its beneficiary from arbitrary arrest and violence.

In 91 B.C.E. Marcus Livius Drusus the Younger, was elected tribune, the office established to protect the interest of the plebeians. Drusus proposed extending citizenship and the vote to all the Italian allies, but the Roman Senate rejected the proposal. Drusus was later assassinated, leaving the Italians frustrated and furious. So began the "Social War" or "War of the Allies." After two years, however, Rome did offer full citizenship to all Italians who had remained loyal and even to those who agreed to put down their arms. It extended full citizenship north as far as the Po River, and partial citizenship up to the Alps Mountains. So, grudgingly, citizenship was offered as an inducement to loyalty. In newly annexed lands, the aristocrats, the group to whom Rome usually granted these rights and obligations, regarded even partial citizenship as attractive.

The policy continued on a limited basis as Rome expanded. Augustus Caesar announced in 14 C.E. that there were 4,937,000 citizens in the empire, about 2 million of them in the provinces. At that time, the total population of the empire was between 70 and 100 million. In 212 C.E., the Emperor Caracalla officially proclaimed citizenship for all free males in the empire, although ambiguous legal restrictions limited the effect. Provincials could occupy the highest offices in the empire: senator, consul, and even emperor. The Emperor Trajan (r. 98–117) was from Spain; Septimius Severus (r. 193–211) from north Africa; Diocletian (r. 284–305) from Dalmatia (modern Croatia).

The development of international law, the *jus gentium* (law of nations; see Source, p. 176), also helped to unite and pacify the empire. After its victory in the first Punic War, 241 B.C.E., Rome interacted more than ever with foreigners and with subjects of Rome who did not have citizenship. To deal with legal cases between Romans and these others, a new official, the *praetor peregrinus* (literally, foreign magistrate), was appointed. The law developed from his judgments was the *jus gentium*. Over time, this law was codified, first by Hadrian, and later, in the east, by the Emperor Justinian (r. 527–565 C.E.).

ECONOMIC POLICIES FOR THE EMPIRE

The empire brought extraordinary benefits to the rulers, but the costs could also be heavy and eventually became oppressive. The Romans levied tribute, taxes, and rents, and recruited soldiers from the peoples they conquered. They settled their own soldiers in captured lands, turning those lands into Roman estates and enslaving millions of people to work on them. They exploited their political power for the economic advantage of their own traders and military and administrative elites. Imperial rule and the opening of imperial markets brought opportunities for economic development and profit in the conquered provinces, although most of these went to the local wealthy elites who possessed the capital and skills to take advantage of them. In general, Roman rulers were solicitous of the upper classes in the provinces, both because of a shared class position and because they believed that the loyalty of these elites was crucial to maintaining Roman hegemony.

The requirements of feeding and provisioning the city of Rome, which had a population of about a million by the time of Augustus, called on vast resources throughout the empire. The most important requirement was grain. Supplies were drawn from Sicily, Egypt and the north African coast, Spain, and the lands surrounding the Black Sea. More specialized products were imported from all parts of the empire: olive oil and wine came from within Italy, Spain, and the Mediterranean shores; pottery and glass from the Rhineland; leather from southern France; marble from Asia Minor; woolen textiles from Britain and northern France, Belgium, and the Netherlands; slaves from many lands. For gladiatorial contests in the Colosseum and for general display in Rome, lions were brought from Africa and Asia, bears from Scotland, horses from Spain, crocodiles and camels from Egypt, and leopards and rhinoceroses from northwest Africa. The transportation of bulk commodities, especially within the empire, was most often by sea.

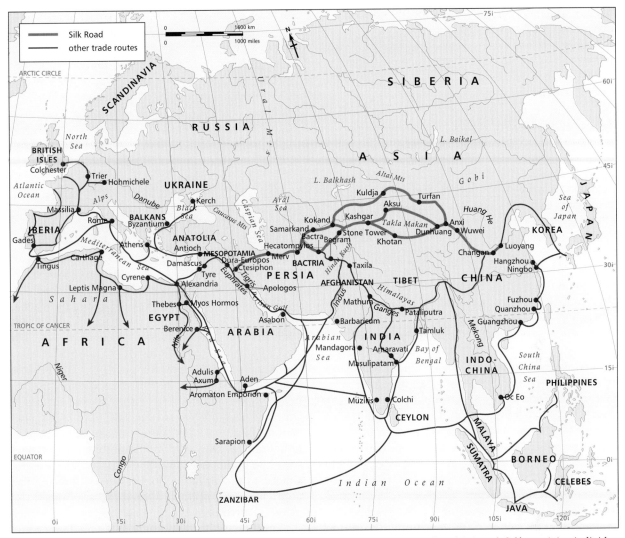

Eurasian trade The commercial links that bound the ancient world were both extensive and sophisticated. Self-sustaining individual networks—the Saharan caravans, the Arab dhows plying the Indian Ocean, the fleets of Chinese junks coasting east Asia, and most famously the Silk Routes traversing central Asia—linked at key entrepots such as Alexandria and Oc Eo by sea, and Ctesiphon and Kashgar by land, to form a truly intercontinental trading system.

A few other extremely large cities, like Alexandria, also needed to import extensively to provide for their hundreds of thousands of inhabitants, but most of the empire was locally self-sufficient. In this pre-industrial age, most people worked on the land, most production was agricultural, and most produce was consumed near the place of production, especially in the newly conquered and settled regions of western Europe. To incorporate these regions into the empire, the Romans constructed and promoted new cities as administrative, military, and financial centers. These included the cores of modern London, Paris, Lyon, Trier, Nimes, Bruges, Barcelona, Cologne, Budapest, and many other European cities. In the

midst of nomadic and migrating peoples, in an empire that rested on agriculture, Rome laid the foundations of a small but potent ruling urban civilization.

At the height of its power, the empire contained more than 5000 civic bodies. The orator Cicero referred to Narbonne, Rome's administrative capital in southern Gaul (from about 118 B.C.E.), as "a colony of Roman citizens, a watch tower of the Roman people, a bulwark against the wild tribes of Gaul" (cited in Mumford, p. 209). Roman rule especially attracted and benefited the urban upper classes in the conquered regions, and helped to urbanize some leaders of the newly arriving immigrant German settlers.

Timgad, North Africa. Timgad, in Algeria, was founded as a military and administrative fortress around 100 C.E. and designed as a perfect square with a grid plan for the streets. The Romans tended to adhere to standard templates of town construction, despite variations in local topography, and Timgad is one of the clearest surviving models of what a provincial headquarters looked like.

People of wealth and power could command specialty goods and generate small but significant streams of intercontinental, long-distance, luxury trade. For such commerce to flourish, trade routes had to be kept safe. The Pax Romana secured the Red Sea routes, which allowed the import of frankincense, myrrh, and other spices from the Arabian peninsula and the Horn of Africa and spices and textiles from India, some of them transshipped from China. By the first century C.E., sailors had discovered that by sailing with the summer monsoon winds they could reach India from Egypt in about four months. They could then return with the winter monsoon, completing the round trip within a year.

Rome's repayment in this exchange was mostly precious metals. Hoards of gold coins from Rome have been discovered in south India, with smaller treasuries in China, southeast Asia, and east Africa. The historian Pliny complained that the trade drained Italy's precious metals, but the profits to be made back home were extraordinary: "In no year does India absorb less than 50,000,000 sesterces of our Empire's wealth, sending back merchandise to be sold with us at a hundred times its original cost" (cited in Lewis and Reinhold, vol. II, p. 120).

For the luxury trades to flourish, the roads had to be maintained and kept safe, so the Pax Romana was essential. The need for safety was most evident in the silk trade, which prospered when Augustan Rome, Parthian Mesopotamia and Iran, Kushan

India, and Han China (see pp. 206–15)—the four empires that spanned the silk routes—were at their peaks. Goods traveled from Luoyang and Xian in China, across the mountains of central Asia, connecting finally at one of the great trading emporia of Begram, Bactra, or Merv. From there, they would continue to the Mediterranean. Silk, light and valuable, was the principal export westward, but lacquerware and bronzes were also carried. A storehouse discovered in 1938 in Begram, which stood at the crossroads of China, India, Persia, and the Mediterranean, revealed some of the principal luxury goods of this intercontinental trade: lacquerwork from China; ivory statues and carvings from India; alabaster, bronze, and glass works from the Mediterranean. Astonishingly, many of the carriers of these treasures seem to have been the steppe nomads of central Asia, the Huns and other "barbarians," who at other times attacked and plundered the empires across which they now traded (see p. 246).

Officially, the Roman upper classes scorned trade as beneath their status. Unofficially, they often entered into contracts with freedmen, their own ex-slaves, to front for their commercial enterprises. Trade was lucrative, and they did not wish to lose the profits. The preferred methods of earning a livelihood were from land ownership, tax collecting for the state, or military conquest, but even generals, like Julius Caesar, profited from the sale of slaves captured in war. Roman traders could be very exploitative. Especially when working in Rome's provinces, they could inspire great hatred. When Mithridates VI, king of Pontus in northern Anatolia, invaded the Roman province of Asia in 88 B.C.E. he encouraged Asian debtors to kill their Roman creditors. Eighty thousand Italian and Italian-Greek businessmen were reported murdered (Grant, p. 184).

In the late second century C.E. internal revolts and external attacks by Gothic peoples brought an end to the Pax Romana and introduced major obstacles to this trade. Roads and markets were no longer secure, and only items that could be consumed locally were worth producing. The production of glass, metals, and textiles in northern Europe, for example, was cut back sharply. Provisioning the city of Rome became more difficult. The population of cities fell, and the cities became less coercive of their suppliers, but as their levels of consumption and the protection they offered declined they also provided less profit and incentive to producers. Trade and productivity faltered. As the Pax Romana began to break down down politically and militarily, trade declined and became more localized.

CULTURAL POLICIES FOR THE EMPIRE

To win and secure allies, Rome not only granted citizenship, codified international law, and built a remarkable physical infrastructure of towns and roads for unifying the empire, it also developed a culture that it brought to the people it conquered. Roman cultural achievements had lagged far behind those of Greece, but as Rome conquered the Greek city-states, it began to absorb the culture of those it conquered. The first prose history of Rome was written in Greek by Fabius Pictor in 202 B.C.E. and the first great historian of Rome was the Greek Polybius (see p. 166). Greek language and literature were adopted by many of the Roman aristocratic classes, as were the architectural, sculptural, and painting traditions of the Greeks. The Romans borrowed from the Greeks as they had earlier borrowed from the Etruscans.

Rome carried this polyglot culture outward in its conquests in Europe and Asia. Its schools in the provinces spread Greek as well as Latin among the tribal Goths and Gauls. Greek was the language of high culture. Latin, however, became the language

The Colosseum, Rome, *c.* **72–80** C.E. Built to house spectacular entertainments, such as mock sea-battles and gladiatorial combats, for audiences of up to 50,000 people, the Colosseum combined Greek decorative traditions with Roman engineering ingenuity, epitomized in the advanced use of concrete as a building material.

Canopus, Hadrian's Villa, Tivoli, *c.* **135** C.E. Rome's wealthy and powerful elites commanded private luxuries beyond the imagination of the average Roman. The Villa of the Emperor Hadrian comprised a series of buildings, gardens, and pools—this one representing a well-known Egyptian canal—laid out on the side of a hill in Tivoli. The complex was designed to bring the more sophisticated pleasures of city life to the country.

of administration. Roman troops constructed amphitheaters, stadiums, and baths wherever they went, the Roman invention of concrete making such constructions feasible. In these settings Roman rulers provided theaters and spectacles modeled on those in Rome.

Rome's sense of superior and inferior, its class consciousness, doubtless encouraged its conquest of other peoples, deemed inferior, and was encouraged, in turn, by the success of those conquests. Rome's greatest epic poem, the *Aeneid*, written by Virgil at the time of the emperor Augustus and singing his praise, exults in this belief in Rome's superiority. At the same time, it upholds the concept of *noblesse oblige*, the duty of the superior to help the inferior:

> . . . Behold the Romans,
> Your very own. These are Iulus' children,
> The race to come. One promise you have heard
> Over and over: here is its fulfillment,
> The son of a god, Augustus Caesar, founder
> Of a new age of gold, in lands where Saturn
> Ruled long ago; he will extend his empire
> Beyond the Indies, beyond the normal measure
> Of years and constellations, where high Atlas
> Turns on his shoulders the star-studded world.
> . . . remember Romans,

> To rule the people under law, to establish
> The way of peace, to battle down the haughty,
> To spare the meek. Our fine arts, these, forever.
> (*Aeneid*, Book VI, 822–31, 893–6; trans. Rolphe
> Humphries)

Coin showing profiles of the Emperor Nero and the Empress Agrippina, 55 C.E. Successive emperors tried to scapegoat the Christians. Nero blamed them for the fire that struck Rome in 64 C.E., and by the end of the first century membership of the Christian community had been made a crime. However, persecution provided the religion with martyrs and increased group unity. (*British Museum, London*)

Religion in The Empire

Officially, Rome celebrated a religion centralized on the person of the emperor-god. After the deification of Augustus at his death, the official priesthood offered animal sacrifices to him and later to his successors, adding these to the traditional sacrifices to the major pagan gods, especially Jupiter, Juno, and Minerva. Birthdays and death anniversaries of the emperors were celebrated as holidays.

Beyond these rituals, however, Roman religious policies allowed a great deal of flexibility. For the most part, as long as the emperor was venerated and the legitimacy of the state was not questioned, diverse religious practices were allowed to flourish. Mithraism, a religion in which Mithras, a Persian

GREEK AND ROMAN GODS

In the second century B.C.E., Greece was absorbed by the Roman Empire. In the process the Romans adopted and adapted many Greek myths, linking their own gallery of gods to Greek legends and deities.

Greek	Roman	
Aphrodite	Venus	Goddess of love and beauty
Apollo, Phoebus	Apollo, Phoebus	Greek god of sun, god of music, poetry, and prophecy
Ares	Mars	God of war
Artemis	Diana	Virgin huntress, goddess of the moon
Asclepius	Aesculapius	God of medicine
Athena (Pallas)	Minerva	Goddess of wisdom and art
Cronus	Saturn	Father of the supreme god: Zeus or Jupiter
Demeter	Ceres	Goddess of the harvest
Dionysus	Bacchus	God of wine and fertility
Eros	Cupid	God of love
Hades, Pluto	Dis	God of the underworld
Hephaestus	Vulcan	God of fire
Hera	Juno	Queen of heaven, wife of Zeus/Jupiter, goddess of women and marriage
Hermes	Mercury	Messenger of the gods, god of roads, cunning, commerce, wealth, and luck
Hestia	Vesta	Goddess of the hearth
Hymen	Hymen	God of marriage
Irene	Pax	Goddess of peace
Pan	Faunus	God of flocks and shepherds
Persephone	Proserpina	Goddess of corn and the spring, goddess of the dead
Poseidon	Neptune	God of the sea
Zeus	Jupiter, Jove	Supreme ruler of gods and men, king of heaven, and overseer of justice and destiny

sun god, was worshiped, emphasized discipline and loyalty. It was especially popular within the military. Sects that challenged the authority of the empire or the emperor, however, were not tolerated. Rome cracked down on worship of the god Bacchus in 186 B.C.E., fearing that lower class members of this cult might turn against the state. The Roman government also clashed with Judaism and with early Christianity, both of which refused to recognize the emperor as divine and generally believed that state power was inferior to God's laws. Indeed, for the first three centuries of the existence of Christianity, many Romans viewed the new religion as atheistic because Christians did not accept the traditional gods, and as treasonable because it spoke of a kingdom of heaven that was distinct from the Roman earthly empire.

Stoicism

Many thoughtful Romans were attracted to Stoicism, a philosophy founded by the Greek Zeno about 300 B.C.E. Stoicism, named for the *stoa* (covered walkway) in Athens where Zeno taught, began with a cosmic theory of the world as a rational, well-ordered, and coherent system, and argued from it to the moral theory that humans should therefore accept, without joy or grief, free from passion, everything that takes place in this world. A corollary of this view stated that people should treat one another with decency because we are all brothers and sisters.

Cicero (106–43 B.C.E.), one of the most important of Roman orators, commentators, and statesmen, was much influenced by Stoic beliefs, and he wrote: "The private individual ought first, in private relations, to live on fair and equal terms with his fellow citizens, with a spirit neither servile and groveling nor yet domineering" (Cicero, *On Duties*, cited in Lewis and Reinhold, vol. I, p. 273). Almost a century later, Seneca (*c.* 4 B.C.E.–65 C.E.), a disciple of Cicero's philosophy, elaborated: "What is the principal thing? A heart . . . which can go forth to face ill or good dauntless and unembarrassed, paralyzed neither by the tumult of the one nor the glamor of the other" (Seneca, *Natural Questions*, cited in Lewis and Reinhold, vol. II, pp. 165–6). Although Stoics did not advocate the end of slavery, they did propose more humane treatment. Writing on the treatment of slaves, Seneca proposed a kind of Golden Rule: "Treat those below you as you would be treated by those above you" (Seneca, *Moral Epistles*, cited in Lewis and Reinhold, vol. II, p. 180).

Stoicism reached the height of its influence a century later with the selection of Marcus Aurelius Antoninus as emperor (r. 161–180 C.E.). He ruled through two decades of almost continuous warfare, economic upheaval, internal revolts, and plague. Through it all, Marcus Aurelius remained courageous and Stoic. He recorded his thoughts in his *Meditations*, one of the most philosophically reflective works ever written by a man in a position of such power:

> Keep thyself then simple, good, pure, serious, free from affectation, a friend of justice, a worshipper of the gods, and help men. Short is life. The universe is either a confusion, and a mutual involution of things, and a dispersion; or it is unity and order and providence . . . If the [latter], I venerate, and I am firm, and I trust in him who governs. (VI:30, 10)

CHRISTIANITY TRIUMPHANT

By the time of Marcus Aurelius, Christianity was making serious inroads into Roman thought. The Stoic philosophy was not far removed from the Christian concept of an orderly world and concern for social welfare. To these beliefs, Christianity added faith in a god actively intervening in human affairs and, specifically, the doctrines of the birth, life, and miracles of Jesus. This combination of beliefs was very attractive to increasing numbers of Romans, and despite severe persecution of Christians under several emperors—Nero (r. 54–68), Marcus Aurelius (r. 161–180), Maximinus I (r. 235–238), Decius (r. 249–251), Valerian (r. 253–260), and Diocletian (r. 284–305)—over the course of three centuries Christianity became acceptable in Rome and flourished. At first it attracted the poor, who were moved by Jesus' concern for the downtrodden, but later, more powerful classes also joined, attracted by both the organization and message of the Church. The Church promoted greater freedom for women, with a few reaching positions of prominence as deaconesses and abbesses, and it began to incorporate some of the sophistication of Greek philosophy, attracting a new intellectual leadership. (For a fuller discussion of early Christianity and its relationship to the Roman Empire, see p. 317.) By the time of Constantine, one out of five inhabitants of the Roman empire was a Christian.

In 313 C.E. the joint emperors, Constantine and Licinius, issued the Edict of Milan, which recognized Christianity as a valid faith, along with paganism. After 324 C.E., when Constantine ruled alone, he favored Christianity as a religion that had brought miraculous benefits to himself personally and to his empire, and he made it the official state religion. Thereafter Christianity spread freely throughout the conquered lands and peoples of northwestern Europe. The network of roads and towns created to facilitate administration also served to transmit the message of Christianity, and members of the Roman Catholic clergy frequently became the bridge between the practices of Christian Rome and those of the "barbarians." After emerging as the official state religion, Christianity succeeded in having government support for pagan cults terminated in 394 C.E. and even the most widespread of them, Mithraism, with its message of loyalty to the emperor, died out. Christianity emerged triumphant.

CONNECTION: The rise of Christianity, pp. 308–30

THE BARBARIANS AND THE FALL OF THE ROMAN EMPIRE

For the Romans, as for the Greeks before them who coined the term, "Barbarian" referred to peoples who spoke unknown foreign languages, were alien, and were usually considered inferior. (It was only later that the word took on connotations of "savage" and "violent.") Rome labeled many of its neighbors on its far-flung borders Barbarians,

including the Celts of central Europe, the various Germanic groups of northern and eastern Europe, and the steppe nomads of central Asia. These peoples did not have cities, written languages, formal government structures, established geographical boundaries, codified laws, or specialization of labor. Some, like the Celts and Germans, lived in villages and carried on settled farming. The steppe peoples were nomadic, spending their lives in their saddles riding, herding, and often fighting among themselves in far-off central Asia. Such peoples, the Romans must have thought, could benefit from the civilizing influences of the empire. Perhaps Virgil had this in mind when he was writing the *Aeneid*.

CELTS

The Celts had arrived in central Europe as early as 2000 B.C.E. Burials indicate their respect for horse-riding warriors and the slow development among them of iron technology in weapons and tools. The Hallstatt cemetery in Austria reveals a greater use of iron by the eighth century B.C.E. and shows trade with Greek civilization. A cemetery at La Tène in Switzerland shows continuing Greek and then Roman influences from the fifth century B.C.E. to the first century C.E. In 390 B.C.E. the Celts sacked Rome, and by 200 B.C.E. Celtic groups had covered central Europe and were pushing outward toward Spain, the British Isles, the Balkans, and Anatolia. Learning from Greek and Roman examples, they built **oppida**, fortified towns, throughout their territories. The largest of these covered more than a half square mile (130 hectares). Ultimately, however,

Funerary bronze couch from the Hallstatt prince's tomb at Eberdingen-Hochdorf, near Stuttgart, Germany, c. 530 B.C.E. This couch demonstrates the remarkable sophistication of some early Celtic art. It was buried in the tomb of a sixth-century B.C.E. Celtic chieftain in Germany, along with other possessions reflecting the wealth and importance of the dead man. (*Württembergisches Landesmuseum, Stuttgart*)

Maiden Castle, Dorset, England. This Iron Age hillfort was the capital of the Durotriges, a Celtic tribe. Despite its massive bank-and-ditch defenses, Maiden Castle, like many other Celtic strongholds, eventually succumbed to Roman assault in the mid-first century C.E.

the Celtic peoples were conquered by Roman armies. They were killed, or assimilated, or fled to Ireland, Scotland, and Wales, where, to some degree, they continue today to preserve the Celtic language and culture.

GOTHS (GERMANIC PEOPLES)

The Goths—Germanic peoples—settled at first in northern Europe outside the Celtic and Roman strongholds. By 600 B.C.E. they had established small villages, and by about 500 B.C.E. they had begun working with iron. With the discovery of richer iron deposits and contact with Greek and Roman technology, the Goths developed more sophisticated tools and weapons. Much of what we know of this early period comes from burials in bogs in northern Germany and Denmark.

Romans and Germans had faced each other along the Rhine since Julius Caesar had conquered Gaul, and along the Danube from the time Augustus had secured that border. They had skirmished, traded, and at times penetrated each other's territories. In 370 C.E., steppe nomads began to invade across thousands of miles from central Asia, bringing pressure to bear on the whole of Europe, and in response to this pressure, the Goths began to migrate westward, pushing more vigorously into Roman territories. These massive Germanic invasions upset the rough balance of power that existed between Rome and the Goths, threatening the stability of the empire. Ultimately, the Goths formed their own states within the imperial territories. (A second Germanic emigration occurred about 500 C.E. as a response to floods in the areas of north Germany and Denmark. Among the emigrant Germanic groups, the Saxons sailed across the North Sea and the English Channel to Britain, where they came to form a substantial part of the population.)

HUNS

The Romans called all the steppe peoples who invaded Europe in 370 C.E. "Huns," but the Huns were, specifically, only one of the principal groups of warrior-nomads who inhabited the flat grasslands from European Russia to Manchuria. They virtually lived on their horses, herding cattle, sheep, and horses as well as hunting. They lived in tents and used wagons to transport their goods as they moved from place to place, especially in their annual shift between summer and winter locations.

THE "BARBARIANS": HOW DO WE KNOW?

The steppe peoples had no written language, and their nomadic life style has left few archaeological remains. We know about them in part from burials,

especially of the Scythians, a group living in southern Russia and in the Altai Mountains of Mongolia. Mostly we know of them from the accounts of the peoples whose lands they invaded: Romans, Greeks, Chinese, and Indians. All these accounts report them as fierce, mobile, swift, and terrifying warriors on horseback, armed with powerful bows, swords, and lances. In more peaceful times, the Huns carried the goods of the overland silk routes through central Asia.

The Huns were not mentioned in Latin histories until Ammianus Marcellinus (330–395 C.E.) described them, but the Chinese historian Sima

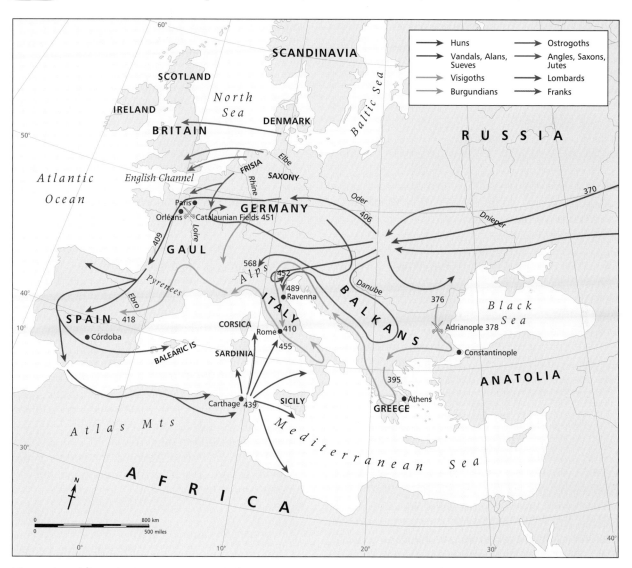

The coming of the Barbarians Rome's control of northern and western Europe declined in the fourth century C.E. as successive waves of Germanic peoples began to migrate and colonize the outer reaches of the empire. When the Huns began to advance westward from central Asia they pushed before them additional Gothic peoples who increased the pressures on Rome. Other Huns were meanwhile pushing south into India and east into China. (For Barbarian invasions into China, see map on p. 208. For invasions into India, see map on p. 244.)

Qian had already depicted them as coarse warriors 500 years earlier:

> During the Ch'ien-yuan reign [140–134 B.C.E.] . . . the Son of Heaven made inquiries among those of the Hsiung-nu [Huns] who had surrendered and been made prisoners, and they all reported that the Hsiung-nu had overcome the king of the Yueh-chih and made a drinking vessel out of his skull. The Yueh-chih had decamped and were hiding somewhere, constantly scheming how to revenge themselves on the Hsiung-nu. (Sima Qian, p. 274)

Further elaboration by Sima delineates several groups of steppe nomads who frequently fought among themselves and sometimes invaded China itself. The Hsiung-nu may not actually have been Huns, but even if not, they were a related group of steppe nomads.

Although they lived in ordo, tent encampments, the Huns' living arrangements and political structures were by no means random. Many groups had chiefs and even governments, and their leaders lived in the most elaborate of the tents. When the Huns invaded Europe, Romans observed emissaries of various peoples enter the tent of Attila, their leader, to conduct political negotiations.

At the time Augustus ruled Rome, groups of steppe nomads were engaged in battles that would ultimately help to topple the Han dynasty in China (see p. 214). They were also beginning the attacks on India that would make two of the groups the rulers of north India: the Kushanas, 150–300 C.E., and the Hunas, 500–550 C.E. (see p. 246). The Huns arrived in Europe in 370 C.E., defeating and displacing the Germanic Alans, Ostrogoths, and Visigoths and pushing them in the direction of Rome.

THE DECLINE AND DISMEMBERMENT OF THE ROMAN EMPIRE

Rome proved vulnerable to the invaders, especially because of a plague that wiped out up to a quarter of the population of some areas in 165–180 C.E. During the reign of Marcus Aurelius (r. 161–180 C.E.), the Goths began to invade the Danube basin. Some penetrated into Greece, and across the Alps and into Italy. "Barbarian" invasions continued for hundreds of years, ultimately leading to the break-up of the Roman Empire.

For seven years, 168–175 C.E., Marcus Aurelius fought against the invaders, but he also recognized that they could be assimilated into the empire for mutual benefit. The Germans wanted to establish settlements, so he offered them land within the borders of the empire that they could develop; they were soldiers, so he offered them positions in Rome's armies. Some of the Gothic groups accepted assimilation into the empire. Others wished simply to plunder and withdraw. Still others wished to seize portions of the empire for themselves and settle. Invaders repeatedly penetrated the borders represented by the Danube and the Rhine. In 248 C.E. the Emperor Decius (r. 249–251) defeated an invasion of Goths in the Balkans, but he was himself killed by another Gothic group. The Goths continued into the Balkans and beyond into Asia Minor. They took to ships and attacked Black Sea commerce, in the process cutting off large parts of Rome's grain supplies. Meanwhile, further west, other nomadic groups, Franks and Vandals, swept across the Rhine into Gaul, Spain, and as far south as north Africa.

The empire struck back. The Emperor Gallienus (r. 253–268 C.E.) created a mobile cavalry, and he moved the imperial military headquarters from Rome to Milan in the north, better to confront invaders into Italy. In a series of battles, Roman armies preserved Italy for the empire. Gallienus died in a plague and was succeeded as emperor by Aurelian (r. 270–275), an even more brilliant and energetic general. In a series of battles, Aurelian protected Rome's western and northern borders, although he abandoned Dacia and pulled back to the Danube.

In the east, too, Rome defeated revolts. The greatest challenge came as the new, expansive Sassanian dynasty in Persia confronted Rome in Armenia and Syria. In 260 C.E. the Roman Emperor Valerian (r. 253–260 C.E.) was captured and held prisoner for the rest of his life. Nevertheless, Rome recaptured its eastern areas, partly because the Sassanians treated the inhabitants of these lands so badly that they revolted. Zenobia, the widow of the leader of semi-independent Palmyra, declared the independence of Syria and Mesopotamia, and annexed Egypt. Her revolt lasted only a few years, and in 273 C.E. Aurelian defeated her and brought her back to Rome in chains.

Continuing warfare forced the decentralization of Rome's power from the capital to distant provincial battlefields, and from civilian control by the Senate in Rome to generals in the field. Soldiers in Gaul, Britain, and Spain declared their general Postumus (r. 259–268 C.E.) the independent emper-

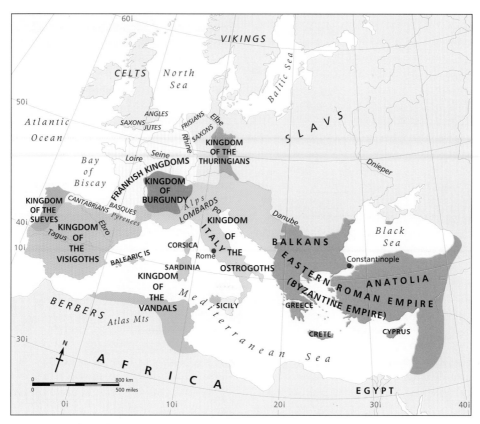

Rome's successors Following the sack of Rome by the Ostrogoths in 455 C.E., a new map of Europe emerged. The Roman power base had shifted east to Constantinople, forming the Byzantine Empire. The steppe invaders, keen to emulate the Romans, had created new kingdoms in Italy, Africa, and Iberia, while Germanic peoples were struggling to create a new power balance in the north.

or of those regions, although their mutiny was defeated by Aurelian in 274 C.E. Militarily, the empire had staged an extraordinary comeback. Thinking that an aura of pomp and majesty would be helpful, the Emperor Diocletian (r. 284–305 C.E.) claimed for himself a sanctity and splendor never before seen in Rome. The expense of his battles and the splendor of his court bankrupted the empire and brought misery to its inhabitants. To cope with the attacks on far distant borders, emperors established subsidiary capitals, and in 330 C.E. Constantine established Constantinople as a secondary capital for ruling the east. After 395 C.E., one emperor in Rome and another in Constantinople formally divided the empire, West and East.

"Barbarian" tribes continued to breach the imperial borders and defenses. Valentinian I (r. 364–375) was the last emperor capable of driving them back effectively. From this time on, driven forward by the invasion of the Huns, the Germans pushed against Roman defenses in increasing numbers. In 378 C.E. Valentinian's brother, the eastern Emperor Valens (r. 364–378), lost two-thirds of the eastern armies—and his life—in battle against the Visigoths at Adrianople. Valens' successor, Theodosius I (r. 379–395 C.E.), who ruled from Constantinople, settled Visigoths within the empire, requiring them to provide soldiers and farmers for the imperial armies and lands. This "federate" status for Goths and other "barbarians" became a common pattern, with Goths, Franks, Alans, and Vandals settling within the imperial borders in increasing numbers. The empire was Roman in name, but was mixed in terms of population, armies, and leadership.

Alaric, the Visigoth (c. 370–410 C.E.), invaded Italy in 401, and in response the Roman Emperor Honorius (r. 395–423 C.E.) removed the capital to Ravenna, a more defensible city on the east coast of Italy. Alaric invaded Italy again in 407, and in 410 he sacked Rome. At the end of 406, combined armies of Goths, Vandals, Suevi, Alans, and Burgundians crossed the Rhine into Gaul and moved into Spain. At first they sacked, looted, and burned, but within a few years they were establishing their own settlements and local kingdoms, displacing or merging with Roman landlords. The Vandal King Geiseric (r. 428–477 C.E.) crossed into north Africa, seizing Carthage and its agriculturally rich hinterlands. Gaining control of a fleet, he challenged Roman control of the Mediterranean. The Romans could not defeat him.

The Huns were building up their own imperial confederacy in central Europe. Their most powerful leader, Attila, who commanded them from 434 to 453 C.E., ruled from the Baltic to the Danube. He invaded Italy in 451 C.E., threatening Rome and withdrawing only on the intervention of Pope Leo I. After Attila's death in 453 C.E., his armies dissolved and never again regained their power.

In 476 C.E., the German general Odoacer deposed the last Roman Emperor in the West, Romulus Augustulus, who was never replaced. Odoacer became the first barbarian king of Italy (r. 476–493), and thus the five-centuries-old Roman Empire came to an end. Some historians argue that the empire lived on in Constantinople, the eastern capital, but the Greek culture of this city, its rule over only the eastern Mediterranean region, and its separation from Rome and the Western Empire made it a very different cultural and political center. By about 600 C.E. the Byzantine Empire, with a political system based on Constantinople, is usually seen as an independent entity rather than merely the continuation of Rome in the east.

In the west, the Roman imperial system continued to function for at least a further two more centuries, although its leadership and its legions were in the hands of Germans and other invading groups. But it is hard to call it either an "empire" when there was no emperor and no allegiance to a central government, or "Roman" when it was led by Germans and Goths and when its capital was no longer in Rome.

CAUSES OF THE DECLINE AND FALL

Structural problems had been visible in the Roman Empire even at the height of its power. Internally, the conflict between the elite and the masses continued, under different names, throughout the history of the Republic and the empire. The cost of sustaining the empire by military force overtaxed the imperial economy, impoverishing the middle classes and the remaining agricultural classes. The yeoman-farmer class, the class that had first built up the Roman republic, was ruined, and although the rich continued to live off their estates in Italy and elsewhere, and the senatorial classes continued to do well, popular support for the imperial ideal had disappeared. In earlier times, an ever-expanding frontier had brought new economic resources to support the empire, but expansion had come to an end in the second century. The empire was overextended.

In addition, the quality of the empire depended on the quality of its emperors, but Rome had no viable system of succession. In the century between Marcus Aurelius and Diocletian, more than eighty men assumed command as emperor, and many of these were assassinated. In the third century C.E., as fighting in the border regions decentralized the empire, competing armies fought to have their generals selected as emperor. The results were devastating to the economy, administration, and morale of the empire.

Rome could no longer win its frontier battles against invaders, but neither could it continue to assimilate Goths and others into its armies and settlements as subordinates. The Roman armies and vast territories of the empire had become heavily Germanic, and when whole tribes of Goths began to serve together in single units under Gothic commanders, questions of the army's loyalty to the empire arose. Romans and Germans saw each other as "other," alien, and the Romans even forbade intermarriage. As Germanic peoples began to take over leading positions, the empire effectively ceased to be Roman.

The rise of Christianity as the principal religion and philosophy of the empire (see pp. 317–18) also suggested that the Roman desire for earthly political power was evaporating. At first, Christianity was accepted by the poor, who used it as a means of expressing their disaffection from the power of the Caesars. Later, however, when Constantine declared Christianity to be a legal state religion in 313 and *the* official state religion in 324, more mainstream Romans converted. Christianity offered an alternative focus for human energy. The eighteenth-century English historian Edward Gibbon argued in *The History of the Decline and Fall of the Roman Empire* that Christianity turned people against this-worldly attractions and power. Later historians regard this as an overstatement, but Christianity did preach that one's eternal salvation was more important than fighting for the empire. It siphoned energy toward more spiritual and humanitarian goals, and toward competition with other religious groups.

More recently, scholars have suggested that

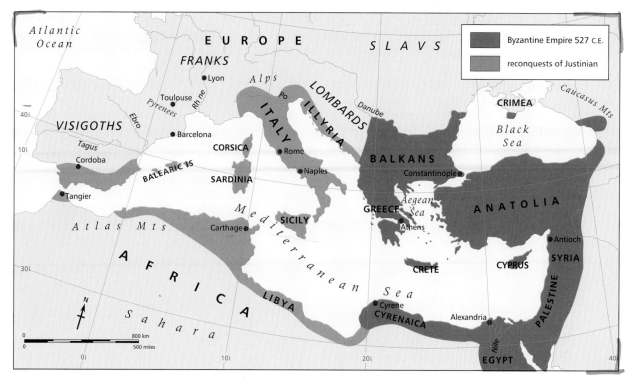

The Byzantine Empire Despite the erosion of Roman power in western Europe by 457 C.E., the East Roman or Byzantine Empire survived with varying fortunes for another thousand years—albeit Greek-speaking and Orthodox Christian—until 1453. Centered on Constantinople, its heartland straddled the crossroads between Europe and Asia. Only briefly, under Justinian (483–565), did it recover control of the western Mediterranean.

climatic change reduced agricultural productivity and the economy. Still others have noted that severe epidemics killed up to a quarter of the population in some imperial centers between 165 and 180 C.E. and again between 251 and 266 C.E. These diseases sapped the empire of manpower and production and left it more open to attack. These biological and ecological arguments complement the more traditional explanations of Rome's fall: overextension; financial and military exhaustion; a failure of leadership; the rise of new, alternative value systems; and the infiltration of Germanic peoples, which fragmented the empire into new, separate, independent states that no longer wished to be subordinated to Rome.

CONNECTION: *The reign of Charlemagne (771–814), pp. 329–30*

THE PERSISTENCE OF EMPIRE IN THE EAST

On May 11, 330, the Emperor Constantine inaugurated the "New Rome which is Constantinople," to share with Rome, as co-capital, the administration of his huge empire. From its inception three elements characterized the new city: Greek language and culture; Roman law and administration; and Christian faith and organization. While the western half of the empire survived only another century and a half, the east continued on its own for another thousand years until 1453 C.E., becoming an empire of its own, called Byzantium after the name of the Greek city around which Constantinople was built.

Like the west, the east had to withstand military attack. Germanic tribes crossed the Danube, but found Constantinople impregnable, defended behind huge walls built by the emperor Theodosius II (r. 408–450). The Byzantine emperor Justinian (r. 527–565) even recaptured many of the western regions including north Africa, southern Spain, Sicily, Italy, and even Rome itself, but the costs in wealth and manpower crippled his empire. After his death most of these western conquests were lost while the Persians constantly warred with the Byzantines in the east.

In religious issues, too, Justinian seemed to over-reach. When many Syrian and Egyptian Christians declared themselves **Monophysites**, believers that Jesus' nature was only divine, not human, Justinian oppressed them in the name of religious conformity and imperial authority. In doing so, he created antagonisms that smoldered for centuries and contributed to the loss of these provinces to the Muslims in the seventh century C.E.

Justinian's legal, administrative, and architectural initiatives produced more lasting results. He had the Roman system of Civil Law codified in four great works known collectively as the Justinian Code, thus helping to perpetuate an administration of great competence. In time, the Code became the basis for much of modern European law. He adorned Constantinople with numerous new buildings, crowned by the Church of Hagia Sophia, the Church of Holy Wisdom. Other churches, forts, and public works were built throughout the empire.

The emperor Heraclius (r. 610–641) defeated the Persian empire, but he and his successors could not hold back the troops which burst out of Arabia after 632 inspired with the religious zeal of newborn Islam (Chapter 11). The Arabs captured much of the land of the Byzantine empire, including Syria and Egypt with their disaffected Monophysites (see p. 339). For centuries, the Christian Byzantine empire based in the Balkans and Asia Minor would confront Islam religiously and militarily. The Byzantine empire organized its armies into **themes**, administrative districts and army units in which peasants were given farms in payment for their military service. These themes and the impregnable fortifications of Constantinople were the empire's bulwark in confronting Arab armies.

The **iconoclastic** controversy, the bitter battle over the use of images, or **icons**, in Christian worship (see Spotlight, pp. 324–5), beginning in 726, further demonstrated the importance of Christian doctrine in the life of the Byzantine empire, and the continuing strain in its political-religious relationship with the Roman church. Indeed the great leaders of the Byzantine empire were known for both their military prowess and their religious leadership. Basil I (r. 867–886) not only kept control of the

Hagia Sophia, Constantinople, 532–7. The Hagia Sophia (Church of the Holy Wisdom), built under the Emperor Justinian, is an imposing visual symbol of the power of the Eastern Empire. The minarets, or pointed towers at the four corners, were added in the fifteenth century when the Ottomans captured Constantinople and the church was converted into a mosque.

Balkans and crushed the Bulgar invaders, and initiated a dynasty which reconquered Crete, Syria, southern Italy, and much of Palestine from the Arabs, but he also healed the religious rift with Rome for a time.

Ultimately, beginning in the late eleventh century C.E., the Byzantine empire was brought down by a combination of religious and political antagonisms. Battered from the north by invading Normans and Slavs, the Byzantines turned to the pope in Rome for help against the Islamic Seljuq Turks from the east who had overrun Asia Minor (Chapters 11 and 14). In response, the pope preached the crusades, but in 1204 crusaders—against the Pope's orders—conquered and sacked Constantinople. The Byzantines recovered the city in 1261 but their empire was irreparably weakened, and in 1453 finally succumbed to the Turks.

How had the Byzantine empire managed to survive for 1000 years after Rome had fallen? The administrative system of the Byzantines deserved much of the credit, as Yale University Professor Deno John Geanakoplos has explained:

> Consisting of a group of highly educated officials trained primarily at the university or, rather "higher school" of Constantinople, the civil service was organized into a hierarchical system of considerable complexity even by today's standards. Taxes were collected regularly, justice was administered, armies were raised and put into the field, and the functions of the state in general were very adequately carried out. It may be said that in its period of greatest power (330–c. 1050) the Byzantine government, despite all its faults (excessive love of pomp and protocol, bureaucratic tendencies, and frequent venality), functioned more effectively, and for a longer period, than virtually any other political organism in history. (Geanakoplos, p. 3.)

The ruling classes were never as isolated and alienated from the common people as in the west. The eastern empire was also less geographically overextended. Even when its more distant territories were lost, it could defend its heartland. Its sources of wealth and military manpower were in Thrace and Anatolia, geographically close to its center of political power in Constantinople, which remained an impregnable fortress for almost 1000 years. In these settled lands, the Byzantine empire had an older and stronger urban tradition than the west, and its cities remained viable centers of commerce long after most cities in the west had all but

disappeared. The fiercest of the invading Gothic tribes turned away from these more settled regions and marched westward toward the more open agricultural lands of the Roman empire. In all these ways, the east was different from the west and was able to survive as an imperial state for another thousand years.

THE ROMAN EMPIRE: WHAT DIFFERENCE DOES IT MAKE?

The Roman Empire laid foundations that have lasted until today in language, law, urban and regional development, and religious organization. Rome's language, Latin, was the official language of the empire, and it persisted as one of the two languages (with Greek) known by all educated Europeans until the seventeenth century, continuing as the language of ritual prayer for the Roman Catholic Church until the mid-twentieth century. Latin formed the base of the Romance languages (Italian, Spanish, Catalan, Portuguese, French, and Romanian) and contributed substantially to English.

Roman law, which developed and was codified over several centuries, inspired the transition to modern, codified law in much of Europe, including the Napoleonic Codes, which the French general and emperor institutionalized wherever he ruled in early nineteenth-century Europe (see Chapter 15). The hundreds of towns that Rome founded and developed as administrative and military centers throughout the empire provided the nuclei around which the urban structure of much of modern Europe and northern Africa developed. The 50,000 miles (80,000 kilometers) of well-paved roads, which connected the cities of the empire, laid the foundation for much of modern Europe's land transportation patterns.

Even after its decline and fall c. 476 C.E. the Roman Empire continued to shape the vision and the administration of hundreds of millions of people. In 330 C.E. the Emperor Constantine inaugurated Constantinople as an eastern, sister capital of the Roman Empire, and that city continued to rule much of the eastern Mediterranean for another thousand years, until 1453 C.E. (see p. 317). Meanwhile in western Europe, during that millennium, the Roman Catholic Church adapted the

Roman imperial administrative organization for its own uses. Much of this organization persists to the present. When the emperor Constantine gave Christianity legal status throughout the empire, and chose it as his own religion, he opened the gates for its unprecedented growth (see p. 305). The Holy Roman Empire, which ruled much of central Europe for some 900 years from 800 C.E., also styled itself a successor to Rome, although the comparison was somewhat remote (see pp. 328–30).

Images of the Roman Empire remain powerful even to our own times. The British Empire, which girdled the globe from the eighteenth to the mid-twentieth centuries, proudly described itself as recreating and extending the imperial military power, administration, legal system, and technological superiority that had characterized Rome. Like the early Romans, the British claimed to have stumbled into their imperial possessions rather than to have actively pursued them (see Chapter 16).

BIBLIOGRAPHY

Andrea, Alfred and James H. Overfield. *The Human Record* (Boston: Houghton Mifflin Co., 3rd ed., 1998).

Antoninus, Marcus Aurelius. *Meditations*, trans. H. G. Long in Whitney J. Oates, ed., *The Stoic and Epicurean Philosophers* (New York: Modern Library, 1940).

Aries, Philippe and Georges Duby, eds. *A History of Private Life: I: From Pagan Rome to Byzantium* (Cambridge: Harvard University Press, 1987).

Boardman, John, Jasper Griffin, and Oswyn Murray, eds. *The Oxford History of the Classical World* (New York: Oxford University Press, 1986).

Brown, Peter. *The Rise of Western Christendom* (Malden, MA: Blackwell, 1996).

Carcopino, Jerome. *Daily Life in Ancient Rome* (New Haven: Yale University Press, 1940).

Clark, Gillian. *Women in Late Antiquity: Pagan and Christian Life Styles* (Oxford: Oxford University Press, 1993).

Cornell, Tim and John Matthews. *Atlas of the Roman World* (New York: Facts on File, 1983).

Cotterell, Arthur, ed. *The Penguin Encyclopedia of Ancient Civilizations* (London: Penguin Books, 1980).

Fantham, Elaine, *et al. Women in the Classical World* (New York: Oxford University Press, 1994).

Finley, M.I., ed. *The Portable Greek Historians* (New York: Viking Press, 1959).

Frank, Andre Gunder and Barry K. Gillis, eds. *The World System: Five Hundred Years or Five Thousand* (New York: Routledge, 1993).

Geanakoplos, Deno John. *Byzantium: Church, Society, and Civilization Seen Through Contemporary Eyes* (Chicago: University of Chicago Press, 1984).

Gibbon, Edward. *The History of the Decline and Fall of the Roman Empire*, abridged by D.M. Low in 3 vols. (New York: Washington Square Press, 1962).

Grant, Michael. *History of Rome* (New York: Scribner's, 1978).

Hunt, Lynn, *et al. The Challenge of the West* (Lexington, MA: D.C. Heath, 1995).

Jones, A.H.M. *Augustus* (New York: W.W. Norton & Co., 1970).

Lewis, Naphtali and Meyer Reinhold. eds. *Roman Civilization: Selected Readings:* Vol I: *The Republic and the Augustan Age*; Vol II: *The Empire* (New York: Columbia University Press, 1990).

Luttwak, Edward N. *The Grand Strategy of the Roman Empire* (Baltimore: Johns Hopkins University Press, 1976).

McNeill, William. *Plagues and Peoples* (Garden City, NY: Anchor Books, 1976).

Mirsky, Jeannette, ed. *The Great Chinese Travellers* (Chicago: University of Chicago Press, 1964).

Mumford, Lewis. *The City in History* (New York: Harcourt, Brace, and World, 1961).

Pantel, Pauline Schmitt, ed. *A History of Women*: Vol I: *From Ancient Goddesses to Christian Saints* (Cambridge: Harvard University Press, 1992).

Parker, Geoffrey, ed. *The (London) Times Atlas of World History* (London: Times Books, 4th ed. 1993).

Past Worlds: The (London) Times Atlas of Archaeology (Maplewood, NJ: Hammond, 1988).

Periplus of the Erythraean Sea, trans. and ed. G.W.B. Huntingford (London: Hakluyt Society, 1980).

Ramage, Nancy and Andrew Ramage. *Roman Art: Romulus to Constantine* (Englewood Cliffs: Prentice Hall, 1991).

Runciman, Steven. *Byzantine Civilization* (Cleveland: World Publishing Co., 1933).

Sima Qian. *Records of the Historian: Chapters from the Shih Chi of Ssu-ma Ch'ien*, trans. Burton Watson (New York: Columbia University Press, 1969).

Time-Life Books. *Time Frame 400 BC–AD 200: Empires Ascendant* (Alexandria, VA: Time-Life Books, 1988).

Time-Life Books. *Time Frame AD 200–600: Empires Besieged* (Alexandria, VA: Time-Life Books, 1988).

Virgil. *Aeneid*, trans. Rolphe Humphries (New York: Charles Scribner's Sons, 1951).

CHAPTER

7

CHINA

220 B.C.E.–910 C.E.

"The August Emperor gave a vigorous display of his authority, and his virtue brought together all the states, and for the first time brought unity and supreme peace."

QIN SHI HUANGDI

FRACTURE AND UNIFICATION: THE QIN, HAN, SUI, AND TANG DYNASTIES

When we last discussed the north China plain in Chapter 4, the Zhou dynasty, 1100–256 B.C.E., was in decline. As the dynasty began to weaken, the powerful, independent states of the region fought among themselves so constantly that China's historians have named the years between 481 and 221 B.C.E. the Warring States period. In 221 B.C.E., after hundreds of years of warfare, the Qin dynasty defeated the others, unifying north China and creating the first Chinese Empire.

This chapter will consider the Chinese Empire during its first 1100 years, from 221 B.C.E. to 907 C.E. The Qin dynasty ended in 206 B.C.E., only four years after the death of its founder. Then the Han dynasty ruled for four centuries, from 202 B.C.E. to 2 C.E. and from 26 to 220 C.E., with a brief twenty-four-year **interregnum** (2–26 C.E.), during which an outsider reigned. For the next three and a half centuries, 220–589 C.E., authority was divided and fractured. Finally China was reunified under another shortlived dynasty, the Sui (581–618), and was ruled for three centuries by the illustrious, expansive Tang dynasty (618–907). During this time China created political and cultural forms that would last for another thousand years, and, as we shall see in Chapter 20, perhaps even to the present.

We begin with a consideration of the sources—How Do We Know? We then examine the key accomplishments under China's imperial rulers—the conquest, consolidation, and confirmation of the empire—and the expansion of China to include "outer China," the distant, conquered provinces inhabited by people not ethnically Chinese. In addition, we outline relationships with peoples to the south and southwest, who were ultimately incorporated into China, and with Korea and Japan, whose cultures were influenced profoundly by China. We close by comparing and contrasting the Chinese Empire with that of Rome.

THE CHINESE EMPIRE: HOW DO WE KNOW?

Our main historical sources for the Shang period are artifacts—such as oracle bones used for divination—uncovered by archaeological excavations. For the succeeding Zhou period, a series of written texts is available. Five of these were later canonized by China's most central political and moral philosopher, Confucius (551–479 B.C.E.), and by his disciples, as especially fine examples of the philosopher's own thought and his concern for history, music, the arts, and rituals:

- the *Book of Documents*, a collection of various statements of early kings and their ministers;

- the *Book of Changes*, the *I Ching*, which details methods of predicting the future through casting sticks;

- the *Book of Songs*, which contains 305 poems, about half of which relate to the everyday lives of ordinary people, half to issues of court politics and rituals;

- the *Spring and Autumn Annals*, which contains brief chronologies from Lu, Confucius' home state;

- *Rites and Rituals* (three texts, grouped together as one), which combines both philosophies and rituals of the court.

In addition to these five, Confucius' own teachings were recorded by his disciples in *The Analects*. A large body of interpretation and commentary grew up around each of these texts.

Other philosophers are also represented in collections from the late Zhou period. **Daoism**, a philosophy of spontaneity in the face of nature and the cosmos, produced two major works: the *Classic of the Way and Its Power*, ascribed to Laozi (Lao-tzu), a sixth-century mystical philosopher, but more probably composed in the third century B.C.E.; and the *Zhuangzi*, written by the philosopher Zhuang Zhou at about the same time. **Legalism**, a philosophy of government characterized by strict laws and strict enforcement, was taught in treatises by Han Feizi (Han-Fei-tzu; d. 233 B.C.E.). There were also several historical texts, often exaggerated and even fabricated, such as the *Intrigues of the Warring States*, from the third century B.C.E. Books of etiquette and ritual reveal the hierarchical and mannered style of proceedings of the state governments. Many of these texts not only cast light on earlier periods but also illuminate the thought and action of the Han dynasty and beyond.

Recording the past was valued both for itself and for the moral principles it was believed to teach. China therefore prepared and transmitted

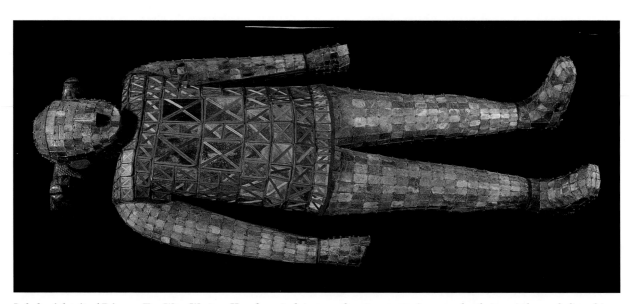

Jade burial suit of Princess Tou Wan, Western Han dynasty, late second century B.C.E. As a very hard stone, jade was believed to be an effective preservative. When the Princess Tou Wan, daughter-in-law of the Emperor Jingdi, died, a burial suit was created for her using 2160 pieces of jade tied together with gold wire.

the most fully and continuously documented history of any ancient empire. Building on this legacy of historical literature, the Han emperor Wudi (r. 141–87 B.C.E.), created a new official position, the Grand Historian of the Han court, with the responsibility of preparing a comprehensive history of the entire Chinese past. The first to hold the post was Sima Tan (d. 110 B.C.E.). He was succeeded by his son Sima Qian (145–85 B.C.E.), one of the greatest historians in world history (see Profile, p. 198). The father began and the son completed the *Shi Qi* or *Records of the Historian*. In 130 chapters it recounted the history of the people of China from mythological times to the first century B.C.E. Sima Qian divided the materials into five sections, which became the pattern for future historians as well. The sections were: "Basic Annals" of the court; "Chronologies" of important events; "Treatises" on such diverse special topics as rites, music, calendar, astronomy, major canals, and economics; "Hereditary Houses" or accounts of major feudal families; and "Memoirs," primarily biographical accounts of famous people in China, including a number of foreigners. In 98 B.C.E., Sima Qian

CHINA–FROM QIN TO TANG

DATE	POLITICAL	RELIGION AND CULTURE	SOCIAL DEVELOPMENT
250 B.C.E.	● Zhou dynasty ends (256) ● Qin Shi Huangdi initiates Qin dynasty (221–206) ● Revolts against Qin (207)	● Han Feizi (d. 233) ● Daoism ● Legalism ● Great Wall	
200 B.C.E.	● Liu Bang (202–195) first emperor of Han dynasty		
150 B.C.E.	● Han Wudi (141–87)	● Confucian Academy established (124)	● Travels of Zhang Qian
100 B.C.E.	● Reign of usurper Wang Mang (9–23 C.E.)	● Sima Qian (145–85) ● Invention of paper	
50 C.E.		● First mention of Buddhism in China	
200 C.E.	● Han dynasty ends (220) ● Age of Disunity (221–331) ● Three Kingdoms (220–280)		
300 C.E.	● Jin dynasty (265–316) ● Northern Wei dynasty (386–534)	● Buddhism expands ● Gu Kaizhi (334–406)	
600 C.E.	● Sui dynasty (581–618) ● Tang dynasty (618–907)	● Invention of block printing ● Grand canal completed (610) ● Buddhist cave art	● Boundaries of empire extended to Mongolia, Turkestan, Afghanistan, Pakistan, and Iran ● Tang briefly held North Korea and Vietnam
650 C.E.	● Empress Wu (684–705)		● First pharmacopoeia
700 C.E.	● Battle of Talas River (751) ● An Lushan rebellion (755–63)	● Wang Wei (701–62) ● Li Bai (701–61) ● Du Fu (712–70) ● Porcelain produced	
800 C.E.		● Repression of Buddhism	
900 C.E.	● Collapse of Tang, leading to disunity (907–960) ● Song dynasty (960–1279)		

PROFILE
Sima Qian
COURT HISTORIAN

Sima Tan (d. 110 B.C.E.) and his son Sima Qian (145-85 B.C.E.) both earned the title of Grand Historian to the Han Emperor Wudi. The position was hereditary. Sima Tan reported to his son "Our forbears were Grand Historians of the Zhou house," but in those days they were "in charge of astronomical matters" and dynastic chronologies. Now father and son transformed the task to one of evaluating the quality of governments and rulers. They created the art of Chinese history as a commentary on politics and ethics.

At the very end of his great work, *Shi Qi*, 130 chapters recounting the history of China from mythological times almost to his own, Sima Qian includes an autobiographical sketch:

> Qian was born at Longmen. He ploughed and kept flocks on the sunny slopes of the mountains near the Yellow River. By the age of ten he was reading aloud the ancient writings. At twenty he journeyed south to the Yangtze and Huai rivers, ascended Kuaiji to search for the cave of Yu, espied Jiuyi, went by water down to Yun and Xiang, journeyed north and crossed the Wen and Si to investigate the traditions in the cities of Qi and Lu, and observed the customs handed down by Master Kong [Confucius], and took part in the archery competition held at Mount Yi in Cou. He suffered distress in Po, Xie, and Pengcheng, and returned home via Liang and Chu. Afterwards Qian served as a palace gentleman, and received orders to be sent on the western expedition to the south of Ba and Shu. Having gone south and captured Qiong, Ze, and Kunming, they returned and made their report on the mission. (Dawson translation, p. xix.)

So his training included farming, literature, travel, adventure, anthropological research, archery, court service, and warfare. If historians improve with their own experience of life, since it enables them to understand more fully the lives of the people they study, then Sima Qian was off to a good start. His father charged him with the historian's task, to be performed at extraordinary standards of excellence:

> When I die, you are bound to become the Grand Historian; and having become Grand Historian, do not forget what I intended to argue and put down in writing. Moreover, filial piety starts in the service of parents, is next to be found in the service of rulers, and finally in the establishment of one's own character. For the most important aspect of filial piety is for your name to be spread abroad in later generations in order to bring glory to your father and mother. (Dawson translation, xix-xx.)

The highlight of Sima Qian's historical writing is its emphasis on biography, a traditional Chinese literary form that he developed into a vehicle for commenting on the political and ethical policies of the state not only in the past but also in his own time. His judgments could be fierce and they sometimes got him into trouble. Personally, his support for his friend General Li Ling at a time when the general was in great disfavor in court led to Sima Qian's castration (see opposite). Later the Han Emperor Wudi was so angered by Sima Qian's account of his father, the Emperor Jingdi, that he had this chapter removed. Sima Qian included in the *Shi Qi* speeches from the Warring States period advocating strategies for one state to gain power over another. The Han government chose to suppress this information as well and "for over a century access to the copy in the imperial library was extremely difficult, as the work and its author were considered unorthodox if not dangerous" (Nienhauser, p. xii). Later, however, imperial feelings apparently mellowed and Sima Qian won the reputation of greatest master of the early Chinese historical tradition.

defended a military leader out of favor with the emperor and the court. As a punishment, he had to choose between execution and castration. He chose castration in order to complete his work:

> It is because I regretted that it had not been completed that I submitted to the extreme penalty without rancor. When I have truly completed this work, I shall deposit it in some safe place. If it may be handed down to men who will appreciate it and penetrate to the villages and great cities, then though I should suffer a thousand mutilations, what regret would I have? (deBary (1999), p. 372)

Sima Qian completed his accounts up to *c.* 100 B.C.E. Ban Biao (3–54 C.E.) added tens of chapters of "Supplementary Chronicles," and his son, Ban Gu (32–92 C.E.), wrote the *Han Shu*, or "History of the Han Dynasty," to 22 C.E. Ban Gu established the tradition of compiling a history of each dynasty, a form continued in the *Hou-Han shu* or "History of the Later Han," and enduring into the twentieth century. In addition, essays, stories, and documents preserved on wood or carved in stone give further evidence of the history of the Han. Similar official dynastic histories and private materials provide our sources for the Era of Division and the Sui and Tang dynasties. For these periods also, there are far more remains of poetry, literature, and art, as well. Later, Sima Guang (1019–86 C.E.) wrote a monumental general history of China from earliest times to his own day, based largely on all these earlier documents and including many that have subsequently been lost.

Because the official histories carry their own biases and focus almost entirely on issues of the central government and its court, unofficial materials from the provinces are especially useful in giving additional viewpoints. Grave sites and tombs yield documents, inscriptions, and engravings, and these often include relief sculptures of the activities of the deceased during his or her life. The burial goods represent in miniature the deceased's house, tools, carriages, boats, farms, and equipment. They often included terra cotta figures or painted frescoes of colleagues from life: entertainers, musicians, servants, and maids.

Archaeologists have uncovered important additional written sources. A cache of documents sealed in a cave in Dunhuang, on the northwest edge of China proper, was discovered by the British archaeologist Aurel Stein in his expeditions in central Asia in 1900–15. They included private and official business documents, contracts, textbooks for students in various fields, instruction in moral education, stories and poems. The cave housed a Buddhist monastery, and many of the documents highlight the Buddhist influence on China at the time. Subsequent Sino-Swedish expeditions in 1927–34 uncovered additional fragments, covering the period 100 B.C.E.–100 C.E. Since the 1960s archaeological sites in central China have continued to yield additional materials.

THE QIN DYNASTY: WHAT DO WE KNOW?

The map on page 208 charts the expansion of the Qin dynasty from its geopolitical base around the confluence of the Yellow and Wei rivers to its control of the whole of north China and a segment of the south. The Qin conquest ended centuries of fighting among the warring dynasties of north China that began with the decline of the Zhou dynasty and lasted through the period of the Warring States, 481–221 B.C.E. The Qin defeated other regional states over the course of perhaps a century, until by 221 B.C.E. they could rightfully claim to have established an empire, the first in China's history and one that has lasted (almost) to the present.

MILITARY POWER AND MOBILIZATION

Armed force was fundamental in the Qin's conquest. Poems from the *Book of Songs*, dating from the early years of the Zhou dynasty, suggest the ubiquity of warfare in early China:

> Which plant is not yellow?
> Which day don't we march?
> Which man does not go
> To bring peace to the four quarters?
>
> Which plant is not brown?
> Which man is not sad?
> Have pity on us soldiers,
> Treated as though we were not men!
>
> We are neither rhinos nor tigers,
> Yet are led through the wilds.
> Have pity on us soldiers,
> Never resting morn or night.

Terra cotta army from the tomb of Qin Shi Huangdi, Qin dynasty, 210 B.C.E. The vastness of the terra cotta army—it comprised 7000 "soldiers"—buried near the tomb of the First Emperor of Qin and the care with which each life-sized figure was molded suggest at once the enormous power of the Qin army and the emperor's concern with the afterlife.

A thick-furred fox
Scurries though the dark grass.
Our loaded carts
Proceed along the Zhou road.　　　　(Ebrey, p. 13)

The Qin not only conquered north China, they also defeated the Xiongnu, or border tribes to the north and west of China proper. They gained authority over northern Korea, and defeated some of the Yue tribes in the south. The first Qin emperor was Qin Shi Huangdi, "the first august emperor of the Qin." (Compare the title of "Caesar Augustus" of Rome.) In 1974 archaeologists digging near his mausoleum discovered a ceramic army of 7000 life-sized soldiers and horses, arranged in military formation and armed with bronze weapons, spears, longbows, and crossbows (a Chinese invention). In 1976, a second excavation uncovered an additional 1400 chariots and cavalrymen in four military units. The next year a much smaller pit was discovered, holding what appeared to be a terra cotta officer corps. These thousands of figures were not mass produced. Each figure was modeled and painted separately, even down to its elaborate hairstyle, which symbolized its specific military office. The figures apparently represented the elite of the imperial troops, and were fashioned to accompany the emperor to his own tomb and afterlife.

The Qin mobilized tens of thousands of men also for enormous public works projects. After conquering the other states of north China they completed the remaining gaps in the 1500-mile (2400-kilometer) Great Wall of China in seven years with a work force of one million laborers. This Wall was to keep the Xiongnu "barbarians" of the north out of China proper and, with its 40-foot (15-meter) high watch towers constructed every few hundred yards, to serve as a first warning in case of attempted invasion. The first emperor conscripted 700,000 laborers to construct his palace, a complex large enough to hold 40,000 people.

ECONOMIC POWER

Some of the enormous public works projects of the Qin were undertaken to increase the economic productivity of the empire. During the centuries of their rise to power, they had built canals and river transport systems in both the Wei River system in the north and the Min River system in Sichuan. In Sichuan they irrigated the region around Chengdu, turning it into a granary for the nation. The transportation and irrigation systems they built in the northern state of Shanxi transformed it into an area so rich in agricultural productivity and the means of transporting it that they could control all of north China from this base. The Qin also captured the richest sources of iron ore and two of China's best ironworking facilities, crucial resources for fashioning both tools and weapons.

Great Wall of China. Begun 214 B.C.E., rebuilt repeatedly. "The seven wonders of the world are not comparable to this work," wrote one awestruck seventeenth-century observer of this most imposing relic of China's past. Faced with brick and stone and averaging 25 feet (7.6 m) high and wide, the wall is studded with towers that serve as signaling stations, warning of the approach of mobile enemies.

EARLY ADVANCES IN WEAPONRY

3000 (B.C.E.) War chariot invented. In Mesopotamia and southeastern Europe first metal swords and shields made (bronze).

2000 First armor made, from bronze scales, in Mesopotamia.

c. **700** The Phoenicians and Egyptians invent galleys— warships powered by oars.

500 Giant crossbows and catapults used by the Greeks and Carthaginians.

200 Hand-held crossbow now being used in China.

300 (C.E.) Stirrups used in China.

950 Gunpowder used by Chinese for signaling devices and fireworks.

1250–1300 Bronze and iron cannon probably used by the Chinese; in Europe, first recorded use of cannon is 1326.

ADMINISTRATIVE POWER

Administratively, Qin Shi Huangdi ruled through a bureaucracy. He did away with the **feudal** system, by which officials had been appointed on the basis of their personal, often family, ties to the court and therefore owed allegiance to the emperor personally rather than to the empire in the abstract. Now people were chosen for office on the basis of ability; their tasks were fixed and governed by systematic, formalized, written rules; and their work was rewarded or punished according to the degree of their efficiency and fidelity. The empire was divided into some forty administrative units called "commanderies." Each commandery was staffed with three leading officials: a civil authority, a military authority, and an inspector representing the emperor. The three officials served as checks and balances to the others' authority: no one individual could assert too much power and threaten the control of the emperor at the center.

The Qin standardized as they centralized. They fixed weights and measures, values of coinage, the size of cart axles and of the roads they traveled. They standardized the legal code. Perhaps most important of all, the Qin standardized the written form of the Chinese language, possibly the most important single act of political and cultural unification in China's history. To this day, despite great variation in the local forms of spoken Chinese, written Chinese is uniform throughout the country, just as the Qin established it.

THE FALL OF THE QIN DYNASTY

Qin Shi Huangdi died in 210 B.C.E. and was buried in the enormous mausoleum he had created, accompanied by the vast ceramic army he had ordered (see p. 200). Within four years his apparently powerful, centralized, productive, well-organized dynasty had collapsed. Despite the apparent strengths, the Qin had oppressed to the breaking point the nation and its peasantry, the 90 percent of the population who paid the taxes, served in the armies, built the public works projects, and the women who quietly supported all these projects through their work at home. Several hundreds of thousands of these peasants were dispatched to fight the Xiongnu in the far north and northwest on both sides of the Great Wall. As the *Han History* later reported:

> The first emperor of Qin sent forth the men of the empire to guard the northern loop of the Yellow River. For more than ten years they were exposed to the rigors of military life, and countless numbers died. . . . He also made the empire transport fodder and grain, beginning with the coastal commanderies of Huang, Qu and Langye, whose inhabitants had to take these commodities to the northern loop of the Yellow River. . . . Although the men toiled at farming, there was not enough grain for rations; and the women could not spin enough yarn for the tents. The common people were ruined. (Cited in Elvin, p. 27)

In addition to these systemic problems, the fight over the succession to Qin Shi Huangdi's throne destroyed the dynasty. A contest for power broke out between a minister, Li Si; another court official, the eunuch Zhao Gao; and the emperor's own son. In the struggle, many supporters of the former emperor were murdered by the son on advice from his minister. Fear and disloyalty flourished. Each person seemed concerned only for his own survival and aggrandizement. Qin Shi Huangdi had instituted bureaucracy in place of personal rule throughout the empire, but personal politics still dominated the imperial court. Finally, Zhao forced the emperor's son to commit suicide, but then he himself was assassinated. While the court was convulsed in these internal struggles, rebels broke into the capital at Xianyang and captured power. Warfare continued until, in 202 B.C.E., the rebel leader Liu Bang emerged victorious and established the Han dynasty.

IDEOLOGIES OF EMPIRE

China's historical record was written and preserved by an official elite trained in philosophy. Perhaps this is the reason for China's profound concern with the philosophy and ideology of empire. Emperors in their public proclamations and writers in their records stress the importance of their philosophy to the actual process of building, sustaining, and guiding the empire.

LEGALISM

During his reign Qin Shi Huangdi set up various inscriptions on stone in various parts of his empire. These proclaimed his values and policies—for example, after he put down a rebellion in the far northeast he inscribed on the city walls:

> Then he mobilized armies, and punished the unprincipled, and those who perpetrated rebellion were wiped out.
> Armed force exterminates the violent and rebellious, but civil power relieves the guiltless of their labors, and the masses all submit in their hearts.
> Achievements and toil are generously assessed, and the rewards even extend to cattle and horses, and his bounty enriches the land.
> The August Emperor gave a vigorous display of his authority, and his virtue brought together all the states, and for the first time brought unity and supreme peace.
> City walls were demolished [suggesting that they were no longer necessary for defense], waterways were opened up, and obstacles were flattened.
> When the physical features of the land had been determined, there was no conscript labor for the masses, and all under heaven was pacified.

> Men take pleasure in their farmland, and women cultivate their tasks, and all matters have their proper arrangement.
> His kindness protects all production, and for long they have been coming together in the fields, and everyone is content with his place.
> (Sima Qian, p. 74)

In another inscription he wrote:

> When the sage of Qin took charge of his state, he first determined punishments and names, and clearly set forth the ancient regulations.
> He was the first to standardize the system of laws, examine and demarcate duties and responsibilities, so as to establish unchanging practices. (Sima Qian, p. 82)

He proclaimed a code of sexual conduct:

> If a man commits adultery, to kill him is no crime, so men hang on to the standards of righteousness.
> If a wife elopes to remarry, then the son will not have a mother, and so everyone is converted into chastity and purity. (Sima Qian, p. 83)

In his rulings Qin Shi Huangdi followed many of the policies of the political philosopher Han Feizi (d. 233 B.C.E.). Han Feizi called himself a Legalist because he believed that strict laws, strictly enforced, were the best assurance of good and stable government. Han Feizi's statements quoted here are quite consistent with the policies actually adopted by Qin Shi Huangdi:

> The intelligent sovereign makes the law select men and makes no arbitrary promotion himself. He makes the law measure merits and makes no arbitrary regulation himself. . . . To govern the state by law is to praise the right and blame the wrong. . . . To correct the faults of the high, to rebuke the vices of the low, to suppress disorders, to decide against mistakes, to subdue the arrogant, to straighten the crooked, and to unify the folkways of the masses, nothing could match the law. . . . If law is definite, the superiors are esteemed and not violated. If the superiors are not violated, the sovereign will become strong and able to maintain the proper course of government. Such was the reason why the early kings esteemed Legalism and handed it down to posterity.

The means whereby the intelligent ruler controls his ministers are two handles only. The two handles are chastisement and commendation. (Han Fei Tzu, I:40,45–7)

DAOISM

This concern for law and order, reward and punishment, recommended by Han Feizi and his school of Legalism, characterizes the regime of Qin Shi Huangdi. There were, however, at least two other major schools of political and ethical thought prominent in China by this time, Daoism and Confucianism. Daoism was a more mystical school, not usually directly applicable to government, but often a solace to public men in their private lives. Daoism is often seen as an inspiration to artists, and, because it advocates a high regard for nature, it is often seen as an inspiration to natural scientists as well. The legendary founder of Daoism and author of its key text, the *Daodejing*, is Laozi (*c.* 604–*c.* 517 B.C.E.), but the school and the book more likely date to the third or fourth centuries B.C.E. Its teachings are cloaked in paradox and mystery:

The Way that can be spoken of is not the constant Way;
The name that can be named is not the constant name.
The nameless is the beginning of Heaven and Earth;
The named is the mother of all things.

Do away with sageliness, discard knowledge,
And the people will benefit a hundredfold.
Do away with humaneness, discard righteousness,
And the people will once more be filial and loving,
Dispense with cleverness, discard profit,
And there will be no more bandits and thieves.
These three, to be regarded as ornaments, are insufficient.
Therefore let the people have something to cling to:
Manifest plainness,
Embrace uncarved wood,
Diminish selfishness,
Reduce desires.

What is softest in the world
Overcomes what is hardest in the world.
No-thing penetrates where there is no space.
Thus I know that in doing nothing there is advantage.
The worldless teaching and the advantage of doing nothing—there are few in the world who understand them.

The more prohibitions there are in the world,
The poorer are the people.
The more sharp weapons the people have,
The more disorder is fomented in the family and state,
The more adroit and clever men are,
The more deceptive things are brought forth.
The more laws and ordnances are promulgated,
The more thieves and robbers there are.
Therefore the sage says:
I do nothing (*wuwei*),
And the people are transformed by themselves.
(deBary, 1999, pp. 79–90)

Finally, the Daoist view of simplicity seems to have little need for government:

Let the state be small and the people be few.
There may be ten or even a hundred times as many implements,
But they should not be used.
Let the people, regarding death as a weighty matter, not travel far.
Though they have boats and carriages, none shall ride in them.
Though they have armor and weapons, none shall display them.
Let the people return once more to the use of knotted ropes [instead of writing; compare the *quipu* of the Incas]
Let them savor their food and find beauty in their clothing, peace in their dwellings, and joy in their customs.
Though neighboring states are within sight of one another,
And the sound of cocks and dogs is audible from one to the other,
People will reach old age and yet not visit one another. (deBary, 1999, p. 94)

CONFUCIANISM

More central to Chinese political as well as ethical thought were the teachings of Confucius (551–479 B.C.E.), a philosopher and political adviser from the small state of Lu in modern Shandong. Confucius began his career as a scholar from a young age. He mastered the six arts of ritual, music, artery, chariot driving, calligraphy, and arithmetic, and then began his career as a teacher. At a time when China was divided into many states, often in conflict, he formulated principles that he thought would bring peace, contentment, dignity, and personal cultural

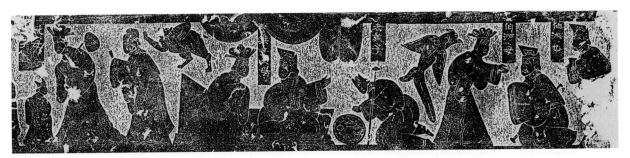

Rubbing of an engraved stone slab depicting Laizi, from the Wu Liang shrine, erected in 151 C.E. at Jiaxiang in Shandong province. Under the Han dynasty, the celebration of filial piety advocated by Confucius took a more exaggerated form, so that men were sometimes appointed to official posts on the basis of their reputation as good sons. Even when he was over seventy years old, Laizi is said to have tried to convince his parents that they were still young by continuing to play with his toys like a boy.

development at least to the elites of his time. Although Confucius was unsuccessful in finding employment as an adviser in any single state, his disciples kept his vision alive, and it has permeated Chinese thought and, often, government policy.

Confucius felt that good government depended on good officials, men of *jen*, or humanity, benevolence, virtue, and culture. Little concerned with the supernatural, he believed that a moral order pervaded the universe and that it could be understood. In contrast to the tumult of his own day, Confucius believed that in the early days of the Zhou dynasty there had been a golden age of peace and order, wisdom and virtue. In those days, political leaders had understood the importance of feudal hierarchy, rituals, music, and art, but the neglect of these elements of humanism and rationalism, and the absence of schools that taught them to new leaders, had reduced China to chaos.

Confucius believed in the essential goodness and educability of each individual, and believed that the virtues of the past could be regained. He believed in the centrality of the "gentleman" (*junzi*), the morally based leader who had the vision to move the society toward peace and virtue. Such a gentleman would and should be concerned about political leadership and the proper ordering of the state. For Confucius, however, gentlemen were not born but made, fashioned through proper education. Believing that character, not birth, was important, he taught whoever would come to him. Confucius' own era was too violent for his teachings to find immediate acceptance.

As we have seen, the Qin dynasty did not welcome his teachings either, but eventually the next dynasty, the Han, did. Under the Han, Confucius' ethical and political values came to dominate the culture and thought of China's scholars and intellectuals. They continued powerful for most of the following 2000 years, also influencing the political thought of Korea, Japan, and southeast Asia. Confucian scholars kept alive the five literary classics of the Zhou dynasty and added to them Confucius' own teachings, *The Analects* (see Source, p. 206).

QIN SHI HUANGDI, THE LEGALISTS, AND THE CONFUCIANISTS

The philosophies of Legalism and Confucianism collided during the Qin dynasty. In direct contrast to the Confucianists' reverence for the past, Li Si, the prime minister, argued that the administration of the Qin was far superior to the government of any earlier time. Li Si argued that "In antiquity all under Heaven was divided and in chaos, and nobody was capable of bringing unity to the rest" (Sima Qian, p. 30). The Qin success was the result of its decision to replace feudal administration with an orderly system of laws and appointment to office on the basis of efficiency in accordance with Legalist principles. Li Si recommended that the Confucian classics be collected and burned so that the past could no longer be held up as an alternative to present policies. In 213 B.C.E. the burning of the books took place. Subsequently, as Confucian scholars continued to oppose Qin Shi Huangdi, he had 460 scholars buried alive. These acts of anti-intellectualism and brutality are reported by Sima Qian, as official historian of the Han government. They leave the Legalist Qin with a dismal reputation. The cruel intrigues and struggles for succession that helped end the Qin confirm that view.

One of the enduring philosophical concepts of Chinese imperial politics was the Mandate of Heaven. Heaven, not a personal god but the cosmic forces of the universe, underpinned rulers of high moral stature and undercut those who lacked it. Heaven conferred its mandate on the moral and revoked it from the immoral. Dynasties were thus held accountable for their actions, and they could not expect to rule forever. The evidence of their loss of cosmic connection would be made manifest, not only in the usual political and economic strife of a weak administration, but also through nature itself going awry in the form of floods, droughts, or other natural disasters. Throughout Chinese history, rebels against an emperor would cite evidence of his having lost the "Mandate," while those supporting new rulers would proclaim their possession of it. Han historians made clear their belief that the Qin dynasty had lost the Mandate of Heaven.

Nevertheless, the Qin had brought China to a new stage of political development: the empire had been founded; an effective bureaucratic administration had been established; and careers had been opened to new men of talent. All these innovations were to last, in changing measures, for 2000 years.

SOURCE
Confucius and The Analects

We have no record of Confucius' writing down his own teachings. *The Analects*, a collection of thoughtful perceptions attributed to him, were apparently recorded and compiled by disciples of his disciples. Because these aphorisms—497 verses in twenty chapters—are brief, unelaborated, unorganized, and written in ideographic form, their exact meaning is not always clear, but these same qualities promote the reader's engagement with and interpretation of the text. *The Analects* have been a part of the education of every Chinese school student for centuries, at least until the Communist revolution in 1949. The selections here represent typical issues for Confucius: the importance of formal, humanistic education in forming proper character; teaching and learning by example; focus on the world of here-and-now; and respect for others, especially for parents and elders.

A young man is to be filial within his family and respectful outside it. He is to be earnest and faithful, overflowing in his love for living beings and intimate with those who are humane. If after such practice he has strength to spare, he may use it in the study of culture.

Lead them by means of regulations and keep order among them through punishments, and the people will evade them and will lack any sense of shame.

Lead them through moral force (*de*) and keep order among them through rites (*li*), and they will have a sense of shame and will also correct themselves.

In education there should be no class distinctions.

Shall I teach you what knowledge is? When you know something, to know that you know it. When you do not know, to know that you do not know it. That is knowledge.

The noble person is concerned with rightness; the small person is concerned with profit.

I am not one who was born with knowledge; I am one who loves the past and is diligent in seeking it.

The Three Armies can be deprived of their commander, but even a common person cannot be deprived of his will.

The wise have no doubts; the humane have no sorrows; the courageous have no fears.

Before you have learned to serve human beings, how can you serve spirits. . . .

When you do not yet know life, how can you know about death?

Look at nothing contrary to ritual; listen to nothing contrary to ritual; say nothing contrary to ritual; do nothing contrary to ritual.

What you would not want for yourself, do not do to others.

Zigong asked about government. The Master said, "sufficient food, sufficient military force, the confidence of the people." Zigong said, "If one had, unavoidably, to dispense with one of these three, which of them should go first?" The Master said, "Get rid of the military." Zigong said, "If one had, unavoidably, to dispense with one of the remaining two, which should go first?" The Master said, "Dispense with the food. Since ancient times there has always been death, but without confidence a people cannot stand."

(deBary, 1999, pp. 45–60)

Throughout Chinese history, some groups rebelled against Confucius' ethical principles. Peasant rebels, a frequent presence throughout the centuries, condemned Confucius' emphasis on order and harmony. In the late nineteenth and twentieth centuries, as China saw itself fall behind the technological and military achievements of the Western world, Confucian traditions were challenged with renewed vigor (see Chapters 17 and 20). Critics argued that Confucianism was incompatible with equality, scientific education, rebellious youth movements, dignity of physical labor, peasant equity, and equal rights for women. The Communist government which ruled China after 1949 attacked Confucius especially bitterly in 1973 and 1974 during the Cultural Revolution, asserting that in his own day Confucius had served as a representative of the slave-owning aristocracy.

THE HAN DYNASTY

When Liu Bang (r. 202–195 B.C.E.) prevailed in the warfare that ended the Qin dynasty, the empire remained intact. One ruling family fell and another took its place and asserted its own control, but the empire itself continued united under a single emperor. The principal Legalist ministers who had guided the Qin were replaced, but the administrative bureaucracy continued to function.

Change came in the leadership style of the new dynasty. Liu Bang was himself a commoner and a soldier, perhaps illiterate, with many years of warfare still ahead of him—he died in battle in 195 B.C.E.—but as his ministers he chose educated men with Confucian principles. Slowly, a new social and political hierarchy emerged, with scholars at the top, followed by farmers, artisans, and merchants. Legalism still influenced the administrative systems, and Daoism's emphasis on nature and emotion continued to be attractive, but Confucius' ethical teachings captured the imagination of the court.

The influence of Confucianism appeared in four other areas. First, history became more important than ever. The appointment of Sima Tan and then of his son Sima Qian as court historians established the tradition of imperial record keeping. The Confucian notion of the importance of tradition and continuity prevailed over the Legalist idea of discounting the past.

Second, in 124 B.C.E. the most powerful and long lived of the Han rulers, Wudi or Emperor Wu (r. 141–87 B.C.E.), established an elite imperial academy to teach specially selected scholar-bureaucrats the wisdom of Confucius and its applicability to problems of governance. The emperor also declared that knowledge of the Confucian classics would be a basis for promotion in the imperial civil service. Although the academy could at first educate only fifty men, it grew in size until in the later Han period it could accommodate 30,000 men. In Han times, the landed aristocracy still gained most of the places in the bureaucracy, but the principle of appointment and promotion based not on birth but on success in an examination in the Confucian classics was finally established during the Tang dynasty (618–907 C.E.).

Third, an imperial conference of Confucian legal scholars was convened in the imperial palace in 51 B.C.E. to codify and establish the principles for applying case law. This established and consolidated the Chinese legal system for centuries to come.

Finally, Confucian scholars, both male and female, began to establish principles of conduct for women. Confucius had spoken of the importance of five relationships in human society: ruler-subject; father-son; husband-wife; older brother-younger brother; and friend-friend. The first four were hierarchical relationships of superior-inferior. Little, however, had been written about the role of women.

ADMONITIONS FOR WOMEN

During the Han dynasty, several authors decided to address this subject (see Spotlight, pp. 212–3). Ban Zhao (45–116 C.E.), sister of the famous court historian Ban Gu, wrote *Admonitions for Women*, a text of advice on the virtues appropriate for aristocratic women, which was divided into seven sections on humility, resignation, subservience, self-abasement, obedience, cleanliness, and industry.

In ancient times, on the third day after a girl was born, people placed her at the base of the bed, gave her a pot shard to play with, and made a sacrifice to announce her birth. She was put below the bed to show that she was lowly and weak and should concentrate on humbling herself before others. Playing with a shard showed that she should get accustomed to hard work and concentrate on being diligent. Announcing her birth to the ancestors showed that she should focus on continuing the sacrifices. These three customs convey the unchanging path for women and the ritual traditions.

Humility means yielding and acting respectful, putting others first and oneself last, never mentioning one's own good deeds or denying one's own faults, enduring insults and bearing with mistreatment, all with due trepidation. Industriousness means going to bed late, getting up early, never shirking work morning or night, never refusing to take on domestic work, and completing

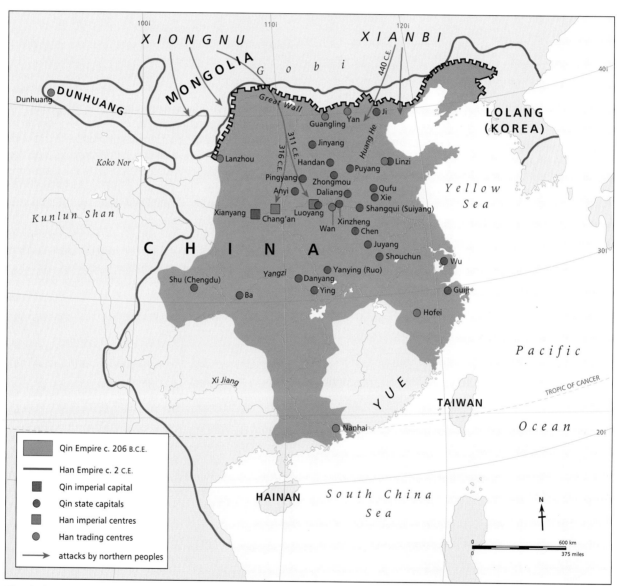

Classical China In 221 B.C.E. two centuries of internecine rivalry—the "Warring States" period—ended with the rise to centralized power of the Qin dynasty, but internal revolt and external pressures on the borders precipitated further civil war. The Han dynasty emerged as the new rulers in 202 B.C.E. They refortified the northern walls, and extended imperial control far to the south and west, deep into central Asia along the silk route, defining a Chinese territorial extent that has been asserted down to the present day.

everything that needs to be done neatly and carefully. Continuing the sacrifices means serving one's husband-master with appropriate demeanor, keeping oneself clean and pure, never joking or laughing, and preparing pure wine and food to offer to the ancestors. (Ebrey, p. 75) (see Spotlight, pp. 212–13)

Placing a similar stress on the virtues of self-sacrificing service, Liu Xiang (79–8 B.C.E.) wrote the *Biographies of Heroic Women*, which recounted the virtues of 125 women. He especially praised the mother of the philosopher Mencius, the greatest of the Confucian scholars. Liu Xiang quotes Mencius' mother telling her son of her concept of women's obligations:

> A woman's duties are to cook the five grains, heat the wine, look after her parents-in-law, make clothes, and that is all! Therefore she cultivates the skills required in the women's quarters and has no ambition to manage affairs outside of the house. The *Book of Changes* says, "In her central place, she attends to the preparation of the food." The *Book of Songs* says, "It will be theirs neither to do wrong nor to do good,/Only about the spirits and the food will they have to think." This means that a woman's duty is not to control or to take charge. Instead she must follow the "three submissions." When she is young, she must submit to her parents. After her marriage, she must submit to her husband. When she is widowed, she must submit to her son. These are the rules of propriety. (Ebrey, p. 73)

(Compare and contrast contemporary Indian perspectives on women's obligations as cited briefly on pp. 237 and 239, and Roman policies on p. 174.)

The pervasive Confucian stress on hierarchy and deference permeates these prescriptions for women's conduct. However, throughout Han times—but not after—women could inherit property, divorce, and remarry after divorce or widowhood. And (see p. 215) even the most highly placed women sometimes rebelled against Confucian ideals.

MILITARY POWER

The Han emperors were no less militaristic than the Qin. Confucian principles of moral rectitude held sway among the educated elites, but the government did not dispense with formal legal systems nor did it forsake offensive or defensive warfare. The standing army numbered between 300,000 and 1,000,000, and all able-bodied men between the ages of twenty or twenty-three and fifty-six were conscripted, serving for one year of training and one year of duty in the capital or in battle on the frontiers. They could be recalled in case of warfare. Throughout the Han dynasty, China was engaged in incessant battles with the Xiongnu and other tribes around the Great Wall (see map opposite). Indeed, as we shall see shortly, the Han forced open a corridor through Gansu in the direction of Xinjiang (Turkestan). One of the reasons for this expansion was to open markets for silk in the west. Parthian traders carried goods on this trade route

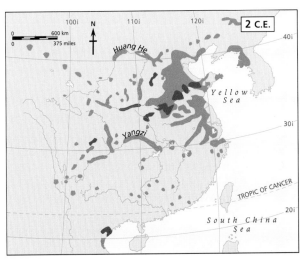

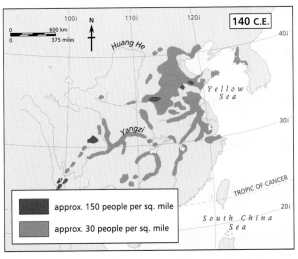

Chinese expansion A substantial shift in Chinese population distribution began during the first two centuries C.E., a fact that can be traced from Han census records. As land-hunger and pressure from the Xiongnu and the Tibetans on the northern border forced migration from the densely populated northeast, and as techniques for rice cultivation in the humid basin of the Yangzi improved, the lands to the south were mastered, and population clusters developed along the river valleys.

as far as Rome (see p. 249). China also wanted to secure a supply of horses from distant Bactria for the military. On the northern borders, where Chinese, Mongol, Tibetan, and Barbarian forces fought, each learned the strengths and weaknesses of the other. A Chinese strength was the crossbow. A very significant Mongol and Tibetan strength was cavalry, mounted on strong, fast horses. To achieve military parity, the Han emperors sought and found a supply of equivalent horses in central Asia. The Gansu corridor served as an access route, and Emperor Wu garrisoned it with 700,000 soldiers. Administrative records written on wooden strips have survived to tell of the lives of these immigrant soldier-colonizers in some detail.

POPULATION AND MIGRATION

The Han dynasty also consolidated its holdings in the comparatively unpopulated south. A population map of China from the year 2 C.E., based on the earliest preserved census in the world, shows the disparity of population distribution. The Chinese heartland was clearly the north; in the south population was sparse, mostly settled along the rivers. In both the south and the border regions, military-agricultural colonies were established to provide military defense and economic development. The Chinese attempted to win the local populations over to Chinese culture, and often succeeded, but

not always. On the borders and in the southeast they met opposition, and rebellions against the Chinese settlers erupted in 86, 83, and 28–25 B.C.E.

In the south, in general, there was little indigenous population and little hostility or resistance to the coming of northerners. The regional Yue or Viet tribes were more often involved in fighting one another, although in 40 C.E. there was a revolt, and violence broke out on at least seven occasions between 100–184 C.E. Perhaps the increased resistance was evoked by the vast increase in the flow of population to the south. Compare the distribution of population in the year 140 C.E., when the second preserved census was taken, with the map showing the population in 2 C.E. The total population had declined from about 58 million to about 48 million, but the regional distribution had shifted from 76 percent in the north and 24 percent in the south, to 54 and 46 percent respectively. The population of the northwest decreased by 6.5 million; of the northeast, by 11.5 million. The likely causes of the population losses on the border were continuing pressure from the Xiongnu and the Tibetans, while in the northeast plain, the great floods caused by the Yellow River breaking its banks and twice changing its course, in c. 4 C.E. and again in 11 C.E., may have affected the population distribution. The military and natural turbulence also impoverished China's civilian population, as the empire allocated more and more resources to support the army, expansionism, and the court in the capital of Chang'an.

ECONOMIC POWER

The economy of Han China grew with the exploitation of new sources of wealth from along the Yangzi River, Sichuan, and the south. New inventions in mining (including salt mining), paper production, the compass, the breast-strap harness for horses, a redesigned plowshare, hydraulic engineering, and the tapping of natural gas increased wealth and productivity. The road through the Gansu corridor to Xinjiang (Turkestan) brought increased knowledge of distant lands and new trade possibilities. In 138 B.C.E. Emperor Wudi dispatched Zhang Qian to inner

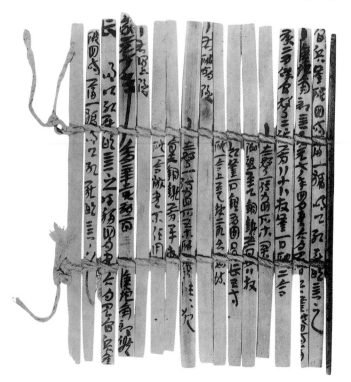

Inventory written on bamboo, 95 C.E. Government bureaucracy expanded with military and economic power under the Han dynasty, producing an enormous number of documents on wooden and bamboo strips. This inventory lists the equipment of two infantry units. (*British Library, London*)

Asia to seek enemies of the Xiongnu who might serve as allies of the Chinese. Zhang returned twelve years later without new alliances, but with precious new information on lands as far west as Bactria, in modern northern Afghanistan. New trade possibilities opened not only in horses, but also in silk. Parthian traders served as intermediaries between the Chinese and Roman Empires. By 57 B.C.E. Chinese silk had reached Rome. The first silk route had been opened. Geography and cartography flourished, and gazetteers began to be published.

The cost of military expeditions and garrisons, and the expenses of the self-aggrandizing court ate up the gains, however. Having dramatically lowered the land revenues when they first took office, the Han emperors began once again to raise them. They also began to nationalize private enterprise, by bringing it under state control, not in order to promote efficiency or honesty but to gain the profits for the state. Although commerce and business were theoretically held in low regard by Confucianists, businessmen flourished under the Han, and Sima Qian praised their enterprise:

> There is no fixed road to wealth, and money has
> no permanent master. It finds its way to the man of
> ability like the spokes of a wheel converging upon
> the hub, and from the hands of the worthless it
> falls like shattered tiles. A family with a thousand
> catties of gold may stand side by side with the lord
> of a city; the man with a hundred million cash may
> enjoy the pleasures of a king. Rich men such as
> these deserve to be called the "untitled nobility,"
> do they not? (Sima Qian, p. 356)

Emperor Wu sought to expropriate some of this wealth to pay for his military ventures and his imperial court. He altered coinage, confiscated the land of the nobility, sold offices and titles, and increased taxes. He established government monopolies in the production of iron, salt, and liquor, and he took over part of the grain trade, arguing that this was a means of stabilizing prices, but actually so that he could secure profits for his government. On his death, his successor, the Emperor Zhao, arranged a debate between his chief minister, who advocated continuing the state monopolies on salt and iron, and a number of Confucian scholars, who opposed them. The minister argued the need:

> We cherish the goal of raising a great army and
> driving the Xiongnu back north. I again assert that

Stone relief of harnessed cattle found at Mizhi, Shaanxi province. Technological advancements, such as the development of the animal-drawn plow, went hand in hand with the increase in the area of cultivated land under the Han dynasty.

> to do away with the salt and iron monopolies and
> equable marketing system would bring havoc to our
> frontier military policies and would be heartless
> toward those on the frontier. (Ebrey, p. 61)

The Confucians opposed the policy of costly military expansion and the government plan to take over businesses in order to finance this expansion. Their argument sounds almost Daoist in its statement that a benevolent king has no enemies:

> The master conqueror need not fight, the expert
> warrior needs no soldiers, and the great commander
> need not array his troops. If you foster high
> standards in the temple and courtroom, you need
> only make a bold show and bring home your troops,
> for the king who practices benevolent government
> has no enemies anywhere. What need can he then
> have for expense funds? (Ebrey, p. 61)

The Confucians distrusted businessmen as self-seeking and corrupt, and they feared that government-run business would multiply that corruption:

SPOTLIGHT
A Han Dynasty Code of Conduct

The poet Zhang Hua (*c.* 232– 300 C.E.) observed his ruler's court with its ministers and courtiers, wives and concubines, and concluded that the traditional Confucian rules of conduct were being violated, especially after the fall of the centralized Han dynasty. To provide a code of conduct, Zhang composed *Admonitions of the Instructress of the Ladies in the Palace.* They define the position of a privileged but highly regulated upper class of women within the rigid, hierarchical Chinese court.

About a century later Gu Kaizhi (c. 334–406), painter at the court of Nanjing, transcribed segments of the *Admonitions* and illustrated them in nine scenes in an elegant scroll painting. Although the original has been lost, a tenth-century copy survives in the British Museum, painted on fine silk weave 137 inches long and 9¾ inches wide (3.48 m by 25 cm).

In **figure 1**, Gu Kaizhi depicts one imperial concubine combing the hair of another in front of a mirror with cosmetic materials arrayed in finely lacquered boxes kept near at hand.

Figure 1 Gu Kaizhi, two concubines in front of a mirror, *Admonitions …*, fourth century C.E.

Opposite her another lady of the court gazes intently into her mirror as she paints her eyebrows. Zhang Hua's text, which inspired the painting, reads:

> Men and women know how to adorn their faces, but there is none who knows how to adorn his character. Yet if the character be not adorned, there is a danger that the rules of conduct may be transgressed. Correct your character as with an axe, embellish it as with a chisel; strive to create holiness in your own nature.

In **figure 2**, Gu has painted a woman in her chamber in conversation with a visiting gentleman who sits on the bench at her bedside. Gu, who was noted for his ability to represent psychological insights through his portraits, has created this scene to illustrate Zhang's Admonition:

> If the words that you utter are good, all men for a thousand leagues around will make response to you. But if you

depart from this principle, even your bedfellow will distrust you.

Gu was also praised for his use of landscape to represent philosophical concepts. His treatment of another of Zhang's Admonitions demonstrates this talent. Zhang wrote:

In nature there is [nothing] that is exalted which is not soon brought low. Among living things there is nothing which having attained its apogee does not henceforth decline. When the sun has reached its mid-course, it begins to sink; when the moon is full it begins to wane. To rise to glory is as hard as to build a mountain out of dust; to fall into calamity is as easy as the rebound of a tense spring.

To illustrate Zhang's perception of the fragility of human accomplishment, and of all of nature as well, Gu has painted a glorious scene of nature in its richness (**figure 3**), a mountain peak alive with wild animals, under a radiant sun and moon, and at the side—a hunter aiming his crossbow.

Artistically, the Admonitions unify the arts of poetry, philosophy, calligraphy, and painting. In the wake of the fall of the Han dynasty they reaffirm the moral, ethical, and aesthetic teachings of Confucius, emphasizing dignity in personal behavior and sensitivity in human relationships. Finally,

Figure 2 Gu Kaizhi, a woman and a gentleman in conversation, *Admonitions …*, fourth century C.E.

although the *Admonitions* are to be delivered to the ladies of the palace by an "Instructress," in fact Zhang, the poet-philosopher, and Gu, the painter-calligrapher, are both males.

Figure 3 Gu Kaizhi, mountain scene, *Admonitions …*, fourth century C.E

The government officers busy themselves with gaining control of the market and cornering commodities. With the commodities cornered, prices soar and merchants make private deals and speculate. The officers connive with the cunning merchants who are hoarding commodities against future need. Quick traders and unscrupulous officials buy when goods are cheap in order to make high profits. Where is the balance in this standard? (Ebrey, p. 63)

The emperor came to accept the Confucian argument and relinquished at least some government-run monopolies.

ADMINISTRATIVE POWER

The bureaucracy of the early Han seemed to run well, and the adoption of Confucian principles tempered some of the harshness of the Legalist codes. In addition, the wars that the Qin had pursued to establish China's borders made fighting somewhat less necessary for the Han. For two hundred years even the problems of succession, problems that had ultimately helped destroy the Qin dynasty, were negotiated effectively, if sometimes quite cruelly. Nevertheless, the absence of clear principles of imperial succession continued, and in 9 C.E. the Han temporarily fell from power because there was no clear successor.

In 1 B.C.E., the Emperor Ping inherited the throne at the age of eight. A regent, Wang Mang, was appointed to run the government during the boy's minority, and when Ping died, Wang Mang became *de facto* ruler, in 9 C.E., declaring himself founder of a new dynasty. His policies, however, alienated virtually everyone. Fighting against the Xiongnu, breaking up large estates, reinstating the prohibition on the sale of land, fixing commodity prices, terminating Han noble status and reducing them to commoners, cutting bureaucratic salaries, confiscating villagers' gold in exchange for bronze—these policies inflamed both rich and poor, nobility and commoners, urban and rural folk. To add to his problems, just at the beginning of Wang Mang's regency, the Yellow River jumped its banks and changed course twice in five years, wreaking immense devastation to property and loss of life. (The Yellow River carries great quantities of silt and has a very shallow bed. It has jumped its banks, and carved out new channels for itself numerous times in China's recorded history.) In 23 C.E., a combination of Xiongnu invasions in the north, the rebellion of Han nobles near the capital, and, after 18 C.E., the revolt of the Red Turbans, a mass movement centered in the Shandong peninsula, which had been most devastated by the river's flooding, brought down Wang Mang and led to the reinstatement of the Han dynasty.

The later Han dynasty, 23–220 C.E., did not have the same strength as the former Han. To cope with continuing incursions, the later Han made alliances with the barbarians, inviting them to settle within the Wall, to provide soldiers for Chinese armies, and even to intermarry with the Chinese. (These policies are similar to Rome's actions in its border regions; see p. 188.) Although this pattern demonstrated the weakness of the Chinese central government, it also contributed to the **sinicization** of the tribal barbarians; they learned the language, culture, and administrative patterns of the Chinese. Reversing the pattern of tribute of the years of strong government, the later Han gave silk cloth to the border tribes so that they would not invade. Later Han emperors also removed the capital from Chang'an eastward to the less exposed Luoyang.

The movement of population to the south increased the wealth of the empire generally, but the increase went largely to merchants and landlords. Peasants continued to be exploited and oppressed by the exactions of these landlords and of the imperial government. As government taxes increased, peasants sold off their private holdings and went to live and farm under the jurisdictions of local landlords. Here, they sought to evade government taxes and military conscription. The landlords themselves faced a dilemma. As members of the governing elites, they were to collect and remit taxes to the central government and to turn over their tenants for conscription, but as landlords and local potentates, it was to their advantage to retain the taxes and the tenants' labor for themselves. Strong central governments were capable of demanding loyalty and collection; the later Han, however, frequently failed. Peasants absconded, the government's tax and labor bases diminished, and provincial notables developed independent power bases.

The beginning of the end of the Han is usually dated to 184 C.E. when a revolt of hundreds of thousands of peasants broke out. The rebellion, called the Yellow Turban revolt for the headgear worn by the rebels, was incited by Zhang Jue, a Daoist healer who proclaimed that a new era would begin with the fall of the Han. It broke out simultaneously in sixteen commanderies throughout the south,

east, and northeast of China. Although this specific revolt was suppressed, it triggered a continuous string of additional outbreaks.

At least four factions struggled for power within the palace—the emperor who, after the death of Emperor Ling in 189, was a young child; the bureaucrats, advisers, palace guards, and regent to the young emperor; the eunuchs in the court, about 2000 castrated men chosen primarily for their direct loyalty to the emperor and the women of the court; and the women of the court and their families. Since each emperor had several wives and consorts, competition among them was fierce, both for their own recognition and for recognition of their sons at court, even as heir to the emperor. After the death of an emperor, his widows and his mother often remained embroiled in court politics to defend their own positions and those of their family.

In the last decades of Han rule, 189–220 C.E., the court was buffeted from the outside and divided on the inside. For example, on September 25, 189 C.E., generals in the court murdered some 2000 eunuchs, destroying their influence on the Han court. By the year 220, when the last Han emperor, Xian, abdicated, the court had no center and the lands of the empire had already been divided among numerous, competing warlords.

THE "THREE KINGDOMS AND SIX DYNASTIES" PERIOD

On the fall of the Han dynasty, China divided into three states: the Wei in the north, ruling over some 29 million people; the Wu in the south, ruling over 11 million; and the Shu in the west, ruling over 7 million. From 265 to 316 C.E. a single dynasty, the Jin, reunited China briefly. Then, for 273 years, 316–589 C.E., China was divided. The most prominent division fell along a north–south axis, with the dividing line approximately following the basin of the Huai River, halfway between the Yellow River to the north and the Yangzi River to the south.

This division was characterized by a number of geographical features. To the north, the top soil is a fine yellow dust called loess. Borne by winds from the west it is 250 feet (75 meters) deep to the north of Chang'an, a region with little irrigation. The agriculture in this area has been dry-field and mostly carried on by owner-operators, and its principal crops are wheat, millet, beans, and turnips. The region is intensely cold in winter. The south, by

contrast, has many waterways, which are useful for both irrigation and navigation. The warmer weather, even subtropical in the far south, makes it possible to grow rice and tea, which were introduced from southeast Asia probably toward the end of the Han dynasty. The area is typically organized into landlord-tenant estates, better able to promote irrigated rice cultivation. During the centuries of imperial division, six successive dynasties governed the south, while a series of non-Chinese barbarian dynasties ruled the north. Warfare and ecological disaster in the north steadily pushed people southward, shifting the balance of population to a southern majority by this period (see map, p. 209). It appeared that the Chinese Empire, like that of Rome, had divided forever.

While China was rent politically, however, its culture and ethical ideologies remained alive and served to maintain its traditions of unity. In the south, especially, the arts, painting, calligraphy, and poetry flourished, frequently with the themes of spiritual survival amid political disarray. The Chinese language, too, continued to unite all literate Chinese as their means of communication. A poem by Tao Yuanming (365–427), who retired from a government post to take up the life of a country gentleman, captured all these elements:

I built my cottage among the habitations of men,
And yet there is no clamor of carriages and horses.
You ask: "Sir, how can this be done?"
"A heart that is distant creates its own solitude."
I pluck chrysanthemums under the eastern hedge,
Then gaze afar toward the southern hills.
The mountain air is fresh at the dusk of day;
The flying birds in flocks return.
In these things there lies a deep meaning;
I want to tell it, but have forgotten the words.

(Cited in Schirokauer, p. 93)

In his paintings of "The Admonitions of the Instructress of the Ladies in the Palace," the painter Gu Kaizhi (334–406) kept alive the Confucian teachings of the Han while developing new artistic traditions for a new age. (See Spotlight, pp. 212–3.)

Meanwhile, in the north, China was open to new social and ethnic syntheses. The barbarians were absorbed into the continuing cultural life of China, and, through intermarriage, into its genetic pool as well. When scholars today note the homogeneity of China's population as "95 percent Han" they are referring to cultural rather than ethnic homogeneity and recognizing the openness of

China toward assimilating and accepting neighboring peoples who accept the culture of the "Han." The Chinese themselves echo the importance of this common culture, referring to all who have accepted it as "people of the Han." The nomadic peoples living on the northern borders and settling within the Great Wall at the invitation of the later Han emperors had already begun to absorb Chinese culture. When they became powerful enough to conquer north China, they found that they needed to enlist Chinese bureaucrats to administer their gains. In many regions, the administrators appointed by the new rulers were descendants of families whom the Han had employed. Thus below the surface of foreign rule a powerful stratum of Chinese elites remained in place.

Hill of the Thousand Buddhas, Jinan, Tang dynasty. The increased power of the Buddhist religious establishment in Tang times is reflected in the growth of cave paintings and sculptures. The merchants and missionaries who brought Buddhism to China along the silk route also brought ideas about the iconography of temples and the depiction of the Buddha (see Spotlight, pp. 288–9).

The most powerful and longest ruling of the nomadic conquerors became the most assimilated. These were the Northern Wei dynasty (r. 386–534), also named the Toba Wei after the tribal group that founded it (called the Xianbei in Chinese). The longer they ruled, the more assimilated they became. In 493–494 they moved their capital from the far west to one of the former Han capitals, Luoyang, so as better to control the northeast. But in Luoyang they wore Chinese dress, adopted Chinese names, and many intermarried. The Toba also made their own contributions to China's administrative practices. In Luoyang they instituted a new pattern of urban organization by wards. Subsequent dynasties used this system in laying out the restored capital of Chang'an (see p. 225). Still later, Japanese imperial planners copied it in Nara (see p. 227). Similarly, in their attempts to keep agricultural populations from fleeing north China, the Toba took over all land ownership for the state and continued to redistribute it in "equal fields" as each generation of cultivators died and new ones inherited the land.

The developing, new aristocracy of mixed Chinese-Xianbei blood alienated the unassimilated Xianbei troops who were garrisoning the frontiers. They finally revolted and defeated the Northern Wei government in 534, opening the way to the Sui dynasty, a family of mixed Chinese-foreign (barbarian) parentage, which reunited China.

BUDDHISM REACHES CHINA

During the Han dynasty Buddhism entered China from its birthplace in India. It is first noted in Chinese historical records in the first century C.E. Siddhartha Gautama, the Buddha, "the enlightened one," (c. 563–483 B.C.E.) introduced a religion of compassion in the face of a world of pain; it is discussed at length in Chapter 9. Here, however, we ask why and how this religion that later died out in its own native soil in India took new root in far off China. Indeed, Confucian scholars and bureaucrats and an institutionalized Daoist establishment often opposed Buddhism's early arrival. Over time, however, its very foreignness may have contributed to its success. The nomadic conquerors who succeeded the Han may have felt comfortable accepting, and even sponsoring a religion which, like themselves, came from outside China.

Second, Buddhism arose in India, to a large degree, as an anti-priestly religion favored by the merchant classes. Later, merchants sponsored Buddhist monasteries, convents, and cave temples along the silk routes between India and China, some of which remain impressive today, and Buddhism arrived in China with Indian Buddhist merchants who traveled these routes. The new religion persevered, securing patronage in several regional courts, capturing the hearts of millions of followers, and ultimately becoming one of the unifying elements in Chinese culture. Eventually Buddhism mixed with Confucianism and Daoism, bringing popular new spiritual, intellectual, cultural, and ritual innovations (see Chapter 9).

REUNIFICATION UNDER THE SUI AND TANG DYNASTIES

Despite almost 400 years of imperial fragmentation, many elements of Chinese unity were potentially at hand: language, ideology, culture, administration at the local level, aristocratic families with deep roots, and sufficient imperial prestige and administrative expertise that even China's conquerors were assimilated to it. To reunite the empire required the restoration of military power, economic productivity, and administrative integration. The Sui dynasty (581–618) provided all three. When the Sui fell, after over-extending itself militarily and economically, the Tang dynasty (618–907) continued and even strengthened these attributes of empire. Moreover the Sui and Tang extended China's reign to truly imperial dimensions—that is, beyond China proper to "outer China," Mongolia, Turkestan, and central Asia as far as the frontiers of modern Afghanistan, Pakistan, and Iran. It also held strong cultural sway over Tibet without direct political control. These lands were larger than all of "inner China" in area, although they held only perhaps 5 percent of its population. In addition, Tang China held northern Vietnam and, briefly, northern Korea. China's cultural influence at this time was extremely strong in Japan as well.

The three centuries of Sui and Tang rule consolidated the theory and practice of Chinese imperial rule even to the present (although today there is no emperor). Since 581 C.E. China has been divided into two administrations only once, in 1127–1275, and fragmented into several regions only twice, in 907–959 and 1916–49. Apart from these three periods, totalling 133 years, the Chinese Empire has stood united for a continuous period of more than fourteen centuries.

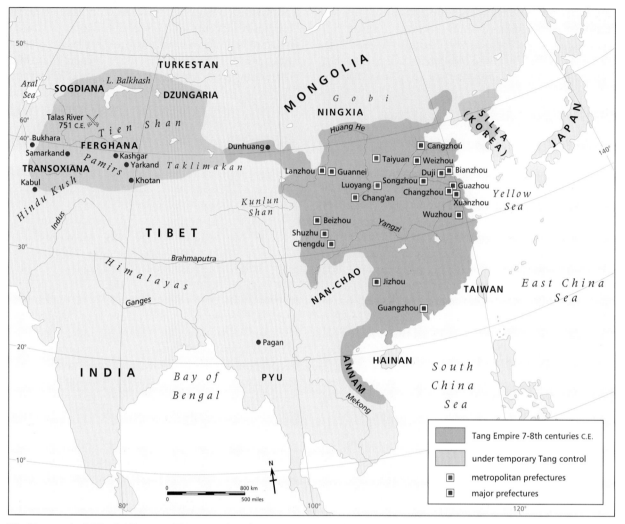

The Tang revival The Sui Dynasty (581–618 C.E.) and its successor, the politically organized Tang, restored the Chinese imperial impulse four centuries after the decline of the Han, extending control along the silk route as far as the Tien Shan mountain range and the arid Ferghana basin. Trade flourished. China finally reached its western limits when its forces were defeated by Arab armies on the Talas River in 751.

The Sui dynasty was founded by the Emperor Wen (581–604), a general of one of the states of north China, who usurped power in his own state and then succeeded in conquering and unifying all of inner China. Militarily he raised the status of the militia, settled them on their own lands, and gave them property rights, thus creating a powerful, committed, and loyal standing army of peasant-farmers. A powerful crossbow, protective body armor, and constant drills to achieve precision in maneuvers and battle made their troops a formidable fighting force. Ideologically, the first Sui emperor and his son, Yang (604–615), who succeeded him, employed a combination of Confucian, Daoist, and Buddhist symbolism and practice in winning popular loyalty.

Administratively, they centralized authority, eliminating a layer of local administrators and transferring their own appointees from one jurisdiction to another every three years to prevent them from establishing their own local power base. They drew up a new centralized legal code which still recognized local customs. Economically, the Sui dynasty completed the Grand Canal from Hangzhou in the south to Kaifeng in the center. The canal linked the Yangzi and Yellow River systems, and extensions connected it to the rebuilt capital in Chang'an and, later, to Beijing. The canal provided for the transportation of the agricultural wealth of the rapidly developing south to the political-military centers of the north.

The expense of mobilizing and dispatching

imperial troops and administrators on their far-flung missions depleted the treasury of the Sui dynasty. The Grand Canal produced many economic benefits, but it cost dearly in manpower. Built in seven years, the canal required the labor of 5.5 million people, and to complete some sections all commoners between the ages of fifteen and fifty-five were pressed into service. Fifty thousand police supervised the construction, flogging and chaining those who could not or would not work, and ordering every fifth family to provide one person to supply and prepare food. In addition to these public works, three disastrous military campaigns in Korea (see pp. 225–6) and in central Asia wasted lives and treasure, and sapped the loyalty of the troops. Finally the leading general of the Sui seized control of the state and under the imperial name Gaozu established the new Tang dynasty in 618 C.E.

Tang policies built on those of the Sui, consolidating and improving them where possible. The Tang dynasty relied more than ever on the imperial examination system to provide its administrators, and in 754 the emperor founded a new Imperial Academy, the Han-Lin Yuan (the Forest of Pens). The arts and technology, often reinforcing one another, flourished under the Tang as never before. The world's first block printing was invented, partly in response to the needs of Buddhists to disseminate their doctrines, for under the Tang the Buddhist religious establishment became increasingly powerful. Buddhist religious art found expression also in further cave sculptures and paintings. New ceramic manufacturing methods led to the production of the first true porcelain, a product of great beauty and durability. For centuries, China alone knew the secret of its manufacture. Millers developed machinery and gears for converting linear and rotary motion, encouraging further development of both water- and windmills. In 659 China produced the world's first pharmacopoeia, or catalog of medicines, listing their contents and uses.

Bridge over the outer moat, a connecting link of the Grand Canal at Suzhou. The engineering feats of the Sui dynasty made significant contributions to the closer integration of the empire. By digging the Grand Canal and building roads in the north China plain, rulers ensured effective communication and the opening of new trade routes between diverse regions.

Finally, Tang era poetry of meditation, nature, politics, fate, suffering, and individual identity transmitted its living legacy even to today's readers in China and beyond. Each of the three most famous Tang poets has been seen as linked to a different cultural tradition: Wang Wei (701–762) to Buddhism; Li Bai (701–761) to Daoism; and Du Fu (712–770) to Confucianism, although each was influenced by all three traditions. Du Fu's "Autumn Meditation" expresses the tension between the high-stakes, hustle-bustle of the imperial court under stress and his own desire for a life of peace within nature:

> I've heard it said Chang'an is like a chessboard, where
> Failure and grief is all these hundred years have brought.
> Mansions of princes and high nobles have new lords.
> New officers are capped and robed for camp and court.
> North on the passes gold drums thunder. To the west
> Horses and chariots rush dispatches and reports.
> Dragon and fish are still, the autumn river's cold.
> My ancient land and times of peace come to my thoughts.

Du Fu's "Ballad of the Army Carts" repeats the heartbreaking pain of war. Du Fu probably wrote it during or following the An Lushan rebellion of 755–763, which the Tang defeated, but from which the dynasty never fully recovered:

> Carts rattle and squeak,
> Horses snort and neigh—
> Bows and arrows at their waists, the conscripts march away.
> Fathers, mothers, children, wives run to say goodbye.
> The Xianyang Bridge in clouds of dust is hidden from the eye.
>
> They tug at them and stamp their feet, weep, and obstruct their way.
> The weeping rises to the sky.
> Along a road a passer-by
> Questions the conscripts. They reply:
> They mobilize us constantly. Sent northwards at fifteen
> To guard the River, we were forced once more to volunteer,

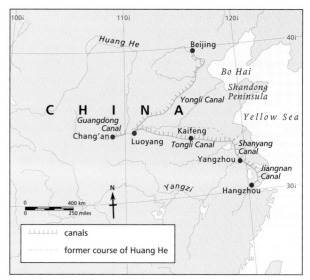

Chinese technology Classical Chinese cultures were administratively and technologically sophisticated. They mastered diplomacy, bureaucracy, navigation, architecture, chemistry, mechanics, astronomy, printing, and, most dramatically, hydrology. Terraced farming, intensive irrigation systems, and the construction of thousands of miles of navigable canals harnessed the often unpredictable rivers of eastern China, and opened up the inland cities to commerce.

> Though we are forty now, to man the western front this year.
> The headman tied our headcloths for us when we first left here.
> We came back white-haired—to be sent again to the frontier.
> Those frontier posts could fill the sea with the blood of those who've died,
> But still the Martial Emperor's aims remain unsatisfied.
> In county after county to the east, Sir, don't you know,
> In village after village only thorns and brambles grow,
> Even if there's a sturdy wife to wield the plough and hoe,
> The borders of the fields have merged, you can't tell east from west.
> It's worse still for the men from Qin, as fighters they're the best—
> And so, like chickens or like dogs, they're driven to and fro.
>
> Though you are kind enough to ask,
> Dare we complain about our task?
> Take, Sir, this winter. In Guanxi
> The troops have not yet been set free.
> The district officers come to press

The land tax from us nonetheless.
  But, Sir, how can we possibly pay?
  Having a son's a curse today.
Far better to have daughters, get them married—
A son will lie lost in the grass, unburied.
  Why, Sir, on distant Qinhhai shore
The bleached ungathered bones lie year on year.
New ghosts complain, and those who died before
Weep in the wet grey sky and haunt the ear.

(Seth)

As Du Fu's poem suggests, the Tang, like the Sui before them, extended their borders too far, pushed the peasants and the conscripts too hard, and, finally, felt the backlash. The Tang dynasty extended China's border farther than any other except the Qing (Manchu), another non-Chinese dynasty from Manchuria, a thousand years later (1644–1912). Its holdings in central Asia flanked and protected the silk route and brought new opportunities for wealth. Ultimately, however, these lands cost more

Ceramic model of a group of musicians seated on a camel, Tang dynasty (618–907 C.E.), excavated from a tomb in the suburb of Xian. The beards, facial features. and costumes of some of the musicians in this group suggest that they are from central Asia. Such models, commonly found in the tombs of the Tang elite, are evidence of a taste for the goods that came along the silk route from the west and the central Asian music that accompanied them.

than they brought in economically and militarily. In 755 An Lushan, one of China's frontier generals of Turkish extraction, revolted, and although the revolt was put down in 763, the cost of the warfare, and the vulnerability it revealed, weakened the Tang dynasty for the entire century and a half leading up to its fall.

The An Lushan revolt came just four years after the Battle of the Talas River in 751. This battle, 2000 miles (3200 kilometers) from Chang'an, on one of the most distant of China's western frontiers, was won by Arab armies. The combined stresses of military losses abroad and revolt at home led the Tang to withdraw from their "outer China" possessions. They found that the border groups—Turks, Uighurs, Khitans, and other ethnic groups—no longer accepted Chinese domination, but continually probed the Tang border fortifications. China ceded control of central Asia to others. One result was that the silk routes soon became passageways of Islam rather than of Buddhism or Confucianism.

Although both agricultural and commercial wealth in China continued to grow, the government could no longer control them for its own imperial purposes. Regional rulers grew in authority and power. In 907 the Tang finally disappeared as China splintered into ten separate states. Yet the imperial idea and pattern held. In 960 the Song dynasty arose, ruling all of China until 1127, and the south until 1279.

CONNECTION: *From the Mongol Empire to the Ming Dynasty*, pp. 383–94.

GREATER CHINA

PROCESSES OF ASSIMILATION

We opened this part on empires by noting that empire signifies rule by one people over another. Let us examine this definition in relation to China.

Caravanserai, Kirghizstan, Tang dynasty, (618–907 C.E.) The silk route led traders through some inhospitable terrain, such as this barren and mountainous region of Kirghizstan in central Asia. This Tang dynasty-era caravanserai, the oldest complete example in existence, would have protected traders from the elements and from preying bandits.

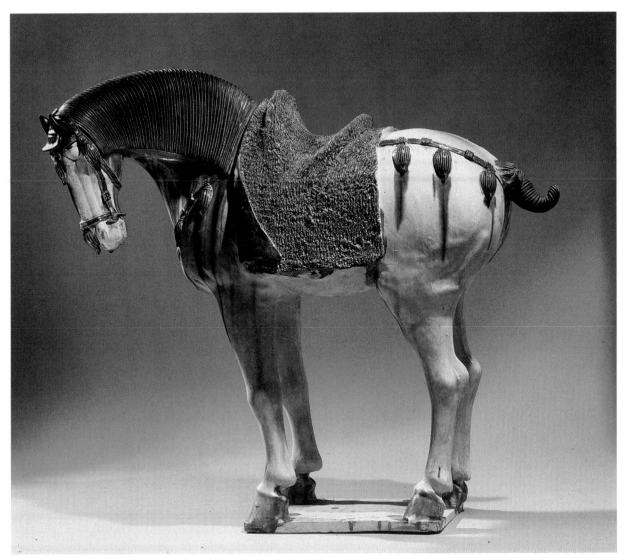

Pottery figure of a Ferghana horse, excavated from a tomb, Tang dynasty (618–907 C.E.). The Tang dynasty opened the Grand Canal, stimulated growth in trade, and expanded the boundaries of the empire. For much of this they were dependent on the mobility of the army, which in turn was dependent for covering great distances on the famed Ferghana horses, immortalized in literature as "the horses that sweated blood." (*Idemitsu Museum of Arts, Tokyo*)

First, within the borders of China, "empire" frequently meant the **assimilation** of others. In the north, many of the tribal groups against which China fought and against which Chinese rulers constructed the Great Wall, nevertheless came to enlist in China's armies, settle its land, assimilate to its culture, adopt its language and calligraphy, and intermarry with its peoples. Both the ethnic Chinese and the Barbarians regarded this process as mutually beneficial. Both also understood the dangers: the "Barbarians" might lose their culture and even find themselves in civil war with others of their ethnic group who rejected assimilation; while the Chinese might be conquered by their new allies.

Indeed, both of these results did occur frequently. Depending on one's point of view, the cultures of both the Barbarians and the Chinese were enriched or diluted by the interchanges.

THE NORTH AND THE NORTHWEST

The most geographically far-reaching of China's expansions beyond the borders of inner China were to the northwest and west. Just as Emperor Han Wudi's expansion into Gansu and beyond did not survive the early Han dynasty, so the Sui–Tang expansion even deeper into central Asia did not survive the Battle of the Talas River and the An Lushan revolt. At other times, China's influence over these regions was cultural and symbolic rather than political, military, or even directly economic.

THE SOUTH AND SOUTHWEST

In south China processes of assimilation took place, but they have made much less of a mark in the records. China as an ethnic, cultural, and political entity developed first in the north, around the Yellow River, but as Chinese peoples moved south of the Yangzi they met people of other ethnic groups. Some moved south to preserve and develop their own separate national identities. The Vietnamese are the clearest example of this pattern. Some remained as distinct, separate tribal groups, usually in remote areas somewhat difficult to access. Occasionally these peoples revolted against the Chinese invasion and take-over of their land. The Miao gave the clearest example of this response. Most of the rest assimilated, including some Vietnamese and Miao, without making a lasting impression on the historical records.

VIETNAM

For a thousand years China held Annam (North Vietnam) as a colony. Conquered by the Han dynasty and incorporated as a province of China in 111 B.C.E., Annam remained part of China until the Vietnamese rebel Ngo Quyen declared himself the king of the independent state of Dai Viet in 939 C.E. after the collapse of the Tang. During and after the Chinese colonization, the Vietnamese were locked in a love-hate relationship with Chinese culture and politics. Chinese scholars and officials, many of them fleeing imperial policies in China, brought to Vietnam their own ideographic script, Confucian ethical principles, and the Confucian literary classics. The Vietnamese adopted them all. Buddhism also arrived in Vietnam via China. The rest of southeast Asia absorbed Buddhism in its Theravada form from India; Vietnam adopted Mahayana Buddhism as it had developed in China, after about the fifth century C.E. These cultural innovations appealed primarily to the upper class aristocracy. At the level of practical technology, the Chinese also introduced a number of valuable agricultural innovations: the collective construction of the huge network of dams and waterworks that protect against the monsoon flooding every year; the use of human excrement as fertilizer; market gardening; and intensive pig farming.

Despite having adopted many Chinese customs, the Vietnamese resented foreign hegemony by the colossus to its north. For example, the two Trung sisters led a military revolt in 39 C.E., succeeded in evicting the Chinese, ruled jointly over Vietnam for two years, and then committed suicide when the revolt was crushed. They are revered in Vietnam to this day. Leaders of numerous, less dramatic revolts that took place during the period of Chinese rule are also viewed as national heroes. Yet the most profound adoption of Chinese administrative reforms took place paradoxically in the fifteenth century, when Vietnam was independent. As a result of Chinese direct rule in the earlier period and Chinese power and proximity during later periods of Vietnamese independence, the country

CHINESE DYNASTIES

Listed below are all the imperial dynasties, starting with the Qin, and the two major pre-imperial ruling houses. Gaps in the date sequences mark those periods when the country was divided between two or more rulers.

Shang	*c.* **1600–1100** B.C.E.
Zhou	*c.* **1100–256**
Qin	**221–206**
Han	**202** B.C.E.–**220** C.E.
Three Kingdoms (Kingdom of Shu Han, Kingdom of Wei, Kingdom of Wu)	**220–65**
Northern and Southern Dynasties	**265–589**
Western Jin	265–317
Eastern Jin	317–419
Northern Wei	424–535
Sui	**202–618**
Tang	**618–907**
Song	**960–1279**
Yuan (Mongol)	**1279–1368**
Ming	**1368–1644**
Manchu (Qing)	**1644–1911**

became a Confucian state, with an examination system, an intellectually elitist administration somewhat aloof from the masses, and an intense desire for independence from China.

KOREA

Korea came under Chinese direct rule only very briefly, but Chinese cultural hegemony profoundly influenced the peninsula. Northern Korea was first conquered by the Emperor Han Wudi in 109–108 B.C.E., along with Manchuria. Military garrisons established Chinese control and influence. Korea, like Vietnam, had borrowed heavily from prehistoric China, including much of Shang technology and, later, iron technology, paper production, printing, lacquerwork, porcelain (although Korean celadon ware had a distinct beauty all its own), wheat and rice agriculture, and the ideographs of written language. (Later, the Koreans developed a written system called *han'gul* based on phonetics.) After the collapse of the Han in 220 C.E., Korea broke free of direct control, although it remained a vassal of the Chinese. Some of China's colonies remained in place, but without military capacity. The Sui dynasty sent three expeditions to conquer Korea, but all ended in disaster. The expansive Tang dynasty also tried to retake Korea in the seventh century, occupying much of the peninsula during 668–676. Ultimately Korea regained and maintained its independence, although it was often forced to accept tributary status.

China's power over Korea can be seen far more in terms of cultural hegemony than in political-military rule. Confucianism, law codes, bureaucratic administration, literature, art, and Mahayana Buddhism all entered Korean life from China, independent of government pressure. In 935 C.E., after the fall of the Tang, Korea's Silla dynasty also fell. The Koryo dynasty, which took its place, built a new capital at Kaesong, just north of today's South Korean capital at Seoul, and modeled it on Chang'an, the Tang capital in China. Both China and Korea spoke of a "younger brother/older brother" relationship between the two countries.

JAPAN

China never conquered Japan, but Japan did accept China's cultural hegemony. Indeed, through the seventh and eighth centuries C.E. Japan actively and enthusiastically attempted to model its state, religion, technology, art, and language on those of

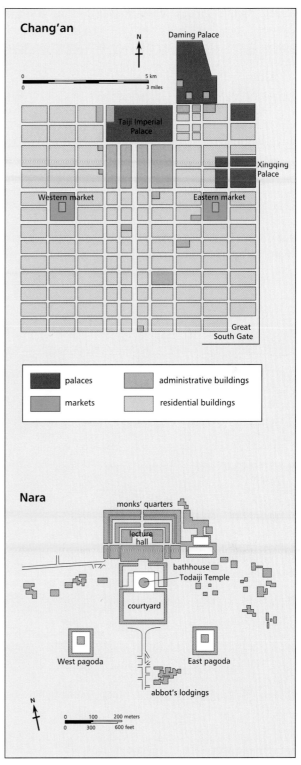

Asian imperial capitals The Tang capital of Chang'an was grid-planned as a massive rectangle over 5 miles (8 km) square, focusing on the imperial quarters and housing about a million people within its walls. The newly centralized Japanese Yamato state built Nara in imitation of Chang'an: a grid plan incorporated the Todaiji Temple complexes.

China. As the Korean peninsula stands between the Chinese mainland and the four major islands of Japan, much of the importation of Chinese forms came through Korea.

Although archaeological records show that Japan was populated by the Jomon people of the coastal regions at least as early as 10,000 B.C.E., rice agriculture, introduced from south China, seems to have begun only about 300 B.C.E. Bronze tools and weapons arrived about the first century B.C.E. and the technology for making iron tools about 200 years later. Waves of immigrants from Korea and China arrived in Japan between *c.* 200 B.C.E. and *c.* 500 C.E. By 500 C.E., about one-third of Japan's nobility claimed Korean or Chinese descent, and many artisans and metal workers in Japan had come from Korea. All was not peaceful between Japan and Korea, however, and invasions and raids broke out in both directions. In 405 C.E. a Korean scribe, named Wani, came to teach the Chinese script, and this became Japan's earliest written language. In this period the Chinese represented the Japanese by an ideograph that means "dwarf." Japan's recorded history begins only in the eighth century C.E., and most of our knowledge of these earlier years comes either from archaeological records or from references in the literatures of China and Korea.

The formation of a state began about the third century C.E., when a clan of people worshiping the sun-goddess established its rule over the Yamato Plain in central Honshu Island. Ultimately, the

The Nandaimon, or "Great South Gate," of the Todai Buddhist temple, 745–752 C.E. The first Japanese Buddhist temples—modeled on the Buddhist temples of China—are among the oldest surviving timber buildings in the world. So faithful and enduring are they that they have become our best examples of *Chinese* architecture for the period (contrast with picture, p. 287).

imperial line of Japan would claim its descent from this group. They used Chinese written characters and accepted elements of both Confucianism and Buddhism to enrich the practices of the indigenous religion, Shinto. After China succeeded in re-establishing its own powerful empire under the Sui and Tang dynasties, the Japanese rulers dispatched numerous delegations of hundreds of members each to China to learn and adopt Chinese models. The Chinese calendar and many methods of government were introduced. In 604 a new seventeen-point "constitution" was introduced, a guide that was modeled on Chinese practice. The document included reverence for Confucianism and Buddhism, and for the sovereign of Japan, and, on a more mundane level, asserted the government's monopoly over the collection of taxes.

Bloody struggles for control of the court in Japan brought Nakatomi no Kamatari to power in 645. He took the surname Fujiwara, and under this name his family dominated the politics of Japan for centuries to come. (One descendant, Prince Konoe Fumimaro, served as prime minister in 1937–9 and again in 1940–1.) Fujiwara adopted Chinese culture, religion, and government as the way to centralize and unify Japan and to assert his own control. He proclaimed the Taika ("great change") reforms in 646, consolidating provincial administration and constructing an extensive road system. The reforms also abolished private ownership of land and, following the Chinese "equal field system," redistributed land at each generational change.

In 710 two acts further consolidated centralized rule. First, a new capital, modeled on Chang'an, was built at Nara. Second, the Japanese ruler now claimed to rule through divine mandate, which, unlike the Chinese concept, could never be revoked. (To this day, the same family occupies the imperial throne, although after World War II, its divinity was officially repudiated; see Chapter 19.) The emperor continued to serve as the chief priest of Japan's Shinto faith, but as Shinto is a religion that worships the gods of nature—streams, trees, rocks—it can be practiced anywhere. Buddhism, by contrast, although it, too, can be practiced everywhere, provides a much more centralized form of organization, through monasteries and temples. Many new Buddhist temples were, therefore, constructed in Chinese form at Nara to centralize worship in Japan. From this time onward Buddhism and Shinto have coexisted in Japan, with millions of Japanese declaring themselves devotees of both faiths.

Following the Chinese model, the Japanese began to record their history for the first time in the *Nihon Shoki*, which was in Chinese, and their legends in the *Kojiki*, written in a mixture of Chinese and Japanese forms. As centuries passed and Japan became more secure in its own political organization and cultural identity, the reliance on Chinese models declined. But in the centuries in which its basic cultural and political identity was formed, Japan had followed carefully and devotedly the hegemonic examples of China, without compulsion or force of any sort.

CHINA AND ROME: HOW DO THEY COMPARE?

DIFFERENCES

Geopolitical

China's heartland was far larger and more cohesive, geographically and culturally, than Rome's. Rome had as its heartland only central Italy, and even after conquering Italy, it held just that single peninsula bounded by the Alps Mountains and the Mediterranean Sea. In the time of Augustus in Rome and the Han dynasty in China, the Roman and Chinese empires each held about 60 million people, but in Rome only a few of these millions were in Italy. In China virtually all were in "inner China," 90 percent of them in the North China Plain.

Ideological

Although Confucian China spoke of a mythological golden age of equality among people in harmony with each other and with nature, realistically the Confucians believed that the best possible government was a well-ordered empire. Imperial Rome knew of its actual, historical republican past and always looked back to it as a golden age. Roman imperial expansion and stratification were often regarded as violations of the earlier republican ideals.

Longevity and Persistence

Rome's empire rose, fell, and was gone, although it lived on as a concept. China's empire has lasted for the last two thousand years. Dynasties have come and gone, and sometimes the empire has broken into fragments, but finally the empire endured as a single political entity. Today, although without an emperor, China's geopolitical unity continues.

Policy and Powers of Assimilation

As China moved both north and south, it assimilated a great number of the peoples it invaded and conquered. Non-ethnic Chinese were absorbed culturally and biologically. Many of the 95 percent of today's Chinese population who are called "Han" are descended from ancestors who were not. The empire was held together by Confucian and Buddhist ideology, supported by the power of the emperor and his armies. Rome's empire was held together by law and backed by military power. Selected non-Romans could gain citizenship under law, but ethnically and culturally the conquered peoples remained "other." Intermarriage with non-citizens was usually forbidden. Rome maintained the cultural distinctions far more than did China.

Language Policy

The Chinese language unified the Chinese Empire across space and through time, to today, far more than Latin did the Roman Empire. Chinese was never subordinated to another language and culture, as Latin was to Greek for many years and in many regions. Nor did Chinese compete with regional languages as Latin ultimately did. Indeed Chinese helped to bring even neighboring countries, Vietnam, Korea, and Japan, together into a single general cultural unit. Latin was gradually supplanted as a spoken tongue by its successor Romance languages: Italian, French, Spanish, Portuguese, Catalan, and Romanian.

Ideology and Cultural Cohesion

China's cultural, Confucian bureaucracy provided a core cultural identity throughout the empire and beyond. Even the alternative political-cultural philosophies of China, such as Daoism, Legalism, and later Buddhism, usually (but not always) served to broaden and augment the attraction of Confucianism. Rome's principal philosophies of paganism, Stoicism and, later, Christianity did not significantly buttress and augment its imperial rule, and the latter two may even have diminished popular loyalty to the empire.

Influence on Neighbors

The Roman Empire influenced the lands it conquered, but had less influence on those outside its boundaries. China exercised lasting hegemonic influence even on neighbors it did not conquer, such as Japan, or conquered only briefly, such as Korea. A considerable part of this legacy was religious and cultural as well as political, economic, and administrative.

SIMILARITIES

Relations with Barbarians

Both empires faced nomadic groups from central Asia who threatened and penetrated their boundaries. Indeed, the Huns, who invaded Europe, and the Xiongnu, who invaded China, may have belonged to the same ethnic group (compare maps on p. 187 and p. 208). Both empires settled the "Barbarians" near their borders and enlisted them in the imperial armies. In both cases, the Barbarians came to hold great power. Ultimately, however, they dismembered the Roman Empire while they were absorbed by the Chinese.

Religious Policies

Both empires incubated foreign religions, especially in times of imperial disorder, but in Rome, Christianity did not save the empire, and by challenging the significance of earthly power it may even have contributed to the empire's weakness. In China, Buddhism was absorbed into Confucianism and Daoism and helped to sustain the national culture in times of political trouble.

The Role of the Emperor

Both empires ascribed divine attributes to the emperor, and both frequently had difficulty in establishing rules for imperial succession. The Romans often attempted to choose their best general, while the Chinese selected a man who could control the imperial family and court. Neither empire believed that a single imperial family should rule forever.

Gender Relationships

Both empires subordinated women to men at all stages of life, and both drew analogies between hierarchies and loyalties in a well-run family and those in a well-run empire. Both empires used marriages as means of confirming political alliances with foreign powers. Both periodically felt that excessive concern with sexual relationships was distracting energy away from the demands of sustaining the empire and instituted strict codes of sexual morality. In China, far more than in Rome, women of the imperial family played an important role in politics behind the scenes, particularly in terms of determining succession. One woman, the Empress Wu (r. 690–705), took the throne herself.

The Significance of Imperial Armies

In both empires, the army was crucial in creating and sustaining the political structure in the face of domestic and foreign enemies. The Roman Empire was established and ruled by generals, as were the Qin, Han, Sui, and Tang dynasties in China. Both empires were periodically threatened and usurped by rebel generals asserting their own authority. The cost of the armies, especially on distant, unprofitable expeditions, often bankrupted the government and encouraged its subjects to evade taxes and military service and even to rise in revolt.

The Deployment of Armies of Colonization

Both empires used colonies of soldier-colonizers to garrison and develop remote areas while simultaneously providing compensation and retirement benefits for the troops.

Overextension

Both empires suffered their greatest challenges in confronting simultaneously the strains of overexpansion and the subsequent internal revolts that were triggered by the costs. In Rome these dual problems, along with the Barbarian invasions, finally precipitated the end of the empire in the west. In China they led to the loss of the Mandate of Heaven and the downfall of dynasties. The external battles against Qin-Jurchen border tribes, for example, combined with the revolt of the Yellow Turbans brought down the later Han; the loss of the distant Battle of the Talas River, combined with the internal revolt of An Lushan, sapped Tang power.

Public Works Projects

Throughout their empire the Romans built roads, aqueducts, public monumental structures, administrative/military towns, and the great capital cities of Rome and Constantinople. The Chinese built the Great Wall, the Grand Canal, systems of transportation by road and water, public monumental structures, administrative/military towns throughout the empire, and several successive capitals, especially Chang'an and Luoyang.

The Concentration of Wealth

In both empires, the benefits of imperial wealth tended to flow toward the center, to the elites in the capital cities. The capitals grew to unprecedented size. Both Chang'an and Rome housed more than one million people.

Policies For and Against Individual Mobility

In order to maintain power and stability in the face of demands for change, both empires periodically bound their peasantry to the soil and demanded that the sons of soldiers follow their fathers' occupations. Both found these policies difficult to enforce. Both offered some individual mobility through service in their armies. In addition, the Chinese examination system provided for advancement within the imperial bureaucracy.

Revolts

Both empires experienced frequent revolts against the emperor and his policies. In Rome, which housed a much larger slave population, many of the revolts were led by slaves. In China they were more typically initiated by peasants. Rome attempted to forestall mass revolts in the capital and other large cities through the provision of so-called "bread and circuses."

Peasant Flight

In both empires, during times of upheaval, peasants sought to evade taxes and conscription by finding refuge as tenants on large, landed estates. In times when imperial government was weak, the largest of these estates challenged the power of the central government.

BIBLIOGRAPHY

Andrea, Alfred and James H. Overfield, eds. *The Human Record:* Vol I (Boston: Houghton Mifflin Co., 3rd ed., 1998).

Blunden, Caroline and Mark Elvin. *Cultural Atlas of China* (New York: Facts on File, 1983).

Bodde, Derk. *Essays on Chinese Civilization*, ed. Charles Le Blanc and Dorothy Borei (Princeton: Princeton University Press, 1981).

Cotterell, Arthur, ed. *The Penguin Encyclopedia of Ancient Civilizations* (London: Penguin Books, 1980).

Creel, H.G. *Confucius: The Man and the Myth* (Westport, CT: Greenwood Press, reprinted 1972 from 1949 ed.).

deBary, William Theodore and Irene Bloom, eds., *Sources of Chinese Tradition, Vol.I: From Earliest Times to 1600* (New York: Columbia University Press, 1999).

Ebrey, Patricia Buckley, ed. *Chinese Civilization: A Sourcebook* (New York: The Free Press, 2nd ed., 1993).

Elvin, Mark. *The Pattern of the Chinese Past* (Stanford: Stanford University Press, 1973).

Fairbank, John K., Edwin O. Reischauer, and Albert M. Craig. *East Asia: Tradition and Transformation* (Boston: Houghton Mifflin, rev. edn, 1989).

Friedman, Edward. "Reconstructing China's National Identity: A Southern Alternative to Mao-Era Anti-Imperialist Nationalism," *Journal of Asian Studies* LIII, No. 1 (February 1994), 67–91.

Han Fei Tzu. *The Complete Works of Han Fei Tzu*, 2 Vols. trans. W.K. Liao (London: Arthur Probsthain, 1959).

Hughes, Sarah Shaver and Brady Hughes, ed. *Women in World History*, Vol. I (Armonk, NY: M.E. Sharpe, 1995).

Lockard, Craig A. "Integrating Southeast Asia into the Framework of World History: The Period Before 1500," *The History Teacher* XXIX, No. 1 (November 1995), 7–35.

McGovern, William Montgomery. *The Early Empires of Central Asia* (Chapel Hill: University of North Carolina Press, 1939).

Murphey, Rhoads. *East Asia: A New History* (New York: HarperCollins, 1997).

Needham, Joseph. *The Shorter Science and Civilization in China*, Vol. I, abridged by Colin A. Ronan (Cambridge: Cambridge University Press, 1978).

Parker, Geoffrey, ed. *The (London) Times Atlas of World History* (London: Times Books, Ltd., 4th ed., 1993).

Past Worlds: The (London) Times Atlas of Archaeology (Maplewood, NJ: Hammond, 1988).

SarDesai, D.R. *Southeast Asia: Past and Present* (Boulder, CO: Westview Press, 3rd ed., 1994).

Schirokauer, Conrad. *A Brief History of Chinese and Japanese Civilizations* (Fort Worth: Harcourt Brace Jovanovich, 2nd ed., 1989).

Schwartz, Benjamin I. *The World of Thought in Ancient China* (Cambridge: Harvard University Press, 1985).

Seth, Vikram. *Three Chinese Poets: Translations of Poems by Wang Wei, Li Bai, and Du Fu* (New York: HarperCollins, 1993).

Sima Qian. *Historical Records*, trans. Raymond Dawson (New York: Oxford University Press, 1994).

Sima Qian. *Records of the Historian: Chapters from the Shih Chi of Ssu-ma Ch'ien*, trans. Burton Watson (New York: Columbia University Press, 1969).

Sullivan, Michael. *The Arts of China* (Berkeley: University of California Press, 1984).

Time-Life Books. *Time Frame. 400 BC–AD 200: Empires Ascendant* (Alexandria, VA: Time-Life Books, 1988).

——. *Time Frame AD 200–600: Empires Besieged* (Alexandria, VA: Time-Life Books, 1988).

——. *Time Frame AD 600–800: The March of Islam* (Alexandria, VA: Time-Life Books, 1989).

Twitchett, Denis and Michael Lowe, eds. *The Cambridge History of China*, Vol. I: *The Ch'in and Han Empires, 221 B.C.–A.D. 220* (Cambridge: Cambridge University Press, 1986).

Twitchett, Denis, ed. *The Cambridge History of China*, Vol. III: *Sui and T'ang China, 589–906*, Part I (Cambridge: Cambridge University Press, 1979).

INDIAN EMPIRES

1500 B.C.E.–1100 C.E.

*" When one king is weaker than the other, he should make peace with him.
When he is stronger than the other, he should make war with him."*

KAUTILYA, *ARTHA–SASTRA*

CULTURAL COHESION IN A DIVIDED SUBCONTINENT

What do we mean by "India"? In this chapter we include the entire sub-continent of south Asia, which includes not only the present-day country of India, but also its neighbors: Pakistan, Afghanistan, Bangladesh, Nepal, and Bhutan. Geographers call the entire region a subcontinent because it is so clearly bounded by powerful natural borders. Along its entire southern perimeter it is surrounded by oceanic waters: the Arabian Sea to the west and the Bay of Bengal to the east. To the north, the Himalayan Mountains, the highest in the world, form an almost impenetrable barrier. To the east and west, spurs of the Himalayas complete the ring of demarcation, but these mountain ranges are lower and more negotiable. Passes through the northwest mountains, like the Khyber Pass, make entrance possible, as does a route through the desert along the western Makran coast. The peoples who came to India before 3000 B.C.E., for whom we have no historical record, seem to have arrived from a variety of approaches, probably including some by sea voyages from Africa, southeast Asia, and the islands of the Pacific. Since then, all the major immigrations have come from the northwest. In modern times British traders and rulers also came by sea (Chapters 13 and 16). They had an important impact on the subcontinent, but they did not stay.

The entire Indian subcontinent has never been unified into a single empire (although in the nineteenth and twentieth centuries, the British lacked only formal control of Afghanistan). Asoka Maurya (r. *c.* 265–38 B.C.E.) was the first person to come close to achieving that goal, but even he never captured the far south. Usually, as today, a variety of rulers controlled different regions of the subcontinent.

India might, in fact, be regarded more as a continent than as a single country. The geographical area of the subcontinent is equal to about half the size of Europe. It is not surprising, then, that Indian empires did not last more than a few hundred years. Yet unlike Rome, and much more like China, India has maintained a persistent cultural unity over several thousand years. In this chapter we will begin to consider why India dissolved politically into many separate states, and in Chapter 9 we will consider the religious and cultural institutions that nevertheless served to bring a loose unity to the subcontinent.

Lion capital of the pillar erected by Asoka at Sarnath, Mauryan, *c.* 250 B.C.E. The polished sandstone columns erected by the Emperor Asoka at places associated with events in the Buddha's life, or marking pilgrim routes to holy places, are of special interest for their 7-foot-tall (2.1 m) capitals. These provide us with the best remaining examples of Mauryan imperial art and are rich in symbolism. For instance, the Buddha was spoken of as a "lion" among spiritual preachers, whose sermon penetrated to all four corners of the world, just as the lion's roar established his authority in the forest.

SETTLEMENT IN SOUTH ASIA

In Chapter 3 we read of the civilization of the Indus valley, which began with the appearance of the first cities of south Asia in about 2500 B.C.E. That civilization began to fade about 1500 B.C.E. for reasons that are not entirely understood. It is thought, however, that as the people of the Indus civilization struggled in and emigrated from their home base in the Indus valley, new waves of "Aryan" immigrants arrived. These new arrivals are named not for their race, but for Sanskrit and the other related **Indo-Aryan** languages they spoke. Archaeologists are not certain of the geographical origins of the new arrivals; some claim they came from central Asia, others from the Iranian plateau, while a few suggest Europe.

In successive waves of immigration, the nomadic and pastoral Aryans, mixing with indigenous peoples, migrated slowly eastward, reaching the Ganges valley about the year 1000 B.C.E. As they settled, they began to build a new urban civilization and to form new states. By about 700–600 B.C.E., numerous political groupings, called *janapadas* (populated territories), began to emerge. The leadership of the territories was centered in specific family lineage groups, and as these lineages grew in size, and as they cleared more forest land to expand their territorial control, the *janapadas* began to take on the political forms of states with urban capitals and political administrations. Some constituted themselves as republics, others as monarchies. By 500–400 B.C.E., about the time the Persian armies of Darius reached the Indus, sixteen large *maha-janapadas* had emerged in northern India. By the time Alexander arrived in 326 B.C.E., four of these large states dominated the rest, and one, Magadha, was beginning to emerge as an imperial power over all. One family dynasty, the Nandas, established limited imperial supremacy at Magadha, but its power lasted for only one generation, from *c.* 364 to 324 B.C.E.

The Maurya family dynasty, which succeeded to the throne of Magadha in 324 B.C.E., remained in power for almost a century and a half, until 185 B.C.E. Its founder, Chandragupta Maurya (r. *c.* 321–297 B.C.E.), may have conceived the idea of an India-wide empire from a possible meeting with Alexander the Great. As we saw in Chapter 5, Alexander had reached the Indus in 326 B.C.E. and had wanted to continue his sweep all the way across the subcontinent to the ocean that he believed to be at the end of the world. His troops, however, mutinied with the famous words of caution: "Sir, if there is one thing above all others a successful man should know, it is when to stop" (cited in Green, p. 410). His army's refusal to go forward forced Alexander to leave India.

Soon thereafter Chandragupta marched his own troops from Magadha into northwest India to fill the power vacuum. Chandragupta's son, Bindusara

INDIAN EMPIRES

DATE	POLITICAL	RELIGION AND CULTURE	SOCIAL DEVELOPMENT
600 B.C.E.	• *Janapadas* established		
500 B.C.E.	• Gandhara and Sind held by Persian Empire (*c.* 518) • *Maha-janapadas* established (500–400)	• Buddha, Siddhartha Gautama (*c.* 563–483) • Puranas written (*c.* 500 B.C.E.– 500 C.E.) • Vedic period ends (1500–500)	
400 B.C.E.	• Nanda dynasty in Magadha (*c.* 364–324)		
300 B.C.E.	• Alexander the Great in south Asia (327–325) • Chandragupta Maurya (*c.* 321–*c.* 297) founds Mauryan dynasty (324–185) in Magadha • Kautilya wrote *Artha–sastra* (*c.* 300)		
250 B.C.E..	• Bindusara Maurya (*c.* 297–*c.* 272) • Asoka Maurya (*c.* 265–238)	• Rock inscriptions of Asoka • Buddhism organized as state religion • Asokan lion column (see p. 232)	• Mauryan empire extended from Afghanistan to Bay of Bengal to Deccan
200 B.C.E.	• Sunga dynasty (185–73) • Mauryan Empire fractures, along with unity of India (185)	• Jain influence increases	
150 B.C.E.		• Sanchi stupa (p. 276) • Menander (Milanda) king of Indo–Greek Empire (*c.* 160–135)	• Trade contacts with S.E. Asia
100 B.C.E.	• First Shaka king in western India (*c.* 94)	• Sangam poetry from Tamil culture	
50 C.E.	• Height of Kushana power under Emperor Kanishka (*c.* 78–*c.* 103)	• Bhagavad-Gita	
100 C.E.		• Gandhara Buddha (pp. 243 and 288) • Rise of Mahayana Buddhism	• Trade flourishes between India and the Central Asian trade routes
200 C.E.		• Beginning of Hindu–Buddhist influence on southeast Asia	

(r. *c.* 297–*c.* 272 B.C.E.), expanded still further the empire that his father had created, and Bindusara's son, Asoka (r. *c.* 265–238 B.C.E.), brought the empire of the Mauryas to its greatest extent, ruling from modern Afghanistan in the northwest to the Bay of Bengal in the east and well into the Deccan penin-sula in the south. By this time India may have held as many as 100 million people.

The record of Asoka's rule, lost for many centuries, was rediscovered by scholars only about a hundred years ago, and today he is considered the greatest of the emperors of the Mauryan dynasty,

INDIAN EMPIRES

DATE	POLITICAL	RELIGION AND CULTURE	SOCIAL DEVELOPMENT
300 C.E.	• Gupta Empire (*c.* 320–540) established by Chandra Gupta (320–*c.* 330)	• Sanskrit used for official business • Hindu ascendancy over Buddhism	• Indian trade contacts with Oc Eo, Funan (300–600)
350 C.E.	• Samudra Gupta (*c.* 330–*c.* 380) expands dynasty throughout north and into south		
400 C.E.	• Chandra Gupta II (*c.* 380–*c.* 415) expands empire to maximum • Kumara Gupta (*c.* 415–455)	• Cultural "golden age" • Panini, Sanskrit grammarian (*fl.* 400) • Faxian, Buddhist pilgrim • Ajanta caves (5th–8th *c.*) (p. 245)	
450 C.E.	• Skanda Gupta (455–467) repulses Huna invasion from central Asia (*c.* 460) • Budha Gupta (467–497)	• Kalidasa composes "Meghaduta" and *Shakuntala*	• Sanskrit in S.E. Asia; Indian gods; Buddhism
500 C.E.	• Hunas gain control of north India	• Classical urban culture declines	
600 C.E.	• Pallavas rise to power at Kanchipuram under Mahendravarman I (*c.* 600–*c.* 611) • Harsha-vardhana (606-647) rules north India from Kanauj • Chalukyas rule central India under Pulakeshin II at Badami (608-642)	• Xuanzang, Buddhist pilgrim	
700 C.E.	• Arabs conquer Sind (712)	• Ellora temple complex (p. 271) (757-790) • Borobudur, Java (p. 250) (778-824) • Khajuraho temple complex (p. 270) (1025-1050) • Vedantic philosophy flourishes	
1100 C.E.	• Cholas defeat Srivijaya Empire, Sumatra	• Angkor Wat, Cambodia (p. 251)	

See also Hinduism and Buddhism timechart, p. 258

the first imperial dynasty to rule over most (but not all) of the Indian subcontinent. Asoka's fame rests not only on his conquests, but also on his conversion to Buddhism and his subsequent activities in spreading that faith throughout India (see Profile, p. 240) and beyond (see Chapter 9).

Following Asoka's death in 238 B.C.E., no emperor was strong enough to maintain centralized power, and the Mauryan Empire went into a half century of decline. The last Mauryan king was assassinated by one of his military commanders in 184 B.C.E., and India subsequently divided among many regional rulers, including some rulers who invaded and seized control of large territories. Finally, the Gupta dynasty brought all of north India under its control in 320 C.E., and presided over a great flowering of Sanskritic and Hindu culture (see Chapter 9). After the collapse of the Gupta dynasty in 497 C.E. the subcontinent was once again politically divided and subject to one wave of invader-rulers after another. These internal divisions and conquests by outsiders continued until the modern independence of India and Pakistan in 1947, and of Bangladesh in 1971.

THE INDIAN EMPIRES: HOW DO WE KNOW?

ARCHAEOLOGY AND PHILOLOGY

Archaeology has contributed greatly to our understanding of the earlier Indus valley. Its sparsely populated desert sites facilitated relatively easy excavation, but the later settlements in the Ganges valley have not been so accessible. This is a humid, subtropical region, where heavy monsoon rains have not allowed ancient settlements to endure. It is also densely settled, making archaeological excavation impracticable if not impossible. The distribution of pottery, painted gray ware dating primarily before 500 B.C.E., and northern black polished ware from after that date, helps us to identify and follow the waves of Aryan immigration into the Ganges valley. The more recently discovered ocher-colored pottery in the western Ganges valley and the presence of black and red ware further east suggest that by the time the Aryans arrived indigenous peoples had already settled on the land. Since the late 1970s archaeological digs have uncovered small settlement sites dating from 1000 to 600 B.C.E. throughout the Ganges valley, but without additional excavations of many other cities and small towns it is difficult to trace archaeologically in any detail the spread and nature of early Aryan civilization. The very large city-site of Taxila (Takshasila), in what is now northwestern Pakistan, which served as a regional capital for Persian, Greek, and Indian rulers, has been extensively and continuously excavated since John Marshall's first expedition in 1913. It is a very rich source of information, but only for a later period.

Philology helps to establish the dispersion of Indo-Aryan peoples by tracking the spread of their languages. The first known remaining specimens of writing in the Ganges valley are Asoka's rock and pillar inscriptions in Brahmi script, which date to the third century B.C.E. To track the oral transmission patterns of earlier centuries, anthropologists study texts that recorded them in written form at a much later time, and compare them with the distribution and evolution of today's spoken languages.

WRITTEN TEXTS

The greatest sources of information for the Aryan invasions, settlements, and empires are written materials, of which there are many. A special group of bards and chroniclers was responsible for collecting and composing these materials, although they did not attempt to establish a direct chronological, interpretive record of the sort found in Greece or Rome (see p. 143 and p. 166–9) or in China (see pp. 196–9). The **Puranas**, or legends and folk tales from earliest times, which were finally collected and written down between c. 500 B.C.E. and 500 C.E., contain genealogical lists of rulers from before the first humans were born to historic times, mixing fact and fable and making no attempt to distinguish between them. The earliest existing source is the *Rigveda*, 1028 hymns composed in Sanskrit about 1500–1200 B.C.E. The **Veda** are religious reflections rather than historical accounts, but to the extent that they refer to the life of the Aryan peoples who wrote them, their accounts are probably reliable. Three other Veda, the *Samaveda*, *Yajurveda*, and *Atharva Veda*, were composed some centuries later. Other religious literature of the Vedic period (1500–500 B.C.E.) include the Brahmanas, which give instructions on rituals and sacrifices, and the Upanishads, which are mystical speculations. These were composed c. 700 B.C.E. and afterwards.

The *Mahabharata* and the *Ramayana*

India's two great epics, the *Mahabharata* and the *Ramayana*, recount events that took place between 1000 and 700 B.C.E., although the texts themselves place the action in earlier mythic times. Neither is a historical account, but both provide valuable information on the social structures, the ways of life, and the values of the time in which they were written. The *Mahabharata* is the longest single poem in the world, some ten times longer than the Bible. Its central story is of a great civil war fought between two branches of the same family. In its tales, subplots, and asides are woven myth, speculation, folklore, moral teaching, and political reflection that are central to India's living culture. The intermingling of the great themes of life, death, family, warfare, duty,

Ahmad Kashmiri, Mughal School, scene from the *Mahabharata*, 1598 C.E. In this painting from an illustrated manuscript, one of the earliest such depictions of the great Indian epic, the god Agni is shown creating fire as a smokescreen to assist his father-in-law, while Arjun quells the flames with magic arrows that release springs of water. (*Oriental & India Office, London*)

and power give the *Mahabharata* continuing universal appeal. In 1985–8 the British theatrical producer Peter Brook produced a nine-hour version of the *Mahabharata* in English and in French and won numerous awards as he staged it in theaters around the world. (It is now available also on video.) The most famous single segment of the *Mahabharata* is the profound religious meditation and instruction called the *Bhagavad-Gita*, or "Song of God." (see Source, p. 266).

The *Ramayana*, which is much shorter, refers to somewhat later times, and there are many versions. The first known written version was in Sanskrit, composed by Valmiki about 700 B.C.E. Its core story tells of the mythical god-king Rama's victory over Ravana, the demon king of Sri Lanka, who had kidnapped his wife, Sita. The diverse versions of the *Ramayana* indicate its great popularity and the variety of its uses. Some focus on the battles between north and south, perhaps a reference to the first Aryan invasions of the south about 800 B.C.E. Some southern versions, however, tend to justify Ravana as defending the south against Rama's invasions from the north. The role of Sita is also told in different ways. Men more frequently praise Sita for her adoration of Rama and her willingness to renounce even her life so that his reputation might remain intact. Women, however, are often critical of Rama for inadequately defending Sita in the first place, then for doubting her fidelity to him during her captivity in Lanka, and, finally, for bowing to public skepticism of her loyalty by exiling her from his royal court.

As Indian sailors, merchants, and priests carried their culture to southeast Asia (see p. 249), the *Ramayana* has become a national epic in several of the countries of that region, especially in Thailand and Indonesia, where it is often dramatized by live actors and through puppetry. In India, the story is retold each year on the holiday of Dussehra, which celebrates the victory of good over evil with great color and pageantry. Broadcast on Indian national television in serialized form for about a year each, the *Mahabharata* and the *Ramayana* drew audiences of hundreds of millions for each weekly episode in the mid-1980s.

Even during the period of our central concern, historical records were not written:

> Throughout the period from the rise of the Mauryan empire in the fourth century B.C. to the establishment of the Gupta kingdom in the fourth century A.D.

Indian School, scene from the *Ramayana*, 1713 C.E. This painting from the *Ramayana* is remarkable for its exquisitely rich gouache illustration. Among the heroes depicted are Rama, his faithful wife Sita, his loyal brother Laxman, and the army of monkey warriors who accompany him in his battle against Ravana, the Lord of Lanka. (*Oriental & India Office, London*)

there is, as far as we know, no evidence of any purely historical writing, and this, in spite of the fact that the period was germane to the evolution of the major political and social institutions in ancient India. (Thapar, *Social History*, p. 271)

Other records do, however, begin to appear that cast light on changes taking place. Codes of law and statecraft, such as the *Artha-sastra*, which is attributed to Chandragupta Maurya's minister Kautilya (*fl.* 300 B.C.E.), and Asoka's own rock inscriptions (see Profile, p. 240), illuminate politics and imperial ideology. Many more such codes appeared in later times, together with Buddhist and Jain texts (see Focus, p. 279), which usually include chronologies and some interpretation.

Visitors from outside also give periodic "snapshot" accounts of India. These include the observations by Megasthenes (*c.* 350–*c.* 290 B.C.E.), a Greek ambassador and historian, sent to the court of Chandragupta Maurya about 300 B.C.E., and Menander (Milinda; *fl.* 160–135 B.C.E.), the Greek king of northwest India, who became a Buddhist. Later, about 400–700 C.E., further observations were recorded by Buddhist pilgrims from China, notably Faxian (Fa-hsien) (*fl.* 399–414 C.E.) and Xuanzang (Hsuan-tsang) (602–664 C.E.).

FAMILIAL, SOCIAL, ECONOMIC, AND RELIGIOUS INSTITUTIONS

Throughout fifteen centuries of decentralized and often weak rule, India nevertheless retained a strong sense of cultural cohesion. The leading Indian historian of the ancient period, Romila Thapar, emphasizes the intermediate familial, social, economic, and religious institutions that brought cohesion to both ancient and modern India:

Indian social history at the moment has one basic pre-occupation: an inquiry into the precise nature of social relationships in the structure of early Indian society. (Thapar, *Social History*, p. 20)

In the following pages, therefore, we analyze not only the two major imperial dynasties of ancient India, the Mauryas and the Guptas, but also the more permanent institutions that mediated between the individual and the state. The religious

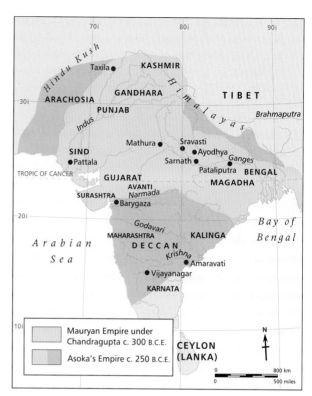

Mauryan India A contemporary of Alexander the Great, Chandragupta Maurya seized control of the kingdom of Magadha and annexed lands to the west, eventually controlling by 300 B.C.E. the strategic trade routes of the Ganges and Indus basins. His grandson Asoka extended the empire west into Seleucid Persia, and south via the wealthy kingdom of Kalinga to gain control of the Deccan by 250.

philosophies and social practices of Hinduism that inspire much of the statecraft of these dynasties are discussed briefly here, and are treated much more fully in Chapter 9. This separation in the discussion of political and religious practices is somewhat artificial, but it allows us to recognize the importance of each system separately as well as to see them interacting in support of one another.

STATECRAFT UNDER THE MAURYAS AND GUPTAS: WHAT DO WE KNOW?

THE MAURYAN EMPIRE

The Maurya dynasty created an imperial government that ruled over or displaced earlier political structures based only on family lineage. Hereditary family lineage did not cease to be important—after all, the imperial ruling dynasty itself was a lineage—but a new state apparatus stood above it in authority and power. The *Mahabharata* told of a large family of cousins falling into intra-family war over issues of inheritance of power, but by the time of the Mauryans, the state stood above such individual families and lineages.

The new empire expressed its theory of politics in the *Artha-sastra*, or science of politics and economics, which has been attributed to Kautilya, the minister of King Chandragupta Maurya. (The date of composition is not certain, and the text may actually have been written down later, but its ideas were current under the Mauryas. The *Artha-sastra* text had been lost to historians and was rediscovered only in 1909.) The text spoke of *danda niti*, translated into English alternatively and provocatively as the "policy of the scepter" or the "policy of the big stick." It had a cut-throat view of inter-state competition. Even in the earlier age of the *janapadas* (smaller political groupings), Indian political thought had already begun to think in terms of *matsyanyaya*, the "justice of the fish"—that is, larger states swallowed smaller ones. The *Artha-sastra* now postulated that every state must be on constant guard against all its neighbors, for all were potential enemies. It counseled that the power of strong states be neutralized through mutual treaties, while weak states should be attacked and conquered. The *Artha-sastra* regarded the immediate circle of neighbors as potential enemies but the next circle beyond them as potential allies, in keeping with the doctrine that the "enemy of my enemy is my friend." In this competitive world of constant warfare, the state had come into its own.

The state had many internal regulatory functions as well. First among these was the requirement to provide a powerful setting in which people had the opportunity to seek the four major goals of life in accord with Hindu philosophy: *artha* (wealth), *kama* (sensual pleasure), *dharma* (the fulfillment of social and religious duties), and *moksha* (the release from earthly existence and union with the infinite power of the universe, achieved, if at all, at the time of death). (see pp. 265–6).

The state helped to enforce rules of behavior between males and females. This relationship charged men with power over women and the responsibility for protecting them, while women were expected to run the household in accordance with the wishes of men and to be available for the pleasure of men. Women's property rights were always very limited, and at some periods they had

none. Hindu views of women's proper role and behavior are discussed briefly on page 281.

The state also regulated the behavior of its subjects in terms of the rules of **caste**. In Hindu belief each person has a social, economic, and ritual position, which was inherited at birth directly from his or her parents. Although this status may, in practice, be changed with considerable difficulty, in theory it remains for life and on into future generations. Caste status not only governs private behavior, it also gives people different, unequal status under law. (The origins and rationale of the caste system as part of Hindu religious belief are discussed in detail on pages 263–4.) It was the task of the state to enforce these caste distinctions, especially their differential rankings, liabilities, and rights in legal proceedings.

The state also regulated religious establishments. The larger Hindu temples and Buddhist monasteries developed considerable economic and political power based on the land and resources that were donated to them by devout followers, especially wealthy landlords, businessmen, and often by kings themselves. They also influenced a wide range of public and private decisions made by their devotees, and the state attempted to regulate the use of this wealth and power.

The state also enforced rules developed by India's **guilds**, associations of businessmen and producers. These mostly urban groups convened to set work rules, prices, and weights and measures, and to enforce quality control. Independent of the state, the guilds could nevertheless call on the state to enforce the regulations they had agreed on. Some students of Indian social structures have asked why the business guilds never seem to have made an attempt to gain direct control of the government in India as they did in medieval Europe (see p. 399). The answer is not entirely clear, but caste distinctions designated some people for government and military careers, others for business, separating those who were permitted to take up the bow and the sword in using force to gain government control from those who could only wield influence through wealth. In Europe businessmen both armed themselves and hired troops; in India, it seems, they did neither.

With so many responsibilities for regulating the interests of conflicting groups internally, and recognizing the need to remain constantly vigilant against powerful neighbors, Chandragupta Maurya and his son Bindusara attempted to build a highly centralized administration with a group of well-

PROFILE
Asoka
INDIA'S BUDDHIST EMPEROR

Until just over a hundred years ago, little was known about Asoka, the Mauryan emperor who held sway over the bulk of the Indian subcontinent from 265 to 238 B.C.E. In the nineteenth century, however, inscriptions that Asoka had made on pillars and rocks to spread his name and ideals were deciphered, and for the first time in modern history Asoka's identity and teachings were understood.

Asoka had constructed at least seven pillar edicts and had inscribed at least fourteen major and numerous minor rock edicts which have been discovered and excavated across many regions of India. Most are written in Brahmi script and are the oldest existing writing in India. The script, although an early variant of Sanskrit, had been lost for centuries until a British official, James Prinsep, redeciphered it in 1837. He also analyzed the collective significance of the rock and pillar edicts discovered up to his time along with materials on Asoka found in early chronicles in Ceylon (modern-day Sri Lanka).

Asoka's famed conversion to Buddhism, a dramatic turning-point in his life, is described in the Thirteenth Major Rock Edict. The carnage he had created in his military victory at Kalinga and the suffering of his victims had left Asoka with a terrible sense of remorse. As reparation for his actions, he proclaimed his renunciation of violence and acceptance of *Dhamma*, the teachings of the Buddha that promote compassion, tolerance, and honesty:

> A hundred and fifty thousand people were deported, a hundred thousand were killed and many times that number perished. Afterwards, now that Kalinga was annexed, the Beloved of the Gods [Asoka] very earnestly practiced *Dhamma*, desired *Dhamma*, and taught *Dhamma*. (Thapar, *Asoka*, p. 255)

He did not however renounce the conquest and annexation of Kalinga, and while he disavowed violence as a general principle, he seemed to retain paid central ministers and bureaucrats, a powerful military, and an efficient system of spies dispersed throughout the empire.

At first Asoka followed similar policies, and he was especially effective at enlarging the empire through military force, but nine years into his administration, he abruptly changed course. In 260 B.C.E. Asoka defeated Kalinga (now Orissa), incorporating this eastern kingdom into his empire. The killing and chaos required to win the victory soured his heart, and he determined to become a different person and a different ruler. He converted to Buddhism, a religion firmly committed to nonviolence, and began to dispatch missionaries throughout his realm as well as to parts of south India beyond his own borders, and to Syria, Greece, Egypt, and, probably, southeast Asia. He sent his own son on a mission to Sri Lanka and the island kingdom permanently converted to Buddhism.

For thirty years after the battle of Kalinga Asoka's reign brought general peace to India and the further expansion of a new, more universalist ethic for a people who were increasingly settling down from nomadism into stable agricultural and urban life. Buddhism, diminishing the importance of the *brahmin* castes, was especially attractive to merchant castes and guilds, and Asoka's patronage was apparently also good for business. But in 185 B.C.E., fifty-three years after Asoka's death, the Mauryan dynasty came to an end, and with it the unity of India. The Mauryas still depended on the power of their lineage as the core of their rule, but they had not continued to produce emperors of the power and charisma of Chandragupta, Bindusara, and Asoka. The Mauryan lineage had not institutionalized its state into a permanent form. India dissolved again into a variety of contesting states.

The core region that remained from Magadha was ruled by the Sunga dynasty, 185–73 B.C.E. With Indian governments faltering, Indo-Greeks, the

it as an option of state policy, especially in dealing with the tribal people of the hills:

the Beloved of the Gods conciliates the forest tribes of his empire, but he warns them that he has power even in his remorse, and he asks them to repent, lest they be killed. (Thapar, *Asoka*, p. 256)

To spread his message and promote a universal faith, Asoka dispatched missionaries throughout his empire and beyond. He also made his own journeys to practice *Dhamma* and help alleviate suffering, especially in rural areas. The Sixth Major Rock Edict proclaims Asoka's dedication to public welfare:

I consider that I must promote the welfare of the whole world, and hard work and the dispatch of business are the means of doing so. Indeed there is no better work than promoting the welfare of the whole world. And whatever

Asoka, as depicted in a nineteenth-century engraving.

may be my great deeds, I have done them in order to discharge my debt to all beings. (Thapar, *Asoka*, p. 253)

Projects implemented by Asoka to improve the welfare of his people included the founding of hospitals, the planting of medicinal plants and trees, and the building of some 84,000 stupas (Buddhist burial mounds) and monasteries. In his bid to create a more tolerant, compassionate society, Asoka granted religious groups outside of Buddhism the freedom to worship, but at the same time encouraged them to respect the beliefs and practices of other sects. The sacrificial use of animals was banned.

Asoka's active contribution to the spread of Buddhism had a lasting impact. His inscriptions offer us tangible evidence of the great influence Buddhism had not only on his own life but on Indian life and thought as a whole.

inheritors of Alexander's empire stationed in Afghanistan and Bactria, invaded in 182 B.C.E., capturing the northwest all the way south to the coastal cities of Gujarat. They produced a hybrid culture

Indo-Greek coin (obverse and reverse), central Asia.
The Indian subcontinent was linked to the silk route by trade routes that passed through Afghanistan and the Kushan Empire and continued westward. These economic connections account for the large quantity of Indo-Greek coinage, like this example showing the Macedonian king Demetrius I (*c.* 337–283 B.C.E.), (see map, p. 272). (*British Museum, London*)

with the Indians they conquered. King Menander (*fl.* 160–135 B.C.E.), an Indo-Greek, carried on a profound conversation with the Buddhist monk Nagasena who introduced the king to his religion. Their dialogue is still studied today as the *Questions of King Milinda*. Gandharan art, synthesizing Greek and Indian contributions, flourished in this period (see Spotlight, p. 242–3), as did the city of Taxila, the great center of trade, culture, and education in the northwest. Finally, large caches of Indo-Greek coinage reflect the importance of trade routes running through the northwest and linking India to the great silk routes of central Asia.

New invaders conquered and displaced the old. In Chapter 7 we read of tribal wars in east Asia, on the borders of China, which pushed Mongol groups westward to Rome. The Shakas, who invaded and ruled parts of northwest and western India for about a century, *c.* 94 B.C.E. to *c.* 20 C.E., were one of these tribal groups. They, in turn, were displaced by

SPOTLIGHT
Gandharan Art

Gandhara, the northern part of Pakistan and northeast Afghanistan, has been a crossroads of warfare, empire, trade, religion, and art at least since the Aryans invaded India, *c.* 1700 B.C.E. Much later, on his way to the Indus Valley, 330 B.C.E., Alexander the Great conquered it, leaving a legacy of Hellenistic influence on local art forms which endured for centuries. **Figure 1** presents one of the most striking examples. This frieze of the Trojan horse, found in northern Pakistan, dates to the second or third century C.E. Cassandra stands in a doorway attempting to block the horse's entry while Laocoön holds a spear to its chest. The subject matter, the draped clothing, and Laocoön's posture derive from Hellenistic culture. The fullness of Cassandra's figure, the form of the chariot wheels, and a general solidity of form reflect local traditions.

As the Greeks left Gandhara, the Mauryan dynasty from the Ganges valley moved in. The emperor Asoka Maurya (265–238 B.C.E.) embraced Buddhism and used his power to broadcast its message. Gandhara was receptive. In addition, many of Buddhism's early supporters were businessmen, some of

Figure 1 Trojan horse frieze, from Mardan district, Gandhara, second to third century C.E. (*British Museum, London*)

Figure 2 "The Bimaran reliquary," Gandhara, first century C.E.

whom must have propagated their faith through Gandhara, for this is the principal corridor linking Indian commerce with the silk routes of central Asia. Gandharan art, as **figures 2** and **3** suggest, became Buddhist art.

Gandharan art began to reach its apogee after Kanishka, emperor of the Kushana invaders, began to rule about 78 C.E. Kanishka, too, was a Buddhist and provided royal patronage to Buddhism. He favored the newly emerging Mahayana form of Buddhism, which for the first time represented the Buddha's human form in artistic images. The Kushanas had migrated from central Asia, and in their travels they had absorbed some Hellenistic perspectives. Their rule within India extended to the Ganges valley as far east as Mathura, Varanasi, and Sarnath, where the Buddha had preached his first sermon. Buddhism and its representation in Hellenistic forms continued through the classical period of the Gupta dynasty (320–480 C.E.). After the "White Huns" invaded, however, at the end of the fifth century, Gandharan art survived only in pockets in Afghanistan and Kashmir until perhaps the eighth century.

Art historians debate the date of the brilliant gold and ruby reliquary, or container for the fragments of Buddhist relics, in **figure 2**. Some argue that its arcade of the Buddha flanked by the gods Indra and Brahma, each in its own arched niche, must be modeled on a style of Roman sarcophagus that did not appear

until the second century C.E. Others assert that Indian artists did not require tutelage from Rome and that it may date from the first century C.E.

Figure 3 from about the third or fourth century C.E. represents the Buddha as rather stiff, his Hellenistic clothing falling in rigid lines, and the expression on his face rather flat. His right hand is posed in the *abhaya mudra* or the hand position

expressing reassurance. His palm shows the Wheel of the Buddha's Doctrine, which enlightens the entire world with its message of the eternal cycle of birth, maturity, and death. Above his head are two *yakshis* or heavenly beings, and to his left and right are Bodhisattvas, newly emerging Buddhas, who, according to Mahayana Buddhism, forsake nirvana to stay on earth and help other humans.

Figure 3 Buddha of the "great wonders," Gandhara, third to fourth century C.E.

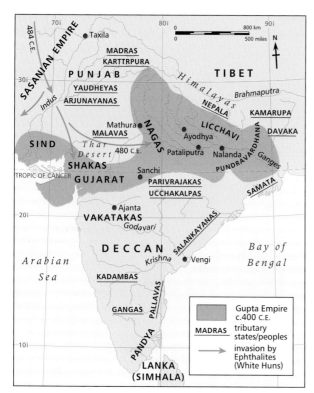

Gupta India In the fourth century C.E. the indigenous Gupta dynasty gained control of the middle Ganges and rapidly built an empire straddling the subcontinent from Sind to the Ganges delta, augmented by a web of treaty and tributary arrangements with neighboring powers. This classical age of Indian civilization was destroyed by invasions of central Asian peoples in the fifth century.

yet another, larger nomadic tribal group from east Asia, known in India as the Kushanas. The geographical extent of Kushana rule is not entirely known, but it seems to have included today's Afghanistan, Pakistan, Kashmir, and India as far south as Gujarat and its ports. The most outstanding Kushana king, Kanishka (r. *c.* 78–*c.* 103 C.E.), seems also to have promoted Buddhism and may have adopted it himself. With a single ruler controlling all these lands, trade between the subcontinent and the central Asian silk routes flourished.

THE GUPTA EMPIRE

In 320 C.E. a new dynasty began its rise to power in the Ganges valley, apparently through a fortunate marriage. The founder, Chandra Gupta I (r. 320–330), came from a dynasty of no historical fame but he married a princess of the powerful Licchavi lineage. Their son, Samudra Gupta (r. *c.* 330–*c.* 380), earned a reputation as one of India's greatest military conquerors. The record of his battles, inscribed on an old Asoka pillar at Allahabad, touches all regions of India: the far south, the east to Bengal and even Assam, the north to Nepal, and the mountain kingdoms of central India, which had often remained independent in their inaccessibility. Samudra's son and successor, Chandra Gupta II (r. *c.* 380–*c.* 415), conquered the Shakas and annexed western India, including prosperous Gujarat and

Plaque of musician with lyre, central India, fifth century C.E. During the Gupta period terra cotta plaques, such as this cross-legged lyre-player, were used to adorn the exterior of temples. It comes from one of the few surviving examples of free-standing brick temples decorated in this way at Bhitargaon in the Gupta heartland. (*British Museum, London*)

Wall-painting illustrating the *Vishvantara Jataka,* Cave 17, Ajanta. Gupta period, fifth century C.E. The rock-cut sanctuaries of Ajanta in northwest Deccan were abandoned for centuries until they were rediscovered in 1817 by British soldiers hunting tigers. The twenty-nine temple caves contain some of the earliest surviving Indian painting and mark the last true flowering of Buddhist art in the subcontinent prior to the ascendancy of Hinduism. This erotic fresco, taken from a folk tale, portrays Prince Vishvantara informing his queen that he has been banished from his father's kingdom.

its Arabian Sea ports, for the first time in five centuries. By marrying his daughter to the head of the Vakataka lineage, he solidified an alliance with his kingdom in central India. Other Gupta alliances were established through marriages with other powerful lineages in the Deccan. The fourth Gupta emperor, Kumara Gupta (r. *c.* 415–455), presided over a great empire now at peace.

Gupta rule was often indirect. Following many of their distant military victories the Gupta emperors abdicated the tasks of administration and withdrew, demanding only tribute payments. Nor did their alliances with other kingdoms and lineages call for direct rule. In the Ganges valley heartland of the empire, the Gupta emperor himself appointed governors at provincial levels, and sometimes even at the district level. At the most local level of the village and the city, however, the Guptas allowed considerable independence to local administrators. The area they administered directly was much smaller than the Mauryan Empire, and the two centuries of Gupta rule and influence are considered India's "golden age" even more for their cultural brilliance than for their political power.

The Guptas presided over a resurgence of Sanskrit literature and Hindu philosophy. The great playwright Kalidasa (fifth century C.E.) composed two epic poems, a lyrical poem "Meghaduta," and the great drama *Shakuntala,* the first Sanskrit drama translated into a western language in modern times. (This 1789 translation by the English judge and Sanskrit scholar William Jones went through five editions in twenty years.) Much of the important literature that had been transmitted orally was now transcribed into writing, including the Purana stories of legend and myth. Further emendations were made to the great epics, the *Mahabharata* and *Ramayana* (see p. 235).

The Gupta Empire began to use Sanskrit for its official correspondence. The great grammarian Panini (*fl. c.* 400 B.C.E.) had fixed the essentials of Sanskrit grammar in *Astadhyayi,* but the Mauryas and most other earlier rulers had used Prakrit, a variant of Sanskrit that was closer to the common language of the people. Now Sanskrit law codes, such as the *Manusmriti,* and principles of statecraft, such as Kautilya's *Artha-sastra,* were studied, revised, and further codified. Many locally powerful officials patronized scholars, humanists, and artists. Important academic centers for Buddhist learning flourished at Taxila in the northwest and Nalanda in the Ganges valley. Chinese Buddhist scholars visited and described these academies, although descriptions of Hindu academies have not been transmitted to the present.

This was especially an age of the resurgence of Hindu religious authority, and major systems of Hindu philosophy were articulated. The most influential, Vedanta, which developed the teachings of the Upanishads, posed a powerful, attractive alternative vision to Buddhism, and in this period Hinduism began to regain ascendancy over Buddhism in India. This was also the period in which the caste system was elaborated and enforced in more detail. *Brahmin* received patronage from rulers, high-level administrators, and wealthy landlords in the form of land grants and court positions. *Brahmin* priests also asserted their role in ritual performance. Buddhism, which had flourished through the patronage of earlier empires, ceded the performance of many of its own rituals to *brahmin* priests, and began to decline (see p. 280).

HUNA INVASIONS AND THE END OF THE NORTH INDIAN EMPIRE

In the fifth century, however, new conquerors came through the passes of the northwest, overthrowing the Gupta Empire and establishing their own headquarters in Bamiyan, Afghanistan. The Hunas were a branch of the Xiongnu, the nomadic Mongol tribes which roamed the regions north of the Great Wall of China. In previous expansions, they had driven other groups west, even into the Roman Empire, as we saw in Chapter 6. Domino fashion, these groups pushed one another westward. The Shakas had invaded India as a result of this sequence in about 94 B.C.E. The Kushanas followed about a century later, driven out of northeast Asia by the Hunas. Now the Hunas themselves arrived in force. These same ethnic peoples were called Huns in the Roman Empire, which they invaded under Attila in 454 C.E.

The first Huna invasions, which occurred about 460 C.E., were repulsed by Skanda Gupta (r. 455–467), but the continuing Huna presence across India's northwest border seems to have disrupted international trade and reduced Gupta wealth. Skanda's successor apparently could not hold the empire together. Regional strongmen began to assert their independence. With central control thus weakened, Huna armies invaded again in about 500 C.E., and for the next half century they fought in, and controlled, much of northern and central India. From their capital in Bamiyan, Afghanistan, the Hunas ruled parts of India as their own imperial provinces. As in Rome, they earned a reputation for great cruelty, reported not only by Indians but also by Chinese and Greeks who visited the region. Huna rule proved brief, however. In 528 C.E. Indian regional princes drove them northwest as far as Kashmir. About a generation later Turkic and Persian armies defeated the main Huna concentrations in Bactria, removing them as a force in India.

Although it was shortlived, the Huna impact on India was considerable. Their invasion further weakened the Gupta Empire, enabling regional powers to dismember it and to declare their own independence. Except for a brief reign by Harsha-vardhana (r. 606–647), king of the north Indian region of Kanauj, no further unification of all of India was ever seriously attempted from inside the subcontinent until the twentieth century. (The Moghul and British empires, discussed in Chapters 14 and 16, were created by invasions from outside, although the Moghuls later settled within the subcontinent.) The urban culture of north India dimmed. The Buddhist monasteries, which the Hunas attacked with especial force, never recovered. By opening up their invasion routes the

Hunas indirectly enriched India's population pool. Gurjaras and Rajputs entered western India more or less along with the Hunas, and settled permanently. The modern Indian states of Gujarat and Rajasthan are named for them and their descendants.

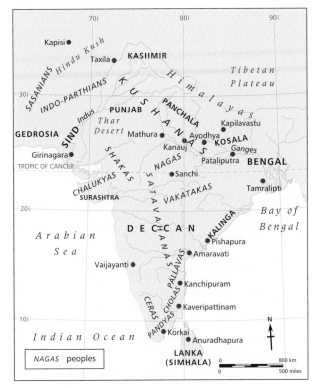

Classical South Asia As kingdoms rose and fell, India had no centralized empire for almost a thousand years. Local powers grew up, often based on different languages and ethnicities. More powerful groups occupied the richest lands, while the weaker were forced into the hills. The roots of today's separate states of India lie in some of these early ethnic kingdoms.

LEGACIES OF THE HUNAS

The legacies of the Hunas in India—the destruction and dismemberment of the Gupta Empire, the reduction in inter-regional trade, the decline of culture, and the introduction of new nomadic groups into already settled imperial lands—quite closely mirror those of their Hun brothers in the Roman Empire. Even the timings were similar, products of the same emigration from east Asia. Of the great empires of the ancient world, only China was capable of defeating or assimilating these invaders without losing its own coherence and identity.

REGIONAL DIVERSITY AND POWER

The history of the Indian subcontinent tends to be written from the perspective of the Ganges valley as the center of political power and influence. (The settlements of the central Indus valley [Chapter 3] did not endure and the region is now a desert.) The Aryans established their centers in the Ganges region; the Mauryans continued the pattern; so did the Guptas; the later Moghuls established their capitals there; the British ultimately followed Moghul patterns by also placing their capital at Delhi; and today's government of independent India has also followed suit. But other regions of India have always been important, too. Even at times when India has been unified, regional powers have regularly challenged the supremacy of the Ganges heartland. In periods such as the

Earthenware sculpture, Nilgiri Hills, south India, early centuries C.E. The Tamil culture of southern India generated not only a separate language and an expressive literary tradition, but also distinctive artifacts. A buffalo cult among the Todas, the largest of the Nilgiri Hills tribal groups, led to the creation of this characterful figurine, made to decorate the lid of an urn containing ashes. (*British Museum, London*)

millennium from 500 C.E. to 1500 C.E., when India had no central empire, the outlying regions asserted their status as independent states.

The major regions of India speak different languages from one another, although imperial rulers have usually introduced a unifying link language for inter-regional communication: Prakrit under Asoka; Sanskrit under the Guptas; and, later, Persian under the Moghuls; and English under the British. Today, two languages are used in India, Hindi and English, while Pakistan uses Urdu and Bangladesh, Bengali. The peoples of different

---

SOURCE
Tamil Culture in Southeast India

The dominant language of the southeast was Tamil and it developed an especially expressive literature. The poetry of the southern Tamilian academies, called *sangam* poetry, written about 100 B.C.E.–250 C.E., set in counterpoint the private, bittersweet play of love against a public atmosphere of warfare and strife. This poetry was lost until it was rediscovered by scholars in the later decades of the nineteenth century. It has been brought to the attention of the English-speaking world by the efforts of the late A.K. Ramanujan.

A King's Double Nature

His armies love massacre,
he loves war,
yet gifts
flow from him ceaselessly.

Come, dear singers,
let's go and see him in Naravu

    where, on trees
    no axe can fell,
    fruits ripen, unharmed
    by swarms of bees,
    egg-shaped, ready
    for the weary traveller
    in the fields of steady, unfailing harvests;
    where warriors with bows
    that never tire of arrows
    shiver
    but stand austere
    in the sea winds
    mixed with the lit cloud
    and the spray of seafoam.

There he is,
in the town of Naravu,
tender among tender women.

Harvest of War

Great king,

you shield your men from ruin,
so your victories, your greatness
are bywords.

Loose chariot wheels
lie about the battleground
with the long white tusks
of bull-elephants.

Flocks of male eagles
eat carrion
with their mates.

Headless bodies
dance about
before they fall
to the ground.

Blood glows,
like the sky before nightfall,
in the red center
of the battlefield.

Demons dance there.
And your kingdom
is an unfailing harvest
of victorious wars.

(trans. by A.K. Ramanujan, pp. 131, 115)

regions have immigrated into the subcontinent from different places and at different times. Throughout their history, when not consolidated into larger empires, they have had their own political-cultural administrations and have often fought one another. The indigenous tribal peoples whose immigration predates any historical records, referred to today as "native Indians" or "**tribals**," generally inhabit less accessible areas, frequently in hilly tracts not easy to farm. They have attempted to protect their independence from outside exploitation by maintaining inaccessibility.

The peoples of Gujarat in the west and of Bengal and Orissa in the east have all seen themselves as distinct when they were ruled from the north, and as independent when that rule was broken. Regional dynasties came and went. The most distinct and separate region was the far south. Here, several lineage and ethnic groups fought to maintain their independence: in the extreme southeast the Pandyas; just north of them along the coast, the Pallavas; still further north, the Colas; and then still further north, along the coast, the Chalukyas. Along the southwest coast, the Perumal and Cera lineages dominated.

SEA TRADE AND CULTURAL INFLUENCE: FROM ROME TO SOUTHEAST ASIA

Imperial governments based inland in the Ganges valley and even further to the northwest tended to draw their economic power from their control over that rich land and from trade through the mountain passes connecting to the silk routes. Many of the regional, coastal powers, on the other hand, traded by sea. This gave them wide ranging external connections to the Roman Empire in the west and to southeast Asia in the east.

Under the Roman emperor Caesar Augustus (r. 27 B.C.E.–14 C.E.) Rome annexed Egypt, opening up a trade route to the east via the Red Sea. Rome controlled enormous wealth, generating a powerful economic demand for goods from Asia. Roman traders learned from the Arabs before them to sail with the southwest monsoon winds from the Red Sea to the west coast of India in about two weeks; about six months later they could sail back with the northeast monsoon. About 50 C.E., a Greek merchant wrote of the Roman trade with Malabar, the southwest coast of India, in his great compendium of trade in the Indian Ocean, *The Periplus of the Erythraean Sea*:

They send large ships to the market-towns on account of the great quantity and bulk of pepper and [cinnamon]. There are imported here, in the first place, a great quantity of coin; topaz, thin clothing, not much; figured linens, antimony, coral, crude glass, copper, tin, lead, wine, not much, but as much as at Barygaza [the flourishing port of Gujarat, further north] . . . There is exported pepper, which is produced in quantity in only one region near these markets. . . . Besides this there are exported great quantities of fine pearls, ivory, silk cloth, spikenard from the Ganges, [cinnamon] from the places in the interior, transparent stones of all kinds, diamonds and sapphires, and tortoise shell. (Cited in Kulke and Rothermund, p. 106)

Numerous hoards of Roman gold coins throughout south India provide archaeological evidence of this trade. Eleven such deposits were found near Coimbatore alone, the area through which trade routes led inland from the Malabar coast, and many others have been discovered near the major ports on the west and east coasts. In 1945, the British archaeologist Sir Mortimer Wheeler discovered the remnants of a Roman trading post at Arikamedu, a fishing village adjacent to Chennai (formerly Madras), and he excavated the brick foundations of large halls and terraces, cisterns, fortifications, and ceramics that had been produced in Italy between 30 B.C.E. and 35 C.E. This outpost suggests that it was likely that the traders actually carrying the goods across the Arabian Sea were foreign rather than Indian: Arabs, Jews, and Romans. Pliny, the Roman historian, complained that Rome was sending around 50 million sesterces a year to India to buy its luxuries, although he noted that they sold in Rome for one hundred times that amount.

CONNECTION: *The Roman Empire and intercontinental trade, pp. 178–81*

SOUTHEAST ASIA: "GREATER INDIA"

Some of the luxuries shipped to Rome were first brought to India from southeast Asia. Indian sailors traveled to all the coastal countries of modern southeast Asia: Myanmar (formerly Burma), Thailand, Cambodia, Vietnam, Malaysia, and Indonesia. To anchor this trade, they established settlements in port cities like Oc Eo in Funan, in the southernmost part of modern Vietnam. *Brahmin* priests and Buddhist monks settled along with the traders, serving the Indian expatriates and attracting local converts at the same time.

At first the impact of Hinduism was more powerful. Both Funan, the present-day Mekong delta region of southern Vietnam and Cambodia, and Champa, further north along the coast of Vietnam, became Hindu kingdoms. Local mythology and Chinese historical records tell quite different stories of the arrival of a *brahmin* priest named Kaundinya. As a result of his activities, Funan adopted Sanskrit as the language of the court and encouraged Hinduism and later Buddhism, as well. But Funan remained an independent state, not an Indian province. Indeed, in the third century C.E. Funan extended its own rule to South Vietnam, Cambodia, central Thailand, northern Malaya, and southern Myanmar from its capital at Vyadhapura, near present-day Phnom Penh. Wherever it went, it encouraged the adoption of Indian culture. Ironically, it infused Indian culture even into states that conquered it. When Champa expanded southward into Funan lands, the kings of Champa began to adopt the cultural, linguistic, and architectural styles of the Pallavas of south India which were then current in Funan. Bhadravarman, a Champa king, built the first Champa temple to the Hindu god Shiva.

Two additional kingdoms under Funan hegemony later established independent states with

Borobudur, Java, late eighth century. This monument, the supreme example of Buddhist art in southeast Asia and Indonesia, is a fantastic microcosm, reproducing in miniature the universe as it was known and imagined in the Mahayana school of Buddhist theology. The relief sculptures, of which there are some 10 miles (16 km), represent the doctrine of karma, the cycle of birth and rebirth, of striving, and release from the Wheel of Life (also shown on the Asokan capital, p. 232).

Angkor Wat, Angkor, Cambodia, early twelfth century C.E. Dedicated to the Hindu god Vishnu, this huge, jungle-bound temple complex once served as the centerpiece of the Khmer Empire, originally founded in 880. Decorated with extensive relief sculpture, the temples of Angkor Wat were intended to emulate mountains in dressed stone.

strong Hindu and Buddhist cultural elements: Java, which was ruled by the Sailendra lineage, and the kingdom of Srivijaya in Sumatra. They, in turn, further spread Indian influences. When the Sailendras attacked the Khmer peoples of present-day Cambodia, the Khmers unified their defenses under King Jayavarman II (r. 790–850). He established a new capital and introduced Hindu temples and philosophies into the whole region around it at Angkor, which was later the location of one of Hinduism's greatest temples constructed by Jayavarman VII (r. 1181–1219). In Java, the Sailendras built an equally extraordinary Buddhist temple at Borobudur in 778–824.

The diffusion of Indian religious and cultural forms continued for centuries throughout southeast Asia. It proceeded almost entirely peacefully, spread by priests and traders, but there were a few exceptions. The Pallava king, Nandivarman III (r. *c.* 844–866), supported a military camp on the Isthmus of Siam in order to protect a group of south Indian merchants who were living and working there. The Chola king, Rajendra I (r. 1014–47), dispatched a fleet to Sumatra and Malaya and defeated the Srivijaya Empire. It appears that his goal was to keep the trade routes open and to support India's shippers on the competitive sea lanes; he claimed no territory. In 1068–9, the

Cholas apparently intervened in a dispute among rival claimants to rule in Malaya, conquered a large part of the region, but then turned it over to their local client. Long before any of these trade ventures, in the third century B.C.E. King Asoka had dispatched missionaries to Sri Lanka and to Myanmar to begin the process of converting these lands to Buddhism.

INDIA, CHINA, AND ROME: EMPIRES AND INTERMEDIATE INSTITUTIONS
HOW DO THEY COMPARE?

SOURCES

Comparing India, China, and Rome is not straightforward. To begin with, in terms of sources of information, India lacks the detailed political, military, economic, administrative, and personal records that would facilitate comparison in any detail. Rome and China compiled official histories as well as a wide variety of personal accounts that have survived to the present. For India, on the other hand, we are often reliant for our best accounts on the observations of foreign visitors. Even the life, writings, and policies of Asoka, now regarded as ancient India's greatest emperor, were lost from historical consciousness for centuries until his rock and pillar edicts were deciphered in the nineteenth century.

ADMINISTRATION

Second, while both Rome and China built institutionalized bureacracies and systems of administration, lasting for centuries in Rome and millennia in China, India's states and empires generally seemed to be extensions of family lineages. Even the most powerful of ancient India's empires, the Mauryan and Gupta, were family holdings. Despite the administrative rigor suggested by Kautilya's *Artha-sastra*, even Chandragupta Maurya's dynasty began to weaken after the death of his grandson Asoka.

INTERNATIONAL RELATIONS

The *Artha-sastra* characterized inter-state relations by the law of the fish, *matsyanyaya*, the large swallow the small. Despite Asoka's renunciation of the excessive use of force, the constant rise and fall of kingdoms and small empires throughout India suggest that Kautilya's view generally prevailed. We do not have records of internal revolts against states and empires in India. Instead, dissidents would abscond to a neighboring state where they felt they could live more freely. Then they might join the official military to fight against their former ruler.

INVASION OF THE HUNAS

Indian empires did not expand beyond the borders of the subcontinent. Indian trade missions in southeast Asia exported cultural and religious innovations along with their material cargo, but almost without exception they made no attempt to establish political rule. On the other hand, outsiders frequently invaded the subcontinent. Remarkably, the one political experience that the empires of India, Rome, and China all shared was invasion and at least partial conquest by the Hunas (Huns, Xiongnu) and by the peoples they displaced. Indeed, all three of these last chapters point to the great importance of the Hunas/Huns in world history, especially from the third through the sixth centuries C.E. Historical records include not only the builders and sustainers of sedentary empire, but also their nomadic challengers. (We will explore this issue further in considering the Mongols in Chapters 12 and 14.)

LOCAL INSTITUTIONS AND THE STATE

In Rome and China, government touched much of the population directly, through taxes, military conscription, imperial service, and aggressive bureaucracies. The state was fundamental to all areas of life. The state in India, on the other hand, seemed to preside over a set of social institutions that had existed prior to it, were more deeply rooted, and were more persistent through time. These institutions included family lineages, aware and proud of their histories; caste groups, each presiding over its own occupational, ritual, and ethnic niche; guild associations, overseeing the conditions of economic production and distribution; local councils, providing government at the village and town level; and religious sects, which gave their members a sense of belonging, identity, and purpose. The state was important in overseeing the activities of all of these groups, but it existed only in the context of their existence. States and empires came and went, but these varied, pervasive institutions carried on in their own rhythms. In the words of historian Romila Thapar:

> The understanding of power in India lies in analyses of the caste and sub-caste relationships and of institutions such as the guilds and village councils, and not merely in the survey of dynastic power. (Thapar, *History*, vol. I, p. 19)

In India political authority was intimately connected, and sometimes subordinated, to familial, cultural, and religious power. In the next chapters on religion in world history, and especially in Chapter 9 on Hinduism and Buddhism, we will explore these connections.

BIBLIOGRAPHY

Allchin, F.R., et al. *The Archaeology of Early Historic South Asia: The Emergence of Cities and States* (Cambridge: Cambridge University Press, 1995).

Basham, A.L. *The Wonder That Was India* (New York: Grove Press, 1954).

Cotterell, Arthur, ed. *The Penguin Encyclopedia of Ancient Civilizations* (London: Penguin Books, 1980).

Craven, Roy C. *A Concise History of Indian Art* (New York: Oxford University Press, n.d.).

Embree, Ainslee, ed. and rev. *Sources of Indian Tradition*, Vol. I: *From the Beginning to 1800* (New York: Columbia University Press, 2nd ed., 1988).

Green, Peter. *Alexander of Macedon, 356–323 B.C.* (Berkeley: University of California Press, 1991).

Hughes, Sarah Shaver and Brady Hughes, eds. *Women in World History*, Vol. I: *Readings from Prehistory to 1500* (Armonk, NY: M.E. Sharpe, 1995).

Kulke, Hermann and Dietmar Rothermund. *A History of India* (Totowa, NJ: Barnes and Noble Books, 1986).

Lockhard, Craig A. "Integrating Southeast Asia into the Framework of World History: The Period Before 1500," *The History Teacher* XXIX, No. 1 (November 1995), 7–35.

The (London) Times Atlas of World History (London: Times Books, 4th ed., 1993).

Past Worlds: The Times Atlas of Archaeology (Maplewood, NJ: Hammond, 1988).

Ramanujan, A.K., ed. and trans. *Poems of Love and War: From the Eight Anthologies and the Ten Long Poems of Classical Tamil* (New York: Columbia University Press, 1985).

Richman, Paula, ed. *Many Ramayanas: The Diversity of a Narrative Tradition in South Asia* (Berkeley: University of California Press, 1991).

Rowland, Benjamin. *The Art and Architecture of India: Buddhist/Hindu/Jain* (New York: Penguin Books, 1977).

SarDesai, D.R. *Southeast Asia: Past and Present* (Boulder, CO: Westview Press, 1994).

Schwartzberg, Joseph E., ed. *A Historical Atlas of South Asia* (Chicago: University of Chicago Press, 1978).

Spodek, Howard, "Studying the History of Urbanization in India," *Journal of Urban History* VI, No. 3 (May, 1980), 251–95.

Spodek, Howard and Doris Srinivasan, eds. *Urban Form and Meaning in South Asia: The Shaping of Cities from Prehistoric to Precolonial Times* (Washington: National Gallery of Art, 1993).

Thapar, Romila. *Ancient Indian Social History* (New Delhi: Orient Longman, 1978).

———. *Asoka and the Decline of the Mauryas* (Delhi: Oxford University Press, 1963).

———. *A History of India*, Vol. I (Baltimore, MD: Penguin Books, 1966).

———. *Interpreting Early India* (New York: Oxford University Press, 1992).

Tharu, Susie and K. Lalita, eds. *Women Writing in India 600 B.C. to the Present*, Vol. I (New York: The Feminist Press, 1991).

The Rise of World Religions

600 B.C.E.–1500 C.E.

NOT BY BREAD ALONE: HOW DO HISTORIANS UNDERSTAND RELIGION IN WORLD HISTORY?

Religion is the sense of human relationship with the sacred, with forces in and beyond nature. Throughout history people have felt the need to establish such relationships with powers that they believed capable of protecting and supporting them and capable of providing a deeper sense of significance to life and the possibility of some form of existence after death. Some people have thought of these forces as abstract and remote; others have regarded them as having personalities, as gods. Some people, of course, do not believe in such powers at all, or they are skeptical.

Mircea Eliade (1907–86), perhaps the leading historian of religion in the mid- and late twentieth century, wrote:

In the most archaic phases of culture, *to live as a human being* was in itself *a religious act*, since eating, sexual activity, and labor all had a sacramental value. Experience of the sacred is inherent in man's mode of being in the world.

When we think of the sacred we must not limit it to divine figures. The sacred does not necessarily imply belief in God or gods or spirits . . . it is the experience of a reality and the source of an awareness of existing in the world. . . . The sacred cannot be recognized "from outside." It is by means of internal experience that each individual will be able to recognize it in the religious acts of a Christian or a "primitive" man. (Eliade, *Ordeal by Labyrinth*, p. 154)

Dome of the Rock, Jerusalem, 692 C.E.

From the earliest human records we have encountered such religious needs. More than 100,000 years ago Neanderthals buried their dead in anticipation of their journey to an afterlife. Archaeologists have found Neanderthal burials with flint tools, food, and cooked meat at Teshik-Tash in Siberia; the burial of a man with a crippled right arm at the Shanidar cave in the Zagros Mountains of Iraq; and graves covered with red ocher powder, including some group burials, in France and central Europe.

Burial rituals—the formal recognition of our common mortality—suggest that the earliest humans thought about the significance of their lives. They hoped that life might continue in some form, even after death, and they must also have dedicated a part of their energies to transmitting values that would continue after they died and to creating institutions to perpetuate those values.

In Part 2 we saw that many early cities and states were dedicated to particular gods or goddesses, sometimes even carrying their names. Gilgamesh, builder of the city of Uruk in Mesopotamia, was two-thirds a god and sought eternal life. In Babylon, Hammurabi transmitted his legal code in the name of the god Shamash. Egyptian hymns proclaimed the divinity of the pharaohs. Chinese of the Shang dynasty used oracle bones to augur the will of transcendent powers. Athens was named for the goddess Athena.

The empires we discussed in Part 3 sought the validation provided by religious leaders and, in exchange, gave financial and political backing to religious institutions. The emperors of Rome and China served also as high-priests for their people. When the Roman emperor Constantine believed that he had been miraculously assisted by Jesus, he transferred his allegiance from paganism to the embattled Christian church. Hinduism and its caste system provided India with a sense of unity and continuity. In several states of south and southeast Asia, Buddhist priests were called upon to validate the authority of rulers. Confucianism, which was discussed in Chapter 7 as one of the pillars of the Chinese imperial system, presents a profound theory of ethical human relationships. Unlike the religions just mentioned, however, Confucianism has very little other-worldly focus.

This part focuses in greater depth on the role of religion in human history. Chronologically, the part spans the entire period, from earliest humans to about 1500 C.E. Its key focus, however, is from *c*. 300 C.E. to *c*. 1200 C.E. In this period Hinduism became more fully defined and systematized throughout India; Buddhism rose to great importance in China, Japan, and southeast Asia; Judaism, exiled from its original home in Israel, spread with the exiles throughout much of west Asia, the Mediterranean basin, and northern Europe; Christianity grew into the great cultural system of Europe; and Islam radiated outward from the pivotal center of Afro-Eurasia to the far corners of the eastern hemisphere. These five religions often confronted one another, sometimes leading to **syncretism**, the borrowing and adaptation of ideas and practices; sometimes to competition; and sometimes to direct conflict.

HINDUISM AND BUDDHISM

9

300 B.C.E.—1200 C.E.

" Empires crumble: Religion alone endures."

JACQUES BENIGNE BOSSUET,

UNIVERSAL HISTORY (1681)

THE SACRED SUBCONTINENT: THE SPREAD OF RELIGION IN INDIA AND BEYOND

This chapter begins with a definition of religion and a description of early religious practices. It proceeds to a brief history of early Hinduism, the most ancient of existing major religions, and analyzes its evolution as the principal cultural system of the Indian subcontinent. Buddhism emerged out of Hinduism in India and spread throughout central, eastern, and southeastern Asia, defining much of the cultural and religious life of this vast region. Its history concludes this chapter.

THE HISTORIAN AND RELIGIOUS BELIEF: HOW DO WE KNOW?

Organized religious groups usually build on the religious experiences proclaimed by their founders and early teachers. All five of the religions we study in this part grew from such experiences, and many of the experiences were miraculous—that is, they are contrary to everyday experience, and they can be neither proved nor disproved. For example, most Hindus believe that gods have regularly intervened in human life as Krishna is said to have done at the Battle of Kurukshetra (see Source, p. 266). They also believe in the reincarnation of all living creatures, including gods. Buddhists believe in the revelation of the Four Noble Truths and the Eightfold Path to Siddhartha Gautama (the Buddha) under the bodhi (bo) tree at Bodh Gaya in northern India; most also believe that Siddhartha was a reborn soul of an earlier Buddha and would himself be born again. Most Jews have believed in special divine intervention in the lives of Abraham and his descendants, a special divine covenant with the Jewish people, and a revelation of divine law at Mount Sinai. Most Christians have believed in the miracle of Jesus' incarnation as the Son of God and his resurrection after death. Most Muslims believe that God revealed his teachings to Muhammad through the angel Gabriel, and that these were later transcribed in the Quran.

[margin annotations: Hinduism; Hinduism Buddhism; Judaism; Christian; Muslim]

Historians, however, cannot study miracles. Historical study seeks proof of events, and such proof is not usually available for miracles. Almost by definition, a belief in miracles is a matter of faith, not of proof. Moreover, history is the study of the regular processes of change over time, and miracles, again by definition, are one-time-only events, which stand outside and defy the normal processes of change.

What can be studied are the manifestations and effects of religious beliefs on people's behavior. Sincere believers in religious miracles restructure their lives accordingly, creating and joining religious organizations to spread the word about these miracles and about their own experiences with them. These new organizations formulate rules of membership, and they infuse their beliefs into everyday life by establishing sacred time, sacred

HINDUISM AND BUDDHISM

DATE	POLITICAL/SOCIAL EVENTS	LITERARY/PHILOSOPHICAL EVENTS
1500 B.C.E.	• Caste system	• *Rigveda* (1500–1200)
900 B.C.E.		• Brahmanas (900–500)
800 B.C.E.		• Upanishads (800–500)
500 B.C.E.	• Siddhartha Gautama (Buddha) (*c.* 563–483) • Mahavir (*b.* 540), Jain teacher	• Buddha delivers sermon on the Four Noble Truths and the Noble Eightfold Path
300 B.C.E.		• *Mahabharata* (300–300 C.E.) • *Ramayana* (300–300 C.E.)
200 B.C.E	• Buddhism more widespread than Hinduismin India (until 200 C.E.); spreading in Sri Lanka • Mahayana Buddhism growing in popularity	
10 C.E	• 4th general council of Buddhism codified Theravada doctrines • Buddhist missionaries in China (65 C.E.)	• Nagarjuna (50–150 C.E.), philosopher of Mahayana Buddhism
300 C.E	• Spread of Hinduism to southeast Asia	
400 C.E.	• Hindu pantheon established • Buddhism declining in India	• Puranas written (400–1000) • Faxian's pilgrimage to India • Sanskrit; Hindu gods, temples, and priests in southeast Asia; Buddhism in southeast Asia
500 C.E.	• Bhakti begun in south India • Buddhist monks to Japan	
600 C.E.	• Buddhist monks to southeast Asia • Buddhism flourishes under Tang dynasty (618–907)	• Xuanzang's pilgrimage to India
700 C.E.	• Hindu temples and shrines begin to appear in India • Buddhism begins to decline in China • Buddhism becoming established in Japan	• Hindu philosopher Shankaracharya (788–820) • Saicho (767–822), Japanese Buddhist priest • Kukai (774–835), Japanese Buddhist priest
800 C.E.	• Hindu priests in southeast Asia • Emperor Wuzong attacks Buddhism in China	• Earliest printed book: (*The Diamond Sutra*) (868)
1000 C.E.	• Muslim invasion of India (1000–1200) • Buddhist institutions close in India	• Hindu philosopher Ramanuja (1017–1137)

See also Indian Empires timechart, pp. 233–4

CHRONOLOGY OF THE WORLD'S RELIGIOUS CULTURES

CULTURE	3000 B.C.E.	2500	2000	1500	1000	500	0	500 C.E.	1000	1500	2000
SUMERIAN	▬▬▬	▬▬	▬								
AKKADIAN/BABYLONIAN			▬▬	▬▬	▬	▬					
HITTITE/HURRIAN			▬	▬							
EGYPTIAN	▬▬▬	▬▬	▬▬	▬▬	▬	▬	▬				
GREEK				· · ·	▬	▬	▬				
ROMAN						▬	▬	▬			
JEWISH			· ·	▬	▬	▬	▬	▬	▬	▬	▬
CHRISTIAN							▬	▬	▬	▬	▬
ISLAMIC								▬	▬	▬	▬
HINDU				▬	▬	▬	▬	▬	▬	▬	▬
BUDDHIST						▬	▬	▬	▬	▬	▬
INCAN									▬	▬	
MAYAN						▬	▬	▬	▬		
AZTEC									▬	▬	
CELTIC						▬	▬	▬			
NORDIC/ICELANDIC								▬	▬		

space, sacred liturgy, and sacred literature and culture. Historically, when religious identity combined with political power, group boundaries became even more important, marking in-group from out-group, separating "us" from "them," sometimes even leading to violent conflict. Historians *do* study these manifestations and effects of religious beliefs:

- **The sanctification of time** Each religion creates its own sacred calendar, linking the present with the past by commemorating each year the key dates in the history of the religion and in the life of its community. It marks dates for the performance of special rituals, celebrations, fasts, and community assemblies. In addition to the community calendar, members of religious organizations create their own individual and family calendars to mark the rites of passage—the great lifecycle events of birth, puberty, marriage, maturity, and death—so that each event has its own ritual observance. Religions especially formulate rules of marriage in an attempt to channel the raw, powerful, mysterious, and often indiscriminate forces of youthful sexuality to conform to the norms of the group.

- **The sanctification of space** Each religion creates its own sacred geography by establishing shrines where miraculous acts are said to have occurred; where saints had been born, flourished, or met their deaths; and where relics from the lives of holy people are preserved and venerated. The most sacred of these sites become centers of pilgrimage. As we have seen in earlier chapters (see for example the Focus, p. 48), whole cities, and especially their sacred quarters, were dedicated to gods and goddesses, and thought to be under their special protection.

- **The sanctification of language and literature** Each religion shapes its own use of language, literature, and artistic imagery. The Hebrew **Bible,** the Greek **New Testament,** the Arabic Quran, the Sanskrit Veda and epics, and the Pali Buddhist **Tripitaka** have provided linguistic and literary canons across the millennia. In translation these texts have given character to new languages. For example, translations of the Bible by Saint Jerome (c. 347–419), William Tyndale (c. 1494–1536), and Martin Luther (1483–1546) have enriched Latin, English, and German, respectively. The retelling in Hindi by Tulsidas (c. 1543–1623) of the Sanskrit Ramayana helped to establish the importance of that modern language in north India. This religious literature usually provides the core of religious liturgy and thus becomes part of the daily expression of faith of the common people. Part 4 quotes religious scriptures extensively because of their centrality to the world's languages, literatures, and imagery.

- **The sanctification of artistic and cultural creativity** Religious sensibilities often inspire specific creative efforts, and religious groups often encourage the creation of art and music to express and enhance their message.

- **The creation of religious organization** As religion moves from individual experience to group membership, organization develops. At one extreme this may be a hierarchical structure with a single leader at the apex and an array of administrative and spiritual orders down to the most local level, the form of the Roman Catholic Church. At another extreme there may be no formal overall organization, and no formal set of rules and regulations, but instead a loose association of local communities related to one another through common beliefs and social structures, the form of Hinduism.

If a religious group grows to include a sizable proportion of the population, some relationship must be negotiated between its organization and the state. We have already noted some examples of close relationships between religion and government—for example, in Sumer (Chapter 2) and in Aryan India (Chapter 8). We shall see more. We shall also see antagonistic relationships between religions and governments. In Chapter 10, for example, we shall see Jewish prophets call Jewish kings to a moral accounting, and in Chapter 11 we shall see Muslim religious authorities fight for their independence from the caliph, the political ruler.

Religious networks and political networks frequently intersected the same geographical space, each growing up in the soil plowed by the other. Both the Roman Catholic and Eastern Orthodox churches, for example, grew up

largely in the territory dominated by the Roman Empire—the Roman church in the west, the Orthodox church in the east. Islam flowered especially in the lands once conquered by Alexander and ruled by his successors, except in the Greek homelands themselves. Buddhism spread across India after the Emperor Asoka made it his state religion, while Hinduism developed as the dominant religion of many of India's subsequent governments. The intersection of major religions with powerful states has created world civilizations of great depth, power, and longevity.

MAJOR RELIGIONS OF THE WORLD, 1998

Religion	Number of followers	Percentage of world population
Christians	1,943,038,000	32.8
Roman Catholics	1,026,501,000	17.3
Protestants	316,445,000	5.3
Orthodox	213,743,000	3.6
Anglicans	63,748,000	1.1
Other Christians	373,832,000	6.3
Unaffiliated Christians	107,686,000	1.8
Muslims	1,164,622,000	19.6
Hindus	761,689,000	12.8
Nonreligious	759,655,000	12.8
Chinese folk religionists	379,162,000	6.4
Buddhists	353,794,000	6.0
Ethnic religionists	248,565,000	4.2
Atheists	149,913,000	2.5
New religionists	100,144,000	1.7
Sikhs	22,232,000	0.4
Jews	14,111,000	0.2
Baha'is	6,764,000	0.1
Confucianists	6,241,000	0.1
Jains	3,922,000	0.1
Shintoists	2,789,000	0.0
Zoroastrians	274,000	0.0

(*Encyclopedia Britannica Book of the Year, 2000, p. 315*).

HINDUISM

THE ORIGINS OF HINDUISM: HOW DO WE KNOW?

Hinduism began before recorded time. The other major religions of the world were inspired by a specific person or event: Abraham's covenant; the Buddha's enlightenment; Jesus' birth; Muhammad's revelation. Hinduism, by contrast, emerged through the weaving together of many diverse, ancient religious traditions of India, some of which precede written records. Hinduism evolved from the experience of the peoples of India. *man-created*

Because Hinduism preserves a rich body of religious literature written in Sanskrit, the language of the Aryan invaders of 1700–1200 B.C.E., scholars believed until recently that Hinduism was a product of that invasion. Even the excavations at Mohenjo-Daro and Harappa, which uncovered a pre-Aryan civilization (see Chapter 3), did not at first alter these beliefs. But as excavation and analysis have continued, many scholars have come to believe that the Indus valley civilization may have contributed many of Hinduism's principal gods and ceremonies. Excavated statues seem to represent the god Shiva (see p. 84), the sacred bull Nandi on which he rides, a man practicing yogic meditation, a sacred tree, and a mother goddess. Archaeologists increasingly argue that the invading Aryans absorbed religious beliefs and practices, along with secular culture, from the Indus valley.

Contemporary anthropological accounts support the idea that Hinduism is an amalgam of beliefs and practices. These accounts emphasize Hinduism's remarkable ability to absorb and assimilate tribal peoples and their gods. Today, about 100 million of India's 1000 million people are officially regarded as "tribals." These peoples were living in India before the arrival of the Aryans, and they have largely attempted to escape Aryan domination by retreating into remote hilly and forested

Gouache illustration from Bhanudatta's *Rasamanjari*, 1685. Krishna, the eighth *avatar* (incarnation) of Vishnu, is always depicted with blue/black skin and is renowned for his prowess as a warrior and a lover. In this scene from one of his amorous adventures, a woman hinders a forester from felling the tree under which she has arranged to meet Krishna for a romantic tryst.

regions, where they could preserve their own social systems. Hindus have, however, pursued them and their lands, building temples in and around tribal areas. These temples recognize tribal gods and incorporate them with the mainstream deities in an attempt to persuade the tribals to accept Hindu religious patterns. Indeed, one of Hinduism's greatest gods, Krishna, the blue/black god, was apparently a tribal god who gained national recognition.

As India's peoples have been diverse, so its evolving religious system is diverse. The concept of "Hinduism" as a unified religion comes from outsiders. Greeks first encountering India, and especially Alexander the Great, who arrived in 327 B.C.E., spoke of India's belief systems and practices collectively as "Hinduism," that is, the ways of the peoples on the far side of the Indus River. When Muslims began to arrive in India, beginning in the eighth century C.E., they adopted the same terminology.

SACRED GEOGRAPHY AND PILGRIMAGE

More than any other religion, Hinduism is associated with a specific territory, India. Almost all Hindus live in India or are of Indian descent. Within India itself a sacred geography has developed. Places visited by gods and by saints, as well as places of great natural sanctity, have become shrines and pilgrim destinations. Pilgrims traveling these routes have created a geography of religious/national integration, and modern transportation, in the form of trains, buses, and airplanes, has increased the pilgrim traffic throughout India. Some of the most important shrines are at the far corners of India, such as Somnath on the far west coast, Haridwar and Rishikesh in the far north on the upper Ganges, Puri on the east coast, and Kanya Kumari (Cape Comorin) at the extreme southern tip. Travel to all of these shrines would thus provide the pilgrim with a "Bharat Darshan," a view of the entire geography of India. Such pilgrimage routes have helped to unify both Hinduism and India.

Each locality in city and village is also knit together by religious shrines, ranging from the simple prayer niche, containing pictures and statues of the gods of the kind found in even the most humble home; through neighborhood shrines, nestled perhaps into the trunk of an especially sacred tree; to local and regional temples.

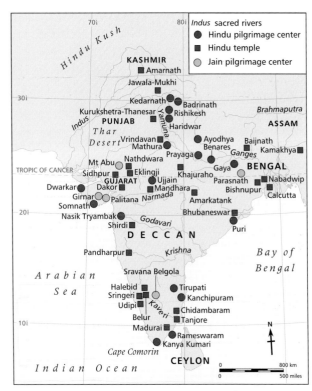

Hindu South Asia Hinduism is the oldest of the world's leading religions, although its geographic range is confined to the peoples of South Asia. Here its impact has been profound, exemplified by the sacred geography of the subcontinent; rivers, mountains, and regions associated with divine mythology are important, and networks of pilgrimage centers and temples provide cultural unity.

THE CENTRAL BELIEFS OF HINDUISM

Hinduism has none of the fixed dogmas of most other world religions, and great flexibility and variety of beliefs exist under the general term "Hindu." Nevertheless, sacred texts do provide a set of beliefs and orientations toward life that are very widely shared. Over time, the introduction of new texts to the Hindu legacy marked the evolution of Hinduism as a living, changing system of beliefs and practices.

The *Rigveda*

Between *c.* 1500 and 1200 B.C.E. Brahmin priests of the nomadic pastoralist Aryan peoples entering India composed the *Rigveda*, a collection of 1028 verses of Sanskrit poetry, the oldest and most venerated of the four books called, collectively, Veda. These verses invoke many early gods, including

Agni, the god of various kinds of fire; Indra, a phallic god of rain and fertility; Surya, god of the sun; and the goddess Dawn, who ushers in the sun each day. They include references to music, dance, and acting as modes of worship. Vedic worship also takes the form of animal sacrifice offered on sacred altars. The *Rigveda* speculates on the creation of the world and on the significance of life in this world, but it pretends to no conclusive answers:

> Who really knows? Who shall here proclaim it? whence things came to be, whence this creation. . . This creation, whence it came to be, whether it was made or not—he who is its overseer in the highest heaven, he surely knows. Or if he does not know . . . ? (X:129, Embree, p. 21)

Prayer room and shrine, India. Nearly every Hindu home in India has a shrine with pictures or small statues of various deities, and many have a special prayer room set aside for their worship. For *puja*, or worship, which is observed every day, ritual purity is emphasized; the time for offerings to the gods is after the morning bath or evening wash.

Caste

The *Rigveda* also introduces the mythic origin and rationale of the caste system, one of the most distinctive features of Hindu life. Caste began, the *Rigveda* suggests, in a primeval sacrifice of a mythical creature, Purusha. He was carved into four sections, each symbolizing one of the principal divisions of the caste system:

> When they divided Purusha, in how many different portions did they arrange him? What became of his mouth, what of his two arms? What were his two thighs and his two feet called? His mouth became the *brahman* [priest]; his two arms were made into the *rajanya* [or *kshatriya*, warrior]; his two thighs the *vaishyas* [business people and farmer/landlords]; from his two feet the *shudra* [person of the lower working class] was born. (X:90 Embree, 18–19)

Apparently, the Aryan invaders were even then thinking of a social system that separated people by occupation and sanctioned that separation through religion. The caste system that developed in India was probably the most rigidly unequal and hierarchical of any in the world. Caste status was hereditary, passing from parent to child at birth. Each caste was subject to different local legal rules, with upper castes being rewarded more generously and punished less severely than lower. Only upper castes were permitted to receive formal education, and the separate castes were not to inter-marry nor even to inter-dine. Their vital fluids were distinct and different, and the blood and semen of one group were not to mingle with those of another. The food fit for one group was not necessarily appropriate for others: *brahmin* priests were to be vegetarians, but *kshatriya* warriors were to eat meat.

Commentators throughout the centuries have searched for additional roots of the caste system, more grounded in social, economic, and political rationales. Many have seen India's caste system as a means of ordering relationships among the multitude of immigrant groups in India's multi-ethnic population, consolidating some at the top and relegating others to the bottom. Others have seen caste as the result of a frozen economic system, with parents doing all they could to make sure that their children maintained at least the family's current occupational status. They sacrificed the possibility of upward mobility in exchange for the security that they would not fall lower on the social scale. Many suggested that the system was

MAJOR HINDU GODS

A shrine with images of one or more of the thousands of gods in the pantheon can be found in every devout Hindu home. Shiva and Vishnu are the two major gods, and we also list others that are widely worshiped.

Brahma The creator god, whose four heads and arms represent the four veda (scriptures), castes, and yugas (ages of the world).

Ganesh The elephant-headed god, bringer of good luck.

Kali Shiva's fierce consort—the goddess of death—is shown as a fearsome, blood-drinking, four-armed black woman.

Krishna The eighth avatar (incarnation) of Vishnu, depicted with blue or black skin. He is honored for his skills as a lover and a warrior; with his consort **Radha**.

Rama The personification of virtue, reason and chivalry; with his consort **Sita**, revered for her loyalty.

Shiva God of destruction, whose dancing in a circle of fire symbolizes the eternal cycle of creation and destruction.

Sitala Mothers traditionally pray to this goddess to protect their children from disease.

Vishnu The preserver, a kindly god, who protects those who worship him, banishes bad luck, and restores good health; with his consorts **Lakshmi**, the goddess of wealth, and **Saraswati**, the goddess of wisdom and the arts.

imposed on the rest of the population by an extremely powerful coalition of *brahmin* priests and *kshatriya* warrior-rulers. Such a dominant coalition is common in world history, and the Indian situation was simply more entrenched than most.

Historians employ the insights of anthropologists as they attempt to understand the historical origins and basis of the caste system. Anthropolog-

ical observation shows that the four castes of the Veda do not exist in practice today. Instead, India has tens of thousands of castes—indeed, there are thousands of different *brahmin* groups alone. In practice, caste is lived in local groupings, in the 750,000 villages, towns, and cities of India. From customary law to dining patterns to marriage arrangements, caste relationships are determined locally, and there is no national over-arching religious system to formulate and enforce rules. In any given village, for example, some twenty to thirty castes may be represented, including all the various craftspeople and artisans. There may be more than one caste claiming *brahmin* status, or *kshatriya*, or *vaishya*, or *shudra*. Anthropologists differentiate between the mythological four *varna* groups of the Vedic caste system and the thousands of *jati* groups through which caste is actually lived in India. Both historians and anthropologists are convinced that the same multitude of castes that they find "on the ground" today existed also in the past.

Throughout Indian history there have been revolts against the hierarchy of the caste system. Throughout the twentieth century the government of India has acted assertively to eliminate the historic discrimination of the caste system (as we shall see in Chapter 20). Nevertheless, through the millennia, caste has usually been more important than government in determining the conditions of life of most people. As historian Romila Thapar has written:

religio n over govt

At the basic level of everyday life interrelationships between the sub-castes within the community were the most influential factor in village life, and this tended to divert attention from political relationships and loyalties to local caste relationships and loyalties. Central political authority became more and more remote. (Thapar, *A History of India*, Vol. I, p. 48)

The Brahmanas and Upanishads

A second collection of Sanskrit religious literature, dating from *c.* 900–500 B.C.E., sets out rules for *brahmins*, including procedures for sacrifice and worship. These scriptures, the Brahmanas, include discussions of the origins of various rituals and myths of the immortal gods. Among the rituals, the *Ashwamedha*, or horse sacrifice, most strongly demonstrates the historic link between *brahmin* priests and *kshatriya* warriors. Truly powerful kings were to allow a horse to roam freely for a year. At the end of the year, the king was to enforce his own authority over all this land, and to sacrifice the horse. Some of India's most powerful rulers actually did perform this ritual, although historians suggest that the horses may have been discreetly guided and restricted in their travels by an accompanying retinue of priests.

The Upanishads, composed about 800–500 B.C.E., are devoted primarily to mystical speculation. They proclaim the oneness of the individual and the universe. The universal spirit, Brahman, and the soul of each individual, *atman*, are ultimately the same substance, just as individual sparks are the same substance as a large fire. In time, each *atman* will be united with the universal Brahman. To reach this unity, each soul will be reincarnated (*samsara*) in a series of bodies, until it is purged of its attachments to the physical world and achieves pure spirituality. Then, at this death of this final body, the *atman* is finally released to its union with the Brahman.

The Upanishads introduce several concepts fundamental to almost all strands of Hinduism. *Dharma* is the set of religious and ethical duties to which each living creature in the universe is subject. These duties are not the same, however, for each creature; they differ according to ritual status. *Karma* is the set of activities of each creature and the effects that these activities have on its *atman*. Each action has an effect on the *atman*; activities in accord with one's *dharma* purify the *atman*; activities in opposition to one's *dharma* pollute it. "Good *karma*," the good effects brought about by actions in accord with *dharma*, will finally enable the *atman* to escape *samsara*, or reincarnation, and reach *moksha*, release from the travails of life on earth and ultimate union with the Brahman. Thus Hinduism sees reward and punishment in the universe as a natural consequence. Good, *dharmic* actions carry their own reward for the *atman*; activities opposed to *dharma* carry their own negative consequences. Activities in this life earn good or bad *karma*.

Hinduism sees life on this earth as *maya*, illusion, compared to the reality beyond, but it also teaches the importance of taking life seriously and living in accordance with *dharma*. Hinduism teaches four goals in life. Two are *dharma* and *moksha*. The other two are *kama*, or physical pleasure, and *artha*, wealth and power (which we considered in Chapter 8). Activity on earth is only *leela*, or play— but the play is important.

The Upanishads also introduce the concept of the lifecycle, with its different duties at each stage. The first stage, *brahmacharya*, is the youthful time of studies and celibacy; the second, *gruhasta*, the householder stage, is for raising a family; the third, *vanaprastha*, literally forest-wandering, is for reflection outside the demands of everyday life; and the last, *sunnyasin*, is for total immersion in meditation in preparation for death and, ideally, for *moksha*.

These early scriptures established a set of principles that constitute the core of Hindu belief: caste, *dharma*, *karma*, life stages, *samsara*, and, ultimately, *moksha*, the union of *atman* and Brahman. They represent a rational system of order in the universe and in individual life. They teach the importance of dharmic activities in this world in order to reach *moksha* in the deeper reality beyond. They are transmitted from *guru*, or teacher, to *shishya*, or student. Although it reveres the *brahmin* priest (not to be confused with the Brahman spirit of the universe), Hinduism is ultimately accessible to each

SACRED WRITINGS OF HINDUISM

Veda The most sacred of the Hindu scriptures, meaning "divine knowledge." They consist of collections of writings compiled by the Aryans: *Rigveda* (hymns and praises), *Yajurveda* (prayers and sacrificial formulas), *Samaveda* (tunes and chants), and *Atharva-Veda* (Veda of the Atharvans, the priests who officiate at sacrifices).

Upanishads Philosophical treatises, centering on the doctrine of Brahma.

Brahamanas Instructions on ritual and sacrifice.

Ramayana An epic poem, telling how Rama (an incarnation of the god Vishnu) and his devotee Hanuman, the monkey god, recover Rama's wife, Sita, who has been abducted by the demon king Ravana.

Mahabharata ("Great Poem of the Bharatas") It includes the *Bhagavadgita* ("Song of God") and consists of eighteen books and 90,000 stanzas.

SOURCE

The Bhagavad-Gita *from the Mahabharata*

The *Bhagavad-Gita* opens on the field of Kuruk-shetra before the final battle between the two branches of the Bharata family, the Kauravas and the Pandavas. Arjun, leader of the Pandavas, despairs of his choices: if he fights, he kills his cousins; if he does not fight, he dies. He turns to his chariot driver, the Lord Krishna, for advice. Krishna's reply incorporates many fundamental principles of Hindu thought. First, Krishna speaks of the duty of Arjun, a *kshatriya* by caste, to fight: "For a *kshatriya* there does not exist another greater good than war enjoined by *dharma*" (II: 31). Each person has a unique *dharma*, largely determined by caste. In this philosophy, changing one's occupational duty is no virtue:

> Better is one's own *dharma* that one may be able to fulfill but imperfectly, than the *dharma* of others that is more easily accomplished. Better is death in the fulfillment of one's own *dharma*. To adopt the *dharma* of others is perilous. (III:35)

Krishna counsels Arjun to action. He notes three kinds of yoga, or discipline, which bring people to spiritual liberation: the yoga of knowledge; the yoga of devotion; and the yoga of action. (The yoga of physical discipline and meditation, known widely today in the West, is yet another form.) In this case, Krishna tells Arjun, the yoga of action is required:

> Do your allotted work, for action is superior to nonaction. Even the normal functioning of your body cannot be accomplished through actionlessness. (III:8)

The key, however, is performing the action because it is right, without concern for its results or rewards:

Action alone is your concern, never at all its fruits. Let not the fruits of action be your motive, nor let yourself be attached to inaction. . . . Seek refuge in the right mental attitude. Wretched are those who are motivated by the fruits of action. (II:49)

Non-attachment is the ideal:

> He who feels no attachment toward anything; who, having encountered the various good or evil things, neither rejoices nor loathes—his wisdom is steadfast. (II:59)
> He who behaves alike to foe and friend; who, likewise is even-poised in honor or dishonor; who is even-tempered in cold and heat, happiness and sorrow; who is free from attachment;
> who regards praise and censure with equanimity; who is silent, content with anything whatever; who has no fixed abode, who is steadfast in mind, who is full of devotion—that man is dear to me. (XII:18–19)

In reply to Arjun's specific anxiety about killing his cousins, Krishna reminds him of the doctrine of reincarnation:

> As a man discards worn-out clothes to put on new and different ones, so the disembodied self discards its worn-out bodies to take on other new ones.
>   Death is certain for anyone born, and birth is certain for the dead; since the cycle is inevitable, you have no cause to grieve! (II:22, 27)

Krishna also assures Arjun of his abiding concern for him, and of the god's power to help him: "If I am in your thought, by my grace you will transcend all dangers" (XVIII:58). Arjun does fight, and wins, and in the end all the warriors who die are reborn.

nevertheless, sparse. *Brahmin* priests appear in the southeast-Asian records only after 800 C.E. It is, therefore, difficult to answer the question: "What brought Indian power and prestige into southeast Asia from about the third century to about the fourteenth century?"

Three theories explaining the appearance of Indian influence in southeast Asia have been suggested. The first two, originally advocated by historian George Coedes in the early twentieth century, argued that Indians initiated contact and attempted to introduce their religion and culture into southeast Asia. His first theory, which stressed the use of military might, is no longer accepted. As noted in Chapter 8, there is very little record of Indian military action in the area, and none suggesting a desire for conquest. His second theory—that Indian traders brought their culture with them—has wider acceptance, but it also encounters serious opposition. Trade connections between India and southeast Asia were numerous, long-standing, and intense. Some cultural and religious influence must have accompanied them, but these contacts were by sea, while much of the Hindu influence was manifest inland.

The third theory, advocated by J.C. van Leur in the 1950s and by O.W. Wolters a generation later, argued that local rulers invited *brahmin* priests to come from India to southeast Asia to build temples, to promote agricultural development on land

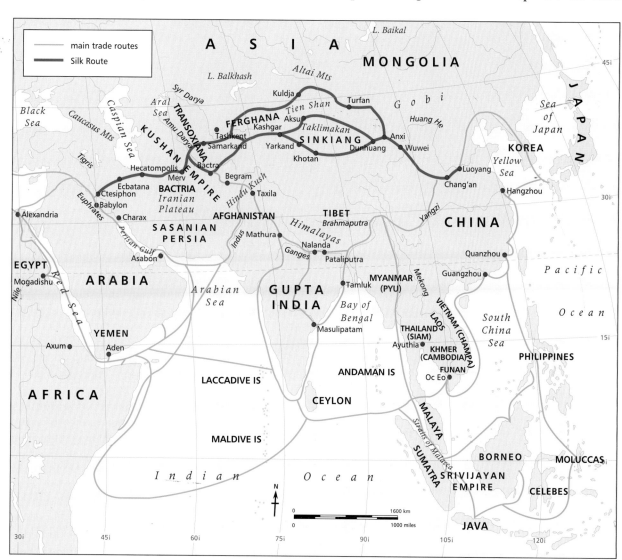

Asian trade Ports along the Indus and Ganges served Arab maritime traders for many centuries, and provided links to the kingdoms of southeast Asia and the South China Sea. To the north, roads following river valleys and passes through the towering Himalayas and the Hindu Kush provided contact with China and the silk route respectively.

Kailasanatha Temple at Ellora, Rashtrakuta, *c.* **757–790** C.E. Carved into an escarpment of volcanic stone, the thirty-three shrines of Ellora have for centuries been a pilgrimage center for Hindus, Buddhists, and Jains (see Focus, p. 279). The monolithic stone shaft in the foreground, 60 feet (18 m) high, would have originally supported a trident symbol of Shiva, to whom this temple is dedicated.

HINDUISM IN SOUTHEAST ASIA

Hinduism did not generally attract, nor seek, converts outside of India, but southeast Asia was an exception. Here, the initiative for conversion grew out of politics, as it had in southern India. The powers of the Hindu temple and the *brahmin* priesthood were imported to validate royal authority in southeast Asia from as early as the third century C.E. to as late as the fourteenth century.

Trade contacts between India and southeast Asia date back to at least 150 B.C.E. Indian sailors carried cargoes to and from Myanmar, the Straits of Malacca, the Kingdom of Funan in modern Cambodia and Vietnam, and Java in modern Indonesia. By the third century C.E., Funan had accepted many elements of Indian culture, religion, and political practice. Chinese envoys reported a prosperous state with walled cities, palaces, and houses. Sanskrit was in use, as was some Indian technology for irrigation and farming. By the fifth century it appears that Sanskrit was in widespread official

use, Indian calendars marked the dates, and Indian gods, including Shiva and Vishnu, were worshiped, as were representations of the Buddha (see Spotlight, pp. 288–9). Hindu temples began to appear with *brahmin* priests to staff them.

[handwritten: use Indian methods - spread]

Hinduism in Southeast Asia: How Do We Know?

Even today the historical stamp of Hinduism endures in southeast Asia in the names of cities like Ayuthia in Thailand, derived from Ayodhya in northern India; in the influence of Sanskrit on several southeast Asian languages; in the popularity of the *Ramayana* and other Hindu literature in the folklore and theater of the region. Moreover, Hindu temples still stand, most spectacularly the Angkor Wat temple complex in Cambodia. Evidence of Hindu influence in southeast Asia appears also in early reports of Chinese visitors, archaeological remains, and **epigraphy** (inscriptions on metal and rock). These records are,

SOURCE

The Bhagavad-Gita *from the Mahabharata*

The *Bhagavad-Gita* opens on the field of Kuruk-shetra before the final battle between the two branches of the Bharata family, the Kauravas and the Pandavas. Arjun, leader of the Pandavas, despairs of his choices: if he fights, he kills his cousins; if he does not fight, he dies. He turns to his chariot driver, the Lord Krishna, for advice. Krishna's reply incorporates many fundamental principles of Hindu thought. First, Krishna speaks of the duty of Arjun, a *kshatriya* by caste, to fight: "For a *kshatriya* there does not exist another greater good than war enjoined by *dharma*" (II: 31). Each person has a unique *dharma*, largely determined by caste. In this philosophy, changing one's occupational duty is no virtue:

caste

> Better is one's own *dharma* that one may be able to fulfill but imperfectly, than the *dharma* of others that is more easily accomplished. Better is death in the fulfillment of one's own *dharma*. To adopt the *dharma* of others is perilous. (III:35)

yoga

Krishna counsels Arjun to action. He notes three kinds of yoga, or discipline, which bring people to spiritual liberation: the yoga of knowledge; the yoga of devotion; and the yoga of action. (The yoga of physical discipline and meditation, known widely today in the West, is yet another form.) In this case, Krishna tells Arjun, the yoga of action is required:

> Do your allotted work, for action is superior to nonaction. Even the normal functioning of your body cannot be accomplished through actionlessness. (III:8)

The key, however, is performing the action because it is right, without concern for its results or rewards: *character is what you do when no one is looking*

Action alone is your concern, never at all its fruits. Let not the fruits of action be your motive, nor let yourself be attached to inaction. . . . Seek refuge in the right mental attitude. Wretched are those who are motivated by the fruits of action. (II:49)

Non-attachment is the ideal:

behavior

> He who feels no attachment toward anything; who, having encountered the various good or evil things, neither rejoices nor loathes—his wisdom is steadfast. (II:59)
> He who behaves alike to foe and friend; who, likewise is even-poised in honor or dishonor; who is even-tempered in cold and heat, happiness and sorrow; who is free from attachment;
> who regards praise and censure with equanimity; who is silent, content with anything whatever; who has no fixed abode, who is steadfast in mind, who is full of devotion—that man is dear to me. (XII:18–19)

In reply to Arjun's specific anxiety about killing his cousins, Krishna reminds him of the doctrine of reincarnation:

reincarnation

> As a man discards worn-out clothes to put on new and different ones, so the disembodied self discards its worn-out bodies to take on other new ones.
>
> Death is certain for anyone born, and birth is certain for the dead; since the cycle is inevitable, you have no cause to grieve! (II:22, 27)

Krishna also assures Arjun of his abiding concern for him, and of the god's power to help him: "If I am in your thought, by my grace you will transcend all dangers" (XVIII:58). Arjun does fight, and wins, and in the end all the warriors who die are reborn.

the end of the year, the king was to enforce his own authority over all this land, and to sacrifice the horse. Some of India's most powerful rulers actually did perform this ritual, although historians suggest that the horses may have been discreetly guided and restricted in their travels by an accompanying retinue of priests.

The Upanishads, composed about 800–500 B.C.E., are devoted primarily to mystical speculation. They proclaim the oneness of the individual and the universe. The universal spirit, Brahman, and the soul of each individual, atman, are ultimately the same substance, just as individual sparks are the same substance as a large fire. In time, each atman will be united with the universal Brahman. To reach this unity, each soul will be reincarnated (samsara) in a series of bodies, until it is purged of its attachments to the physical world and achieves pure spirituality. Then, at this death of this final body, the atman is finally released to its union with the Brahman.

The Upanishads introduce several concepts fundamental to almost all strands of Hinduism. Dharma is the set of religious and ethical duties to which each living creature in the universe is subject. These duties are not the same, however, for each creature; they differ according to ritual status. Karma is the set of activities of each creature and the effects that these activities have on its atman. Each action has an effect on the atman; activities in accord with one's dharma purify the atman; activities in opposition to one's dharma pollute it. "Good karma," the good effects brought about by actions in accord with dharma, will finally enable the atman to escape samsara, or reincarnation, and reach moksha, release from the travails of life on earth and ultimate union with the Brahman. Thus Hinduism sees reward and punishment in the universe as a natural consequence. Good, dharmic actions carry their own reward for the atman; activities opposed to dharma carry their own negative consequences. Activities in this life earn good or bad karma.

Hinduism sees life on this earth as maya, illusion, compared to the reality beyond, but it also teaches the importance of taking life seriously and living in accordance with dharma. Hinduism teaches four goals in life. Two are dharma and moksha. The other two are kama, or physical pleasure, and artha, wealth and power (which we considered in Chapter 8). Activity on earth is only leela, or play—but the play is important.

The Upanishads also introduce the concept of the lifecycle, with its different duties at each stage. The first stage, brahmacharya, is the youthful time of studies and celibacy; the second, gruhasta, the householder stage, is for raising a family; the third, vanaprastha, literally forest-wandering, is for reflection outside the demands of everyday life; and the last, sunnyasin, is for total immersion in meditation in preparation for death and, ideally, for moksha.

These early scriptures established a set of principles that constitute the core of Hindu belief: caste, dharma, karma, life stages, samsara, and, ultimately, moksha, the union of atman and Brahman. They represent a rational system of order in the universe and in individual life. They teach the importance of dharmic activities in this world in order to reach moksha in the deeper reality beyond. They are transmitted from guru, or teacher, to shishya, or student. Although it reveres the brahmin priest (not to be confused with the Brahman spirit of the universe), Hinduism is ultimately accessible to each

SACRED WRITINGS OF HINDUISM

Veda	The most sacred of the Hindu scriptures, meaning "divine knowledge." They consist of collections of writings compiled by the Aryans: *Rigveda* (hymns and praises), *Yajurveda* (prayers and sacrificial formulas), *Samaveda* (tunes and chants), and *Atharva-Veda* (Veda of the Atharvans, the priests who officiate at sacrifices).
Upanishads	Philosophical treatises, centering on the doctrine of Brahma.
Brahamanas	Instructions on ritual and sacrifice.
Ramayana	An epic poem, telling how Rama (an incarnation of the god Vishnu) and his devotee Hanuman, the monkey god, recover Rama's wife, Sita, who has been abducted by the demon king Ravana.
Mahabharata	("Great Poem of the Bharatas") It includes the *Bhagavadgita* ("Song of God") and consists of eighteen books and 90,000 stanzas.

individual, even to those of low caste. Despite the hierarchy of the caste system, Hinduism allows enormous spiritual scope to each individual. It has no core dogma that each must affirm. Each individual Hindu frequently has his or her own sense of spirituality. This universal accessibility of Hinduism is most clear in three later forms of literature that have become a kind of folk treasury (in contrast to the Veda, Brahmanas, and Upanishads, which are the province of the *brahmin* priests).

In the last chapter (see p. 235) we discussed India's two great epic poems, the *Ramayana* and the *Mahabharata*. The latter's central story revolves around the civil war between two branches of the family of the Bharatas (from whom India derives its current Hindi name, Bharat). Like the *Ramayana*, the *Mahabharata* presents moral conflicts, the dilemma of taking sides, and the necessity of acting decisively. At its center stands the *Bhagavad-Gita* ("Song of God"; see Source, opposite), a philosophical discourse on the duties and the meaning of life and death.

The *Bhagavad-Gita* summarizes many of the key doctrines of Hinduism. Lord Krishna promises to help people who do their duty, and points the way toward spiritual fulfillment. The text demonstrates considerable assimilation within Hinduism, for the Lord Krishna is a dark-skinned, non-Vedic, non-Aryan tribal god, perhaps from the south. His centrality in this most revered Sanskrit text suggests the continuing accommodation between the Aryans and the indigenous peoples of India.

The two epics generally also reflect greater prestige for women than did earlier Sanskrit texts. In the *Ramayana*, Sita is presented as a traditionally subordinate wife to Rama: her commitment to honor and duty surpasses even his; she defends Rama's honor even when he fails to defend hers. She is more heroic than he, although her heroism is defined by her role as dutiful wife. Rama is implicitly criticized for his inability to defend her both from Ravana and from the gossip of his own subjects. In some versions, the criticism is made explicit. In the *Mahabharata*, by contrast, Draupadi is the wife of all five of the Pandava brothers, and she protects, defends, and inspires them in their struggles, going far beyond the subservient role that women play in the majority of Aryan literature. In the epics, the female force, *shakti*, has gained recognition.

Scene from a dramatization of the ***Ramayana.*** During the north Indian festival of Dussehra, the Ram-leela, the play of the Lord Rama, is enacted in huge public spectacles. Scenes from the *Ramayana*, with its epic tale of the victory of good over evil, are performed by exotically costumed actors, and giant effigies of demons from the epic are dramatically burnt to the delight of the crowds.

The Puranas

The Puranas, ancient stories, are eighteen major and eighteen minor collections of folk tales of the people. These are legends of gods and kings, of the creation and destruction of the universe. Here emerge in central positions the most popular of the gods of Hinduism, Vishnu and Shiva. Here, too, appear female goddesses, often as consorts of the principal gods, such as Lakshmi and Saraswati with Vishnu; and Parvati, Durga, and Kali with Shiva. These goddesses also help to balance the rather suppressed position of females evident in the earlier Aryan literature. The Puranas were transmitted orally, usually in popular vernacular languages, until, beginning about 450 C.E., in recognition of their popularity, they were translated and recorded in Sanskrit and became part of Hinduism's informal literary canon.

TEMPLES AND SHRINES

By the seventh century C.E. fundamental changes had taken place in the form of Hindu worship. Personal prayer, often addressed to representations of the gods in statues and pictures, displaced sacrifice. Temples of great beauty were built. The caves at Ellora in western India were fashioned into temples in the eighth century, reflecting the early importance of caves in Hindu worship. Within the temples, sculpture and painting demonstrate the artistic development in religious worship. The bas reliefs and artwork in the temples at Kanchi and Mahabalipuram in the south, also built in the eighth century, continue to dazzle viewers today. Sexual passion and the union of male and female entered into forms of worship, symbolically representing passion for, and union with, god, as the temple sculptures at Khajuraho in north India about 1000 C.E. illustrate.

Magnificent temples flourished everywhere in India, but especially in the south of the subcontinent. University of Chicago anthropologist Arjun Appadurai writes of the diverse array of temples that mark the Indian landscape:

> In many ways the Hindu temple is the quintessentially South Indian institution. . . . Temples come in every size and scale, from small family shrines to village temples, to lineage temples, to regional temples, to great pan-regional pilgrimage centers. (pp. 8–9)

Bronze sculpture of Vishnu, early Chola period, first half of tenth century. Vishnu is beloved as the tender, merciful deity—the Preserver—and as the second member of the Hindu trinity he complements Brahma the Creator and Shiva the Destroyer. He is said to come to earth periodically as an *avatar*, an incarnation in various forms, to help humankind in times of crisis. (*Metropolitan Museum of Art, New York*)

FOCUS
Bhakti: The Path of Mystical Devotion

About 500 C.E., beginning in south India and spreading northward, a powerful new strand of mystical devotion enriched Hinduism. It continues today in the multitudes of devotional prayer meetings in every corner of India. Bhakti built on classical texts such as the *Gita* that promised: "No one devoted to me is lost. . . . Keep me in your mind and devotion, sacrifice to me, bow to me, discipline your self toward me, and you will reach me." (IX:31, 34)

Bhakti was a revolt within Hinduism against formality in religion, against hierarchy, and against the power of the *brahmin* priesthood. It often found expression in poetry composed in the everyday vernacular local language by common people, including washermen, potters, fishermen, hunters, and producers of home-made liquor, as well as by a few kings and princes.

Basavanna (1106–68), declaring that "Love of Shiva cannot live with ritual," left his home at the age of sixteen and wandered until he received a message from Shiva at a place "where three rivers meet." He devoted himself to the Lord Shiva, advocated equality, spoke for the poor, attacked orthodox Brahminism, and founded the Virashaiva movement dedicated to these principles. He composed his poetry in Kannada, one of the vernacular languages of south India. Here it is translated by A.K. Ramanujan in his beautiful, brief anthology of four south Indian Bhakti poets, *Speaking of Siva*:

The rich
will make temples for Shiva.
What shall I,
a poor man,
do?

My legs are pillars,
the body the shrine,
the head a cupola
of gold.

Listen, O lord of the meeting rivers,
things standing shall fall,
but the moving ever shall stay.

(Ramanujan, p. 88)

Some of the most inspired and popular of the Bhakti poets, like Mahadeviyakka in twelfth-century south India and Mirabai in sixteenth-century west India, were women who expressed their religious passion in overtly sexual terms. Mahadeviyakka wrote in the Kannada vernacular of her longing for God: "Night and day in your worship I forget myself."

He bartered my heart,
looted my flesh
claimed as tribute
my pleasure,
took over
all of me.

I'm the woman of love
for my lord, white as jasmine.

(Ramanujan, p. 125)

Mirabai, who left a marriage with a prince in order to follow her religious passion, wrote in Hindi of her love for Lord Krishna:

Let us go to a realm beyond going,
Where death is afraid to go
Where the high-flying birds alight and play,
Afloat in the full lake of love.   (Embree, p. 369)

Writing also in a Hindi dialect, also in the sixteenth century, the blind poet Surdas sang of Krishna's steadfast concern for each person:

Listen, ingrate, who then do you think has stayed
   by you both day and night,
Befriending you—though you long ago forgot, if
   ever, that is, you knew?
Even today he stands at your side, ready to bear
   your birth-born shame,
Always wanting for life to go well, and loving you
   as his own.   (Embree, 360–61)

Priests persuaded tribal to worship Hindu Gods → became wealthier

RELIGION AND RULE

Temples were often patronized by wealthy land-owners and rulers who sought validation of their power and rule through the prestige of *brahmin* priests. As in many religions, rulers supported priests, while priests affirmed the authority of the rulers. This was especially true in the south. At least as early as the eighth century, new rulers who seized lands occupied by indigenous tribal peoples often imported *brahmin* priests to overawe the tribals with their learning, piety, and rituals. The priests were to persuade the tribals of the proper authority of the king. In order to pacify the tribals, their gods might be incorporated into the array of gods worshiped in the temple by the priests, just as the tribal peoples would begin to worship the major gods of Hinduism. Anthropologists describe this process as an interplay between the "great" national tradition and the "little" local tradition. As new lands were opened, and tribals were persuaded to accept the new ruling coalition, the temples grew larger and more wealthy.

In exchange for their support, kings rewarded priests with land grants, court subsidies, and temple bequests. *Brahmin* priests and Tamil rulers prospered together. Historian Romila Thapar reports the temples "financing various commercial enterprises and acting as banker and money-lender to village assemblies and similar bodies" (*History of India*, p. 211). Hindu colleges, rest-houses for pilgrims, centers of administration, and even cities grew up around some of these temples.

Life revolved around temples

Kandariya Mahadeo Temple at Khajuraho, Chandela, *c.* 1025–1050 C.E. The twenty surviving temples at Khajuraho, though maimed by time, are still among the greatest examples of medieval Hindu architecture and sculpture in north India. Beneath the soaring towers, multilayered bands of sculptures writhe in a pulsating tableau of human and divine activity. The depictions of athletic lovemaking, which so scandalized nineteenth-century European travelers, can be linked to Tantric sects of Hinduism, then prevalent in the Chandela region.

specially granted to them, to invoke the Hindu gods to validate the authority of the rulers, and to convince the local population of this divine validation. In the words of historian Kenneth R. Hall, these priests were to serve as "development planners." They brought with them from India principles of government, religious law, administration, art, and architecture. In promoting these religious/political practices through the priests, southeast Asian rulers were emulating the policies of the Pallava and Chola kings of southern India. But Hinduism did not survive in southeast Asia. It was superseded by Buddhism and, later, by Islam.

HINDUISM AND BUDDHISM IN SOUTHEAST ASIA

Buddhist monks as well as Hindu priests were invited to southeast Asia to help establish and consolidate the power of local kings, and southeast Asian rulers found the Buddhist monks as useful as the Hindu *brahmins*, for they served similar political and administrative functions, but in the name of Buddhism. For example, the ruler of the Srivijaya Empire in the East Indies welcomed 1000 Buddhist monks to his kingdom in the late seventh century C.E. Jayavarman VII, the Buddhist ruler of the Khmer kingdom at the end of the twelfth century, added Buddhist images in the great temple of Angkor Wat, which had been built earlier in the century to honor the Hindu god Vishnu.

By about the fourteenth century, Hinduism had died out in southeast Asia, while Buddhism continued to thrive. In India, on the other hand, Buddhism withered away, while Hinduism flourished. In fact, except for its temporary success in southeast Asia, Hinduism has never attracted, nor welcomed, many converts outside of India and its neighbor, Nepal. Buddhism, on the contrary, became an enormously successful proselytizing religion throughout Asia.

BUDDHISM

Buddhism was born in India, within the culture of Hinduism, and then charted its own path. Like Hinduism, it questioned the reality of this earthly world and speculated on the existence of other worlds. Unlike Hinduism, however, Buddhism had a founder, a set of originating scriptures, and an order of monks. In opposition to Hinduism, it renounced hereditary caste organization and the supremacy of the *brahmin* priests. Budhism spread to southeast Asia along with Hinduism, but Buddhism became more popular, gaining acceptance as the principal relgion of Myanmar, Thailand, Cambodia, Laos, Vietnam, Sri Lanka, and Tibet until today. It won multitudes of adherents throughout the rest of Asia as well, in Sri Lanka, Tibet, China, Korea, and Japan. Yet in India itself, Buddhism lost out in competition with Hinduism and its priesthood, virtually vanishing from the subcontinent by about the twelfth century C.E.

Bronze Dancing Shiva, eleventh century. Shiva is a god of destruction whose frenzied dancing—usually, as here, enacted on the body of a dwarf demon—symbolizes the eternal cycle of creation and destruction. Craftworkers of the South Indian Chola dynasty molded bronze into forms of exquisite grace and power (see also picture, p. 268). (*Musée Guimet, Paris*)

THE BUDDHA

Born about 563 B.C.E. as a prince, Siddhartha Gautama was shielded from normal life until at the age of twenty-nine he emerged from his palace and confronted for the first time the reality of the pain of everyday life. He identified human suffering as the key problem of life and sought a means of emancipation from it. Following a long quest, he found his enlightenment through meditation, becoming the Buddha, the enlightened one, and began to preach his new understanding. The source of suffering, he taught, was personal desire and passion; they could be overcome by proper living. A new consciousness could be achieved by a combination of disciplining the mind and observing ethical precepts in human relationships. In the face of continuing rebirths into the pain of life, the Buddha taught that right living could bring release from the cycle of mortality and

[margin annotations: freedom from suffering; moksha]

pain, and entry into *nirvana*, a kind of blissful nothingness. On the metaphysical plane, the Buddha taught that everything in the universe is transient; there is no "being." There exists neither an immortal soul nor a god, neither *atman* nor Brahman. The Buddha's teachings about the illusion of life and about rebirth and release were consistent with Hindu concepts of *maya*, *samsara*, and *moksha*, but the Buddha's denial of god put him on the fringes of Hindu thought. His rejection of caste as an organizing hierarchy and of the Hindu priests as connoisseurs of religious truth, won him powerful allies—and powerful opponents. A band of disciples, monks, the *Sangha*, gathered around him to learn his message and to teach it.

The three-fold motto of all devout Buddhist was: "I seek refuge in the Buddha; I seek refuge in the Doctrine; I seek refuge in the Sangha (order of monks)."

SOURCE
The Address to Sigala: Buddhism in Everyday Life

[margin annotation: 10 commandments]

Much of the Buddha's moral and ethical instruction is directed to the monks of the Sangha. In the Address to Sigala, however, he speaks to laypeople about their relationships and responsibilities toward one another. The address includes practical advice to husbands and wives, friends, employers, and employees. The lengthy address is translated and summarized here by A.L. Basham.

Husbands should respect their wives, and comply as far as possible with their requests. They should not commit adultery. They should give their wives full charge of the home, and supply them with fine clothes and jewellery as far as their means permit. Wives should be thorough in their duties, gentle and kind to the whole household, chaste, and careful in housekeeping, and should carry out their work with skill and enthusiasm.

A man should be generous to his friends, speak kindly of them, act in their interest in every way possible, treat them as his equals, and keep his word to them. They in turn should watch over his interests and property, take care of him when he is "off his guard" [i.e., intoxicated, infatuated, or otherwise liable to commit rash and careless actions], stand by him and help him in time of trouble, and respect other members of his family.

Employers should treat their servants and workpeople decently. They should not be given tasks beyond their strength. They should receive adequate food and wages, be cared for in time of sickness and infirmity, and be given regular holidays and bonuses in times of prosperity. They should rise early and go to bed late in the service of their master, be content with their just wages, work thoroughly, and maintain their master's reputation. (Digha Nikaya, iii:161; cited in Basham, p. 286)

PROFILE

Siddhartha Gautama

THE BUDDHA

A.L. Basham (1914–86), the most influential interpreter of ancient India of his generation, wrote that all we know of the Buddha's life and teaching comes from much later accounts, embellished by his followers. "Much doubt now exists as to the real doctrines of the historical Buddha, as distinct from those of Buddhism" (p. 256). The accounts that exist tell the following story.

Siddhartha Gautama was born *c.* 563 B.C.E. in the foothills of the Himalayan mountains of what is now Nepal. His father, a *kshatriya* warrior caste chief of the Shakyas, a republican tribe, received a prophecy that Siddhartha would become either a great emperor or a great religious teacher. Hoping that his son would follow the former vocation, the chief sheltered him as best he could so that he would experience neither pain nor disillusionment.

At the age of twenty-nine, Siddhartha started to grow curious about what lay beyond the confines of his father's palace. Leaving his wife, Yasadhara, and their son Rahula, he instructed his charioteer to take him to the city. Here he came across a frail, elderly man. Never having encountered old age, Siddhartha was confused. His companion explained that aging was an inevitable, and painful, part of human experience. As Siddhartha took further excursions outside the palace he soon came to see that pain was an inevitable part of life, experienced in illness, aging, death, and even birth.

On his fourth and final trip he met a wandering holy man who had shunned the trappings of wealth and material gain. Siddhartha decided to do likewise. Bidding farewell to his family for the last time, he set out on horseback in search of an antidote to sorrow and a means of teaching it to others.

For six years Siddhartha wandered as an ascetic. Nearing starvation, however, he gave up the path of asceticism. Determined to achieve enlightenment, he began to meditate, sitting under a tree at Bodh Gaya near modern Patna, in India. His concentration and fortitude were tested by Mara, the spirit of this world, who tempted him to give up his meditation with both threats of punishment and promises of rewards. Touching the ground with his hand in a gesture, or *mudra*, repeated often in sculptures of the Buddha, Siddhartha revealed these temptations to be illusions. On the forty-ninth day of meditation he reached enlightenment, becoming the Buddha, He Who Has Awakened. He had found an antidote to pain and suffering. He proceeded to the Deer Park at Sarnath, near Banaras, where he delivered his first sermon setting forth the Four Noble Truths and the Noble Eightfold Path (see Source, p. 276).

Although much of the Hindu priesthood opposed the Buddha's teachings, the kings of Magadha and Koshala, whose territories included most of the lower Gangetic plain, befriended and supported him and the small band of followers gathered around him. The Buddha taught peacefully and calmly until about 483 B.C.E., when, at the age of eighty, he died, surrounded by a cadre of dedicated monks and believers, the original Buddhist Sangha (order of monks).

Teaching Buddha, **from Sarnath, India, Gupta dynasty, fifth century** C.E. *(Archeological Musem, Sarnath)*

SOURCE
The Four Noble Truths and the Noble Eightfold Path

1. This is the Noble Truth of Sorrow. Birth is sorrow, age is sorrow, disease is sorrow, death is sorrow, contact with the unpleasant is sorrow, separation from the pleasant is sorrow, every wish unfulfilled is sorrow—in short all the five components of individuality are sorrow.

2. And this is the Noble Truth of the Arising of Sorrow. [It arises from] thirst, which leads to rebirth, which brings delight and passion, and seeks pleasure now here, now there—the thirst for sensual pleasure, the thirst for continued life, the thirst for power.

3. And this is the Noble Truth of the Stopping of Sorrow. It is the complete stopping of that thirst, so that no passion remains, leaving it, being emancipated from it, being released from it, giving no place to it.

4. And this is the Noble Truth of the Way which Leads to the Stopping of Sorrow. It is the Noble Eightfold Path—Right Views, Right Resolve, Right Speech, Right Conduct, Right Livelihood, Right Effort, Right Recollection and Right Meditation. (Basham, p. 269)

Great Stupa, Sanchi, third century B.C.E.–first century C.E. With its four gloriously carved gates and majestic central hemisphere, the Great Stupa of Sanchi is the most remarkable surviving example of the 84,000 such Buddhist burial mounds reputedly erected by the emperor Asoka during the Mauryan Empire. This "world mountain," oriented to the four corners of the universe, contained a holy relic, the object of pilgrims' devotion, and is topped by a three-tiered umbrella representing the Three Jewels of Buddhism: the Buddha, the Law, and the community of monks.

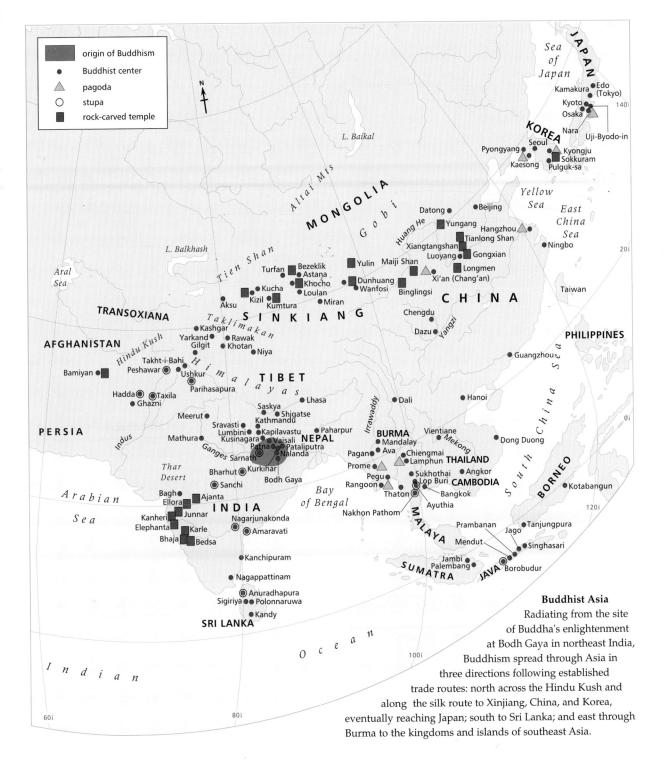

Buddhist Asia

Radiating from the site of Buddha's enlightenment at Bodh Gaya in northeast India, Buddhism spread through Asia in three directions following established trade routes: north across the Hindu Kush and along the silk route to Xinjiang, China, and Korea, eventually reaching Japan; south to Sri Lanka; and east through Burma to the kingdoms and islands of southeast Asia.

The Sangha and the Doctrine

The Sangha was open to all men regardless of caste and thus drew the antagonism of *brahmins*, although some did join. For a time, women were permitted to form their own convents, but only under special restrictions. (Today Buddhist nuns exist only in Tibet.)

The monks wore saffron robes and shaved their heads. They practiced celibacy and renounced alcohol, but no vow of obedience to the order was required. The monks were intellectually and spiritually free. Decisions were made through group discussion, perpetuating the pattern of the early republics of the north Indian hills. Monks studied, disciplined their spirits, meditated, and did the physical work of their monasteries. At first, they were to wander, begging for their living, except during the rainy months of the monsoon, but as monasteries became richer through donations of money and land, the monks tended to settle down. They also tended to give up begging, which diminished their contact with the common people to some degree.

A series of general councils began to codify the principles, doctrines, and texts of the emerging community. The first, convened shortly after the Buddha's death, began the continuing process of collecting his teachings. The second, about a century later, began to dispute the essential meaning of Buddhism. The third, convened at Pataliputra, Asoka's capital, revealed more of the differences that would soon lead to a split over the question of whether the Buddha was a human or a god. By this time an array of Buddhist *caityas*, or shrines, was growing. In addition to monasteries, great *stupas*, or burial mounds, of Buddhist relics were built at Barhut, Sanchi, and Amaravati. Between 200 B.C.E. and 200 C.E. there were more Buddhist than Hindu shrines in India. Theological discussion flourished, with a heavy emphasis on *metta*, or benevolence; non-violence; *dharma*, or proper behavior, although not related to caste since Buddhism rejected hereditary caste; and tolerance for all religions.

Mahayana Buddhism

The fourth general council, convened in the first century C.E. in Kashmir, codified the key doctrines of Buddhism as they had developed from earliest times. These were the principles of the Theravada ("Doctrine of the Elders") branch of Buddhism, which we have been examining and which is today the prevailing form in Sri Lanka and southeast Asia, except for Vietnam. But by now a newer school of Mahayana Buddhism had been growing for perhaps two centuries and had become a serious challenge to Theravada. Mahayana means "the Greater Vehicle," and its advocates claimed that their practices could carry more Buddhists to nirvana because they had bodhisattvas to help. A bodhisattva was a "being of wisdom" on the verge of achieving nirvana but so concerned about the welfare of fellow humans that he postponed his

entrance into nirvana to remain on earth, or to be reborn, in order to help others.

In addition, Mahayana Buddhism taught that religious merit, achieved through performing good deeds, could be transferred from one person to another. It embellished the concept of nirvana with the vision of a Mahayana heaven, presided over by Amitabha Buddha, a form of the Buddha who had lived on earth and had now become a kind of father in heaven. Subsequently, Mahayanists developed the concept of numerous heavens with numerous forms of the Buddha presiding over them. They also developed the concept of the Maitreya Buddha, a suffering servant who will come to redeem humanity.

Some theologians note the similarity of the concept of this Maitreya Buddha to the Christian

SACRED WRITINGS OF BUDDHISM

Tripitaka	"The Three Baskets": **Vinaya**, on the proper conduct of Buddhist monks and nuns; **Sutta**, discourses attributed to the Buddha; and **Abhidhamma**, supplementary doctrines. Written in Pali.
The Mahayanas	(Mahayana is Sanskrit for "Greater Vehicle.") The body of writings associated with the school of Buddhism dominant in Tibet, Mongolia, China, Korea, and Japan. Includes the famous allegory, the Lotus Sutra, the Buddhist Parable of the Prodigal Son.
Milindapanha	Dialogue between the Greek king Milinda and the Buddhist monk Nagasena on the philosophy of Buddhism.
Buddha's Four Noble Truths	Suffering is always present in life; desire is the cause of suffering; freedom from suffering can be achieved in nirvana (perfect peace and bliss); the Eightfold Path leads to nirvana.

FOCUS

Jainism

India has given birth to several religions, and Jainism is one of the oldest still existing. It shares many characteristics with Buddhism. At about the time of the Buddha, the teacher Mahavir (b. *c.* 540 B.C.E.), the twenty-fourth in a long lineage of Jain religious leaders, guided the religion into its modern form. The religion takes its name from Mahavir's designation *jina*, or conqueror. Like Theravada Buddhists, Jains reject the caste system and the supremacy of *brahmin* priests, postulating instead that there is no god, but that humans do have souls that they can purify by careful attention to their actions, and especially by practicing non-violence. If they follow the eternal law of ethical treatment of others and devotion to the rather austere rituals of the faith, Jains believe they will reach nirvana, which is an end to the cycle of rebirths rather than a rewarding afterlife.

Jainism's emphasis on non-violence is so powerful that Jains typically do not become farmers lest they kill living creatures in the soil. In a country overwhelmingly agricultural, Jains are usually urban and often businessmen. Jainism did not spread outside India, and its 4 million adherents today live almost entirely in India. Because Jains, like earlier Buddhists, employ *brahmin* priests to officiate at their lifecycle events, and because Jains intermarry freely with several Hindu *vaishya* (business) sub-castes, some consider them a branch of Hinduism, although they do not usually regard themselves as Hindus. One of the regions of Jain strength in India is western Gujarat, the region where Mahatma Gandhi grew up (see Chapter 20). The Mahatma attributed his adherence to non-violence in large part to the influence of Jainism.

Jainist nuns on their way to worship. Although most Jains are laypersons, important monasteries house priests and nuns. These nuns wear mouth-cloths to prevent injury to insects that might otherwise be inhaled.

Messiah, and some suggest that the Buddhists may have borrowed it. They also suggest that Christians may have borrowed the narratives of the virgin birth of the Buddha and of his temptation in his search for enlightenment, and applied them to Jesus. There are significant similarities in the stories of these two men/gods and their biogra-

phies. Further, Mahayanists spoke of three aspects of the Buddha: Amitabha, the Buddha in heaven; Gautama, the historical Buddha on earth; and the most revered of all the bodhisattvas, the freely moving Avalokiteshvara. Theologians ask: To what degree do these three Buddhist forms correspond to the Father, Son, Holy Spirit of Christianity as it was developing at the same time? How much borrowing took place between India and the Mediterranean coast, and in which direction?

Within India, Mahayana Buddhism began to challenge Hinduism more boldly than Theravada had. Wishing to compete for upper caste and upper class audiences, Mahayanists began to record their theology in Sanskrit, the language of the elites, rather than the more colloquial Pali language, which Theravada had preferred. Mahayana theologians, most notably Nagarjuna (*fl. c.* 50–150 C.E.), began to elaborate Buddhist philosophy and debate directly with *brahmin* priests. Buddhist monasteries established major educational programs, especially at Nalanda in Bihar, where the Buddha had spent much of his life, and at Taxila, on the international trade routes in the northern Punjab.

To spread the new faith, Buddhist missions traveled to southeast Asia and, increasingly, overland via the silk routes to central Asia and China. The first Buddhist missionaries are mentioned in Chinese records about 65 C.E. They established their first monastery at Luoyang. Over the centuries, many more were built within China and along the silk route. Chinese pilgrims traveled the silk route in the opposite direction to visit and study in the land of the Buddha, and some, most notably Faxian, who visited in 399–414, left important records of their observations. Thousands came from throughout the Buddhist world to study at Taxila and Nalanda.

THE DECLINE OF BUDDHISM IN INDIA

From its beginnings in India, Buddhism's strongest appeal had been to *kshatriya* rulers and *vaishya* businessmen, who felt that *brahmin* priests did not respect them. The Buddha himself came from a *kshatriya* family, and his early friendship with the *kshatriya* kings of Magadha and Koshala had ensured their early support for his movement. Later kings and merchants also donated huge sums of money to support Buddhist monks, temples, and monasteries. Many people of the lower castes, who felt the weight and the arrogance of all the other castes pressing down on them, also joined the newly forming religion. They were especially attracted by the use of the vernacular Pali and Magadhi languages in place of Sanskrit, and the absence of the financial demands of the *brahmins*. (In the 1950s, almost a thousand years after Buddhism's demise in India, about 5 million "out-castes," people whose caste ranked below the bottom, revived Buddhism in India in protest at the inequalities of the caste system and declared their allegiance to the old/new religion. These "neo-Buddhists" are virtually the only Buddhists to be found in India today [see Chapter 20].)

By the fifth century C.E., however, the Chinese Buddhist pilgrim Faxian noted weaknesses in Indian Buddhism. The religion continued to exist in India for another six centuries, so his observation was hardly definitive, but Buddhism did die out in India, losing strength from the time of the decline of the Gupta Empire (*c.* 320–550 C.E.; see p. 246). Regional rulers began to choose Hinduism over Buddhism, and alliances with priests rather than with monks. Perhaps such choices strengthened the rulers' standing with their subjects, since Hinduism always seemed closer to the common people. Also, without imperial assistance, merchants' incomes may have decreased within India, reducing their contributions to Buddhist temples. Trade with southeast Asia continued to be lucrative, however, and the Buddhist presence there remained strong.

At the popular level, lower castes who had found the anti-caste philosophy of Buddhism attractive, apparently also began to shift their allegiances back toward more orthodox Hinduism as an anchor in a time of political change. In any case, Mahayana Buddhism, with its many god-like Buddhas and bodhisattvas inhabiting a multitude of heavens, seemed so close to Hinduism that many Buddhists must have seen little purpose in maintaining a distinction. Finally, Buddhists throughout their history in India had relied upon Hindu *brahmin* priests to officiate at their lifecycle ceremonies of birth, marriage, and death, so Hindu priests could argue that they always had a significant claim on Buddhist allegiance.

Readers who are accustomed to the monotheistic pattern of religions claiming the undivided loyalty of their followers will recognize here a very different pattern. Many religions, especially polytheistic religions, expect that individuals will incorporate diverse elements of different religions into their personal philosophy and ritual. We will see more examples of this personal syncretism and loyalty to multiple religions as we examine Buddhism's relationship with Confucianism in China and with both Confucianism and Shinto in Japan.

As Hinduism evolved, it became more attractive to Buddhists. Theologians like Shankaracharya (788–820) and Ramanuja (1017–1137) advanced philosophies based on the Vedic literature known to the common people and built many temples and schools to spread their thought. Hindu *bhakti* devotionalism (see Focus, p. 269) also attracted followers to its mystical, ecstatic forms. At the same time, Hinduism, following its tradition of syncretism, incorporated the Buddha himself within its own polytheistic universe as an incarnation of Vishnu. A devotee could revere the Buddha within the overarching framework of Hinduism. Finally, although neither Buddhism nor Hinduism gave much scope to women within their official institutions of temples, schools, and monasteries, for Hinduism the home was much more central than the public institution, and here women did have a central role in worship and ritual. Buddhism was much more centered on its monasteries and monks. The comparative lack of a role for women, and the comparative disinterest in domestic life generally, may have impeded its spread.

The end of Buddhism in India came with the arrival of Muslims during the first two centuries of their major invasions into India, between 1000 and 1200 C.E. Muslims saw Buddhism as a competitive proselytizing religion, unlike Hinduism, and did not wish to coexist with it. Because Buddhism was, by this time, relatively weak and relatively centralized within its monasteries and schools, Muslims were able to destroy the remnants of the religion by attacking these institutions. Buddhist monks were killed or forced to flee from India to centers in southeast Asia, Nepal, and Tibet. Hinduism was equipped to survive the challenge because it was much more broadly based as the religion of home and community and far more deeply rooted in Indian culture.

Guanyin, Buddhist deity, Northern Song dynasty, China, *c.* **1200 C.E.** Guanyin, a bodhisattva, or enlightened being, who remains in this world to relieve human suffering, was a very popular subject in Chinese art: this painted-wood example is particularly sensuous and refined. Buddhist deities are considered to have the spiritual qualities of both genders and by this date the feminine qualities were accentuated. (*Nelson-Atkins Museum of Art, Kansas City, Missouri*)

BUDDHISM IN CHINA AND JAPAN

common people

more people involved

Early Buddhism Outside India: How Do We Know?

Because Buddhism has no single central organization, our knowledge of its spread is gained by studying the works of the monks, missionaries, poets, architects, and sculptors who spread the faith. This decentralization and vast geographical diffusion mean that Buddhism has taken on different forms from place to place, time to time, and state to state. It arrived in foreign form, but over time each regional culture has put its own stamp on Buddhism. We must, therefore, examine the faith and practice of Buddhism in each region separately.

Arrival in China: The Silk Route

The thin line of communication over which pilgrims and missionaries carried the message of the

Diamond Sutra, 868 C.E.
This superb frontispiece, showing the Buddha preaching to an elderly disciple, comes from the *Diamond Sutra*, a Sanskrit tale transmitted along the silk route and translated into Chinese in the fifth century. Produced by woodblock to a high standard of technical and artistic achievement, the 17-foot-long (5.2 m) sutra is the world's earliest dated printed book. (*British Library, London*)

Buddha from India to China and beyond was the silk route, the same route that carried luxury products between China and India and then on to the West. Several of the pilgrims who traveled these routes, especially Faxian, in the early years of the fifth century C.E., and Xuanzang, in the early years of the seventh, brought back both Buddhist texts and important first-hand information from India and the lands along the silk routes. Turning north from India through Kashgar, and then east to Khotan, Turfan, Dunhuang, and on to Chang'an in the heart of China, Buddhist pilgrims improved these trade routes with rest-houses (see picture, p. 222), temples, and monasteries, some built into caves.

Although Buddhism first appeared in China in the first century C.E., at the height of the Han dynasty, it took firmer root after the dynasty fell (see p. 217). Confucianism, China's dominant philosophy, was intimately tied to the fate of the imperial government, and only after this central political structure collapsed could Mahayana Buddhism find a place. The mystical character of Mahayana Buddhism especially attracted Daoists. To some degree, the two beliefs competed, but some of the competition eventually led to each validating the other. For example, some Daoists claimed that the Buddha was actually Laozi as he appeared in his travels in India. Many Buddhists, in turn, accorded to Laozi and Confucius the status of bodhisattva. In this way, competition sometimes turned into mutual recognition.

As a foreign religion, Buddhism also had special appeal for some of the rulers of northern China in the third through the sixth centuries, since they, too, were outsiders. The Toba rulers of the Northern Wei dynasty (386–534) occasionally persecuted Buddhists as a threat to the state, but mostly they felt some kinship to this religion of outsiders. They patronized Buddhist shrines and monks, but they also regulated them.

In the south, with its abundance of émigrés from the northern court, Confucianism was crippled by the severance of its connection with the government. In contrast, newly arriving Buddhists won followers by proposing an organized, aesthetic philosophy for coping with the hazards of life in semi-exile. In southern China Buddhist arts of poetry, painting, and calligraphy flourished, and monasteries in the south offered refuge to the men who might have been part of the governing Confucian aristocracy in other times. In the southern state of Liang, the "Emperor" Wu (r. 502–549) declared Buddhism the official state religion, built temples, sponsored Buddhist assemblies, and wrote Buddhist commentaries.

Doctrinally, Buddhism had important differences from Confucianism, but the two world perspectives seem to have reached mutual accommodation. For example, Confucianism encouraged family cohesion and the veneration of ancestors, while Buddhist monks followed lives of celibacy; but Buddhist laypeople also valued family (see Source, p. 274), and the monks themselves venerated the Buddha and bodhisattvas as their spiritual ancestors. Nevertheless, tension between the two belief systems and organizations never completely dissipated. Confucians thought in terms of government order and control, while Buddhists tended toward decentralized congregational worship within a loose doctrinal framework. In many areas of China, as Buddhist monasteries became wealthy from the donations of local magnates and landlords, Confucian governments moved to regulate their power.

Buddhism's network of pilgrims and monks crisscrossed China, helping to integrate the nation. Through almost four centuries of division in China, from the fall of the Han (220 C.E.) to the rise of the Sui (581), Buddhism continued to grow in both north and south. Indeed, the founder of the Sui dynasty, a Buddhist himself, also patronized Confucianism and Daoism, seeing all these belief systems as vital to earning legitimacy for his government. The Tang extended this veneration. The only woman ever to rule China in her own name, the "Emperor" Wu, was a great patron of Buddhism. First ruling indirectly through the Emperor Gaozong (d. 683), whose concubine she was, and then, after his death, through two of their sons, in 690 she proclaimed herself the emperor of a new dynasty, the Zhou. She patronized Buddhism as a means of legitimizing her rule, declaring herself a reincarnation of Maitreya, the Buddha of future salvation. The empress built temples in every province of China. Before she was deposed in 705, she had overseen the warfare that expanded the Tang to its greatest geographical extent, including Xinjiang and Tibet.

Buddhism under the Tang Dynasty

Under the Tang dynasty (618–907) the intellectual, spiritual, and artistic life of Buddhism flourished. Eight major sects developed, each with a different interpretation of the original message of the Buddha, the importance of rules and regulations, rituals, meditation, scholarship, disciplinary exercises, and devotion. Among the larger and more significant schools was the Pure Land Sect. Its devotees believed that anyone could reach the Pure Land of paradise after death through faith in the Buddha Amitabha, the presiding authority in that realm. Members of the sect demonstrated their faith by continuously repeating the name Amitabha. Devotees also meditated on the Bodhisattva Guanyin, the bodhisattva of mercy (see picture, p. 281).

Another sect, Chan Buddhism, taught the importance of meditation. Some followers believed in lengthy disciplines of meditation, which would gradually lead to enlightenment; others in spontaneous flashes of insight, which would lead to the same goal. Both Pure Land and Chan were adopted in Japan as well, where the meditative exercises of Chan became known as Zen.

Buddhists are credited with inventing woodblock printing as a means of reproducing their sacred texts. The earliest woodblock print known is an illustrated copy of the *Diamond Sutra* from 868 C.E., discovered in the Dunhuang Caves. Most of the Buddhist art and architecture of Tang China was destroyed in later persecution, confiscation, and warfare. Its leading representations are now seen in Japan, which at just about this time adopted much of Chinese Buddhism as its own and then modified it (see pictures, pp. 226 and 286).

Political and military defeats started Buddhism on its decline in China. In far-off central Asia Muslim forces defeated Chinese forces in the decisive Battle of the Talas River in 751. Four years later, the revolt of General An Lushan in northeast China occupied the imperial armies for eight years. China's power in central Asia was broken, and with it the power of Buddhism in these regions. Islam would become the world religion of most of central Asia (see Chapter 11).

Almost a century later, the Tang emperor, Wuzong (r. 840–846), attacked Buddhism and its monasteries. Wuzong was a Daoist, personally opposed to Buddhism. He feared the power of the Buddhist establishment, the wealth and influence of its various monasteries especially when the Tang had been weakened by external defeats and internal revolts. Wuzong confiscated the lands and wealth of the Buddhist monasteries. He forced monks and nuns to leave the monasteries, claiming that he personally had defrocked 260,500 monks and nuns. He destroyed sacred texts, statues, and shrines, leaving only 49 monasteries and 800 monks in all of China. Later rulers alternated between reversing and re-imposing Wuzong's policies, and although Buddhism has remained a presence in China, even to today, it never recovered its numbers, vitality, or influence.

Buddhism in Japan

Long before "The Way of the Buddha" arrived in Japan, c. 552 C.E., the people of Japan followed "The Way of the *Kami*," later called Shinto. *Kamis* were the powers and spirits inherent in nature. Found everywhere, they could be called upon to help in time of human need. Shrines to the *kami* were built everywhere, always including a mirror in tribute to the sun-goddess, a sword, and a jewel. According

SOURCE

The Transience of Life: A Woman's Perspective from the Tang Dynasty

This anonymous poem of the Tang dynasty, discovered in the Dunhuang cave and translated by Patricia Ebrey and Lily Hwa, illuminates the Buddhist sense of the transience of life as experienced by a woman of high status.

A Woman's Hundred Years

At ten, like a flowering branch in the rain,
She is slender, delicate, and full of grace.
Her parents are themselves as young as the rising moon
And do not allow her past the red curtain without a reason.

At twenty, receiving the hairpin, she is a spring bud.
Her parents arrange her betrothal; the matter's well done.
A fragrant carriage comes at evening to carry her to her lord.
Like Xioshi and his wife, at dawn they depart with the clouds.

At thirty, perfect as a pearl, full of the beauty of youth,
At her window, by the gauze curtain, she makes up in front of the mirror.
With her singing companions, in the waterlily season,
She rows a boat and plucks the blue flowers.

At forty, she is mistress of a prosperous house and makes plans.
Three sons and five daughters give her some trouble.
With her lute not far away, she toils always at her loom.
Her only fear that the sun will set too soon.

At fifty, afraid of her husband's dislike,
She strains to please him with every charm.
Trying to remember the many tricks she had learned since the age of sixteen.
No longer is she afraid of mothers- and sisters-in-law.

At sixty, face wrinkled and hair like silk thread,
She walks unsteadily and speaks little.
Distressed that her sons can find no brides,
Grieved that her daughters have departed for their husbands' homes.

At seventy, frail and thin, but not knowing what to do about it,
She is no longer able to learn the Buddhist Law even if she tries.
In the morning a light breeze
Makes her joints crack like clanging gongs.

At eighty, eyes blinded and ears half-deaf,
When she goes out she cannot tell north from east.
Dreaming always of departed loves,
Who persuade her to chase the dying breeze.

At ninety, the glow fades like spent lightning.
Human affairs are no longer her concern.
Lying on a pillow, solitary on her high bed,
She resembles the dying leaves that fall in autumn.

At a hundred, like a cliff crumbling in the wind,
For her body it is the moment to become dust.
Children and grandchildren will perform sacrifices to her spirit.
And clear moonlight will forever illumine her patch of earth.

(Ebrey, p. 104)

to the earliest Japanese records, the *Kojiki* (712 C.E.) and *Nihon shoki* (720 C.E.), the highest of the *kami* were Amaterasu, the sun-goddess and her obstreperous brother Susa-no-o. Amaterasu's grandson Niniqi descended to earth and set out to conquer Japan. He established himself as Japan's first emperor in 660 B.C.E., and all subsequent emperors trace their lineage directly back to this mythological founder. With the later arrival of Buddhism, the *kami* continued to have a distinguished and venerated position, often as minor Buddhas or bodhisattvas. Conversely, the Buddhas and bodhisattvas were accepted as especially powerful and exalted *kami*, capable of helping those in adversity. The royal family in Japan knew that the Emperor Asoka in India had adopted Buddhism and they emulated his decision.

BUDDHISM'S ARRIVAL IN JAPAN: HOW DO WE KNOW?

The semi-mythological *Nihon shoki* and *Kojiki* give a basic history of early Japan, but these records—and all accounts of Buddhist saints—must be read with some caution since they blend myth with factual record: Chinese histories occasionally discuss conditions in Japan; temples in Japan are themselves models of the development of Buddhism in the nation; and the treasures of art and documents housed in the temples enhance that perspective. For example, inside the Todaiji Temple in Nara, the Shosoin storehouse is one of the world's great repositories of art, holding several thousand treasures from the eighth century, including paintings, sculptures, calligraphy, textiles, ceramics, jade, metal and lacquer work, masks for drama, and musical instruments. Some were imported from regions throughout Asia and demonstrate Japan's position as eastern terminus of one great trans-Asian silk route. For later times, after the eighth century C.E., literature as well as personal diaries and records help to fill out the more formal accounts.

BUDDHISM'S ARRIVAL IN JAPAN: WHAT DO WE KNOW?

Buddhism first came to Japan from China via the Paekche kingdom of southwest Korea in 552 C.E. The *Nihon shoki* tells of the Paekche king sending Buddhist texts and statues and asking help in a war against another Korean kingdom, the Silla. From the very beginning, Buddhism had political as well as religious implications. Clans close to the Japanese emperor were divided in their reception of the foreign religion, with those who accepted it regarding Buddhism as a force for performing miracles, especially healing the sick, and many Buddhist monks were especially skilled in medicine. A minority, however, thought the new religion ought to be banned.

Buddhism found acceptance at a political level in Japan a half century later under Prince Shotoku Taishi (573–621). The prince effectively ruled the country as the regent to the ruler of the Yamato Plain, the western region of Japan. An enthusiastic Buddhist, Shotoku built many temples, including the Horyuji in the capital city of Nara. A scholar of Buddhist theology, he invited Buddhist clergy from Korea, and dispatched four Japanese missions to Sui China to learn more about Buddhism, both as a religious system and as a model for centralizing his political rule. At this time China was the premier state of eastern Asia, and Buddhism was seen as one of the principal constituents of its power. In 604, Prince Shotoku introduced a kind of constitution to centralize and strengthen the Japanese government. Among its seventeen articles, the first promoted Confucian principles of social organization and the second declared that the Japanese people should "Sincerely reverence the three treasures . . . the Buddha, the Law, and the Monastic orders" (Embree, p. 50).

A century later, in 710, the ruling clans of Japan moved their capital to Nara, then called Heijo. Continuing to regard China as the model state of their day, the Japanese rulers copied much of the Chinese structures of authority and administration. They used Chinese ideographs as their written language, and adopted Chinese patterns of bureaucracy, tax systems, architecture, and land reforms. They modeled their new capital on the city plan of Chang'an, building a smaller version of that Chinese capital at Nara. Within Nara they built numerous Buddhist temples, including several of national significance. They encouraged the creation of a system of monasteries and convents throughout the provinces, with the Todaiji monastery, built by the Emperor Shomu (r. 724–749), at the apex. Buddhism became a pillar in the structure of national unity and administration. Buddhism did not replace Shinto, the indigenous worship of spirits, especially spirits of nature. Rather, it complemented the indigenous system. The emperor performed the official rituals of both Shinto and Buddhist worship.

Buddhism introduced a measure of centralization. Shinto, a looser system of belief and worship, had spread throughout all of Japan with no need of a central shrine for its worship of nature. By contrast, the Horyuji Temple near Nara became a central shrine for all of Japan. In 741 the rulers ordered that a Buddhist temple and pagoda be established in each province. Buddhism and Shinto co-existed in Japan in a pattern that continues even today.

As in China, the power and wealth of Buddhist monasteries and temples in Japan, and especially in Nara, alarmed some members of the court. To reduce the power of the Buddhist clergy and to increase the power of his own lineage, the Emperor Kammu (r. 781–806) moved the capital again, from Nara to Heian (modern Kyoto) in 794. This move initiated the Heian period in Japanese history and coincided with the decline of the Tang Empire in China. The Japanese government dispatched its last official mission to China in 838. With Japan on the ascendant and China in decline, Japan's Buddhism developed along its own paths, helped by substantial imperial patronage. The Emperor Kammu himself patronized two young Japanese monks who founded the Tendai and Shingon schools of Buddhism, the two most powerful and enduring Buddhist movements in Japan.

The Buddhist priesthood itself became increasingly Japanese, no longer reliant on priests from the mainland. It also entered more profoundly into politics. The priest Saicho (767–822) studied Tiantai (*Tendai* in Japanese) Buddhism in China and introduced it into Japan. Based on the Lotus Sutra, Tendai taught that each person could achieve enlightenment through sincere religious devotion. On Mount Hiei, northeast of Kyoto, Saicho built the Enryakuji monastery, which grew rapidly and steadily into one of the most important temple communities in Japan.

Horyuji Temple, Nara, Japan, 670 C.E. Through the seventh and eighth centuries the Japanese court enthusiastically welcomed Chinese political and artistic forms (Chapter 7). This is Japan's earliest surviving example of Buddhist architecture, which was adopted along with Chinese writing, painting, and sculpture. It became a central shrine for all of Japan.

Hoodo (Phoenix Hall), Byodoin Temple, Uji, Japan, eleventh century. The Phoenix Hall of the Byodoin Temple, with its jauntily uplifted roof-corners, indicates how over time the Buddhist style took on a distinctively Japanese flavor and shed its Chinese influence (contrast with picture, p. 286).

Saicho had intended his monastery to remain aloof from politics, and he therefore built it far from the national capital in Nara. Ironically, however, when the capital was moved to Kyoto, the monastery again found itself geographically close to the national political center. Saicho encouraged the monks to add teaching, administration, and social work in the service of the nation to their religious duties, merging Confucian and Buddhist value systems. His monastery grew to house tens of thousands of monks in some 3000 buildings. By the eleventh century, an era of deep and violent political fissures in Japanese political life, many Shinto and Buddhist temples supported standing armies to protect themselves and their extensive land holdings and branch temples. Troops from the Mount Hiei monastery began to enter the capital, demanding additional lands and thus completely reversing Saicho's original wishes. The Buddhist clergy thereafter became increasingly intertwined with Japanese politics.

Kukai (774–835), another Japanese Buddhist priest who studied in China, also returned home to preach a new form of Buddhism. He became abbot of the monastery of the great Toji temple at Kyoto, where he introduced Shingon ("True Word") Buddhism. Shingon emphasizes the repetition of mystic incantations or **mantras**; meditation on col-

orful, sometimes stunning, geometrically ordered religious paintings, called **mandalas**, of Buddhas and bodhisattvas in their heavens; complicated rituals; music; and ecstatic dancing. Because the transmission of these forms was closely guarded among believers, Shingon was also called Esoteric Buddhism. Creating more accessible forms as well, Kukai introduced rituals, such as the austere and beautiful tea ceremony, in which a formal ritual surrounding the serving and drinking of tea invites deep meditation. Kukai is also credited with inventing the *kana* **syllabary**, a Japanese script in phonetic letters rather than **ideograms**. These innovations, in addition to mysterious, secret rituals, use of herbal medicines, and the elegant pageantry of Shingon, gave Kukai's monastery great popularity and power.

Another Chinese form of Buddhism that deeply influenced Japan was dedicated to Amida, or, in Sanskrit, Amitabha, the Buddha of the Infinite Light. In the tenth century, two priests, Kuya (903–972) and Genshin (942–1017), popularized this sect, which taught the importance of chanting the mantra *nembutsu*, "Praise to Amida Buddha." Amidism grew in subsequent generations through the organizational abilities of a series of monks, including Ryonin (1072–1132), who taught the counting of rosary beads to accompany the

SPOTLIGHT
Images of the Buddha

Monks and merchants carried the Buddha's message throughout Asia. He had taught that humans could cope with the suffering of life, illness, aging, and death by cultivating proper understanding of these normal processes and by curbing excessive expectations and desires for unrealistic alternatives. This message remained the core of Theravada Buddhism, the form practiced in Sri Lanka and southeast Asia. Other devotees accepted this profound message of simplicity but elaborated it into new forms. The greatest theological change, the development of Mahayana Buddhism, introduced the concept of the Bodhisattva, the saintlike person so dedicated to humanity that he would choose to be reborn to help others rather than enter nirvana (see picture, p. 281). For Mahayanists the Buddha himself was seen as a Bodhisattva who had lived on earth before his known lifetime, 563–483 B.C.E., and would be reborn again. This and related new concepts were transmitted across the silk route to China, Korea, and Japan and proved attractive to hundreds of millions of people. The three pictures in this Spotlight illustrate the increasing elaboration of the message of the Buddha in its manifestations across two millennia of time and a continent of space. Because they all represent the same event, the death of the Buddha, we can compare these transformations directly.

Figure 1 from Gandhara in northern Pakistan–Afghanistan in the second century C.E. (see Spotlight, pp. 242–3) gives one of the early representations of the Buddha in human form. Previously art had represented him through the icon of a wheel, a reference to his message of the wheel of life, death, and rebirth. Here he is shown dying, surrounded by a small group of grieving monks and devotees. The Buddha has a halo around his head. The Gandharan artist fuses Hellenistic styles, as in the clothing, with Indian, as in the forms of the bodies.

Figure 2 is a painting from a wall in the Buddhist cave complex at Dunhuang (Cave 428) from the early sixth century C.E. Monks and merchants transmitting the message of the Buddha along the silk route and into China constructed numerous monasteries and caravan halts along the way. Dunhuang, situated just west of the end of the Great Wall, marked the ecological boundary

Figure 1 Dying Buddha, Gandhara, Afghanistan, second century C.E.

between the great Lop and Taklamakan deserts to the west and the Gansu corridor leading into China to the east and provided the site for one of the most important of these complexes. The walls of 460 of its caves are painted with Buddhist scenes. In **figure 2** many devotees, as well as the Buddha, are crowned with halos, suggesting their bodhisattva status. The artwork differs sharply from the one from Gandhara, with the faces and bodies far more sketchy, and the background as well as the facial markings far more abstract and enchanted.

As Buddhism reached Japan in the seventh century C.E., the elaboration of immortal beings continued to multiply along with representations of a heavenly life. **Figure 3**, a Japanese painting on silk from the seventeenth/eighteenth century, portrays the dying Buddha in a grove of sal trees, attended by human disciples, bodhisattvas, grieving animals, and representatives of other worlds. From across the river, another disciple leads the Buddha's mother and her retinue down from heaven to attend his last teaching. The specific mixture of populations as well as the aesthetic style of this picture, quite different from those at Dunhuang and Gandhara, are products of the Japanese imagination. This variety is the mark of a living, expanding, diversifying religious system engaging the needs of its growing population across time and space.

Figure 2 Dying Buddha, Cave 428, Dunhuang, China, early sixth century C.E.

Figure 3 Dying Buddha, Japanese scroll, seventeenth to eighteenth century C.E.

repetition of the *nembutsu*, a practice that spread to most sects of Japanese Buddhism. By the late twelfth century Amidism established its independence of other Buddhist sects and at last reached a mass audience for whom its message of uncomplicated, universal access to salvation had great appeal.

Three other elements gave Buddhism a prominence and significance in Japanese life that has continued till today. First, Japanese Buddhism cultivated an especially pure aesthetic dimension, which we have seen here in the representations of the Buddha and bodhisattvas and of the architecture and art of the Japanese Buddhist temples. This appreciation of artistic creativity is apparent throughout Japan in formal gardens, in painting and calligraphy, and in the art of presentation of everything from self, to gifts, to tea, to food. Second, Buddhism's emphasis on the transience of all life has inspired much of the greatest Japanese literature, from the *Tale of Genji*, written by Lady Murasaki (*c.* 978–*c.* 1015) at the Japanese court a thousand years ago, to the novels of Mishima Yukio (1925–70), who committed *seppuku*, ritual suicide, immediately after completing his last novel. Third, Buddhism has coexisted and even merged to some degree with indigenous Shinto worship and belief.

By the twelfth century Japan had entered its Buddhist Age. Despite occasional attacks on Buddhism as a foreign religion and as an excessively wealthy and powerful organization, Buddhism has remained one of the two national religions of Japan. Most Japanese continue to mingle Buddhism and Shinto in their aesthetic and spiritual lives as well as in their ritual practices.

HINDUISM AND BUDDHISM: HOW DO THEY COMPARE?

Hinduism and Buddhism have undergone enormous transformations through their thousands of years of history. Geographically, Hinduism spread across the Indian subcontinent from its roots in the encounter between Aryan invaders and the indigenous peoples of the Indus valley and north India. It extended briefly even to southeast Asia (where a single Hindu outpost still remains on the Indonesian island of Bali). Buddhism spread from the Buddha's home region in the Himalayan foothills throughout India, where it subsequently died out, and most of east and southeast Asia, where it flourishes (see map, p. 277). Buddhism's array of monasteries and temples, and its venera-

tion of the homeland of the Buddha himself, mark its sacred geography.

Both religions established their own sacred calendars and their control over lifecycle events. In this, Hindu priests took a commanding position since even Buddhists employed them to officiate. Within India this continuing role of the *brahmin* priests ultimately helped Hinduism to absorb Buddhism. Outside India, where no other major religion was already in place, Buddhist priests performed their own rituals, and came to predominate.

Both groups developed sacred languages. Buddhists felt that Sanskrit was narrowly limited to Hindu priests and so used Pali, a language closer to the vernacular. Over time, as the common people expressed their own religious feelings in their own languages, the leaders of both religions responded by also using the vernacular. Both religions inspired extensive literatures, including philosophy, mystical poetry, drama, and folk tales. Both generated their own artistic traditions in painting, sculpture, and temple architecture.

Organizationally, Buddhism, especially in its early Theravada form, was seen as a religion of its monks. Many of the common people found comfort and meaning in their philosophy and supported them, but ultimately they turned to *brahmin* priests for their ritual needs. Within Hinduism the caste system structured all classes and occupations into a single framework of relationships, with *brahmins* and *kshatriyas*, and, in a few more commercial locations, *vaishyas*, predominating. Buddhism's later Mahayana form, with its multitudes of gods, bodhisattvas, and heavens, did reach out to more people ritually as well as emotionally.

The evolution of Hinduism and Buddhism demonstrates the flexibility of great world religions. A small sect may define itself narrowly, proclaiming a core set of principles and practices and adhering to them rigidly. For its small membership, these restrictions may be the very attraction of the sect. But for a religion to grow in numbers, it must be open organizationally, doctrinally, and ritually to the varied spiritual, psychic, and social needs of diverse peoples. Like the empires we studied in Part 3, a world religion must be able to accommodate, satisfy, and absorb people of various languages, regions, classes, and previous spiritual beliefs and practices. World religions expand their theologies and practices to incorporate ever more members, until they reach their limits of flexibility.

Finally, religions and governments have been historically interdependent. Buddhism flourished thanks to the early support of the Buddha's royal allies and later through the backing of the Emperor Asoka. It spread to southeast Asia and to Japan as kings offered their support in exchange for Buddhist legitimation. In China, Buddhism found its opening after Confucian dynasties fell and people searched for new belief systems and new leaders. Hinduism flourished as kings in India struck their own agreements with *brahmin* priests. Conversely, when governments turned against particular religious groups, they could devastate them. And when sizable religious groups shifted their support away from a ruler, they undermined his authority. We shall find more of this mutual antagonism in the next chapters.

We turn now to three religions—Judaism, Christianity, and Islam—which have been militantly monotheistic. Although Judaism has remained quite small, Christianity and Islam have been aggressive in their desire to win converts, and have become today the largest of the world's religions, with almost two billion and one billion followers, respectively. Their relationships with the governments alongside which they exist have been checkered. Their impact on spiritual, cultural, social, and aesthetic life has been immense.

BIBLIOGRAPHY

Allchin, F.R., *et al. The Archaeology of Early Historic South Asia: The Emergence of Cities and States* (Cambridge: Cambridge University Press, 1995).

Andrea, Alfred and James Overfield, eds. *The Human Record.* Vol. I (Boston: Houghton Mifflin Company, 3rd ed., 1998).

Appadurai, Arjun. *Worship and Conflict under Colonial Rule* (Cambridge: Cambridge University Press, 1981).

Basham, A.L. *The Wonder That Was India* (New York: Grove Press, 1954).

Berger, Peter L. *The Sacred Canopy* (New York: Anchor Books, 1967).

Bhagavad Gita, trans. Barbara Stoler Miller (New York: Bantam Books, 1986).

Bhattacharya, Haridas, ed. *The Cultural Heritage of India.* Vol. III: *The Philosophies* (Calcutta: The Ramakrishna Mission Institute of Culture, 1953).

Holy Bible, New Revised Standard Version (Grand Rapids, MI: Zondervan Publishing House, 1989).

Blunden, Caroline and Mark Elvin. *Cultural Atlas of China* (New York: Facts on File, 1983).

Bodde, Derk. *Essays on Chinese Civilization*, ed. Charles Le Blanc and Dorothy Borei (Princeton: Princeton University Press, 1981).

Britannica Book of the Year 2000 (Chicago: Encyclopedia Britannica, Inc., 1999).

Conze, Edward. *Buddhist Scriptures* (New York: Penguin Books, 1959).

Cotterell, Arthur, ed. *The Penguin Encyclopedia of Ancient Civilizations* (London: Penguin Books, 1980).

Craven, Roy C. *A Concise History of Indian Art* (New York: Oxford University Press, n.d.).

deBary, William Theodore and Irene Bloom, eds., *Sources of Chinese Tradition, Vol. I: From Earliest Times to 1600*

(New York: Columbia University Press, 2nd ed., 1999).

The Dhammapada, trans. by Juan Mascaro (New York: Penguin Books, 1973).

Dimmitt, Cornelia and J.A.B. van Buitenen, ed. and trans. *Classical Hindu Mythology* (Philadelphia: Temple University Press, 1978).

Eberhard, Wolfram. *China's Minorities: Yesterday and Today* (Belmont, CA: Wadsworth Publishing, 1982).

Ebrey, Patricia Buckley, ed. *Chinese Civilization: A Sourcebook* (New York: The Free Press, 2nd ed., 1993).

Eliade, Mircea. *Ordeal by Labyrinth* (Chicago: University of Chicago Press, 1982).

——. *The Sacred and the Profane* (New York: Harper Torchbooks, 1959).

——. *Yoga: Immortality and Freedom* (Princeton: Princeton University Press, 1969).

Elvin, Mark. *The Pattern of the Chinese Past* (Stanford: Stanford University Press, 1973).

Embree, Ainslee, ed. and rev. *Sources of Indian Tradition*, Vol. I: *From the Beginning to 1800* (New York: Columbia University Press, 2nd ed., 1988).

Friedman, Edward. "Reconstructing China's National Identity: A Southern Alternative to Mao-Era Anti-Imperialist Nationalism," *Journal of Asian Studies* LIII, No. 1 (February 1994), 67–91.

Green, Peter. *Alexander of Macedon, 356–323 B.C.* (Berkeley: University of California Press, 1991).

Hall, Kenneth R. *Maritime Trade and State Development in Early Southeast Asia* (Honolulu: University of Hawaii, 1985).

Hall, Kenneth R. and John K. Whitmore, eds. *Explorations in Early Southeast Asian History: The Origins of Southeast Asian Statecraft* (Ann Arbor: Center for South and Southeast Asian Studies, University of Michigan, 1976).

Honour, Hugh and John Fleming. *The Visual Arts: A History* (Englewood Cliffs, NJ: Prentice-Hall, 1995).

Hopfe, Lewis M. *Religions of the World* (New York: Macmillan Publishing Company, 5th ed., 1991).

Hughes, Sarah Shaver and Brady Hughes, eds. *Women in World History*, Vol. I: *Readings from Prehistory to 1500* (Armonk, NY: M.E. Sharpe, 1995).

Kulke, Hermann and Dietmar Rothermund. *A History of India* (Totowa, NJ: Barnes and Noble Books, 1986).

Lockard, Craig A. "Integrating Southeast Asia into the Framework of World History: The Period Before 1500," *The History Teacher* XXIX, No. 1 (November 1995), 7–35.

Martin, Rafe. *The Hungry Tigress: Buddhist Legends and Jataka Tales* (Berkeley, CA: Parallax Press, 1990).

McGovern, William Montgomery. *The Early Empires of Central Asia* (Chapel Hill: University of North Carolina Press, 1939).

McManners, John, ed. *The Oxford Illustrated History of Christianity* (New York: Oxford University Press, 1990).

Murphey, Rhoads. *A Brief History of Asia* (New York: HarperCollins, 1992).

Needham, Joseph. *The Shorter Science and Civilization in China*, Vol. I, abridged by Colin A. Ronan (Cambridge: Cambridge University Press, 1978).

Nelson, Lynn and Patrick Peebles, eds. *Classics of Eastern Thought* (San Diego: Harcourt Brace Jovanovich, 1991).

Parker, Geoffrey, ed. *The (London) Times Atlas of World History* (London: Times Books, 4th ed., 1998).

Past Worlds: The (London) Times Atlas of Archaeology (Maplewood, NJ: Hammond, 1988).

Ramanujan, A.K., ed. and trans. *Poems of Love and War: From the Eight Anthologies and the Ten Long Poems of Classical Tamil* (New York: Columbia University Press, 1985).

Ramanujan, A.K., trans. *Speaking of Síva* (Harmondsworth, England: Penguin Books, 1973).

Richman, Paula, ed. *Many Ramayanas: The Diversity of a Narrative Tradition in South Asia* (Berkeley: University of California Press, 1991).

Rowland, Benjamin. *The Art and Architecture of India: Buddhist/Hindu/Jain* (New York: Penguin Books, 1977).

SarDesai, D.R. *Southeast Asia: Past and Present* (Boulder, CO: Westview Press, 3rd ed., 1994).

Schirokauer, Conrad. *A Brief History of Chinese and Japanese Civilizations* (Fort Worth: Harcourt Brace Jovanovich, 2nd ed., 1989).

Schwartz, Benjamin I. *The World of Thought in Ancient China* (Cambridge: Harvard University Press, 1985).

Schwartzberg, Joseph E., ed. *A Historical Atlas of South Asia* (Chicago: University of Chicago Press, 1978).

Seth, Vikram. *Three Chinese Poets: Translations of Poems by Wang Wei, Li Bai, and Du Fu* (New York: HarperCollins, 1993).

Sima Qian. *Historical Records*, trans. Raymond Dawson (New York: Oxford University Press, 1994).

Sima Qian. *Records of the Historian: Chapters from the Shih Chi of Ssu-ma Ch'ien*, trans. Burton Watson (New York: Columbia University Press, 1969).

Smart, Ninian. *The World's Religions* (Cambridge: Cambridge University Press, 1989).

Spodek, Howard. "Studying the History of Urbanization in India," *Journal of Urban History* VI, No. 3 (May, 1980) 251–95.

Spodek, Howard and Doris Srinivasan, eds. *Urban Form and Meaning in South Asia: The Shaping of Cities from Prehistoric to Precolonial Times* (Washington: National Gallery of Art, 1993).

Ssu-ma Ch'ien. *The Grand Scribe's Records, Vol. I: The Basic Annals of Pre-Han China*, ed. William H. Nienhauser, jr., trans. Tsai-fa Cheng, *et al* (Bloomington: Indiana University Press. 1994).

Stein, Burton. *Peasant State and Society in Medieval South India* (New Delhi: Oxford University Press, 1980).

Sullivan, Michael. *The Arts of China* (Berkeley: University of California Press, 1984).

Thapar, Romila. *Ancient Indian Social History* (New Delhi: Orient Longman, 1978).

——. *Asoka and the Decline of the Mauryas* (New Delhi: Oxford University Press, 1963).

——. *A History of India*, Vol. I (Baltimore, MD: Penguin Books, 1966).

——. *Interpreting Early India* (New York: Oxford University Press, 1992).

Tharu, Susie and K. Lalita, eds. *Women Writing in India 600 B.C. to the Present*, Vol. I (New York: The Feminist Press, 1991).

Tsunoda, Ryusaku, William Theodore deBary, and Donald Keene, comps. *Sources of Japanese Tradition* (New York: Columbia University Press, 1958).

Twitchett, Denis and Michael Lowe, eds. *The Cambridge History of China*, Vol. I: *The Ch'in and Han Empires, 221 B.C.-A.D. 220* (Cambridge: Cambridge University Press, 1986).

Twitchett, Denis, ed. *The Cambridge History of China*, Vol. III: *Sui and T'ang China, 589–906*, Part I (Cambridge: Cambridge University Press, 1979).

Warren, Henry Clarke. *Buddhism in Translations* (New York: Atheneum, 1963; first published Cambridge: Harvard University Press, 1896).

Weins, Herold J. *Han Expansion in South China* (N.P.: The Shoe String Press, 1967).

Zimmer, Heinrich. *Philosophies of India* (New York: Meridian Books, 1956).

JUDAISM AND CHRISTIANITY

600 B.C.E–1100 C.E

"Love your neighbor as yourself."

LEVITICUS 19:18, MATTHEW 19:19

"Love the Lord your God with all your heart, and with all your soul, and with all your might."

DEUTERONOMY 6:5, MARK 12:33

PEOPLES OF THE BIBLE: GOD'S EVOLUTION IN WEST ASIA AND EUROPE

JUDAISM

The story of Judaism begins some 3800 years ago with one man's vision of a single, unique God of all creation. God and Abraham sealed a covenant stating that Abraham's descendants would forever revere and worship that God, and God, in turn, would forever watch over and protect them. From then until now Judaism has remained a relatively small, family-based religion, focused in part in Israel, the land promised by God to Abraham, with branches throughout the world. Today there are only about 14 million Jews worldwide, but their role in world history has been disproportionate to their numbers.

The Jewish belief in one god, **monotheism**, was not simply a reduction in the number of gods from many to one. Historian–theologian Yehezkel Kaufmann explains that monotheism presented "a new religious category . . . of a God above nature, whose will is supreme, who is not subject to compulsion and fate,

who is free of the bonds of myth and magic" (p. 227). Into a world that believed in many gods who often fought with one another and interfered capriciously in human life, Abraham and his family introduced and perpetuated the concept of a single god whose rule was both orderly and just. (The Pharaoh Akhenaten in Egypt had proposed a single god [see Profile, p. 70], but later rulers obliterated his teachings and institutions.) In contrast with paganism's many gods of diverse temperaments, the new monotheism provided a much more definitive statement of right and wrong. At the same time it demanded much greater conformity in both faith and action, calling for adherence to a strict code of ethics within a community governed by laws proclaimed by God.

Although the number of Jews has always been small, many of Judaism's core beliefs were later incorporated into Christianity and Islam, the two great monotheistic faiths that have come to

JUDAISM AND CHRISTIANITY

DATE	POLITICAL/SOCIAL EVENTS	LITERARY/PHILOSOPHICAL EVENTS
1700 B.C.E.	• Abraham travels from Mesopotamia to Israel (c. 1750)	
1600 B.C.E.	• Hebrew slavery in Egypt	
1200 B.C.E.	• Moses (?1300–?1200) • Exodus from Egypt; legal codes formulated; return to Palestine; tribal government under Judges	
1000 B.C.E.	• Period of Kings begins with Saul, David, and Solomon • First temple in Jerusalem	
900 B.C.E	• Jewish kingdom divides into Israel and Judaea	
800 B.C.E.	• Prophets exhort Jewish nation (800–500) • Assyrians conquer Israel and exile Jews (721)	• Numbers (850–650) • Genesis (mid 8th century) • Prophets Isaiah, Amos, Micah
700 B.C.E.		• Josiah begins to write down Torah (640) • Deuteronomy (mid 7th century) • Leviticus (mid 7th century) • Jeremiah
600 B.C.E.	• Babylonians conquer Judaea, exile the people, and destroy the first temple (586) • Jews permitted to return to Judaea and rebuild the temple (538)	• Book of Job (600)
300 B.C.E.		• Books of TaNaKh (the Torah) edited and canonized
100 B.C.E	• Birth and death of Jesus (c. 4 B.C.E.–30 C.E.)	
10 C.E.	• Rome captures Jerusalem (63) • Christianity emerges from Judaism • St. Paul, Saul of Tarsus, organizes early Christianity (d. c. 67) • Rome destroys second temple (70)	• Gospels (70–100) • Acts (70–80) • Epistles of Paul (50–120)
100 C.E.	• Rome exiles Jews from Judaea; Jewish diaspora throughout Mediterranean basin and west Asia (135) • Rabbinical tradition developed (1st to 4th century)	

include half the world's population today. Judaism, however, has tenaciously maintained its own particular rituals and its own sense of family, setting it apart as a distinct religious community. We begin this chapter with a study of Judaism and then proceed to Christianity, which emerged from it, and challenged it. In the next chapter we explore Islam and the interactions among all three of these closely related, but often bitterly antagonistic, monotheistic religions.

EARLY JUDAISM: HOW DO WE KNOW?

Our knowledge of early Jewish history comes from the scriptures known collectively as the **TaNaKh**: Torah (the Five Books of Moses), Nevi'im (the Books of the Prophets), and Ketuvim (additional historical, poetic, and philosophic writings). Christians have incorporated the entire TaNaKh into their Bible, referring to these scriptures

JUDAISM AND CHRISTIANITY

DATE	POLITICAL/SOCIAL EVENTS	LITERARY/PHILOSOPHICAL EVENTS
200 C.E.	● Christians presecuted under Severus, Decius, and Diocletian	● Babylonian and Jerusalem Talmuds edited and published (200–500)
300 C.E.	● Christianity legalized (313) and then declared the official religion of the Roman Empire (392) ● Council of Nicea (325)	● Augustine's *The City of God* and *Confessions*
400 C.E.	● Council of Chalcedon (451)	
500 C.E.	● Monasticism in Europe ● Clovis converted to Christianity ● St. Benedict founds monastery of Monte Cassino	
600 C.E.	● England converted to Christianity	● Venerable Bede, Ecclesiastical *History of the English People*
700 C.E.	● Iconoclastic controversy	
800 C.E.	● Coronation of Charlemagne (800) ● St. Cyril and St. Methodius convert Russia, translate the Bible, and create the Cyrillic alphabet	● Einhard, *Life of Charlemagne*
900 C.E.	● Missionaries proliferate among the Vikings	
1000 C.E	● Christians capture Toledo from Muslim control and begin *reconquista* (1085) ● Split of Western and Eastern Christianity (1054) ● 1st Crusade (1095–9))	
1100 C.E.	● 2nd Crusade (1147–9) ● 3rd Crusade (1189–92)	
1200 C.E.	● 4th Crusade (1202–04) ● Children's Crusade (1212) ● Crusaders capture Constantinople (1204–61) ● 5th–8th Crusades (1218–91)	
1300 C.E.	● Monastic orders proliferate	
1400 C.E.	● Christians capture Granada, Spain, complete the *reconquista* (1492), expel Jews and Muslims	

collectively as the "Old Testament." Because the New Testament is written in Greek and the Old Testament in Hebrew, the TaNaKh is often referred to as the Hebrew Bible. For centuries, Jews and Christians believed that these earliest books of the Bible, which describe the creation of the world and the earliest history of the Jewish people, were the literal word of God. Some still hold to this belief, but during the past two centuries scholarship has undermined it and has given us a new

sense of the historical place of these books. Today historians ask: When and where were the books of the Hebrew Bible composed and how valid are they as historical documents?

Modern scholarly analysis of the TaNaKh texts became a prominent academic enterprise in Germany during the early nineteenth century. The founders of "biblical criticism" argued persuasively that the decision to begin to edit and write down the oral texts that had been passed from

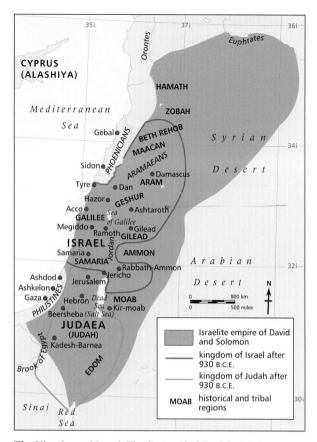

The Kingdom of Israel The first unified Jewish state in Palestine emerged around 980 B.C.E. under King David. He united the tribes of Israel during a period of decline among their more powerful neighbors—Egypt and the Hittites. After the death of his son Solomon (926 B.C.E.), tribal rivalries divided the empire into the kingdoms of Judah and Israel, but the sense of cultural unity survived.

Exodus, Leviticus, and Numbers. Together with Deuteronomy, these books formed the Torah or "Five Books of Moses."

With the ravages of time, older copies of the Torah, written in Hebrew on parchment scrolls, began to perish and new ones were copied out. The oldest existing Hebrew manuscripts of the entire Torah date only to the ninth to the eleventh centuries C.E., but fragments dating to as early as the second century B.C.E. have been discovered. Stored in caves near the Dead Sea in Israel, these Dead Sea Scrolls have been rediscovered only since 1947. Another very early edition of the Torah is a Greek translation from the Hebrew, the Septuagint. It was prepared for the Greek-speaking Jews of Egypt in the third and second centuries B.C.E. It still exists and is consistent with the Hebrew texts of our own time. In short, the written text of the Torah appears to have been preserved with great fidelity for at least 2600 years. The oral texts on which the written scriptures were based date back much further.

The narratives of the five books of the Torah abound with miracles, as God intervenes continuously in the history of the Jews. The Torah begins with God's creating the world and contracting his covenant with Abraham. Over the next several generations, the Torah continues, famine struck Canaan, the land God promised to Abraham. Abraham's grandson and his family traveled to the Nile valley of Egypt in search of food. At first invited by the Pharaoh to remain as permanent residents, they were later enslaved. After 400 years of slavery, about 1200 B.C.E., the Jews won their freedom and escaped from Egypt under the leadership of Moses through the miraculous intervention of God. During their journey back to Israel through the wilderness of the Sinai Desert, the contentious group of ex-slaves was forged into a small but militant nation. The Torah records a dramatic miracle at Mount Sinai in which God revealed a set of religious and civil laws for them to follow.

The Torah remains one of the greatest examples of mythistory. Its stories are not necessarily to be read as literal, historical records, but their version of events gave birth to the Jewish people's concept of itself and helped to define its character and principal beliefs. The mythological stories of the Torah tell us what the Jewish people, and especially its literate leadership, have thought important about their own origins and mission. They also define images of God that have profoundly influenced the imagination and action of Jews, Christians, and Muslims for millennia.

generation to generation was made by Josiah, the king of the Jewish state of Judah (r. 640–609 B.C.E.). The story of Josiah's reign is told in the biblical book of II Kings, chapters 20–21. Struggling to survive in the face of the powerful Assyrian Empire, Josiah was anxious to promote allegiance to the state and its religion. He centralized Jewish worship in the national temple in Jerusalem and collected and transcribed the most important texts of his people. Josiah regarded adherence to the laws laid down in these scriptures as fundamental to the maintenance of the Jewish religion, the Jewish people, and his own Jewish kingdom. From existing literary fragments, folk wisdom, and oral history he had the book of Deuteronomy, the fifth book of the TaNaKh, written down. Soon, additional literary materials from at least three other major interpretive traditions were also woven together to create the books of Genesis,

ESSENTIAL BELIEFS OF JUDAISM IN EARLY SCRIPTURES

The Torah fixes many of the essential beliefs and principles of Judaism:

- A single caring God, demanding obedience, who administers rewards and punishments fairly and in accordance with his fixed laws:

  Hear, O Israel, the Lord is our God, the Lord alone. You shall love the Lord your God with all your heart, and with all your soul, and with all your might. (Deuteronomy 6:4–5)

  Know therefore that the Lord your God is God, the faithful God who maintains covenant loyalty with those who love him and keep his commandments, to a thousand generations, and who repays in their own person those who reject him. (Deuteronomy VII:9–10)

- A God of history, whose power affects the destiny of individuals and nations:

  I am the Lord your God who brought you out of Egypt, out of the land of slavery. (Exodus 20:2–3)

- A community rooted in a divinely chosen family and ethnic group:

  Now the Lord said to Abram, "Go from your country and your kindred and your father's house to the land that I will show you. I will make of you a great nation, and I will bless you, and make your name great, so that you will be a blessing." (Genesis 12:1–2)

Dead Sea Scrolls, Isaiah scroll 1Q Is. 9 verses 58.6–63.4. The five hundred or so documents that make up the Dead Sea Scrolls— which date between about 250 B.C.E. and 70 C.E.—appear at one time to have formed the library of a Jewish community. As well as providing evidence of the accuracy of Hebrew biblical texts, they give information about the life of the community itself. (*Israel Museum, Jerusalem*)

- A specific, "promised," geographical homeland:

  When Abraham reached Canaan, God said to him: "Raise your eyes now, and look from the place where you are, northward and southward and eastward and westward; for all the land that you see I will give to you and to your offspring forever." (Genesis 13:14–15)

- A legal system to guide proper behavior: religious, familial, sexual, commercial, civic, ethical, and ritual. The introduction to this code was the Ten Commandments, revered as the heart of the revelation to Moses at Mount Sinai (see p. 323).

To ground the mystical beliefs and forge the Jewish people into a "kingdom of priests and a sacred nation," rules issued in the name of God forbade intermarriage with outsiders; prohibited eating animals which do not have cloven hooves and chew their cud, and fish which do not have scales and fins (Deuteronomy 14 and Leviticus 11); and centralized worship in the hands of a priestly aristocracy. Animal sacrifices were to be offered, but only by the hereditary priests and only in a single national temple in Jerusalem.

The Jewish Calendar

Jewish religious leaders reconstituted earlier pagan nature celebrations into a calendar of national religious celebration. A spring festival of renewal was incorporated into Passover, the commemoration of the exodus from Egypt; an early summer festival of first harvest was subsumed into Shavuot, a rejoicing in the revelation of the Ten Commandments at Sinai; and an early fall harvest festival became part of Sukkot (Succoth), a remembrance of the years of wandering in the desert. All these festivals were to be celebrated, if possible, by pilgrimage to the central, national temple in Jerusalem. Celebrations of nature, history, and national identity were fused together.

SOURCE
The Ten Commandments

I am the Lord your God who brought you out of Egypt, out of the house of slavery.
You shall have no other gods before me.
You shall not make for yourself an idol, whether in the form of anything that is in heaven above, or that is on the earth beneath, or that is in the water under the earth.
You shall not bow down to them or worship them; for I the Lord your God am a jealous god, punishing children for the iniquity of parents, to the third and fourth generation of those who reject me, but showing steadfast love to the thousandth generation of those who love me and keep my commandments.
You shall not make wrongful use of the name of the Lord your God, for the Lord will not acquit anyone who misuses his name.
Remember the sabbath day, and keep it holy. Six days you shall labor and do all your work. But the seventh day is a sabbath to the Lord your God; you shall not do any work—you, your son or your daughter, your male or female slave, your livestock, or the alien resident in your towns. For in six days the Lord made heaven and earth, the sea, and all that is in them, but rested the seventh day; therefore the Lord blessed the sabbath day and consecrated it.
Honor your father and your mother, so that your days may be long in the land that the Lord your God is giving you.
You shall not murder.
You shall not commit adultery.
You shall not steal.
You shall not bear false witness against your neighbor.
You shall not covet your neighbor's house; you shall not covet your neighbor's wife, or male or female slave, or ox, or donkey, or anything that belongs to your neighbor.

(Exodus 20:2–17; see also Deuteronomy 5)

Moses, mosaic in San Vitale, Ravenna, Italy, sixth century C.E. After he had led the Israelite slaves out of Egypt by the miracle of parting the Red Sea (see picture, p. 302), Moses ascended Mount Sinai. There he received from God the Torah, or sacred teachings, beginning with the two tablets of the Ten Commandments. He led his quarrelsome people across the Sinai desert but died at the border of the promised land.

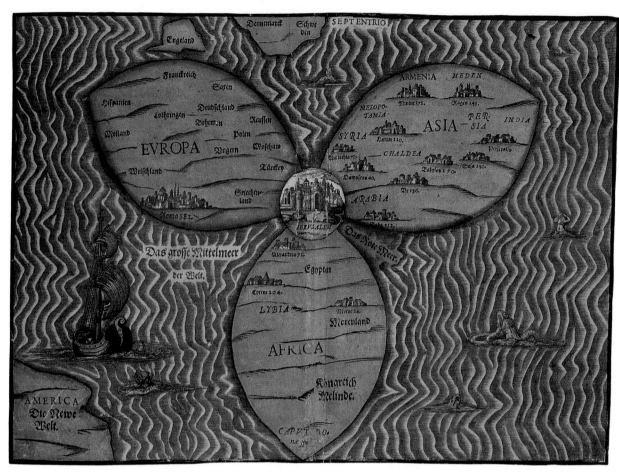

Map of the world by Heinrich Bunting, 1585. Many peoples believed that their capital city was the cosmo-magical axis of the universe (see pp. 48 and 92). This map, shaped like a clover leaf, places Jerusalem at the center, uniting Africa, Asia, and Europe.

THE EVOLUTION OF GOD

The Torah portrays God as an evolving moral force in dialogue with humans. In God's early interactions with humans, his nature is still malleable. Disgusted at human disobedience, he destroys almost all humankind through a flood, but he then pledges never to be so destructive again, creating a rainbow as a kind of treaty of peace with humanity (Genesis 6–8). Still fearful of the collective power of humanity, God confounds their inter-communication by dividing them into separate language groups at the Tower of Babel (Genesis 11). While deciding the fate of the sinful cities of Sodom and Gommorah, God listens to Abraham's plea for the defense: "Far be it from thee to do this—to kill good and bad together; for then the good would suffer with the bad. Far be it from thee. Shall not the judge of all the earth do what is just?" (Genesis 18–19). God apparently bans child sacrifice when he stops Abraham from killing his son Isaac. (The Muslim Quran reports this to be Abraham's son Ishmael; see p. 336.)

When asked by Moses to identify himself by name, God replies enigmatically and powerfully, "I am who I am" (Exodus III:14). The Hebrew designation for God's name is YHWH, "Being." Because Jews have regarded this name as too sacred to pronounce, only the consonants are written; the vowels are unknown. English-speaking readers have usually rendered it either Jehovah or Yahweh. Slowly, God becomes more secure in his own power and more available to dialogue with humans.

In Jewish theology, God is almighty but still accessible through prayer and even through dialogue. Indeed, humans and God come to understand each other by arguing with one another in a process that the contemporary rabbi Arthur Waskow has called "Godwrestling." If Jews are to be God's people and to follow his will, he, in turn, is expected to be a compassionate and attentive ruler. This view challenged the pagan beliefs in self-

Beliefs of Other Contemporary Peoples

Recent academic findings of the past 150 years situate Jewish core beliefs in the geography of the Fertile Crescent. For example, as we know from earlier chapters, some of the pharaohs, notably Amenhotep IV, known also as Akhenaten (see Profile, p. 70), who ruled Egypt at just about the time that the Torah places the Jewish captivity there, also proclaimed a belief in one god:

O sole god, like whom there is no other!
Thou didst create the world according to thy desire,
Whilst thou wert alone:
All men, cattle, and wild beasts,
Whatever is on earth, going upon (its) feet,

And what is on high, flying with its wings.

(Pritchard, p. 370)

And, as we read in Chapter 2, Hammurabi of Mesopotamia had already issued a law code in the name of his god, Shamash, by the year 1750 B.C.E., 500 years before the Torah reported that Moses received the Ten Commandments and the beginnings of the Jewish code of law. These historic precedents must have inspired many of the early Jewish beliefs and practices. Through the centuries, however, the beliefs of Akhenaten and the legal system of Hammurabi were lost, even within their own nations, while Jews kept themselves and their beliefs alive.

willed gods, but it left Judaism with no strong answer to the eternal problem of evil in the universe: "If there is a single God, and if he is good, why do the wicked prosper and the righteous suffer?" One biblical response is found in the Book of Job (c. 600 B.C.E.). To the questions of the innocent, suffering Job, God finally responds with overwhelming power:

Who is this whose ignorant words cloud my design
in darkness?
Brace yourself and stand up like a man; I will ask
the questions, and you shall answer.
Where were you when I laid the earth's
foundations?
Tell me, if you know and understand.
Who settled its dimensions? Surely you should
know. . . .
Is it for a man who disputes with the Almighty to be
stubborn?
Should he that argues with God answer back?
(Job 38:2–5; 40:2)

But while God lectures Job for his brashness in questioning his authority and power, he understands Job's anguish at the apparent injustice in the world and ultimately rewards Job with health, a restored family, and abundance for his honesty in raising his questions.

THE LATER BOOKS OF JEWISH SCRIPTURE

The later volumes of the TaNaKh, the books of Nevi'im and Ketuvim, carry the history of the Jewish people to about the fifth century B.C.E. God continues as a constant presence in these narratives, but he intervenes less openly and less frequently. These later records can generally be cross-checked against the archaeology of the region and the history of neighboring peoples, and they seem generally consistent.

These volumes continue the history from about the year 1200 B.C.E., as the Jews returned to Canaan, or Israel, the land promised to them, and made it their home. The biblical account in the Book of Joshua tells of continuous, violent, political and religious warfare between the invading Jews and the resident Canaanite peoples. Modern scholarship suggests, however, that re-entry into the land of Israel was a gradual process, with fewer, more localized battles, and considerably more cultural borrowing among all the groups in the region.

Arriving in Canaan, the Jews first organized themselves in a loose tribal confederacy led by a series of "Judges," ad hoc leaders who took command at critical periods, especially at times of war. Later, despite warnings that a monarchy would lead to increased warfare, profligate leaders,

Crossing the Red Sea, *c.* 245 C.E. **Fresco from the synagogue at Dura Europos**. The Old Testament tells of God's miraculous intervention in helping Moses and the people of Israel escape enslavement in Egypt. Hotly pursued by Pharaoh's soldiers to the banks of the Red Sea, Moses saw the waves draw back in front of him to allow the Jews to pass. When the Egyptians tried to follow, the sea engulfed them and they were drowned. (*National Archaeological Museum, Damascus, Syria*)

extortionate taxes, and the impressment of young men and women into royal service, the Jews anointed a king. For three generations, strong kings, Saul, David, and Solomon (*c.* 1020–950 B.C.E.), ruled and expanded the geographic base of the people. They established a firm national center in Jerusalem, where they united political and religious power by building both palace and temple, exalting both king and priest. The earlier warnings against royal excesses, however, proved correct. Unable to sustain Solomon's legendary extravagances in expenditures and in relationships with 700 wives, many of them foreign princesses, and 300 concubines, the kingdom split in two.

THE TEACHINGS OF THE PROPHETS: MORALITY AND HOPE

Continuing despotism by their kings and greed on the part of their wealthier citizens ripped apart the social fabric of the two splinter kingdoms of Judah and Israel. A group of prophets emerged, demanding reform. In powerful and sublime language these men called for a reinstitution of justice, compassion, and ethics. They introduced permanently into the conscience of mankind their voices, speaking in the name of God and of the people against the hypocritical misuse of religious and political power. The prophet Isaiah, in the eighth century B.C.E., led the charge:

> When you stretch out your hands, I will hide my
> eyes from you;
> even though you make many prayers, I will not
> listen;
> your hands are full of blood.
> Wash yourselves; make yourselves clean;
> remove the evil of your doings
> from before my eyes;
> cease to do evil,
> learn to do good;
> seek justice,

rescue the oppressed,
defend the orphan,
plead for the widow. (Isaiah 1:15–17)

At about the same time, Amos was equally severe and equally eloquent in confronting the northern kingdom of Israel just before its destruction:

You that turn justice upside down and bring righteousness to the ground! . . .
you that hate a man who brings the wrongdoer to court
and loathe him who speaks the whole truth:
for all this, because you levy taxes on the poor and extort a tribute of grain from them,
Though you have built houses of hewn stone, you shall not live in them, though you have planted pleasant vineyards, you shall not drink wine from them. . . .
Hate evil and love good; enthrone justice in the courts. (Amos 5:7–15)

A century later, Jeremiah continued in the same spirit of moral outrage, rebuking the rulers and people of Judah, the remaining southern kingdom:

You keep saying, "This place is the temple of the Lord, the temple of the Lord, the temple of the Lord!" This catchword of yours is a lie; put no trust in it. Mend your ways and your doings, deal fairly with one another, do not oppress the alien, the orphan, and the widow, shed no innocent blood in this place, do not run after other gods to your own ruin. (Jeremiah 7: 4–6; Oxford New English Bible translation)

So even at the time that Israel and Judah developed powerful kingdoms, ironically, the prophets remembered that the beginnings of the Jewish people were in slavery and that a significant part of its mission was to identify with and help the downtrodden. As power and excess multiplied, they echoed the words of Deuteronomy 16:20: "Justice, and only justice, you shall pursue, so that you may live and occupy the land that the Lord your God is giving you." When destruction came, the prophets interpreted it as punishment not *of* their God, as earlier peoples had often done, but *by* their God. Destruction of a corrupt nation indicated not the weakness of its God, but his ethical consistency.

Finally, the prophets not only harangued, blamed, and condemned, they also held up visions of a future to inspire their listeners. They saw God transforming human history. He offered rewards as well as punishments. He offered hope. Micah's prophecy, also in the eighth century B.C.E., is one of the most exalted, and perhaps utopian:

JEWISH FESTIVALS AND FAST DAYS

Hebrew date	Gregorian date	Name of festival
1–2 Tishri	Sept–Oct	Rosh Hashana (New Year)
10 Tishri	Sept–Oct	Yom Kippur (Day of Atonement)
15–21 Tishri	Sept–Oct	Sukkot (Feast of the Tabernacles)
22 Tishri	Sept–Oct	Shemini Atzeret (8th Day of the Solemn Assembly
23 Tishri	Sept–Oct	Simchat Torah (Rejoicing of the Law)
25 Kislev–2–3 Tevet	Nov–Dec	Hannukah (Feast of Dedication)
14–15 Adar	Feb–Mar	Purim (Feast of Lots)
14–20 Nisan	Mar–Apr	Pesach (Passover)
5 Iyar	Apr–May	Israel Independence Day
6–7 Sivan	May–Jun	Shavuot (Feast of Weeks)
9 Av	Jul–Aug	Tisha be–Av (Fast of 9th Av)

For out of Zion shall go forth instruction, and the word of the Lord from Jerusalem.

He shall judge between many peoples, and shall arbitrate between strong nations far away; they shall beat their swords into plowshares, and their spears into pruning hooks; nation shall not lift up sword against nation, neither shall they learn war any more;

but they shall all sit under their own vines and under their own fig trees, and no one shall make them afraid; for the mouth of the Lord of hosts has spoken. (Micah 4:1–4)

Micah closed with a vision of great Jewish religious commitment, balanced by equally great tolerance for the diversity of others:

For all the peoples walk each in the name of its god, but we will walk in the name of the Lord our God forever and ever. (Micah 4: 5)

Gender Relations

The God of the Hebrew Bible is male and alone. His words establish a patriarchal society through Abraham and his descendants. The Torah grants women fewer civil and religious rights (and obligations) than men. They are regarded as ritually unclean each month at times of menstruation and in childbirth. Men may be ritually unclean as a result of wet dreams or sexual diseases (Leviticus 15), but these occur with less regularity. The regulation of sexuality is a fundamental issue in Jewish law, as it is in most religions. Marriage is regarded as the norm, with a strong emphasis on bearing children. Homosexual behavior is strongly rejected. (Today, however, some branches of Judaism have revised gender rules and discarded prohibitions on homosexuality.)

A few women are credited with heroic roles. Sarah, Abraham's wife, forced him to choose her son as his proper successor, and gained God's approval (Genesis 16). Deborah led Israel in peace and war, during the period of conquering the land of Israel (Judges 4–5). Ruth, a convert, taught the importance of openness to the outside world, and became an ancestor of King David and, therefore, in Christian belief, of Jesus (Book of Ruth). Esther, in the Persian diaspora, was married to the king and used her position to block the attempts of a court minister to kill the Jews of the Persian Empire (Book of Esther). Although none of these stories can be authenticated externally, nor dated exactly, they speak to the significance of individual, exceptional women at turning points in Jewish history, and in the collective mind of the Jewish people.

DEFEAT, EXILE, AND REDEFINITION

Jews represent both an ethnic community and a universal religion. This dual identity became especially clear as Jews were exiled by foreign conquest out of the land of Israel as part of a plan to encourage their assimilation and to open up the land of Canaan to foreign immigration. First, the northern kingdom of Israel was exiled by Sennacherib of Assyria in 721 B.C.E. These exiles drifted into assimilation and were subsequently referred to as the "Lost Ten Tribes of Israel." In 586 B.C.E., the temple in Jerusalem was destroyed, and thousands of Jews from the southern kingdom of Judah were exiled to Babylon, but this group remained loyal to its unique identity as a separate community, remembering its homeland:

By the rivers of Babylon—there we sat down and wept when we remembered Zion. . . .
Our captors asked us for songs: "Sing us one of the songs of Zion!"
How could we sing the Lord's song in a foreign land?
If I forget you, O Jerusalem, let my right hand wither!
Let my tongue cling to the roof of my mouth if I do not remember you, if I do not set Jerusalem above my highest joy. (Psalm 137)

When they were permitted to return to Judaea some sixty years later, many Jews left Babylonia, returned to Judaea, rebuilt their temple and reconstructed national life. But many did not. Those who stayed behind did not assimilate into the Babylonian culture, however. They reconstituted their religion, replacing the sacrificial services of the temple with meditation and prayers offered privately or in synagogues. They substituted teachers and rabbis, positions earned through study and piety, for the hereditary priesthood. In academies at Sura and Pumbeditha, towns adjacent to Babylon, rabbis continued the study of the Torah. They interpreted and edited Jewish law based on its teachings, and they elaborated stories and myths, which often conveyed moral principles. The multivolumed recording of their proceedings, the Babylonian Talmud, was completed about 500 C.E.

So distinguished was the scholarship of Babylonia, that this Talmud was considered superior in coverage and scholarship to the Jerusalem Talmud that was produced at about the same time in academies in Israel.

For several centuries Jews lived in substantial numbers both in Israel and in the diaspora. A census of the Roman Empire undertaken by the Emperor Claudius in 48 C.E. showed 5,984,072 Jews. This figure suggests a total global Jewish population of about 8 million (Baron, pp. 170 and 372, n. 7). At the time, the population of the Roman Empire was perhaps 60 million, and that of the Afro-Eurasian world about 170 million. Most Jews outside Israel seemed to have continued to look to Jerusalem as a spiritual center, and they sent funds to support the temple until its second destruction by the Romans in 70 C.E. The Roman philosopher Seneca (4 B.C.E.–65 C.E.), resentful of the Jewish presence, exaggerated their power: "The customs of this accursed race have gained such influence that they are now received throughout all the world. The vanquished have given laws to their victors" (*De superstitione*, cited in Crossan, p. 418).

The second (Herod's) temple (model), 20 B.C.E. The temple at Jerusalem was originally built in the tenth century B.C.E. by King Solomon as a symbol of national unity and as a religious pilgrimage center. Razed by the Babylonians in 586 B.C.E., it was rebuilt sixty years later. It was finally destroyed by the Romans in 70 C.E. as part of the campaign to crush Jewish rebellion.

Jews were driven out of their promised land into exile several times: by the Assyrians in 721 B.C.E., by the Babylonians in 586 B.C.E., and, following anti-imperial revolts, by the Romans in 135 C.E. In addition, many Jews traveled willingly, by free choice, throughout the trade and cultural networks that had been established by the Persians in the sixth century B.C.E., enhanced by Alexander the Great in the fourth century B.C.E., and extended by the Roman Empire.

The Roman exile of 135 C.E., however, fundamentally and permanently altered Jewish existence. It removed all but a few Jews from their political homeland until the twentieth century. This final exile established the principal contours of Jewish diaspora existence from then on: life as a minority group; dispersed among various peoples of the entire world; with distinct religious and social practices; united in reverence for sacred texts and their teachings; usually dependent on the widely varying policies of the peoples among whom they lived; and sometimes forced to choose between religious conversion, emigration, or death. Jews preserved their cohesion through their acceptance of the authority of the TaNaKh and the importance of studying it, and their persistence in seeing themselves as a special kind of family even in dispersion.

MINORITY–MAJORITY RELATIONS IN THE DIASPORA

In general, Jews remained socially and religiously distinct wherever they traveled. This identification was imposed partially from the outside by others, partially by internal discipline and loyalty to the group, its traditions, and laws. Jewish history becomes a case study also of tolerance and intolerance of minorities by majority peoples around the world. The Book of Esther, written about (and probably during) the Persian diaspora, 638–333 B.C.E., captures the vulnerability of minority existence. A royal minister sees his chance to advance his career and profit and argues to the king:

> There is a certain people, dispersed among the many peoples in all the provinces of your kingdom, who

Menorah procession, Arch of Titus, Rome, c. 81 C.E. The Romans put down the Jewish revolt of 70 C.E. by recapturing Jerusalem, destroying the temple, and looting its sacred objects. This relief from Emperor Titus' triumphal arch shows Roman soldiers with the temple *menorah*, a seven-branched candelabrum, which today serves as an official emblem of the state of Israel.

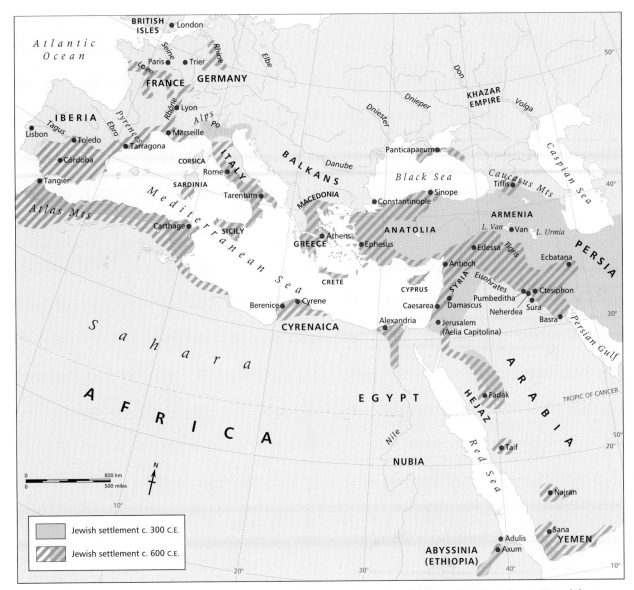

The Jewish diaspora Following the Jewish Revolt in 66 C.E., the Roman destruction of the temple in Jerusalem in 70, and the defeat of the Bar-Cochba revolt in 135, the Roman government expelled the Jews from Judaea. These migrations spread Judaism north into Mesopotamia and Anatolia, followed trade routes throughout the Mediterranean and the Red Sea, and eventually resulted in Jewish communities being established as far afield as northwest Europe and Ethiopia.

keep themselves apart. Their laws are different from those of every other people; they do not keep your majesty's laws. It does not befit your majesty to tolerate them. If it please your majesty, let an order be made in writing for their destruction; and I will pay ten thousand talents of silver to your majesty's officials, to be deposited in the royal treasury. (Esther 3:8–9; Oxford New English Bible)

The king accedes: "The money and the people are yours; deal with them as you wish" (Esther 3:11; Oxford translation). A pattern of official xeno-

phobia and greed, repeated frequently in Jewish history—and in the history of many minorities—is captured in biblical literature.

There were many contrary examples, however. Jewish life in the diaspora survived and often flourished. For example, Rabbi Benjamin of Tudela, Spain, visited Muslim Baghdad in 1160–70 C.E. and reported: "In Baghdad there are about 40,000 Jews, and they dwell in security, prosperity, and honor under the great Caliph, and amongst them are great sages, the heads of Academies engaged in the study of the law. In this city there are ten Academies . . .

and twenty-eight Jewish synagogues" (cited in Andrea and Overfield, pp. 248–9).

CHRISTIANITY EMERGES FROM JUDAISM

At about the time of the destruction of the temple in 70 C.E., a splinter group within the Jewish people was forming around the person and teachings of Jesus of Nazareth. Disdained by segments of the Jewish religious establishment as a heretic and feared by the Roman imperialists as a potential revolutionary, Jesus was exalted by his followers as one specially chosen and anointed by God (*Messiah* in Hebrew, *Christos* in Greek). Jesus said that he had come not to abolish the Jewish law but to fulfill it. His followers ultimately accepted much of the moral core of Jewish teachings but rejected most parts of its legal and separatist covenant. They proclaimed Jesus to be the source of eternal life and accepted him as a miracle-worker and the son of God. Beginning with the early missionary activities of St Paul, they built an entirely new organizational structure and spread the new faith of Christianity among one-third of humankind.

CHRISTIANITY

Jesus Christ (*c.* 4 B.C.E.–*c.* 30 C.E.), the founder of Christianity, was born to an unmarried Jewish woman and her carpenter fiancé in a manger in Bethlehem, 10 miles (16 kilometers) from Jerusalem, some 2000 years ago. Jesus grew into an astonishingly powerful preacher, who promised eternal life and happiness to the poor and downtrodden people of colonial Judaea if only they would keep their faith in God. As Jesus' fame spread, and came to include a reputation for curing the blind and lame, and even raising the dead, the Jewish religious authorities and the Roman colonial administrators feared his attacks on their establishments. To prevent any potential rebellion, the Roman government crucified him when he was thirty-three years old.

But death did not stop Jesus' message. His disciples, and especially Paul, a newcomer to the faith who was converted through a miraculous encounter with the dead Jesus, took his message of compassion, salvation, and eternal life to Rome. Although Jesus had avoided the question during his life, his followers now claimed that he was indeed the son of God, born to his mother Mary through a virgin birth. The upper classes of proud

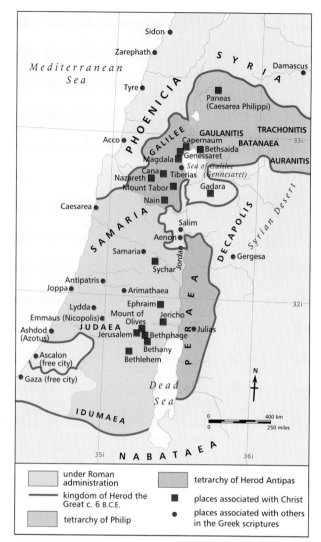

Palestine at the time of Jesus Christianity first emerged as a sect within Judaism when Roman control of Palestine was increasing. Shortly before Jesus' birth, Rome had granted Herod the Great the Kingdom of Judaea as a client ruler. Upon his death in 4 B.C.E. the kingdom was divided among his sons, and Judaea itself came under direct Roman military rule.

Rome scoffed at first, but more and more of the simple people believed. Despite early persecution, Christianity increased in influence, until it became the official religion of the empire. Spread through the networks of the empire, it ultimately became the most important organizing force in post-Roman Europe. The message of compassion and exultation and the organization of the church expanded throughout the world. Today almost 2 billion people, one-third of the world's population, spread among numerous different churches and denominations, declare themselves followers of this son of God, the simple preacher from Judaea.

MYTHISTORY:
HOW DO WE KNOW?

The search for the historical Jesus has become something of a scholarly industry:

> Historical Jesus research is becoming something of a scholarly bad joke . . . There is Jesus as a political revolutionary by S.G.F. Brandon (1967), as a magician by Morton Smith (1978), as a Galilean charismatic by Geza Vermes (1981, 1984), as a Galilean rabbi by Bruce Chilton (1984), as a Hillelite or proto-Pharisee by Harvey Falk (1985), as an Essene by Harvey Falk (1985), as an eschatological prophet by E.P. Sanders (1985).
> (Crossan, p. xxvii–xxviii)

And as a prophet, exorcist, miracleworker, and marginal Jew by J.P. Meier (1991). It remains inconclusive because the only records of Jesus' life are the four gospels, "the good news accounts," of the New Testament, and they are neither unbiased nor contemporary. These four books are the opening segment of the New Testament, the second section of the Christian Bible, which recounts the life, teachings, and disciples of Jesus. Mark, probably the oldest of the four gospels, dates to 70 C.E., forty years after Jesus' death. Like the later gospels attributed to Matthew, Luke, and John, Mark assembles a collection of traditions about Jesus as they were transmitted among his followers. Despite the gospels' accounts of Jesus' multitudes of followers, he is not discussed in either Roman or Jewish records of the time.

External histories do indicate, however, that Jesus' times were turbulent and difficult. Judaea was a colony of the Roman Empire, taxed heavily and suppressed economically and politically. Jesus' nation, the Jewish people, was divided into at least four conflicting groups. The largest of these groups, the Pharisees, identified with the masses of the population, resented the Roman occupation, and sought comfort in keeping alive and re-interpreting Jewish religious traditions. The Jesus of the gospels wanted much more rapid and radical religious reform and frequently referred to the Pharisees as hypocrites. The more elite Sadducees, the temple priesthood and their allies, had become servants of the Roman state and preached accommodation with it. A much smaller, militant group of Zealots sought, quixotically, to drive out the Romans through violence. A fourth, still smaller group, the Essenes, lived a prayerful existence by the shores of the Dead Sea and preached the imminent end of the world as they knew it. Predictions of a radical reversal of fortune had also been common among the Jewish prophets centuries before, and Jesus' emphasis on the coming of the kingdom of God resonated strongly with these beliefs in a coming apocalypse.

JESUS' LIFE, TEACHINGS, AND DISCIPLES

According to the four gospels, which were written about 70–100 C.E., Jesus' life and message inspired a core of devoted disciples who embraced his concern for the poor and downtrodden and believed that he had accomplished miracles in feeding the multitudes, curing the sick, and even restoring the dead to life. They believed Jesus to be at least in part divine, the son of God, born miraculously through Mary, a virgin betrothed to Joseph, a carpenter from Nazareth. When asked, Jesus did not contradict their assumptions about his identity. After Jesus' death, his followers believed that he had arisen from the grave and ascended to heaven to join God. Their belief contained equal measures of admiration for his message of compassion and salvation and for his ability to perform miracles.

The four gospels present only a sketch of Jesus' life. They chart more fully his teachings and his charismatic power over his disciples, the men and women who created the religious community of Christianity. Despite conventional dating, Jesus must have been born no later than 4 B.C.E., for Herod, king at the time of his birth, died in that year. Jesus' family had been living in Galilee, where his father was an artisan. Taken to Jerusalem when he was twelve years old, Jesus asked precocious and disturbing questions of the temple priests. In Galilee, the beautiful and lush northern region of Judaea, only recently converted to Judaism, he continued his unorthodox search for truth. Toward the end of his life, perhaps frustrated by a lack of success at home, he turned his attentions to Jerusalem, the religious heartland of Judaea. There he continued his preaching, angering both the Jewish religious establishment, which viewed him as a heretic, and the Roman imperial government, which feared his rabble-rousing. The Roman governor of Judaea, Pontius Pilate, had Jesus crucified to avoid possible rebellion.

The Sermon on the Mount: The Beatitudes

Jesus' teaching, powerful in direct address, in parable, and in allegory, established his identification with the poor and oppressed, his disdain for the Roman authorities, and his scorn for the Jewish religious leadership of his time. He sounded much like a latterday Jewish prophet calling his people to reform. The Beatitudes, a list of promises of God's rewards for the simple, righteous people, the first of Jesus' great sermons recorded in the New Testament, was delivered from the top of a hill in Galilee.

Blessed are the poor in spirit, for theirs is the kingdom of heaven.
Blessed are those who mourn, for they will be comforted.
Blessed are the meek, for they will inherit the earth.
Blessed are those who hunger and thirst for righteousness, for they will be filled.
Blessed are the merciful, for they will receive mercy.
Blessed are the poor in heart, for they will see God.
Blessed are the peacemakers, for they will be called children of God.
Blessed are those who are persecuted for righteousness' sake, for theirs is the kingdom of heaven. (Matthew 5:3–10).

He promised that religious sincerity would be rewarded:

Ask, and it will be given you; search, and you will find; knock, and the door will be opened for you. For everyone who asks receives, and everyone who searches finds, and for everyone who knocks, the door will be opened. (Matthew 7:7–8).

He prescribed a form of prayer:

Pray then in this way:
Our Father in heaven, hallowed be your name. Your kingdom come. Your will be done, on earth as it is in heaven.
    Give us this day our daily bread.
    And forgive us our debts, as we also have forgiven our debtors.
    And do not bring us to the time of trial, but rescue us from the evil one. (Here biblical accounts differ, some adding: "For the kingdom, and the power, and the glory are yours forever. Amen.") (Matthew 6:9–13)

Adapting Rituals and Philosophies

Jesus' form of prayer and the Beatitudes that he preached (see Source above) were fully in accord with Jewish tradition, but baptism was marginal to Judaism. By accepting baptism from the desert preacher John the Baptist, Jesus prepared the way for adapting an existing practice and giving it new meaning for his followers. A minor practice within Judaism, baptism would later become in Christianity the central sacrament of purification enjoined on all members. As we have seen, newly forming religions often adapt rituals and philosophies from already existing religions, as, for example Buddhism adapted the concept of dharma from Hinduism, and both Buddhists and Jains employed Hindu priests. This borrowing and adaptation can be attractive to members of the existing religion who wish to join the new one, for it assures them that their spiritual customs will be maintained. At the same time, a new interpretation gives the ritual a new meaning for the new faith. At his "last supper," a Passover ritual meal, Jesus had eaten unleavened, flat bread as a symbol of slavery in Egypt, and he had drunk wine that accompanies all Jewish festivals as a symbol of joy. He offered the bread and wine also to his disciples, with the words, "This is my body … this is my blood." Thus he introduced the **Eucharist**, or Holy Communion, a central sacrament, a mystery through which the invisible Christ grants communion to those who believe in him.

In his teachings, Jesus also addressed political and social issues, staking out his own often ambiguous positions in relationship to the contesting philosophies of the day. When Jesus, following John, taught, "Repent; for the kingdom of heaven has come near" (Matthew 4:17), he was not explicit in describing that kingdom or its date of arrival. But in metaphor and parable he preached that life as we know it on earth would soon change dramatically, or even come to an end. His advice was not for a middle-class, bourgeois audience planning carefully for the future:

Therefore I tell you, do not worry about your life, what you will eat or what you will drink, or about your body, what you will wear. Is not life more than food, and the body more than clothing? Look at the birds of the air; they neither sow nor reap nor gather into barns, and yet your heavenly Father feeds them. Are you not of more value than they? And can any of you by worrying add a single hour to your span of life? And why do you worry about clothing? Consider the lilies of the field, how they grow; they neither toil nor spin,

Silver crucifix from Birka, Sweden, *c.* **900** C.E. The cross—signifying Christ's crucifixion—was adopted by Christians as a symbol of their faith as early as the second century. Making "the sign of the cross" was believed powerful in warding off evil, and, in later centuries, crusaders were said to "take the cross" when they set off on crusade (a word itself derived from the Latin for cross, *crux*). (*Historiska Museet, Stockholm*)

yet I tell you, even Solomon in all his glory
was not clothed like one of these.
(Matthew 6:25–9)

Jesus' words must have been especially welcome to
the poor, as he spoke repeatedly of the "Kingdom
of Heaven" in which the tables would be turned:

It will be hard for a rich person to enter the kingdom
of heaven. Again I tell you, it is easier for a camel to
go through the eye of a needle than for someone
who is rich to enter the kingdom of God.
(Matthew 19:23–4)

In that Kingdom, Jesus promised much to his
devoted followers:

At the renewal of all things, when the Son of Man is
seated on the throne of his glory, you who have
followed me will also sit on twelve thrones, judging
the twelve tribes of Israel. And everyone who has
left houses or brothers or sisters or father or mother
or children or fields, for my name's sake, will receive
a hundredfold, and will inherit eternal life.
(Matthew 19:28–9)

The apocalypse would be violent. Jesus had
declared that the most important commandment

The four evangelists, from the *Gospel Book of Charlemagne*, early ninth century. With the exception of the cross, the best-known symbols in early Christianity were associated with the four gospels. Based on a text in the Book of Revelation (4:7), Matthew was represented by a man, Mark by a lion, Luke by a winged ox, and John by an eagle. (*Cathedral Treasury, Aachen, Germany*)

was to "Love the Lord your God with all your heart, and with all your soul, and with all your mind," and the second was "Love your neighbor as yourself," both directly cited from the TaNaKh, Deuteronomy 6:7 and Leviticus 19:18. Indeed he had carried these principles to new dimensions, declaring "Love your enemies and pray for your persecutors" (Matthew 5:44). But he also proclaimed a very contrary battle cry: "He that is not with me is against me" (Matthew 12:30):

> Do not think that I have come to bring peace to earth; I have not come to bring peace, but a sword. I have come to set a man against his father, and a daughter against her mother, and a daughter-in-law against her mother-in-law; and one's foes will be members of one's own household.
> (Matthew 10: 34–6)

He reversed Isaiah's prophecy of a world at peace:

> Nation will make war against nation, kingdom upon kingdom; there will be famines and earthquakes in many places. With all these things the birth-pangs of the new age begin. (Matthew 24:7–8; compare Mark 13:8 and Luke 21:10–11)

Jesus and the Jewish Establishment

The gospels depict Jesus' attitude toward Jewish law as ambivalent but often condescending, his relationship toward the Jewish religious leadership as confrontational. He scoffed at Jewish dietary laws: "It is not what goes into the mouth that defiles a person, but it is what comes out of the mouth that defiles" (Matthew 15:11). He constantly tested the limits of Sabbath restrictions, declaring that: "The Sabbath is made for man, not man for the Sabbath." He restricted divorce, announcing that: "If a man divorces his wife for any cause other than unchastity he involves her in adultery; and anyone who marries a divorced woman commits adultery" (Matthew 5:32).

Miracle and Mystery: Passion and Resurrection

Throughout his ministry Jesus had performed miracles—healing the sick, restoring sight to the blind, feeding multitudes of followers from just a few loaves and fishes, walking on water, calming storms, even raising the dead. These miracles, perhaps even more than his ethical teachings, brought followers flocking to him. The gospel narrative of Jesus' Passion, his suffering on the cross, presenting himself at this final moment of his life as both human and divine in one personage, and finally his miraculous resurrection from the grave, his appearances to his disciples, and his ascent to heaven, complete the miracle and the majesty.

The stories of Jesus' life and death, message and miracles, formed the basis for Christianity, at first a new sect located within Judaism. Although different followers attributed more or less divinity and greater or lesser miracles to him, apparently all accepted Jesus as a new, reforming teacher. Many saw him as the long-awaited "messiah," a messenger and savior specially "anointed" by God. His apostles, especially Paul of Tarsus (d. 67), now refocused Jesus' message and built the Christian sect into a new, powerful religion. The apostles' preaching, organizational work, and letters to fledgling Christian communities fill most of the rest of the New Testament.

CHRISTIANITY ORGANIZES

The Early Disciples

Peter, described in the gospels as Jesus' chosen organizational leader, first took the Christian message outside the Jewish community (Acts 10). Declaring circumcision unnecessary for membership, he welcomed gentiles into the new church. James, Jesus' brother and leader of the Christian community of Jerusalem, abrogated most of the Jewish dietary laws for the new community (Acts 15). These apostles believed that the rigorous ritual laws of Judaism inhibited the spread of its ethical message. Instead, they chose to emphasize the miraculous powers of Jesus and his followers. They spoke little of their master's views on the coming apocalypse, but stressed his statements on the importance of love and redemption.

Paul Organizes the Early Church

Tensions continued to simmer between mainstream Jewish leaders and the early Christians. One of the fiercest opponents of the new sect, Saul from the Anatolian town of Tarsus, was traveling to confront the Christian community in Damascus, when he experienced an overpowering mystical vision of Jesus that literally knocked him to the ground. Reversing his previous position, Saul now affirmed the authenticity of Jesus as the divine

Son of God. In speaking within the Jewish community, he had preferred his Hebrew name Saul. Now, as he took his new message also to gentiles, he preferred his Roman name Paul. He dedicated himself to establishing Christianity as an independent, organized religion. Jewish by ethnicity and early religious choice, Roman by citizenship, and Greek by culture, Paul was ideally placed to refine and explicate Jesus' message. He became the second founder of Christianity.

To link the flourishing, but separate, Christian communities, Paul undertook three missionary voyages in the eastern Mediterranean, and he kept in continuous communication through a series of letters, Paul's "Epistles" of the New Testament. He advised the leadership emerging within each local church organization: the presbyters, or elders; the deacons above them; and, at the head, the bishop. He promised eternal life to those who believed in Jesus' power. He declared Jewish ritual laws an obstacle to spiritual progress (Galatians 5:2–6). Neither membership in a chosen family nor observance of laws or rituals was necessary in the new religion. Faith alone was sufficient.

> The law was our disciplinarian until Christ came, so that we might be justified by faith. But now that faith has come, we are no longer subject to a disciplinarian, for in Christ Jesus you are all children of God through faith. (Galatians 3:24–6)

Paul proclaimed a new equality in Christianity:

> There is no longer Jew or Greek, there is no longer slave or free, there is no longer male or female; for all of you are one in Christ Jesus. (Galatians 3:28)

Recalling Jesus' resurrection, Paul's greatest promise was eternal life, the miraculous triumph over death. All Christians could achieve it:

> Listen, I will tell you a mystery! We will not all die but we will all be changed, in a moment, in the twinkling of an eye, at the last trumpet. For the

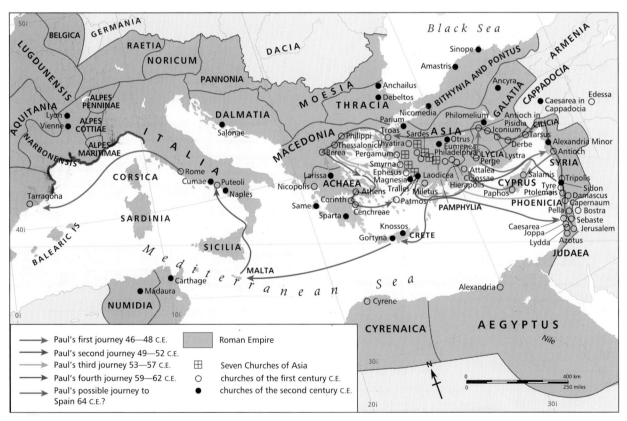

Paul's missionary journeys Following Jesus' trial and crucifixion, about 29 C.E., his disciples, notably the Roman convert Paul, set out to convert non-Jews or gentiles. Paul's journeys took him throughout the Greco-Roman east Mediterranean, and beyond. These journeys and the epistles Paul wrote began to weave struggling Christian groups into a new religious organization, the Roman Catholic Church. Paul died in Rome, apparently a martyr to the Emperor Nero.

trumpet will sound, and the dead will be raised
imperishable, and we will be changed. For this
perishable body must put on imperishability,
and this mortal body must put on immortality.
(1 Corinthians 15:51–3)

Paul formulated a new concept of "original sin"
and redemption from it. Jews had accepted the
Genesis story of Adam and Eve's disobedience in
the Garden of Eden as a mythical explanation of
some of life's harsh realities: the pain of childbirth,
the struggle to earn a living, the dangers of wild
beasts, and, most of all, human mortality. Paul now
proclaimed that Adam and Eve's "original sin"
could be forgiven. Humanity could, in a sense,
return to paradise and eternal life. Jesus' death on
the cross was atonement for original sin. According
to Paul, those who believed in Jesus and accepted
membership in the new Christian community
would be forgiven by God and "saved." Although
they would still be mortal, at the end of their
earthly lives they would inherit a life in heaven,
and, much later, would even be reborn on earth
(Romans 5–6).

Paul re-affirmed existing mystical rights, like
baptism, and created new ones like the eucharist,
the ritual eating of unleavened bread and drinking
of wine. The eucharist recalled Jesus' last supper
with his disciples at the Passover Seder meal before
he was taken to his final trial and crucifixion. Many
Christians said the eucharist represented the body
and blood of Jesus himself, now consumed and
incorporated by his followers. (Some pagans satiri-
cally called it cannibalism.)

The Christian Calendar

Pagans had celebrated the winter solstice;
Christians now fixed the observance of Jesus' birth,
Christmas, at that time of year, although no one
knew the actual date of his birth. Good Friday, at
about the time of Passover, mourned Jesus' crucifixion and death; three days later his resurrection
was celebrated in the joyous festival of **Easter**.
Corresponding to the Jewish holiday of **Pentecost**,
the anniversary of receiving the Ten Commandments
fifty days after the Passover, Christianity introduced
its own holiday of Pentecost. It commemorates the
date when, according to the book of Acts, chapter 2,
the "Holy Spirit," the third element of the Trinity
along with God the Father and Jesus the son, filled
Jesus' disciples and they "began to talk in other
tongues, as the Spirit gave them power of utterance,"

MAJOR CHRISTIAN FESTIVALS

January 6	Epiphany
February–March	Shrove Tuesday, or Mardi Gras (day before Ash Wednesday)
February–March	Ash Wednesday (first day of Lent)
February–April	Lent
February 2	Candlemas Day
March–April	Easter
March 25	Feast of Annunciation
April–June	Ascension (40 days after Easter)
May–June	Pentecost/Whit Sunday (50 days after Easter)
May–June	Trinity Sunday (Sunday after Pentecost)
November–December	Advent
December 24	Christmas Eve
December 25	Christmas Day

enabling them to preach to the various peoples of the
world. (Modern day Christian Pentecostals "speak in
tongues," praying and uttering praises ecstatically,
healing through prayer and laying on of hands, and
speaking of experiencing spiritual miracles.)

Special saints' days were designated to mark the
lives and deaths of people who helped to spread
the new religion. The new Christian calendar,
which has become the most widely used in the
world, fixed its first year at the approximate date of
Jesus' birth. The Jewish Sabbath, a weekly day of
rest and reflection, was transferred from Saturday
to Sunday.

Gender Relations

Although Paul had proclaimed that in Jesus "There
is no longer male or female," he seemed to distrust
sexual energies. Like Jesus he was unmarried. He
recommended celibacy and, for those unable to

meet that standard, monogamous marriage as a means of sexual restraint:

> It is well for a man not to touch a woman. But because of cases of sexual immorality, each man should have his own wife and each woman her own husband. The husband should give to his wife her conjugal rights, and likewise the wife to her husband. (1 Corinthians 7:1–3)

In addition, Paul moved to subordinate women, first at home:

> I want you to understand that Christ is the head of every man, and the husband is the head of the wife. . . . he is the image and reflection of God; but woman is the reflection of man. Indeed, man was not made from woman, but woman from man. Neither was man created for the sake of woman, but woman for the sake of man. (1 Corinthians 11:3–9)

Then in the church:

> Women should be silent in the churches. For they are not permitted to speak, but should be subordinate, as the law also says. If there is anything they desire to know, let them ask their husbands at home. (1 Corinthians 14:34–5)

On the other hand, women served as deaconesses and abbesses in some of the early churches, and Paul welcomed them warmly and treated them respectfully. So it is difficult to understand the relationship between Paul's theory and his practice with regard to women in the Church.

Slavery

Paul had also declared that spiritually "There is no longer slave or free," but in practice he accepted slavery, saying, "Slaves, obey your earthly masters with fear and trembling." He did urge masters to be kind to slaves and to "stop threatening them for you know that both of you have the same Master in heaven, and with him there is no partiality" (Ephesians 6:5–9).

Struggle for Survival in Rome

Having established the central doctrines of the new religion, and stabilized its core communities, both Peter and Paul moved to expand its geographical scope. Both saw Rome as the capital of empire and the center of the international communication network of the time. Both traveled to Rome to preach and teach, and tradition holds that both were martyred there in the persecutions of the Emperor Nero, about 67 C.E. and that both are entombed and enshrined there.

In this capital of empire, Christianity appeared as one of several mystery religions, all of which were based on beliefs in supernatural beings. They included the religion of Mithras, a Persian sun god; Demeter, a Greek goddess; YHWH of the Jews; and an eclectic mixture of beliefs called Gnosticism. Romans seemed to be in search of a more inspiring, other-worldly faith than paganism provided, but at the time of the deaths of Peter and Paul, Christianity was still a relatively weak force.

Paradoxically, because they refused to worship the Emperor or to take oaths in his name, Christians were viewed by official Rome as atheists. Their emphasis on other-worldly salvation and their strong internal organization were seen as threats to the state's authority. Official treatment of Christianity was erratic but was often marked by severe persecution. The first Christians, Jews by nationality, were scorned as provincial foreigners. Some Roman authorities thought that Christian beliefs in resurrection and an afterlife undermined pride in citizenship and willingness to serve in the army. About the year 100, the historian Tacitus wrote of:

> a class of persons hated for their vices whom the crowd called Christians. Christus, after whom they were named, had undergone the death penalty in the reign of Tiberius, by sentence of the procurator Pontius Pilate, and the pernicious superstition was checked for a moment only to break out once more, not only in Judaea, the home of the disease, but in the Capital itself, where everything horrible or shameful in the world gathers and becomes fashionable. (Tacitus, *Annales* XV:44, cited in Honour and Fleming)

Nero (r. 54–68) scapegoated the Christians, blaming them for the great fire in 64, apparently executing both Peter and Paul among his victims, and sending hundreds of Christians to die in public gladiatorial contests and by burning. Edicts of persecution were issued by Emperors Antoninus Pius (r. 138–161), Marcus Aurelius (r. 161–180), Septimius Severus (r. 193–211), and Diocletian (r. 284–305). In 257 the Emperor Valerian (r. 253–

260) was prepared to launch a major persecution of Christians, but he was captured in battle by Persians. In these early years of persecution, thousands of Christians suffered martyrdom.

CHRISTIANITY TRIUMPHANT

Despite the scorn and the persecution, Christianity continued to grow. Its key doctrines and texts were written, edited, and approved by leaders in the network of Christian churches. The contents of the New Testament were agreed upon by about 200, and by 250 the city of Rome alone held about 50,000 Christians among its million inhabitants. Most were of the lower classes, attracted by Jesus' message to the poor, but middle- and upper-class Romans had also joined. In particular, Christianity proved attractive to the wives of Roman leaders, perhaps drawn by its emphasis on monogamy. Many brought their husbands into the Church. About the year 200, the Church leader Tertullian exulted, with some exaggeration, "We are but of yesterday, and already we have filled your world: cities, islands, fortresses, towns, marketplaces, the camp itself, tribes, companies, the palace, the senate, the forum. … We have left you nothing but your temples only!" (*Apology* 37.4, cited in Kee (1995), p. 213). By the reign of Constantine, one out of five inhabitants of the Roman Empire was a Christian.

The Conversion of Constantine

Helena, the mother of the Emperor Constantine (r. 306–337), had churches built in Asia Minor and the Holy Land and traveled to Jerusalem, seeking the cross on which Jesus died. In 313, Constantine himself had a vision in which a cross with the words *in hoc signo vinces* (in this sign you will be victorious) appeared to him the night before he won the critical battle that made him sole emperor in the Western Empire. He immediately declared Christianity legal. He funded Christian leaders and their construction of churches while he withdrew official support from the pagan churches, making Christianity the *de facto* official religion of the Roman Empire. Constantine sponsored the Council of Nicea in 325, the largest assembly of bishops of local Christian churches up to that time. He convened the Council primarily to establish the central theological doctrines of Christianity, but it also established a Church organization for the Roman Empire, a network of urban bishoprics

Marble head of Constantine, Palazzo dei Conservatori, Rome, 313 C.E. This gigantic bust—the head is over 8 feet (2.4 m) tall—exhibits a stark and expressive realism that verges on caricature. Coming after Diocletian (r. 284–305) insisted on being worshiped as divine, the bust represents a returning awareness that people—even Roman emperors—are humans not gods.

grouped into provinces, with each province headed by the chief bishop of its largest city. In 337, on his deathbed, Constantine accepted baptism.

In 392, the Emperor Theodosius (r. 379–395) declared Christianity the official religion of the Roman Empire. He outlawed paganism and severely restricted Judaism, initiating centuries of bitter Christian persecution of both traditions.

How Had Christianity Succeeded?

How had Christianity, once scorned and persecuted, achieved such power? Christian believers attributed the success to divine assistance. Historians seek more earthly explanations. Let us consider two approaches.

Beginning in 1776, Edward Gibbon began the publication of his six-volume masterpiece, *The History of the Decline and Fall of the Roman Empire*. A child of the enlightenment philosophy of his time, which rejected supernatural explanations (see Chapter 15), Gibbon rather sarcastically presented five reasons for Christianity's victories. But beneath his sarcasm Gibbon revealed the profound strengths of the new religion:

- Its "inflexible and intolerant" zeal, derived from its Jewish roots.

- Its promise of resurrection and a future life for believers, soon augmented by the threat of eternal damnation for nonbelievers; Cyprian, Bishop of Carthage (d. 258) declared, for example, "Outside the church there is no salvation." (McManners, p. 37)

- Its assertion of miraculous accomplishments, including exorcisms. Gibbon, always seeking the exaggeration, cited the paradoxical claim of Tertullian: "I believe because it is absurd!" (Gibbon, p. 206)

- The austere morals of the first Christians. The Christian search for spiritual perfection, monogamous sexual code, rejection of worldly honor, and general emphasis on equality attracted many converts. In the extreme case, martyrdom won admiration, sympathy, and followers. Tertullian asserted "The blood of martyrs is seed." (McManners, p. 43)

- The Church generated a state within a state through the decentralized leadership of its local bishops and presbyters, the structure Paul had begun to knit together. As imperial structures weakened, the Church provided an alternative community. This Christian community distributed philanthropy to needy people within and even outside the Church. It also publicized its message effectively—in Greek, the language of the eastern part of the empire.

Many historians of our own time accept the thrust of Gibbon's explanations, but tend to emphasize more the importance of community within the Church.

"From the outset, the major goal of the Jesus movement was to call into existence a new kind of inclusive community that might arch over all the ordinary human distinctions of race and religion," writes Howard Clark Kee (1991, p. 2). Kee analyzes five different kinds of community that were active in the Roman world during the first two centuries of the Christian era and suggests that Christianity developed an appeal to each of them: The community of the wise, seeking special knowledge of the future; the community of the law-abiding, seeking appropriate rules of guidance in the present; the community where God dwells among his people, seeking assurance that it was specially selected and cared for; the community of mystical participation, influenced by the mystery religions of the time; and the ethnically and culturally inclusive community, outsiders seeking a place of belonging. Different aspects of the Christian message, developed by different Church leaders, spoke to each of these communities and succeeded in drawing them in (Kee, 1995).

Historical sociologist Michael Mann cites the psychological and practical rewards of the growing Christian "ecumene," the worldwide community of the Church, with its comprehensive philosophy for living and organizing. Although much of Christianity's message targeted the poor, Mann notes that the religion also drew a large following of urban artisans, whom the aristocratic Roman Empire devalued. Excluded from political power, these working-class people were in search of a comprehensive and welcoming community. They wanted to recreate an earlier, simpler, more participatory era and they became Christians. As imperial power became increasingly centralized, remote, insensitive, and later unstable, "In many ways Christianity represented how Rome liked to idealize its republican past" (Mann, p. 325).

PROFILE
St. Augustine
BISHOP OF HIPPO

With the declaration that "the true philosopher is the lover of God," Augustine (354–430) aptly described his own position within the early Christian Church. Brought up by a devout Christian mother and pagan father in the Roman province of Numidia (modern-day Algeria), Augustine displayed a devotion to intellectual pursuits from an early age. In Carthage, where he was a student, he became deeply involved in Manichaeism, a philosophy that combined Christianity with elements of other religions and encouraged its adherents to a life of asceticism and celibacy. Unfortunately, Augustine was only permitted to join the lower order of the Manichaean Church because of his romantic attachment to a woman of low birth, with whom he had a son, and it was not long before he decided to look elsewhere for intellectual and spiritual fulfilment. An official professorship at Milan brought Augustine into contact with the writings of Plotinus, the third-century philosopher and founder of Neoplatonism. According to Neoplatonic thought, the way to experience ultimate reality or truth was by returning to one's inner self. Through such an act of introspection Augustine discovered God. The incident, which is described in terms of a mystical experience in the *Confessions*, came about just as Augustine was bemoaning his past actions:

> I was saying these things and weeping in the most bitter contrition of my heart, when lo, I heard the voice of a boy or girl, I know not which, coming from a neighbouring house, chanting, and oft repeating, "Take up and read; take up and read." Immediately my countenance was changed. . . . I rose up, interpreting it no other way than as a command to me from Heaven to open the book, and to read the first chapter I should light upon

> [Augustine, *Confessions*, I; ed. J. G. Pilkington, 1896]

The book that Augustine opened was the New Testament Letters and the first words he read were from the Letter of Paul to the Romans: ". . . put ye on the Lord Jesus Christ, and make not provision for the flesh, to fulfil the lusts thereof." Knowledge of God, Augustine discovered, only became possible through a renunciation of the body and a profound identification with one's own soul—an idea that fused Christian theology with Platonic philosophy.

Shortly after his conversion to Christianity—he was baptized in 386 with his son—Augustine returned to Tagaste in North Africa, the place of his birth, and established a small religious community. In 396 he became Bishop of Hippo, a role that necessitated his active participation in the struggle to end the schism in the African Church and control the various heretical schools. Augustine's belief that all moral activity was ultimately dependent on the grace of God was deemed extreme by some of his contemporaries and his personal understanding of the doctrines of original sin and free will was never fully accepted by the Church. Despite this, Augustine's enormous literary output continued as a significant source of inspiration for later generations of theologians and his legacy to Christian thinking on the relationship between politics and religion was profound.

Augustine died on August 28, 430 just as Rome's dominance in north Africa was drawing to its close.

St. Augustine of Hippo as represented by El Greco, 1590. (*Museum of Santa Cruz Toledo*)

DOCTRINE: DEFINITION AND DISPUTE

As it grew after receiving official recognition, institutional Christianity refined its theology. The most influential theologian of the period, Augustine (354–430), Bishop of Hippo in north Africa, wrote *The City of God* to explain Christianity's relationship to competing religions and philosophies, and to the Roman government with which it was increasingly intertwined. Despite Christianity's designation as the official religion of the empire, Augustine declared its message to be spiritual rather than political. Christianity, he argued, should be concerned with the mystical, heavenly City of Jerusalem rather than with earthly politics. His theology supported the separation of Church and state that came to characterize western Europe fourteen centuries later, after the French Revolution (see Chapter 15).

Augustine built philosophical bridges to Platonic philosophy, the dominant system of the Hellenistic world of his time and place. Christianity envisioned Jesus, God's son, walking the earth and suffering for his people. He was, literally, very down to earth. God, the Father, had more transcendent characteristics, but they were less emphasized in Christian theology at the time. Plato (*c.* 429–*c.* 347 B.C.E.; see p. 145) and later **Neoplatonic** philosophers, however, provided the model of a more exalted, more remote god, a god that was more accepted among the leading thinkers of Augustine's time. According to Augustine, Plato's god was:

> the maker of all created things, the light by which things are known, and the good in reference to which things are to be done; . . . we have in him the first principle of nature, the truth of doctrines, and the happiness of life. (p. 253)

In addition, Plato's god existed in the soul of every person, perhaps a borrowing from Hinduism (see Chapter 9).

Augustine married these Platonic and Neo-Platonic views to the transcendent characteristics of God in Christian theology. This provided Christianity with a new intellectual respectability, which attracted new audiences in the vast Hellenistic world. He also encouraged contemplation and meditation within Christianity, an important element in the monastic life that was beginning to emerge. Augustine himself organized a community of monks in Tegaste (now Souk-Ahras), the city of his birth.

Augustine believed that Christians should subordinate their will and reason to the teachings and authority of the Church:

> Man was made upright that he might not live according to himself, but according to Him that made him—in other words, that he might do His will and not his own. (p. 445)

Judgment and salvation were in the hands of God alone.

> The source of man's happiness lies only in God, whom he abandons when he sins, and not in himself, by living according to whom he sins. (p. 445)

Some Church theologians, such as Pelagius (*c.* 354–after 418), feared that Augustine's elevation of the majesty and authority of the Church would devalue both public service for the poor and private initiative by less disciplined Christians, but Augustine's views prevailed.

Original Sin, Sexuality, and Salvation

In his earlier *Confessions*, Augustine had written of his personal life of (relatively mild) sin before his conversion to Christianity. Now he warned Christians that Adam and Eve's willfulness had led to original sin; sin had unlocked the forces of lust, turning the flesh against the spirit; and lust had called forth a death sentence on all humans in place of the immortality originally intended for them:

> As soon as our first parents had transgressed the commandment, divine grace forsook them, and they were confounded at their own wickedness. . . . They experienced a new motion of their flesh which had become disobedient to them, in strict retribution of their own disobedience to God. . . . Then began the flesh to lust against the Spirit. . . . And thus, from the bad use of free will, there originated the whole train of evil . . . on to the destruction of the second death, which has no end, those only being excepted who are freed by the grace of God. (p. 422–3)

For Augustine, and for the Church, sexuality was perilous and woman suspect. In Roman Catholic theology, profane flesh and divine spirit confronted each other uneasily.

Church Dogma: Discipline and Battles

Some theological disputes led to violence, especially as the Church attempted to suppress doctrinal disagreement. The most divisive concerned the nature of the divinity of Jesus. The theologian Arius (c. 250–336) taught that Christ's humanity limited his divinity; God the father, wholly transcendent, was more sacred than the son who had walked the earth. The Council of Nicea, which was convened in 325 to resolve this dispute, issued an official statement of creed affirming Jesus' complete divinity and his indivisibility from God. The Arian controversy continued, however, especially on the fringes of empire, where Arian missionaries converted many of the Gothic tribes to their own beliefs.

Pope Leo I (440–461) demanded unquestioning obedience: "Truth, which is simple and one, does not admit of variety" (Grant, *Rome*, p. 458). Wars between the new Arian converts and the Roman Church ensued, until finally Arianism was defeated in battle. Of these struggles the historian Ammianus Marcellinus (c. 330–395) wrote, "No wild beasts are such enemies to mankind as are most of the Christians in the deadly hatred they feel for one another" (Grant, *Rome*, p. 457). A recent (1999) book by Richard L. Rubenstein, *When Jesus Became God*, explores the Arian controversy and the use of violence to suppress dissent within the early Church.

In the eastern Mediterranean, bitter and violent conflicts broke out among rival Christian theological factions, again, over the precise balance between Jesus' divinity and his humanity. Persecution of dissidents by the Orthodox Church in Carthage, Syria, and Egypt was so severe that the advent in the seventh century of Muslim rule, which treated all the Christian sects equally, was often welcomed as a respite from the struggles (Matthew, p. 49).

OFFICIAL CHRISTIANITY IN THE WAKE OF EMPIRE

Christianity spread to western and northern Europe along the communication and transportation networks of the Roman Empire. Born in Judaea under Roman occupation, Christianity now spread throughout the empire, spoke its languages of Greek and Latin, preached the gospel along its trade routes, and constructed church communities in its cities. As the empire weakened and dissolved, Christianity emerged and flourished.

Thanks to official recognition and patronage, the Church grew steadily. As the Roman imperial government weakened (see pp. 185–90), it enlisted the now official Church as a kind of department of state. Roman Catholic bishops now came "from the ranks of the senatorial governing class . . . they stood for continuity of the old Roman values. . . . The eventual conversion of the barbarian leaders was due to their influence" (Matthew, p. 21). Through a variety of educational institutions the churches, monasteries, convents, and bishops kept Rome's culture alive in northern and western Europe. In more remote areas these were virtually the only centers of literacy and through them Christianity spread its message aggressively and effectively: "None of the major Germanic peoples who entered the Roman provinces in the fourth and fifth centuries remained pagan for more than a generation after they crossed the frontier" (Mann, p. 335). About 507 Clovis, chief of the Merovingian Franks, converted to Christianity, the first barbarian to accept the religion of the empire. He established his capital in Paris and had thousands of his tribesmen converted, for, in general, followers accepted the religion of their leader.

Monasteries and Missionaries

Decentralized Leadership Christianity spread in urban areas through its bishops in their large churches. In rural and remote areas, monks, acting as missionaries, carried the message. Monasteries, which were small, isolated communities, each under the local control of a single abbot, modeled the spirituality and simplicity of the earliest Christian communities. Because sexual activity was ruled out, monasticism became as accessible to women in convents as to men in monasteries, and was equally valued by both. Many monasteries contained both men and women, each living in celibacy. The most famous of the early monastics, St. Benedict (c. 480–547), founded a monastery at Monte Cassino, about 100 miles (160 kilometers) southeast of Rome. The writings of Pope Gregory I (r. 590–604) give us the most detailed information on the life, regulations, and discipline of that exemplary institution, although each monastery had its own variations in administration and practice.

Gregory saw the usefulness of the monasteries and monks in converting and disciplining the barbarians, and he began to direct their activity from Rome. By the year 600 there were about

200 monasteries in Gaul alone, and the first missionaries dispatched by Rome arrived in England *c.* 597. By 700 all of England had been converted. Linguistic and cultural development accompanied the Church's teaching; in Northumbria, for example, the Venerable Bede (*c.* 673–735) translated the gospels into English and wrote *The Ecclesiastical History of the English People*. In the ninth, tenth, and eleventh centuries, missionary activity was directed toward the "Northmen," the Vikings, from Scandinavia, who raided and traded for goods and slaves from North America and Greenland, through the North Sea and the Baltic, down the Volga River, across the Caspian Sea, and on as far as Baghdad. The Vikings came into the Christian fold with only a tenuous link to Rome and a strong admixture of pagan ritual.

By this time Christians had far surpassed Jews in numbers, geographical spread, power, and influence. Christian missionaries continued their attempts to convert Jews, often by coercion. In 576, for example, a Gallic bishop gave the Jews of his city the choice between baptism and expulsion (McManners, p. 85), a pattern that was repeated periodically, although Jews had not yet immigrated into western Europe in large numbers.

In much of rural western Europe local authorities valued the monks both as the only literate people in the region and as the most capable persons in administering land and agriculture. These authorities also sought an alliance with the prestige and power of the Church. They granted land and administrative powers to nearby monasteries, transforming them into important local economic forces. (Compare the administrative roles of Hindu priests and Buddhist monks in south and southeast Asia; Chapter 9.) Monks became courtiers and bishops as well as missionaries as they expanded the geographic, social, and economic dimensions of the Church. Until the Lateran Declaration of 1216 under Pope Innocent III (r. 1198–1216), monasteries could form and dissolve at local initiatives, so we have no record of their exact numbers in the early centuries. A history of the very decentralized Church of this time would have to be written from the bottom up.

The Church in the West was decentralized partly because the Roman Empire was decentralized, having lost its administrative power. There was no longer an emperor in Rome. The Church and what was left of the government groped toward a new mutual relationship. In 496, Pope Gelasius I (r. 492–496) saw the mutual dependence of Church and state, and he wrote: "Christian emperors would need priests for attaining eternal life and priests would avail themselves of imperial regulations in the conduct of temporal affairs" (Tierney, p. 15). Gelasius, who wanted each institution to keep to its own domain, supported St. Augustine of Hippo in advocating an early separation of Church and state.

The Church East and West

In the far more literate and sophisticated Byzantine Empire, political leaders did not relinquish their power to Church authorities. Indeed, the emperor at Constantinople served as administrative head of the Church, a pattern that had been set by Constantine when he presided over the Council of Nicea, outside Constantinople.

Today, Eastern Orthodoxy and Roman Catholicism share the same fundamental faith and scripture and they maintain official communication with each other, but they developed many historic differences over church organization, authority, aesthetics, and language. In the East, the Church remained far more urban, as did the entire region. The West had so few roads and so little trade that it was held together organizationally by its urban military and ecclesiastical strongholds. The Council of Chalcedon (451) recognized four centers of church organization, or sees: Antioch, Jerusalem, Alexandria, and Constantinople, with Constantinople predominating—and having the same leadership role in the East as Rome had in the West. Rome, still under its own emperor, and with its own bishop, was deemed an entirely separate administrative center.

Rome and Byzantium have remained divided over the authority of the bishop of Rome to the present. From the sixth century, he has claimed to be pope, *pappa*, father of the (Roman) Catholic Church, the direct organizational successor of the apostle Peter. Eastern Orthodox Christianity, however, has never recognized the pope's claim to preeminent authority. Also, unlike the Roman practice, all but the highest clergy in Eastern Orthodoxy are permitted to marry, so here again the two clergies have not accepted each other's authority. The language of Rome is Latin, while the East uses Greek and the various Slavic languages of eastern Europe. Their aesthetics for religious art are also different (see Spotlight, pp. 324–5). Friction between the two groups has waxed and waned over time, with the most direct confrontation coming in 1204, when crusaders dispatched by Rome to fight against Muslims in Jerusalem (see pp. 360–3) turned northward and sacked Constantinople instead.

As in the West, monastic life flourished in the Byzantine Empire, with exemplary institutions at remote, starkly beautiful sites such as Mount Sinai and Mount Athos. The greatest missionary activity of the Eastern monks came later than in the West. Hemmed in by the Holy Roman Empire and the barbarians to the west and by the growing power of Islam to the east after about 650, Byzantium turned its missionary efforts northward, toward Russia. The brothers St. Cyril (c. 827–869) and St. Methodius (c. 825–884) translated the Bible into Slavonic, creating the Cyrillic alphabet in which to transcribe and publish it. When Russia embraced Orthodox Christianity in the tenth century it also adopted this alphabet. In the late fifteenth century, after the fall of Constantinople to the Turks (1453), Moscow began to refer to itself as the "Third Rome," the spiritual and political heir to the Caesars and the Byzantine Empire.

Monastery of St. Catherine, Mount Sinai, 557 C.E. According to the Torah, Moses received the tablets of the law from God on Mount Sinai. It was for this reason that the Byzantine emperor Justinian I (r. 527–565) chose to found the monastery of St. Catherine here. The remote beauty of the place also made it ideal for spiritual meditation.

SPOTLIGHT
Icons and Iconoclasm

"What the written word is to the literate, the icon is to the illiterate. What speech is to the ear, the icon is to the eye." With these words St. John of Damascus (*c*. 657–*c*. 749) explained the importance of **icons** in Eastern Orthodox Christianity. Icons—sacred images of Jesus, Mary, angels, and saints, often paintings on gold backgrounds—are of central importance in Eastern Orthodox Christian worship. Incense is offered to them, candles are lit before them, they are carried in processions in the church and accorded a place of honor in the home. Legends report that Christ and the Virgin Mary appeared after their deaths to St. Luke so that he might paint them and thus provide an accurate representation of their likeness. **Figure 1**, an icon of Mary holding the infant Jesus in her lap, flanked by SS. Theodore and George and overseen by angels, was probably painted in Constantinople in the sixth or seventh century and is one of the oldest

remaining icons.

This heritage from the earliest icons to their central position today might appear to be a straight-line development, but, in fact, for more than a century, between 726–843, fierce controversy over the place of icons divided Eastern Orthodoxy

Figure 1 Icon of Mary, Jesus, and SS. Theodore and George, St Catherine's Monastery, Israel, sixth to seventh century C.E.

and created tensions with the Roman Church as well. In 726 the Emperor Leo III took the side of the **iconoclasts**, the breakers of icons, in ordering the destruction of all images that depicted Jesus, Mary, saints, or angels in human form. The representation of Christ was especially targeted.

Those who kept such icons were to be physically punished. **Figure 2** from an eleventh-century manuscript portrays an iconoclast destroying an image of Jesus.

Historians cite multiple reasons underlying the emperor's order. Theologically, iconoclasts argued that Jesus' divine nature could not be painted. **Iconodules**, people who venerated the icons, replied that Christ's human presence was real and significant, and paintings were needed to capture it. Politically, Emperor Leo III was asserting his power in a struggle with Church authorities. Culturally, iconoclasts were accepting the Islamic (and Jewish) reading of the biblical prohibition against creating images of humans or gods for worship. From its founding in 622 C.E. (see Chapter 11), Islam defeated a series of Christian armies and was gaining whole nations of converts, while the Byzantine empire itself was reduced to Constantinople, its European provinces, and Asia Minor. Some Church leaders may have reasoned that biblical bans against the use of images in worship should be enforced. As in Islam, Eastern Orthodoxy did continue to produce an abundance of art that did not reproduce the human figure. The western regions of the empire did not cease creating religious images, and the pope and Western Christendom repudiated the edict altogether.

Figure 2 Iconoclast churchmen spearing an image of Christ, illumination, The Chludov Psalter, eleventh century C.E.

Iconoclasm raged for over a century as art forms became the focal center of theological, political, and cultural struggles. In 843 the Empress Theodora restored the use of icons in an act called "The Triumph of Orthodoxy," an event still celebrated in the Eastern Church on the first Sunday in Lent. **Figure 3**, an icon entitled "The Triumph of Orthodoxy," painted in Constantinople in the late fourteenth or early fifteenth century, commemorates the victory. In the top center stands the Virgin Mary holding the infant Jesus; on the left, Theodora and her young son, the emperor Michael III; to the right, the Patriarch of Constantinople, Methodius, and three supporters of the iconodule position. The lower register includes eleven additional iconodules.

Figure 3 Icon of the "Triumph of Orthodoxy," Constantinople, late fourteenth/early fifteenth century C.E.

The spread of Christianity The disciples and early missionaries established Christian communities in southwest Asia, Greece, Italy, north Africa, and India. On the other hand, Roman persecution, the decline of western Rome, and the rise of Islam (see map, p. 341) hindered its dissemination. The Orthodox Church of Constantinople converted eastern Europe, penetrating Russia; Rome became reestablished as a powerful center; and Celtic missionaries traveled throughout northwest Europe.

In other regions of east-central Europe, Rome and Byzantium competed in spreading their religious and cultural messages and organizations. Rome won out in Poland, Bohemia, Lithuania, and Ukraine; the Eastern Church in Bulgaria, Romania, and Serbia. In the Great Schism of 1054 the two Churches divided definitively into the Latin or Roman Catholic Church, predominant in western Europe, and the Greek Orthodox Church, which prevailed in the east. Other national Churches, among the world's oldest, had also grown up beyond Rome's jurisdiction, including the Armenian, the Coptic in Egypt, and the Ethiopian. They now asserted their independence from

Constantinople as well, creating a pattern of distinct national Churches that the Protestant Reformation would later adopt (see Chapter 13).

CHRISTIANITY IN WESTERN EUROPE

The abrupt, dramatic rise of Islam throughout the Middle East and into the Mediterranean, which we will examine in the next chapter, had an immediate and profound influence on Christianity. By the year 700, Islam had won the eastern Mediterranean and the north coast of Africa, key regions of both Christianity and the former Roman Empire. The Muslim Umayyad dynasty pushed on into Spain and crossed the Pyrenees. Stopped only in southern France by Charles Martel (c. 688–741) at the Battle of Tours in 732, the Umayyad forces returned to Spain. Muslim troops captured segments of the southern Italian peninsula, Sicily, and other Mediterranean islands. Geographically cut off from the lands of its birth and early vigor, Christianity became primarily a religion of Europe, where many of its members were recently converted warrior nobles.

In western Europe outside of Rome, Christianity developed a multitude of local institutions. Churches, monasteries, and convents were established, and leadership was decentralized. In regions which lacked organized government and administration, local church leaders and institutions provided whatever existed of order, administration, and a sense of larger community. For several centuries, "Christendom was dominated by thousands of dedicated unmarried men and women" (McManners, p. 89), the clergy of the Church. Among lay people as well as among the clergy, the period from the sixth through the tenth centuries was a lengthy era of faith, prayer, and meditation. Quiet piety and spiritualism gave meaning to life. Christians

Christ triumphing over evil, Frankish terra cotta plaque, Merovingian era.
It was not unusual for western Europeans to represent Christ in contemporary local costume (compare the Spotlight on Buddhas, pp. 288–9). Here, dressed as a member of the German warrior nobility, he treads the serpent, an emblem of the devil, underfoot. (*Musée des Antiquités, St-Germain-en-Laye, France*)

sought eternal salvation within the Church, and feared eternal damnation outside it. Missionary activity continued enthusiastically, now turned northward toward the Vikings and the Slavs, as other geographical doors had been forcibly shut.

In the Byzantine Empire, the state became in effect an armed force. In Rome, the pope felt surrounded by the hostile powers of Constantinople and Islam to the east and south, and several Gothic kings to the north and west. Seeking alliances with strongmen, he turned to a Frank, Charles (Carolus) Martel, who gave his name to the Carolingian family. As we have seen, Martel had repulsed the Muslims at Tours in 732. In 754 his son Pepin III (r. 751–768) answered the call of Pope Stephen II (r. 752–757) for help in fighting the Lombard Goths who were invading Italy and threatening the papal possessions. Pepin secured a swath of lands from Rome to Ravenna and turned them over to papal rule. In exchange, the pope anointed Pepin and his two sons, confirming the succession of his family as the royal house ruling the Franks.

THE CAROLINGIAN DYNASTY

751	Pepin III "the Short" becomes King of the Franks
755	Franks drive Lombards out of central Italy; creation of Papal States
768–814	Charlemagne rules as King of the Franks
774	Charlemagne defeats Lombards in northern Italy
800	Pope Leo III crowns Charlemagne
814–840	Louis the Pious succeeds Charlemagne as "emperor"
843	Treaty of Verdun partitions the Carolingian Empire
870	Treaty of Mersen further divides Carolingian Empire
875–950	New invasions of Vikings, Muslims, and Magyars
962	Ottonian dynasty succeeds Carolingian in Germany
987	Capetian dynasty succeeds Carolingian in France

Bronze and gilt statuette of Charlemagne, *c.* 860–870 C.E. Charlemagne's ceaseless warfare spread Christianity and Frankish rule across western Europe, while repelling barbarian intruders and enemies of Rome. In 800 C.E. Pope Leo III showed his gratitude by crowning him Holy Roman Emperor. (*Louvre, Paris*)

Charlemagne

Pepin's son Charles ruled between 771 and 814 as Charles the Great, Charlemagne, and was crowned Roman Emperor by Pope Leo III on Christmas Day 800, in Rome. Emperor and pope set out to attempt to reconstruct the historic Roman Empire, and to achieve this goal Charlemagne spent all his adult lifetime in warfare (see Source below), continuing the military expeditions of his father and grandfather. He reconquered the north-eastern corner of Spain from its Muslim rulers, defeated the Lombard rulers of Italy and relieved their pressure on the pope, seized Bavaria and Bohemia, killed and looted the entire nobility of the Huns in Pannonia (modern Austria and Hungary), and subdued the German Saxon populations along the Elbe River after thirty-three years of warfare. Himself a German Frank, Charlemagne offered the German Saxons a choice of conversion to Christianity or death. With Charlemagne's victories the borders of his kingdom came to match the borders of the dominance of the Church of Rome, except for the British Isles, which he did not enter. The political capital of western Europe passed from Rome to Charlemagne's own palace in Aix-la-Chapelle (Aachen) in modern Germany. Although Charlemagne was barely literate, he established within this palace a center of learning that attracted Church scholars from throughout Europe, initiating what historians call the Carolingian Renaissance.

"For good or ill, a peculiarly determined form of Catholic Christianity became the mandatory faith of all the regions, Mediterranean and non-Mediterranean alike, that had come together to form a post-Roman western Europe." (Brown, p. 17)

SOURCE
Charlemagne and Harun-al-Rashid

Charlemagne spent his lifetime fighting in the name of the pope and on behalf of Christianity. In 777 he invaded Muslim Spain and by 801 had captured Barcelona. (His campaigns in Spain gave rise to the epic poem *The Song of Roland* about the defeat of his rearguard in the pass of Roncesvalles. This became the most celebrated poem of medieval French chivalry.)

Yet Charlemagne carried on a valued diplomatic friendship with the most powerful Muslim ruler of his day, Harun-al-Rashid, Caliph of Baghdad (r. 786–809). Charlemagne's adviser, friend, and biographer Einhard (c. 770–840) describes the friendship:

> With Harun-al-Rachid [*sic*], King of the Persians, who held almost the whole of the East in fee, always excepting India, Charlemagne was on such friendly terms that Harun valued his goodwill more than the approval of all the other kings and princes in the entire world, and considered that he alone was worthy of being honoured and propitiated with gifts. When Charlemagne's messengers, whom he had sent with offerings to the most Holy Sepulchre of our Lord and Saviour and to the place of His resurrection, came to Harun and told him of their master's intention, he not only granted all that was asked but even went so far as to agree that this sacred scene of our redemption should be placed under Charlemagne's own jurisdiction. When the time came for these messengers to turn homewards, Harun sent some of his own men to accompany them and dispatched to Charlemagne costly gifts, which included robes, spices and other marvels of the lands of the Orient. A few years earlier Harun had sent Charlemagne the only elephant he possessed, simply because the Frankish King asked for it. (Einhard, p. 70)

Einhard does not note what gifts Charlemagne might have sent to Baghdad in return, nor does he comment on the political benefits of this interfaith diplomacy between the two great empires—empires that flanked, and confronted, the Byzantine Empire lying between them.

Charlemagne's coronation challenged the authority of the Eastern emperor in Constantinople, but during the next years Charlemagne managed, through negotiation and warfare, to gain Constantinople's recognition of his title. There were once again two emperors, east and west.

The Carolingian family remained powerful until about the end of the century, but then could no longer fight off the new invasions of the western Christian world by Magyars (Hungarians), Norsemen, and Arabs. Internally, regional administrators, emboldened by weakness at the center, began to act independently of the emperor's authority. Only after yet another century could militarily powerful leaders begin to cobble together loosely structured kingdoms in northwest-ern Europe. Meanwhile, political leadership in Europe was generally decentralized in rural manor estates controlled by local lords. Religious leadership in the cathedrals, churches, monasteries, and convents filled the gap, providing a greater sense of overall community and order. In this era, 600–1100 C.E., the Church gave Europe its fundamental character and order. The Magyar and Norse invaders, like the Germans before them, converted to it. By the end of the eleventh century, the Roman Catholic Church, as well as the political authorities of western Europe, were preparing to confront Islam.

CONNECTION: *The Crusades (1095–1291), pp. 360–3*

TRANSITIONS

During the European high middle ages Christianity completed its first millennium. It had originated in the eastern Mediterranean and spread throughout Europe. It had begun with the teachings of one man preached by a handful of disciples and institutionalized through the zeal of a single missionary, and had flowered into two separate, far-flung Church hierarchies and several localized Church structures. It had begun with a membership of downtrodden Jews, added middling-level gentiles, attracted some of the elites of Rome, and finally converted multitudes of Europe's invading barbarians. It had expanded its own organizational establishment via the network of transportation, communication, and trade put in place by the Roman Empire, and when that empire dissolved and contracted it maintained and consolidated its position within the remains of those old Roman administrative and market centers. As European society became more rural, Christian monasteries and convents were founded in the countryside and often took on administrative and developmental roles alongside their spiritual missions. In short, the Church, like the empire, was much transformed.

The transformations of both the Christian religious world and the European political world continued after 1000 with extraordinary developments in crusading vigor, trade and commerce, urbanization, intellectual and artistic creativity, and religious reform. We will explore these transformations in Chapter 12. (Readers who wish to follow those events may skip ahead to that chapter.) First, however, we turn to equally startling and revolutionary

Laon Cathedral, west front, *c.* 1190–95. Gothic architecture was the dominant style in Europe after the twelfth century and was based on northern European models. Gothic churches were built to communicate, announcing the glories of heaven with their confident mastery of space and light and, at the same time, heralding the wealth and power of the Church.

developments that had created another world religion, originating in the Arabian peninsula only a few hundred miles from the birth place of both Judaism and Christianity. By the year 1000 it had spread across north Africa, northward into Spain, throughout the Middle East, and on through Iran and Afghanistan into India. Our study of Islam in Chapter 11 will complete our introduction to the origins and early life of the three major monotheistic religions.

BIBLIOGRAPHY

Andrea, Alfred and James Overfield, eds. *The Human Record*, Vol. I (Boston: Houghton Mifflin Company, 3rd ed., 1998).

Armstrong, Karen. *A History of God* (New York: Knopf, 1993).

Augustine. *The City of God*, trans. Marcus Dods (New York: Modern Library, 1950).

Baron, Salo Wittmayer. *A Social and Religious History of the Jews*, Vol. 1 (New York: Columbia University Press, 1952).

Brown, Peter. *The Rise of Western Christendom* (Malden, MA: Blackwell Publishers, 1996).

Holy Bible. New Revised Standard Version (Grand Rapids, MI: Zondervan Publishing House, 1989).

Crossan, John Dominic. *The Historical Jesus. The Life of a Mediterranean Jewish Peasant* (San Francisco: HarperCollins, 1991).

de Lange, Nicholas. *Atlas of the Jewish World* (New York: Facts on File, 1984).

Einhard and Notker the Stammerer. *Two Lives of Charlemagne*, trans. Lewis Thorpe (Harmondsworth, England: Penguin Books, 1969).

Eliade, Mircea. *Ordeal by Labyrinth* (Chicago: University of Chicago Press, 1982).

——. *The Sacred and the Profane* (New York: Harper Torchbooks, 1959).

Gibbon, Edward. *The History of the Decline and Fall of the Roman Empire*, 3 vols., abridged by D.M. Low (New York: Washington Square Books, 1962).

Grant, Michael. *History of Rome* (New York: Charles Scribner's Sons, 1978).

——. *Jesus: An Historian's Review of the Gospels* (New York: Touchstone, 1995).

Halpern, Baruch. *The First Historians: The Hebrew Bible and History* (San Francisco: Harper and Row, 1988).

Honour, Hugh and John Fleming. *The Visual Arts: A History* (Englewood Cliffs, NJ: Prentice-Hall, 4th ed., 1995).

Hopfe, Lewis M. *Religions of the World* (New York: Macmillan Publishing Company, 5th ed., 1991).

Kaufmann, Yehezkel. *The Religion of Israel* (Chicago: University of Chicago Press, 1960).

Kee, Howard Clark. *Who Are The People of God: Early Christian Models of Community* (New Haven: Yale University Press, 1995).

Kee, Howard Clark, *et al. Christianity: A Social and Cultural History* (New York: Macmillan Publishers, 1991).

Mann, Michael. *A History of Power from the Beginning to A.D. 1760* (Cambridge: Cambridge University Press, 1986).

Matthew, Donald. *Atlas of Medieval Europe* (New York: Facts on File, 1983).

McManners, John, ed. *The Oxford Illustrated History of Christianity* (New York: Oxford University Press, 1990).

Meier, John P. *A Marginal Jew: Rethinking the Historical Jesus* 2 vols. (New York: Doubleday, 1991, 1994).

Momigliano, Arnaldo. *On Pagans, Jews, and Christians* (Hanover NH: University Press of New England for Wesleyan University Press, 1987).

The New English Bible with the Apocrypha. Oxford Study Edition (New York: Oxford University Press, 1970).

Palmer, R.R. and Joel Colton. *A History of the Modern World*, 8th ed. (New York: Knopf, 1984).

Pritchard, James B., ed. *Ancient Near Eastern Texts Relating to the Old Testament* (Princeton: Princeton University Press, 3rd ed., 1969).

Rosenberg, David and Harold Bloom. *The Book of J* (New York: Grove Weidenfeld, 1990).

Rubenstein, Richard L. *When Jesus Became God* (New York: Harcourt Brace, 1999).

Smart, Ninian. *The World's Religions* (Cambridge: Cambridge University Press, 1989).

Smart, Ninian and Richard D. Hecht, eds. *Sacred Texts of the World: A Universal Anthology* (New York: Crossroad Publishing, 1982).

Smeltzer, Robert M. *Jewish People, Jewish Thought* (New York: Macmillan Publishing Co., Inc., 1980).

Tierney, Brian. *The Crisis of Church and State 1050–1300* (Englewood Cliffs; Prentice-Hall, 1964).

CHAPTER
11

ISLAM

570 C.E.–1500 C.E.

"For much of the period from the eighth to the eighteenth century the leading civilization on the planet in terms of spread and creativity was that of Islam."

FRANCIS ROBINSON

SUBMISSION TO ALLAH:
MUSLIM CIVILIZATION BRIDGES THE WORLD

Islam, in Arabic, means submission. Islam teaches submission to the word of the one God, called "Allah" in Arabic. Muslims, those who submit, know God's word primarily through the Quran, the Arabic book that records the teachings of God as they were transmitted through the angel Gabriel to the Prophet Muhammad (570–632). Stories of Muhammad's life, words, and deeds (*hadith*) carefully collected, sifted, and transmitted over many generations, and the biography of the Prophet compiled by Ibn Ishaq (d. 767) and revised by Ibn Hisham (d. 833–4), provide models of the righteous life and how to live it. Muhammad was the most recent, and the final, prophet of God's message of ethical monotheism. Devout Muslims declare this belief in prayers, which are recited five times each day: "There is no God but God, and Muhammad is his Prophet."

As Christians begin the year 1 of their calendar with an event in the life of Jesus, so Muslims begin theirs with an event in the life of Muhammad. The event, however, is not the birth of Muhammad, nor the revelation to him of the Quran, but his **hijra**, the journey from the city of his birth, Mecca, where he was harassed for his beliefs, to

Medina some 200 miles (320 kilometers) away. City leaders in Medina invited Muhammad to establish a new form of government. For Islam the teachings of the Quran and of Muhammad's life are fulfilled only with the creation of a community of believers, the **umma**, and its proper regulation through political structures. The *hijra* and Muhammad's assertion of governmental leadership in Medina therefore mark the year 1 on the Muslim calendar, corresponding to the year 622 on the Christian calendar.

Through its early centuries, Islam established administrative and legal systems in the areas to which it spread: Arabia, western Asia, northern Africa, and Spain. As Islam spread later to eastern Europe, central Asia, south Asia, and sub-Saharan Africa, it arrived sometimes with government backing, sometimes without. Islam is considered in this part on the spread of world religions, but because it often unified government and religion into a single system, it may also be compared with the materials in Part 3 on the expansion of world empires. After the twelfth century, Islam extended into China and southeast Asia as a religious and cultural system without government support. In this chapter, however, we shall trace the growth and spread of Islam as a religious, governmental, and cultural system. We shall also examine its encounters with other religions and empires.

PERSPECTIVES ON ISLAM: HOW DO WE KNOW?

A 1993 essay by Richard Eaton, historian at the University of Arizona, explores many of the key historiographical problems in Islamic history. Eaton notes that much of the historical writing on Islam is based on orthodox Islamic sources or, conversely, on the writings of their opponents. Such sources are not unbiased. In addition, several key documents were written down long after the events they describe, allowing possible alterations in the text.

The Quran itself, for example, was compiled some fifty years after Muhammad received his first revelation. The first Arabic biography of the Prophet was written by Muhammad ibn Ishaq (d. 767) more than a century after the Prophet's death. Moreover, Islam suffered three civil wars in its first 120 years, and considerable internal fighting thereafter, and many of the "official" histories were prepared in support of one position or another. Finally, as Islam confronted other religious civilizations, the accounts of its history were frequently tendentious, again supporting one side or another.

In their search for unbiased information, recent historians have made use of sources that were not recorded as historical narratives but that provide data from which history can be written:

The new generation of historians thus uncovered an impressive variety of sources: commercial

ISLAM		
DATE C.E.	**POLITICAL/SOCIAL EVENTS**	**LITERARY/PHILOSOPHICAL EVENTS**
500	● Muhammad (570–632)	
600	● Hijra (622) ● Muslim conquest of Mecca ● Orthodox or Rightly Guided Caliphs (632–661) ● Muslim conquest of Iraq, Syria, Palestine, Egypt, western Iran (632–642), Cyprus (649), and Persian Empire (650s) ● Umayyad caliphate (661–750); capital in Damascus ● Muslim conquest of Carthage (698) and central Asia (650–712) ● Husayn killed at Karbala (680); Sunni–Shi'ite split	● Revelation of the Quran to Muhammad (610) ● Persian becomes second language of Islam
700	● Muslim conquest of Tunis (700), Spain (711–716), Sind and lower Indus valley ● Muslim defeat at Battle of Tours (732) ● Muslims defeat Chinese at battle of Talas River (751) ● Abbasid caliphate (750–1258) ● Baghdad founded (762)	● Biography of Muhammad by Ibn Ishaq (d. 767) ● Formulation of major systems of Islamic law
800	● Divisions in Muslim Empire (833–945) ● Fez founded (808)	● al–Tabari, *History of Prophets and Kings* ● al–Khwarazmi develops algebra ● Abbasid caliphate establishes "House of Wisdom" translation bureau in Baghdad ● Sufi tariqat
900	● Persians seize Baghdad (945) ● Cairo founded (969)	● Ferdowsi, *Shah Nama* ● al–Razi, *Encyclopedia of Medicine* ● Turkish becomes third language of Islam ● Mutazilites challenge Islamic orthodoxy

ISLAM

DATE C.E.	POLITICAL/SOCIAL EVENTS	LITERARY/PHILOSOPHICAL EVENTS
1000	• Seljuk Turks dominate Abbasid caliphate (1038) • Almoravid dynasty in north Africa and Spain (1061–1145) • Battle of Manzikert (1071) • 1st Crusade (1095–9)	• Ibn Sina (Avicenna), philosopher, produces "Canon of Medicine" • al–Biruni writes on mathematics and astronomy (d. 1046)
1100	• Almohad dynasty rules north Africa and Spain (1145–1269) • 2nd Crusade (1147–9) • Salah al-Din (Saladin) recaptures Jerusalem (1187) • 3rd Crusade (1189–92)	• al–Ghazzali (d. 1111), Muslim philosopher and theologian • Ibn Rushd (Avarroes; 1126–98) • Maimonides (1135–1204), Jewish physician, philosopher, and theologian
1200	• 4th Crusade (1202–04) • Sultanate of Delhi (1211–1526) • Children's Crusade (1212) • 5th–8th Crusades (1218–91) • Crusaders driven from west Asia (1291) • Fall of Baghdad to Mongols (1258); end of Abbasid Caliphate	• Jalal al–Din Rumi, *Mathnawi* • al–Juvaini, *History of the World Conquerors* • Rashid al–Din, *World History*
1300	• Mansa Musa's pilgrimage to Mecca (1324) • Conversion of Malayans and Indonesians to Islam	• Ibn Battuta (1304–68), traveler • Ibn Khaldun, *Universal History*
1400	• Ottoman Turks conquer Constantinople (1453) • Christians capture Granada, Spain, and complete the *reconquista* (1492)	

documents, tax registers, official land grants, administrative seals, census records, coins, gravestones, magical incantations written on bowls, memoirs of pilgrims, archeological and architectural data, biographical dictionaries, inscriptional evidence, and, more recently, oral history. (Eaton in Adas, p. 4)

From these records has emerged a deeper understanding of the culture of Muhammad's homeland in Arabia and of the adjacent Byzantine and Sassanian Persian Empires. These records suggest that Islam did not develop within a national vacuum. It incorporated religious, cultural, and social structures that were already present among its neighbors. Further, in contrast to the view that Islam was spread by the sword, new information suggests that the early rapid military expansion of the Islamic Empire was not motivated by a desire to win converts to the new faith but rather by political, economic, and military goals. Indeed, at first non-Arabs were not encouraged to join the ranks of Muslim believers.

People converted to Islam not primarily under threat of the sword, nor even necessarily because of devout belief in the Muslim creed, but because participation in Islam widened their religious, political, social, economic, and cultural horizons. To convert to Islam was to access world civilization. (On p. 318 we noted a similar rationale inspiring the spread of Christianity.) Islam was not only a faith, not only a system of government, not only a social and cultural organization, but a combination of all four. For ten centuries Islam represented the world's most cosmopolitan civilization.

Another area of intense concern and reinterpretation is the status of women in early Islam. Here, Eaton's insights are supplemented by those of scholars such as Judith Tucker, Nikki Keddie, Beth Baron, and Leila Ahmed, who have enriched our understanding of gender roles in pre-Islamic Arabia. These scholars differ in their evaluations of the impact of early Islam on women because they differ in their evaluation of the status of women in Arabia and in the neighboring Byzantine and Sassanian Empires in the period before

Muhammad. Some see the treatment of women advocated by Muhammad as an improvement in that status, some as a decline. All, however, agree that the status of women was affected less by the teachings of Muhammad, which are ambiguous, than by contact with the Sassanian and Byzantine Empires. Seclusion from men, the wearing of the veil, practices of marriage and divorce, and the legal and economic status prescribed for women were adapted from these areas of conquest.

THE PROPHET: HIS LIFE AND TEACHING

Born in 570 to parents eminent in the Quraysh tribe of Arabia, Muhammad was a deeply meditative person, retreating regularly to a nearby hill to pray and reflect. In 610, when he was forty years old, his reflections were interrupted by the voice of the angel Gabriel, who instructed him: "Recite: In the name of the Lord who created Man of a blood-clot." For the next two decades, God continued to reveal his messages to Muhammad through Gabriel. Muhammad, who could not write, dictated these messages to a scribe. During the Prophet's lifetime, the verses were written down on palm leaves, stone, and other materials. The collection was completed during the rule of Umar, the second caliph (r. 634–644), and under Uthman, the third caliph (r. 644–656), an officially authorized edition was issued. By the middle eighth century, as Arab armies defeated Chinese forces in central Asia, the Muslim victors learned from their prisoners of war the technology of papermaking. By the end of the eighth century Baghdad had a paper mill; Egypt by 900; Morocco and Spain by 1100. Turks brought the art of papermaking to north India in the twelfth century. One use of paper was, of course, in the administration of the government bureaucracy. Another, perhaps even more important, was in the printing and diffusion of the Quran.

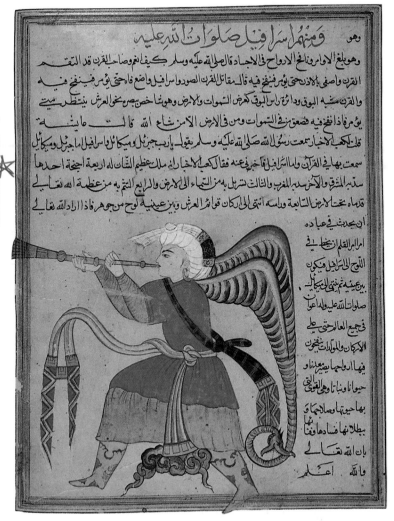

Trumpet call of the archangel Gabriel. Muhammad's religious career as a prophet seems to have been inspired by his early supernatural experiences. Once, he encountered a mighty being, the archangel Gabriel, on the horizon, who commanded him to recite . . . This was the first *surah* (section from the Quran) revealed to humanity, and is symbolized here by Gabriel's blowing on a trumpet. (*British Library, London*)

Approximately the length of the Christian New Testament, the Quran is considered by Muslims the absolute, uncorrupted, word of God. Composed in poetic form, the Quran helped to define the literary standards of the Arabic language. Muslims chant and study its text in Arabic, considering each syllable sacred. Even today many Muslims reject translations of the Quran into other languages as inadequate. (In this text we follow the translation of A.J. Arberry, the version most acceptable to Muslim scholars. The translation by N.J. Dawood is somewhat more accessible and reads more smoothly.) Reverence for the language, poetry, and message of the Quran brings unity to all Muslims throughout the world. The Quran provides the basis not only of the Islamic faith but also of its principles of government, law, and social cohesion.

According to the Quran, Muhammad was only a messenger of God, not the originator of a new doctrine. Indeed, he was not even the founder of Islam. Several prophets came before him, including Adam, Noah, Abraham, Moses, and Jesus:

> We believe in God, and in that which has been sent down on us and sent down on Abraham, Ishmael, Isaac and Jacob, and the tribes, and that which was given to Moses and Jesus and the Prophets, of their Lord; we make no division between any of them, and to Him we surrender. (Quran, 2:130–32)

Muslims claim Abraham, the father of Jewish monotheism, as the first Muslim: "Abraham in truth was not a Jew, neither a Christian; but he was a Muslim and one of pure faith" (Quran, 3:60).

The teachings of each of the earlier prophets, however, were corrupted over time by their followers. Christians, for example, mistakenly considered Jesus to be the son of God, and perverted the message of pure monotheism. The Quran deplored this heresy, declaring, "It is not for God to take a son unto Him" (19:36). The Jews' error was in refusing to accept the Quran as a revised and updated version of the truth already given to them:

> When they were told, "Believe in that God has sent down," They said, "We believe in what was sent down on us"; and they disbelieve in what is beyond that. (2:85)

The message delivered to Muhammad was final, uncorrupted, and true. Muhammad did not formulate this message; he only transmitted it as received. In the chain of prophets, Muhammad is the last and final link.

THE FIVE PILLARS OF ISLAM:

The Quran reveals the "five pillars" of Islam, the five ritual expressions that define orthodox Muslim religious belief and practice:

- Declaration of the creed, "There is no god but God, and Muhammad is his Prophet"

- Prayers to be recited five times daily while facing Mecca (2:144), and, if possible, to be recited in public assembly at midday each Friday

- Alms to be donated to the poor in the community, especially to widows and orphans (2:212 ff.), later recommended at 2½ percent of income

- The month of Ramadan to be observed by fasting each day, although eating is permitted at night, with a major feast marking the month's end (2:179–84)

- The *hajj*, a pilgrimage to Mecca to be undertaken, where possible, at least once in a lifetime (2:185 ff.).

A sixth pillar, **jihad**, or sacred struggle (2:187), was less stringently required and has been interpreted in different ways. Some scholars interpret *jihad* as a call to physical warfare to preserve and extend the **dar al-Islam**, the political rule of Islam. Even then, *jihad* should be pursued only in self-defense, for "God loves not the aggressors" (2:187). Others understand *jihad* as a call to internal spiritual struggle to live Islam as fully as possible. The Quran gives a capsule description of this proper life:

> True piety is this: to believe in God, and the Last Day, the angels, the Book, and the Prophets,
> to give of one's substance, however cherished, to kinsmen, and orphans, the needy, the traveller, beggars, and to ransom the slave,
> to perform the prayer, to pay the alms.
> And they who fulfil their covenant, and endure with fortitude misfortune, hardship and peril, these are they who are true in their faith, these are the truly godfearing. (2:172–3)

Finally, the Quran promises repeatedly that those who observe Islam faithfully will find their reward in paradise:

> And those that believe, and do deeds of righteousness,
> them We shall admit to gardens underneath which rivers flow, therein dwelling forever and ever; therein for them shall be spouses purified, and We shall admit them to a shelter of plenteous shade. (4:60)

On the other hand, those who reject the opportunity to fulfill the teachings of Islam will burn in Hell:

> Who earns evil, and is encompassed by his transgressions—those are the inhabitants of the Fire; there they shall dwell forever. (2:75)

[handwritten margin notes: "everyone will claim him"; "but Jesus is God"; "can justify everything and terrorism"; "wow... nice"]

"Celebration of the End of Ramadan," from *The Maqamat (The Meetings), c.* **1325–50** C.E. At the end of Ramadan, the month of fasting, Muslims don new clothes, throng the congregational mosques, and share their mingled senses of joy, relief, and achievement. Here a cavalcade, brandishing flags bearing religious inscriptions, unites in celebration. (*Bibliothèque Nationale, Paris*)

Humans are to choose between doing good and evil, but the Quran asserts that our free will is limited: "God has power over everything" (4:87).

Historian Michael Morony demonstrated that many of Islam's beliefs and practices were consistent with the rituals of peoples in the regions into which Islam spread, and this made acceptance of the new religion easier. For example, regular prayer times and recitals of creed were also central to Judaism and Christianity, as was institutionalized charity. Animal sacrifice was a part of pagan and Zoroastrian religions, as it was of Islam. Ritual slaughter of animals for food mirrored Jewish practice, as did male circumcision. Ritual washing before public prayers was also practiced by Zoroastrians. In this sense, Islam fit into its cultural setting, facilitating assimilation in both directions.

WOMEN: DEBATES OVER THE EFFECTS OF ISLAM

The Quran speaks extensively of women, establishing a pattern of gender relations that clearly places men above them.

> Men are the managers of the affairs of women for that God has preferred in bounty one of them over another, and for that they have expended of their property. Righteous women are therefore obedient, guarding the secret for God's guarding. And those you fear may be rebellious admonish; banish them to their couches, and beat them. If they then obey you, look not for any way against them; God is All-high, All-great. (4:38)

Women are placed on earth, in part, to satisfy men's sexual desires:

> Your women are a tillage for you; so come into your tillage as you wish. (2:223)

Women are also considered sexually seductive, and the Quran therefore urges the Prophet to

> Say to the believing women, that they cast down their eyes and guard their private parts, and reveal not their adornment save such as is outward; and let them cast their veils over their bosoms, and not reveal their adornment save to their husbands [close relatives, and the very old and very young]. (24:31)

As witnesses in legal matters, the testimony of two women is equal that of a single man (2:282). Similarly in matters of inheritance, "to the male the like of the portion of two females" (4:11).

Despite these apparently demeaning exhortations, some modern scholars assert that Islam actually introduced "a positive social revolution" (Tucker, p. 42) in gender relations. Compared to what came before, Islam introduced new rights and security in marriage. Islamic law, **shari'a**, safeguarded the rights of both partners in marriage through contractual responsibilities: it insisted on the consent of the bride; it specified that the dowry, or bridal gift, go to the bride and not to her family; and it spelled out the husband's obligations to support his wives and children. Although men were allowed to take up to four wives, the Quran added, "if you fear that you will not be equitable, then one only" (4:3), so in practice only one wife was normally permitted. These scholars note also that in the life of Muhammad, three women played exemplary roles: his first wife, Khadija, who supported him economically and emotionally when the revelations he received brought him scorn from others; Aisha, the most beloved of the wives he took after Khadija's death, and the daughter of Abu Bakr, Muhammad's successor as **caliph** or leader of the Muslim community; and Fatima, the daughter of the Prophet and wife of the fourth caliph, Ali. Nevertheless, these women drew their importance from their service to prominent men, and were criticized when they asserted more independent roles.

Other scholars have argued that Islam made the plight of women worse than it had been before. These scholars argue that in pre-Islamic Arabia, women could initiate marriage, they could have more than one husband, they could divorce their husbands, they could remain in their parents' home area and have their husbands come to live with them, and they could keep custody of their children in case of divorce. In pre-Islamic Arabia, some pagan goddesses were worshipped, suggesting that there was considerable respect for females.

Of those scholars who feel that the position of women declined under Islam, some put the blame on Islam itself, but others suggest that the teachings of Islam were actually comparatively liberal. These scholars argue that it was contact with the Byzantine and Sassanian Empires that reduced their status. Tribal, nomadic Arabia treated women with relative equality, but the neighboring empires, with their settled, urban civilizations, veiled women and kept them home under male domination. The Arabs adopted these practices. In effect, this group of scholars is also saying that the more liberal Quranic rules regarding women were reinterpreted after contact with societies outside Arabia.

MUHAMMAD IN WAR AND PEACE

Muhammad created the original *umma* or Muslim community. In his home town of Mecca, Muhammad became the leader of a sect of about 100 followers, but many people thought Muhammad mad because of his reports of revelations from God, and some apparently tried to assassinate him. Then, in 622, the elders of the city of Medina, some 200 miles (320 kilometers) to the north, invited him to adjudicate bitter disputes among local tribes and to take over the reins of government. Muhammad accepted, confirming the principle that the teachings of Islam were best implemented under an Islamic government, a *dar al-Islam* ("an abode of Islam"). In Medina Muhammad promulgated Quranic business ethics as well as family laws of marriage, divorce, and inheritance.

After establishing his authority in Medina, Muhammad turned his ambition and his troops back towards Mecca. In 624 he successfully raided a large Meccan caravan train, reducing Mecca's prosperity by cutting important trade routes and winning local fame for himself. In 625 the Meccans fought back, defeating Muhammad at Uhud. In 627 the two sides fought to a draw at the Battle of the Ditch, but Muhammad's reputation grew as he stood up to the proud and powerful Meccans. In 630, following a dispute between the tribes of the two cities, Mecca surrendered to Medina.

Christian Arabs remained largely aloof from Muhammad's alliances, while some Jews actively opposed his political goals and rejected his claims to religious prophecy. Disappointed in his wish to unite the members of the two monotheistic religions of the region under his leadership, and especially infuriated that some Jewish families had even joined the Meccan enemy in war, he had the Jewish men of the Banu Qurayza clan executed, and the women and children enslaved. On the other hand, in other parts of Arabia Jews and Christians, though subject to a special tax, were free to practice their religion.

By the time he died in 632, Muhammad was well on his way to creating from the warring tribes an Arabia-wide federation dedicated to the faith and the political structure of Islam.

SUCCESSION STRUGGLES AND THE EARLY CALIPHS

When the Prophet died leaving no male heir, the Muslim community feared that the *umma* and its political organization would break up. To preserve them, the Muslim leadership elected Abu Bakr (r. 632–634), one of Muhammad's closest associates and the father of his wife Aisha, as caliph—that is, successor to the Prophet and head of the Muslim community. The next three caliphs were similarly elected from among Muhammad's relatives and companions, but amidst much more dissension.

Abu Bakr mobilized to prevent Muslims from deserting their new religion and the authority of its government, attacking those who tried. Arabia was convulsed in tribal warfare. The contending tribes fought for power and looted one another. Their battles spilled over the borders of the Arabian peninsula, as did their search for allies. The Byzantine and Sassanian Empires saw the Arab troops encroaching on their territories and fought back, but in the Battle of Ajnadayn (634), in southern Palestine, the Arab clans combined to form a unified army and defeated the Byzantine army.

> With this victory their ambitions became boundless; they were no longer raiders on the soil of Syria seeking booty, but contenders for control of the settled empires. What began as large-scale intertribal skirmishing to consolidate a political confederation in Arabia ended as a full-scale war against the two empires. (Lapidus, p. 39)

Conquest followed conquest—Damascus in 636; Jerusalem in 638. But the northward march stopped as Byzantine troops held fast at the borders of the Anatolian peninsula. The Byzantine Empire defended its Anatolian borders for another four centuries, and its Balkan territories for eight. But the Sassanian Empire collapsed almost immediately. In 637 Arab armies defeated the Persians in battle, seized their capital, Ctesiphon, and forced the last emperor to flee. Meeting little opposition, Arab armies swept across Iraq, Iran, Afghanistan, and central Asia. Other Arab armies now turned toward northern Africa, taking Egypt in 641–643 and Tripoli in 643.

The second caliph, Umar I (r. 634–644), established the early principles of political administration in the conquered territories. The troops were not to interfere with the way of life of the conquered populations. The early caliphs did not encourage conversion to Islam, lest the political and social status of conqueror and conquered become confused. Also, since Muslims were exempted from land taxes and poll taxes, the conversion of the conquered peoples would cause considerable loss of tax revenue to Umar's government. To prevent the armies and the administrators from interfering with the economy and the social traditions of the newly conquered territories, Umar ordered the occupiers to live in garrison cities somewhat apart from the conquered populations. New garrison cities, such as Basra, Kufa, Fustat, and Merv, were built, and new neighborhoods for the foreign troops and administrators were added to existing cities. Local systems of taxation and administration were largely left in place, and incumbent personnel often kept their jobs, but lands that had been owned by the state and its officials were confiscated and claimed for the new government.

These new arrangements proved unstable. In the new garrison cities, conqueror and conquered lived side by side, and they could not effectively be segregated socially and culturally. In addition, the troops soon argued that their pay was not adequate. Their incomes lagged, even as the new conquests enriched the top-level administrators. What had become of Islam's call for a more egalitarian society? In essence, the imperial aims of the ruling class and the religious goals of Islam were pulling in opposite directions.

THE FIRST CIVIL WAR; UMAYYAD VICTORY

The jockeying for power among various political, economic, tribal, and religious interest groups precipitated a series of civil wars. The third caliph, Uthman (r. 644–656), was assassinated by a contingent of Arab troops from Egypt, who complained that their governors were cruel, their pay was inadequate, and that class divisions were destroying Arab unity. Uthman's successor, Ali (r. 656–661), was assassinated by a group that found him too soft on the Umayyad family, which was claiming the caliphate for itself. After Ali's assassination, the Umayyad leader, Mu'awiya, declared himself caliph and began the ninety-year rule of the Umayyad caliphate. Moving the capital out of Arabia to Damascus, Syria, Mu'awiya (r. 661–680) distanced himself from the original Muslim elite of the Arabian peninsula. He opened Islam to more cosmopolitan influences and a more professional style of imperial administration.

Life in the cities was eroding the solidarity of tribal society. A new social structure was developing that would divide the Arab upper and lower classes while mixing together the Arab and non-Arab elites. The caliphs looked to Islam as the glue that could bind the emerging society together, and they abandoned the policy of Muslim Arab rule over non-Muslim, non-Arab peoples. Instead they sought to assimilate the conquered peoples into a single Muslim *umma*. By the middle of the eighth century, conversions to Islam were increasing among the urban populations, as was the use of Arabic as the language of administration, literature, and everyday speech. These changes in religion and language had not yet affected the rural areas very deeply.

Stone statue of the caliph al-Walid II, Khirbat al-Mafjar, Syria, *c.* eighth century. Arab conquerors, as rulers of west Asia, could pick and choose between the artistic styles of the region. Artworks from the palaces built by Umayyad princes in the Syrian desert combine Iranian and Byzantine influences, as can be seen in this statue of an early caliph. (*Israel Antiquities Authority, Jerusalem*)

THE SECOND CIVIL WAR; SUNNI, SHI'A, AND ISMAILI DIVISIONS

Tension nevertheless remained high among the various religious and tribal factions, and war broke out again on Mu'awiya's death in 680. His son, Yazid I (r. 680–683), claimed the caliphate, but Husayn, the son of Ali, took the field against him. When Husayn was killed in battle at Karbala, Iraq, in the year 680, he joined his father as the second martyr of the Shi'a ("partisans" of Ali; also Shi'ite) branch of Islam. The Shi'as, who stressed the importance of religious purity, wanted the caliph to represent Islam's religious principles rather than imperial aspirations. They felt that Ali had represented that purer orientation and they would recognize only descendants of Ali as **imam**, or rightful caliph. From this time onward, Shi'as campaigned for the appointment of their imam to fill the position of caliph.

One after another, all of the first eleven imams were assassinated. After the death of the eleventh imam in 874 and the disappearance of his son, the hereditary line ended. From this time onward, "twelver" Shi'as have looked forward to the reappearance of the "hidden" twelfth imam, referred to as the **mahdi**, or the "rightly guided one," a messiah, to usher in a new age of Islam, truth, and justice. Meanwhile, they have usually been willing to accept the authority of the current government, while stressing matters of the spiritual rather than the temporal world.

An earlier split had occurred among the Shi'as at the death of the sixth imam in 765. While most accepted the accession of his younger son, Musa al-Kazim, a minority called "seveners" followed the elder son Ismail. These Ismailis led active proselytizing campaigns among tribals and peasants in Arabia, Syria, Iraq, central Asia, and northern Africa, and in the towns of Iran. They led frequent rebellions against the caliphate. This group, too, later split. One branch of Ismailis lives on today, revering the Aga Khan as its leader.

The great majority of Muslims, however, regarded the caliph as primarily a political official, administering the empire of Islam, and they accepted the

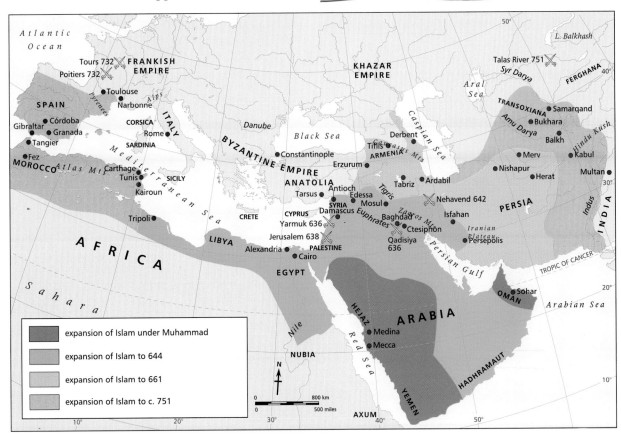

The expansion of Islam The Muslim faith spread with astonishing speed from its center at Mecca, exploiting the vacuum left by the collapse of Rome and Seleucid Persia. Within a century of the death of the Prophet Muhammad in 632 C.E., Arab armies had reached the Atlantic coast in the west, and the borders of India and China in the east.

rule of the Umayyads. They called themselves Sunnis, or followers of "the Prophet's example." The division between Sunni and Shi'a, which began over the proper succession to the caliphate, has continued to the present, long after the caliphate has ceased to exist, as the principal sectarian division within Islam. Some 83 percent of the world's Muslims today are Sunnis, 16 percent Shi'as. The split is largely geographical with Shi'as forming 95 percent of the population of Iran and about 60 percent of Iraq. Ismailis, a branch of Shi'as, are found mostly in Pakistan and India. Elsewhere Sunnis are the overwhelming majority.

THE HEIGHTS AND DEPTHS OF THE UMAYYAD DYNASTY

After the succession struggle on Mu'awiya's death, the Umayyads consolidated their rule and embarked on wars of imperial conquest. Arab armies conquered the entire northern coast of Africa by 711. They crossed the Straits of Gibraltar and completed the conquest of Spain between 711 and 756. Raiders into France were pushed back south of the Pyrenees in 732, however, by the armies of Charles Martel at the Battle of Tours. Other armies marched eastward, capturing large parts of central Asia, and raiding repeatedly in the Indus valley region of Sind.

To symbolize their imperial power, the Umayyad caliphs constructed elegant, monumental mosques in Jerusalem in 691 (the Dome of the Rock; see picture below); in Medina, 706–710; Damascus, 706–714; and, again, Jerusalem (the al-Aqsa), 709–715. They began also to create an imperial bureaucracy which owed its allegiance to the state rather than to the current ruler personally.

The Umayyads copied the imperial structures of the Byzantine and Persian Empires: wars of imperial conquest, bureaucracy in administration, monu-

The exterior of the Dome of the Rock, Jerusalem, first constructed in 692 C.E. The first Umayyad caliph, Abd al-Malik (r. 685–705) built this shrine as the first major monument in Islamic history. It celebrates the triumphal conquests of the Umayyad dynasty as it emerged from Arabia and defeated both the Byzantine and Persian empires to carve out a new empire of its own.

mentality in architecture, and regal opulence at court. They used Arabic as their language of administration. Under Caliph Umar II (717–720), the Umayyads turned to Islam to provide the spiritual and ideological glue of their empire. Recognizing that they could no longer administer so large and sophisticated an empire from their narrow base as foreign conquerors, they encouraged their subjects to convert to Islam and create a universal empire based on a common faith. Arabs and non-Arabs would be equal in the eyes of Islam. Access to both military and civilian office would be equalized, as would taxes.

The Umayyads were raising conflicting aspirations. Worse, Umar's successors were not so committed to the program of equality under Islam as he was, so implementation was inconsistent and various interest groups were frustrated by the vagaries of their changing fortunes. Many Sunni religious leaders, although pleased with the new emphasis on Islam, were offended by the imperial pomp of the Umayyads, and their use of religion for blatantly political purposes. Many Shi'as continued to nourish the hope that one of their imams would displace the Umayyads and take his rightful place as caliph. In Kufa, Iraq, Shi'as revolted in 740, but the revolt was suppressed, and its leaders were executed. Non-Arab Muslims whose taxes were not lowered, or were lowered only temporarily, railed against the government that had not delivered on its promises. Arabs were unhappy that their own taxes were being raised to compensate for the reductions offered to others.

The Umayyad armies were overextended and exhausted and began to lose major battles. The Turks drove them from Transoxiania, central Asia; the Khazars stopped them in Armenia in 730; the Greeks destroyed a major Syrian army in Anatolia in 740; Charles Martel halted the Umayyad advance in France in 732; in north Africa Berber rebels, although defeated in 742, destroyed a Syrian army of 27,000 in the process. Umayyad forces did win the critical Battle of the Talas River in 751, halting the advance of Chinese forces westward and opening central Asia and its silk routes to Islamic religious and cultural missions, but they did not push forward. Military advances stopped. Pulled in many conflicting directions, without the strength to reply, the caliphate was drawn into the third civil war.

THE THIRD CIVIL WAR; ABBASID VICTORY

The Abbasid clan in northern Iran—descended from an uncle of Muhammad named Abbas, and also claiming support from descendants from the line of Ali—revolted against the Umayyads. Supported by Arab settlers in Iran who were protesting against high and unjust taxes, by Shi'as who were seeking their own rule, and also by a faction from Yemen, they overthrew the Umayyad caliphate. In 750, Abu al-Abbas al-Saffah initiated the new Abbasid caliphate, which ruled in reality for a century and a half and in name until 1258. Signaling new policy directions, the new Abbasid caliph built a new capital, Baghdad, 500 miles (800 kilometers) to the east of Damascus, along the banks of the Tigris River, in the heart of the historic Fertile Crescent.

THE ABBASID CALIPHATE

The Abbasid caliphs continued the tasks of the Umayyads in trying to bring order and unity to an empire of heterogeneous peoples, and they followed many of the principles attempted by Umar II. They used Arabic as a unifying language of official communication and administration, and they continued to urge non-Muslims to convert. They recruited widely among all the peoples of the empire to fill admin-

Clay figurine of a female slave from Khirbat al-Mafjar, Syria, c. eighth century. Female slaves had their place in the world of the Umayyad dynasty and beyond. Often the objects of passionate love, many were accomplished singers and highly educated.

istrative and military positions. As the bureaucracy expanded Nestorian Christians, Jews, Shi'as, and numerous ethnic groups were prominent in their administration.

For a century the Abbasids succeeded—to a surprising degree—in solving the problems of administering large empires. They kept their administration cosmopolitan and centralized, yet at the same time in touch with local communities. They rotated their officers so that none could become entrenched and semi-independent in a distant posting. They regularized taxes. They employed spies as well as troops of soldiers and armed police. They also attempted to maintain good relations with the local notables, such as village headmen, large landowners, *qadis* or judges, officials of local mosques, religious teachers, moneylenders, accountants, merchants, and family patriarchs, who were the critical sources of information and power in the villages and towns.

STRESS IN THE CALIPHATE

Difficulties in the caliphate became apparent early on, however. The process of choosing a successor to the caliph remained unresolved. At the death of Caliph Harun-al-Rashid (786–809), his two sons fought for the throne, provoking a fourth civil war. Recruiting troops proved an even bigger problem. Throughout the empire, local strongmen were invited to ally their troops to the caliph's armies, but these military contingents naturally owed their allegiance not to Baghdad but to the local potentate.

The caliphs expanded sharply the use of slave troops in their armies. The Umayyads and some peripheral administrations had already set the example of using slaves to staff their armies, but slave troops were often poorly disciplined. Sometimes various contingents turned on one another, and reliance on slaves isolated the caliphs from their own civilian populations. The rulers became increasingly remote from the people they ruled—the more imperial the caliphate, the more distant it became from the original Islamic ideals of equality and simplicity.

THE EMERGENCE OF QUASI-INDEPENDENT STATES

At the same time the civilian bureaucracy became more corrupt and more distant from the general population, and tax collection was increasingly turned over to exploitative, semi-independent tax farmers. In 868 Ahmad ibn Tulun, a Turkish commander, established a virtually independent dynasty ruling over Egypt and Syria, until the caliph, al-Muktafi (r. 902–908), brought them back into line in 905. The slaves in the salt mines of southern Iraq waged a successful revolt for fifteen years, 868–883. In 867, frontier troops in central Iran revolted and won control of southern and western Iran.

Ismaili and Shi'a religious leaders organized revolts throughout the empire. Denying the legitimacy of Abbasid claims to rule and highlighting the exploitation of the village and tribal masses by the distant and corrupt administration in Baghdad, they won many victories in the name of their own views of Islam. Inspired by the Ismailis, peasant and Bedouin raiders raided Mecca, briefly carrying away the sacred Ka'aba stone, the most venerated shrine in the holy city.

The Fatimid clan, claiming to be the rightful successors of the Prophet, conquered Egypt and much of northern Africa. They broke openly with Baghdad, declaring themselves the legitimate caliphs. In Iraq, other rebels took control first of the regions around Baghdad and then, in 945, of Baghdad itself. The caliph was permitted to continue to rule in name, but in effect the empire as a unified, centralized administration was finished.

ISLAM EXPANDS

The functional end of the caliphate did not mean the end of the spread of Islam. Quite the contrary. Regional rulers, finding themselves more independent, pursued policies of political and military expansion while proclaiming the religion and culture of Islam as their own. Sometimes they claimed to act in the name of the caliph; sometimes they claimed complete independence.

INDIA

In northern Iran and Afghanistan, a government run by slave soldiers who had earned their freedom established itself in Ghazni, Afghanistan, in 962. These Ghaznavids launched raids into north India, 999–1026, and finally established their rule over the Punjab, 1021–1186. They were followed by the Ghurids, who were also at first more raiders from Ghur than rulers of India. In 1211, however, the Ghurid general who conquered Delhi declared himself an independent sultan, initiating a series of five dynasties, which are known collectively as the

Portrait of Mahmud of Ghazni, from Rashid al-Din's *World History*, 1306–7. Mahmud (998–1030), a Sunni Muslim prince, is shown putting on the traditional diplomatic gift of a robe of honor, bestowed by the Abbasid caliph. Regional rulers sometimes declared their independence from central control, but Mahmud of Ghazni was careful to include the caliph's name on his coinage, thereby presenting himself as a loyal subject. (*Edinburgh University Library*)

Sultanate of Delhi (1211–1526). By 1236 they controlled north India; by 1335, almost the entire subcontinent. When Delhi's power dimmed, numerous Muslim rulers controlled other regions of India. These regional governments, in particular, stayed close to their subjects, encouraged the development of regional languages, and provided new opportunities to **Sufis**, Muslim mystics and teachers, to introduce and practice Islam in new areas. In 1526, temporarily, and in 1556, more permanently, a mixture of Mongol and Turkish Muslim invaders conquered India, heralding the start of a new era, the Mughal Empire.

Most, but not all, of the Muslim rulers recognized the importance of a respectful religious accommodation with the overwhelming Hindu majority. The first Muslim invaders in Sind in the

The rise of the Delhi Sultanate The Muslim Afghan Ghaznavid Empire was the first of a number of Afghan and Turkic powers who, exploiting divisions among local Hindu rulers, established their hegemony in northern India. Based at Delhi, six successive Muslim dynasties commanded varying territorial extents, but only briefly in the mid-fourteenth century did they completely control the Deccan.

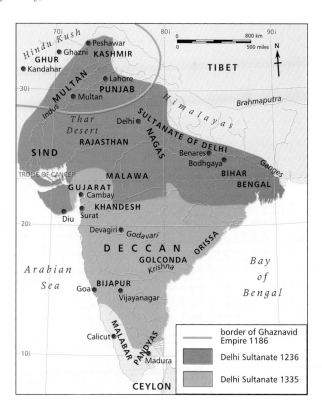

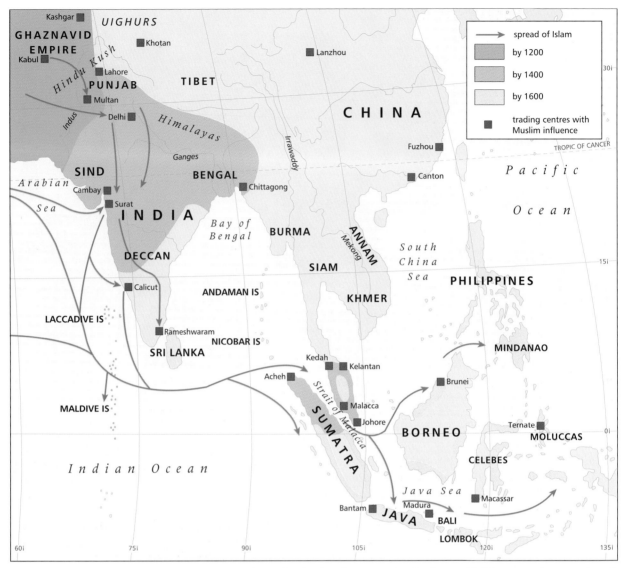

Islam in south and southeast Asia The disruption of centralized political power in the Muslim world did not stop the expansion of Islam in Africa and southern Asia. Arab maritime traders carried their faith to the shores of India and onward throughout maritime southeast Asia. The Indian heartland was conquered by successive waves of Muslim invaders, who, by 1400, secured the key Indo-Gangetic plain.

eighth century extended **dhimmi** status (see Focus, p. 361) to Hindus, arguing that behind the many forms of god in Hinduism there was just one reality, and also recognizing that warfare against so large a majority of Hindus was impossible. Muslims often did deface Hindu and Buddhist shrines. For example, they destroyed the famous Shaivite temple at Somnath, western India, in 1024, and the Turkish forces occupying Bengal and Bihar also destroyed the last remaining libraries and monasteries of Buddhism in that region, delivering the final death blow to a religion that had already seen most of its following in India disappear.

The Muslim conquest of India opened the subcontinent to Persians, Afghans, Turks, and Mongols seeking jobs with the new governments (see Chapter 14). This immigration brought a variety of Islamic practices to India, where no single orthodoxy prevailed. Diverse Muslims coexisted with diverse Hindus, venerating some saints and sharing some devotions in common. India's population became 20–25 percent Muslim. Many were descendants of Muslim immigrants near the top of the social hierarchy; others were converts, escaping untouchability at the bottom of the caste system. The majority of India's population, however, remained Hindu.

SOUTHEAST ASIA

The beginning of mass conversions of southeast Asians to Islam came in the fourteenth and fifteenth centuries, and today, Malaysia and Indonesia are overwhelmingly Muslim. Ocean traders and Sufis from India seem to have accomplished most of the missionary work. The traders offered increased economic opportunities to local people who would adopt Islam, while the Sufis and the regional kings of southeast Asia exchanged support for one another in a familiar pattern of interdependence between religious and political leaders. We will consider this further in Chapter 12.

MOROCCO AND SPAIN

The Arab Umayyads had carried Islam across northern Africa and into Spain by 711. In north Africa, after initial resistance, most of the conquered Berbers converted to Islam. At one extreme, conversion was accompanied by intermarriage, and some of the Arab conquerors and Berber peoples intermingled to the point where it was no longer possible to distinguish among them ethnically. In other cases, whole tribes converted. They became part of the Islamic world, but they remained in their tribal groupings. Often they conducted their own internal administration like a small state.

In 786 Idris (d. 791), a descendant of Ali and Fatima, in rebellion against the Umayyads, led an Arab-Berber coalition and founded the first Moroccan-Islamic state. Other small Berber-Muslim states also sprang up. In the tenth century a coalition of Muslim Berbers founded the Almoravid dynasty. They conquered Morocco, crossed the Straits of Gibraltar, and captured southern Spain, which had been ruled by the Umayyads but was now threatened by Christian powers. By the mid-twelfth century the Almoravids weakened. A new dynasty, the Almohads, followed, also rooted in ascetic Islam and imposing a religious hierarchy on a tribal society. They conquered both Morocco and Spain, but were driven from Spain by Christian forces in 1212 and collapsed in Morocco in 1269, leaving the region with localized governments.

SUB-SAHARAN AFRICA

As in southeast Asia, Islam was carried to sub-Saharan Africa by traders and Sufis from the north. The Arab conquest of north Africa multiplied contacts between Arab and Black Africans, and south

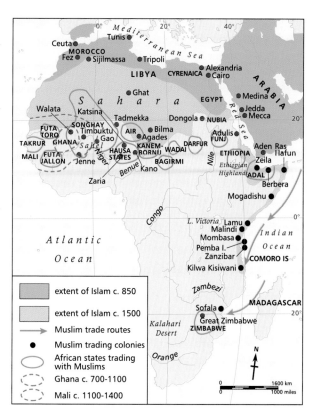

Islam in Africa Islam entered sub-Saharan Africa as a result of trade. Trans-Saharan caravans from Egypt, Libya, and Morocco gradually introduced the faith overland among the trading kingdoms of west Africa, while the Arab traders of the Indian Ocean carried the message south by sea along the east coast of the continent.

of the Sahara new kingdoms were growing, their power derived from their control of the trade routes across the desert. The southern states sent gold, slaves, hides, and ivory to the north in exchange for copper, silver, dried fruit, cloth, and salt. The largest of the states, Ghana, had been founded about 300 C.E., and by the tenth century it was both a partner and a rival of the Berbers for control of the trade. Other nearby states, including Kawkaw, Takrur, and Bornu also participated in this trade. All of them invited Muslim administrators from the north to join their courts. Traders from the north invited their southern counterparts to adopt their religion, and Sufis came to establish new communities of faith and good works. Although the common people were not much affected until the nineteenth century, leading traders and rulers began to convert to Islam, and many participated in both Islamic and indigenous religious practices. Throughout the region, Islam served commercial and administrative as well as religious purposes.

From about 1200 to about 1600, Mali succeeded Ghana as the dominant state of sub-Saharan Africa, and as the center of Islam in the region. Mali's most famous ruler, Mansa Musa (r. 1307–32), made the *hajj* (pilgrimage) to Mecca in 1324, disbursing legendary amounts of gold along the way. By this time, Muslim rulers sought prestige through public affiliation with, and support for, Islamic institutions. They built up Timbuktu, the most important trading city on the Niger River, at its northern bend near the Sahara, into a major center of Arabic and Muslim studies. Through the eighteenth century, Timbuktu remained the focus of Islamic scholarship in sub-Saharan Africa.

SELJUK TURKS AND THEIR SULTANATE

In the seventh and eighth centuries, the consolidation of the Tang dynasty in China revived the pressure on the pastoral, nomadic peoples of inner Asia, pushing them westward, just as the Han had done centuries before (see Chapters 7 and 8). This time the pastoral nomads encountered peoples who had been converted to Islam. As a result of contacts with Muslim scholars and mystics, many of the nomadic peoples converted as well. One of these groups, the

Turkish-speaking Qarluq peoples, gained control of Bukhara (992) and Samarqand (999) in modern Uzbekistan. They propagated Islam and began to sponsor the development of the Turkish language and a Turkish-Islamic civilization.

Another Turkish-speaking group, led by the Seljuk (or Saljuq) family, entered central Asia, conquered Afghanistan and Iran, and seized Baghdad in 1055. They proceeded to defeat the Byzantine Empire at Manzikert in 1071, opening Anatolia to further invasion.

In Baghdad, the Seljuk Turks kept the caliph on his throne and ruled in his name. They titled themselves sultans, claiming authority over the secular side of government, while leaving the administration of religious affairs to the caliph. Several of the provincial governments that had already won effective control over their own affairs now also called themselves sultanates. The unity of the Abbasid state dissolved, although the nominal authority of the caliph was still accepted everywhere.

MONGOLS, TURKS, AND THE DESTRUCTION OF THE CALIPHATE

In Karakorum, Mongolia, Temujin (*c.* 1162–1227), later called Genghis Khan ("Universal Ruler"),

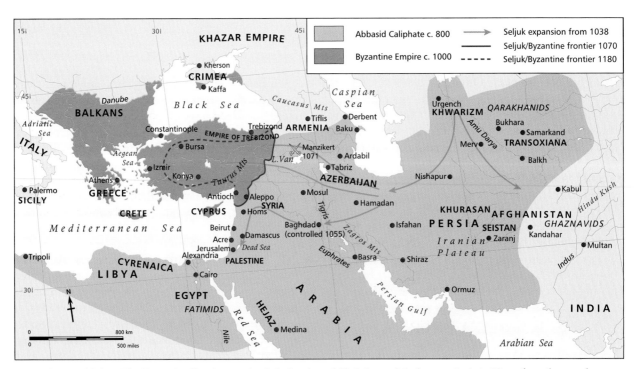

Byzantium and Islam The Byzantine Empire remained the bastion of Christian political power in Asia Minor for a thousand years after the fall of Rome. A powerful new force for Islam, the Seljuk Turks, appeared out of central Asia in the eleventh century. After invading Persia and Syria, they defeated a Byzantine army at Manzikert in 1071 and began to infiltrate the Byzantine heartland.

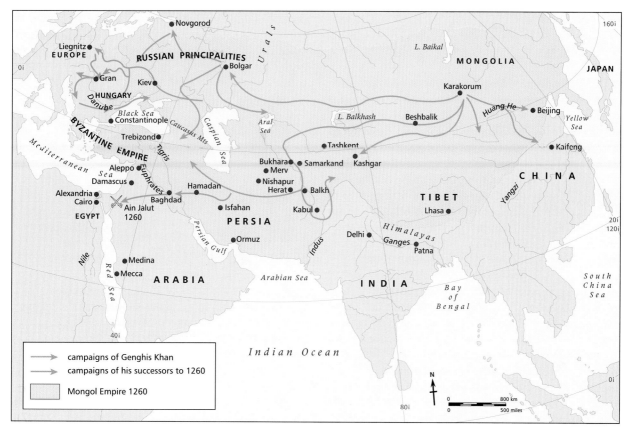

The Mongol world The irruption across Eurasia of the Mongols, an aggressive steppe nomad people, remains one of the most successful military undertakings of all time. Within thirty years the campaigns of Genghis Khan took the Mongol cavalry east to the Chinese heartland and west to Kievan Russia, the Caucasus, and Persia. His immediate successors consolidated China, entered Europe, and went on to establish a network of trans-Asian empires.

forged a confederation of Mongol and Turkish peoples which rode outward, east and west, creating the largest land-based empire in history. The story of the Mongol expansion is told in Chapter 12. Muslims whose lands he conquered felt especially devastated. An eyewitness observer, Ibn al-Athir, records his response to the early waves of invasions in 1220–1:

> For some years I continued averse from mentioning this event, deeming it so horrible that I shrank from recording it. To whom, indeed can it be easy to write the announcement of the death-blow of Islam and the Muslims, or who is he on whom the remembrance thereof can weigh lightly? O would that my mother had not born me, or that I had died and become a forgotten thing ere this befell. …

> These [Tartars] spared none, slaying women and men and children, ripping open pregnant women and killing unborn babes. … For these were a people

who emerged from the confines of China, and attacked the cities of Turkistan, like Kashghar and Balasahun, and these advanced on the cities of Transoxiana, such as Samarqand, Bukhara, and the like …

> Therefore Islam and the Muslims have been afflicted during this period with calamities wherewith no people hath been visited. (McNeill and Waldman, pp. 249–51).

In 1258, Genghis' grandson Hülegü (*c.* 1217–65) conquered Baghdad and executed the caliph, ending the Abbasid empire. The Mongols might have continued further on their conquests in west Asia, but the death of Hülegü's brother in China diverted their attention. Meanwhile, the sultan in Cairo defeated the Mongol troops at the Battle of Ain Jalut (1260), near Nazareth, ending their threat of further advance. Mongol rule in west Asia continued, however, until 1336.

SPIRITUAL, RELIGIOUS, AND CULTURAL FLOWERING

When the caliphate fell, the universal Muslim community, the *umma*, seemed to fall with it. Its central political focus was destroyed. Earlier historians have therefore characterized 1258 as a downward turning point, ushering in a protracted decline. More recent writers, however, especially Marshall Hodgson, in his monumental three-volume *The Venture of Islam*, emphasize the continuing growth of Islam outside the Arab world. After 1258 Islam "as a belief system *and* as a world civilization, grew among the peoples of Asia and Africa" (Eaton, p. 24). The descendants of the Mongols themselves converted to Islam within a century of their arrival in Islamic lands. Muslim scholars, mystics, and merchants carried Islam throughout the entire region of the Indian Ocean by sea, and along the length of the silk routes by land. When Timur the Lame (Tamerlane or Tamburlane; 1336–1405) led his Turkish invaders along many of the routes and in many of the same kinds of campaigns as Genghis Khan had done, sacking or capturing Delhi (1398), Aleppo (1400), Damascus (1401), Ankara (1402), and Bukhara (1402), he had the support of Islamic scholars (*ulama*) and mystics (Sufis). Timur's descendants patronized Islamic scholarship and within a century Samarqand and Bukhara had become major capitals of Islamic culture. They also patronized Turkish as a literary language, encouraging its development as the third language of Islam along with Arabic and Persian.

Today, approximately 17 percent of the world's Muslim population lives in southeast Asia, an area never subject to the rule of the caliphate; 30 percent lives in south Asia, where conversion took place almost entirely after its fall; 12 percent lives in sub-Saharan Africa, again virtually untouched by the caliphate. In short, some 60 percent of today's Muslims are descended from peoples who had no connection to the Abbasid caliphate in Baghdad. In the following pages we consider the factors that enabled Islam to flourish and spread as a religion and a civilization even after its historic political center collapsed.

LAW

First, the legal systems of Islam, *shari'a*, lived on. For Muslims, as for Jews, law expresses in formal terms the standards of proper conduct. Law sup-

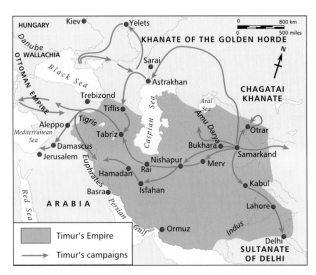

The Empire of Timur The final stage of Mongol power was inspired by Timur's ambitions. Originating in Samarqand, his armies struck east to India, north to the Khanate of the Golden Horde, and west against the Ottoman and Egyptian Mameluke empires. Despite brilliant, brutal, early successes, the empire was unable to sustain its internal dynamics, and its collapse saw the exit of Mongol power from the world stage.

ports the fundamental Islamic duty of *hisba*, "to promote what is right and to prevent what is wrong" (Musallam in Robinson, p. 175). Muslims encounter their legal system in the regulation of public life; in family matters of marriage, divorce, parental responsibilities, and inheritance; and in the *shari'a*'s advice on daily activities such as eating, dressing, and housekeeping. As the early caliphs and the Abbasids began to confront legal questions, they appointed *qadis*, or judges, to resolve them. The *qadis* searched the classical texts of the Quran, the *hadith,* and biographies of the Prophet for their core teachings, and then relied on a combination of local custom and their own deliberation and judgment (*ijtihad*) in rendering final decisions.

Seeking to overcome wide differences in local practices, four great legal scholars of the eighth and ninth centuries formulated the major systems of Islamic law that endure till today: the system of Abu Hanifah (699–767) is in use mostly in the Arab Middle East and south Asia; of Malik ibn Anas (*c.* 715–795) in north, central, and west Africa; of Muhammad al-Shafii (767–820) in east Africa, southern Arabia, and southeast Asia; and of Ahmad ibn Hanbal (780–855) in Saudi Arabia. Although most localities have followed one or another of these systems since about the tenth century, the existence of multiple systems has allowed flexibility in interpretation. Under certain circumstances, local legal experts have the option of drawing on any of the four texts. Because Shi'a maintain different traditions of authority, encompassing the teachings of Ali and the early imams, they have also developed different schools of law. The most widespread is that of Jafar al-Sadiq (d. 765).

The *Ulama*: the Scholars and Jurists of Islam

The personnel of the legal system are the **ulama** (singular *alim*), the religiously trained scholars of Islam who interpret and implement the law. The *ulama* constitute a class that includes *qadis* and their assistants, Quran reciters, prayer leaders, and preachers. The *ulama* are sometimes trained in formal theological schools or, more frequently, are simply apprenticed to senior *ulama*. Islam has no formal hierarchical, bureaucratic institution of *ulama*—indeed, it has no official church. Informal networks of respected *ulama* have provided cohesion, stability, and flexibility within Islam, regardless of the changing forms of government.

Ideally, *ulama* and ruler worked together to decide and implement religious policy, but when Caliph al-Mamun (r. 813–833) proclaimed that he had the right to give authoritative interpretations of the Quran, the *ulama* mobilized the population of Baghdad against him. He responded with an inquisition to root out these opponents. The only major leader who stood up to him was Ahmad ibn Hanbal, the greatest *hadith* scholar of his generation, who argued that only the scholars had the authority to interpret Quranic text. The people supported him, and to escape the continuing popular protest, Caliph al-Mutasim (r. 833–842) moved his capital from densely populated Baghdad to Samarra, 60 miles (97 kilometers) away.

In 848–849 the Caliph al-Mutawakkil (d. 861) withdrew the claim of caliphal authority in religious matters. The *ulama* had won, but the battle had so embittered relations between caliph and *ulama* that their spheres of influence were forever separated: the caliph had authority over matters of state; the *ulama* over matters of religion. The caliphs came to represent the imperial aspirations of the state, while the *ulama* represented the everyday needs and wishes of the people. Losing touch with their own people, caliphs employed armies of slaves and of Turkish mercenaries. Over time, such departures from popular accountability cost them the caliphate. But the *ulama* endured, in touch with the people, and serving as their guides.

SUFIS, THE MYSTICS OF ISLAM

Law brings order to life. It makes concrete the responsibilities of one individual to another and to society in general. In Islam it also fixes the formal

Divorce proceedings. A scribe records the accusations of a husband and wife as they petition for a divorce in front of a *qadi*, or judge. A woman had limited rights to divorce her husband, but a man could divorce his wife without stipulating a reason, though in practice matters were rarely this simple. A *qadi* would bring to bear the combined wisdom of scriptural knowledge, local custom, and his own judgment in making an adjudication. (*Bibliothèque Nationale, Paris*)

Delivering a lecture. A traditional saying—"Kings are the rulers of the people, but scholars are the rulers of kings"—indicates the esteem in which learning is traditionally held by Muslims. Moreover, the transmission of knowledge was deemed a major act of piety. A well-stocked library serves as the backdrop for a lecture, in which a teacher would first dictate a text, then discourse upon it. (*Bibliothèque Nationale, Paris*)

obligations due to God; the *ulama* convey and interpret this message.

Sufis, on the other hand, reveal the inner, mystical path to God. Early Sufis found and transmitted the inner disciplines of mind and body, the purifications of the heart that enabled their followers to experience God directly as the ultimate reality. They usually disdained worldly pleasures. One of the earliest of the Sufis, Hasan al-Basri (643–728), concluded: "This world has neither worth nor weight with God, so slight it is" (cited in Esposito, p. 102). Though most Sufis were men, some, like Rabi'a al-Adawiyya (d. 801), were women. Rabi'a, like the Hindu Mirabai (see p. 269), rejected marriage to devote herself to God: "Love of God hath so absorbed me that neither love nor hate of any other thing remain in my heart" (Embree, p. 448).

As we have seen throughout this part, every theistic religion has an aspect of devotional love of god, spontaneous prayer, private meditation, fasting and asceticism, and, often, of physical disciplines, music, dance, and poetry. In Islam these aspects were adopted by the Sufis, who also absorbed influences from the mystics of other religions, especially monasticism from Christianity and Buddhism, and ecstasy in prayer (bhakti, see Source, p. 269) from Hinduism.

Through their lives of exemplary devotion to God and people the Sufis enhanced the message of Islam, as J.S. Trimingham has written in *Sufi Orders in Islam*. They attracted people through the simplicity of their piety, their personal love of God, and their dedication to the needs of others. Some developed reputations for magical powers.

these twentieth-century questions in Chapters 19 through 23. Those countries that have achieved high levels of industrialization—mostly the countries of Europe and their daughter civilizations overseas; Japan; and now some of the countries of East Asia (see Chapter 19)—have experienced a wide range of fundamental changes, akin to many of those that Britain experienced.

THE SECOND STAGE OF INDUSTRIALIZATION 1860–1914

NEW PRODUCTS AND NEW NATIONS

Between 1860 and the outbreak of World War I in 1914, a "second industrial revolution" further transformed world productivity, the ways in which humans lived their lives, and the power balances among the major nations and regions of the world. The principal technological advances came in steel, chemicals, and electricity, and these were supported by organizational breakthroughs in shipping, banking, and insurance.

Steel and Chemical Industries

The invention of new technologies—the Bessemer steel converter (1856) in Britain followed by the Siemens–Martin open-hearth method of production (1864) in Germany—soon allowed iron ore to be converted to steel cheaply and abundantly. Germany, united as a country in 1871 under Otto von Bismarck (see p. 580), forged ahead. By 1900 it was producing more steel than Britain, 6.3 million tons to 5.0 tons; in 1913, on the eve of World War I, Germany's lead had grown to 17.6 million tons against 7.7 tons. Germany also led in the invention of a number of additional new technologies, especially the internal combustion engine, the diesel engine, and the automobile.

Chemical industries grew especially after 1870 as synthetic substances, notably derivatives from coal, began to augment and replace the earlier reliance on natural substances from the vegetable world, such as alkalis and dyes. Now, synthetic, aniline dyes were made from coal tar. Both fertilizers and explosives could be made from synthetic nitrogen and phosphates. Artificial fertilizers added to a revolution in agricultural productivity,

MAJOR DISCOVERIES AND INVENTIONS—1830–1914

1831	Dynamo: Michael Faraday
1834	Reaping machine: Cyrus McCormick
1836	Revolver: Samuel Colt
1837	Telegraph: Samuel Morse
1839	Vulcanized rubber: Charles Goodyear
1852	Gyroscope: Léon Foucault
1853	Passenger elevator: Elisha Otis
1856	Celluloid: Alexander Parkes Bessemer converter: Henry Bessemer Bunsen burner: Robert Bunsen
1858	Refrigerator: Ferdinand Carré Washing machine: Hamilton Smith
1859	Internal combustion engine: Etienne Lenoir
1862	Rapid-fire gun: Richard Gatling
1866	Dynamite: Alfred Nobel
1876	Telephone: Alexander Graham Bell
1877	Phonograph: Thomas Edison
1879	Incandescent lamp: Thomas Edison
1885	Motorcycle: Edward Butler Electric transformer: William Stanley Vacuum flask: James Dewar
1887	Motorcar engine: Gottlieb Daimler/Karl Benz
1888	Pneumatic tire: John Boyd Dunlop Kodak camera: George Eastman
1895	Wireless: Nikola Tesla X-rays: Wilhelm Roentgen
1896	Radioactivity: Antoine Becquerel
1897	Diesel engine: Rudolf Diesel
1898	Submarine: John P. Holland Radium and polonium: Pierre and Marie Curie
1902	Radio-telephone: Reginald Fessenden
1903	Airplane: Wilbur and Orville Wright
1905	Theory of relativity: Albert Einstein
1911	Combine harvester: Benjamin Holt
1914	Tank: Ernest Swinton

SPOTLIGHT
Through the Camera's Lens

Photography has dramatically altered the way we see and represent our world. The earliest photographic processes, developed by Louis J.M. Daguerre (1787–1851) and then by William Henry Fox Talbot (1800–77), pioneered the process and later inventions brought photography to ever wider audiences. Faster lenses (1840s), the changeover from "wet" (1851) to "dry" (1871) glass and metal plates, and then the use of film (about 1900) as the medium for the exposure process were key technical developments.

In 1888 George Eastman invented the "Kodak," the first camera which could be mass-produced. Amateurs could now take their own photographs, leaving the processes of developing and printing them to commercial laboratories. Photography became a mass hobby.

The invention of more sensitive plates and faster shutter speeds enabled the photography of rapid motion. In 1878 Eadweard Muybridge captured the beauty of a galloping horse in twelve shots from a racetrack (**figure 1**), and invalidated forever the classical representation of horses racing with all four legs extended off the ground. By providing exact images of what the eye could see, photography also challenged the fine arts, especially painting; photographers could capture scenes with an accuracy that no artist could hope to match. In creative response, painters sought new ways of representing reality: Impressionism and, later, the various schools of abstract art evolved in large part because the camera usurped the traditional role of painting.

Photography also became a medium for telling stories, and the power of photo-journalism was realized at a very early date. In 1855 the British government dispatched Roger Fenton to photograph the Crimean War and bring home pictures that might disprove reports of blundering military commanders. The American Civil War was widely photographed, most strikingly by Mathew Brady and his corps of about twenty cameramen. They chose to show the horrors and the grimness of the war (**figure 2**) rather than its heroism. Brady hoped to turn

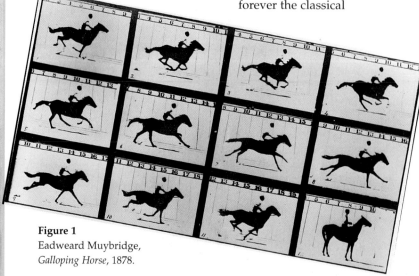

Figure 1
Eadweard Muybridge,
Galloping Horse, 1878.

The mosques where they lived and prayed, and the mausolea in which they were buried, were revered as sacred shrines (see Focus, p. 359). Eaton cites such a Sufi saint in a sixteenth-century folk ballad of eastern Bengal:

At that time there came a Mahomedan *pir* [Sufi] to that village. He built a mosque in its outskirts, and for the whole day sat under a fig tree. . . . His fame soon spread far and wide. Everybody talked of the occult powers that he possessed. If a sick man called on him he would cure him at once by dust or some trifle touched by him. He read and spoke the innermost thoughts of a man before he opened his mouth. . . . Hundreds of men and women came every day to pay him their respects. Whatever they wanted they miraculously got from this saint. Presents of rice, fruits, and other delicious food, goats, chickens, and fowls came in large quantities to his doors. Of these offerings the *pir* did not touch a bit but freely distributed all among the poor. (Adas, pp. 21–2)

Individual mystics appeared in Islam from its earliest days, drawing their inspiration directly from the Quran: "I am near to answer the call of the caller, when he calls to Me" (2:182); "We indeed created man; and We know what his soul whispers within him, and We are nearer to him than the jugular vein" (L:15). Centuries later, they began to form **tariqas**, or mystical brotherhoods, often located at the mosque or mausoleum of an especially revered saint. Some *tariqas*, like that attributed to Abu Yazid al-Bistami (d. 874), emphasized ecstatic practices; others, like that of the even more famous Abu'l Qasim al-Junayd (d. 910), were more sober and meditative. The *tariqa mawlawiya* was founded by Jalal-al-Din Rumi (1207–73) in Konya, Turkey. Rumi is most famous for his expression of ecstatic worship through dance. Rumi's Persian language text, the *Mathnawi*, expressed in rich and evocative lyrics his love of God: "The result of religion is nothing but rapture" (Rumi, *Mathnawi* 1:312, cited in Vitray-Meyerovitch, p. 83).

The more solemn *ulama* and the more emotional Sufis were often suspicious of one another. Deeply

Whirling Dervishes. Sufism represents the mystical, contemplative strand of Islam—a strand that is captured vividly by the "Whirling Dervishes," a religious order closely linked to the teachings of the thirteenth-century Persian poet Jalal al-Din Rumi. Their slow, revolving dance helps to create higher states of consciousness, while being a ceremonial ritual in its own right.

PROFILE
Al-Ghazzali
"RENEWER OF ISLAM"

Born and educated in Iran, Abu Hamid Muhammad al-Ghazzali (1058–1111) was appointed at the age of thirty-three to teach philosophy at the leading *madrasa*, or theological institute, in Baghdad. During four years there Ghazzali began to doubt the role of rationality in life and searched for more holistic ways of experiencing the world. Torn between holding his prestigious tenure at the *madrasa* or giving it up to pursue new roads toward truth, Ghazzali was on the verge of breakdown:

> For nearly six months . . . I was continuously tossed about between the attractions of worldly desires and the impulses towards eternal life. In that month the matter ceased to be one of choice and became one of compulsion. God caused my tongue to dry up so that I was prevented from lecturing. One particular day I would make an effort to lecture in order to gratify the hearts of my following, but my tongue would not utter a single word nor could I accomplish anything at all. This impediment in my speech produced grief in my heart, and at the same time my power to digest and assimilate food and drink was impaired; I could hardly swallow or digest a single mouthful of food.
> (al-Ghazzali, p. 57)

In 1095 Ghazzali resigned his post. He traveled to Damascus, Jerusalem, and Mecca, and then returned to his home town, where he lived the monastic life of a Sufi mystic, for ten years:

> I learnt with certainty that it is above all the mystics who walk on the road of God; their life is the best life, their method the soundest method, their character the purest character. (p. 60)

During his time of contemplation, Ghazzali wrote a great number of philosophical and theological works, including the influential *Revival of the Religious Sciences,* exploring the relationship between religion and reason. He asserted the importance of mystical experience and a direct, personal understanding of God, while at the same time defending the doctrine and authority of the Islamic faith.

In 1106 Ghazzali was persuaded to return to teaching, now proclaiming the complementarity of Sufism and rationality:

> Just as intellect is one of the stages of human development in which there is an "eye" which sees the various types of intelligible objects, which are beyond the ken of the senses, so prophecy also is the description of a state in which there is an eye endowed with light such that in that light the unseen and other supra-intellectual objects become visible. (p. 65)

By the end of his life, Ghazzali's reconciliation of Sufism and rationality within Islam had earned him the title "Renewer of Islam."

---

disturbed by the tension between the two perspectives, almost to the point of emotional and psychological breakdown, Abu Hamid Muhammad al-Ghazzali (1058–1111) finally formulated a synthesis of the intellectual and the mystical sides of Islam that has proved satisfying to Muslims ever since (see Profile above).

INTELLECTUAL SYNTHESES

As the *ulama* provided order to the social structures of Islam, and the Sufis spread its spiritual powers, other intellectuals further enriched its cultural depth. The historian and theologian al-Tabari (*c.* 839–923) introduced formal historical writings

with his *History of Prophets and Kings*. The segment on prophecy recorded the contributions from Abraham through Muhammad; the record of kings covered rulers from biblical times to his own and included eyewitness reports of relatively recent events.

With the conquest of Iran in the mid-seventh century, Persian became the second language of Islam. (The arrival of the Turks in 923 introduced Turkish as the third.) The Persian poet Ferdowsi (940–1020) wrote an epic poem on the mythical origins of the Persian peoples, in which one of his central themes is the tragedy that befalls "a good man whose king is a fool."

The Mongols also supported historical writing, including al-Juvaini's (1226–83) *History of the World Conquerors,* which told of Genghis Khan's conquests, especially in Iran. Rashid al-Din (1247–1318) wrote *World History,* which many regard as the first attempt at a history of humanity, as it integrates Chinese, Indian, European, Muslim, and Mongol history into a single cosmopolitan perspective.

Ibn Khaldun (1332–1406) of Tunis is often viewed as the first to apply social science theory to the study of history. His *Universal History* stressed a cyclical theory of history, in which vigorous nomadic peoples regularly conquered urban peoples who were settled, cultured, and contented, took over their cities, settled into lives of luxury, and then themselves fell prey to the next round of invasion from more robust nomads. The theory seemed to fit the coming and going of invaders from Arabia, Mongolia, and central Asia that characterized his times. Among Ibn Khaldun's other interpretive themes that still seem insightful today are: "The differences between Easterners and Westerners are cultural [not innate]"(p. 51); "The differences between peoples arise principally from the differences in their occupations" (p. 80); and, perhaps, "Scholars are of all men those least fitted for politics and its ways" (p. 64).

Theology and philosophy had been regarded as inferior to revelation in early Islam, but as Muslims came into contact with the philosophies of the Hellenistic and Indian worlds, they were drawn to concepts of Platonism and Neoplatonism in particular. The caliphate established in Baghdad a "house of wisdom," a translation bureau under Hunayn ibn Ishaq (d. 873). In the next 200 years some eighty Greek authors were translated, including Aristotle, Plato, Galen, and Euclid. So, too, were writings from Syriac, Sanskrit, and Persian.

A group of Islamic philosophers, called *Mutazilites,* "those who keep themselves apart," began to challenge orthodox Islamic belief, arguing that the attributes of God in the Quran were not literal but metaphorical, that human actions and life were not pre-determined, and that the Quran had not existed eternally. Their style of rational argument, called *kalam,* was deeply suspect among most Muslims. One of these men, al-Ashari (873–935), began in the *Mutazilite* camp, but when he was about forty years old, he turned to the orthodox belief that the Quran was indeed the revealed word of God, that only authentic traditions about the Prophet were trustworthy, and that, while rationality was useful within certain limits, it could not equal the truths revealed by God.

Other *Mutazilites* rejected this position. Al-Farabi (*c.* 870–950) argued that philosophical knowledge gained through study and thought was of higher value than revelation from God. Similar notions of the supremacy of philsophy were expressed by al-Kindi (d. 870), Ibn Sina (Avicenna; d. 1037), and Ibn Rushd (Averroes; 1126–98). Such philosophical speculation was marginal to mainstream Islamic thought and actually found more resonance among Christian and Jewish philosophers of the time.

The European Christian thinkers were indebted to the Muslims for keeping alive the Hellenistic traditions, for with the fall of the Roman Empire in the West the intellectual traditions and resources of Christianity had been neglected and forgotten. Now, thanks to Arabic translations and Islamic thought, Christian and Jewish philosophers grappled both with the original texts from Greece and India, and with the newer concepts introduced by Muslim thinkers.

The intersection of intellectual traditions also enriched mathematics, astronomy, and medicine. Indian scholars brought their texts on astronomy to Baghdad as early as 770. The caliph had them translated into Arabic, which was becoming the common language of scholarship throughout the empire. Arabs adopted and transmitted Hindi numerals and the decimal system, including the zero, throughout the empire and on into Europe, where they were (mis)named "Arabic" numerals. A few decades later, al-Khwarazmi (d. *c.* 846) used Indian texts in conjunction with scholarship from Greece and Iran to develop algebra (from the Arabic *al-jabr,* "restoration"). (The word algorithm comes from al-Khwarazmi's name.) Al-Biruni (d. 1046) wrote extensively on number theory and

computation, and later scholars developed the trigonometry we study today. Al-Biruni also wrote *al-Qanun al-Mas'udi*, a compendium of Islamic astronomy, which incorporated findings from throughout the empire. Arabic mathematical and astronomical theories apparently informed Copernicus as he proposed a **heliocentric** universe in the sixteenth century (see Chapter 13).

Medical wisdom and herbal remedies were transmitted from one end of the empire to the other. Al-Razi (d. 925) compiled an encyclopedia of medicine, *al-Hawi,* giving the views of Greek, Syrian, Indian, Iranian, and Arab writers on each disease, and including his own clinical observations and opinions. The book was translated into Latin as *Continens.* Ibn Sina, noted above for his contributions to philosophy, produced the even more encyclopedic *Qanun fi'l-tibb* ("Canon of Medicine"), which included volumes on the pharmacology of herbs, the functioning of organs, fevers, and surgery. The *Qanun* was translated into Latin and dominated medical thinking for 300 years.

THE GLOBAL TRANSMISSION OF TECHNOLOGY

By 751, at the end of the Umayyad dynasty, Islam served as a network of communication that linked all the major civilizations of Eurasia. For example, as we noted above on p. 335, Muslims learned paper-making from the Chinese and transmitted the technology throughout their domain. European Christians learned the art from Muslims in Spain.

Andrew Watson's *Agricultural Innovation in the Early Islamic World* discusses the agricultural exchanges and innovation that enriched the world of Islam. Between the eighth and tenth centuries Arabs brought from India hard wheat, rice, varieties of sorghum, sugarcane, bananas, sour oranges, lemons, limes, mangoes, watermelon, coconut palm, spinach, artichokes, eggplants, and the key industrial crop, cotton. All these crops were introduced throughout the empire, wherever climatic conditions were favorable. Watson suggests that this was the largest agricultural exchange in world history up to that time. Because most of these crops from India were warm weather crops, many of them facilitated summer cropping in areas that had previously lain fallow in that season. To replicate the monsoon climate of India, Muslim officials improved existing forms of irrigation (underground water canals and water-lifting mechanisms) and invented new ones (certain kinds of cisterns).

Agricultural productivity diversified and increased, encouraging population increase in general and urban growth in particular.

CITY DESIGN AND ARCHITECTURE

Muslim governments built great cities and adorned their public spaces lavishly and often exquisitely. The largest of the cities were the political capitals. Baghdad was built along the west bank of the Tigris River in 762 to serve as the capital of the Abbasid dynasty, and it served that purpose for almost 500 years. In the ninth century, with between 300,000 and 500,000 people in 25 square miles (65 square kilometers), Baghdad became the largest city in the world west of China. As the caliphate declined, and Baghdad with it, regional capitals grew in importance: Bukhara, Nishapur, and Isfahan in the east, and Cairo, Fez, and Cordoba in the west. The Fatimid rulers of Egypt began their administration in Fustat and expanded that already existing city into al-Qahira, Cairo, in 969. In Morocco, Idris II (r. 791–828) built Fez in 808 as the capital of the Idrisid dynasty, which had been founded by his father. A later dynasty, the Almoravids, built their capital Marrakesh in 1070. In Andalusia, southern Spain, the Umayyads developed Cordoba into one of the most cosmopolitan cities of the Islamic world. It achieved its greatest splendor in the mid-tenth century, but was sacked by Berbers in 1013 and never fully recovered.

The architecture of these cities proclaimed the splendor of Islam and the power of the Muslim ruler. Although the daily prayers in Islam may be performed privately, Friday noon prayers require collective assembly, so all cities and most neighborhoods within cities also construct mosques for public services. Wealthy rulers proclaimed their power and piety by building monumental central mosques, as they did early on in Jerusalem, Medina, and Damascus. The Abbasids constructed an enormous central mosque in Baghdad, and during the years that Samarra served as their capital a huge mosque was constructed there, too (848–52). Great mosques were also built at Qayrawan in Tunisia, Fez in Morocco, and Cordoba in Spain.

As the Seljuk Turks conquered and then joined the world of Islam, they built an especially monumental mosque at Isfahan in the late eleventh century, and then rebuilt it fifty years later after Ismaili Shi'as burned it down. Ottoman architects, most notably Hoja Sinan (1490–1578), constructed magnificent mosques, such as the Selimiye at Edirne

Mihrab **in the Great Mosque, Cordoba, Spain,** *c.* **961–976.** Under the Umayyads, Cordoba grew to be by far the most prosperous city in western Europe, second only to Baghdad in the Islamic world. At its height, the city is said to have contained some 300 public baths and 3000 mosques within its walls. Shown here is the most important surviving example. Great attention was lavished on the decoration of the Great Mosque, and the *mihrab*, a small domed chamber indicating the direction of Mecca, is considered unique for its horseshoe-shaped doorway, a stylistic innovation of the Muslims in Spain.

The Great Mosque and minaret of al-Mutawakkil, Samarra, Iraq, 848–52. Though now only a shadow of its former glory, this 1150-year-old mosque remains the largest of its kind in the world. The three essential elements of simple mosque architecture emerge clearly through the ruins: a central courtyard or atrium, a (formerly) covered sanctuary inside the perimeter walls, and a minaret, or tower, from which the *muezzin* (crier) summons the community to worship.

and the Sulaymaniye in Istanbul, and other public buildings which incorporated Byzantine and Islamic forms. When Islam crossed the Sahara desert, a new architectural form developed, the Sahelian mosque. When Mansa Musa returned from his trip to Mecca in 1325 (see p. 348), he brought with him an Arab architect to supervise the construction of mosques and **madrasas** (theological schools) especially in Timbuktu.

The public architecture of mosques, mausolea, and, to a lesser extent, the royal and governmental buildings that frequently adjoin them, anchored the formal religious and political institutions of the Islamic city. The bazaar, or market area, was home to the business activities. Business in Islam was an honored profession. Muhammad himself had been a caravan operator, and his first wife, Khadija, had been a businesswoman. Even today mosques often control the land immediately adjacent to them and lease it out to businesses so that the rents can support the mosques. Islamic cities were, in effect, nodes on international trade routes linking the Islamic world from China to Morocco and Spain. These trade routes enabled the movement not only

of goods but also of people and ideas from one end of Eurasia to the other (see Chapter 12). The *hajj* (pilgrimage) to Mecca was also instrumental in creating a communication network among the regions and peoples of Islam.

The *Rihla* or travelogues of Ibn Battuta (1304– c. 1368; see Source, p. 360) demonstrate the opportunities for travel open to a person of culture. In thirty years of traveling from his home in Tangier, he traversed approximately 73,000 miles (117,000 kilometers) of territories that today belong to some fifty different countries. Thanks to his mastery of Arabic and his knowledge of *shari'a*, he found a welcome reception, and frequently temporary employment and gifts of wives and wealth in the lands he traversed. Muhammad Tughluq, sultan of Delhi, appointed him a *qadi* and, later, his envoy to China. Ibn Battuta's tales of adventure reflect the unity of the Islamic world. Despite its diversity, this world was held together by reverence for the Quran, the *shari'a*, the Arabic language (supplemented by Persian and Turkish), the rulers who ruled in its cities, and the scholars and merchants who traveled through them.

FOCUS
Mausolea in Islam

Because Islam teaches that all the dead should be honored, and that the saintly among them could confer blessings, mausolea have a special significance and sanctity. The followers of Timur (Tamerlane), for example, built for him an enormous tomb at Samarqand in 1405. Some mark personal love and devotion. Perhaps the best known of all Islamic buildings, the Taj Mahal in Agra, India, was built by the Emperor Shah Jahan as a mausoleum for his wife Mumtaz Mahal, who died giving birth to their fifteenth child. At a much more humble level, simple tombs of local saints are found throughout the Islamic world, attracting followers, especially women, who pour out their hearts in prayer, trusting that the sanctity of the saint will carry it to God.

The Taj Mahal, Agra, India, 1632–48.

Bronzesmith, Isfahan bazaar, Iran. In Islam religion and business are integrally linked, in that the land adjoining mosques is often leased to market traders whose rents support the buildings and their activities. Here a bronzesmith works outside his shop in the bazaar at Isfahan, which has been thriving since the third century C.E.

RELATIONS WITH NON-MUSLIMS

ISLAM AND THE SWORD

Early Islamic governments spread by the sword. As a result, popular belief in the West has held that the religion of Islam spread in the same way. Although conversion by force was practiced occasionally, by and large it was not. For example, as we have noted, the early "rightly guided" caliphs and the early Umayyads did not seek to convert the people they conquered. They wanted to rule as Arab Muslim conquerors over non-Arab, non-Muslim subjects. Only when the later Umayyads feared that they could not continue minority rule over so large a majority, did they decide actively to seek

SOURCE

Ibn Battuta's Observations on Gender Relations

Ibn Battuta (1304–c. 1368) learned his concepts of gender relations in the Arab heartland of Islam. As he traveled he was often astonished, and sometimes shocked, by the status of women in other Islamic countries. In the Turkish and Mongol regions between the Black and Caspian Seas, wives of local, ruling khans (sultans) owned property. When the senior wife appeared at the khan's residence, Ibn Battuta observes, the khan (sultan)

> advances to the entrance to the pavilion to meet her, salutes her, takes her by the hand, and only after she has mounted to the couch and taken her seat does the sultan himself sit down. All this is done in full view of those present, and without any use of veils. (Dunn, p. 168)

In the Maldive Islands, in the Indian Ocean, Ibn Battuta was even more scandalized:

> Their womenfolk do not cover their hands, not even their queen does so, and they comb their hair and gather it at one side. Most of them wear only an apron from their waists to the ground, the rest of their bodies being uncovered. When I held the *qadiship* there, I tried to put an end to this practice and ordered them to wear clothes, but I met with no success. No woman was admitted to my presence in a lawsuit unless her body was covered, but apart from that I was unable to effect anything. (McNeill, p. 276)

In Mali, west Africa, female slaves and servants went publicly into the ruler's court completely naked. When Ibn Battuta found a scholar's wife chatting with another man, he complained to the scholar and was put in his place,

> The association of women with men is agreeable to us and a part of good conduct, to which no suspicion attaches. They are not like the women of your country. (Dunn, p. 300)

Ibn Battuta left immediately and never returned to the man's home.

---

conversion of, and alliance with, the conquered peoples. A principal goal of conquest, however, remained the creation of a *dar al-Islam*, a rule under which Islam could be practiced freely. This did not mean that the people of the land were forced to become Muslims, only that the Muslims among them must have the freedom to practice their religion and sustain their culture.

Later, when many Muslims lived under non-Muslim governments, the *ulama* declared that any government that permitted freedom of religion to Muslims could be a *dar al-Islam*. The alternative was a *dar al-Harb*, an "abode of war," which had to be opposed because it restricted the practice of Islam.

THE CRUSADES

At opposite ends of the Mediterranean, Muslims and Christians fought each other in war. The crusades (1095–1291) were perhaps more political and economic than religious in motive. After Arab armies captured Jerusalem in 638, they built new, glorious mosques to indicate their own dominance, but they allowed Christians to continue their religious practices without hindrance and permitted Jews to return to Jerusalem officially for the first time since their exile by the Romans in 70 C.E. (see p. 304). Only centuries later, after Muslim Turkish armies won the Battle of Manzikert in 1071 and opened Anatolia to conquest, did the Byzantine emperor, Alexius I, call on Pope Urban II to help fight the Muslims and to recapture Jerusalem and the "Holy Land." The pope seized this opportunity to unite western Europe and its various rulers under his own banner in the name of religion.

FOCUS
Dhimmi Status

Non-Muslims were offered three choices. The first was to convert to Islam. The second was to accept "protected," *dhimmi*, status as worshipers of one God who accepted Muslim rule. All the monotheistic "peoples of the book," were eligible for this status, including Christians, Jews, and Zoroastrians. Later, Islamic governments in India also extended *dhimmi* status to Hindus. The *dhimmi* were often required to pay a special poll tax, but they could follow their own religion and their own personal law regarding marriage, divorce, and inheritance, and they were to be protected by the Muslim government. The third option was to fight against the Muslim state, an option that was chosen least often.

The status of the *dhimmi* was spelled out in "The Pact of Umar," a document ascribed to Umar II (r. 634–644). This document prescribed second-class status for the *dhimmi*. They were not to build new houses of worship nor to reconstruct old ones. They were not to convert anyone to their religion. They were not to wear the same clothing as Muslims, but to wear distinguishing garments. The sounds of their prayers, their calls to prayer, and their funeral processions were to be muted. Their houses were not to be higher than the houses of Muslims. The poll tax, however, was not mentioned in this document. Perhaps designed to encourage non-Muslims to gain first-class citizenship by converting, these rules were nevertheless not crippling to life, and, indeed, they were often not implemented. Travelers throughout the Muslim world noted that Jews and Christians often held some of the highest positions in public and private life and were self-governing in their religious life (see below).

THE CRUSADES

First Crusade (1095–9)	Proclaimed by Pope Urban II, the crusade was motivated by the occupation of Anatolia and Jerusalem by the Seljuk Turks. The crusaders recaptured Jerusalem and established several Latin kingdoms on the Syrian coast.
Second Crusade (1147–9)	Led by Louis VII of France and the Holy Roman Emperor, Conrad III, this was a disaster from the crusaders' point of view.
Third Crusade (1189–92)	Mounted to recapture Jerusalem, which had been taken by Saladin in 1187. Personal rivalry between the leaders, Philip II Augustus of France and Richard I of England, undermined the crusaders' unity.
Fourth Crusade (1202–04)	This crusade against Egypt was diverted, at the instigation of the Venetians, to sack and divide Constantinople, which led to half a century of western rule over Byzantium.
Children's Crusade (1212)	Thousands of children crossed Europe on their way to Palestine. Untold numbers were sold into slavery in Marseilles, France, or died of disease and malnutrition.
Fifth Crusade (1218–21)	King Andrew of Hungary, Cardinal Pelagius, King John of Jerusalem, and King Hugh of Cyprus captured, then lost, Damietta, Egypt.
Sixth Crusade (1228–9)	The Holy Roman Emperor, Frederick II (r. 1212–50), led the crusade that, through negotiation with the sultan of Egypt, recovered Jerusalem. The city was finally lost in 1244.
Seventh Crusade (1249–54) and Eighth (1270–91)	Both led by Louis IX of France (r. 1226–70), who was inspired by religious motives, but both were personal disasters. Louis was later canonized.

Illustration of the Second Crusade (1147–9). Lance-bearing Christian forces face a Muslim army in this scene from the Second Crusade. The fleur-de-lys emblem, here sported on his shield by the French king, Louis VII, was adopted at almost the same time by his opponent, the ruler of Aleppo. (*British Library, London*)

Christian rulers, knights, and merchants were also driven by their own political and military ambitions and by the promise of trade opportunities that would accompany the establishment of a Latin kingdom in the Middle East (Esposito, p. 60).

At first, the European Christian crusaders were successful and brutal. In 1099 they captured Jerusalem, killing all its Muslim residents, men, women, and children. They turned the Dome of the Rock into a church and the adjacent al-Aqsa mosque into an official residence. At the time, Muslim leadership in the region was divided and did not respond. Then Salah al-Din (Saladin) (*c.* 1137–93), who had established a new dynasty in Egypt, recaptured Jerusalem in 1187. But more crusades followed, often revealing very worldly motives. When Richard I, the Lion-Heart (r. 1189–99), captured Acre on the Mediterranean coast in the Third Crusade (1189–92), he also massacred its men, women, and children. By 1291, however, Muslim forces had reconquered Acre and all other crusader outposts. Although four minor crusades followed, none succeeded in capturing and holding any outposts in the Holy Land.

The crusader soldiers themselves were largely mercenaries who sought their own benefit and who attacked many in their path for their own profit. As early as 1096, *en route* overland to Jerusalem on the First Crusade, they paused to slaughter Jews. In 1204, during the Fourth Crusade, Roman Catholic armies, acting against the direct orders of the pope, attacked the city of Zara in Croatia and Constantinople, the capital of the Byzantine Empire, their presumed ally. Instead of uniting Christianity and defeating the Muslims, the crusaders had divided Christianity and were defeated by the Muslims.

CONNECTION: *Europe during the Middle Ages and the Renaissance, pp. 394–407*

A GOLDEN AGE IN SPAIN

At the other end of the Mediterranean, in Spain, Islam flourished, and with it the Christian and Jewish communities of the peninsula. Through a century of immigration, conquest, administration, and intermarriage, Umayyad and Berber invaders brought Islam to a central position in Spain. They also revitalized trade by breaking the monopoly of Byzantine control over the western Mediterranean. They introduced new crops and new irrigation techniques from west Asia (see p. 356). Abd al-Rahman III (912–961) asserted his separation from the Abbasids by declaring himself a caliph rather than just a sultan. A series of rulers expanded the ornate mosque at Cordoba, making it one of the architectural showcases of Islam.

Eastern scholars of law and philosophy immigrated to the flourishing court. Poets developed new styles, based in Arabic but also influenced by local Spanish and Latin styles. Greek philosophical and medical treatises were translated into Latin as well as Arabic, thus opening intellectual communication with the educated classes in Christendom. Although some Christians revolted against Islamic and Arabic inroads, and were killed in battle (850–859), many more adopted Arabic lifestyles.

By 1030, the caliphate in Spain had disintegrated. Various armed struggles broke out between the provinces and the capital, townsmen and rural Berber immigrants, and converts and Arabs. The conflicts did not, however, impede the spread of Islam. As in the eastern Mediterranean, provincial administrations replaced the central caliphate and brought the culture of their courts closer to the general population. Sufis spread their ascetic and devotional teachings.

The vacuum in the central government did, however, provide an opening to various Christian forces to begin the *reconquista*, the reconquest of Spain. In 1085 Alfonso VI (r. 1065–1109) captured Toledo. Two successive Arab/Berber dynasties invading from Morocco, the Almoravids and Almohads, could not stem the Christian advance. By the mid-thirteenth century all of Spain with the exception of Granada was in Christian hands. Granada fell in 1492 to the unified kingdom of Ferdinand and Isabella. Muslim rule in Spain was broken.

During the years of the *reconquista*, culture continued to flourish. The Almohads, for example, patronized Ibn Rushd (known to Christians as Averroes; 1126–98), who linked rationalist thought in Islam with that of earlier Greeks and contemporary Christians. But the Almohads did persecute others, including the family of the Jewish physician, philosopher, and theologian Moses Maimonides (1135–1204), forcing them to flee until they finally found a home in Cairo, where Maimonides became court physician to the sultan Salah al-Din.

Until the mid-thirteenth century, Christian rulers in Spain patronized the rich, hybrid culture. They translated the Bible, the Talmud, and the Quran into Castilian. Arabic texts on astrology and astronomy, and the philosophical works of Muslim thinkers, including al-Kindi, al-Farabi, and Ibn Sina (Avicenna), were translated into Castilian and Latin, as was Maimonides' philosophy. Spain was the entry-way into western Europe for classical writings and their reworking through the prism of Islamic civilization.

By the fourteenth century, however, Christianity became triumphal and intolerant. In 1391, Jews were forced to accept baptism. In 1480 the Roman Catholic Church in Spain established an inquisition to hunt down Jews and Muslims who had not converted. (Later it also attacked Protestants.) In 1492 the Jewish population was expelled from Spain, and in 1501 Muslims had to choose between exile and conversion to Christianity. In 1566 Arabic was banned in Spain, and in 1609 all Muslims were

SPOTLIGHT
The Alhambra

The peculiar charm of this old dreamy palace is its power of calling up vague reveries and picturings of the past, and thus clothing naked realities with the illusions of the memory and the imagination.
(Cited in Grabar, p. 203.)

So wrote American author Washington Irving of the Alhambra in Granada, Spain, as he saw it in the early 1800s. The fourteenth-century Spanish complex of buildings called in Arabic "Qalat al-hamra," the red citadel, had conveyed a lasting vision of illusion and reality intertwined.

With the fall of Seville to the Christian *reconquista* in 1248, Granada remained as the only Islamic kingdom in Spain. Nestled on a spur of the Sierra Nevada mountains in the south, the city flourished thanks to an influx of talented Muslims fleeing the advancing Christian armies, and the enterprise and vigor of its rulers. Two of them, Kings Yusuf I (1333–54) and Muhammad V (1354–9, 1362–91) of the Nasrid dynasty, had most of the buildings of the Alhambra that still stand today built to serve as their home, a city within a city. Their legacy is today the best-preserved palace of medieval Spain, referred to by art historian Oleg Grabar as the "perfect expression of a unique regional tradition" (p. 205).

The Old Royal Palace, the heart of the Alhambra complex, is an ensemble of courtyards flanked by arcades and connected by "secret passageways and small doors [that] led . . . from one marvelous architectural setting to the next"

Figure 1 The Court of the Lions.

(Grabar, p. 114). Among the most elegant of the courts are the Hall of the Ambassadors, where the king's throne may have been placed for public audiences; the Court of the Myrtles, a rectangular court, 120 by 77 feet (36.6 x 23.5 m), centered on a 24 ½ foot (7.15 m) wide pool running almost its full length; and the Court of Lions with its central fountain encircled by a dozen stone lions whose mouths are water spouts (**figure 1**). The geometry of design of the courtyards finds its counterpoint in the richness of ornamentation for which the Alhambra is equally famous, for example in its many "stalactite" domes like the one in the Hall of the Two Sisters (**figure 2**). The adjoining gardens and pools within the walls of the Alhambra (**figure 3**) and in the Generalife gardens about 656 feet (200 m) distant, all meticulously arranged in accord with Islamic traditions of landscaping, complete a regal composition of fantasy and elegance.

In 1492, Granada fell, ending all Islamic rule in Spain, and in 1501 Muslims were forced to convert or to leave. The old era had passed. Patronage for new architectural ventures would henceforth come from Christian rulers and, indeed, in 1526 King Charles V gave orders for the construction of his own royal palace, built to a very different aesthetic, which today stands immediately adjacent to the Old Royal Palace within the walls of the Alhambra. The old order had come to an end.

Figure 2 Stucco decoration in the Hall of the Two Sisters.

Figure 3 Pools and pavilions in the Alhambra gardens.

expelled from Spain. The golden age of religious tolerance and cultural exchange was over.

CONVERSION AND ASSIMILATION: HOW DO WE KNOW?

Only in the last two decades has serious research been done on conversion to Islam, asking exactly how the process worked. Three works stand out. Nehemia Levtzion edited a set of studies on *Conversion to Islam* in 1979 examining the motives of converts. Levtzion argued that "assimilation" was a better term than "conversion" for describing the process of becoming a Muslim. People in conquered areas, especially, were not so much overwhelmed by political conquest as they were impressed with the richness of the culture that Islam brought to them. They found that their lives were enriched by the rituals, philosophy, art, and sense of belonging to a world system that came with joining the *umma*, the Islamic community.

Richard Bulliet's *Conversion to Islam in the Medieval Period: An Essay in Quantitative History* demonstrates that conversion took place at different rates of speed in each of the six societies he examines: Arabia, Egypt, Iraq, Syria, Iran, and Spain. He notes the problems of finding data to understand the process, since "medieval Islam produced no missionaries, bishops, baptismal rites, or other indicators of conversion that could be conveniently recorded by the Muslim chronicler" (p. 4). For data, Bulliet examines the speed of adoption of Muslim names in each of the six societies. He concludes that rapid acceptance of Islam went hand in hand with a breakdown in central political rule. As centralized Islamic rule broke down, paradoxically, Sufis carried the word of Islam more freely and with more backing from local governments.

We also know of the very large-scale assimilation to Islam by the Mongol successors of Genghis Khan and of the followers of Timur the Lame (Tamerlane). These ruling groups were assimilated by Islam because the new civilization they encountered offered them cultural, political, social, economic, and spiritual rewards that were not available in the religions and cultures of their birth. Their biological and cultural descendants helped to establish the great Islamic empires of the fifteenth through the eighteenth centuries: the Ottomans based in Turkey, the Safavids in Iran, and the Mughals in India (see Chapter 15).

Richard Eaton's *The Rise of Islam and the Bengal Frontier: 1204–1760* compares records of land development with records of religious assimilation. Eaton finds that in eastern Bengal (modern Bangladesh) Islam was most successful in frontier areas being brought under cultivation for the first time. In such areas several factors encouraged the assimilation of Islam: first, no world religion had already captured the field; second, a government headed by Muslims encouraged settlers to develop the frontier and favored Muslims in disbursing titles to the land and in tax policies; third, Muslim land developers, sometimes, but not always, very devout in their practices, came to develop and farm the land and in the process introduced the message of Islam to this new region; and, fourth, local peoples who had not been integrated into the Hindu system came to work the land under the direction of Muslims and, following their example, began to assimilate Islam into their own lives. Eaton points out that conversion was not instantaneous, but a process that occurred gradually through two or three generations. Families integrated more and more Islamic ideas and practices into their lives until, finally, they accepted Islam fully.

Finally, the great assimilation that took place outside the heartlands of Islamic conquest, in sub-Saharan Africa and southeast Asia, was carried by traders and later supported by Sufis and *ulama*. In both these huge areas, the trade networks by land and sea were so densely worked by Muslims that indigenous traders began to assimilate Islam into their lives, either from religious conviction or from the promise of trade advantage. They stayed to join in one of the world's richest and most wide-spread civilizations, the *umma* of Islam. By 1500, despite its losses in Spain, Islam dominated much of the eastern hemisphere as a world religion, a polity, a people, and a civilization.

JUDAISM, CHRISTIANITY, AND ISLAM: WHAT DIFFERENCE DOES IT MAKE?

As monotheistic religions, sharing common ancestors, belief in divinely given written scriptures, and common rituals and practices, such as regular prayer and charity; valuing pilgrimage and sharing many common holy places; promising that behavior will receive its proper rewards and punishments in the future, on earth and in an afterlife; balancing and integrating strands of mysticism, legalism, and pious devotion; the three religions of Judaism, Christianity, and Islam would appear to be naturally suited to co-existence and even to mutual reinforcement. And indeed at times, notably in Spain, during much, but not all, of the period from about 750 to about 1250, the three faiths coexisted and gladly learned from one another. But such warm, reciprocally beneficial coexistence has been the exception rather than the rule.

Perhaps two factors can explain the hostility that has often characterized the relationships among these religions. First all three have been proselytizing religions—although Judaism abandoned this practice early in the Christian era—and their very closeness has made them bitterly competitive. Each has had some feeling that it has come the closest to the essential truths of God and the world, and that the others have somehow failed to recognize this. Both Christianity and Islam, for example, accuse Judaism of stubbornly refusing to accept later revelations that modify and update its original truths. Both Judaism and Islam accuse Christianity of a kind of idolatry in claiming that God begat a son who was actually a form of God and who walked the earth in human form. Both Judaism and Christianity argue that God did not give a special, final revelation to Muhammad. In each case these religions have looked at one another and said that, despite elements of deep commonality, there exist also fundamental heresies. Indeed within each of these religions, at various times, splits have turned one group against another amidst cries of heresy and calls to armed opposition. Truth was to be maintained, asserted, and defended through the force of arms. (Religions with less insistence on doctrinal correctness, such as Hinduism and Buddhism, have had less, and less bitter, religious warfare.)

Second, as each religion developed, it sought the support of government. It often sought to be the government. Truth was to be reinforced by power. Basic competition over spiritual and philosophical truths spilled over into competition also for tax monies, office, land, and public acceptance of specific ritual and architectural symbols, and suppression of opposition. When they could, these religions marched through the world armed. The idea that the state and religion should be separated appeared as early as Augustine; but until recently, in the lands where these three religions predominated, the state and religion were usually intimately bound up with one another, and in many places the religion of the leader of the state was expected to be accepted as the religion of his subjects, or at least to be given preferred treatment over others.

Historically, Christianity came to dominate the European lands formerly held by the Roman Empire and, as we shall see, traveled with its European faithful to the New World. Islam dominated North Africa and the Asian lands formerly held by the Persian and Alexandrine empires, and it traveled with armies, saints, and traders to India and southeast Asia (see maps, pp. 345 and 346). Judaism, which lost out to its younger successors both in numbers and in gaining the support of governments, remained everywhere a minority religion, dependent on the tolerance of others. (This identification of different religions with particular parts of the world was typical also of Hinduism, identified with India and, to a much lesser extent, with southeast Asia; and of Buddhism, identified with the Indian subcontinent, east and southeast Asia, and the routes connecting them.)

Nevertheless, amidst the carving up of the world into zones of religious dominance backed by supportive governments, and frequent warfare among religious groups, there were also times of mutually beneficial co-existence, sharing of cultures, and recognition of the commonalities of these religions and of the common humanity of their faithful. In many regions like the Middle East, and in cities along the various trade routes all over the world, members of different religions lived side-by-side, often developing mutual understanding, respect, and trust. And always the voice of the mystic, like that of Jalal al-Din Rumi, called out for recognition of the oneness of God and the unity of God's universe:

> What is to be done, O Moslems? for I do not
> recognize myself.
> I am neither Christian, nor Jew, nor Gabr
> [Zoroastrian], nor Moslem.
> I am not of the East, nor of the West, nor of the land,
> nor of the sea;
> I am not of Nature's mint, nor of the circling
> heavens.
> I am not of earth, nor of water, nor of air, nor of fire;
> I am not of the empyrian, nor of the dust, nor of
> existence, nor of entity.
> I am not of India, nor of China, nor of Bulgaria, nor
> of Saqsin;
> I am not of the kingdom of Iraqain, nor of the
> country of Khorasan.

I am not of this world, nor of the next, nor of
Paradise, nor of Hell;
I am not of Adam, nor of Eve, nor of Eden and [the
angel] Rizwan.
My place is the Placeless, my trace is the Traceless;

'Tis neither body nor soul, for I belong to the soul of
the Beloved.
I have put duality away, I have seen that the two
worlds are one;
One I seek, One I know, One I see, One I call.

(McNeill and Waldman, p. 242)

BIBLIOGRAPHY

Adas, Michael. *Islamic and European Expansion* (Philadelphia: Temple University Press, 1993).

Ahmed, Leila. *Women and Gender in Islam* (New Haven: Yale University Press, 1992).

Bulliet, Richard W. *Conversion to Islam in the Medieval Period: An Essay in Quantitative History* (Cambridge: Harvard University Press, 1979).

Dunn, Ross E. *The Adventures of Ibn Battuta* (Berkeley: University of California Press, 1986).

Eaton, Richard M. "Islamic History as Global History," in Adas, *op. cit.*, 1–36.

Eaton, Richard M. *The Rise of Islam and the Bengal Frontier, 1204–1760* (Berkeley: University of California Press, 1993).

Embree, Ainslee T., ed. *Sources of Indian Tradition*, Volume I: *From the Beginning to 1800* (New York: Columbia University Press, 2nd ed., 1988).

Esposito, John. *Islam: The Straight Path* (New York: Oxford University Press, 1991).

Ferdowsi. *The Legend of Seyavash* (London: Penguin Books, 1992).

al-Ghazzali. *The Faith and Practice of al-Ghazali*, trans. W. Montgomery Watt (London: Allen and Unwin, 1953).

Grabar, Oleg. The Alhambra (Cambridge: Harvard University Press, 1978).

Hodgson, Marshall G.S. *Rethinking World History: Essays on Europe, Islam, and World History*, ed. Edmund Burke III (Cambridge: Cambridge University Press, 1993).

——. *The Venture of Islam*, 3 vols. (Chicago: University of Chicago Press, 1974).

Ibn Khaldun. *An Arab Philosophy of History*, ed. Charles Issawi (London: John Murray, 1950).

Ikram, S.M. *Muslim Civilization in India* (New York: Columbia University Press, 1964).

Johns, Jeremy. "Christianity and Islam," in John McManners, ed. *The Oxford Illustrated History of Christianity* (Oxford: Oxford University Press, 1990), 163–95.

Keddie, Nikki R. and Beth Baron, eds. *Women in Middle Eastern History* (New Haven: Yale University Press, 1991).

The Koran trans. N.J. Dawood (London: Penguin Books, 1990).

The Koran Interpreted trans. A.J. Arberry (New York: Macmillan Publishing Co., 1955).

Lapidus, Ira M. *A History of Islamic Societies* (Cambridge: Cambridge University Press, 1988).

Levtzion, Nehemia, ed. *Conversion to Islam* (New York: Holmes and Meier, 1979).

Lewis, Bernard, ed. and trans. *Islam from the Prophet Muhammad to the Capture of Constantinople*, 2 vols. (New York: Oxford University Press, 1987).

Lewis, Bernard. *Islam and the West* (New York: Oxford University Press, 1993).

McNeill, William H. and Marilyn Robinson Waldman, eds. *The Islamic World* (Chicago: University of Chicago Press, 1983).

Morony, Michael. *Iraq after the Muslim Conquest* (Princeton: Princeton University Press, 1984).

Nashat, Guity. "Women in the Middle East, 8000 B.C.–A.D. 1800," in *Restoring Women to History*, eds. Cheryl Johnson-Odim and Margaret Strobel. (Bloomington: Organization of American Historians, 1988).

Robinson, Francis, ed. *The Cambridge Illustrated History of the Islamic World* (Cambridge: Cambridge University Press, 1996)

Seltzer, Robert M. *Jewish People, Jewish Thought* (New York: Macmillan Publishing, 1980).

Time-Life Books. *Time Frame AD 1200–1300: The Mongol Conquests* (Alexandria, VA: Time-Life Books, 1989).

——. *Time Frame AD 1300–1400: The Age of Calamity* (Alexandria, VA, 1989).

Trimingham, John S. *Sufi Orders in Islam* (Oxford: Oxford University Press, 1971).

Times Atlas of World History, ed. Geoffrey Barraclough (London: Times Books, 1979).

Tucker, Judith. "Gender and Islamic History," in Adas, *op. cit.*, pp. 37–74.

Vitray-Meyerovitch, Eva de. *Rumi and Sufism* (Sausalito, CA: Post-Apollo Press, 1987).

Watson, Andrew. *Agricultural Innovation in the Early Islamic World* (Cambridge: Cambridge University Press, 1983).

Map of Venice and the lagoon from the Kitab-I Bahriye ("Book of Seafaring") of Piri Reis, written in 1521. By the early 1500s, seafarers and navigators shared information even across competitive civilizational boundaries. Piri Reis, an Ottoman Turkish Muslim admiral made extensive use of Arab, Portuguese, and Spanish maps and charts as he prepared his own navigational texts. Here he has produced a map of Venice, the greatest of the European, Christian ports on the Mediterranean. On another of his maps, from 1513, America appears on the Atlantic almost exactly as Columbus charted it. Within a few years America appeared also on Chinese maps. *(The al-Sabah Collection, Dar al-Athar al-Islamiyyah, Kuwait)*

5

World Trade

CHANNELS OF COMMUNICATION: THE EXCHANGE OF COMMODITIES, DISEASES, AND CULTURE

In earlier parts of this book we have touched on economic systems and the importance of trade in regional and world economies. Trade linked the oldest centers of urban civilization—Mesopotamia, the Indus valley, and the Nile valley—as we noted in Part 2. In Part 3 we saw that empires sought to secure the principal transportation routes and that the imperial rulers usually controlled a substantial part of their trade. Finally, in Part 4 we noted that world religions spread along the same routes as trade, and that religions were often carried by the merchants themselves as well as by more formal official representations. Both Buddhism and Islam spread to eastern Asia via the overland silk routes, and to southeast Asia via the shipping lanes of the Indian Ocean. The exchange of commodities went hand in hand with the exchange of ideas.

In this part we will look more closely at the traders, the trade routes, and the importance of trade and economics in world history between 1100 and 1776. This part has two chapters, divided about the year 1500, when a series of voyages by Christopher Columbus, Ferdinand Magellan, and other explorer-traders demonstrated conclusively that the world was a globe; revealed that there were continental land masses in both the western and the eastern hemispheres; and linked these hemispheres in continuous relationships of economic and cultural exchange.

The first chapter of this part describes the patterns and the philosophies of world trade prior to this linkage. It indicates the importance of the pre-1500 networks in the establishment of the later systems.

12 ESTABLISHING WORLD TRADE ROUTES

1100—1500 C.E.

"A growing mountain of hard evidence ... indicates indubitably that the whole of Eurasia was culturally and technologically interconnected [by about 1500 B.C.E.]"

VICTOR H. MAIR

"Stadtluft macht frei" –"City air makes one free."

GERMAN PROVERB

THE PATTERNS AND PHILOSOPHIES OF EARLY ECONOMIC SYSTEMS

TRADE AND TRADERS: GOALS AND FUNCTIONS

Today long-distance, international trade forms a substantial part of the world's commerce and includes even the most basic products of everyday food and clothing. In earlier times, long-distance trade was only a small fraction of overall trade, mostly supplying luxury goods for the upper classes: silks, gold, spices, and the like (see Spotlight, pp. 386–9). Because these goods were valuable relative to their weight, merchants could carry them over long distances and still sell them for handsome profits. The buyers were mostly wealthy, for only they could afford such luxuries. Some commercial goods, like raw wool and cotton, were also traded over medium distances, a few hundred miles. The transportation costs were justified as these goods became more valuable after importation when they were manufactured into finished products.

The largest part of the exchange economy was in local transactions—food crops traded for local hand manufactures or raw materials. These goods were necessities but they had little value in relationship to their weight; the cost of transportation was a substantial part of their final price. They were, therefore, traded only over short distances. Often, they were bartered in exchange for other local goods rather than sold for money in more distant markets. This exchange of local goods is a fundamental part of local and regional history, but the study of world history focuses on long-distance exchange and its importance in knitting together distant regions of the world. Trade provides an index of economic vitality. It also stimulates economic growth; people produce goods

Marco Polo, from *Romance of Alexander,* *c.* 1340.

The second chapter examines the changes in world trade patterns and economic philosophies from 1500 to 1776, when the publication of Adam Smith's *Wealth of Nations* signaled the arrival of a new philosophy of world trade and economics, later called capitalism. Smith applauded the work of private businesspeople who were pursuing their own profit, and proclaimed them the chief engine of progressive change in world history. He opposed governmental and religious control of trade, the pattern we shall most frequently encounter before 1500. Smith's word was not final, and the philosophy of capitalism is still debated today, reviled by some, extolled by others, but significant to virtually all debates over the larger questions of economics and to many questions of politics, culture, and religion as well. Debates over the capitalist system versus other forms of economic organization open this chapter and reappear frequently in Parts 7 and 8.

and provide services only if markets exist for them. (Anyone who has ever looked for a job has experienced this. If jobs exist, they work; if jobs do not exist, they remain unemployed and economically unproductive.)

WORLD TRADE: AN HISTORICAL ANALYSIS

Historians studying world trade seek to understand its purposes, conditions, and regulations. We ask about social as well as economic values. For example: What benefits are achieved by each different system of trade? Which systems benefit which members of society? Which systems harm which members of society? What are the trade-offs in benefits and losses under each system?

Some of the most provocative explorations of the history of trade originated in public policy debates in the United States and Europe following the Great Depression. That economic collapse of the 1930s, discussed in Chapter 18, challenged the advocates of market-based, free-trade economies. Traders in a **free market economy** seek personal

\multicolumn{4}{c}{**MEDIEVAL WORLD TRADE**}
DATE C.E.	**POLITICAL/ SOCIAL EVENTS**	**TRADE DEVELOPMENTS**	**EXPLORATION**
1050	• Normans under William I invade England (1066) • Seljuk Turks take Baghdad • Franks invade Anatolia and Syria and found Crusader states • Almoravids destroy Kingdom of Ghana (1067)	• Venice dominates Adriatic; trading ports set up throughout eastern Mediterranean (1000–1100)	
1100		• Age of Great Zimbabwe in southern Africa • Wool trade flourishing between England and Flanders	
1150	• Salah al-Din, sultan of Turkish Syria and Egypt, retakes Jerusalem (1187) • St. Francis of Assisi (1181–1226) • St. Dominic (1170–1221) • St. Clare of Assisi (1194–1253)	• Market fairs in the Champagne region, France • Paper-making spreads from Muslim world	
1200	• Foundation of first Muslim empire in India • Genghis Khan establishes Mongol Empire (1206–1405) • Collapse of Mayan civilization in Central America; rise of Incas in Peru • Rise of Mali, west Africa	• Rise of craft guilds in towns of western Europe • Foundation of Hanseatic League (1241)	
1250	• Osman I founds Ottoman dynasty in Turkey (1290–1326) • Emergence of Empire of Benin, Nigeria • Mongols fail to conquer Japan (1281)	• Increasing Venetian links central Asia and China (1255–95) • Revolt of craftspeople in Flanders	• Marco Polo arrives in China (1275)

MEDIEVAL WORLD TRADE

DATE C.E.	POLITICAL/ SOCIAL EVENTS	TRADE DEVELOPMENTS	EXPLORATION
1300	• Hundred Years War between England and France (1337–1453) • Height of Mali (Mandingo) Empire under Sultan Mansa Musa • Bubonic plague in Europe (1346–1350)	• West Africa provides two-thirds of the gold of the eastern hemisphere	• Ibn Battuta's travels in east Asia and Africa (c. 1330–60)
1350	• Ghettoization of Jews in western Europe • Ashikaga Shoguns dominate Japan (1338–1573) • Ming dynasty in China (1368)	• Revolts of urban workers in Italy and Flanders	
1400	• Ottoman Turks establish foothold in Europe at Gallipoli	• Great Chinese naval expeditions reach east coast of Africa and India under Zheng He • China reconstructs and extends Grand Canal	• Portugal's Prince Henry the Navigator sponsors expeditions to west Africa
1450	• Printing of Gutenberg's Bible (1455) • War of the Roses in England (1453–85) • Turks capture Constantinople (1453) • Jews driven from Spain (1492) • Treaty of Tordesillas (1494)	• Decline of Kilwa and Great Zimbabwe in southeast Africa (c. 1450) • Medici family in Florence: Giovanni, Cosimo, Lorenzo	• Bartholomeu Dias sails round Cape of Good Hope (1488) • Columbus reaches the Americas (1492) • Vasco de Gama reaches the Malabar coast, India (1498)
1500	• Machiavelli, *The Prince* (1513) • Muslims in Spain forced to covert or leave • Zenith of Songhay Empire of the middle Niger region (1492–1529) • Hernán Cortés and Spanish conquistadores defeat Aztecs and seize Mexico (1519–21) • Francisco Pizarro and Spanish conquistadores defeat Incas and seize Peru	• Portugal sets up trading port of Goa, in India (1502); Portuguese ships armed with cannon	• Ferdinand Magellan's voyage round globe (1519–22)

economic profit by buying goods at a lower price and selling them at a higher price. In their quest for economic profit, however, businesspeople also risk economic loss because conditions and prices in the market change constantly. In completely free market economies conditions of trade would not be regulated at all. Prices would vary only in terms of the relationship between the **supply** of goods and the economic **demand** for them, and businesspeople would be free to seek their fortune as they choose. All societies, however, do regulate trade to some degree in order also to serve the non-economic goals of the society. Business may be more or less regulated, but it is never completely unregulated.

The questions asked in the 1930s were: Had the freedom given to private businesspeople been too extensive? Had excessive freedom ultimately devastated the economies of the world in the 1930s? Should governments be given more control over the regulation and planning of national economies? As the debate continued, scholars searched the past for relevant experience.

Karl Polanyi, a historical anthropologist at Columbia University, argued that market economies, private profit seeking, and capitalism were a peculiar and unnatural way of structuring an economy. Market economies had not existed in the distant past. Although they had captured the imagination of many people in Polanyi's own time, they were, in fact, historical oddities. With an interdisciplinary team of colleagues, Polanyi examined the past and found that:

> Prehistory, early history, and . . . the whole history apart from those last centuries, had economies the organization of which differed from anything assumed by the economist. . . . They possessed no system of price-making markets. (p. 241)

> Not before the third century B.C. was the working of a supply-demand-price mechanism in international trade noticeable. (p. 87)

The earlier systems had been different because their goals had been different. In the ancient Mediterranean, at least until the time of Aristotle, not private profit, but "community, self-sufficiency and justice . . . were the frame of reference . . . on all economic matters" (p. 80).

> The human economy . . . is embedded and enmeshed in institutions, economic and noneconomic. The inclusion of the noneconomic is vital. For religion or government may be as important for the structure and functioning of the economy as monetary institutions or the availability of tools and machines. (p. 250)

Polanyi argued that the exchange of goods was not carried out primarily in trade-for-profit, but in reciprocal gift-giving between individuals and in redistribution carried out by government and religious institutions claiming to serve the common good. Exchange for profit had been frowned upon or even forbidden because it requires and engenders unhealthy competitiveness, "an attitude involving a distinctive antagonistic relationship between the partners" (p. 255). Economies were to serve the purposes of establishing social cohesion and satisfying the basic needs of all members of the society—rather than serving the private interests of a few.

Polanyi and his colleagues backed their argument with a series of accompanying historical sketches of "Marketless Trading in Hammurabi's Time," "Mesopotamian Economic History," and "Ports of Trade in the Eastern Mediterranean," and then added studies of contemporary non-market economies from India and Africa, both north and south of the Sahara. Some recent anthropological studies have supported Polanyi's analyses of early economies. Yale University anthropologist James Scott, for example, has found in many peasant villages a "moral economy," a mandate that everyone within the village be fed before any individual is permitted to sell surplus food outside the village for private profit.

Other scholars differed sharply from this historical analysis, citing different data from different kinds of economic systems. In *Cross-Cultural Trade in World History*, Philip Curtin, Professor of History at Johns Hopkins University, presents considerable evidence of market economies based on private profit throughout the world from earliest times. Curtin agrees with Polanyi that trade is embedded in deeper political, social, religious, and moral structures of society, but he notes that more independent trade for private profit exists as well, with equally deep historic roots. Long-distance trade for private profit has flourished in major port cities around the world for millennia. The merchants who carried this trade were often foreigners, with some independence from local political and social structures. They tended to occupy marginal positions in the host society, but central positions in the international trade networks.

> Trade communities of merchants living among aliens in associated networks are to be found on every continent and back through time to the very beginning of urban life. They are . . . one of the most widespread of all human institutions over a very long run of time. (Curtin, p. 3)

These communities were composed of "stranger merchants . . . cross-cultural brokers, helping and encouraging trade between the host society and people of their own origin who moved along the trade routes" (p. 2). They formed "trade diasporas . . . a whole series of trade settlements in alien towns . . . an interrelated net of commercial communities forming a trade network" (p. 2). These trade diasporas appear in the archaeological record as early as 3500 B.C.E. The visiting merchants who carried the trade were marginal to their host societies rather than embedded within them. They were not entirely unregulated by the hosts, but neither were they totally subordinated. They were expected to take at least a reasonable profit; sometimes they took more. "St. Nicholas was the patron saint of thieves and merchants alike" (Curtin, p. 6). To illustrate his argument, Curtin sketches a series of trade diasporas around the world in a variety of time periods.

TRADE NETWORKS: 1250–1500

The historical sociologist Janet Abu-Lughod advances a similar argument and traces eight interlocking trade circuits connecting the commerce of the eastern hemisphere in the period 1250–1350. Her synthesis, *Before European Hegemony: The World System A.D. 1250–1350*, analyzes and maps six trade routes based on sea travel, primarily in the Indian Ocean; the thousands of miles of overland silk routes across central Asia; and a comparatively short land and river route within western Europe. In *Europe and the People without History* historical anthropologist Eric Wolf also proposes a similar outline of trade linkages, and includes three regions omitted by Abu-Lughod: west Africa south of the Sahara, connected to the Mediterranean by camel caravan; the valley of Mexico with its ties to the Yucatán; and the Andes Mountains of Latin America, with its links to the Pacific coast.

Abu-Lughod and Wolf, separately, reach several conclusions of fundamental importance:

- **Before 1500:** Asian and African trading systems were already well established by the time Europeans sailed into the Indian Ocean to trade in their own ships in 1498.

- **At 1500:** European traders established a permanent connection between the eastern and western hemispheres for the first time following Columbus' four voyages, 1492–1506.

- **After 1500:** As European traders grew more powerful, they attempted to subordinate pre-existing systems to their own centralized control from European headquarters. European control increased as northwestern Europe industrialized after 1750 (see Chapter 16).

WORLD TRADE PATTERNS, 1100–1500:
WHAT DO WE KNOW?

THE AMERICAS

In the Andes Mountains of South America, a major hub of civilization grew up after 600 C.E. (see pp. 105–112). By the time the Incas consolidated their empire in the early fifteenth century, the mountain peoples generated extensive trade, connecting settlements over hundreds of miles north to south and linking together a political nation of some 32 million people. Trade was important up and down the mountain sides. With peaks rising up to 20,000 feet (over 6000 meters), these mountain slopes hosted several different ecological zones, encouraging product differentiation and trade. The valleys below provided sweet potatoes, maize, manioc, squash, beans, chili peppers, peanuts, and cotton. The hills above produced white potatoes, a cereal grain called quinoa, coca, feathers, animal skins, and medicines. The highlands people specialized in manufacture and crafts, including gold working. Trade between the ecological zones was controlled by the state and its semi-divine rulers. Under Inca rulers, from the early 1400s until the Spanish conquest in 1535, many of the best of the 15,000 miles (24,000 kilometers) of roads through the Andes were open only to government officials.

In the Yucatán of Central and North America, the Mayan peoples had flourished from 200 B.C.E. to 900 C.E. (see pp. 100–5). Archaeologists Linda Schele and David Freidel tell us that Mayan traders flourished rather independently, amassing a disproportionate share of wealth. "In a culture which regarded the accumulation of wealth as an aberration, this turn of events created unease and social strife" (p. 97). So ultimately the traders were brought under the control of the hierarchical state, creating a new set of unequal relations dominated by kings rather than merchants.

By the time the Spanish arrived in the 1520s, the Maya had weakened in the Yucatán, and the Aztecs dominated the valley of Mexico. The Spanish conquistadores wrote vivid accounts of the great market place of the Aztec capital, Tenochtitlán. William Prescott's classic *History of the Conquest of Mexico* summarizes:

> On drawing near to the . . . great market, the Spaniards were astonished at the throng of people

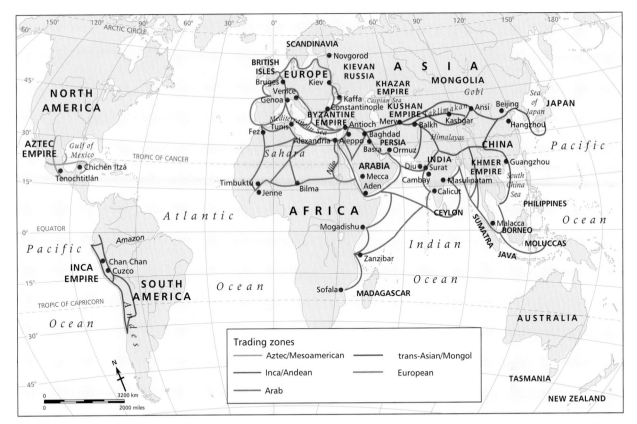

World trade routes Between 1100 and 1500 a relay system of trade by land and sea connected almost all populous regions of Eurasia, as well as north and east Africa. Long-distance traders carried goods along their own segments of these routes, and then turned them over to traders in the next sector. The western hemisphere was still separate, and had two major trade networks of its own.

pressing towards it, and, on entering the place, their surprise was still further heightened by the sight of the multitudes assembled there, and the dimensions of the inclosure, thrice as large as the celebrated square of Salamanca [Spain]. Here were met together traders from all parts, with the products and manufactures peculiar to their countries; the goldsmiths of Azcapozalso; the potters and jewellers of Cholula, the painters of Tezcuco, the stone-cutters of Tenajocan, the hunters of Xilotepec, the fishermen of Cuitlahuac, the fruiterers of the warm countries, the mat and chair-makers of Quauhtitlan, and the florists of Xochimilco—all busily engaged in recommending their respective wares, and in chattering with purchasers. (p. 328)

The market met every fifth day, with perhaps 40,000 to 50,000 merchants swarming in, rowing their canoes across the lake in which Tenochtitlán was built. Prescott compares the market to "the periodical fairs in Europe, not as they exist now, but as they existed in the Middle Ages, when . . . they served as the great central marts for commercial intercourse" (p. 331).

But how independent were these Tenochtitlán merchants? The Spanish described the city's market as being under tight government control. In addition to officers who kept the peace, collected taxes, and checked the accuracy of weights and measures, a court of twelve judges sat to decide cases immediately (p. 331).

A guild of traders, called *pochteca*, carried on long-distance trade, which expanded steadily through the fifteenth century. They led caravans for hundreds of miles, carrying city-crafted obsidian knives, fur blankets, clothes, herbs, and dyes, and brought back such raw materials as jade, seashells, jaguar skins, feathers from forest birds, and, in the greatest volume, cotton from the Gulf coast. They were to marry only within the guild, and, though they were commoners, they could send their sons to temple schools and they had their own courts.

They often gathered both goods and military intelligence for the ruling families. They were protected by royal troops, and sometimes attacks on

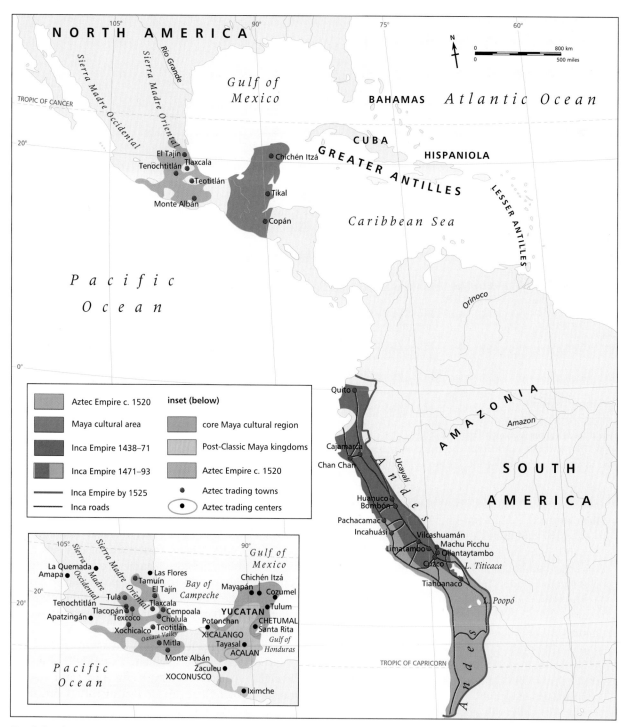

Pre-Columbian America Pre-Columbian America had two great regions of trade and political power. In the north, the Aztec kingdom, centered on Tenochtitlán, dominated. The adjacent Maya of central America were in decline. In South America, about 1500, the Inca dominated the Andes mountain regions, linking them together through an extensive system of roads.

traveling *pochteca* were returned by troops, who used the attacks as a justification for punishing the attackers and confiscating their lands. Curtin notes that the *pochteca* lived in their own wards in the towns, had their own magistrates, and supervised the markets on their own. Their main god, Yiacatecutli, seemed akin to the Toltec god Quetzalcoatl, and this, too, suggests that they were to some degree foreigners living in a trade diaspora. Curtin credits the *pochteca* with a high degree of

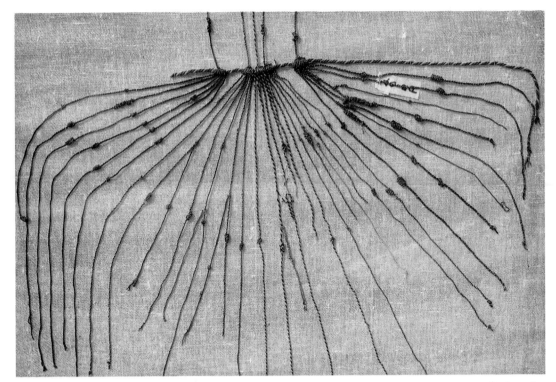

Photograph of a *quipu*. In the Inca empire, which extended from Ecuador to central Chile, trading was facilitated by an extensive road network. This *quipu*, a device of knotted string used to record dates and accounts, would have been a handy aid to the traveling South American businessman of the early 1400s.

independence from the state and temple (Curtin, 85–7).

As the American Indian nations had not invented the wheel, goods were carried by pack animals and humans. Along the South American coast, near the equator, the Incas sailed boats constructed of balsa wood. The Mayans paddled canoes through the river systems of the Yucatán. The two major civilizational hubs functioned independently of one another and both were, of course, virtually completely cut off from Afro-Eurasia. When Europeans arrived in the sixteenth century brandishing new weapons, commanding new military organizations, and transmitting new diseases, the American residents were unprepared for the challenges.

SUB-SAHARAN AFRICA

West Africa

The introduction of the camel in the second to fifth century C.E. opened the possibility of regular trans-Saharan trade. Oases provided the necessary rest and watering points for their caravans, and produced dates, a major commodity of trade. The earliest written records of this trade begin with the arrival of Islamic traders in the eighth century.

For the most part, African political units were local, but three large empires were forged successively around the northern bend in the Niger, near Timbuktu, where the **sahel**, the arid fringe of the desert, meets the vast Sahara itself. These three empires were: Ghana, about 700 to about 1100; Mali, about 1100 to about 1400; and Songhay, about 1300 to about 1600, when the kingdom was destroyed in battle by the Beni Marin tribes of Morocco. These kingdoms kept the trade routes open and secure. In contrast with almost all other governments, which amassed their wealth and power by controlling land and agriculture, these empires drew their power from their control over trade, traders, and trade routes.

Gold, slaves, cloth, ivory, ebony, pepper, and kola nuts (a stimulant) moved north across the Sahara; salt, dates, horses, brass, copper, glassware, beads, leather, textiles, clothing, and foodstuffs moved south. Gold was the central attraction. Up to *c.* 1350, the gold mines of west Africa "furnished about two-thirds of the gold circulating in the economy of the hemisphere" (Wolf, pp. 38–9). In 1324, when the Muslim emperor of Mali, Mansa Musa

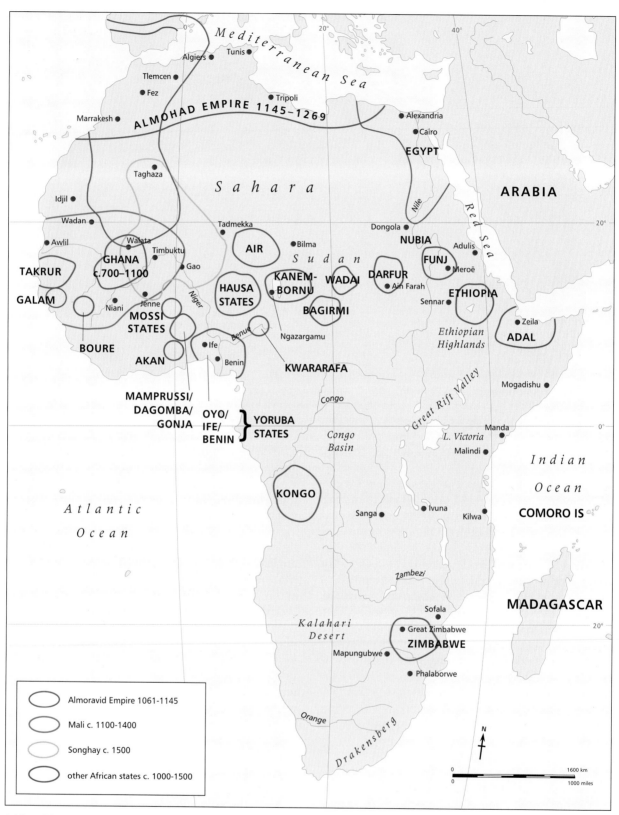

African kingdoms Many states appeared in 1000–1500 in northern and western Africa, their power based on control over long-distance trade—gold, ivory, and slaves moving north; metalware, textiles, and salt carried south. Ghana, Mali, and Songhay are discussed in the text. These states, protected from marauders by the Sahara, could usually maintain their independence.

Mosque at Jenne, Mali, first built fourteenth century C.E. The spectacular mud-brick mosques found in the major towns of the African savanna states, such as Jenne and Timbuktu, point to the acceptance of Islam by the merchant and ruling classes in the thirteenth and fourteenth centuries. The mud, which washes away in the rain, needs continual renewal—hence the built-in "scaffolding" of the structure.

(r. 1307–32), passed through Cairo on his way to Mecca, he dispensed so much gold in gifts to court officials and in purchases in the bazaar that "the value of Cairo's currency was depressed for many years." A European map of 1375 showing a seated Mansa Musa as ruler of Mali is captioned as follows: "So abundant is the gold found in his country that he is the richest and most noble king in all the land" (see also p. 348).

There were many natural break-points for the north–south trade: From the Mediterranean coast to the northern fringe of the desert, trade was borne by pack horse; across the desert, via oases, by camel; across the arid sahel and the grassy **savanna** lands again by pack animal; and finally through the tropical forest, afflicted with the lethal tsetse fly, it was borne by human porters. For the most part, the trade was carried from one market center to the next in short relays by locally dominant trade groups. A few trading communities, however, notably the Soninke and, especially, their Mande-speaking Dyula branch, established trade diasporas which negotiated with the rulers.

Thus, Africa south of the Sahara was not the isolated, backward area of European imagination, but an integral part of a web of relations that connected forest cultivators and miners with savanna and desert traders and with the merchants and rulers of the North African settled belt. This web of relations had a warp of gold. (Wolf, p. 40)

Great Zimbabwe. The biggest and most celebrated of several stone enclosures in east Africa dating from the tenth to fifteenth centuries, Great Zimbabwe provided raw materials for trade at the coastal settlements, especially gold, copper, tin, and iron and was also a trading post for luxury goods—Islamic pottery and cowrie shells were dug up at the site.

East Africa, south of the Horn, came into the trade system of the Indian Ocean through the voyages of Arab merchants in the ninth century. The first major port had been Manda, succeeded in the thirteenth century by Kilwa. The ruling Arab dynasty seized control also of the port of Sofala, which lay to the south. Through local African traders they traded with the interior, especially at Great Zimbabwe (Curtin, p. 34).

The gold, ivory, horns, skins, tortoiseshell, and slaves collected from the interior were traded to Arabia and India for spices, pottery, glass beads, and cloth. Under the Mahdali dynasty, trade became a Kilwan monopoly, but both previously and later it was apparently more open. Arab traders carried most of the Indian Ocean commerce, but there were exceptions. In the early 1400s, the Chinese admiral Zheng He, a Muslim, reached Kilwa several times, seeking tribute for the Ming Empire (see p. 393). More frequently, Chinese goods were shipped via India by intermediary Arab merchants.

THE INDIAN OCEAN

Four of Abu-Lughod's routes include Indian Ocean ports. Sea lanes provided alternatives to the overland silk route. They linked eastern, southern, and western Asia and Africa. During the height of its empire, traders from Rome itself plied these waters, and on rare occasions continued all the way to China. They were not, however, ethnically Roman:

They were descendants of the same people who had been trading to the East before the Roman Empire came into existence: Jews from Egypt and the Fertile Crescent, Greek-speaking Egyptians, and other Levantines from the ecumenical and Hellenized world of Mediterranean commerce. (Curtin, p. 100)

Roman trade left a permanent heritage of diaspora traders, in the form of small religious communities of Jews and Christians, living along the southwest coast of India long after the fall of Rome.

During the period of Tang-Abbasid control over the silk route, Jews had again emerged as a preeminent trading community of the diaspora.

For a brief period centered on the eighth and early ninth centuries, a Jewish trade diaspora became the most important trade group over the whole network of routes linking Europe and China. The Jews who ran this trade were called *Radaniyya* in Arabic . . . [probably from] Persian *rha dan*, meaning "those who know the way." (Curtin, p. 106)

The religious diaspora of the Jews facilitated their trade connections. Charlemagne's ninth-century empire (see p. 329) used them for carrying trade in France. Babylon, astride many of the key trade routes in western Asia, held the most prominent Jewish community in the world at the time, but there were also small Jewish communities in Calicut and Cochin in south India and in Kai-feng, China. When the Portuguese explorer Vasco da Gama reached Calicut in 1498, a local Jewish merchant was able to serve as interpreter. Cairo, one of the world's great trade centers, also sheltered a very significant Jewish community.

How Do We Know?

Information on all Middle Eastern cultures from the ninth through the twelfth centuries has come to historians from the Cairo Genizah (Hebrew for a repository of old papers), studied by Solomon Goitein from the 1950s through the 1970s. Jewish law requires that religious writings not be destroyed; the Genizah was the storage point in Cairo for these documents for three centuries. It also included massive bundles of notes and manuscripts on secular and sacred aspects of life, on society in

Statuette of Semitic trader, Chinese, tenth century. Traders from the Roman Empire traveling the silk routes were likely to be Jews from the Fertile Crescent, Greek-speaking Egyptians, and other Levantines. They and their descendants eventually settled along the trans-Asian routes, which most likely explains the Chinese derivation of this glazed porcelain Jewish (?) peddler, made during Tang dynasty times. *(The Seattle Art Museum)*

general, and on the Jewish community in particular. The centuries-old manuscripts have proven to be a gold mine for historians.

Muslim Traders

With the rise of Islam (see Chapter 11), and especially after the Abbasids shifted their capital to Baghdad, Muslim traders, Arabs and Persians, dominated the routes through the Indian Ocean.

> In the broadest perspective of Afro-Eurasian history, in the period from about 750 A.D. to at least 1500, Islam was the central civilization for the whole of the Old World. . . . it was also the principal agency for contact between the discrete cultures of this period, serving as the carrier that transmitted innovations from one society to another. . . . The Muslim religion was also carried as part of a broad process of culture change—largely by traders, not conquerors. (Curtin, p. 107)

Islam encouraged trade. Muhammad himself had been a trader and caravan driver and he came from a trading town. The *hajj* (pilgrimage), encouraged for every Muslim at least once during his or her lifetime, demanded international travel; trade connections flourished with it. A Muslim trade colony had operated in Sri Lanka from about 700 C.E. Arab traders sailed with the monsoon winds first to India, then on to southeast Asia, and some, even on to the southeast coast of China. Catching the proper seasonal winds in each direction, and using their **lateen**, triangular, sails to maximum effect, sailors could complete a round trip from Mesopotamia to China in less than two years. Carried not by military power but by traders, Islam came to be the dominant religion in Indonesia (the largest Muslim country in the world today), and to attract tens of millions of Chinese adherents. The entire length of the Indian Ocean littoral, from east Africa through India and on to Indonesia, housed a Muslim, largely Arab, trading diaspora. The stories of Sinbad the Sailor, preserved in the tales told by Scheherezade in the *Thousand and One Nights*, reflect the importance of this Muslim trade network.

THE SILK ROUTES AND THE MONGOLS

The great central Asian silk route had declined after the ninth century along with the Abbasid and Tang dynasties which had protected and encouraged it.

Under the Mongol Empire, 1206–1405, the largest land empire ever known, it was reborn. The 2 million Mongols who inhabited the plateau region of central Asia were divided into several warring tribes, each led by a *khan*. The land was poor and the climate harsh. The Mongols shepherded their cattle, sheep, and goats in a circular pattern of migration called **transhumance**: in the brief summers they moved northward; in winter they turned back south. They spent most of their waking hours on horseback and mastered the art of warfare from the stirrups, with bow and arrow as well as sword by their side.

Genghis Khan

Temujin, later Genghis Khan, was born about 1162 into one of the more powerful and more militant Mongol tribes. His father, chief of his tribe, was poisoned by a rival tribe. About three generations before Temujin's birth, one of his ancestors, Kabul Khan, had briefly united the Mongols, and to reunify them became Genghis' own mission. He conquered the surrounding tribes, one by one, and united them at Karakorum, his capital. Although skilled at negotiation, Temujin was infamous for his brutality. Historian Rashid al-Din reports Genghis Khan's declaration:

> Man's greatest good fortune is to chase and defeat his enemy, seize all his possessions, leave his married women weeping and wailing, ride his gelding, and use the bodies of his women as a nightshirt and support, gazing upon and kissing their rosy breasts, sucking their lips which are as sweet as the berries of their breasts. (Cited in Ratchnevsky, p. 153)

Temujin defeated the Tatars and killed all surviving males taller than a cart axle. He defeated the Taichi'ut and boiled alive all their chiefs. In 1206, an assembly of all the chiefs of the steppe regions proclaimed him Genghis Khan ("Universal Ruler"). He organized them for further battle under a pyramid of officers leading units of 100, 1000, and 10,000 mounted warriors, commanded, as they grew older, by his four sons. Promotion within the fighting machine was by merit. Internal feuding among the Mongols ended. A new legal code, based on written and recorded case law, called for high moral standards within the Mongol nation.

Genghis turned east toward China. *En route* he captured the Tangut kingdom of Xixia, and from

Chinese engineers he mastered the weapons of siege warfare: the **mangonel** and **trebuchet** that could catapult great rocks; giant crossbows mounted on stands; and gunpowder that he could launch from longbows in bamboo-tube rockets. In 1211 he pierced the Great Wall of China, and in 1215 he conquered the capital, Zhongdu (modern Beijing), killing thousands. Genghis' officials and successors continued south until they captured all of China, establishing the Mongol dynasty, 1276–1368. They conquered Korea, large parts of southeast Asia as far as Java, and attempted, but failed, to take Japan as well. The planned assault on Japan in 1281 was stopped by *kamikaze*, divine winds, which prevented the Mongol fleet from sailing.

Genghis also turned west, conquering the Kara-Khitai Empire that included the major cities Tashkent and Samarqand. He turned southward toward India, reaching the Indus River and stationing troops in the Punjab, but he was unable to penetrate further. Turning northwest, he proceeded to

conquer Khwarizm. In the great cities of Bukhara, Nishapur, Merv, Herat, Balkh, and Gurgan, millions were reported killed, an exaggeration, but an indication of great slaughter. Genghis went on to capture Tabriz and Tbilisi. When he died in 1227 his four sons continued the expansion relentlessly. In the northwest they defeated the Bulgars along the Volga and the Cumans of the southern steppes and then entered Russia. They took Moscow, destroyed Kiev, overran Moravia and Silesia, and set their sights on the conquest of Hungary. In 1241, Genghis' son Ogedei (Ögödei; 1185–1241) died, and during the succession dispute the Mongols withdrew east of Kiev. They never resumed their westward movement. Central and western Europe remained untouched.

In the southwest, under Genghis' grandson Hulegu (c. 1217–65), the Mongols captured and destroyed Baghdad, ending the five-century-old Abbasid dynasty by killing the caliph. Meanwhile Mongke, Genghis' grandson and the fourth and last

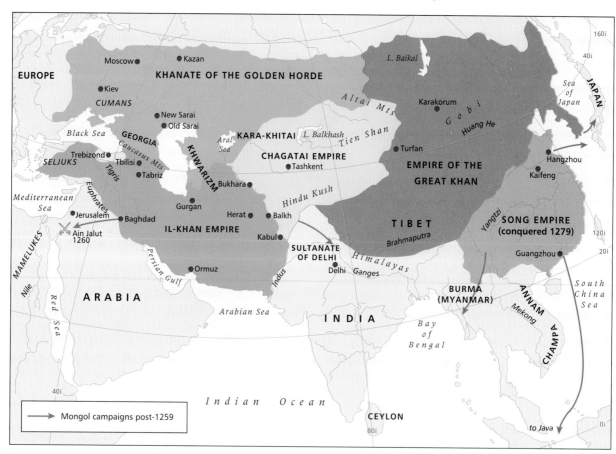

The Mongol successor states After the death of Genghis Khan's grandson Mongke in 1259, the Mongol world devolved into four successor states. Kublai Khan's emerged as the most powerful, but only after a long struggle with Song China. In central Asia, the Chagatai dominated the eastern steppe; the Golden Horde became established in southern Russia; and the Il-Khan in Persia ruled from Kabul to Anatolia.

Genghis Khan, from Rashid al-Din's world history, thirteenth century. Genghis Khan's conquests had as much impact on west Asia as they did on China. This Persian illustration of Genghis pursuing his enemies comes from a history, which some consider to be the first world history, written by Rashid al-Din (1247–1318), a Persian administrator employed by Mongol Il-Khans in Iran. *(Bibliothèque Nationale, Paris)*

successor to his title as "Great Khan," died while campaigning in China and many of the Mongol forces withdrew to attend a general conclave in Karakorum to choose his successor. A small force, however, proceeded to Ain Jalut, in modern day Jordan, and were defeated in battle. The Mongols never pressed further westward. The empire divided permanently into four separate *khanates*, or empires. At their apogee, 1279–1350, the Mongols ruled all of China, almost all of Russia, Iran, Iraq, and central Asia.

Mongol rule was extensive but brief. The Mongols could not govern their empire from horseback, and they were soon absorbed by the peoples they had conquered. They intermarried freely with the Turks who had joined them as allies in conquest. In Russia, Mongols and Turks merged with Slavs and Finns in a new Turkish-speaking ethnic group, the Tartars. In Persia and China they assimilated into local culture, converting to various religions, including Christianity, Buddhism, and Confucianism. In most of the areas inhabited by Muslims, the Mongols and their Turkish allies typically converted to Islam.

After such transformations, the four segments of Genghis' empire went their own separate ways. Slowly they were driven from their conquests. By 1335 the male line of Genghis and his grandson Hulegu died out in the Il-Khan Empire in Persia. The Ming dynasty defeated and evicted the Mongol (or Yuan) rulers in 1368. The Russians pushed out the Golden Horde (named not, as one might think, for their numbers, but for their tents, *Ordu* in Turkish). The Chagatai Khanate was destroyed by Timur the Lame (Tamerlane) after 1369. The last Mongol state in the Crimea was conquered only in the eighteenth century.

Cultural historians credit the Mongols with very little permanent contribution—they were absorbed into other, more settled and sophisticated cultures—but they did establish, for about a century, the "Pax Mongolica," the Mongolian Peace, over a vast region, in which intercontinental trade could flourish across the reopened silk route. Reports from two world travelers, Ibn Battuta (1304–68) of Morocco and Marco Polo (1254–1324) of Venice, give vivid insights into that exotic trade route.

World Travelers: Ibn Battuta and Marco Polo

In Chapter 11 we noted Ibn Battuta's observations on the variety of Islamic practices he encountered during his thirty years and 73,000 miles (117,000 kilometers) of travel (see p. 358). He also commented

SPOTLIGHT
The Ships of Trade

From the late seventh century ships sailed from the Red Sea and Persian Gulf ports all the way to China, returning with silk, porcelain, and jade. Sometimes they traveled part of the way, exchanging their west Asian cargo for Chinese goods at an intermediate port, perhaps in the Malayan archipelago. As trade increased along these routes, the ports grew in size by servicing the ships and crews. They became homes to cosmopolitan business communities that financed and directed the voyages. Al-Masudi, noting the pattern of trans-shipments in his encyclopedia of 916, describes Muslim merchants who had married and settled in the Indian ports.

Regional shipping routes were linked into this oceanic, intercontinental trade, and the Oman–Basra route through the Persian Gulf, connecting Mesopotamia and the Indian Ocean, was one of the most important of them. **Figure 1** depicts a boat that plied this route. The illustration accompanied the twelfth-century *Maqamat*, or tales of

Figure 1 Arab trader, illustration from the *Maqamat* of al-Hariri, twelfth century.

fiction, of al-Hariri and portrays Arab passengers with a crew apparently from India and perhaps Africa.

Europeans bought the silks of China, the spices of south and southeast Asia, and the textiles of India in ports much closer to home, such as Alexandria, where the Arab traders transported them. But travel accounts of more distant civilizations, especially the reports by Marco Polo from his travels across Asia in 1271–95, excited Europe's imagination, as the painting on p. 390 suggests. **Figure 2** is a fanciful depiction of Cambay, the principal port of the northwest coast of India, in an illustration from the *Livre des Merveilles* (*The Book of Wonders*) (1410). Cambay's walls, buildings, and even ships are more European than Indian. The painter had heard wondrous tales, but had not actually seen the port with his own eyes.

Figure 2 Trade in the Gulf of Cambay, India, from the *Livre des Merveilles*, 1410.

With the seven official expeditions of Admiral Zheng He between 1405 and 1433, the Chinese government dispatched foreign diplomatic and trade missions all the way to the Persian Gulf and the east coast of Africa. Inland trade, however, was much more typical. China held one-fifth of the world's population and its internal markets were huge. River traffic at festival time in Kaifeng, the capital of the northern Song dynasty (**figure 3**), show well-developed channels of trade plied by a multitude of Chinese junks. The picture is a section taken from a twelfth-century scroll painting by Zhang Zeduan.

Figure 3 River traffic at Qing Ming festival, Kaifeng, by Zhang Zeduan, Song dynasty scroll. (*National Palace Museum, Taiwan*)

PROFILE
Marco Polo
AND HIS FABULOUS TRAVELS

Almost everything we know about Marco Polo's life (1254–1324) is based on the colorful account he left us of his travels through Asia. Little is known of his childhood years in Venice or his education. Marco's father and uncle, both Venetian merchants, traveled from their home in 1260 on a trade mission as far as Bogara and Sarai, at the northern end of the Caspian Sea. War broke out, and their route back home was blocked. But the route eastward was open, and the brothers finally traveled as far as Beijing, where Ghenghis Khan's grandson, Kublai Khan (1215–94), ruled. The Great Khan invited the men to return with more information on Christianity and a delegation from the pope. The information and delegation never materialized, but in 1271 the two brothers, along with the seventeen-year-old Marco, set out for China again. They arrived in 1275 and remained there for seventeen years. How exactly they occupied themselves during this time is unclear from Marco's account, but it was not uncommon for foreigners to find employment in the Mongol state. Kublai Khan, it appears, was so enchanted by Marco's tales of foreign lands that he sent him on repeated reconnaissance trips throughout the empire.

The Polos eventually set off for home in about 1292, reaching Venice in 1295. Relatives and friends had apparently thought the men long since dead and the reunion was emotional. Soon after his homecoming, Marco was captured in a battle in the Mediterranean by Genoese sailors and imprisoned. He dictated the tales of his travels to his fellow-prisoner Rustichello (Rusticiano), a writer of Romances. The language Rustichello employed was Franco-Italian, a composite language popular in the thirteenth and fourteenth centuries. Europe now had its most complete and consistent account up to that date of the silk route and of the fabulous Chinese empire of Kublai Khan. Marco's *Travels* was soon translated into several European languages, intro-

extensively on conditions of travel and trade. In central Asia Ibn Battuta encountered a military expedition of Oz Beg Khan (d. 1341), the ruler of the khanate of the Golden Horde:

> We saw a vast city on the move with its inhabitants, with mosques and bazaars in it, the smoke of the kitchens rising in the air (for they cook while on the march), and horse-drawn wagons transporting the people. (Dunn, p. 167)

The tents of this camp/city were Mongol **yurts**. Made of wooden poles covered with leather pelt, and with rugs on the floor, the yurts could be disassembled quickly for travel.

Later, Ibn Battuta was granted his request to travel with one of Oz Beg Khan's wives along the trade route as she returned to her father's home in Constantinople to give birth to her child. The princess travelled with 5000 horsemen under military command, 500 of her own troops and servants, 200 slave girls, 20 Greek and Indian pages, 400 wagons, 2000 horses, and about 500 oxen and camels (Dunn, p. 170). They crossed from Islamic Mongol territory to Christian Byzantium.

Marco Polo was a merchant in a family of merchants (see Profile above), and his account of his travels to and in China was thus particularly attuned to patterns of trade. His numerous descriptions of urban markets support Curtin's concept of an urban-centered trade diaspora. For example, consider Marco Polo's description of Tabriz in northwest Persia:

> The people of Tabriz live by trade and industry; for cloth of gold and silk is woven here in great quantity and of great value. The city is so favourably situated that it is a market for merchandise from India and Baghdad, from Mosul and Hormuz, and from many other places; and many Latin merchants come here to buy the merchandise imported from foreign lands. It is also a market for precious stones, which

ducing to Christian Europe a new understanding of the world. In the following extract Marco explains in vivid terms how central Asian routes challenged travelers and their animals:

> For the merchants of these parts, when they travel from one country to another, traverse vast deserts, that is to say dry, barren, sandy regions, producing no grass or fodder suitable for horses, and the wells and sources of fresh water lie so far apart that they must travel by long stages if their beasts are to have anything to drink. (Polo, p. 61)

For seven centuries scholars have hotly debated the authenticity of Marco Polo's account. No original copy of *The Travels* exists and scholars have been faced with some 140 manuscript versions that were copied in various languages and dialects from scribe to scribe before the invention of printing. Recently, Frances Wood, head of the China Department at

the British Library, has asked, *Did Marco Polo Go to China?* (1996). Wood notes that Marco did not mention any of the phenomena that should have caught his attention during his reported time in China: Chinese writing, tea, chopsticks, foot binding, the Great Wall. Despite his claims to frequent meetings with the Kublai Khan, Marco Polo is not mentioned in any Chinese records of the time. Wood concludes that Polo's work is actually based on materials gathered from others, that he himself never traveled beyond the Black Sea. As a travel narrative, Wood asserts, the book was a fabrication, but as an account of what was known of China at the time, it was a very rich and very influential source of information. The debate over authenticity of authorship continues.

Marco Polo, title page of first printed edition of *The Travels of Marco Polo*, 1477.

are found here in great abundance. It is a city where good profits are made by traveling merchants. The inhabitants are a mixed lot and good for very little. There are Armenians and Nestorians, Jacobites and Georgians and Persians; and there are also worshippers of Mahomet, who are the natives of the city and are called Tabrizis. (Polo, p. 57)

Central Asian routes challenged travelers and their animals. Despite the Pax Mongolica, merchants still had to be prepared to defend themselves from attack:

> Among the people of these kingdoms there are many who are brutal and bloodthirsty. They are for ever slaughtering one another; and, were it not for fear of the government, that is, the Tartar lordship of the Levant, they would do great mischief to travelling merchants. The government imposes severe penalties upon them and has ordered that along all dangerous routes the inhabitants at the

request of the merchants shall supply good and efficient escorts from district to district for their safe conduct on payment of two or three groats for each loaded beast according to the length of the journey. Yet, for all that the government can do, these brigands are not to be deterred from frequent depredations. Unless the merchants are well armed and equipped with bows, they slay and harry them unsparingly. (Polo, p. 61)

Bubonic Plague and the Trade Routes

In addition to commerce and religion, the bubonic plague also traveled the trade routes. William McNeill's masterly *Plagues and Peoples* argues persuasively that "Mongol movements across previously isolating distances in all probability brought the bacillus *Pasteurella pestis* to the rodents of the Eurasian steppe for the first time" (p. 134). The infection apparently entered China in 1331 and decimated its population.

The best estimates show a decrease from 123 million about 1200 (before the Mongol invasions began) to a mere 65 million in 1393 . . . . Even Mongol ferocity cannot account for such a drastic decrease. Disease assuredly played a big part in cutting Chinese numbers in half; and bubonic plague . . . is by all odds the most likely candidate for such a role. (p. 144)

Along the silk routes, after the mid-fourteenth century, the presence and the role of the Mongols declined, probably also a result of plague deaths. The plague reached the Crimea in 1346. There, plague-infested rats boarded ships, disembarking with the disease at all the ports of Europe and the Near East.

In Europe, where the plague was new and people had no natural immunity, one-third of the population died. The ravages of the plague foreshadowed further, even worse, epidemics that would sweep across the continent, as groups of people who had not previously been exposed to one another's diseases began to meet for the first time (see Chapter 14).

CHINA AND THE SOUTH CHINA SEA

Marco Polo reported being overwhelmed when he finally arrived in China in 1275. He described its

ruler, Kublai Khan, as "the mightiest man, whether in respect of subjects or of territory or of treasure, who is in the world today or who ever has been, from Adam our first parent down to the present moment" (p. 113). Polo correctly informed the West that China in the late 1200s was the richest, most technologically advanced, and largest politically unified country in the world. Certain elements leading to the creation of wealth had been in place for centuries. In the ninth century, under the Tang, wood block printing had been invented. From that time onward, ideas could spread in China more rapidly than anywhere else. One of the first uses of print was to conserve and spread religious concepts; the oldest printed book extant in the world is a copy of the Buddhist *Diamond Sutra* from 868 (see picture, p. 282). The government also used print to spread information on new farming methods.

The great luxury products of China—silk, porcelain, and tea—continued to attract the merchants of the world as they had since Tang times. Foreign merchants were housed in the suburbs of the capital, each nationality with its own accommodations. Lombards, Germans, and French from Europe were among them. A huge service industry grew up to attend them, Polo noted, in particular, an army of prostitutes:

I assure you that there are fully 20,000 of them, all serving the needs of men for money. They have a captain general, and there are chiefs of hundreds and of thousands responsible to the captain. This is because, whenever ambassadors come to the Great Khan on his business and are maintained at his expense, which is done on a lavish scale, the captain is called upon to provide one of these women every

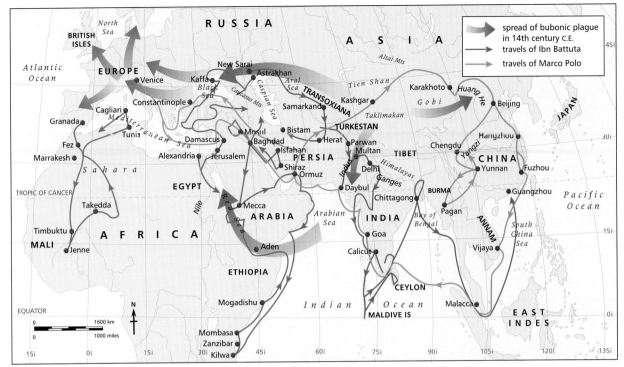

The routes of the plague The central and east Asian stability imposed by Mongol rule—the "Mongol peace"—brought mixed benefits. Trade flourished, and travelers such as Ibn Battuta and Marco Polo were able to write remarkable accounts of the lands they visited. At the same time, however, vectors for other travelers, such as the rats that carried bubonic plague, also opened up. The Black Death, originating in central Asia, was one of a succession of plagues that followed the trade routes by land and sea, decimating parts of Europe and China.

night for the ambassador and one for each of his attendants. They are changed each night and receive no payment; for this is the tax they pay to the Great Khan. (Polo, p. 129)

The international merchants were at the peak of a highly integrated national system of trade and commerce. Market towns sprang up throughout China, enabling virtually every rural family to sell its products for cash and to buy city goods. In turn, the small market towns were linked to larger cities, which provided more specialized products and access to government administrators. At the apex of this national system of urbanization were regional capitals, such as Kai-feng and Hangzhou. Geographer William Skinner's extensive presentation on the geography and functioning of market towns in China demonstrated the significance of this dense network of towns. Here, families could buy and sell, arrange a marriage, determine the latest government rulings, hear about new farming possibilities, learn the dates and the results of academic examinations. "By late traditional times, markets had so proliferated on the Chinese land-

scape and were so distributed that at least one was accessible to virtually every rural household" (Skinner, p. 6).

At the base of the economic system were the rural families, struggling to survive by producing commodities demanded by the traders. Hand manufacture, especially of cotton cloth, often supplemented farm production in rural areas. The producers were integrated into the market system either through direct, personal access or through brokers who supplied raw materials and bought the finished product. Dong Xianliang's "Weaving Song," written during the Ming dynasty, summarizes the industrial organization:

He tends his cotton in the garden in the morning,
In the evening makes his cloth upon the loom.
His wife weaves with ever-moving fingers;
His girls spin with never-ceasing wheels.
It is the humid and unhealthy season.
When they finish the last of the cotton from their garden.
Prices go up and up, if outside merchants come to buy;

So if warp's plentiful a lack of weft brings grief.
They therefore buy raw cotton and spin it night after night.

> (Elvin, p. 273)

Women were the chief producers in this supplemental rural industry. They also carried the finished product to market. Conditions both of production and of marketing could be savage. Xu Xianzhong's "Prose Poem on Cotton Cloth" presents the harshness of both aspects:

> Why do you ignore their toil? Why are you touched
> Only by the loveliness that is born from toil?
> . . .
> Shall I tell you how their work exhausts them?
> By hand and treadle they turn the rollers of wood and iron,
> Feeling their fibre in between their fingers;
> The cotton comes out fluffy and the seeds fall away.
> The string of the cotton bow is stretched so taut
> It twangs with a sob from its pillar.
> They draw out slivers, spin them on their wheels

> To the accompaniment of a medley of creakings.
> Working through the darkness by candlelight,
> Forgetful of bed. When energy ebbs, they sing.
> The quilts are cold. Unheard, the waterclock flows over.
> . . .
> When a woman leaves for market
> She does not look at her hungry husband.
> Afraid her cloth's not good enough,
> She adorns her face with cream and powder,
> Touches men's shoulders to arouse their lust,
> And sells herself with pleasant words.
> Money she thinks of as a beast its prey;
> Merchants she coaxes as she would her father.
> Nor is her burden lifted till one buys.

> (Elvin, pp. 273–4)

From Mongol to Ming: Dynastic Transition

Marco Polo reported that the economy did not serve everyone equally well. He told of especially bitter poverty and class division in south China:

> In the province of Manzi almost all the poor and needy sell some of their sons and daughters to the rich and noble, so that they may support themselves on the price paid for them and the children may be better fed in their new homes. (Polo, p. 227)

Polo also understood that the Mongol rulers were resented as foreign colonial masters:

Ink and watercolor print showing silk manufacture, Chinese, early seventeenth century. During the Song dynasty (960–1279), long-distance trade across central Asia dwindled. Maritime trade, with its very much safer and cheaper routes, now offered a viable alternative, and silk, along with porcelain and tea, continued to attract the merchants of the world. Unwinding filaments from silkworm cocoons in order to make yarn was considered women's work, as this Ming dynasty print suggests. (*Victoria & Albert Museum, London*)

All the Cathayans hated the government of the Great Khan, because he set over them Tartar rulers, mostly Saracens, and they could not endure it, since it made them feel that they were no more than slaves. Moreover the Great Khan had no legal title to rule the province of Cathay, having acquired it by force. (Polo, p. 133)

During the ninety years of Mongol rule, 1279–1368, China's population plummeted from a high of 100 million to just over 50 million. Revolution ensued, and in 1368 the Ming dynasty replaced the Mongols and ruled for almost three centuries, until 1644.

Under the Ming dynasty, the population increased sharply. By 1450 it had reached 100 million again, and by 1580 the population was at least 130 million. Mark Elvin estimates it in that year as "somewhere between 160 and 250 million" (p. 129). Plagues and rebellions again caused the population to fall back to 100 million by 1650, but from that trough it rose consistently into present times.

The population settled new territories as it grew. The origins of the Chinese Empire had been in the Yellow River valley in the north (see Chapter 4). At the time of the Han dynasty, upward of 80 percent of the population of China lived north of the Yangzi valley. Under the late Tang dynasty the population was divided about equally between north and south. Warfare with the Mongols in the north drove the migrants south. At the height of the Mongol dynasty up to 90 percent of the population lived in the south. Economically, the south produced rice, cotton, and tea, three of China's most valuable products, not available in the northern climate. Closer to the southeast Asian and Indian Ocean sea lanes, the south also developed China's principal ports for international commerce. After the Mongols were defeated, however, migration began to reverse. By about 1500, 75 percent lived in the south, and northward movement was continuing.

International Trade and Government Intervention

China's ports, as Marco Polo had described them, hosted traders from around the world. Their Chinese counterparts were both private traders and traders in government service. In the early fifteenth century, the Ming Emperor Yongle commissioned a series of seven spectacular ocean voyages under the Muslim eunuch, Admiral Zheng He. The first voyage set out in 1405 with sixty-two large junks, 100 smaller ships, and 30,000 crew. The largest ships were 450 feet (140 meters) long, displaced 1600 tons, held a crew of about 500, and were the largest ships built anywhere up to that time. They carried silks, porcelains, and pepper. The first expedition sailed as far as Calicut, near the southwest tip of India. In six further missions between 1407 and 1433, Zheng He sailed to ports all along the Indian Ocean littoral, at least twice reaching the east African ports of Mogadishu, Brava, Malindi, and Kilwa. The Emperor Yongle seemed most pleased with a giraffe sent to him by the sultan of Malindi on the fourth voyage, 1416–19.

Why did China halt the voyages? Why did China not dispatch its own missions to Europe, and even to the western hemisphere, rather than only receive voyages from Europeans, beginning with the Portuguese in 1514? Many answers appear possible: The Ming turned their energies inward, toward consolidation and internal development. At first they pushed the Mongols further north from the wall, but an invasion of Mongolia failed in 1449. Thereafter, the Ming limited their military goals, rebuilt the wall, and restricted their forces to more defensible borders.

In 1411 the Ming reconstructed and extended the Grand Canal from Hangzhou in the south to Beijing in the north. The canal was the cheapest, most efficient means of shipping the grain and produce required by the northern capital. The manmade inland waterway also reduced the importance of coastal shipping, enabling the Ming emperors to turn their backs on the seas and ocean. The faction of eunuchs, dedicated court servants like Zheng He, who urged the government to continue its sponsorship of foreign trade, lost out in palace competition to other factions that promoted internal development. International private shipping was also curtailed.

The government limited contacts with foreigners and prohibited private overseas trade by Chinese merchants. The Ming dynasty went further by promulgating a series of acts to curtail overseas private trade. In 1371, coastal residents were forbidden to travel overseas. Then, recognizing that smuggling resulted, the government issued further prohibitions in 1390, 1394, 1397, 1433, 1449, and 1452. The continuing prohibitions reveal that smuggling did continue, but, for the most part, private Chinese sailors were cut off from foreign trade.

The government defined the expeditions of Zheng He as political missions that sought tribute to China from outlying countries. Although products were exchanged on these voyages, officially trade was not their goal. So, while both private and government trade flourished in the interior of China, and while thousands of Chinese emigrated to carry on private businesses throughout southeast Asia, China's official overseas trade virtually stopped. The Zheng He expeditions proved to be spectacular exceptions to generally restrictive policies.

The costs of these decisions to limit China's international trade, both official and private, proved enormous. Chinese society became introverted, and although economic growth continued, it was with no "fundamental breakthrough in technique" (Elvin, p. 95). New "invention was almost entirely absent. ... The dynamic quality of the medieval Chinese economy disappeared. This seems to have happened some time around the middle of the fourteenth century" (p. 203).

Military technology improved but then stagnated. China had invented gunpowder before 1000 C.E., but used it only sporadically. Ming cannon in the early fifteenth century were at least equal to those anywhere in the world, but metal was in short supply, limiting further development. The Ming fought few battles against fortress cities, where cannon were most useful, so they also saw little need to invest further in developing heavy weaponry. No enemies appeared against whom it would have been useful or necessary. In fighting against invasions from the north, the crossbow was of more importance to the infantrymen, who made up China's armies of a million and more soldiers. At first, when China was itself very advanced, these decisions seemed not so consequential. Later, they rendered the country vulnerable. China rested content with its accomplishments and stagnated in what Elvin has called a "high level equilibrium trap" (p. 203).

EUROPE AND THE MEDITERRANEAN, 700–1500

The popularity of Marco Polo's accounts of his travels suggests that western Europeans were paying more attention to international trade by the mid-1200s. The remote western fringes of Eurasia were emerging from the agrarian, localized, **manorial economy** and other-worldly spirit which had marked the Middle Ages, the period from about 700 to about 1350 C.E.

The Middle Ages were named in the fifteenth century when western Europeans were reviving and reintegrating lost Greek and Roman urban culture back into their lives. They saw this new movement as a **Renaissance** or rebirth, and disparaged the previous era from the decline of Greek and Roman "classical" culture until their own time as an in-between time, **medieval**, a middle age, between the greatness that had been and the greatness that they felt was now returning. Scholars today, however, are not so dismissive of this rich and innovative period.

The Early Middle Ages

During medieval times, there had been no political force able to protect trade, build and maintain roads, and provide consistent standards of currency and law. Moreover, with the rise of Islam along its eastern and southern coasts, the Mediterranean had become a zone of armed conflict. Trade in western Europe plummeted and cities declined. Rome's population, more than a million during its days as an imperial capital, dwindled to 50,000 in 700 C.E. Even so it was the largest city in western Europe's new era. Charlemagne (742–814) created an empire centered on his capital in Aix-la-Chapelle (Aachen) in northwest Germany, but the structure did not last (see pp. 329–30). Charlemagne's descendants could not preserve it from internal decay and external attack. Norsemen from the north, Magyars (Hungarians) from the east, and Arabs and Berbers from the south invaded and plundered throughout the ninth century.

In the absence of central government, urban administration, and protected trade routes, two responses emerged. One addressed the need for authority and order across large territories. The other provided a new localized means of production and consumption. Each of these systems of organization, one for government, one for economics, has been called "**feudal**" (having to do with land control) by later historians. Let us examine both, first the governmental, then the economic. Men capable of enforcing law and order by virtue of their military might—their ability to fight as armed horsemen and to gather other armed cavalry under their leadership— ranked themselves by relative military power. They then swore allegiance to one another, those with greater power serving as lords, those with lesser serving as vassals. The mounted horsemen among the vassals were called knights. The ranking was hierarchical, but just as those below owed responsibilities to those above, so those above owed (different) responsibilities to those below. The system thus combined and reinforced legal obligations with personal obligations. At the highest levels, kingdoms might emerge from the feudal relationships. The most powerful lords of France chose Hugh Capet to be their king, and agreed to serve as his vassals in 987. Hugh's descendants occupied the French throne for 800 years, until the French Revolution.

But most people were not lords, vassals, or knights in this military-political system. Most life in Christian western Europe—excluding Muslim Spain—centered on rural manors (see Source below). These relatively self-contained estates,

SOURCE
"Capitulare de Villis"– The Rules of Manor Life

In this list of instructions, Louis the Pious (r. 814–840), son of Charlemagne, outlines the administration of his own estates in Aquitaine. The document dates to about the year 800, and relates to an unusually large and efficiently managed estate, but it provides useful insights into general principles for administering a self-contained rural manor.

1. We wish that our estates which we have instituted to serve our needs discharge their services to us entirely and to no other men.
2. Our people shall be well taken care of and reduced to poverty by no one.
3. Our stewards shall not presume to put our people to their own service, either to force them to work, to cut wood, or to do any other task for them. And they shall accept no gift from them. . . .
4. If any of our people does injury to us either by stealing or by some other offense he shall make good the damage and for the remainder of the legal satisfaction he shall be punished by whipping, with the exception of homicide and arson cases which are punishable by fines. . . .
5. When our stewards ought to see that our work is done—the sowing, plowing, harvesting, cutting of hay, or gathering of grapes—let each one at the proper season and in each and every place organize and oversee what is to be done that it may be done well. . . .

6. We wish our stewards to give a tithe [10 percent] of all our products to the churches on our domains and that the tithe not be given to the churches of another except to those entitled to it by ancient usage. And our churches shall not have clerics other than our own, that is, of our people or our place.
31. They shall set aside each year what they ought to give as food and maintenance to the workers entitled to it and to the women working in the women's quarters and shall give it fully at the right time and make known to us what they have done with it and where they got it.
36. Our woods and forests shall be well taken care of and where there shall be a place for a clearing let it be cleared. Our stewards shall not allow the fields to become woods and where there ought to be woods they shall not allow anyone to cut too much or damage them.
43. For our women's work-shops the stewards shall provide the materials at the right time as it has been established, that is flax, wool, woad, vermilion dye, madder, wool-combs, teasels, soap, grease, vessels and other lesser things which are necessary there.
49. The women's quarters, that is, their houses, heated rooms, and sitting rooms, shall be well ordered and have good fences around them and strong gates that our work may be done well.

(Introduction to Contemporary Civilization in the West, pp. 5–13)

dominated by locally powerful landowners, provided most of their own domestic production and consumption and did very little trading with the outside world. Many of the residents of the manors were **serfs**, people bound to the land by personal status and offering to the lord of the manor their labor and services, or a cash rent, in exchange for the right to work the land, a share in its product, or just administration within the manor, and protection from outside attack. While the system was hierarchical and restrictive, especially for the serfs, it also gave them some degree of control over the land.

The other-worldly Christian ethic that was prevalent at the time frowned on such fundamental business practices as trade for profit, interest on loans, and amassing private wealth. St. Augustine's fifth-century observations carried the day: "Business is in itself an evil, for it turns men from seeking true rest, which is in God" (cited in *Introduction to Contemporary Civilization in the West*, Vol. I, p. 65). By the eighth century, Europe had become a trade backwater of relatively self-sufficient rural manors.

The High Middle Ages

By about the year 1000 signs of economic revival had begun in agriculture and population growth. Lords of the manors began to farm in a three-field system instead of two. That is, each year they left fallow one-third of their land instead of one-half, immediately raising production potential by 33 percent. New harnesses were developed that could yoke horses more efficiently to heavier plows with iron plowshares capable of digging more deeply into the soil and facilitating the expansion of farming into new areas. Up to about 1000, four-fifths of northwestern Europe was covered by dense forests. Peasants then began to clear and cultivate the forests of northeastern France. Germans colonized the Rhineland and Black Forest areas. Scandinavians and East Slavs moved eastward into the great plains of central Europe and even further into the great flat, sprawling steppes of Russia. On the basis of such data as the annual growth rings of trees and pollen counts in bogs, historians now believe that the European climate also changed, becoming warmer and promoting greater agricultural productivity. Population increased and spread. The population

The girding-on of swords, thirteenth-century manuscript. In the feudal system, vassals pledged allegiance to lords in exchange for property and protection: the relationship was invested with religious significance because the ladder of hierarchy from serfs, vassals, lords, and the king was seen as extending to heaven. This manuscript shows the girding-on of swords, part of the formal ritual associated with the making of a knight. Hands clasped above the head was the typical posture of prayer in the Middle Ages. (*British Museum, London*)

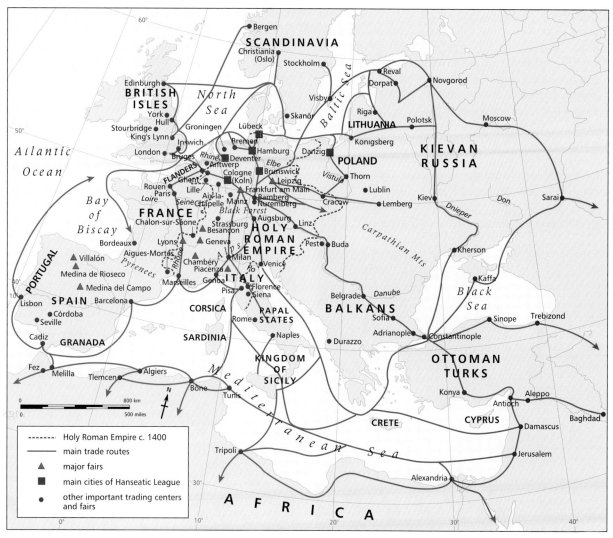

Medieval European trade Four important sets of trade routes emerged by about 1200 in Europe: the ports of the Mediterranean, led by Venice and Genoa; the North Sea and the Baltic, dominated by the Hanseatic League of merchants; a regular system of fairs along the north–south routes between northern Italy and the mouth of the Rhine; and the river systems of Russia, where Scandinavian sailors carried their goods.

of Europe is estimated at 30 million in 1000, 40–45 million in 1150, and 70 million in 1300.

The Rise of an Urban Middle Class

In eastern Europe, Mongol raids limited economic growth. In the thirteenth century the Mongols, moving westward, blocked the Slav advance. In the later fourteenth century, although they withdrew as a conquering power, the nomadic Mongols periodically swooped in to plunder. Their presence inhibited the development of urban areas and trade in Russia's eastern regions. In central Europe, eastern Germany in particular, landed aristocrats blocked the rise of new commercial classes, who

might have built independent cities of trade. The region's economy and government were dominated by a military aristocracy.

In western Europe, on the other hand, cities and an urban, middle-class business community (the **bourgeoisie**—from "burg" or "town"), began to flourish. The restoration of trade, trade routes, and urban market centers, and the increasing importance of businessmen—and some business-women, usually widows—marked the later medieval period.

The cities of Italy, preserving some of Rome's urban heritage, and persisting in a measure of Mediterranean trade, had never entirely lost their cohesion and their control over the adjacent countryside. Now, in the cities of northern and coastal Italy—Venice, Genoa, Pisa, Florence, Milan—and along the North Sea coast—Bruges and Ghent—commerce and manufacture combined to propel economic growth. Woolen textile manufacture in Flanders in the north, and cotton and woolen textile production in Florence in the south, began to create industrial classes, comfortable merchants, and thriving markets. Venice, and to a lesser extent Genoa and Pisa, traded across the Mediterranean, bringing to Europe luxury goods from the Middle East and farther Asia.

By 1150 periodic market fairs in the Champagne region provided points for the exchange of Flemish cloth, French wines, and goods from Asia. Henri Pirenne, in his book *Medieval Cities*, hailed the long-distance, traveling merchants who (re)opened these international trade routes as courageous sires of a new age of commerce, wealth, and intellectual cross-fertilization, and the towns they built as homes of innovation and growth. Pirenne notes that these new heroes of commerce often grew from somewhat unsavory roots to positions of distinction through unremitting attention to business matters and, later, through religious devotion.

The new towns contained several classes: the church officials, bishops in the largest of the cities, who had continued through the most difficult times

Aerial view of present-day Delft, west Netherlands. Here, gabled medieval townhouses are seen surrounding the bustling market square in Delft. Since the late 1500s the town has been famous for its pottery and porcelain known as delftware. Dutch products began to compete in European markets with porcelain imports from China.

Painting of 's-Hertogenbosch, Netherlands, 1530. Compare today's photograph of a medieval square on market day (opposite) with this view of a cloth market in another Dutch town painted in 1530. The layout and construction of the stalls are virtually identical.

to maintain churches, cathedrals, monasteries, and convents; artisans and small-scale manufacturers, who were attracted by markets for both labor and finished products; shopkeepers, who traded mostly in locally produced commodities and everyday necessities; and now the adventurous long-distance merchants. By 1200, the largest of the Italian towns had populations of 50,000 to 80,000; in northern Europe, 25,000 to 30,000.

The merchants, both long-distance traders and local guild members, needing both physical and legal protection from attack and looting, began to organize the townspeople to demand charters of independence from regional rulers. They sought codes of law to safeguard them against arbitrary confiscation and taxation; to provide adequate space for markets; to enforce official standards of weights, measures, coinage, currency, and laws; and the construction of protective walls around the cities. To achieve these institutional goals, the merchants and most other citizens swore oaths of allegiance to one another to protect and defend their new urban institutions, by force if necessary. The early modern western European city, the home of the merchant class, took on an entirely new organizational and institutional structure.

Guilds and City-States Confront Rural Aristocrats

As business increased, local traders and manufacturers formed trade organizations called **guilds**, which regulated the quality and quantity of production and trade, prices, wages, and the recruitment, training, and certification of apprentices, journeymen, and masters. The guilds also represented their members in town governments and thus helped to keep industrial and commercial interests at the forefront of the civic agenda. Guild members were mostly males, but widowed heads of households and workshops were also included among the voting members. Most guilds were organized locally, within their home towns, but international traders organized international guilds corresponding to their commercial interests. The Hanseatic League, though lacking the social and religious dimensions of a true guild, was founded in 1241 to represent the interests of leading shippers of the cities of Germany and nearby northern Europe. The League dominated the commerce of their region.

West European cities, organized internally through associations of their guilds and often supported by local clergy, won their political independence from surrounding landed aristocrats. The city-states were strongest where commerce was most firmly established—in north Italian cities, such as Venice, Genoa, Pisa, and Florence, and in Flanders, in Bruges, Ghent, and Antwerp. City-states also asserted political control over surrounding suburbs and the nearby rural areas, which were needed for their food and supplies. They claimed personal liberty from the lord of the surrounding countryside and asserted their own right to govern fiscal and judicial matters. In some parts of Germany rural serfs who managed to escape their manors and survive in a city for a year won their freedom from the land. *"Stadtluft macht frei* (City air makes one free)," they declared.

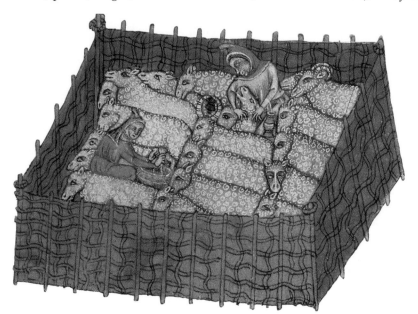

Sheep in pen being milked, Luttrell Psalter, fourteenth century. Woolen-cloth merchants had congregated at Flanders from an early stage, and by the twelfth century the industry there needed English wool to function to capacity. Prior to medieval times overland traders could transport only small and valuable objects over long distances; by the fourteenth century the emergence of sea routes meant that bulk goods, such as wool and grain, could be traded internationally. (*British Library, London*)

In the face of urban cohesion and organization, territorial princes were often forced to relinquish their control. Sometimes these lords were bought off; occasionally they were defeated in open warfare, as the citizens of Bruges, Ghent, and other Flemish cities defeated the king of France, albeit temporarily, at the Battle of Courtrai in 1302. Clergy, who also stood to gain from the independence of towns in which their major churches were located, often mediated between urban and rural interests, usually in favor of the city. The merchants of the city, and the long-distance merchants who traveled through on business, gained freedom to conduct business and earn profits free from princely interference and exactions. By the early 1300s, traders had achieved an independent political status backed by armed force as well as wealth, a status unknown elsewhere in the world.

Economic and Social Conflict Within the City

In two regions of western Europe, north Italy and Flanders, industrialization in the textile industries had proceeded so far by 1300 that latent class antagonisms between employer and employee occasionally broke out in open conflict. Between 200 and 300 workshops in Florence produced a total of 100,000 pieces of woolen cloth each year and provided a livelihood for one-fourth of the city's population.

Other cities of northern Italy, though smaller, had similar industrial patterns. Flanders and the neighboring regions of northern France and Belgium were even more industrialized and felt perhaps the greatest tension between employer and employee. Capitalist traders organized the industry by transmitting the demands for production and supplying the raw materials and equipment to meet it. Below them, the class structure was neither simple nor without the possibility of upward mobility. Guild masters, and the aspiring journeymen and apprentices within the guilds, held the best positions among the manual workers: shearing the sheep; fulling the cloth (that is, shrinking and thickening it by moistening, heating, and pressing it); and dyeing the wool. Weavers, carders, and combers were lower on the pay and social scales, and of these, only the weavers were likely to organize a guild. Below all these, an army of poor people washed, warped, and spun the wool. Female and child laborers, employed at even lower pay and in worse conditions than the men, enabled working families to survive.

Revolts at the end of the thirteenth century broke out in the Flemish cities of Douai, Tournai, Ypres, and Bruges. The leaders were usually craftsmen, and the immediate goal was usually participation in government for members of the craft guilds. The proletariat, the workers outside the guild organizations, could hope only that increased

Italian School, The Oar Makers, eighteenth-century painting of a medieval guild sign. By the thirteenth century, as the advantages of corporate organizations over individual enterprise loomed larger, specific craftsmen's guilds began to appear—in this case, that of the oar makers. Guilds issued regulations that covered everything from protecting the welfare of deceased members' families to ensuring quality of production. (*Museo Correr, Venice*)

wages, shorter hours, and better conditions of work might follow.

In the fourteenth century, increasingly impoverished workers, suffering also from plagues, wars, and bad harvests, confronted increasingly wealthy traders and industrialists. Workers were forbidden to strike and, in some towns, forbidden even to assemble. Nevertheless, a limited class consciousness was growing, especially in Florence, the greatest industrial center of western Europe. Finally, the *Ciompi* (named for the neighborhood of Florence in which they lived), the lowest class of workers, who were not affiliated with guilds, joined by lower level artisans, revolted. They understood the risks: in 1345 ten wool-carders had been hanged for organizing workers. In 1378 the *Ciompi* presented their demands to the officials of Florence. They wanted open access to the guilds, the right to unionize, a reduction of worker fines and punishments, and the right "to participate in the government of the City." They gained some of their goals, but the powerful business leaders of the city ultimately triumphed. By 1382 the major guilds were back in control, and soon a more dictatorial government under the Medici family (see below) was installed. Similar revolts occurred in Flanders, but on a smaller scale, and with no more success.

The Church Revises its Economic Policies

In establishing its independent power, the urban, trading, middle-class community was fighting the two most powerful groups of the time, Church clergy and landed aristocrats. From its earliest times, the Church had taken a dim view of the quest for profit and wealth. St. Augustine, as we noted (see p. 320), perpetuated the disdain. In the High Middle Ages theologians seriously debated whether it was possible for a merchant to attain salvation.

The taking and giving of interest on loans was forbidden to Christians, and for this reason much of the business of moneylending was carried out by Jews, who were so much a part of the merchant classes in early medieval northern Europe that a traditional administrative phrase referred to "Jews and other merchants" (Mundy and Riesenberg, p. 47). Jewish prominence in trade and urban life was, in part, a product of church laws forbidding their ownership of land. By the end of the thirteenth century, Christian rulers were also forcing Jews to live in ghettos, specific areas of the cities to which they were confined each night. Stigmatized four times over as alien by religion, foreign by ancestry, moneylenders by occupation, and segregated by residence, Jews were nevertheless tolerated as an economically vital trade diaspora until local people mastered the intricacies of business. After that, Jews were often persecuted, sometimes murdered, and repeatedly exiled—from England in 1290, from France in 1394, from Spain in 1492, and from many German cities.

Ironically, the Church had encouraged the rebirth of trade. In Chapter 11 we noted the religious and political dimensions of the crusades. These expeditions, from 1095 to the thirteenth century, were perhaps even more important for their economic influence. In the process of launching the First Crusade in 1095, Pope Urban II not only asserted the military and political importance of the papacy but also promoted the commercial and naval power of the Italian city-states, especially Venice. Fleets from the major commercial cities of Italy boarded commercial cargo along with the crusader soldiers. The expeditions whetted European appetites for the luxury products of Asia, which had been difficult to obtain.

As commerce flourished, the Church built up its urban churches and cathedrals. By the thirteenth century the Church itself had become a great property holder and a borrower and lender. As the Church also sought the patronage of the rising merchant classes, it began to modify some of its earlier denunciations of business and its practices and to turn a blind eye to the charging of interest. The greatest of the medieval Church theologians, St. Thomas Aquinas (1225–74), addressed the issue directly in his *Summa Theologica*.

Aquinas justified commerce: "Buying and selling seem to be established for the common advantage of both parties" (*Contemporary Civilization*, Vol. I, p. 67). He wrote of a "just" price, determined by negotiation between buyer and seller. Neither church nor government needed to regulate prices: "The just price of things is not fixed with mathematical precision, but depends on a kind of estimate, so that a slight addition or subtraction would not seem to destroy the equality of justice" (pp. 67-–8). Profit was allowed if its uses were deemed appropriate: "Nothing prevents gain from being directed to some necessary or even virtuous end, and thus trading becomes lawful." Traders were allowed compensation for their labor: "A man may take to trade . . . and seek gain, not as an end, but as payment for his labor" (p. 74). Aquinas elaborated similar interpretations to allow interest on commercial loans.

Renaissance: Intellectual and Cultural Transformation

On the basis of merchant wealth in the cities, a Renaissance, a rebirth, in thought, literature, art, manners, and sensibilities, arose throughout central and western Europe. The Renaissance began in the middle 1300s and continued for about two centuries. Proclaiming that the proper study of man is man, Renaissance **humanism** assigned to God a less overwhelming, less intimidating role in human life and concerns. Asserting the importance of the individual, it challenged the monopoly of the Church over the interpretation of cultural life. In his *Oration on the Dignity of Man*, Giovanni Pico della Mirandola (1463–94) places in the mouth of God himself the most succinct statement of this humanistic perspective of the Renaissance:

I have given you, Adam, neither a predetermined place nor a particular aspect nor any special prerogatives in order that you may take and possess these through your own decision and choice. The limitations on the nature of other creatures are contained within my prescribed laws. You shall determine your own nature without constraint from any barrier, by means of the freedom to whose power I have entrusted you. . . . I have made you

SOURCE

The Realpolitik of Niccolò Machiavelli

Humanism included perspectives on how people actually behaved, as well as on how they ought to behave. In political thought this perspective yielded studies in *realpolitik*, a very down-to-earth, even cynical view of human behavior that argued that ends justify means. Its principal exponent, Niccolò Machiavelli, had held several high-ranking posts in the government of his native Florence before the Medici family came to power in 1512 and dismissed him as a potential enemy of the new administration. Until the end of his life, Machiavelli wrote on the philosophy of government, hoping that his instructions on "good" government would guide some future leader to restore Italy to its former glory.

From this arises the question whether it is better to be loved more than feared, or feared more than loved. The reply is, that one ought to be both feared and loved, but as it is difficult for the two to go together, it is much safer to be feared than loved . . . For it may be said of men in general that they are ungrateful, voluble dissemblers, anxious to avoid danger, and covetous of gain; as long as you benefit them, they are entirely yours; they offer you their blood, their goods, their life, and their children, as I have before said, when the necessity is remote; but when it approaches, they revolt . . . Men have less scruple in offending one who makes himself loved than one who makes himself feared; for love is held by a chain of obligation which, men being selfish, is broken whenever it serves their purposes; but fear is maintained by a dread of punishment which never fails. . . .

A prudent ruler ought not to keep faith when by so doing it would be against his interest, and when the reasons which made him bind himself no longer exist. If men were all good, this precept would not be a good one; but as they are bad, and would not observe their faith with you, so you are not bound to keep faith with them . . . But it is necessary to be able to disguise this character well, and to be a great feigner and dissembler; and men are so simple and so ready to obey present necessities, that one who deceives will always find those who allow themselves to be deceived . . . It is not, therefore, necessary for a prince to have all the above named [virtuous] qualities, but it is very necessary to seem to have them. I would even be bold to say that to possess them and always to observe them is dangerous, but to appear to possess them is useful.

(Machiavelli, pp. 60–65)

neither heavenly nor earthly, neither mortal nor immortal so that, like a free and sovereign artificer, you might mold and fashion yourself into that form you yourself shall have chosen. (Cited in Wilkie/Hurt, p. 1571)

Masaccio, *Trinity with the Virgin, St. John, and Donors*, 1427. During the Renaissance, people began to rethink their relationship to God and the world around them; at the same time, artists were developing a new means of depicting reality. According to some art history scholars, Masaccio's monumental fresco is the first painting created in correct geometric perspective (the single vanishing point lies at the foot of the cross). (*S. Maria Novella, Florence*)

DATING THE RENAISSANCE: WHAT DIFFERENCE DOES IT MAKE?

We have presented the Renaissance in the context of the rise of trade and the increasingly favorable emphasis placed upon the profit motive in western Europe. In this framework, especially, the 1300s are a good date to introduce it, and this is the date most historians prefer. But the Renaissance marks a shift in religious as well as secular values, and historians of the Church often see this change beginning as early as the mid-eleventh century. (Historians also speak of the Carolingian Renaissance in the age of Charlemagne, but that cultural transformation collapsed along with his empire, while the intellectual shift of 1050 marked a continuous line of development.)

Church historian Carter Lindberg charts some of these early changes. In philosophy, three thinkers in particular suggested that pure faith is not enough to attain salvation. St. Anselm (1033–1109) introduced the concept of *fides quaerens intellectum*, "faith seeking understanding"; Peter Abelard (1079–1142) sought self-knowledge in a way that presaged the later emphasis on individualism, and Peter's physical as well as emotional love for the forbidden Eloise demonstrated the intensity of that quest; St. Bernard of Clairvaux (1090–1153) sought to combine love and spirituality along with faith.

The same era witnessed an intellectual opening to the Arab world especially through links in Spain. Scholars began the systematic translation of Arabic texts into Latin, re-establishing the link with the ancient Roman and Greek literature texts that the Arabs had preserved and developed, and that the European world had lost. The works of Avicenna (Ibn Sina), Averroes (Ibn Rushd), as well as the Jewish philosopher Maimonides helped restore the emphasis on logic and philosophy that Aristotle had taught.

Universities were founded. Most had practical emphases: medical studies at Salerno, Italy; legal studies at Bologna, Italy; theological studies at Paris. Students and professors from Paris seeking more intellectual freedom crossed the English Channel and founded the University of Oxford about 1200, with Cambridge following shortly afterward. By 1300 there were about a dozen universities in western Europe; by 1500, nearly one hundred. The teaching within the universities had to be approved by the Church, and most often centered on theology, but it included grammar, dialectic, rhetoric, arithmetic, music, geometry, and astronomy. And no matter how rigorous the rules, the assembly of dozens of young men in a small area led to challenges to authority and quests for individualism, as demonstrated by the "Goliard Poets," who took their name from the biblical Goliath, a kind of early anti-Christ.

> The writers of the poems rejoiced in the name, for they spoke in behalf of youth and pleasure and were the enemies of sobriety, propriety, and piety. Their output was varied. They wrote parodies of religious literature, irreverent, blasphemous, sometimes obscene – a *Drunkard's Mass*, an *Office of the Ribalds*, a *Glutton's Mass*. Their poetry is filled with mocking allusion to the most sacred solemnities; a Credo in which the poet professes, "I believe in dice... and love the tavern more than Jesus"; a benediction "Fraud be with you." (*Introduction to Contemporary Civilization*, p.105)

Art continued to emphasize religious themes, but it too began to become more earthly, more earthy, and more influenced by business. Masaccio's painting of *Trinity with the Virgin* (1427; see p. 403) demonstrates the evolution of *geometric perspective* in painting, suggesting not only a new artistic technique but also a new relationship of humans to space. (Compare the similar use of perspective in Van Eyck's *Wedding Portrait* (see above) and contrast it with other paintings in this chapter, for example *The Romance of Alexander* (p. 371) and the market scene at 's-Hertogenbosch (p. 398).

By the fifteenth century, intellectual and bourgeois sensibilities had joined together. *The Arnolfini Wedding Portrait*, painted in 1434 in Flanders by Jan van Eyck, depicts in realistic setting and clothing the marriage of a businessman, probably an Italian stationed in Flanders, and his, perhaps already pregnant, wife. Renaissance artists frequently merged their concerns for secular business affairs with their concerns for spiritual life.

Because of its increasing financial success, however, the Church suffered attack from within and without. Orders of priests and of nuns—Franciscans following the teachings of St. Francis of Assisi (1181–1226), Dominicans following St. Dominic (1170–1221), and "Poor Clares" following St. Clare of Assisi (1194–1253)—had challenged the Church to live up to its early ideals of compassion for the poor and simplicity in everyday living. During the Renaissance, however, clergy, landown-

Jan van Eyck, *The Arnolfini Wedding Portrait,* **1434.** Giovanni Arnolfini, a wealthy Italian merchant living in Flanders, commissioned the Flemish artist van Eyck to produce this pictorial record of his marriage. On the far wall, van Eyck has written in Latin "Jan van Eyck was here," much in the way that a notary would sign a legal document. (*National Gallery, London*)

ing warriors, and business entrepreneurs established a hierarchy of three social orders, analogous to similar systems in China and parallel to the caste system of India, and coordinated their efforts to mold the shape of western European society.

The richest fruits of Renaissance creativity matured in Florence (home of the *Ciompi* revolt), where the illustrious Medici family provided lavish patronage. The family's fortune had been built by the merchant-banker Giovanni de' Medici (1360–1429), and enhanced by his son, Cosimo (1389–1464), and grandson, Lorenzo (1449–92). Here creative artists like Michelangelo (1475–1564), painter of the Sistine Chapel ceiling; Leonardo da Vinci (1452–1519), scientific experimenter and painter of the *Mona Lisa*; and Niccolò Machiavelli (1469–1527), author of *The Prince*, which proposed a new, harsh, and hard-nosed philosophy of government (see Source, p. 402), developed and expressed their genius. At the same time, the general population of the city enjoyed high standards of literacy and expressiveness.

Creativity flourished in the practical as well as the fine arts and contributed substantially to the rise of merchant power. Many innovations came from amalgamating local techniques with those encountered in the course of trade, especially with Arab civilization. Improvements in sailing technology included a new design in the ships themselves. In the thirteenth century the caravel of the Mediterranean, with its triangular, or lateen (Latin) sails, used mostly by Arab sailors, was blended with the straight sternpost and stern rudder of northern Europe. The caravel could also be rerigged with a square sail for greater speed in a tail wind. The astrolabe, again an Arab invention, helped determine longitude at sea. The rediscovery in the early fifteenth century of Ptolemy's *Geography*, written in the second century C.E., and preserved in the Arab world, helped to spark interest in proper mapping. (An error in longitude in Ptolemy's map led Columbus to underestimate the size of the globe and think he could reach east Asia by sailing across the Atlantic.)

Cannon, especially when mounted on ships, gave European merchants firepower not available to others. Although the Chinese had invented gunpowder centuries before (see p. 394), the Europeans applied the invention in the fourteenth century to become the masters of gun-making. By the early 1400s they were using cannonballs. The Ottoman Turks employed Christian west Europeans to build and operate the cannon they used to besiege and conquer Constantinople. By the late 1400s European warring powers were competing energetically in an "arms race" to develop the most powerful and effective cannons and guns. Leonardo and others worked on the mathematics of the projectiles. (So did Sir Isaac Newton in the seventeenth century, and his labors led to his invention of the calculus; see Chapter 15.) When Portuguese ships began to sail into Asian waters after 1498, claiming the right to regulate commerce, their guns and cannons enabled them to sink all challengers.

The Chinese had also invented the principle of movable type and the printing press, but, again, European technology surpassed them in implementation. Movable type was better suited to Europe's alphabetic languages than to Chinese ideographs. By 1455, in Mainz, Germany, Johannes Gutenburg (*c.* 1390–1486) had printed the first major book set in movable type, the Bible. By the end of the century at least 10 million individual books in some 30,000 different editions had been produced and distributed.

Of specific use to merchants in fourteenth-century Italy, two centuries after the decimal system had been absorbed from India via the Arab world, businesspeople began to develop double-entry bookkeeping. It facilitated accurate recording of transactions and efficient tracking of business profits and losses. In 1494 Luca Pacioli (*c.* 1445– *c.* 1514), a Franciscan friar and mathematician, first published the method in systematic form.

Ironies of the Fourteenth Century: Plague and War

The Renaissance in culture and invention seems to have been limited mostly to the upper classes, for in many respects the fourteenth century in western Europe was catastrophic. The area was plunged into famine, plague, and civil, international, and intercontinental warfare, which halted its economic prosperity and population growth for a century. A great famine struck 1315–17 and may have left the population generally so weakened that when bubonic plague reached Europe by way of trading ships in 1348, it killed off a third of Europe's population, reducing it from 70 million in 1300 to only 45 million in 1400. Giovanni Boccaccio (1313–75) captured the horror of the plague in the introduction to his otherwise droll and humanistic classic of the era, *The Decameron*:

> In the year of Our Lord 1348 the deadly plague broke out in the great city of Florence. . . . At the onset of the disease both men and women were afflicted by a sort of swelling in the groin or under the armpits which sometimes attained the size of a common apple or egg. Some of these swellings were larger and some smaller, and all were commonly called boils. From these two starting points the boils began in a little while to spread and appear generally all over the body. Afterwards, the manifestation of the disease changed into black or livid spots on the arms, thighs, and the whole person. . . . Neither the advice of physicians nor the virtue of any medicine seemed to help. . . almost everyone died within three days of the appearance of the signs – some sooner, some later. . . .
>
> Let alone the fact that one man shunned the other and that nobody had any thought for his neighbor;

even relatives visited their folks little or never, and when they did, they communicated from a distance. The calamity had instilled such horror into the hearts of men and women that brother abandoned brother, uncles, sisters and wives left their dear ones to perish and, what is more serious and almost incredible, parents avoided visiting or nursing their very children, as though these were not their own flesh. . . . (xxiii–xxvii).

Paradoxically, the complete dissolution of the norms of everyday life inspired a reassessment of fundamental values and institutions that may have helped carry Renaissance values of individualism and a humanistic perspective to the common people as well as the elites. "Out of sheer necessity, therefore, quite different customs arose among the survivors from the original laws of the townspeople." (p. xxvii).

The Triumph of Death, **French, 1503.** This sixteenth-century work recalls the enormous loss of life caused by the Black Death of 1348. Brought back from east Asia by Genoan merchants, the bubonic plague is estimated to have killed between 20 and 50 percent of Europe's inhabitants. Contemporary medicine was impotent in the face of the disease, whose onset meant certain death. (*Bibliothèque Nationale, Paris*)

The peasants who survived the plague benefited from the labor shortages that followed, gaining higher wages and access to more land, freedom from labor services, and geographical mobility. They began to form a new class of property-owning peasants. With the urban industrial workers and guild members who were similarly confronting their employers, they rioted more frequently and more boldly against kings and nobles who attempted to raise taxes for the incessant warfare of the time.

England and France fought the so-called Hundred Years War, 1337–1453. During this time, France also experienced civil warfare between the followers of the Dukes of Burgundy and Orleans. England saw its barons fight among themselves, Scotland invade, and Wales revolt. When defeat by the French in 1453 pushed the English from almost all the land they had held on the Continent, a civil war, the War of the Roses, broke out at home, 1453–85. Henry VII won out, establishing the Tudor dynasty (1485–1603). The wars at home and abroad created a new sense of national identity in both England and France and helped to strengthen their "new monarchies" in centralizing their administrations (see Chapter 13).

While western Europe was establishing the frameworks of new economic, cultural, and political organizations, in eastern Europe the Byzantine Empire collapsed. Already weakened internally, it could not withstand the advancing Ottoman Turks. The Turks captured Gallipoli in 1356, Adrianople in 1361, Kosovo in 1389, Nicopolis in 1396, and Constantinople itself in 1453. By the mid-sixteenth century, the Ottomans ruled not only the Balkans and Anatolia, but also Hungary, the Crimea, Mesopotamia, Syria, Egypt, and most of northern Africa. They permitted access to the trade routes of the eastern Mediterranean to Muslim traders, but virtually closed them to Christians.

ATLANTIC EXPLORATION

The loss of access to the eastern Mediterranean and its Asian trade pushed western Europeans to explore for alternative routes. Prince Henry the Navigator (1394–1460), a member of Portugal's ruling family, fostered continuous exploration of the west African coast in search of a southern passage around Africa to Asia. Portugal founded small ports and entrepots all along the Atlantic coast of Africa. Portuguese traders carried out extensive trade in slaves and gold, taking some 150,000 slaves from Africa in the half-century 1450–1500. The Portuguese had already captured Ceuta on the Mediterranean coast of Morocco in 1415, giving them (and later the Spanish) a toe-hold in Africa.

In 1488 Bartholomeu Dias (c. 1450–1500) rounded the Cape of Good Hope and sailed into the Indian Ocean. Pushing further on that route, with the help of local navigators, in 1498 Vasco da Gama (c. 1460–1524) reached India's Malabar coast. On a second voyage in 1502, da Gama captained an armed fleet of twenty-one ships and fought against local Arab sailor-merchants who were backed by a coalition of Egyptians, Turks, and Venetians opposed to the new interloper. Their ships and guns gave the Portuguese the advantage, and they established their Indian Ocean headquarters at Goa on the west coast of India, and a chain of fortified ports as far as Indonesia and China. By 1504, an average of a ship a month sailed from Lisbon to Asia. In the process the Portuguese earned a reputation for violence and arbitrary authority.

Spain, despite its geographical position, had not been among Europe's leading traders. In the late fifteenth century, however, emerging state power and religious conviction joined with Spain's desire to exploit new commercial opportunities. Spain's two major regional kingdoms were united in the 1469 marriage of Ferdinand of Aragon with Isabella of Castile, both devout Catholics. Spanish forces, strengthened by the unification and inspired by the Church, completed the *reconquista* in 1492, driving Muslims out of Granada, their last remaining outpost in Spain, and expelling Jews who refused to convert. In the same year, convinced by the Italian ship captain Christopher Columbus (1451–1506) that a western passage to China and India was possible across the Atlantic, the Spanish crown sponsored his voyages of exploration.

Most professional cartographers believed that the world was a globe, but their calculations had severely underestimated its size, and they had no idea that two continents occupied the opposite hemisphere. Reaching the Americas in 1492, Columbus did not understand that he had not arrived in "The Indies." Ferdinand Magellan (c. 1480–1521) more clearly established the general dimensions of the earth's sphere by initiating a three-year circumnavigation of the globe 1519–22 a voyage that altered forever the intellectual, commercial, and demographic horizons of the world. In the process Magellan also established the basis for Spain's claim to the Philippines, later named for King Phillip II of Spain. Magellan himself was killed in the Philippines and did not complete the voyage.

In 1493 a proclamation by the pope charged Spain and Portugal with evangelizing their new discoveries, and by the 1494 Treaty of Tordesillas Rome divided the newly accessible worlds of Asia and the western hemisphere between the Spanish and Portuguese. By persuasion and by force Spanish and Portuguese missionaries converted millions of people all over the world.

Other, more economically advanced European powers did not compete seriously with Spain and Portugal in overseas trade for another century. They were embroiled in their own religious and civil wars and were still integrating their internal economies. By 1600, however, the merchants and rulers of the Netherlands, France, and England were ready for new endeavors. They followed the Spanish and Portuguese and, in many areas, displaced them. They saw the oceans of the world as new arenas of competition in trade, migration, and colonization. They thoroughly reorganized the networks of world trade. The interactions of these trading powers among themselves and with the other great powers of the world through the period 1500–1750 are the principal subject of the next chapter.

BIBLIOGRAPHY

Abu-Lughod, Janet L. *Before European Hegemony: The World System A.D. 1250–1350* (New York: Oxford University Press, 1989).

Adas, Michael, ed. *Islamic and European Expansion* (Philadelphia: Temple University Press, 1993).

Aquinas, St. Thomas. *Summa Theologica* (excerpts) in *Introduction to Contemporary Civilization in the West*, cited below.

Bentley, Jerry H. *Old World Encounters* (New York: Oxford University Press, 1993).

Bloch, Marc. *Feudal Society*, 2 vols. (Chicago: University of Chicago Press, 1961).

Boccaccio, Giovanni. *The Decameron*, trans. Frances Winwar (New York: Modern Library, 1955).

Braudel, Fernand. *Capitalism and Material Life, 1400–1800*, trans. from the French by Miriam Kochan (New York: Harper and Row, 1973).

Chaudhuri, K. N. *Asia Before Europe* (Cambridge: Cambridge University Press, 1990).

—. *Trade and Civilization in the Indian Ocean: An Economic History from the Rise of Islam to 1750* (Cambridge: Cambridge University Press, 1985).

—. *Introduction to Contemporary Civilization in the West*, Vol. I (New York: Columbia University Press, 2nd ed., 1954).

Crosby, Alfred W. *Ecological Imperialism: The Biological Expansion of Europe, 900–1900* (Cambridge: Cambridge University Press, 1986).

Curtin, Philip. *Cross-Cultural Trade in World History* (Cambridge: Cambridge University Press, 1984).

Dunn, Ross. *The Adventures of Ibn Battuta* (Berkeley: University of California Press, 1986).

Elvin, Mark. *The Pattern of the Chinese Past* (Stanford: Stanford University Press, 1973).

Frank, Andre Gunder and Barry K. Gills, eds. *The World System: Five Hundred Years or Five Thousand?* (London: Routledge, 1993).

Ghosh, Amitav. *In an Antique Land* (New York: Knopf, 1993).

Goitein, Shelomo Dov. *A Mediterranean Society: The Jewish Communities of the Arab World as Portrayed in the Documents of the Cairo Genizah*, 6 vols. (Berkeley: University of California Press, 1967–83).

Hohenberg, Paul M. and Lynn Hollen Lees. *The Making of Urban Europe, 1000–1950.* (Cambridge: Harvard University Press, 1985).

Kee, Howard Clark, *et al. Christianity: A Social and Cultural History* (New York: Macmillan, 1991).

Levathes, Louise. *When China Ruled the Seas: The Treasure Fleet of the Dragon Throne, 1405–33* (New York: Oxford University Press, 1996).

Levenson, Jay A. *Circa 1492: Art in the Age of Exploration* (Washington: National Gallery of Art, 1991).

Lindberg, Carter. "The Late Middle Ages and the Reformations of the Sixteenth Century," in Kee, *et al. Christianity*, pp. 257–423.

Machiavelli, Niccolò, trans. by Luigi Ricci. *The Prince and the Discourses* (New York: Modern Library, 1950).

Mair, Victor H. "Mummies of the Tarim Basin," *Archaeology* XLVIII, No. 2 (1995), 28–35.

McNeill, William H. *The Age of Gunpowder Empires, 1450–1800* (Washington: American Historical Association, 1989).

—. *Plagues and Peoples* (Garden City, NY: Anchor Press/Doubleday, 1976).

Mundy, John H. and Peter Riesenberg. *The Medieval Town* (New York: Van Nostrand Reinhold Company, 1958).

Nicholas, David. *The Evolution of the Medieval World* (New York: Longman, 1992).

Pirenne, Henri. *Medieval Cities* (Princeton: Princeton University Press, 1925).

Polanyi, Karl, Conrad M. Arensberg, and Harry W. Pearson, eds. *Trade and Market in the Early Empires* (Chicago: The Free Press, 1957).

Polo, Marco. *The Travels*, trans. from the French by Ronald Latham (London: Penguin Books, 1958).

Prescott, William H. *History of the Conquest of Mexico and History of the Conquest of Peru* (New York: Modern Library, n.d.; 1st ed., *c.* 1844–7).

Ratchnevsky, Paul. *Genghis Khan: His Life and Legacy*, trans. and ed. by Thomas Nivison Haining (Oxford: Blackwell, 1991).

Raychaudhuri, Tapan and Irfan Habib. *The Cambridge Economic History of India.* Vol. I: *c.* 122–*c.* 1750 (Cambridge: Cambridge University Press, 1982).

Reynolds, Susan. *Fiefs and Vassals* (Oxford: Clarendon Press, 1994).

Schele, Linda and David Freidel. *A Forest of Kings: The Untold Story of the Ancient Maya* (New York: William Morrow and Co., 1990).

Scott, James C. *The Moral Economy of the Peasant* (New Haven: Yale University Press, 1976).

Skinner, G. William. "Marketing and Social Structure in Rural China," *Journal of Asian Studies* XXIV, No. 1 (November 1964), 3–43.

Scheherezade: Tales from a Thousand and One Nights. Trans. by A.V Arberry (New York: New American Library, 1955).

The (London) Times Atlas of World History ed. Geoffrey Parker (London: Times Books Ltd., 4th ed., 1993).

Tuchman, Barbara. *A Distant Mirror: The Calamitous Fourteenth Century* (New York: Knopf, 1978).

Wilkie, Brian and James Hurt, eds. *Literature of the Western World*, Vol. I (New York: Macmillan, 1984).

Wills, John E., Jr. "Maritime Asia, 1500–1800: the Interactive Emergence of European Domination," *American Historical Review* XCVIII, No. 1 (February 1993), 83–105.

Wolf, Eric. *Europe and the People without History* (Berkeley: University of California Press, 1982).

Wood, Frances. *Did Marco Polo Go to China?* (Boulder, CO: Westview Press, 1996).

THE UNIFICATION OF WORLD TRADE

CHAPTER 13

1500–1776

" Civil government, so far as it is instituted for the security of property, is in reality instituted for the defense of the rich against the poor."

ADAM SMITH

THE INVISIBLE HAND REACHES OUT: A CAPITALIST WORLD SYSTEM APPEARS

CAPITALISM AND THE EXPANSION OF EUROPE

This chapter opens in 1500, at a time when ocean voyages of exploration and trade were linking the eastern and western hemispheres and initiating a new phase of world history. It closes almost three centuries later as most of the regions of the world were beginning to enter into a single system of trade and exchange. This emerging system, later called **capitalism** was based on the private ownership of wealth and the means of production and on the pursuit of private economic profit. Capitalism allowed individuals to exchange their products and labor in a free, unregulated market. It had little place for the restrictive rules of church and government. Free market exchange would decide the prices of goods and labor by reaching a balance between supply and demand. The lure of the market would encourage people to invest their capital, or accumulated wealth, in economic activities that might earn profits (or suffer losses).

In Chapter 12 we saw the business people of Europe expanding their enterprises. Trading centers such as Venice, Florence, Genoa, Milan, Bruges, Antwerp, Paris, Lyon, and London grew ever larger as the headquarters of the new commerce. After 1500, European enterprise also expanded into already existing networks in Asia and began to restructure them. In the Americas, too, it created new networks. This global expansion of European enterprise provides an important focus for organizing our understanding of the period 1500–1776. The economic encounter of African and Asian societies with the new European commercial practices provides another focus which demonstrates the exceptional powers claimed by the merchant-traders of northwestern Europe, and the extraordinary support they received from their governments.

EUROPEAN COLONIZATION AND THE EXPANSION OF TRADE: WHAT DIFFERENCE DOES IT MAKE?

In earlier chapters we have usually been concerned with the question of "How Do We Know?" and the search for adequate sources of information. By 1500, sources become increasingly abundant, and our concern turns increasingly to selecting interpretive frameworks for understanding the significance of historical events. Two fundamentally different interpretive frameworks have inspired fierce debate over the significance of world trade between 1500 and 1776.

The first interpretive framework seeks to relate economic systems to culture systems. It asks: From whose point of view should we tell the story of the creation of a global trade network? To what degree should we emphasize Western European creativity as the driving force promoting this increased level of global exchange? Conversely, to what degree should we focus on ancient and proud civilizations of Asia, Africa, and the Americas as they re-examined their own institutions in light of the new European arrivals? Is it possible for historians to become polycentric, or multi-centric, holding in our minds multiple perspectives that can encompass the varied ways in which global economic exchange has been seen?

The second interpretive framework focuses on identifying winners and losers in the new, capitalist system of global economic exchange. Advocates of capitalism saw in this new economic philosophy the potential for a world of vastly increased economic productivity and wealth that would ultimately benefit everyone. Critics acknowledged the increased productivity and wealth, but they feared that business people would hoard these benefits for themselves. The advantages would not "trickle down" to the common people. The gulf between the rich and the poor would widen.

Critics also noted that capitalism tended to break the personal, emotional, and social ties that linked upper and lower classes to one another as patron to client, regardless of their economic relationships. These social ties could be restrictive, especially for the client, but they also provided the promise of protection in time of economic difficulty. By comparison, capitalism, which spoke only of the "bottom line" of profit and loss, seemed at once more free and more ruthless.

Academics in our own day refer to the first, optimistic perspective, stressing the productivity of capitalist enterprise, as the theory of development or of modernization. They refer to the second, pessimistic theory, stressing the mal-distribution of wealth, as the theory of dependency or the **development of underdevelopment**. We shall be alert to these conflicting interpretations throughout this chapter and in Chapter 16 which considers the industrial revolution and imperialism.

SPAIN'S EMPIRE

Critics who claim that Europe's wealth was built on the exploitation of people overseas have some justification, but the experiences of Spain and Portugal demonstrate that exploitation alone was not enough. To build and sustain wealth, countries must be able to use wealth effectively. They must conceive and implement policies of economic growth. They require banks and instruments of exchange to store and transmit money. They need commercial intelligence to create and evaluate strategies for investing capital sensibly and profitably. They must develop efficient means of transporting goods and people. Both Spain and Portugal lacked these facilities. Both countries built enormous global empires in the sixteenth century based on their ocean explorations (see Chapter 12), but by the end of the sixteenth century both these empires were on the wane, first challenged and then surpassed by the Netherlands, France, and England, countries that established successful commercial communities.

NEW WORLD CONQUESTS

The four voyages of Christopher Columbus between 1492 and 1504 revealed to the Spanish crown some of the opportunities for agricultural development, religious conversion, and exploitation of resources in gold and silver to be found in the Americas. Spanish settlers began to colonize the islands of the Caribbean and the north coast of South America. Spanish *conquistadors* marched inland to conquer what they could. In 1519 Hernán Cortés began his expedition from Vera Cruz with 600 Spaniards, joined by hundreds more Native Americans from the various states through which he passed, to overthrow the powerful Aztec empire at Tenochtitlán, modern day Mexico City. They conquered the capital city in 1521 after a bitter four-

THE INTERCONNECTING WORLD

DATE	EUROPE	THE AMERICAS	ASIA AND AFRICA
1500	• Communero revolt in Spain (1520/1) • Luther excommunicated (1521)	• Four voyages of Christopher Columbus (1492–1504) • Cortés conquers Tenochtitlán (1521)	• Portuguese establish trading posts in East Africa (1505) • Portugal captures Goa, India (1510) • Portuguese missionaries arrive in China (1514)
1525	• Henry VIII becomes head of new Anglican church (1534) • First stock exchange in Antwerp (1538) • Calvin establishes Presbyterian theocracy in Geneva (1541)	• Pizarro captures Inca emperor Atahualpa (1532) • Potosí silver mine discovered (1545)	• Mughals invade India (1526) • St. Francis Xavier arrives in Japan (1549)
1550	• Council of Trent (1545–63) • End of Hundred Years' War (1558) • Tobacco first introduced into Europe (1559); potato (c. 1565)	• Portuguese begin sugar cultivation in Brazil (c. 1560)	• Akbar consolidates Mughal Empire (1556–1605) • Spanish capture Manila, Philippines (1571) • Portuguese establish colony in Angola (1571)
1575	• Spanish Armada defeated by England (1588) • Henry IV of France issues Edict of Nantes (1598)		• Matteo Ricci arrives in China (1582) • Japan invades Korea (1592)
1600	• Dutch, English, and French East India companies founded • Holland wins independence from Spain; Bank of Amsterdam established (1609)		• Tokugawa shoguns begin consolidation of Japan (1603) • Christianity outlawed in Japan (1606) • Dutch found Batavia (Jakarta), Indonesia (1619)
1625	• Portugal declares independence from Spain (1640) • Russia captures Siberia (1649)		• Manchus conquer China and form Qing dynasty (1644)
1650	• English Navigation Act (1651) • Louis XIV of France, the "Sun King" (1643–1715)		• Dutch capture Cape of Good Hope (1652)
1675	• War of the League of Augsburg (1688–97) • Bank of England created (1694)		• Qing dynasty establishes "Canton system" (1683)
1700	• Peter the Great founds St. Petersburg (1704) • War of the Spanish Succession (1702–13) • Act of Union creates Great Britain (1707)		• Edo, Japan, has 1 million people
1725	• War of Austrian Succession (1740–8)		
1750	• Seven Years' War (1756–63) • Adam Smith, *The Wealth of Nations* (1776)	• War of American Independence (1775–81)	• After English victory at Plassey, English gain Bengal (1757)

Emperor Atahualpa arrested by Francisco Pizarro in 1532.
When Pizarro landed on the northern coast of Peru on May 13, 1532 he brought with him a force of 200 men with horses, guns, and swords. The Inca Emperor Atahualpa, backed up by thousands of troops, felt he had little to fear from the Spanish and, as this contemporary Peruvian drawing shows, he accepted Pizarro's seemingly friendly invitation to meet accompanied only by his bodyguards. It was a trap, and Pizarro arrested and later executed him.

month siege and the empire fell to them. In the next few years they captured the Yucatán and most of central America. Cortés became ruler of the Kingdom of New Spain, re-organized in 1535 as the Vice-Royalty of New Spain.

In South America, the Inca Empire of the west coast and Andes Mountains became accessible to Spanish conquistadors after Vasco Nuñez de Balboa found a portage across the Isthmus of Panama in 1513. The Spanish could now transport their ships from the Atlantic coast overland across the Isthmus and then sail south along the Pacific Coast to Peru. Rumors of great stores of gold encouraged these voyages. In 1532, Francisco Pizarro, leading a force of some two hundred men, captured the Inca Emperor Atahualpa. Although given a room full of gold as ransom for his life, Pizarro nevertheless feared a revolt and killed the emperor. In 1533 he captured the Inca capital, Cuzco. The Spanish conquistadors fought among themselves for years until Spain established the Vice-Royalty of Peru in mid-century as the South American counterpart to the Vice-Royalty of New Spain in the north.

How had a few hundred Spanish soldiers and their Indian allies succeeded in overthrowing the two largest empires in the Americas? The conquered Native Americans had:

- divided and fought among themselves;

- lacked the Spaniards' military technology and organization;

- despaired when their commanders-in-chief, Montezuma in Mexico and Atahualpa in Peru, were captured;

- succumbed to European diseases, such as smallpox (see Focus, p. 457).

MAKING THE CONQUESTS PAY

After the conquests, the Spanish began to reorganize the economies of the Americas. They established the *encomienda* system, assigning the taxes and the labor of local Indian populations to Spanish colonists who were also to convert them to Roman Catholicism, if possible. The Indians were virtually enslaved under conditions of great cruelty. The *encomienda* system was first established on the island of Hispaniola, where in twenty years the Indian population fell from several million to 29,000. Humane voices, especially of priests such as Bartolomé de Las Casas, opposed the *encomienda* system, but it continued until so many Indians died that it could function no longer. In most of Mexico and Peru the system ended by the late 1500s, but it continued for another century in Venezuela; for another two centuries, until 1791, in Chile; and until the very early 1800s in Paraguay.

The replacement systems were not much more humane. The *repartimiento* system in central Mexico and the similar *mita* system in Peru forced Indians into low paid or unpaid labor for a portion of each year on Spanish-owned farms, in mines and workshops, and on public works projects. These systems, too, were forms of unofficial slavery. Not all labor was coerced, however. Spanish-owned **haciendas**, agricultural estates producing commercial crops and livestock, employed both free and indentured labor. The haciendas often produced commercially the newly imported products of the eastern hemisphere—wheat, cattle, pigs, sheep, chickens, horses, and mules—in addition to the indigenous local crops of maize, potatoes, and manioc (cassava). Silver mines, too, often used paid labor at very low wages. The immense Potosí mine

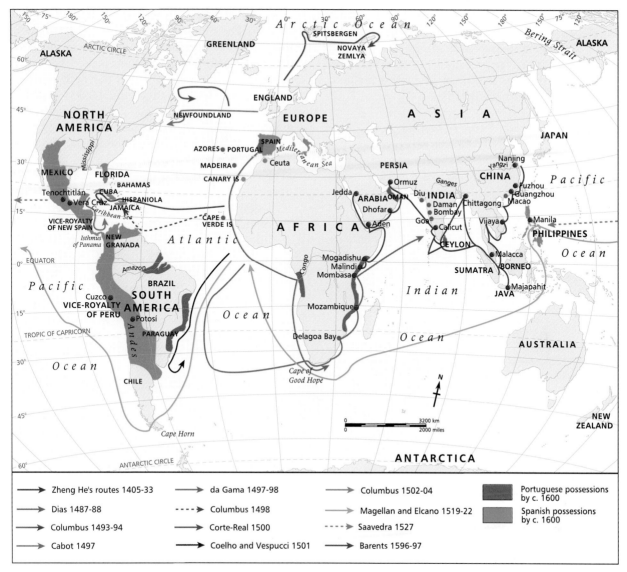

→ Zheng He's routes 1405-33	→ da Gama 1497-98	→ Columbus 1502-04	■ Portuguese possessions by c. 1600
→ Dias 1487-88	---→ Columbus 1498	→ Magellan and Elcano 1519-22	■ Spanish possessions by c. 1600
→ Columbus 1493-94	→ Corte-Real 1500	---→ Saavedra 1527	
→ Cabot 1497	→ Coelho and Vespucci 1501	→ Barents 1596-97	

World exploration The closure of sea routes through the Middle East drove the trading nations of Western Europe to seek alternate maritime passages to Asia. European navigators and cartographers rapidly built a map of the globe which included, by sailing west, the "New World" of the Americas and, by sailing south, a passage around Africa, linking with the Arab trading routes of the Indian Ocean. The voyages of the Ming Chinese admiral Zheng He were undertaken to demonstrate China's strength even more than for trade.

in Upper Peru (today's Bolivia) employed 40,000 Indian miners in the seventeenth century. On the other hand, as sugar plantations were introduced into the Caribbean islands and into Brazil, Indian laborers were unable or unwilling to perform the gang labor of the cane fields, so slaves were imported by the millions from Africa (see pp. 463–70). African slaves also worked the tobacco, cacao, and indigo plantations.

From the Spanish perspective, the most valuable products of the Americas throughout the sixteenth century were gold and silver. The mine at Potosí, discovered in 1545, was the largest silver mine in the world. Smaller mines were opened in Mexico in 1545 and 1558. In 1556 a new method of separating silver from ore by using mercury, available from Almaden in Spain, was discovered. Between 1550 and 1800 Mexico and South America produced more than 80 percent of the world's silver and more than 70 percent of its gold. The precious metals were exported each year from Latin America eastward to Europe and westward to the Philippines, where the Spanish had captured Manila in 1571 and established their chief trade center for East Asia.

They were ultimately used to pay for European purchases of silks, tea, textiles, and spices from India and China. Between one-third and one-half of all American silver produced between 1527 and 1821 found its way to China. The Mexican peso became a legal currency in China.

MERCHANT PROFITS

The gold and silver mines of the Americas brought virtual enslavement to the Native Americans, and they benefited the Spaniards less than the merchants of Antwerp, Genoa, Amsterdam, London, and Paris. The Spanish did not have the commercial infrastructure to employ the new resources in profitable investments, and they lacked the ships to carry the trade generated by the new finds of gold and silver. Indeed, they often lacked even the ships to carry the precious metals themselves in the armed and escorted flotillas that set sail each year from the Caribbean to Europe, and from the west coast of Mexico to Manila.

The experienced merchants of the trade cities of Europe organized the necessary commercial services. They exchanged the raw metals for cash and bills of exchange, provided loans to tide over the period from the arrival of one shipment of silver to the next, arranged the purchase of goods needed by the Spanish, and supplied the necessary shipping. The most important of these commercial centers was Antwerp (Belgium), with its extraordinarily skilled and wealthy merchant families, such as the Welsers and the Fuggers.

WARFARE AND BANKRUPTCY

Two powerful kings ruled Spain for most of the sixteenth century: Charles V (r. 1516–56) and his son Philip II (r. 1556–98). Both ruled much more than Spain. Many regions of Europe at this time were "owned" by particular families who had the responsibility to protect them, and the right to tax them and to bequeath them to others. Charles inherited Spain and the Spanish colonies in Africa, the Americas, Naples, and Sicily from his mother's parents, Ferdinand and Isabella. From his father's family, the House of Burgundy, he inherited the Netherlands and the German lands owned by the Habsburg family. Charles was the most powerful ruler in Europe.

Charles V had been raised in Flanders by his father's family of the House of Burgundy. He knew no Spanish, and in his pride and his foreignness he alienated Spain. He appointed foreign courtiers from Flanders to offices in Spain, and he used Spanish wealth to fund his political programs in central European territories. Spaniards revolted. The nobles wanted to stop the drain of money to central Europe and the assignment of offices to foreigners. They wanted Charles to return to Spain. As civil order broke down, artisans and business classes in Castile revolted

Plan of Potosí and the Cerro Rico (Rich Hill), Upper Peru. This seventeenth-century painting shows Potosí and the hills in which the lucrative silver mines were located. The mines at Potosí employed some 40,000 poorly paid Indian laborers and tens of thousands of horses—shown in this painting ascending and descending the hills—to transport the material and drive the machinery.

against the great landholders in the Communero revolt of 1520–21. The revolutionaries held conflicting goals, and as they fought one another to exhaustion Charles easily retained his hold on government.

But when Charles entered into wars against the Ottoman Turkish empire in eastern Europe and on the Mediterranean, and into the Christian religious wars of Catholic versus Protestant in northern and central Europe (see next section on the Protestant Reformation and the Catholic Counter-Reformation), he bankrupted even the silver-rich treasury of Spain. After Charles's abdication in 1556, his son Philip II continued the politics of warfare and suffered many of the same results. Even his military victories were financial defeats.

TRADE AND RELIGION IN EUROPE: THE PROTESTANT REFORMATION AND THE CATHOLIC COUNTER-REFORMATION

Charles V and his son Philip II fought against Protestant countries in wars explicitly devoted to matters of faith and commitment to specific religious communities. These wars siphoned off the vast treasures which Spain brought from the Americas, and so diverted her from economic and commercial growth. Here we take a moment to analyze the basis for the schism between Catholics and Protestants that so divided Europe in the sixteenth

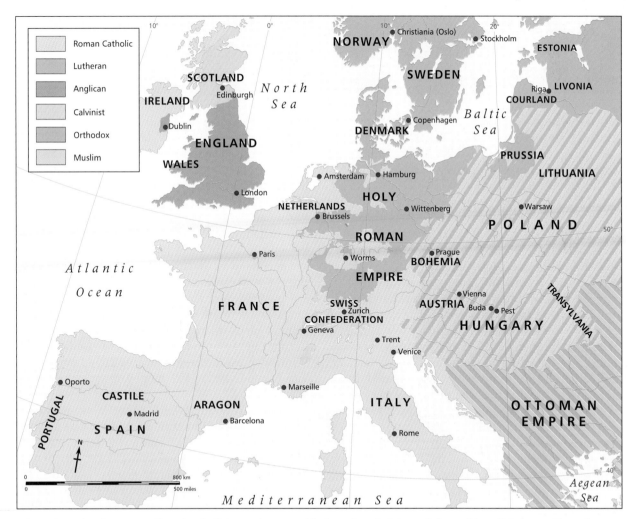

The Reformation in Europe The tide of religious reform was felt throughout Europe and changed its political map. The early commitment of most of northern Europe to Calvinism, Lutheranism, or Anglicanism was counterbalanced by the recovery to Catholicism of France and Poland. Counter-Reformation zeal, combined with political confrontation and dynastic rivalry, culminated in the Thirty Years' War (1618–48), fought across Europe's heartland at enormous cost.

John Calvin weighing the Bible against Popish Pomp. Calvin had studied the writings of the first generation of reformers such as Martin Luther and accepted without question the idea of justification by faith alone and the biblical foundation of religious authority. This contemporary woodcut shows him weighing what he saw as the extraneous ceremonial trappings and overweening bishops of the Catholic church against the simple truth of the Bible.

and seventeenth centuries. We will also consider scholarly arguments over the extent to which specific religious philosophies have direct impact on national economic development.

THE REFORMATION

Roman Catholicism had won the hearts, spirits, and tithes of the overwhelming majority of the population of western and central Europe. By 1500 it had become so wealthy and powerful in the process that several reformers charged the church with straying too far from Jesus' early simplicity and his message of compassion for the poor.

Martin Luther (1483–1546), a pious German monk who lived in a monastery in Wittenberg and taught in the university there, shared these criticisms of the church's wealth and further asserted that it claimed too much power over individual conscience. Luther doubted the importance of church sacraments and authority. He kept his doubts private, however, until in 1517 a friar came to Wittenberg selling **indulgences,** exemption from punishment for sins in exchange for donations to the church. Outraged, Luther posted on the door of the castle church ninety-five theses asserting the importance of faith and grace alone. Priests, he wrote, were not needed to mediate between humans and God. Pressed to recant, Luther

refused, declaring "it is neither right nor safe to act against conscience."

Excommunicated by the Pope, Luther was protected by several local rulers in Germany, who used the occasion to assert their independence of the Holy Roman Emperor, Charles V. From this time, Lutheranism, as the newly emerging denomination was called, often aligned itself with local rulers. When a revolt of peasants against their landlords swept Germany in 1524, Luther urged the local princes to suppress the revolt by force, and thousands were killed. Lutheranism was adopted by the kings of Denmark and Sweden and many of the princes of Germany, and this region of northern Europe became the heartland of Lutheranism. Printing presses using movable type, introduced into Europe about 1450, helped to spread the new message.

In Geneva, Switzerland, John Calvin (1509–64) preached another doctrine of reform. Like Luther, Calvin spoke of justification by faith and the supremacy of individual conscience. He denied the authority of the church. Calvin went beyond Luther in arguing that God grants his grace to whomever he chooses, regardless of individual behavior. Unlike Luther, Calvin rejected alliances with government, although he did create a religious community which dominated the city government of Geneva. Calvinism spread widely without the patronage of any political authority. (In the United States Calvinism is the dominant faith of Presbyterianism, named for its elected leaders or presbyters.)

A third major strand of reform arose in England, where King Henry VIII (r. 1509–47) broke from the church not for reasons of doctrine, but to claim authority for England over the entire Roman Catholic establishment within the country—churches, monasteries, and clergy—and to gain for himself a divorce, which the church had forbidden, from the first of his six wives. Henry had no doctrinal quarrel with Rome. He simply wanted to head the English church himself, and in 1534 Parliament named him "Protector and Only Supreme Head of the Church and Clergy of England," a title passed on to later English sovereigns. In England, Henry's new church was called Anglican. (Its followers in the United States are called Episcopalians.) Each of the three reform movements permitted their clergy to marry.

THE COUNTER-REFORMATION

Its religious monopoly challenged, the Roman Catholic church countered with the Council of Trent, which met irregularly for eighteen years, 1545–63. The Council reaffirmed the basic doctrines of Catholicism, including the celibacy of the clergy, and encouraged greater religious devotion among

PROTESTANT REFORMATION AND COUNTER-REFORMATION—KEY EVENTS

c. 1170	Waldensians in France reject church doctrines including transubstantiation and purgatory
1244	Catholic church crushes Albigensians in southern France
14th century	Lollards dispute church doctrine and want ecclesiastical property put to charitable use
1419	Hussites in Bohemia wage war against the Holy Roman Empire
1517	Martin Luther protests against sale of indulgences at Wittenberg
1519	Ulrich Zwingli leads Reformation in Switzerland
1524	German peasants revolt; Luther urges princes to suppress them
1529	The first known use of the word "Protestant"
1534	Henry VIII of England renounces papal supremacy and proclaims himself head of the "Church of England"
1534	Ignatius Loyola founds Society of Jesus (Jesuits); Luther's German translation of Bible published
1541	John Calvin establishes Presbyterian theocracy in Geneva, Switzerland
1545–63	Council of Trent initiates Catholic Counter-Reformation
1549–51	St. Francis Xavier travels in Japan
1555	Peace of Augsburg empowers princes within the Holy Roman Empire to choose faith (either Catholic or Lutheran) for the people of their realms
1559	John Knox returns from exile to found the Church of Scotland
1562	French Wars of Religion begin
1572	Approximately 25,000 French Huguenots killed in Massacre of St. Bartholomew
1588	Spanish Armada against England fails
1598	Henry IV of France enacts Edict of Nantes, granting religious freedom to Huguenots
1648	Thirty Years' War ends with split between Protestant and Catholic countries of Europe established
1685	Revocation of Edict of Nantes by Louis XIV forces some 400,000 French Huguenots to flee to Protestant countries

them. New religious orders arose to purify the church and transmit its teachings. St. Ignatius Loyola (1491–1556) founded the Society of Jesus, which was especially dedicated to education, secular as well as religious, and to carrying the message of the church around the world. St. Francis Xavier (1506–52) introduced the Jesuit vision to India, Indonesia, and Japan, baptizing thousands of new Catholics. In Paris, St. Vincent de Paul (1581–1660) began his work among the wretched of the slums, a humanitarian mission that continues around the world today.

The Roman Catholic church was fighting for an international, universal vision of the world under its own leadership, while the various Protestant movements encouraged separate national states. In return, several of the new national states encouraged the Protestant movement.

SOURCE
Don Quixote of La Mancha

Miguel de Cervantes Saavedra (1547–1616) experienced the heights and depths of Spain's rise and fall. He fought for Spain in its naval victory over the Ottomans in the Battle of Lepanto (1571) (p. 446), although he himself was captured and held prisoner for five years. Later, he helped to provision the ill-fated Spanish Armada against England. Cervantes felt both the majesty of Spain's aspiration to save and rule Europe in the name of Catholicism and the bitterness of its defeats. In *Don Quixote of La Mancha*, often considered the most outstanding novel ever written in Spanish, Cervantes created two figures who represented these two perspectives: Don Quixote, the romantic knight with his head in the clouds, and Sancho Panza, his squire with his feet firmly rooted on earth. The Don's famous encounter with a cluster of windmills—which he mistakes for hostile giants—represents the poignant, if humorous, confrontation between noble aspiration and harsh reality.

> Just then they came in sight of thirty or forty windmills that rise from the plain, and no sooner did Don Quixote see them than he said to his squire: "Fortune is guiding our affairs better than we ourselves could have wished. Do you see over yonder, friend Sancho, thirty or forty hulking giants? I intend to do battle with them and slay them. With their spoils we shall begin to be rich, for this is a righteous war and the removal of so foul a brood from off the face of the earth is a service God will bless."

> "What giants?" asked Sancho Panza.

> "Those you see over there," replied his master, "with their long arms; some of them have well-nigh two leagues in length."

> "Take care, sir," cried Sancho. "Those over there are not giants but windmills, and those things that seem to be arms are their sails, which when they are whirled around by the wind turn the millstone."

> "It is clear," replied Don Quixote, "that you are not experienced in adventures. Those are giants, and if you are afraid, turn aside and pray whilst I enter into fierce and unequal battle with them."

> Uttering these words, he clapped spurs to Rozinante, his steed … and rammed the first mill in his way. He ran his lance into the sail, but the wind twisted it with such violence that it shivered the lance in pieces and dragged both rider and horse after it, rolling them over and over on the ground, sorely damaged.

> "God help us!" cried Sancho. "Did I not tell you, sir, to mind what you were doing, for those were only windmills? Nobody could have mistaken them unless he had windmills in his brain."

> "Hold your peace, good Sancho," replied Don Quixote. "The affairs of war are, above all others, subject to continual change."

Cervantes' novel gives us the adjective *quixotic*: impractically idealistic, marked by rash, lofty, romantic ideals.

RELIGIOUS BELIEFS AND CAPITALIST PRACTICE
WHAT DIFFERENCE DOES IT MAKE?

The noted social scientist Max Weber, writing *The Protestant Ethic and the Spirit of Capitalism* in the early twentieth century, suggested that Protestantism's emphasis on individual achievement and divine grace tended to promote economic enterprise and capitalism. Protestants, Weber claimed, would assert and demonstrate their virtue through devotion to thrift, discipline, industriousness, and business. Subsequent authors, however, notably the British social historian R.H. Tawney, countered that capitalist thought and practice had preceded Protestantism and that some Catholic areas, such as northern Italy and parts of France, were strongly capitalistic, while some Protestant areas, notably in north Germany, were not. Tawney argued that it was difficult to show any consistent correlation between religious doctrines and economic policy. Debates over the relationship between religious doctrine and business practice continue unabated and unresolved until today in relation to all major religions. (Today when East Asian economies are flourishing, Confucian traditions are praised for encouraging development. During the previous century the same traditions, interpreted differently, had been blamed for a lack of development.)

PROTESTANT CHALLENGES FROM THE DUTCH REPUBLIC AND ENGLAND

Inspired by Protestant doctrines and chafing under Spanish rule, the Netherlands, including today's regions of both Holland and Belgium, rose in revolt. Although geographically small, they were among the wealthiest of Philip's possessions. They were offended by the excessive quantity and deficient quality of the Spanish administrators sent to govern them. They also feared that Philip would extend the Spanish Inquisition and its persecution of non-Catholics to the Netherlands. Many of the peoples of the Netherlands had left Catholicism for new Protestant movements, and many Protestants from other countries had come seeking asylum. In the Netherlands, Protestants and Catholics had reached an accommodation and neither community wished to see that harmony destroyed by the Inquisition. Philip's government refused to pay attention, and the Netherlands erupted in fury. A civil war ensued in which thousands were killed, property was destroyed, and churches were desecrated. By 1576, however, the Netherlands had suffered enough, and representatives of all the Netherlands united across religious lines to expel the Spanish.

In the same year, Queen Elizabeth of England (r. 1558–1603), the daughter of Henry VIII, officially and publicly aligned her country with the rebels in the Netherlands and began to pursue a policy of alliance with Protestant forces throughout Europe. In reply, Philip II prepared to invade England. In 1588 the Spanish Armada set out for England with 130 ships, 30,000 men, and 2400 pieces of artillery. The Armada was destroyed by the English and by a fierce storm, called at the time "the Protestant wind."

Spain entered a century-long decline. The northern Netherlands, Holland, won its independence in 1609. In 1640 Portugal, which had been united with Spain since 1580, declared its independence once again, and constituent units of Spain, especially Catalonia in the northeast, fought costly, if unsuccessful, wars for independence. Philip III (r. 1598–1621) and Philip IV (r. 1621–65) were incompetent rulers; Charles II (r. 1665–1700) was mentally incapable of ruling. And finally, about mid-century, the stream of silver from the Americas dried up, dwindling from 135 million pesos in the decade 1591–1600 to 19 million in 1651–60. Spain had squandered a fabulous windfall of silver and gold. England and the Netherlands emerged as the rising powers of Europe; their self-confidence and their economies flourished; and their merchant classes organized to travel the world.

PORTUGAL'S EMPIRE

The rulers of Castile and Aragon, Isabella and Ferdinand, married and united their thrones, creating modern Spain in 1492, but the western third of the Iberian peninsula, Portugal, remained a separate state. For sixty years, from 1580 to 1640, it was incorporated into Spain, but otherwise it has remained separate until today. In terms of worldwide exploration and trade, Portugal had entered the field earlier and more vigorously than Spain, but it, too, fell under the commercial domination of Genoa and Antwerp. In addition, Portugal's population was too small and diffused to sustain the trading empire it created.

SUGAR, SLAVES, AND FOOD

Portugal sought souls for Christianity, gold for its national treasury, grain and fish to supplement its domestic food supply, and slaves for its new plantations. Recognizing the economic potential of the sugar plantations, which they had seen in the eastern Mediterranean, Portuguese entrepreneurs transplanted them to Madeira and other islands in the Atlantic Ocean. (Spanish landlords and businessmen did the same in the Canary Islands.)

In 1415 Portugal captured Ceuta on the Moroccan coast of North Africa, one of the major points of the trans-Saharan trade in gold and slaves. Then to get closer to the sources of supply, Portuguese ships, supported by the crown, sailed down the coast of West Africa, rounding Cape Bojador in 1434 and continuing on to the Gold Coast in 1472. Bartholomeu Dias reached the Cape of Good Hope and continued northward a few hundred miles up the east coast of Africa in 1488. As the Portuguese explored they also built fortresses—such as El Mina in modern Ghana—as assembly and shipping points for their purchases of slaves and gold. The crown also claimed some of these lands, including Angola in 1484. By 1500, Lisbon was receiving some 1500 lbs (700 kg) of gold and 10,000 slaves each year from west Africa. The slave trade was of minor importance at the time. In the next century, however, the Portuguese would develop an enormous plantation-based sugar industry in the New World, which would exploit the labor of millions of slaves. The importance of these slaves, in terms of both trade and the enforced migrations of people, is considered in detail in the next chapter.

The fortress of São Jorge da Mina (later called El Mina), African Gold Coast, 1482. Built at the order of King John II of Portugal in 1482, this fortress—like many others—provided a fortified trading post designed both to protect Portuguese trade from rival Europeans and to serve as a supply base. At the beginning of the sixteenth century trade was in gold and kola nuts with imports of American crops such as maize and cassava, and trans-shipment of slaves. It was not until the late seventeenth century that the export of slaves became the main trade on the Gold Coast.

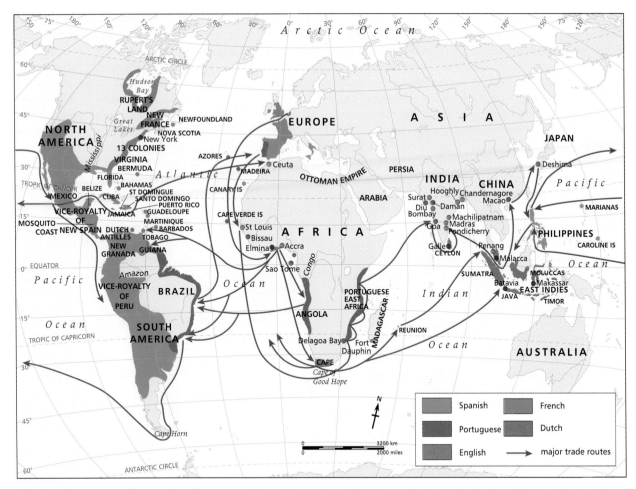

The first European trading empires European seaborne intercontinental trade was dominated by Spain and Portugal in the sixteenth century. The Spanish rapidly colonized Central America, the Andes mountain regions, and the Philippines. The Portuguese concentrated on the coasts of Brazil, east and west Africa, and the Arabian Sea ports of India. A century later the Dutch, English, and French followed, establishing settler colonies in North America and South Africa and fortified trading posts along the coasts elsewhere.

THE INDIAN OCEAN: ADVANCING PORTUGAL'S COASTAL EXPLORATIONS OF AFRICA

In 1498 Vasco da Gama extended Portugal's voyages of exploration. Departing from Africa with the assistance of a local pilot who knew the route, he sailed into one of the world's liveliest arenas of trade, the Indian Ocean and the west coast of India (see Chapter 12). Almost immediately the Portuguese introduced armed violence into trade relations that had been peaceful. In 1500 a Portuguese expedition under Pedro Alvarez Cabral, on its way to founding a fort at Cochin, India, was instructed to sink Muslim ships on sight. When da Gama returned on his second voyage in 1502 he came with twenty-one armed ships to assert Portuguese power in the Indian Ocean.

Seven years later, at the Battle of Diu, Portuguese cannon devastated a combined Egyptian-Gujarati-Calicut fleet. Under Governor Afonso de Albuquerque (1509–15) Portugal captured Goa in 1510, Malacca in 1511, and Hormuz in 1515. At the height of their Indian Ocean power, Portugal held some fifty ports. Portuguese trade boomed.

THE DUTCH REPUBLIC

In the early seventeenth century, the Dutch had the most efficient economic system in Europe. The Dutch Republic bordered the North Sea, reclaimed land from its waters, and lived from its largesse. Fishing was the Republic's great national industry. One out of every four Dutch persons was reliant on the herring industry—catching, salting, smoking, pickling, selling—and others depended on cod fishing and whaling. With their windmills and their dikes, the Dutch also reclaimed land from the sea: 364,565 acres (147,539 hectares) between 1540 and 1715 and another 84,638 acres (34,253 hectares) from inland lakes. With such an investment of capital and energy, the Dutch worked their land carefully and efficiently (see Focus, pp. 430–1). They developed new methods of crop rotation, planting turnips in the fall to provide winter food for humans and sheep. At other times of year they raised peas, beans, and clover to restore nitrogen to the soil. With these cropping patterns, the Dutch no longer had to leave one third of their land fallow each year. They farmed it all, increasing productivity by 50 percent. In addition, the Dutch built one of the largest textile industries in Europe, based on wool from their own sheep and huge quantities imported from England.

On the sea and in the rivers, the Dutch sailed 10,000 ships as early as 1600, and for the next cen-tury they dominated the shipping of northern Europe. From the Baltic they brought timber and grain to Amsterdam and Western Europe. In exchange, from the ports of Portugal, Spain, and France they carried salt, oil, wool, wine, and, most of all, the silver and gold of the New World. Often they warehoused in Amsterdam the trade goods *en route* to other ports, earning additional profits on the storage. They used substantial amounts of the timber themselves to build the most seaworthy, yet economical, ships of the day.

The Dutch also developed the commercial institutions to underpin their dominance in trade. The bourse, or stock exchange, was opened in Amsterdam in the mid-sixteenth century as the Dutch were gaining control of the Baltic trade, and it was reopened in 1592 as they captured a dominant role in supplying grain to Mediterranean countries. In 1598 they initiated a Chamber of Insurance; in 1609 the Bank of Amsterdam was established. This bank accepted coins from all over

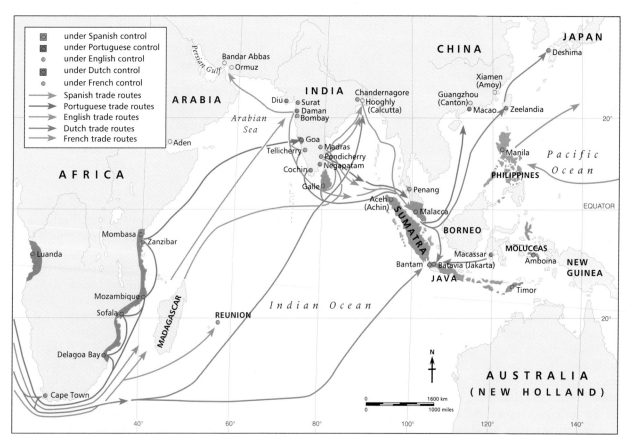

Indian Ocean Trade in the seventeenth century Prior to the sixteenth century, Arabs and other local traders had dominated Indian Ocean commerce. When the Portuguese arrived in 1498, however, European nations entered directly into these trade routes in armed ships. Controlled from headquarters in Europe, they established coastal trade enclaves throughout the region. They began to battle each other for supremacy, projecting European competition into these distant waters and shores.

the world, assessed their gold and silver content, and exchanged them for gold florin coins that were fixed in weight and value and became the standard everywhere. The Dutch government guaranteed the safety of deposits in the national bank, attracting capital from throughout Europe. Depositors were able to draw checks on their accounts. For two centuries, until the French Revolution in 1789, Amsterdam was the financial center of Europe.

At the time, the northern Netherlands was a union of seven provinces, each a republic led by prosperous businessmen, and the Dutch Republic won its independence from Spain through more than four decades of warfare, from 1566 to 1609. The basis of the war was both political and religious. The southern ten provinces of the Netherlands were Catholic, and they remained as the Spanish Netherlands, today's Belgium.

In 1602 Dutch businessmen founded the Dutch East India Company, a joint stock company dedicated to trade in Asia (see Focus, pp. 424–5). The Company captured several Portuguese ports, but concentrated on the most lucrative of all the East Asian centers, Java and the Moluccas, or the Spice Islands of today's Indonesia. Here "their economic leadership of the world was finally consolidated" (Braudel, vol. 3, p. 211). In 1619 the Dutch East India Company founded Jakarta, which served as its regional headquarters until Indonesia won its independence in 1950. In 1623 the Dutch seized Amboina in the Moluccas, killing a group of Englishmen they found there, and forcing the English back to India. In 1600 a group of Dutch traders had reached Japan. Even after all other foreigners were expelled in 1641 (see p. 439), the Dutch were permitted a small settlement on Deshima Island, off Nagasaki, and for two centuries they were the only European traders allowed in Japan. In 1652 the Dutch captured the Cape of Good Hope from the Portuguese and established the first settlement of Afrikaners, South Africans of Dutch descent, who remain powerful there.

In the Americas, the Dutch West India Company raided the shipping of the Spanish and the Portuguese, and then founded their own rich sugar plantations in Caracas, Curaçao, and Guiana. For a few decades they held Bahia in Brazil, but the Portuguese drove them out in 1654. In North America they established New Amsterdam on Manhattan Island. The English, however, conquered and annexed it and in 1664 renamed it New York.

For all their commercial skill and success, the Dutch could not ultimately retain their supremacy. Beginning with the English Navigation Act of 1651, which permitted imports to England and its dependencies only in English ships or in those of the exporting country, the English attempted to restrict Dutch shipping. Three indecisive wars followed, 1652–74. Years of warfare on land against France also exhausted Dutch resources. In 1700 the Dutch Republic had a population of 2 million people; at this time the population of the British Isles was 9 million, and that of France 19 million. An aggressive small country simply could not continue to compete with two aggressive large countries.

FRANCE AND ENGLAND

France and England competed for dominance in world trade. For two centuries each pursued its own strategy—France by land and England by sea—and leadership finally went to the mistress of the waves.

FRANCE: CONSOLIDATING THE NATION

In the second half of the sixteenth century, France endured four decades of civil warfare because the crown was unable to control the various antagonistic factions, religious groups, and regions of the country. Struggles between Catholics and Protestants, called Huguenots in France, helped to fuel the warfare. So, too, did the desire of the nobles to have more independence from the king. In 1589 Henry of Navarre, a Huguenot, came to the throne as Henry IV (r. 1589–1610). Recognizing the importance of Catholicism to the majority of the French people, he became a Catholic with the apocryphal comment, "Paris is worth a Mass." In 1598 Henry issued the Edict of Nantes, which gave Protestants the same civil rights as Catholics and thus helped to heal the religious schism between them. He was not entirely successful, however, and, indeed, was assassinated by a Catholic militant. His successor, Louis XIII (r. 1610–43), following the advice of his chief minister, the Cardinal Richelieu, encouraged nobles to invest in trade by land and sea, built up France's armies, and cultivated allies among France's neighbors.

Louis XIV, in an extraordinarily long and forceful reign (1643–1715), "made France the strongest country in Europe" (p. 161), according to R.R.

Palmer, a leading historian of France and Europe. Under the Sun King, as Louis was known, France set the standard throughout Europe for administration, war, diplomacy, language, thought, literature, architecture, fashion, cooking, and etiquette. Although they had been slower to enter transoceanic trade, the French now began to trade in India and Madagascar, the American Great Lakes and Mississippi River; to establish colonies in the West Indies; and to stake a claim to Canada. By 1690 Louis XIV had raised an army of 400,000 men, equal to the combined armies of England, the Habsburg Empire, Prussia, Russia, and the Dutch Republic. At this time, the French navy was also larger than the English, with 120 ships of the line compared to the English navy's 100. Also, as we have seen, in 1700, France had a population of 19 million, more than double that of the British Isles.

Louis XIV boasted *"L'état, c'est moi"*—"I am the state"—by which he meant that the powers of the state rested in him alone. His leading religious adviser, Bishop Jacques-Bénigne Bossuet (1627–1704), linked the king's power to divine right, asserting that "Royalty has its origin in the divinity itself" (Columbia University, *Contemporary Civilization*, p. 705). Louis XIV continued the right of the king to appoint the Catholic clergy in France, and he revoked the Edict of Nantes in the belief that a single, dominant religion was more important than the toleration of minorities within his kingdom.

Economically, Louis XIV's chief economic advisor, Jean-Baptiste Colbert (1625–96), pursued a

FOCUS
The Joint Stock Companies in Asia

In the early 1600s financiers in the Dutch Republic, England, France, and elsewhere invested in national joint stock companies for trading overseas. They invested in expectation of the great profits that might come from successful shipping ventures. Their potential losses were limited to the value of their investment.

In India, the English, French, and Dutch East India Companies set up trading posts, usually called "factories," within towns. The English, for example, started to trade at Machilipatnam on the southeast coast, and in 1613 at Surat on the west coast. In 1615 they fortified the Surat position and set up inland trading centers at Agra, Burhanpur, and Patna. The French established themselves at Pondicherry and the Dutch also at Machilipatnam. Until the end of the century, the Mughals and local government generally welcomed the foreign traders as means of stimulating the economy through trade and enriching the government through taxes.

In the Indian Ocean, pepper was a large part of the companies' trade. Between them, the English and Dutch East India Companies carried 13.5 million pounds (6 million kilograms) of pepper to Europe in the peak year of 1670, although a sizeable portion of the Dutch share came from Indonesia. Other goods included indigo, raw silk, saltpeter, and, increasingly, Indian textiles. By 1684, the English East India Company alone imported 1,760,315 pieces of cotton cloth. There were also large-scale exports of textiles carried by Europeans from India to Africa in payment for slaves going to the Caribbean.

As the companies' ships traveled armed, and as their representatives established fortresses and trading centers on the coasts of Asia and of the Americas, the companies became, in effect, miniature governments. Malachy Postlethwayt's *Universal Dictionary* of 1751 wrote that the Dutch East India Company

makes peace and war at pleasure, and by its own authority; administers justice to all; … settles colonies, builds fortifications, levies troops, maintains numerous armies and garrisons, fits out fleets, and coins money. (Cited in Tracy, *The Political Economy of Merchant Empires*, p. 196)

Following its victories at Plassey in 1757 and Buxar in 1765, the British East India Company became the *de facto* government of Bengal in India, and continued to expand until it was effectively the ruler of almost all of India. The British government regulated the East India Company from its founding in 1600, and finally disbanded it and took over direct rule of India after the Indian revolt of 1857.

policy of **mercantilism**—fostering the economic welfare of one's own nation against all others—by strengthening the economic power and control of the state over the national economy, even more aggressively than had Richelieu. To facilitate trade, he abolished local taxes on trade throughout central France (a region as large as England), although his government was not powerful enough to do away with these internal tariffs throughout the entire country. Colbert established a Commercial Code to unify business practice throughout the country. To improve communication and transportation, he built roads and canals, including a link between the Bay of Biscay and the Mediterranean. He set quality standards for hand manufacturers to improve their marketability and gave financial incentives to the French manufacturers of such luxury goods as silks, tapestries, glass, and woolens. Meanwhile the needs of the army created huge national markets for uniforms, equipment, and provisions.

The growth of French military and economic strength disturbed the balance of power in Europe and precipitated a series of wars. The War of the League of Augsburg, 1688–97, and the War of the Spanish Succession, 1702–13, reduced France's power and she ceded to Britain the American colonies of Newfoundland and Nova Scotia and all French claims to the Hudson Bay territory. Britain began to pull ahead in overseas possessions. (The names of Britain and England are often used interchangeably in everyday usage. Formally, however, before the 1707 Act of Union, England and Wales

Andries van Eertvel, *The Return to Amsterdam of the Fleet of the Dutch East India Company*, 1599. The Dutch East India Company was founded in 1602 to create a monopoly over Dutch trade and to seize control of the Portuguese trade routes in the Indian Ocean. The company owned a fleet of ships armed with cannon which carried pepper, indigo, raw silk, saltpeter, and textiles from India to western Europe. In the later 1600s, large-scale exports of textiles were also carried from India to Africa in payment for slaves going to the Caribbean. (*Johnny Van Haeften Gallery, London*)

were one country, Scotland another. By the 1707 Act they were united into the single country of Great Britain.)

BRITAIN: ESTABLISHING COMMERCIAL SUPREMACY

In the same wars, Britain won from Spain the *asiento*, the right to carry all the slave cargoes from Africa to Spanish America, plus one shipload of more conventional goods each year to Panama. These officially recognized trading rights also provided cover for British ships to engage illegally in the business of piracy and smuggling that flourished in the Caribbean. Control of transoceanic colonies and trade had become a prized objective. In reality in the eighteenth century the most valued properties in the Americas were the sugar-producing islands of the Caribbean, and the most valuable trade was in human cargo—that is, the slaves who worked the sugar plantations. In Asia, control of sea lanes and of the outposts established by the var-

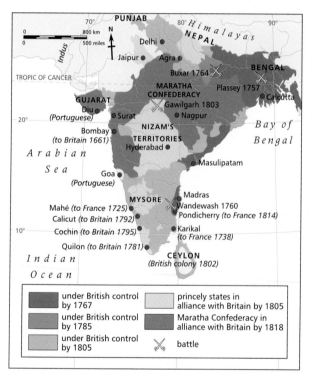

British power in India to 1818 The weakening of the Mughal Empire created a situation which was exploited by the English and French East India companies. They created strategic alliances with local independent princes and competed for power on land and sea. With Clive's victory at Plassey (1757) the English gained Bengal, a power base which allowed them to expand steadily, but their control over India was not secure until their final defeat of the Maratha confederation in 1818.

ious East India companies was the prize; the winner had not yet emerged.

Competition for dominance between the French and the British continued through four more wars in the eighteenth century: the War of Austrian Succession, 1740–48; the Seven Years' War, 1756–63; the War of American Independence (the American Revolution), 1775–81 (see pp. 491–5); and the wars of the French Revolution and Napoleon, 1792–1815 (see pp. 495–506). These wars demonstrated the importance of sea power, and here the British triumphed. Paul Kennedy supplies data (p. 99) that demonstrate the supremacy of the French on land but the British at sea: Around 1790, the French population outnumbered the British 28 million to 16 million, and French armies outnumbered the British by an even greater ratio, 180,000 to 40,000. But the British navy had 195 ships of the line compared with France's 81.

Suffering defeats at sea, the French retreated from their colonial positions. In the Peace Settlement at Paris in 1763 at the end of the Seven Years' War, they turned over their immense, but thinly populated, holdings in North America east of the Mississippi to the British and those west of the Mississippi to Spain. They kept their rich, sugar-producing islands in the Caribbean: Saint-Domingue (Haiti), Guadeloupe, and Martinique. In India, although they lost out in other locations, they kept Pondicherry on the southeast coast and a few additional commercial locations. The French navy was deployed against the British in America during the American Revolution, but it was competely crushed during the Napoleonic Wars. The British, though they lost the thirteen colonies of the United States in 1783, triumphed everywhere else because of the great strength of their navy. They held Canada. They held their islands in the Caribbean. They increased their holdings in India (see Focus, pp. 424–5), and they dominated the sea lanes both across the Atlantic Ocean and through the Indian Ocean.

The British Triumph in Overseas Trade and Colonization:

What Do We Know and How Do We Know It?

How did Britain achieve supremacy in world trade and colonization? How can we understand the process? Fernand Braudel's epic three-volume *Civilization and Capitalism 15th–18th Century*, which surveys the entire process of the rise of capitalism, stresses a comparative approach. Braudel compares, for example, England's early success in achieving a single unified national market throughout its island kingdom with the far more limited success of France, which managed to integrate economically only about one-third of its territories before the French Revolution in 1789. A further comparative advantage for England was its geography. As an island with many navigable rivers, England's ports and markets were numerous and easily accessible. More than virtually all other countries, except perhaps the Netherlands, England concentrated on building its navy and merchant marine, and, in comparison, England was far larger than the Netherlands. Ironically, England made its decision to concentrate on the sea after it lost its territories on the European continent to France in the Hundred Years' War, 1453–1558. France, by comparison, divided its interests between the Continent and the seas.

Institutionally, England surpassed all others, even the Netherlands, in supporting sophisticated economic enterprise. Recognizing the importance of a stable currency, England fixed the value of the pound sterling in 1560–61 at 4 ounces (114 grams) of silver, and maintained that valuation until after World War I. The Bank of England, created in 1694, could transact its business with a currency of fixed value. Moreover, England never defaulted on its debts and so she earned the trust of the international financial community. In times of war as well as of peace, England could borrow whatever sums she needed. "England, by dethroning Amsterdam, had become the point of convergence of all the world's trade—and all the world so to speak settled its accounts in London" (Braudel, p. 364). Politically, England developed a new system of constitutional monarchy after 1688 which gave strong support to private commercial interests, as we shall see in Chapter 15. The French later ridiculed Britain as "a nation of shopkeepers," but geographically, militarily, institutionally, politically, and agriculturally, the British were building the capacity to become the most effective businessmen in the world.

CAPITALISM

By the late eighteenth century, European economies were expanding and had become the subject of discussion and debate not only among business-people and political leaders, but among philosophers as well. Adam Smith (1723–90) had already established his reputation as a moral philosopher before he turned to writing what became his most famous work. In 1776 Smith published *The Wealth of Nations*, a book of a thousand pages, the first systematic explanation of a newly emerging philosophy of economics, later called capitalism. In contrast to the mercantilist views of his day, Smith argued that national wealth was not to be measured by treasuries of precious metals, but rather by quantities of productivity and of trade. He opened his great work with an illustration from a pin factory where a division of labor into specialized tasks of production increased output dramatically. Smith further argued that when workers specialize in what they do best, and then exchange their products in the market, productivity increases. The competitive free market guides production: Goods that consumers demand to buy attract higher prices, and producers supply them in order to earn good profits; unwanted goods earn no profits, and producers stop producing them. This law of **supply and demand** in the market leads to the production of the amounts and kinds of goods that suit the wishes of consumers and the capacity of producers. According to Smith's Law of Accumulation, profits will then be reinvested in further production.

Smith reached a new and surprising conclusion: wealth comes not from the command of a ruler, nor the regulations of the clergy, nor the altruism of members of the community, but as a result of people pursuing their own economic self-interest, and exchanging the fruits of their labor in the market.

> It is not from the benevolence of the butcher, the brewer, or the baker that we expect our dinner, but from their regard to their self-interest. We address ourselves, not to their humanity, but to their self-love, and never talk to them of our necessities, but of their advantages. (p. 14)

Although Smith did not use the term, today we call the system he analyzed capitalism—that is, most wealth, or capital, rests in private, non-governmental hands, and economic decisions on price, supply, and demand are made through the free market rather than by government decision. Critics of this capitalist market system, in which buyer and seller negotiate freely over prices, equated capitalism's self-interest with greed, but Smith explained how competition transformed self-interest into community benefit. If a greedy producer charges too much

SPOTLIGHT
The European "Other" in Art

Early encounters between peoples of different cultures quickly made their way into art. Artistic representation, like the three examples here, transports us back to earlier times and places, and invites the modern viewer to add contemporary understandings to those of the artist. Here we focus on portrayals of Europeans by indigenous artists from Nigeria, India, and the Andes, respectively. The artworks all date from the middle to the late seventeenth century, by which time the colonial presence was firmly established in all three continents. A strong sense emerges, nevertheless, of the alien, the "other," appearance and manners of these Westerners through the eyes of those engaged in depicting them.

Figure 1 shows leopard hunters returning with their catch on a brass plaque typical of the artistic craft of Benin City in today's Nigeria. The dress, helmets, daggers, and firearms of the hunters, and what we can see of their faces, suggest that they are Portuguese. The plaque itself decorated the palace of the Obas, or rulers, of Benin, and suggests the magnitude of the impact of the early Portuguese traders and visitors. Mostly known to us for their trade in slaves, apparently the Portuguese had additional, though similarly violent, interests on the West African coast.

By contrast with our first example, the Indian cotton textile in **figure 2** provides a much more detailed portrayal of Dutch traders greeting each other. Painted on cotton cloth in the late seventeenth century, it suggests that the Dutch have come from far across the seas and trade in a rich array of goods. The

Figure 1 Brass plaque from Benin City (Nigeria), seventeenth century.

whiskers, wide-brimmed hats, ornate doublets and pantaloons, and buckled shoes of the Westerners are painstakingly rendered, and the artist was clearly keen to contrast their appearance with that of the bemused Indian gentleman (far right). The doffing of caps and handshakes must appear strange to this onlooker, who would be accustomed to greeting others by joining his own palms in the "namaste" salute. The Indian artist has painted the faces of the Dutch in careful, realistic detail, suggesting a more intimate knowledge of the European subjects.

The painted Inca ritual drinking vessel made of wood, known as a *kero*, in **figure 3**, represents people of *three* different cultures: to the left, an Inca dignitary; in the center a Spaniard playing a trumpet; and, on the right, one of the earliest (*c.* 1650 C.E.) depictions of a black African in South America, a man playing a drum. The similar postures, dress, and hats of the Spaniard and the African, as well as their instuments, suggest that they are of roughly similar status, and engaged in a common enterprise. This is not the representation of slavery that contemporary viewers might have expected. In this way the art resulting from cross-cultural encounters reminds us to take nothing for granted but to keep our eyes alert to the unusual.

Figure 2 Indian cotton cloth, late seventeenth century.

Figure 3 Inca–Spanish wooden drinking vessel, Peru, *c.* 1650.

FOCUS

Agriculture in Economic Growth

Commercial agriculture underpins the growth of cities and trade networks (see Part 2), and Britain and the Dutch Republic had the most productive and efficient commercial agriculture in the world. The Netherlands, as noted above, farmed with special care, treating its land as a precious resource. Meanwhile British farmers introduced new equipment such as iron plows and Jethro Tull's seed drill. They initiated huge irrigation and drainage projects to make new land available.

New laws regarding land ownership changed fundamentally the relationships between tenants and landlords. In Britain (and the Netherlands) peasants began to pay rent to landowners in a business relationship, rather than performing services for them as client to patron. Moreover, lands that had been held in common by the village community and had been used for grazing sheep and cattle by shepherds and livestock owners who had no lands of their own were now parcelled out for private ownership through a series of enclosure acts. Enclosures had begun in England in very limited measure in the late 1400s. In the eighteenth century the process resumed and the pace increased. In the period 1714–1801, about one-fourth of the land in Britain was converted from community property to private property through enclosures. The results were very favorable to landowners, and urban businessmen now bought land as agricultural investment property. Agricultural productivity shot up; landowners prospered. But hundreds of thousands of farmers with small plots and cottagers who had subsisted through the use of the common lands for grazing their animals were now turned into tenant farmers and wage laborers. Many left the land altogether and headed for the growing cities. The results were revolutionary, and profoundly disturbing, as economic historian Robert Heilbroner explains:

> Where before there was a kind of communality of ownership, now there is private property. Where there were yeomen now there are sheep ... As early as the middle of the sixteenth century riots had broken out against it; in one such uprising, 3,500 people were killed. (Heilbroner, p. 30)

Seed drill, 1701. Jethro Tull (1674–1741) is a key figure of the eighteenth-century agricultural revolution, which saw new technology harnessed to farming techniques. Tull's machine drill employed a rotary mechanism that sowed seeds in rows, permitting cultivation between the rows and thus reducing the need for weeding.

for his goods, someone else will undercut him and lower prices will result; if he pays his employees too little, they will abandon him and seek work elsewhere. Out of the conflicting self-interests of individual members of the society, paradoxically, social harmony will emerge. Smith, who was a professor of moral philosophy at the University of Edinburgh, disagreed with those who said that rulers or priests must regulate the economy in order to achieve equity. Like an "invisible hand," he believed, the impersonal market would do the job.

Believing that the market would correct most economic imbalances, Smith opposed government intervention in the market. He argued for a hands-

The process continued until the mid-nineteenth century (beyond our time period here):

In 1820 … the Duchess of Sutherland dispossessed 15,000 tenants from 794,000 acres of land, replaced them with 131,000 sheep, and by way of compensation rented her evicted families an average of two acres of submarginal land each. (Heilbroner, p. 30)

For better and for worse, the capitalist market system had come to the English countryside and to the Netherlands. Other areas of Europe lagged far behind in turning land into commercial property and in transforming the relationships between landowners and those who worked the land into commercial arrangements.

Enclosure Acts. This aerial photograph of the village of Padbury in Buckinghamshire, England, shows the ridge and furrow of former open field agriculture. The straight hedges were established after the Enclosure Acts of the late eighteenth century. Single crops would have been grown in these large fields and exchanged at market for a range of goods. The concentric circles (lower right) mark the site of a former windmill.

off government policy of *laissez-faire* toward the market—that is, let people do as they choose. But he did recognize that some necessities for economic growth were beyond the powers of any single, small producer. "The erection and maintenance of the public works which facilitate the commerce of any country, such as good roads, bridges, navigable canals, harbors, et cetera, must require very different degrees of expense" (vol. V, p. 1), and therefore Smith urged government to promote these public works. He believed that education was fundamental to economic productivity. Private education, because it was more accountable, was more effective than public education, but government-supported public education was better than none.

Smith recognized, of course, that the market did not always do its work of balancing supply and demand. Huge businesses that formed virtual **monopolies** could control whole industries and manipulate market forces. Their size gave them unfair leverage and Smith wanted them broken up. *The Wealth of Nations* attacked the East India Company, the joint stock company that monopolized virtually all of Britain's trade in Asia and had even become the acting government of Bengal in India. Smith argued that its monopoly should be broken. His plea, however, failed.

Capitalism was the prevailing economic philosophy in Britain in the years of its economic supremacy in the nineteenth century (see Chapter 16), and the new system spread to many other countries as well. As we shall see in the following chapters, many critics blamed capitalism for the inhumanity and cruelty of the slave trade, the seizure of colonies overseas, and the vulnerability of workers at home. Smith understood these problems, but argued that they were corruptions of the market system rather than natural products of it. He condemned slavery as a form of kidnapping and theft of human beings, rather than a free market exchange. Similarly he deplored the European destruction of the native American states and populations as a violation of human ethics:

> The savage injustice of the Europeans rendered an event which ought to have been beneficial to all ruinous and destructive to several of those unfortunate countries. (p. 416)

On the issue of vulnerability of workers, Smith was less understanding. Critics noted that the balance between supply and demand took time to emerge and in the meantime workers suffered. The business cycle was wrenching. Producers increased supplies until the market was glutted and then they stopped. Jobs were plentiful and then were cut back. In the long run balance might result, but in the short run the economy was a roller-coaster. Moreover as the Industrial Revolution began at the end of the eighteenth century, business firms multiplied in size, leaving the individual worker powerless to bargain for wages and working conditions.

CONNECTION: *The Industrial Revolution (1740–1914),* pp. 517–56

DIVERSE CULTURES; DIVERSE ECONOMIC SYSTEMS

The global expansion of Western European countries between the sixteenth and the eighteenth centuries provides only one perspective on trade in this period. Now we examine other trading groups around the globe, analyzing differences and similarities among them, and also noting the results of their mutual encounters. African export trade, for example, was reoriented geographically to the coastal ports established by European traders, and the slave trade sent millions of Africans to the western hemisphere as human cargo. These developments, although important in considerations of trade, will be discussed at length in the next chapter on migration patterns. Here we will consider the trade patterns of Russia and Asian powers. The history of the migration of Asian imperial conquerors will also find its place in the next chapter.

Russia

At the end of the seventeenth century Russia had little direct contact with the market economies of northwestern Europe. The country was geographically remote by land, and by sea the only port was Archangel at the extreme north, on the White Sea, iced in for most of the year. The foreign trade that did exist was carried by foreign ships traveling Russia's river system. Russia belonged to the Greek Orthodox branch of Christianity, so communication with the Church of Rome and its Western European networks was also limited.

Russia had begun to take its modern form only after Ivan III (1462–1505) overthrew the domination of the Mongols in 1480. Muscovy, the territory around Moscow, became the core of an expanding independent state. At first, Russia expanded southeastward, defeating the khanate of Astrakhan in 1556 and capturing the Volga River basin south to the Caspian Sea and its access to the silk trade of Persia. It also expanded eastward to the Pacific (1649), capturing Siberia and its rich population of fur-bearing animals. Russia had only a tiny urban trading class and very few big city markets. As late as 1811, only 4 percent of its population was urban. The overwhelming majority of its people lived in serfdom, a virtual slavery. Occasional serf uprisings, like that led by Stepan Razin (Stenka Razin; d. 1671) in 1667, were brutally suppressed, and the gulf between free persons and serfs increased.

PROFILE
Peter the Great

BRINGING RUSSIA INTO EUROPE

Unpopular in his time and controversial after, Peter the Great resolved to make Russia into a great Western power. Initially, as a child of the second marriage of Czar Alexey, Peter was consigned to the background of Russian court politics. In 1682, at age ten, he was designated to co-czar with his half-brother, the feeble-minded Ivan, but Sofia, Peter's half-sister, held real power. Dispatched with his mother to a village outside Moscow, Peter caroused in the capital's foreign quarter, played war games with his friends, developed a passion for boats, and became obsessed with Western military technology and practice, especially in navigation, artillery, engineering, and shipbuilding.

Peter the Great in armor.

In 1689, using troops that he had drilled during his childhood games, Peter blocked a plot to crown Sofia as empress, and when Ivan V died seven years later Peter at last became sole czar of Russia. In 1697 he embarked upon his "Grand Embassy of Western Europe." Traveling under an assumed name to evade royal protocol, the czar and his party explored the Baltic ports, the Holy Roman Empire, Holland, and England, searching for allies in Peter's wars against the Turks and gathering information on the economic, cultural, and military-industrial practices of the Western powers.

Peter envied Europe's international trade routes, and spent much of his reign fighting against the Ottoman Empire and Sweden in order to gain control of warm water ports on the Black and Baltic Seas. In 1704, he founded St. Petersburg, his new capital on the Baltic, as Russia's "window on the west," commercially, geographically, and architecturally.

In the process of orienting Russia toward the West, Peter established naval forces, reorganized the army along Western lines, brought the Church under state control, and streamlined local and central government. He required Western-style education for all male nobles, introduced "cipher schools" for teaching basic reading and arithmetic, established a printing press, and funded the Academy of Sciences, which opened a year before his death in 1724. Peter wanted service to himself and to the state to count more than birth or seniority, and in 1722 he introduced a new Table of Ranks that automatically gave noble status to officials who reached the eighth position out of fourteen.

Peter strengthened the position of the ruling classes, the landowners, and the rising bourgeoisie, economically and politically as well. He demanded that aristocrats acquire the dress, morals, and tastes of Europe's elites, driving a cultural wedge between the nobility and the great mass of Russians. He allotted to the nobility some 175,000 serfs and 100,000 acres of land in the first half of his reign alone. Meanwhile he exploited the peasantry ruthlessly. Conscription, programs of forced labor, a poll tax, and indirect taxes on everything from bee-keeping to salt provoked two major uprisings in the Russian interior between 1705 and 1708. The czar suppressed them brutally. An iron-willed autocrat, Peter brought his nation into Europe and made it an important military power, but millions of Russians paid a terrible price for his vision of modernization.

When Peter the Great (r. 1682–1725; see Profile p. 433) became emperor, he saw Sweden as his principal enemy. Sweden already held Finland and the entire eastern shore of the Baltic, bottling up Russia without any Baltic port. Then, in a crushing blow, 8000 Swedish troops defeated 40,000 Russians at the Battle of Narva in 1700. Humiliated, Peter set out to construct in Russia a powerful state based on a powerful army and navy. As a young man, Peter had traveled through Western Europe, especially in England and the Netherlands, working for several months as a ship's carpenter in Amsterdam. Impressed by the military strength of the Western European countries, Peter invited to Russia military experts from the west to train and lead his troops after he became emperor. He bought the artillery of Western Europe and copied it. In 1709, when Sweden invaded Russia, Peter was prepared. He retreated until the Swedes fell from the exhaustion of pursuing him through the severe Russian winter. Then, holding his ground at Poltava in south Russia, he defeated the remainder. The Swedish army was finished as an imperial force, and Russia began to seize Baltic possessions.

Bartolomeo Carlo Rastrelli, *The Founding of St. Petersburg,* **Russia, 1723.** This bronze relief commemorates the founding of St. Petersburg in 1704. Peter the Great intended his capital to be an all-weather port and a "window on the West." As part of his drive for Westernization he decreed that the aristocracy must abandon their Russian dress in favor of European clothes. The garb of the men depicted here indicates clearly that the edict was already in place. (*Hermitage, St. Petersburg*)

By 1703–04 Peter had started to build a new capital, an all-weather port and "window on the West," in St. Petersburg. He promoted mining, metallurgy, and textile manufacture, largely as means of supplying his troops. As labor, he used serfs. He created a new system of administration with himself as head. He subordinated the Eastern Orthodox clergy to his own leadership. He created a new "state service," including both civil and military officials, and made appointments to it completely without regard to family status. The move was revolutionary, but it did not survive long after Peter's death. Peter established and edited the first newspaper in Russia. He forced the westernization of the nobility and gentry, established schools for their children, and sent many to study in Western Europe. He made them abandon their Russian dress in favor of the clothing of Western Europe, and forced the men to shave or trim their beards in Western style.

Peter achieved many of his goals, establishing a strong central administration, a powerful military, some commercial enterprise, international trade connections, and diplomatic contact with the nations of Western Europe. He did not, however, free Russia's merchants to carry on the kinds of independent economic activity characteristic of West European commerce. And he kept the largest enterprises, like weapons manufacture and shipping, in the hands of the state. Considered an **enlightened despot**—a ruler who advanced new concepts of intellectual inquiry and legal rights, at least for the nobility, but who held on to power for himself—Peter died in 1725. Since he had killed his own son rather than permit him to sidetrack reforms, Peter was succeeded for two years by his wife and then by other family members. In 1762 Catherine the Great assumed the throne and ruled for thirty-four years. At least as despotic as Peter, Catherine won especially important victories over Poles and Turks, expanding the borders of Russia to the Black Sea. After brutally suppressing a revolt by hundreds of thousands of serfs led by Yemelyan Pugachev (1726–75), she reduced Russia's serfs to a position of virtual slavery.

OTTOMANS AND MUGHALS

At the beginning of our period, two enormous empires, the Ottomans and the Mughals, were rising in Asia just as Spain and Portugal were in Europe. Indeed there was some connection. The Ottoman conquest of Constantinople in 1453, and its control of the eastern Mediterranean trade, encouraged the Atlantic countries to seek new routes to Asia, inspiring Columbus' and Vasco da Gama's voyages of exploration. The Mughals, a land-based empire, began their rise to power a little later, beginning their invasion of India in 1526.

By 1600 all four empires were approaching the height of their powers. By 1700 all were in severe decline because of overextension, draining warfare, weak state systems and lack of attention to technological improvements, especially in the military. All four also allowed control of their economic affairs to fall into the hands of foreigners. By the end of our period, all were subordinated to greater or lesser degree under the power of the newly risen French and British.

The Ottomans did not control their own trade and its profits. At first, because of political alliances with France, only French ships were allowed to trade with the Ottomans. After 1580 trade opened more widely and the English and Dutch entered the trade, along with Jews, Armenians, Venetians, and Genoese. The situation came to resemble Spain's, in which the empire's new riches went into the hands of foreign merchants. A shift in the balance of trade also weakened the central government. The Otto-mans imported more manufactured goods and exported more raw materials, increasing the wealth of the landed estate holders and enabling them to break free of central control.

In India, between 1556 and 1605, the Mughal emperor Akbar established one of the great empires of the world. Akbar's administrative reforms brought change in trade and economies as well. Village India joined the cash economy while city markets encouraged the production of luxury goods for the court and everyday goods for the common people. A series of studies by scholars of the Mughal period, such as Irfan Habib, Shireen Moosvi, and Hamida Khatoon Naqvi, and by scholars of the early years of English penetration of the Indian markets, notably Tapan Raychaudhuri and Chris Bayly, have examined the workings of these urban markets.

The markets contained a wide array of craftsmen, shopkeepers, and higher level specialists. Moneylenders and moneychangers were active throughout the urban system, enabling the smooth transfer of funds across the empire. Their *hundis* (bills of exchange) were accepted throughout the empire, and these financial instruments facilitated the work of government officials in collecting and

Merchants with their camel caravans in Asia, 1575. As this French woodcut indicates, the Ottomans allowed the French to trade with them, and camel caravans were used to transport the raw materials and goods to the ships.

transmitting the land revenue in cash. Indian cities boasted very wealthy business financiers and important guild organizations. The guilds, much like the contemporary European guilds, regulated and supervised the major trades in cities. Contrary to popular beliefs sometimes mistakenly held about India as an other-worldly culture, business flourished and prospered. After all, among the multitude of India's castes (see Chapters 8 and 9), were *baniyas* or *vaishyas* who were charged specifically with carrying on business.

Indian traders were highly mobile, and therefore had some independence from the political fortunes of the rulers of the time. If a particular ruler could not defend his territory against foreign invasion, or maintain internal law and order, or tried to extort excessive taxes, the merchant communities left for other cities more amenable to their pursuits. Conversely, rulers who wanted to improve their commercial prospects lured these footloose merchants with offers of free land and low taxes. Thus, even in the event of political decline or catastrophe, India's business might continue.

Indian businessmen continued to carry on coastal and ocean-going trade, but the imperial government could not support these ventures very effectively. They had no navy. In 1686, for example, the English blocked Indian trade between Bengal and Southeast Asia and even seized ships belonging to the officers and family members of the Mughal rulers. The Emperor Aurangzeb replied by land, forcing the English out of their settlement at Hoogly. But the English relocated at a new town, Calcutta, and continued their maritime commerce and armed competition. Furthermore, despite sophisticated economic institutions developed within family-held firms, Indian merchants did not develop impersonal business firms like the European joint stock companies. When the European joint stock companies arrived on the subcontinent, they opened a new scale of overseas operations.

"Idris giving instruction to mankind on the art of weaving," Mughal period, c. 1590. In the Islamic tradition, the mythical Idris gives instruction and protection to pious and skilled weavers. Here weavers wash, dry, spin, skein, and weave their wool, while courtiers present rolls of cloth for inspection. Most production was localized, as suggested here, although a few examples of large, well organized workshops, with wage labor and centralized management, mostly under the control of Mughal courts, also existed. When pressured, weavers organized in boycotts and strikes to resist the exactions of rulers and merchants, and to defend the honor of their religion.

MING AND QING DYNASTIES IN CHINA

The Ming dynasty in China, as we saw in Chapter 12, had largely closed China to foreign trade in favor of developing the internal economy and of defending the northern borders against Mongol and Manchu attack. They repaired the Great Wall and extended it an additional 600 miles (965 kilometers).

Having limited the size and power of their navy, the Ming were harassed by Japanese and Chinese pirates on their coasts. In reply, they avoided the sea and revived the system of inland transportation by canals. The pirate attacks increased and became minor invasions of the mainland, even up the Yangzi River. Following national unification at the end of the sixteenth century, the new Japanese government brought the pirates under control, but then Japan invaded Korea in 1592 intending ultimately

Portuguese ships and sailors, lacquer screen, Chinese, seventeenth century. The faces of the sailors and the ship itself are not depicted as hostile, although at the beginning of the previous century the Portuguese had been expelled for aggressive actions and by mid century were restricted to coastal enclaves.

to invade China. Warfare continued for years, mostly within the Korean peninsula, but also within north China, until Japan finally withdrew in 1598.

The Western presence was very limited at this stage. The few Portuguese who arrived in China after 1514 were mostly Jesuit missionaries whose influence was felt far more in the culture of the court than in the commerce of the marketplace. Matteo Ricci (1552–1610), one of the most prominent of the Jesuit missionaries to China, shared with government officials in Beijing his knowledge of mathematics, cartography, astronomy, mechanics, and clocks, while he mastered the Chinese language and many of the Confucian classics. The Jesuits concentrated their efforts on winning the elites of China, and by 1700 some 300,000 Chinese had converted to Christianity.

Despite the shutdown of most international trade, China's economy expanded, at least until about 1600. China, after all, contained one-fifth of the world's population and generated an immense internal economy. The canal system encouraged north–south trade. Using kaolin clay, Chinese artisans created a porcelain more beautiful and stronger than ever. Weaving and dyeing of silk continued and expanded near Suzhou; cotton textiles flourished at Nanjing; Hebei specialized in iron manufacture. In the late Ming period, private sea-going trade with Southeast Asia began to flourish again, often carried by families who had sent emigrants to the region and thus had local contacts. Within China, this trade was regulated by local authorities on the south China coast. Fascinating research by Wang Gungwu on the success of overseas Chinese merchants suggests that had the Chinese government supported its own traders at home, instead of restricting them, they too might have been effective in building overseas merchant empires:

> There is also the difference between merchants barely tolerated by a centralized empire and those whose rulers and governments used them for their imperial cause … they could, in terms of entrepreneurship and daring, do everything that the various Europeans could do. But they were helpless to produce the necessary institutional change in China to match European or even Japanese power. They were never the instruments of any effort by Ming or Qing authorities to build merchant empires; nor could they hope to get mandarin or ideological support for any innovative efforts of their own. (p. 401)

When Europeans came to trade, the Chinese government restricted them to coastal enclaves. The Ming dynasty limited the Portuguese to Macao in 1557 (where they remained until 1999 under agreement with the current Chinese government). By the time the Dutch and British arrived in the 1600s, the Ming had weakened internally and the Mandate of Heaven (see Chapter 7) passed to the Qing, Manchus from north of the Great Wall who captured the government of China in 1644. The Qing finally secured the southeast coast in 1683. They established the "Canton system," restricting European traders to the area around Canton (Guangzhou), and entrusting their supervision and control to a monopoly of Chinese firms called the Cohong. Because of these restrictions, and because of the vast size of China, the European merchants had little effect on China. The silver they brought, however, enriched the Chinese economy. As noted above (see pp. 413–14), between a third and a half of all the silver of the New World ultimately went to China to pay for purchases of silk, porcelain, tea, and other products. Merchants became wealthy, but the government did not. The quality of the Ming administration grew weaker, undermining the dynasty and preparing an opening for the succession of the Qing (see p. 453).

CONNECTION: *China, 1800–1914, pp. 544–9*

TOKUGAWA JAPAN

The Japanese experience of Europeans united religious and economic aspects. The first to make a significant impact was the Jesuit priest St. Francis Xavier, who arrived in 1549. Like Matteo Ricci in China, he, too, adapted to local cultural practices in dress, food, residence, and, of course, language. For their religious ideas, their culture, and trade, Europeans were at first warmly welcomed. Among their contributions were tobacco, bread, playing cards, and deep-fat frying, which inspired the Japanese specialty of tempura. Christianity found a foothold in Japan, and by 1614, as in China, there were over 300,000 converts.

The Japanese government, apprehensive about so large a group of elite converts, and consolidating its own power in a new **shogunate**, or military administration, began to crack down. In 1597, after a Spanish ship captain boasted of the power of his king, and after Spain had colonized Manila, the **shogun** Hideyoshi crucified six Franciscan missionaries and eighteen Japanese converts. In 1606 Christianity was outlawed, and in 1614 the new shogun Tokugawa Ieyasu began to expel all Christian missionaries. Three thousand Japanese Christians were martyred. In 1623 the British left Japan; in 1624 the Spanish were expelled; in 1630 Japanese were forbidden to travel overseas. In 1637–8, in reaction to a revolt that was more a rural economic protest than a religious uprising, 37,000 Christians were killed. The Portuguese were expelled. Only a small contingent of Dutch traders was permitted to remain, confined to Deshima Island off Nagasaki. A limited number of Chinese ships continued to visit Japan each year and some diplomatic contact with Korea continued, but Japan chose to live largely in isolation.

As in China, the suppression of contact with outsiders did not cripple Japan. Its process of political consolidation continued under the three Tokugawa family shoguns from the 1600 battle of Sekigahara until 1651. The country was unified and peaceful. Guns were virtually banned. Agriculture thrived as the area of land under cultivation doubled, and the production of cash crops, such as indigo, tobacco, sugar cane, and mulberry leaves as food for silk worms, increased. The population almost doubled, from 18 million in 1600 to 30 million by the mid-1700s, at which point it stabilized temporarily. The new government was in the hands of the **samurai** warrior classes, who made up about 7 percent of the population. They benefited most from the improved conditions, and there were sometimes violent protests against the increasing disparities in income, but standards of living and of education generally improved. City merchants, *chonin*, emerged as a newly wealthy and powerful class, dealing in the new cash commodities of farm and hand manufacture. They supplied banking, shipping, loans, and other comercial services, and founded family businesses, some of which endure today. The Tokugawa capital Edo (Tokyo) grew to a million people by 1700, among the largest cities in the world at the time.

CONNECTION: *Japan, 1867–1914, pp. 582–9*

SOUTHEAST ASIA

Southeast Asia was one of the great prizes of international commerce throughout our period, and foreign merchants from China, Japan, India, Arabia, and Europe were active in its markets. Yet the merchants of the region did not themselves become major factors in the international side of the trade. Foreign traders began their activities on the coast and then moved inland, taking control of local markets. They also fought among themselves. The Dutch East India Company, for example, ousted from the Indonesian archipelago not only the local merchants but also European competitors by 1640. By this time, the spice trade was beginning to level off, and the Dutch were in the process of restructuring the economies of Southeast Asia, especially Indonesia, to produce such commercial crops as sugar, coffee, and tobacco. In the Philippines, the Spanish asserted similar power.

Local rulers entered into commercial agreements with the foreign traders that enriched themselves, but not their merchant communities. Commercial profits were repatriated from Southeast Asia back to Europe, creating ever more serious imbalances of power and wealth. Capitalist enterprise in the hands of merchants, backed by the state and by military power, was radiating outward from Europe; Southeast Asia had become a participant in this new system, and a victim of it.

CONNECTION: *Southeast Asia and Indonesia, 1795–1880, p. 542*

WHAT DIFFERENCE DOES IT MAKE?

As we close this exploration of world trade in 1776, we have witnessed enormous changes from 1100, when we began, and even from 1500, when European explorers began their oceanic voyages. During these centuries, an entirely new set of trade networks opened, crisscrossing the Atlantic Ocean. Major elements in these new trade relationships included the export from the western hemisphere of enormous quantities of gold and silver to Europe (and to Asia, across the Pacific), and the taking of millions of people in slavery from Africa to the plantations of the Americas. The earlier center of ocean trade, the Indian Ocean, continued important, but now European traders—Portuguese, followed by Dutch, British, and French—gained control of the intercontinental segments of that trade. The variety of traders in coastal port cities around the world increased, with some exceptions, as in Japan, and the trade outposts, "factories," of the Europeans were fortified militarily. Within Europe, the power of nation-states and of private traders increased, in large part because of the profits of international trade and because of the perceived need to support it with ocean-going fleets and navies. Competition increased in the technology of shipping, the sophistication of commercial strategies, the manufacture of armaments, and the training and disciplining of armed forces at home and overseas. Leadership passed from the Spanish and Portuguese to the Dutch, French, and British. Through most of these centuries, the most powerful and wealthy of the world's empires were in Asia, but by the end of our period, Europeans, fired by a desire for profit, and often by a desire to spread the gospel of Christianity, were fashioning overseas empires of unprecedented extent and complexity.

BIBLIOGRAPHY

Andrea, Alfred and James Overfield, eds. *The Human Record.* (Boston: Houghton Mifflin, 2nd ed., 1994).

Austen, Ralph A. "Marginalization, Stagnation, and Growth: the Trans-Saharan Caravan Trade in the Era of European Expansion, 1500–1900," in Tracy, *The Rise of Merchant Empires*, 311–350.

Bayly, C.A. *Indian Society and the Making of the British Empire* (Cambridge: Cambridge University Press, 1988).

Braudel, Fernand. *Capitalism and Material Life 1400–1800*, trans. by Miriam Kochan (New York: Harper and Row, 1973).

—. *Civilization and Capitalism 15th–18th Century.* Vol. 2: *The Wheels of Commerce*, trans. by Sian Reynolds (New York: Harper and Row, 1986).

—. *Civilization and Capitalism 15th–18th Century.* Vol. 3: *The Perspective of the World*, trans. by Sian Reynolds (New York: Harper and Row, 1986).

—.*The Mediterranean and the Mediterranean World in the Age of Phillip II*, 2 vols, trans. by Sian Reynolds (New York: Harper Torchbooks, Vol. 1: 1972; Vol. 2: 1973).

Cervantes Saavedra, Miguel de. *Don Quixote of La Mancha*, trans. by Walter Starkie (New York: New American Library, 1957).

Chaudhuri, K.N. "Reflections on the Organizing Principle of Premodern Trade," in Tracy, ed., *The Political Economy of Merchant Empires*, 421–2.

—. *Trade and Civilization in the Indian Ocean* (Cambridge: Cambridge University Press, 1985).

Cipolla, Carlo. *Clocks and Culture 1300–1700* (New York: W.W. Norton, 1978).

Columbia University. *Introduction to Contemporary Civilization in the West*, 2 vols. (New York: Columbia University Press, 2nd ed., 1954).

Cross, Harry E., "South American Bullion Production and Export 1550–1750," in J.F. Richards, ed., *Precious Metals in the Later Medieval and Early Modern Worlds*, 397–423 (Durham, NC: Carolina Academic Press, 1983).

Curtin, Philip, Steven Feierman, Leonard Thompson, and Jan Vansina. *African History from Earliest Times to Independence* (New York: Longman, 2nd ed. 1995).

Curtin, Philip D., ed. *Africa Remembered: Narratives by West Africans from the Era of the Slave Trade* (Madison: University of Wisconsin Press, 1967).

—. *The Rise and Fall of the Plantation Complex* (Cambridge: Cambridge University Press, 1990).

Dale, Stephen Frederic. *Indian Merchants and Eurasian Trade, 1600–1750* (Cambridge: Cambridge University Press, 1994).

Das Gupta, Ashin and M.N. Pearson, eds. *India and the Indian Ocean 1500–1800* (Calcutta: Oxford University Press, 1987).

Ebrey, Patricia Buckley. *Cambridge Illustrated History of China* (Cambridge: Cambridge University Press, 1996).

—. ed. *Chinese Civilization: A Sourcebook* (New York: Free Press, 2nd ed., 1993).

Elvin, Mark. *The Pattern of the Chinese Past* (Stanford: Stanford University Press, 1973).

Fairbank, John K., Edwin O. Reischauer, and Albert M. Craig. *East Asia: Tradition and Transformation*, revised ed. (Boston: Houghton Mifflin, 1989).

Gungwu, Wang, "Merchants without Empire: the Hokkien Sojourning Communities," in Tracy, *The Rise of Merchant Empires*, 400–21.

Habib, Irfan, "Merchant Communities in Precolonial India," in Tracy, *The Rise of Merchant Empires*, 371–99.

Heilbroner, Robert. *The Worldly Philosophers*, 4th ed. (New York: Simon and Schuster, 1972).

Hirschman, Albert O. *The Passions and the Interests*, 20th anniversary ed. (Princeton: Princeton University Press, 1997).

Kathirithamby-Wells, Jeyamalar, "Restraints on the Development of Merchant Capitalism in Southeast Asia before *c.* 1800," in Anthony Reid, ed., *Southeast Asia in the Early Modern Era*, 123–48.

Kennedy, Paul, *The Rise and Fall of the Great Powers* (New York: Vintage Books, 1987).

Klein, Herbert, "Economic Aspects of the Eighteenth-Century Atlantic Slave Trade," in Tracy, *The Rise of Merchant Empires*, 287–310.

Kulke, Harmann and Dietmar Rothermund. *A History of India* (Totowa, NJ: Barnes and Noble, 1986).

Lapidus, Ira. *A History of Islamic Societies* (Cambridge: Cambridge University Press, 1988).

McNeill, William H. "The Age of Gunpowder Empires, 1450–1800," in Michael Adas, ed., *Islamic and European Expansion* (Philadelphia: Temple University Press, 1993), 103–9.

Mauro, Frederic, "Merchant Communities, 1350–1750," in Tracy, *The Rise of Merchant Empires*, 255–86.

Mintz, Sidney W. *Sweetness and Power: The Place of Sugar in Modern History* (New York: Penguin Books, 1985).

Northrup, David, ed. *The Atlantic Slave Trade* (Lexington, MA: D.C. Heath, 1994).

Palmer, R.R. and Joel Colton. *A History of the Modern World* (New York: Knopf, 8th ed., 1995).

Pannikar, K.M. *Asia and Western Dominance 1498–1945: A Survey of the Vasco da Gama Epoch of Asian History* (London: Allen and Unwin, 1953).

Parker, Geoffrey, "Europe and the Wider World, 1500–1700," in Tracy, ed., *The Political Economy of Merchant Empires*, 161–195.

Pearson, M.N., "Merchants and States," in Tracy, ed., *The Political Economy of Merchant Empires*, 41–116.

Reid, Anthony. *Southeast Asia in the Age of Commerce 1450–1680*. Vol 1: *The Land Below the Winds*; Vol 2: *Expansion and Crisis* (New Haven: Yale University Press, Vol. 1: 1988; Vol. 2: 1993).

—. ed. *Southeast Asia in the Early Modern Era: Trade, Power, and Belief* (Ithaca: Cornell University Press, 1993).

Richards, John F. *The Mughal Empire* (Cambridge: Cambridge University Press, 1993).

Robinson, Francis, ed. *The Cambridge Illustrated History of the Islamic World* (Cambridge: Cambridge University Press, 1996).

Rothermund, Dietmar. *Asian Trade and European Expansion in the Age of Mercantilism* (Delhi: Manohar, 1981).

Schama, Simon. *The Embarrassment of Riches* (New York: Knopf, 1987).

Schirokauer, Conrad. *A Brief History of Chinese and Japanese Civilizations*. (Fort Worth: Harcourt Brace Jovanovich, 2nd ed., 1989).

Smith, Adam. *An Inquiry into the Nature and Causes of the Wealth of Nations* (New York: Modern Library, 1937).

Spence, Jonathan D. *The Memory Palace of Matteo Ricci* (New York: Penguin Books, 1985).

Steensgaard, Niels. *The Asian Trade Revolution of the Seventeenth Century* (Chicago: University of Chicago Press, 1973).

Tawney, R.H. *Religion and the Rise of Capitalism* (New York: Harcourt, Brace, & Co., 1926).

The [London] Times Atlas of World History, ed. Richard Overy (London: Times Books Ltd., 5th ed., 1999).

Thornton, John. *Africa and Africans in the Making of the Atlantic World, 1400–1680* (Cambridge: Cambridge University Press, 1992).

Tracy, James D., ed. *The Political Economy of Merchant Empires* (Cambridge: Cambridge University Press, 1991).

—. ed. *The Rise of Merchant Empires* (Cambridge: Cambridge University Press, 1990).

Wallerstein, Immanuel. *The Modern World System* 3 vols. (San Diego: Academic Press, Inc., Vol. 1: 1974; Vol. 2: 1980; Vol. 3: 1989).

Weber, Max. *The Protestant Ethic and the Spirit of Capitalism*, trans. by Talcott Parsons (London, 1930).

Williams, Eric. *Capitalism and Slavery* (Chapel Hill: University of North Carolina Press, 1994).

Wolf, Eric. *Europe and the People without History* (Berkeley: University of California Press, 1982).

Wrigley, E.A. "A Simple Model of London's Importance in Changing English Society and Economy 1650–1750," in Philip Abrams and E.A. Wrigley, eds., *Towns in Societies* (Cambridge: Cambridge University Press, 1978).

Migration: Free People and Slaves

1300–1750

"BE FRUITFUL AND MULTIPLY, FILL UP THE EARTH AND SUBDUE IT": DEMOGRAPHIC CHANGES IN A NEW GLOBAL ECUMENE

From the beginning, historians have chosen most frequently to write about great individuals, major institutions, and the politics and wars of particular peoples. In the twentieth century, however, and especially in its second half, historians began to examine demographics, that is, human populations viewed collectively and usually represented in quantitative terms. They asked such questions as: When and why do populations grow and decline? What are the impacts on population of disease, war, famine, and more efficient farming methods? We have already touched on some of these issues beginning with the migration of *Homo sapiens* around the globe. In this part we shall examine demographic data specifically concerned with migration, the movement of large groups of people across geographical space, from one region to another, and between countryside and city.

New topics in the study of the past are often inspired by new experiences in the present. In our own time, demographic shifts are dramatically altering our world, both in the population explosion which has doubled the earth's population in the last thirty years and in the migrations of hundreds of millions of people both from one region to another and from rural areas to cities. These demographic transformations evoke comparisons with earlier historical eras, especially the period 1500–1750 when the population of whole continents was restructured as new peoples immigrated and native populations perished. At the same time,

François Biard, *The Slave Trade*, 1840. (*Kingston-upon-Hull City Museums and Art Galleries*)

great capital cities, some of them newly founded, also experienced enormous population growth.

There is another reason for choosing to study aggregate populations instead of individual lives. Such studies are often the closest we can come to understanding the lives of average people. They may not have left written records—most were not literate—so we are not able to know their individual biographies, but through demographic studies of aggregate groups we may be able to gain a better understanding of the societies in which they lived and died.

Finally, new kinds of research often require new kinds of tools; sometimes the research is motivated by the availability of these new tools. Population history requires quantitative information and the statistical tools to work with it. Within the last generation demographers have made great strides in methodology, some of it as a result of new computers and data processing capabilities. Their quantitative researches provide additional, new replies to the question "How Do We Know?"

14 DEMOGRAPHY AND MIGRATION

1300–1750

"The world is divided and organized according to the force of numbers..."

FERNAND BRAUDEL

THE MOVEMENT OF PEOPLES AROUND THE EARTH

This chapter introduces both important migration events and important scholars who have studied them. Among the events are the migrations of conquering nomadic groups as they swept into new lands: the Ottomans, Safavids, and Mughals who invaded and occupied southeastern Europe and western and southern Asia, and the Manchus who invaded and conquered China. We turn to the Americas to see Europeans invade and settle, and later import millions of people from Africa to work as slaves, while up to 90 percent of Native Americans succumbed to new diseases and died. We will find that similar proportions of the indigenous populations died off when European settlers arrived in Australia and New Zealand. The final event we examine is the construction and reconstruction of great national and imperial capitals which attracted vast numbers of urban immigrants.

DEMOGRAPHY: WHAT DO WE KNOW? HOW DO WE KNOW? WHAT IS ITS SIGNIFICANCE?

In studying these events we will examine the work of four major demographic historians. In looking at the consequences of European expansion we will consider the work of Fernand Braudel, the great French historian of the *longue durée* (historical change over long periods of time), who examined "the weight of numbers," the overall shift in human population from one area of the world to another (see Focus, pp. 454–5). Carl Sauer and others of the "Berkeley School" tried to gauge with greater accuracy the death rates of Amerindians as Europeans invaded and migrated to their lands. In our study of the slave trade from Africa to the Americas we will focus on the quantitative study of Philip Curtin. Finally in our examination of the changing demography of London we will draw on the work of E.A. Wrigley and others of the Cambridge [England] Group for the History of Population and Social Structure, who used available population data to analyze major changes in social structures, especially of Europe.

These demographic historians examine aggregate human populations in quantitative terms. They ask about total population and its components: age groups, gender, household size. They utilize life expectancy and other "vital statistics" such as birth rates, death rates, and marriage rates. They may analyze the average age at marriage; rates of childbirth, legitimacy and illegitimacy; the quantitative impacts on population of epidemics, natural catastrophes, and war; class size and composition. Through large-scale analyses of such data demographers seek to understand and interpret patterns of change and, although the statistics may sometimes seem dry, they tell stories of fundamental structures and changes in human society. Today, in recognition of the importance of these data, most governments gather the information as a matter of course. To find information on earlier periods that lack such systematic official data collection, historians search for other sources. Church registers of birth and death, travelers' estimates of populations and of catastrophes, ships'

records of passengers and cargo, for example, have all proved valuable sources.

ASIAN MIGRATIONS 1300–1750

Between 1300 and 1750, successive waves of new migrants within Asia created three new empires and several new ruling dynasties within already existing empires. Turkish invaders founded the Ottoman, Safavid, and Mughal Empires, while the Manchus in China and the descendants of Genghis Khan in central Asia introduced new dynasties to existing empires.

THE OTTOMAN EMPIRE 1300–1700

The Ottoman Empire, named for Osman whose military victory in 1301 laid its foundation in northwest Anatolia, expanded from his small holding to become a world power. It rose to prominence at the same time as Spain and Portugal did in western Europe (see Chapter 13) and was at its height in 1600. By 1700, however, it was in decline. The Ottomans began by expanding outward from their

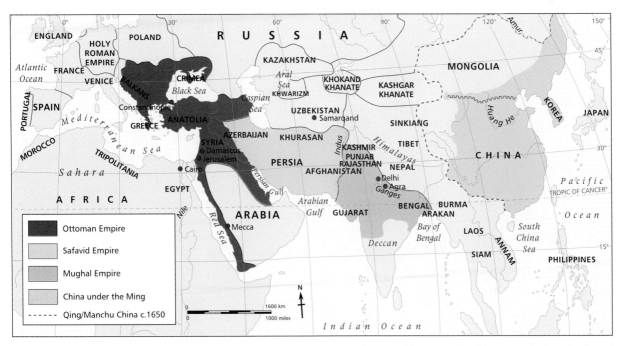

Eurasian empires, 1300–1700 Eurasia on the eve of European expansion was dominated by a complex of huge, interlocking, land-based empires, linked by overland trade routes, and by the Arab trading ecumene of the Indian Ocean. The four empires highlighted here were land-based, inward-looking, and ill-prepared for the challenge of European imperialism that would arrive by sea and, over the next four hundred years, effectively undermine them.

early home in Anatolia, confronting the Byzantine empire to the west and the Seljuq Turks to the east. Through the thirteenth and fourteenth centuries the Ottomans captured much of Anatolia, crossing into Europe to take Gallipoli in 1354. Three groups led and sustained the Turkish invasions: **gazis**, Turkish warriors inspired by Islam to conquer territories and bring them under Dar-ul-Islam, the rule of a state hospitable to Islam; **Sufis**, members of reli-

Siege of Beograd (Belgrade) by Mehemmed II, sixteenth-century Persian manuscript. After the setback of defeat by central Asian conqueror Tamerlane in 1402, the Ottoman Empire rebuilt, consolidated, and extended its power. A major watershed was passed when Sultan Mehemmed II conquered Constantinople (Istanbul) in 1453, making it the third and last Ottoman capital city. This Turkish empire endured for 600 years (1300–1922) and at its height spanned three continents. (*Topkapi Palace, Istanbul*)

gious orders, often practicing mystical and ecstatic rituals, who accompanied the troops and introduced Islam within the conquered regions; and **janissaries**, slaves captured or bought from among the conquered populations, usually from among the Christians of the Balkans, to be converted to Islam and serve in the elite Turkish armies and, occasionally, in the administration. In 1527 the slave infantry numbered about 28,000. In conquering Anatolia, Turks displaced the local agricultural communities and became the majority population.

Having established a foothold in Europe, the Ottomans invited Turkish warriors into the Balkans and occupied northern Greece, Macedonia, and Bulgaria. At the Battle of Kosovo in 1389 they secured Serbia, and established control of the western Balkans. Demographically, however, the invaders were not so numerous in this region nor did they force widespread conversion. A census of 1520–30 showed that about one-fifth of the Balkan population was Muslim, about four-fifths was Christian, and there was a small Jewish minority.

Under Mehemmed (Mehmed) II, "The Conqueror" (r. 1451–81), the Ottomans moved on to conquer Constantinople in 1453 and then the remainder of Anatolia, the Crimea on the north side of the Black Sea, and substantial areas of Venice's empire in Greece and the Aegean. They began the process of rebuilding Constantinople into a great capital city, and by 1600 it had become one of the largest cities in Europe, with 700,000 inhabitants. The capital attracted a great influx of immigrant scholars to its **madrasas**, religious schools, and its bureaucratic jobs, which required Islamic learning and knowledge of the law.

Selim I (r. 1512–20) defeated decisively the Shi'a Safavid empire in Persia at the 1514 Battle of Chaldiran. Turning next against the Mameluke Empire of Egypt, he conquered its key cities of Aleppo, Damascus, and its capital in Cairo. These victories gave the Ottomans control of the holy cities of Jerusalem, Mecca, and Medina, and of both coasts of the Red Sea. Suleiman (Süleyman) I, "the Magnificent" (r. 1520–66), returned to battle in Europe, adding Hungary to his empire and pushing to the gates of Vienna. As they entered central Europe, the Ottomans confronted the Habsburg Empire. Alliances here crossed religious lines, with Catholic France sometimes joining with the Muslim Ottomans in alliance against the Catholic Habsburgs. In a series of battles, which collectively formed a kind of world war, the Ottomans were defeated at sea in 1571 at Lepanto off the coast of

Greece, by a coalition of the papacy, Venice, and the Habsburgs. Finally, in 1580, a peace treaty confirmed the informal boundaries that endure in the Mediterranean until today between predominantly Christian Europe to the north and west, and predominantly Muslim North Africa and West Asia to the south and east.

Battles on land continued until 1606, when the peace treaty of Zsitva Torok confirmed Ottoman rule over Romania, Hungary, and Transylvania, but recognized the Habsburgs as their equals. Financially and militarily drained by two centuries of warfare with the Habsburgs in the Balkans and southeastern Europe, the Ottomans halted their expansion into these areas in 1606. In 1683, a last attempt to seize Vienna failed. North of the Black Sea, where Russia, Poland, and the Ottomans fought, the empire had greater success, taking control of substantial parts of the Ukraine in 1676. These victories, however, marked the maximum extent of Ottoman dominance in the region. Russia, its military power built under Peter the Great and consolidated under Catherine the Great, pushed the Ottomans back. Throughout the late 1700s, the

Ottomans once again brought in Western European experts to retrain their military, as they had in capturing Constantinople, but this effort was too little, too late. The Ottoman Empire had fallen too far behind the Western Europeans and the Russians economically and militarily; they could no longer catch up.

Through both immigration and natural increase, the population of the Ottoman Empire seems to have more than doubled, from 12–13 million in 1520–30 in the early years of the rule of Suleiman I (a time when Spain may have had 5 million inhabitants; England 2.5 million; Portugal 1 million) to 17–18 million in 1580, to possibly 30–35 million by 1600 (Braudel, *The Mediterranean*, Vol. 1, p. 410). This doubling, or even tripling, of the empire's population was consistent with the general population increase of the Mediterranean basin, which rose from about 30 or 35 million in 1500 to 60 to 70 million in 1600.

CONNECTION: *The Ottoman Empire, 1829–76,* pp. 541–2

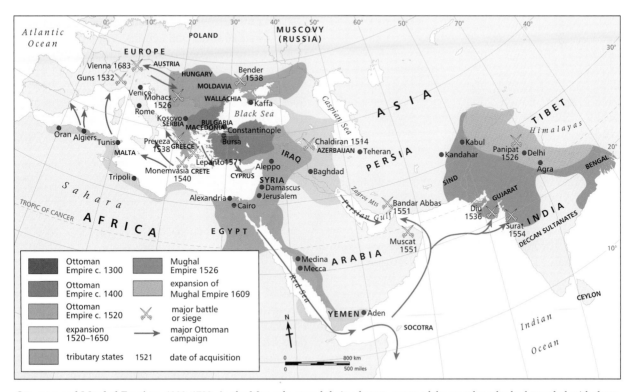

Ottoman and Mughal Empires, 1300–1700 As the Mongols ceased their advance, some of the peoples who had traveled with them began to assert their power. The Ottoman Turks began to establish their new empire, which conquered Constantinople in 1453 and thrust into southeastern Europe as well as the Mediterranean coast. Babur, a Mughal, began the conquest of India in 1526 and his grandson Akbar proceeded to construct one of the largest, most powerful, and most cultured empires of his day.

INDIA: THE MUGHAL EMPIRE
1526–1750

The Mughals, a mixture of Mongol and Turkish peoples from Central Asia, rose to power a little later than the Ottomans, beginning their invasion of India in 1526. Under four generations of commanding emperors—Akbar (r. 1556–1605; see Profile opposite), Jehangir (r. 1605–27), Shah Jahan (r. 1627–58), and Aurangzeb (r. 1658–1707)—they dominated most of the subcontinent, ruling it from splendid capitals that they built in the north, and from mobile tent-cities that they occupied while fighting throughout the subcontinent. Although they continued to rule in name until 1858, the Mughals began to decline as a result of Aurangzeb's extended military campaigns which wasted the financial and human resources of his empire, and also antagonized the Hindu majority population over whom the Mughals, who were Muslims, ruled.

The Mughals were only the most recent of peoples to invade India. From prehistoric times, India had experienced wave after wave of immigration. Most of the migrants arrived from the northwest, crossing the passes between today's Afghanistan and Pakistan. The Indo-Aryans, who established the cultural and social foundations of the subcontinent, arrived via this route about 1700 B.C.E (see pp. 77–85 and 232–5). The archaeological evidence as well as their literature suggest that they fought and conquered the resident people of the Indus Valley civilization. Greeks, Scythians, and Huns were among the later immigrant groups who also crossed the passes to make India their home (see p. 246).

In 711–713, in an exception to the usual pattern, Muslim Arabs invaded along the Makran Coast of the Arabian Sea, and conquered and settled Sind. But the overwhelming Muslim invasions came overland through the mountain passes from Afghanistan. The Muslim sultan in Afghanistan, Mahmud of Ghazna (971–1030), began the Muslim conquest of India about the year 1000 C.E. A dynasty from Ghur followed in 1186, and one of its generals conquered Delhi in 1206, declaring himself the Sultan of Delhi and beginning three hundred years of the Delhi sultanate. His dynasty and its successors were of the Afghan Turkish elite. The problem for all these rulers, and perhaps for the subcontinent to this day, was how to integrate into a single, stable society the Turkish warlords; the accompanying Muslim scholars, bureaucrats, and holy men;

and the Hindu majority population that often resisted the invaders.

In 1523 Babur (Zahir-ud-Din Mohammad, 1483–1530), a descendant of Timur on his father's side and of Genghis Khan on his mother's side, invaded India and conquered the Delhi rulers. In 1526 he established himself as Sultan. His son, Humayan, was defeated in battles with Afghans and driven out of India, but he fought his way back through Afghanistan and into north India before his death. The task of continuing the conquest and consolidating its administration fell to Humayun's son Akbar (1542–1605), perhaps India's greatest ruler.

In a half century of rule, 1556–1605, Akbar established one of the great empires of the world. He extended his dominions over about two-thirds of the subcontinent—from his northwestern base in Afghanistan, Kashmir, Punjab, and the upper Ganges, southward to encompass Rajasthan and Gujarat, and eastward all the way through Bengal. His great-grandson, and third successor, Aurangzeb (Alamgir, 1658–1707), continued the conquest almost to the southern tip of the country. But Aurangzeb forsook Akbar's tolerance. He imposed a poll tax on Hindus and desecrated their shrines and statues, antagonizing them and fomenting resentment. Aurangzeb's military adventures in the south overextended his armies and overtaxed the peasantry to the point of revolt. Hindu Marathas in western India and Sikhs in the north, as well as the Afghan Nadir Shah, who invaded from Iran in 1739, rose against the Mughal Empire. By the middle of the eighteenth century, the empire lay weak and open to new invaders from Western Europe— the British and the French.

CONNECTION: *India, 1858–1914, pp. 543–4*

AKBAR'S REIGN:
HOW DO WE KNOW?

A Muslim ruling over a vast Hindu majority, Akbar incorporated into his military leadership many Hindu **rajas**, and brought into his harem the daughters of many Rajput rulers. Two-thirds of his civil and military officers were foreigners: Afghans, Turks, Iranians, Arabs, and others. Between 20 and 25 percent of India's population became Muslim, most through conversion, the rest the result of immigration from outside. The popular religious culture of India, especially of north India, became

PROFILE *Akbar*

WINNING AND KEEPING AN EMPIRE

Born in 1542, Akbar was reared in exile with his father, the Mughal ruler Humayun, in the rugged terrain of Afghanistan. His childhood was dominated by physical pursuits, and he grew up without learning to read and write, although he loved to have others read to him. Akbar's father Humayun succeeded in returning to India and re-establishing his authority in Delhi when he fell down a staircase and died. Akbar acceded to the throne at age fourteen.

Four years later, he began to govern on his own as absolute monarch. Raised on stories of his ancestors Timur the Lame and Genghis Khan, and of his grandfather Babur who had established Mughal rule in north India, Akbar now set about creating an empire of his own. He showed no mercy to those who would not submit to his rule. In 1568 protracted fighting in the Mewar district culminated in a siege of the historic fortress of Chitor and ultimately the massacre of its entire population of 30,000 inhabitants. In 1572 Akbar conquered Gujarat, gaining control of its commercial networks and its resources of cotton and indigo. Then came Bengal to the north, with its rice, silk, and saltpeter. Kashmir to the north, Orissa to the south, and Sind to the west followed. Each new conquest brought greater riches. With his minister Todar Mal, Akbar established a system of bureaucratic administration based on land control and systematic assessment that endured throughout Mughal times and even into the British period. Mughal officials, aware that their wealth would revert to the emperor at death, lived a life of lavish consumption.

Sixteenth-century engraving of Akbar.

Akbar understood immediately that as a foreigner and a Muslim in an overwhelmingly Hindu country, he would have to temper conquest with conciliation. He allowed the fiercely independent Hindu Rajputs, who controlled the hilly territory of Rajasthan, to keep their ancestral lands and he offered them roles in his government and armies. In return they paid tribute to him, supplied him with troops, and gave him their daughters in marriage alliances. He appointed Hindus to a third of the posts in his centralized administration, although two-thirds went to Muslims who immigrated in large numbers from Iran, Afghanistan, and Central Asia to the expanding Mughal court. In 1562 Akbar discontinued the practice of enslaving prisoners of war and forcing them to convert to Islam. In 1563 he abolished a tax on Hindu pilgrims traveling to sacred shrines. The next year, most importantly, he revoked the *jizya*, the head tax levied on non-Muslims.

He encouraged and participated personally in religious discussions among Muslims, Hindus, Parsis, and Christians. Indeed, Jesuits mistook his enquiries into Catholic doctrine as a willingness to convert. In 1582 he declared a new personal religion, the Din-i-Ilahi, or Divine Faith, an amalgam of Islamic, Hindu, and Parsi perspectives. He also incorporated some concepts of Divine Rights, declaring himself the vice-Regent of God and appointing himself ultimate arbiter on disputes concerning Islamic law. Elaborate ceremonials at court emphasized the emperor's supremacy, and he was careful to encourage reverence among the common people as well. Orthodox Muslims saw Akbar's pronouncements as heresies and went into opposition. Several were jailed.

During a reign which spanned half a century, Akbar presided over a glittering court, in which the fine arts, literature, and architecture flourished. He transformed himself from conquering despot of a foreign religious minority to respected emperor of all Hindustan.

Abul-Fazl presenting his book of the Akbarnama to Akbar, c. 1600. Surrounded by his courtiers, the emperor Akbar receives from his principal administrator, Abul-Fazl, the Akbarnama, an array of Mughal miniature paintings which illustrate the military, diplomatic, economic, and administrative life of Akbar's empire and government. Note the diversity in appearance and dress of the courtiers. Abul-Fazl himself was an Indian Muslim educated in Persian fashion, while Akbar was a soldier of Turkish and Mongol descent. At its best, such diversity was a mark of strength in the Mughal court. (*Chester Beatty Library, Dublin*)

MIGRATION 1370–1930

1370–1405	Timur the Lame's victories over Iran, northern India, Anatolia, and northern Syria
c. 1450	Portugal begins to trade in slaves from the West African coast
1500–1888	About 9.6 million slaves are transported to the Americas
1521–35	Hernán Cortés captures most of Mesoamerica and the Yucatán for Spain
1533	Francisco Pizarro defeats Incas; establishes Spanish colony in South America
1565–1605	Akbar establishes Mughal Empire, gaining dominion over two-thirds of India
1600	Ottoman Empire population (c. 30–35 million) has more than doubled in sixty years
1619	First African slaves brought to British North America
1620	*Mayflower* sets sail for New World
c. 1640	Russia gains control over most of North Asia
1652	Dutch settlers set up a base at Cape Town, South Africa
1680–1800	Chinese imperial expansion to most of central Asia
1788	British settlement of Australia
1840	Britain annexes New Zealand
1820–1930	50 million Europeans migrate to North and South America, Australia, and New Zealand

a mixture of Hindu and Muslim practices. Sufis spread their message in Hindi, a modern derivative of Sanskrit, the sacred language of Hindus. At the same time they inspired the creation of the Urdu (camp) language, the language of common exchange between the invaders and the resident population. Urdu used the syntactical structure of Hindi, the alphabet of Arabic and Persian, and a vocabulary of words drawn from Sanskrit, Persian, and Arabic. Akbar, in particular, encouraged cultural **syncretism** and the mixing of groups. In his court, he encouraged representative spokesmen of numerous religions to explain and argue their doctrines; he incorporated Hindus into about one-fourth of his governmental positions; and he himself brought Hindu as well as Muslim brides into his harem.

A great conqueror, Akbar spent years on the move with his troops, but he also built new capitals for himself, first at Agra, later at Fatehpur Sikri nearby. With his chief revenue officer, Todar Mal, he established an administrative bureaucracy modeled on a military hierarchy. He surveyed each region of India down to the village level, evaluated its fertility, and thus established the land revenue each was to pay. His administrators collected the payment in cash. These reforms brought village India into a cash economy, while city markets encouraged the production of luxury goods for the court and everyday goods for the common people.

In 1600, at the height of Akbar's rule, the population of India was 140–150 million, with about 110 million contained within the Mughal Empire, about the same population as China and twice that of the Ottoman Empire at its largest. Irfan Habib, Professor of History at the Aligarh Muslim University, arrived at this estimate by analyzing land revenue records of the amount of land under cultivation, along with other records indicating the tax payments on agricultural production. He then estimated the number of persons needed to cultivate such amounts of land and raise crops of such value. The population increase that occurred all over Afro-Eurasia at this time affected India as well, and Habib estimates the population of the subcontinent in 1800 at about 200 million.

SAFAVID PERSIA
1400–1700

In the thirteenth century the Mongols and Turks first devastated and then repopulated Persia. At first the invaders systematically exterminated the populations of the cities they confronted; others, hearing of the massacres, fled. The invading Mongols and Turks then settled on the land, reduced to serfdom those who remained behind, and taxed them into poverty. By the end of the century, however, the invaders began to assimilate Persian ways, rebuilding the cities, redeveloping the irrigation works, supporting agriculture and trade, including the silk routes to China, and adopting both the religion of Islam and the culture of Persia, with its monarchical traditions.

In 1370 the successor to the Chaghatay branch of the Mongols, Timur the Lame (Tamerlane, as Europeans called him; c. 1336–1405) came to power, ruling Iran, and much of northern India, Anatolia, and northern Syria from his capital in Samarqand until his death in 1405. With this further set of invasions, Turkish peoples came to constitute about one-fourth of Iran's population, which is the ratio today. The Mongol/Turkish invaders were pastoral peoples, and under their rule substantial agricultural land reverted to pasturage and villagers turned to nomadic existences, farming in valley bottoms and herding sheep in nearby mountain highlands.

The Defeat of Pir Padishah by Shah Rukh in 1403, Persian, 1420–30. Shah Rukh, son of Timur the Lame, was a direct ancestor of the Safavid Persians. During his reign, he had to deal with several rebellions, including one by the Sarbadars, a brigand community in Khurasan. Leading the decisive charge, Shah Rukh's army commander beheads one of the rebel cavalrymen. (*Victoria & Albert Museum. London*)

Some of the Turks, as well as other ethnic groups in Iran, later came to accept the militantly religious teachings of Shaykh Safi al-Din (1252–1334). His followers, called **Safavids**, claimed political as well as religious authority. In 1501, a disciple of the teachings of Safi, Shah Isma'il (1487–1524) declared himself the hidden imam, the long-awaited political/religious messiah of Shi'ite Muslims. He occupied Tabriz and proclaimed himself the Shah of Iran.

The Safavids found it difficult to bring together the very diverse peoples and interests of Iran. The greatest achievement was by Shah Abbas (1588–1629), who built up the military capacity of the country. He did this, in part, by importing European weapons, equipment, technicians, and advisers. He acquired and built muskets and artillery that were capable of matching the Ottomans. Like other Safavid rulers, he brought slaves from Georgia, Armenia, and Turkish lands to form the core of his armies. Abbas also built a great, new capital city at Isfahan. He encouraged trade and commerce there by inviting Armenian merchants as well as many artisans, including ceramicists who could produce "Chinese" porcelains. He invited some Chinese potters to teach Iranians their trade, and some of them remained and settled in Isfahan. Abbas, however, murdered competing religious leaders and groups, including other Shi'a groups as well as Sunnis and Sufis. His successors in the middle of the century gave official sanction to efforts to convert both Jews and Zoroastrians to Islam by force. But they did not succeed in bringing all the powers of his decentralized realm into a centralized monarchy.

By the end of the seventeenth century, the Safavid army was unraveling, its central administration was failing, regional powers were reasserting themselves, and Iran was in anarchy. Despite the occasional brilliant military conqueror, such as Nadir Shah (1688–1747), another Turkish/Mongol immigrant who took the throne in 1736, Iran was already moving toward partition, first internally, and later at the hands of Europeans and Russians.

Attacks on the borders by land and sea. Through the fifteenth and sixteenth centuries, the Ming dynasty was bedeviled by raids and attacks from the Mongols and other barbarian peoples on China's northern frontiers. The Great Wall underwent major reconstruction in this period. Meanwhile coastal residents were forced to take to their boats to battle the pirates who attacked their settlements. (*Historiographical Institute, University of Tokyo*).

CHINA: THE MING AND MANCHU DYNASTIES 1368–1750

In 1211 Genghis Khan invaded and conquered China, destroying the Qin and Song dynasties in the process. His descendants established the Yuan dynasty, which ruled for a century (1271–1368) until the Ming dynasty drove them out and established its own long and successful rule (1368–1644). (See Chapter 12.)

By 1600 China's economy was flourishing and the country contained one-fifth of the world's population, about 150 million people. Ming border policy was to pacify and to accommodate the Mongol peoples of the north. The emperors stationed large numbers of troops there and rebuilt the Great Wall. Ming anxieties were well founded. In 1644 China was again conquered by invaders from the north, as the Jurchen, or Manchus, of Manchuria established a new dynasty, the Qing (1644–1911). The Manchu invasions undercut China's power and sophistication, and contributed—along with natural disasters, virulent epidemics, and the failure of irrigation systems—to a catastrophic fall in China's population. The Mandate of Heaven had surely passed from the Ming.

The Qing expanded the borders of China, more than doubling the size of the country. They conquered and controlled Tibet, Xinjiang, Outer Mongolia, and the Tarim Basin, the heartland of the old silk routes. One of their most important European contacts was with Russia, and disputes between the two empires were negotiated in the Treaty of Nerchinsk, 1689, the first Chinese–European treaty negotiated on terms of equality. The treaty facilitated trade between China and Russia and delimited their border along the Amur River, although the border between Mongolia and Siberia was not fixed.

The country's population began to grow again in the eighteenth century. This was made possible by the introduction of new crops into China from the New World. Sweet potatoes, for example, were widespread in coastal China by the mid-eighteenth century, while maize and the Irish potato became common in the north and in the southwest at the same time. Peanuts had spread rapidly in south and southwestern China in the late Ming, and were also becoming an important crop in north China by the end of Qianlong's reign (r. 1736–95). All these crops helped to improve the health of China's rural workers and, because the crops also grew well even in poor and hilly land, they enabled the population to increase rapidly.

GLOBAL POPULATION GROWTH AND SHIFT

From 1500–1750 internal developments within Europe began to increase its influence in the world.

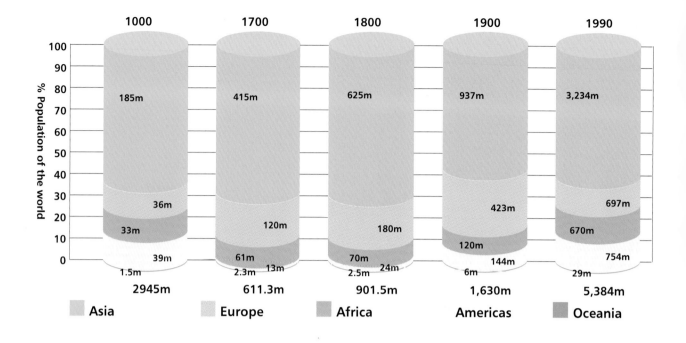

	1000	1700	1800	1900	1990
Asia	185m	415m	625m	937m	3,234m
Europe	36m	120m	180m	423m	697m
Africa	33m	61m	70m	120m	670m
Americas	39m	13m	24m	144m	754m
Oceania	1.5m	2.3m	2.5m	6m	29m
	2945m	611.3m	901.5m	1,630m	5,384m

% Population of the world

Asia   Europe   Africa   Americas   Oceania

FOCUS

Fernand Braudel and The Annales School of History

The historian's task of gathering data often requires long hours of solitary research industy archives. But in evaluating and interpreting these data, historians engage one another, and sometimes the general public, in discussion and debate. In these processes they sometimes form into "schools," groups of historians who share common perspectives in terms of problems to be addressed or interpretative frameworks to be employed. Some perspectives are so widely shared that they are too large to be labeled as a single school, for example feminist readings that stress the importance of gender relations or Marxist readings that stress the importance of class. Sometimes, however, "schools" form around groups of perhaps five to fifty historians.

In the closing years of the nineteenth century social scientists in France such as the sociologist Emile Durkheim and the geographer Paul Vidal de La Blanche emphasized the potentials of interdisciplinary study. Each discipline would add its special insights to research on a common problem. Lucien Febvre (1878–1956) and Marc Bloch (1886–1944) built on this perspective in creating the *Annales* school. Both emphasized interdisciplinary study: geography; *mentalités*, the collective perspective of masses of people; and the balance between the individual and the entire society. Both minimized what most other historians of the time considered the core of the discipline: political history, biography, and international relations.

Febvre's greatest disciple, Fernand Braudel (1902–85), helped administer the Centre des Recherches Historiques (established by Febvre) and publish the journal. After Febvre's death in 1956, Braudel succeeded him in the leadership of both institutions.

Braudel's first great historical work was his study of *The Mediterranean and the Mediterranean World in the Age of Philip II*, in two volumes, first published in 1949. Here Braudel worked out in practice his concept of three time frames always operating simultaneously: most

World population totals and distribution: In the last 1,000 years, the world's population has multiplied twenty times from less than 300 million to 6,000 million (the United Nations estimate as of October 1999). Moreover, the distribution of that population by geographical origins has shifted. For most of the millennium, the proportion of people in Europe grew fastest, but in the last century, that trend reversed. Since 1900, the percentage of people in Africa, the Americas, and Oceania has grown fastest. The decline in population in the Americas, 1000–1700, represents the death of American Indians; the rise after 1700 represents, in large part, immigration from Europe and Africa. In all time periods Asia has held by far the largest proportion of the world's population.

Many of these developments were discussed in Chapter 13:

- changing balances of trade;

- increasing powers of the traders in the diaspora cities of trade around the globe;

- increasing power of European nation states and their support for overseas trade;

- shifting of trade to the Atlantic (rather than the Indian Ocean);

- increasing pace of technological invention in Europe, especially in guns and ships;

- increasing discipline and order within European armies;

- importing of immense quantities of gold and silver from the New World;

- exploiting the labor of millions of slaves taken from Africa to work the plantations of the New World;

- and the inspirational message of aggressive Christianity.

---

deeply rooted, the *longue durée*, extending back even to geologic time and establishing the fundamental conditions of material life, states of mind, natural environment, and geography; the middle time frame of social, economic, and political organization; and the short term, the time of an individual life, the time frame of most conventional historical study of events, or *l'histoire événementielle*. Implementing this concept of diverse time frames, Braudel begins with the physical and human geography of the Mediterranean basin, goes on to its political systems, and ends with the specific policies of Philip II and other rulers of his time. His work revolutionized the way many historians understood their discipline.

For our own purposes in this chapter, Braudel's three-volume study of *Civilization and Capitalism: 15th–18th Century* (1967–79) is even more important. The first volume sets out such issues of the *longue durée* as global population figures; the everyday food that people ate in different parts of the world; the houses they lived in, the clothes they wore, the fashions they affected; the technology they used; their money and media of exchange; and the cities they built and used. Volume two focusses principally on economic systems, especially in Europe, and, by comparison, elsewhere as well. Volume three follows the transformations of that economy from the establishment of a capitalist system of trade through the beginning of the industrial revolution. Braudel gives us a history of the economy of the world as an integrated whole, though clearly from a European focus. In both of these major works, Braudel omitted the study of popular attitudes, *mentalités*, so important to his mentors Febvre and Bloch, and only in the second edition (1966) did he employ quantification as a significant tool.

Some of the school's influences have been noted in Chapter 13, for example K.N. Chaudhuri's analyses of Indian Ocean trade, so reminiscent of Braudel's studies of the Mediterranean; Immanuel Wallerstein's studies of the World-System, following Braudel's researches in the global spread of capitalism; and the volumes on merchant trade and empires edited by James Tracy, which build on both studies. Today the school has a multitude of international links with cultural historians such as Peter Burke, Robert Darnton, Natalie Zemon Davis, Carlo Ginzburg, and Lawrence Stone. The influence of the school has spread in the English-speaking world especially since the translation of Braudel's *Mediterranean* in 1972. By now, the contributors to and readers of the *Annales* are so diverse and so integrated with other forms of interdisiplinary history that they have outgrown their distinction as a separate school.

Here, however, our emphasis is on the sheer demographic force of numbers in European expansion, and the creation of "New Europes" worldwide. The shifting weight of numbers helped cause, and also reflected, the shifting power relationships.

Demographers estimate that Europe's population more than tripled between 1000 and 1700, with the greatest growth coming after the Black Death of 1348–51. The plague killed off perhaps a third of Europe's population, but it soon increased again to its former levels and then continued to multiply. The "New World" across the Atlantic provided a new home to some of the increased millions.

Meanwhile, the population of Asia held its own, while that of Africa was reduced, in part by the loss of some 10 million slaves. The native populations of the Americas were decimated, with up to 90 percent of the native Indian populations lost, although numbers were slowly augmented by European migrants. In the most sweeping terms, and based on very high levels of guesswork, the demographic shift in regions of the world is represented by the pie charts on page 454.

Asia held about two-thirds of the world's population, with the proportion actually growing from 63 percent to 69 percent of the total between 1000 and 1800. Europeans, however, increased even faster. They multiplied not only within Europe but, in the words of Alfred Crosby, a leading scholar on the demographic effects of European expansion, they also "leapfrogged around the globe [to found] Neo-Europes, lands thousands of kilometers from Europe and from each other" (Crosby, p. 2). In 1800 North America held almost five million whites, South America about 500,000, Australia 10,000, and New Zealand a few thousand. "These numbers were not yet very large, but they laid the foundation for 'the deluge.' Between 1820 and 1930, well over fifty million Europeans migrated to the Neo-European lands overseas ... approximately one-fifth of the entire population of Europe at the beginning of that period" (Crosby, p. 5). The number of peoples of European ancestry who settled outside Europe grew from 5.7 million in 1810 to 200 million in 1910. These nineteenth-century figures take us into the times of the Industrial Revolution and its massive transformations, which are covered in the next part (see p. 530), but the demographic spread across the world had already begun by 1800.

The expansion of Europe was not unique in world history, yet it was probably the most numerically sizeable and geographically widespread mass migration ever seen; a migration across vast expanses of water; creating permanent links among continents of the world that had been almost entirely separate; and bringing European dominion over three continents besides its own.

THE EXPANSION OF EUROPE 1096–1750

Some historians trace the modern emigration of Europeans outward for purposes of conquest and settlement back to the series of Crusades that lasted from 1096 until just after the last crusader kingdom was destroyed in 1291. Those expeditions were launched for religious purposes: to seize and settle the "Holy Land." Trade, however, was another important factor. Along with the military campaigns, Europeans established commercial centers astride the land and sea silk routes to China and on the coast of Africa, where European textiles and metal products were exchanged for gold and slaves. Most of these European settlements also housed at least some missionaries.

As we have seen in Chapter 13, in the sixteenth century both Spain and Portugal built enormous global empires. The voyages of Columbus revealed gold and silver reserves in the Americas and many Europeans who followed him were prepared to kill Native Americans and to take over their lands. Cortés conquered the Aztec nation of Mexico in 1519 and Pizarro the Incas in 1533. The death and destruction were monumental, but warfare was not the greatest killer; disease was even more deadly (see Focus, opposite).

By the early 1600s, however, Spanish supremacy was being challenged by the Dutch Republic, England, and France. All three had developed expertise in the construction of high quality ships, and all three fostered business groups skilled in trade and motivated by profit, with strong ties to political leadership. At first, all three concentrated on the Caribbean, and its potential for profits from plantations. They seized and settled outposts: England most notably in the Bahamas and Jamaica, France in Saint-Domingue (today's Haiti), and the Dutch along the Brazilian coast and in Curaçao. Later they turned to the North American mainland.

NORTH AMERICA

North America had its own attractions for farmers, artisans, laborers, and agricultural workers who

FOCUS

The Columbian Exchanges of Plants, Animals, and Disease

The peoples of the eastern and western hemispheres had no sustained contact for thousands of years. Columbus's voyages therefore ushered in a new era of interaction. This "Columbian Exchange" brought in its wake both catastrophe and new opportunities. The catastrophe befell the Amerindians who had no resistance to the diseases carried by the Europeans. The new opportunities came with the intercontinental exchange of new plants and animals. Historian Alfred Crosby evaluates both sets of consequences, following the systematic efforts begun by the "Berkeley School" in the 1930s.

Crosby cites the lowest currently accepted estimate of the Amerindian population of 1492 as 33 million, the highest as perhaps 50 million. By comparison, Europe at the time had a population of 80 million. The death of millions of Amerindians followed almost immediately after Europeans began to arrive. At their lowest points after the coming of Europeans, the populations of the western hemisphere dropped to 4.5 million. "The conclusion must be that the major initial effect of the Columbian voyages was the transformation of America into a charnel house" (Crosby, p. 160).

The biggest killers were not guns, but diseases: smallpox, measles, whooping cough, chicken pox, bubonic plague, malaria, diphtheria, amoebic dysentery, and influenza. The populations of the New World, separated by thousands of years and thousands of miles from those of the Old, had little resistance to its diseases. Up to 90 percent of the population died.

Ironically, and more happily, links between the hemispheres also brought an exchange of food sources, which later facilitated the multiplication of human lives. From South America, the cassava spread to Africa and Asia and the white potato to northern Europe. Sweet potatoes traveled to China as did maize, of which China is today the second largest producer after the United States. Today, the former Soviet Union produces ten times more potatoes by weight than does South America; Africa produces almost twice as much cassava as does South America.

The migration of flora and fauna went from east to west as well. Wheat was the leading Old World crop to come to the New World, but perhaps an even greater contribution came in domesticated animals: cattle, sheep, pigs, and goats. Domesticated horses, too, were imported from the Old World to the New. In the long run, these exchanges of food sources did much to increase the population of the world more than ten times, from about 500 million in 1492 to about 6 billion today. But not everyone participated in this growth. There were demographic winners and losers. Peoples of the European continent in 1492 were the biggest winners; Asians generally did well; Amerindians were among the biggest losers.

came to settle. Some of the earliest settlers were pushed out of Europe by the "price revolution" created by the availability of New World silver. The influx of the precious metal into Europe, and into the European trade networks in Asia, inflated prices; wages did not keep pace. People living at the margins of European society sought the opportunity of new frontiers in North America.

Later, through the seventeenth and early eighteenth centuries, the European invaders into the New World came in different waves and appropriated different regions for their purposes. In Virginia they came at first looking for gold, beaver furs, deer skin, and a northwest passage to Asia. They failed in these goals, and at first they failed even to survive. Of the first 900 colonists arriving 1607–09, only sixty were alive at the end of the two years. Some 9000 came between 1610 and 1622; at the later date, only 2000 were alive. After 1618 the crown-appointed administrators of the colony offered fifty acres to any settler who would come, and by this date Virginia's tobacco crop became the staple product of its economy. Settlers continued to come, but the life was difficult, attractive mostly to people of the lower social classes. Many signed on as indentured laborers, three-fourths of them male, and most aged between fifteen and twenty-four. Since their masters cared little for them, they were bought and sold, and often worked to death, not much different than slaves. With life so cheap, at the whim of both man and nature, the massacre of Native Americans, who were seen as alien, savage, non-Christian, and an obstacle to European invasion and expansion, became a way of life for the land-hungry settlers.

Maryland also grew tobacco, but its goals included more than mere economic profit. The land had been given by the British crown to George Calvert, Lord Baltimore, and he established here a religious refuge for Catholics, an oppressed minority in England. Catholics formed a minority of the population of the colony, but they were legally protected. Their relationships with the Native Americans, however, were also murderous.

In New England, the first collective settlement of Europeans was the Pilgrim colony founded in 1620. Dissenters from the official doctrines of the Church of England, the Pilgrims also sought a religious haven in the New World. Their community was bound together by the Mayflower Compact, an agreement they drafted on board ship to the New World, establishing a governing body "for the general good of the colony; unto which, we promise all due submission and obedience." Of the 102 Pilgrims who landed at Plymouth, fewer than half survived the first year, but with the help of Native Americans who befriended the settlers, the colony took root.

In 1630 a new group of settlers, the Puritans, arrived in New England. The Pilgrims wished to separate from the Church of England; the Puritans wished only to purify it. They were richer and better educated than the Pilgrims. Many had some college education. King Charles I, eager to get them out of England, gave them a charter to establish the

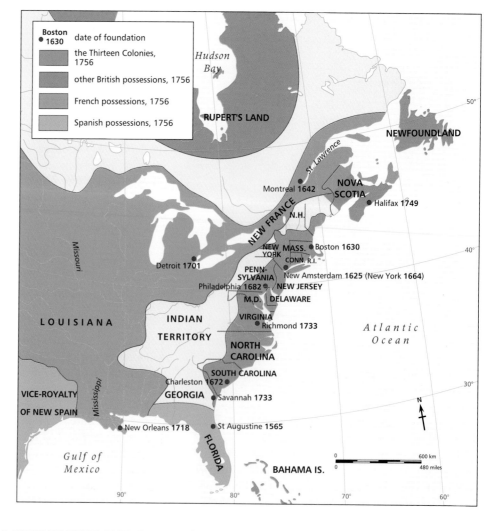

European settlement in eastern North America. Along the Atlantic coast of North America, Britain established an array of colonies. Thirteen of them revolted in 1776 to form the United States, but the northern areas remained loyal. The British restricted settlement across the Appalachian Mountains so that land was held by Indian nations and, still further west, claimed by the French. Florida was held by the British, 1763–83, but otherwise was a Spanish possession until invaded and conquered by the US in 1818.

EUROPEAN MIGRATION TO NORTH AMERICA

1565	Spanish settle in Florida
1604	Nova Scotia settled by French
1607	First permanent English settlement at Jamestown, Virginia
1608	"New France" in Canada settled by French
1611	Dutch settle on Manhattan Island
1620	*Mayflower* sails from Plymouth, England, with Pilgrim Fathers to found first colony in New England, at Plymouth, Massachusetts
1622	Maine settled by English
1624	New York settled by Dutch
1630	Massachusetts settled by Massachusetts Bay Co.
1634	English Catholics found Maryland
1635–8	Connecticut settled by English
1638	Rhode Island settled by groups from Massachusetts
1638	Delaware settled by Swedes
1663	Carolina settled by English
1670	Rupert's Land claimed by Hudson Bay Co.
1681	Pennsylvania settled by English Quakers
1682	French claim Mississippi area
1713	British sovereignty over Newfoundland recognized

flee. The Puritans were narrow in their outlook, but fiercely devoted to community, discipline, work, education, and spreading their view of religion. They scorned Indians, fought them, and confiscated their land with little compunction.

The Dutch had settled the area around New Amsterdam until the British seized it in 1664 and, after a brief loss, recaptured it in 1673. The British renamed it New York, and the area developed its own polyglot, pragmatic, tolerant business ethic instituted by the Dutch.

Perhaps the most inspiring settlement was the Quaker colony of Pennsylvania founded by William Penn, a British aristocrat who had joined the Society of Friends, as Quakers were called formally, inspired by a lecture on the Society's basic principles of freedom of conscience, non-violence, and **pacifism**. Pennsylvania and its first capital, Philadelphia (whose name means "brotherly love"), became known throughout western Europe for its religious toleration and people of many countries and faiths immigrated here: English, Scots, French, Germans, Irish, Welsh, Swedes, Finns, and Swiss; Mennonites, Lutherans, Dutch Reformed, Baptists, Anglicans, Presbyterians, Catholics, Jews, and a few hermits and mystics (Nash, p. 59). Indeed, even Native Americans immigrated to flee the violence against them that was endemic elsewhere. Unfortunately the non-Quaker immigrant-invaders did not share Penn's early commitment to tolerant, peaceful inter-racial relationships with the Native

Puritans arrive in New England. Religious freedom and economic opportunity were the two great attractions for European immigrants to the New World. Many of the immigrants from England were dissenters from the established official church. Their independence was a background factor that later helped to inspire the American Revolution in 1776. Some of the dissenters, however, like the Puritans, were themselves intolerant toward others who settled in their communities, forcing them to conform or to leave.

Company of the Massachusetts Bay. By the end of the year 1000 had settled; within a decade, 20,000. Many more emigrated to the sugar plantations of the Caribbean islands.

The Puritans had left England for their own religious freedom, but they now denied it to others. People like Roger Williams, a minister who wanted the separation of Church and state, were forced to

Americans, regulated by legal contracts and personal contacts. After Penn's death, they too pushed Indians off the land, although with less violence than elsewhere.

While the British founded numerous, diverse, thriving colonies along the Atlantic Coast, from Newfoundland to South Carolina, and inland on Hudson's Bay, the French settled, lightly, the inland waterways of the St. Lawrence River, the Great Lakes, and the Mississippi River, as well as Gulf Coast Louisiana. During the global warfare between Britain and France, the Seven Years' War of 1756–63, British military forces conquered the North American mainland from the Atlantic to the Mississippi. Their victory ensured that North America would be English speaking. French cultural influences and migration, however, continued strong in the region of Quebec, and have maintained a French-speaking province there until today. By 1750, about four million people of European origin inhabited North America.

THE ANTIPODES: AUSTRALIA AND NEW ZEALAND 1600–1900

Crossing the Atlantic became relatively quick and easy, but reaching Australia and New Zealand, on the opposite side of the globe, was quite a different matter. Even their neighbors had established only minimal contacts with them. There had been some landings by Asians in the sixteenth century. They came to the north coast in search of a sea slug, which looked like a withered penis when smoked and dried and which was Indonesia's largest export to the Chinese, who valued the slugs as an aphrodisiac.

Spanish copies of Portuguese charts suggest that Portuguese sailors had landed on and mapped the northern and eastern coasts of Australia, and that the Spanish may have known about them, but no continuing contact resulted. In the early 1600s, a few Dutch sailors reached parts of the coast, several wrecking their ships in the process. Between 1642 and 1644, under commission from the Dutch East India Company, the Dutch commander Abel Tasman (c. 1605–59) began the systematic exploration of New Zealand, the island that was later named Tasmania, and the north coast of Australia. He reported "naked beach-roving wretches, destitute even of rice … miserably poor, and in many places of a very bad disposition" (cited in Hughes, p. 48). With such unpromising descriptions reaching England, and the general decline of Spanish, Dutch, and Portuguese power, Australia remained virtually untouched by Europeans for a century and a half, and the pattern of immigration from Europe lags behind the pattern going to the Western hemisphere by a similar amount of time.

In 1768, the English Captain James Cook (1728–79) set out on a three-year voyage, which took him to Tahiti to take astronomical observations; to Australia to determine the nature of the

Captain James Cook's crew refitting H.M.S. *Endeavour* **at the Endeavour River on the East Coast of Australia, June 1770**. In the course of his great explorations of the South Pacific Ocean, Cook made the first European landing on Australia, which he claimed for Britain under the name of New South Wales. Convicts were later banished in droves to the new colony to ease overcrowding in British jails.

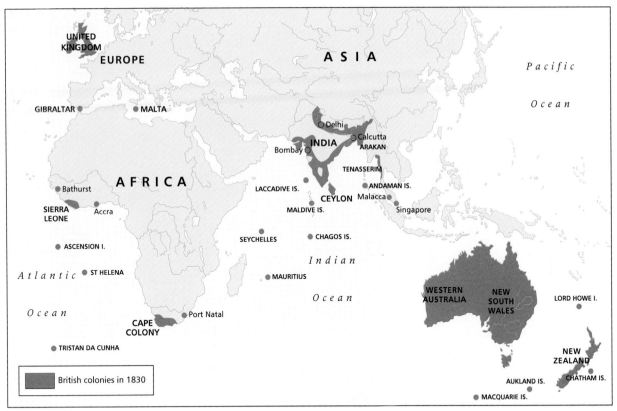

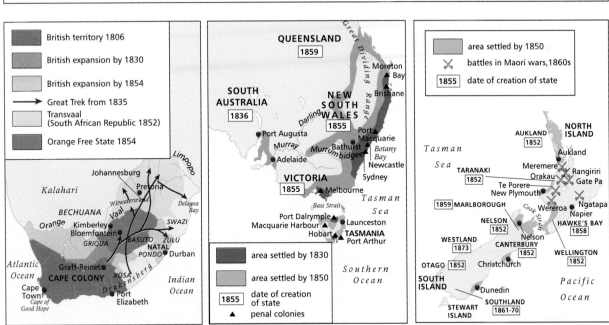

British settlement in Australia, New Zealand, and South Africa British expansion in the scramble for empire, driven by land hunger and mineral wealth, was unparalleled. Outside the riches of India, British colonists ousted the Dutch from Cape Colony, grasped the habitable littoral of southeast Australia (initially colonizing it with prisoners and other social outcasts), and laid claim to the world's most southerly inhabitable territory, New Zealand, as a promised land for its burgeoning early nineteenth-century population.

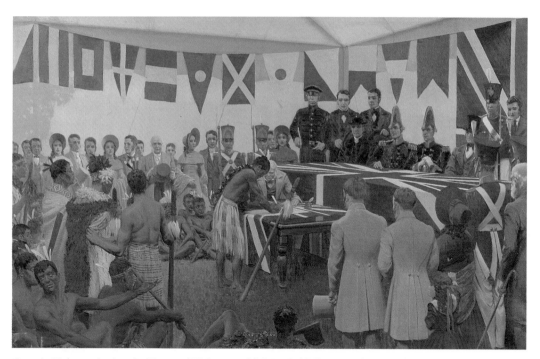

Captain Hobson signing the Treaty of Waitanga with Maori chiefs, 1840. The treaty was intended to secure the annexation of New Zealand to the British government, while guaranteeing the constitutional rights of the Maoris. But language difficulties and cultural differences caused misinterpretation of the fine print and the settlers' sense of racial superiority over the "natives" eventually precipitated wars and the forfeiture of Maori lands.

"Southern Continent" reported by Tasman; to map New Zealand; and, thanks to the zeal of a young amateur botanist, Joseph Banks, to report on the natural resources of all these distant lands. The success of Cook's three-year voyage was made possible by discoveries of proper food supplements to prevent scurvy among the sailors and of new instrumentation to chart longitude and thus establish location at sea. Cook's descriptions of the people he encountered in Australia differed markedly from those of Tasman:

> in reality they are far happier than we Europeans, being wholly unacquainted not only with the superfluous but the necessary conveniencies so much sought after in Europe, they are happy in not knowing the use of them. They live in tranquility which is not disturb'd by the Inequality of Condition. (Hughes, p. 54)

On the basis of Cook's report, the British government decided that Australia could serve as the "dumping ground" it had been seeking for the prisoners who were overcrowding the jails at home. British settlement in Australia thus began in the form of penal colonies, first at Botany Bay and then at other points along the southeast coast, the best watered and most fertile part of Australia. Because mountains flanked close against the coast and fresh water was scarce, progress inland was problematic, and settlement by Europeans was slow, based on commercial agriculture in wool, dairy cattle, and sugar cultivation. In the 1850s and again in the 1890s, however, gold was discovered and newcomers rushed in. The advent of faster shipping stimulated wheat exports, and refrigeration increased the frozen meat trade after 1880. Even so, the population in 1861 was only 1,200,000; by 1901 it had climbed to 3,800,000.

The coming of Europeans, even in small numbers, destroyed the fragile ecology of aboriginal civilization. It survived only in the center and far north of the continent. In 1788, when Europeans first arrived to settle Australia, there had been perhaps 300,000 aborigines. By 2000, the 19 million inhabitants of Australia were 92 percent European, 7 percent Asian, 1 percent aboriginal (*New York Times 2000 Almanac*, p. 532). Today, most of Australia's 50,000 full-blooded aborigines, and many of its 150,000 part-aborigines live on reservations in arid inland regions.

The devastation caused by the arrival of British settlers was repeated in New Zealand. The Maori, an East Polynesian people, had arrived and settled in New Zealand about 750 C.E. They had lived there for almost a thousand years, probably in isolation, until Tasman, sailing past Australia, reached New Zealand's west coast in 1642. The Maori killed four members of his party and prevented his landing. On his voyage more than a century later, James Cook further explored New Zealand for four months and found the Maori brave, warlike, and cannabalistic. Joseph Banks, the botanist who was on the voyage, wrote: "I suppose they live intirely [sic] on fish, dogs, and enemies" (Hughes, p. 52).

The people may have been fierce, but the seals and whales in the coastal waters, and the flax and timber on land, attracted hunters and traders from Australia, America, and Britain. The first missionaries came in 1814 to convert the Maori. Warfare against and among the Maori was made more deadly by weapons introduced by Europeans. Diseases accompanying the European arrival, especially tuberculosis, venereal diseases, and measles, cut the Maori population from about 200,000 when Cook arrived to perhaps 100,000 in 1840 and to 42,000 by the end of the century. In 1840, British settlers signed a treaty with a group of Maori chiefs that gave sovereignty to the British crown. Although they declared equal rights under law for Maoris and Europeans, in practice they enforced racial inequality. The British confiscated Maori lands on North Island and precipitated wars that drove the Maori from some of New Zealand's richest lands.

SOUTH AFRICA 1652–1902

The first European settlers were sent to South Africa by the Dutch East India Company in 1652 to set up a base at Cape Town for shipping between Europe and Asia. The Company soon invited Dutch, French, and German settlers to move inland and to establish ranches in Cape Colony. By 1700, the Europeans held most of the good farmland in the region; by 1795, they had spread 300 miles (480 kilometers) north and 500 miles (800 kilometers) east of Cape Town. The colony then had a total population of 60,000, of which one-third were whites. Most of the African peoples were of two main ethnic groups—the Khoikhoi herdsmen and the San hunters—with some slaves from other African groups, and some peoples of mixed ancestry.

In 1795, the British took control of the Cape Colony from its Dutch settlers to prevent it from falling to France, which had conquered Holland during the Wars of the French Revolution (see

pp. 495–501). In 1814, the Dutch formally gave the Cape to the British, and the first British colonists arrived in 1820. The continuing struggle for land and power among the British, Dutch, and Africans is discussed in Chapter 16.

SLAVERY: ENFORCED MIGRATION 1500–1750

Most of the migrations of Europeans discussed so far were of free peoples, who moved by choice. But throughout the seventeenth and eighteenth centuries, Africa contributed more immigrants to the New World than did Europe. These Africans came as slaves, taken as captives and transported against their will (see Spotlight, pp. 466–7).

The slave trade was not new. As we have seen in Chapter 12, camel caravans had carried gold and slaves northward across the Sahara, and European cotton and woolen textiles, copper, and brass southward from the Mediterranean since about the seventh century C.E. On its east coast, Africa had been long integrated into the Indian Ocean trade by Muslim and Arab traders. They exported from Africa gold, slaves, ivory, and amber and imported cotton and silk cloth.

Portuguese and later European trading reoriented the trade routes of Africa to the Atlantic coast. Caravans continued to cross the desert, but far more trade now came to the new coastal town fortresses, which were constructed at such places as St. Louis, Cape Coast, Elmina, São Tomé Island, Bonny, Luanda, and Benguela. Here, Africans brought gold and slaves to trade to the European shippers. The number of slaves rose from under a thousand a year in 1451–75, when Portugal began to trade in slaves from the West African coast, to about 7,500 a year in the first half of the seventeenth century, to about 50,000 a year throughout the eighteenth and first half of the nineteenth centuries. In all, the transatlantic slave trade carried some 10 million people from Africa to the western hemisphere to work as slaves, generally on sugar, tobacco, and cotton plantations.

The slaves took on economic importance in direct proportion to the expansion of the sugar plantation economy of the Caribbean after 1650. In the 1700s, the plantations reached their maximum productivity and profitability. Between 1713 and 1792 Great Britain alone imported £162 million of goods from the Caribbean, almost all of it sugar.

This was half again as much as all British imports from Asia during the same period. France held the richest single sugar colony in the Caribbean, Saint-Domingue in Haiti (see p. 506).

HOW MANY SLAVES? HOW DO WE KNOW?

The landmark study on the demographics of the slave trade remains Philip Curtin's *The Atlantic Slave Trade: A Census*, published in 1969. Curtin examined carefully the existing estimate of 15 million as the number of slaves carried from Africa to the New World and concluded that it had been hastily accepted with little basis in research. Curtin undertook a fundamental investigation of the numbers. He limited himself to data already published rather than undertaking original archival searches of his own. The accounts included import records of specific African and American ports, shipping records, and projections based on historical slave populations in the Americas. On this basis, Curtin produced the first systemic analysis of the quantity of slaves from Africa landed in the Americas.

First he analyzed the structure of the plantation economy that produced the sugar, and stressed six key points:

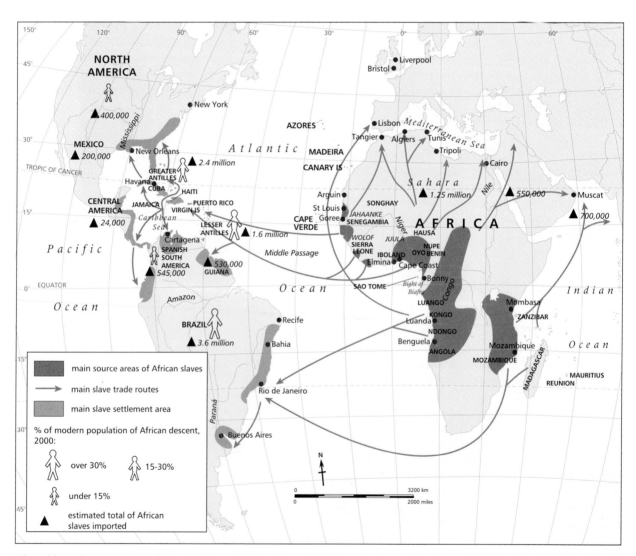

The African slave trade A trade in sub-Saharan African slaves dated from the Roman Empire, and had been lucratively developed by Arab merchants from the eighth century. But the impact of Western European entrepreneurs, seeking cheap labor for the Americas, was unparalleled. The millions of Africans who survived the Middle Passage by boat from Africa to the Americas between about 1550 and the late nineteenth century formed a new African diaspora in the New World.

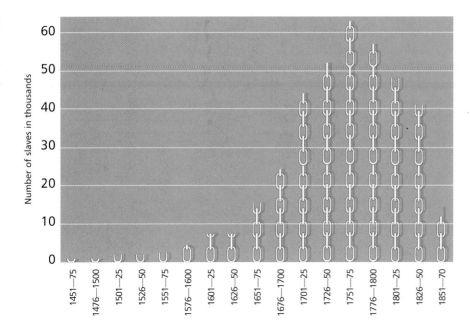

Major trends of the Atlantic slave trade in annual average number of slaves imported. Sixty percent of all slaves delivered to the New World arrived between 1721 and 1820; 80 percent between 1701 and 1850. The British abolition of the slave trade in 1807 had some effect, but it did not stop the trade. (Source: Curtin, *The Atlantic Slave Trade*)

- it relied on slave labor;

- it was organized as an early large-scale capitalist enterprise with gangs of laborers;

- its owners held "feudal," legal rights over the workers;

- it supplied a crop for export to distant European markets but often did not grow its own food; it was completely reliant on international trade for profits and for necessities;

- "political control over the system lay on another continent and in another kind of society" (Curtin);

- in its organization, the sugar plantation was a forerunner of factory labor.

Curtin begins his analysis with the importation of slaves into Europe, including Sicily, Portugal, Spain, and Italy, as well as to the sugar-producing islands off the coasts of these countries. Evaluating and revising the statistics of previous demographers for the period 1450–1500, Curtin estimates that 50,000 Africans were imported as slaves into Europe and 25,000 into the Atlantic islands of Madeira, Cape Verde, and the Canaries. Another 100,000 were transported off the African coast to São Tomé.

Based primarily on the records of *asientos*, shipping licenses issued to foreign firms between 1521

and 1773, and government records, especially from Great Britain, Curtin estimates that up to 1865 the entire import of Africans to Spanish America was 1,552,000, with 702,000 of these going to Cuba. For the entire period from 1640 to 1807 (when the British outlawed the slave trade), Curtin estimates that 1,665,000 people were imported as slaves to the British West Indies. To the French West Indies between 1664 and 1838, Curtin estimates that 1,600,200 were imported and that in Portuguese America, these numbers were more than double. To Brazil alone, with its massive sugar plantations in Bahia, Curtin accepts the estimates of two earlier demographers of about 3,646,800. To the Dutch West Indies, 500,000 people were imported as slaves; to the Danish West Indies, now the American Virgin Islands, 28,000. Imports to the United States and pre-1776 North America totalled about 399,000.

Thus, Curtin's 1969 estimate for the total importation of slaves to the Americas was 9,566,000. Overall, "more Africans than Europeans arrived in the Americas between, say, 1492 and 1770" (p. 87). Curtin noted that, although his estimates could well be off by as much as 50 percent, they were, nevertheless, "correct enough to point out contradictions in present hypotheses and to raise new questions for comparative demography and social history" (p. 93)

One of Curtin's findings, for example, was that the USA and Canada imported only 4.2 percent of all the slaves imported into the Americas, about 400,000 out of 9,566,000.

SPOTLIGHT
Slavery:
THE PLANTATION SYSTEM

Artistic representations of slavery and the slave trade carry their own editorial comment. W. Clark's "Ten Views of Antigua" (1823), from which **figure 1** is taken, presents the plantation system under a bright blue sky. Two images predominate: the white gentleman making his rounds upon his horse, benignly chatting with one of his charges, and the long line of cane cutters

stretching as far as the eye can see. The healthy-looking workers resemble free employees more than slaves. Harvesting appears as hard, productive labor, performed by strong, surprisingly heavily clothed workers. Two overseers, one in the lower left and another near the center of the painting, convey an impression of careful management and tight, almost industrial organization.

The Slave Trade (**figure 2**), by François Biard, paints a very different, deeply disturbing picture, deliberately emphasizing the sadism of the traffic in humans, as people are inspected, purchased, branded, and whipped. To the rear right of the market, located on the African coast, are shackled rows of slaves awaiting their turn on the block. This scene has little to do with economic productivity; to the

Figure 1 W. Clark, *Slaves Fell the Ripe Sugar, Antigua*, 1823. (*British Library, London*)

extent that economics is involved in this view of slavery, it is in the intense bargaining over the price of the slave in the center of the picture who is bound, prodded, and whose teeth are being checked by a crew member. The artist exposes the brutal indifference toward human suffering that was an intrinsic part of the slave trade. Many of the slaves are women, especially those undergoing the most brutal treatment and responding with the most pain, and a powerful undercurrent of sadistic sexuality permeates the image. Whites are not alone in enjoying the infliction of pain. Blacks and whites are equally intent on bargaining over the price of the bound slave in the center; and while a white man brands one female slave, a black man whips another. Despite its touches of voyeurism and pornography, Biard's painting unequivocally condemns the entire system of slavery.

To the left of the painting, slaves are forced on board ships that would carry them across the Atlantic to the plantations of the Caribbean and North America.

Figure 2 François Biard, *The Slave Trade*, 1840.

The "tight packing" of the slave ship *Brookes* in 1789, depicted here in an engraving from the time (**figure 3**), condemns the slave trade by straightforwardly exposing a different side of its economics. The desire to use every inch of space for transporting live human cargo saw people squashed together so tightly that they hardly had room to turn over. Each man was allowed a space 6 feet long by 16 inches wide, and usually 2½ feet high; each woman 5' 10" by 16"; each boy 5' by 14"; each girl 4'6" by 12". So densely packed were the ships that contagious diseases spread like wildfire, leading to significant loss of life, and later the shippers were forced to reduce the crowding. Objective descriptions of the conditions of the slave trade, such as this one, helped inspire its abolition in England in 1807.

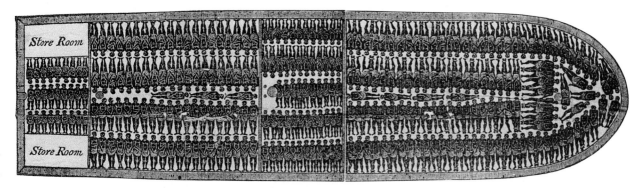

Figure 3 Copper engraving of *Brookes* slave ship, Liverpool, 1789.

Rather than sustaining the regular excess of deaths over births typical of tropical America, the North American colonies developed a pattern of natural growth among the slaves … By the end of the eighteenth century, North American slave populations were growing at nearly the same rate as that of the settler populations from Europe … Historians have neglected [this] almost completely, even though it has an obvious and important bearing on such recent historical problems as the comparative history of slavery in the New World. Nor have demographic historians yet produced a complete or satisfactory explanation of this phenomenon. (p. 73)

The sex ratio of men to women among African-Americans sustains the argument that North American slave owners must have treated their human property in ways that allowed them to live and reproduce, in contrast to slave owners resident in the Caribbean:

Since many more men than women were shipped from Africa in the illegal slave trade [a ratio of about two to one], substantial imports would have influenced the sex ratio of the North American slave population. Yet, the census of 1861 actually shows the number of Negro women slightly exceeding the number of Negro men in the United States … Contrary to the parochial view of history that most North Americans pick up in school, the United States was only a marginal recipient of slaves from Africa. The real center of the trade was tropical America, with almost 90 percent going to the Atlantic fringe from Brazil through the Guianas to the Caribbean coast and islands. (p. 74)

Curtin's work initiated continuing statistical research. Paul Lovejoy's careful study, published in 1982, generally supported Curtin. Lovejoy indicated that the distribution of ports of departure and ports of arrival may need some re-examination, but "My synthesis of the partial totals supports Curtin's total estimate for imports into the Americas and the islands of the Atlantic basin" (in Northrup, p. 55). The debate continues, but we now have a clear, empirical basis for understanding the dimensions of three centuries of Atlantic trade in human beings.

Two additional demographic inquiries have followed Curtin's *Census*. First, historians have sought to locate the geographical source of slaves exported from Africa. Lovejoy, for example, finds that of the

5.5 million exported in the hundred years between 1701 and 1800, the three largest sources were west central Africa, with 2 million, the Bight of Biafra, with 814,000, and the Senegambia, with 201,000 (Lovejoy, p. 50).

After a careful assessment of the locations of the trade along the coast, Curtin sees the law of supply and demand at work, creating cycles of rising and falling prices. When slaves were plentiful, often because of warfare and the seizing of captives who could be sold into slavery, prices fell; then more European slavers arrived to take advantage of the low prices, increasing demand, raising prices, and encouraging European slavers to look elsewhere. The marketplace shifted as prices oscillated. The result seems to be that no area was constantly a supplier, but that each area had time to recover some of its population losses. Curtin also points out that only about one-third of the slaves sold overseas were women, so that population losses to the next generation in Africa were somewhat limited.

The second demographic inquiry concerns the new sources and new methods of obtaining cheap, highly controlled labor for the plantations after the slave trade was abolished and suppressed, beginning with legislation in Great Britain in 1807. As Curtin points out, the British and French developed schemes to coerce Africans to emigrate to the West Indies. Asia also became a source of supply. Between 1845 and 1914, nearly 450,000 contract workers emigrated from India to the British West Indies and French Caribbean. Private planters, with the cooperation of the government of British India, also began developing systems of **indentured, contract labor** to bring workers from India to the Indian Ocean (French) colonies of Mauritius and Réunion. The Dutch brought Javanese workers to their plantations in Surinam. Cuba imported some 150,000 Chinese contract workers between 1849 and 1875.

REINTERPRETING THE SLAVE TRADE

From the fifteenth to the nineteenth centuries, many individual states were taking form on the African continent. The largest, like the Songhay empire of West Africa, was about the size of France or Spain. Medium-sized states, the size of Portugal or of England, were more numerous, including the Oyo Empire in Nigeria, Nupe, Igala, and Benin in the lower Niger Valley, the Hausa states of northern

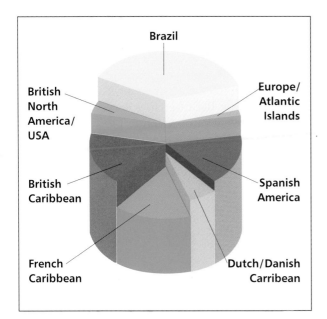

Destinations of the Atlantic slave trade by importing regions, 1451–1870. Historian Philip Curtin estimated that 9.6 million slaves were imported to the Americas alone, with the largest number being shipped to Brazil to work its huge sugar plantations in Bahia. (Source: Curtin, *The African Slave Trade*)

Nigeria, and Kongo, in central Africa. Slavery and the slave trade were important to the rise and decline of these states. First, in a region where land was not privately owned, slaves represented the main form of wealth. A rich state held many slaves. Second, the slaves were a source of labor, a means for their owners to increase wealth. Third, the trade in slaves was a means of still further increasing wealth, either for the state itself or for private traders.

A turn-about in the interpretation of the slave trade is underway. Africans are emerging as active businessmen who helped build up this important trade. John Thornton's revisionist study, *Africa and Africans in the Making of the Atlantic World, 1400-1640*, surveys the early years of the trade, before it became a flood, and stresses this African commercial participation. Long before Europeans arrived on the Atlantic coast, slavery was big business in Africa. When European traders offered new opportunities, African businessmen joined in, continuing to control the trade up to the water's edge.

My examination of the military and political relations between Africans and Europeans concludes that Africans controlled the nature of their interactions with Europe. Europeans did not possesss the military power to force Africans to participate in any type of trade in which their leaders did not wish to engage. Therefore all African trade with the Atlantic, including the slave trade, had to be voluntary. Finally, a careful look at the slave trade and the process of acquisition of slaves argues that slaves had long been used in African societies, that African political systems placed great importance on the legal relationships of slavery for political purposes, and that relatively large numbers of people were likely to be slaves at any one time. Because so much of the process of acquisition, transfer, and sale of slaves was under the control of African states and elites, they were able to protect themselves from the demographic impact and transfer the considerable social dislocations to poorer members of their own societies. (p. 7)

Europeans possessed neither the military strength nor the immunity to disease to enter the interior of the continent. They stayed in coastal enclaves, while Africans captured the slaves and brought them to be purchased. Occasionally, African rulers attempted to limit the trade, but both African and European traders seemed beyond their control.

The lure of profit increased as the demand for slaves multiplied in the next two centuries. Some of the trading communities of Africa, ethnic groups that traditionally facilitated and controlled trade, probably profited, including the Jahaanke of the Gambia–River Niger region; the Juula of northern Ghana, Côte d'Ivoire, and Upper Niger River; the Wolof of Senegal; and the Awka and Aro of Iboland in Nigeria. A new community of African–Portuguese traders was also born as Portuguese and Africans along the coast bonded and had children.

The effects of the slave trade on the total economy of Africa remain much disputed. Some scholars, following the pioneering work of Walter Rodney in his *How Europe Underdeveloped Africa* (1972), continue to cite dire economic consequences. Some more recent writers, however, like David Eltis, suggest that the slave trade, despite its enormous absolute size, was small relative to the total size of Africa's population and internal economy. This debate over size and significance continues.

No one, of course, can estimate the lost opportunities for African development represented by the export of so many millions of its strongest and most resilient men and women. Crosby points out ironically that, as part of the Atlantic exchange, Africa received new crops such as maize, manioc, and cassava, which became staple foods and may actually have increased the population more than the export of population depleted it. And, of course, slavery established a new population of African Americans throughout the western hemisphere.

CONNECTION: *The Haitian revolution and the abolition of slavery, pp. 506–9*

CITIES AND DEMOGRAPHICS

Studies of population movement analyze not only migration across global regions, but also the movement from rural to urban areas, and from one urban area to another. Because cities serve as centers for rule, administration, economic production, trade, and cosmopolitan philosophy and art, migration into (or out of) the cities tells us something of the

SOURCE
Ibn Khaldun on Urban Life in the Fourteenth Century

The process of transition from nomadic to sedentary and urban forms, and the "softening" of the invaders that had occurred, had been remarked upon by the great social philosopher Ibn Khaldun of Tunis (1332–1406) in his observations of contemporary Arab life. Ibn Khaldun presents an early philosophy of the flowering and decline of civilization.

It is rare that the age of the state should exceed three generations, a generation being the average age of an individual, that is forty years or the time necessary for full growth and development.

We said that the age of the state rarely exceeds three generations because the first generation still retains its nomadic roughness and savagery, and such nomadic characteristics as a hard life, courage, predatoriness, and the desire to share glory. All this means that the strength of the solidarity uniting the people is still firm, which makes that people feared and powerful and able to dominate others.

The second generation, however, have already passed from the nomadic to the sedentary way of life, owing to the power they wield and the luxury they enjoy. They have abandoned their rough life for an easy and luxurious one. …

As for the third generation, they have completely forgotten the nomadic and rough stage, as though it had never existed. They have also lost their love of power and their social solidarity through having been accustomed to being ruled. Luxury corrupts them, because of the pleasant and easy way of living in which they have been brought up. As a result, they become a liability on the state, like women and children who need to be protected. …

… the rulers of a state, once they have become sedentary, always imitate in their ways of living those of the state to which they have succeeded and whose condition they have seen and generally adopted.

This is what happened to the Arabs, when they conquered and ruled over the Persian and Byzantine empires … Up until then they had known nothing of civilization. (Ibn Khaldun, pp. 117–19)

Ibn Khaldun's depiction of nomadic conquerors being ultimately absorbed and assimilated into the civilizations they conquer is a frequently repeated process in world history. We have seen the barbarian conquests of Rome and China in Chapters 6 and 7. His portrait of the decadence and decay of civilizations does not, however, fit all cases. In India, for example, Aurangzeb provoked fatal rebellions when he tried to rule too strictly over too many people, from too remote a location. Aurangzeb's fatal flaw was not decadence but excessive zeal.

transformation of society. Here, we combine demographic data with our information on the nature of the city or cities under study to assess these transformations. The movement from nomadic to urban society is one of the most striking examples (see Source, opposite).

As we know from Part 2, we expect urban occupations, diversity of population, and rates of innovation to be very different from those of the countryside. What then was happening in the various regions of the world we have been examining in terms of rural–urban movement? Although an examination of capital cities is not decisive, it is informative, especially for an era in which specific accurate population data may not be available. We expect, however, that capitals of strong states will attract large and vibrant populations.

DELHI/SHAH JAHANABAD

Each Mughal emperor built his own capital. The sultans immediately preceding them had ruled from Delhi. Akbar ruled primarily from Agra, about 100 miles (160 kilometers) south of Delhi, but in 1569 he built a new capital, about 20 miles (32 kilometers) from Agra, at Fatehpur Sikri to honor a Sufi saint who had prayed there for a male heir for the emperor. By the end of the century, however, a shortage of water at the beautiful, archi-

tecturally eclectic capital forced Akbar to abandon the city and return to Agra. His son, Jahangir, preferred to rule from Lahore and he built up that Punjabi city as his capital. Akbar's grandson Shah Jahan rebuilt Delhi as his own capital and gave it his own name.

Built in a semicircular shape, with a radius of 10–12 miles (16–20 kilometers), Shah Jahanabad apparently had a population reaching 2 million. As a newly rebuilt city, almost all its residents were immigrants. The merchant and artisan population, in particular, was composed of foreign merchants such as Armenians, Persians, Central Asians, and Kashmiris.

Stephen Blake in his study *Shahjahanabad* describes the Delhi of Shah Jahan as recapturing the spirit of imperial authority vested in it over centuries, most recently by the Delhi Sultanate. It served also as a religious center, a place of pilgrimage revered throughout India for its tombs and graves of saints and holy men. The inner city was encircled by a massive stone wall, 3.8 miles (6 kilometers) long, 27 feet (8 meters) high, 12 feet (3.6 meters) thick. At the convergence of the main streets stood the palace-fort, the home of the emperor, the administrative center of the Mughal Empire. The city had its splendors. The poet Amir Khusrau inscribed on the walls of the private audience hall of the emperor, above the peacock throne:

Shah Jahan leaving the Great Mosque at Delhi by elephant, seventeenth century. Akbar's grandson Shah Jahan restored and rebuilt Delhi in the 1600s to serve as the capital of the Mughal Empire. In 1739 the Persian emperor Nadir Shah conquered the city and looted its treasures, including the famous Peacock Throne. Today, with neighboring New Delhi, it is India's capital and third largest city.

"If there is a paradise on earth, it is here, it is here, it is here." Opposite it, a thousand yards west, set on a small hill, rose the *masjid-i-jami*, the Friday mosque, or chief public mosque of the city. In keeping with Islamic architectural principles, gardens with streams of water running through them to delight the eye and the ear were included in the landscaping.

The larger city housed an assembly of military camps, each under the leadership of one of the emperor's leading generals. M. Gentile, a visiting Frenchman in the mid-eighteenth century wrote: "There are many mansions of the nobles, which one can compare to small towns and in which reside the women, equipment, and bazars (or public markets) of the nobles" (Blake, p. 179). The twentieth-century historian Percival Spear referred to Shah Jahanabad's "nomadic court and its tents of stone" (Toynbee, p. 237), the architecture reminding the viewer that the Mughals "had started as nomads in the central Asian steppes, and until their last days they never forgot their origin" (p. 238). Each nobleman also built his own mosque. But the main function of the city was as the center of administrative and military power. Visitors to India observed that in reality the largest city in India was the military camp led by the emperor in the field. When he went to war, as Aurangzeb did for years at a time, hundreds of thousands of soldiers and camp followers accompanied him; Delhi itself was deserted.

ISFAHAN

In Iran, Shah Abbas (1537–1628) made Isfahan his capital in 1598. One of the largest and most beautiful cities of its time, it contained perhaps a half million people in its 25-mile (40-kilometer) circumference. Its two most monumental features were a 2½-mile (4-kilometer) long elegant promenade, the Chahar Bagh, lined by gardens and court residences encouraged by Shah Abbas and, in the center of the city, the **maidan**, a large public square a third of a mile (536 meters) long by a tenth of a mile (160 metres) wide. The maidan was lined on one side by two tiers of shops, on the other sides by the royal palace, the royal mosque, and the smaller Lutfullah mosque. The maidan served as marketplace, meeting place, and even as a sportsfield where polo was played.

Shah Abbas fostered increased artisanal production and trade, and Isfahan welcomed merchants and craftsmen from around the world. In the extended bazaar, which stretched for 1½ miles

(2.4 kilometers) from the maidan to the main mosque, were located shops, factories, and warehouses, as well as smaller mosques, madrasas (Islamic schools), baths, and **caravanserais** (travelers' hostels). Up to 25,000 people worked in the textile industry alone. Chinese ceramicists were imported to train workers in Chinese porcelain manufacture, and carpets and metalwork were also anchors of Isfahan's craft production.

Despite their differences in religion, Shah Abbas and the European powers shared a common political and military opposition to the Ottoman Empire, which lay between them. In the early 1600s Shah Abbas allowed both the English and the Dutch to open trade offices in Isfahan. He also practiced religious tolerance, perhaps for practical reasons. Augustinian, Carmelite, and Capuchin missions were established. Christian Armenians, forced by Shah Abbas to immigrate from their earlier home in Julfa to expand Isfahan's commerce, built their own suburb, called New Julfa, appropriate to their status as prosperous merchants. A Jewish quarter also grew up in the northwestern part of the city, but later in Shah Abbas' reign Jews were persecuted and forced to convert to Islam or to leave.

Shah Abbas maintained absolute command and imported soldiers who were totally loyal to him. He also kept his forces supplied with up-to-date weapons, for he understood that Iran's status and survival depended upon them, surrounded as it was by the hostile Ottoman Empire on the west, continuing threats from nomads to the north, and a powerful, if friendly, Mughal Empire on the east. In a report of 1605 to Pope Paul V, the friar Paul Simon described the Shah as ruthless, dictatorial, and militarily prepared with forces recruited from far and near:

> His militia is divided into three kinds of troops: one of Georgians, who will be about 25,000 and are mounted; the second force … is made up of slaves of various races, many of them Christian renegades: their number will be as many again … The third body consists of soldiers whom the great governors of Persia are obliged to maintain and pay the whole year; they will be about 50,000. (Andrea and Overfield, pp. 91–92)

ISTANBUL/CONSTANTINOPLE

Constantinople had been the capital of the much reduced Byzantine Empire when Sultan Mehemmed II captured it and made it his own capital in 1453. He renamed the city Istanbul and began to recast it as the administrative center of the Ottoman Empire, which he was rapidly enlarging. In 1478 Istanbul had about 80,000 inhabitants; between 1520 and 1535, there were 400,000; and some Western observers estimated a population of 700,000 by 1600. Istanbul had become a city of Turks—58 percent of the population in the sixteenth and seventeenth centuries—but there were also Greeks, Jews, Armenians, and Tziganes.

The vast conurbation was composed of three major segments plus numerous suburbs. Central Istanbul housed the government center, with trees, gardens, fountains, promenades, and 400 mosques; sprawling, uneven bazaars where luxuries as well as day-to-day necessities could be purchased; and the Serai, near the tip of the peninsula, where the government officials lived in their palaces and gardens. Across the small waterway, called the Golden Horn, were the ports and major commercial establishments of Galata. Here the Western ships came; here were the Jewish businessmen; the shops and warehouses; cabarets; the French ambassador; Latin and Greek merchants dressing in the Turkish style and living in grand houses. On Galata, too,

were the two major arsenals, that of Kasim Pasha and the Topkhana, marking the Ottoman commitment to military power. On the Asian side of the Straits of the Bosphorus was the third part of Istanbul, Üsküdar, a more Turkish city, and the terminus of the great land routes through Asia.

Fernand Braudel sees in Istanbul the prototype of the great modern European capitals that would arise a century later. Economically these cities produced little, but they processed goods passing through, and were the "hothouses of civilization" (p. 351), where new ideas and patterns arose and created an order. Braudel remarks that cities that were only capitals would not fare well in the next century; those that were economically productive would. Beginning in the late sixteenth century, the economy of Istanbul was undercut by changes in the world economy. As trade shifted to the Atlantic and to European powers that carried their own commerce around the African continent instead of through the Middle East, the Ottoman Empire and its capital were left as a backwater. Trade deserted them. The vast amounts of silver and gold entering European markets from the Americas in the 1500s also inflated and subverted Istanbul's economy.

Map of Constantinople (Istanbul), late sixteenth century. Byzantine-ruled Constantinople harked back to the great ancient cities of Rome and Athens, whose cultural achievements it rivaled. Under the Ottomans, who renamed it Istanbul, it resumed its role as one of the great early modern centers—a city of diverse peoples and trade in goods and ideas.

LONDON

By comparison with the Asian and East European capitals, London had a very different pattern of immigration and employment. While Delhi, Isfahan, and Istanbul all declined during the late seventeenth and early eighteenth centuries in response to negative political and economic factors, London grew, primarily because of economic factors.

E.A. Wrigley, one of the founding members of the Cambridge Group for the History of Population and Social Structure, has examined the changing demography of London between 1650 and 1750 to analyze the city's relationship with English society and economy. Wrigley begins with London's extraordinary population growth, from 200,000 in 1600, to 400,000 in 1650 and 575,000 by 1700, when it became the largest city in Western Europe, to 675,000 in 1750 and 900,000 in 1800. London dominated the development of all of England. In 1650 London held 7 percent of England's total population; in 1750, 11 percent.

Before the twentieth century, as a general rule, large cities everywhere in the world were so unsanitary that death rates exceeded birth rates. So London's extraordinary population growth reflects not only births within the city, but also extraordinary immigration to compensate for high death rates. Wrigley estimates that by the end of the 1600s, 8,000 people a year were migrating into London. Since the entire population of England at this time was only 5 million, London was siphoning half of England's population growth into itself.

With so high a proportion of England's population living in London, or at least visiting the city for a substantial part of their lives, Wrigley suggests that this contact must have had significant influence on the country as a whole. He suggests that the high levels of population growth in London in the seventeenth century may have been a significant factor in giving birth to the industrialization of the eighteenth.

Wrigley suggests several relevant causal relationships. The first group concerns economics: London's growth promoted the creation of a national market, including transportation and communication facilities; evoked increasing agricultural productivity to feed the urban population; developed new sources of raw materials, especially coal, to provide for them; developed new commercial instruments; and increased productivity and purchasing power. Demographically, London's high death and immigration rates kept England's rate of population growth relatively low. Sociologically, London's growth disseminated new ways of thinking about economics and its importance. Londoners placed increasing value on production and consumption for the common person, encouraging higher levels of entrepreneurship throughout the country.

Wrigley does not here discuss the political variables, but without them London's growth could have simply led to parasitism, with the urban ruling elites commandeering the production of the countryside for their own good. Such parasitism was common in imperial capitals elsewhere. In London, however, values of production and increased consumption for the common person were reinforced by a government increasingly dominated by commercial classes.

CONNECTION: *New patterns of urban life, 1800s, pp. 557–65*

WHAT DIFFERENCE DOES IT MAKE?

Wrigley's study of London addresses squarely the relationship between demographic shifts and changes in politics, economics, and social life. In Part 5 we saw the early economic transformation in the trade of England as it began to build a global trade empire. Here we have seen demographic growth and complexity in the capital city that closely match that economic growth and complexity. Wrigley makes clear that these transformations have important implications for fundamental political restructuring, industrialization, and social change (which we will analyze in Part 7).

Numbers count. The historical demographers whom we have studied in this chapter demonstrate that demographic shifts are important in themselves and that they are critical causes of and reactions to great global transformations. Braudel emphasized this in his study of global commerce; Curtin in his study of the Atlantic slave trade; Sauer in his study of the decimation of the native American Indian population; and Habib in his study of "Population" in the Mughal Empire. Wrigley's study of London's changing demography reaffirms this view of the importance of demographics. His work, and the work of other historical demographers, prepares us to study in Part 7 some of the revolutionary legacies of these demographic changes.

BIBLIOGRAPHY

Andrea, Alfred J. and James H. Overfield, eds.,
The Human Record: Sources of Global History, Vol. II
(Boston: Houghton Mifflin Co., 3rd ed., 1998).

Blake, Stephen P. *Shahjahanabad*
(Cambridge: Cambridge University Press, 1990).

Braudel, Fernand. *Capitalism and Material Life 1400–1800*,
trans. by Miriam Kochan (New York: Harper & Row,
1973).

— . *The Mediterranean and the Mediterranean World in the
Age of Philip II*, 2 vols., trans. by Sian Reynolds
(New York: Harper and Row, 1973).

Crosby, Alfred W. *Ecological Imperialism:
The Biological Expansion of Europe, 900–1900*
(Cambridge: Cambridge University Press, 1986).

Curtin, Philip D. *The Atlantic Slave Trade: A Census*
(Madison: University of Wisconsin Press, 1969).

— . *The Rise and Fall of the Plantation Complex:
Essays in Atlantic History* (Cambridge: Cambridge
University Press, 1990).

Eltis, David, "Precolonial Western Africa and the
Atlantic Economy," in Barbara Solow, ed.
Slavery and the Rise of the Atlantic System
(Cambridge: Cambridge University Press, 1991),
97–119, excerpted in Northrup, pp. 161–173.

Frykenberg, R.E., ed., *Delhi through the Ages:
Essays in Urban History, Culture and Society*
(Delhi: Oxford University Press, 1986).

Gates, Henry Louis, Jr. *Wonders of The African World*
(New York: Knopf, 1999).

Habib, Irfan, "Population," in *The Cambridge Economic
History of India*, Vol. 1: c. 1200–c. 1750, eds. Tapan
Raychaudhuri and Irfan Habib (Cambridge:
Cambridge University Press, 1982), 163–171.

Henige, David, "Measuring the Immeasurable:
The Atlantic Slave Trade, West African Population
and the Pyrrhonian Critic," *Journal of African History*
XXVII.2 (1986), 303–13.

Hughes, Robert. *The Fatal Shore. The Epic of Australia's
Founding* (New York: Knopf, 1986).

Ibn Khaldun. *An Arab Philosophy of History*, trans. by
Charles Issawi (London: John Murray, 1950).

Inalcik, Halil. *The Ottoman Empire: The Classical Age*,
trans. by Norman Itzkowitz and Colin Imber
(New York: Praeger Publishers, 1973).

Inikori, Joseph E. and Stanley L. Engerman, eds.,
The Atlantic Slave Trade (Durham: Duke University
Press, 1992).

Keegan, John. *A History of Warfare* (New York: Knopf,
1993).

Lapidus, Ira M. *A History of Islamic Societies*
(Berkeley: University of California Press, 1988).

Lovejoy, Paul E., "The Volume of the Atlantic Slave
Trade: A Synthesis," *Journal of African History* XXIII
(1982), 473–500.

McNeill, William H. *The Pursuit of Power:
Technology, Armed Force, and Society since 1000 A.D.*
(Chicago: University of Chicago Press, 1983).

Mintz, Sidney W. *Sweetness and Power: The Place of Sugar
in Modern History* (New York: Penguin Books, 1985).

Naqvi, Hamida Khatoon, "Shahjahanabad: The Mughal
Delhi, 1638–1803: An Introduction," in *Delhi through
the Ages*, ed., R. E. Frykenberg (Delhi: Oxford
University Press, 1986), 143–51.

Nash, Gary, *et al. The American People. Creating a Nation
and a Society* (New York: Harper and Row, 4th ed.,
1998).

New York Times 2000 Almanac (New York: Penguin, 1999).

Northrup, David, ed. *The Atlantic Slave Trade*
(Lexington, MA: D.C. Heath, 1994).

Past Worlds: The [London] Times Atlas of Archaeology
(Maplewood, NJ: Hammond, 1988).

Robinson, Francis. *Atlas of the Islamic World since 1500*
(New York: Facts on File, Inc., 1982).

Rodney, Walter. *How Europe Underdeveloped Africa*
(Washington: Howard University Press, 1972).

Sauer, Carl Ortwin. *Sixteenth Century North America:
The Land and People as Seen by the Europeans*
(Berkeley: University of California Press, 1971).

Schwartzberg, Joseph, ed., *A Historical Atlas of South Asia*
(Chicago: University of Chicago Press, 1978).

Spence, Jonathan D. *The Search for Modern China*
(New York: W.W. Norton and Co., 1990).

The [London] Times Atlas of World History ed. Geoffrey
Parker (London: Times Books, 4th ed, 1993).

Thornton, John. *Africa and Africans in the Making of the
Atlantic World, 1400–1640* (Cambridge: Cambridge
University Press, 1992).

Tosh, John. *The Pursuit of History* (New York: Longman,
1984).

Toynbee, Arnold. *Cities of Destiny* (New York:
Weathervane Books, 1967).

Willigan, J. Dennis and Katherine A. Lynch.
Sources and Methods of Historical Demography
(New York: Academic Press, 1982).

Wolf, Eric. *Europe and the People without History*
(Berkeley: University of California Press, 1982).

Wrigley, E.A. *Population and History*
(New York: McGraw-Hill Book Company, 1969).

— . "A Simple Model of London's Importance in
Changing English Society and Economy 1650-1750,"
Past and Present XXXVII (1967), 44–70.

Social Change

1688–1914

WESTERN REVOLUTIONS AND
THEIR EXPORT

An unprecedented ferment in global exploration, commerce, and migration began in the thirteenth century (see Parts 5 and 6). By the seventeenth century accommodations to these transformations were needed in political, economic, and social philosophy and organization. These accommodations first took form in Europe and the Americas. Later, through political colonialism, economic imperialism, and Christian missionary activity, they spread to the rest of the world. The new forms percolated into everyday life and consciousness everywhere, but each society adapted in its own way. The results were, as one might expect, diverse and quite often unexpected.

Explosive events, "revolutions," punctuated the changes through the years 1688–1914. One cluster of revolutions—in England, North America, France, Haiti, and Latin America—promoted new political philosophies and introduced new political structures. Many historians, such as R.R. Palmer, refer to them collectively as constituting "The Age of Democratic Revolution." Beginning about the same time, a series of innovations in economic organization and the uses of machinery dramatically increased the quantity and quality of economic productivity. Most historians name this transformation the "Industrial

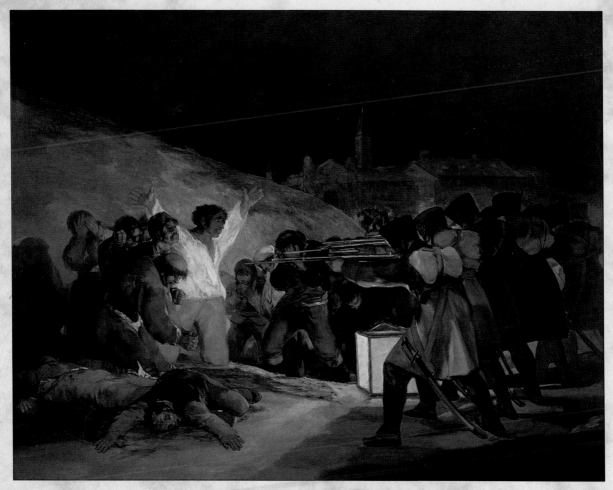

Francisco Jose de Goya, *Execution of the Defenders of Madrid, 3rd May, 1808,* **1814.** (*Prado, Madrid*)

Revolution." These revolutions in politics and economics were accompanied by equally dramatic social changes, which affected the individual, the family, the neighborhood, and the community. Many of these transformations originated in Western Europe, but ultimately people all over the world were affected and formulated their own varied responses, adaptations, and rejections. For purposes of analysis, this part will consider these three transformations sequentially: political change in this chapter, industrial change in Chapter 16, and social change in Chapter 17.

15 POLITICAL REVOLUTIONS IN EUROPE AND THE AMERICAS

1688–1850

"The aim of every political association is the preservation of the natural and imprescriptible rights of man; these rights are liberty, property, security, and resistance to oppression."

FRENCH DECLARATION OF THE RIGHTS OF MAN AND THE CITIZEN

THE BIRTH OF HUMAN RIGHTS IN THE AGE OF ENLIGHTENMENT

POLITICAL REVOLUTION

A revolution is a fundamental and often rapid change in the way systems operate—whether political, economic, intellectual, or social. A political revolution, for example, not only removes some people from office and replaces them with others, it also changes the fundamental basis on which the new leaders come to power, the authority they claim, and their mission in office. Leaders of revolutions usually state their goals in terms of high, uncompromisable principles. As revolutionary struggles unfold and as different groups rise and fall, however, they may lurch from one political position to another relatively swiftly and often violently.

In a major revolution several groups may participate and cooperate in the struggle to replace an existing government. Each group may have its own goals, and these goals may be in conflict. As their joint movement appears to be nearing success and it becomes likely that a new government will replace the old, the struggle among the various participating groups will emerge. Each group will seek fiercely to incorporate its own programs and personnel into the new government and even to dominate it. This struggle to control the new government may be even more brutal, violent, chaotic, and unpredictable than the battle to overthrow the old. The stakes are high. Major revolutions can have significant, lasting consequences, not only for participants in that place and time but also for people of later generations and far-flung locations.

The first three political revolutions we will consider all share these characteristics of major revolutions. The "Glorious Revolution" of 1688 in England, the revolt of the

THE AGE OF REVOLUTIONS

DATE	EUROPE	NORTH AMERICA	LATIN AMERICA
1640	• Galileo dies; Newton is born (1642) • Civil wars in England (1642–6; 1647–9) • Execution of King Charles I of England (1649) • Restoration of English monarchy (1660) • Royal Society of London founded (1662)		• Portugal takes Brazil from the Dutch (1654)
1670	• The "Glorious Revolution" in England (1688) • The English Bill of Rights (1689) • John Locke's *Second Treatise on Government* (1689) • *Philosophes:* Diderot (1713–84); Voltaire (1694–1778); Rousseau (1712–1778); Montesquieu (1689–1755)		
1760	• Tennis Court Oath (June 20, 1789) • French Revolution (1789–99) • "March of the Women" (1789) • "Great Fear" (1789) • "Second French Revolution" (1791–99)	• British levy taxes on Americans in the Stamp Act (1765) • American Declaration of Independence (1776); War (1775–83) • Constitution (1789)	• Revolts against European rule in Peru, Colombia, and Brazil (1780–98) • Tupac Amaru revolt, Peru (1780)
1790	• "Reign of Terror" (1793–95) • Napoleon seizes power (1799); Emperor (1804) • Napoleon issues Civil Code (1804) • Napoleon invades Russia; finally defeated (1812)	• Bill of Rights ratified (1791) • Louisiana Purchase from France (1803)	• Toussaint L'Ouverture leads slave revolt against French in Saint-Domingue (Haiti) (1791) • Haiti proclaims independence (1804) • Joseph Bonaparte, King of Spain (1808) • Bolívar and San Martin lead revolts against Spain (1808–28) • Paraguay declares independence (1810–11)
1820	• Congress of Vienna (1814–15) • Reform Act extends voting franchise in Britain (1832) • Britain abolishes slavery in its empire (1833)	• President Andrew Jackson evicts Cherokee Indian Nation: "Trail of Tears" (1838) • Warfare with Mexico ends in victory for America (1848) • United States abolishes slavery (1863, 1865)	• Mexico wins independence (1821) • Prince Pedro declares Brazil independent (1822)

American colonies against British rule in 1776, and the French Revolution of 1789 removed one set of rulers and replaced them with another; changed the basis of authority of the state and its relationship to its citizens; and proposed new missions for the state. When we refer here to the "state" we mean the entire mechanism of government, its officers, its institutions, and its organization. All of these revolutions were fought in the name of principle. The English revolution was considered "bloodless," although it was the culmination of a lengthy period of national violence and civil warfare. The American and French Revolutions precipitated lengthy wars.

All three of these revolutions have been characterized as "democratic" because they increased the participation of more (but not all) of the people in government. All of them at some time tried to balance two additional, competing goals: they sought to protect the rights of propertied people while increasing the power of the state (although not of the king). These goals were not, and to this day are not, fully compatible. Individual rights, property rights, and the rights of the state often conflict. So we must be careful in our understanding of the "democracy" that emerged from these revolutions.

Collectively, for Europeans and Americans, the revolutions that occurred in the hundred years between 1688 and 1789:

- situated the authority of government on earth rather than in heaven and thus increased the influence of the secular over the other-worldly;

- rejected the theory that governments were based on a **divine right of king**s in favor of the theory that governments derive their just powers from the consent of the governed;

- encouraged the creation of an effective bureaucracy to administer the affairs of government;

- emphasized the principle of individual merit, of "a career open to talent," rather than promoting people on the basis of personal and hereditary connections;

- helped to solidify the nation-state as the principal unit of government;

- extended effective power over the state to classes of people hitherto excluded, especially to men of the professions and business;

- encouraged the growth of business and industry for private profit;

- inspired the revolutionary leaders to export their new ideologies and methods to new geographical areas, sometimes by force; and

- precipitated wars of heretofore unknown degrees of military mobilization, geographical extent, and human destructiveness.

"Liberty," "equality," "fraternity," "natural rights," "the pursuit of happiness," "property," and "no taxation without representation" were the battle cries of these various revolutions. As frequently happens, the results were often unintended, unanticipated, and ironic. The political forms that actually resulted did increase human freedom for many people in many countries, but they often coexisted with slavery, patriarchy, colonialism, and warfare.

To understand these ironies more fully, we examine two further revolutions that were inspired in part by these first three. In 1791, the slaves of Haiti, a French colony, revolted and abolished slavery. The French reluctance, and later refusal, to sanction this revolution against slavery demonstrated serious shortcomings in their own revolution. Then, in the first three decades of the nineteenth century, all the colonies of Spain and Portugal in Latin America fought for and won their independence. But the triumphant generals of the revolution fought among themselves as their dreams of vast, unified, powerful nations dissolved into the reality of smaller, weaker states. And the triumphant **creole** elite—the descendants of the European settlers in these colonies—suppressed indigenous peoples, people of mixed Spanish-Amerindian ancestry (*mestizos*), and African-Americans, thereby spreading disillusionment throughout the continent.

ENGLAND'S GLORIOUS REVOLUTION 1688

PHILOSOPHICAL RATIONALES

The philosophy justifying England's "Glorious Revolution" developed over many years. Thomas Hobbes (1588–1679), one of England's leading political philosophers, seemed to justify the enormous, existing power of the king over the citizens. In his most influential work, *Leviathan*, of 1651, he declared: "Nothing the sovereign representative can do to a subject, on what pretence soever, can properly be called injustice, or injury." But Hobbes was simultaneously providing a rationale for limiting the king's power. He declared that the king could claim his authority not by virtue of special,

An Eyewitness Representation of the Execution of Charles I, **by Weesop, 1649.** Charles's belief in the divine right of kings and the authority of the Church of England led eventually to a civil war with Parliament—which he and his supporters lost. At his subsequent trial, the king was sentenced to death as a tyrant, murderer, and enemy of the nation and beheaded at Whitehall, London, on January 30, 1649. (*Private Collection*)

personal rights, nor of representing God on earth, but because "Every subject is author of every act the sovereign doth." In other words, the king has authority to the extent that he represents the will of the people.

HOBBES AND "THE STATE OF NATURE"

Hobbes, like others of his time, was trying to understand the English monarchy in terms of its origins. He postulated the myth of a prehistoric, individualistic, unruly, "state of nature," which people had rejected in order to create a society that would protect them individually and collectively. Uncontrolled by law and a king, Hobbes wrote, "the life of man [is] solitary, poor, nasty, brutish, and short … During the time men live without a common power to keep them all in awe, they are in that condition which is called war; and such a war, as is of every man against every man." To escape such lawlessness, men had exchanged their individual liberties for social and political order. Their (mythical) **social contract**, not divine appointment, had created monarchy in order to serve the people.

At about the time Hobbes was writing, England was in continuing revolt against its sovereigns.

Religion was a burning issue, and it seemed that no sovereign could satisfy all the conflicting wishes of dissenters—Roman Catholics, Presbyterians, Puritans, and Quakers—and the official Anglican church. Frustrations simmered but had no focus until both James I (r. 1603–25) and his son Charles I (r. 1625–49) ran out of money to administer their governments, especially the naval and military departments, and therefore convened Parliament to request additional funds. Members of Parliament—landowners, increasingly wealthy city merchants, lawyers, Puritans and other religious dissenters, as well as Anglican clergy—were not inclined to give the kings the money they requested. They challenged royal authority, proposed increased power for an elected legislature, promotion by merit in government jobs, and, most of all, religious tolerance in private and public life. When Charles I nevertheless attempted to levy taxes without its sanction, the Parliament he had convened in 1640 came to open warfare with him and ultimately, under the leadership of Oliver Cromwell (Lord Protector of England, 1653–8), executed him. Cromwell, an ardent Calvinist (see p. 416) and military genius, ruled in rather arbitrary fashion until he died in 1658. Neither Cromwell nor Parliament had been able to achieve a new form of effective government and the monarchy was restored in 1660.

THE BILL OF RIGHTS 1689

Charles II (r. 1660–85) and his brother James II (r. 1685–90) continued to claim more powers than the Parliament wished to sanction. James II, a Catholic, favored Catholics in many of his official appointments. When, in his old age, a son was born to James, leading nobles feared that James and his successors might reinstitute Catholicism as England's official religion a century and a half after Henry VIII had disestablished it in favor of the Church of England (see p. 417). They invited James II's daughter, Mary, and her husband William of Orange, ruler of the United Provinces of the Netherlands, both resolute Protestants, to return to England and assume the monarchy. In 1688 William and Mary arrived in England and confirmed their new rule by defeating the troops still loyal to James II at the Battle of the Boyne in Ireland in 1690.

Although the new king and queen had been invited primarily to resolve religious conflicts, their ascension to the throne also brought resolution to the power conflict between king and Parliament. The Bill of Rights that was enacted by Parliament in 1689 created a kind of contract between the monarchy and people. It stipulated, among other clauses, that no taxes could be raised, nor armies recruited without prior Parliamentary approval; no subject could be arrested and detained without legal process; and no law could be suspended by the king unilaterally. The Glorious Revolution thus not only displaced one monarch in favor of another but also limited the powers of the monarch under constitutional law. After all, this new monarch had been selected by noblemen and confirmed by Parliament. The Anglican church remained the established Church of England, but the Toleration Act of 1689 granted Puritan Dissenters—but not Roman Catholics—the right of free public worship. Parliament did not yet revoke the Test Act which reserved military and civil offices for Anglicans only. Nevertheless, these settlements brought some resolution to the issues of religion in politics that had beset England for so long.

LOCKE AND THE ENLIGHTENMENT

This formal, public renegotiation of the tacit contract between king and people recalls the philosophy of Hobbes, but it went beyond Hobbes' bleak view of human political nature. The philosophical accomplishments of the Glorious Revolution are even more closely associated with the writings of John Locke (1632–1704), who had fled England in 1683 for the Netherlands, returning only after the revolution was complete. While he was in the Netherlands, Locke wrote his most important essay on political philosophy, *Second Treatise on Government*, although it was not published until 1689, after the Glorious Revolution had been implemented and Locke felt it safe to return to England. Since Locke's philosophy parallels not only the English revolution but also many subsequent ones, his arguments deserve attention.

Like Hobbes, Locke argued that government is a secular compact entered into voluntarily and freely by individuals. If there are to be kings, they too must live under the constitution. Locke, like Hobbes, based his argument on a mythical, prehistoric, "state of nature," which people forsook in order to provide for their common defense and needs. He, however, stressed the importance of common consent in the earlier mythical contract. The legitimacy of the contract continues only as long as the consent continues. If they no longer consent to the contract, the people have the right to terminate it. Going beyond Hobbes, Locke explicitly proclaimed the right of revolution in his *Second Treatise on Government*:

> There remains still in the people a supreme power to remove or alter the legislative, when they find the legislative act contrary to the trust reposed in them. For all power given with trust for the attaining of an end, being limited by that end, whenever that end is manifestly neglected, or opposed, the trust must necessarily be forfeited, and the power devolves into the hands of those that gave it, who may place it anew where they shall think best for their safety and security. (p. 92)

Locke postulated the "equal right that every man hath to his natural freedom, without being subjected to the will or authority of any other man" (p. 33). "Absolute monarchy, which by some men is counted the only government in the world, is indeed inconsistent with civil society" (p. 53). Majority rule is Locke's basis of government: "the act of the majority passes for the act of the whole, and of course determines as having by the law of nature and reason, the power of the whole" (p. 59).

GOVERNMENT BY PROPERTY OWNERS

Locke was not, however, proposing radical democracy; he was not advocating one person–one vote. For Locke, government was for property owners. "Government," Locke proclaimed, "has no other end but the preservation of property" (p. 57). "The great and chief end therefore, of men's uniting into commonwealths, and putting themselves under government, is the preservation of their property" (p. 75). Indeed, after the initial, mythical social contract had established the government's authority, succeeding generations had signalled their continuing acceptance of that contract by allowing their property to be protected by the government. "The supreme power cannot take from any man any part of his property without his own consent. For the preservation of property being the end of government, and that for which men enter into society, it necessarily supposes and requires, that the people should have property" (p. 85). (Contrast the view of common soldiers in the Source box below.)

Taxes, therefore, cannot be levied unilaterally or arbitrarily. "If anyone shall claim a power to lay and levy taxes on the people, by his own authority, and without such consent of the people, he thereby invades the fundamental law of property, and subverts the end of government" (p. 87).

Hobbes had already indicated the growing importance of property and industry to seventeenth-century England. Without peace and stability, he wrote:

> there is no place for industry; because the fruit thereof is uncertain; and consequently no culture of the earth; no navigation, nor use of the commodities that may be imported by sea; no commodious building; no instruments of moving, and removing, such things as require much force; no knowledge of the face of the earth; no account of time; no arts; no letters; no society. (p. 895)

Hobbes wanted a society of economic productivity achieved through industry, commerce, and invention. Locke saw private ownership of property and private profit as the means to achieving that end. He saw the property-owning classes of England, the men who made the Glorious Revolution, as the nation's proper leaders and administrators, and he asserted the importance of the enclosure acts by which England was dividing up the common lands

SOURCE

Universal Suffrage vs. Property Rights

E.P. Thompson, the twentieth-century British historian, emphasized the contributions of common people to history. In his ground-breaking *The Making of the English Working Class* (pp. 22–3), Thompson cites statements made in 1647 at an army council meeting that attempted to find a constitutional solution to the struggle between the king and Parliament and to determine the role of the common people in electing the Parliament.

Oliver Cromwell's son-in-law, General Ireton, proposed extending the franchise, but only to men of property, fearing that private property might otherwise be abolished: "No person hath a right to an interest or share in the disposing of the affairs of the kingdom ... that hath not a permanent fixed interest in this kingdom. ... If you admit any man that hath a breath and being, Why may not those men vote against all property?"

The common soldiers replied more democratically and more bitterly. One asserted: "There are many thousands of us soldiers that have ventured our lives; we have had little propriety in the kingdom as to our estates, yet we have had a birthright. But it seems now, except a man hath a fixed estate in this kingdom, he hath no right. ... I wonder we were so much deceived." If we are asked to fight on behalf of the government, we should have a voice in its election.

of each village, turning them into private property, and selling them. These enclosure acts were creating a new, wealthier landlord class, which turned its energies to increasing agricultural productivity. At the same time the acts forced rural people, who had owned no land of their own but who had been grazing their animals on the commons, to give up their independence. Most found work with more prosperous landlords and some moved to the cities in search of new jobs.

Locke is today usually criticized for overlooking the situation of the non-propertied classes. In his mythical state of nature land had been abundant—available for the taking—and anyone could become a property owner. But in both Locke's time and our own, access to unclaimed, unowned property is not so easy. Indeed, when Locke notes that "the turfs my servant has cut ... become my property" (p. 19), he credits the labor of the landless servant to his landed master. In practice, Locke's theory justified the government of England by Parliament under constitutional law which limited the power of the king and transferred it to the hands of the proper-tied classes—the system which was evolving in his time. Locke's is the voice of the improving land-lords and the rising commercial classes who made the Glorious Revolution.

For its time the Glorious Revolution may have been democratic because it placed the king under constitutional rule. But until 1820 fewer than 500 influential men in all of Britain, it has been estimated, could control the election of the majority of the Parliament. The 1832 Reform Act expanded the actual electorate in the British Isles from about a half million to about 800,000. Not until 1867 and 1884 did Reform Acts extend the vote to the middle and lower classes as well as to Catholics, Dissenters, and Jews. By that time the Industrial Revolution had created an entirely new class of occupations and workers who could successfully demand representation, as we shall see in the next chapter. Women got the vote in Britain only in the twentieth century.

INTELLECTUAL REVOLUTIONS IN SCIENCE AND PHILOSOPHY

During the time between the two English political revolutions of the seventeenth century, the Royal Society of London was founded in 1662. The study of science was beginning to be institutionalized,

both as knowledge for its own sake and as techno-logical application to practical problems. In some ways, our brief survey of the advancement of science therefore belongs more appropriately to Chapter 13 on advances in global commerce or to Chapter 16 on the industrial revolution. But changes in scientific thinking proceeded step-by-step with changes in politics so we examine them here in the midst of the revolution in political thought.

HOW DO WE KNOW?

In his 1985 book *Revolution in Science*, Harvard University historian of science I. Bernard Cohen writes that the study of the history of science is a surprisingly new field. Although some of the scientists we shall consider here—Copernicus, Pascal, Galileo, Descartes, Newton, Harvey, Leeuwenhoek, and Linnaeus—spoke of their find-ings as revolutionary, the first academic historian to write of a scientific revolution seems to have been a Ph.D. candidate at Columbia University, Martha (Bronfenbrenner) Ornstein. In her 1913 dissertation she summarized the importance of the array of sci-entific discoveries and inventions that included the telescope, which "utterly revolutionized the science of astronomy," "revolutionary changes in optics," "Linnaeus's revolutionary work" in plant and ani-mal classification, "the revolution in the universi-ties" toward systematic, empirical research, and the role of scientific societies as carriers of culture, "much as the universities had been before the sci-entific revolution." There had been, she wrote, "a revolution in the established habits of thought and inquiry, compared to which most revolutions regis-tered in history seem insignificant" (p. 21, cited in Cohen, p. 392).

In 1948, in a series of lectures, one of the most distinguished of professional historians, Herbert Butterfield, wrote that the scientific revolution of the seventeenth century "overturned the authority in science not only of the Middle Ages but of the ancient world. ... [It] outshines everything since the rise of Christianity and reduces the Renaissance and Reformation to the rank of mere episodes, mere internal displacements, within the system of medieval Christendom" (Butterfield, p. vii, cited in Cohen, p. 390). Butterfield refrained from calling this transformation a one-time revolution, since he saw it as a kind of "continuing historical, or history making force acting right up to the pre-sent time" (Cohen, p. 398). Beginning in the 1950s, especially in *The Copernican Revolution* (1957) and *The Structure of Scientific Revolutions* (1962, 3rd ed., 1996), Thomas Kuhn turned his attention to the process of scientific investigation as a method of thought and research that constantly challenges conventional thinking and stands ready to overthrow it. Kuhn argued that most scientific research is based on small, incremental advances in human knowledge. Kuhn called this "normal science." "Revolutionary science" occurs when scientists break completely with existing explanations of their field, finding them inadequate, and create new theories that are better able to account for all the data available. Galileo and Newton created such great revolutions.

WHAT DO WE KNOW?

What then was this revolution in seventeenth-century science? First, the seventeenth century marked the move from the individual scientist working alone to the creation of a community of scientists, in touch with one another, sharing knowledge and ideas, and building a collective structure of thought and method. It would still be possible for a scientific genius like Leonardo da Vinci (1452–1519) to die with his work unrecognized, and even unknown, but this would be less likely. Leonardo, most famous for his paintings of *The Last Supper* and the *Mona Lisa*, also carried out research in human anatomy through the dissection of cadavers; he wrote of the circulation of the blood through the body and of the path of the earth around the sun; he drew sketches for inventions such as submarines and airplanes. But he did not circulate these scientific and technological ideas. At the time of his death they remained confined to his own notebooks and were not discovered until the twentieth century. The creation of scientific academies in the seventeenth century made it much less likely that such genius would remain hidden.

Second, science added four new dimensions to its methods: mathematical formulations; **empiricism**; technological innovation; and freedom of inquiry. All of these are found in the great revolution in astronomy and physics from Copernicus through Kepler and Galileo, and on to Newton, one of the most studied revolutions in the history of science. Indeed, many historians would call this *the* scientific revolution of the seventeenth century.

Nicholas Copernicus (1473–1543), an outstanding Polish astronomer, was commissioned by Pope Paul III to devise a new calendar that would correct the errors of the Julian calendar. The Julian calendar was based on a 365¼-day year, while the actual time it takes the earth to circle the sun is eleven minutes and fourteen seconds less. So the calendar year was continuously losing time, about ten days

Map of the heavens according to Nicholas Copernicus, c. 1543. Copernicus placed the sun in the middle of his solar system with the earth circling around it. He also demonstrated the tilt and rotation of the earth's axis as it traveled in its yearly orbit. In these findings he differed from Ptolemy, the second century C.E. Greek astronomer, but he did continue to see the solar system as bounded, with an array of fixed stars and constellations marking its outer limits.

Newton experiments with light. Newton's first published papers were in optics. Here he worked as an experimental scientist rather than as a theoretical mathematician. By passing the rays of the sun through a prism he demonstrated that white light was an amalgam of colored rays. Using this information he built a reflecting telescope, using a mirror to focus light and thus to avoid the chromatic aberration that appeared in a refracting telescope.

by the sixteenth century, and holidays, like Christmas and Easter, began to slip backward into different seasons. The Pope commissioned Copernicus to analyze the astronomy underlying the calendar.

In the sixteenth century, people accepted the model of the second century C.E. Greek astronomer Ptolemy showing the earth at the center of the universe. The sun, the moon, the planets, and the stars went around it. As a mathematician, Copernicus began tracking the movements of all these bodies. He was able to fashion a mathematical system that showed the earth at the center of the universe, as accepted belief had it, but he also found a much simpler, though still complicated, formula that showed the sun, not the earth, at the center of the solar system. His new formulation also showed the earth turning on its axis every twenty-four hours rather than having the entire cosmos revolve around the earth (see picture, p. 485). As a rule,

scientists faced with more than one workable explanation choose the simpler, and with his new, simpler model of a solar system Copernicus could explain the calendrical difficulties that had been his principal assignment. But this new explanation would land him in serious trouble with the church, and he knew it.

The concept of the earth at the center of the universe, as taught by Ptolemy had been adopted as the official doctrine of the Catholic church because it was consistent with Biblical passages (Joshua 10:13; Ecclesiastes 1:4-5) that spoke of the sun's circle around the earth. The consequences of challenging that belief frightened Copernicus, as he wrote to the Pope in his letter of transmission introducing his findings:

> I may well presume, most Holy Father, that certain people, as soon as they hear that in this book about the Revolutions of the Spheres of the Universe I ascribe movement to the earthly globe, will cry out that. . . I should at once be hissed off the stage. . . . Thinking therefore within myself that to ascribe movement to the Earth must indeed seem an absurd performance on my part to those who know that many centuries have consented to the establishment of the contrary judgment, namely that the Earth is placed immovably as the central point in the middle of the Universe, I hesitated long whether, on the one hand, I should give to the light these my Commentaries written to prove the Earth's motion . . . . These misgivings and actual protests have been overcome by my friends . . . [one of whom] often urged and even importuned me to publish this work which I had kept in store not for nine years only, but to a fourth period of nine years. . . . They urged that I should not, on account of my fears, refuse any longer to contribute the fruits of my labors to the common advantage of those interested in mathematics. . . . Yielding then to their persuasion I at last permitted my friends to publish that work which they have so long demanded. (Kuhn, 1957, pp. 137–38.)

In the end, Copernicus stuck to the principles of his mathematical commitments and his conscience. He presented the truth as he understood it, but he published his complete findings only on his deathbed. They created much less stir than might have been expected, since they were published as a mathematical study, comprehensible only to most learned astronomers and mathematicians of his day. They became the object of technical study more than of theological debate.

The greatest astronomer of the next generation, Tycho Brahe (1546–1601), reexamined the mathematics of Copernicus and propounded a new schema that showed the sun and moon circling the earth in the middle of the solar system, and all the other planets circling the sun. It was a more complicated model, but one consistent with the data. The breakthrough that enshrined the sun-centered universe was made by Johannes Kepler (1571–1630). Kepler worked with Brahe toward the end of Brahe's life. For ten years he worked through the rich data he inherited, and finally reached a new understanding. The sun was at the center of the solar system and the planets, including earth, moved around it, but their orbits were not circles but ellipses, and they moved not at a fixed speed, but at a varying speed depending on their position at any time on the ellipse. With these new insights, Kepler designed a model of the solar system that was simple, comprehensive, and mathematically consistent with the data available. He published his results in 1609 in *On the Motion of Mars*.

The theological argument was now most clearly drawn. As Kuhn writes, "Copernicanism required a transformation in man's view of his relation to God and of the bases of his morality" (1957, p. 193). The earth was no longer the center of God's creation. There was no longer a fixed, heavenly location for God's throne. The perfection of the universe—with the earth at the center of a series of fixed, concentric, crystalline circles in which the planets traveled—was contaminated. Protestant leaders, believing in the literal word of Bible, and led by Luther himself, had attacked the heliocentric universe of Copernicus as early as 1539. The Catholic church, at first allowing much more latitude to individual belief in this matter, was much slower to condemn, but in 1610 the church officially designated the Copernican model a heresy, and in 1616, *De Revolutionibus* and all other writings that affirmed the earth's motion were put on the Index, a list of writings that were forbidden to be taught or even read.

For many years the split between the mathematical astronomers and the church continued rather quietly, with the mathematicians generally winning out among educated audiences. Then, in 1609, Galileo Galilei (1564–1642), the Italian astronomer, turned the newly invented telescope skyward and changed forever what we know about the heavens, how we know it, and its significance in the eyes of the non-specialist, general public. Galileo added new empirical evidence and new technology to the toolkit of astronomy, opening new avenues of knowledge and popularizing them. The telescope had been created in the Netherlands; Galileo was the first to turn it toward the skies, and he made one discovery after another: The Milky Way is not just a dull glow in the sky but a gigantic collection of stars; the moon's surface is irregular, covered with craters and hills; the moon's radiant light is a reflection from the sun; the sun has imperfections, dark spots which appear and disappear across its surface; the earth is not the only planet with moons—Galileo observed at least four satellites circling Jupiter.

Galileo wrote, "We shall prove the earth to be a wandering body [in orbit around the sun] ... This we shall support by an infinitude of arguments drawn from nature" (Galileo, *Starry Messenger*, p. 45) Over and over Galileo stressed the validity of his own empirical observations. "With the aid of the telescope this has been scrutinized so directly and with such ocular certainty that all the disputes which have vexed the philosophers through so many ages have been resolved, and we are at last freed from wordy debates about it" (p. 49). "One may learn with all the certainty of sense evidence" (p. 28); "All these facts were discovered and observed by me not many days ago with the aid of a spyglass which I devised, after first being illuminated by divine grace" (p. 28); "our own eyes show us" (p. 57). Galileo's appeal to sense evidence, to direct observation, to empirically based information, and to its complete accessibility to anyone who looks through a telescope, found enormous resonance. He wrote for a general audience, not for university scholars; he wrote in Italian, not in Latin. The publication of Galileo's discoveries increased public interest in astronomy, and that public interest gradually turned into general acceptance.

The church, deeply enmeshed in its cold war with Protestantism, finally turned against him. In 1633 Galileo was tried by the Roman Inquisition and found guilty of having taught his doctrines against the orders of the church. Under threat of torture, the sixty-nine-year-old scientist recanted his beliefs and was sentenced to house arrest in his villa near Florence for the rest of his life. (In 1992, 359 years later, Pope John Paul II officially and publicly spoke of the ruling of the Inquisition as a "sad misunderstanding which now belongs to the past," and suggested that there is no incompatibility between "the spirit of science and its rules of research on the one hand, and the Christian faith on the other" (*Philadelphia Inquirer*, November 1, 1992).

In the same year as Galileo's death Isaac Newton was born in England, on Christmas Day, 1642. He studied at Cambridge University and became a professor of mathematics there at age twenty-six. In the course of his research, he discovered the calculus, a discovery he shared, separately, with the German mathematician Gottfried Wilhelm Leibnitz (1646–1716). A mathematical system especially useful in calculating motion along curved lines, the calculus was immediately valuable in predicting the celestial course of planets and the earthly trajectory of artillery shells. Another area of Newton's early research was in optics, focusing on the spectrum of light as it passed through a prism. Then he turned his attention to the new issues raised by Copernicus, Kepler, and Galileo: Why do heavy bodies always fall toward earth even as the earth is moving through space? What moves the earth? What moves the planets and what keeps them in their orbits? Before Copernicus, Ptolemy's view of the fixed spheres of the universe answered those questions. But without those fixed spheres, how should we understand the movements of the heavens?

In finding the universal law of gravity, Newton showed that the laws of planetary motion that Kepler formulated, and the laws of earthly movement that Galileo discovered in his later career, along with additional principles of inertia of motion discovered by the French mathematician and philosopher René Descartes (1596–1650), were all consistent. The universal principle of gravitation, coupled with the principle of inertia—that a body once set in motion tends to continue moving at the same speed in the same direction—gives a form for understanding the means by which the universe holds together. Moreover, these forces of inertia and gravity are universal, operating in the same way on earth as in the wider universe. Asserting the principle of the universal law of gravity was the imaginative leap of Newton's new discovery; working out the mathematics was the toil of genius, and he produced it in 1687 in his *Mathematical Principles of Natural Philosophy*. He worked out the formula for the pull of gravity: all matter moves as if every particle attracts every other particle with a force proportional to the product of the two masses, and inversely proportional to the square of the distance between them. This force is universal gravitation.

Like all later scientists, Newton did not try to explain why this force worked, only how it worked. This new law had enormous philosophical implica-tions, for it explained the "glue" in the Copernican system of the universe. It also had very practical consequences in the understanding and prediction of the tides. The great advances in mathematics underpinned not only theoretical research, but also practical invention in the form of time-keeping, mapping, and processes that required accuracy such as the aiming of artillery and the construction of steam engines. In light of his revolutionary contributions, Newton was named President of the Royal Society in 1703.

The discoveries in astronomy, physics, and mathematics were the leading sectors in the scientific revolution of the seventeenth century, but they were not alone. In England, William Harvey published *On the Movement of the Heart and Blood*, based on years of laboratory research and vivisection of animals, demonstrating the circulation of blood through the body. In the Netherlands, Anthony van Leeuwenhoek (1632–1723) improved the newly invented microscope, the other great advance in optics along with the telescope, to see and then create drawings of blood corpuscles, spermatozoa, and bacteria. His observations enabled him to argue that reproduction even among tiny creatures was through sexual mating, not spontaneous generation. Leeuwenhoek was a businessman in the cloth trade, not specially educated in the sciences, and his election as a Fellow of the Royal Society of London in 1680 demonstrated that amateurs were entering avidly into this new research.

Leeuwenhoek's researches expanded the knowledge of the number and variety of tiny, microscopic creatures. Carolus Linnaeus (1707–78) developed a system of classification for these and all other known creatures in nature, *Systema Naturae* (1735), including an analysis of sexual reproduction in plants. The further evolution of eighteenth-century science was well underway.

The new science both reduced and expanded human powers and self-understanding. Some, frightened, agreed with Blaise Pascal, a devout Christian French mathematician: "I am terrified by the eternal silence of these infinite spaces." But more took heart along with Alexander Pope, that a brave, new world was dawning:

> Nature and nature's law lay hid in night;
> God said, "Let Newton be," and all was light.

The new world of science swept away much superstition, at least for the time, and suggested that rationality and science could create a new world in which people would trust their senses to gather empirical information and to act upon it, a world in which the laws of nature could be discovered and calculated, a world in which science would inspire technological invention in the practical arts of making human life more productive and more comfortable. Throughout the eighteenth century, this vision of natural law and the power of human reason spilled over from science and technology to philosophy and political theory.

THE *PHILOSOPHES* AND THE ENLIGHTENMENT IN THE EIGHTEENTH CENTURY

In the century between the Glorious Revolution in England and the American and French revolutions, a movement in philosophic thought emerged called the Enlightenment. Its intellectual center was in France, although key participants lived in America, Scotland, England, Prussia, Russia, and elsewhere. The French leaders of the Enlightenment were called **philosophes** and their philosophy helped inspire the American and the French revolutions.

Following on the scientific revolution of the seventeenth century the *philosophes* believed in a world of rationality, in which collected human knowledge and systematic thought could serve as powerful tools for finding order in the universe and for solving key problems in political and economic life. Their concerns for clarity of thought, combined with the desire to solve practical problems in public life, gave them considerable influence over the restructuring of new political institutions in their age of revolution. The authors of the American Declaration of Independence and of the French Declaration of the Rights of Man and the Citizen drew much of their inspiration from the *philosophes*. The *philosophes* believed in order, but also in freedom of thought and expression. For them, public discussion and debate were the means toward finding better ideas and solutions. Indeed, the *philosophes* were in constant dialogue and debate with one another.

Travel influenced the *philosophes'* thought, opening them to a wider range of ideas. Charles de Secondat, the Baron de Montesquieu (1689–1755), traveled widely himself and presented satiric criticism of French institutions, including the monarchy and the Catholic church, in the form of *Persian Letters*, supposedly dispatched by two visitors to France writing their observations to readers at home. Twenty-seven years later, in 1748, Montesquieu wrote his most influential work, *The Spirit of Laws*, in which he recognized that different countries need different kinds of governments, and advocated a separation of powers based on his (mis)understanding of the British system. The authors of the United States constitution later acknowledged their debt to Montesquieu's thought.

The Philosophers at Supper by Jean Huber, 1750. Voltaire (1), Condorcet (5), and Diderot (6) are among the figures depicted in this engraving, a visual checklist of important Enlightenment thinkers. Seeing the Western world as emerging from centuries of darkness and ignorance, these Frenchmen promoted reason, science, and a respect for humanity— ideas that would underpin the intellectual case for the French Revolution of 1789. (*Bibliothèque Nationale, Paris*)

In terms of spiritual and religious beliefs, most *philosophes* were deists. They allowed that the world may have required an original creator, like Aristotle's prime mover, but once the processes of life had begun, he had withdrawn. Their metaphor was that of a watchmaker who built the mechanism, started it moving, and departed. Humanity's fate thereafter was in its own hands.

In contrast to such Catholic doctrines as original sin and the authority of the church over human reason, the *philosophes* argued that human progress was possible through the steady and unrestricted expansion of knowledge or "enlightenment." Jean-Antoine-Nicolas de Caritat, Marquis de Condorcet (1743–94), author of the *Sketch of the Progress of the Human Mind* (published in 1795), proclaimed "the perfectibility of humanity is indefinite" (Andrea and Overfield, p. 153). The most famous academic product of the *philosophes* and the Enlightenment was the *Encyclopedia, or Rational Dictionary of the Arts, Sciences, and Crafts*, compiled by Denis Diderot (1713–84) and containing articles by leading scholars and *philosophes*. The *Encyclopedia* reaffirmed this faith in human progress based on education:

> The aim of an Encyclopedia is to collect all the knowledge that now lies scattered over the face of the earth, to make known its general structure to the men among whom we live, and to transmit it to those who will come after us, in order that the labors of past ages may be useful to the ages that will follow, that our grandsons, as they become better educated, may become at the same time more virtuous and more happy, and that we may not die without having deserved well of the human race. (Columbia University, *Contemporary Civilization*, pp. 988–9)

Diderot called for further social and political revolution. "We are beginning to shake off the yoke of authority and tradition in order to hold fast to the laws of reason" (p. 992). Challenging authority meant being open to multiple perspectives rather than holding a single truth, and Diderot built this concept into the structure of his volumes.

> By giving cross-references to articles where solid principles serve as foundation for the diametrically opposed truths we shall be able to throw down the whole edifice of mud and scatter the idle heap of dust. ... If these cross-references, which now confirm and now refute, are carried out artistically according

to a plan carefully conceived in advance, they will give to the Encyclopedia the ... ability to change men's common way of thinking. (p. 996)

The *Encyclopedia* ultimately filled seventeen volumes of text and eleven of illustrations.

Another *philosophe*, François-Marie Arouet, better known as Voltaire (1694–1778), spoke out with courage and wit. His *Elements of the Philosophy of Newton* (1738) explicated new scientific evidence of the rational order and the human ability to comprehend the universe; *Philosophical Letters on the English* (1734) argued for freedom of religion, inquiry, and the press; *Essai sur les moeurs* (1756), translated as *Universal History*, gave a humanistic context to historical development and placed responsibility in human hands. Voltaire cried *"Ecrasez l'infame!"*— "crush the infamy" of superstition, intolerance, and the power of the clergy.

The *philosophes* were not, however, committed to popular democracy. Voltaire preferred benevolent and **enlightened despotism** to badly administered self-rule. In the best of all possible worlds, there would be an enlightened ruler like Frederick II, the Great, of Prussia (r. 1740–86), at whose court Voltaire lived for several years, or Catherine II, the Great, Empress of Russia (r. 1762–96), of whom he was a close friend, or Joseph II, Emperor of Austria (r. 1765–90). All three ruled countries in which the administration was efficient, taxes were reasonable, agricultural and handicraft production was encouraged, freedom of expression and religion was allowed, the military was strengthened, and powerful empires resulted. The enlightened despot acted in disciplined ways, subject in his or her mind to the law of nature. But the population at large had no say or vote in the administration.

Skepticism regarding democratic government was carried further in the works of Jean-Jacques Rousseau (1712–78), perhaps the most enigmatic and ambiguous of all of the eighteenth-century French thinkers. Rousseau questioned the primacy of intellect and human ingenuity. Like Hobbes and Locke, he wrote of the "state of nature," but, unlike them, he seemed, in some ways, to wish to return to it. His *Social Contract* (1762) lamented, "Man is born free; and everywhere he is in chains." In his *Discourse on the Origin of Inequality* (1755) he wrote:

> There is hardly any inequality in the state of nature; all the inequality which now prevails owes its strength and growth to the development of our

faculties and the advance of the human mind, and becomes at last permanent and legitimate by the establishment of property and laws. (Columbia University, *Contemporary Civilization*, p. 1147)

Rousseau proposed a democracy far more radical than that of the other *philosophes* yet he also seemed to justify a repressive tyranny of the majority. Like Locke and Hobbes, Rousseau mythologized an original social contract transforming a state of nature into a community, and he attributed great power to that community: "Each of us puts his person and all his power in common under the supreme direction of the general will" (Columbia University, *Contemporary Civilization*, p. 1151). "Whoever refuses to obey the general will shall be compelled to do so by the whole body. This means nothing less than that he will be forced to be free" (p. 1153). Political philosphers have argued for more than two centuries over the paradox of Rousseau's "general will." How is the citizen "forced to be free"? Is this a proclamation of freedom, justification for suppressing minorities, or a proposal for creating a totalitarian state?

Adam Smith, whose economic ideas we have already examined (see pp. 427–32), is sometimes group-ed with the *philosophes*, with whom he carried on extensive discussions and correspondence. Like Locke, Smith believed it was normal for people to want to "better their condition" materially. He saw that this attempt was not always successful, but suggested:

> it is well that nature imposes upon us in this manner. It is this deception which rouses and keeps in continual motion the industry of mankind. It is this which first prompted them to cultivate the ground, to build houses, to found cities and commonwealths, and to invent and improve all the sciences and arts, which ennoble and embellish human life. (*Moral Sentiments*, IV. 1.10)

Much less optimistically, Smith recognized that private enrichment would engender jealousy and envy. Private property, therefore, needed to be protected and this, he agreed with Locke, was the task of government:

> Civil government, so far as it is instituted for the security of property, is in reality instituted for the defense of the rich against the poor, or of those who have some property against those who have none at all. (Smith, *The Wealth of Nations*, p. 674)

At the time of the American and French revolutions these arguments for enlightenment, rationality, experimental science, secularism, private profit and ownership, "fellow feeling," and limitations on the power of government all clamored for changes in politics, economics, and social life. But what would be the substance and direction of those changes? How would they be implemented and by whom?

REVOLUTION IN NORTH AMERICA, 1776

As English settlers began to colonize North America, Australia, and South Africa in the seventeenth and eighteenth centuries, they assumed that they shared in the rights of all Englishmen. By the 1760s, however, North American settlers were beginning to resent the control over their political and economic life exerted by rulers in Britain. British control over American trade, restrictions on the development of American shipping, and the resulting limitations on the development of certain kinds of manufacture, were as galling as the issue of taxation. The 1763 British victory over the French in the Seven Years' War in North America, concluding a global cluster of wars between the two powers for commercial and naval supremacy (see pp. 423–6), ended the threat of attacks by French or Indians, and freed the American colonists from further need of British troops. However, the British decided to maintain a large army in North America and to tax the colonies directly to pay for it. The 1765 Stamp Act levied taxes on a long list of commerical and legal documents. It was vigorously protested by the colonists and only reluctantly repealed by Parliament because of serious rioting and boycotting of British goods.

Additional grievances against further imperious decrees of King George III built up until finally the Americans declared themselves an independent country in 1776 and fought to end British rule over them. The American Declaration of Independence set out a list of these "injuries and usurpations." It reflected the American resolve to secure the same legal rights as Englishmen had won at home almost a century earlier. It charged the king with "taking away our Charters, abolishing our most valuable Laws, and altering fundamentally the Forms of our Governments." It declared the social contract that bound the colonies to Britain had been broken. It declared, ultimately, the right of revolution.

Signing of the Declaration of Independence, July 4, 1776 **by John Trumbull, 1786–97.** What began as a protest against colonial trade restrictions and the limiting of political liberty grew into a revolutionary struggle and the birth of a nation. The Declaration of Independence enshrined the principles underlying the new United States and later influenced freedom-fighters all over the world. (*Capitol Collection, Washington*)

The American Revolution went further in establishing political democracy than had the Glorious Revolution in England. It abolished the monarchy entirely, replacing it with an elected government. Having declared that "all men are created equal," with unalienable rights not only to life and liberty, but also to the vague but seductive "pursuit of happiness," the revolutionaries now set out to consolidate their commitments in a new legal structure. Their leaders, men like George Washington, Benjamin Franklin, Thomas Jefferson, and James Madison, were soldiers, entrepreneurs, and statesmen of considerable erudition, common sense, restraint, and balance.

THE CONSTITUTION AND THE BILL OF RIGHTS 1789

After the Americans won their war for independence, 1775–81, and in 1783 achieved a peace treaty with Britain, political leaders of the thirteen colonies met in Philadelphia to establish a framework for their new nation. They drafted a new Constitution in 1789, and a Bill of Rights, which was ratified in 1791. The American Bill of Rights, the first ten amendments to the Constitution, guar-

anteed to Americans not only the basic rights enjoyed by the British at the time, but more: freedom of religion (and the separation of church and state), press, assembly, and petition; the right to bear arms; protection against unreasonable searches and against cruel and unusual punishment; and the right to a speedy and proper trial by a jury of peers. The Americans established a federal system of government. The states individually set the rules for voting and many, but not all, removed the property requirements. By 1800 Vermont had instituted universal manhood suffrage, and South Carolina, Pennsylvania, New Hampshire, and Delaware extended the vote to virtually every adult white male taxpayer.

Historians of the early United States situate the more radical American approach to political liberty in at least four factors: religious, geographic, social, and philosophical. First, a disproportionate share of the settlers coming to America from England and Europe were religious dissenters seeking spiritual independence outside the established churches of their countries. Their widespread, popular beliefs in the importance of individual liberties carried over from religion into politics.

Second, the availability of apparently open land presented abundant individual opportunity to the new Americans (as they dispossessed Native Americans). Later, the historian Frederick Jackson Turner would extend this "frontier thesis," arguing that the relative freedom and openness of American life was based psychologically as well as materially on the presence of seemingly endless open frontier land. Third, the absence of landed and aristocratic privilege, and the strength of artisan classes in the urban population increased the demand for democracy. Finally, eighteenth-century political thought had generally grown more radical, especially among the *philosophes* in France. By the time the Americans wrote their Bill of Rights, the French Revolution was well underway.

THE FIRST ANTI-IMPERIAL REVOLUTION

The American Revolution, in addition to securing British rights for Americans, was also, and perhaps more importantly, the first modern anti-colonial revolution. The trade and taxation policies imposed by Britain had pushed businessmen and artisans into opposition to British rule. Other nations, notably France, eager to embarrass Britain and to detach its most promising colonies, provided financial and military support, which helped the Americans to win their independence.

One of the goals of the Revolution was to open the North American continent west of the Appalachian Mountains to settlement. The British

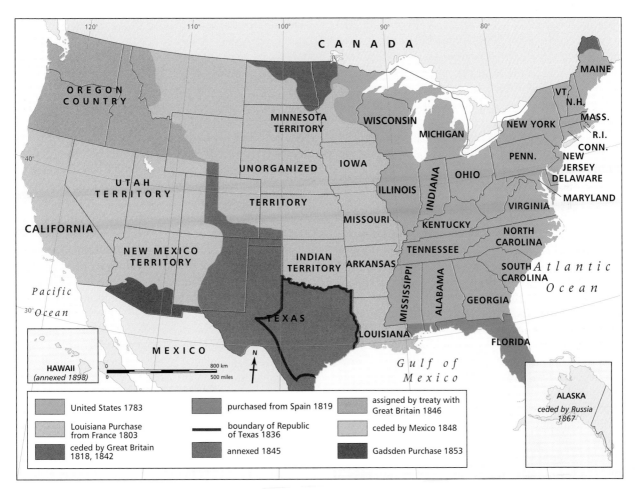

The growth of the United States The westward expansion of the United States was effected by territorial cession, acquisition, and conquest. Following independence in 1783, the Louisiana Purchase from France (1803) and the annexations of West and East Florida from Spain, doubled the nation's size. Another doubling occurred with the annexation of Texas (1845), the acquisition of Oregon (1846), and military victory over Mexico (1848), which brought the southwest. Alaska was purchased from Russia (1867). Hawaii was annexed in 1898. In all cases, European immigrants and their descendants displaced Native Americans, and in less than a century the United States had become one of the world's largest nations.

prohibition on this westward movement had stood in stark contrast to Spanish and Portuguese settlement policy in Latin America. As the newly independent Americans migrated westward, annexing land as they went, they began to develop imperial interests that were expressed in the mystique of "Manifest Destiny." This popular belief in America's natural growth across the continent was consolidated with the huge Louisiana Purchase from France in 1803. Texans were encouraged to assert their independence from Mexico in 1836 and were then absorbed into the American Union in 1845. Warfare with Mexico in 1846–8 ended in victory for the United States and the annexation of the southwest. Other annexations of land in North America took place more peacefully, with negotiations with Britain for the Oregon country in 1844–6 and with Russia for the purchase of Alaska in 1867. (Offshore expansion began in 1898, see pp. 663–6, 792.)

Over the centuries America served as an inspiration to anti-colonial forces. Jawaharlal Nehru, leading India's twentieth-century struggle for independence from Britain, cited the American Revolution as a model for his own country: "This political change in America was important and destined to bear great results. The American colonies which became free then have grown today [1932] into the most powerful, the richest, and industrially the most advanced country in the world" (p. 355).

The American Revolution, however, did not bring democracy to everyone. The greatest shortcoming was the American perpetuation of slavery. The system was finally ended only by the American Civil War, 1861–5, the bloodiest in the history of the nation. Even afterward, racial discrimination characterized American law until the 1960s and continues to mark American practice up to the present. The status of the Native American population actually worsened after the Revolution, as settlers of European extraction headed west, first by wagon train and later by railroad. They slaughtered American Indians, pushed them out of the way, confined them to remote, semi-barren reservations, destroyed the buffalo herds on which their nomadic existence depended, and discouraged the preservation of their separate cultures and languages. For the indigenous Indians the effects of the Revolution were exactly opposite to those of the settler-invaders: expansion became contraction, democracy became tyranny, prosperity became poverty, and liberty became confinement.

The hypocrisy of democratic statements, on the one hand, and atrocities against Indians, on the other, peaked in the presidency of Andrew Jackson (1829–37). Jackson fought against economic and political privilege and to extend opportunity to the common man, yet he ordered the United States Army to evict the Cherokee Nation from their lands in Georgia and to drive them to the "Great American Desert" in the west in direct defiance of the Supreme Court of the United States. About one-fourth of the 15,000 Indians forced onto this "Trail of Tears" died *en route*.

How did America reconcile its ideals of equality and liberty with the enslavement of blacks and the confinement of Indians at home? It did so by considering non-whites and non-Europeans as "other" —that is, as not quite equal biologically. Race was often used as a definition, usually made by a quick, if approximate and sometimes inaccurate, visual measure, and often as a legal standard. The fixing of legal identity by race, which had been heretofore a flexible category, became especially common in the southern United States in dealing with slaves, ex-slaves, and free blacks. For many years, racial definition was used as a legal standard in excluding Asians from immigrating as well. If non-whites were considered not quite equal biologically, the unalienable right to liberty could be abridged. Once the revolutionary principle of equality was accepted in America and elsewhere, the battle was drawn between those who wished to narrow its application to an "in-group" while excluding "others" and those who wished to apply it to all peoples. That battle continues today, in law and in practice, in the United States and around the globe.

THE FRENCH REVOLUTION AND NAPOLEON 1789–1812

The American Revolution, with its combined messages of colonial revolt, constitutional government, individual freedom, and equality under law, inspired many peoples at the time and over the centuries. But in comparison with European countries and their experiences, America and its Revolution were unique. At the end of the eighteenth century, America was a country of four million people on the fringes of a continental wilderness, without traditions of class and clerical privilege, and founded in large measure by dissidents. Building on already existing British freedoms and fighting a war (with the support of several international allies) against a distant colonial government, the leaders of the Revolution were an educated, comfortable elite. The French Revolution, on the other hand, was an internal revolt against entrenched feudal, clerical, and monarchical privilege within the most populous (24 million people) and most powerful European state of its time. It unleashed powerful, combative internal factions, none of which could control the direction or the velocity of revolutionary events inside or outside of France. The French Revolution immediately affected all of Europe, most of the western hemisphere, and indeed the whole world. Some would argue that the battles over its central principles continue even today. The twentieth-century Chinese leader Zhou Enlai, when asked to assess the effects of the French Revolution, allegedly replied: "It's too soon to tell."

ORIGINS OF REVOLUTION

The French Revolution, like the English Civil Wars of the 1640s, was triggered by the king's need for funds. Much like Charles I, King Louis XVI (r. 1774–92) decided to solicit these funds by convening leaders of the French people through the "Estates-General" in 1789.

From this point on, political, social, and ideological change proceeded very rapidly as political institutions, social classes, and philosophical beliefs challenged one another in a continuous unfolding of critical events. France was divided, hierarchically, into three "Estates": the clergy, numbering about 100,000 and controlling perhaps 10 percent of the land of France; the nobility, perhaps 300,000 men, who owned approximately 25 percent of the land; and everyone else. This third estate included a rising and prosperous group of urban merchants and professionals (estimated at 8 percent of the total population), as well as working-class artisans, and the four-fifths of France who were farmers. The wealth that the king wished to tap was concentrated in the first two estates and the **bourgeoisie**, or leading urban professional and commercial classes, of the third.

THE REVOLT OF THE THIRD ESTATE

The Estates-General had not been convened since 1614 and the procedures for its meeting were disputed, revealing grievances not only against the king, but also among the representatives. The nobles wished to seize the moment to make the Estates-General into the constitutional government of France, with the king subordinate to them. They wanted guarantees of personal liberty, freedom of the press and speech, and freedom from arbitrary arrest. They also wanted minimal taxation, but they might have conceded this point in exchange for greater political power. Under their proposed constitution, the Estates-General would meet in three separate chambers: one for the nobility; one for the clergy, in which the nobility also had a powerful voice; and a third for everyone else.

The Third Estate, which had long regarded the nobility as parasitic and resented their multitude of special privileges, viewed the new proposals with suspicion. The members of the Third Estate drew their inspiration for a more democratic, representative, inclusive, and accountable government from the writings of the *philosophes*, and the experience of the revolutions in England and, especially, in America. Their local spokesman and leading pamphleteer was actually a clergyman, the Abbé Emmanuel-Joseph Sieyès (1748–1836), who wrote *What Is the Third Estate?* (1789). The tract opened with a catechism of three political questions and answers: "(1) What is the third estate? Everything. (2) What has it been in the political order up to the present? Nothing. (3) What does it demand? To Become Something." The leaders of the Third Estate asked for an end to the privileges that had enriched and empowered the clergy and the nobility while reducing the opportunities available to everyone else and impoverishing the French Crown. Many saw the king as an ally in the struggle against the nobility. They proposed that the entire Estates-General meet in a single body, since the king had granted them as many representatives as both of the other two Estates combined.

When the Parlement of Paris ruled that the three Estates should meet separately, as the nobility had wished, the Third Estate was enraged. For six weeks its members boycotted the Estates-General when it was convened in May 1789. On June 13 a few priests joined them and four days later the Third Estate, with its allies, declared itself the "National Assembly." The king locked them out of their meeting hall. On 20 June they met on a nearby indoor tennis court and swore the "Oath of the Tennis Court," claiming legal power, and declaring that they would not disband until a new constitution was drafted. Louis XVI, frightened by these events, and unwilling or unable to assert his own leadership, called up some 18,000 troops to defend himself from possible attack at his palace in Versailles where all these events were taking place.

THE REVOLT OF THE POOR

Meanwhile, in Paris, 12 miles (19 kilometers) away, and throughout France, mobs of people were rising against organized authority. The harvest had been poor, and the price of bread in 1789 was near record heights. Some farmers refused to pay their taxes and their manorial dues, and many city people were hungry. Beggars and brigands began to roam the countryside and move toward Paris.

The Oath of the Tennis Court **by Jacques-Louis David, 1790.** In this dramatic composition, David captures the moment when the Third Estate asserted their sovereignty as the elected representatives of France. The merchants, professionals, and artisans who attended the hastily convened meeting swore to remain in session until they had drawn up a new constitution—one that would end the vested interests of the nobility and clergy. (*Musée Carnavalet, Paris*)

Contemporary colored engraving showing women marching to Versailles on 5 October 1789. Angered by reports of a luxurious banquet staged by the king, a large crowd of Parisians, mostly women, stormed Versailles and laid siege to the royal palace. Louis XVI and his family, though later executed, were at this point saved only by the intervention of the French general the Marquis de Lafayette.

In the capital, mobs stormed the Bastille, which was a combination of jail and armory. Meeting violent resistance, they murdered the governor of the Bastille, the mayor of Paris, and a number of soldiers. In an attempt to contain these revolutionary disorders, the king, in Versailles, recognized the National Assembly, the new group formed by the Third Estate and its allies, as representatives of the people and authorized it to draft a new constitution.

The National Assembly abolished what was left of feudalism and serfdom, the tithe for the church, and the special privileges of the nobility. It issued the "Declaration of the Rights of Man and the Citizen" with seventeen articles, including:

1. Men are born and remain free and equal in rights; social distinctions may be based only upon general usefulness.

2. The aim of every political association is the preservation of the natural and inalienable rights of man; these rights are liberty, property, security, and resistance to oppression.

3. The source of all sovereignty resides essentially in the nation. …

6. Law is the expression of the general will. … All citizens, being equal before it, are equally admissible to all public offices, positions, and employments, according to their capacity, and without other distinction than that of virtues and talents. …

13. For the maintenance of the public force and for the expenses of administration a common tax is indispensable; it must be assessed equally on all citizens in proportion to their means. …

15. Society has the right to require of every public agent an accounting of his administration.

The Declaration further affirmed freedom of thought, religion, petition, and due process under law. It represented a triumph for the doctrines of the *philosophes*.

Meanwhile, hungry mobs in Paris continued toward insurrection. In October, led by a demonstration of housewives, market women, and revolutionary militants protesting the high price of bread, 20,000 Parisians marched to the royal palace in Versailles. This "March of the Women" broke into the palace, overwhelmed the National Guard, and forced the royal family to return to Paris where they could be kept under surveillance. In the meantime, in the countryside, peasants felt an (unfounded) "Great Fear" that landlords were attempting to block reform by hiring thugs to burn the harvest. In response, peasants attacked the estates of the nobility and the clergy, and their managers.

Over the next two years, the National Assembly drew up a constitution, which called for a constitutional monarchy; did away with titles and perquisites of nobility and clergy; introduced uniform government across the country; disestablished the Roman Catholic clergy and confiscated the property of the church; and convened a new Legislative Assembly, for which about one-half of adult, male Frenchmen were entitled to vote, essentially by a property qualification. Protestants, Jews, and agnostics were admitted to full citizenship and could vote and run for office if they met the property qualifications. Citizenship would be based not on religious affiliation but on residence in the country and allegiance to its government. Except for the radical—and polarizing—anti-clerical position, the actions of the French Revolution thus far seemed quite similar to those of England and America. They were consistent with the optimistic and activist world-view of the *philosophes*. The new Constitution was finally promulgated in September 1791 following a wave of strikes and an official ban on labor organizations.

INTERNATIONAL WAR, THE "SECOND" REVOLUTION, AND THE TERROR 1791–9

In June 1791 Louis XVI and his queen Marie-Antoinette attempted to flee France but were apprehended and, thereafter, held as virtual prisoners in the royal palace. Shocked and frightened, thousands of aristocrats emigrated to neighboring countries that were more respectful of monarchy and aristocracy. News of the abolition of feudal

The Hall of Mirrors, Palace of Versailles, c. 1725. This opulent royal palace, 12 miles (19 kilometers) southwest of Paris, is closely associated with Louis XIV, the Sun King. His belief in the absolute power of kings finds its expression at Versailles. During the reign of his grandson, Louis XVI, its aristocratic splendor fueled the anger of the poor peasants and revolutionaries.

privilege and of the Civil Constitution of the Clergy filled the nobility and clergy across Europe with dread. Leopold II, the Habsburg Emperor (r. 1790–92) and brother of Marie-Antoinette, entered into discussions with other rulers to consider war against the new French government. The French National Assembly, meeting under the new constitution, began to mobilize both in response to this threat and in anticipation of extending the revolution. In April 1792 it declared war on the Austrian monarchy, and for the next twenty-three years, France would be at war with several of the major countries of Europe.

Events careered onward at a revolutionary pace. The war went poorly and mobs stormed the royal palace attempting to kill the king and beginning the "Second French Revolution." Louis sought protection in the National Assembly and was imprisoned; all his official powers were terminated. The Assembly disbanded and called for a new National Convention—to be elected by universal male suffrage—to draw up a new constitution. Amid mob violence, the new Convention met in September 1792. Its leaders were *Jacobins*, members of a nationwide network of political clubs named (ironically) for a former convent in Paris where they had first met. They divided into the more moderate *Girondins*, named for a region of France and in general representing the provinces, and the *Montagnards*, representatives mostly from Paris, who drew their name from the benches they occupied on the uppermost left side of the assembly hall. By 361 to 359 votes, the Convention voted to execute the king in January 1793. The "Second Revolution" was well underway.

Outside the Assembly, the Paris Commune, the government of Paris, represented the workers, merchants, and artisans of the city, who were generally more radical than the Convention. They were called the *sansculottes*, "without breeches," because the men wore long trousers rather than the knee breeches of the middle and aristocratic classes. In June 1793, the Commune invaded the National Convention and forced the arrest of thirty-one *Girondins* on charges of treason, leaving the more radical *Montagnards* in control.

To govern in the midst of the combined international and civil warfare, the Convention created a Committee of Public Safety, which launched a Reign of Terror against "counter-revolutionaries." It executed about 40,000 people between mid-1793 and mid-1794. At Nantes, in the Vendée region of western France, the center of the royalist counter-

revolution, the Committee intentionally drowned 2000 people. To wage war abroad it instituted a *levée en masse*, or national military draft, which raised an unprecedented army of 800,000 men, and mobilized the economic resources of France to support it.

The Committee intensified the campaign against feudal privilege, rejecting the payment of compensation to the manor lords, who lost their special rights over their tenants. It promoted instruction in practical farming and craft production, spoke of introducing universal elementary education, and abolished slavery throughout France's colonies. It introduced a new calendar, counting Year 1 from the founding of the French Republic in 1793, giving new names to the twelve months, and dividing each month into three weeks of ten days each. The most important leader of the Committee, Maximilien Robespierre (1758–94), introduced in 1794 the Worship of the Supreme Being, a kind of civic religious ritual that alienated the Catholic majority in France.

By July 1794, however, French armies were winning wars against the other European powers, and the domestic economy seemed to be recovering. The members of the Convention, partly out of fear for their own lives, managed to end both the mob-inspired violence and the official Terror. The Convention outlawed and guillotined Robespierre. It relaxed price controls and, when working-class mobs threatened the Convention, called in the troops and suppressed the revolt. In 1795 it instituted yet another constitution, this time calling for a three-stage election of a representative government. Almost all adult males could vote for electors who, in turn, chose a national legislative assembly composed of men who did have to meet property qualifications and who, in turn, chose an executive of five Directors. When the 1795 elections were threatened by insurrection, the Convention called upon General Napoleon Bonaparte (1769–1821) to protect the process.

The Directory, as the executive body was called, governed from 1795 to 1799. With the execution of the monarch, the manorial system and the privileges of the nobility and clergy had come to an end, and the Directory ratified the new peasant and commercial landowners in the possession of their new property. However, the Directory itself was unpopular and unstable, and the greater freedom benefited its opponents while at the same time enabling the Catholic church to make a strong comeback. The elections of Directors in 1797, 1798,

FRENCH REVOLUTION—KEY EVENTS

1789
May   Meeting of Estates-General called by Louis XVI to discuss financial reforms; nobles oppose reform
June   Third Estate (commoners) demands to meet together with First and Second Estates (clergy and nobility); King refuses
Tennis Court Oath: Third Estate, joined by some members of First and Second, declares itself to be a National Assembly
July   Hunger and anger at authority stirs the poor; "Great Fear" seizes; mobs storm Bastille in Paris
August   Declaration of the Rights of Man and the Citizen; abolition of feudal privileges
October   Women's March on Versailles; forces Louis to relocate to Paris; National (Constituent Assembly) begins drafting constitution, through 1791: abolishes hereditary titles; extends franchise to about half adult males, based on property; decentralizes government but makes it uniform; disestablishes clergy and confiscates Church property; bases citizenship on residence, not religion; abolishes guilds

1790   Work of Constituent Assembly continues; Civil Constitution of the Clergy splits the clergy into "constitutional" and "refractory" groups and divides their followers

1791
June   Wave of strikes; Labor organizations forbidden by Le Chapelier law; Louis flees Paris, is apprehended in Varennes and returned
September   New Constitution promulgated
October   New Legislative Assembly meets, divided between Jacobins and Girondins

1792
January   Girondins forms government but are undermined by Jacobins
April   France declares war on Austria; 23 years of war begin
August   "Second French Revolution"; working class uprising in Paris establishes Commune, imprisons king and royal family, forces abrogation of Constitution and preparation of new constitution by new National Convention
September   Mob violence in Paris, 1100 executed; National Convention, dominated by Jacobins, elected on basis of universal suffrage, proclaims a republic

1793
January   Louis XVI guillotined by vote of 361–359
April   National Convention establishes Committee of Public Safety, dominated by Maximilien Robespierre; Reign of Terror begins (40,000 executed, 1793–4); levée en masse military draft; revolutionary calendar
October   Marie-Antoinette guillotined

1794   Military victories; decline in mob violence; end of official Terror
July   Robespierre and 21 supporters guillotined

1795
May   Mob insurrection suppressed by army
October   Directory of five members as chief executive of the government

1795–9   Directory confirms new rights of peasants and commercial landlords, but is politically unstable

1799
November   Directory overthrown in coup led by Napoleon; consulate of three members with Napoleon as first consul is established, effectively ending the Revolution

---

and 1799 were disputed, and on each occasion army officers were called in to dismiss the Directors, until, in 1799, Bonaparte, acting with the Abbé Sieyès, staged a *coup d'état* and had himself appointed First Consul. In 1802 his position was upgraded to consul for life and, in 1804, to emperor. Losing the right of free elections, France itself became a benevolent despotism. The process that historians usually call the French Revolution (see Focus, opposite) was over.

FOCUS
The Historiography of the French Revolution

The study of the French Revolution remains the pre-eminent subject of French historiography, producing a seemingly endless variety of interpretations. Three approaches, however, have predominated. The first emphasizes the importance of ideas, stressing the *philosophes* as the precursors of revolution. This interpretation tends to focus on the first three months of the Revolution and the significance of the "Declaration of the Rights of Man and the Citizen." R.R. Palmer's *The Age of the Democratic Revolution* (1959), for example, favors this reading. A second interpretation stresses the significance of class interests in the Revolution, and tends to highlight the next chronological stage, as urban workers and rural peasantry escalated their protests and demonstrations. George Lefebvre's *The Coming of the French Revolution* (1939) represents this position. A more recent interpretation (influenced by literary theory) speaks of the revolution as "discourse," an interplay of ideas and interest groups that constantly shifts, or "skids," as events unfold. As the direction of the Revolution changed irrevocably with each new event, for example the execution of Louis XVI, ideas were reassessed and classes reshuffled themselves into new alignments. François Furet's *Interpreting the French Revolution* (1978) is the leading statement of this point of view. Our narrative, including the discussion of the *philosophes* on pp. 489–91, incorporates elements of all three interpretive perspectives.

There is a broader issue, too. Historians sometimes envision events as part of a long sweep of related trends. Sometimes they see them as contingencies, occurring because of circumstances that are unique and unpredictable. The French Revolution presents both aspects. On the one hand, it was an outgrowth of larger trends, the ideals of the *philosophes* and the legacies of the British and American revolutions. On the other hand, specific events unfolded day-by-day in ways which were quite unpredictable; had they turned out differently—for example had the one vote majority to guillotine the king been reversed—the outcome of the Revolution might have been quite different. To understand the French Revolution, both these perspectives—the grand sweep and the contingency—are necessary.

NAPOLEON IN POWER
1799–1812

As head of government, Napoleon consolidated and even expanded many of the innovations of the Revolution. To maintain the equality of classes and to systematize the administration of justice, he codified the laws of France. The Code Napoléon or Civil Code, which was issued in 1804, pressed for equality before the law and the principle of a "career open to talents," that is, all people should have access to professional advancement according to their ability, rather than by birth or social status. Uniform codes of criminal, commercial, and penal law were also introduced. The administration was organized into a smoothly functioning service throughout France.

Fearing a counter-revolution led by the church, Napoleon reached a **Concordat** with the Pope. The French government continued to hold the former church lands, but agreed in exchange to pay the salaries of the clergy (including Protestants and others) and to allow the Pope to regain authority over the appointment and discipline of the Roman Catholic clergy. Protestants, dissenters, Jews, and others were reaffirmed in full citizenship, with all the rights and obligations that such status entailed, as long as they swore their allegiance to the state. In many conquered cities, including Rome and Frankfurt, French armies pulled down the ghetto walls that for centuries had segregated Jews. The government hired a large bureaucracy to administer the state. It selected personnel mostly on the Revolutionary principle of a "career open to talent," hiring the best-qualified personnel rather than those with personal or hereditary connections.

This openness of opportunity suited Napoleon very well. He had come from Corsica, of a modest

Napoleon Crossing the Alps **by Jacques-Louis David, c. 1800.** Having chronicled the Revolution with his brush, David became Napoleon's official painter. The heroic style of the portrait projects the Emperor's enormous confidence as he heads for military glory in the Italian campaigns of 1796–7. The truth of the journey was rather different: Napoleon crossed the Alps on a docile but footsure mule, not a fiery stallion. (*Palace of Versailles, near Paris*)

family, and made his mark as a military officer. He had no respect for unearned authority. Nor was he formally religious. He earned his power through his military, administrative, and leadership skills. In a striking exception to the principle of advancement by merit, however, Napoleon appointed his brothers as kings of Spain, Holland, and Westphalia, his brother-in-law as king of Naples, and his stepson as viceroy of the kingdom of Italy. He himself continued to lead the forces of France in military victories over the powers of Europe.

NAPOLEONIC WARS AND THE SPREAD OF REVOLUTION 1799–1812

As a son of the Revolution, Napoleon sought to spread its principles by force of arms. By 1810 he had conquered or entered into alliances with all the major powers and regions of Europe except Portugal, the Ottoman-held Balkans, and Britain. In each conquered state, Napoleon introduced the principal legal and administrative reforms of the Revolution: an end to feudal privilege, equality of rights, religious toleration, codified law, free trade, and efficient and systematic administration, including statistical accounting, registration of documents, and the use of the metric system. In many areas of Europe, Napoleon was welcomed for the reforms he brought.

There were, however, flaws in Napoleon's policies, and they finally brought his rule to an end. First, Napoleon attempted to conquer Britain, and ultimately the naval power of that island nation and the land forces of its allies, especially those of Russia, proved too strong. Napoleon could not

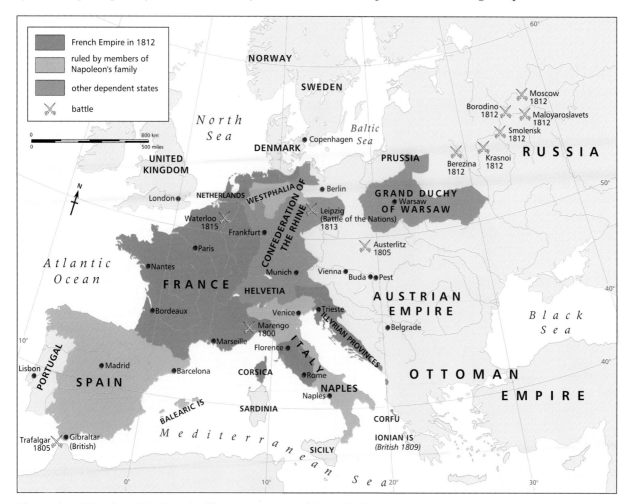

The empire of Napoleon Napoleon, fired by revolutionary zeal, fought brilliantly to bring much of Europe under his dominion, often installing relatives as rulers. Napoleonic institutions were introduced to Italy, the Low Countries, Germany, and then Poland by force of arms. By 1812 Napoleon seemed invincible, but Britain's strength at sea and Napoleon's disastrous losses on land in his invasion of Russia (1812) led to his downfall.

SPOTLIGHT
Francisco Goya:
REVOLUTIONARY REALITY AND RHETORIC

The *philosophes* of the Enlightenment proclaimed that human reason and learning could initiate a new age of peace, prosperity, happiness, and personal development. Many radicals put their faith in the French Revolution to usher in this new era, although its leaders admitted that the process might, unfortunately, be bloody. The Spanish painter Francisco Goya (1746–1828), while siding with the revolutionary cause, created dazzling, cynical critiques of these claims that continue to trouble us two centuries later.

Goya studied painting in Madrid. In the 1790s he produced a series of etchings, "Los Caprichos," which are considered among the most powerful since those of Rembrandt van Rijn (1606–69). One of them, *The Sleep of Reason Produces Monsters* (**figure 1**), created a terrifying scene that apparently challenged a key tenet of the Enlightenment. The title is included within the painting itself and would seem to suggest that when the mind's defenses are down, as in sleep, we are prey to internal monsters. These

psychological insights into the frailties of the human mind precede Sigmund Freud's (1856–1939) concept of the unconscious (see p. 617) by a century. Goya later added a subtitle echoing the faith of the Enlightenment: "Imagination abandoned by reason produces impossible monsters; united with her, she is the mother of the arts." But the etching itself

Figure 1 Francisco Goya, *The Sleep of Reason Produces Monsters*, 1799.

continues to question whether reason will ever be powerful enough to subdue all the demons which beset us.

Goya did not, however, defect to the side of traditional inherited privilege. Commissioned to paint the family of the Spanish King Charles IV, who had joined with other European monarchs in war against the young French republic, Goya produced a canvas of psychological revelations just as devastating in its own way as *The Sleep of Reason*. In *Charles IV and His Family* (**figure 2**), painted in 1800, the clothing of the royal family is regal enough, as is the setting in one of the picture galleries of the palace; Goya's technique of illuminating his subjects is incandescent and the medium is an enormous, opulent, 9-by-11-foot (2.8 × 3.4m) oil painting. But the vulgar postures and faces of the subjects betray an unimaginative, harsh, hollow, and frightened family. Royalty was no more exempt from Goya's attacks than was reason.

Goya's *Execution of the Defenders of Madrid* (**figure 3**)

Figure 2 Francisco Goya, *Charles IV and His Family*, 1800. (*Prado, Madrid*)

depicts yet another betrayal. Many Spaniards had hoped that Napoleon's victory over Spain would bring a new era of enlightenment and progress. But the French troops were barbaric, and the Spanish resistance was savage. The crushing of the rebellion culminated in the execution of Spanish martyrs on May 3, 1808. In another huge canvas, Goya illuminated this defeat with the intensity of a religious martyrdom, focussed on the Christlike pose of the firing squad's victim. For Goya, royal power had been a sham, but neither had reason nor revolution fulfilled their promise of creating an enlightened world.

Figure 3 Francisco Goya, *Execution of the Defenders of Madrid, 3rd May, 1808*, 1814. (*Prado, Madrid*)

break the British hold on continental shipping and he was defeated at sea by Lord Nelson at the Battle of Trafalgar in 1805. When the Russian emperor supported Britain, Napoleon invaded Russia in 1812 and mired his army irretrievably in the vastness of that country during the bitterness of its winter. During that campaign, 400,000 of Napoleon's troops died from battle, starvation, and exposure; another 100,000 were captured.

Finally, the nations Napoleon conquered began to experience the stirrings of nationalism and the desire to rule themselves. Haiti, which had achieved virtual independence in the 1790s, resisted Napoleon's attempt to re-impose French rule and re-institute slavery in the island (see below). Some 50,000 French troops perished in Haiti, most by diseases such as yellow fever, but many at the hands of revolutionary slaves. European peoples, too, did not want their countries to be colonies of France. By 1813 Napoleon had been defeated by his disastrous losses in Russia and by a coalition of European armies; the French were driven back to their borders. In 1814 Napoleon abdicated and Louis XVIII (r. 1814–15; 1815–24) assumed the throne of France. Napoleon escaped from exile on the Mediterranean island of Elba only to be defeated and exiled again in 1815, this time to St. Helena in the South Atlantic. The Napoleonic era was over. The Congress of Vienna, an assembly of representatives of all the powers of Europe, led by the most influential states, concluded diplomatic agreements that established a **balance of power** among them and redrew the post-war map of Europe (see p. 578). Political conservatism enveloped France and Europe for a generation.

CONNECTION: *Nationalism, pp. 575–82*

HAITI: SLAVE REVOLUTION AND RESPONSE 1791

The formal philosophy and rhetoric of enlightenment and revolution (see p. 480) proclaimed the natural desire of all humans to be free, and in the slave plantations of the Caribbean local slave revolts were common, feared, and ruthlessly suppressed. In the western sector of the island of Hispaniola in the colony of Saint-Domingue (modern Haiti), French planters had established one of the most brutal of the slave plantation systems. By 1791, 500,000 black slaves formed the overwhelming majority of the population, with 40,000 whites, many of them owners of plantations and slaves, and 30,000 free people of color, both **mulatto** and black. For decades, the slaves had escaped psychologically and culturally through the practice of **vodoun** (voodoo), a religion that blended the Catholicism of their masters with religious practices brought from Africa. Physically, they had escaped through *maroonage*, flight from the plantations to the surrounding hills. Sometimes the escaped slaves, maroons, established their own colonies. In the 1750s one of the maroons, François Makandal, built among the maroon colonies a network of resistance to slavery. Inspired to independence by vodoun beliefs and using poison to attack individual plantation owners, Makandal apparently planned to poison the water supply of Le Cap,

French lithograph of Pierre Dominique Toussaint L'Ouverture, early nineteenth century. The colony of Saint-Domingue (present-day Haiti) in the West Indies had made a fortune for the French through sugar plantations worked by African slaves. In the 1790s, under the leadership of Toussaint L'Ouverture, it became the site of a slave revolution that eventually led to independence. The former slave acquired his surname because of the ferocity with which he made an opening ("ouverture") in the enemy ranks.

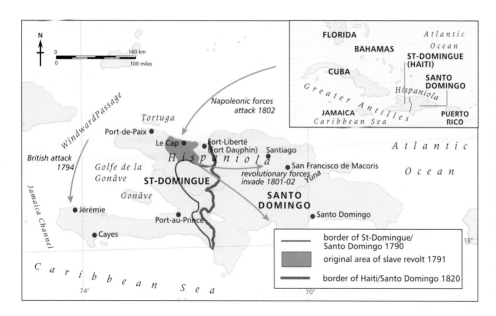

The revolution in Haiti
One of the most dramatic revolutions occurred on the Caribbean island of Hispaniola. A slave revolt in 1791 in the French region, Saint-Domingue, spread rapidly, briefly penetrating and uniting with the Spanish sector, Santo Domingo. Despite interventions by French and British forces, and the incarceration of its leader, Toussaint L'Ouverture, in 1803, Haiti gained its independence from France in 1804, the first successful slave revolt in history.

the main town of northern Saint-Domingue, but he was captured and burned at the stake in 1758.

In 1791, slave revolts broke out across Saint-Domingue. The inspiration seems to have been the natural desire for freedom, perhaps abetted by news of the American and French Revolutions. One of the earliest rallying cries, delivered by the poet Boukman Dutty in Haitian-French patois, *"Coute la liberté li pale nan coeur nous tous"*—"Listen to the voice of liberty which speaks in the hearts of all of us," implied no knowledge of the European and American revolutions.

The revolt spread. From guerrilla warfare by maroon bands, it grew to general armed struggle and civil warfare. In the western part of Saint-Domingue, white planters welcomed the support of British troops who came as allies to suppress the slave revolt and also to drive out the French. The mulattoes—those of mixed race parentage— were free people, and some of them owned slaves. They now sought their own rights of representation and were divided over the issue of slavery. In the eastern part of Saint-Domingue, a new leader, Toussaint L'Ouverture (c. 1743–1803), a freed black, established an alliance with the Spanish rulers against both the slave system in Saint-Domingue (but not in the Spanish part of the island) and the French. Toussaint incorporated the rhetoric of the French Revolution into his own. In 1794, under Robespierre, the French National Assembly abolished slavery in all French colonies. In response, Toussaint linked himself to France as he continued his war against slaveowners, who were now

aligned with the British and who resisted the new French decree. By May 1800 Toussaint had become the effective ruler of Saint-Domingue.

When Napoleon came to power in 1799 he reversed French policy on slavery. He dispatched 20,000 French troops to recapture the island and to reinstitute slavery as he had done in Guadeloupe in 1802. Napoleon's representative deceived Toussaint into suspending his revolution. Toussaint was imprisoned in 1802 and exiled to France, where he died the next year. Nevertheless, unified black and mulatto armies, now under many different cooperating leaders, continued the struggle against France, drove out its forces, and, once again, abolished slavery. As many as 50,000 French troops died of yellow fever, and thousands more became military casualties. On January 1, 1804, Saint-Domingue at last proclaimed its independence and its new name of Haiti, the Carib name for mountain. This completed the only known successful slave revolution in history.

ABOLITION OF SLAVERY AND THE SLAVE TRADE: HISTORIANS DEBATE THE CAUSES

Initially, the British tried to assist in putting down the slave rebellion in Haiti. When they failed, their subsequent decision to limit the spread of slavery by abolishing the slave trade in 1807 reflected, in part, their fear of further revolts. In 1833 Britain abolished slavery throughout its Empire. The United States, a slave-holding country which feared that the Haitian slave revolt might spread northward, prohibited all trade with Haiti in 1806. In 1808, following Britain's lead, America outlawed participation in the international slave trade, although it abolished internal slavery only with the Civil War (1861–5). It recognized Haiti as an independent country also during that war, in 1862. Slavery was not the only issue at stake in the United States' Civil War, but each of the other issues was linked to it. Would the United States follow the model of the Northern states and become an urban, free-labor, industrial nation, or follow the Southern pattern with its rural, slave-holding plantation economy? As the North grew more populous and wealthier, the South began to feel itself an internal colony within the United States and grew increasingly resentful and rebellious. An even more central question was states' rights: Did individual states have the right to secede from the Union? The question arose primarily because the slave-holding Southern states preferred secession rather than face the possibility of abolition. When Abraham Lincoln was elected President in 1860, they feared the worst and began to secede. Lincoln, a man who would have preferred peace, recognized that to preserve the Union he would have to go to war. The American Civil War saw more than one-half million dead, the bloodiest war in the history of the country. In the midst of the war, in 1863, Lincoln issued the Emancipation Proclamation declaring free all slaves in areas that had seceded and were fighting against the Union. In 1865, after the Union victory and Lincoln's assassination, the Thirteenth Amendment to the Constitution officially abolished slavery throughout the country. No compensation was paid. As a class, the southern slave owners were ruined. Their way of life was finished. Elsewhere, however, the Atlantic slave trade continued at about three-quarters of its highest volume (p. 465). That trade did not end effectively until slavery was abolished in 1876 in Puerto Rico, in 1886 in Cuba, and in 1888 in Brazil.

Why were the slave trade, and then slavery itself, abolished in the Atlantic countries? To what extent was the spread of democratic revolution responsible? Analyses differ. Historians who emphasize the significance of the Haitian Revolution, as C.L.R. James and David Nicholls do, stress the fear that the uprising of the slaves engendered among slave owners. In the lands of the Caribbean, including northeastern Brazil, black slaves working the high-mortality plantations formed up to 90 percent of the population. Local rebellions already occurred frequently, and large-scale revolution now appeared as a real possibility. The abolition of the slave trade provided some limit on the size of the slave population, although total abolition—a much more expensive act for the slave owners—would come only later.

A second school of thought, shared by historians such as David Brion Davis and Orlando Patterson, stresses the importance of compassion as a motive. Davis emphasizes the increasing influence of humanitarian sentiment in European Christian thought from the seventeenth century:

> The philosophy of benevolence was a product of the seventeenth century, when certain British Protestants, shaken by theological controversy and the implications of modern science, looked increasingly to human nature and conduct as a basis for faith. In their impatience with theological dogma, their distaste for the doctrine of original sin, their appreciation for human feeling and sentiment, and their confidence in man's capacity for moral improvement, these Latitudinarians, as they were called, anticipated the main concerns of the Enlightenment, and laid an indispensable foundation for social reform. (pp. 348–49)

The emphasis on compassion increased in reaction against the growing scale and unprecedented cruelty of slavery in the New World. Among Christian groups opposing slavery, Quakers and Methodists stood out. The birth and growth of both these denominations—Quakerism under the leadership of George Fox (1624–91) and Methodism under John Wesley (1703–91)—were contemporary with the development of mass slavery in the Americas. Other branches of Christianity had long since made peace with the institution of slavery, contenting themselves with promising a gentler existence in life after death. Quakers and Methodists, however, had to confront the reality of slavery for the first time in one of its cruelest, New World, forms. In Britain, William Wilberforce (1759–1833), a philanthropist and member of the Clapham Sect—a group of well-to-do Evangelicals—played a major part in the antislavery movement. As a Member of Parliament, he led the campaign to abolish the slave trade and to emancipate existing slaves.

The *philosophes* argued a third, similar but more intellectual position against slavery. They argued that slavery violated the law of nature; it was inconsistent with the nature of humankind. Montesquieu

(1689–1755), in his assessments of the nature of laws and government, argued that "the call for slavery was the call of the wealthy and the decadent, not for the general welfare of mankind" (cited in Davis, p. 408).

Finally, an economic critique began to develop in the eighteenth century. Slavery was not profitable to the society, certainly not to the slave, and not to the development of a more productive economy in the long run. In *The Wealth of Nations* Adam Smith argued that slavery, like all examples of monopoly and special privilege, inhibited economic growth. Lacking the opportunity to acquire wealth and property for himself, the slave would find it in his interest to work as little as possible. Slave-owners advocated their system not so much for its economic benefits but for the power it gave them over others, despite economic losses. The leading exponents of this rationale for abolition in recent times have been Marxists, led by Eric Williams in his classic *Capitalism and Slavery* (1944). Many economic historians disagreed with this analysis, most notably Robert Fogel and Stanley Engerman, who published *Time on the Cross* in 1974, an elaborate two-volume statistical study linking economics with statistics (**econometrics**) to show the profitability of slavery. Opposing these earlier econometricians, Seymour Drescher argued bluntly (1977) that abolition was "econocide," economic disaster, for Britain. Drescher sided with the humanitarian assessment: abolition was implemented despite its economic costs.

What to do without slaves? The successor system to slavery was not free labor. Indentured labor, supplied in large part by vast contract immigration from India and China, filled the labor needs of the post-slavery Caribbean as well as those of new plantation economies in the Indian Ocean in Fiji, Mauritius, and Réunion, and in south and east Africa. Although not quite slaves, indentured servants traded many of their basic economic and political rights for a number of years in exchange for employment.

Finally, with the export of slave labor from Africa banned, European entrepreneurs began in the later 1800s to explore the possibilities of shifting the production of primary products to Africa itself and to employ on-site personnel to perform the necessary work. Although this system sounded like free labor, in fact the wages were so low and conditions so abysmal, that many observers saw these economic initiatives as a newer form of slavery transplanted back to Africa.

THE END OF COLONIALISM IN LATIN AMERICA: INDEPENDENCE AND DISILLUSIONMENT 1810–30

In the period 1810 to 1826 virtually all the countries of Latin America expelled their European colonial rulers and established their independence. Latin Americans drew inspiration from the intellectual and political legacies of the American, French, and Haitian revolutions, although few wanted to move so far toward democratic rights as the Europeans had done, and many were frightened by the events in Haiti.

The revolts of the early nineteenth century were led, for the most part, by creole elites, American-born direct descendants of Spanish settlers. A series of earlier revolts, however, had been led by Amerindians and *mestizos*. In 1780, in Cuzco, Peru, Tupac Amaru, a *mestizo* with Inca ancestors, led 70,000 rebels against Spanish rule. Creoles did not join in this revolt and Tupac Amaru was captured and executed in 1783. The entire revolt was brutally crushed. The Comunero Revolt in Colombia in 1781 drove the viceroy from Bogotá but ended with some concessions by the Spanish and internal fighting among the rebels. A conspiracy among bureaucrats, intellectuals, and miners in Minas Girais, Brazil, was discovered in 1788, and its leaders were arrested and hanged. Mulattoes led a revolt in Bahia, Brazil, in 1798. At the time of all these revolts, Spain and Portugal were still independent, powerful countries and, with the aid of creoles and *mazombos* (American-born direct descendants of Portuguese settlers), they suppressed the revolts. In general, the creoles and *mazombos* saw their fate linked more to the Spanish and Portuguese rulers than to the Amerindians or to those of mixed parentage. The Napoleonic wars in Spain, however, gave the colonies the opportunity to declare their independence, with the creoles leading the way. The revolts were bloody and successful.

In virtually every revolt, leadership was provided by a creole elite. Such men as Father Miguel Hidalgo (1753–1811) in Mexico, Simón Bolívar (1783–1830; see Profile, p. 512) in Venezuela and northern South America, and José de San Martín (1778–1850) in Argentina and southern South America, were all creoles, as were their leading generals, administrators, and supporters. They were familiar with European traditions and events,

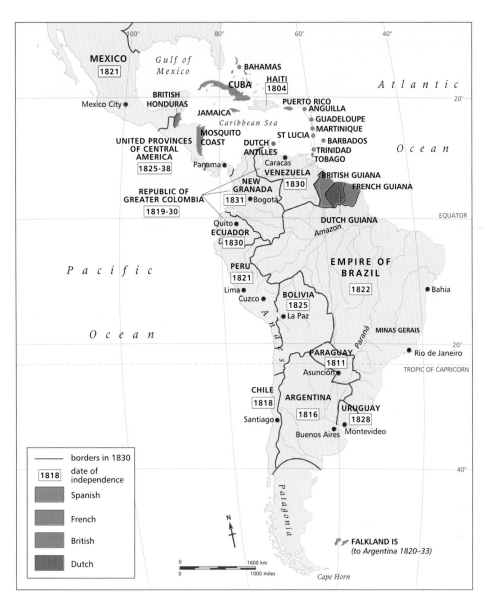

Liberation movements in Latin America The collapse of Iberian rule in Latin America was virtually complete by 1826. Sustained campaigns by Simón Bolívar and Antonio José de Sucre demolished Spanish control of Venezuela, Colombia, and Peru while, from the south, José de San Martin led the Argentine and Chilean Army of the Andes north to Lima. Liberation brought many internal power struggles and divisions, leaving the present-day South American map with an array of some twenty republics.

and many of them had studied in Europe. Indeed many of the revolutions seemed to be fought for the benefit of the creoles, who actually formed less than 5 percent of the total population. Other Latin Americans, *mestizos* and Amerindians, gained little. On the Caribbean islands of Cuba and Puerto Rico there were no rebellions. Here the elites, frightened lest the slave revolt of Haiti be repeated on their own islands, remained loyal to Spain.

MEXICO

Father Miguel Hidalgo led the first wave of Mexico's revolt until he was executed in 1811. Father José María Morelos (1765–1815) then took command of the revolutionary movement. Morelos sought to displace the Spanish and creole elites, to abolish slavery, and, unlike Hidalgo, to revoke the special privileges and landholdings of the church. The Spanish captured and executed him in 1815. By the time Mexico won its independence in 1821, its revolution was controlled by its most conservative creole elite. For two years Mexico was ruled as a monarchy, but in 1823 it was proclaimed a republic. Military leaders, businessmen, and foreign powers all struggled for control and Mexico remained unstable for decades. Its size was also reduced by half. Central American regions, after years of rebellions, broke away from Mexico and formed a union; it dissolved in internal regional antagonisms in 1838. Texas, with waves of immigrants entering from the United States, and encour-

aged by the United States government, declared its independence from Mexico in 1836. Nine years later the United States annexed Texas, precipitating the Mexican-American war. In the peace settlement, America gained the territories of its current southwestern States.

BRAZIL

Brazil, the largest country in Latin America in terms of both geography and population, had a different method of achieving independence, and this helps to explain why it did not break apart after independence. When Napoleon invaded Portugal in 1807, the Portuguese royal family, assisted by Britain, fled to Rio de Janeiro and ruled the Portuguese Empire from the Brazilian capital for thirteen years. King Dom João (John) VI (r. 1816–26) raised Brazil's legal status to equal that of Portugal and expanded Rio as a center of trade, administration, education, and cultural institutions.

In 1821 João returned with his court to Lisbon, but left his son and heir, Prince Pedro, in Rio. When the Parliament, or Cortes, in Lisbon attempted to cut Brazil and Rio back to size, the American-born Brazilian elite, the *mazombos*, counseled defiance. In 1822 Pedro declared Brazil independent, and Portugal did little to stop the move. Pedro was soon crowned "Constitutional Emperor and Perpetual Defender of Brazil," but the effective rulers of Brazil were its *mazombo* elites. Brazil was thus spared the warfare, disintegration, and *caudillismo*, or rule of local strongmen, characteristic of Spanish Latin America, but it was ruled by very similar American-born descendants of Iberian families. While the former Spanish colonies became republics, Brazil became a monarchy under a member of the Portuguese royal family.

PARAGUAY: THE NEW HISTORIOGRAPHY

Tiny landlocked Paraguay, with a population of 150,000, declared its independence in 1810–11 from the viceroyalty of La Plata as well as from Spain and defeated an Argentine army which had been sent to subdue it. Its Dictator, José Gaspar Rodríguez de Francia, who governed until his death in 1840, has been characterized very negatively by historians of several nations, including his own. But new revisionist studies by historians such as Richard Alan White portray Francia as a revolutionary who led his country to a period of

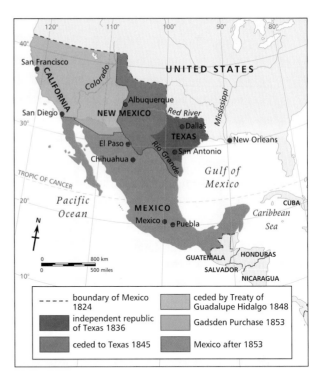

Mexico, 1824–53 In 1821 the Viceroyalty of New Spain, with its capital in Mexico City, won its independence from Spain. By 1823, the Central American counties seceded, leaving Mexico with its current southern border. Then, piece by piece, the northern areas were lost to the United States: Texas through secession from Mexico (1836) and annexation by the US (1845); some territories through warfare (1846–48); and some through purchase (1853).

exemplary economic and cultural independence. They suggest that Francia's negative evaluations resulted from his harsh treatment of creole elites, and his autocratic policies, but that his concern for economic development helped the Amerindians of Paraguay by keeping them isolated from exploitative world markets.

Paraguay based its revolution on self-government and land redistribution. For a half century, rulers redistributed lands of the government, the church, and private large-scale landowners to the masses of *mestizo* and Indian cultivators. Paraguay became self-sufficient in food production. The government established a simple but effective education system which virtually eliminated illiteracy. The state established iron works, textile mills, and livestock industries. It did not accept foreign investment or entanglement. Paraguay's achievements in political independence, economic growth, self-reliance, and raising the standards of its native and *mestizo* populations, engendered envy in its neighbors and apprehension among foreign financiers.

PROFILE
Simón Bolívar
THE LIBERATOR

As soldier, diplomat, general, administrator, visionary, newspaper publisher, law giver, national president, dictator, lover, and disillusioned revolutionary, Simón Bolívar dominated public life in Latin America for most of two decades, from 1810 until his death in 1830. Son of a Venezuelen Creole aristocrat, Bolívar studied in Europe from age sixteen to nineteen, primarily in Spain. On return to Caracas, his chosen bride died in their first year together and Bolívar vowed to devote his life to politics. He returned to Europe for travel and continued

Nineteenth-century engraving of Simón Bolívar.

study of the *philosophes*. Returning to Venezuela in 1807 he joined in the movements for independence that swept the region, especially after Napoleon's troops invaded Spain, undercutting Spanish authority and power in the Americas.

In many of his early efforts he failed. Assigned to diplomatic duty in England, he was unable to gain recognition and material support for the Venezuelan revolution. In 1811, when Venezuela lost its independence within a year of declaring it, he was serving as an army officer. In 1813 he captured Caracas and reasserted Venezuelan independence, but he was defeated and exiled in 1814. In defeat, however, he wrote visionary documents. His *Manifesto of Cartagena*, 1812, was a rallying cry for revolutionary forces to continue the struggle against Spain. His *Letter from Jamaica* of September 1815, written in exile, underlined not only Latin America's political suppression, but also its economic servitude.

Bolívar renewed his military expeditions and began to earn fabulous success. In 1819 his forces defeated the Spanish and established the Republic of Colombia with himself as president and mili-

tary dictator. Within two more years they liberated Venezuela and Ecuador, filling out the borders of the federation. In Quito, Ecuador, he met Manuela Saenz, who left her husband to join Bolívar and remain by his side to the last day of his life, despite his numerous affairs and the public scandal of their own relationship. By 1825, through brilliant military action he crossed the Andes mountains and captured Peru and Upper Peru, later named Bolivia in his honor, and became president of both.

Just as his dreams of a single united region seemed to reach fruition, however, they dissolved in warfare among his generals, who now fought for the independence of each of the constituent units. Bolívar tried to hold the federation together through dictatorial rulings, but his high-handedness further alienated his former supporters and he narrowly escaped an assassination attempt in 1828 as Manuela Saenz covered his exit.

Bolívar withdrew from political leadership in 1830. A few months later he died in the agony of tuberculosis, indebted and disillusioned. Gabriel Garcia Marquez, Colombia's Nobel laureate novelist recaptures Bolívar's life in *The General in His Labyrinth* (1990), especially the consummate sadness of his last journey across Colombia. Witnessing scenes of devastation from years of warfare, he exclaims, "What a price we've had to pay for an independence that's not worth shit!" And recognizing the hatred that now meets him from former allies, he laments, "The day I die the bells in Caracas will ring in jubilation." So ended the life of the Liberator, the greatest hero of Latin America's liberation struggle, but a catastrophic failure in guiding its post-independence agenda.

From 1865 to 1870 Argentina, Brazil, and Uruguay, backed by loans from Britain, fought against Paraguay to destroy its populist policies. After the invaders won, they killed off the majority of Paraguay's adult male population, dismantled its political institutions, and opened its economy to foreign investment and control. Paraguay's unique experiment was over.

AFTER INDEPENDENCE

The continent was wrested from Spain by the sword. The greatest of the revolutionary leaders, Simón Bolívar of Venezuela in the north, José de San Martín of Argentina in the south, Antonio José de Sucré of Ecuador, and Bernardo O'Higgins of Chile combined military excellence with intellectual, administrative, and diplomatic accomplishments. Many other commanders were essentially military figures. Once the Spanish were defeated, the generals began to fight among themselves.

Bolívar grew disillusioned as "Gran Colombia" dissolved into Colombia, Venezuela, and Ecuador. Further south, the Spanish viceroyalty of La Plata dissolved into Argentina, Paraguay, Uruguay, and Bolivia. For a decade, 1829–39, under General Andrés Santa Cruz, a *mestizo*, Peru and Bolivia were united, but then broke apart, to the relief of some of their neighbors. Chile, isolated by the Andes to its east, and open to the outside world via the Pacific Ocean to its west, also became a separate, independent nation. In total, eighteen nations emerged from Spanish America.

Warfare among many of the new states and violent repression of the Indian and African-American populations (one-fourth of Brazil's population in 1850 were slaves) gave prominence and power both to national armies and to private military forces throughout Latin America. The military strongmen, or *caudillos*, came to control local areas and even national governments. Personal rule, only minimally controlled by official codes of law or by formal election procedures, prevailed in many countries up to the late twentieth century. (See Pablo Neruda's epic history of Latin America in verse, p. 514.)

RELIGIOUS AND ECONOMIC ISSUES

Many of the new nations of Latin America wished to increase their own power by breaking the authority and wealth of the Catholic church. Many confiscated church lands, refused the official collection of tithes to fund the church, demanded a voice in the selection of church clergy, and limited church control over educational facilities. To some degree, these crusades against church power reflected also Indian pressures for a greater appreciation of indigenous cultures, both outside of Christianity and in syncretic movements to join Christian practices to existing indigenous beliefs and rituals. Mexico, which had a large Indian and *mestizo* population, was most eager to limit church power, and its continuing struggles were the bloodiest. Over time, in each country, individual accommodations were made between church and state, and to this day they continue to renegotiate their positions.

Economically, until at least 1870, Latin America remained overwhelmingly agrarian, with the hacienda, a kind of feudal estate, continuing as the principal institution for organizing production and labor. The vast majority of the hacienda owners were creole, while the peasant workers were overwhelmingly Indian and *mestizo*. Many Indians remained in villages, where their participation in any larger, external, national economy was marginal. Since ancestry counted so profoundly for each group, the ethnic and racial composition of the population, whether native-born or foreign-born, whether Indian, African, *mestizo*, or Caucasian, in large measure determined the fate and the culture of each colony.

As production for foreign markets increased, new forms of foreign domination, "**neo-colonialism**," arose. The principal new power was Britain, and its method was economic investment and control. By 1824, there were 100 British commercial firms functioning in Latin America staffed by 3000 British citizens. Shipping to and from Latin America was carried primarily by British ships. Britain's economic domination of Latin American economies increased with the growing productivity and profitability of its industrial revolution at home.

In the mid-nineteenth century, Latin America was home to a mixed amalgam of philosophies and practices. From the United States and France, it inherited a legacy of revolution in the name of representative democracy and individual freedom. It inherited from Spain and Portugal a loyalty to more conservative, religious, hierarchical traditions. From its own history of settlement it received a diverse mix of peoples from three continents, often in uneasy relationship to one another. From the international economy Latin America inherited

SOURCE

An Epic Verse History of Latin America

The Chilean writer Pablo Neruda (1904–73), a recipient of the Nobel Prize for Literature in 1971, advanced a critical and disillusioned vision of Latin America in its first century of independence. In *Canto General* (1950), Neruda's epic poem of Latin American history, he paints the Spanish settlement of the land as a harsh and tawdry process.

> The land passed between the entailed estates,
> doubloon to doubloon, dispossessed,
> paste of apparitions and convents
> until the entire blue geography was
> divided into haciendas and encomiendas.
> The mestizo's ulcer, the overseer's
> and slaver's whip
> moved through the lifeless space.
> The Creole was an impoverished specter
> who picked up the crumbs,
> until he saved enough
> to acquire a little title
> painted with gilt letters.
> And in the dark carnival
> he masqueraded as a count
> a proud man among beggars,
> with his little silver cane. ...

The *conquistadors* of the sixteenth century had been expelled by the *libertadors* of the early nineteenth century, but the infrastructure of shopkeepers, clergy, administrators, and hangers-on that had become established in Latin America remained in place as the real inheritors of the revolution. Neruda scowled:

> Soon, undershirt by undershirt,
> they expelled the conquistador
> and established the conquest
> of the grocery store.
> Then they acquired pride
> bought on the black market.
> They were adjudged
> haciendas, whips, slaves,
> catechisms, commissaries,
> alms boxes, tenements, brothels,
> and all this they called
> holy western culture.

Neruda singles out the petty businessmen as the new, but unworthy, elite of Latin America. In more enterprising regions bigger businessmen and investors occupied the leadership positions. These men of practical affairs combined with craftsmen on the one hand, and with government policy makers on the other, to introduce limited industrial development in the twentieth century (see Chapter 23).

a subordinate position, dependent on outside supply, demand, and control.

CONNECTION: *Latin America, 1870–2000, pp. 774–97*

WHAT DIFFERENCE DOES IT MAKE?

Charles Dickens opened *A Tale of Two Cities*, his novel set against the background of the French Revolution, with the famous passage, "It was the best of times. It was the worst of times ... it was the season of Light, it was the season of Darkness, it was the spring of hope, it was the winter of despair ..." Having examined the unfolding of this period of political revolution we can better understand Dickens's paradoxical characterization. We began with the successes of the English revolutions in establishing constitutional government. That revolution slowly expanded to include ever larger segments of the population, and to include freedom of religion among its guarantees. But that same

government refused to grant the rights of Britons to its American subjects, provoking the American War for Independence. It did abolish the slave trade and slavery, but only in the early nineteenth century, and by that time, as we shall see in Chapter 16, Britain had captured extensive, non-settler colonies overseas.

The *philosophes* spoke of human perfectibility and advocated human reason. They provided rationales that inspired the American, French, and Latin American revolutions, yet many of them preferred benevolent despotism as more efficient. One of the greatest of the *philosophes*, Rousseau, has been interpreted variously as espousing a variety of government alternatives, from radical democracy to totalitarian dictatorship. And later experience would test the limits of the power of rationality in the governance of human affairs (see Spotlight on Goya, pp. 504–05.)

The War for Independence in North America freed Britain's thirteen colonies and created the United States. It introduced a limited democracy that nonetheless sanctioned attacks on Indians and permitted slavery. The most profound of all the revolutions of its time, the French Revolution, ended in class antagonism, with the monarchy restored, after much of Europe had been convulsed in more extensive warfare than it had ever seen before. Yet in the course of Napoleon's conquests, he abolished feudal privileges throughout Europe and introduced new codes of law and bureaucracies recruited on the basis of merit. Ironically, Napoleon's imperialism also provoked new nationalism among the peoples he conquered. In Haiti, in response to the slave revolt, Napoleon reversed France's stated opposition to slavery, and lost tens of thousands of soldiers to battle and disease. Haiti's successful slave revolt became a successful war for independence. Wars for independence in Latin America freed that continent from direct, political control from overseas, but power was seized by creole and *mazombo* elites who lorded it over the Native American multitudes. In addition, the new nations soon fell into economic dependence on their former colonizers.

As the revolutionary era cooled, Western Europe and North America had created new centers of democratic ideals and practices, although vulnerable and limited, and Latin America had followed this lead, although in still more limited fashion. In the next chapter we see how the advent of a different kind of revolution—in industrial production and organization—intersected with these already complex trends.

BIBLIOGRAPHY

Andrea, Alfred and James Overfield, eds. *The Human Record*, 2 vols. (Boston: Houghton Mifflin Co., 2nd ed, 1994).

Archer, Leonie, ed. *Slavery and Other Forms of Unfree Labor* (London: Routledge, 1988).

Bayly, Christopher Alan. *Indian Society and the Making of the British Empire* (Cambridge: Cambridge University Press, 1988).

Boorstin, Daniel. *The Discoverers* (New York: Random House, 1983).

Bronowski, Jacob. *The Ascent of Man* (London: British Broadcasting Corporation, 1973).

Burns, E. Bradford. *Latin America* (Englewood Cliffs, NJ: Prentice Hall, 6th ed, 1993).

Cohen I, Bernard. *Revolution in Science* (Cambridge, MA: Harvard University Press, 1985).

Curtin, Philip. *The Rise and Fall of the Plantation Complex* (New York: Cambridge University Press, 1989).

Columbia College, Columbia University. *Contemporary Civilization in the West*, Vol 2. (New York: Columbia University Press, 1954).

Davis, David Brion. *The Problem of Slavery in the Age of Revolution, 1770–1823* (Ithaca: Cornell University Press, 1975).

—. "Looking at Slavery from Broader Perspectives," *American Historical Review* 105:2 (April, 2000), 452–66.

de Bary, Wm. Theodore, *et al. Sources of Indian Tradition* (New York: Columbia University Press, 1960).

Drescher, Seymour. *Econocide* (Pittsburgh: University of Pittsburgh Press, 1977).

—. *The Problem of Slavery in Western Culture* (New York: Oxford University Press, 1966).

Fick, Carolyn E. *The Making of Haiti* (Knoxville: University of Tennessee Press, 1990).

Fogel, Robert William and Stanley L. Engerman. *Time on the Cross*, 2 vols (Boston: Little, Brown, 1974).

Foner, Eric, ed. *The New American History* (Philadelphia: Temple University Press, 1990).

Foucault, Michel. *Discipline and Punish: The Birth of the Prison*, trans. by Alan Sheridan (New York: Vintage Books, 1979).

Furet, François. *Interpreting the French Revolution*, trans. by Elborg Foster (Cambridge: Cambridge University Press, 1981).

Galilei, Galileo. *Discoveries and Opinions of Galileo*, trans. by Stillman Drake (New York: Anchor Books, 1957).

Genovese, Eugene. *From Rebellion to Revolution* (Baton Rouge: Louisiana University Press, 1979).

Halévy, Élie. *England in 1815* (New York: Barnes and Noble, 1961).

Hanke, Lewis and Jane M. Rausch, eds. *People and Issues in Latin American History* (New York: Markus Weiner, 1990).

Hobbes, Thomas. *Selections*, ed. Frederick J.E. Woodbridge (New York: Charles Scribner's Sons, 1958).

Hobsbawm, Eric. *The Age of Empire 1875–1914* (New York: Vintage Books, 1987).

—. *The Age of Revolution 1789–1848* (New York: New American Library, 1962).

James, C.L.R., *The Black Jacobins* (New York: Random House, 1963).

Kolchin, Peter. *American Slavery 1619–1877* (New York: Hill and Wang, 1993).

Knight, Franklin W. "The Haitian Revolution," *American Historical Review* 105:1 (February 2000), 103–115.

Kuhn, Thomas S. *The Copernican Revolution* (Cambridge, MA: Harvard University Press, 1957).

—. *The Structure of Scientific Revolutions* (Chicago: University of Chicago Press, 3rd edn, 1996).

Lefebvre, Georges. *The Coming of the French Revolution*, trans. by R.R. Palmer (Princeton: Princeton University Press, 1947).

Locke, John. *Second Treatise on Government* (Arlington Heights, IL: Crofts Classics, 1982).

McClellan III, James F. and Harold Dorn. *Science and Technology in World History* (Baltimore: Johns Hopkin University Press, 1999)

Márquez, Gabriel Garcia. *The General in His Labyrinth*. trans. by Edith Grossman (New York: Knopf, 1990).

Mintz, Sidney W. *Sweetness and Power: The Place of Sugar in Modern History* (New York: Viking Penguin, 1985).

Murphey, Rhoads. *A History of Asia* (New York: HarperCollins, 1992).

Nash, Gary B., *et al.*, eds. *The American People*, 2 vols. (New York: Harper and Row, 1986).

Nehru, Jawaharlal. *Glimpses of World History* (New Delhi: Jawaharlal Nehru Memorial Fund and Oxford University Press, ed. 1982).

Neruda, Pablo. *Canto General*, trans. by Jack Schmitt (Berkeley: University of California Press, 1991).

Nicholls, David, "Haiti: Race, Slavery and Independence (1804–1825)," in Archer, ed., *Slavery*, pp. 225–38.

Northrup, David, ed. *The Atlantic Slave Trade* (Lexington, MA: D.C. Heath and Company, 1994).

Palmer, R.R. *The Age of Democratic Revolution* (Princeton: Princeton University Press, 1959).

Patterson, Orlando. *Freedom in the Making of Western Culture* (New York: Basic Books, 1991).

Raychaudhuri, Tapan. *Europe Reconsidered: Perceptions of the West in Nineteenth-century Bengal* (Delhi: Oxford University Press, 1988).

Rousseau, Jean-Jacques. *The Social Contract*, trans. by Maurice Cranston (New York: Viking Penguin, 1968).

Smith, Adam. *The Theory of Moral Sentiments* (Charlottesville, VA: Lincoln-Rembrandt Publishers, 6th ed., 1986).

—. *The Wealth of Nations*, Books I–III (New York: Viking Penguin Classics, 1986)

Spear, Percival, ed. *The Oxford History of India* (Oxford: Clarendon Press, 3rd ed., 1961).

Thompson, E.P. *The Making of the English Working Class* (New York: Vintage Books, 1966).

Thompson, Vincent Bakpetu. *The Making of the African Diaspora in the Americas 1441–1900* (New York: Longman, 1987).

The [London] *Times Atlas of World History* ed. Geoffrey Parker (London: Times Books, 1981, 4th ed., 1993).

Tocqueville, Alexis de. *The Old Regime and the French Revolution*, trans. by Gilbert Stuart (Garden City, New York: Doubleday Anchor Books, 1955).

Turner, Frederick Jackson. *The Frontier in American History* (New York; Henry Holt, 1920).

Ward, David. *Cities and Immigrants* (New York: Oxford University Press, 1971).

Weinberg, Albert Katz. *Manifest Destiny* (Chicago: Quadrangle Books, 1963).

White, Richard Alan. *Paraguay's Autonomous Revolution, 1810–1840* (Albuquerque: University of New Mexico Press, 1978).

Wilentz, Sean. *Chants Democratic: New York and the Rise of the American Working Class, 1788–1850* (New York: Oxford University Press, 1984).

Williams, Eric. *Capitalism and Slavery* (Chapel Hill: University of North Carolina Press, 1944).

THE INDUSTRIAL REVOLUTION

CHAPTER 16

"Our wealth has gone into the hands of foreigners. . . . Introduce industry from countries abroad and achieve mastery of the modern machinery."

DALPATRAM KAVI

THE GLOBAL CONSEQUENCES OF INDUSTRIAL EXPANSION AND IMPERIALISM

THE INDUSTRIAL REVOLUTION: WHAT WAS IT? WHAT WAS ITS SIGNIFICANCE?

The industrial revolution which took place in the eighteenth and nineteenth centuries changed far more than the machinery we use and the organization of our work. It also changed the locations of our workplaces and homes, the size and composition of our families and the quality and quantity of the time we spend with them, the educational systems we create, the wars we fight, and the relationships among nations. This chapter examines the industrial revolution as a process with deep roots and lasting consequences—a process extending backward and forward in time, and touching most areas of life. It also views the industrial revolution as a global process, restructuring not only the workshops of production, but also the procurement of raw materials in the fields and mines of the world, and the sales of manufactured products in far-flung marketplaces.

The masters of the new industrial productivity took this comprehensive view, and it often led them into global ventures, which sometimes became imperial in their scope. This chapter therefore begins with the invention of new machinery and concludes with an analysis of the relationship between the industrial revolution and imperialism. The social effects of the industrial revolution on urbanization, gender and family relationships, and new personal and national identities are considered in the following chapter.

BRITAIN 1740–1860

The industrial revolution began in Britain and 1740–1860 is usually considered the crucial era of its arrival. In this period the British cotton textile industry grew into the world's most productive; its railway network became the nation's principal means of inland transportation and communication; and a new fleet of steam-powered ships enabled Britain to project its new productivity and power around the globe.

INDUSTRIALIZATION IN THE WEST

DATE	BRITAIN	REST OF EUROPE	NORTH AMERICA
1760	• James Watt improves Newcomen's steam engine (1763) • James Hargreaves introduces spinning jenny (1764)		
1780	• Combination Act forbids workers to unionize (1799); repealed 1824		• Eli Whitney invents cotton gin (1793)
1800	• Luddite riots (1810–20) • Peterloo Massacre, Manchester (1819)		
1820	• George Stephenson's locomotive *Rocket* (1829) • Factory Act forbids employment of children (1833) • Chartist movement calls for universal male suffrage (1838)	• Invention of photography in France by Louis Jacques Mandé Daguerre (1839) • Worker revolts in Paris, Prague, Vienna, and Russia (1830)	• First transatlantic steamship lines in operation (1838) • Revolver invented by Samuel Colt (1836)
1840	• Sir Edwin Chadwick issues report on the Poor Laws (1842) • Friedrich Engels, *The Condition of the Working Class in England* (1845) • Repeal of the Corn Laws (1846) • Bessemer steel converter (1856) • Samuel Smiles, *Self Help* (1859)	• Year of Revolutions—in France, Austria, and Prussia (1848) • Marx and Engels, *Communist Manifesto* (1848) • Siemens-Martin open-hearth steel production, Germany (1864)	• Invention of the sewing machine (1846)
1860	• Under Prime Minister Gladstone, Liberal government begins to provide universal state-supported education (1870) • Liberals under Gladstone and Tories under Disraeli compete for workers' votes • Trade Union Act guarantees right to strike (1871)	• Growth of chemical industries (after 1870) • Massacre of the Paris Commune (1871) • Bismarck unifies Germany (1871) • Germany's SPD is first working-class political party (1875)	• American Civil War (1861–65) • Richard Gatling invents the machine gun (1861) • Thomas Edison invents early form of telegraph (1864) • Invention of the typewriter (1867) • Canada becomes unified Dominion (1867) • Edison establishes private industrial development lab (1876)
1880	• London Dock strike (1889)	• Labor unions legalized in France (1884) • May 1 recognized in France as annual "Labor Day" (1890)	• American Federation of Labor founded (1886) • Kodak camera (1888) • Homestead Steel strike (1892)

A REVOLUTION IN TEXTILE MANUFACTURE

Until the mid-eighteenth century, the staple British textile had been woolens, but then India's light, colorful, durable cotton textiles began to displace woolens in the market. Britain responded by manipulating tariffs and import regulations to ban Indian cottons, while British inventors began to produce new machinery which enabled Britain to surpass Indian production in both quantity and quality. In 1733, John Kay (1704–64) invented the "flying shuttle," which allowed a single weaver to send the shuttle forth and back across the loom automatically, without the need of a second operator to push it. The spinners could not keep up with the increased demand of the weavers until, in 1764, James Hargreaves (d. 1778) introduced the spinning jenny, which could run eight spindles at once; by 1770, sixteen; by the end of the century, 120. Machines to card and comb the cotton to prepare it for spinning were also developed.

Thus far, the machinery was new, but the power source was still human labor, and production was still concentrated in rural homes and small workshops. In 1769, Richard Arkwright (1732–92) patented the "water frame," a machine that could spin several strands simultaneously. Powered by water, it could run continuously. Samuel Crompton (1753–1827) patented a "mule," a hybrid that joined the principles of the spinning jenny and the water frame to produce a better quality and higher quantity of cotton thread. Now British cloth could rival that of India.

Meanwhile, in the coalfields of Britain, mine owners were seeking more efficient means of pumping water out of mine shafts, enabling deeper

digging. By 1712, Thomas Newcomen (1663–1729) had mastered the use of steam power to drive these pumps. In 1763, James Watt (1736–1819), a technician at the University of Glasgow, was experimenting with improvements to Newcomen's steam engine, when Matthew Boulton (1728–1809), a small manufacturer, provided him with the capital necessary to develop larger and more costly steam engines. By 1785 the firm of Boulton and Watt was manufacturing new steam engines for use in Britain and for export. In the 1780s Arkwright substituted a new Boulton and Watt steam engine in place of water power. From this point, equipment grew more sophisticated and more expensive. Spinning and weaving moved from the producer's home or small workshop adjacent to a stream of water, to new steam-powered cotton textile mills, which increased continuously in size and productivity. New power-looms, invented to cope with increased spinning capacity, had become commercially profitable by about 1800, and were introduced on a large scale after the Napoleonic wars of 1812–15.

The new productivity of the machines transformed the economy of Britain. Hand spinners in India required 50,000 hours to produce 100 pounds (45 kilograms) of cotton yarn. Crompton's mule could do the same task in 2000 hours; Arkwright's steam-powered frame, available by 1795, took 300 hours; and automatic mules, available by 1825, took 135 hours. Moreover, the quality of the finished product steadily increased in strength, durability, and fine texture. The number of mule spindles rose from 50,000 in 1788 to 4.6 million in 1811. Cotton textiles became the most important product of British industries by 1820, making up almost half of Britain's exports.

The new productivity and structure of the cotton textile industry also affected the millions of spinners and weavers who continued to work at home on much simpler machines. As late as 1815 owners of new weaving mills also continued the putting-out system, providing weavers with cotton thread and paying them for the finished, woven product. When

James Hargreaves's spinning jenny. Named for his daughter, Hargreaves's invention was a spinning machine that prepared natural fibers for weaving. It thus made possible the expanded production of cotton cloth. The industrial revolution was built on relatively simple innovations like this jenny and the even earlier "flying shuttle" of John Kay, 1733.

cutbacks in production were necessary, the home workers could be cut, while the large factories continued to run. The burden of recession could be shifted to the shoulders of the home producer, leaving the factory owners and laborers relatively unscathed. In 1791, home-based workers in the north of England burned down one of the new power-loom factories in Manchester. Machine-wrecking riots followed for several decades, culminating in the Luddite riots of 1810–20. Named for their mythical leader, Ned Ludd, the rioters wanted the new machines banned. Thousands of soldiers were called in to suppress these riots.

The textile revolution also generated spin-off effects around the world. India's industrial position was reversed as she became a supplier of raw cotton to Britain and an importer of machine-manufactured cotton textiles from Britain. Britain's new mills required unprecedented quantities of good-quality cotton. In the United States, the invention of the cotton gin by Eli Whitney (1765–1825) in 1793 meant that a worker could clean 50 pounds (23 kilograms) of cotton in the time it had taken to clean one. This solved part of the problem. The plantation economy of the United States revived and expanded, providing the necessary raw cotton, but, unfortunately, giving slavery a new lease on life. American cotton production rose from 3000 bales in 1790 to 178,000 bales in 1810; 732,000 bales in 1830; and 4,500,000 bales in 1860 (Fogel and Engerman, p. 44). Industrialization in Britain was reshaping the world economy.

CAPITAL GOODS: IRON, STEAM ENGINES, RAILWAYS, AND STEAMSHIPS

The textile industry began with a consumer product that everyone used and that already employed a substantial handicraft labor force; it mechanized and reorganized the production process in factories. Other industrial innovations created new products. Many were in the capital goods sector of the economy—that is, they produced tools to expand production rather than goods for private consumption. Britain's iron industry, which had been established since the mid-1500s, at first used charcoal to heat iron ore, but by about 1750 new processes of mining provided coal more abundantly and cheaply. About 1775, the iron industry relocated to the coal and iron fields of the British Midlands. A process of stirring the molten iron ore at high temperatures was introduced by Henry

Cort (1740–1800) in the 1780s. This "puddling" encouraged the use of larger ovens and integrated the processes of melting, hammering, and rolling the iron into bars of very high quality. Productivity increased dramatically. As the price of production dropped and the quality increased, iron was introduced into building construction. The greatest demand for the metal came, however, with new inventions. The steam engine, railroad track and locomotives, steamships, and new urban systems of gas supply and solid and liquid waste disposal all depended on iron for their construction. Britain produced 25,000 tons of pig iron in 1720, 125,000 tons in 1796, and 250,000 tons in 1804. Its world market share was 19 percent in 1800 and 52 percent in 1840—that is, Britain produced as much manufactured iron as the whole rest of the world.

With the new steam engine and the increased availability and quality of iron, the railroad industry was born. The first reliable locomotive, George Stephenson's *Rocket*, was produced in 1829. It serviced the Manchester–Liverpool route, reaching a speed of 16 miles (26 kilometers) per hour. By the 1840s a railroad boom swept England and crossed the Atlantic to the United States, where it facilitated the westward expansion of that rapidly expanding country. By the 1850s most of the 23,500 miles (37,820 kilometers) of today's railway network in Britain were already in place, and entrepreneurs found new foreign markets for their locomotives and tracks in India and Latin America.

The new locomotives quickly superseded the canal systems of Britain and the United States which had been built mostly since the 1750s as the favored means of transporting raw materials and bulk goods between industrial cities. Until the

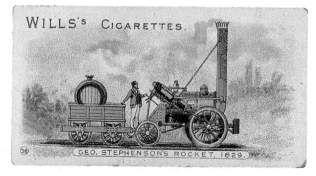

George Stephenson's locomotive *Rocket*, 1829, from a chromolithographic cigarette card of 1901. On October 14, 1829, the *Rocket* won a competition for an engine to haul freight and passengers on the Manchester–Liverpool Railway. The success of Stephenson's invention stimulated a boom in locomotive construction and track laying around the world.

The industrial revolution In the early nineteenth century the industrial revolution spread throughout the trading nations of Western Europe (and enmeshed their colonies, which provided both raw materials and markets). The earlier use of water power gave way to steam engines; coal became the power source. Canal transportation was superseded by railways, driven by steam.

coming of the steam-powered train, these canals had been considered the transportation wave of the future. (The speed with which the newer technology displaced the older provides one reason why historians resist predicting the future. Events do not necessarily proceed in a straight-line process of development, and new, unanticipated developments frequently displace older patterns quite unexpectedly.)

Steamships, using much the same technology as locomotives, were introduced at about the same time. The first transatlantic steamship lines began operation in 1838. World steamship tonnage multiplied more than 100 times, from 32,000 tons in 1831 to 3,300,000 tons in 1876. With its new textile mills, iron factories, and steam-driven transportation networks, Britain soon became the "workshop of the world."

WHY DID THE INDUSTRIAL REVOLUTION BEGIN IN BRITAIN?
HOW DO WE KNOW?

Historians have long debated the origins of the industrial revolution. The term itself was used at least as early as 1845, in the opening of Friedrich Engels' *The Condition of the Working Class in England*:

> The history of the English working classes begins in the second half of the eighteenth century with the invention of the steam engine and of machines for spinning and weaving cotton. It is well known that these inventions gave the impetus to the genesis of an industrial revolution. This revolution had a social as well as an economic aspect since it changed the entire structure of middle-class society.

Arnold Toynbee (uncle of the twentieth-century historian Arnold Toynbee) was apparently the first professional historian to use the term. In a set of lectures delivered in 1880–81, Toynbee identified 1760 as the beginning of the process. He chose this date in recognition of the inventions we have been discussing here. In 1934, John Nef, economic historian at the University of Chicago, argued that the iron industry had already been in place by the mid-sixteenth century and that date was a more

SOURCE

Conflicting Images of Early Industrial Life: The English Romantic Poets

In the century 1750–1850, Britain was transformed by industrialization. Factories, cities, and the working classes all multiplied. One response to the turmoil created by these changes was Romanticism, a new international movement in literature and the arts, which opposed the rationalism of the Enlightenment and which glorified emotion. Poets in Britain, such as William Wordsworth (1770–1850) and Samuel Taylor Coleridge (1772–1834), turned away from the belief in modern progress through science and rational knowledge toward nature, history, and their own inner feelings. They saw a great vision of a new aesthetic beauty emerging. Others, such as the poet William Blake (1757–1827), who were closer to the lives of working-class people, saw the great suffering caused by industrialization. Devoutly religious and nationalistic, Blake nevertheless condemned the people, the government, and the Church of England, for tolerating "a land of poverty" in the very midst of "a rich and fruitful land."

The following two conflicting perspectives are based on views of London about 1800.

Upon Westminster Bridge, September 3, 1802

Earth has not anything to show more fair:
Dull would he be of soul who could pass by
A sight so touching in its majesty;
This City now doth, like a garment, wear
The beauty of the morning; silent, bare,
Ships, towers, domes, theatres, and temples lie
Open unto the fields, and to the sky;

All bright and glittering in the smokeless air.
Never did sun more beautifully steep
In his first splendour, valley, rock, or hill;
Ne'er saw I, never felt, a calm so deep!
The river glideth at his own sweet will:
Dear God! the very houses seem asleep;
And all that mighty heart is lying still!

William Wordsworth

London

I wander thro' each charter'd* street,
Near where the charter'd Thames does flow,
And mark in every face I meet
Marks of weakness, marks of woe.

In every cry of every Man,
In every Infant's cry of fear,
In every voice, in every ban,
The mind-forg'd manacles I hear.

How the Chimney-sweeper's cry
Every blackning Church appalls;
And the hapless Soldier's sigh
Runs in blood down Palace walls.

But most thro' midnight streets I hear
How the youthful Harlot's curse
Blasts the new-born Infant's tear**,
And blights with plagues the Marriage hearse.

William Blake

*charter'd = licensed by the government, controlled, owned
**the infant is blind at birth, from venereal disease transmitted by the parent

Interior of Crystal Palace, designed by Joseph Paxton for the Great Exhibition of 1851 in London. This glass-and-iron exhibition hall, a landmark of early modern architecture, was a celebration of the powerful Victorian economy and an expression of British technological accomplishment and imperial might.

appropriate choice. More recent historians, such as Fernand Braudel, have also seen the roots of the industrialization process stretching back for centuries. They have stressed the underlying economic, political, social, intellectual, and scientific transformations that we have discussed in the last few chapters. All these processes coalesced in the British economy in the late eighteenth century to create the industrial revolution:

- increasing productivity in agriculture;

- new merchant classes in power, and the evolution of a capitalist philosophy of economics which justified their power;

- a powerful state that supported economic development, despite the pure capitalist doctrine of *laissez-faire* that called for the state to stay out of business;

- the rise of science, with its new, empirical view of the world, and of technology, with its

determination to find practical solutions to practical problems;

- a social structure that allowed and even encouraged people of different classes to work together, especially artisans who worked with their hands and financiers, who provided capital;

- more intense patterns of global trading for buying raw materials and for selling manufactured products;

- an expanding population which increased both the labor supply and the demand for more production;

- slave labor in plantation economies, which brought more than a century of exceptional capital accumulation;

- the discovery of massive deposits of gold and silver in the New World, which also increased capital accumulation; and

- "proto-industrialization"—that is, early forms of industrial organization that introduced new skills to both management and labor, paving the way to large-scale factory production.

Is this question of the origins of the industrial revolution purely academic, simply one of those debates over dates that historians enjoy? In fact, the debate carries serious implications for planning industrial development in today's world. As many newly independent nations with little industry seek to industrialize, they ask: Does industrialization mean simply the acquisition of machinery and the adaptation of advanced technology? Or must a nation also experience a much wider range of agricultural, economic, philosophical, scientific, political, and social changes? How, and under what terms, can it raise the capital necessary to begin? What are the tasks confronting a government wishing to promote industrialization? We shall examine

A canal connects two oceans. The construction of the Panama Canal in 1905, linking the Atlantic and Pacific Oceans, ranks as one of the greatest engineering feats of all time. The task involved removing about 175 million cubic yards (143 million cubic meters) of earth as well as sanitizing the entire area, which was infested by mosquitoes that spread yellow fever and malaria.

MAJOR DISCOVERIES AND INVENTIONS—1640–1830

1640	Theory of numbers: Pierre de Fermat
1642	Calculating machine: Blaise Pascal
1650	Air pump: Otto von Guericke
1656	Pendulum clock: Otto von Guericke
1665–75	Calculus: Isaac Newton and Gottfried Leibnitz (independently)
1698	Steam pump: Thomas Savory
1712	Steam engine: Thomas Newcomen
1714	Mercury thermometer: Gabriel Fahrenheit
1733	Flying shuttle: John Kay Seed drill: Jethro Tull
1752	Lightning conductor: Benjamin Franklin
1764	Spinning jenny: James Hargreaves
1765	Condensing steam engine: James Watt
1768	Hydrometer: Antoine Baumé
1783	Parachute: Louis Lenormand
1785	Power loom: Edmund Cartwright
1789	Combustion: Antoine Lavoisier
1793	Cotton gin: Eli Whitney
1800	Electric battery: Alessandro Volta
1807	Steamboat: Robert Fulton
1815	Miner's safety lamp: Humphry Davy
1818	Bicycle: Karl von Sauerbrun
1823	Digital calculating machine: Charles Babbage
1824	Portland cement: Joseph Aspdin
1825	Electromagnet: William Sturgeon
1826	Photograph: Joseph Niépce
1828	Blast furnace: James Neilson
1829	Steam locomotive: George Stephenson

Figure 2 Mathew Brady, Battery ready for action at Richmond, Virginia, 1864.

the North even more solidly
against the South for having
precipitated the war, but time has
blunted the overt political message.
His pictures are now read as a
general testimony to the universal
hardships of war.

Jacob Riis turned his camera
on the slums of New York City
(**figure 3**) to create his book *How the
Other Half Lives*. Riis's images
of the crowding, poverty, and
harshness of tenement life served
as a powerful voice in campaigns
for social reform. Some critics
noted, however, that the pictures
were too composed and self-
consciously "artistic" to evoke
genuine horror on the part of the
viewer, and while the camera could
blankly record images of urban
blight, it could neither explain its
causes nor formulate its cures.

Figure 3 Jacob A. Riis, *Bandits' Roost, New York*, 1888.

while explosives helped in the construction of engineering feats, such as the new tunnels through the Alps in Europe, the Suez Canal in North Africa, and the Panama Canal in Central America. Soda, made from the coal by-product of ammonia, was used in manufacturing both soap and glass. New drugs, insecticides, perfumes, and cosmetics were produced and made their way to the marketplace. Plastics, produced from coal tar acids, became available in the late nineteenth century.

Electricity

Electrical inventions sparked one another throughout Europe and across the Atlantic to the United States, as well. In 1831 Michael Faraday (1791–1867) in Britain first demonstrated the principle of electromagnetic induction by moving a metal conductor through a magnetic field to generate electricity, a process repeated regularly today in high school classrooms. By 1850 several companies were producing simple electric generators. In the 1860s Ernst Werner von Siemens (1816–92) in Germany developed a practical dynamo. In the United States in the 1880s Nikola Tesla (1856–1943) invented methods to transmit the power effectively over long distances, patenting the alternating current generator in 1892.

The best-known inventor of the age was the American Thomas Alva Edison (1847–1931), who acquired more than one thousand patents for new innovations, 225 of which were patented between 1879 and 1882, for incandescent light bulbs, fuses, sockets, switches, circuit breakers, and meters. Others included an early form of telegraph in 1864; the stock ticker in 1870; the phonograph based on a metal cylinder in 1877; and the wax cylinder recorder in 1888, forerunner of the vinyl record player; and the kinetoscope in 1889, a forerunner of the moving picture. More important than any single invention, however, was Edison's establishment in 1876 of (probably the first) private industrial development laboratory in Menlo Park, New Jersey, a rural area halfway between New York and Philadelphia. Until this time, invention had been largely an individual achievement, based on the skills and luck of the individual inventor. Edison's new research facility institutionalized the process of invention.

FACTORY PRODUCTION

Production, too, was concentrated into immense, impersonal corporations. The second industrial revolution corresponded to the era of big business. In Germany, the rising power in Europe, two large **cartels**, collaborative business associations, were formed for the production of electronic equipment: Siemens–Schuckert and Allgemeine Elektrizitäts Gesellschaft (AEG). Two others, specializing in chemical production, later merged into I.G. Farben (1925). For steel production, each major producing

Machine shop, West Lynn works, USA, c. 1898. The United States led the way in mass production of household goods. In the nineteenth century, people immigrated to the big cities from rural America and from overseas to work in factories—often for low pay, with long hours and in hot, noisy conditions. The factory system expanded hugely after 1913 when Henry Ford introduced assembly-line technologies to motor-car production.

country had its own giants: Krupp in Germany, Schneider–Creusot in France, Vickers–Armstrong in Britain, and, largest of all, the United States Steel Corporation. These huge corporations integrated the entire process of production from raw material to finished product. They owned their own coal and iron mines, produced steel, and manufactured such final products as ships, railway equipment, and armaments.

Industrial concentration displaced the artisan in favor of mass-production and mass-consumption. In these mass-market innovations, the United States was frequently the leader, producing the sewing machine (invented by Elias Howe in 1846); the typewriter (1867); clocks and watches, the everyday timekeepers of the new office and factory routines; the telephone, phonograph, and cinema; the bicycle, invented in its modern form in Britain by James Starley in 1885; and small arms, like the revolver, invented by Samuel Colt in 1836, and the rifle, invented by Oliver Winchester, and improved to a repeating rifle by Christopher Spencer in 1860.

WARFARE AND INDUSTRIALIZATION

Warfare and industrialization went hand-in-hand. In the United States, for example, the Civil War (1861–5) not only preserved a political union but also marked the victory of the industrializing, urban, free-labor north over the rural, plantation economy, slave-holding south. It marked a transformation that soon placed the United States among the leaders of world industrialization. Wars of white immigrants against native American Indians, which soon turned to slaughters and forcible relocations to reservations, accompanied the new cross-continental railroads. Wars against Mexico completed the borders of the contiguous United States, and wars against Spain brought the United States its first overseas colonies.

The machine gun, invented by Richard Gatling in 1862, was improved several times. In 1883 it took on the name of Maxim gun, for the American Hiram Maxim who created a gun that had a range of almost 1½ miles (2.4 kilometers) and could shoot eleven rounds per second. The Maxim won its greatest fame in Africa, where Europeans found it indispensable in their colonization efforts (see p. 553). In Germany, the Krupp family of steel manufacturers concentrated on producing the heavy armaments that enabled Prussia to defeat France in 1870, to forge a united Germany (see Chapter 17),

and to prove a formidable combatant in both World Wars (see Chapter 18).

THE EFFECTS OF THE SECOND INDUSTRIAL REVOLUTION WORLDWIDE

Profits from all these businesses, civilian and military, spilled over into finance capital, the purposeful reinvestment of capital into new business to reap new profits. Financiers sought new opportunities in far-flung regions of the world. The industrial development of the Americas offered huge opportunities, and Britain became the largest investor. From the 1840s, for example, the railway networks of both North and South America were in large part financed by British investors. The availability of such investment capital made the task of industrial and urban development easier in the Americas, because the needed sums could be borrowed and repaid later.

These borrowings, and the industrialization and urbanization that came from them, encouraged the immigration that helped increase the population of North America from 39 million in 1850 to 106 million in 1900, and that of South America from 20 million to 38 million in the same period. The United States absorbed these investments without losing political control of its own internal development and became the most industrialized of all countries. South America, however, became an early example of neo-colonialism—in which foreign economic control leads to indirect foreign political control as well.

Canada enjoyed internal self-government within the British Empire from 1840 and became a unified Dominion, including Ontario, Quebec, Nova Scotia, and New Brunswick, in 1867. It attracted increasing immigration and investment, especially after the United States' frontier was filled in with its own immigrants. Nova Scotia and New Brunswick had joined the original provinces of Quebec and Ontario on condition that a railroad be built to link them with Quebec. More dramatically, the Canadian Pacific Railway was completed in 1885, spanning all of Canada from east to west. Between 1900 and 1916, 73 million acres (29.5 million hectares) of land were planted with wheat and other commercial agriculture. $400 million per year was invested in this sector and in the mining of coal, gold, lead, zinc, nickel, and copper.

In Russia and the Ottoman Empire, the largest investments came from France. For the six decades leading up to World War I, Russia's industrial output grew at the rate of 5 percent per year. It produced more steel than France, Italy, or Japan and by 1914 it had 46,000 miles (74,000 kilometers) of railroad track and was the world's fourth largest industrial power. It could not, however, keep up with the industrial advances of the United States and Germany. Similarly, Russia's railway mileage seems less adequate when the immense expanse of the country, by far the largest in the world, is considered. The proportion of Russian industrial production remained at about 8 percent of the world total from 1880 to 1914, and most of its heavy industry was owned by foreigners.

Total foreign investment in the Ottoman Empire was much less, about $1.2 billion in 1914, and the empire's industrial base became progressively less competitive than those of Western European nations. Increasingly, the Ottoman Empire was seen as the "sick man of Europe" (see p. 541).

Overall global investments were immense, with Britain far in the lead. By 1914 Britain had invested some $20 billion, France about $8.7 billion, and Germany about $6 billion. The global age of finance capital was in full swing.

SOCIAL CHANGES: THE CONDITIONS OF WORKING PEOPLE

WHAT DO WE KNOW AND HOW DO WE KNOW IT?

So far we have concentrated on the immense new productivity of industrialization, of the abundance and the wonders of new products. But how did the workers fare? What were the conditions of life for those who worked the machines that produced this new wealth? Reports from the early years in Britain, the birthplace of the industrial revolution, relate with horrifying regularity the wretched conditions of the working class. Popular literature, official government reports, political tracts, and the cries of labor organizers repeat the same theme: In the midst of increasing national wealth, workers suffered wracking poverty and degradation. On the other hand, by the end of our period (1914), the condition of working-class people in Western Europe and the United States, at least, was becoming comfortable. What had changed? How? What was the significance of the change? These questions

remain important today as increasingly sophisticated machines continue to produce more abundant and more sophisticated products and more anxiety in the life of workers. (For the effects of industrialization on gender relations, see pp. 569–74.)

DEMOGRAPHIC CAUSES AND EFFECTS OF THE INDUSTRIAL REVOLUTION

Many demographic shifts suggest that levels of population and industrialization increased together. The population of Europe almost doubled between 1750 and 1850, from 140 million to 265 million, and then jumped another 50 percent to 400 million by 1900. At the same time, emigration carried an additional 50 million people overseas, especially to the Americas, Australia, and South Africa. Much of this increase occurred before the introduction of machinery. Also, the increase seems to have been worldwide; China's population multiplied four times between 1650 and 1850. Historians now believe the main cause was the availability of new foods, such as maize, provided by the "Columbian exchange" (see Focus, p. 457).

Demographers note two waves of change that followed the industrial revolution: first, death rates fell as people ate better and kept cleaner, and as public health measures increased the safety of the water supply, improved the sanitation of cities, combatted epidemics, and taught new standards of personal hygiene. Then birth rates went down. Parents began to realize that improved health increased the likelihood that their children would live to adulthood, and that it was not necessary to produce numerous children to insure that two or three or four would survive. They began to practice family planning. The old "Iron Law of Wages" had argued that as income increased people would simply use the surplus to have more children; this did not happen. Population growth in industrialized countries began to stabilize.

WINNERS AND LOSERS IN THE INDUSTRIAL REVOLUTION

New entrepreneurs, men creating successful new industrial enterprises, often profited handsomely in this era. Their literary representative was Samuel Smiles (1812–1904), whose *Self Help*, published in 1859, advocated self-reliance as the key to "a harvest of wealth and prosperity." Smiles described the careers of many of these self-made new men, the

Putters or trolley boys, from *Mines and Miners* by L. Simonin, early nineteenth century. Until the reforms of the 1870s, owners of factories and mines were able to force children as young as five and six to work up to sixteen hours a day—often in hazardous conditions. Orphans and pauper children were especially vulnerable since capitalists merely had to keep them fed and sheltered in return for their services. The resulting disease, industrial injury, and illiteracy tended to make poor families even poorer.

"industrial heroes of the civilized world," for example Josiah Wedgwood, a potter, son and grandson of potters, who created a new form of pottery that still bears his name. Wedgwood pottery transformed the British industry, earning great profits for Wedgwood and providing employment in his own factories for 20,000 workers. As industries of all sorts expanded, each nation had its own examples of "captains of industry"—for example, four generations of the Friedrich Krupp family, manufacturers of steel and weapons in Germany; Andrew Carnegie, also in steel manufacture, and J. Pierpont Morgan in investment banking in the USA.

Not everyone benefited. Handicraft workers were displaced by the new mechanization. In 1820 there were 240,000 handloom weavers in Britain; in 1840, 123,000; in 1856, 23,000. Some of these workers found jobs running the new power-looms, but many could not make the transition and fell into poverty.

While attending his father's factory in England, Friedrich Engels (1820–95) compiled devastating accounts of *The Condition of the Working Class in England* (1845). Engels' description of the St. Giles slum in London demonstrates the moral outrage that led him to join with Karl Marx in calling for revolution:

Heaps of garbage and ashes lie in all directions, and the foul liquids emptied before the doors gather in stinking pools. Here live the poorest of the poor, the worst paid workers with thieves and the victims of prostitution indiscriminately huddled together ...

[T]hey who have some kind of shelter are fortunate in comparison with the utterly homeless. In London fifty thousand human beings get up every morning, not knowing where they are to lay their heads at night.

Government reports, although more restrained in tone, sustained these horrific views. They called for, and got, remedial legislation. Official committees studied working-class conditions in the factories and neighborhoods of Britain's growing industrial cities and in its mines. In 1831, a committee chaired by the Member of Parliament Michael Thomas Sadler (1780–1835) investigated the conditions of child labor in cotton and linen factories. It found children beginning work at the age of six, usually for twelve- and thirteen-hour days. They were often given food so wretched that, despite their hunger, they left it for pigs to eat. Workplaces were cramped and dirty all year long, and were especially damaging to health during the long nights of winter, when gas, candles, and oil lamps added their soot and smoke to the air of the factory. Still worse conditions were revealed by the Committee on the Conditions in Mines that was appointed in 1842 and was chaired by Anthony Ashley Cooper, 7th Earl of Shaftesbury. Children worked for fourteen hours underground each day. Legally, they could work from the age of nine, but parents needing extra income frequently brought even younger children.

Sir Edwin Chadwick (1800–90), an investigator for the Royal Commission on the Poor Laws, issued his *Inquiry into the Condition of the Poor* in 1842 after taking abundant testimony from workers in factories and mines, homes and workplaces.

Chadwick noted that the British government had already begun legislating the conditions of child labor and of tenement construction. He now urged further legislation to provide for sewage, drainage, sanitation, and a clean water supply. His Report suggested that not only the poor workers but also their employers, the community, and the government would benefit. Chadwick's report helped inspire broad public support for the Public Health Act of 1848 and the creation of a Board of Health.

POLITICAL REACTION IN BRITAIN AND EUROPE 1800–1914

POLITICAL RESPONSES IN BRITAIN

Britain had a growing urban, industrial population, which demanded political change. The government, recognizing that industrialization was transforming Britain and fearful of the consequences, responded initially by trying to repress the movement for reform. The *Peterloo Massacre* at St. Peter's Fields in Manchester in 1819 demonstrated the government's position. A huge, but peaceful demonstration by 80,000 people called for universal male suffrage, the annual election of the House of Commons in Parliament, and the abolition of the Corn Laws. The Corn Laws had raised the tariff on grain to levels that effectively banned importation, thus keeping the price of basic foodstuffs high, favoring landowners and farmers at the expense of the growing urban, industrial population. Soldiers fired on the demonstrators, killing eleven and wounding some 400. The government applauded the soldiers and passed further legislation to restrict free expression.

The mood of Parliament had changed by 1832, partly because of revolutions on the European continent, and partly because of riots in England. Fearing the possibility of revolution, the Whig party in Parliament forced through the Reform Bill of 1832. Its most significant provision was to shift 143 seats in Parliament from rural constituencies, which were losing population and were often dominated by single families, to expanding urban

constituencies. The number of voters increased by about 60 percent but still totalled only about 800,000 in all of Britain. A far greater proportion of the new voters, however, were professionals: doctors, lawyers, businessmen, and journalists. The benefits of the 1832 reforms went to the middle classes, but soon the two main parties, conservative Tories and more liberal Whigs, jockeying for power, began to craft new programs to protect and enfranchise urban working people in an attempt to gain more votes. (For contrasting views on the 1832 Bill, see Focus, opposite.)

The Factory Act of 1833 not only forbade the employment of children under the age of nine in textile mills, it also, for the first time, provided for paid inspectors to enforce the legislation. In 1842 the employment of women and of children under the age of ten was forbidden in the coal mines. The Ten Hour Act of 1847 extended this ruling to cover factories and limited the hours of work for women. In practice, men's hours were also soon reduced.

Parliament abolished slavery in the British Empire in 1833 (see p. 507) and passed a new Poor

The Chartists. As this contemporary cartoon implies, the sheer weight of support received by the Chartists was a powerful argument in favor of voting rights being extended to all men (though not yet women). Parliament rejected increasingly large charters, or petitions, on three occasions and it was not until 1918 that universal male suffrage was adopted in Great Britain.

Law in 1834, which provided assistance just adequate to sustain life. The law required that recipients live in government workhouses and participate in government-created work projects, but this provision was not usually enforced. In 1835 it enacted a Municipal Corporations Act, which reformed elections and administrations in large cities, enabling them to cope more successfully with the problems of growth and industrialization.

On some fundamental issues Parliament moved slowly and sometimes it refused to move at all. The Chartist movement presented a Charter with more than a million signatures to Parliament in 1838 calling for universal male suffrage, an end to property qualifications for members of parliament, and equal electoral districts. Despite, or perhaps because of, a wave of violence instigated by some of the Chartists, the House of Commons rejected the petition. When it was resubmitted in 1842, with more than 3.3 million signatures, the Charter was rejected again, overwhelmingly, by 287 votes to 49. Parliament feared that universal suffrage would bring an end to the sanctity of property and the capitalist economic system.

In 1846, however, under a Tory government led by Robert Peel, Parliament did repeal the Corn Laws, signalling the victory of the urban constituencies and the triumph of free trade. Britain gave up its policy of self-sufficiency in food and entered fully into the international trade system to

FOCUS
Labor Organization and Parliament: Contrasting Views

The growth of an organized labor movement had a great influence on Parliament, yet different historians discuss this relationship between labor and Parliament from very different perspectives. Most stress the wisdom and flexibility of Parliament in yielding increasing power to a wide variety of new urban industrial interest groups, including laborers, even as early as 1832. Compare, for example, R.R. Palmer writing on the Reform Bill:

> Great Britain in 1830 was probably nearer to real revolution than any country of Europe—for the revolutions of 1830 on the Continent were in reality only insurrections and readjustments. In Britain a distressed mass of factory workers, and of craft workers thrown out of employment by factory comptetition, was led by an irate manufacturing interest, grown strong by industrial changes and determined no longer to tolerate its exclusion from political life. Had these elements resorted to general violence a real revolution might have occurred. Yet there was no violent revolution in Britain. The reason probably lies first of all in the existence of the historic institution of Parliament, which, erratic though it was before the Reform Bill, provided the means by which social changes could be legally accomplished and continued, in principle, to enjoy universal respect. (p. 462)

The 1832 Bill did not, however, actually vest power with industrial laborers, and E. P. Thompson charges that the working classes felt betrayed. They had struggled heroically and now would have to continue their struggle.

> Again and again in these years working men expressed their resentment: "they wish to make us tools", or "implements", or "machines". A witness before the parliamentary committee enquiring into the hand-loom weavers (1835) was asked to state the view of his fellows on the Reform Bill:
>
> Q: Are the working classes better satisfied with the institutions of the country since the change has taken place?
>
> A: I do not think they are. They viewed the Reform Bill as a measure calculated to join the middle and upper classes to Government, and leave them in the hands of Government as a sort of machine to work according to the pleasure of Government. (pp. 831–2)

purchase its food and sell its manufactured goods. A second Reform Bill in 1867, passed by the Tory government of Benjamin Disraeli, doubled the electorate to about 2 million, about one-third of all adult males. The Bill enfranchised most urban working men.

The two major political parties, Liberals and Tories, now competed directly for the favor of the industrial workers. In 1870, the Liberal government of William Gladstone began to provide universal, state-supported education and, in the next year, it formally legalized labor unions. The Tories, under Disraeli's second administration, 1876–80, extended the acts regulating public sanitation and conditions of labor in factories and mines. They also regulated the conditions of housing for the poor. In 1884, under Gladstone, a third Reform Bill doubled the electorate again. In 1918 Great Britain adopted universal male suffrage and extended the vote to women over the age of 30.

LABOR ORGANIZATION

Social historian E.P. Thompson identifies the London Corresponding Society founded in 1792, as perhaps "the first definitely working-class political organisation formed in Britain" (Thompson, p. 20). Unions were forbidden to unionize under the Combination Act of 1799, but in 1824 these laws were repealed. Small trade unions took root, usually finding their greatest success among the better-off "aristocracy of labor," the machinists, carpenters, printers, and spinners. Sometimes they would go on strike; politically they organized for suffrage campaigns; and some helped organize cooperative enterprises. Only under the Trade Union Act of 1871 was the right to strike recognized officially. Unskilled workers began increasingly to join into unions, with miners and transport workers usually in the lead. They drew encouragement from the Fabian Society, a group of intellectuals centered in the Bloomsbury section of London that sought to make government and society more receptive to working-class interests without violence. They supported the London Dock strike of 1889, which demonstrated working-class strength by closing that great port. They formed the core constituency of the new Labour Party. The Party won only two seats in the 1900 elections, but in 1906 it captured twenty-nine seats and began its permanent role in parliamentary politics in Britain. By 1914, 4 million Britons held membership in trade unions.

LABOR ORGANIZATION OUTSIDE BRITAIN

Karl Marx and Theories of Worker Revolution

In Britain workers created their own organizations and pulled political party leaders in their wake. Elsewhere, political leaders and intellectual theoreticians attempted to give leadership in organizing much smaller groups of workers. Foremost among the theoreticians was Karl Marx (1818–83). A well-educated and trained German journalist of Jewish ancestry, Marx called for a worker-led revolution. He organized revolutionary socialists through active campaigning, polemical tracts calling for revolution, such as the *Communist Manifesto*, which he wrote with Friedrich Engels, and three volumes of scholarly analysis and critique of the capitalist system called *Das Kapital*.

Marx began his studies in Berlin at a time when western and central Europe were alive with revolutionary sentiments—both of workers seeking new rights and of nationalists seeking greater political representation. In 1848, many of these revolutionary pressures came to a head—and were crushed. In France, a revolt against the monarchy of Louis Philippe (r. 1830–48) and the proclamation of a provisional republic was followed by the establishment of government-sponsored workshops to provide employment for the poor. A new, far more conservative government was elected in April, however, and it closed the workshops in Paris. The poor people of the city took to the barricades, and the army was called out. More than 10,000 people were killed or injured in the ensuing street riots.

In Austria, protesting students and workers took control of Prague and Vienna and were crushed in both cities by regular forces of the Austrian army at the cost of thousands of casualties. In Prussia, in the same year, worker demands for more democracy and more worker rights joined with demands for a new constitution that would lead toward the merger of Prussia with the many small German-speaking states of the former Holy Roman Empire into a new country of Germany. At first it appeared that the Prussian king Frederick William IV (r. 1840–61) would grant these demands, and a Constituent Assembly was convened in Frankfurt to write a new German constitution. In the end, however, the king reasserted his divine right to rule and rejected the constitution. Under these circumstances the smaller states refused to join in a unified government. With conservative forces in the ascendant, Marx moved to London where he spent the rest of his life, much of it in active scholarship in the British Museum.

Marx believed that wealth is produced not so much by capitalists, who control the finances, but by the **proletariat**—the laborers—who do the actual physical work of production. Because this is not recognized, workers do not receive proper returns for their contributions. Violent revolution is the only recourse "to raise the proletariat to the position of ruling class, to establish democracy" (*Communist Manifesto*, p. 30). In a stirring call to this revolution, Marx and Engels declare the Communist party as its leader:

> Let the ruling classes tremble at a Communist revolution. The proletarians have nothing to lose but their chains. They have a world to win. Workingmen of all countries, unite! (p. 44)

Until the revolution would take place, Marx and Engels called for many shorter term legislative goals, including: "a heavy progressive or graduated income tax, … free education for all children in public schools … and … abolition of child factory labor in its present form." Many other labor groups shared these goals and they were subsequently adopted in virtually all industrialized countries.

After the revolution would occur, Marx and Engels called for the establishment of a very powerful, worker-led government to assume control of the economy, and they looked forward to a still later time when the state would be unnecessary and would wither away. They identified the state as "the organized power of one class for oppressing another," so when workers ruled the state there would be no need for further oppression and the state would vanish. Marx and Engels gave no further description of this utopia, but it finally rested on their most central and most radical tenet:

> The theory of the Communists may be summed up in the single sentence: Abolition of private property. (p. 23)

Marx's theory included a view of history that saw class struggle as perpetual: "The history of all hitherto existing society is the history of class struggles." The current form of the struggle was bourgeoisie vs. proletariat. The bourgeoisie themselves had created the proletariat by organizing the new factories which employed them. Marx condemned the sexual ethics of the bourgeoisie. Despite their official reverence for the family, Marx accused them of sexual abuse of their workers, economic perpetuation of prostitution, and wife-swapping among themselves: "Our bourgeois, not content with having the wives and daughters of their proletarians at their disposal, not to speak of common prostitutes, take the greatest pleasure in seducing each other's wives." Marx heaped scorn on religion, charging the bourgeoisie with using it as an opiate to divert the proletariat from its fundamental economic concerns. Marx was a materialist, arguing that economics is the basis of life; ideas and intellectual life are derivative of economic status: "Man's consciousness changes with every change in the conditions of his material existence, in his social relations and in his social life. … The ruling ideas of each age have ever been the ideas of its ruling class."

The proletarian revolution predicted as inevitable by Marx and Engels did not take place in the nineteenth century. (In Chapter 19 we will consider the extent to which the 1917 Russian revolution was proletarian and Marxist. As we have seen in Britain, three factors worked toward a different resolution of class tensions. First, workers' unions began to win their demands for higher pay, shorter hours, and better working conditions. Second, political institutions expanded to assimilate the new worker organizations and accommodate many of their demands. Third, legislation favorable to workers was passed, the franchise was extended, and a labor party took its place in Parliament.

In retrospect, some of Marx and Engels' most enduring interpretations have been cultural even more than economic. They identified four critical areas of social-cultural tension during the height of the industrial revolution:

- the challenge of coping with rapid change, observing in the *Communist Manifesto* that "all that is solid melts into air";

- the alienation of factory workers from their work, as they became insignificant cogs in great systems of production;

- the alienation of workers from nature, as farmers left the countryside to find jobs in urban industries; and

- the dominance of the husband over the wife in the modern family and the need to create real equality between them.

Germany 1870–1914

A wave of labor unrest and strikes swept across Europe in the late 1860s and early 1870s, signaling the growing strength of labor. In Germany chief minister Otto von Bismarck (1815–98) pursued diverse and sometimes conflicting strategies to keep working people allied to his government. He extended universal male suffrage to the North German Confederation in 1867 and then to all of Germany when he unified the country in 1871. But he limited the power of the legislature and diluted the power of the vote since the government ministers were responsible to the king, not to Parliament. When Germany's opposition Social Democratic Party became Europe's first political party based on the working classes in 1875, Bismarck sharply restricted its organizational activities. On the other hand, declaring "I too am a socialist," he passed legislation providing workers' disability and accident insurance and, in the 1880s, the first compulsory social security system in Europe. This legislation, however, covered only male industrial workers, not women or children. Thanks to government policies, worker militancy, and its learning from Britain's earlier painful experiences, Germany did not repeat the worst conditions of child and female labor, and of excessive hours and brutal conditions of industrial work.

The United States 1870–1914

In the United States, labor began to organize especially with the industrialization that began after the Civil War (1861–5). A number of craft unions joined together to form the National Labor Union in 1866, but although it claimed 300,000 members by the early 1870s, it did not survive the depression of 1873. The Noble Order of the Knights of Labor, founded as a secret society in 1869, grew into a mass union, open to all workers, with 700,000 members in 1886. The leadership of the Knights of Labor could not control its membership, however, and various wildcat strikes broke out, some of them violent, alienating much of the rest of the membership. America's most successful labor organization was the American Federation of Labor, a union of skilled craft workers, founded in 1886 by Samuel Gompers (1850–1924). Its membership grew to 1 million by 1900 and 2 million by 1914. Women were not allowed to join, but in 1900 the International Ladies Garment Workers Union (ILGWU) was formed—with males dominating its leadership.

A series of strikes in America throughout the 1890s led to violence. Hired detectives, local police, and even army troops attacked strikers and were attacked in return. Near Pittsburgh, steel workers lost the Homestead Steel strike in 1892 as the Governor of Pennsylvania sent in 8000 troops. The American Railway Union under Eugene Debs lost a strike at the Pullman Palace Car Company in Chicago when the Governor of Illinois obtained a court injunction to force the workers back to their jobs. Violence ensued, leaving scores of workers dead. In resolving a 1908 strike of hat makers, the United States Supreme Court ruled that trade unions were subject to the Sherman Anti-Trust Act, leaving their members personally liable for business losses suffered during strikes. Until this ruling was reversed in the 1930s, militant unionism was virtually dead, although the small Industrial Workers of the World (IWW), representing a radical perspective on labor organization, did form in 1905.

The United States did develop powerful labor organizations, mostly in the twentieth century, but it never produced a significant political party based primarily on labor. Labor organization in the United States was fragmented into craft-specific unions. In this nation of immigrants, workers also held multiple identities; their ethnic identities frequently inhibited them from building union solidarity with those of other ethnic groups. Many immigrants came to America to earn money and return home; these workers did not usually have a commitment to active unionization. Pay scales and working conditions in the United States were significantly better than in Europe, further muting worker grievances. Finally, the capitalist ideology of the country discouraged class divisions, and the government restricted labor organization.

France 1870–1914

In France, much of the potential leadership of a workers' movement was wiped out in 1871 by the massacre of the Paris Commune, an uprising of urban leaders in Paris. At least 20,000 people were killed by the French national government and another 10,000 were exiled. Ten years later, when some of the exiles from the Paris Commune returned, organization began again. In 1884 *syndicats*, labor unions, were legalized. Two competing federations were formed, one calling primarily for mutual help, the other for political action. Together, they numbered 140,000 members in 1890,

Massacre of the Paris radicals. The slaughter meted out to the Paris Commune of 1871 is graphically depicted by the Post-Impressionist painter Edouard Manet. Left-wing urban leaders tried to set up their own state-within-a-state, but the communards were put down brutally by the national government. At least 20,000 were summarily executed and over 40,000 were taken prisoner. (*Museum Folkwang, Essen*)

a figure that more than tripled to 580,000 by the end of the century. By 1909, an umbrella group, the Confédération Génerale de Travail, numbered nearly a million. In 1890, May 1 was recognized as an annual "Labor Day." French politics, however, was dominated by the wealthier business leaders. Industrial workers organized, but they commanded less influence than farmers, shopkeepers, and small businessmen.

COMPETITION AMONG INDUSTRIAL POWERS: THE QUEST FOR EMPIRE

Britain pioneered the industrial revolution, but by the mid-nineteenth century rivals had begun to appear. The United States emerged from its Civil War in 1865 with a rapidly growing immigrant population moving westward by railway across a continent that was abundant in resources, removing Indians who blocked their way, and building an industrial base of production that surpassed

Britain's by 1900. Germany unified its constituent states into a single country under Kaiser Wilhelm and Prime Minister Otto von Bismarck in 1871, and also surpassed Britain in the early years of the twentieth century. In addition, Germany's population at 67 million was almost 50 percent greater than Britain's, and was growing faster. France produced only half the industrial output of Britain or Germany, but nevertheless ranked third among European powers.

The greatest competition took place overseas, beyond the borders of Europe, in the quest for imperial power. Empires were not new, of course, but the use of advanced technology and new strategies of financial and economic dominance gave them new power over others in the late nineteenth and early twentieth centuries. By 1914, peoples of Europe and of European ancestry had settled and ruled, directly or indirectly, 85 percent of the earth's land surface: Canada, the United States, large parts of Latin America, Siberia, Australia, New Zealand, and substantial parts of South Africa by invasion, settlement, and conquest; most of India, Southeast Asia, and Africa by direct rule over

Assertions of European Supremacy and Obligation

Rudyard Kipling's famous poem, "The White Man's Burden," proclaims Britain's superiority—racial, moral, political, economic, and religious—over the peoples it conquered. Kipling represents the breach between the white colonial and the sullen, "Half-devil and half-child" peoples he governed as unbridgeable. He laments the plight of the poor white man, who gives his all to help ungrateful heathen peoples. In the hey-day of imperialism, Kipling does not note any benefits to the colonizers nor does he suggest the role of military power and violence in producing and maintaining the empire. Kipling dedicated the poem to the United States as a warning as it began its colonial rule of the Philippines in 1899.

The White Man's Burden

Take up the White Man's burden—
Send forth the best ye breed—
Go bind your sons to exile
To serve your captives' need;
To wait in heavy harness,
On fluttered folk and wild—
Your new-caught, sullen peoples,
Half-devil and half-child.

Take up the White Man's burden—
In patience to abide,
To veil the threat of terror
And check the show of pride;
By open speech and simple,
An hundred times made plain,
To seek another's profit,
And work another's gain.

Take up the White Man's burden—
The savage wars of peace—
Fill full the mouth of Famine
And bid the sickness cease;

And when your goal is nearest
The end for others sought,
Watch Sloth and heathen Folly
Bring all your hope to nought.

Take up the White Man's burden—
No tawdry rule of kings,
But toil of serf and sweeper—
The tale of common things.
The ports ye shall not enter,
The roads ye shall not tread,
Go make them with you living,
And mark them with your dead.

Take up the White Man's burden—
And reap his old reward:
The blame of those ye better,
The hate of those ye guard—
The cry of hosts ye humor
(Ah, slowly!) toward the light:—
"Why brought ye us from bondage,
Our loved Egyptian night?"

Take up the White Man's burden—
Ye dare not stoop to less—
Nor call too loud on Freedom
To cloak your weariness;
By all ye cry or whisper,
By all ye leave or do,
The silent, sullen peoples
Shall weigh your Gods and you.

Take up the White Man's burden—
Have done with childish days—
The lightly proferred laurel,
The easy, ungrudged praise.
Comes now, to search your manhood
Through all the thankless years,
Cold, edged with dear-bought wisdom,
The judgment of your peers!

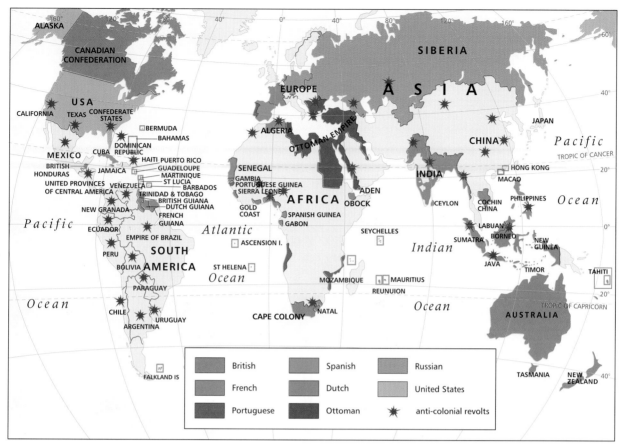

European imperialism 1815–70 By the middle of the nineteenth century, revolutions had brought independence to most of the Americas. With Africa largely impenetrable, European imperialists now focussed on Asia. Russia had spread across Siberia to the Pacific, and the United States extended from the Atlantic to the Pacific, while Britain controlled India, South Africa, Australia, and New Zealand. In 1867 Canada achieved "dominion" status, virtual political independence.

indigenous populations; China by indirect rule. Much of Latin America, although politically independent, was dominated internally by elites of European ancestry and externally by European financial investors and their governments. Some states, like Russia and the Ottoman Empire, were dominated in large part by capital from northwestern Europe, but also held their own colonial areas. In terms introduced by the historian Fernand Braudel and the sociologist Immanuel Wallerstein, northwest Europe and the United States had become the *core* regions of world economic and political power; most of the rest of the world, excepting Japan, was incorporated and subordinated into their *periphery*.

The leading states of Western Europe had achieved their power through their "dual revolutions," political and industrial. Politically and socially they had achieved, or seemed to be in the process of achieving:

- consolidated nation-states;

- parliamentary democracies;

- bureaucratic administrations;

- freedom of the press, assembly, and religion;

- freedom from wrongful arrest and torture;

- increased levels of literacy and general, public education;

- high levels of trade and international exchange;

- high levels of economic entrepreneurship and legal protection of property;

- humanitarian perspectives;

- thriving artistic life.

THE WORLD BEYOND THE INDUSTRIALIZED WEST

DATE	OTTOMAN EMPIRE	INDIA, S-E ASIA & CHINA	AFRICA
1800		• Sir Stamford Raffles establishes Singapore for the British (1819)	• British forces drive Napoleon from Egypt (1801); Muhammad Ali assumes rule (1807) • Shaka seizes leadership of the Zulu kingdom near the Cape Colony (1816)
1820	• Greece wins independence; Serbia, Wallachia, and Moldavia gain autonomy (1829) • French gain control of Algeria from empire (1830) • Muhammad Ali renders Egypt effectively independent (1832)	• Java War, Dutch vs. Indonesians (1825–30) • Dutch introduce cultivation system in Indonesia (1830) • First Opium War (1839–42): China cedes Hong Kong to the British	• Great Trek north by the Boers (Afrikaners) (1834–41) • French invade Algeria (1830); warfare with al-Qadir (1841)
1840	• Crimean War (1853–4) • Westernization encouraged in the Hatt-i Humayun edict (1856)	• Taiping Rebellion begins (1850); suppressed 1864 • "First War for National Independence" in India (1857) • Russians seize Amur River region (1858) • Second Opium War (1856–60): Beijing occupied by French and British	• David Livingstone lands along Angola coast for first African expedition (1841)
1860	• Young Turks go into exile (1876) • Russian attack through the Balkans reaches Istanbul (1877)	• Russian seize Maritime Provinces (1860) and Ili valley in Turkestan (1871–81)	• Suez Canal opens (1869) • Diamonds and gold discovered in the Cape Colony region • Egyptian *khedive* forced to add European representatives to his cabinet (1878)
1880		• France seizes all of Indochina (1883–93) • Germany annexes Eastern New Guinea and the Marshall and Solomon Islands (1880s) • Japan defeats China in warfare (1894–5) • Boxer Rebellion (1898–1900)	• Bismarck's Berlin Convention apportions Africa among competing powers (1884) • General Kitchener retakes Sudan in Battle of Omdurman (1898) • Rhodesia (now Zimbabwe and Zambia) named after Cecil John Rhodes (1898) • Boer War (1899–1902) • Ethiopia defeats Italian forces at Adowa (1896)
1900	• Italy takes Libya from weakened empire (1911)	• India's first steel mill at Jamshedpur, Bihar (1911) • Subcontinent has 35,000 miles of railroad track (1914)	• Maji-Maji revolt against German rule in Tanganyika (1905–07) • Belgian Parliament takes over control of the Congo (1908) • British form Union of South Africa (1910) • Natives Land Act closes 87 percent of South African land to African ownership (1913)

Economically and industrially, they had achieved or seemed to be in the process of achieving:

- high levels of productivity;

- competence in new methods of science and technology;

- relatively high levels of health and of medical care;

- an integrated world economy; and

- powerful weaponry.

Western Europeans, especially Britons, began to define themselves as people who had mastered these qualities; in contrast to the peoples whom they were colonizing and dominating, who lacked them. Soon after Charles Darwin published *On The Origin of Species* in 1859, the philosopher Herbert Spencer (1820–1903) (mis)represented the concept of "survival of the fittest" as a doctrine explaining and justifying the rule by the strong over the weak. Spencer's "social Darwinism" argued that those who were strong deserved their superiority, the weak deserved their inferiority. Spencer also believed that the European races were more advanced than those of other regions. The social-political order that confirmed wealthy, powerful, white, male Europeans in positions of dominance was as it ought to be. Rudyard Kipling's "White Man's Burden" enshrined these beliefs in poetic form (see Source, p. 538).

THE OTTOMAN EMPIRE: THE "SICK MAN OF EUROPE" 1829–76

As the colonizing powers of the world built their empires, they surveyed the weaknesses in many of the formerly powerful empires around them. The closest geographically, the Ottoman Empire, had been in continous decline since it had lost control of Hungary in 1699. With the joint backing of the British, French, and Russians in 1829, Greece won its independence, and three Balkan states—Serbia, Wallachia, and Moldavia—were recognized as autonomous, although still formally under the Ottoman Empire. In the aftermath of these imperial defeats, Muhammad (Mehemet) Ali seized his

Florence Nightingale, Turkey, c. 1854. During the Crimean War "the Lady of the Lamp" established and supervised efficient nursing departments at Scutari and Balaklava. Her unflagging efforts ensured that the mortality rate among the injured was greatly reduced. The effect of her reforms would transform nursing from the realm of menial drudgery into a skilled medical profession with high standards of education.

opportunity to make Egypt effectively independent in 1832 (see p. 549); the Saud family had already won similar autonomy for Arabia; and the French began their occupation of Algeria in 1830. The Ottoman Empire had become the "sick man of Europe."

The Ottoman Empire ruled its subjects, in large part, through their religious communities. Each community administered its own legal system and even collected its own taxes. Different religious groups within the empire looked outward for protection, if necessary, by their co-religionists in other countries. The Greek Orthodox, in particular, looked toward Russia; the Roman Catholics looked to France; Protestants to Britain. Religious missions from these countries received special protection within the Ottoman Empire, and often served as bases for trade and intelligence-gathering as well. Moreover, foreigners trading within the empire were permitted the right to trial by judges of their own nation. Ottoman theory and practice of the state was quite different from that of Western Europe, where the unified nation-state was becoming the norm. In addition, the Ottomans had not kept up with the industrial development of the rest of Europe. In the 1840s Sultan Abdul Mejid enacted the *Tanzimat* (Restructuring) reforms to bring the Ottoman legal code and its social and educational standards into closer accord with those of Western European states, but with very limited success.

The Crimean War of 1853–4 demonstrated the weakness of the Ottoman system. Here on the north shore of the Black Sea, the major powers of Europe confronted one another in a conflict which tested their abilities both to fight and to negotiate settlements. The war began as Russia probed Ottoman strength by attacking Turkey in the Crimean peninsula. Turkey was saved only through the assistance of France and Britain, which pushed back the Russian assault, restoring Crimea to the Ottomans. Austria seized the opportunity to occupy Wallachia and Moldavia, and the final peace treaty recognized both Romania and Serbia as self-governing principalities, under the protection of other European powers.

In an attempt to remedy its weaknesses, the Ottoman government issued the Hatt-i Humayun edict in 1856. This ushered in numerous changes to conform to Western European standards, including equality under a common law for all citizens, tax reform, security of property, the end of torture, more honest administration, and greater freedom of the press. The "Young Turks," a group of mod-

ernizing intellectuals, were delighted, and nationalistic Armenians, Bulgars, Macedonians, and Cretans hoped for greater autonomy. A change of sultan in 1876, however, brought a reverse of all these policies and aspirations. The Young Turks went into exile, and Bulgarian and Armenian nationalists were massacred.

A weak Ottoman Empire left a power vacuum in southeast Europe, which invited continuing foreign intervention and competition. A new Russian attack through the Balkans reached Istanbul itself in 1877. Britain threatened to go to war with Russia, but Bismarck convened an international conference in Berlin in 1878 to resolve the conflict through diplomacy. Warfare was averted for the moment, but the mixture of Ottoman weakness, aggressive expansionism on the part of other European countries, assertive nationalism in the Balkans, and increasing militarization with increasingly powerful weapons threatened a later, larger war. It arrived in 1914 (see pp. 602–6).

CONNECTION: *The end of the Ottoman Empire, 1914–23, p. 715*

SOUTHEAST ASIA AND INDONESIA 1795–1880

In southeast Asia, the colonial competition that had marked the period from 1500 to 1750 continued. The British established a settlement at Penang, Malaya; took Malacca from the Dutch in 1795; and, under Sir Stamford Raffles, established Singapore in 1819. In a series of wars, the British took control of Burma and turned it into a major exporter of rice, timber, teak, and oil, and developed the port of Rangoon to handle the trade. Tin was discovered in Malaya, and its rubber plantations became the world's largest producers.

France began its conquest of Indochina in 1859, completing the takeover by 1893, ostensibly to protect French Catholic missionaries. In dislodging Vietnam from China's tributary sphere, the French interrupted a centuries-old relationship. Vietnam's leading products for export were rice and rubber. Germany, entering late into the colonial competition, annexed Eastern New Guinea and the Marshall and Solomon Islands in the 1880s.

Sharing in the expansionist spirit of the times, the Netherlands decided to annex the entire Indonesian archipelago, building on its administrative center at Batavia (Jakarta) in Java and the trading posts it already occupied. The Dutch wished to dissuade other European powers from intruding and to add the profits from rubber, oil, tin, and tobacco from the other islands to those from sugar, coffee, tea, and tobacco from Java. The Dutch ruled through especially high levels of violence and cruelty. The Java War, 1825–30, had many background provocations and finally erupted when the Dutch built a highway through property housing the tomb of a Muslim saint. In five years of brutal combat between Dutch and Javanese, 15,000 government soldiers were killed, including 8000 Dutch. Some 200,000 Javanese died in the war and in the famine and disease that followed.

In 1830 the Dutch introduced a new, particularly exploitative economic policy called "the cultivation system," *Kulturstelsel*. The Indonesian peasants were forced to devote one fifth of their land to the production of cash crops, especially coffee, sugar, and indigo, to be turned over to the Dutch for export to the Netherlands as a kind of taxation. From 1840 to 1880 the estimated profits equaled one-fourth of the total budget of the Netherlands.

INDIA 1858–1914

The British East India Company had come to India in the seventeenth century to buy spices and hand-made cotton textiles in exchange for bullion, wool, and metals. As a result of British commercial policies in the eighteenth century, the importation of Indian textiles was stopped, and as a result of the British industrial revolution, British machine-made cotton textiles flooded India's markets. India was

---

SOURCE

"The Attack of King Industry"

Communities in India that were already active in business provided many of the new industrialists. Indian financiers became industrialists by importing the new industrial machinery ready-made from Europe. In Ahmedabad, the capital of Gujarat, local businessmen, led by an administrator with close ties to British entrepreneurs, followed Bombay in establishing a local cotton textile industry in 1861. A few years earlier Dalpatram Kavi, a local poet and intellectual leader, had called on his fellow countrymen to recognize the importance of industry to their future. His Gujarati poem, "Hunnarkhan-ni Chadayi"— "The Attack of King Industry," presents a far-reaching agenda for reform centering on industrial change and proposes social restructuring as well. It suggests that the British had brought much of value to India and that Indians were prepared to absorb and implement some of this legacy, but without the British imperial presence and its costs.

Fellow countrymen, let us remove all the
  miseries of our country,
Do work, for the new kingdom has come.
  Its king is industry.

Our wealth has gone into the hands of
  foreigners. The great blunder is yours
For you did not unite yourselves—fellow
  countrymen.

Consider the time, see for yourselves. All our
  people have become poor,
Many men of business have fallen—fellow
  countrymen.

Put away idleness. Fill the treasuries with
  knowledge.
Now awake and work new wonders—fellow
  countrymen.

With kith and kin keep harmony. Do not enter
  into debt.
Limit the dinners for your caste—
  fellow countrymen.

Introduce industry from countries abroad and
  master the modern machinery.
Please attend to this plea from the Poet Dalpat—
  fellow countrymen.

(trans. by Chimanbhai Trivedi and Howard Spodek)

transformed into the model colony, importing manufactured goods from Britain's industries and exporting raw materials such as cotton, jute (mostly for making bags), leather, and enormous quantities of tea. India displaced China as the leading provider of tea to Europe. Two-thirds of India's imports from Britain throughout the second half of the nineteenth century and the first years of the twentieth century were machine-manufactured textiles. Iron and steel goods came second. About one-fifth of all overseas British investment in the late nineteenth century was in India. India's own taxes, however, paid for the building and maintenance of the Indian railway system. By 1914 the subcontinent had 35,000 miles (56,000 kilometers) of track. The railway made possible increased commerce, the movement of troops, the relief of famine, the spread of political dissidence, and pilgrimage visits to religious shrines.

India began its own industrial revolution with cotton textiles, primarily in Bombay. This textile industry was started by local Gujaratis, who had long family histories of involvement in business. The need to found new industries found expression even in local poetry, as "The Attack of King Industry" (see Source, p. 543), makes clear. (In Calcutta, where jute textiles were produced, industry was largely pioneered by British investors.) Mining began in the coal fields of Bengal, Bihar, Orissa, and Assam, and in 1911 the Tata family of Bombay built India's first steel mill at Jamshedpur, Bihar. At the start of World War I, factory employment in all of India had reached about 1 million (out of a total population of about 300 million). While employment in large, mechanized factories was increasing, many hand craftsmen were being displaced, so the actual percentage of people earning their living by manufacturing of all sorts stayed approximately the same, at about 10 percent of the workforce (and has continued about the same till today).

The British ruled India directly, and therefore British influence was felt throughout the administrative and educational systems of the country. Concepts based on European political revolutions were introduced, and imperialism confronted its internal contradiction: How could an imperial power teach the values of self-rule and democracy while maintaining its own foreign rule? Finally, as we shall see in Chapter 20, this contradiction forced Britain to leave India in 1947.

India's reception of British imperialism was quite ambivalent. In 1857 a revolt swept across north India. The British called it an army mutiny but later Indian historians designated it "The First War for National Independence." In fact, the 1857 revolt involved far more than mutinous troops, but far less than the masses generally; it lacked unified leadership and direction. When more organized movements for independence began in the late nineteenth century, their leaders first had to evaluate British rule and to find a balance between acceptance and rejection of its political, economic, social, and cultural models. By the early twentieth century, most politically conscious Indians had come to believe that the British should go home and allow India to choose its own direction.

CONNECTION: *India, 1914–2000, pp. 693–711*

CHINA 1800–1914

China was already a colony and also possessed colonies of its own at the time Europeans began to challenge its power. The Qing dynasty, which governed China from 1644 to 1911, was headed by Manchu invaders from southeastern Manchuria. Even before they invaded and ruled China, the Manchus had established a state in Manchuria, made Korea a vassal state, and made Inner Mongolia a dependency. After establishing their rule in China, the Qing expanded westward. In the eighteenth century they annexed new lands equal to the size of China itself in Outer Mongolia, Dzungaria, the Tarim Basin, Eastern Turkestan, Tsinghai, and Tibet. They also subordinated the peoples of southeast Asia into tributary relationships. Revolts broke out against Manchu rule, but until 1800 they were mostly at the periphery of the empire and posed no serious threat to the dynasty.

By the early 1800s, however, a continuously rising population put pressure on resources and government administrative capacity. The 100 million people of 1650 tripled to 300 million by 1800 and reached 420 million by 1850. More land was needed. Allowing the settlement of Manchuria seemed a suitable reply to the problem, but the Manchus would not permit Chinese settlement in their homeland. Nor did the Manchus increase the size of their bureaucracy to service the rising population, preferring to delegate administrative responsibilities to local authorities, a response that was inadequate. Finally, the Europeans trading with China, especially the British, had discovered that China would accept opium in payment for its tea, silk, and porcelains. Indeed, the opium trade was another example of the growth of multinational commerce: the British had the crop grown cheaply in their Indian colony and carried it from the ports of Bombay, Calcutta, and Madras to Canton in China. The centuries of paying for Chinese exports with silver and gold came to an end. By the 1820s China was purchasing so much opium that it began to export silver!

The Opium Wars 1839–42 and 1856–60

Seeking to staunch the drain of silver and to stop the importation of opium, the Chinese attempted to ban and resist its the import in 1839. It was too late. By now the British proclaimed the ideology of "free trade," and in support of this position British shipboard cannon destroyed Chinese ships and port installations in the harbor at Guangzhou (Canton). This Opium War of 1839–42 was no contest. China ceded to Britain the island of Hong Kong as a colony and opened five Treaty Ports in which foreigners could live and conduct business under their own laws rather than under the laws of China—a condition known as **extraterritoriality**. France and the United States soon gained similar concessions.

Foreign settlements were established in the new treaty ports and became the centers of new industry, education, and publishing. The focus of international trade began to relocate from Guangzhou to Shanghai, at the mouth of the Yangzi River, a more central location along the Chinese coast.

Still China did not establish the formal diplomatic recognition and exchange that European powers had demanded. A second set of wars followed in 1856–60, and these led to the occupation of Beijing by 17,000 French and British soldiers and the sacking of the imperial Summer Palace. More treaty ports were opened, including inland centers along the Yangzi River, now patrolled by British gunboats. Europeans gained control over the administration of China's foreign trade and tariffs. The opium trade continued to expand. Christian missionaries were given freedom to travel throughout China. Some Chinese worked with the foreigners as *compradors*, or intermediaries in business and administration.

As the Manchu government weakened in the last decades of the nineteenth century, revolts broke out, foreign powers continued to seize parts of the country and its tributaries, and there were more calls for internal reform. (The Chinese situation showed similarities with events in the Ottoman

The steamer *Nemesis* destroying eleven Chinese junks at Cherpez Canton, China, by E. Duncan, 1843. The two separate wars fought between Britain and China in the 1840s and 1850s began when the Chinese government tried to halt British merchants from illegally importing opium. The victorious British, here recording an early harbor skirmish, exacted harsh commercial penalties and annexed Chinese territory, including Hong Kong. (*National Maritime Museum, Canada*)

Empire at about the same time.) The greatest of the internal revolts, the Taiping Rebellion, began in 1850 led by Hong Xiuquan, a frustrated scholar who claimed visions of himself as the younger brother of Jesus Christ. The main demands of the Taiping leaders, however, were quite concrete: an end to the corrupt and inefficient Manchu imperial rule, an end to extortionate landlord demands, and alleviation of poverty. Beginning in the southwest, the Taiping came to dominate the Yangzi valley and established their capital in Nanjing in 1853. The imperial government was unable to respond effectively, but regional military leaders, equipped with more modern weapons, finally defeated the revolt, winning more power for themselves. By the time the Taiping Rebellion was suppressed in 1864, some

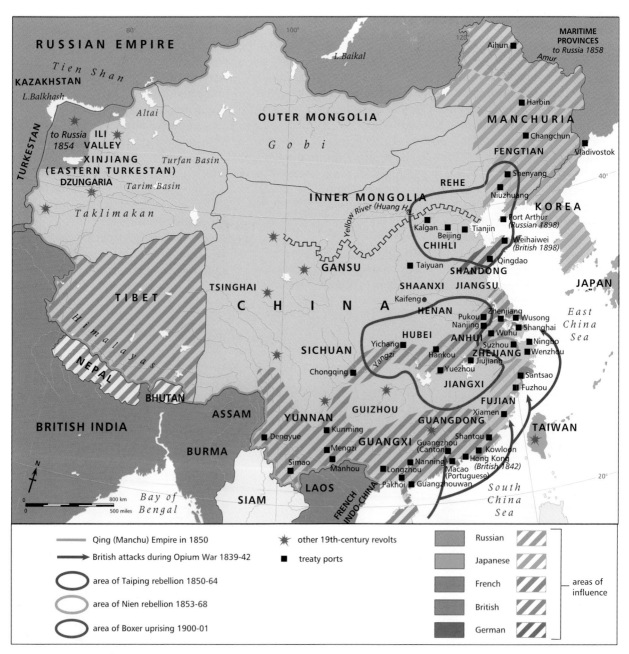

The decline of the Qing dynasty During the course of the nineteenth century, the authority of the Qing (Manchu) dynasty in China was undermined. Beset by the aggressive actions of European colonial powers, the Qing granted extensive trade and territorial concessions. Internally, a series of increasingly violent rebellions, both within the Chinese heartland and in the western (often Muslim) regions, brought the dynasty to the verge of collapse by the turn of the century.

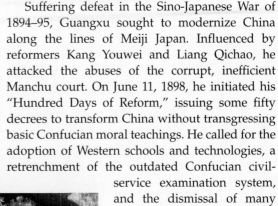

PROFILE
Empress Dowager Cixi
CHINA'S "DRAGON LADY"

If we cannot rely upon…supernatural formulas, can we not rely upon the heart of our people? If we lost it, how can we maintain our country? (Haldane, p. 180).

With these words, Empress Dowager Cixi, one of only three women ever to rule China, sanctioned the Boxer Rebellion, a broad-based peasant movement aimed at eliminating all Western influences in China. Invoking supernatural powers, the Boxers killed over 200 foreign citizens, prompting Austria-Hungary, France, Great Britain, Italy, Japan, Russia, and the United States to send in their troops. Thousands of Chinese were killed, the Qing court fled Beijing, and China was forced to pay substantial reparations. The once-mighty Celestial Empire was humiliated yet again.

Portrait of Cixi from 1908 photograph. (private collection)

History has not been kind to Empress Dowager Cixi, who ruled from 1861 until her death in 1908. Born in 1835, Cixi was the only concubine of Emperor Xianfeng to give birth to a son. She delivered Tongzhi in 1856, securing her a prestigious position within the walls of the Forbidden City. In 1861 Tongzhi ascended the throne and Cixi began to earn her reputation as a ruthless despot. She seized control over her son, away from his regents, and became the Empress Dowager. When Tongzhi died two years later, Cixi was rumored to have killed her daughter-in-law and unborn grandchild, placing her nephew Guangxu on the throne to maintain her own status. In 1889, she retired to her Summer Palace, but was eventually recalled to Beijing to advise the young Emperor.

Suffering defeat in the Sino-Japanese War of 1894–95, Guangxu sought to modernize China along the lines of Meiji Japan. Influenced by reformers Kang Youwei and Liang Qichao, he attacked the abuses of the corrupt, inefficient Manchu court. On June 11, 1898, he initiated his "Hundred Days of Reform," issuing some fifty decrees to transform China without transgressing basic Confucian moral teachings. He called for the adoption of Western schools and technologies, a retrenchment of the outdated Confucian civil-service examination system, and the dismissal of many high-ranking officials—possibly the Empress Dowager herself. With the help of her loyal advisors, Cixi reasserted her power and Guangxu spent the rest of his life under house arrest. The modernization movement was crushed just weeks after it began and only months before the Boxer Rebellion.

Cixi might not have been the "dragon-lady," the "iron-willed, oversexed Manchu concubine" of popular lore, but she became the most powerful person in China. She did not hesitate to exercise her authority over either Tongzhi or Guangxu, and was thus responsible for thwarting much-needed reforms. Inadvertently she paved the way for the 1911 Revolution. Yet, as historian Sterling Seagrave recently pointed out, Cixi did not make her decisions alone. A coterie of officials counseled her, wanting to protect not only traditional Chinese values against Western interference, but also their own positions within the Empire. After 1900, Cixi was forced to accept reform, but for China her efforts were too few and too late.

20 million people had been killed. At about the same time, additional rebellions broke out among tribal peoples near Guangzhou, among the Miao tribals in Guizhou, and among Muslims in Yunnan and Gansu. The largest of all the rebel groups, the Nien, controlled much of the territory between Nanjing and Kaifeng. Collectively, these rebellions cost another 10 million lives.

With the central government fully occupied with these internal revolts, foreign imperialists began to establish their territorial claims as well. Russians seized border areas in the Amur River region (1858), the Maritime Provinces (1860), and, for ten years, the Ili valley in Turkestan (1871–81). France defeated Chinese forces in a local war and seized all of Indo-China (1883–84). Most humiliating of all, Japan defeated China in warfare in 1894–5. China ceded Taiwan to Japan, granted it the right to operate factories in the treaty ports, and paid a huge indemnity. Korea passed to Japanese control, although formal colonial rule did not follow until 1910. The historic relationship of China as teacher and Japan as disciple, which dated back at least to 600 C.E., had been abruptly reversed. The new industrial age had introduced new values and new power relationships.

The Boxer Rebellion 1898–1900

In the last years of the nineteenth century, China was in turmoil. In Beijing, a group of nationalists, called "Boxers" by the Europeans, enraged by foreign arrogance in China, burned Christian missions, killed missionaries, and laid siege to the foreign legations for two months. The imperial powers of Europe and the United States put down this revolt and exacted yet another exorbitant indemnity. The Europeans and Americans did not, however, wish to take over the government of China directly. They wanted to have a Chinese government responsible for China. They wanted to preserve China as a quasi-colony, and they therefore supported the Manchus in the formalities of power, even as they steadily hollowed out the content of that power.

A group of Chinese modernizers began to organize new industries, beginning with textiles, but the government, now in the hands of an aging dowager empress who controlled the heir apparent until she died in 1908, blocked their reforms (see Profile, p. 547). Frustrated nationalists called for revolution. Their leading organizer was Sun Yat-sen, a Cantonese educated in Honolulu, where he became a Christian, and in Hong Kong, where he became a doctor.

Boxers on the march. The mostly poor peasants who formed the Boxer Rebellion of 1898–1900 blamed hard times on foreign interference and Christian missionaries. Renowned for the ferocity of their attacks, the rebels terrified Western residents as they marched into Tianjin (pictured). A 20,000-strong force, comprising soldiers from different colonial powers, finally crushed the revolt in Beijing.

Sun called for a two-fold anti-colonial revolution: first, against the Manchus and then against the European, American, and Japanese powers. Only after the first revolution was successful in overthrowing Manchu rule in 1911 did Sun begin to push against the Western powers and Japan. The story of that struggle is told in Chapter 20.

CONNECTION: *China, 1856–1911, p. 581*

AFRICA 1652–1912

Once equipped with the technology to enter and subdue the continent of Africa, Europeans began to covet it for many diverse reasons. Napoleon invaded Egypt in 1798 because he saw it as a route to India and a means of dislodging the British from that colony. The hinterlands behind its trading ports offered good lands for farming and so South Africa, first desired as a way station on the long routes between Europe and Asia, soon became a comfortable and fruitful farming colony. Discovered by outsiders only in the second half of the nineteenth century, the mineral wealth of central and southern Africa—diamonds, gold, and copper—soon became one of its richest attractions for capitalist investment. Equatorial Africa was also rich in tropical products. Finally, as the possession of colonies began to be seen in Europe as a status symbol of nationalism, the major nations of Europe carved up the continent of Africa, each taking a share.

EGYPT 1798–1882

The earliest European expansion into Africa in modern times, beyond the coastal enclaves that had been established for trade, took place at the extreme north and south of the continent. Napoleon's forces invaded Egypt in 1798 and held it until British forces drove them out in 1801. After both European powers had withdrawn, Muhammad (Mehemet) Ali (1769–1849) took over actual rule in 1807, even though he was nominally a viceroy of the Ottoman Empire. He built new irrigation works, encouraged the cultivation of cotton for Europe's booming textile industry, and introduced some new industries, including Egypt's own textile mills. He modernized the army and administration and built a system of secular state schools to train administrators and officers. He introduced a government printing press, which in turn encouraged translations into Arabic. Militarily, he marched his newly equipped armies up the Nile, captured the Sudan, and built the city of Khartoum to serve as its capital in 1830. He also gained control of the holy cities of Mecca and Medina in Arabia to counter the power of the militantly Islamic Wahabi movement there. He occupied Syria and Palestine and threatened Istanbul itself until Britain and France stood in his way, offering him, instead, recognition as the hereditary ruler of Egypt. Muhammad Ali's son commissioned a French firm to build the Suez Canal, which was opened in 1869. His grandson expanded Egyptian territorial holdings both along the coast of the Red Sea and inland toward the headwaters of the Nile.

Egypt entered the international economy based in Europe, but soon was spending more on imports, military modernization, and beautification projects in Cairo than it was earning in exports. As Egyptian debts rose, European creditors pressured their governments to force the *khedive* (the title given to Muhammad Ali and his successors) to appoint European experts as Commissioners of the Debt in 1876. In 1878 the *khedive* was forced to add a French and a British representative to his cabinet. Even so, in 1881 the European powers had the Ottoman sultan dismiss the *khedive*, Muhammad Ali's grandson. When an Egyptian military revolt then seized power, Britain sent in its forces, primarily to protect the Suez canal, and stayed on as the power behind the throne until the 1950s. For Egypt, entanglement with Europe had proved a two-edged sword.

CONNECTION: *Egypt, 1882–2000, pp. 720–5*

ALGERIA 1830–71

The French invaded Algeria in 1830 to suppress piracy, as the Americans had done at Tripoli, and to collect debts. Once arrived, they remained in control of Algiers and two other ports. Resistance swelled under Abd al-Qadir, head of a rural Muslim brotherhood, who began to build a small state with its own administration and a modernized army of 10,000 men trained by European advisers. At first, the French avoided confrontation with al-Qadir, who stayed south of their holdings, but in 1841 bitter warfare broke out. Before the French won, they had committed 110,000 troops to the war and had attacked neighboring Morocco to block reinforcements to their enemy. Revolts

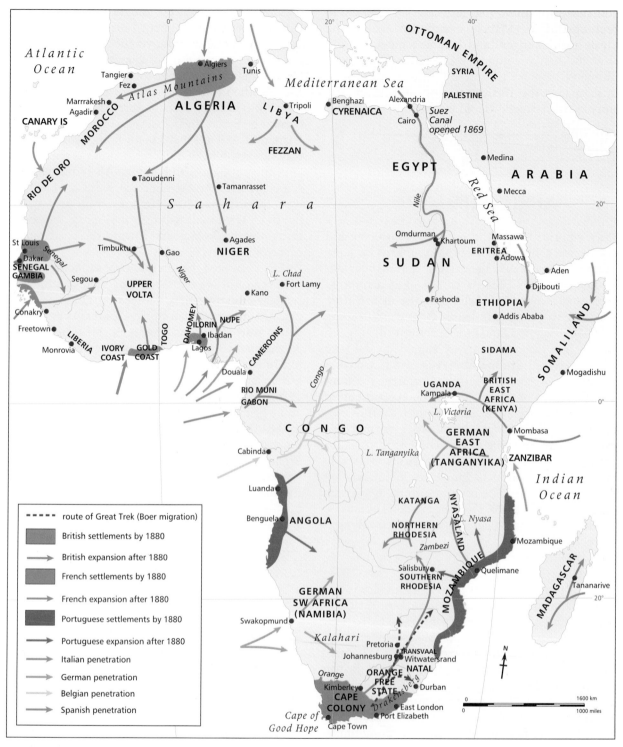

European expansion in Africa Steamboats, machine-guns, and quinine (to combat malaria) all gave Europeans new access to the interior of Africa in the later nineteenth century, and they intensified their nationalistic competition. The British pursued the dream of linking their possessions from Cape Town to Cairo, while France seized much of North and Central Africa. Bismarck's Berlin Conference of 1884 tried to apportion the spoils among all the competing powers.

continued to simmer, with the last and largest repressed in 1871. French armies took over rural areas, opening them for French settlement.

CONNECTION: *Algerian independence, pp. 733–6*

SOUTH AFRICA 1652–1910

The Dutch had established a colony at the Cape of Good Hope in South Africa in 1652 as a way station *en route* to India and the Spice Islands. The settlement grew slowly, and immigrants from other European countries also joined it. The expansion of the European Cape Colony further destabilized a region already passing through an *mfecane*, or time of troubles.

In 1816, Shaka (c. 1787–1828) seized the leadership of his small Zulu kingdom just to the north and east of the Cape Colony. Shaka organized a standing army of 40,000 soldiers, rigorously trained and disciplined, housed in stockades separate from the rest of the population, and armed with newly designed short, stabbing spears, which gave them enormous power over their enemies in hand-to-hand combat. By 1828, when Shaka was assassinated by two half-brothers, his kingdom had expanded, forcing the Soshagane, Nguni, Ndebele, Sotho, Ngwane, and Mfengu peoples to flee their lands. Some moved into the Cape Colony, but the vast majority turned north and west, displacing other peoples in turn.

European expansion at the Cape had similar disruptive effects on local populations. As the Dutch and the British set out to the rural areas to farm, they displaced the Khoikhoi people who had been resident in the area. The Khoikhoi chiefdoms dissolved in the face of warfare, displacement, and catastrophic smallpox epidemics that decimated their numbers. Some of the Khoikhoi, along with other African peoples, were taken as slaves to fill the labor needs of the Europeans.

As a result of their victories in the Napoleonic Wars, military and legal control of the Cape Colony passed to the British. British laws and social practices were instituted, including freedom of the press and of assembly, the development of representative government, the abolition of the slave trade, and the emancipation of slaves. Nevertheless Europeans controlled the best land of the region, leaving their former slaves to be wage workers rather than land-owners and farmers. Property restrictions on voting effectively kept Africans out of power, and the Masters and Servants Act limited the freedom of movement of black workers.

In a great migration, some 8000 people of Dutch descent, unhappy with the increasingly British customs of the colony, and seeking new land for farming, departed on a great march, or trek, northward in the years between 1834 and 1841. These people, usually called Boers (meaning farmers in Dutch), or Afrikaners (for the African dialect of Dutch they spoke), ultimately founded two new republics, the Orange Free State and the Transvaal. Meanwhile, the Cape Colony expanded eastward, annexing Natal in 1843, partly to keep the Boers out. As they migrated, the Boers fought, displaced, conquered, and restricted to reservations the African peoples they encountered. Seeking labor to work the land, they often captured and virtually enslaved Africans living around them.

When the Suez Canal restructured the shipping routes between Asia and Europe in 1869, South Africa might have become a quiet colonial backwater. But in the 1870s diamonds were discovered at Kimberley, and in the 1880s the world's largest known deposit of gold was found at Witwatersrand. Competition for this new wealth intensified the general hostility between the Boers and the British into full-scale warfare. The British army of 450,000 men finally defeated the Boer army of 88,000 in the three-year-long Boer War, 1899–1902. In 1910, the British consolidated their own two colonies (Cape and Natal) with the two Boer republics into the Union of South Africa, which became a self-governing country. After 1913 South Africa had the same sorts of political institutions and rights as Australia and Canada. It was considered a white settler colony despite its black majority.

Labor Issues:
Coercion and Unionization

Throughout Africa, Europeans confronted the problem of finding labor for their new farms and enterprises. By confiscating African land and redistributing it among themselves, Europeans took farms away from Africans and produced a new wage-labor force. The 1913 Natives Land Act of South Africa closed 87 percent of South African land to African ownership; the remaining 13 percent was the most marginal land. The newly displaced labor force was especially vital for the new coffee plantations in the highlands of east Africa. In the farming areas of Kenya, Northern Rhodesia, Nyasaland, and Angola a system of tenancy without wages developed, a kind of share-cropping system. Within their colonies in Angola and Mozambique, the Portuguese used intimidation to coerce labor, but the Africans often fled or otherwise subverted the plans of their colonizers. The British colonies, which used the carrot of (low) wages seemed more successful in eliciting production. Along the coast, indentured laborers from India, China, and southeast Asia were imported by the thousands to work in the sugar plantations.

The greatest problem was finding labor for the South African diamond and gold mines (and later for the great copper mines in the Congo as well). Taxation was introduced that had to be paid in cash, forcing all Africans to find some way of raising the money. Jobs in the mines were one alternative. Because the Europeans feared the revolutionary potential of a stable African labor force in the mines, they usually recruited workers on contracts for only one or two years at a time. They split up families, housing the male workers in barrack-like accommodations near the mines while exiling their families to distant reservations where the women and children carried on limited farming and craft production. The mine owners did not pay the workers enough to support their families so the farming and handicrafts of the women in effect subsidized the workers' salaries.

Trade unions in the mines organized only the white skilled workers and kept Africans out of these jobs. In 1906, when the mines employed 18,000 whites, 94,000 Africans, and 51,000 Chinese indentured laborers, the white skilled workers went on strike to protest their being squeezed out by the Chinese and the Blacks. Owners broke this strike through the use of Afrikaner strike breakers, but ultimately the Chinese miners were repatriated and the skilled jobs were reserved for whites. Race thus trumped both the free markets of capitalism and the solidarity of labor unions.

EUROPEAN EXPLORERS IN CENTRAL AFRICA

The area of the continent least known to Europeans was central Africa. David Livingstone (1813–73), a

Stanley tracks down explorer. "Dr Livingstone, I presume?" Before journalist Henry Stanley, on assignment for the *New York Herald*, tracked down the Scottish missionary in the heart of the African interior, the latter had been feared dead. Livingstone, who campaigned against slavery, was the first European explorer to reach Lake Tanganyika, the great Victoria Falls, and parts of the Congo.

Scottish missionary who was fascinated by exploration and eager for the opportunity to provide medical assistance, landed at Luanda along the Angola Coast in 1841 and crossed equatorial Africa to Quelimane, spending fourteen years in this expedition. Two subsequent trips in equatorial Africa lasted a total of thirteen years, until Livingstone died in the course of his explorations. Livingstone captured the imagination of Europe, and in 1871, the *New York Herald* dispatched Henry Morton Stanley (1841–1904) to try to find him on his third expedition. Not only did Stanley locate Livingstone, he also carried out expeditions of his own through the Lake District of East Africa and along the Congo River. On Stanley's return through Europe, King Leopold II of Belgium engaged him to establish trading stations along the Congo River. Unlike Livingstone, Stanley was motivated by personal profit and he accepted the king's proposal. The colonization of central Africa was beginning.

Stanley, representing the king and his International Association for the Exploration and Civilization of Africa, negotiated treaties with hundreds of local chiefs. The treaties gave him the power to establish a Confederation of Free Negro Republics, an estate of some 900,000 square miles (2.3 million square kilometers), which functioned as a kind of slave plantation within Africa for the economic benefit of King Leopold. In this enterprise, Leopold was actually acting as a private investor rather than as king of Belgium.

THE SCRAMBLE FOR AFRICA

As European powers colonized central Africa, they came into direct competition with each other. Fearing the consequences of this competition, Bismarck again employed diplomacy to defuse European conflict, as he had done a few years earlier in the Balkans. He convened a conference in Berlin in 1884–5 to determine the allocation of Congo lands and to establish ground rules for fixing borders among European colonies in Africa. The Berlin Conference assigned the administration of the Congo, an area one-third the size of the continental United States, to Leopold II personally as a kind of company government. The Congo became, in effect, his private estate, eighty times larger than Belgium itself. Its economic purpose was, first, the harvesting of natural rubber, the sap of the rubber tree, and, later, the exploitation of the Congo's rich mineral reserves, especially copper. Laborers were forced to work as slaves

at the point of a gun. Company agents killed and maimed workers who offered resistance. In 1908, recognizing both the cruelty and the economic losses of the Congo administration, the Belgian Parliament took over control of the colony from the king, but the Congo remained one of the most harshly administered of all the African colonies.

The Conference also divided up the lands of Africa on paper, generally apportioning inland areas to the European nations already settled on the adjacent coast. These nations were then charged with establishing actual inland settlements in those regions, and they quickly did so, dispatching settlers in a "scramble for Africa." Portugal added to its domains in Angola and Mozambique. Italy captured a piece of Somaliland at the horn of Africa and Eritrea on the Red Sea. It also attempted to conquer proud Ethiopia, but King Menelik II (r. 1889–1913) had purchased sufficient guns and

THE RHODES COLOSSUS
STRIDING FROM CAPE TOWN TO CAIRO.

The Rhodes Colossus. Cecil John Rhodes became one of the main champions of British rule in southern Africa, promoting colonization "from Cape Town to Cairo." The statesman and financier divided his time between diamond mining and annexing territories to British imperial rule. Rhodesia (now Zimbabwe and Zambia) was named for him in 1894.

trained his forces well enough to defeat Italy at the Battle of Adowa in 1896. Italy did succeed, however, in taking Libya from the weakened Ottoman Empire in 1911. Germany established colonies in German East Africa (Tanganyika), the Cameroons, Togo, and German Southwest Africa (Namibia). The Germans, like the British and French before them, established treaties with African chiefs who often did not understand the significance of the documents they ratified but nevertheless found their power over their people strengthened. The chiefs frequently became, in effect, the agents of Europeans for recruiting labor and collecting taxes. In exchange, the Europeans protected the chiefs from resistance and rebellion.

On the occasions when Africans resisted these one-sided agreements, Europeans responded with force. Between 1884 and 1898, the French put down the rebellion of the Mande peoples under the Muslim Samori Toure. The British finally quelled a series of Asante revolts in the Gold Coast in 1900. The Germans crushed perhaps the greatest of the unsuccessful rebellions, the Maji-Maji revolt of 1905–7 in Tanganyika. Led by Kinji-kitile Ngwele, who claimed to have magic water (*maji*), which would turn German bullets to water, the rebels had refused to perform forced labor on the cotton plantations. The uprising ended with 70,000 rebels dead, including those who succumbed to disease and malnutrition. Other less spectacular revolts were similarly suppressed with violence.

A decade after the Berlin Conference, France and Britain, the two largest colonial powers, found themselves on a collision course in the Nile valley. From the north, British troops were moving up the Nile valley to fight the troops of a Muslim militant state, which challenged them near Khartoum. Muhammad Ahmed had proclaimed himself as the **Mahdi**, "the guided one of the Prophet," and began to build a state in the Sudan. In 1885 he defeated an Egyptian force commanded by British General Charles Gordon at Khartoum. For some time Britain did not respond, but a decade later it sent another force under General Horatio Herbert Kitchener to retake the Sudan for Egypt. At Omdurman, Kitchener's army destroyed the Mahdists, killing 11,000 men and wounding 16,000 in a single battle on 2 September 1898, while losing just forty of its own soldiers. The British forces had machine guns while the Mahdists believed they were impervious to bullets.

As English forces began to connect the north–south route, French forces were proceeding from their huge holdings in west Africa to link up with their small toehold in the east at French Somaliland. In 1898 General Kitchener confronted French Captain Jean-Baptiste Marchand at Fashoda. War threatened, as provocative correspondence and news accounts were issued on both sides. In the end, the heavily outnumbered French backed down, and France retreated to its substantial holdings in Algeria, and to Morocco, which it later divided with Spain in 1912.

WHAT DIFFERENCE DOES IT MAKE?

The industrial revolution in Western Europe and the United States ushered in an era of imperialism that brought most of the world's land under European political control. Why did the industrializing nations assert their powers in this way? To some extent, the answer seems obvious: They relished the power, wealth, and prestige that apparently came with imperial possessions. They also claimed to welcome the opportunity to serve others. Further, the industrial system that they were building seemed to take on a life of its own, requiring ever-increasing sources of raw materials and more markets in which to sell. But why was trade alone not enough? Why did the industrialists feel it was necessary to take political control as well? Were there additional motives behind imperialism? And did the results of imperialism match the aspirations of the imperial rulers?

We cannot answer all these questions fully, but a recent (April 1997) article by Patrick Wolfe in *The American Historical Review*, "History and Imperialism: A Century of Theory, from Marx to Postcolonialism," helps us to review and sort out some of the most prominent explanations.

Karl Marx deplored the exploitation of colonialism, but, as a European, he valued some of its contributions. Britain, he emphasized, brought to India a new economic dynamism, with railroads, industrial infrastructure, and communication networks. Ultimately this transformation would lead to capitalism and then socialism. Marx wrote in 1853: "Whatever may have been the crimes of England, she was the unconscious tool of history in bringing about that revolution" (Marx and Engels, *First Indian War*, p. 21).

J.A. Hobson, a British economist writing in 1902, and V.I. Lenin, the leader of the Communist revolution in Russia (see Chapter 19), writing in 1916, agreed that the desire to control raw materials and markets drove imperialism. Hobson pointed out that the profits of the imperial system went mostly to the rich. He believed that if imperialism were ended overseas, a concentration on investment and industry at home would provide greater opportunities to the working classes in Europe. M.N. Roy, a founder of the Communist Party of India, disagreed with Hobson, arguing that the profits of imperialism did provide workers at home in Europe with economic gains. The revolt against the imperial, and capitalist, system would begin among the workers in the colonies who were more exploited.

Several analysts have tried to grasp the imperial system as a whole, understanding the impact of colonizer and colonized upon one another. Some, like Marx, above, saw the system introducing valuable modernization into the colonies. Most, like Immanuel Wallerstein and the American economists Paul Baran and Paul Sweezy, argued that the imperial power would always seek to keep the colonies in a position of dependency and underdevelopment. The imperial power might introduce some technological innovations, such as railways that were necessary for their trade, but they had no interest in enabling the colonies to become economic and technological rivals. Indeed, one reason for imposing imperial domination was to prevent the colony from taking control of its own economic policies.

Ronald Robinson and John Gallagher, British historians writing in the 1960s, and French anthropologist Louis Althusser, writing in the 1970s and 1980s, stressed the need to evaluate imperialism on a case-by-case basis. British imperialism in Egypt, for example, was quite sophisticated and benign compared with the raw cruelty of Belgian imperialism in the Congo. Even within individual colonies, imperialists treated different regions and groups differently, for example incorporating educated urban groups into the administration while treating plantation workers almost like slave labor. Imperial rule also varied considerably depending on the administration in power in the imperial country and also on the local imperial representatives on the scene. All three scholars eschewed generalizations and emphasized the complexity of the imperial enterprise.

Finally, some of the most recent scholarly analyses of imperialism—often referred to as postcolonial analyses—have stressed the cultural impact of imperialism on both colonized and colonizer. Imperial rulers usually drew a sense of pride from their conquest and exalted their own culture for possessing colonies. Colonized peoples, on the other hand, had to re-examine their historic cultural traditions and identities in light of the fact that they had been conquered by foreigners. The postcolonial literature that analyzes this cultural confrontation is expanding rapidly at present, with contributions by literary critics such as Edward Said, Homi Bhabha, and Gayatri Chakravorty Spivak. Indeed, as industrialization has brought peoples of the world into ever closer contact, and political philosophies have collided with one another, questions of personal and group identity have increased everywhere. In the next chapter we examine three areas of cultural identity—urban identity, gender identity, and national identity—in the age of revolution.

BIBLIOGRAPHY

Abu-Lughod, Janet and Richard Hay, Jr., eds., *Third World Urbanization* (Chicago: Maaroufa Press, 1977).

Adas, Michael, ed. *Islamic and European Expansion* (Philadelphia: Temple University Press, 1993).

—. *Machines as the Measure of Men* (Ithaca: Cornell University Press, 1989).

Andrea, Alfred and James Overfield, eds., *The Human Record*, Vol. 2, (Boston: Houghton Mifflin, 3rd ed., 1998).

Bairoch, Paul. *Cities and Economic Development*, trans. by Christopher Braider (Chicago: University of Chicago Press, 1988).

Braudel, Fernand. *Civilization and Capitalism 15th–18th Century: The Perspective of the World*, trans. by Sian Reynolds (New York: Harper and Row, 1984).

Briggs, Asa. *A Social History of England* (New York: Viking Press, 1983).

Burns, E. Bradford. *Latin America: A Concise Interpretive History* (Englewood Cliffs: Prentice Hall, 6th ed., 1993).

Cameron, Rondo. *A Concise Economic History of the World* (New York: Oxford University Press, 1989).

Cobban, Alfred. *A History of Modern France*, Vol. 2: *1799–1945* (Harmondsworth: Penguin Books, 1961).

Curtin, Philip, *et al. African History from Earliest Times to Independence* (Longman: London, 2nd ed., 1995).

Dalpat-Kavya Navnit (Selections from Dalpat the Poet), in Gujarati, ed. Deshavram Kashiram Shastri (Ahmedabad: Gujarat Vidyasabha, 1949).

Davis, Lance E. and Robert A. Huttenback. *Mammon and the Pursuit of Empire* (New York: Cambridge University Press, 1989).

Deane, Phyllis. *The First Industrial Revolution* (Cambridge: Cambridge University Press, 2nd ed., 1979).

Engels, Friedrich. *The Condition of the Working Class in England*, trans. by W.O. Henderson and W.H. Chaloner (Stanford: Stanford University Press, 1968).

Fogel, Robert and Stanley L. Engerman. *Time on the Cross*, 2 vols (Boston: Little, Brown, 1974).

Grinker, Roy Richard and Christopher B. Steiner, eds. *Perspectives on Africa* (Oxford: Blackwell, 1997).

Haldane, Charlotte. *The Last Great Empress of China* (Indianapolis: Bobbs-Merrill, 1965).

Hanke, Lewis and Jane M. Rausch, eds. *People and Issues in Latin American History* (New York: Markus Wiener Publishing, 1990).

Headrick, Daniel R. *The Tools of Empire* (New York: Oxford University Press, 1981).

Hobsbawm, Eric. *The Age of Capital 1848–1875* (New York: Vintage Books, 1975).

—. *The Age of Empire 1875–1914* (New York: Vintage, 1987).

—. *The Age of Revolution 1789–1848* (New York: New American Library, 1962).

Hughes, Thomas P. *American Genesis* (New York: Viking, 1989).

Kennedy, Paul. *The Rise and Fall of the Great Powers* (New York: Random House, 1987).

Laslett, Peter. *The World We Have Lost* (New York: Charles Scribner's Sons, 1965).

Lenin, V.I. *Imperialism, the Highest Stage of Capitalism* (Peking: Foreign Languages Press, 1965).

Magraw, Roger. *France 1815–1914: The Bourgeois Century* (Oxford: Oxford University Press, 1983).

Marx, Karl and Frederick Engels. *The Communist Manifesto* (New York: International Publishers, 1948).

—. *The First Indian War of Independence 1857–1859* (Moscow: Foreign Languages Press, n.d., *c.* 1960).

Moore, Barrington, Jr. *The Social Origins of Dictatorship and Democracy* (Boston: Beacon Press, 1966).

Murphey, Rhoads. *A History of Asia* (New York: Addison Wesley Longman, 3rd ed., 1999).

Palmer, R.R. and Joel Colton. *A History of the Modern World* (New York: McGraw Hill, 8th ed., 1995).

Perlin, Frank. *The Invisible City: Monetary, Administrative and Popular Infrastructures in Asia and Europe, 1500–1900* (Brookfield, VT: Variorum, 1993).

Perrot, Michelle. *Workers on Strike; France, 1871–1890*, trans. by Chris Turner with Erica Carter and Claire Laudet (Leamington Spa: Berg, 1987).

Revel, Jacques and Lynn Hunt, eds. *Histories: French Constructions of the Past*, trans. by Arthur Goldhammer *et al.* (New York: New York Press, 1995)

SarDesai, D.R. *Southeast Asia Past and Present* (Boulder, CO: Westview Press, 3rd ed., 1994).

Seagrave, Sterling, with Peggy Seagrave. *Dragon Lady: The Life and Legend of the Last Empress of China* (New York: Knopf, 1992.)

Seal, Anil. *The Emergence of Indian Nationalism* (Cambridge: Cambridge University Press, 1968).

Stearns, Peter N. *The Industrial Revolution in World History* (Boulder, CO: Westview Press, 1993).

Thompson, E.P. *The Making of the English Working Class* (New York: Vintage, 1966).

Time-Life Books. *Time Frame AD 1850–1900: The Colonial Overlords.* (Alexandria, VA: Time-Life Books, 1990).

Wallerstein, Immanuel. *The Modern World-system 1: Capitalist Agriculture and the Origins of the European World-economy in the Sixteenth Century* (San Diego: Academic Press, 1974).

Wilentz, Sean. *Chants Democratic: New York City and the Rise of the American Working Class, 1788–1850* (New York: Oxford University Press, 1984).

Wolf, Eric R. *Europe and the People without History* (Berkeley: University of California Press, 1982).

Wolfe, Patrick, "Imperialism and History: A Century of Theory, from Marx to Postcolonialism," *American Historical Review* CII, No. 2 (April 1997), 388–420.

SOCIAL REVOLUTIONS

1830–1914

"Social progress and historic changes occur by virtue of the progress of women toward liberty, and decadence of the social order occurs as the result of a decrease in the liberty of women."

CHARLES FOURIER

URBANIZATION, GENDER RELATIONS, AND NATIONALISM WEST AND EAST

People's everyday lives and the social structures in which they lived changed dramatically as a result of the political and industrial revolutions. The increasing authority of the nation-state, struggles for participatory democracy, abundant increases in productivity, restructuring of the labor market, and the shifting international power relationships were not remote abstractions. They changed the day-to-day lives of ordinary people. In this chapter we examine three areas of that transformation: urban life, gender relations, and nationalism. We ask: How did local communities change? How did relationships between men and women change? And how did people re-imagine their roles as citizens and subjects?

We conclude the chapter with special attention to the transformation of Japan in the second half of the nineteenth century. Japan was the first non-European country to industrialize successfully, alter its internal political structures, and enter the international competition in conquering colonies. At the farthest eastern edge of Eurasia, Japan seemed to be following, in its own way, patterns established at the farthest west.

NEW PATTERNS OF URBAN LIFE

Cities from the eighteenth century began a period of growth that has continued without break until today. In the largest cities this process included large-scale suburbanization, which was made possible by the new railroad transportation systems for goods and passengers. Automobiles later enlarged the system to ever-greater dimensions. Growth was both geographic and demographic. Cities grew because they served new functions for more people. One of these functions, which brought about much of the early growth, was the increasing importance of centralized government. The political and administrative functions of many cities have continued to expand not only in the great capitals of industrialized nations like Washington, Canberra, and Paris, but also in the capitals of nations that are not heavily industrialized such as New Delhi, Beijing, Jakarta, Lagos, and Abidjan. Nevertheless, most economists believe that urbanization based primarily on government jobs is economically and socially problematic. Cities tend to grow on the basis of economic productivity.

Indeed, much of the urban growth in the nineteenth century was a direct result of industrialization. The steam engine, which could be constructed anywhere, made the location of industries more flexible. Factories sprang up near port facilities, at inland transportation hubs, in the heart of raw materials resource centers like the Midlands of Britain, or Silesia in central Europe, and in large concentrations of consumers, like the great cities of Paris and London. New industrial metropolises dotted the map.

Immigrants streamed into the new cities for jobs. Farmers became factory workers and the balance between urban and rural populations tilted continuously cityward. Within cities, the children of artisans became factory workers. Both farmers and artisans found the new industrial city shocking. They were exchanging the styles of life of farm and workshop for regimes of routinization, standardization, and regulation. The skills that they had previously mastered were of little use here. At the same time, opportunities beckoned: cultural, educational, recreational, social, and, most important, economic. In the early years of the industrial revolution, conditions of labor and of public health were abysmal; later, as productivity increased, workers organized, employers and governments paid heed, and conditions started to improve.

"City lights" began to appear more attractive. The nineteenth century began the global age of urbanization.

THE CONDITIONS OF URBANIZATION: HOW DO WE KNOW?

Primary Documents of the Time

"The most remarkable social phenomenon of the present century is the concentration of population in cities." These words open Adna Ferrin Weber's *The Growth of Cities in the Nineteenth Century*, published in 1899, the first comprehensive quantitative study of the subject. Weber's research began as a Ph.D. dissertation in demographic statistics in 1898 at Columbia University and was published the next year in book form. A century later it remains an invaluable introduction to the central issues.

In Chapter 16 we saw a small sampling of the poetry, political polemics, and government reports tracking the phenomenon of nineteenth-century urbanization as it was occurring. Here, we will examine a few of the scholarly approaches to the subject that were also appearing, and Weber's book is a good starting point. Weber called attention to the breakdown of boundaries between city and country. Institutionally, cities were becoming the

18 Back Queen Street, Deansgate, Manchester. As this *Illustrated London News* drawing of housing conditions of the Manchester Cotton Operatives in 1862 shows, accommodation in this city could be spartan. Manchester in particular, with its high mortality rate, desperately needed the attentions of voluntary agencies that were attempting to better the living conditions of those who had been drawn to work in the new industries. Despite the fact that many workers emigrated to the United States or to British colonies overseas, the population continued to grow at a great rate, with adverse consequences for public health and housing.

Paris, a Rainy Day **by Gustave Caillebotte, 1876–77.** An Impressionist's-eye-view of life in an urban setting. Although a number of studies suggest that the burgeoning urban development of the turn of the century ground down the lives of the poor, for the bourgeoisie, with leisure time on their hands, cities provided a backdrop for pleasure. (*Musée Marmottan, Paris*)

cockpits of modern life; geographically, they were already spawning suburbs that would later be derided as "urban sprawl."

> In the last half-century [1848–98], all the agencies of modern civilization have worked together to abolish this rural isolation; the cities have torn down their fortifications, which separated them from the open country; while the railways, the newspaper press, freedom of migration and settlement, etc., cause the spread of the ideas originating in the cities and lift the people of the rural districts out of their state of mental stagnation. Industry is also carried on outside of the cities, so that the medieval distinction between town and country has lost its meaning in the advanced countries. (pp. 7–8)

To critics of urbanization, Weber replied that cities and industry were needed to absorb the surplus growth of rural population. In most of Europe, except France, he writes, "the rural populations, by reason of their continuous increase, produce a surplus which must migrate either to the cities or foreign lands" (p. 67). Without cities and industrial jobs, what would happen to this surplus population? This rhetorical question implied by Weber continues to our own day.

As befits his discipline, Weber began with a statistical summary and an analysis of levels of urbanization in his own time, and traced it back through the nineteenth century. As part of his doctoral research, Weber attempted global coverage and he gathered his data from official government publications as well as unofficial population estimates from around the world. In general, he found industrialization the main reason for city growth. England and Wales, 62 percent urban, were by far the most industrialized and the most urbanized countries on earth. The next closest were Australia, at 42 percent, and the various parts of Germany, at about 30 percent. In general, the largest cities were growing fastest. London, the world's largest city in 1890, held 4.2 million people; New York, the second largest, 2.7 million. The least industrialized countries were the least urbanized—below 10 percent—but most of these countries did not maintain statistical records. Besides industry, Weber cited other important reasons for the growth of cities:

- the general improvement in public health regulation, which improved longevity, especially in densely crowded cities;

- the agricultural revolution, still taking place before Weber's eyes, that was freeing an enormous workforce to migrate to cities, and supplying adequate food to nourish them all;

- the growth of government, centralized in cities;

- the growth of commerce, the life blood of cities;

- rising standards of living and attractive personal opportunities in education, amusements, and social interaction and stimulation.

In contrast to the gloom of poverty and oppression pictured by Marx and Engels a half century earlier, Weber radiated optimism. Weber's projection included increasing collective action, achieved through peaceful means, and increasing levels of domesticity and personal comfort.

> But there will still be left a large field for private associations, whose activities have already added to the comforts of city life. Consider the conveniences at the disposal of the *fin de siècle* [end of the century] housewife: a house with a good part of the old-fashioned portable furniture built into it, e.g., china cabinets, refrigerators, wardrobes, sideboards, cheval glasses [full-length, swivel mirrors], bath tubs, etc; electric lights, telephones and electric buttons in every room, automatic burglar alarms, etc....[Weber then quotes another urban advocate:] Thus has vanished the necessity for drawing water, hewing

> wood, keeping a cow, churning, laundering clothes, cleaning house, beating carpets, and very much of the rest of the onerous duties of housekeeping, as our mothers knew it. (pp. 218–20)

A judicious scholar, Weber did not omit the many negative aspects of city life at the end of the nineteenth century. Although death rates in the city had been declining steadily, urban death rates in 1899 remained higher than rural ones in most countries. In one of the worst examples, during the decade 1880–90, when the expected length of life at birth for all of England and Wales was forty-seven years, in Manchester, one of the greatest centers of the early industrial revolution, it was twenty-nine. Industrialization exacted its costs. Nevertheless, Weber reviewed the public health measures such as water and sewage systems and the provision of clinics that had already been effective in other places, strongly advocated more of them, and remained optimistic—if urbanites could cooperate for the common good.

Weber's pioneering work gives us a flavor of the end of the nineteenth-century view of urbanization. His work finds a place among a multitude of other studies and meditations on the industrial city, for this was one of the most critical areas of study of the time. For example, Charles Booth (1840–1916) led a team of researchers in London, which produced the seventeen volumes of *Life and Labour of the People in London*. Between 1886 and 1903, Booth and his colleagues systematically visited thousands of homes throughout London, interviewing workers to discover how the working people of the metropolis labored and lived. An enterprising English businessman, with interests in the United States as well, and a political and social reformer, Booth funded the survey himself in order to understand from on-the-ground investigation what might be done to resolve the persistent problem of poverty in the midst of wealth.

Although not an academic, Booth plunged into the empirical research with a zeal born from the methods of his business affairs and the influence of the newly emerging discipline of sociology. His investigations, which earned world-wide attention, found that 30.7 percent of London's population lived below the poverty line—that is, they received incomes too low to support themselves and their families in health. Poverty was especially severe among the elderly, and Booth began to lobby intensively for old-age pensions (introduced by the Liberal Party in 1906). Although he never developed a theoretical framework for understanding his data, Booth was a pioneer in understanding the actual workings of the metropolis.

Not all studies of the city were so empirically based. The most eminent poets, like Charles Baudelaire in France and Walt Whitman in the United States, cried of the city's lonely despair and sang of its collective enthusiasms (see Source, p. 562). Philosophical speculation on the nature of the city also flourished. In Germany, Max Weber (1864–1920) began a series of essays and books attempting to understand the world changing around him, helping also to establish the new discipline of sociology. His essay, "The City," published in 1922, a decade after our period, analyzed the modern industrial city as a new creation. Weber was less interested in the economics of urban life than in its institutional structure. He contrasted the new urban institutions with the close-knit guilds and political and religious associations of earlier self-governing European cities, especially medieval cities (see Chapter 12). Weber concluded that the sprawling industrial city, open to any immigrant who wished to come, embedded within a nation-state that controlled its life and politics, was not the self-contained city of earlier times. Europe, at least, was living in a new era.

Georg Simmel (1858–1914), a social psychologist in Germany, wrote in 1903 of the destabilizing effects of these new cities:

> The individual has become a mere cog in an enormous organization of things and powers which tears from his hands all progress, spirituality, and value in order to transform them from their subjective form into the form of a purely objective life. … the metropolis is the genuine arena of this culture which outgrows all personal life. Here … is offered such an overwhelming fullness of crytallized and impersonalized spirit that the personality, so to speak, cannot maintain itself under its impact. (Sennett, pp. 58–9)

Two factors were breaking down the individual personality. First, the division of labor was turning the individual into a

Guaranty Building in Buffalo, New York, designed by Louis Henry Sullivan, 1894–96. Sullivan's designs for steel-frame construction of large buildings—made possible because steel was now readily available and the elevator had been invented—were the forerunners of today's skyscrapers. A glance at the skyline of any large American or European city will confirm that Sullivan greatly influenced twentieth-century architecture, particularly in the United States. Sullivan's working principle that form follows function applied to the tall buildings (up to ten stories in the late nineteenth century) that he designed. It was important to maximize the limited space in city centers, and the idea of carrying buildings upward instead of outward met the need.

SOURCE

Poets of the City: Baudelaire and Whitman

The nineteenth-century city attracted not only scholars with empirical data, and philosophers with speculations, but also poets with profound feelings. In the last chapter we cited the English Romantic poets Blake and Wordsworth. Here we compare two very different poets. Charles Baudelaire (1821–67) lived a difficult life emotionally and financially. He observed with melancholy and resignation the life of Paris and the Parisians, and yet identified with and loved what he saw. Here, as in most of his poetry, Baudelaire observes the worn, little people to be seen under the surface glitter of Europe's most cultured city.

The Twilight of Dawn

Here and there chimneys begin to smoke.
Women of pleasure, their eyelids bleary,
Their mouths open, sleep only half awake;
Beggar women, their thin, cold breasts sagging,
Breathe onto burning embers, then onto their
   fingers.

It was the hour when, amidst the cold and the
   grind,
The pain of women in childbirth deepens;
Like a sob cut short in a clot of blood,
The crow of a rooster, far off, cuts through the
   hazy air.
A sea of fog bathes the buildings.
Men in agony in the workhouses
Heave their dying breath in undignified gasps.
The debauched return home, broken by their
   work.
The shivering dawn robed in pink and green
Advances slowly along the deserted Seine,
And somber, aging Paris, rubbing its eyes,
Picks up its tools, and sets to work.

(trans. by Howard Spodek)

In the United States, Walt Whitman (1819–92) sang a more optimistic, vigorous song of American life and its seemingly endless immigrant variety. A few of his poems touch on city life. Here he exults in the growth of Manhattan, abounding in human creations but still set in nature. Whitman calls the island by its Native American name.

Mannahatta

I was asking for something specific and perfect
   for my city,
Whereupon lo! upsprang the aboriginal name.

Now I see what there is in a name, a word,
   liquid, sane, unruly, musical, self-sufficient,
I see that the word of my city is that word from
   of old,
Because I see that word nested in nests of water-
   bays, superb
Rich, hemm'd thick all around with sailships and
   steamships, an island sixteen miles long,
   solid-founded,
Numberless crowded streets, high growths of
   iron, slender, strong, light, splendidly uprising
   toward clear skies,
Tides swift and ample, well-loved by me, toward
   sundown,
The flowing sea-currents, the little islands, larger
   adjoining islands, the heights, the villas,
The countless masts, the white shore-steamers,
   the lighters, the ferry-boats, the black sea-
   steamers well-model'd,
The down-town streets, the jobbers' houses of
   business, the houses of business of the ship-
   merchants and money-brokers, the river-streets,
Immigrants arriving, fifteen or twenty thousand
   in a week,
The carts hauling goods, the manly race of
   drivers of horses, the brown-faced sailors,

The summer air, the bright sun shining, and the sailing clouds aloft,
The winter snows, the sleigh-bells, the broken ice in the river, passing along up or down with the flood-tide or ebb-tide,
The mechanics of the city, the masters, well-form'd, beautiful faced, looking you straight in the eyes,

Trottoirs throng'd, vehicles, Broadway, the women, the shops and shows,
A million people—manners free and superb—open voices—hospitality—the most courageous and friendly young men,
City of hurried and sparkling waters! city of spires and masts!
City nested in bays! my city!

specialist and leading to the loss of a sense of personal or community wholeness. Second, the sheer multitude of people and experiences in the city was also forcing the individual to retreat into a small, private niche. The urban dweller was evolving into a person swift of intellect but lacking integration.

Based on a similar conception of nature and the city, Oswald Spengler (1880–1936), philosopher of history, went the next step and declared that the enormous "world-cities" of his day were inevitably destroying the spirit of the folk peoples that had built them. He titled his famous book *The Decline of the West* (1918–22) and argued that the cycle of urban growth and decay had occurred before in other civilizations:

> This, then, is the conclusion of the city's history; growing from primitive barter-center to culture-city and at last to world-city, it sacrifices first the blood and soul of its creators to the needs of its majestic evolution, and then the last flower of that growth to the spirit of Civilization—and so, doomed, moves on to final self-destruction. (cited in Sennett, p. 85)

Spengler's writing, and others like it, had painful consequences, for in the cultural contest between city and countryside, it stigmatized the cosmopolitan life and people of the city. German cities had not experienced the same rise and liberation of the merchant classes as had England, the Netherlands, and France. German traditions of urban freedom and creativity were weaker and less valued (despite the fact that its cities were becoming industrial powerhouses). A generation after Spengler, Germany would turn inward, filled with praise for the traditional values of "the Volk, the People," meaning the native, rural people, and scorn the more diverse, cosmopolitan urbanites.

In the United States, the "Chicago School of urban ecology" was just getting underway about the time of World War I. Sociologists Robert Park (1864–1944) and Louis Wirth (1897–1952) guided teams of scholars at the University of Chicago in studying their own city, the world's fastest-growing industrial metropolis of the day. To some degree, they philosophized and speculated as did the Germans. To a larger degree they launched empirical studies of conditions in the city, similar to those carried out by Booth, and they studied neighborhoods within the city as well as the metropolis as a whole.

The Chicago School argued that urbanites did not live their lives downtown, as so many previous scholars had implied, but in local neighborhoods, each of which had its own characteristics. People's lives were not so disconnected, isolated, or alienated as it might appear. At the end of the day, most people went back to their own homes in their own neighborhoods, places where they had a strong sense of self and community. These neighborhoods interacted with each other, and with the commercial areas of the city, in their own ways. The variety of social and economic lifestyles multiplied with the size of the city and the diversity of its functions. Neighborhoods reflected this diversity.

The commercial areas themselves were also increasing in size, complexity, and facilities. By the 1870s, department stores, coffeehouses, pubs, and restaurants had added urbanity to the central business district, attracting retail shoppers, window shoppers, and people with some leisure time. Theaters, concert houses, museums, the press and publishing houses, libraries, clubs, and a multitude of new voluntary associations provided culture and entertainment. They also created a "public sphere"—a setting in which the people of a nation form and circulate their most influential civic ideas, goals, and aspirations. Here was the modern analogue of the ancient Greek agora.

A new transportation system made possible this specialization of commercial, cultural, industrial, and residential neighborhoods within the city. London opened its first underground railway system in 1863, the first major subway system in the world, and others followed. From the 1870s, commuter railways began to service new suburbs, and electric trolleys came into service after 1885. The first skyscrapers rose in the 1880s, beginning with ten-story buildings in Chicago. The availability of steel at commercial prices made their construction possible, and the invention of elevators made them accessible.

URBAN SPRAWL: HOW DO WE KNOW?

One of the central problems of the industrializing city of the early nineteenth-century was crowding. Poor ventilation, inadequate sanitation, unclean water, alienation from nature, poor health, and tuberculosis resulted as densities in urban cores reached, and even surpassed, 100,000 people per square mile (2.5 square kilometers). By the last decades of the century the electric trolley cars and commuter railways offered the means to suburbanize, and the city expanded in area as never before. At first the densities in the center did not appear to diminish, for the stream of new immigrants to the city matched and even exceeded those who were suburbanizing. Slowly, however, the highest densities did come down.

We know that urban sprawl had become a problem by the late 1800s because town planners began seeking solutions to the new problem: How to provide space for population increase, allow for geographical expansion, yet continue to provide green space, while fostering participation in both the local community and the metropolis as a whole? The British reformer Ebenezer Howard (1850–1928) provided one of the first proposals in his book *Tomorrow: A Peaceful Path to Real Reform* (1898), later revised and reissued as *Garden Cities of Tomorrow* (1902). Howard's schematic plan for a "Group of Slumless Smokeless Cities" illustrates his provocative concept of a region of about 250,000 people on 66,000 acres (26,700 hectares). This would be far too miniature to cope with the problems of a London or a New York. Its intense control over the planning process also demanded political decisions that might not be possible within a participatory democracy. Nevertheless, the **garden city** concept of a core city ringed by separate suburbs, each set in a green belt, linked to one another by rapid transit,

provided provocative, creative, somewhat utopian thinking for one of the new urban problems dawning with the new century.

THE NON-INDUSTRIAL, NON-EUROPEAN CITY

The cities of Europe were different from those of Africa and Asia even before industrialization. Asian and African cities usually functioned primarily as political, religious, and cultural capitals, and they were controlled by leaders of those sectors, while Western European cities, beginning in the twelfth century, began to give greater emphasis to economics and were controlled far more by leaders of commerce (see pp. 470–74). The rise of industrialization in Western Europe intensified that contrast.

What kind of new colonial cities did European businessmen and governments establish in Asia and Africa, in Bombay and Calcutta, Singapore and Hong Kong, St. Louis (Senegal) and Dakar? First, these cities were built along the coast, to accommodate European ships and commerce. Second, they grew beyond their early role as centers for export trade, increasingly emphasizing government and administration. Third, to the extent that new commerce or industry was introduced, it was usually initiated and owned by European colonialists. These foreigners ran the businesses for the benefit and profit of their countries and themselves. Fourth, the urban plan usually encouraged a segregation of populations by ethnicity. European residents lived in sections of the cities largely reserved for them. In the Chinese port cities—beginning with Shanghai, Guangzhou, Xiamen, Fuzhou, and Ningbo—each colonizing power—British, French, German, Japanese, American—had a sector in which its own law ruled. They also segregated local populations by ethnicity. The British rulers of Singapore, for example, established separate areas of the city for British and other Europeans, Chinese, Malays, Indians, and Bugis (see map opposite).

Rather than promoting integration and national development, such cities fostered local political fragmentation, low levels of industrial development, and increased European control. Yet these cities were also the entry point for European business, industry, education, philosophy, manners, and culture, in however limited and restricted a way. Throughout the Asian and African worlds, these segregated, controlled, profit-taking cities were also windows on another world, repulsive to some, but seductive and attractive to others. As we

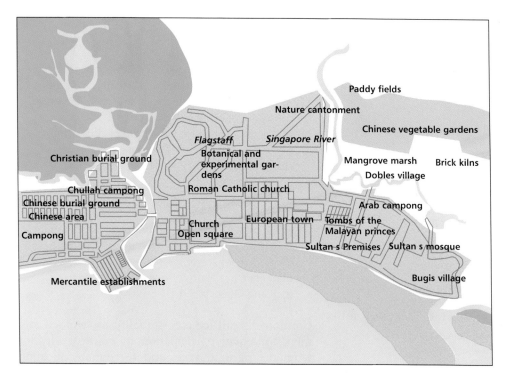

A map of the town and environs of Singapore, from an actual survey by G.D. Coleman, 1839. Singapore was not an indigenous town that gradually grew up around a bustling port; it was purposely founded in 1819 on the site of a fishing village by Sir Stamford Raffles, who saw its potential as a trading center. The British actively encouraged immigration to the new port, and divided the thriving city into separate areas for the different ethnic groups that lived and worked there. The divisions can be seen clearly on the map.

shall see in Part 8, these cities were both the centers of the colonial enterprise and the incubators of anticolonial movements. (See Frantz Fanon's *Wretched of the Earth*, cited below, p. 735.)

GENDER RELATIONS: THEIR SIGNIFICANCE IN AN AGE OF REVOLUTIONS

Many events in history are "gendered"—that is, they affect men and women differently. Increasingly historians analyze these differences to enrich our understanding of the past. In addition, people in search of forms of relationships between men and women different from those that exist at present study past events to find possible alternatives. The knowledge that these relationships are not fixed and inevitable, not governed by biological determinism, can be very liberating for people attempting to fashion new ways of living.

THE MOVEMENT TOWARD EQUALITY

The political and industrial revolutions that occurred between 1688 and 1914 were certainly "gendered" events. The Enlightenment and the political revolutions, especially in Britain, the United States,

and France, stressed individualism. The individual was to be seen on his or her own merits, rather than in terms of hereditary or group identities. Careers were to be open to merit, not restricted to particular families, classes, or castes. But women did not gain such recognition as individuals, and many commentators remarked on this discrepancy between revolutionary goals for men and more modest aspirations for women. In Britain, for example, the *Commentaries on the Laws of England* (1765–9) prepared by the jurist William Blackstone (1723–80), which served for more than a century as the basic introduction to the English legal system, explained:

> By marriage, the husband and wife are one person in law: that is, the very being or legal existence of the woman is suspended during the marriage, or at least incorporated and consolidated into that of the husband: under whose wing, protection, and cover, she performs every thing. … (Bell and Offen, p. 33)

Blackstone expressed the prevailing principle that a married woman is represented by her husband. All important decisions for her are made by him. Nevertheless, under civil law, she might hold property in her own name.

In France in the midst of the tumult of the French Revolution, in July 1790, the Marquis de Condorcet (1743–94), a philosopher and an elected member of the Legislative Assembly, had proposed

WOMEN'S EMANCIPATION
1790–1928

c. 1790 Olympe de Gouges writes the polemical *Declaration of the Rights of Woman and the Citizen*

1792 Mary Wollstonecraft writes *A Vindication of the Rights of Woman*, regarded as the first manifesto of the women's movement in Britain

1794 Condorcet writes of the desirability of establishing equality of civil and political rights for men and women in *Progrès de l'esprit*

1829 *Sati* (ritual suicide by Hindu widows) banned in India

1848 Elizabeth Cady Stanton and Lucretia Mott organize first women's rights convention at Seneca Falls, New York

1850 Beginnings in Britain of national agitation for women's suffrage

1857–72 Married Women's Property Acts allow British women to keep their own possessions on marriage

1866 Mott founds American Equal Rights Association

1868 First public meeting of women's suffrage movement held in Manchester, England

1869 In Britain women rate-payers may vote in municipal elections; Cady Stanton is first president of US National Woman Suffrage Association

1890 Footbinding beginning to die out in China

1903 Emmeline Pankhurst founds Women's Social and Political Union

1906 Pankhurst and her daughters launch militant campaign in Britain

1913 Suffragettes protest in Washington, D.C.; International Women's Peace Conference held in the Netherlands

1914–18 Women assume responsibilities outside the home during World War I

1918 British women householders over 30 years granted the vote

1919 Constance de Markiewicz the first woman elected to Parliament in Britain

1920 19th amendment to the Constitution gives US women the vote

1928 British women over 21 years granted the vote

"The Admission of Women to the Rights of the City":

> [Philosophers and legislators] have they not every one violated the principle of the equality of rights, in tranquilly depriving the half of the human race of that of assisting in the making of law; in excluding women from the right of citizenship? … Now the rights of men result only from this, that men are beings with sensibility, capable of acquiring moral ideas, and of reasoning on these ideas. So women, having these same qualities, have necessarily equal rights. Either no individual of the human race has genuine rights, or else all have the same; and he who votes against the right of another, whatever the religion, color, or sex of that other, has henceforth abjured his own.
> (Bell and Offen, p. 99)

Condorcet's call for civic equality for women and men, for equal participation in political life, for women's right to vote, and for equal education ("Instruction should be the same for women and men") was rejected by the Assembly.

Writing under the pen name Olympe de Gouges, Marie Gouze (1748–93) directly appropriated the language of the Revolution's *Declaration of the Rights of Man and the Citizen* (1789). Her *Declaration of the Rights of Woman and the Citizen* exposed its lack of concern for the rights of women:

> Article I. Woman is born free and remains equal in rights to man. Social distinctions can be founded only on general utility. …
> Article XVII. The right of property is inviolable and sacred to both sexes, jointly or separately. …
> (Bell and Offen, pp. 105–6)

Gouges addressed this document to the French queen, Marie-Antoinette, urging her to adopt this feminist program as her own and thus win over France to the royalist cause. In 1793 the radical Jacobins in the Assembly, condemning Gouges for both royalism and feminism, had her guillotined.

Napoleon's Civil Code of 1804, article 213, declared: "A husband owes protection to his wife; a wife obedience to her husband" (Bell and Offen, p. 39). In principle, husbands controlled property held jointly by the couple, but the two could enter into separate contracts to allow wives to control property of their own, and many did so.

The French Revolution did not achieve legal equality between the genders, but it did encourage

feminism, a word coined by the French merchant and philosopher Charles Fourier (1772–1837) to denote efforts towards gender equality. In 1808, Fourier urged reform, and argued that:

> The best nations are always those that accord women the greatest amount of liberty. ... Social progress and historic changes occur by virtue of the progress of women toward liberty, and decadence of the social order occurs as the result of a decrease in the liberty of women. ... In summary, the extension of women's privileges is the general principle for all social progress. (Bell and Offen, I: 41)

A half century later, in 1848, at Seneca Falls, New York, an assembly of three hundred women led by Lucretia Mott (1793–1880), one of the many Quakers active in the movement for women's rights, and Elizabeth Cady Stanton (1815–1902)

SOURCE
"Declaration of Sentiments"
Seneca Falls Convention, July 1848

The first women's rights convention held in the United States met at Seneca Falls, New York in 1848. Under the leadership of Lucretia Mott and Elizabeth Cady Stanton the convention issued a "Declaration" modeled on the "Declaration of Independence," but with a very different set of charges and objectives.

> We hold these truths to be self-evident: that all men and women are created equal. ... The history of mankind is a history of repeated injuries and usurpations on the part of man toward woman, having in direct object the establishment of an absolute tyranny over her. To prove this, let facts be submitted to a candid world.
>
> He has never permitted her to exercise her inalienable right to the elective franchise.
>
> He has compelled her to submit to laws, in the formation of which she had no voice. ...
>
> He has made her, if married, in the eye of the law, civilly dead.
>
> He has taken from her all right in property, even to the wages she earns.
>
> In the covenant of marriage, she is compelled to promise obedience to her husband, he becoming, to all intents and purposes, her master ...
>
> He has so framed the laws of divorce, as to what shall be the proper causes, and in case of separation, to whom the guardianship of the children shall be given, as to be wholly regardless of the happiness of women ...
>
> He closes against her all the avenues to wealth and distinction which he considers most honorable to himself. As a teacher of theology, medicine, or law, she is not known.
>
> He has denied her the facilities for obtaining a thorough education, all colleges being closed against her.
>
> He allows her in Church, as well as State, but a subordinate position, claiming Apostolic authority for her exclusion from the ministry, and, with some exceptions, from any public participation in the affairs of the Church.
>
> He has endeavored, in every way that he could, to destroy her confidence in her own powers, to lessen her self-respect, and to make her willing to lead a dependent and abject life. ...
>
> In entering upon the great work before us, we anticipate no small amount of misconception, misrepresentation, and ridicule; but we shall use every instrumentality within our power to effect our object. We shall employ agents, circulate tracts, petition the State and National legislatures, and endeavor to enlist the pulpit and the press in our behalf. We hope this Convention will be followed by a series of Conventions embracing every part of the country. (Bell and Offen, pp. 252–4)

SOURCE

Feminist Frustrations: Living in "A Doll's House"

A Doll's House (1879), by Norwegian playwright Henrik Ibsen (1828–1906), catapulted feminist frustrations onto the public stage. A student of human behavior and a moralist, Ibsen was concerned with social problems and contemporary issues. In his dramas, many of which shocked the public with their controversial subjects, Ibsen explored the themes of conflict between the individual and society, between husband and wife, and between love and duty. *A Doll's House* traces a middle-class woman's realization that her role in life has been meaningless. At the climax of the play, as the heroine Nora walks out of her home, leaving her husband and children, she explains to her husband:

> You've always been so kind to me. But our home's been nothing but a playpen. I've been your doll-wife here, just as at home I was Papa's doll-child. And in turn the children have been my dolls. I thought it was fun when you played with me, just as they thought it fun when I played with them. That's been our marriage, Torvald. … There's another job I have to do first. I have to try to educate myself. You can't help me with that. I've got to do it alone. And that's why I'm leaving you now … I have to stand competely alone, if I'm ever going to discover myself and the world out there. So I can't go on living with you.

Asked by her husband about her marriage vows, Nora continues:

> I have other duties equally sacred. … Before all else, I'm a human being, no less than you—or anyway, I ought to try to become one. … I have to think over these things myself and try to understand them.

Asked about her religious convictions, Nora replies:

> I only know what the minister said when I was confirmed. He told me religion was this thing and that. When I get clear and away by myself, I'll go into that problem too. I'll see if what the minister said was right, or, in any case, if it's right for me.

Asked about her moral conscience, Nora concludes:

> It's not easy to answer that. … I simply don't know. I'm all confused about these things. I just know I see them so differently from you. I find out, for one thing, that the law's not at all what I'd thought—but I can't get it through my head that the law is fair.

appropriated the language of the American Declaration of Independence in a similar way, to call attention to the lack of women's rights in the United States. They, too, began with a demand for political rights, but went much farther to call for equality in marriage and divorce, in custody of children, in employment, in education, and in church (see Source, p. 567).

In Britain, Mary Wollstonecraft (1759–97) wrote *A Vindication of the Rights of Woman* in 1792 in which she argued for equal opportunites for all in educa-

tion. She insisted that women should have the right to participate in economic and political life on an equal basis with men. Over sixty years later, the distinguished economist and political philosopher John Stuart Mill (1806–73) brought to Parliament in 1866, as part of the debate over the extension of voting rights, a petition asking that women, too, be granted the right to vote. His motion failed. Mill nevertheless persisted in his efforts. In addition to *On Liberty* (1859), his most famous argument for freedom generally, he wrote extensively on

The Great Procession, June 18, 1910. Not only women campaigned for their right to vote: in this procession of the WSPU (Women's Social and Political Union) a hunger strikers' banner is hoisted aloft by male supporters. Emmeline Pankhurst, an English barrister frustrated that politicians would not pass legislation to allow women to vote, organized the WSPU and began a militant campaign to secure women's suffrage in Britain. She used assaults on public property to call attention to her cause, and spent time in prison where she and other jailed suffragettes went on hunger strike.

behalf of women's equality in particular, notably *The Subjection of Women* (1869). Mill based his argument for equality not only on legal and moral principles, but also on the assertion that equality among adults was essential to warm emotional ties of mutuality, the basis of rewarding family life and of all civilized life.

The women's movement pursued many goals, especially property rights, access to education, access to jobs and fair pay, and rights in divorce and child custody. At first suffrage was just one of these goals, but soon feminists came to believe that without the vote, women could not easily achieve any of their other goals. On the other hand, they feared that the majority of women were more religious and more conservative than they were. If women had the vote, feminists feared, the majority would vote conservatively. By the turn of the century in Britain, however, as the Labour Party began to form and, as workers became increasingly active politically, the women's movement grew larger and more militant. In the early 1900s, up to World War I, feminist leaders, such as the barrister Emmeline Goulden Pankhurst (1858–1928) and her daughters, adopted the tactics of direct action: breaking windows, destroying mail, cutting telegraph wires. When arrested, they went on hunger strikes, which the government countered with force feeding (see Profile, p. 570).

Despite the fact that these tactics brought immense public attention to the suffragettes, they did not win the vote before the war. During the war suffragettes suspended their activities, plunging themselves into supporting the war effort. The quality and devotion of their work in factories, as nurses, as ambulance drivers, won the admiration of British political leaders, and in 1918, British women over the age of thirty who had higher educational degrees or some property were granted the vote, and, after 1928, it was extended to all women aged twenty-one and older. Norway had been the first European country to grant female suffrage in 1910; Germany in 1918; (the United States in 1920); France in 1945. By the time these victories came, they seemed almost anti-climactic. For many years, women voted more or less as did men of the same class. The vote did, however, give women more leverage in addressing other issues. The area of greatest feminist concern shifted to the workplace and the home.

GENDER RELATIONSHIPS AND THE INDUSTRIAL REVOLUTION

By creating factories, the industrial revolution drove a wedge between the home and the workplace that dramatically affected both. Wives who had been accustomed to working alongside, or at least in proximity to, their husbands on the farm or in the shop or workshop now found that the major source of employment was away from home. The industrial revolution, perhaps even more than the political revolutions, forced redefinitions of identities. What should the woman's role and place be now? How should motherhood and work be balanced? In a world that expected most females to be under the protection of males, how were single women to define, and fend for, themselves? In what voice should the feminist movement address these complex issues?

As the industrial revolution began in semi-rural locations, its labor force was drawn primarily from young, (as yet) unmarried women, frequently daughters of local farmers. Some of the early factory owners built boarding houses for the women and treated them protectively, as young wards. Francis Cabot Lowell (1775–1817) built his mills at Waltham, Massachusetts, on this principle. He promised the women hard work, with pay adequate to help their families and to save towards marriage. After his death, his partners extended his example by establishing a new town, Lowell, with the largest cotton mill built to that date. By the 1840s, about half the mills in New England followed this model. Factory work had its demands of order, discipline, and the clock, and the dormitory-boarding houses were somewhat crowded, but labor historian Alice Kessler-Harris quotes approvingly the very warm assessment of the Lowell experience from one of its workers in the 1830s: It was "the first field that had ever been open to her outside of her own restricted home. … the first money they earned! When they felt the jingle of silver in their pocket, there for the first time, their heads became erect and they walked as if on air" (Kessler-Harris, p. 34).

As new machinery became heavier, as factory work became more prevalent, and as economic

PROFILE

Emmeline Pankhurst

BRITISH FEMINIST AND SUFFRAGETTE

"The argument of the broken pane of glass is the most valuable argument in modern politics" declared Emmeline Pankhurst, militant champion of the woman suffrage movement in Britain. Since the 1860s, societies campaigning for the enfranchisement of women had sprung up throughout Britain, but as a series of major suffrage bills met defeat in Parliament, frustration mounted and many suffragists resorted to more direct and increasingly violent actions.

Born in Manchester, England, in 1858, Emmeline Pankhurst (née Goulden) had studied in Paris where she had been impressed by the work of French feminists. In 1879 she married Richard Marsden Pankhurst, a friend of John Stuart Mill and a radical barrister who was the author of the first woman suffrage bill in Britain in the late 1860s and the Married Women's Property Acts of 1870 and 1882. Ten years into her marriage Mrs Pankhurst founded the Woman's Franchise League which obtained for married women the right to vote in elections to local offices. In 1903 she established the Women's Social and Political Union (WSPU) with her eldest daughter Christabel, a lawyer by training.

Attracting a large number of followers, mostly middle-class and aristocratic women, the WSPU became the most renowned of Britain's suffrage movements. Pankhurst led mass demonstrations and rallies and zealously campaigned against politicians who refused to back the suffragist cause. Her rather fragile demeanor belied a headstrong temperament and a talent for oratory.

In 1906 the WSPU embarked on a campaign of extreme militancy, drawing on disruptive tactics employed by other political activists such as the Irish nationalists. Taunted by their detractors and labeled rather derisively as "suffragettes," to distinguish them from the nonmilitant suffragists, Pankhurst and her followers set fire to public buildings, smashed windows, sabotaged mailboxes, slashed paintings in London's National

depression pressed down on both American and British economies, the workforce shifted. Men, often farmers and immigrants, moved into the factories, displacing the women. The men demanded higher pay, which factory owners had previously-hoped to avoid by hiring women. The culture of the industrializing world of that time, primarily in Britain, called for men to support their families. A young, unmarried woman might earn just enough for herself and that would be adequate. A man required a "family wage." The rising productivity of constantly improving machinery made this "family wage" possible, and it became the baseline standard for industry.

Women were thus displaced from factory work and brought back to the home. By the second half of the nineteenth-century, "domesticity" became the norm for middle- and even working-class women and their families. As we noted above (see p. 560), at just this time living standards began to rise and generally continued to rise into the early twentieth century. Life expectancy for women, a basic index of well-being, rose rapidly in Britain from forty-four years in 1890, to fifty-two in 1910, to sixty in 1920. At the same time family size decreased. Child-bearing became less frequent, freer from infection thanks to antisepsis, less painful with the use of anesthesia, and safer with the professionalization of the practice of medicine. Free, compulsory education in the 1830s and 1840s began to take children out of the home. Some women began to use their time to enter into the array of white collar jobs that were opening. The most respectable jobs provided satisfying work which also fit the cultural perception of women as care givers and nurturers: teaching in the new school systems and nursing in the new hospitals. Other women worked as secretaries and clerks in the new offices, although this was primarily a male occupation in the nineteenth century, and as sales personnel in the new

Gallery, and pelted government officials with eggs. Pankhurst explained, "There is something which governments care for more than human life and that is the security of property, and it is through property that we shall strike the enemy."

The government stood its ground. In 1908–09, Emmeline Pankhurst was jailed three times, once for urging people to storm the Houses of Parliament. In prison, Pankhurst, like other convicted suffragettes, undertook repeated hunger strikes. The authorities reacted by force-feeding her, attaching metal clamps to her jaw and pouring gruel down her throat. These grotesque measures backfired, increasing support for the suffragette movement in Britain and abroad. The government resorted to the "Cat and Mouse" Act in 1913 by which hunger-striking prisoners were released for a time and then reimprisoned once their health returned. Within a year Emmeline Pankhurst was released and reincarcerated twelve times.

With the outbreak of World War I, Emmeline Pankhurst called a halt to the suffrage campaign and many suffragettes channeled their energies into the war effort. This did much to soften the government's attitude to the feminist cause and in 1918 British women aged thirty or over received the complete franchise. During the war, and for some years after, Emmeline Pankhurst toured the United States, Canada, and Russia and worked for the industrial mobilization of women. On her return to England in 1926 she was selected as Conservative candidate for an east London constituency but by this point her health was failing and she was never elected. A few weeks before her death in 1928, The Representation of the People Act was passed in Britain and women gained voting rights equal to those of men.

Emmeline Pankhurst with her daughter Christabel, 1908.

SPOTLIGHT
Women's Bodies
and Reform

In the nineteenth century, four separate movements combined to introduce deep reforms in the way women's bodies were presented, viewed, and treated: rationalism, which subjected numerous traditional habits and practices to greater scrutiny; humanitarianism, which encouraged greater kindness and compassion in social relations; feminism, which demanded better, more egalitarian, treatment for women; and colonialism, which often sought changes in the treatment of women in colonized areas, partly in order to improve the women's lives, partly in order to underline the alleged superiority of the status of women in Europe.

Figure 1 shows a woman on a funeral pyre, prepared to commit her body to flames in order to accompany her husband in his death. This act of ritual suicide, called *sati* (suttee), had been practiced by a very small group of upper-caste women in India for centuries. In the late eighteenth century, the British government began to campaign against the practice, finally banning it in British India in 1829 Many Indians, like Raja Rammohun Roy (1772–1833), supported the British and urged them to enact the legislation, but others resented the colonizers' interference. The British presented their motives as simply humanitarian, but more recently historians have suggested that the British emphasis on outlawing *sati* served as a means of proclaiming their own moral superiority over the Indians and justifying imperialism. These historians note that the British were introducing very little structural change in the lives of Indian women, by providing education or jobs for widows for example, that might encourage them to go on living. British legislation against *sati* was generally effective, but not completely. The act of *sati* in figure 1 took place in 1946, and the practice still occurs on rare occasions in today's India.

Footbinding in China had been practiced among the upper classes since the tenth century.

Figure 1 *Sati* ceremony, Allahabad, India, 1946.

Figure 2 Bound feet, compared with a shoe and a tea cup, late nineteenth century.

In "A Correct View of the New Machine for Winding up the Ladies" (**figure 3**), the cartoonist ridicules the practice of waist-binding among European women in the nineteenth century. Upper-class women wore corsets, devices made of whalebone which constricted the waist painfully, making it appear as tiny as possible and, by contrast, accentuating the hips, buttocks, and breasts. The corsets were often so tight that they interfered with women's ability to breathe properly and encouraged "swooning." Still, the practice of corseting continued until around the end of the century, at which time gains in female emancipation forced it out of fashion.

Parents tightly bound the feet of their girl children at about the age of five so that they did not grow longer than five or six inches. The tiny foot that resulted (**figure 2**) was regarded as beautiful and the restrictions on mobility were considered a mark of upper-class elegance. The vast majority of Chinese women, peasants, were not subjected to footbinding; they had to work the fields. Under the influence of foreign colonial powers in China, anti-footbinding societies began to arise in the 1890s, and the image of the bound foot changed from delicate to grotesque. By the 1930s footbinding was no longer practiced in China, except in isolated cases. Once again foreign pressure had been a combination of rationalism, humanitarianism, feminism, and a desire to assert European moral superiority.

Figure 3 Anon., "The New Machine for Winding up the Ladies," English cartoon, c. 1840.

department stores (where they also shopped). A very few went on to professions.

Most women spent a great deal of time caring for their families and homes. The industrial revolution, with its new productivity and its new systems of ventilation, central heating, lighting, indoor plumbing, and running hot and cold water, contributed to domestic comfort and made life easier for those who could afford these services.

While domestic concerns and new technological wonders engaged the middle classes, and were desired by the working classes, for a great number of people they were out of reach. The 15-20 percent of adult females who had to work as principal breadwinners for themselves and their families confronted more basic problems of earning a living. The value placed on domesticity as the proper role for females, and the concommitant view that men should earn a "family wage" but that women needed only supplementary income, made the plight of the working woman doubly difficult. These women, often immigrants, desperately poor, and without male support, were no longer seen, as the first industrial women workers had been, as proud and independent, but as unfortunate objects of sympathy and pity.

They found jobs where they could. Domestic service was most common, employing two to three times as many women as industry, even in industrialized countries. On the margins of society, other women earned a living through prostitution. In the second half of the nineteenth century, censuses in the largest cities, London and Paris, routinely reported tens of thousands of prostitutes walking the streets, serving in brothels, or, occasionally, employed in more comfortable settings by more prosperous clients. These women were often condemned by more conventional society, but at the same time they earned some respect for their independence. Most of them worked only until about the age of twenty-five, by which time they usually found other work or were married.

The socialist wing of the feminist movement understood that class differences often inhibited solidarity among women. Karl Marx spoke of the difference between the bourgeois and the proletarian family (see p. 534). He wrote of the conflict between roles of mother and of worker. With Engels, Marx condemned the "double oppression" of women by both capitalism and the family, but he praised capitalism for freeing women from being regarded as property. He encouraged women in their struggle for citizens' rights and economic independence. In *The Origin of the Family, Private Property and the State* (1884), Engels argued that the form of the family was not fixed. It had evolved substantially in the past, and he proposed further, revolutionary change:

> The peculiar character of the supremacy of the husband over the wife in the modern family, the necessity of creating real social equality between them and the way to do it, will only be seen in the clear light of day when both possess legally complete equality of rights. Then it will be plain that the first condition for the liberation of the wife is to bring the whole female sex back into public industry, and that this in turn demands that the characteristic of the monogamous family as the economic unit of society be abolished. (Engels, 137–38)

In Germany, the Social Democratic Party (SPD) created a separate organizational structure for women that enlisted 174,751 women members by 1914, the largest movement of women in Europe. The number reflects, however, not only women seeking independent expression, but also women who sought to ally themselves with their husbands as members of the party. Working women's organizations were undercut by the opposition of male unionized workers who feared that the women would take away their jobs or, at least, increase the labor pool and thus drive wages down.

GENDER RELATIONSHIPS IN COLONIZATION

The Europeans who travelled overseas to trade beginning in the sixteenth century were almost invariably males and they frequently entered into sexual liaisons with local women. As the men stayed longer, these relationships became increasingly important for business and administration as well as for social and sexual pleasure. One example was the **signares**, concubines of French traders in the Senegambia, present-day Senegal and Gambia. As the Senegal Company forbade its traders to marry locally, the men found concubines among the local Wolof and Lebou peoples. These women helped the men to negotiate local languages, customs, and health conditions.

In India, the **nabobs**, the successful traders who became wealthy, frequently took local women in much the same way. Not forbidden to marry, they fathered Anglo-Indian children who came to form a small but important community of their own, espe-

Christmas in India, **a sketch by E.K. Johnson**, *The Graphic*, **1881.** Just as, for the most part, European men did not socialize or form a solidarity with the men whose country they had colonized, so, too, the women kept themselves apart and their lives centered on their families and their European friends. The wife would oversee the running of the household as she was accustomed to doing at home. Here the *ayah* looks after the youngest child in much the same way that Nanny would have back in England.

cially in the large port cities of Bombay, Madras, and Calcutta.

As Europeans began to establish colonies, and as women began to travel to these colonies, usually with husbands, or in search of husbands, they began to draw inward, establishing more rigid boundaries between themselves and the local populations. Earlier historians had attributed this increasing distance to the restrictive attitudes of the European women who wished to prevent their husbands' mixing with the local women. More recent, feminist scholarship has attributed the responsibility for the increased distance to both husband and wife. Both exhibited racism. Both usually wished to keep local men from intimate contact with European women. As colonial settlements increased in size and stability, each family tended to view itself as a representative of the rulers, a colonial outpost in miniature.

Did the colonizing women form a solidarity with their colonized sisters? Most contemporary historians think not. The colonizers tended to fasten on flaws in the gender relations among the colonized peoples, and then set out to introduce reforms. In India the British outlawed *sati*, the practice of widows burning themselves to death on their deceased husbands' funeral pyres (see Spotlight, pp. 572–3); they introduced a minimum age of marriage; they urged widow remarriage despite upper-caste Hindu resistance. In Africa they sought to end polygamy. In each case, the colonial government emphasized the superiority of its own practices, and the good fortune of the colo-

nized to have the Europeans there to save them from themselves. The European colonizers pointed to their interventions in gender relations to justify and praise their own colonial rule. The colonizing women did the same.

The colonial presence did, however, introduce new patterns of gender relations into the colonies, based on the European models. At least some of the colonized peoples chose to move toward a more European style of gender relations, including more education for women, more freedom of choice in marriage, more companionate marriage, an end to *sati* in India, to polygamy in parts of Africa, and to footbinding in China (see Spotlight, pp. 572–3). Sometimes new paths were adopted because they seemed better, sometimes because they won favor for the colonized peoples with the colonizing masters. (Later, as nationalism took root, foreign practices were sometimes rejected because of their colonial associations.)

NATIONALISM: WHAT DO WE KNOW?

For most people in today's world, nationality is an important part of personal identity and historians have turned to nationalism as a central issue. Some stress the significance of particular forms of nationalism, others argue that national identity is, and can be, constantly shaped and reshaped. In this sense historians of national identity are similar to historians of gender identity: they not only wish to understand where we have been, they also want to consider alternative futures.

One of the first historians and philosophers of nationalism, the Frenchman Joseph-Ernest Renan (1823–92), in his 1882 lecture "What is a Nation?", captured the twofold nature of nationalism. Nationalism requires fundamental shared elements in the lives of the citizen, but these alone are not enough for constructing a nation. That task requires also a vision of what the nation might become, and a political commitment to constructing such a future. Further, in considering the nation as a "spiritual principle," Renan asserted his belief that in his time nationalism was displacing religion as a central concern:

A nation is a spiritual principle, the outcome of the profound complications of history; it is a spiritual family not a group determined by the shape of the earth. We have now seen what things are not [by themselves] adequate for the creation of such a spiritual principle, namely, race, language, material interest, religous affinities, geography, and military necessity. What [else] then is required? …

A nation is therefore a large-scale solidarity, constituted by the feeling of the sacrifices that one has made in the past and of those that one is prepared to make in the future. It presupposes a past; it is summarized, however, in the present by a

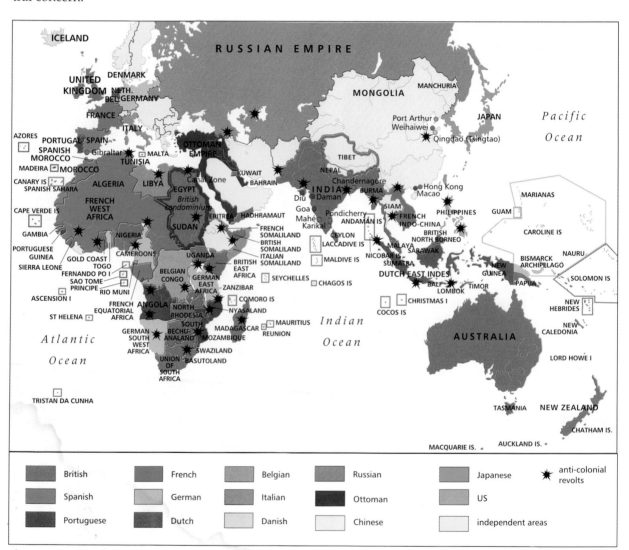

European empires in 1914 By the beginning of World War I, European imperialism had reached its zenith, with four-fifths of the globe under the direct political control of Europeans or people of European ancestry. Only Antarctica remained unclaimed. Although this power was sustained by technological, naval, and military superiority, insurrections were widespread and increasingly well organized. Imperial trade established a global economic system and spread European cultural values.

tangible fact, namely, consent, the clearly expressed desire to continue a common life.

In this essay, Renan overlooked two additional elements that later historians added to their concept of modern nationalism. First, at least since the French Revolution, the modern nation exists in a world of nations, frequently competitive with one another. Second, at least since the French Revolution and the industrial revolution, the nation has been the vehicle for the spread of trade networks and capitalism throughout the world.

FRENCH NATIONALISM

The ideology and actions of the French Revolution gave a new definition to the concept of the nation, and introduced new political and cultural loyalties. In 1789, the members of the National Assembly, declaring themselves "The representatives of the people of France," proclaimed in the *Declaration of the Rights of Man and the Citizen*: "The source of all sovereignty is located essentially in the nation; no body, no individual can exercise authority which does not emanate from it expressly." This Declaration encapsulated ideas that had been present in France for decades. It proclaimed that the people of France were forging a social contract, swearing allegiance not to a ruler, religion or language/ethnic group but to all the people of the nation—a common political group. The Declaration seemed to take for granted the primordial elements of French nationality—a common language, history, and geography—and with the vision of what the French people might become. It ratified a new national identity for France.

As we have seen (pp. 501–06), the power of France's new nationalism swept across Europe with its armies between 1791 and 1815, not only to conquer others, but also to promote its idea of nationalism. The French state took to itself new, unprecedented powers. It had the authority to tax in the name of the nation, the very authority that Louis XVI had sought for himself when he had convened the Estates General. Having the authority to draft virtually the entire adult male population of the country for the army in the new *levée en masse*, France conscripted an army numbering hundreds of thousands. French armies imposed their imperial governments on the nations they conquered, and, after the promulgation of the Napoleonic codes in 1804, they imposed their legal system as well. The new message seemed clear: A people organized under a national banner of its own making could act with unprecedented power to tax, to fight, to legislate, to conquer, and to rule.

NATIONALISM IN THE UNITED STATES

The United States had also established itself as a nation based on an oath binding citizens to the common good. Americans declared in their Constitution:

> We, the People of the United States, in Order to form a more perfect Union, establish Justice, insure domestic Tranquility, provide for the common defence, promote the general Welfare, and secure the blessings of Liberty to ourselves and our Posterity, do ordain and establish this Constitution for the United States of America.

The American Constitution also illustrated the degree to which a nation was constituted by the will of its leaders, rather than by primordial historical legacies. Indeed, foreign observers like Alexis de Tocqueville (1805–59) commented on the newness of America and its lack of history. A substantial proportion of America's institutions, and of its population, was drawn from Britain, but immigrants came from all over the world. Some were excluded from full citizenship: African-American slaves, native American Indians, and women lacked civil liberties. But the pattern for future inclusion was also being set. New immigrants could join this nation, and, after slaves were freed, so could they, although racism remained powerful. Native Americans remained torn between allegiances to Indian nations and the American nation. The United States declared that the nation was not necessarily an array of people who shared a common history, geography, language, race, ethnicity, religion, and language. A nation could be formed on the basis of a new vision of the present and future and adherence to a common law.

Nationalism in the United States maintained itself by force of arms in the face of secession by the eleven Confederate States of America in 1861. The Confederacy claimed greater rights for constituent states, especially the right to sanction slavery, and it favored agrarian rather than industrial economic policies. Some 500,000 men were killed in the Civil War on both sides. Immediately following the war, the victorious central government instituted policies favoring reconciliation (often at the expense of the recently freed ex-slaves), although later these policies became more punitive. After the war, the industrial and economic expansion of the United States set a pace exceeding that of any other nation.

NATIONALISM ON THE PERIPHERY OF WESTERN EUROPE

Nationalists elsewhere also attempted to implement the new message. At first they succeeded only on the periphery of Western Europe. On pages 509–14 we noted the revolutions in Latin America, and their transformation from transcontinental revolts into individual national movements, destroying the unifying visions of Simón Bolívar and José de San Martín. The Latin American events underscored the dominant importance of leadership. Nationalism spoke in the name of the people, but it spoke in the voice of specific leaders and classes of leaders: lawyers, journalists, teachers, and military officials.

In Canada, the Report to the British government by the Earl of Durham in 1839 led to the unification of mostly English-speaking Upper Canada, today's Ontario, with mostly French-speaking Lower Canada, today's Quebec. Durham urged responsible government over domestic affairs and the rapid development of railways and canals to consolidate the nation. The Durham Report was quickly accepted and implemented. In 1867 the Dominion of Canada was established, increasing the scope of parliamentary democracy and adding the eastern maritime provinces to the core of Quebec and Ontario. Tensions between the British and French regions of Canada diminished, but they did not disappear. They continue to surface periodically to the present.

Also on the periphery, but within Europe, revolts in the Balkans broke out from 1815 onward in the name of individual nationalities. The first successful revolt was of the Greek peoples against the Ottoman Empire. Greece won its independence in 1829 with the backing of military forces dispatched by England, France, and Russia. At the same time, other Ottoman possessions also gained autonomy: Serbia, Wallachia and Moldavia in present-day Romania, and Egypt. The European powers supported this aggressive nationalism in the Balkans and northeast Africa because it diminished the power of the Ottoman Empire, while increasing their own leverage within the region.

Nationalism always had two faces. As a positive force, it promised to empower the masses of a nation with freedom and evoke their collective participation in building new futures. As a negative power, it threatened to force the masses to serve the state and to turn one nation against another in destructive warfare. The Balkans saw both these faces. Some nationalist movements won independence and the possibility of greater freedom and creativity. On the other hand, a century of simmering nationalism throughout the region climaxed in 1914 when a Serbian nationalist assassinated the Crown Prince of Austria-Hungary in Sarajevo. The major powers of Europe soon took sides and World War I began (see Chapter 18).

ITALY AND GERMANY

Before 1870 neither Italy nor Germany existed as we now know them. Each was divided up into many regions under the control of different rulers. In Italy, the largest single state was the kingdom of Sardinia-Piedmont, but other states were controlled by other rulers. The area around Venice was controlled by Austria and the region around Rome by the Pope. Most of the small states of Germany had been included within Charlemagne's empire, founded in 800 C.E., and then within its successor institution, the Holy Roman Empire. Each of these states had its own ruler and even its own system of government. The largest, Austria, was in itself a significant state. The smallest had only a few thousand inhabitants. In addition, to the east lay Prussia, a powerful state which was beginning to think of itself as the leader of the German-speaking peoples.

As nation-states formed in Western Europe and demonstrated the economic, political, military, and cultural power that came from unity, regional leaders in Italy and Germany also sought unification for themselves. A common language and clearly demarcated geographical borders were considered vital elements in national unity, and were helpful to Italy in consolidating its peninsular nation. Germany, however, lacked clear natural geographic boundaries and faced the question as to which German-speaking states would be included within the new country and which would be excluded.

In the heart of Europe, nationalism grew in hard soil. The great powers of Austria, Prussia, Russia, France, and Britain suppressed new national uprisings by peoples within their empires. At their meeting to draft the peace settlements at the Congress of Vienna in 1814–15 after the Napoleonic Wars, they set limits on national movements in central Europe. Led by Prince Clemens von Metternich (1773–

1859), foreign minister of Austria, they were successful for a generation, quelling powerful uprisings in Poland, Prussia, Italy, and Hungary between 1846 and 1849. (Belgium did gain national independence, from the Dutch, in 1830.) Only in the 1850s did nationalism win major victories in lands under these empires. Then Italy and Germany began successfully to unite their several divided regions to form new nations. In each country, cultural nationalism preceded political mobilization.

Giuseppe Mazzini (1805–72) provided a prophetic vision for Italy. In 1831 he founded Young Italy, a secret association urging Italian unification and independence from foreign control by the French, Austrians, and Spanish. Mazzini's *On the Duties of Man* expressed his nationalistic, democratic, and humanistic views:

O my brothers, love your Country! Our country is our Home, the House that God has given us, placing

therein a numerous family that loves us, and whom we love; a family with whom we sympathize more readily, and whom we understand more quickly, than we do others; and which, from its being centred round a given spot, and from the homogeneous nature of its elements, is adapted to a special branch of activity. (*Contemporary Civilization*, p. 570)

When Mazzini's cultural view was joined by the political organization of Camillo Cavour (1810–61), Prime Minister of Sardinia-Piedmont in 1852 under King Victor Emmanuel II, the nationalist movement was poised for political victory. Cavour formed a brief alliance with Napoleon III of France against Austria, which enabled the annexation of Lombardy. The adjacent regions of Parma, Modena, and Tuscany joined by **plebiscite**. Giuseppe Garibaldi (1807–82) led 1150 followers, wearing red shirts, into the south Italian Kingdom of the Two Sicilies, which collapsed and subsequently also

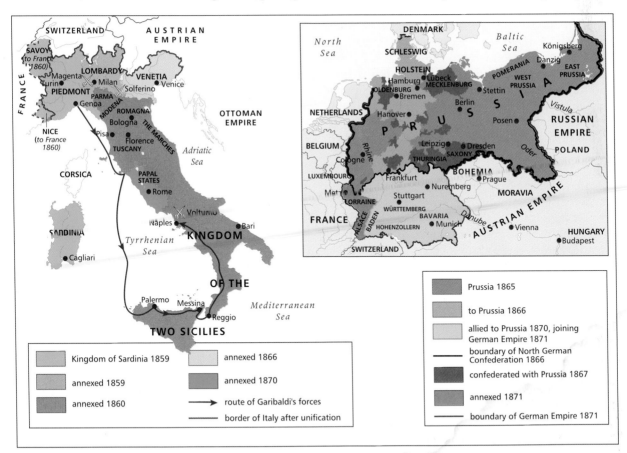

The unification of Italy and Germany The middle years of the nineteenth century saw popular forces drawing together the disparate territories of central Europe into modern nation states. In Germany the political, military, and economic strength of Prussia had been growing for over two centuries, and Bismarck's wars with Denmark (1864), Austria (1866), and France (1870) eventually secured the union. In Italy the expansion of Piedmont–Sardinia into Lombardy, the Veneto, and Rome, and Garibaldi's march through the south, united the nation.

joined Piedmont after a plebiscite. The Veneto was added after a war in which Italy allied with Prussia against Austria. Finally Rome was annexed in 1870 after French troops were withdrawn to fight against Prussia. Through the various contributions of Mazzini, Cavour, Garibaldi, Victor Emmanuel II, Napoleon III, war, and popular votes, Italy had become a unified nation.

At about the same time, Prime Minister Otto von Bismarck of Prussia (1815–98) was unifying the multitude of small German states into a single German nation under William I (King of Prussia 1861–88, Emperor of Germany 1871–88). The cultural basis of German unity was solidly established. The brothers Jakob and Wilhelm Grimm, founders of the modern science of linguistics, analyzed the various dialects of German and collected fairy tales from all parts of the region, publishing them in 1812 as a unifying folklore for the nation. A series of philosophers and historians, including J.G. von Herder (1744–1803), J.G. Fichte (1762–1814), Georg Wilhelm Friedrich Hegel (1770–1831), Leopold von Ranke (1795–1886), and Heinrich von Treitschke (1834–96) urged Germany to fulfill its natural destiny, just as Mazzini had urged Italy to fulfill its.

From 1828 a series of customs unions, *zollverein*, had already established an economic foundation for unification. Increasing industrialization provided the financial and military underpinnings for it. Now Bismarck instituted a policy of "Blood and Iron." Two wars were the key. In 1866 Bismarck defeated Austria and formed the North German Confederation without her. In 1871 he defeated France, annexing Alsace and Lorraine. In light of these victories the southern states of Germany— Bavaria, Baden, and Württemberg—also joined the newly formed nation.

THE RISE OF ZIONISM IN EUROPE

One of the last of the nationalist movements to arise in nineteenth-century Europe was Zionism, the movement to recreate a Jewish homeland. Jews had been dispersed into Europe even during the time of the Roman Empire. By the turn of the twentieth century, their principal European locations were in Poland, Russia, and the Ukraine. Through the centuries Jews had prayed for a return to Zion, the ancestral homeland in modern Israel. In the second half of the nineteenth century, under the influence of various European nationalist movements, some philosophers proposed going beyond prayer. They looked forward to an actual return and the establishment of a state.

The move from prayer to political organization took thirty-five years. On assignment in Paris to report on the trial of Alfred Dreyfus, a Jewish officer in the French army accused of treason, the Viennese Jewish journalist Theodor Herzl (1860– 1904) encountered fierce anti-Semitism. Shocked to find such ethnic and religious hatred in the capital of the liberal world, Herzl concluded that Jews could be free, independent, and safe only in a country of their own. In 1897 he founded the Zionist movement. Because Palestine, the goal of most of the early Zionists, was already the home of 600,000

French cartoon portraying Prince Otto Eduard Leopold von Bismarck, Prime Minister of Prussia, 1870. Political figures have traditionally been treated irreverently by cartoonists, but this caricature is savage. The French were outraged by Bismarck's ambitions to get the Prussian prince Leopold on to the Spanish throne—a key factor in the war between the two countries.

Arabs, Jewish nationalism simultaneously took the form of a colonizing movement originating in Europe. The consequences of this nationalistic/colonizing effort are traced in Chapter 21.

CHINA 1856–1911

European nationalism grew out of competition and warfare among nations. Especially in the 1800s, after the Napoleonic wars, European nations attempted to achieve a balance of power among themselves. In this view, to be a nation was to participate in an international system of nations. Imperial China was, by contrast, considered to be a nation in isolation—until European and American intervention brought her into the global arena of contesting powers in the mid-nineteenth century.

Despite China's powerful historical tradition, linguistic homogeneity, and folkloric and religious traditions, many historians have omitted China from discussions of nationalism. Partly, this omission arises from a **Eurocentricity**, which has overlooked non-European countries. Partly, it represents a view that Chinese nationalism was different from that of Europe. But China did create its own nationalism, as earlier segments of this text have argued and as Prasenjit Duara has emphasized in his recent study *Rescuing History from the Nation*. Throughout its history, China did face hostile neighbors, especially to the north. It negotiated with them; it fought them; it built and rebuilt the Great Wall to keep them out. Nevertheless, China was periodically invaded and conquered by foreigners. Marco Polo found a descendant of Genghis Khan sitting on the throne in Beijing (see Profile, pp. 388–9). From 1644 to 1911, during the height of European penetration of China, the country was ruled by Manchus, foreigners from the north. China did have international relations, sometimes tributary, often hostile, with its neighbors. China's genius was its ability to assimilate the foreigners to its own culture so fully that 95 percent of China's population considered themselves "People of Han"—that is, descendants of that early Chinese dynasty. The Chinese sense of national identity was one of the most powerful in the world, and it was the result of purposeful political and cultural decisions implemented over 2000 years.

The series of defeats at the hands of the Europeans in the Opium Wars (see p. 545), the devastating loss of Korea and Taiwan to the Japanese in the war of 1894–5, and the crushing of the Boxer Rebellion in 1898 (see p. 548) profoundly disturbed China's sense of identity. European and Japanese powers controlled her port cities and became focuses for the introduction of foreign culture, education, commerce, and industry. In response, many Chinese intellectuals began to propose changes in such fundamental, historic Chinese institutions as the examination system, the centrality of Confucian learning, the non-industrial economic system, and even the system of imperial rule. As the Manchu government appeared unwilling to implement these changes, Chinese reformers turned to revolution, seeking the overthrow of the Manchus as the first step toward evicting the European and Japanese foreigners. The revolution of 1911 achieved this first goal, and opened the way to the next two tasks: removing European power over China and charting new paths for the Chinese nation consistent both with its past and with the new military, political, and economic challenges and opportunities facing it.

ANTI-COLONIAL REVOLTS 1857–1914

By 1911, the authors of the Chinese revolution looked forward to modernizing the country. A series of earlier revolts throughout the countries colonized by Europe had, however, mostly looked backward to their own traditions. Colonized peoples had revolted to throw out the foreigners and return to the pre-colonial past. The 1857–8 revolt in India took this position; as did the Mahdist revolt on the upper Nile (1881–98); so, too, did Shamil, "ruler of the righteous and destroyer of the unbeliever," against Russia in the Caucasus (between 1834 and 1859); Emilio Aguinaldo against the United States in the Philippines (1898–1902); peasant warfare against the Dutch in Bali and Lombok, Indonesia (1881–94), and in Sumatra (1881–1908). Throughout sub-Saharan Africa local ethnic groups fought European invasion and occupation: Ethiopia defeated Italy at Adowa in 1896; the Bunyoro resisted the British in Uganda (1890–98), as did the Matabele and Mashona in Rhodesia (1896). The Maji-Maji revolt opposed German rule in Tanganyika (1905–7); the Mande under Samori Toure fought the French in west Africa (1884–98); and the Asante fought the British in the Gold Coast (1900). Revolts against the Portuguese in Angola broke out in 1913.

Later, armed revolts and non-violent political movements against colonial rule became more forward-looking. Their leaders sought not a simple return to the past, but a newly restructured nation, usually incorporating significant elements of the past with new goals based in part on innovations introduced by colonial powers. In India, the Indian National Congress, founded in 1885, proposed a pattern of parliamentary democracy for India, often (but not always) with an admixture of Hindu reformism. In 1907, in Egypt, Saad Zaghlul (1857–1927) founded the Hizb al-Umma or People's Party, which, in turn, became the core of the nationalist Wafd party after 1919. The Young Turk party, formed in 1878 in patriotic anger against the Ottoman defeats in the Balkans, grew into a revolutionary party by 1908. The Young Turks, like the Chinese nationalists, saw as their first task the removal of the ruling government, the Ottomans, before going on to further reforms. Indonesia's first nationalist association, the Budi Utomo, was formed in 1908; South Africa's National Congress in 1912; and Viet Nam's Viet Nam Quang Phuc Hoi in 1913.

Each of these organizations had a conception of the future nation it was constructing, modelled in part on European military, economic, political, and administrative forms, but also incorporating its own cultural, religious, and social dimensions.

JAPAN: FROM ISOLATION TO EQUALITY 1867–1914

In terms of nationalism, Japan was unified by race, with a national mythistory and a single dynasty of emperors that relates back to the founding of the nation in the seventh century B.C.E., a single national language, an integrated national political structure, and an island-based geography. Japan's insular nature was intensified in the early 1600s when the government closed the country to foreign, especially European, contact. Rather than accept the European model of contesting nation-states, Japan at this point chose relative isolation. With the challenge from Western nations in 1853, however, Japan recognized the need to transform itself militarily, economically, diplomatically, politically, and culturally. The history of Japan after 1853 charts its move from isolation to full, prominent participation in the world of nation-states.

THE END OF THE SHOGUNATE

By 1639, Japan had shut down commerce and contact with the European world, except for a Dutch outpost, virtually quarantined on Deshima Island in Nagasaki harbor, which was allowed to receive one ship each year. The Chinese were also permitted to trade at Nagasaki, but only under severe restrictions. Some trade could also pass through the Ryukyu Islands to China, under the guise of "tribute," and Korea could trade through the islands of Tsushima. Otherwise, Japan was isolated. In the late 1700s and early 1800s, an occasional European ship would attempt to establish contact, but they were turned away.

In 1853, however, Commodore Matthew Perry (1794–1858) was dispatched from the United States with a small squadron, including three steam frigates, to force Japan open to trade as China had been opened in the Opium War a decade before. Japan lacked the means to resist the Americans and the European powers that soon followed into Japanese waters, and over the next few years she opened more ports, at first on the periphery, but then at Nagasaki, Kobe, and Yokahama. Japan opened Edo (Tokyo) and Osaka to foreign residence, and then granted the foreigners extra-territorial legal rights. Foreigners were permitted to stipulate Japan's tariff policies. In 1863 and 1864, in the face of firing on their ships, British, French, Dutch, and American naval forces demolished Japanese coastal forts and and supplies and forced Japan to pay an indemnity. Like China, Japan seemed headed toward control by foreigners.

Unlike China, however, young, vigorous leaders seized control of the government of Japan, forcing a dramatic restructuring of the nation's politics, administration, class structure, economy, technology, and culture. These leaders, for the most part young samurai warriors in the *hans* (feudal estates) of Choshu and Satsuma at the southern extreme of Japan, decided that Japan's current government was not capable of coping with the European threat. Great diversity of opinion flourished among the approximately 250 different *han* in Japan, but the most powerful regional leaders felt that the shogun, who ruled Japan in the name of the emperor, should be removed and the emperor himself should be restored as the direct ruler of Japan. The young samurai, members of Japan's hereditary military elite, should formulate the policies of the new administration.

The samurai were able to employ some of the technological information introduced by the Dutch from their station in Nagasaki harbor. "Dutch learning" had been available for a century. Indeed, in 1811 the shogunate had established an office for translating Dutch material, and it was expanded into a school for European languages and science in 1857. Some of the *han* did the same, including Satsuma, Choshu, and Mito. By 1840, some Japanese were already casting Western guns and artillery. Sakuma Zozan (1811–64), one of the advocates of adopting Western military methods, coined the motto of the movement: "Eastern Ethics; Western Science." Japan could adopt Western technology, he counseled, especially military technology, while still maintaining its own culture.

Sakuma believed that opening the country was both necessary and beneficial. Not everyone agreed, however, and in 1860 a group of samurai from the conservative *han* of Mito argued a contrary position: "Revere the Emperor; Expel the Barbarian." The lines of conflict were sharpening. Political violence increased as exponents of the opposing positions attacked each other. Sakuma was assassinated in 1864 by Mito loyalists, who then assassinated yet another leader and committed ritual suicide. Attacks on foreigners taking up residence and conducting business in Japan also increased.

In 1865 a group of young samurai in Choshu attacked and defeated their *daimyo*, the ruler of their *han*, establishing control of the government of Choshu. Next year, the armed forces of Choshu confronted and defeated those of the shogun while the other *daimyo* sat out the contest. In 1868 the forces of Choshu and Satsuma, joining with those of several other more remote *han*, seized control of the emperor's palace in Kyoto and declared the shogunate ended, the lands of the shogun confiscated, and the emperor restored to imperial power. Most of the fighting was over by November, although naval battles continued into early 1869. The **Meiji restoration** ended the power of the shogunate forever and brought the *daimyo* and their young samurai to power in the name of the Emperor Meiji (r. 1867–1912). The emperor assumed the throne at the age of fourteen and reigned over a national transformation of astonishing speed.

POLICIES OF THE MEIJI GOVERNMENT

On April 8, 1868, the revolutionary leaders issued a Charter Oath in the name of the Emperor Meiji. The fifth and last article proved the most important: "Knowledge shall be sought throughout the world so as to strengthen the foundations of imperial rule." The new goal was "A rich country and a

THE MEIJI RESTORATION AND INDUSTRIALIZATION IN JAPAN

1853	Commander Perry sails into Edo Bay, ending 250 years' isolation
1854	Treaty of Kanagawa gives US trading rights with Japan
1860s	Series of "unequal treaties" gives US, Britain, France, Russia, and Netherlands commercial and territorial privileges
1868	Tokugawa shogun forced to abdicate. Executive power vested with emperor in Meiji restoration
1871	Administration is overhauled; Western-style changes introduced
1872	National education system introduced, providing teaching for 90 per cent of children by 1900 First railway opened
1873	Old order changed by removal of privileges of samurai class
1876	Koreans, under threat, agree to open three of their ports to the Japanese and exchange diplomats
1877	Satsuma rebellion represented last great (unsuccessful) challenge of conservative forces
1879	Representative system of local government introduced
1884	Western-style peerage (upper house) is created
1885	Cabinet government introduced
1889	Adoption of constitution based on Bismarck's Germany
1889	Number of cotton mills has risen from 3 (1877) to 83
1894–5	War with China ends in Japanese victory
1902	Britain and Japan sign military pact
1904–5	War with Russia ends in Japanese victory
1914	Japan joins World War I on side of Allies

strong military." The new leaders had already begun to search the world for new political, economic, and military models that might be adapted to Japan's needs.

After treaty agreements had been signed in 1858, the shogun had already dispatched embassies to the United States in 1860 and to Europe in 1862, beginning official exchanges of information. Now a two-year overseas goodwill mission, headed by Prince Iwakura Tonomi (1825–83), set out in 1871 to deepen relationships with the heads of state of the treaty powers, to discuss future treaty revisions, and to enable Japanese leaders to experience the West at first hand. Fifty-four students accompanied the mission. A ministry of education was estab-lished in 1871 and its first budget (1873) included funds for sending 250 students abroad to study. Many of these students became leaders in the new Japan. Foreign instructors were also brought to Japan. The late shogun's government had employed some foreigners in industrial enterprises, but the Meiji rulers imported far more. They set out to develop Hokkaido and brought in American experts, who introduced large-scale farming practices to the northern island. By 1879 the ministry of industry employed 130 foreigners. Doctors were brought from Germany to teach medicine, and from America to teach natural and social sciences. After a few years, however, the cost of importing foreign experts outweighed the benefits, and fewer were

SOURCE

Fukuzawa Yukichi: Cultural Interpreter

Born into the lower levels of the feudal aristocracy in Kyushu, Fukuzawa Yukichi (1834–1901) had a thirst for knowledge that took him to Osaka, Nagasaki (for Dutch learning), to the United States in 1860 with the very first Japanese official mission (and again in 1867), and to Europe in 1862. Fukuzawa rejected government office, the usual alternative, in favor of private life as a journalist and teacher. He earned a reputation as the foremost interpreter of the West to Japan and his books describing the West as he understood it sold in the hundreds of thousands to a nation hungry for such observation and interpretation. He founded a school in Tokyo that later became Keio University, the training ground of many of Japan's business leaders. The following excerpts are from Fukuzawa's *Autobiography*, published in 1899. He states his goal of interpreting the West fairly, even though he knows that he will face opposition.

The final purpose of all my work was to create in Japan a civilized nation, as well equipped in both the arts of war and peace as those of the Western world. I acted as if I had become the sole functioning agent for the introduction of Western culture. It was natural then that I would be disliked by the older type of Japanese, and suspected of working for the benefit of foreigners. ... I regard the human being as the most sacred and responsible of all orders, unable in reason to do anything base. ... In short, my creed is that a man should find his faith in independence and self-respect. (p. 214)

He investigates the style of Western institutions:

For instance, when I saw a hospital, I wanted to know how it was run—who paid the running expenses; when I visited a bank, I wished to learn how the money was deposited and paid out. By similar first-hand queries, I learned something of the postal system and the military conscription then in force in France but not in England. A perplexing institution was representative government. ... For some time it was beyond my comprehension to understand what they [political parties] were "fighting" for, and what was meant, anyway, by "fighting" in peace time. "This man and that man are 'enemies' in the House," they would tell me. But these "enemies" were to be seen at the same table, eating and drinking with each other. (p. 134)

employed. Missionaries, who came at their own expense, were an important exception.

RESTRUCTURING GOVERNMENT

The emperor was brought from his home in Kyoto to Edo, the former capital of the Shogun, which was renamed Tokyo ("Eastern Capital") in 1868. In 1869, the *daimyo* of four of the most important *han*—Choshu, Satsuma, Tosa, and Hizen—turned over their estates to the emperor, setting the pattern for other *daimyo*. At first they were appointed governors, but two years later their domains were abolished and reorganized among the other prefectures of Japan. The *daimyo* retained certain rights of tax collection, which kept them financially well off, and stipends were paid to the samurai to avoid outright revolt. Nevertheless, a decade of samurai revolts in Choshu, Kyshsu, Hizen, and, by far the largest, in Satsuma did challenge the new government. In Satsuma 40,000 troops, under the reluctant leadership of Saigo Takamori, confronted the government and were crushed. Japan's national government held firm.

The core of the central government's new army, 10,000 men drawn from Satsuma, Choshu, and Tosa, was established in 1871. In 1878, the army was reorganized and money was invested in modern equipment, much of it manufactured in Japan. An army staff college began to train an officer corps along a German model, while the navy adapted a British model, often purchasing its ships from Britain. Service in the armed forces introduced Japanese conscripts to new ways of life, some travel, reading and writing, Western-style uniforms and shoes, nationalism, and reverence for the emperor. Japan was becoming the most powerful nation in east Asia.

RESTRUCTURING THE ECONOMY

Recognizing an economic principle that underlay the industrial revolution in Britain, Japan first built up its agriculture. It needed the profits, and it needed the food and manpower which an effective agriculture would make available for urban industry. New seeds, fertilizer, and methods were introduced throughout the islands and Hokkaido was opened to farming. Agricultural colleges spread the new techniques and information. In the 1880s, agricultural production went up by about 30 percent, and from 1890 to 1915 by 100 percent. This production

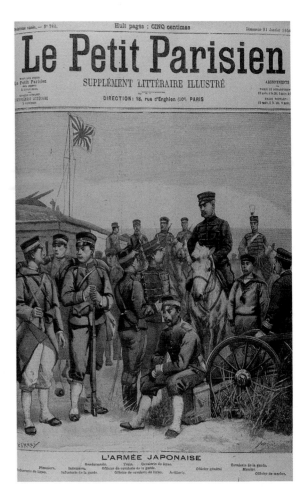

East wears West. The Japanese troops pictured on the front of this French magazine are a perfect example of the detail to which the government of Japan was willing to go in their efforts to fit into the modern world of early twentieth-century politics and fashions.

included not only food crops but also tea, cotton, and silk, mostly for the export market. The profits from increased agricultural production did not go to the peasants but to the landlord, who invested them in commerce or industry. Poorer peasants were squeezed off the land by high rents and all peasants were heavily taxed to fund the large expenses of industrialization and militarization.

In large-scale industrialization, the government was the entrepreneur. It built the first railway line, between Tokyo and Yokohama, in 1872. In two decades about 2000 miles (3200 kilometers) of track followed. Within the cities, trolleys and *rikishas* (rickshaws) supplemented the train lines. Telegraph lines linked all the major cities by 1880. The government financed coal mines, iron mines, a machine-tool factory, cement works, glass and tile factories, wool and cotton textile mills, shipyards, mines, and weapons manufacture. In 1873 it established the Imperial College of Engineering. But the industry that contributed the most, silk, which accounted for more than 40 percent of all of Japan's exports, was developed largely by private entrepreneurs.

URBANIZATION

Under the Tokugawa Shogunate, 1603–1867, each *daimyo* had his own capital. As a result, Japan had a rich array of administrative towns and cities spread throughout the country. During the Meiji Restoration, they provided the network for the diffusion of new cultural patterns. Some cities stood out. Kyoto, the home of the emperor, was the center of traditional culture; Osaka was the most important business center; and Edo (Tokyo) was, by the mid-1800s, the largest and most flourishing of the major cities, with a population of a half million to a million people.

Tokugawa urban culture had mixed strains. At the center of business life were merchants dedicated to making money. Yet they liked entertainment and found it outside their homes. Homes were for wife, children, and household duties. The amusement quarters of the city were for restaurants, theater, artistic culture, the female companionship of *geisha* personal entertainers, and prostitutes.

Social networks based on neighborhoods, shrines, guilds, and civic needs such as firefighting provided a sense of community, and cities grew relatively slowly in the first generation of the Restoration. By 1895 only 12 percent of Japan's population of 42 million lived in cities. Industrialization in large factories had barely begun. In 1897 only 400,000 workers in all of Japan were working in factories employing more than five workers. By the turn of the century, however, the institutional and economic changes of the Restoration were taking effect, and urban populations multiplied, so that by the mid-1930s 45 percent of the 69 million people of Japan were living in cities. The industrial labor force reached 1.7 million in 1920 (and 6 million by 1936).

The culture of the cities changed dramatically. Japanese cities, crowded and subject to fire and earthquake, changed not only with cultural and technological innovations, but also with the necessity to rebuild from time to time. Edward

Advertisement throwaway from the Mitsui dry-goods store (later Mitsuoki Department Store), Tokyo, *c.* 1895. Retail outlets were obvious signs of the drive to embrace industrialized Western culture, as this "before" and "after" picture aptly demonstrates. The traditional first floor (bottom), with its legions of clerks haggling over material, has been augmented by the new-fangled second floor (top), where a more serene atmosphere and slick glass display cases proclaim a new style of consumerism.

The expansion and modernization of Japan
Responding to the threats of foreign gunboats, Japanese samurai leaders overthrew the long-established Tokugawa shogunate and restored imperial power under the Emperor Meiji in 1868. Within fifty years, industrial development, growing international trade, and territorial expansion made Japan a world power. Initially asserting its control of neighboring islands, and then taking advantage of Manchu decline, its victories over China (1894–95) and Russia (1904–05) established Japanese control over Taiwan, Korea, and Karafuto (southern Sakhalin), and its dominant influence over Manchuria and even parts of mainland China.

Seidensticker's remarkable study of Tokyo between 1867 and 1923, *Low City, High City*, describes a double transformation. The old heart of Tokyo, the low city, developed bigger businesses, more raucous entertainment, and newer fashions, but it remained rooted in the plebeian culture of the Tokugawa period of Edo. The high city, built literally on somewhat higher ground, was developed later, with modern buildings, more refinement of a Western sort, and a more modernist culture.

CULTURAL AND EDUCATIONAL CHANGE

Western cultural styles, superficial and profound, proliferated in Meiji Japan (see Source, p. 585). The

Gregorian calendar and the seven-day week, with Sunday as a holiday, were adopted in 1882, and the metric system in 1886. Samurai men began to prefer Western haircuts to the traditional shaved head and topknot. The military dressed in Western-style uniforms, and in 1872 Western dress became mandatory at all official ceremonies. Meat eating was encouraged, despite Buddhist ethics, and *sukiyaki* was developed as part of Japanese cuisine.

Japanese readers turned avidly to Western texts. Philosophers of the Enlightenment drew attention to individual rights, and Utilitarians such as John Stuart Mill (see p. 568) were read and appreciated. The more combative social Darwinism of Herbert Spencer (see p. 541) proved attractive as a justification for Japan's sense of its growing power and coming imperialism and Samuel Smiles' emphasis on *Self Help* (see p. 530) also found a receptive readership.

Tokugawa Japan had valued formal education. Samurai had attended Confucian-based schools run by the *han*; commoners had studied in schools located in Buddhist temples. At the time of the Restoration, an estimated 45 percent of adult males and 15 percent of adult females could read and write, about the same proportions as in advanced European countries. Building on this base, the government introduced a highly centralized system of education and then mandated compulsory attendance. By 1905, over 90 percent of both boys and girls of primary school age were attending school. The schools were recognized for high quality, for providing public education superior to private schools, and for helping move Japan from the feudal, hierarchical society of Tokugawa Japan to a more egalitarian system than that of most European countries. At the university level, a series of excellent institutions were established throughout Japan, beginning with Tokyo University in 1886.

GENDER RELATIONS

The Meiji Restoration opened up entirely new arenas of public life and achievement for Japanese men, and, for a few years before marriage, some women also found new opportunities in education, factory employment, and a handful of new cultural opportunities. For the most part, however, women's public options were restricted. As the emperor's position was restored, so was male dominance in the home reinforced. Police Security Regulations of 1890, Article 5, prohibited women and minors from joining political organizations and holding or attending meetings in which political speeches or lectures were given. (The vote was granted to women only after World War II; see p. 666.) The 1898 Civil Code reinforced patriarchy within the family, granting the male head of the family unquestioned authority. Women had few legal rights. At marriage, control over her property passed to her husband. Fathers held exclusive right to custody over children. Concubinage was abolished in 1880, but society sanctioned prostitution and the discreet keeping of mistresses. As high school education was extended to women, the Girls' High School Law of 1899 declared its goal to be "good wives and wise mothers." Within the home, women held great authority and respect, but they were allowed virtually no place in the public life of Japan.

WAR, COLONIALISM, AND EQUALITY IN THE FAMILY OF NATIONS

From the beginning of the Meiji Restoration, Japan sought to end the demeaning provisions of extraterritoriality and also to regain control of its own tariffs. These goals provided the rationales for introducing new legal systems, more consistent with those of Western countries. If Japan's laws were in accord with those of Europe, there would be no justification for continuing extraterritoriality. The British relinquished extraterritoriality in 1899 when the new legal codes took effect. Other nations followed suit, and Japan reciprocated by allowing foreigners to establish residences outside the treaty ports. Additional treaties returned full control over tariffs to Japan in 1911.

War and colonization also seemed important to full membership in the European community of nations. Yamagata Aritomo (1838–1922), the chief proponent of the law of universal conscription in 1873 and the chief architect of Japan's new army, argued this position, and turned his attention to the conquest of Korea. Japan had forced the establishment of a legation in Korea in 1876. As political leaders in that country divided over policy issues, some sought support from more conservative China, others from more progressive Japan. When fighting between the groups broke out in 1894, both China and Japan sent in troops and war began between the two powers. On land, Japanese armies seized all of Korea and pushed on into Manchuria. At sea, they defeated the Chinese fleet, captured Port Arthur, the naval base in southern Manchuria,

and the port of Weihaiwei on Shandong. Peace negotiations gave Japan Taiwan and the Pescadores Islands, and Japan supplanted China as the dominant nation of East Asia. Korea was formally recognized as independent, but Japan held sway there nonetheless. Japan was also to receive control over the Liaotung Peninsula, but an international diplomatic consortium led by Russia forced it to withdraw, despite Japan's resentment.

In the first years of the twentieth century, two further engagements with the West ratified Japan's arrival among the powers of the world. First, in 1902, Britain and Japan signed an alliance, the first military pact on equal terms between a European and a non-Western country. It brought together the most powerful navies of Europe and of East Asia. It blocked Russian aspirations, and it further secured semi-colonial control over China. Second, in response to continuing Russian penetration of Manchuria and increasingly hostile diplomacy, Japan attacked the Russian fleet in Port Arthur in 1904 and declared war. Fighting far from the center of their country, the Russian army was defeated. A Russian fleet dispatched from the Baltic was intercepted and annihilated by the Japanese in 1905 as it crossed the Straits of Tsushima.

An Asian power had defeated a European power for the first time since the victories of the Ottomans in eastern Europe in the seventeenth century. (In Russia, the defeat precipitated the revolution of 1905.) In the peace conference convened by American President Theodore Roosevelt, Japan was given a protectorate over Korea, predominant rights over southern Manchuria (including the Liaotung Peninsula) and control of the southern Sakhalin Island. In 1910, with no European power protesting, Japan formally annexed Korea. Japan had reached the international status it had desired—less than a half century after embarking on its quest. Nationalism, technological innovation, and imperialism had become supreme in Japan as in Europe.

WHAT DIFFERENCE DOES IT MAKE?

The democratic and industrial revolutions affected day-to-day life in profound ways. The location of work shifted from rural agriculture to urban industry, and population followed. In addition the location of work and of home split apart as old principles of community weakened and new ones began to take shape. The struggles for political freedom and the new economic opportunities of the

RUSSO-JAPANESE WAR 1904–5—KEY EVENTS

The war arose from conflicting ambitions in Manchuria and Korea, in particular the Russian occupation of Port Arthur (1896) and Amur province (1900).

May 1904	Battle of Yalu River: the Russians are defeated by the Japanese in the vicinity of Antung (now Dandong), Manchuria. The river forms the border with Korea, and the Japanese army forces a crossing against light opposition. Quickly overcoming the Russians, who retreat north, the Japanese move to besiege Port Arthur (Lushun).
May 1904–January 1905	Siege of Port Arthur: the Japanese fleet blockades the harbor, keeping the Russian fleet bottled up, while the army launches a series of minor attacks. Japanese eventually overcome garrison, which surrenders, after heavy losses. Japanese lose some 58,000 men.
February–May 1905	Battle of Mukden (Shenyang): Japanese defeat Russians outside the capital city of Manchuria, in the last major engagement of the war, in which 41,000 Japanese were killed and wounded and the Russian dead and wounded totalled more than 32,000. The czar is finally persuaded to accept US mediation. Russia's Baltic Fleet is annihilated in the Tsushima Straits.
August 1905	Peace agreement: Russia surrendered its lease on Port Arthur, ceded South Sakhalin to Japan, evacuated Manchuria, and recognized Japanese interests in Korea. For the first time in more than two centuries an Asian power had defeated a European power. US president Theodore Roosevelt mediated the agreement and was awarded the Nobel Prize for peace (1906).

city challenged gender identities, leading women and men to begin to see their relationships in new perspectives. The power of the nation-state also emerged clearly as countries that were independent sought to compete with one another, and those that were not sought to win independence from their colonial conquerors. In both cases, nationalism flourished and people defined their own personal identities in terms of their country.

New movements arose for new political structures to provide more personal freedom; for increased economic productivity and more equitable distribution; for more livable cities with a reborn sense of community; for a revised, more equitable balance of responsibilities and rewards between men and women in both public and private life; and for a nationalism that might secure the rights of each citizen and discourage the brutal competition that led to war and oppressive colonialism. Between around 1750 and 1914 these opportunities and challenges took shape in Europe and North America and then spread to the rest of the world largely through colonialism and the threat of colonialism. Optimists believed that progress would result; pessimists had their doubts. When world war (1914–1918) opened the twentieth century, the pessimists seemed to be winning.

BIBLIOGRAPHY

Abu-Lughod, Janet and Richard Hay, Jr., eds. *Third World Urbanization* (Chicago: Maaroufa Press, 1977).

Adas, Michael, ed. *Islamic and European Expansion* (Philadelphia: Temple University Press, 1993).

Anderson, Benedict. *Imagined Communities* (London: Verso, 1983).

Anderson, Bonnie and Judith Zinsser. *A History of Their Own*, 2 vols. (New York: Harper and Row, 1988).

Andrea, Alfred and James Overfield, eds. *The Human Record*, Vol 2 (Boston: Houghton Mifflin, 3rd ed. 1998).

Bairoch, Paul. *Cities and Economic Development*, trans. by Christopher Braider (Chicago: University of Chicago Press, 1988).

Baudelaire, Charles. *Les Fleurs du Mal*, trans. by Richard Howard (Boston: Godine, 1983).

Bell, Susan Groag and Karen M. Offen, eds. *Women, the Family, and Freedom*, Vol. 1, 1750–1880 (Stanford: Stanford University Press, 1983).

Bernstein, Gail Lee, ed. *Recreating Japanese Women, 1600–1945* (Berkeley: University of California Press, 1991).

Braudel, Fernand. *The Identity of France*, trans. by Sian Reynolds (New York; Harper and Row, 1988).

Bridenthal, Renate, Claudia Koonz, and Susan Stuard, eds. *Becoming Visible: Women in European History* (Boston: Houghton Mifflin, 2nd ed., 1987).

Booth, Charles. *On the City*, ed. by Harold W. Pfautz (Chicago: University of Chicago Press, 1967).

Burton, Antoinette. *Burdens of History* (Chapel Hill: University of North Carolina Press, 1994).

Casey, James. *The History of the Family* (Oxford: Blackwell, 1989).

Chatterjee, Partha. *The Nation and Its Fragments* (Princeton: Princeton University Press, 1993).

Collcutt, Martin, Marius Jansen, and Isao Kumakura. *Cultural Atlas of Japan* (New York: Facts on File, 1988).

Columbia College, Columbia University. eds. *Contemporary Civilization in the West* (New York: Columbia University Press, 2nd ed., 1954).

Cooper, Frederick and Ann Laura Stoler, eds. *Tensions of Empire* (Berkeley: University of California Press, 1997).

Di Giorgio, Michela, "The Catholic Model," in Fraisse and Perrot, eds. *Emerging Feminism*, pp. 166–197.

Duara, Prasenjit. *Rescuing History from the Nation* (Chicago: University of Chicago Press, 1995).

Eley, Geoff and Ronald Grigor Suny, eds. *Becoming National* (New York: Oxford University Press, 1996).

Engels, Friedrich. *The Origins of the Family, Private Property and the State,* ed. by Eleanor Burke Leacock (New York: International Publishers, 1973).

Fairbank, John K., Edwin O. Reischauer, and Albert Craig. *East Asia: Tradition and Transformation* (Boston: Houghton Mifflin, rev. ed., 1989).

Fraisse, Genevieve and Michelle Perrot, eds. *A History of Women in the West: Emerging Feminism from Revolution to World War*, Vol. IV (Cambridge, MA: Belknap Press, 1993).

Frederick, Christine. *The New Housekeeping* (Garden City, NY: Doubleday, 1914).

Fujimura-Fanselow, Kumiko and Atsuko Kameda, eds. *Japanese Women* (New York: Feminist Press, 1995).

Gluck, Carol. *Japan's Modern Myths* (Princeton: Princeton University Press, 1985).

Hibbert, Christopher. *London* (Harmondsworth, Middlesex: Penguin Books Ltd., 1977).

Hertzberg, Arthur, ed. *The Zionist Idea* (New York: Meridian Books Inc. and Philadelpia: Jewish Publication Society, 1960).

Hirschmeier, Johannes. *The Origins of Entrepreneurship in Meiji Japan* (Cambridge, MA: Harvard University Press, 1964).

Hobsbawm, Eric. *The Age of Capital, 1848–1875* (New York: Vintage Books, 1975).

—. *The Age of Empire, 1875–1914* (New York: Vintage, 1987).

—. *The Age of Revolution, 1789–1848* (New York: New American Library, 1962).

Hohenberg, Paul M. and Lynn Hollen Lees. *The Making of Urban Europe, 1000–1950* (Cambridge, MA: Harvard University Press, 1985).

Hutchinson, John and Anthony D. Smith, eds. *Nationalism* (New York: Oxford University Press, 1994).

Ibsen, Henrik. *A Doll's House*, trans. by Rolf Fjelde in *Literature of the Western World Vol. II: Neoclassicism Through the Modern Period*, ed. by Brian Wilkie and James Hurt (New York: Macmillan Publishing Co., Inc., 1984), pp. 1304–57.

Kaneko, Sachiko, "The Struggle for Legal Rights and Reforms: A Historical View," in Fujimora-Fanselow and Kameda, eds. *Japanese Women*, pp. 3–14.

Kennedy, Paul. *The Rise and Fall of the Great Powers* (New York; Random House, 1987).

Kessler-Harris, Alice. *Out to Work* (New York: Oxford University Press, 1982).

Knibiehler, Yvonne, "Bodies and Hearts," in Fraisse and Perrot, eds., *Emerging Feminism*, pp. 325–68.

Marx, Karl and Frederick Engels. *The Communist Manifesto* (New York: International Publishers, 1948).

Morris-Suzuki, Tessa. *The Technological Transformation of Japan* (Cambridge: Cambridge University Press, 1994).

Mumford, Lewis. *The City in History* (New York: Harcourt Brace & World, 1961).

Procida, Mary A. "Married to the Empire: British Wives and British Imperialism in India, 1883-1947" (University of Pennsylvania: Ph.D. dissertation, 1997).

Renan, Ernest, "What is a Nation?" in Eley and Suny, pp. 42–55.

Restoring Women to History (Bloomington, IN: Organization of American Historians, 1988).

Rousseau, Jean-Jacques. *The Social Contract*, trans. by Maurice Cranston (Harmondsworth, Middlesex: Penguin Books, 1968).

Rybczynski, Witold. *Home* (New York: Penguin Books, 1987).

Said, Edward W. *Culture and Imperialism* (New York: Vintage Books, 1993).

Schirokauer, Conrad. *A Brief History of Chinese and Japanese Civilizations* (Fort Worth: Harcourt Brace Jovanovich, 2nd ed., 1989).

Scott, Joan Wallach. *Only Paradoxes to Offer* (Cambridge, MA: Harvard University Press, 1996).

—. "The Woman Worker," in Fraisse and Perrot, eds., *Emerging Feminism*, pp. 399–426.

Seidensticker, Edward. *Low City, High City* (Cambridge, MA: Harvard University Press, 1991).

Sennett, Richard, ed. *Classic Essays on the Culture of Cities* (Englewood Cliffs: Prentice Hall, 1969).

Spivak, Gayatri Chakravorty, "Subaltern Studies: Deconstructing Historiography," in Ranajit Guha and Gayatri Chakravorty Spivak, eds., *Selected Subaltern Studies* (New York: Oxford University Press, 1988), pp. 3–32.

Strobel, Margaret, "Gender, Sex, and Empire," in Adas, pp. 345–375.

Thomas, Ray and Peter Cresswell. *The New Town Idea* (Walton Hall, Milton Keynes: Open University Press, 1973).

Tilly, Louise, "Industrialization and Gender Inequality," in Adas, pp. 243–310.

Times [London] *Atlas of World History* (London: Times Books, 5th ed., 1999).

Tocqueville, Alexis de. *Democracy in America*, 2 vols (New York: Knopf, 1945).

Tsunoda, Ryusaku, Wm. Theodore de Bary, and Donald Keene, comps. *Sources of Japanese Tradition* (New York: Columbia University Press, 1958).

Uno, Kathleen S., "Women and Changes in the Household Division of Labor," in Gail Lee Bernstein, ed., *Recreating Japanese Women, 1600–1945* (Berkeley: University of California Press, 1991), pp. 17–41.

Wakakuwa, Midori, "Three Women Artists of the Meiji Period (1868–1912): Reconsidering Their Significance from a Feminist Perspective," in Fujimura-Fanselow and Kameda, eds., *Japanese Women*, pp. 61–74.

Walkowitz, Judith, "Dangerous Sexualities," in Fraisse and Perrot, eds., *Emerging Feminism*, pp. 369–98.

Warner, Sam Bass, Jr. *The Private City* (Philadelphia: University of Pennsylvania Press, 1987).

Weber, Adna Ferrin. *The Growth of Cities in the Nineteenth Century* (Ithaca: Cornell University Press, reprint 1963).

Weber, Max. *The City*, trans. by Don Martindale and Gertrud Neuwirth (New York: Free Press, 1958).

Whitman, Walt. *Complete Poetry and Collected Prose* (New York: The Library of America, 1982).

Wollstonecraft, Mary. *Vindication of the Rights of Woman* (London: Penguin Books, 1975).

Yukichi, Fukuzawa. *The Autobiography of Yukichi Fukuzawa*, trans. by Eiichi Kiyooka (New York: Columbia University Press, 1966).

PART 8

Exploding Technologies

CONTESTED VISIONS OF A NEW INTERNATIONAL ORDER

The twentieth century began with great promise. The political and industrial revolutions of the previous two centuries encouraged western Europeans to believe that they were mastering the secrets of securing a long, productive, comfortable, and meaningful life for the individual and the community. They believed that they were transmitting these benefits around the globe through their colonial policies, and that their colonial possessions would continue long into the foreseeable future. Polish poet Wislawa Szymborska captured the optimism:

Our twentieth century was going to improve on others. . . .
A couple of problems weren't going to come up anymore:
Hunger, for example, and war, and so forth.

The first world war, global economic depression, the second world war, the Cold War, and revolts throughout the colonial world shattered many of these European illusions. "Anyone who planned to enjoy the world is now faced with a hopeless task," Szymborska wrote. (For the complete poem, "How Should We Live," see p. 615.)

What had gone wrong? Technology can produce catastrophe as well as creativity. Optimists at the beginning of the century had overemphasized its positive potentials. They had underestimated the problems of deciding its purposes, uses, and controls in a world of competition among nations, ethnic groups, and ideologies.

Atomic weapons test in the Marshall Islands, 1950.

The first half of the century saw technology put to use more in warfare than in peace, but the second half brought a resurgence of optimism; the United Nations emerged as a needed venue for conflict resolution and international bargaining; the cold war was contained as an armed truce and then came to an end virtually without bloodshed (although many **proxy wars** had been fought in its name). Technology—especially information and communication technology and biotechnology—was once again promising beneficial revolutions globally and in every day life.

The world had heard such promises before and once again the voices of caution were loud and clear: prosperity and opportunity were not trickling down to billions of impoverished people, not in poor countries and not in rich ones; identity conflicts remained powerful and unresolved and ethnic and religious violence broke out repeatedly around the globe; issues of gender identity, growing more powerful throughout the twentieth century, continued to expose tensions in family and public life; and technologies of destruction continued to multiply side-by-side with technologies of productivity.

The era at the dawn of the twenty-first century had not yet claimed a name and identity of its own. Academics often referred to it as "post-modern," understanding that many of its attributes had been seen a century before, some were new and required new perspectives, and no one could see with clarity how the mix would turn out.

CHAPTER 18

TECHNOLOGIES OF MASS-PRODUCTION AND DESTRUCTION

1914–2000

"Our twentieth century was going to improve on others… A couple of problems weren't going to come up anymore: hunger, for example, and war, and so forth."

WISLAWA SZYMBORSKA

WHAT IS A TECHNOLOGICAL SYSTEM AND WHY IS IT IMPORTANT?

TECHNOLOGICAL SYSTEMS

The first part of this chapter will introduce technology in its more benign mode—that is, those technological developments that encourage life and make it more productive, enjoyable, and perhaps meaningful. The second part will introduce the destructive aspect of technology, manifest especially in violence and warfare. The final segments discuss attempts, often frustrating and conflict-filled, but nevertheless continuing, to build institutions to harness technology for humane uses.

"Technology" includes not only inventions but also the systems that produce and sustain them. Thomas Hughes, a historian of science and technology, explains this comprehensive definition:

> In popular accounts of technology, inventions of the late nineteenth century, such as the incandescent light, the radio, the airplane, and the gasoline-driven automobile, occupy center stage, but these inventions were embedded within technological systems. Such systems involve far more than the so-called hardware, devices, machines and processes, and the transportation, communication, and information networks that interconnect them. Such systems consist also of people and organizations. An electric light-and-power system, for instance, may involve generators, motors, transmission lines, utility companies, manufacturing enterprises, and banks. Even a regulatory body may be co-opted into the system. (p. 3)

The technological enterprise grew into the most pervasive characteristic of the twentieth century and continues to grow. It has dramatically altered:

- the number, longevity, and health of the people who inhabit the globe;

- the size and organization of families;

- the location, design, and equipment of homes, neighborhoods, and workplaces;

- the nature and organization of work and the training necessary to do it;

- the quantities and varieties of food people eat as well as the regions of the globe from which they come;

- clothing;

- travel for business and pleasure;

- recreation;

- the strategies and destructive potentials of wars;

- the complexity and structure of economic, social, and governmental organizations; and

- the ecology, that is, the interaction of the life systems, of the earth.

DEMOGRAPHIC SHIFTS

Improvements in technology have changed our relationship to life and death, health and sickness. Biological and health advances have included new drugs such as sulfa-based medicines (1930s), penicillin and antibiotics (from the 1940s), hormonal and mood-altering chemicals (from the 1950s), and new methods of contraception, especially the birth control pill (1950s), that have changed sexual attitudes and practices around the globe. Organ transplants, including eyes (1940s), kidney (1954), liver (1963), heart (1967), and bone marrow (1970s) have given millions of people a new lease of life. Individuals, families, and nations have struggled with the problems of paying for these new medical miracles.

Public health services, the fortunate linking of medical knowledge with government responsibility, have increased, especially in the provision of safe drinking water and sewage offtake (although not always and everywhere as quickly as new needs have arisen). Vaccines have eliminated the fear of many childhood diseases. Polio was tamed in the 1950s, and smallpox, a disease of historically epidemic proportions, has been eradicated through the World Health Organization's vaccinating virtually all humans in areas of the world infected with the disease in the 1960s and 1970s. The last known case was in Somalia in 1977. The once-feared smallpox virus lives today only in laboratory specimens kept for research.

The progress of technology and its application often collided with other ecological constraints. In the 1950s and 1960s, for example, the chemical insecticide DDT seemed to offer a weapon against the malaria-bearing anopheles mosquito, but DDT proved toxic to human and animal life and was generally banned. Mosquitoes returned to places from which they had been temporarily eradicated and quinine-based drugs returned as the principal defense and treatment against malaria.

New farm technology. The American Burger tractor, invented in 1889, was the first to install an internal-combustion engine. With the introduction of automated farm machinery huge tracts of land around the world were brought under cultivation and food productivity soared. Here, in 1917, a woman from Vassar College in Poughkeepsie, New York, plows a field as part of the war effort.

Food productivity multiplied. More land was brought under cultivation. New machinery, notably the tractor and combine, facilitated the opening of the American and Canadian Midwest, the Argentinian pampas, the steppe land of Russia, and the economically developing continent of Australia. Between 1950 and 1990 the use of commercial fertilizer increased globally six times. Irrigated cropland around the world tripled, as did world grain production. Agricultural education spread up-to-date scientific information directly to farmers. Plant breeding and genetics produced new, higher-yielding varieties, a breakthrough given special recognition when Barbara McClintock, a botanist and plant breeder who specialized in the genetics of corn, was awarded the Nobel Prize in Physiology or Medicine in 1983, at the age of 83.

By the end of the twentieth century, although some scientists questioned the wisdom of manipulating the basic designs of life, new biotechnology and genetic engineering were creating breakthroughs in kinds and totals of crop production. In 1997 scientists succeeded in cloning a sheep and were experimenting with producing blood in the bodies of animals that could be used for human transfusions. Scientists, clergy, ethicists, and political leaders continue to grapple with the implications of these discoveries (see Focus, opposite).

In the developing nations of the **third world**, beginning in the 1960s, new seeds and fertilizers, engineered in part under the auspices of the philanthropic Rockefeller Foundation, increased the productivity of land under wheat cultivation by up to five times. For his work with "miracle" wheat seeds, Norman Borlaug was awarded the Nobel Prize for Peace in 1970. Experimentation with additional crops, such as rice, led to similar breakthroughs. Land that was already fully populated and under intense cultivation became increasingly productive. For example, although India's population doubled between 1966 and 1991, the "green revolution" enabled the country to achieve self-sufficiency in food during those years.

Distribution and equity, however, presented problems. At first many critics noted the increasing income disparities created by the revolution in productivity. Wealthier farmers could most easily afford the new seeds and the additional fertilizer, pesticides and irrigation water required to cultivate them. The green revolution made the rich richer as it increased productivity. Did it make the poor poorer? This debate raged for many years. At present the World Bank argues, on the basis of a twenty-year survey in South India, that the incomes of the smallest farmers and the landless peasants have increased sharply, as has their intake of calories and protein, as high-yielding, labor intensive cultivation has created more and better jobs for them.

Everywhere new farm machinery reduced the need for labor and rural population ratios dropped sharply—in America from 72 percent in 1900 to 24 percent in 1995; in Europe, quite similarly, from 70 percent to 26 percent; for the world as a whole from 84 percent to 55 percent. Farmers left the countryside in droves to search for urban jobs.

Developments in health and food technology facilitated a population explosion. More people were born and they lived longer. Despite dire predictions of famine, four times as many people live on the earth in the year 2000 than in the year 1900, and a greater percentage of them had access to adequate food. The population *added* between 1980 and the year 2000, 1.5 billion, was almost the total population of the earth in 1900. Life expectancy at birth in the USA rose from fifty-four years in 1920 to seventy-seven years in 1996. In India it increased from thirty years at Independence in 1947 to fifty-four years in 1981 to sixty-two years in 1996. In China it reached sixty-nine years and in Japan eighty.

Demographers, seeking to explain the differential population growth, postulate two successive demographic shifts. First, as health conditions and food supply improved, death rates dropped while birth rates remained high and population increased. This has happened all over the world. Later, as parents saw that the mortality rates had fallen and that their children were likely to survive to adulthood, they chose to plan their family size through the use of contraception. Birth rates then dropped, as death rates had earlier. This second stage, of family planning, has occurred in the wealthier regions of the world, where death rates were lowest. In some of these countries, birth rates have actually dropped below death rates and the overall population of some countries in Europe—Germany in the late twentieth century, France periodically—is actually declining. In poorer countries where death rates are still relatively high, however, the second stage of declining birth rates has not (yet) occurred, and population continues to rise. Demographers suggest that the best way to reduce population growth is to improve health measures to help assure parents that their babies and children will live; then parents will plan fewer of them. Parents will also plan the births during a relatively short, specific time during the mother's life.

FOCUS

Genetic Engineering and the Human Genome Project

In the 1950s biochemists James Watson, Francis Crick, and Maurice Wilkins uncovered the structure of DNA, a very long molecule found in each cell of every living being. DNA is an "information bearer" (Lewontin). Its component chemicals, and the order in which they appear, give the blueprint for each form of life, and of each individual. The discovery has profound practical applications. Biologists and biochemists have learned how to substitute one gene for another, yielding astonishing new hybrids of grains that have multiplied food productivity and animals that are more productive of meat, milk, and even certain chemicals useful in medicine. Genetic engineering in humans promises to cure certain genetically based illnesses like cystic fibrosis, muscular dystrophy, and Huntington's chorea. It carries the promise, and the threat, of creating humans who are taller or shorter, heavier or lighter, blue eyed or brown.

The long-term consequences of genetic engineering are as yet unknown, but they are permanent, transmitted to every subsequent generation of their recipients, so the procedures are the subject of intense scrutiny and debate. In 1990 the United States Government initiated the Human Genome Project to identify all the approximately 100,000 genes in human DNA, and to "map" the sequences of the 3 billion chemical bases that make it up. In June 2000 it announced success as did a private research laboratory. The next task is to understand the functioning of each component. Here, too, private laboratories are also working aggressively on these puzzles for the new technology promises great wealth to its masters, although the costs to consumers are not yet known.

In addition to voluntary programs of family planning within individual families, many nations have undertaken official population policies. Many European countries, like France, in light of declining birth rates, have adopted policies that encourage more births by extending economic support to families with young children. To fill needs for labor they have invited immigrants from poorer countries and created new ethnic mixtures and new political and social issues. Many less wealthy and more crowded countries have promulgated policies to discourage large families. Most drastically, China since the 1980s has attempted to limit families to just one child. Implementation, however, has been difficult. A family wanting a male child, the usual preference, may break the law to have a second child if the first is a female, or may even kill a first-born female. In India, ruthless and thoughtless enforcement of rigid sterilization quotas by the government of Prime Minister Indira Gandhi cost her the 1977 elections. Government family planning programs have been restrained ever since. The powerful state and the individual family have clashed here over values and implementation; policies that may benefit the state and the society may not be seen as beneficial by the individual family.

GENDER RELATIONS

Changes in technology helped inspire profound changes in gender relationships. Films brought Mae West, Greta Garbo, and Marlene Dietrich to audiences around the world. Fashions changed. Flappers in Europe and the United States "abandoned their corsets, bobbed their hair, hiked up their skirts, wore skimpy bathing costumes at the beach, started wearing makeup, and smoked in public" (Rosenberg, p. 64). The title of Beth Bailey's book captured one of the unintended changes engendered by the automobile: *From Front Porch to Back Seat: Courtship in Twentieth Century America*. Margaret Sanger in the USA, Marie Stopes in Britain, and Theodore van de Velde in the Netherlands published marriage manuals emphasizing the enjoyment of sex by both women and men in marriage and, at the same time, advocating

Indian squatter settlement. In the huge cities of the underdeveloped world, shanty towns have sprung up—a makeshift solution to endemic poverty and overcrowding. This squatter settlement in Bombay (population: 11.5 million) might be unsightly, but represents one answer to the acute housing shortage in urban India.

family planning. The father of modern psychiatry, Sigmund Freud, called sex the primal driving force in life, and introduced new ammunition in the battle of the sexes with his claim that women suffered from "penis envy." Another psychoanalyst, Karen Horney, reversed this argument-from-biology: Men suffered feelings of inadequacy because they could not bear children. Anthropology added its insights as Margaret Mead brought back new observations from New Guinea of aggressive women and passive men reversing the conventional stereotype in the West. Mead argued that sex traits were cultural and malleable, not biological and fixed.

Not everyone agreed with the new sexuality or the new gender identities. The differences in values became clearer as World War II put new demands on the labor force. Different combatant countries followed different family policies. The Allies—the United States, Great Britain, and the USSR—encouraged women to join the wartime workforce. The Axis powers—Germany, Italy, and Japan—kept them in the home despite the needs of the war (see

p. 612). In China, the communists encouraged women to join in the struggle directly; the nationalists kept them at home (see p. 686).

After the war, feminism found new voices. Simone de Beauvoir published *The Second Sex* in France in 1949 furthering the argument that while sex is biological, gender, the behavioral traits associated with each sex, is learned. "One is not born, but rather becomes, a woman." In the United States, Betty Friedan's *The Feminine Mystique* (1963) challenged women to ask if their life as homemaker in suburbia was adequately fulfilling, to consider working outside the home, and to push for equal conditions in that work.

In Europe and the United States the new feminism became a powerful, if controversial force. In other parts of the world, the concept of new roles for women outside the home and community was more disputed. Often the very fact that new concepts of gender relations came from the West, from colonial powers, influenced their reception, making them more attractive to some, more suspect to others. We consider these responses below, in each regional analysis.

URBANIZATION AND MIGRATION

The world's growing population moved steadily into cities. We have seen (p. 430) that mechanization of agriculture was one of the factors that pushed people away from the countryside. In addition, jobs in manufacture, bureaucracy, and service industries pulled them to the cities (see Focus, below). At the beginning of the century, urbanization was still linked to industrial growth; by the end of the century, however, the most rapidly growing cities, and, increasingly, the largest of them, were in the poorer, less industrialized areas of the world—for example, Mexico City and São Paulo in Brazil, each with about 16 million in 1995; Mumbai (Bombay) and Calcutta in India; Buenos Aires in Argentina; Seoul in South Korea; Shanghai and Beijing in China; Lagos in Nigeria; and Rio de Janeiro in Brazil, each with between 10 and 15 million people.

In many of the richer countries, however, in a process termed **counterurbanization**, cities turned inside out, and central city populations declined. Poorer citizens remained in the center as the richer availed themselves of the new means of transportation and of communication via phone, fax, and the World Wide Web to relocate to the suburbs. Businesses, too, recognizing a new freedom of movement, left the central cities, partly to reduce their overhead costs. Multinational corporations crossed international boundaries to relocate their factories, removing them from high-wage urban centers in the **first world** to new sites offering cheaper labor in the third.

Following the building of the first aircraft in 1903 by Wilbur and Orville Wright, and the first solo flight across the Atlantic in 1927 by Charles Lindbergh, international and intercontinental flights became commonplace for business and pleasure, and tourism became one of the world's largest

---

FOCUS
Cities and Crowds: Ants and Industry

A poem composed by the Marathi language poet Mardhekar, who comes from Mumbai (Bombay), captures what his translator, A.K. Ramanujan, calls "the vision (or cliché) of the modern city-dweller's city, the city as nightmare, its crowds, its faceless anomie, its clock-bound materialism":

I am an ant,
He is an ant, you are an ant, she is an ant,
A handful are foreign, a handful native;
A thousand have crowded, a million, a billion,
Trillions and trillions of ants;
Innumerable uncountable all have crowded here,
Many from the anthills, many others fugitive!
Some are fat and black, some red, some white;
Some are the winged ants of the monsoon,
Some are the big bold ones of summer,
Some are careful and walk in a file;
Some are silly and eat sugar wherever they find it;
Some stick and sting;
Some live feeding honey to others;

And some fertilize the Queen,
Smart enough to please!
Who will usurp
All these ants
One by one
To become King?
Who will carry
The summa of matter
To the spiritual realm?
—Ants, ants, cheaper by the dozen, ants for sale ...
This flood of ants comes, open the gates!
The suburban train
Of ten past ten
Has arrived emptying its sigh ...

Ramanujan notes a modern transformation in this image of the city and its population squeeze: "Premodern ants were extolled for their industry, not denigrated." And as we saw in Chapter 4, pre-industrial cities had been proclaimed as centers of religious and cultural life (p. 92).

---

industries. The World Tourism Organization reported total global receipts from international travelers at $445 billion in 1998. In the same year 46 million people visited the USA, spending $74 billion. Students, in particular, traveled around the globe for formal and informal study and work opportunities.

In contrast, many others traveled out of economic necessity and fear of repression—often on foot. Millions of political refugees from Vietnam, Afghanistan, Tibet, Iraq, the former USSR, Central America, Mozambique, Ethiopia, and numerous other African states sought refuge and asylum in neighboring countries. "Guest workers," also by the millions, traveled in search of jobs from southern Europe, North Africa, and Turkey to northern Europe; from the entire world to the oil-rich Persian Gulf areas; and, often illegally, from Asia and Latin America to the United States.

DOMESTIC CHANGE

Twentieth-century technology transformed the quality of daily life as well as its location and density. Within the home, washing machines, vacuum cleaners, dishwashers, refrigerators, and sewing machines relieved some of the tedium and labor of housework. The automobile, bus, truck, train, airplane, and jet affected transportation for almost all citizens of the world. The revolution in the means of communication—telegraph, telephone, copier, fax machine, modem, internet, radio, phonograph, various kinds of sound reproduction, photography, motion pictures, television, satellite transmission, and cable—opened visions of the whole world to potentially all its citizens.

These new technologies totally transformed work and play as well as the distribution of these activities in geographical space. Air-conditioning not only changed standards of comfort, but opened many warmer areas of the world (including the southern United States) to increased immigration and development.

First developed after World War II, early computers were huge machines, designed to solve mathematical problems. At the end of the century, they were found in homes and offices worldwide and were small enough to be easily portable. The computer not only affected each one of the above revolutions in transportation and communication, but also transformed data processing, office work, and the further development of large-scale organizations, science, and commerce. With the advent and spread of the World Wide Web in the 1990s participants worked, shopped, and communicated electronically with friends and family from within their homes.

Civil aviation. A steward serves passengers on board a KLM Fokker F18 in 1932. In the 1920s, the popularity of aerial circuses and flying clubs, run by former World War I pilots, combined with rapid improvements in technology, heralded a new age of civil aviation. By the 1930s a worldwide network of commercial routes had developed. In these early years the high cost of air travel created an aura of glamor and exclusivity.

New technological systems such as the automated assembly line production of Henry Ford's automobile factories, the more recent introduction of robotics, and the management techniques of Frederick Taylor changed the nature of work and the efficiency of production. Scientific research facilities were established by private industry, like Bell Laboratories, by philanthropic corporations, like the Rockefeller and Ford Foundations, and, most of all, by national governments all over the world. They changed the concept and mode of creativity. No longer needing to rely on experienced, gifted artisans tinkering in small shops, twentieth-century technology systematized invention and promoted an increasing demand for ever more sophisticated and expensive research facilities.

Synthetic fabrics and dyes changed wardrobes. Plastics were the most important new, man-made material of the twentieth century, replacing metals, rubber, and glass in many uses. They also increased the world's reliance on petroleum, a non-renewable fossil fuel, from which plastics are synthesized.

ENERGY

Twentieth-century technology demanded ever-increasing supplies of inanimate energy. Among its most central symbols were the electric power gen-erator, the internal-combustion engine, the hydro-electric dam, the oil well, and the nuclear reactor. Gaining access to energy resources was a key issue for all countries. Some were richly endowed and began with a large advantage. Others, such as Japan, possessed few energy resources and had to seize or buy them, or tap the natural energy of sun, wind, and water, or generate new forms of energy by unlocking the atom. Many countries of Western Europe were seriously dependent on oil, although they had other energy resources, especially coal, and introduced new forms of more accessible energy. The United States, despite vast natural resources, relied on large energy imports to build and support its economy.

Some countries, especially those in the Middle East, had fossil fuel energy resources (oil) far beyond their current needs. Because of the need for oil, the five countries in the world with the largest known crude oil reserves—Saudi Arabia, Iraq, the United Arab Emirates, Kuwait, and Iran—were all been subject to greater or lesser degrees of foreign competition for control and colonization. They were at the center of international power struggles for control of that oil wealth. Since 1973, they have banded together with other oil-rich member states of the Organization of Petroleum Exporting Countries (OPEC) to gain better econom-

Before the silicon chip. Immediately after World War II, when the first practical computers were constructed, advances in information theory and the invention of the transistor gave birth to such hulking monsters as ENIAC, developed at the University of Pennsylvania in 1946. It weighed 50 tons and occupied 2000 square feet of floor space.

ic terms and more political power in exchange for their oil, restructuring the terms of world trade and power in the process. The **geo-politics** of oil supply and demand were crucial issues in twentieth-century history (see p. 726).

Atomic power was first developed for military uses, but it also provided significant amounts of the world's commercial energy supply. Despite the ecological problems of safety and nuclear waste disposal, the meltdown of the Soviet nuclear reactor in Chernobyl, Ukraine, in 1986, and the near meltdown in 1979 of the American reactor at Three Mile Island in Pennsylvania, many countries continue to expand their nuclear generating capacities. In France, for example, nuclear power supplies 75 percent of electricity production.

The hunger for energy drove technological development and vice versa. The increasingly sophisticated technology generated increasing demands for investment capital and skilled personnel. These demands forced increased educational requirements on labor forces everywhere. Sometimes they led to tensions and even violent competition among nations. The desire to be competitive technologically sometimes fostered warfare; and much modern technology, in turn, was devoted to the design and production of arms.

NATIONAL IDENTITY AND WORLD WAR

The twentieth century began with the promise of ever more astonishing and beneficial advances in technology. But technology follows human direction, and other motives intruded, undermining the promise of peace and prosperity, and yielding instead two world wars separated by a world-wide depression and followed by a "cold war." For much of the century, many of the best efforts of technology were redirected from butter to guns, from the production of civilian, consumer goods to the production of weapons and war materiel.

Competition among nations over technological advances, productivity, and markets helped to instigate both world wars. From the late eighteenth century, Britain's technological supremacy was unchallenged, and, from her position of industrial and military strength, she imposed a Pax Britannica, which kept the world safe from major war for more than half a century. By 1900 the United States had overtaken Britain, but distance

and American isolationism muted the competition. As Germany also surpassed Britain in technological capacity, however, competition for industrial markets and prestige brought increasing tension (see pp. 537–41).

This economic competition was embedded in still larger issues of nationalism, a powerful force in early twentieth-century Europe (see Chapter 17). People's reverence for their nation-states, and for their shared language, history, ethnicity, and aspirations within those states, had grown so passionate that they were willing to fight and die for them. Cynics argued that the masses of the population were being manipulated to the battle-front by industrialists in each country who stood to profit from war production, but the national feelings were powerful in themselves. Indeed they seemed just as strong among smaller, newer states with little economic base in military production.

Even the most powerful nations believed that they could strengthen their security by forming defensive alliances. In the late nineteenth century these countries created a system of alliances that led in the early years of the twentieth century to a Europe divided into two potentially hostile camps—the Triple Alliance of Germany, Austria-Hungary, and Italy; and the Triple Entente of France, Russia, and Britain.

WORLD WAR I 1914–18

World War I (called the Great War until World War II surpassed it in magnitude) began on June 28, 1914 when a Serbian nationalist, eager to gain from the Austro-Hungarian empire certain territories with heavily Serbian populations, assassinated Archduke Francis Ferdinand, heir to the Austro-Hungarian throne. A month later, Austria-Hungary declared war on Serbia, triggering a domino effect among other European powers, Japan, and the Ottoman Empire. Under the system of alliances built up over the preceding three decades, countries now came to the aid of one another. Russia mobilized its armies to defend Serbia. Germany declared war on Russia and France, and invaded Belgium. Britain declared war on Germany as did Britain's ally Japan.

In November, the Ottoman Empire joined Germany and the Austro-Hungarian Empire in an alliance called the Central Powers. On the other side the British, French, and Russians, joined by the Italians in 1915, formed an alliance called the Allied Powers (Allies). The Central Powers won early vic-

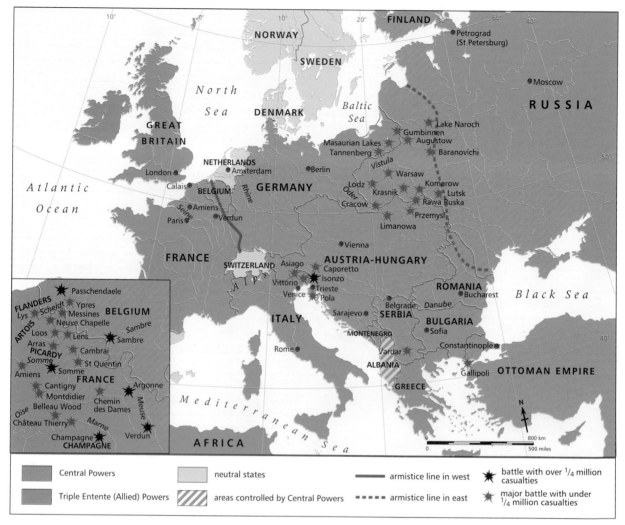

World War I European rivalries for political and economic superiority, within Europe and throughout its imperial holdings, erupted in 1914. A fragile system of alliances designed to contain the ambitions of Germany and Austria-Hungary (the Central Powers) collapsed, resulting in a conflict of horrific proportions. Turkey joined the Central Powers. In France and Belgium a stalemate war of attrition developed. In the east a war of thrust and counter-thrust caused enormous popular dissent and exhaustion, eventually bringing the collapse of the Turkish, Russian, and Austrian empires alike. In all, 20 million people died.

tories in Belgium and Poland but in September the German advance was stopped by the Allies at the first Battle of the Marne. Along the western front the opposing armies then continued to fight in two facing trench systems that stretched 500 miles (805 km) from the English Channel to the border of Switzerland. On the eastern front Russian armies lost over a million men in combat against the combined German and Austrian forces.

The United States remained neutral until 1917, selling weapons and material to both sides. Then, with Russia in collapse, Germany turned its attention to the western front. To choke off American supplies to the British and French, Germany began intensive submarine warfare against American shipping. Germany gambled that the Allies would collapse before the United States responded—and lost. After German submarines began sinking unarmed passenger ships, the United States declared war in April 1917. Once the United States began providing its abundant supplies and fresh troops, the Allies moved toward victory. The fighting finally ended with an armistice on November 11, 1918.

The war introduced new weapons. The machine gun, first used extensively in this war, and the tank, invented in 1914, helped define the nature of World War I. Hundreds of thousands of soldiers dug into trenches on each side, faced each other with very little movement for months at a time and then

charged in human waves. Tens and even hundreds of thousands were slaughtered by machine guns. Erich Maria Remarque captured the horrors of this trench warfare in his novel *All Quiet on the Western Front*. In addition, Germany introduced poison gas in World War I, leading to subsequent international bans against its use (although many nations still continue to store poison gas in their armories).

Submarine warfare and aerial bombardment, initiated at the end of World War I, also marked the military campaigns. None of the combatants had expected a war like this, so long and so deadly. By its end a total of 20 million soldiers and civilians had been killed.

The victory of the Allies over the Central Powers seemed to promise lasting peace in a new world order in which colonialism would give way to the independence of all nation-al groups. The American President Woodrow Wilson declared that the goal of the Allies was to "make the world safe for democracy." The voices of all peoples should be heard. Allied war aims, as expressed by Wilson in his "Fourteen Points," called for:

A free, open-minded, and absolutely impartial adjustment of all colonial claims, based upon a strict observance of the principle that in determining all such questions of sovereignty the interests of the population concerned must have equal weight with the equitable claims of the Government whose title is to be determined. (cited in Hofstadter, pp. 224–5)

Life in the trenches. World War I became notorious for its trench warfare, in which combatants dug themselves into positions but made few territorial gains. The horrifying drudgery, the cold, the wet, the shelling, the machine gun fire, the nervous tension, the smell of corpses and mustard gas lasted for years. By 1918, the end of the conflict, around 8.5 million soldiers had lost their lives.

The Paris Peace Settlement of 1919

The peace conference convened in Paris in 1919 amidst great hope. In the redrawing of national borders and the settling of financial accounts, each major power sought its own benefit. Representatives of colonies and of sub-national ethnic groups, encouraged by Wilson's doctrine of self-determination of nationalities, sought recognition and some measure of independence and sovereignty. Among the combatants who participated, Japan sought to maintain control over the East Asian possessions of Germany that it had captured during the war. Prince Faisal represented Arabs who had contributed to victory over the Ottoman Empire and now sought the creation of new, independent states. W.E.B. DuBois, an African-American scholar and activist, called for racial justice on behalf of the Pan-African Congress, a group of fifty-eight delegates from Africa and the African diaspora who convened in Paris. In the end, the American, British, and French delegations were most critical to the post-war negotiations.

Two empires, the Austro-Hungarian and the Ottoman, were dissolved. Austria-Hungary was reduced and divided into two separate states. From its former territories Czechoslovakia and Yugoslavia were created. The Ottoman Empire disappeared; its core region in Anatolia and the city of Istanbul became the new nation of Turkey. From the remainder, Romania and Greece were expanded; Syria and Lebanon were created as new proto-nations, temporarily **mandated** to France for tutelage until they were considered ready for independence; Palestine and Iraq were similarly created and mandated to Britain. During the war the Russian Empire had also collapsed, its government replaced by a communist revolution. From the former empire, the new states of Poland, Finland, Estonia, Latvia, and Lithuania were created. The negotiators hoped the new borders would protect hostile ethnic groups from each other and from external domination. Legal safeguards for minorities were also enacted in new state constitutions.

Germany lost Alsace-Lorraine to France, large areas in the east to Poland, and small areas to Lithuania, Belgium, and Denmark. Germany was ordered to pay heavy **reparations**, although in practice not much was paid. Most gallingly for Germany, it was forced to accept total responsibility for causing the loss and damage of the war. Germany signed the Treaty of Versailles concluding the war, and left humiliated, resentful, but, despite the loss of lands and the financial reparations, potentially still powerful.

FOCUS
War Experiences Subvert Colonialism

Colonial powers employed their colonial armies in fighting both World Wars, transporting them from one battle front to another. Military service overseas often transformed the soldiers, making them skeptical of the advantages of European civilization. Some European soldiers came to realize that at least some of the people they colonized did not respect them but rather feared and hated them. A young journalist from India, serving briefly as a World War I correspondent in Iraq, wrote of his growing realization of the resentment Arabs felt for British colonization. He saw Arab women in particular transmitting their resentment by asserting their religious and cultural conventions. He began to understand more fully the opposition to colonialism that both peoples shared:

We understood … that in the entire region Arabs regarded the English as their enemies. Bitter antagonism dripped from their eyes. They moved about like lost undertakers, joking among themselves but stopping the moment they saw the British. They talked with the foreigners mechanically, speaking only when it was completely unavoidable. They took their few cents in pay, and otherwise behaved like defeated and dependent enemies. Their dignified women hid themselves in burkhas, which covered them from head to foot. The white soldiers must have sensed their independent temper, however, and therefore their military superiors issued strict orders not to talk with the local women. (Yagnik, p. 262, translated from the Gujarati by Devavrat Pathak and Howard Spodek.)

The League of Nations was created by the European powers as part of the Paris Peace Settlement in the hope of eliminating warfare and fostering international cooperation. But disillusionment soon followed. The League was crippled by three congenital defects. First, its principal sponsor, the United States, refused to join because of Congressional opposition. The world's most powerful technological, industrial, financial, and military power, the United States withdrew back into the isolation of its ocean defenses.

Second, the League did nothing about colonialism in Asia and Africa. In fact, the treaties of 1919 enlarged colonial rule through the grant of mandatory powers to Britain and France over Middle Eastern lands conquered from the Ottoman Empire and to Japan over parts of China previously held by Germany. In India, the British fell short on their wartime promise to expand self-rule; on the contrary it restricted freedoms of the press and assembly. The League effectively died when it failed to counter Japan's invasion of China, Italy's invasion of Ethiopia, Germany's re-armament, and the outbreak of the Spanish Civil War. The war in Spain, from 1936 to 1939, saw right-wing insurgent forces led by General Francisco Franco (1892–1975) overthrow the leftist constitutional government. Germany and Italy sent tens of thousands of troops in support of Franco; the USSR sent military equipment, technicians, and advisers in support of the government; the liberal democracies refused to intervene and sent no assistance, although thousands of volunteers, the International Brigade immortalized in Ernest Hemingway's *For Whom the Bell Tolls*, came to fight for the government. Many analysts saw this confrontation as a dress rehearsal for World War II. Franco's victory turned Spain into a dictatorship that lasted until he died.

Third, the League failed to resolve the complex issues of national identities. In accord with the principle of national self-determination, ten new states were born, or reborn, as a result of the Paris Peace accords, and fourteen states were specifically charged with protecting racial, religious, and linguistic minorities within their borders, assuring those minorities of equal rights with all citizens, including the right to primary school instruction in their mother tongue. In central Europe, however, nationality groups were widely dispersed, and many minorities continued to feel aggrieved. German minorities in Czechoslovakia, for example, protested their treatment, and Germany annexed the German-speaking areas of Czechoslovakia in 1938. Britain and France chose a policy of appeasement rather than confronting Germany and possibly going to war. The League was not able to resolve conflicting claims peacefully, and it commanded no armed forces of its own. Armed nationalism had triumphed over unarmed internationalism.

BETWEEN THE WARS, 1920–39: ECONOMIC DEPRESSION AND THE EXPANSION OF THE WELFARE STATE

Worldwide economic **depression** further destabilized domestic and international politics. Depression is a severe economic downturn in production and consumption that continues over a significant period of time, at least several months. Depression was considered normal in a free-market economy as the forces of supply and demand periodically fell out of step and then came back into line. But the Great Depression was far more extreme in its extent and duration. On October 29, 1929—"Black Tuesday"—the New York stock exchange crashed, ending five years of relative prosperity and marking the beginning of a worldwide economic depression which would continue until the outbreak of World War II in 1939.

The United States had emerged from World War I as a creditor nation. To pay the reparations from the war, Germany depended on loans from several nations, especially the United States. With the crash of the stock market, however, American financiers called in these loans, undercutting the European economy. In addition, farmers who had produced at record levels during the war had difficulty cutting back production, resulting in huge, unsold surpluses and a depression in agriculture. Faced with such economic difficulty, each country, and especially the United States, closed its borders to imports, so that it could sell its own products internally without competition. But as each country raised its barriers, international markets contracted, increasing the depression.

Mass unemployment swept Britain, America, and Germany. Latin American countries, notably Argentina, which had been approaching a European living standard, found their economies devastated, turned away from European markets, and sought to salvage what they could through domestic development (see pp. 787–8).

Communist Russia, standing somewhat apart from the world economy, had introduced central-

ized national planning in 1928, emphasizing heavy industrialization. Its factories flourished, but agriculture was devastated and levels of private consumption plummeted (see p. 647).

In 1921 there were 2 million unemployed in Britain. They collected unemployment insurance in accord with an act that had been passed a decade earlier. The government also implemented an old age pension system, medical aids, and subsidized housing. But the world depression increased this unemployment to almost 3 million. Unemployment payments multiplied, while tax collections dropped. The welfare state expanded and government remained stable, but the Depression ground on.

America, the country most dedicated to private enterprise and "rugged individualism," and therefore most reluctant to expand government social welfare programs, saw national income drop by half between 1929 and 1932. Almost 14 million people were unemployed. Elected in 1932, in the midst of national despair, Democratic President

Franklin Delano Roosevelt rallied the nation with charismatic optimism. Declaring that "The only thing we have to fear is fear itself," he instituted social welfare programs as a means of preserving the capitalist foundation. He provided financial relief for the unemployed, public works projects to create construction jobs, subsidies to farmers to reduce production and eliminate surpluses, and federal support for low-cost housing and slum clearance. A Civilian Conservation Corps was established, ostensibly to promote conservation and reforestation, but mostly to provide some 3 million jobs to youth. The Tennessee Valley Authority created an immense hydroelectric program, combining flood control with rural electrification and regional economic development.

Roosevelt increased the regulation of business and promoted unions. The Securities and Exchange Commission, created in 1929, regulated the stock exchange. The National Recovery Administration encouraged regulation of prices and production

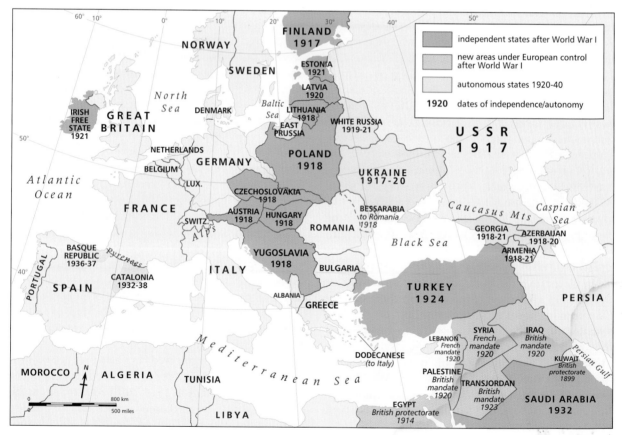

The new post-war nations In the wake of World War I, old empires fell and new states and colonies (euphemistically called mandates and protectorates) were created. The Austro-Hungarian and Ottoman Empires were eradicated. A belt of nation-states was established throughout Central and Eastern Europe; some had brief lives and were soon annexed by Russia. The core of the Ottoman Empire became Turkey, while other segments were mandated to Britain and France as quasi-colonies.

until it was judged unconstitutional in 1935. The Social Security Act of 1935 introduced unemployment, old age, and disability insurance—policies already in place in parts of Western Europe well before World War I. Child labor was abolished. Forty hours of work was set as the weekly norm. Minimum hourly wages were fixed. Union organization was encouraged and union membership grew from 4 million in 1929 to 9 million in 1940. The most capitalist of the major powers thus accepted the welfare state. Throughout the century, the scope of welfare expanded and contracted with different governments, philosophies of government, and budgetary conditions, but the principle that the state had a major role in protecting and advancing the welfare of its people persisted.

In Germany, the world depression followed on the heels of catastrophic inflation. In the 1920s the Government induced hyperinflation to pay the resented war reparations thus wiping out the savings of the middle classes and amplifying resentment over the punitive Versailles Treaty, including its emphasis on German war guilt and insistence on Germany's disarmament. By 1924 industrial production had recovered but then the Depression wiped out the gains. The new government, called the Weimar Republic, was perceived by many as a weak and precarious experiment in constitutional democracy in a nation accustomed to a military monarchy. Exciting new movements in art and architecture that were responsive to new technological potential for creativity, notably the Bauhaus school of architecture, were threatened and ultimately driven out of the country. Anti-democratic forces and political ideologies, backed by thugs on the streets, triumphed over aesthetic and cultural creativity.

WORLD WAR II 1939–45

The strains of the 1930s ultimately triggered World War II. Germany, Italy, and Japan all sought to alleviate the suffering of the Depression by building up armaments and seeking new conquests. In Germany, Adolf Hitler (1889–1945) led a new party, the National Socialists, or Nazis. The party used violence to intimidate the opposition, but finally came to power legally in 1933 on a platform of extreme nationalism, construction of public works, expansionism, and virulent anti-Semitism, all of which Hitler had spelled out in his manifesto, *Mein Kampf,* ("My Struggle," 1925). Some business and military leaders supported him as a counter-weight to communism. As leader of the largest party in the German parliament in 1933, with 38 percent of the popular vote, Hitler became Chancellor. He quickly suppressed all other parties, revoked the citizenship of Jews, and rearmed Germany. He intensified each of these programs over the next few years and in 1936 he moved troops into the Rhineland (the region of Germany west of the Rhine River) in

WORLD WAR II—KEY EVENTS

1935–36	Italy conquers Ethiopia
1936–39	Spanish Civil War
July 7, 1937	Japanese troops invade China
September 1938	Appeasement in Munich; Germany annexes Sudetenland
September 1939	Nazi-Soviet Pact: Germany invades Poland; Britain and France declare war; Poland partitioned between Germany and Russia
Mar–Apr 1940	*Blitzkrieg*: German forces conquer Denmark and Norway
May–June	Italy declares war on Britain and France; German forces conquer France, the Netherlands, and Belgium
June 1940– June 1941	Battle of Britain; Britain holds firm against German bombing attacks
June 21, 1941	German forces invade USSR
Dec 7	Japanese bomb US Navy, Pearl Harbor
Jan-Mar 1942	Indonesia, Malaya, Burma and the Philippines are conquered by Japan
June	US Navy defeats Japanese at the Battle of Midway
1942–43	End of Axis resistance in North Africa; Soviet victory in Battle of Stalingrad
1943–44	Red Army slowly pushes Wehrmacht back to Germany
June 6, 1944	Allies land in Normandy (D-Day)
Feb 1945	Yalta conference: Churchill, Roosevelt, and Stalin discuss post-war settlement
March 1945	US planes bomb Tokyo
May 7	Germany surrenders
August 6, 9	US drops atom bomb on Hiroshima, and then on Nagasaki
August 14	Japan surrenders

violation of the Versailles Treaty. In 1938 Hitler annexed Austria and the German-speaking areas of Czechoslovakia. On September 1, 1939 he invaded Poland, and finally met resistance from the great powers who until this time had appeased his aggressions. Britain and France declared war.

In Italy, Benito Mussolini (1883–1945) had become prime minister in 1921 as leader of a party of 300,000 members who threatened to march on Rome if he were not appointed. His party was called **fascist**, meaning that it represented extreme nationalism, the power of the state over the individual, the supremacy of the leader over the party and nation, and a willingness to use intimidation and violence to achieve its goal. Mussolini asserted:

> War alone brings up to its highest tension all human energy and puts the stamp of nobility upon the peoples who have the courage to meet it. … Thus a doctrine which is founded upon this harmful postulate of peace is hostile to Fascism … all the international leagues and societies … as history will show, can be scattered to the winds when once strong national feeling is aroused by any motive. (Columbia College, p. 1151)

In 1935, preceding Hitler's moves, Mussolini conquered Ethiopia while other nations responded feebly even though Ethiopia belonged to the League of Nations. Mussolini did not share Hitler's anti-Semitism, but in other respects he was an appropriate partner in Hitler's aggressive plans. When civil war broke out in Spain in 1936, both Hitler and Mussolini sent assistance to the right-wing Nationalists. At this point their two nations formed an alliance called the Axis.

In East Asia, as we shall see in the next chapter, Japan also moved aggressively against its neighbor, China. Following the successes of the Meiji Restoration (see p. 583), Japan had become the strongest military power in East Asia, and had cultivated political philosophies to justify invading and taking over neighboring countries. Like Germany, it too had a rapidly rising population, reaching 62 million by 1928, and felt confined. Japan was technologically more sophisticated than its neighbors but it needed to import most of its raw materials. In 1931, Japanese military forces seized Manchuria. The Japanese government had forbidden this action, but acquiesced after the fact. The League of Nations condemned the invasion but imposed no real sanctions, and the condemnation moved Japan to ally with Germany and Italy. In

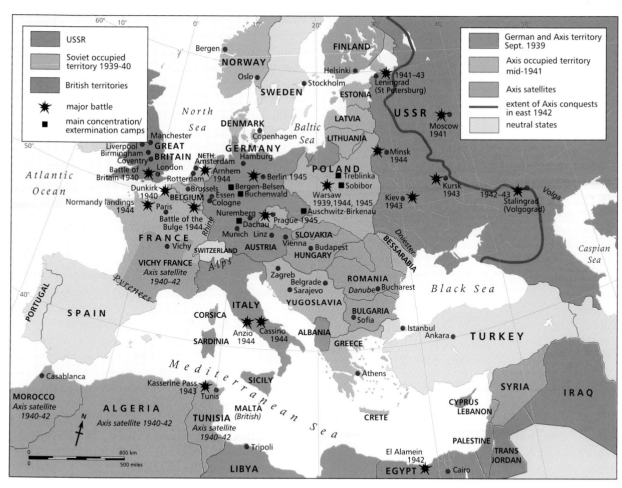

World War II in Europe Fighting began in 1939 with a "blitzkrieg," or lightning war, by Germany and her Italian ally. By late 1942 they controlled most of Europe. But Germany's invasion of Russia in 1941 brought the power of that huge state into opposition and enmeshed Germany into exhausting land war. Britain held out defensively and then began to fight back, especially after the United States entered the war, bringing in air power and material support. By early 1944, the tide had turned.

1937 Japan invaded China, and the Pacific War, as the Japanese call World War II, had begun. Japan became a member of the Axis powers from December 1941.

CONNECTION: *The Pacific War, 1930–45, pp. 663–6*

Until Germany's invasion of Poland the democratic nations which had been victorious in World War I had observed all these separate aggressions and done little. The League of Nations had all but collapsed in the wake of Italy's invasion of Ethiopia. Britain and France had acquiesced in Germany's earlier moves. America had retreated to isolation. These nations had not caused World War II, but by their inaction they had done nothing to prevent it.

After their declaration of war, France and Britain took no immediate military action against Germany and a brief period of "phony war" followed during the winter of 1939-40. In April 1940 Hitler again went on the offensive and Germany invaded Denmark and Norway. On May 10 it invaded Belgium and advanced into France. British forces were evacuated from Dunkirk, France at the end of May and on June 22 the French signed an armistice with Germany. Germany now turned its attention to Britain and heavy bombing of London and other strategic cities in England took place throughout the autumn. Despite heavy losses, including 20,000 dead in London alone, the British held firm, thanks to the Royal Air Force, the invention of radar, and success in cracking German secret codes. Germany abandoned the "Battle of Britain" and turned its forces eastward against Russia. By 1942 Germany

and its allies had conquered most of western and central Europe, almost half of European Russia and much of North Africa.

As the war progressed the alliance of Britain, the Free French (an exile government based in London), the Soviet Union, and some twenty allied countries slowly evolved. With the Japanese bombing of the American naval base in Pearl Harbor in December 1941, America entered the war sending combat forces to both Europe and the Pacific. (The war in the Pacific is discussed below, pp. 663–6.) By the end of 1942 the Allied counter offensive began. Under General Eisenhower, allied forces invaded Algeria and Morocco and pushed eastward. By the spring of 1943 they were met by British forces moving westward from Egypt under General Montgomery and north Africa was recaptured. In the winter of 1942–3, the Russians held out against German troops at the battle of Stalingrad, in which hundreds of thousands died on both sides. General Zhukor led the Russian counter-attack and then began pushing the Germans westward. In 1943 Mussolini's government fell and Italy joined the Allies. D-Day, June 6, 1944, brought the largest military operation in history as Allied forces invaded Normandy and began the push eastward. On the first day, 130,000 men landed, 1 million within a month. The war in Europe finally ended on May 7, 1945 with Germany's surrender. In the Pacific the United States dropped an atomic bomb on the city of Hiroshima, Japan, on August 6 and three days later another atomic bomb on the city of Nagasaki (see p. 666). On August 14 Japan surrendered and the Pacific War was also over.

World War II is called a "total war" because it involved the entire populations and economies of the nations that fought it. The distinction between military and civilian disappeared. Non-combatants were bombed and killed on both sides. It is estimated that about 45 million people died—30 million of them civilians. The heaviest fighting was in the Soviet Union, which lost more people than any other country—about 20 million. Japan lost about 2 million people and Germany just over 4 million. Britain and the United States each lost about 400,000. Six million Jews died in Nazi concentration camps.

Technology in the War

World War II witnessed a dramatic increase in the use of technology—tanks, submarines, and aircraft—as well as the number of troops.

The mobilization of so many personnel and so much equipment opened new visions of life. People who served overseas and who saw for the first time new modes of life, as well as death, were changed in the process. Women's lives were deeply affected.

Nazi Party rally. Over 750,000 Nazi Party workers, soldiers, and civilians greeted Adolf Hitler at the 1934 Nuremberg conference. Against the backdrop of a giant swastika, the German chancellor proclaimed that the Third Reich would last for the next thousand years. Ironically, the trial of Nazi war criminals by the victorious Allied powers would take place in the same city eleven years later.

"Rosie the Riveter," symbol of World War II American women workers, on a poster from the War Production Coordinating Committee.

Horrors of the War

Two horrors distinguished World War II from all others that came before. Massive warfare had been known before. So too had leaders bent on conquest, from Alexander and Genghis Khan to Napoleon. But the decision by the Nazis to obliterate an entire people—the Jews—from the world, without any ostensible economic or territorial goal, and mobilizing the full resources of the state against an unarmed opponent to carry out the task, constituted a new goal, executed by new technology.

Anti-Semitism was not new in Europe, but the Nazi program was unprecedented. First, it reversed the trend of acceptance and civic equality for Jews advanced a century and a half earlier by the French Revolution. Second, it targeted Jews as an ethnic or racial group rather than as a religious community. This was not a policy for conversion or even for exile. Anyone with a Jewish grandparent was considered Jewish under Nazi laws and marked for death.

Although born of an Austrian father and raised in Vienna, Adolf Hitler, the leader of Germany, declared the "Aryan" Germans at the top and the Jews at the bottom of a racial hierarchy that included the British and other northern Europeans near the top, Poles and other Slavs in the middle, and Africans and other peoples of color near the bottom.

Intending to exterminate these "lesser peoples," he built concentration camps where prisoners were used as slave labor before being gassed and cremated. Millions of Jews were brought to the camps by a railway network specially constructed for this purpose. Even in the closing days of the war, when Germany clearly had been defeated, Hitler ordered the trains and the crematoria to continue operations. By 1945, some 6 million Jews accompanied by millions from other "inferior" races, especially gypsies and Poles, joined also by homosexuals and handicapped people, had been murdered. The Holocaust, as this butchery was named, made World War II into a conflict of good versus evil even in the eyes of many Germans after the war. The moral crisis and the appalling devastation of the Holocaust are impossible to fully comprehend, but

The demands of keeping factories running full blast during the war while putting millions of soldiers onto the battlefields required a larger labor force. During World War I millions of women began to work outside the home for pay, and the stereotypes of "men's work" and "women's work" began to erode. This experience contributed to the achievement of women's suffrage in the United States and in Western Europe. After World War I the majority of women did not remain in the workforce, but after World War II women continued in unprecedented numbers to work in industrial and unconventional jobs. The mobilization of women was, however, culturally specific: German and Japanese women were encouraged to continue to stay at home, despite the exigencies of war; women served actively in Russian factories; Britain conscripted some women in World War II.

the writing of survivors such as Elie Wiesel (see p. 617) helps us to understand them. (See also the importance of the Holocaust experience in the founding of the State of Israel on p. 736–7.)

The atomic bombs dropped by America on Hiroshima and Nagasaki, Japan, introduced a new weapon ultimately capable of destroying all life on earth, changing both the nature of war and peace as well as humanity's conception of itself. At the first test of the bomb, as the fireball rose over the testing grounds at Alamogordo, New Mexico, J. Robert Oppenheimer, architect of the bomb and director of the $2 billion Manhattan Project that produced it, quoted from the Hindu *Bhagavad Gita*: "I am become as death, the destroyer of worlds." Of the 245,000 people living in Hiroshima on August 6, 75,000 died that day, perhaps another 100,000 thereafter, while still others suffered radiation poisoning, cancer, and genetic deformation. Three days later, a second bomb was dropped on Nagasaki, and on August 14 Japan submitted its unconditional surrender. Today, despite years of continuing efforts toward arms control, there are tens of thousands of nuclear bombs and warheads on missiles, submarines, and airplanes capable of destroying human life many times over.

In retrospect, debate has raged over the wisdom and purpose of using the atomic bomb to end the war in the Pacific. Critics see the act as racist, pointing out that this weapon was not used in Europe (although the bomb had not yet been prepared at the time Germany surrendered in May 1945). Cynics suggest that its real purpose had less to do with defeating Japan than with demonstrating American power to Russia on the eve of the Cold War (see p. 622). Those who justify the use of the bomb suggest that losses of life on both sides would have been higher had the Allies invaded Japan's home islands. The use of the bomb certainly saved Allied lives, and may even have saved Japanese lives. The casualties in the battles for Pacific islands had been in the hundreds of thousands, and war in Japan itself might have cost a million Allied troops and even more Japanese. Finally, they argue, in a

The liberation of Belsen. Shocked British soldiers liberating Belsen concentration camp in 1945 found 40,000 Jews and other victims of the Holocaust dying of starvation, typhus, and tuberculosis. Many prisoners had been used for medical experiments. Framed by an open grave, a Dr Klein is shown speaking to Movietone News. His experiments included injecting benzine into his victims to harden their arteries. He was responsible for thousands of deaths.

war of such scope and brutality, combatants inevitably use the weapons that are available.

Some of the war technology, however, had by-products of use to civilians. Radar, which Britain developed to protect its island kingdom from Germany in the Battle of Britain, 1940, was valuable in commercial aviation. Nuclear energy could be employed under careful supervision for peaceful uses in power generation and medicine. Drugs, such as sulfa and penicillin, entered the civilian pharmacopeia. But the technology of warfare drew the lion's share of the scientific and technological budgets of many nations, including the largest industrial powers, the USA and USSR, and of many developing countries, as well.

THE IMAGE OF HUMANITY

Until the eve of World War I, the Western idea of human progress through rationalism, science, and technological progress had been widely accepted. There had been no war between the great European powers since the 1871 conflict between France and Germany, and even that had been relatively small and contained (although 250,000 people died). Democracy seemed both progressive and in the ascendant. Life expectancy and quality seemed to be improving steadily.

The colonial dominance of Europe over ancient Asian and African civilizations had the effect of reaffirming Europeans' belief in the supremacy of their technology and political systems. Students from all over the world were coming to Europe's universities to study Western sciences and arts. If machines were "the measure of man," European civilization measured best of all, and was gaining ground.

Some contrary voices, however, were already breaking through the self-congratulation. Mohandas Gandhi (1869–1948) of India, writing in 1906 in *Hind Swaraj or Indian Home Rule*, caricatured and re-evaluated Western accomplishments from a different perspective.

> Formerly when people wanted to fight with one another, they measured between them their bodily strength; now it is possible to take away thousands

A-bomb devastation. On August 6, 1945, the "Enola Gay" Super-Fortress aircraft released the first atom bomb ever used in warfare over Hiroshima, an important Japanese military base and seaport. Over 130,000 people were killed or injured and the city was largely flattened. The USA took the action—and again, three days later at Nagasaki—in a (successful) bid to end the Pacific War.

SOURCE
How Should We Live?

The Polish poet Wislawa Szymborska, winner of the Nobel Prize for Literature in 1996, reflects upon the disillusionment of the twentieth century and assumes that life should and must go on nevertheless. "How should we live?" she asks at the close of one of her most poignant poems, written in the 1970s. In this poem, however, she offers no answers:

> Our twentieth century was going to improve on
> the others.
> It will never prove it now,
> now that its years are numbered,
> its gait is shaky,
> its breath is short.
>
> Too many things have happened
> that weren't supposed to happen,
> and what was supposed to come about
> has not.
>
> Happiness and spring, among other things,
> were supposed to be getting closer.
>
> Fear was expected to leave the mountains and
> the valleys.
> Truth was supposed to hit home
> before a lie.
>
> A couple of problems weren't going
> to come up anymore:

> hunger, for example,
> and war, and so forth.
>
> There was going to be respect
> for helpless people's helplessness,
> trust, that kind of stuff.
>
> Anyone who planned to enjoy the world
> is now faced
> with a hopeless task.
>
> Stupidity isn't funny.
> Wisdom isn't gay.
> Hope
> isn't that young girl anymore,
> et cetera, alas.
>
> God was finally going to believe
> in a man both good and strong,
> but good and strong
> are still two different men.
>
> "How should we live?" someone asked me in a
> letter.
> I had meant to ask him
> the same question.
>
> Again, and as ever,
> as may be seen above,
> the most pressing questions
> are naive ones.

of lives by one man working behind a gun from a hill. This is civilization. Formerly, men worked in the open air only as much as they liked. Now thousands of workmen meet together and for the sake of maintenance work in factories or mines. Their condition is worse than that of beasts. They are obliged to work, at the risk of their lives, at most dangerous occupations, for the sake of millionaires. Formerly, men were made slaves under physical compulsion. Now they are enslaved by temptations of money and of the luxuries that money can buy. … This civilization takes note neither of morality nor of religion. Its votaries calmly state that their business is not to teach religion. Some even consider it to be a superstitious growth. Others put on the cloak of religion, and prate about morality. … Civilization seeks to increase bodily comforts, and it fails miserably even in doing so. …

Gandhi concluded, "This civilization is such that one has only to be patient and it will be self-destroyed."

New, non-representational, or abstract, art also seemed to question the significance of rationality. The most innovative and honored of its creators, Pablo Picasso (1881–1973; see Spotlight, pp. 618–19), drew from African "primitive" art to create new forms of his own. Through these African-inspired

PROFILE
Charlie Chaplin
THE "TRAMP"

Charlie Chaplin's *Modern Times* is one of the most beloved motion pictures ever made. Upon its release in 1936, however, it was a commercial failure. The classic slapstick humor of Chaplin's trademark character the "Tramp"—with his bowler hat, baggy pants, oversized shoes, twitching mustache, mournful smile, and comic waddle—was accompanied by a biting critique of American capitalism during the Depression era. The film opens with a startling and hilarious

Photograph of Charlie Chaplin, 1910s.

jump-cut from sheep being herded in the fields to workers hurrying from subway cars into factories for hours of mind-numbing routine. The Tramp works feverishly on an assembly line, but cannot keep up with the relentless pace. His bumbling antics cost him his job, but he eventually triumphs, evading the authorities while managing to find food, clothing, shelter, and love along the way.

Charles Spencer was born on April 16, 1889 in the slums of South London. After his father died in 1901, Charlie's mother spent the rest of her life in and out of mental institutions. Charlie and his brother were shuttled between orphanages and boys' schools before they joined a well-known London vaudeville troupe. Charlie sang and danced his way into local acclaim, honing his distinctive brand of expressive comedy.

In 1910, he toured the United States, where he was attracted to the growing motion picture industry. He signed a contract with the Keystone Film Company, completing his first black-and-white, silent movie in 1914. Thereafter, Chaplin's star rose quickly. During his fifty-year career, Chaplin made over eighty films and the Tramp became an icon recognized throughout the world. With fellow celebrities Douglas Fairbanks and Mary Pickford, Chaplin organized the United

Artists production company in 1919 to conquer the attempt of commercial production companies to monopolize the industry.

As Chaplin's fame grew, so did the controversies that surrounded him. His personal life, his radical political views, and his love life became front page news. He dated a string of young, beautiful starlets, marrying four times. In 1943, the year he wed Oona O'Neill, a former lover filed a paternity suit against him. Although a blood test proved negative, a California court rejected the evidence and forced Chaplin to support the child. Chaplin was never afraid to voice his opinions—far more humanitarian than political—in his films. In *The Great Dictator*, he parodied the megalomania and racism of Adolf Hitler. He began the film in 1937, when appeasement of the dictator was the order of the day, and he was warned by critics not to proceed. By the time the film was completed in 1940, however, World War II had begun and Chaplin was hailed as a genius.

In the 1940s and 1950s, Chaplin was labeled a Communist and placed under FBI surveillance by J. Edgar Hoover. Still a British subject, he was denied permission to re-enter the United States after a 1952 trip to Europe. He lived the rest of his life in exile with O'Neill in Switzerland, returning to the United States only briefly in 1972 to receive an extraordinary award from the American Academy of Motion Picture Arts and Sciences. He died on Christmas Day, 1977.

A critic of economic and social inequities, Charlie Chaplin utilized modern technology to protest "modern times." The tramp encouraged millions of viewers to understand their own problems, and to identify with those of others, through a lens that was serious, compassionate, and funny all at the same time.

innovations, he demonstrated that the West had much to learn from the naturalism and spirituality cultures that it dominated politically, economically, and militarily.

At about the same time in Vienna, in the heart of central Europe itself, Sigmund Freud's (1856–1939) new art of psychoanalysis ascribed humanity's most profound moving force not to rationality, the pride of European science and technology, but to sexuality. He argued that people did not understand their own deepest drives; these were hidden in the unconscious. He, too, questioned the ability of European civilization to survive:

> There are two tenets of psychoanalysis which offend the whole world and excite its resentment … The first of these displeasing propositions of psychoanalysis is this: that mental processes are essentially unconscious . … [the] next proposition consists in the assertion that … sexual impulses have contributed invaluably to the highest cultural, artistic, and social achievements of the human mind. … Society can conceive of no more powerful menace to its culture than would arise from the liberation of the sexual impulses and a return of them to their original goal. (*General Introduction*, pp. 25–7)

World War I confirmed the apprehensions of these critics. Freud feared for human life itself, and questioned its meaning and direction. In 1930 he wrote:

> During the last few generations mankind has made an extraordinary advance in the natural sciences and in their technical application and has established his control over nature in a way never before imagined. … But … this subjugation of the forces of nature, which is the fulfilment of a longing that goes back thousands of years, has not increased the amount of pleasurable satisfaction which they may expect from life and has not made them feel happier. (*Civilization*, p. 34–5)

He saw a great struggle between Eros and Thanatos, Love and Death, and remained apprehensive about the future results:

> Men have gained control over the forces of nature to such an extent that with their help they would have no difficulty in exterminating one another to the last man. They know this, and hence comes a large part of their current unrest, their unhappiness and their mood of anxiety. And now it is to be expected that the other of the two "Heavenly Powers,"

Eternal Eros, will make an effort to assert himself in the struggle with his equally immortal adversary. But who can foresee with what success and with what result? (*Civilization*, pp. 34–5)

Voices of despair multiplied. Consider "The Second Coming," written in 1921 shortly after World War I and the Russian Revolution (see pp. 643–6) by the Irish poet and playwright William Butler Yeats (1865–1939):

> Turning and turning in the widening gyre
> The falcon cannot hear the falconer;
> Things fall apart; the centre cannot hold;
> Mere anarchy is loosed upon the world,
> The blood-dimmed tide is loosed, and everywhere
> The ceremony of innocence is drowned;
> The best lack all conviction, while the worst
> Are full of passionate intensity.

Yeats held out no hope in rationality, nor in science, nor in progress, but rather in mystical religious experience:

> Surely some revelation is at hand;
> Surely the Second Coming is at hand.

His only hope was for an unknown, different future, no continuation of twentieth-century ways, and he, too, closed in speculation:

> And what rough beast, its hour come round at last,
> Slouches towards Bethlehem to be born?
> (cited in Wilkie and Hurt, p. 1655)

With the far greater destruction of World War II and its atomic bombs and genocide, humanity seemed to touch rock bottom. At the age of twelve, in 1941, Elie Wiesel had immersed himself in the practices of **chasidic**, orthodox, devotional Judaism in Sighet, Hungary. In reply to the question, "Why do you pray?" he had said, "Why did I pray? A strange question. Why did I live? Why did I breathe?" But in 1944, after three years in a Nazi ghetto, he arrived in Birkenau, the gateway to Auschwitz, the hungriest of the concentration camps.

> Not far from us, flames were leaping up from a ditch, gigantic flames. They were burning something. A lorry drew up at the pit and delivered its load—little children. Babies! Yes, I saw it—saw it with my own eyes … those children in the flames. (Is it surprising that I could not sleep after that?

SPOTLIGHT
Icons of War

Twentieth-century wars have been the bloodiest in history. Twenty million civilians and soldiers died in World War I; 45 million in World War II; tens of millions more in local wars and civil wars, conventional wars and guerrilla wars, around the globe. Weapons of mass destruction have multiplied in number and power, including lethal gas, chemical and biological weapons, as well as nuclear weapons, which threaten all human existence.

How can an artist desiring peace focus world attention on the destructiveness of these weapons? Pablo Picasso

(1881–1973), probably the twentieth century's most influential painter, faced this problem after German squadrons supporting Franco in the Spanish Civil War (1936–9) carried out the first aerial bombardment against unarmed civilians in history at the unprotected Basque village of Guernica on April 28, 1937. Picasso replied with *Guernica* (**figure 1**), a painting in black and white depicting the anguish, pain, and suffering of men, women, children, and animals. The exact symbolism is not entirely clear even today, but the vision of terror includes a fallen warrior, a

despairing woman carrying a wounded child, maimed individuals, and a horse writhing in agony. From the moment of its creation in 1937, *Guernica* has commanded a unique position in anti-war protest. The republican Spanish government immediately displayed the painting in its official pavilion at the Paris International Exhibition of 1938 to call for support against the opposition nationalist forces and their German allies. After the nationalist–fascist forces won the civil war, Picasso refused to allow the picture to hang in Spain. It was placed in the Prado Museum in Madrid only after

Figure 1 Pablo Picasso, *Guernica*, 1937.

Figure 2 Children fleeing from Trang Bang, South Vietnam, June 8, 1972.

the end of Franco's fascist government in 1975.

Picasso brought a single remote air attack to global attention. By contrast, during the American war in Vietnam, a multitude of photo-journalists captured the horror vividly and transmitted it around the world instantaneously. Perhaps the most wrenching image to emerge from the fighting—one that had a critical influence in turning Western opinion against America's involvement in the conflict—came from Trang Bang village, when an accidental napalm bombing forced residents to flee, and a little girl was photographed running away from the flames, naked, her flesh on fire (**figure 2**).

The atomic bomb posed a new problem for human comprehension. Hiroshima and Nagasaki (see p. 613) revealed the destructiveness of its explosive power and poisonous radiation. **Figure 3**, from an atomic test in the Marshall Islands in 1950, ignores those bitter realities for a moment, glorifying the bomb's awesome power and even beauty. It recalls the subtitle of Stanley Kubrick's brilliant anti-war film *Dr. Strangelove: or How I Learned to Stop Worrying and Love the Bomb* (1964).

Figure 3 Atom bomb test in the Marshall Islands, 1950.

Sleep had fled my eyes.)

So this was where we were going. A little farther on was another and larger ditch for adults.

I pinched my face. Was I still alive? Was I awake? I could not believe it. How could it be possible for them to burn people, children, and for the world to keep silent? No, none of this could be true. It was a nightmare.

Wiesel soon becomes aware of someone reciting the Kaddish, the Jewish prayer for the dead.

For the first time, I felt revolt rise up in me. Why should I bless His name? The Eternal, Lord of the Universe, the All-Powerful and Terrible, was silent. What had I to thank Him for?

Long-cherished images of humanity and of the gods it had held sacred perished in the Holocaust. Yet Wiesel found the courage to make of his experiences in the death camps the stuff of literature and the basis of a new morality:

Never shall I forget that night, the first night in camp, which has turned my life into one long night, seven times cursed and seven times sealed. Never shall I forget that smoke. Never shall I forget the little faces of the children, whose bodies I saw turned into wreaths of smoke beneath a silent blue sky.

Never shall I forget those flames which consumed my faith forever.

Never shall I forget that nocturnal silence which deprived me, for all eternity, of the desire to live. Never shall I forget those moments which murdered my God and my soul and turned my dreams to dust. Never shall I forget these things, even if I am condemned to live as long as God Himself. Never. (*Night*, pp. 41–3)

To transmit this horrible personal history, to warn humanity of its own destructiveness, and to proclaim the need to preserve life became Wiesel's consuming passion. The award of the Nobel Peace Prize in 1986 recognized his mission.

From Japan, which suffered from the world's first and only nuclear explosions used in war, came similar meditations of anguish and despair, followed later by a commitment to prevent such catastrophe in the future. A student in Hiroshima Women's Junior College, Artsuko Tsujioka, remembered the atomic attack on her city in which 75,000 people were killed instantaneously and tens of thousands lingered on to die later or to be mis-

shapen and genetically damaged from the persistent radiation:

It happened instantaneously. I felt as if my back had been struck with a big hammer, and then as if I had been thrown into boiling oil. ... That first night ended. ... My friends and the other people were no longer able to move. The skin had peeled off of their burned arms, legs and backs. I wanted to move them, but there was no place on their bodies that I could touch ... I still have the scars from that day; on my head, face, arms, legs and chest. There are reddish black scars on my arms and the face that I see in the mirror does not look as if it belongs to me. It always saddens me to think that I will never look the way I used to. I lost all hope at first. I was obsessed with the idea that I had become a freak and did not want to be seen by anyone. I cried constantly for my good friends and kind teachers who had died in such a terrible way.

My way of thinking became warped and pessimistic. Even my beautiful voice, that my friends had envied, had turned weak and hoarse. When I think of the way it was then, I feel as if I were being strangled. But I have been able to take comfort in the thought that physical beauty is not everything, that a beautiful spirit can do away with physical ugliness. This has given me new hope for the future. (cited in Andrea and Overfield, pp. 417–19)

On a national scale, Japan's peace parks at both Hiroshima and Nagasaki record the nuclear destruction as well as subsequent commitments to seeking international peace. Since World War II, Japan has been committed to keeping nuclear arms out of Japan and intensely involved in the efforts of the United Nations to work for peace. Its increased wealth, coupled with the relative decline of the United States as a military power in the Pacific, however, put stresses on Japan's anti-militaristic patterns at the turn of the twenty-first century.

The French **existentialist** author Albert Camus (1913–60), perhaps the most influential voice in European literature in his time, wrote in 1940, the year France fell to Germany: "There is but one truly serious philosophical problem, and that is suicide. Judging whether life is or is not worth living amounts to answering the fundamental question of philosophy." Perhaps, however, rock bottom had been reached, or perhaps hope is part of the human condition, even in conditions of apparent hopelessness, for Camus answered his own question in *The*

Myth of Sisyphus (1942) with an affirmation, which he repeated in 1955:

> This book declares that even within the limits of nihilism it is possible to find the means to proceed beyond nihilism. ... Although *The Myth of Sisyphus* poses mortal problems, it sums itself up for me as a lucid invitation to live and to create, in the very midst of the desert. (p. 3)

THE LEVIATHAN STATE AND THE UNITED NATIONS

Throughout the twentieth century war was often the justification for investing the nation-state with unprecedented powers. Conscription (the draft) gave governments the power to send soldiers off to war and possible death. During the years of World War I the Allies mobilized 40,700,000 people, the Central Powers 25,100,000; of these 8.5 million were killed, along with 10 million civilians. In World War II, the Allies mobilized 62 million men and women, the Axis powers 30 million; in the war, 15 million soldiers were killed, and approximately 30 million civilians died.

In warfare the state took over increasing control of the economy and technology, and bureaucracies mushroomed. Total war expenditures of the Allies in World War I (in 1913 dollars) was $57,700 million; of the Central Powers, $24,700 million. The state determined levels of production, the allocation of raw materials, rationing of consumer goods, including food, and the regula-

tion of international trade. To pay for the war, states sold huge bond issues, which bound them for years with unprecedented levels of debt. They further destabilized their economies by printing money. The available technologies of communication were commandeered for spreading government propaganda, both officially and unofficially. The press, the movies, and the public schools told the government's side of the war and did not report that of the enemy. Governments in this way limited the freedom of speech.

World War II, much greater in scope, had repeated and intensified the administrative experiences of 1914–18, and increased the powers of government still more. Total costs of the war were estimated at $1,150,000,000,000. Statesmen, political philosophers, and common people sought to create a global institution that could counterbalance the destructive power of the **leviathan** state.

Bombers on a raid. By World War II aircraft of all kinds were poised for aerial combat. Here an SAAF/BAF Beaufighter fires three-inch RPs during an attack on German positions in the Yugoslavian town of Zuzemberg in 1945. The astronomical cost of bombs and aircraft contributed to the Allies' wartime expenditure of $1,150,000,000,000.

DEFENSE EXPENDITURE*

	USA	USSR	China	Germany	UK	Japan
1930	.699	.722	–	.162	.512	.218
1938	1.13	5.43	–	7.41	1.86	1.74
1950	14.5	15.5	2.5	–	2.3	–
1970	77.8	72.0	23.7	6.1	5.8	1.3
1987	293.2	274.7	13.4	34.1	31.5	24.2
1997	273.0	64.0 (Russia)	36.6	33.4	35.7	40.9

* In billions of current dollars

Defense expenditure. Fueled by the conflict and the Cold War, massive expenditure by the USA and USSR on military hardware has kept them neck and neck. A new trend, since 1960, has been the rapid militarization of the developing nations. Sources of data: Paul Kennedy, *The Rise and Fall of The Great Powers* and *New York Times 2000 Almanac*.

The founding of the United Nations was a life-affirming political response to humanity's horror at its own destructiveness. In 1945, fifty nations, mostly of Europe and the Americas, recognizing that "disregard and contempt for human rights have resulted in barbarous acts which have outraged the conscience of mankind," joined together to establish the United Nations Organization "to save succeeding generations from the scourge of war." The UN sought to establish among all nations mutual commitments to world peace and human rights, to arbitration and negotiation rather than arms in the resolution of conflict, and to the promotion of health, welfare, and the advancement of education and science.

COLD WAR 1945–85

The United Nations has experienced three major stages of development. The first was mediation during the Cold War. In the first years after the massive destruction of World War II in Europe and Asia, the United States provided a kind of **Pax Americana** to a war-weary world. Through the $12 billion investment of the Marshall Plan it encouraged the reconstruction of Western Europe along democratic and mixed capitalistic–socialistic patterns. In Japan, during seven years of military and political occupation, America outlawed the divine status attributed to the emperor, promulgated a democratic constitution and educational system, and introduced new concepts of business management (see pp. 666–8).

The USSR, as leader of the communist world, feared American capitalist hegemony and military power, and despite the devastation it had suffered during World War II, it challenged American military and economic supremacy. First it built a wall of allied states as a defensive buffer to its west, using its powers of post-war military occupation to install favorable governments. Great Britain's Winston Churchill declared ruefully, "An iron curtain has descended across the continent." In reply, the United States created the North Atlantic Treaty Organization (NATO) in 1949. NATO included democratic countries with capitalist, socialist, and mixed economies: Great Britain, France, Italy, Canada, Denmark, Norway, Iceland, Belgium, the Netherlands, and Luxembourg. Portugal, though not a democracy, was also a charter member. In 1952 both Greece and Turkey joined, as did West Germany in 1955. The USSR then formally established the Warsaw Pact among the nations of Bulgaria, Czechoslovakia, East Germany, Hungary, Poland, and Romania, which were communist in their politics and economics. (See map, p. 650, and discussion, pp. 650–1.) Forty years of "cold war" competition had begun.

The United States had exploded the world's first atomic bomb in 1945; the USSR followed in 1949 (Britain in 1952, France in 1960, China in 1964, India in 1974, and Pakistan in 1998). The USA's first hydrogen bomb in 1952 was matched by the USSR in the next year. The heavens, too, became a field of contest as Russia put the first satellite, the *Sputnik*, in space orbit in 1957 followed by the first manned satellite in 1961. America landed the first man on the moon in 1969.

Each side provoked the other, sometimes to the brink of war. Following World War II, Germany had been divided east and west by the allied victors and in 1948 the USSR blockaded land access to West Berlin, an area held by the US, Britain, and France, but situated deep within Soviet-held territory. American President Harry Truman responded with the Berlin airlift of supplies and personnel and after a few months the blockade was lifted. Germany remained a divided country, however, until 1989. In East Germany (1953), Hungary (1956), Czechoslovakia (1968), and Poland (1981), the USSR crushed democratic revolts; NATO protested but did not intervene.

Following a revolution in 1959, Cuba became a communist country "only 90 miles off the coast of Florida" (see pp. 795–9), threatening America's self-confidence and its hold over Latin America. In 1961, President Kennedy backed an invasion of the island by Cuban refugees in the United States; it failed catastrophically. In 1962 he announced evidence that the USSR had installed missiles on the island and demanded their removal. In fear of imminent Armageddon, the world watched the face-off until, a few days later, Nikita Khrushchev announced that the USSR would remove the missiles in exchange for American promises not to invade Cuba again and to remove its own missiles from Turkey.

Despite, or perhaps because of, the destructive power of their arsenals, the European and North American powers exercised restraint. The Cold War never turned hot within their borders. But in **client states** in Africa, Asia, and Latin America, warfare did break out repeatedly. Here the Great Powers could sell or give away their older weapons and test the newer ones in countries whose leaders were only too eager to receive them.

Proxy wars were fought in Africa—in Congo (Zaire), Nigeria, Ethiopia, Angola, and Mozambique—sometimes with Cuban troops. In Central American guerrilla wars in Guatemala, Nicaragua, and El Salvador, the United States and the USSR supported opposing parties. In the Middle East, Israel was widely viewed as a client of the United States and in response many Arab states turned to the USSR for economic aid and military assistance. Some, however, played both sides diplomatically to get what benefits they could from the Cold War competition.

Sometimes the USA and the USSR did enter directly as combatants. Korea had been divided at the end of World War II. The north was allied with Russia and China, the south with the USA. In 1950 the north attacked the south. The response of an American-led UN army was so aggressive that China felt its own borders threatened and entered the war, which was then fought to a draw. By war's end in 1953, 115,000 soldiers, including 37,000 Americans, and a million civilians had died in the south. The north did not release statistics.

Vietnam proved even more bloody with some quarter million war dead in the south alone, including 58,000 Americans. After World War II, the French attempted to re-establish

"A great step for mankind ..." Edwin ("Buzz") Aldrin, the second man on the moon, clambers down the ladder of the Apollo II lunar module "Eagle" in July 1969. Neil Armstrong had set foot on the moon moments earlier. The race for supremacy in space between the superpowers was fueled by the Cold War.

colonial rule but they were forced to withdraw after their military defeat at Dienbienphu in 1954. Vietnam then divided north and south. Civil war engulfed the south. The north, under a communist government, called repeatedly for reunification of the country and supported the Vietcong insurgents against the government of the south. America, tragically misreading an essentially nationalist civil war as a Cold War battle, and unskilled in fighting guerrilla warfare, committed increasing numbers of its own troops to supporting the government of the south in an ultimately doomed cause, and finally evacuated its troops in ignominious defeat in 1975.

The USSR suffered its "Vietnam" in Afghanistan. In 1979 the USSR sent troops to support a communist coup and fought on doggedly against opposition forces, supported in part by the USA, until the Soviets were forced to withdraw in 1988–9. The casualties were far fewer than those in Vietnam, but Afghanistan was thoroughly destabilized, and even at the turn of the century was still embroiled in civil war.

The costs of this military-technological competition were astronomical. In 1960 the governments of the world spent $413 billion on military expenses. People everywhere were alarmed by such a massive concentration of power in the military. In his 1961 farewell address as President of the United States, Dwight Eisenhower, a five-star general who had served as Supreme Commander of Allied Forces in Europe during World War II, now warned his nation against the dangers of the "military-industrial complex":

In the councils of government, we must guard against the acquisition of unwarranted influence, whether sought or unsought, by the military-industrial complex. The potential for the disastrous rise of misplaced power exists and will persist. We must never let the weight of this combination endanger our liberties or democratic processes. We should take nothing for granted. Only an alert and knowledgeable citizenry can compel the proper meshing of the huge industrial and military machinery of defense with our peaceful methods and goals, so that security and liberty may prosper together. (cited in Johnson, p. 424)

Eisenhower's warning went unheeded. The military build-up continued. Military expansion and the concomitant expansion of the state after World War II proceeded, proportionately, even more rapidly in the less developed nations in Latin America, Asia, and Africa. While public expenditures for the military doubled in the **developed world** of North America and Europe from $385 billion in 1960 to $789 billion in 1988, in the **developing world** they multiplied almost five times from $28 billion to $134 billion. Between 1960 and 1988 the number of soldiers in the developing nations doubled from 8 million to 16.5 million, though in the developed nations it remained stationary at 10 million.

In 1985, in the face of the massive spending for armaments by President Ronald Reagan, the Soviet Union under Mikhail Gorbachev gave up the arms race and began new policies of *perestroika*, restruc-

America evacuating its last personnel from Saigon in defeat, April 30, 1975. More than a decade of warfare in Vietnam convulsed America in bitter disagreements at home, and exposed its inability to understand nationalist guerrilla warfare overseas.

Dismantling of the Berlin Wall, 1989. In 1961, the Soviet Union constructed a wall dividing Berlin east and west, and sealing an embarrassing point of illegal emigration. In 1989 the people of Berlin dismantled the wall, removing one of the most poignant symbols of the Cold War and beginning the reunification of Germany.

David Wolff, director of the Cold War International History Project (CWIHP) at the Woodrow Wilson Center in Washington begins his optimistic description of the opening of Russian records on the Cold War as he observed the beginning of that process in 1997–8. The opening took place as part of the *glasnost* initiatives of Mikhail Gorbachev when he assumed power in the USSR in 1985. Four archives were beginning to open. One "contains the largest collection in the world of Stalin's memoranda of conversations with foreign leaders." But Stalin spoke little, since "He did not have to explain his policy to anyone. All he had to do was ordain it and monitor execution." Another archive contains the transcripts of the Politburo/Presidium, the highest executive board in the nation, but this archive is closed to all but the best-connected scholars. Two other Communist Party archives are also opening somewhat slowly. Army archives are virtually closed, although some scholars have had access to records of the KGB, the secret police.

Wolff concludes that as one nation opens its archives others are more inclined to open theirs, in order to make sure that their views are also represented. He ends in optimism that historians will gain even more access to records in the USA as well, because "Only when comparable materials are available on both sides can the international history of the conflict be written."

turing its politics and economics, and of *glasnost*, greater openness in domestic and international affairs (see p. 657). The Warsaw Pact, the political-military alliance in eastern Europe led by the USSR, dissolved and its member nations became independent. East and West Germany were re-unified. By 1991 the Soviet Union itself disintegrated into independent nations (see p. 658). In response, the American-led North Atlantic Treaty Organization (NATO) softened its military edge. The Cold War seemed over. Despite the extraordinary armaments, sabre rattling, and confrontations, the superpowers had avoided direct warfare for four decades.

THE COLD WAR
HOW DO WE KNOW?

"What war, conflict, or indeed relationship could possibly be described accurately from only one side's perspective?" With this rhetorical question,

DECOLONIZATION AND NEW NATIONS

At its creation, the United Nations Organization included fifty-one nations and its agenda was dominated by Cold War competition. By the year 2000, it had multiplied to 188 members, as nations that had been under colonial rule became independent and joined, bringing their new voices and new concerns to the Organization. The process of decolonization was in large part a legacy of the world wars and the global depression, 1914 to 1945 (see Focus, p. 605). These cataclysms had left the colonizing powers depleted of manpower, financial resources, and moral status. They were unable to hold on to their colonies, especially as many of the colonies began to demand independence. The colonized peoples, and many of the colonizers as well, no longer believed in the "White Man's Burden", or the *mission civilizatrice*. These myths of the superiority of the colonizers now

First World, Second World, Third World

In the period after World War II, many commentators spoke of three worlds, or styles of development: the first world consisted of the wealthy, capitalist, democratic countries of Western Europe and the United States; the second world of Russia and its eastern European allies, with their Communist Party states; and the third world of poorer nations, just emerging from colonization and now seeking their appropriate place in the world.

Today the term "third world" is frequently used with a negative, and much resented, connotation to designate poor, technologically backward, inefficiently organized nations. When the term first came to be used in the 1950s, however, it carried more inspirational connotations. In the first wave of decolonization following World War II, newly independent nations emerged into a world bitterly and expensively polarized into two hostile, belligerent blocs. The United States mobilized a group of Western European nations, which were mostly wealthy or in the process of regaining their wealth after the war, following primarily capitalistic free-market economic principles, and practicing democratic politics. The USSR mobilized an opposing group of nations in Eastern Europe; these were less wealthy but possessed the basic material necessities of life under an economy commanded by the state, which was ruled by the Communist Party. These two blocs, the North Atlantic Treaty Organization (NATO) and the Warsaw Pact, respectively, confronted each other, heavily armed and actively competing in developing and testing nuclear weapons and delivery systems. They competed, too, for the support and alliance of the newly independent nations.

Many of the newly independent nations, however, advocated a third alternative, a "third world." Many wished to be non-aligned, to avoid taking sides. They felt that Europe and America put little value on human life, as two world wars had demonstrated.

They urged disarmament, especially nuclear disarmament, at a time when the first two worlds were locked in an arms race to build first the atomic bomb, then the hydrogen bomb, and ever more powerful rockets to launch them. They advocated state investment in such basic human needs as food, clothing, shelter, medical care, and small, "appropriate" scale technology, often through international assistance, rather than in the purchase of weapons.

With independence, each of these former colonies entered the United Nations, changing the size and complexion of that organization. Although race was not usually mentioned overtly in third world advocacy, almost all members of the "third world" were peoples of color, while the overwhelming majority of both first and second world groups were white. In 1955, third world representatives convened by Jawaharlal Nehru (1889–1964) of India, Gamal Abdel Nasser (1918–70) of Egypt, and Marshal Tito (1892–1980) of Yugoslavia met at Bandung, Indonesia, to launch their collective entry into international politics.

Some first and second world leaders, especially the American Secretary of State John Foster Dulles (1888–1959), saw these third world positions as immoral refusals to take sides in what they regarded as the great ideological, quasi-religious struggles of the Cold War. But, generally, in the 1950s the term "third world" had a positive connotation. The French academic Alfred Sauvy claimed to have coined the term as a parallel to the Third Estate in the French Revolution, which claimed to represent the vast majority of the nation that up to then had been ruled only by the first and second estates of clergy and nobility (see p. 495). The French journal of international economic and political development, *Cahiers du Tiers Monde* ("Journal of the Third World"), established in 1956, also chose its title as a proud call to a new global order.

appeared completely hollow. Chapters 20 to 23 detail specific anti-colonial movements in each region of the world. Here we summarize some of the principal steps.

India, the largest of all the colonies, and one that had begun to organize a national movement from 1885, won its independence from Great Britain in 1947, although it was partitioned into two nations, India and Pakistan (including East Pakistan, which became Bangladesh in 1971) (p. 704). In 1948 Yugoslavia broke with the USSR, wrestling free from Soviet control. In the same year Israel won its independence from Great Britain, also following a partition that separated the Jewish state from its Arab neighbors in Palestine (p. 737). In 1949, the communist revolutionaries in China led by Mao Zedong captured the state and closed down the foreign holdings in the treaty ports, asserting China's control over its own destiny. (The anti-communist, nationalist Chinese fled to the island of Taiwan, leaving China divided as well) (p. 686). In 1952, Gamal Abdel Nasser led a successful coup in Egypt and in 1956 he nationalized the Suez Canal, clearly establishing Egypt's independence from Great Britain's control (p. 721). In 1957 Ghana became the first black African country to win its independence, from Great Britain, and dozens followed in the next decade (p. 751). Algeria, which held a million French settlers, won independence in 1962 after a long and bitter struggle that threatened to plunge France itself into civil war (p. 733). Portugal held on longer than any other major colonial power, giving up Mozambique and Angola, and some smaller holdings as well, only after lengthy colonial wars as well as a government coup at home in 1974 (p. 754). In claiming their national independence, individual countries stressed such diverse values as bourgeois democracy, workers' socialism, Islamic resurgence, and indigenous nationalism, often in various combinations.

Even among the colonizers, colonialism was no longer considered an appropriate form of government, except in rare cases of tiny dependencies. As new countries became independent, however, the two blocs of the Cold War tried to win them over and often involved them in proxy wars, as we have seen, and will see further below. One reaction against such interference from the USA and the USSR was the formation of a third bloc, a third world (see Focus, opposite), of non-aligned nations. The first step was taken in 1955 when leaders of twenty nations of Africa and Asia convened in Bandung, Indonesia, to articulate a post-colonial agenda. They called for a global reduction in military expenditure and ideological confrontation, and an increase in expenditure for economic development, health, education, welfare, and housing. The representatives at Bandung were not all from Africa and Asia—Tito represented Yugoslavia; nor were they all non-aligned—Zhou Enlai represented China; nor did any permanent organization emerge; but for the first time, non-Western leaders had assembled to articulate their own vision of a new world order. Within the United Nations, their constantly increasing numbers gave them a powerful voice. In the 1960s, the UN began a series of "Development Decades" initiatives devoted to third world issues.

THE UNITED NATIONS TODAY

At the end of the Cold War and with formal decolonization virtually complete, international alignments have become more fluid and the United Nations seems to be entering a third stage, serving as a forum for international action in containing regional conflicts. The UN has sent troops and negotiators to Ethiopia, Somalia, Angola, the Persian Gulf, Southeast Asia, Haiti, and Bosnia, and it has helped negotiate *ad hoc* international crises, such as hostage situations. Gorbachev called the United Nations a "unique instrument without which world politics would be inconceivable today," but it lacks the sovereignty of a government. It commands only such powers as its constituent members choose to vest in it.

With 188 sovereign nation members, and commensurately diverse ideologies, the United Nations' decisions and activities are subjected to a constant stream of criticism from one point or another on the political spectrum. Yet, within that highly politicized framework it goes on with its work providing a forum where nations can meet, discuss common goals, and negotiate disagreements. It does not always succeed, but such a forum is invaluable.

Ecological Issues

By 1990 the United Nations was also involved in organizing against global ecological destruction (see Focus, pp. 628–9). Many concerns dominate the agenda, but the main ones are:

- the depletion of the ozone layer through the introduction into the environment of chlorofluo-

FOCUS
Ecology

Ecology refers to the relationship of plants, animals, and humans to their environment and to one another. Throughout history, humans have stood in terror and supplication before potentially destructive forces of nature: flood, fire, storm, earthquake, volcano, disease, famine. But from the earliest historical times we have also recognized our capacity for inflicting damage on the eco-system. The 5000-year-old *Epic of Gilgamesh*, which we noted in Chapter 2, described the resentment of Humbaba, the supernatural Lord of the Forest, at the arrogance of Gilgamesh and Enkidu, who chopped down his trees for their urban construction projects in Uruk. The industrial revolution, beginning in the late eighteenth century,

as we have seen in Chapter 16, introduced a new dimension of human intervention in the world's ecology as industrial wastes polluted air and water so thoroughly that life spans were cut short and disease flourished. Many nations and localities responded in self-defense with legislation to protect the natural environment and safeguard human health and welfare. In our own century, the human potential to destroy the ecological balance has reached startling proportions, transcending local and national borders.

Rachel Carson's *Silent Spring* (1962) exposed the devastating effects on humans, wildlife, and plants caused by the use of toxic chemicals—pesticides, fungicides, and herbicides—in everyday farming and insect control throughout the world. By virtue of its combination of scientific rigor and journalistic vividness, *Silent Spring* is frequently credited as

The UN's Food and Agriculture Organization sponsors ecological projects in poor regions of the world. In Senegal, West Africa, a father and son plant seedlings to protect their village's multipurpose garden from the wind and sun. The blue plastic (collected from village waste) covers the soil near the roots, helping to retain the moisture.

rocarbons, a principal chemical in aerosol sprays and in most coolants, such as refrigeration and air conditioning units;

• global warming, or the greenhouse effect, caused primarily by the introduction into the environment of carbon dioxide, which traps heat in the earth's lower atmosphere, raising temperatures around the globe;

• The destruction of the marine environment through ocean dumping, ship pollution, and the absorption of chemicals into the water table;

• acid rain, the pollution of the atmosphere with chemical pollutants that descend with rainfall;

• deforestation, especially in the tropics, where at least 25 million acres of trees are cut down yearly;

the founding statement of the ecological movement in the twentieth century.

> The most alarming of all man's assaults upon the environment is the contamination of air, earth, rivers, and sea with dangerous and even lethal materials. This pollution is for the most part irrecoverable; the chain of evil it initiates not only in the world that must support life but in living tissues is for the most part irreversible. In this now universal contamination of the environment, chemicals are the sinister and little recognized partners of radiation in changing the very nature of the world—the very nature of its life....Chemicals sprayed on croplands or forests or gardens lie long in the soil, entering into living organisms, passing from one to another in a chain of poisoning and death. Or they pass mysteriously by underground streams until they emerge, and through the alchemy of air and sunlight, combine into new forms that kill vegetation, sicken cattle, and work unknown harm on those who drink from once-pure wells. (Carson, pp. 23–4)

Carson's powerful voice evoked responses. For example, after she revealed that DDT, one of the most powerful chemicals used to combat mosquitoes and, thus, malaria, was also poisonous to humans, governments thoughout the world generally banned its use. "Green" parties, with strong platforms on ecological issues, began to organize in many countries, especially in Western Europe, and more mainstream parties began to adopt some of their programs. Citizens founded organizations such as the World Wildlife Fund and Greenpeace in order to protect the environment. Some farmers began to use natural means of pest control in place of chemicals, and consumers began to seek out "natural" or "organic" foods raised without the use of chemical fertilizers and pesticides.

As the ecological movement grew it emphasized the unity of the global environment and thus the need for coordinated global action. Ecological issues transcended national borders. In 1972 the United Nations Conference on the Human Environment met in Stockholm and moved to establish the United Nations Environment Program (UNEP) to "protect the environment by distributing education materials and by serving as a coordinator and catalyst of environmental initiatives." In 1983 the United Nations General Assembly established a World Commission on Environment and Development (WCED), chaired by Norway's prime minister Gro Harlem Brundtland The WCED was to propose political and technological plans for achieving a healthier environment consistent with greater economic growth which would also preserve the natural environment. Its recommendations covered the challenges of population growth; food security; species and ecosystems (the original concerns of ecologists like Rachel Carson); energy; industry; and urbanization. In addition, it made recommendations for institutional and legal changes to achieve these goals.

To prepare for implementation, the United Nations sponsored a conference on Environment and Development (UNCED), the "Earth Summit" in Rio de Janeiro, 1992, that was attended by delegates from over 175 countries, including 100 heads of state, the largest such gathering in history. Ecology had become a permanent part of the international agenda.

The political issues remain thornier than the technological:

> The Earth is one but the world is not. We all depend on one biosphere for sustaining our lives. Yet each community, each country strives for survival and prosperity with little regard for its impact on others. Some consume the Earth's resources at a rate that would leave little for future generations. Others, many more in number, consume far too little and live with the prospect of hunger, squalor, disease, and early death. (Carson, p. 28)

- at a more local level, polluted air, contaminated water, and cigarette smoke are now clearly associated with carcinogens.

In general, more developed countries tend to place the blame for ecological problems on the increase in global population, an increase most marked in the less developed countries. The less developed countries, in response, blame the more developed as the source of the industries that create the pollution. On the issue of world hunger, the developed countries again point to population pressures on food supplies in the less developed countries, while the less developed blame flaws in the world economy and food distribution mechanisms, both controlled by the wealthier countries. Agreement is emerging on the need for international cooperation in a stronger UN Environment

UNITED NATIONS AGENCIES

The primary focus of attention in the United Nations has been on peace and war, but its various programs and agencies, many concerned with technology, have provided forums for the resolution of other issues and the promotion of international welfare. The United Nations' key agencies include:

- International Court of Justice (World Court) has dealt with issues such as territorial rights, territorial waters, rights of individuals to asylum, and territorial sovereignty

- Food and Agriculture Organization (FAO), monitors information for improving food supply and distribution

- World Trade Organization (WTO), oversees international trade, settles trade disputes, and negotiates trade liberalization

- World Bank provides financial assistance to developing nations

- United Nations Educational, Scientific, and Cultural Organization (UNESCO), sponsors research and publication

- United Nations Children's (Emergency) Fund (UNICEF), establishes programs for family welfare

- World Health Organization (WHO), monitors and researches health conditions

- International Labor Organization (ILO), promotes employment and seeks to improve labor conditions and living standards

- World Intellectual Property Organization, protects the interests of the producers of literary, industrial, scientific, and artistic works

- Commission on Human Rights, gathers information and formulates policy on the rights of persons belonging to national, ethnic, religious, and linguistic minorities, including indigenous peoples

Program, but for the present the United Nations lack sovereign power. It can gather information, carry out research, make recommendations, hold conferences, and provide counsel, but it has no powers of enforcement. Implementation depends upon the decision of member nations.

THE NATION-STATE, INTERNATIONAL ORGANIZATION, AND THE INDIVIDUAL

As problems of ecology, arms control, and economic regulation transcended national borders, pressures for international organization grew. The post-war period saw the emergence of regional international organizations with common aims, such as the League of Arab States (1945), the Organization of American States (1948), the Organization of African Unity (1963), the Association of Southeast Asian States (1967), the South Asian Association for Regional Cooperation (1983), and the Commonwealth of Independent States (1991), which was formed by twelve of the fifteen former members of the USSR immediately after its dissolution.

Important inter-regional coalitions for specific purposes also took shape, and three of the most important of these helped to change the direction of the world economy. The so-called Group of 77 (which now includes over 100 members) formed around the United Nations First Conference on Trade and Development (1964) to present the agenda of the lesser developed nations, and it continues in that function today. More dramatically, the Organization of Petroleum Exporting Countries (OPEC) cartel, founded in 1960 and led by Saudi Arabia, shocked the industrial world by forcing sudden, sharp rises in oil prices in 1973 and for several years thereafter. OPEC splintered internally and declined as an economic force by 1980, but it illustrated the capacity of third world nations to draw attention to their needs and their power. The six industrial nations that convened in 1975 to coordinate their response to OPEC—the USA, Britain, France, West Germany, Italy, and Japan—have continued to meet yearly to maintain a system of international cooperation. When Canada joined, this group became known as the G-7, or group of seven. In 1997 Russia also joined, making it the G-8.

WESTERN EUROPE

Ironically, following the suffering of its wars, Western Europe set the most promising example of regional cooperation and even unification. In 1947, Winston Churchill had described Europe as "a rubble heap, a charnel house, a breeding ground for pestilence and hate." But out of the wreckage came several "economic miracles," many of them the result of cooperation between recent enemies. In 1950, French Foreign Minister Robert Schuman and West German Chancellor Konrad Adenauer agreed to form the European Coal and Steel Community, to place these economic key elements under an independent international authority. The ECSC was born in 1952 with the addition of Italy and the Benelux (Belgium, Netherlands, Luxembourg) countries. Its success led to the Treaties of Rome in 1957 that established the European Economic Community (EEC), or Common Market, to lower, and ultimately remove tariffs among member countries; to foster the free movement of goods, labor, and capital; and to establish a single external tariff. The treaties also established Euratom to create common policies for the peaceful development of atomic energy. Agreement on agricultural policy was more difficult because it involved issues of national self-reliance in food, the mystique of family farms, and the need to accommodate rural and urban interests. Nevertheless, in 1962, a Common Agricultural Policy was also negotiated.

In 1965 the Brussels treaty merged the ECSC, the EEC, and Euratom, and created the basis of a West European economic administration with a commission, council, parliament, and court. Additional nations were admitted, including Great Britain, Ireland, and Denmark in 1973, Greece in 1981, and Spain and Portugal in 1986. Western Europe was moving toward a "Europe without frontiers."

In 1991, the Treaty of Maastricht created a monetary union and paved the way to the creation of a European Central Bank and a European currency called the euro, introduced in 1999. When ratified in 1993 the treaty converted the European Community into the European Union (EU). In 1995 the EU added Austria, Finland, and Sweden, creating in Western Europe the world's largest integrated market with over 370 million people in fifteen nations. Maastricht also called for the creation of common policies in foreign and security matters, and cooperation in issues of justice and home affairs, but these initiatives have not yet been implemented. In 1999, the European Council of Foreign Ministers agreed to develop a common defense policy, which implied also a common armed force independent of NATO. In the same year the EU was considering applications for membership from Cyprus and from ten countries in eastern Europe that had been part of the USSR. The dream of a unified, peaceful, prosperous, democratic Europe seemed within reach.

Pessimists, however, noted the inability of the EU to respond effectively to warfare and "ethnic cleansing" in the former Yugoslavia. There, in the southeastern corner of Europe, Yugoslavia divided into six republics in 1989 following the death of

The Atomium, Euratom headquarters, Brussels. As European countries that had fought each other for centuries began to forge institutions of cooperation after 1945, collaboration in the peaceful development of atomic energy took on both practical and symbolic importance. The 1957 Treaty of Rome that established the European Economic Community (EEC) also created Euratom to create joint policies. The Atomium at Euratom headquarters in Brussels symbolized this new commitment.

long-time leader Marshal Tito and the collapse of his communist government. Following the division, Serbian forces were brutal in attempting to control areas of Croatia and Bosnia in which Serbs were dominant and to drive out Croats and Bosnians. The fighting began in 1991 and ended only in 1995 with the signing of accords, brokered in the United States and backed by United Nations peacekeeping forces. In 1998, ethnic Albanians in the Kosovo Province of Serbia began a campaign to withdraw from Serbia and join Albania. In response, Serbian forces drove 700,000 ethnic Albanians from their homes until finally NATO forces intervened, bombing Serbia into submission. The fighting ended in June 1999. As the ethnic Albanians returned to their homes, however, they began taking revenge by attacking local Serbs. Numerous commentators noted that the prosperity and technological progress of Europe at the opening of the twentieth century had been destroyed by national and ethnic violence that had begun in Serbia, and now at the end of the century, Europe was dragged into war, albeit a small, localized war, in the same place and for some of the same reasons. Ethnic identity remained an explosive force.

THE UNITED STATES

In the United States in the second half of the twentieth century, ethnic and racial identity also remained a critical issue. The nation continued to grow through substantial immigration, 25 million people from 1951 to 1997. In 1997 about 10 percent of the American population, 26 million people, were foreign-born. About half of them had immigrated from Central America, South America, and the Caribbean. Seven million had been born in Mexico, 6.5 million in Asia. The complexion of America, previously some 85 percent European and 12 percent African in origin in 1950, was changing.

The most stirring movements of popular protest in America in these decades were for the civil rights and economic and social advancement of African-Americans and other ethnic minorities, and of women. President Truman racially integrated the entire American armed forces for the first time after World War II. Although the Eisenhower presidency was generally viewed as tranquil, during these years (1953–60) the country echoed with protests in the streets and in the courts to integrate public facilities from water fountains in public places, to lunch

Martin Luther King's "I have a dream" speech, Washington Mall, 1963. Dr. Martin Luther King's 1963 "dream" for an integrated America touched the hearts of hundreds of thousands of listeners on the national mall in Washington and, ultimately, millions in America and around the world. Awarded the Nobel Prize for Peace in 1964, King was revered by moderates for his Gandhian non-violence. Later he became more radical, and more despairing, but always non-violent.

counters and dining halls, to schools and colleges, to buses and other public transportation facilities. Reluctantly Eisenhower backed these protests with National Guard protection to ensure that the peace was maintained and the law enforced.

In the 1960s President Kennedy used the "bully pulpit" of the White House to support the escalating struggle for civil rights. A black Baptist minister, the Rev. Martin Luther King, Jr., captured the public imagination with his non-violent protest marches and sit-ins, a strategy that he adapted from India's Mahatma Gandhi (see pp. 695–9). King's brilliant oratory, his public sermons like his "I have a dream" speech delivered at the Washington Mall in 1963, transformed public opinion. Both the president (1963) and the civil rights leader (1968) were assassinated, but the struggle continued. President Lyndon Baines Johnson sponsored the Voting Rights Act of 1965 that secured and protected the vote for all citizens, capping a struggle that had been waged by civil rights advocates in the southern states. Legal barriers to equality fell, but the struggle to end racial discrimination in economic and social life was still continuing at the end of the century.

The civil rights battles linked America to the world in several ways. First, the presence of minorities who did not have equality in law or in practice called into question America's credentials as the world's oldest democracy. Data indicating that conditions of life in America's worst slums were equivalent to those in third world nations—in terms of infant mortality and hunger, for example—further tarnished America's reputation. Second, America's civil rights leaders were part of a worldwide movement. Earlier in the century, African-American academic activist W.E.B. DuBois (see p. 748) left the United States to live his last years in Africa, and several African-American authors such as Langston Hughes, Richard Wright, and James Baldwin lived for years as expatriates in Paris. Martin Luther King drew his inspiration and strategy from India's Mahatma Gandhi. More militant Malcolm X (1925–65) converted to Islam and described in his *Autobiography* how his participation in the *hajj* pilgrimage to Mecca showed him for the first time that blacks and whites could live together as equals. African-American civil rights leaders and leaders of Africa's anti-colonial movements identified with each other.

The feminist movement (see pp. 565–75) forged links domestically to the civil rights movement and internationally to global movements for women's rights. The struggle for equal rights, equal pay, equal access to jobs was similar everywhere, but, in comparison to third world countries, the American struggle was perceived as more middle class. Authors like Betty Friedan in *The Feminine Mystique* and Gloria Steinem in *Ms. Magazine* were addressing American homemakers who were beginning to seek jobs and careers outside the home, while feminists in third world countries were protesting widow burnings in India (see p. 708), genital mutilation in Africa, and calling everywhere for programs to increase female literacy, rights to property, control over family planning, and rights to participate in public life. Global sisterhood had many elements of solidarity, but it was not a homogeneous movement.

In the 1960s and early 1970s, the civil rights and feminist movements coalesced with the nationwide protest against the war in Vietnam, creating a vibrant, creative, colorful, shrill, and sometimes violent culture conflict that convulsed the country with its excesses on both sides. Publicly and privately, within millions of families, citizens struggled with questions of the appropriate length of hair, legitimacy of draft dodging, use of drugs, and degree of sexual freedom. President Johnson (1963–8), buffeted by the anti-Vietnam War movement, declined to run for a second term. President Nixon (1969–74) felt so beleaguered by political "enemies" that he misused the power of his office to spy on them, and finally resigned rather than face impeachment.

Global affairs, and especially affairs in the third world, continued to play a central part in domestic politics. President Carter (1977–80) lost his bid for re-election in large part because the OPEC oil cartel decreased the availability of oil, increased its price, and forced a contraction in the American economy (p. 732). In addition, Carter was powerless to respond effectively when militants in Iran captured the American embassy in Tehran and held its workers hostage (see p. 729).

By 1980, a new style, more tranquil and much more conservative, settled over America's political and cultural life. The Vietnam War ended in 1973. The legal struggle for civil rights had been won, and the social and economic struggles continued more quietly. President Ronald Reagan (1981–8) adopted a costly policy of military escalation. The Soviet Union bankrupted itself in trying to keep up with his "Star Wars" Strategic Defense Initiative, much as Reagan had hoped. Soon the entire communist system collapsed, leaving the US unchallenged as a global military "superpower".

EUROPE AND THE UNITED STATES		
DATE	POLITICAL	SOCIAL AND CULTURAL
	• World War I (1914–18) • United States enters war (1917) • Paris Peace Settlement (1919)	
1920	• New York stock market crashes (1929)	• Adolf Hitler, *My Struggle* (1925) • First solo flight across the Atlantic by Charles Lindbergh (1927) • Erich Maria Remarque, *All Quiet on the Western Front* (1929)
1930	• President Roosevelt launches New Deal (1933) • Nazi Party comes to power in Germany under Adolf Hitler (1933) • Spanish Civil War (1936–9) • World War II in Europe; holocaust (1939–45)	• Pablo Picasso, *Guernica* (1937)
1940	• Japan bombs Pearl Harbor; USA enters the war (1941) • US airforce drops atomic bomb on Hiroshima, Japan (1945) • United Nations founded (1945) • India and Pakistan win independence from Great Britain (1947) • Berlin blockade; Cold War begins (1948) • Yugoslavia gains freedom from USSR control (1948) • Israel wins independence from Great Britain (1948) • NATO founded (1949)	• Ernest Hemingway, *For Whom the Bell Tolls* (1940) • Development of penicillin and antibiotics • Albert Camus, *The Myth of Sisyphus* (1942) • Simone de Beauvoir, *The Second Sex* (1949)

The same military expenditures also threw the United States budget into unprecedented deficit expenditure and forced sharp cutbacks in spending for social policies. In reducing taxes and social expenditure Reagan was following the initiative undertaken by Margaret Thatcher in Great Britain. Both leaders called into question the premises of the activist welfare state that had governed policy throughout most of the century. They reduced the role of government outside the military, looked to private business as the generator of wealth and benefits, and lowered taxes, especially taxes on the rich. Even Reagan's more liberal Democratic successor Bill Clinton (president 1993–) announced "the day of big government is over," and the first non-Conservative successor to Thatcher in Britain, Labour Party leader Tony Blair, elected in 1997, adopted a similar philosophy. The search continued for a proper triangular balance between the freedom of the individual, the legitimate activities of government, and the humane control of technology.

GLOBALIZATION

Increasing technology and decreasing government regulation made "globalization" the buzzword of the closing years of the twentieth century. Technologies, markets, and nations were being brought together, as *New York Times* journalist Thomas Friedman writes,

> in a way that is enabling individuals, corporations and nation-states to reach around the world farther, faster, deeper and cheaper than ever before, and in a way that is also producing a powerful backlash from those brutalized or left behind by this new system. (Friedman, pp. 7–8.)

Globalization means increased tourism, the creation of more world music, as well as new dimensions of international economic investment. Pessimists argue that globalization threatens to homogenize the world's cultures into a single

DATE	POLITICAL	SOCIAL AND CULTURAL
1950	● Korean War (1950–3) ● Egypt nationalizes Suez Canal, establishing independence from Great Britain (1956) ● Treaties of Rome (1957) lead to establishment of European Community ● Ghana wins independence from Great Britain (1957)	● Contraceptive pill becomes available in the late 50s
1960	● Cuban missile crisis (1962) ● Algeria wins independence from France (1962) ● Group of 77 forms (1964) ● America involved in Vietnam War (1964–73) ● Lyndon Johnson sponsors Voting Rights Act (1965) ● US Defense Department creates internet (1969)	● Rachel Carson, *Silent Spring* (1962) ● Betty Friedan, *The Feminine Mystique* (1963) ● Martin Luther King delivers "I Have a Dream" speech in Washington Mall (1963) ● Stanley Kubrick, *Dr Strangelove* (1964) ● Malcolm X assassinated (1965) ● Apollo II lands on moon (1969)
1970	● Formation of OPEC (1973) ● Watergate affair forces resignation of President Nixon (1974)	● United Nations conference on the Human Environment (1972) ● Near meltdown of nuclear reactor at Three Mile Island, Penn. (1979)
1980	● "Star Wars" Strategic Defense Initiative, proposed by President Reagan (1981–8)	● World Wide Web created (1989)
1990	● Maastricht Treaty (1991) ● Bosnian War (1991–5) ● Russia joins the Group of Seven, forming the G-8 (1997) ● War in Kosovo (1998–9)	● United Nations "Earth Summit" in Rio (1992) ● Around 10 percent of the US population are foreign-born (1997) ● Internet connection worldwide rises from 3 million people in 1993 to 200 million in 1999 ● Protests in Seattle, Washington, against the World Trade Organization (1999)

"McDonald's" culture and undercut its many languages with a single, dominant global language, English. Optimists assert that globalization provides communication networks that allow small, niche cultures, languages, and organizations to flourish.

The driving force behind globalization is free-market capitalism, often seen to be headquartered in the United States, and spread not only by its businesses, but also by its effective control over the World Bank and related global financial institutions. Investment capital is traveling around the globe at unprecedented rates. In 1990, total private capital for investment going from the United States, Japan, and the European Union totaled $43.9 billion; in 1997, $299 billion. According to the World Trade Organization, total exports of merchandise and commercial services world wide reached $6.5 trillion.

THE GLOBAL CRIMINAL ECONOMY

A substantial proportion of this trade is illegal. Sociologist Manuel Castells categorizes the participants and estimates the value and the diversity of the global criminal economy:

Crime is as old as humankind. But global crime, the networking of powerful criminal organizations, and their associates, in shared activities throughout the planet, is a new phenomenon that profoundly affects international and national economies, politics, security, and ultimately, societies at large. The Sicilian Cosa Nostra (and its associates, La Camorra. Ndrangheta, and Sacra Corona Unita), the American Mafia, the Colombian cartels, the Mexican cartels, the Nigerian criminal networks, the Japanese Mafiyas, the Turkish heroin traffickers, the Jamaican Posses, and a myriad of regional and local criminal groupings in all countries [including the Chinese Triads and the Japanese Yakuza whom he discusses later], have come together in a global, diversified network that permeates boundaries and links up ventures of all sorts. While drugs traffic is the most important segment of this worldwide industry, arms deals also represent a high-value market. (Castells, III: 166–7)

Other trade activities include: trafficking in nuclear materials, especially from the Russian nuclear weapons industry; smuggling of illegal immigrants; trafficking in women and children; trafficking in body parts for medical transplants; and, underpinning all the rest, a huge investment in money-laundering to allow illegal profits to be used and reinvested in the legal economy.

The 1994 United Nations Conference on Global Organized Crime estimated that global trade in drugs amounted to about $500 billion a year; that is, it was larger than the global trade in oil. Overall profits from all kinds of activities were put as high as $750 billion a year. … In a very conservative estimate, the G-7 Financial Task Force declared in April 1990 that at least $120 billion a year in drug money was laundered in the world's financial system. (Castells, III, 169)

This illegal economy is driven primarily by the demand for its products, especially the demand for drugs in the United States and Western Europe. It funds political corruption, violence, and instability around the world, eroding the legitimacy of governments and, in some countries, totally undermining them.

THE INTERNET AND THE WORLD WIDE WEB

The technologies of globalization are computerization, satellite communication, the internet and the World Wide Web. The growth of these communication networks is astounding. The first modern, practical computers were created during and immediately after World War II, at first based on vacuum tubes and then in the late 1950s on transistors. The first integrated-circuit based computer was marketed by IBM in 1965. The internet was created by the United States Defense Department in 1969 as an intricate web of tens of thousands of computer networks linked by telephone lines to expedite communication within the government and related agencies, and to provide emergency backup in case other communication means failed.

Commercial service began in the 1980s when the US National Science Foundation created facilities for connecting private computer networks to government networks. In 1993 some 3 million people were connected to the internet worldwide; by mid-1999, 200 million. "Today the Internet is the world's largest communications network. … It is the fastest growing form of media in history" (*New York Times Almanac*, 2000, p. 816). Within the internet, the World Wide Web is a vast network of information first created in 1989 and made accessible to mass use with the creation in 1994 of the **web browser**, a computer program access key. With the internet and World Wide Web, shopping, research, and accessing documents can all be done while sitting in front of a computer at home or in an office, or even from a portable computer while traveling. E-mail, another facility of the internet, makes instantaneous global communication available at nominal cost.

The speed and depth of the transformation in people's private and business lives made possible, and sometimes forced, by this new technology recalls similar processes from the beginning of the twentieth century, before they were interrupted by war, depression, and cold war. At that time, economist Joseph Schumpeter called capitalism a process of "creative destruction," in which new and more efficient products and services displaced older, less efficient ones. As economist Christopher Freeman reminds us,

The transition, however, is a painful one, involving the decline of older, established industries, techniques, firms, skills, and other social institutions as well as the rise of new ones. A truly pervasive new technology leads to a new skill profile, a new generation of capital equipment, a new infrastructure, new management procedures and organization, and even a new lifestyle and *weltanschauung*—a new way of looking at the world—or in [economist Joseph] Schumpeter's phrase, a "wave of creative destruction." (Freeman in Bulliet, p. 328)

Many people lose their jobs to more efficient and cost-effective technology-based organizations, and many with less education are threatened by economic organizations that require ever more training. In the United States and globally, the new technologies have increased the separation between rich and poor, as those who access and guide the technological transformation do well, but many others are left behind. Poor nations are also left far-ther behind as the rich nations, notably the United States, get richer. Moreover, because the new technologies are dependent on research laboratories, these facilities, especially in the United States, continue to attract talented, skilled persons, draining them from less technologically sophisticated nations. To some degree this is offset by new employment opportunities. New, communications-related jobs are foot-loose, and many high-skilled jobs can be located in third world countries, where salaries are lower. For example, Bangalore and Hyderabad, cities in India, have become miniature "Silicon Valleys" through the investments of multi-national companies like IBM, Texas Instruments, and Microsoft, and through the entrepreneurship of local information technology experts. Here, highly skilled personnel earn salaries far higher than most local salaries, yet substantially below those of the US, EU, and Japan. These salary differentials help drive the constant flow of investment capital, goods, and labor around the globe.

DISPARITIES, DISRUPTIONS, AND CRISES OF IDENTITY

Average living standards around the world are improving, but the disparities between rich and poor are increasing, as often happens when new sources of wealth become available for private development. In 1996, the poorest 20 percent of the world's population received 1.4 percent of the world's income, down from 2.3 percent in 1966; the richest 20 percent received 85 percent, up from 70 percent (statistics from *United Nations Development Report*, cited in Castells, III, p. 80). Apprehension in the face of rapid, continuous, unabating change is normal and widespread, and many commentators note that "Our world, and our lives, are being shaped by the conflicting trends of globalization and identity" (Castells, II, p. 1). In the face of change, people seek to protect their identity and sometimes to create new identities mediating between past and future. They may assert these identities—religious, national, ethnic, territorial/

World Trade Organization protest, Seattle, 1999. Protesters against the World Trade Organization demonstrated in Seattle in 1999 against many new technologies. Genetically engineered crops, for example, might ultimately provide food for all the world's growing population with no harmful effects, as American seed companies proclaimed as they produced new varieties; or they might cause unknown and unprecedented problems, as European governments and consumers feared as they banned these products. Scientific and technological disputes turned into international economic and political tensions.

local, gender, or occupational—sometimes peacefully, sometimes in disruptive and even violent forms. (Studies like Manuel Castells' three-volume *The Information Age: Economy, Society, and Culture* trace many examples of such organizations and their programs.)

In December 1999, the World Trade Organization (WTO), the United Nations' agency for setting the terms of international trade, met in Seattle, Washington. Protestors blocked the streets of this normally tranquil city and demonstrated dramatically their apprehensions at the increasing tempo of World trade and their demands for more regulation by national governments and by the United Nations. Many of the protestors argued that they favored world trade, but they wanted protection for the environment, human rights, labor, and children's welfare. They feared that the demands for profits would overrun these humanitarian concerns, and they saw trade restrictions as a means of securing the protection they wished. Similarly, many national and religious groups fear that the spread of powerful global communications systems will overwhelm their unique cultures. Few such groups wish to stop globalization entirely, but they seek limits and restraints that will protect the identities and interests that are special to themselves.

Some world-scale capitalists also view unregulated global capitalism as a threat to the stability of the world's economy. George Soros, a billionaire investor and philanthropist, cautions,

> We live in a global economy, but the political organization of our global society is woefully inadequate. . . . International law and international institutions, insofar as they exist, are not strong enough to prevent war or the large-scale abuse of human rights in individual countries. Ecological threats are not adequately dealt with. . . . Market forces, if they are given complete authority even in the purely economic and financial arenas, produce chaos and could ultimately lead to the downfall of the global capitalist system . . . The world has entered a period of profound imbalance in which no individual state can resist the power of global financial markets and there are practically no institutions for rule making on an international scale. Collective decision-making mechanisms for the global economy simply do not exist. . . . In short we need a global society to support our global economy. A global society does not mean a global state. To abolish the existen e of states is neither feasible nor desirable; but inso ar as there are collective interests

that transcend state boundaries, the sovereignty of states must be subordinated to international law and international institutions. (Soros, pp. xix–xxx)

At the dawn of the twenty-first century, we are witnessing a global balancing act between rapidly expanding technological capabilities, the desire for economic profits, the need to protect human rights, a passion to preserve group identities, and the fluctuating power of the state to intervene on behalf of those contentious interests. The balancing act in itself is not new, but its global pervasiveness is.

READING CONTEMPORARY HISTORY: WHAT DIFFERENCE DOES IT MAKE?

Here the work of the historian changes from analyzing the past to considering its implications for the future. Contemporary history challenges our ability to be objective, to evaluate the consequences of events still in process, and to make sense of data so abundant that we cannot absorb it all. One of the most important criteria used by the historian—the consequences of events—is not available. These are events in progress. Here we use historical information, and our own value judgments, to think about paths into the future: How should we cope with technological creativity? How should we preserve and negotiate our identities? What institutions enable us to find paths into the future? What institutions may block us? We need to keep up with the changes as they are occurring around us, and to evaluate their significance in light of what we know about the results of technological change and of identity preservation in the past. Tensions sometimes lead to conflict, but they may also stimulate unexpected creativity. This chapter has laid down some of the issues, and some examples of previous failures and successes in dealing with them. It has used primarily European and American examples. The final five chapters of the book travel the world, examining how other cultures and states have coped with issues of twentieth-century war, economic depression, Cold War, decolonization, independence, and an increasingly sophisticated technology. They give us comparative studies in how peoples with diverse identities and states with differing levels of power, have been meeting these challenges.

BIBLIOGRAPHY

Andrea, Alfred and James H. Overfield, eds. *The Human Record*, Vol 2 (Boston: Houghton Mifflin, 3rd ed., 1998).

Bulliet, Richard W., ed., *The Columbia History of the 20th Century* (New York: Columbia University Press, 1998).

Camus, Albert. *The Myth of Sisyphus* (New York: Vintage Books, 1959).

Carson, Rachel. *Silent Spring* (New York: Penguin Books, 1965).

Castells, Manuel. *The Information Age: Economy, Society, and Culture* 3 Vols. (Oxford: Blackwell, 1997, 1999).

Chafe, William H. and Harvard Sitkoff, eds. *A History of Our Time* (New York: Oxford University Press, 3rd ed., 1991).

Columbia College, Columbia University. *Introduction to Contemporary Civilization in the West: A Source Book*, Vol. 2 (New York: Columbia University Press, 2nd ed., 1954).

Fox, Richard G., ed. *Urban India: Society, Space and Image* (Durham, NC: Duke University Program in Comparative Studies on Southern Asia, 1970).

Franck, Irene and David Brownstone. *The Green Encyclopedia* (New York: Prentice Hall, 1992).

Freeman, Christopher. "Technology and Invention," in Bulliet, pp. 314–44.

Freud, Sigmund. *Civilization and its Discontents* (New York: W.W. Norton and Co., 1961).

—. *A General Introduction to Psychoanalysis* (New York: Pocket Books, 1952).

Friedam, Betty. *The Feminine Mystique* (New York: Dell, 1963).

Friedman, Thomas. *The Lexus and the Olive Tree* (New York: Farrar, Straus, Giroux, 1999).

Gandhi, Mohandas Karamchand. *Hind Swaraj or Indian Home Rule* (Ahmedabad: Navajivan Press, 1938).

Goncharov, Sergei N., John W. Lewis, and Xue Litai. *Uncertain Partners: Stalin, Mao, and the Korean War* (Stanford: Stanford University Press, 1993).

Hemingway, Ernest. *For Whom the Bell Tolls* (New York: Scribner, 1940).

Hofstadter, Richard, ed. *Great Issues in American History: A Documentary Record* (New York: Vintage Books, 1959).

Howard, Michael and William Roger Louis, eds. *The Oxford History of The Twentieth Century* (New York: Oxford University Press, 1998).

Hughes, Thomas. *American Genesis* (New York: Viking, 1989).

Johnson, Paul. *Modern Times* (New York: Harper and Row, 1983).

Kennedy, Paul. *The Rise and Fall of the Great Powers* (New York: Random House, 1987).

Lewis, David Levering. *W. E. B. Du Bois: Biography of a Race 1868–1919* (New York: Henry Holt, 1993).

Lewontin, Richard. *It Ain't Necessarily So: The Dream of the Human Genome Project and Other Illusions* (New York: New York Review of Books, 2000).

Pickering, Kevin T. and Lewis A. Owen. *An Introduction to Global Environmental Issues* (New York: Routledge, 1994).

Ramanujan, A.K. "Towards an Anthology of City Images," in Fox, pp. 224–42.

Remarque, Erich Maria. *All Quiet on the Western Front* trans. A.W. Wheen (Boston: Little, Brown, 1958).

Rosenberg, Rosalind, "The 'Woman' Question," in Bulliet, pp. 53–80.

Sivard, Ruth Leger. *World Military and Social Expenditures 1996* (Washington: World Priorities, 16th ed., 1996).

Soros, George. *The Crisis of Global Capitalism* (New York: Public Affairs, 1998).

Specter, Michael, "The Pharmageddon Riddle." *New Yorker* (April 10, 2000), 58–71.

Szymborska, Wislawa. *View with a Grain of Sand* (San Diego: Harcourt Brace, 1995).

United Nations. *Declaration of the Universal Rights of Man*.

Watson, James D. *The Double Helix* (New York: Atheneum, 1968).

Wiesel, Elie. *Night* (New York: Bantam Books, 1962).

Wilkie, Brian and James Hurt, eds. *Literature of the Western World*, Vol. II (New York: Macmillan, 1984).

Wolff, David. "Coming in From the Cold," *Perspectives* Vol. 37 No. 7 (October 1999), 1, 15–20.

World Almanac and Book of Facts 1991 through 2000 (Mahwah, NJ: World Almanac Books, 1990 through 1999).

World Bank. *World Development Report 1999: Development and the Environment* (New York: Oxford University Press, 1999).

World Commission on Environment and Development. *Our Common Future* (New York: Oxford University Press, 1987).

Yagnik, Indulal. *Autobiography*, Vol. 1 (in Gujarati) (Ahmedabad: Ravaani Publishing House, 1955).

CHAPTER

19

THE SOVIET UNION AND JAPAN

1914–2000

"We must no longer lag behind."

JOSEPH STALIN

"Europe is not the only model. We can be a model too."

NATSUME SOSEKI

PLAYING TECHNOLOGICAL CATCH-UP WITH THE WEST

THE CONTRASTING EXPERIENCES OF THE SOVIET UNION AND JAPAN

Throughout the twentieth century, two powerful countries dedicated themselves to catching up with, and even surpassing, the technological power of Western Europe and North America. Russia and Japan began from different geo-political and cultural–religious bases. Russia had expanded over several centuries to become the largest country in the world, with access to all the natural resources of eastern Europe and northern Asia. Japan was a small island nation, about the size of California, with few natural resources and a rapidly growing population pressing on available land. Culturally, Russia was the home of the Eastern Orthodox Christian Church, as well as the recipient of influences from its earlier waves of Mongol immigrants from the

east and Scandinavian immigrants from the west. Japan maintained a homogeneous population, united in its dedication to emperor and nation, and had reached a peaceful accommodation among its Shinto, Buddhist, and Confucian cultural and religious heritages.

The encounters of Russia and Japan with Western technology had also been different. Following the eighteenth century example of Peter the Great (see p. 433), some of Russia's czars had embraced the new technology, but others had not. Japan had kept Western technology and culture out of its islands for more than two centuries (see pp. 438–9), but both nations were forced to confront the increasingly aggressive Western Europeans and Americans in the mid-nineteenth century. Russia had attacked the Ottoman Empire in the Crimea and was defeated by a coalition led by Britain, France, and their allies. Japan was threatened by the frigates of the United States fleet under Matthew Perry in 1853. These two events made Russia and Japan realize their need to catch up with Western European and North American military technology and both saw that government initiatives were required to achieve this. But how should they go about it? The two governments developed different policies to play the technological game. The two halves of this chapter trace their separate trajectories.

RUSSIA 1914–2000

The Russian Revolution of 1917 challenged the capitalist order by instituting communism. As we noted in Chapter 16, communism advocated the abolition of private property and control of the economic resources by the state. It argued that the Communist Party should spearhead this system by the use of violence if necessary. Leaders of the party believed that Russia could telescope the development process and catapult itself into the ranks of the wealthy and powerful. The Bolshevik Party, renamed the Communist Party in 1918, asserted the importance of its own official dominance over the politics, economy, and society of Russia. Through the worldwide organization of the Communist International, it proposed itself as a model for, and leader of, colonized and backward countries in overthrowing foreign control and capitalist economic development. It argued that poor nations had been intentionally "underdeveloped" by, and for, the rich. The new communist system established by the Russian Revolution endured through years of hardship and of war, both civil and international. After World War II, Russia imposed its own system on many of its neighbors in eastern Europe by military invasion. At about the same time, elements of the Russian example were accepted more willingly by other nations—notably China—and by many new nations emerging from colonial rule. But since the early 1990s, ironically, Russia's own leaders have repudiated the philosophy of state-run communism. Revolutionary changes that have occurred in Russia since the late 1980s provide an opportunity for re-examination of the rhetoric and reality of communist rule.

Geographically and politically Russia has one foot in Europe, another in Asia. As we have seen, Peter the Great (r. 1682–1725) turned westward, founding St. Petersburg as his capital, port, and window on the west. Catherine II, the Great (r. 1762–96) further nurtured the European Enlighten-

ment at the Russian court. Stunned by his defeat in the Crimean War (1853–6) at the hands of Britain and France in alliance with Turkey, Czar Alexander II (r. 1855–81) adopted a more liberal policy. He freed Russia's serfs in 1861, instituted the **zemstvo** system of local self-government in 1864, reduced censorship of the press, reformed the legal system, encouraged industrialization, and promoted the construction of a nationwide railway system. Czar Nicholas II (r. 1894–1917) furthered heavy industrialization under two progressive ministers, Count Sergei Witte (1849–1915) and Peter Stolypin (1862–1911), and allowed the birth of some representative political institutions, but he rejected the democratic reforms demanded by intellectuals, workers, and political organizers.

THE BUILD-UP TO REVOLUTION 1914–17

On the eve of World War I, Russia lagged far behind the Western European countries economically and

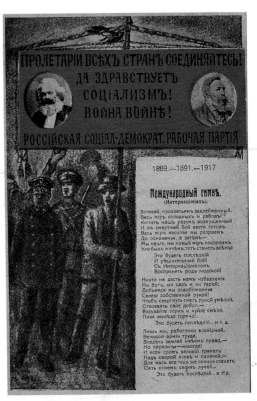

Poster commemorating "The Internationale," the rallying anthem of the Communist movement. Karl Marx (left) and Friedrich Engels (right), who appear at the top of this poster, collaborated in developing the theoretical principles underlying "scientific socialism" and in organizing a working-class movement dedicated to revolting against capitalism.

THE SOVIET UNION AND JAPAN

DATE	SOVIET UNION	JAPAN
1900	• Defeated by Japan in war (1904–05) • "Bloody Sunday"; insurrection ruthlessly suppressed by Czarist troops (1905) • *Duma* forces czar to abdicate, beginning revolution (March 1917) • Communist Party seizes control of the revolution (Nov. 1917) • Leaves Great War by signing Treaty of Brest-Litovsk with Germany (1918) • Civil War (1918–22) between Red Army (led by Trotsky) and anti-revolutionary White Russians; Red Army victorious	• Colonizes Taiwan and Korea; defeats Russia in war (1904–05) 1910 • Is assigned control over Liaotung Peninsula in north China by Paris Peace Settlement (1919) • Gross national income rises by 40 percent during World War I • Urban riots break out, triggered by rising price of rice (1918)
1920	• Lenin establishes State Commission for Electricity (1920) • Lenin's death in 1924 ushers in power struggle between Trotsky and Stalin – who wins • Stalin's Five-Year Plans (1928) • Stalin collectivizes agriculture (1929)	• *Zaibatsu* (conglomerates) come to control economy; industrial production rises by two-thirds (1920–30)
1930	• Famine causes deaths of millions in Kazakhstan and Ukraine (1932–4) • Great Purge: millions executed or sent to gulags in Siberia (1936–8)	• Prime Minister Osachi Hamaguchi assassinated (1931) • Major Industries Control Law encourages large companies to form cartels (1931) • Japan invades China; Pacific War (1937–45) • The "Rape of Nanjing" (1937)
1940	• Annexes Lithuania, Latvia, and Estonia (1940) • Deaths of some 20 million people during World War II (1939–45) • Imposes communist governments on Czechoslovakia, Romania, Bulgaria, Poland, Hungary, and East Germany (1945/8) • Berlin blockade; Cold War begins (1948–89)	• Signs Tripartite Pact, aligning itself with Germany and Italy (1940) • Signs neutrality pact with Soviet Union (1941) • Bombs American Pacific fleet at Pearl Harbor (1941) • America drops atom bombs on Hiroshima and Nagasaki (1945) • Allied Powers occupy Japan; political, economic, and social restructuring (1945–52)

industrially. Its population of 175 million was about 75 percent more than that of the United States, more than two and a half times that of Germany, and four times that of Britain; its energy consumption was one-tenth the USA's, 30 percent of Germany's, and one-fourth of Britain's. Its share of world manufacturing was 8 percent compared with America's 32 percent, Germany's 15 percent, and Britain's 14 percent.

Nicholas II had made great strides in increasing industrial production. Energy consumption had increased from 4.6 metric tons equivalent in 1890 to 23 million in 1913; railway mileage from about 22,000 miles (35,400 kilometers) in 1890 to 31,000 miles (50,000 kilometers) in 1900 to 46,000 miles (74,000 kilometers) in 1913; and the per capita level of industrialization doubled from 1880 to 1913. But during that same period, 1880–1913, the USA's per capita level of industrialization quadrupled, Germany's rose three and one-half times, and France's, Italy's, Austria's, and Japan's all slightly more than doubled (Kennedy, p. 200). In a rapidly industrializing world, Russia had to race much faster just to keep up.

Since Russia lacked the capital to build the industries it wanted, it invited foreign investment. In 1917 foreigners held nearly 50 percent of the Russian national debt. Russia was Europe's largest debtor.

Russia's agriculture was unproductive and its technology was primitive, but economic productivity had little bearing on the power over land and

THE SOVIET UNION AND JAPAN

DATE	SOVIET UNION	JAPAN
1950	• At the 20th Party Congress Nikita Khrushchev officially exposes Stalin's tyranny (1956) • Khrushchev crushes Hungarian uprising (1956) • Soviet space program puts first rocket, Sputnik, into space (1957)	• Economic benefits from American participation in the Korean War (1950–53)
1960	• Alexander Solzhenitsyn, *A Day in the Life of Ivan Denisovich* (1962) • Cuban missile crisis (1962) • Leonid Brezhnev puts down Czech revolt, or "Prague Spring" (1968)	• Admitted to Organization for Economic Cooperation and Development (OECD) (1964) • Bullet train inaugurated (1964) • Hosts Olympics (1964)
1970	• Lech Walensa begins to organize independent trade union federation, or Solidarity, in Poland (1978) • Pope John Paul II visits Poland (1979)	• Economy hit badly by "oil shocks" (1973)
1980	• Mikhail Gorbachev institutes policies of *glasnost* and *perestroika* on coming to power (1985) • Partial meltdown of Chernobyl nuclear power plant (1986)	• Trade frictions with United States and Europe • Equal Employment Opportunity Act (1986) • Death of Emperor Hirohito (1989) • Hit by recession (1989)
1990	• Coup attempt aginst Gorbachev by die-hard communists fails (1991) • USSR dissolves into fifteen independent states of which Russia is largest (1991) • Boris Yeltsin convenes Constitutional Assembly that produces new constitution for Russia (1993) • Russia accorded associate status in NATO (1997) • Yeltsin resigns as president (1999)	• Becomes world's largest donor of foreign aid—$14 billion (1994) • East Asian financial collapse (1997)

peasantry held by Russia's wealthy elites. An exploited peasantry living in **mirs** (village collectives) had neither the economic incentive nor the technical training to produce more. The small parcels of land they farmed privately were subdivided into tiny plots, as sons in each generation shared equally in dividing the inheritance of their fathers. Finally, the government forbade the sale of village land to outsiders. This did prevent exploitation by absentee landords, but it blocked the investment from outside the village that might have funded agricultural improvement through new technology. Productivity stagnated. The sharp class divisions between the peasants and the gentry persisted, marked by differences not only in wealth and education, but in dress and manners. More-

over, the costs of industrialization and the repayment of foreign loans had to be squeezed out of the agricultural sector. The result was a mass of peasants impoverished, technologically backward, despised by the wealthy elite, and suffering under the weight of a national program of industrialization for which they were made to pay.

LENIN AND THE BOLSHEVIK REVOLUTION

Several revolutionary groups attacked these conditions, each offering a different plan. The Social Democrats followed George Plekhanov (1857–1918), an orthodox Marxist thinker, who saw the need for more capitalist development in Russia to

Distribution of Bolshevik leaflets in Petrograd, Russia, 1917. The seeds of revolution germinated with astonishing speed in the 35-degree-below-zero Soviet winter: long-suffering bread queues suddenly erupted and bakeries were looted; workers, whose factories lacked coal, went on strike; and demonstrators carried banners saying "Down with the German woman"—a reference to Czar Nicholas's wife. Lenin called for "Peace, Land, Bread," seeking withdrawal from war. The Russian monarchy abdicated on March 16, 1917.

create new urban working and middle classes. Plekhanov's party would then organize the new industrial workers to overthrow the bourgeoisie. A lawyer, Vladimir Ilyich Ulyanov (1870–1924), later calling himself Lenin, stressed the need for the party to provide leadership for the revolution:

> Not a single class in history has reached power without thrusting forward its political leaders, without advancing leading representatives capable of directing and organizing the movement. We must train people who will dedicate to the revolution, not a spare evening but the whole of their lives. (Kochan and Abraham, p. 240)

In 1902, in a pamphlet entitled "What Is to Be Done?", Lenin again underlined the need for an absolutely dedicated core of leaders to carry out the revolution: "Give us an organization of revolutionaries and we will overturn Russia!" In January 1905, with revolutionary feelings running high, some 200,000 factory workers and others in St. Petersburg, led by a priest, Father Gapon, assembled peacefully and respectfully to deliver to the czar, who was not in the city, a petition for better working conditions, higher pay, and representative government. On that "Bloody Sunday," January 22, troops fired on the demonstrators, killing several hundred and wounding perhaps a thousand. The government's lack of moral authority was

unmasked. By the end of the month almost 500,000 workers were on strike, joined by peasant revolts, mutinies of soldiers, and protests by the intelligentsia of doctors, lawyers, professors, teachers, and engineers.

Before this domestic turmoil erupted, the czar had committed Russia to war with Japan but defeats at sea and on land (see p. 589) further revealed Russia's inadequacies in both technology and government organization. This defeat in the Russo–Japanese war, domestic tax revolts in the countryside, and strikes in the industrializing cities forced the czar to respond. Yielding as little as possible, he established the first *duma*, or parliament, representing peasants and landlords, but allowing workers only scant representation. The czar limited the powers of the *dumas*, frequently dismissed them, sometimes jailed their members, and chose their class composition selectively to divide the principal revolutionary constituencies, workers and bourgeoisie. The *dumas* endured as a focus for democratic organization and aspiration, but they were unable to work cooperatively, and the czar was able to stave off revolution for a decade.

World War I, with its 2 million Russian casualties, finally united the many forces of opposition and brought down the monarchy. In the midst of revolutionary ferment, in February 1917, 10,000 women in St. Petersburg marched to protest the rationing of bread and demanded the czar's

THE RUSSIAN REVOLUTION—KEY EVENTS

1898	Social democratic Party (SDP) formed by George Plekhanov (1857–1918) and Vladimir Ilyich Lenin (1870–1924)
1903	Split in SDP at party's second congress into Bolsheviks (the "majority") and Mensheviks (the "minority")
1905 January	"Bloody Sunday" when repression of workers at St. Petersburg leads to strikes and "1905 Revolution"
1905	Japan defeats Russia in warfare
1917 March	Riots in St. Petersburg; czar abdicates; provisional government formed; power struggle between government and soviet (council of workers and soldiers) in St. Petersburg
April	Lenin in St. Petersburg demands transfer of power to soviets, end of war, land to peasants, and worker control of industry
July	Bolsheviks try to seize power; Leon Trotsky (1879–1940) arrested and Lenin goes into hiding. Aleksandr Kerensky (1881–1970) heads provisional government
November	Bolshevik revolution: Red Guards seize government offices; all members of provisional government arrested; Council of Peoples' Commissars established as new government, led by Lenin, with Trotsky as commissar for war and Joseph Stalin (1879–1953) as commissar for national minorities; land distributed to peasants; banks nationalized; national debt repudiated
1918 March	Treaty of Brest-Litovsk
July	Czar Nicholas II and family murdered at Yekaterinburg in Siberia

Looters, St. Petersburg, 1905. Small pockets of revolutionary fervor flared up prior to 1917. In 1905, the year these peasants are depicted looting bosses' houses, twenty officers and 230 guards were arrested in St. Petersburg when a plot to assassinate the czar was uncovered.

abdication. Despite government orders, the army refused to fire on them (Rosenberg, p. 62).

In the first revolution of March 1917, the *duma* forced the czar to abdicate and established a new provisional government under Aleksandr Kerensky. But the war persisted. The turmoil of mutiny and desertion in the army, food shortages, farm revolts, and factory strikes ground on. More radical groups sought to seize control. Lenin, with the assistance of the Germans who wanted to sow discord in Russia, returned from exile in Switzerland. He called for an immediate withdrawal from the war, land for the peasants, and a government-run food distribution system. "Peace, Land, Bread," was his motto. Lenin organized an armed takeover of the government headquarters, the railway stations, power plants, post offices, and telephone exchanges. On November 7 (October 25 on the old, Julian calendar), this revolutionary coup succeeded, and the communists seized power. Confounding Marxist doctrine, the revolution had occurred not in one of Europe's most capitalistic and industrialized countries, but in one of the least. In March 1918, signing the Treaty of Brest-Litovsk

Lenin and Joseph Stalin at Gorki, Russia, 1922.
After Lenin's premature death two years after this photograph was taken, Stalin battled to eliminate his rivals (Leon Trotsky was banished abroad and eventually assassinated in Mexico) before emerging as supreme dictator of the Communist Party in 1929. He soon abandoned Lenin's New Economic Policy in favor of a series of brutal five-year plans to enforce the collectivization of agriculture and industry.

allowed peasants to sell their products on the open market and middlemen to buy and sell consumer goods at a profit. The central government, however, controlled the "commanding heights" of the economy: finance, banking, international trade, power generation, and heavy industry.

STATE PLANNING 1920–53

Lenin sought the industrial transformation of Russia. In 1920, as he established the State Commission for Electrification, he declared: "Communism is Soviet power, plus electrification of the whole country." Lenin invited German and American technicians to Russia to improve productivity by harnessing capitalist means to communist goals. He took special interest in the system of scientific management and time studies in the workplace introduced by the American Frederick Taylor.

Lenin's death in 1924 ushered in a bitter power struggle, from which Joseph Stalin (1879–1953) emerged triumphant over Leon Trotsky (1879–1940) —and then adapted Trotsky's programs. Trotsky, a brilliant, ruthless man, who had organized the Red Army, had argued that through careful but bold planning a technologically backward country could leapfrog stages of growth and, through the "law of combined development," quickly catch up to the more advanced. Having defeated Trotsky, Stalin now implemented Trotsky's program. He declared his driving nationalist passion that Russia must no longer lag behind the more developed nations.

with Germany, the communist government took Russia out of the Great War.

Civil war between communist revolutionary "Red" and anti-revolutionary "White" forces enveloped the country. Contingents of troops from fourteen countries (including a small number of Americans in the Baltic and 8000 at Vladivostok) joined the Whites. The Bolshevik government took over ownership of land, banks, the merchant marine, and all industrial enterprises. It confiscated all holdings of the church and forbade religious teaching in the schools. It established the **Cheka** (security police) and instituted a reign of "Red Terror" against its opponents' "White Terror." In Yekaterinburg, the local soviet executed the czar, his wife, and their children. By 1920 the communists, as the Bolsheviks now called themselves, were victorious in the civil war. In 1921 they banned all opposition, even dissenting voices within the party, and made the central committee, under Lenin's control, the binding authority in the government.

World war and civil war, followed by even more devastating drought, famine, and economic dislocation convinced Lenin of the need for economic stability and an incentive to produce. In 1921 he implemented the New Economic Policy (NEP) that

those who fall behind get beaten. But we do not want to be beaten. No, we refuse to be beaten! One feature of the history of old Russia was the continual beatings she suffered for falling behind, for her backwardness. She was beaten by the Mongol Khans. She was beaten by the Turkish beys. She was beaten by the Swedish feudal lords.

She was beaten by the Polish and Lithuanian gentry. She was beaten by the British and French capitalists. She was beaten by the Japanese barons. All beat her—for her backwardness: for military backwardness, for cultural backwardness, for political backwardness, for industrial backwardness, for agricultural backwardness. She was beaten because to do so was profitable and could be done with impunity. …

That is why we must no longer lag behind.
(Andrea and Overfield, p. 398)

Stalin's rhetoric would appeal not only to his immediate audience in Russia, but also to a more global audience of poorer states and colonies beginning to protest against their subordination and to seek independence and development.

To achieve this "combined development," Stalin in 1928 instituted nationwide, state-directed five-year plans that covered the basic economic structure of the whole country. In place of capitalism, in which market forces of supply and demand determine production goals, wages, profits, and the flow of capital, labor, and resources, Stalin instituted government planning to make those decisions from the large-scale national macro-level to the small-scale local micro-level.

Where could Russia find capital to invest in industrial development, especially with most world capital markets closed to the communist state? Stalin turned to his own agricultural sector and peasantry. By artificially lowering the prices for agricultural production and raising the prices for agricultural tools and materials, Stalin used his planning apparatus to squeeze both capital and labor out of agriculture into industry. But he squeezed so hard that agricultural productivity fell, and peasants withheld their crops from the artificially deflated market. State planning was not working.

Class struggle. "Liquidate the Kulaks as a Class" reads this banner held aloft by farm workers in 1930. Between 1929 and 1933, Stalin aimed to convert the whole of the Soviet rural economy to collective farms and agricultural cooperatives. Kulaks were wealthier peasants who had benefited under the former system and were now regarded as oppressors and class enemies.

Nevertheless, in 1929 Stalin increased the role of the state still further. He **collectivized** agriculture. More than half of all Soviet farmers were compelled to give up their individual fields and to live and work instead on newly formed collective farms of 1000 acres (approximately 400 hectares) or more.

STALIN'S SOVIET UNION— KEY EVENTS

1912	Stalin is appointed by Lenin to the Bolshevik central committee
1922	Becomes general secretary of central committee
1924	Lenin's death leaves Stalin and Trotsky in power struggle
1928–9	Stalin engineers Trotsky's exile and achieves supreme power, which he exercises with brutality
1928–38	First two five-year plans involve forced industrialization to develop heavy and light industry and collectivization of agriculture, policies that required deportation and caused famine
1932–4	Famine causes deaths of millions in Ukraine and Kazakhstan
1936–8	Great Purge carried out, in which opposition in both party and army is eliminated in show trials; millions killed or sent to gulags in Siberia and elsewhere
1939	Pact with Hitler gives USSR Baltic states, eastern Poland, and Bessarabia, but Stalin taken by surprise when Hitler invades USSR (1941)
1941–5	Russia withstands German invasion, despite 20 million dead
1945	Victory in war encourages Stalin to take the cult of personality to new lengths and the policy of terror continues
1945–8	Eastern Europe brought under Soviet control
1953	After Stalin's death his role is denounced by Khrushchev and other members of ruling elite

The communist government increased the use of heavy machinery and large-scale farming operations, stipulated the goods to be produced and their sales prices, encouraged millions of peasants to leave the farms for work on the state's new industrial enterprises, and eliminated wealthier peasants and middlemen.

Although some farmers were living better in 1939 than 1929, many others were not. The most industrious and talented farmers were killed or imprisoned. Hundreds of thousands of better-off peasants, **kulaks**, who refused collectivization were murdered; millions were transported to labor camps in Siberia. Peasants who owned animals preferred to slaughter them rather than turn them over to collectives. There had been over 60 million head of cattle in the USSR in 1928; by 1933 there were fewer than 35 million. Initiative shrivelled as the more entrepreneurial farmers were turned into a kind of rural proletariat. The government continued to collect high proportions of the agricultural production to pay for the imports of foreign technology and machinery for its industrial programs. Although few developing countries today are willing to reduce private consumption below 80 percent of the national product, Russia reduced it to little over 50 percent. The political coercion and chaos introduced by these policies, combined with bad harvests in southeast Russia, led to the tragic and wasteful deaths of between 2 and 3 million peasants by 1932.

While the peasants suffered enormous hardship, industry flourished as never before. At first, Russia hired foreign technology and imported foreign machinery. Despite ideological differences with the United States, Stalin, like Lenin before him, saw the necessity of importing materials, machinery, and even some organizational programming from there. In 1924 Stalin declared:

> American efficiency is that indomitable force which neither knows nor recognizes obstacles; which continues on a task once started until it is finished, even if it is a minor task; and without which serious constructive work is inconceivable. … The combination of Russian revolutionary sweep with American efficiency is the essence of Leninism. (Hughes, p. 251)

Meanwhile, the Russian government was training its own personnel and learning to construct its own massive industrial plants. At the falls of the Dnieper River, the communist state constructed

Dnieprostroy, which, when it opened in 1932, was the largest hydroelectric power station in the world. In the early 1920s, the USSR had imported tens of thousands of tractors, most of them Fords and International Harvesters from the United States. By the 1930s, however, Russia constructed a giant plant at Stalingrad to manufacture its own tractors. At Gorki (Nizhny Novgorod) the government built a plant based on the American Ford model at River Rouge, Michigan. At Magnitogorsk, in Siberia, they constructed a steel complex based on US Steel's plant in Gary, Indiana.

From 1928 to 1938, the per capita level of industrialization nearly doubled. From 1928 to 1940, the production of coal increased from 36 to 166 million tons, of electricity from 5 to 48 billion kilowatt hours, and of steel from 4 to 18 million tons. Stalin explained: "The independence of our country cannot be upheld unless we have an adequate industrial basis for defense" (Kochan and Abraham, p. 368). The planners began to convert a nation of peasants into a nation of industrial workers, as the urban population of the country increased three and one-half times from 10.7 million in 1928 to 36.5 million in 1938, from 7 percent of the country's population to 20 percent.

Most dramatically, the Soviet increases came when Western Europe and North America were reeling under world depression. The communist system won new admirers in the West. The American political comedian Will Rogers commented: "Those rascals in Russia, along with their cuckoo stuff have got some mighty good ideas. … Just think of everybody in a country going to work." Journalist Lincoln Steffens wrote: "All roads in our day lead to Moscow." British political critic and historian John Strachey exclaimed: "To travel from the capitalist world into Soviet territory is to pass from death to birth."

WOMEN WORKERS IN THE SOVIET UNION

For women, too, the Soviet system led to great change, but perhaps less thorough than promised. As elsewhere, World War I brought women into factories, fields, and even the armed forces, and the civil war continued the pattern. Over 70,000 women served in the Red Army. In 1921, 65 percent of Petrograd's factory workers were women. In 1917, the first Soviet marriage law constituted marriage as a civil contract and provided for relatively easy divorce and child maintenance procedures.

The government ordered equal pay for equal work, but the provision was not enforced. To bring law into line with practice, and recognizing the lack of availability of effective birth-control methods, abortion on demand was granted as a right; so was maternity leave with full pay. When the men returned from the wars, they wanted their jobs back and their women at home, but Russian women retained most of the benefits they had won and "legally speaking, Russian women were better off than women anywhere in the world" (Kochan and Abraham, p. 337). Over the next decades women entered professions so rapidly that they became the majority in medicine and teaching—care-giving occupations—and a substantial minority in engineering, technical occupations, and law.

In practice, however, women bore the "double burden" of continuing the major responsibility for running their homes and caring for their families while working full time. With the introduction of state-planned heavy industrialization after 1929, the double burden on women increased.

Russian poster for women chemical workers, 1930. Despite the government's difficulties in enforcing "equal pay for equal work," women's rights improved markedly under the communist system. This poster appears to idealize full-time employment combined with raising a family.

The factories invited their labor, while shortages of foodstuffs forced them to spend more time and energy in ration lines and in the search for food. Abortion became so common that it was once again outlawed for a time after 1936. The struggle to balance the new legal equality and protection with older social and family traditions continued (and continues today).

Political leaders of countries under European colonial control saw the Russian example—telescoped development, state planning, rapid industrialization, the transformation of the peasantry into an urban labor force, emphasis on education and health services, national enthusiasm in rebuilding a nation along scientific lines—as just what they needed. As a political prisoner in British India in July 1933, Jawaharlal Nehru, future first prime minister of independent India, wrote to his daughter:

> People often argue about the Five Year Plan. …
> It is easy enough to point out where it has failed. …
> [but] One thing is clear: that the Five Year Plan has

completely changed the face of Russia. From a feudal country it has suddenly become an advanced industrial country. There has been an amazing cultural advance; and the social services, the system of social, health, and accident insurance, are the most inclusive and advanced in the world. In spite of privation and want, the terrible fear of unemployment and starvation which hangs over workers in other countries has gone. There is a new sense of economic security among the people … further … this Plan has impressed itself on the imagination of the world. Everybody talks of "planning" now, and of Five-Year and Ten-Year and Three-Year plans. The Soviets have put magic into the word. (*Glimpses of World History*, pp. 856–7)

EXPORTING THE REVOLUTION

Soviet leaders wished to spread their revolution throughout the world and had established in 1919 the Third Socialist International, or Comintern, to serve that function. Indeed, the succession struggle

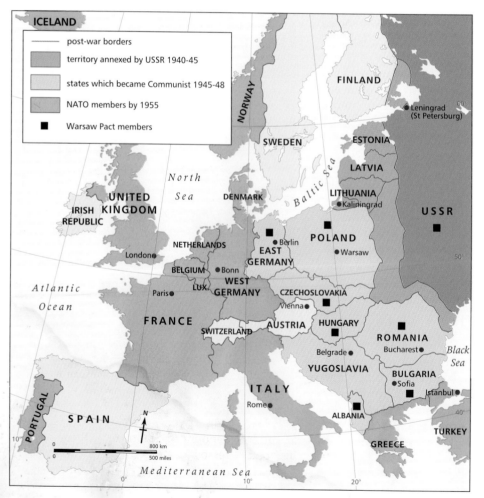

Post-war Europe Western and eastern bloc competition, following their alliance in crushing Nazi Germany, crystallized in the Cold War. The Soviet Union annexed invaded territories in the Baltic states and eastern Poland and set up a string of puppet communist states as the Warsaw Pact alliance, from East Germany to Bulgaria. The Western Allies formed the countervailing NATO alliance. The stalemate continued for forty years.

of 1924, at Lenin's death, had partly turned on the question of how quickly to spread the revolution. Leon Trotsky, who lost, had argued for its rapid export. Joseph Stalin, who won, argued for securing the revolution at home before projecting it abroad. To some nations devastated by World War II, and to others just emerging from colonialism and seeking a model for rapid, government-sponsored modernization, Russia's successes appeared attractive. Russia's ability to survive ferocious punishment in World War II, to fight back, and to win through despite untold material damage and the deaths of some 20 million people—the most severe losses of any combatant nation—earned its people and its government great respect in the world community.

On the other hand, Russia turned to building an empire of its own by armed force. After the war between 1945 and 1948 Russia imposed communist governments controlled from Moscow on Czechoslovakia, Romania, Bulgaria, Poland, Hungary, and Eastern Germany—adding them to the northern nations of Lithuania, Latvia, and Estonia, which Russia had annexed in 1940. Russia then ordered the economies of these satellite nations to serve its own, having them produce goods needed by Russia and selling them to Russia at artificially low prices. Despite its anti-imperial rhetoric, Russia had kept control of the czar's empire and was now adding to it.

COLD WAR

Western European nations and the United States condemned these actions. Britain's Winston Churchill deplored Russia's construction of an "iron curtain" separating Europe into two mutually hostile ideological/political/economic/military blocs. But many nations newly emerging from imperial rule themselves, and fearing American military and economic dominance in the post-war world, were willing to overlook Russian suppression of her neighbors—and of internal opposition—and instead applauded the Russians for providing some balance of power. From 1947 until 1991 much of the world was entangled in the Cold War between the Western nations, which formed the North Atlantic Treaty Organization (NATO), and Russia and its allies organized in the Warsaw Pact. The costs of that Cold War were discussed on p. 625. Some observers saw limited benefits in the Cold War: an opening for new, poor, recently independent nations to play one side against the other

for aid and assistance. Most neutral observers, however, criticized the sheer volume of military expenditure, and they blamed both NATO and the Warsaw Pact for encouraging the new nations, too, to waste their resources and energies in unnecessary military exercises.

RUSSIAN STATE POWER AND OPPRESSION

Weighing most heavily against the considerable communist accomplishments within the Soviet Union, however, were some catastrophic failures. The extraordinary power of the party left no room for opposition, discussion, or debate. It allowed no political freedom. As early as 1902, Lenin had called for the party to be "the vanguard fighter … guided by the most advanced theory." The party now controlled the state, the army, the Cheka (later the KGB), or secret police, and the Gosplan or planning commission. Its control stretched into the deepest recesses of the economic, political, social, and cultural life of the country (see Spotlight, pp. 652–3).

Through the party "purges" of the 1930s, Stalin eradicated any potential opposition to himself and his policies. In 1933, a third of the members of the Communist Party were expelled. Thousands were tried and, after submitting forced confessions, executed. Millions more were imprisoned in a nationwide network of prison camps later called the **Gulag** (see below).

KHRUSCHEV (1953–64)

After Stalin's death in 1953, Party General Secretary Nikita Khrushchev (1894–1971) began to disclose and reject some of the coercive powers of the state. At the Twentieth Party Congress in 1956, Khrushchev exposed officially the extent of Stalin's tyranny:

> Arbitrary behavior by one person encouraged and permitted arbitrariness in others. Mass arrests and deportations of many thousands of people, executions without trial and without normal investigation created conditions of insecurity, fear, and even desperation. (Kochan and Abraham, p. 447)

In 1961, at the Twenty-second Party Congress, Khruschev denounced Stalin more fully and had his body removed from Lenin's Mausoleum. Khruschev released a number of political prisoners of conscience, permitted publication of many

SPOTLIGHT
Soviet Socialist Realism

Every state has its own policy for culture, expressed in such elements as school curricula, support for artists and the arts, exhibitions in public museums and galleries, and rules on what may and may not be broadcast through the media and printed in the press. These policies reflect the values and goals of the state, and have enormous influence on the cultural messages received by citizens, on what they get to read, hear, see, and evaluate. In countries where individual expression is protected, the arts and culture will flourish in many forms and directions and artists feel free to produce what they wish, although even here they are alert to emphases suggested by funding resources. In countries where the state imposes its will, at least by controlling the financial supports, at most by forbidding certain expression altogether, the arts and culture are highly controlled. In severe cases, the punishment for breaking with official policy may

range from the cut-off of state funding, to restrictions on the right to exhibit cultural productions, to imprisonment or exile, and even to execution.

The art of revolutionary Russia began by glorifying its

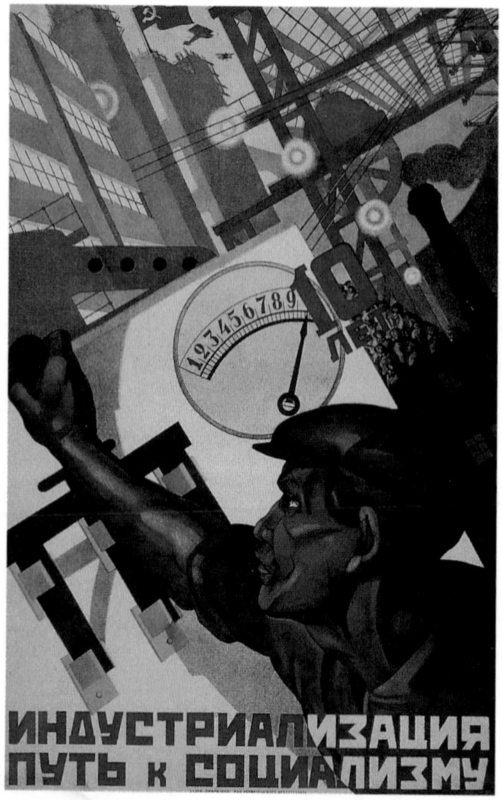

Figure 1 Russian poster, "Industrialization Is the Path to Socialism," 1928.

socialist goals, yet official freedom of expression allowed a wide variety of forms. In 1928, the Communist Party instituted the Cultural Revolution to "proletarianize" the arts, that is to create expressions that would be understood immediately by the masses and inspire them to carry out the goals of the revolution. In 1932, all artistic groups other than those sanctioned by the government were smothered, and in 1934 Socialist Realism was left as the only officially sanctioned approach. Avant-garde or "progressive" art was decried as bourgeois and irrelevant to the people, and painters were instructed to depict real events and people in an idealized, optimistic way that provided a glimpse of the glorious future of the Soviet Union under communism. The three posters in this Spotlight demonstrate the results.

In a visual pun with the gauge in the center, **figure 1**, "Industrialization Is the Path to Socialism" (1928), celebrates the tenth anniversary of the October Revolution in 1917 and shows a worker pulling the switch to inaugurate the first Five Year Plan. Few would call this important art according to the usual canons of artistic expression, but it uses artistic forms to transmit its message to the masses.

Figure 2, "Transportation workers," is a factory poster from 1932 designed to inspire workers to redouble their efforts. The banners call to achieve the Five Year Plan in just four years. It draws attention to the

importance of the railway network to the success of Russia, by far the largest country in the world in terms of geographical size. The poster also proclaims the engineering accomplishments of the Soviets and celebrates the importance of the union of mental and physical labor.

Figure 3 declares "Long live the great banner of Marx, Engels, and Lenin" and attempts to inspire the Soviet people in any forthcoming war (although Stalin had just signed a non-aggression pact with the Nazis). Set in

Moscow, it musters many of the central icons of Russian history and the Revolution—the walls of the Kremlin, St. Boris' cathedral, Lenin's tomb—and it reassures the people that Russian military might will be adequate to the coming battle. Most of all it establishes Joseph Stalin as the leader who will ensure victory. Many critics would regard these posters as propaganda rather than art, for aesthetic values take a back seat to the need to excite and persuade the viewer of the truth of the political message.

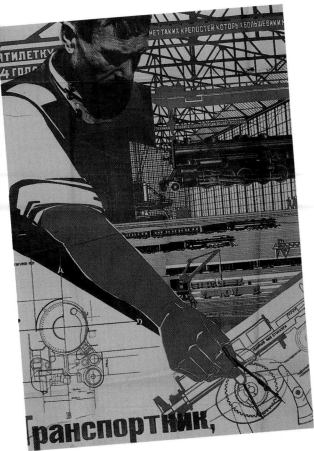

Figure 2 Russian poster, "Transportation Workers…," 1932.

Figure 3 Russian poster, "Long Live the Great Banner of Marx, Engels, and Lenin," 1939.

politically banned works, and moderated Stalin's plans for heavy industrialization in favor of greater production of consumer goods. The Soviet government itself gradually began to portray Stalin as a political monster.

Under Khrushchev, the Soviet Union continued to attempt to catch up to the West—and in some competitions even to surpass it. The Soviet space program put the first space satellite, the Sputnik, into orbit in 1957 and tried, unsuccessfully, to develop more of the "virgin lands" of Kazakhstan and Siberia. Agriculture continued to lag and consumer goods continued to be limited, but Russia seemed on a par with the United States militarily and industrially. The question would later arise whether the relatively backward economy could continue to support the national investment in heavy military industries. At the time, however, the Russian government claimed to be surrounded and threatened by the United States and its allies, and, having endured two world wars, saw no choice but to continue preparing its defenses.

Khrushchev maintained Russia's domination of Eastern Europe. He crushed the Hungarian uprising of 1956. He stationed nuclear-tipped missiles in Cuba, Russia's ally in the Caribbean—until forced to withdraw them in 1962 in confrontation with the USA. He allowed the East Germans to build the Berlin Wall in 1961 to close escape routes to the West. Nonetheless the Soviet Party leadership considered Khrushchev reckless and removed him from power in 1964. He was followed by almost two decades of bureaucratic stagnation under Leonid Brezhnev (1906–82).

Struggling for Historical Truth under Communist Dictatorship
What Do We Know? How Do We Know?

Winston Churchill remarked in 1939: "I cannot forecast to you the action of Russia. It is a riddle wrapped in a mystery inside an enigma." Russian novelist Alexander Solzhenitsyn (b. 1918) added

Moscow power parade. At the height of the Cold War, the arms race against the West saw Russian leaders Khrushchev and Brezhnev pouring colossal sums of money into military hardware. This parade shows tanks moving through Red Square, Moscow, to mark the sixty-sixth anniversary of the 1917 October Revolution. Lenin keeps watch.

SOURCE
The Gulag Archipelago

Alexander Solzhenitsyn (b. 1918) spent years in Soviet prison camps and characterized them as the crucial institution in perpetuating Stalin's totalitarian rule. Millions were sentenced to these camps located throughout the Soviet Union. Solzhenitsyn, who first revealed their existence publicly in the 1960s, called them the *Gulag Archipelago*. The camps administered tortures, which reached their peak when prisoners were interrogated:

> But the most awful thing they can do with you is this: undress you from the waist down, place you on your back on the floor, pull your legs apart, seat assistants on them (from the glorious corps of sergeants!) who also hold down your arms; and then the interrogator (and women interrogators have not shrunk from this) stands between your legs and with the toe of his boot (or of her shoe) gradually, steadily, and with ever greater pressure crushes against the floor those organs which once made you a man. He looks into your eyes and repeats and repeats his questions or the betrayal he is urging on you. If he does not press down too quickly or just a shade too powerfully, you still have fifteen seconds left in which to scream that you will confess to everything, that you are ready to see arrested all twenty of those people he's been demanding of you, or that you will slander in the newspapers everthing you hold holy. (pp. 127–8)

Jailers as well as prisoners were dehumanized in the process, though in dramatically different ways:

> If you could just get one of them to resist! "I love strong opponents! It's such fun to break their backs!" said the Leningrad interrogator Sitov to G. G———v.
>
> And if your opponent is so strong that he refuses to give in, all your methods have failed, and you are in a rage? Then don't control your fury! It's tremendously satisfying, that outburst! Let your anger have its way; don't set any bounds to it! Don't hold yourself back! That's when interrogators spit in the open mouth of the accused! And shove his face into a full cuspidor! That's the state of mind in which they drag priests around by their long hair! Or urinate in a kneeling prisoner's face! After such a storm of fury you feel yourself a real honest-to-God man! (p. 150)

Solzhenitsyn's *Gulag Archipelago* was smuggled out of the USSR and published in Paris in 1973. For revealing its horrors, and demonstrating that they were not an aberration introduced by Stalin, but a fundamental institution introduced by Lenin himself, Solzhenitsyn was exiled from the Soviet Union. He took up residence in Cavendish, Vermont. Finally in 1990, during the Gorbachev era, Solzhenitsyn's citizenship was restored. Constant in his love for Russia, and repelled by the materialism and consumerism of the West, he returned home in 1994.

more bluntly in 1973, "It has always been impossible to learn the truth about anything in our country" (p. 92, n.48). Assuming that to control knowledge is to control power, the communist government of Russia limited and tampered with the supply of information. (Turn to pp. I–10 and I–11 of this textbook for an example of its doctoring of photographs of historical events.)

Following the death of Stalin, however, Khrushchev began to open the record, publicly revealing Stalin's atrocities. In the new climate of openness, Solzhenitsyn was able to publish *A Day in the Life of Ivan Denisovich*, a realistic novel depicting conditions in one of the gulags. Khrushchev fell from power in 1964, however, and Solzhenitsyn could publish his next two novels—*The First Circle*, set in a prison, and *Cancer Ward*, set in a hospital—only in editions smuggled out of Russia. Internally his writing circulated illegally in **samizdat** ("self-published"), privately copied formats. In 1970 the novelist was awarded the Nobel Prize for Literature but he did not travel to Stockholm to receive the

PROFILE
Pope John Paul II
COSMOPOLITAN, CONSERVATIVE, ANTI-COMMUNIST

On June 2, 1979, Pope John Paul II's jet liner landed at Warsaw's Okecie Airport. Poland's native son, Karol Jozef Wojtyla, had been named supreme pontiff of the Roman Catholic Church just several months before and his first trip home was marked by tremendous celebration. To most Poles, Catholics governed by a Communist regime, Pope John Paul II's journey behind the Iron Curtain brought hope amidst political repression and economic depression. It also marked the start of a turbulent decade within Eastern Europe, one that witnessed the rise of the Solidarity movement in Poland and ultimately the demise of the Soviet Union. Pope John Paul II was a key participant in both events.

Karol Jozef Wojtyla was born on May 18, 1920 in Wadowice, Poland. In 1939, the Second World War interrupted his academic training at Jagiellonian University in Krakow, and from 1940 to 1944, Karol worked as a manual laborer in Krakow, thereby avoiding deportation to a Nazi work camp. This work experience inspired his lifelong concern for the welfare of the laboring poor. His dedication to this cause, coupled with his scathing critique of Communism, formed the backbone of his religious ideology in later years.

In 1948, Karol was ordained a priest. He earned a doctorate in theology and wrote several important theses on Catholic ethics and philosophy. He attended the meetings of the Second Vatican Council in 1962, articulating in the midst of that liberal assembly his more conservative positions regarding abortion, birth control, clerical celibacy, and women's roles in the Catholic Church. In 1963, he was named Archbishop

Pope John Paul II dressed in the traditional robe of a Masai chief, Nairobi, 1995.

of Krakow, and four years later he became Cardinal Wojtyla. On October 16, 1978, he was elected Pope, taking the name John Paul II. As pope, his steadfast refusal to modify traditional Church doctrine came under increasing attack by liberal Catholics. His opposition to the "liberation theology," with its Marxist philosophy of class struggle, articulated by many Latin American priests, further estranged the left wing of the Church.

As an active leader, and fluent in several languages, the Pope has traveled the globe to meet with Catholics in the Americas, Africa, and Asia. In the early 1980s, he was both the inspiration for and the ultimate protector of the Solidarity movement against Communism in Poland, spearheaded by union leader Lech Walesa. Indeed, the Pope's role in the fall of Communism in Eastern Europe re-affirmed the geo-political power of the papacy and gave a belated reply to Joseph Stalin's sarcastic question "The Pope! How many divisions has *he* got?"

While the Pope was a firm opponent of Communism during the 1980s, he did not embrace capitalism. His stand was more complex. In his 1987 encyclical *Sollicitudo Rei Socialis* (*On Social Concern*), he pointed to the danger of the ever-widening gap between the rich and poor in all countries. He preached "the right of every individual to the full use of the benefits offered by science and technology" for the good of all people. John Paul argued that the Catholic Church must transcend the economic, political, and social ideologies that have divided the world in order to minister to the masses who are often caught beneath them.

award, fearing that he would be denied re-entry to the Russia he loved, despite its political problems.

Solzhenitsyn courageously took it upon himself to go beyond *Ivan Denisovich*, to reveal fully the extent of the gulag, the nationwide archipelago of prison labor camps spread throughout the country, most of them in cold, vast, remote Siberia.

> This Archipelago crisscrossed and patterned that other country within which it was located, like a gigantic patchwork, cutting into its cities, hovering over its streets. Yet there were many who did not even guess at its presence and many, many others who had heard something vague. And only those who had been there knew the whole truth. (p. x)

As many as 8 million citizens were imprisoned at any given time, and some 20 million may have died in the Gulag (see Source, p. 655).

BREZHNEV (1964–82)

Brezhnev ruled the Soviet Union from 1964 to 1982 as head of the government and General Secretary of the Communist Party. In 1968 Czechoslovakia tried to escape Russian control and establish an independent government. Brezhnev ended the hopes of this "Prague Spring" by declaring that the Soviet Union would intervene in the affairs of its satellites to prevent counter-revolution, a policy later named the "Brezhnev doctrine." He sent in Soviet troops to crush the Czech revolt. In the first years of his administration, Brezhnev built up the armed forces of the USSR, although later he made cutbacks.

Despite the Brezhnev doctrine, unrest simmered in Eastern Europe, most strongly in Poland. Here the Roman Catholic Church remained a powerful voice critical of communist rule and when Karol Wojtyla, the Polish archbishop of Krakow, was elected Pope in 1978, dissidents throughout Poland took heart (see Profile, opposite). Lech Walensa, a shipyard worker in Gdansk, began to organize what ultimately became Solidarity, an independent trade union federation with a membership of more than 10 million industrial and agricultural workers. Solidarity demanded not only lower prices and higher wages, but also the right to strike, freedom for political prisoners, an end to censorship, and free elections. At Moscow's bidding, the Polish government jailed Walensa and other Solidarity leaders and declared martial law. The Pope, however, supported Solidarity and the United States imposed economic sanctions. In 1982 Brezhnev died, martial law ended, and Walensa was freed. In 1983 he received the Nobel Peace Prize. Pressure on the Polish government, and on the Moscow government behind it, continued to build.

GORBACHEV (1985–91)

More fundamental reform of the Soviet system began in 1985, with the coming to power of Mikhail Gorbachev (b. 1931) and his policies of *glasnost* (political and cultural openness) and of *perestroika* (economic restructuring). The USSR could no longer afford the arms race. Its economy was neither producing nor distributing goods effectively. Its growing professional classes protested the restrictions on freedom. The churches continued to seek greater freedom of expression. In the satellite countries of Eastern Europe and in the non-Russian states of the USSR itself—especially the Baltic states and in the states of Central Asia which were culturally, linguistically, and religiously different from Russia—nationalist groups sought greater independence. In its haste to industrialize the Russians had allowed technology to get out of control, as evident in the massive pollution of air and sea, most frighteningly in the Aral Sea, and in the partial meltdown of the nuclear power plant at Chernobyl, Ukraine, in 1986, which spread radiation over several European nations.

Gorbachev withdrew the USSR from the arms race and began a fundamental reorganization of its technological institutions and economic priorities. He terminated control over the governments of Eastern Europe, which Russia had put into place and supported militarily during and after World War II. With the removal of Russian armies, all six nations—East Germany, Poland, Hungary, Czechoslovakia, Bulgaria, and Romania—became independent. Divided by the Allied occupying powers at the end of World War II, East and West Germany re-united, tearing down the Berlin Wall that had marked their division. Gorbachev resisted the right of constituent republics of the USSR to declare independence and leave the union, but many now declared their independence: the Baltic states of Estonia, Latvia, and Lithuania; the Slavic states of Belarus and Ukraine; the peripheral states of Armenia and Georgia, and the Muslim majority states in central Asia. With government control uncertain, historic ethnic tensions re-emerged within and between these states, and violent clashes marked the end of the empire.

The break-up of the Soviet Union The Soviet experiment with Marxist ideology crumbled, after seventy years, at the end of the 1980s. President Gorbachev's policy of *glasnost* (1985) allowed the nations of Eastern Europe to move, largely bloodlessly, toward independence and economic reform, but in the Caucasus mountains and Central Asia reform was often accompanied by an insurgence of nationalism, organized crime, and power struggles. In 1991 these nations also became independent—except for Chechnya, where fighting continued for years.

In August 1991 a coup attempt against Gorbachev, led by die-hard communists, failed, largely because Boris Yeltsin, the elected president of the Russian Republic, opposed it, courageously climbing atop an armored troop carrier to make his position clear. On December 24, 1991, however, the USSR dissolved itself into fifteen independent states, each proclaiming its national identity; Gorbachev no longer had a state to rule; Yeltsin's Russia was by far the largest surviving state.

YELTSIN (1991–99)

Yeltsin convened a Constitutional Assembly that produced a new constitution in 1993. But the Russian economy continued to sputter, and Yeltsin and the parliament came into direct, violent conflict. Following battles in which about 150 people were killed, Yeltsin reasserted his power as president. He was reelected in nationwide multiparty elections in 1996 that reaffirmed Russia's commitment to democracy.

In the decade 1991 to 2000, however, the Russian gross domestic product dropped by 50 percent, the life span of citizens fell by two and a half years, the birthrate dropped by a third, and the mortality rate rose by a quarter, while a small class of entrepreneurs made great profits. The government privatized its economic holdings, selling them off at bargain rates to its supporters. Petty crime became commonplace and organized criminal gangs flourished. In a face-off with government, "robber capitalists," wielding huge economic power, refused to pay taxes, bringing the nation to near bankruptcy.

Internationally, Yeltsin's greatest success may have been winning the confidence and support of foreign financial institutions and governments that continued to keep Russia's floundering economy afloat through investments, loans, and debt rescheduling. In 1997 Russia was accorded associate status in NATO, its former arch enemy, while the Czech Republic, Poland, and Hungary were invited as full members. His greatest embarrassment was the continuing war in the remote breakaway province of Chechnya where all the technology of the once proud Russian army could not defeat the nationalist rebels, nor could the Russian government negotiate a graceful retreat. On December 31, 1999, Yeltsin resigned as President of Russia. Vladimir Putin was elected his successor.

Base camp, near Urus-Martan, Chechnya. With the breakup of the USSR, most of the former Soviet satellites states gained independence through peaceful means, but Muslim-majority Chechnya was not offered that alternative. When it attempted to secede in 1994 Russian troops suppressed the revolt in two years of warfare, and returned in force in 1999 when resistance resumed. Despite Russia's overwhelming military strength, armed guerrilla conflict continues in Chechnya.

Russian beggar, Moscow. The introduction of capitalism in Russia enabled a few to become enormously wealthy, especially those who could buy up state-assets at discount prices. But generally the economy and society were plagued with new problems of adjusting to free enterprise and a market economy. At the bottom, the safety net no longer functioned, and heartbreaking scenes of beggars outside posh new boutiques became common in Moscow.

JAPAN: FRAGILE SUPERPOWER

BEFORE WORLD WAR I

Like Russia, Japan feared domination by the West. Confronted by foreign warships in the mid-nineteenth century (see pp. 582–9), the Japanese responded with the restoration program under the Emperor Meiji, an astonishingly rapid reorganization of government, administration, economy, industry, and finances.

As we have seen in Chapter 17, Japan, following Western examples, asserted a sphere of influence in China and seized colonies for itself. It defeated China in Korea in 1895 and became the dominant nation of east Asia, reversing its previous student–teacher relationship with China. Japan made Korea and the island of Taiwan into colonies and defeated Russia by land and sea in East Asia, in 1904–5, after signing a military alliance with Britain in 1902. For the first time in modern history, an Asian country had defeated a European one.

World War I touched East Asia only slightly. Nevertheless, Japan was seated as one of the victorious Five Great Powers at the 1919 peace conference in Paris—the only non-Western nation accepted as an equal at the proceedings—and was assigned control over Germany's Pacific colonies, including the Liaotung Peninsula in north China, which Japan had seized in 1914.

FOCUS
Economics in the Comic Books

In Japan, the comics, like television, have become a powerful medium for entertainment, for the transmission of knowledge, and for the diffusion of values. Indeed the term "comics" is a misnomer. Most *manga* (the generic term for cartoons, narrative strips, and animated films) are not at all funny. The most ambitious strive to achieve artistic and intellectual responsibility.

With these words, Peter Duus, Professor of History at Stanford University, introduces *Japan Inc.: An Introduction to Japanese Economics (The Comic Book)* published in translation in 1988 from the 1986 Japanese original by Shotaro Ishinomori. Weekly "comic books" sell in the hundreds of thousands of copies;

the record is 4 million. Some 550,000 copies of *Japan Inc.* were sold in less than a year. The six chapters of the *manga*, "comic," include quite serious issues: Trade Friction, Countering the Rise of the Yen, Industrial Structure, Deficit Finance, Monetary Revolution, and an Epilogue, which stresses the importance of human and humane relations in business. The two pages reproduced here depict a debate between two executives with different perspectives within a single company as they weigh the effects on small subcontractors of the company's decision to close a local automobile factory and relocate its production to the United States. In the end, Kudo's more compassionate position does win out. (*Japan Inc.* pp. 12–13)

A spread from *Japan Inc.: An Introduction to Japanese Economics* by Shotaro Ishinomori. Not all animation is so serious. Most is oriented toward entertainment. In translation Japanese animated productions have swept world markets as the commercial success of the film *Pokemon* and its associated merchandise demonstrated in 1999.

World War I had presented Japan with an unprecedented economic opportunity. While other industrialized countries were occupied with war in Europe, Japan developed its industries relatively free from competition. Between 1914 and 1918 Japan's gross national income rose by 40 percent, and for the first time Japan began to export more than she imported. Heavy industry showed particularly impressive growth. Manufacturing increased 72 percent while the labor force expanded only 42 percent, indicating the growing use of machinery. Transport increased 60 percent. Between 1914 and 1919 Japan's merchant marine almost doubled, to 2.8 million tons. The production and export of consumer goods also advanced. In the first decades of the twentieth century, Japan's greatest exports were textiles, primarily silk, of which 80 percent was produced by women.

As a late-comer, Japan could take advantage of technology already developed in the West (the path that Trotsky was preaching in Russia). Japanese industries practiced three different patterns in importing that technology. Some signed agreements with foreign firms to establish branches in Japan; some negotiated for licenses to use the new technologies; and some practised "reverse engineering," analyzing foreign machinery and reproducing it with adaptations appropriate to Japanese needs. Adaptation produced innovations, for example by applying chemical research to agricultural and even ceramics production. Most of the foreign technology was imported by private firms, but the government also encouraged research by funding state universities, laboratories, and the development of military technology.

Japan bridged the "dual economy," the separation between large-scale and cottage industries that has inhibited growth in many countries. In a "dual economy," one sector consists of large, highly capitalized, technically advanced factories employing thousands of workers producing modern products; the other sector includes small-scale workshops, with relatively low capitalization and less up-to-date equipment, often employing fewer than thirty workers, producing traditional goods. In most countries, the small-scale sector tends to shrivel, its workers consigned to low wages and poor conditions, as larger firms achieve economies of scale and put it out of business. Governments, too, as we have seen in Russia, often invest their resources in large industries, neglecting the small sector. But in Japan, the smaller factories adopted appropriate scale, new technologies, and began to produce new goods needed by the larger industries. From the early years of the century, Japan evolved systems of subcontracting between the large and small sectors which made them interdependent and complementary.

Today, even the largest Japanese industries rely on small factories to supply parts of their final, assembled products (a process of "outsourcing" increasingly adopted today in the United States). Particularly under the pressure of war, 1937–45, Japanese business developed cost-effective systems of precisely timed (*kamban*, "just in time") deliveries so that large firms did not need to keep large inventories of parts, but ordered and received them just when they were needed. Under this "just-in-time" system, needed changes in production are usually carried out by the smaller industries. The strain of periodically changing the mix of industrial production is borne disproportionately by the individual small factories, affecting relatively few people, while the larger industries and the economy as a whole are spared.

SOCIAL CONSEQUENCES OF WAR-TIME INDUSTRIAL GROWTH

Because of poor harvests in 1918 the price of rice, Japan's staple food, rose sharply. In response, massive riots broke out in hundreds of cities and towns, involving some 700,000 people, lasting fifty days, and resulting in 25,000 arrests and 1000 deaths. The government responded by importing rice and other staples from its colonial territories in Korea and Taiwan.

The riots represented the growth of Japan's urban voice as the urban proportion of the population rose from over 10 percent in 1890 to close to 50 percent in the 1920s (to 78 percent in the 1990s). Labor was increasingly organized and the citizenry politicized. In 1925 all male subjects over the age of twenty-five, 12.5 million people, were given the vote.

The riots also reminded Japan of its increasing dependence on its colonies for daily commodities. In the later 1920s Taiwan and Korea provided four-fifths of Japan's rice imports and two-thirds of its sugar. For industrial raw materials, such as minerals, metals, petroleum, fertilizers, and lumber, Japan had to shop further afield, and this would lead it into fatal colonial adventures.

In the 1920s, industrial production increased by two-thirds and the *zaibatsu* (huge holding companies or conglomerates) came to control much of the Japanese economy. The four largest—Mitsui,

Samurai warrior. The ancient and proud warrior class of the samurai worshipped athletic prowess, swordsmanship, and fierce loyalty to the emperor. In 1877 the last 400,000 samurai were pensioned off to become *shizoku*, Japanese gentry, but their virtues lived on in the country's psyche. In times of crisis, the warriors' values turned Japanese nationalism into a potent force.

Mitsubishi, Sumitomo, and Yasuda—were controlled by individual families, and each operated a bank and numerous enterprises in a variety of industries, ranging from textiles to shipping and machinery. A Mitsubishi mining company, for example, would extract minerals, which would then be made into a product by one of the Mitsubishi manufacturing companies. This product would be marketed abroad by a Mitsubishi trading firm and transported in ships of another Mitsubishi affiliate. The whole process would be financed through the Mitsubishi bank.

The *zaibatsu* combined large size with an ability to shift production to meet demands. The *zaibatsu* families also held considerable influence in government, both through the money they controlled and their close family links with prominent politicians. The Major Industries Control Law of 1931, for example, encouraged large companies in key industries to join in cartels to regulate production and prices (Morris-Suzuki, p. 139).

MILITARISM

International respect, growing wealth, rising urbanization, increasing industrialization, high rates of literacy, universal male suffrage, and the institutionalization of political parties suggested that Japan was embracing liberal democracy. But the political power of the *zaibatsu* undermined people's faith in democratic practice, and the military held extraordinary power, both under law and in popular opinion. In contrast to most democratic countries, in which the civilian government controls the military, Japanese law specified that the ministers of war and of the navy had to be active generals or admirals. Conversely, the formal powers of the Diet were restricted. In theory, the emperor held

the ultimate political authority for the country and, although he never did govern actively, political leaders speaking in his name dominated public policy. Japan's traditional Shinto religion (see Chapter 9) emphasized the emperor's divinity and asserted the leading role of Japan's samurai warrior ethic.

Many of these military elites began to claim expanded powers for the armed forces. They wished to protect Japan, a resource-poor island nation, especially vulnerable to shifts in international trade and its regulation. The world depression of 1929 shocked the Japanese economy as the value of exports dropped 50 percent between 1929 and 1931. Unemployment rose to 3 million, with rural areas hardest hit. Many civilians seemed to agree with the military: the future would look brighter if Japan could reorganize and control the economy of East Asia for its own benefit. When Prime Minister Osachi Hamaguchi over-rode his navy and accepted a 1930 international agreement with the United

States and Britain, effectively limiting the size of the Japanese navy, a right-wing fanatic murdered him. Similar assassinations followed in the 1930s.

THE RUN-UP TO THE PACIFIC WAR 1930–37

On the night of September 18, 1931 the Japanese army blew up a section of the South Manchurian Railroad, deliberately provoking military confrontation with China. Following this "Manchurian incident" the Japanese army began to set its own agenda, without regard to Tokyo's instructions.

The army sought to control all of Manchuria both for its mineral wealth and for its geo-political position as a buffer against Russia. After completing the military takeover of Manchuria, Japan established a puppet state there, Manchukuo, and installed its hand-picked emperor, Pu Yi. When the League of Nations censured Japan, it left the organization. Mired in economic depression, the major powers did nothing. The Japanese civilian government, which had attempted to rein in the army, lost public support and fell. The next prime minister was assassinated and henceforth the military dominated the government.

Strategic and commercial concerns began to converge. As Morris-Suzuki notes, Japan's "technologies of peace and war were, above all else, interrelated" (p. 125). The government encouraged and protected infant industries, especially those that could be quickly converted to military production: chemicals, automobiles, aircraft, and shipping. In the two decades from the end of World War I to 1937, Japan's industrial production tripled. Technological advances included the production of new artifical fibers, such as rayon, of which Japan became a major exporter; chemical improvements in fertilizers; and improved machine tools. By 1935, 89 percent of Japanese households had access to electric lighting (compared with 68 percent in the United States). Consumer goods, such as refrigerators, which were becoming common in the wealthier Western countries, were priced beyond the means of the average Japanese consumer. Okochi Masatoshi, director of Japan's Institute for Physical and Chemical Research, saw clearly the close relationship between commercial and military industrialization. He wrote in 1937: "In the final analysis future wars will not be wars of military might versus military might. They will be wars involving the entire nation's scientific knowledge and industrial capacity" (Morris-Suzuki, p. 127). With the onset of World War II, Japan's industries shifted from civilian to military production.

THE PACIFIC WAR 1937–45

In 1937 a clash between Chinese and Japanese troops at the Marco Polo Bridge near Beijing triggered a full-scale war with China, which marked the beginning of the Pacific War (World War II). The

Summary executions in the Pacific. Japanese soldiers were notoriously brutal in their treatment of prisoners during World War II. British servicemen captured in the Pacific theater were forced to construct the Burma Railway and many died of starvation and disease in the process. Some were murdered in cold blood, as here, the imminent execution of three Allied fighters before open graves.

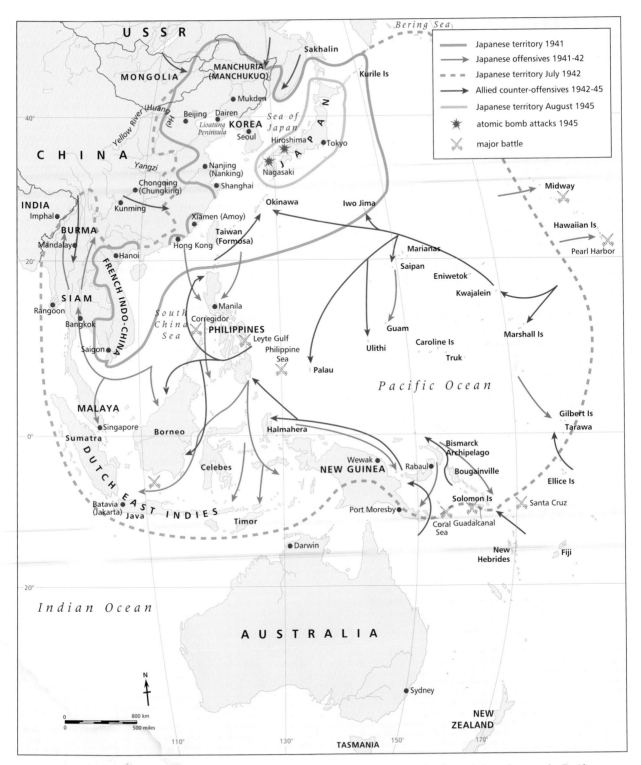

World War II in the Pacific Japan mounted combined operations in 1941 in East Asia, Southeast Asia, and across the Pacific, opening a war front from the borders of India to Hawaii. This supremely aggressive move was meant to secure the resources and markets needed to sustain the "Greater East Asia Co-Prosperity Sphere." It proved impossible to defend: Chinese resistance, a daring US island-hopping campaign in the Pacific—culminating in the explosion of atomic bombs over Hiroshima and Nagasaki—and Soviet assaults on Manchuria defeated Japan completely.

Japanese had not expected the fierce resistance of the Chinese. Planning to end the "China probem" with a single quick victory that would terrify the enemy into suing for peace, the Japanese army launched a full-scale attack on Nanjing (Nanking), capturing the city in December. Japanese troops murdered, raped, and pillaged in what is now generally known as "the Rape of Nanjing." Twelve thousand noncombattant Chinese were killed in the first two or three days after Nanjing was captured, and about 20,000 cases of rape were reported in the first month. In the first six weeks some 200,000 civilians and prisoners of war were killed in and around the city. The atrocities set an ugly precedent for later Japanese cruelty toward many of the peoples it defeated throughout Asia during the war.

In the face of repeated Japanese advances, the Chinese government retreated to Chongqing (Chungking), on the upper Yangzi River deep in the interior of the country. The Chinese, like the Russians retreating before the Germans, followed a scorched-earth strategy, leaving little in their wake that the enemy could use. The war in China became a stalemate. Even in 1945, when Japan itself was under attack, about a million Japanese soldiers were still fighting in China, and another 750,000 in Manchuria. China's sheer persistence helped wear out the Japanese.

The war in Europe had begun in September 1939 (pp. 608–14), and in September 1940 Japan signed the Tripartite Pact, formally aligning itself with Germany and Italy as the "Axis Powers." Axis plans however were not well coordinated. Japan could have joined in their war against the USSR, opening a second front from Manchuria, as Germany wished. Instead, it signed a neutrality pact with the Soviet Union in April 1941 and turned southward to capture French Indo-China, putting it on a collision course with the USA.

Isolationist pressure in America had thus far kept the USA out of armed warfare, but America did respond to Japanese aggression in China and Southeast Asia by placing an embargo on trade with Japan and by freezing its assets in July 1941. Resource-poor Japan, fearing for its supplies of oil and other raw materials, now had to choose between pulling back or confronting the United States in open warfare. Many resented American resistance to Japan's growing power as just another example of white man's colonialism, of a piece with European colonialism throughout Asia. On December 7, Japan bombed the American Pacific fleet at Pearl Harbor, Hawaii. America declared war

the next day. In Britain, Winston Churchill immediately understood the consequences:

> Hitler's fate was sealed. Mussolini's fate was sealed. As for the Japanese, they would be ground to powder. All the rest was merely the proper application of overwhelming force. (Kennedy, *Rise and Fall*, p. 347)

Before American industrial power and troop mobilization could move into high gear, however, Japan conquered the Philippines, the Malay peninsula and Singapore, Indonesia, parts of New Guinea, Indochina, Thailand, and Burma. In the Pacific, it reached almost to Australia. Designating the conquests as the "Greater East Asia Co-Prosperity Sphere," Japan attempted to build an imperial system that would provide raw materials for its industries and markets for its finished products and that would willingly adopt Japanese cultural practices as well. The plan did not work. The colonial economies could not produce and deliver the supplies that Japan wanted, and, more crucially, Japan could not absorb the agricultural products they could produce. Market structures based on the existing integration of world trade systems were not easily re-organized.

Instead of implanting its culture, Japan's occupations generally evoked nationalistic opposition. Japan's treatment of conquered peoples and prisoners of war was notably harsh and earned it a reputation for cruelty. The brutalizing of thousands of Korean, Chinese, and Filipina women to serve as "sex slaves" for Japanese soldiers came to international attention, along with the demand for financial reparation and public apologies, half a century after the war was over.

Japan's victories over European colonizers provided a double shock. Asians had never before seen Asians defeat Europeans. As these victories enhanced the image of Japanese power, they undermined the image of the Europeans. After the war, when the European colonizers attempted to return —the British to Burma and Malaya, the French to Indochina, the Dutch to Indonesia—local nationalist groups rose in protest, sometimes armed, and eventually achieved independence. In this sense, the Japanese victories were responsible for ending European colonialism in the Pacific region.

Once America entered the war with its full industrial and technological strength, the tide turned. In June 1942, American naval forces won their first battle at Midway Island. Then, from bases

US servicemen in the Pacific. Landing in Higgins boats from a base in Australia, American troops of the 163rd Infantry Regiment, 41st Division, hit the beach running during the invasion of Wake Island, May 18, 1944. Two months earlier, the United States had begun firebombing Japanese cities.

in Australia, they moved northwestward, taking Guadalcanal and New Guinea, recapturing the Philippines and the Pacific island chains. During the spring of 1945 they captured Okinawa after three months of brutal fighting. As early as March 1944 the Americans had begun firebombing Japanese cities. Japan had expected Americans to become tired of the war and negotiate a peace, but instead America demanded unconditional surrender.

The firebombing intensified. On March 9, 1945, 83,793 people were killed, 40,918 injured, and 267,000 buildings destroyed in Tokyo alone. Burning and starving—caloric intake had dropped from a daily standard of 2200 to 1405 by 1944—Japan fought on. Finally, America dropped the atomic bomb on Hiroshima on August 6, 1945 (see p. 614). On August 8, the USSR invaded Manchuria and Korea. On August 9, America dropped a second atomic bomb, this time on Nagasaki. On August 15, 1945 Japan offered its unconditional surrender.

Japan lay in ruins. Some 3 million Japanese had died in the war, a fourth of Japan's national assets were destroyed, industrial production was at barely 10 percent of pre-war levels, millions of homes had been destroyed, and Japan had lost all its colonial holdings. Mass starvation was prevented only by food imported by the occupation authorities.

THE OCCUPATION 1945–52

Japan awaited an uncertain future under American occupation headed by Supreme Commander for the Allied Powers (SCAP), General Douglas MacArthur. The occupation lasted until 1952 and focused on four goals: punishing some Japanese leaders as war criminals; establishing democratic institutions and practices; reviving the devastated Japanese economy; and enlisting Japan as an ally in the new Cold War against the USSR. All four goals were achieved.

Some 200,000 wartime leaders were barred from office. Twenty-five of the top leaders were tried for starting the war, and seven were hanged. The emperor was no longer to be regarded as sacred, nor would he wield political power. His role would be as a constitutional monarch. The preservation of the emperor as a symbol probably made Japanese acceptance of the occupation less difficult.

The colonial empire was dissolved, and 5.5 million expatriate Japanese were returned to Japan. The military was completely demobilized. State support for Shinto was ended. Police authority was reduced. Freedom of speech was reintroduced. Political prisoners were freed. A new constitution, issued in 1947, granted universal adult suffrage to everyone over the age of twenty, including women

for the first time. The Diet became an elected, British-style parliament, with two houses. The judiciary was independent, headed by a supreme court. Guarantees of freedom of assembly, the press, "life, liberty, and the pursuit of happiness," and the "right to maintain the minimum standards of wholesome and cultural living" were also written into the constitution (Fairbank, p. 821).

Economically, the Occupation Authority pushed ahead on four fronts. First, it redistributed agricultural land. Land held by absentee landlords and land in excess of 10 acres (4 hectares) per family had to be sold to the government at low rates, and the government, in turn, sold it to small farmers

who prospered and felt strong allegiance to the government.

Second, the largest *zaibatsu* were dissolved into their constituent companies and anti-monopoly legislation was passed. Over the next decades, new conglomerates, called **keiretsu**, grew up with many qualities of the *zaibatsu*, but they were less restrictive, and they allowed more scope for the start-up of new companies.

Third, the Occupation Authority encouraged the formation of labor unions, legalizing the right to organize, bargain, and strike. Within three years the unions had grown to several million members, and had begun to turn communist. The Occupation

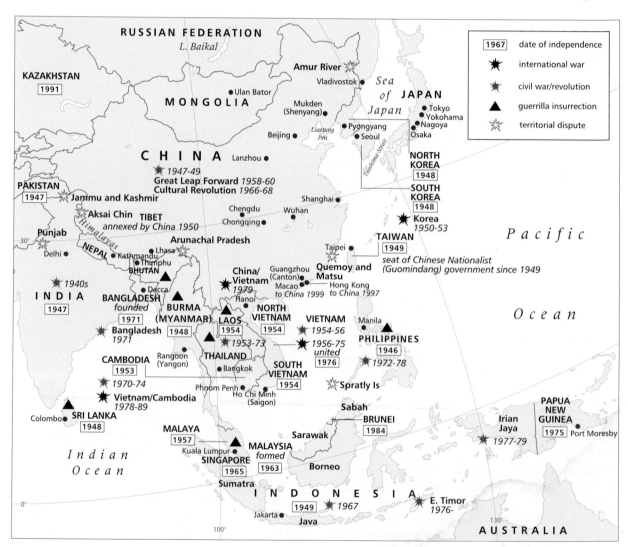

East Asia since 1945 China, the most populous nation in the world, completed one of the greatest revolutions in history, as a communist government displaced an empire which had endured for more than two millennia and then reunified the country after forty years of civil war. Japan recovered from catastrophic war losses and became rich and powerful. Most nations of the region emerged from Japanese wartime colonialism and claimed independence from European colonialism as well. In such tumultuous times, stability was constantly threatened by war and insurrection.

Authority then passed new laws to restrict the unions and purge their communist leaders. Unionization and strikes declined, but labor unions, which work closely with management, remained important in Japan's socio-economic life.

Finally, the Occupation Authority restructured the educational system (see Focus, below). Middle school students increased from 2.4 to 4.3 million; high school students from 380,000 to 1.2 million by 1952 to 4.3 million by 1975. By 1995, 90 percent of the appropriate age group graduated from high school. University students increased from 84,000 to 2.5 million in 1995, one-third of the university-age group.

Ironically, within five years of the end of World War II, the United States enlisted Japan as its ally in the Cold War against China and Russia. Japan's post-war constitution limited its military commitments, but a United States–Japanese Security Treaty did allow the United States to maintain military bases throughout Japan and to retain Okinawa until 1972. Under this treaty Japan was protected militarily by the United States.

Meanwhile, Japan became a principal supplier of materials and support services to the Americans fighting in neighboring Korea. The Korean War (1950–3) was an economic boon to Japan, providing a jump-start to the new growth. During the war, America bought $4 billion worth of military manufactures and tens of thousands of American troops were stationed in Japan. Between 1950 and 1973, Japan's economy grew at a phenomenal average rate of 10.5 percent a year. The gross national product grew from $24 billion in 1955, to $484 billion in 1975, to $4.3 trillion in 1994.

The American occupation introduced to Japan many management training experts. The most influential was W. Edwards Deming, who brought the concept of quality control systems, or "TQM," Total Quality Management, involving all workers throughout the entire process of production. Japanese businessmen adopted this concept more fully than Americans did. Japanese workers were encouraged to feel themselves a valued part of the production process, their suggestions solicited and taken seriously, their job security ensured to the extent possible, their pay and benefits kept at high levels.

Japanese consumer goods, produced through this system of personal dedication combined with the highest technological efficiency, earned a reputation for excellent quality and began to take over large shares of the world market, challenging more established producers, including the Americans.

CONTINUITIES 1952–73

By charging government with the coordination of the national economy, Japan set a path different from both the *laissez-faire* American pattern and the state control of the USSR. Japan's Ministry for International Trade and Industry (MITI) had charge of national tax and investment policies and encouraged industries in allied fields to share technological information. MITI decided which industries would be permitted access to capital for investment

FOCUS
Historical Revisionism in Japan

The study of history was transformed under American occupation: The contents of school textbooks were dramatically revised to remove much of the emperor-centered, nationalistic wartime ideology. Even today, older Japanese can vividly recall their shock and disbelief at being directed by their teachers, on occupation orders, to take a brush and black ink to wipe out whole pages of their textbooks until new books were available (Spodek, p. 15).

History is still being revised as Japan attempts to decide how to tell the story of its participation in World War II. Does it stress only the end of the war, the atomic bombing of Hiroshima, and Japan's suffering? Or should it also discuss the beginning of the war and Japan's aggression? Should stress be placed on the American embargoes that forced Japan to choose between retreat and war, or on Japan's choice of war? These questions are still alive in educational circles, in public debate, museum displays at Hiroshima and Nagasaki, and in television serials on the war.

and, in the early post-war years, to imports of scarce foreign machinery, materials, and technology.

Japan had found a way of development that was neither fully capitalist and competitive nor fully state-controlled. It blended private enterprise with state guidance in a competitive, high-technology economy, manufacturing exports for a global economy. Until the 1970s, Japan still imported and adapted much of its new technology. Sony, for example, acquired a patent to produce the newly invented transistor in 1954, solved the problem of using it to broadcast the human voice, and began to produce transistor radios. The number of researchers employed by private companies multiplied seven times between 1952 and 1975. Japan's research capacity was dispersed in numerous small research centers, which gave the country enormous flexibility in research and production. (In the 1980s some twenty-five industrial research towns, called **technopolises**, were added to the mix, although some critics argued that Japan needed more concentration of technical expertise, not less.)

Japan gained increasing international recognition for its economic and technological gains. In 1964, a number of symbolic events marked this coming of age. In April, Japan was admitted to the Organization for Economic Cooperation and Development (OECD), which until then had included only European and North American governments. Later in the year, the Shinkansen, or "bullet train," began carrying passengers between Tokyo and Osaka at speeds of 125 miles (200 kilometers) an hour, the fastest in the world. In the same year, Tokyo played host to the summer Olympics, winning universal praise for its new architecture, stadia, hotels, and ability to accommodate and please both the participants and the throngs of spectators.

In the 1960s, in recognition of its increasing economic strength, Japan began to produce more consumer goods. From 1957 to 1965 the percentage of non-agricultural homes with black-and-white television sets rose from 7.8 percent to 95 percent; and the homes with refrigerators from 2.8 percent to 68.7 percent. Consumer demand increased in sophistication and in buying power.

THE OIL SHOCKS OF 1973 AND 1979

Japan's response to the "oil shocks" of 1973 and 1979 demonstrated both her vulnerability and flexibility. In October 1973, as war broke out between Israel and its Arab neighbors (see pp. 737–40), Arab producers raised the price of oil worldwide by two-thirds and restricted its availability (see p. 732). All industrial nations were hard hit, but Japan, which imported 86 percent of its energy needs, mostly oil from the Middle East, was especially affected. In response, Japan intensified the search for conserving energy, and through increased industrial efficiency reduced its dependence on oil by 25 percent; it sought oil imports from new sources; and it began to shift into even more knowledge-intensive industries, such as electronics and computers, which are much less energy-dependent.

When Arab nations again raised the price of oil dramatically in 1979, Japan was better able to cope than other industrial countries. Its productivity did not decline significantly. From the oil shock of 1973 until 1988, Japan's technology and its economy tell two stories: on the one hand, the rate of growth has declined, averaging 5 percent a year (Ito, p. 3), less than half that of the previous two decades; on the other hand, this performance was better than that of any other major power.

CONTROLLING POLLUTION

Rapid industrialization and urbanization brought problems of pollution to Japan. By the 1960s, daytime skies in Tokyo were grey, Tokyo Bay was filled with industrial sludge, and traffic policemen suffered from lead poisoning, even though they worked on two-hour rotations. Specific cases of industrial pollution drew worldwide attention. In the small city of Minamata, on the island of Kyushu, mercury dumped into the bay by a large chemical plant was leading to deformities and deaths among the local population. By 1958 government research pointed to mercury poisoning as the cause of the disease, but the report was not publicly released.

In 1968 and 1969 lawyers filed four separate suits against polluters: in Minamata, in a similar case in Niigata, in Yokkaichi, where the issue was air pollution, and in Toyama, where the problem was cadmium poisoning. These "Big Four" cases progressed through the courts for the next few years. "By 1973, when the Minamata plaintiffs won the largest tort award in Japanese history, the anti-pollution movement ignited by the Big Four was being described as a radically new form of Japanese political action" (Upham, p. 342).

The issue of industrial pollution underlined by these cases had moved to the top of Japan's politi-

Legacy of pollution. In Minamata, mercury poisoning killed forty-three people and maimed many others between 1953 and 1956. The disease, causing tumors, paralysis, and bone deformities, was contracted by eating fish contaminated by dimethyl mercury seeping from a local PVC factory. In this famous image, Eugene Smith captured the poignancy of a mother bathing her stricken son.

cal agenda. Ruling and opposition parties agreed on legislation and implementation to produce a clean Japan. "Japan went from being clearly the most polluted of the major industrial countries to comparing favorably on those indexes of pollution related to human health" (Upham, p. 343).

INTERNATIONAL INVESTMENT FINANCE 1989–2000

Japan continued to earn colossal trade surpluses, reaching $163 billion in 1996. Much of this surplus was invested overseas. For example, all the major Japanese automobile manufacturers established production plants in the United States between 1980 and 1985: Nissan in Tennessee; Honda in Ohio; Toyota in California; Mazda in Michigan. Cars produced in these plants were sold in America without import or tariff restrictions, although their profits are expatriated back to Japan. Even more overseas investment was placed in developing countries, especially in nearby Asian countries. In 1999, Matsushita Electrical Industrial had fifty-eight factories in Southeast Asia, fourteen of them in Malaysia. Japan became the world's largest donor of foreign aid, giving about $14 billion in 1994. The aid helped the recipient and also provided a climate receptive to Japanese business and investment.

On the other side, forces inhibiting growth included three major problems. First, Japan's enormous trade surpluses created "trade frictions" with debtor countries. For example, the American trade deficit with Japan in 1986 reached $62 billion and,

despite increasing competitiveness from America, it was still $57 billion in 1997. In Southeast Asia, Japan had a trade surplus of approximately $20 billion in 1997–8, although it dropped the next year by 60 percent. Western nations urged Japan to impose "voluntary self-restrictions" on exports, to open its own markets to increased imports, and to consume more. Japan agreed, and by 1985 these voluntary restrictions had cut 40 percent of potential exports. Nevertheless, the balance of trade continued dramatically in Japan's favor. In an ongoing dispute, the United States and some European countries further claimed that unfair trade practices kept foreign products out of Japanese markets.

Second, the off-shore investments in nearby countries—Korea, Taiwan, Hong Kong, Singapore, Thailand, and China—were led both to increased competition from their new products and to a loss of jobs to their lower-wage economies. Japan experienced the same "hollowing out of industry" as did the United States, as industries closed at home and factories and jobs moved off-shore. Meanwhile, the Asian nations receiving the investment were going through the same processes of technological development as Japan had in its post-war years. They competed with Japan internationally and even within the Japanese home market in industries such as textiles, chemicals, iron and steel, and electrical products. In response Japanese financiers and industrialists began to invest more at home in computer technology (although Japan seriously lagged behind the United States) and to restructure personnel policies to link employment, wages, and benefits more directly to performance and productivity, while reducing job security.

Finally, in 1989 an economic "bubble" burst in Japan and the country slipped into an unexpected recession. In a "bubble" economy, prices for stocks and investments rise as investors bet on the future, anticipating continually improving economic performance. If these expectations outrun reality, however, prices will suddenly collapse. In Japan in 1989–90 land values plummeted by two-thirds. (The total land of Japan had been valued at four times the total value of land in the United States.) The Nikkei stock market index followed, plummeting by 60 percent from 1989 to 1992. Billions of dollars in paper wealth were wiped out, and Japan fell into a long-term depression. This depression curtailed Japan's economic and technological growth and its power in the international economy. The Japanese government that had been credited with masterminding forty years of continuous growth was now blamed for economic recession.

GENERATIONAL SHIFTS, 1989–2000

Politics

Emperor Hirohito died in 1989, ending a reign of sixty-three years. Many Japanese saw his passing as symbolic of deep changes in their political system. During the occupation, Japan's prime minister Yoshida Shigeru had set the country's economic and political policies on three pillars: a dominant political party, an efficient bureaucracy, and a Cold War alliance with the United States. By the late

1980s "all three of Yoshida's premises were in ruins" (Gibney, p. 388).

The dominant Liberal Democratic Party (LDP), after guiding the country for forty years, seemed "derailed" (Duus, 1998, p. 354). Disgusted by its corruption—politicians had been bought by big business and had joined in league with organized crime—voters in 1993 returned a multiparty government that formed its cabinet without the LDP. The LDP remained the largest party in the Diet (parliament), and returned to power as head of a coalition government in 1996, but voters remained disaffected with the LDP in particular and with politicians in general. The bureaucracy, too, did not sustain its reputation for efficiency and honesty. It had won much of its praise as guide and monitor of Japan's economic success; now it took much of the blame for the recession.

Finally, with the end of the Cold War Japan searched for a new international position. Should it continue to build its international policy primarily on an alliance with the United States, or should it attempt to provide a separate leadership to the nations of East and Southeast Asia? Militarily, Japan's budget had grown to the third largest in the world (about $41 billion in 1996), but it was bound by its post-war constitution not to send its troops overseas. In 1992 the Diet made an exception, allowing troops to serve in United Nations Peace Keeping Operations in non-combatant roles, such

Toyota factory, Japan. In this fully automated factory robots fit windshields to a production-line car. Robots are not only cheaper than humans, but in Japan, with its low birthrates and long life spans, they also compensate for labor shortages.

as engineering roads and bridges in Cambodia (1992), and settling refugees in Mozambique (1993). Japan's wealth and industriousness had thrust it into a position in international politics and diplomacy, as in economics, for which its experience as a homogeneous island nation had not given it much preparation. It wrestled with its new responsibilities.

The Work Ethic

Devotion to work had enabled Japan to achieve high levels of productivity, but it also constricted people's personal lives and their enjoyment of the products of their hard work. In the early 1990s, despite the longest life-spans in the world, middle-aged Japanese executives began to fear *karoshi* (literally, death from overwork), high levels of stress-related illness among senior businessmen, and, indeed, some middle-level managers in their forties did collapse and die of heart attacks and other diseases.

The younger generation, however, those in their thirties and below, seemed to be a "new breed," *shinjinrui*. They seemed less devoted to work than their parents. They had grown up in smaller families, often as only children, more self-centered and self-contained, wealthier and more interested in consumption and individualism than those born before, during, and immediately after the War. Some searched for a spiritual side of life in new religious sects. Historian Peter Duus, in his discussion of these new traits among Japanese youth, nevertheless notes that they had been raised in a rigorous regimen of education and preparation for careers in corporate society, and "by comparison with youth in the Western industrial countries, the 'new breed' were much more likely to see work as their main interest in life" (p. 365). Lifestyles were changing, but within limits.

An Aging Society

Japan's population is aging. Its life spans are the longest in the world. At birth, women's life expectancy is eighty-three years, that of men is seventy-seven. The birth rate has fallen below replacement level. With the aging population, social security benefits become more costly and the proportion of working people to retired people becomes much smaller. All industrialized countries will face this prospect; Japan is confronting it now. One of the solutions has been robotics, in which Japan is far-and-away the world's leader, with more industrial robots than the entire rest of the world combined. Japan has developed whole factories run by computers, lasers, and robots, which almost eliminate the need for human workers. Another solution has been the importation of foreign workers, but Japan has not wanted these foreigners to remain as citizens and serious frictions are emerging (as they have in Europe) between the Japanese and their "guest workers."

Women in the Workforce: How Do We Know?

In a recent essay on the status of women in postwar Japan, historian Kathleen Uno speculates that the Meiji ideal of "Good Wife, Wise Mother" was changing. "This ideal defined women as managers of domestic affairs in households and nurturers of children" (Uno, p. 294). By the 1980s, most women still saw their primary role in the household while men's was outside, but perspectives on gender roles were changing, as more women worked outside the home and more shared in housework.

Sandra Buckley, Professor of East Asian studies at McGill University, Montreal, agrees. Economic pressures on the family, the extraordinary long life-expectancy of Japanese women, and the fact that most women have only one or two children, encourage women to enter the labor force. Nevertheless, the overwhelming majority seem to view their primary responsibility as the home, and most work part time rather than full time. Japanese women tend to follow an M-curve of employment, taking jobs after schooling, quitting at the birth of their children, returning when they are grown, and perhaps quitting again when their aging parents (and their husband's parents) need care.

The legal system supports this emphasis on the wife/mother at home. Moreover, Buckley writes, Japanese women seemed to view higher education as a means to a better marriage rather than a better job:

> The more educated a woman was, the less likely she was to enter full-time employment and the shorter her average periods of stay in the work force. The reason behind this trend appears to have been the differing value attached to education for men and women. For the male each educational achievement was a qualification for future employment, whereas

for the female each educational achievement was a potential qualification for a better marriage match. The more economically secure the marriage she made, the less likely a woman was to need to enter or remain in the workplace to supplement family income. The higher the social and economic status of her partner, the more pressure a woman was under to leave full-time employment. Certain specializations were seen as better qualifications for a particular category of future spouse. Pharmacology was popular in the 1980s as a possible entree to a marriage match with a doctor. Certain women's universities regularly supplied graduating lists to hospitals. One well-known Tokyo women's college was renowned as a source of wives for career diplomats. (p. 362)

Frank Upham, Professor at Boston College Law School, on the other hand, attributed the low employment rate of university-trained women to the employers rather than to the women. Employers discriminated against university-trained women because they were likely to stay on as full-time employees; the employers preferred women who would quit during child-bearing ages and could, therefore, be kept as part-time, lower paid employees. Japan passed an Equal Employment Opportunity Act (EEOA) in 1986 and women could work at night, at part-time employment and low-wage jobs, just like men. Women's work opportunities were increasing (Upham, p. 337). Japanese patriarchy was under some challenge. With the passage of the EEOA, the employment rate for female university graduates reached 75.2 percent, compared with the male rate of 78.8 percent.

JAPAN AS A MODEL:
HOW DO WE KNOW?

Japan's economic growth at home, and its investments in the region, made it a model of development in much of East and Southeast Asia. The model emphasized: a state-guided economy with a national bureaucracy directing the investments of both public and private enterprise; high levels of (rote) education; a disciplined, industry-friendly labor force; high rates of savings and investments; concentration on industrialization and high technology production; and dedication to the nation. With most nations of the region adopting this model, growth was extraordinary: Between 1965 and 1996, the average annual growth of the GNP for the world as a whole was 3.1 percent. For South Korea it was 8.9 percent; Singapore, 8.3 percent; Hong Kong, 7.5 percent; Thailand, 7.3 percent; Indonesia, 6.7 percent; Malaysia, 6.8 percent; the Philippines, 3.5 percent. Japan's growth had slowed after its 1989 recession, but still averaged 4.5 percent. China, which we treat separately in the next chapter, grew at 8.5 percent. "Before July 2, 1997 the Asian Pacific was considered, rightly, to be the world's success story of economic development and technological modernization of the past half-century" (Castells, III, p. 206).

Then the currency of Thailand fell sharply, as investors recognized that the national economy was not expanding as rapidly as incoming investment and loans, and the country had a mounting trade deficit. The values of land and industry on which the loans and investments had been based

East Asian cityscape. Neon, symbol of the hi-tech economy, rises vertically into the night sky above a teeming city street in the Ginza district of Tokyo, Japan.

were artificially high, and they collapsed, as did the value of Thai currency. Investments stopped and loans were recalled, first from Thailand and then from neighboring countries with similar financial problems. South Korea, Thailand, Indonesia, Malaysia, and the Philippines, which had seen $93 billion in net investments enter their countries in 1996, saw $12 billion leave in 1997.

> In a few months, in 1997 and 1998, entire economies collapsed (Indonesia, South Korea), others went into a deep recession (Malaysia, Thailand, Hong Kong, the Philippines), and the leading economy, Japan, the second largest in the world, was shaken by financial bankruptcies, prompting the international downgrading of Japanese bonds and stocks.
> (Castells, III, p. 207)

What had happened? The Asian economies were actually doing many things right. They had budget surpluses, low inflation, high rates of savings, and substantial exports. But they had taken on more loans, especially short-term loans, than their productivity justified, and as collateral they had presented real estate that was dramatically and unrealistically overpriced. Beyond this, their internal financial systems were not "transparent," that is, not open to external analysis and evaluation. (These problems had also surfaced in Japan after the 1989 "bubble" burst.) Corrupt politicians, bureaucrats, bankers, and organized crime leaders were guiding investments inappropriately, for their own benefit, and covering up their actions. Meanwhile investment money and loans poured in from overseas. The monies were misused, pocketed, or poorly invested in speculation, until finally the economies collapsed.

The governments, which had been so helpful as their economies had grown, were now not strong enough to bail out the failing banks and industries. (In the United States, in the 1980s, the government had spent $250 billion bailing out savings and loans associations which had made bad investments.) The system of government direction which had produced economic miracles now left a wake of recession and depression. Those which had relied less on international funds, and which had paid more attention to basic business fundamentals—like Taiwan and Singapore—had fewer troubles; those which had taken in the most foreign loans and investments, and had invested least prudently, were most affected—like South Korea, Indonesia, and Thailand.

What could be done? The International Monetary Fund came to the rescue in some countries with massive loans, but the very arrival of the IMF frightened off other investors and encouraged them to withdraw their funds. Also the IMF was more concerned with recovering the loans and investments than with the economic health of the defaulting country. It virtually took over control of the economy of the defaulting country and usually demanded a regimen of economic austerity so severe that it jeopardized the health and welfare of the citizens of the country. This was the experience in South Korea in 1997, which accepted a bail-out loan of $58 billion, the largest ever in the history of the IMF.

Some international bankers, like billionaire George Soros, saw the need for countries to be more honest and more transparent. They argued that state guidance and regulations should be cut back as national economies grew, and that private enterprise be given more scope. But they also argued that some regulation was needed at the international level. Trillions of dollars in investment funds were swirling around the globe greedily, without guidance or tracking or common purpose, battering the economies of all but the largest states. The East Asian collapse was one result. (Compare Russia, p. 658, Mexico, p. 785, and Brazil, p. 789.) Capital markets had become global, but the national and international institutions for keeping them honest and transparent had not. This was the great institutional deficiency now exposed by the experience of East and Southeast Asia.

WHAT DIFFERENCE DOES IT MAKE?

Both Russia and Japan had set out to chart new paths of technological development not only for themselves but for others as well. The paths had been different. Russia's had imploded, with many of its methods discredited: government control of the total economy; comprehensive medium range (five year) planning; suppression of individual rights and the creation of a vast prison system "for the good of the state"; concentration on heavy industry to the detriment of both medium-sized industry and agriculture; industrial development without adequate concern for ecology; and direct control over smaller neighbors to subordinate their economies for the benefit of the imperial power. Russia had also invested immense resources in the technology of military development and space research. The Russian government saw this investment not in economic terms but as a necessity of living in a world of aggressive states. It had cost Russia dearly, but it also enabled the country to survive the German invasion of World War II and to combat American capitalism and imperialism, the perceived enemy, during the Cold War. Russia's technological accomplishments were impressive, and had enabled the country to achieve its goals as it understood them. At the century's end, however, Russia did not seem to be an example to any other country, and it was itself trying to find new paths of development.

Japan's economy, on the other hand, had become a startling success and its methods were studied and sometimes copied by other countries, especially its East Asian neighbors: state guidance and coordination of the economy; concentration on appropriate scale technologies; integration of large, medium, and small sectors of the economy; concentration on export markets; high standards of education; and quality control at all levels of production. Japan, too, had embarked on periods of imperial expansion and of subordination of individual rights to those of the state, and these policies had backfired. An island nation with a long history of isolation, Japan became a world economic and technological leader that was learning to integrate its economic and technological needs with those of others. It was also a pioneer in developing international investment policies, but these had not all worked out well, as the economic crises in several East and Southeast Asian countries demonstrated with startling abruptness. At the end of the twentieth century Japan also seemed to be lagging in computer and biological technologies. Some observers blamed the nation's education system for favoring rote learning over more creative problem-solving.

In the end it appeared that no nation, no matter how successful, could provide a ready-made model for others. Each nation had its own history, culture, geography, and range of goals. Technological and investment policies would have to be individually tailored and international institutions would have to be created to cope with the new, uncontrolled global markets. In the next chapters we will examine some of the alternative courses chosen by other countries and regions.

BIBLIOGRAPHY

Andrea, Alfred and James Overfield. *The Human Record*, Vol. 2 (Boston: Houghton Mifflin, 3rd ed., 1998).

Baum, Gregory and Robert Ellsberg, eds. *The Logic of Solidarity: Commentaries on Pope John Paul II's Encyclical "On Social Concern"* (Maryknoll, NY: Orbis Books, 1989).

Beasley, W.G. *Japanese Imperialism 1894–1945* (New York: Oxford University Press, 1987).

Buckley, S. "Altered States: The Body Politics of 'Being-Woman'," in Gordon, ed., *Postwar Japan*, 342–72.

Buruma, Ian. *God's Dust: A Modern Asian Journey* (New York: Farrar, Straus and Giroux, 1989).

Castells, Manuel. *The Information Age: Economy, Society and Culture* 3 Vols. (Malden, MA: Blackwell, 1996–98).

Clark, Ronald. *Lenin: The Man behind the Mask* (London: Faber and Faber, 1988).

Duus, Peter. *Modern Japan* (Boston: Houghton Mifflin, 2nd ed., 1998).

Fairbank, John K., Edwin O. Reischauer, and Albert M. Craig. *East Asia: Tradition and Transformation* (Boston: Houghton Mifflin, rev. ed., 1989).

Gibney, Frank. *Japan: The Fragile Superpower* (Tokyo: Charles E. Tuttle, 3rd rev. ed., 1996).

Gordon, Andrew. *Labor and Imperial Democracy in Prewar Japan* (Berkeley: University of California Press, 1991).

—. ed. *Postwar Japan as History* (Berkeley: University of California Press, 1993).

Harris, Nigel. *The End of the Third World* (New York: Viking Penguin, 1987).

Hughes, T. *American Genesis* (New York: Viking, 1989).

Ishinomori, Shotaro. *Japan Inc.: An Introduction to Japanese Economics*, trans. by Betsey Scheiner (Berkeley: University of California Press, 1988).

Ito, Takatoshi. *The Japanese Economy* (Cambridge, MA: MIT Press, 1992).

Johnson, Chalmers, *MITI and the Japanese Miracle* (Stanford: Stanford University Press, 1982).

Kamata, Satoshi. *Japan in the Passing Lane* (New York: Pantheon, 1982).

Kennedy, Paul. *Preparing for the Twenty-first Century* (New York: Random House 1993)

—. *The Rise and Fall of Great Powers* (New York: Random House, 1987).

Kochan, Lionel and Richar Abraham. *The Making of Modern Russia* (London: Penguin Books, 1983).

Lewin, Moshe. *Russian Peasants and Soviet Power* (New York: W.W. Norton, 1968).

Malia, Martin. *The Soviet Tragedy* (New York: The Free Press, 1994).

Morris-Suzuki, Tessa. *The Technological Transformation of Japan* (Cambridge: Cambridge University Press, 1994).

Myers, Ramon H. and Mark R. Peattie, eds. *The Japanese Colonial Empire, 1895–1945* (Princeton: Princeton University Press, 1984).

Nehru, Jawaharlal. *Glimpses of World History* (New Delhi: Oxford University Press, 1982).

Reed, John. *Ten Days That Shook the World* (London: Penguin Books, 1960).

Reischauer, Edwin O. *The Japanese Today* (Cambridge, MA: Harvard University Press, 1988).

Remnick, David. *Lenin's Tomb: The Last Days of the Soviet Empire* (New York: Vintage Books, 1994).

Rosenberg, Rosalind, "The 'Woman Question,'" in Richard W. Bulliet, ed. *The Columbia History of the 20th Century* (New York: Columbia University Press, 1998).

Samuels, Richard J. *The Business of the Japanese State* (Ithaca: Cornell University Press, 1987).

—. *"Rich Nation, Strong Army"* (Ithaca: Cornell University Press, 1994).

Sivard, Ruth L. *World Military and Social Expenditures, 1991.* (Washington: World Priorities, 14th through 16th eds., 1991–96).

Smith, Dennis B. *Japan since 1945: The Rise of an Economic Superpower* (New York: St. Martin's Press, 1995).

Smith, Headrick. *The New Russians* (New York: Random House, 1990).

Solzhenitsyn, Alexander. *The Gulag Archipelago*, 3 vols. (New York: Harper and Row, 1974–78).

Soros, George. *The Crisis of Global Capitalism* (New York: Public Affairs, 1998).

Spodek, Susannah R. "On the History of Japan: World War I to the Present," (unpub. manuscript, 1996).

Stavrianos, L.S. *Global Rift* (New York: W. Morrow, 1981)

The [London] Times Atlas of World History. Ed. Richard Overy (London: Times Books Ltd, 5th ed., 1999).

Trotsky, Leon. *The Russian Revolution* (Garden City, New York: Doubleday Anchor Books, 1959).

Tsunoda, Ryusaku, Wm. Theodore de Bary, and Donald Keene, comps. *Sources of Japanese Tradition* (New York: Columbia University Press, 1958).

United Nations Development Program. *Human Development Report 1998* (New York: Oxford University Press, 1998).

Uno, Kathleen S. "Women and Changes in Household Division of Labor," in Gail Lee Bernstein, ed., *Recreating Japanese Women, 1600–1945* (Berkeley: University of California Press, 1991), 17–41.

Vogel, Ezra. *The Four Little Dragons: The Spread of Industrialization in East Asia* (Cambridge, MA: Harvard University Press, 1991).

— . *Japan as Number One* (Cambridge, MA: Harvard University Press, 1979).

World Almanac and Book of Facts 2000 (Mahwah, New Jersey: World Almanac Books, 1999).

World Bank. *World Development Report*, annual (New York: Oxford University Press, 1992 through 1998/9).

CHAPTER
20
CHINA AND INDIA

"All power to the Peasant Association"

MAO ZEDONG

"Hunger is the argument that is driving India to the spinning wheel."

M.K. GANDHI

THE GIANT AGRARIAN NATION-WORLDS

Home to some of the most ancient and influential civilizations, China and India are almost worlds in themselves. Both are vast and densely populated countries: China, with 1.2 billion people, contains about one-fifth of the world's population, and India, with another billion inhabitants, contains one-sixth. Each is four times larger than any other country on earth. (The United States is the third largest country in terms of population, with "only" about 270 million inhabitants.) Although their urban populations are growing rapidly, both China and India remain predominantly agricultural countries; China's current population is 71 percent rural; India's is 73 percent.

Politically, until 1947, India was administered as a colony of Britain, and British India included the regions that became today's independent states of Pakistan and Bangladesh. China was not administered directly by foreign powers, but Britain, France, Russia, Germany, and Japan had great economic and cultural influence over the huge nation. Between 1931 and 1945

Japan seized substantial areas of China (see pp. 663–6).

Because of British colonial policies, India was, despite its diverse ethnicities, languages, religions, and castes, partially unified as a political unit throughout the twentieth century, with the enormous exceptions of the partitions of Pakistan and Bangladesh into separate countries. China, on the other hand, despite the relative unity of its culture and ethnicity, was without an effective central government through most of the first half of the century, suffering both civil war and invasion from Japan.

India and China attained modern statehood at about the same time. India won independence from England in 1947. After Japan was defeated in World War II, China continued its nationwide communist revolution that drove out foreign powers and unified almost the entire country in 1949 (except for Taiwan, Hong Kong, and Macao).

The two countries then chose different strategies of development. Influenced by British colonial legacies and by its own heterogeneity, India chose democratic elec-

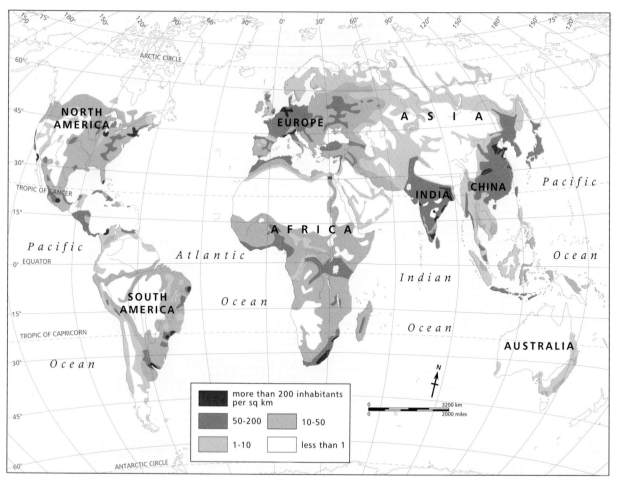

World population distribution today While the bulk of the world's population lives, as always, in coastal regions or along river valleys, the rapid rise in urbanism over the last century has created enormous imbalances as cities attract economic migrants from their hinterlands and from abroad. Some areas, like Europe, are so urbanized that their entire surface has high densities; others like China and India are so packed that even rural areas house urban densities. The only areas with low densities are those ecologically difficult for human life—deserts, mountains, frozen regions.

toral politics and a mixed socialist-capitalist economy. China, on the other hand, was dominated both politically and economically by its victorious communist army and government. Since the 1980s, both countries have introduced more capitalistic economies that are more open to participation in the global economy, and both countries have developed a variety of technological policies in response to the varied needs of their immense populations and their status as regional and world powers.

CHINA 1911–2000

THE PRELUDE TO REVOLUTION

The 1911 revolution that ended China's 2000-year-old empire climaxed the nation's first set of res-

ponses to Europe's nineteenth-century military and technological invasions. As we have seen in Chapter 16, Britain's gunboat assaults in the opium war of 1839–42 had forced open the sea and river ports of China to opium and Western manufactures, imposed unequal treaties, established foreign concessions, and granted extraterritorial legal rights to Europeans (see p. 545). Following further defeats and dismemberment in the Arrow War of 1859–60, the Sino-Japanese war of 1894–5, and the Boxer Rebellion in 1899–1900 (see p. 548), China lay supine before European and Japanese control. With the central government in confusion, peasant revolt simmered. To suppress the Taiping peasant revolt of 1850–64 had required fourteen years of warfare in which millions died.

Imperial officials attempted to shore up the government by adopting two methods from the

West: "self-strengthening" of industrial and military capacities and restructuring of the official civil service examinations, with greater infusions of science and technology. Both movements encouraged more hopes for change than they could satisfy. China was industrializing, but only slowly; in 1911 there were one million industrial workers—of a total population of 400 million. Most industry was small-scale, much of it in textiles. Faith in the viability of Confucian traditions and in the government that was to implement them was dying. After seventy years of military defeat, colonial subordination, peasant revolt, and intellectual contentiousness, China was ripe for revolution. The Mandate of Heaven was passing from the Manchu dynasty.

THE 1911 REVOLUTION

A bomb explosion in the Wuhan area in October 1911 had triggered a series of army mutinies and civilian revolts. Within a month, the Manchu government had promulgated a civil constitution and convened a provisional national assembly. Yuan Shihkai (1859–1916), the most powerful military official in China, was elected premier. In January 1912, the boy emperor, Puyi (r. 1908–12), abdicated, ending 2000 years of China's imperial tradition, and Yuan received full powers to organize a provisional republican government. But he exceeded his mandate. In January 1916 Yuan took the title of emperor, provoking widespread revolt. Under severe military attack and critically ill, Yuan died in June. With no effective governing center, China entered a decade of rule by **warlords**, regional leaders who had their own independent militias.

Some of the warlords controlled whole provinces, others only a few towns or segments of railway line; some had formal military training, others were simply local strongmen; some sought to play a role in forming a powerful national government, others to continue China's division. Many were rapacious. In many parts of China, old, painful proverbs took on new reality: "In an age of chaos, don't miss the chance to loot during the fire" and "In the official's house, wine and meat are allowed to rot, but on the roads are the bones of those who starved to death" (Ebrey, pp. 374–5).

Two groups emerged as the most powerful and the most likely to subdue the warlords and consolidate a national government: the Guomindang (GMD, National People's Party) and the communists. Both looked to Sun Yat-sen (1866–1925) as a founding mentor. Although raised in a peasant household, Sun received his secondary education in a missionary school in Hawaii and his medical training in Hong Kong. He spent most of his adult life in China's port cities or abroad.

In 1895, Sun's attempt at a coup in Guangzhou (Canton) failed and he was exiled. He was in the United States organizing for revolution when the 1911 uprising began. He returned to help found the GMD and to be elected first president of the United Provinces of China, but then was exiled by a jealous and fearful Yuan in 1913. He returned to Guangzhou in the early 1920s, and led his movement from that port city, but he never regained power.

Sun's "Three People's Principles" included a heavy admixture of Western thought. The first, nationalism, called for revolution against foreign political control, beginning with the ousting of the

Founder of the GMD. Sun Yat-sen (Yixian), photographed here in Western dress as was his custom, is considered the "father of the nation" even though he spent much of his life abroad and never achieved his own political ambitions. He was a revolutionary and helped to found the Guomindang, and although unable to stay in power himself, he influenced China's most important figures of the next generation: Chiang Kai-shek and Mao Zedong.

CHINA AND INDIA

DATE	CHINA	INDIA
1900	• Boxer Rebellion against Western influence is suppressed by foreign troops (1900)	• Mohandas Karamchand Gandhi publishes *Hind Swaraj*, or *Indian Home Rule* (1909)
1910	• 1911 Revolution ends Manchu dynasty and 2000 years of imperial rule • Yuan Shihkai elected premier (1911); dies 1916 • Warlords battle throughout China • May 4th Movement (1919)	• Gandhi returns from South Africa and establishes new *ashram* in Ahmedabad (1915) • Government of India Act creates dual British/Indian government (1919) • British crack down on freedom of the press and assembly in the Rowlatt Acts (1919) • Amritsar (Jalianwala Bagh) massacre (1919)
1920	• Chinese Communist Party formed (1921) • Sun Yat-sen dies (1925) • Guomindang (GMD) and Communists vie for power (1925–49) • Chiang Kai-shek captures Beijing (1927–8); rules from Nanjing • Mao's Report on Hunan Peasant Movement (1927)	• Non-cooperation campaign boycotts British interests (1920–2) • Gandhi fasts for twenty-one days to promote Hindu–Muslim unity (1924)
1930	• Mao Zedong leads Communists on the Long March, from Jiangxi to Yan'an (1934) • Japanese seize Manchuria (1931) and go on to invade China proper (1937) • Communists kidnap Jiang to gain cooperation in the war against Japan (1936)	• Salt March campaign (1930–2) • Gandhi outflanks socialists by persuading Jawaharlal Nehru to postpone land redistribution • Congress appoints National Planning Commission (1938)
1940	• Japan surrenders; civil war resumes (1945) • Foundation of the Communist People's Republic of China (1949) • Foreigners expelled (1949)	• "Quit India" campaign (1942) • Independence from Great Britain is followed by partition of the subcontinent (1947)

Manchus from China, and against foreign economic control, which had rendered China.

> the colony of every nation with which it has concluded treaties; each of them is China's master. China is not just the colony of one country, but the colony of many countries. We are not just the slaves of one country, but the slaves of many countries ... Today we are the poorest and weakest nation in the world, and occupy the lowest position in international affairs ... other men are the carving knife and serving dish; we are the fish and the meat ... we must espouse nationalism and bring this national spirit to the salvation of the country. (de Bary, pp. 769)

His second principle, democracy, emphasized a predominantly Western political model: "Since we have had only ideas about popular rights, and no democratic system has evolved, we have to go to Europe and America for a republican form of government." He did, however, claim the separation of powers as an ancient Chinese tradition (Andrea and Overfield, p. 350).

The third principle, under the heading "People's Livelihood," revealed Sun's ambivalence toward Western technology and organization. He proclaimed the need for new technology:

> First we must build means of communication, railroads and waterways, on a large scale. Second we must open up mines. Third we must hasten to develop manufacturing. Although China has a multitiude of workers, she has no machinery and so cannot compete with other countries. Goods used throughout China have to be manufactured and

CHINA AND INDIA

DATE	CHINA	INDIA
1950	• China invades and colonizes Tibet (1950) • Korean War (1950–3) • "100 Flowers Campaign" briefly permits some freedom of expression (1956–7) • Mao initiates "Great Leap Forward" experiment (1958–60)	• Policy of protective discrimination reserves jobs for untouchable castes (1955) • Hindu Marriage Act (1955) and Hindu Succession Act (1956) increase rights for women
1960	• Diplomatic relations with Russia are severed (1961) • Sino-Indian border war (1962) • Cultural Revolution initiates party purges and reignites revolutionary zeal; formation of Red Guard (1966)	• Death of Nehru (1964)
1970	• China joins United Nations (1971) • Groundbreaking visit to China by President Nixon (1972) • Mao dies; "Gang of Four" arrested (1976) • Deng Xiaoping comes to power; economic liberalization (1979) • One family, one child policy (1980)	• Civil war leads to creation of Bangladesh on land of East Pakistan (1971) • Prime Minister Indira Gandhi asserts dictatorial powers during "Emergency Rule" (1975–7) • Policy of forced sterilization (1975–7)
1980	• China joins World Bank and the International Monetary Fund (1980) • Students demonstrating in Tiananmen Square are killed by soldiers (1989)	• Indira Gandhi assassinated (1984)
1990	• Hong Kong reverts to Chinese sovereignty after 155 years as a British colony (1997) • Macao returned to China by Portugal (1999) • China voted "most favored nation" trading status by US (2000)	• Rajiv Gandhi assassinated (1991) • Prime Minister P.V. Narasimha Rao lowers tariffs and begins to welcome foreign investments (1991) • Pakistan and India test nuclear devices in violation of international treaties (1998) • Population reaches 1 billion (1999)

imported from other countries, with the result that our rights and interests are simply leaking away. (de Bary, p. 778)

But Western-style industrialization was not his chosen model:

> With the invention of modern machines, the phenomenon of uneven distribution of wealth in the West has become all the more marked. ... On my tour of Europe and America, I saw with my own eyes the instability of their economic structure and the deep concern of their leaders in groping for a solution. (Andrea and Overfield, p. 351)

Fearing "the expansion of private capital and the emergence of a great wealthy class with the consequent inequalities" in China, Sun called for a different path: state ownership and "state power to build up these enterprises." But he thought Marxism irrelevant for China: "In China, where industry is not yet developed, Marx's class war and dictatorship of the proletariat are impracticable" (de Bary, pp. 778–9). China's economic problem was not unequal distribution but lack of production.

Chinese of all political parties revered Sun, but they could not implement his plans. Sun, however, inspired the two leaders who contested for dominance in China for a quarter century following his death in 1925: the GMD's Chiang Kai-shek (Jiang Jieshi) (1887–1975) and the communists' Mao Zedong (1893–1976). Chiang began as a military commander and later sought to build a government; Mao began as a Communist Party organizer and later built an army. Both learned that "in a country ruled and plundered by marauding warlord armies, it was naked military power that was crucial in determining the direction of political events" (Meisner, p. 21). In Mao's blunt words: "political power grows out of the barrel of a gun."

POWER STRUGGLES 1925–37

Chiang had studied in a Japanese military academy, fought for the 1911 revolution, and rose to command China's own new military academy, established with Russian financing, near Guangzhou. After Sun's death, he succeeded to the leadership of the GMD. A staunch advocate of the neo-Confucian New Life movement in the 1930s, Chiang wrote *China's Destiny* in 1943 to re-affirm the conservative virtues of China's indigenous, hierarchical, genteel culture. Yet he also became a Methodist, as Sun had. Each man married a Chinese Christian woman (both were sisters of T.V. Soong, a wealthy industrialist), and valued contributions of foreign Christians in China's economic modernization.

Chiang maintained close personal, professional, and financial connections with Shanghai underworld figures, Russian Comintern agents, Western businessmen, and Christian missionaries. As China dissolved into warlordism, Chiang was named commander-in-chief of the GMD's National Revolutionary Army, and for a quarter of a century he fought to unify China under his own control against three powerful enemies: the warlords; the Japanese, who seized Manchuria in 1931 and went on to invade China proper in 1937 (see p. 663); and the communists.

Foreign powers in the treaty ports monitored China's shifting fortunes with considerable self-interest. In 1931, foreigners had a total of US$3243 million invested in China, slightly more than double the amount of 1914; which was, in turn, slightly more than double that of 1902. Foreign loans financed Chinese railways and heavy industry, and foreigners held three-fourths of all investments in shipping, almost half of the cotton spindles, and 80–90 percent of the coal mines. Through the early 1920s politicization and unionization of industrial workers encouraged many strikes, and the employers, many of them foreigners, often responded with violence. They wanted a compliant government that would help break the strikes. Most of the foreign investors aided, and sought to manipulate, Chiang as the leader closest to their interests. During the period 1929 to 1937, they lent him much of the money needed to cover the GMD government's annual deficits of 12 to 28 percent a year.

Foreign-based Christian missionaries and educational institutions also supported the GMD, attracted partly by Chiang's own Christian affiliation. The YMCA movement claimed 54,000 members in 1922. In the early 1920s, some 12,000 Christian missionaries, slightly more Protestants than Catholics, served in China. Christian and foreign colleges enrolled 4000 of the 35,000 students in Chinese colleges in 1922, and 9 percent of their students were women. Much of Western culture and literature was incorporated in the new curricula of China's universities. Chinese students and intellectuals were eager to hear voices from the West and East, and such luminaries as Bertrand Russell, John Dewey, Albert Einstein, and Rabindranath Tagore visited and lectured widely.

With the support of Western business and cultural leaders, and the Russian Comintern as well, Chiang undertook to defeat the warlords and to re-establish a viable central government. Through the great northern expedition from Guangzhou, Chiang captured Beijing in 1927–8, established his own capital in Nanjing on the lower Yangzi River, and began to consolidate GMD power over China. Despite these early military victories, however, Chiang ultimately failed. His government, permeated by corruption, alienated the peasantry by forging alliances with exploitative landlords. High officials sold off provisions intended to feed and clothe its starving armed forces. When the Japanese invasion of 1937 forced Chiang's retreat into the remote mountainous reaches of Chongqing (Chungking), the communists persuaded the Chinese peasants that they, not the GMD, could best fight off the Japanese and represent peasant interests in a free China.

MAO ZEDONG AND THE RISE OF THE COMMUNIST PARTY FROM 1921

The communist leader, Mao Zedong (1893–1976), Sun's other principal successor, shared the goals of a strong, united, independent China and the improvement of the people's livelihood, but his background was quite different. First, the 1911 revolution, in which he participated, was over by the time he was eighteen, and was therefore no longer an issue. Second, Mao's personal experience was limited to China. Although he read widely in Western as well as Chinese literature and philosophy, Mao's first travel outside China, a visit to Russia, came only in 1949. He had helped other

对伟大导师毛主席心怀一个"忠"字
对伟大毛泽东思想狠抓一个"用"字

Poster from 1960 showing Mao Zedong and supporters of the Cultural Revolution, each holding a copy of Mao's teachings, the "Little Red Book." Mao realized early on that the peasantry could carry forward the ideals of communism, even when the workers' movement was destroyed by Chiang Kai-shek. Mao was determined to eliminate "foreign dogmatism" and was against copying the Soviet blueprint for communism. His unique application of Marxism to China's needs gave rise to a mass following.

Chinese students travel to Europe during World War I, but for himself, he later told reporter Edgar Snow, "I did not want to go to Europe. I felt that I did not know enough about my own country, and that my time could be more profitably spent in China" (Snow, p. 149).

Third, Mao had little experience of the Western business and missionary establishments in China. His own formative experiences were in the countryside and in educational institutions. Compared with both Sun and Chiang, Mao cared little for China's reputation in the West but much for the quality of life of the Chinese peasant. Mao had grown up on his father's farm in Hunan province, where he learned at first hand of the exploitation of the peasant, sometimes, he said, through the oppressive strategies of his father, who rose from poverty to become a middle-level farmer and small-scale trader. Mao later recounted that he left this life to become an athletic, serious, politically committed student, reading widely, and consolidating a core group of similarly inclined young men: "My friends and I preferred to talk only of large matters—the nature of men, of human society, of China, the world, and the universe! ... We also became ardent physical culturists" (Snow, p. 146).

By 1919, Mao's educational quests had brought him to Beijing (Peking) University, just as China's resentment against foreign imperialism was boiling over. The peace treaties of World War I assigned Germany's holdings in the Shandong Peninsula of north China to Japan rather than returning them to China. In Paris, Chinese protestors physically blocked their nation's delegates from attending the signing ceremonies, and thus China never did sign the peace agreements. Within China, protests against the treaties by students and others began on May 4, 1919, engendering a continuing critique of China's international humiliation, the apparent bankruptcy of its historical traditions, and the content of its cultural links to the West. The "May Fourth Movement" also helped to sow the seeds of the Chinese Communist Party (CCP), which came to fruition in 1921 following discussions between Chinese revolutionaries and representatives of the newly formed Comintern of the USSR (see p. 650).

At that time, Mao was a participant in the study group of Li Dazhao, chief librarian of Beijing University and one of the founders of the CCP.

Li had already proclaimed the importance of the peasantry and called on the university students to help mobilize them:

> Our China is a rural nation and most of the laboring class is made up of peasants. If they are not liberated, then our whole nation will not be liberated … Go out and develop them and cause them to know [that they should] demand liberation, speak out about their sufferings, throw off their ignorance and be people who will themselves plan their own lives. (Spence, p. 308)

When Mao joined the party he began organizing workers in the industrial plants of the Wuhan region, but in 1925 he was re-assigned to peasant organization in his native Hunan. Despite the orthodox Marxist doctrines of Comintern advisors, Mao in Hunan came to see the Chinese peasantry, rather than the proletariat, as China's revolutionary vanguard. In terms of technology, he abandoned the emphasis on large-scale industrial planning and sought instead local solutions to local problems through locally developed, appropriate rural technologies. Mao's enthusiastic and influential, but polemical and doctrinaire, 1927 report on the Hunan peasant movement updated Li's more rural emphasis:

> the broad peasant masses have risen to fulfill their historic mission … the democratic forces in the rural areas have risen to overthrow the rural feudal power. The patriarchal-feudal class of local bullies, bad gentry, and lawless landlords has formed the basis of autocratic government for thousands of years, the cornerstone of imperialism, warlordism and corrupt officialdom. To overthrow this feudal power is the real objective of the national revolution. … The leadership of the poor peasants is absolutely necessary. Without the poor peasants there can be no revolution. (de Bary, p. 869)

This revolution required violence: the peasants had to use their strength to overthrow the authority of the landlords.

Mao's enemies had their own tools of violence. While Mao was organizing peasants in the 1920s, Chiang was massacring the core of the revolutionary proletariat in Shanghai, Wuhan, and Guangzhou. As Chiang completed the northern expedition and consolidated his control over the warlords, he turned, in alliance with the international business community, and without excessive objection from the Comintern, to murdering thousands of communist industrial workers in the spring of 1927. In Changsha, local military leaders joined with the GMD and local landlords to slaughter thousands of peasants who had recently expropriated the land they worked from its legal owners. By the summer of 1928, according to Zhou Enlai, one of the most sophisticated communist leaders, only 32,000 union members in all of China remained loyal to the Communist Party. By 1929, only 3 percent of the Party members could be counted proletarians. Mao's peasant alternative was, of necessity, the communists' last resort.

When the GMD put down the Hunan Autumn Harvest Uprising in 1927, Mao's core group retreated to the Jinggangshan border area between Hunan and Chiangxi. Other communist leaders, driven from the cities, joined them. They built up a **soviet**, a local communist government, redistributing land, introducing improved farming methods, and instituting new educational systems spreading literacy and dispensing political indoctrination. They recruited and trained a guerrilla army. Mao himself formulated its tactics: "The enemy advances, we retreat; the enemy camps, we harass; the enemy tires, we attack; the enemy retreats, we pursue" (Spence, p. 375).

The guerrillas could exist only with the cooperation of the peasantry whom they wished to mobilize. Appropriate, rather revolutionary rules were established to govern soldiers' behavior: "prompt obedience to orders; no confiscations whatever from the poor peasantry; and prompt delivery directly to the Government, for its disposal, of all goods confiscated from the landlords" (Snow, p. 176). These were later elaborated to include: "Be courteous and polite to the people and help them when you can. … Be honest in all transactions with the peasants. … Pay for all articles purchased" (Snow, p. 176).

GENDER ISSUES

Mao's principles of women's rights recognized the changes already taking place. Feminism had begun to flourish in China by the 1920s with the formation of such organizations as the Women's Suffrage Association and the Women's Rights League. Its constituency was mostly Western-influenced urban intellectuals. *New Youth* magazine, for example,

occupied by Japan 1933

area of Japanese influence 1932-37

Communist strongholds to 1935

Long March Oct. 1934–Oct. 1935

Communist base 1935-45

occupied by Japan by 1944

Communist controlled by 1945

The Communist Revolution in China Chinese communists and Nationalists (GMD) united briefly to subdue the warlord factions which emerged after the collapse of the Manchu (Qing) dynasty, and to consolidate a national government. After 1927 Nationalist repression forced the communists to retreat to remote areas, focussing in the northwest after the Long March of 1934–5, where guerrilla warfare continued. With the Japanese invasion of China proper in 1937, China was torn by both international and civil war. After Japan's defeat in 1945, the communists turned to defeating the GMD as well.

often critical of Confucius for his emphasis on patriarchy and obedience to authority, had translated and published Ibsen's *A Doll's House* in 1918 (see p. 568). Pa Chin's novel *Family*, one of the key works of China's reformist New Culture Movement, transplanted Ibsen's advocacy of women's equality and independence into a modern Chinese setting. Margaret Sanger, American feminist and advocate of contraception, had toured and lectured throughout China in 1922. There were also some 1,500,000 women working outside their homes for pay in light industrial factories, mostly textiles, in China's cities. Now Mao refocused feminist attention on the countryside and the peasantry:

the authority of the husband ... has always been comparatively weak among the poor peasants, because the poor peasant women, compelled for

financial reasons to take more part in manual work than women of the wealthier classes, have obtained more right to speak and more power to make decisions in family affairs. In recent years the rural economy has become even more bankrupt and the basic condition for men's domination over women has already been undermined. And now, with the rise of the peasant movement, women in many places have set out immediately to organize the rural women's association; the opportunity has come for them to lift up their heads, and the authority of the husband is tottering more and more every day.
(de Bary, p. 872)

Communist policies took two complementary directions. The first, and more effective, restructured the labor and military forces, giving more scope and power to women. Building the Chinese soviet and fighting guerrilla battles required the support of every available resource. While women did not usually participate in warfare directly, the increased need for production and personnel brought them out of the house into new jobs, effectively raising their status. Then, after the revolution had succeeded in 1949, the communists issued a new marriage law forbidding arranged marriages, stopping all purchase and sale in marriage contracts, and encouraging free choice of marriage partners. This law met strong resistance. Men who had already bought their wives objected; so did mothers-in-law, who ruled over each household's domestic labor force. The traditional Chinese family provided for old age security, child care, medical facilities, and the production and consumption of food, clothing, and shelter. The new communist marriage law seemed to threaten this structure without providing any alternative. The law was not widely enforced. In *The Unfinished Liberation of Chinese Women, 1949–1980* Phyllis Andors points out that this pattern would continue in China for decades: Restructuring of the labor force to include more women working for remuneration outside the home would raise women's status and be accepted if it was part of the task of building the nation; direct restructuring of the family as an end in itself would meet resistance. The leadership of the Party remained conspicuously male.

THE LONG MARCH AND THE RISE TO POWER 1934–49

Chiang sent five successive military expeditions against the Chiangxi soviet, beginning with 100,000 men and leading up to one million. By 1934, the communists could no longer hold out. Mao led

Women of Shanghai with tiny, bound feet working at frames for sorting tea leaves. From the early years of the twentieth century urban women had begun to leave the confines of home to work in light industry. The move from home to workplace gave women more status, which was further strengthened by the reforms of the communist government when it came to power. The abandonment of footbinding in all but the most outlying areas of China did much to enhance the freedom of women.

some 80,000 men and thirty-five women out of the siege and began the Long March, a 370-day, 6000-mile (9650-kilometer) strategic retreat, by foot, under constant bombardment and attack from Chiang's forces, across rivers, mountain ranges, marshes, and grasslands, westward to Guizhou and then northward to a final new base camp in Yan'an. Some 20,000 men finally arrived in Yan'an, of whom about half had marched since the beginning, the rest having joined *en route*. The courage, comradeship, commitment, and idealism of this march, in the face of seemingly insurmountable natural obstacles and human opposition, were the formative experience of a generation of Chinese communist leaders. At the front, Mao now became the unquestioned leader of the movement, party, and army.

Mao established his capital at remote, impoverished Yan'an and rebuilt his soviet structure, nurturing his army, inducting its soldiers into agricultural assistance work, redistributing land, encouraging handicrafts, establishing newspapers and schools, an arts and literature academy, and medical programs for training paramedical "barefoot doctors." The Chinese communist program developed more fully here: a peasant-centered economy, administered and aided by guerrilla soldiers, capped by a dictatorial but comparatively benevolent communist leadership, encouraging literacy accompanied by indoctrination in communist ideology. Tension built up, however, between ideological goals and practical implementation, between being "Red" and being "expert."

Although Yan'an was remote from the main fighting, and was subject to GMD attacks, the communists launched guerrilla action against the Japanese after their invasion of China proper in 1937. By comparison, Chiang seemed less nationalistic. He appeared willing to compromise with the Japanese and more eager to pursue the Chinese communists than to fight the foreign invaders. Mao, on the other hand seemed willing to join forces with Chiang to unite China against the foreigner. Following the "Xi'an incident," the bold kidnap of Chiang by dissident generals in 1936, Chiang moved toward temporary cooperation with the communists.

At first, the Japanese had hoped to rule China with the help of Chinese collaborators, as they had Manchuria, but their cruelty after the capture of Nanjing in December 1937 ended those hopes (see p. 665). The Chinese vowed to fight back. The communists fought a rearguard guerrilla war from their northern base in Shaanxi, while Chiang led a **scorched-earth** retreat to a new headquarters far up the Yangzi River in Chongqing. Soldiers and civilians suffered catastrophically.

By the early 1940s, nationalist cooperation began to unravel as communists and GMD forces jockeyed for temporary power and future position. America supported the GMD. After a temporary respite in 1945, full-scale civil war resumed. The USA extended help to Chiang in training his troops, airlifting them to critical military locations, and turning over to them war material. The Soviet Union, fighting for its life against Germany, observed neutrality with Japan until the last week of the war. Then it entered Manchuria, stripping for itself a great deal of that region's military and industrial equipment, while turning over some of it to the Chinese communists. As China's civil war continued after 1945, communist forces, well disciplined and warmly supported by peasants in many parts of the country, defeated the ill-disciplined and ill-provisioned GMD forces, whose rations and materials were often sold off for private profit without ever reaching them. By the fall of 1949, the communists had driven the GMD completely out of mainland China to the island of Taiwan. The Communist People's Republic of China was born.

REVOLUTIONARY POLICIES 1949–66

For Mao and the guerrilla veterans who dominated the new government, the principal fears were foreign domination, internal chaos, and the lingering power of the wealthy classes and the large-scale landholders. The new rulers modeled much of their new government on the experiences of the Long March and the Yan'an soviet, and returned to them for inspiration in difficult times as long as they lived, even up to the early 1990s. Important policies included:

- redistribution of land;

- women's rights to hold land;

- appropriate technology;

- production and equal distribution of basic necessities for everyone;

- universal literacy (reaching 81 percent by 1997, 73 percent for females and 90 percent for males).

The government mobilized tight-knit, local, social networks not only for suppressing such vices as opium addiction and prostitution but also for enforcing rigid political indoctrination and conformity, including the informing by one family member against another and the use of coercion in extracting personal confessions of political deviance.

Land redistribution was a top priority. During this class revolution, perhaps half the peasantry of China received at least some benefits while as a many as 1 million landlords were killed. Lacking experience in urban economic affairs, the communist government at first invited the cooperation of businessmen, both Chinese and foreign. But policies changed abruptly as China entered the Korean War in October 1950 (p. 623). Threats, expropriation, and accusations of espionage—sometimes justified—against businessmen and Christian missionaries forced almost all foreigners to leave China by the end of 1950. Numerous campaigns against counter-revolutionaries; the confiscation and redistribution of private property; hundreds and even thousands of executions; intensive public, group pressure to elicit confessions from those perceived as enemies of the revolution; and regular confrontations between workers and owners, now incorporated into the processes of labor relations, destroyed the large capitalist sector in China. Many countries, led by the United States, refused to recognize the new government. The Russian communist government, on the other hand, maintained a strong alliance and helped to draft and implement China's first five-year plan between 1952 and 1957.

Communist policies on urbanization and industrialization were more ambivalent. The communists had come to power as an anti-urban, peasant movement. The large cities, especially Shanghai, had fostered the foreign enclaves, extraterritorial law, and colonial behavior which flagrantly insulted the Chinese in their own country, but they also

Trial of a landlord. Most such trials ended with a confession and a promise to reform; some with a bullet for the accused. In its first moves toward collectivization, the communist government instituted a number of land reforms that gave the arable land to the peasants who worked it and did away with the landlords—literally.

housed China's industrial base, military technology, administration, and cultural life. As the communists began to capture the nation's cities, Mao began to re-evaluate their potential:

> From 1927 to the present the center of gravity of our work has been in the villages—gathering strength in the villages, using the villages in order to surround the cities, and then taking the cities. The period for this method of work has now ended. The period of the city leading the village has now begun. (Spence, p. 508)

Policies and results, however, were both uneven. To restrain urban growth, the government promulgated severe limitations on internal migration, but movement from the countryside continued steadily, if slowly. China's population, which had been 10.6 percent urban in 1949 and 16.3 percent in 1958, reached 29 percent urban in 1997. In sheer numbers this was an increase from 57 million to 361 million people. As time went by, the cities again challenged communist ideological purity—Guangzhou promoted capitalism; Beijing, political protest; Shanghai, internationalism. Chinese leaders had to balance conflicting claims on behalf of urban, bureaucratic, centralized, "expert" industrialization against those for rural, grass-roots, "Red" populism. To some degree, the leaders contended among themselves, with a group around Liu Shaoqi and Deng Xiaoping in the former camp; Mao and Lin Piao in the latter. Some, like Zhou Enlai, sought compromise and synthesis.

Militarily, the communists extolled the spirit of the guerrilla warrior over high-tech weaponry, and taunted America, the world's most heavily armed country, as a "paper tiger." Indeed, China itself fought the United States to a draw in Korea, 1950–3 (see p. 623), and then saw the American superpower withdraw in defeat from Vietnam in 1973. Nevertheless, China bought, produced, or purloined up-to-date military technology. In 1964, China exploded its first atomic bomb; in the mid-1970s it followed with hydrogen bombs; in 1980 it tested missiles with a range of 7000 miles (11,200 kilometers) and in 1981 launched three space satellites. It began to manufacture and sell sophisticated missiles, submarines, and chemical weapons to other developing countries by the 1980s. Nevertheless, its military expenditure dropped from 12 percent of its total gross national product in 1960 to 5.7 percent in 1997. China was betting its future power on a developed economy leading its military rather than vice versa (Kennedy, p. 384; *New York Times 2000 Almanac*, p. 510).

Economically, China adopted a five-year plan based on the USSR model. It called for multiplying the value of industrial output between 1952 and 1957 almost two and one-half times, and claimed at the end to have overachieved the target by 22 percent. By the end of the plan, even democracy seemed a possibility. In 1956–7, Mao's call, "Let a hundred flowers bloom, let a hundred schools of thought contend," opened the gates of public expression and even criticism of government. In Beijing, students and others posted their thoughts on what became known as Democratic Wall. By late 1957, however, fearing uncontrolled, growing protest, the government shifted its policies and jailed protesters, sent them to labor camps, and exiled them to remote rural farms. Economically, it implemented the "Great Leap Forward," grouping virtually all of rural China into communes, "sending down" city people to villages, virtually terminating whatever small private enterprises had survived, and attempting to downscale and disperse industry by establishing local, small-scale enterprises, referred to generically as "backyard steel mills." The Great Leap Forward, administered by powerful, distant government officials who attempted to restructure the entire economy of the nation according to communist ideology led to economic catastrophe including millions of deaths by starvation.

THE CULTURAL REVOLUTION 1966–9

The government relaxed for a few years, but then reinstated similar and perhaps even more extreme ideological and economic policies in the Great Proletarian Cultural Revolution in 1966. Mao sought through this revolution to purge the party of time-serving bureaucrats and to reignite revolutionary fervor. Those who responded most enthusiastically were the army and students, who, with Mao's encouragement, organized themselves into the Red Guard. Teachers were denounced by their students and by party officials; professors and intellectuals were exiled to remote villages and forced to undertake hard labor.

The Long March was now thirty years in the past, yet nostalgia for its ideological zeal still motivated China's aging leaders. Mao was venerated as their last hope to restore the intensity of those early days of the revolution. Key quotations from his statements were published in millions of copies of *The Quotations of Chairman Mao*, often called the Little Red Book, because of its size and the color of its cover. (See picture, p. 683.) These were circulated and read publicly throughout the country. Economic chaos and starvation on the one hand and the total stifling and destruction of intellectual and academic life on the other brought China to a standstill. For three years, 1966–9, militant, committed anarchy reigned.

RECOVERY

As the damage became clearly visible, China reversed its policy in yet another example of "fang–zhou," "loosening up–tightening down." The People's Liberation Army was given the task of putting down the Red Guards, the youth and student cadres who had wrecked chaos in the name of Mao. New international respectability was sought, most dramatically by the normalization of relations with the United States after President Nixon visited China in 1972. Domestically, attention refocused on the economy and the restoration of productivity. Imports and exports, which had held roughly flat for several years at slightly over $2 billion each through the late 1960s, rose steadily until, in 1978, each registered $10 billion. One fourth of the imports were machinery and equipment, including complete plants—6934 of them in 1978—built entirely by foreigners (Spence, p. 641). Almost all of these new factories were in heavy industries, especially petrochemicals and iron and steel. By 1980, China was producing more steel than Britain or France.

Maurice Meisner, Professor of History at the University of Wisconsin, in his assessment, *Mao's China and After*, underlines the ironic imbalance in strong support for industry and weak agricultural results under Mao, the leading apostle of peasant revolution. "Between 1950 and 1977 industrial output grew at an average annual rate of 13.5 percent … the highest rate of all developing or developed major nations of the world during the time and a more rapid pace than achieved by any country during any comparable period of rapid industrialization in modern world history" (pp. 436–7). Meanwhile, agriculture was upended, collectivized, and relatively neglected in terms of investment. As Meisner points out, the agonizingly slow growth of agriculture at 2.3 percent a year from 1952 to 1977 could barely keep pace with population growth of 2 percent a year.

AFTER MAO: THE ERA OF REFORM

On September 9, 1976 Mao died. By the end of the year, the "Gang of Four," the four leaders who claimed to be closest to Mao, including his wife Jiang Qing, were under arrest. They had been among the most militant of the high level officials responsible for the Cultural Revolution. China was in the midst of a struggle for succession. By December 1978 it became apparent that Deng Xiaoping (1904–1997) and his allies had achieved control of the party and its agenda. They remained in control for the next two decades.

Born in Sichuan Province, Deng spent formative years, from the age of sixteen to twenty-one, studying, doing factory work, and organizing on behalf of the communist party among the expatriate Chinese. After a few months' visit in Moscow, he returned to China as a political and military organizer of soviets in southwest China. On the Long March he became a close companion of Mao. As an army officer, he shared the military command of as many as 300,000 troops. In 1952 Mao called him back to Beijing, and his star continued to rise until 1966 when he appeared too moderate for the leaders of the Great Cultural Revolution and was stripped of his offices and exiled to a tractor repair factory in an infantry school in southern China. He was recalled to Beijing by Mao only in 1973.

Deng advocated economic liberalism, but within a state firmly controlled by the communist party. By the time of his death, Deng and his colleagues had sold off about half of the state's economic holdings leaving only 18 percent of the workforce in state employment, down from 90 percent in 1978. He welcomed foreign investment, which reached $42 billion in 1997, and loans, reaching a total of $130 billion in foreign debt. Exports rose to account for 25 percent of total production. Per capita income quadrupled. Deng also shifted more investment to agriculture, ended collectivization, and introduced a "private responsibility system," unleashing enormous productivity gains of 9 percent a year in the early 1980s. The growth in China's total gross domestic product (GDP) led the world, averaging 11.2 percent per year, 1986–97. Health standards improved. Life expectancy reached seventy.

The new leaders also faced directly the problems of population growth. Government programs for "small family happiness," beginning in 1974, culminated in the 1980 policy of one family, one child. The party set birth quotas for each county and city, established a nationwide system for distributing contraceptive devices, enforced regulations against early marriage, provided incentives for having only one child and disincentives for having more. The bureaucracy monitored pregnancies and births carefully and abortions were frequently coerced if necessary (Rosenberg, p. 70). Fertility rates dropped to 2.3 per hundred women in the 1980s, indicating considerable success. The enormous coercive power of the state evoked massive unrest, evasion, and, in some case, female infanticide, as couples preferred their one child to be male. The smaller families, however, led to a dramatic reduction in the responsibilities of child care and encouraged greater freedom for women in the home and greater equality and participation in work and public life outside. By the year 2000, the birth rate had dropped so low that the government began considering relaxation of the policy.

The liberalization of the economy, however, also brought problems. Environmental degradation, including the pollution of air and water, increased dramatically. The social safety net was punctured and unemployment rose. The World Bank classified 65 million people, 7 percent of the population, as "absolutely poor" in 1995. China's "floating population," rural people who shifted to China's cities in search of jobs, grew to more than 100 million. Previously government regulations had forbidden such internal migration. Now these new urbanites, still without legal permits for long-time residence, formed up to one-third of the population of some of China's cities. They were blamed for increases in crime and social unrest. Of course they also provided low cost labor for China's growing economy—when they could find jobs.

At higher levels of the economy, white-collar crime and corruption became major problems. As in Russia (see p. 658), as the government liberalized, state assets were often sold to the party faithful at bargain prices. Meanwhile the lure of new profits, a relaxation in law enforcement, and a rise in bribery created

> a new class of privately wealthy moguls. China witnessed a rapid recrudescence of quasi-illegal night spots, gangsterism, drug dealing, secret societies, prostitution, and gambling, much of it owned and run by the police and military. (Schell, 1999, p. 394).

HUMAN RIGHTS AND INTERNATIONAL RELATIONS

Despite these admitted problems, Deng's government could speak proudly of its accomplishments in the "four modernizations" of agriculture, science and technology, industry, and defense. Critics, however, called for the "fifth modernization"— democracy. In 1989, tens of thousands of demonstrators, mostly students, assembled in Tiananmen Square, demanding democracy as the antidote to a government ruled by old men, infested with corruption, and no longer in touch with the grass roots. The government called in the army to clear the square. In the process, as many as 2000 demonstrators were killed, and more injured. The students' protests were tragically validated, but their proposed solution would have to wait.

In terms of international relations, also, China implemented a series of dramatic turnabouts. In the

President Nixon meets with Communist Party Chairman Mao Zedong in Beijing, during his groundbreaking 1972 visit to China. The Chinese government, clearly worried by aggressive Soviet policy in Czechoslovakia, took steps to improve relations with the United States. Four years after the Sino-Western rapprochement, begun in 1971, foreign trade with China had tripled, and by 1980 China had joined the International Monetary Fund and the World Bank.

first decade of communist rule, its chief ally was the USSR, which helped the new communist state design its five-year plan, train and provision its armed forces, and build factories, transportation facilities, urban neighborhoods, and administrative centers. But in the mid-1950s, the USSR under Khruschev began to moderate its own militant policies both domestically and internationally. China, however, remained more "Red," and the two countries quarrelled bitterly over ideology, as they had in 1927. In the summer of 1960, the USSR recalled all of its technical advisors in China, including those working on atomic energy projects. Diplomatic relations were severed in 1961. In China's border disputes with India, which spilled over briefly into warfare in 1962, the USSR backed India's claims and entered into defense alliances with China's opponent.

Armed conflicts with the USSR arose over borders in northern Manchuria and Xinjiang province. Fighting in 1969 caused about 100 Russian and 800 Chinese casualties. At considerable expense, China then concentrated its defense forces in these border areas. Only after 1985, under Gorbachev's new policies of *glasnost* (political and cultural openess) and *perestroika* (economic restructuring) in the Soviet Union, were diplomatic relations between the two countries normalized. Still, the two powers remain wary and armed across thousands of miles of shared borders.

Relations with the United States also oscillated. For almost two decades, America lamented and resented the "loss" of China and continued to support Jiang's **irredentist** forces on Taiwan after 1949. Communist policies thoroughly alienated capitalist business people and Christian religious communities, both of which had invested in China. The Chinese government's use of "brain-washing" tactics to convert their internal opponents through unremitting propaganda, group pressure, and official coercion, scandalized Americans. China's "liberation" of Tibet in 1950, and the ruthless suppression of the Tibetan Buddhist revolt in 1959, seemed to confirm the militaristic, brutal nature of the government, although no one moved to aid the Tibetan resistance. The Korean War, provoked by North Korea's invasion of the south in 1950, led to the three-year engagement of American and United Nations forces against those of China, fought to a deadlock. Against the advice of its closest overseas allies, the USA lobbied to keep the People's Republic of China out of the United Nations; the Chinese people were represented by the government of Taiwan.

Tiananmen Square, June 5, 1989. Tanks traveling down Changan Boulevard, in front of the Beijing Hotel, are confronted by a brave Chinese man who pleads for an end to the killing of demonstrating students. This photograph has come to symbolize the struggle of the Chinese people to reassert their dignity and gain democracy in the face of the huge and powerful communist regime.

In the early 1970s, however, the diplomatic scene changed dramatically. Mao and his new advisors, retreating from the economic catastrophe of the Cultural Revolution, sought assistance from abroad. President Nixon and his Secretary of State, Henry Kissinger, also favored more pragmatic policies. In 1971, the USA did not stand in the way of China's joining the United Nations, and in the next year, Nixon visited China, advancing the normalization of relations between the two countries. While the USA still formally protests the 1989 Tiananmen Square crackdown on democracy, relations are improving and top-ranking American government officials visit Beijing regularly, on Chinese terms. In 2000 the United States Congress voted to grant China permanent "most favored nation" trade status despite opposition to China's persistent and extreme human rights abuses.

Within its own area of the world, China for 2000 years has viewed itself as the dominant, central power, and has sought that recognition from its neighbors with mixed success. In many of these countries, China was a feared and resented neighbor, not an uncommon relationship for a regional superpower. China invaded and colonized Tibet. It backed the murderous Khmer Rouge Party and its leader Pol Pot in the vicious civil wars in Cambodia, even committing troops briefly to combat. In several nearby states, Chinese minorities were viewed with suspicion as possible fifth column infiltrators, both for the Chinese nation and the Communist Party. In anti-Chinese and anti-communist riots in Indonesia in 1965 thousands of Chinese were murdered, and hundreds of thousands more were exiled. The startling economic success of Korea and Taiwan, not to mention that of Japan, has challenged both China's regional supremacy and its communist path of development. In 1997 the island of Hong Kong, and the tiny strip of adjacent territories on the mainland, which had been a colony of the British empire since 1842, reverted to Chinese sovereignty. (Two years later tiny Macao was returned to China by Portugal.) Commercial and political observers wait and watch to see the policies that China will implement in this historic outpost of capitalism.

Finally has been China's relationship with India. When India became independent in 1947 and China completed its revolution in 1949, they chose dramatically different social, political, and economic paths, and both saw themselves as leading the third world in new patterns of development. At the Bandung Conference in 1955, both offered leadership to nations newly emerging from colonialism.

China became a model for agrarian guerrilla revolt throughout Southeast Asia and beyond, while India's non-violent path inspired others, especially in Black Africa. India did not protest China's takeover of Tibet in 1950, and consistently backed China's petition to enter the United Nations. But differences over border demarcations in the mountainous regions of Leh and Ladakh finally led to open warfare in 1962. The Chinese decisively defeated Indian troops, penetrated through the mountain passes to within striking distance of India's heartland, and then withdrew voluntarily to the borders they had claimed. In this war, the concept of third world solidarity suffered a mortal blow, which rhetoric could not cover up. India's testing of nuclear devices in 1974 and 1998 increased the mutual suspicion.

WHAT DIFFERENCE DOES IT MAKE?

China demonstrated the inevitability of each huge nation of the world finding its own developmental path. China might for a time take guidance from one foreign ideology or another, and it might enter into alliances with various powers at one time or another, but finally it sought a path appropriate to its own size, geography, power, technology, and historical experience. Chinese at home and abroad, including many who disapproved of current government policies, took pride in the newfound unity, power, and independence of the Central Kingdom. China might make mistakes, but they would be its own mistakes. Leaving behind a century of humiliating colonialism and devastating civil war, today's China would kowtow to no one.

INDIA 1914–2000

At the end of World War I, India's demand for independence ignited a mass movement that bore many similarities to China's. With the vast majority of its population in rural areas, India, like China, was rooted in agriculture and its peasantry. Like China's Mao Zedong, India's Mohandas Karamchand Gandhi (better known as the Mahatma or "great soul"; 1869–1948) mobilized this rural constituency. Both leaders created new social and economic institutions for greater equity and also emphasized the need for new technologies appropriate to their agrarian, impoverished societies. Both saw their methods and solutions as models for others to copy.

Fifty years after ending colonialism, both countries could point to significant accomplishments including: cumulative and growing economic expansion, more rapid in China, slower in India; political cohesion; social transformation in accord with their differing agendas; and dominance in the politics of their separate regions of the world. They also shared the similar challenge of maintaining national agreements on common agendas after the unifying enemy of colonialism had been defeated.

The differences between the two mammoth countries were at least equally significant. Unlike China, which had no functioning central government between 1912 and 1949 and had been carved into numerous European and Japanese spheres of influence, India had a central government, which was under British colonial control until independence in 1947. Political disputes evolved through generally peaceful, constitutional processes. India's nationalist leaders, unlike those of China, welcomed businessmen and professionals along with the peasantry in their struggle. Unlike China, in its independence movement India pursued an extraordinary strategy of non-violent mass civil resistance. It fought no civil war nor did World War II significantly touch its borders. When Independence came, relationships with colonial Great Britain continued harmonious, and India retained membership in the Commonwealth of Nations. Even the partition of the subcontinent into two, India and Pakistan, in 1947, followed constitutional processes, although the subsequent transfers of population were enormously violent. The 1971 creation of the independent country of Bangladesh on the land of East Pakistan was the product of civil war, in which India aided Bangladesh against West Pakistan, but violence was usually contained.

After 1947, as an independent country, India chose a pattern of political democracy and a mixed economy, balancing a "socialist pattern of society," with considerable allowance for private ventures. India confronted enormous, persistent challenges from both its own social structure and the colonial heritage: hierarchical caste restrictions, especially discrimination against ex-untouchables; conflict between religious communities, especially Hindus and Muslims; tensions among regional and linguistic groups; renewed oppression of women; hunger and poverty in an economy of scarcity; and continuing massive population growth. In these struggles, India followed its own unique policies for development, including technological policies of great diversity.

THE INDEPENDENCE STRUGGLE 1914–47

Throughout World War I, resistance to British rule generally took the form of constitutional protest and was concentrated in the hands of men who were educated in British ways, through British-run schools, sometimes in Britain itself. The Indian National Congress, established in 1885 at British initiative as a vent for Indian nationalist criticism, had become the focal institution for nationalist organization. Somewhat more than a third of its membership was trained in the legal profession. In 1835, T.B. Macaulay, law member of the British Government of India, had declared the intent of the government's educational policies to create a class "Indian in blood and colour, but English in taste, in opinions, in morals, and in intellect" (Hay, p. 31); the Congress leadership reflected the results.

In 1917, the British Secretary of State for India, Edwin Montagu, announced the goal of British policy to be "increasing association of Indians in every branch of the administration, and the gradual development of self-governing institutions, with a view to the progressive realisation of responsible government in India as an integral part of the British Empire." A series of constitutional reforms had already established official councils with substantial Indian membership, elected by very limited elites, to advise the government. The Government of India Act, 1919, expanded provincial and central legislatures and created a dual government, or **dyarchy**, transferring powers over agriculture, public works, education, local self-government, and education to Indian elected legislators at the provincial level.

This half-way house proved unstable; Britain had trouble deciding whether it wished India to be a democracy or a colony. Each new issue revealed the contradiction. When commodity prices rose sharply, virtually doubling between 1914 and 1920, the government seemed unable or unwilling to control them. When the post-war years increased the demands for political independence, the government responded with repression. Against the advice of all of the elected Indians in the Imperial Legislative Council, in 1919 the government cracked down on freedom of the press and assembly by passing the Rowlatt Acts. In Amritsar, Punjab, a British general, Reginald Dyer, ordered his troops to fire, to disperse an unarmed protest rally. Blocking the only exit, the soldiers turned the outdoor meeting-place of Jalianwala Bagh into a

SOURCE

Gandhi's First Experience with Racism in South Africa

Mahatma Gandhi published his *Autobiography* originally as a series of newspaper articles. Many of the episodes also carried a moral message for readers. The story of his first encounter with racism in South Africa implies that he had never experienced such severe discrimination, neither in colonial India nor during his law school days in London.

On the seventh or eighth day after my arrival, I left Durban. A first class seat was booked for me. … The train reached Maritzburg, the capital of Natal, at about 9 P.M. … A passenger came next, and looked me up and down. He saw that I was a "colored" man. This disturbed him. Out he went and came in again with one or two officials. They all kept quiet, when another offical came to me and said, "Come along, you must go to the van compartment."

"But I have a first class ticket," said I.

"That doesn't matter," rejoined the other. "I tell you, you must go to the van compartment."

"I tell you, I was permitted to travel in this compartment at Durban, and I insist on going on in it."

"No you won't," said the offical. "You must leave this compartment, or else I shall have to call a police constable to push you out."

"Yes, you may. I refuse to get out voluntarily."

The constable came. He took me by the hand and pushed me out. My luggage was also taken out. I refused to go to the other compartment and the train steamed away. I went and sat in the waiting room, keeping my hand bag with me, and leaving the other luggage where it was. …

It was winter, and winter in the higher regions of South Africa is severely cold. Maritzburg being at a high altitude, the cold was extremely bitter. My overcoat was in my luggage, but I did not dare to ask for it lest I should be insulted again, so I sat and shivered. There was no light in the room. A passenger came in at about midnight and possibly wanted to talk to me. But I was in no mood to talk.

I began to think of my duty. Should I fight for my rights or go back to India, or should I go on to Pretoria without minding the insults, and return to India after finishing the case? It would be cowardice to run back to India without fulfilling my obligation. The hardship to which I was subjected was superficial—only a symptom of the deep disease of color prejudice. I should try, if possible, to root out the disease and suffer hardships in the process. (Jack, p. 29–30)

---

gruesome shooting gallery, killing 379 people and wounding 1100. The government forced the general to resign, but a popular outpouring of support for him in Britain thoroughly alienated Indian moderates. World War I had already exposed a murderous brutality within European civilization; now it appeared in India as well, thoroughly laced with racism. From this point onward in the eyes of even moderate Indians, British colonial rule had forfeited its legitimacy.

NEW POLITICAL DIRECTIONS AND REFORM: GANDHI

At this juncture Mohandas Karamchand Gandhi— Mahatma Gandhi—emerged as a leader offering new political directions, new moral perspectives, and new programs of internal reform as well as anti-colonial mobilization. Gandhi called India to find strength and courage in its own peasant roots and spiritual traditions. His success had limitations, but all political activity until well past independence, almost to the present, would revolve around the Congress, which he now reconstructed into a mass movement.

Gandhi's family had been advisors to local rulers in western India for several generations, and his uncle felt that if Mohandas were to maintain the family tradition under British rule, he must travel to Britain to study law. Gandhi emerged from three years of study in London with a deeply considered re-affirmation of his Indian heritage in Hinduism, in religious openness, and in an appreciation of localized, small-scale organizations. Two days after completing his legal training and one day after being admitted to the bar, Gandhi returned to India. He practised law without distinction for a year and then accepted the case of an Indian emigrant business firm in South Africa. There, apparently for the first time, Gandhi suffered racist persecution repeatedly.

The Indian community in South Africa had mostly come there to work as indentured laborers. The South African government wanted them to return home at the end of their service and instituted laws to make their long-term status untenable. Indians were required to carry identification cards at all times and to pay heavy head taxes. Then the government nullified all marriages not performed by Christian clergy, rendering illegitimate the children of almost all the Indian immigrants. Although he had arrived as the lawyer for a wealthy Indian Muslim client, Gandhi identified with the pain and humiliation of his less privileged countrymen and, indeed, suffered it himself as he was physically evicted from public facilities (see Source, p. 695) and threatened with beatings and even death for asserting his rights. Heretofore a rather private person, Gandhi began to organize a protest movement.

Instead of leaving at the end of his year's employment, Gandhi remained in South Africa for twenty-one years, 1893–1914, inventing new methods of resistance: *satyagraha*, "truth force," manifested in self-sacrificing, non-violent mass demonstrations, demanding that the persecutors recognize the immorality of their own position and redress the suffering of the oppressed; *ahimsa*, non-violence in the face of attack; civil disobedience against unjust laws, with a willingness to suffer the legal consequences, including imprisonment, and frequently illegal consequences, such as beatings; the establishment of a headquarters, modeled on the Hindu religious *ashram*, providing living and working quarters for himself, family, and closest allies in his campaigns; the creation of a press for publishing the principles of his movement. Because he renounced violence, Gandhi, in accord with Hindu traditional practices, called these methods "passive resistance," but they were actually systems of "militant non-violence." These techniques were later adopted by leaders of resistance movements around the world from Martin Luther King (1929–68) in the USA to Nelson Mandela (b. 1918) (p. 755) in South Africa itself.

In South Africa, working with Indians from across the regional, linguistic, religious, and caste diversity of the subcontinent, Gandhi gained a breadth of experience of India that would have been difficult for a leader from within a single Indian region. Concurrently his reputation also spread throughout India.

In 1909, Gandhi published *Hind Swaraj, or Indian Home Rule*. Banned in India, it championed India's own civilization, exhorting Indians to conquer the feelings of fear and inferiority inherent in their colonial situation and to attack British hegemony courageously.

> We have hitherto said nothing because we have been cowed down ... it is our duty now to speak out boldly. We consider your schools and law courts to be useless. We want our own ancient schools and courts to be restored. The common language of India is not English but Hindi. You should, therefore, learn it. We can hold communication with you only in our national language. ...
>
> We cannot tolerate the idea of your spending money on railways and the military. We see no occasion for either. ... We do not need any European cloth. We shall manage with articles produced and manufactured at home. You have great military resources. ... You may, if you like, cut us to pieces. You may shatter us at the cannon's mouth. If you act contrary to our will, we shall not help you; and without our help, we know that you cannot move one step forward. (Jack, pp. 118–9)

Gandhi's success in South Africa was limited to short-term compromises with the government, but he earned the esteem of his countrymen in both South Africa and India. They eagerly awaited his political initiatives when he returned home and established a new *ashram* in Ahmedabad in 1915.

Popular discontent with British rule already existed; Gandhi gave it new leadership and direction. By 1907, the extremist wing of Congress, led by Bal Gangadhar Tilak (1856–1920), called for the British to leave India immediately. Tilak and the extremists employed the idioms and festivals of Hinduism as the basis for Indian nationalism. Economically, *swadeshi* campaigns for the use of indigenous products, especially after 1905, had demonstrated the degree to which voluntary boycotts of imports could spur Indian industrial productivity and profits. How much more effective legal control over tariffs would be once the British left! Businessmen and industrialists also resented British reluctance to share industrial secrets, restrictions on industrial and infrastructural investment, removal of tax monies from India back to Britain in the form of "home charges," and limits on career advancement for Indians.

Several peasant movements which Gandhi would come to direct began with local organization, as in Champaran in Bihar, 1917; in Kheda, 1917 and Bardoli, 1922 and 1928, in Gujarat. Peasants from these areas asked Gandhi to provide more sophisticated and effective leadership to advance their own initial activities. Millworkers in Ahmedabad, too, had already organized themselves (against local employers, not against the British), when they asked Gandhi to take charge of their strike in 1919. Gandhi recognized India's smoldering grass-roots anger, inflamed by postwar economic hardship and political repression. He reconstituted the Congress into a mass organization with millions of dues-paying members, a standing executive committee to keep the organization functioning between annual meetings, and a program of mass civil disobedience, *satyagraha*.

INDIAN INDEPENDENCE—KEY FIGURES

Rabindranath Tagore (1861–1941) Indian poet, painter, and musician from Bengal, who translated his own verse into English. He received the Nobel prize for literature in 1913. An ardent nationalist and advocate of social reform, he resigned his knighthood (granted in 1918) in protest against British repression in India.

Mohandas Karamchand Gandhi (1869–1948) Indian political and spiritual leader, who fought against anti-Indian discrimination in South Africa before returning to India in 1914. He became leader of the Indian National Congress in the 1920s. Gandhi maintained non-violent ideals through civil disobedience campaigns and was imprisoned in 1922, 1932, 1933, and 1942 for anti-British activities. He played a crucial part in the negotiations leading to partition and Independence.

Muhammad Ali Jinnah (1876–1948) The founder of Pakistan. A member of the Indian National Congress, at first he advocated cooperation between Hindus and Muslims. Later, he transformed the Muslim League from a cultural to a political organization. In 1940 Jinnah demanded the partition of British India into separate Muslim and Hindu states. Jinnah achieved his goal, but he had to accept a smaller state than he had demanded. He became governor-general of Pakistan in 1947 and died in office.

Jawaharlal Nehru (1889–1964) Indian nationalist politician and prime minister, 1947–64. Before partition, he led the socialist wing of the Congress Party and was regarded as second only to Gandhi. Between 1921 and 1945 he was imprisoned by the British nine times for political activities. As prime minister he developed the idea of non-alignment (neutrality toward the major powers), established an industrial base, and sustained a parliamentary democracy based on the rule of law.

Subhas Chandra Bose (1897–1945) Indian nationalist leader (known as "Netaji"—"Respected Leader"), who called for outright Indian independence. Frequently imprisoned, he became president of the All-India Congress (1938–9). He supported the Axis powers (Germany, Italy, and Japan) during World War II and became commander-in-chief of the Japanese-sponsored Indian National Army. He was reported killed in a plane crash during his military career, adding to his stature as a martyr for his nation.

Identifying with the multitudes, Gandhi chose an ever simpler and more basic public presentation. Already a vegetarian and owning few possessions, he now rejected Western dress and reduced his clothing to a bare minimum, usually wearing just a loincloth and, in cold weather, a shawl, and simple wooden sandals—a powerful fashion statement. To his nation and to his wife, without discussion, he announced his choice of celibacy at the age of thirty-seven. Oppressed peoples throughout the world have historically feared that their leaders might sell them out, but Gandhi's ascetic and quasi-religious idiom re-assured and captured India's masses. He lived his *satyagraha* and *ahimsa* principles of self-suffering and militant non-violence through fasting, "courting" arrest, and putting his life on the line in leading his public protest movements. Although his countrymen began calling him Mahatma, "great soul," Gandhi said that he was not a saint trying to work in politics, but rather a politician trying to become a saint. Many of his British opponents, and some Indian opponents as well, nevertheless saw him as a canny politician manipulating the symbols of sainthood. Winston Churchill scornfully dismissed Gandhi as a "half-naked fakir."

Gandhi knit together India's enormous size and diversity by cultivating personal and political alliances with the major regional leaders. His most analytic and thorough biographer, Judith Brown, praises his skill in winning the allegiance of such regional giants as C. Rajagopalachari (1879–1972) in Madras; Rajendra Prasad (1884–1963) in Bihar, later the first president of independent India; Vallabhbhai Patel (c. 1873–1933) in Gujarat, who went on to become chairman of the entire Congress Party; and Jawaharlal Nehru (1889–1964) in Uttar Pradesh (then called United Provinces), who became the first prime minister of independent India in 1947, a post he held until his death.

Gandhi was not successful everywhere, however. He did not capture the leadership nor the

Gandhi and Nehru. Mahatma Gandhi, wearing his customary dhoti, and Jawaharlal Nehru are deep in conversation at the All-India Congress Committee Meeting in Bombay, July 6, 1946, where Nehru took office as President of the Congress. Gandhi and Nehru were the charismatic figures who led the Indian National Congress, a broad-based political organization which was the vehicle for the nationalist movement for independence.

rank and file of the large eastern state of Bengal. In Calcutta, Subhas Chandra Bose (1847–1945) often opposed Gandhi as too ascetic in his personal life, too narrow in his intellectual interests, too dictatorial in his political authority, and too compromising with business and landlord interests in consolidating his power. Left-wing socialists throughout India also found Gandhi too cozy with big business and landlord interests. When the Congress socialists advocated land redistribution in the 1930s, Gandhi successfully won over the highly respected, usually socialist, Nehru, and the issue was deferred until after Independence. Despite valiant efforts, Gandhi failed to capture the most important Muslim leadership. Mohammed Ali Jinnah (1876– 1948), leader of the movement for a separate Pakistan, found Gandhi's style both too ascetic and too Hindu. As Independence neared, Jinnah did not trust Gandhi's Congress to deal equitably with Muslims.

INTERNAL PROBLEMS

Nevertheless, across India, key leaders praised Gandhi for redirecting them back to the rural, peasant center of Indian life. At the opposite end of the political/moral spectrum from Mao in his evaluation of means and ends, Gandhi nevertheless paralleled the Chinese leader in pointing to the problems, and the potentials, of the peasantry. When the Mahatma spoke of *swaraj*, self-rule, he intended not only freedom from colonialism, but internal self discipline as well. He stressed five principal domestic programs, each fundamental to India's twentieth-century development:

Hindu–Muslim Unity

Gandhi attempted to hold Hindus and Muslims together in a secular, egalitarian India. After World War I, he supported Muslim international religious concerns through the the Khilafat Movement, supporting the Muslim Caliphate of the Ottoman Empire against British designs, even after the fall of the Ottoman Empire. In 1924, Gandhi fasted for twenty-one days to promote Hindu–Muslim unity. During the partition riots in 1947, he walked through violence-torn areas to advocate peace. Muslims, however, doubted their fair treatment in a majority Hindu country and saw even Gandhi's political idiom as excessively Hindu. The partition of India into two nations, India led by Gandhi and the Congress and Pakistan led by Jinnah and the

Muslim League, was his greatest failure, Gandhi felt, and he refused to participate in independence celebrations. In 1948, Gandhi was assassinated by a Hindu fanatic who found him soft on Muslims. The Hindu–Muslim breach remains a problem today, both in tensions across the international border between India and Pakistan and in domestic conflict between Hindus and Muslims.

Abolition of Untouchability

Gandhi worked to end untouchability. He was not opposed to the general concept of the caste system, seeing differences among people, even by birth, as a part of social reality, but he fought the designation of about 15 percent of India's Hindu population as outcastes, humiliated and oppressed. Declaring, "It has always been a mystery to me how men can feel themselves honored by the humiliation of their fellow beings," Gandhi coined for the **untouchables** a new name, *harijan*, "children of God." In 1932, Gandhi undertook a fast-unto-death against separate electorates for the "depressed classes." He approved of reserving places in elected assemblies—even more places than the untouchables had asked and the government had been willing to allocate. But he wanted all voters to select from among the untouchable candidates lest the untouchables begin to form a political nation-within-a-nation, as Muslims were beginning to do. After a week, the untouchables' leader, B. R. Ambedkar (1893–1956), a lawyer trained partly at Columbia University, acceded in Gandhi's demands. At the same time Hindu leaders, their consciences touched, began to push for an end to restrictions on untouchables and opened many Hindu temples to them.

The effects of Gandhi's campaign were mixed. Though he appeared far ahead of public opinion, many untouchable leaders thought Gandhi patronizing and restrictive, offering too little, too late. They called *harijan* a euphemism and preferred the more blunt designation *dalit*, oppressed. In 1955 the government began a policy of protective discrimination, reserving a limited percentage of places in government jobs, universities, and elected offices only for the "scheduled castes," those castes that were listed on an official schedule as formerly untouchable. The issue of reservations for scheduled castes has continued as a hot, sometimes violent topic since Independence. But over the years the question of how many places should be reserved, for whom, under what categories, and for how long has not been resolved.

Cultural Policies

In developing pride in India's heritages, fostering the development of regional languages and literatures, and more efficient schooling through the vernacular, Gandhi rejected the use of English in India's public life and schools. In his first major address after returning to the subcontinent he argued:

> Suppose that we had been receiving, during the past fifty years, education through our vernaculars ... we should have today a free India, we should have our educated men, not as if they were foreigners in their own land but speaking to the heart of the nation; they would be working among the poorest of the poor, and whatever they would have gained during the past fifty years would be a heritage for the nation. (Jack, p. 131)

Over the years since Independence, Indian vernaculars have increasingly displaced English as the language of instruction in India's educational institutions all the way through university level. Yet English remains one of the two official languages of India; the other is Hindi. Parents who have aspirations for their children's career prospects usually encourage them to study English, and the widespread knowledge of English among India's educated classes has kept the country in touch with world developments.

Prohibition

Gandhi led a temperance movement to ban alcoholic drinks. His argument was based primarily on concern for the effects of alcohol abuse on working-class families, especially when the husband/breadwinner spent his earnings on drink. After Independence, many states of India chose to restrict or prohibit the use of liquor, but by the later 1980s only Gandhi's home state of Gujarat retained almost total prohibition—and it had enormous problems of bootlegging and of collusion between politicians and bootleggers.

Appropriate Technology

Because of Gandhi's concern for appropriate technology, the Congress Party made the spinning wheel its emblem; hand-spun, hand-woven cloth its dress; and the production of a daily quota of hand-spun yarn a requirement for membership.

Gandhi expressed his early denunciation of modern machinery in *Hind Swaraj* in a mystical religious idiom. Later he demanded small-scale, labor-intensive, alternative technologies for economic and humanitarian reasons:

> Hunger is the argument that is driving India to the spinning wheel. ... We must think of millions who are today less than animals, who are almost in a dying state. The spinning wheel is the reviving draught for the millions of our dying countrymen and countrywomen. ... I do want growth. I do want self-determination. I do want freedom, but I want all these for the soul. ... A plea for the spinning wheel is a plea for recognizing the dignity of labor.

THE DEBATE OVER TECHNOLOGY

Again, not everyone agreed with Gandhi. His most powerful disciple, Jawaharlal Nehru, advocated equally adamantly the importance of modern machinery and technology. Nehru could see both sides of the technological debate (see Spotlight, pp. 702–3). He had been educated in England, but Gandhi had introduced him—as he had introduced a generation of India's leaders—to the reality of India's 500,000 villages, where 85 percent of its population lived a technologically simple, generally impoverished existence:

> He sent us to the villages, and the countryside hummed with the activity of innumerable messengers of the new gospel of action. The peasant was shaken up and he began to emerge from his quiescent shell. The effect on us was different but equally far-reaching, for we saw, for the first time as it were, the villager in the intimacy of his mud-hut, and with the stark shadow of hunger always pursuing him. We learnt our Indian economics more from these visits than from books and learned discourses. (Nehru, p. 365)

In the end, however, Nehru came down unequivocally in favor of large-scale industry:

> It can hardly be challenged that, in the context of the modern world, no country can be politically and economically independent, even within the framework of international inter-dependence, unless it is highly industrialized and has developed its power resources to the utmost. ... Thus an attempt to build up a country's economy largely on the basis

of cottage and small-scale industries is doomed to failure. It will not solve the basic problems of the country or maintain freedom, nor will it fit in with the world framework, except as a colonial appendage. (p. 414)

Nehru, who had become a socialist as a result of his study at Harrow, Cambridge, and the Inns of Court law school, advocated the need for planning to guide proper uses of high technology, and in 1938, the Congress appointed its own National Planning Commission, the forerunner of the official planning commission established after Independence.

Gandhi is praised by most Indians as the father of the new nation, but his influence on the actual winning of independence and of new policies of the new government has been widely questioned. India's transformation into an independent state was no simple moral victory, but an exercise in *realpolitik*, a response by Britain to enormous losses in the global economic depression and World War II, as much as to Gandhi's politics. Gandhi led three massive, nationwide *satyagraha* campaigns. The non-cooperation campaign of 1920–22 boy-

cotted British colonial schools, law courts, administrative positions, manufactures, and imports. In a few localities, Indians refused to pay taxes. The Congress began to construct a parallel government. A decade later, in the salt march campaign of 1930–32, Gandhi mocked the government salt monopoly by marching to the sea and manufacturing salt from sea water. This simple action initiated a nationwide campaign of civil disobedience and law breaking, which focused world attention on the colonial government's lack of authority and respect in the eyes of most Indians. After another ten years, the "Quit India" campaign of 1942 refused Indian political support to Britain's efforts in World War II unless Independence was granted. (The Indian army, however, did fight loyally under British command.) Despite these three massive, nationwide campaigns, the British did not finally concede independence until 1947.

INDEPENDENCE AND AFTER

At Independence, despite Gandhi's efforts to maintain unity, the subcontinent was partitioned

The Salt March. Mahatma Gandhi begins the symbolic 240 mile, 27-day walk from Ahmedabad to Dandi on the coast, where he collected sea salt and thus technically broke the salt law—the Government's monopoly on salt production. Civil disobedience did not win independence immediately, but it did discredit the moral and political authority of the colonial government.

SPOTLIGHT
The Dam Technology Controversies

In the 1930s, colossal dams for hydroelectric power, irrigation, and flood control captured the technological spotlight around the world. Russia completed Dnieprostroy on the Dnieper River (see p. 649); the United States built the Hoover Dam; in colonial India new Canal Colonies were created through irrigation systems along the Indus River. Later, as new nations gained independence, they, too, saw huge dams as their destiny. Prime Minister Nehru called them the "Temples of Modern India." Egypt opened the Aswan Dam in 1970 with great fanfare and great hope (see p. 721).

By the 1980s, however, new evidence altered perspectives everywhere. Silt that would have washed downstream to enrich soils was clogging dams instead. Irrigation water was depositing saline residues and, as water tables rose, they too brought more salt to plant roots. River flows diminished sharply, cutting into the productivity of river deltas and seas. Millions of people were displaced, creating

Figure 1 Narmada Dam, Manibeli, India, 1994.

massive problems of relocation, and, frequently, scandals of government inaction and corruption.

The Narmada River dam (**figure 1**) was undertaken in 1987 for the benefit of arid areas of western India. Opposition mobilized, however, against environmental damage and the lack of compensation provided for displaced persons. The Japanese government withdrew its financial support in 1990; the World Bank in 1994. The federal government of India and the State Government of Gujarat, however, vowed to push on. In 1994, a neighboring state that was to get few of the benefits but many of the displaced persons called for a revised settlement and in 1995 India's Supreme Court suspended construction. In 1999 the Court allowed the dam to add 5 meters to its height, but this brought it to only a little more than half its projected height.

In China, the Three Gorges Dam on the Yangzi River (**figure 2**) was commissioned in 1992 for completion in 2009 as potentially the world's largest hydro-electric project. It, too, drew profound criticism for: cost, currently estimated at $28 billion; number of displaced persons, estimated at between 1.1 and 1.6 million; environmental impact, including the flooding of nearby cultural antiquities and historical sites; and fear of corruption leading to potentially catastrophically shoddy construction.

As the mystique of large dams evaporated, conservation experts advocated more appropriate-scale technologies: very small, low cost, locally controlled irrigation projects that pose minimal ecological and social risks, and keep control close to home. Two of the most common are drip irrigation which delivers water in precise quantities directly to crop roots, and various methods of "rain harvesting," capturing and storing natural rainfall in local check dams (**figure 3**) for direct use, or in percolation ponds from which it seeps into the soil recharging underground sources of water.

Figure 2 Three Gorges Dam, Yangtze River, China, 1992–.

Figure 3 Eight-meter-high micro-dam checks water erosion and provides water for drinking and irrigation.

into Hindu-majority India, governed by a generally secular Congress Party, and Muslim-majority Pakistan, under an officially Muslim government. The creation of Pakistan responded to Muslim cultural-religious claims, like those of the poet Muhammad Iqbal, for a nation governed according to Islamic principles, and to Muslim political-economic claims, like those of Muhammad Ali Jinnah, Pakistan's first president, for an equitable distribution of national positions and patronage. Pakistan's peculiar geography, with two wings, east and west, separated by some 800 miles (1280 kilometers) of hostile Indian territory, reflected the distribution of Muslim majorities in the subcontinent. An estimated 12 million people shifted their homes—6 million Hindus and Sikhs from east and west Pakistan, 6 million Muslims from India. In the process, between 200,000 and one million people were killed. Nevertheless, a sizeable Muslim minority, 10

percent of India's population, remained within India. While Hindus and Muslims mostly cohabit the land peacefully, under a secular constitution, tensions between them remain and are sometimes exploited by political leaders.

Relations between India and Pakistan have remained tense since partition, and have been further inflamed by disputes over the proper political affiliation for the Kashmir region They broke into open war in 1947, 1965, and 1971. The 1971 war was triggered by the break-up of the two wings of Pakistan and the formation of the new nation of Bangladesh in the east. India had always maintained that religion alone could not be the basis of a state, and, with everyone else, regarded the union of Urdu-speaking, arid, West Pakistan, with 800-mile (1280-kilometer) distant, Bengali-speaking, marshy, East Pakistan peculiar and unstable. When civil war broke out in 1971, India chose to ally itself

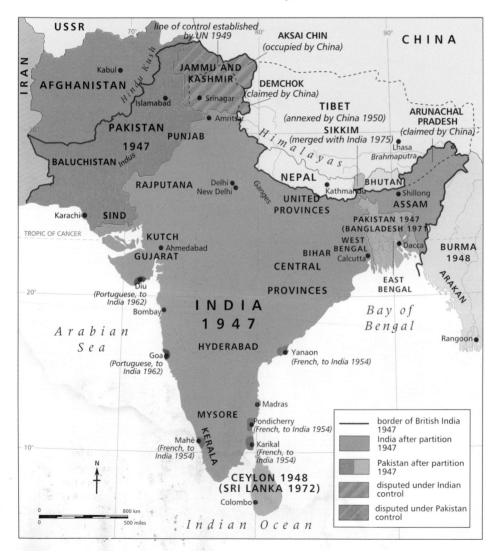

Political change in South Asia after 1947 At Independence in 1947, British India was partitioned into secular, but Hindu-majority, India and Muslim Pakistan amid enormous violence and migration. Disputes over Kashmir continue until today. In 1971 the east wing of Pakistan fought, with Indian assistance, a war of independence against the west and became Bangladesh.

with the newly emerging nation of Bangladesh, an impoverished, densely populated, deltaic country of 125 million people. In 1998 India and Pakistan both tested nuclear weapons, increasing tensions.

Despite Gandhi's quixotic vision of transforming the Congress into a non-official, social service institution, the party members quickly took over the new government of India. Although often called a "soft-state," not always able to implement its will and legislation, early moves by the independent government quickly consolidated the country. Britain had governed about one-third of India's landmass indirectly, through local rulers. Legally, these 562 "princes" maintained direct relations with the British Crown and at Independence had the (theoretical) power to declare merger with India, or Pakistan, or independence. Fears of a **Balkanization** of the subcontinent, its break-up into numerous, separate, small states, were countered by the carrot-and-stick offers of the Home Minister, Vallabhbhai Patel, who prevailed on the princes within India's borders to accede. Dispute over the legitimacy of Kashmir's accession has remained the sole, but contentious, exception.

Other threatened Balkanization was also averted. Gandhi had organized the Congress by linguistic regions and after Independence, the Congress government created new states in accordance with these linguistic borders. Despite fears of separatism, the states have stayed together in the Indian union. Strong separatist movements continue, however, in Punjab, based on discontent within the Sikh religious community; in Muslim-majority Kashmir; and in the far distant and ethnically Mongoloid northeast Himalayan regions of Assam. But thus far, a combination of political bargaining and armed force has kept the country together.

Gandhi's Congress generally respected constitutional process, and the democracy proposed by British rulers has become a reality in India since Independence. Except for two years of "Emergency Rule," 1975–7, during which Prime Minister Indira Gandhi (1917–84) asserted dictatorial powers (see Profile, p. 706), India has functioned democratically and constitutionally as a union of some thirty states and territories, with universal adult franchise and guaranteed freedoms of press, assembly, speech, religion, and an independent judiciary. Despite imperfections, India prides itself on being the world's largest democracy. It also has seen numerous freely elected state communist governments functioning within a democratic framework, first in Kerala in 1957 and later in West Bengal.

Since the 1950s, small groups of revolutionary guerrillas, named Naxalites, for the village of Naxalbari in Bihar where they began their activities, have also been a presence. But India has not given strong support to militant communism. The reasons may be India's generally religious orientation, skepticism about a philosophy and organization so tied to foreign governments, recognition of communism's origin as a proletarian rather than a peasant movement, and state repression of revolutionary organizations.

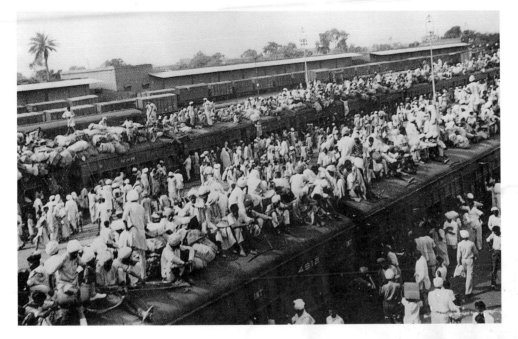

Mass migration. The partition of India at independence created an unprecedented transfer of population in two directions: Hindus fled Pakistan for the safety of India, and Muslims living in India struggled to get safely over the border into their new homeland. This packed train, groaning with refugees from Pakistan, arrives in Amritsar, just over the Indian border, on October 16, 1947.

Until recently, *laissez-faire* capitalism fared even less well. Only one party ever directly espoused a capitalist philosophy of development, and it had limited success and a short life. Indians, including much of the business community, seemed to view capitalism as excessively individualistic and materialistic, based on a philosophy of self-interest often seen as greed, and associated with colonialism in the past and the return of a neo-colonial economic dominance in the present. Despite a large free-enterprise sector in the economy, especially in agriculture, most major Indian parties have advocated socialism, on the grounds of its stated concern for the common good. Nehru, in particular, espoused "a socialist pattern of development." A change in this policy began in 1991 as India moved to open its economy to international markets. Threatened with an inability to meet its foreign debts, India modified its economic policies in the directions suggested by the World Bank. Prime Minister P.V. Narasimha Rao, with Finance Minister Manmohan Singh, lowered tariffs and began to welcome foreign investments.

Through the first four decades of Independence, India's democracy was dominated by one party, the Congress, and the party's leadership was dominated by one family, the Nehru dynasty. Jawaharlal Nehru, prime minister from Independence until his death in 1964, was soon succeeded by his daughter, Indira Gandhi (no relation to the Mahatma), who was prime minister in 1967–77 and from 1980 until her assassination in 1984. She was followed by her son, Rajiv, in 1984–9. With Rajiv's assassination in 1991, India moved clearly into a period of multi-party maneuvering and coalition governments that increasingly looked at issues from regional, communal, linguistic, and personal—rather than national—perspectives. A respected political commentator noted bitterly:

> People openly spoke of political parties becoming mafia gangs, legislatures having many members,

PROFILE
Indira Gandhi
PRIME MINISTER OF INDIA

In Indian political circles, the Nehru-Gandhi family is often referred to as "The Dynasty." Established by one of the country's most successful lawyers and early modern nationalists, Motilal Nehru (1861–1931), it was continued by his son Jawaharlal (1889–1964). The younger Nehru was educated in elite institutions in England. Then, at the age of twenty-seven he entered into an arranged marriage with Kamala Kaul, a sixteen-year-old woman from a much more modest family. Their only child, Indira, saw that her father's driving, nationalist ambition left little time for his wife, and she felt her young mother's painful isolation.

Sickly and withdrawn as a child in this atmosphere of high aspirations, Indira grew up a wary, self-protective woman. She left her college studies in India to nurse her tubercular mother who died in 1936. She began studies at Oxford University in England but left after one year, at the outbreak of the World War. Her marriage to Feroze Gandhi, a Parsi, unrelated to the Mahatma, proved rocky as her husband, a journalist and politician, began to oppose her political beliefs and flaunted his relationships with other women.

When he was elected Prime Minister, Jawaharlal asked Indira to preside over his official residence in New Delhi, and at his death she was named Minister of Information and Broadcasting. Two years later she was chosen to be Prime Minister by senior party officials who thought that they could control her. She charted her own course, however, and her choice of labor leader V.V. Giri as President of India split the party. In elections in 1970, her wing of the party, Congress (I), for Indira, campaigned on the slogan "Down with Poverty!" and captured 350 of the 515 seats in the lower house of Parliament. In 1971 Indira ordered troops into East Pakistan to support its revolt against West Pakistan. Their joint victory created the independent country of Bangladesh. In 1974 India tested an atomic bomb

Indira Gandhi, prime minister of India (1966–77; 1980–84), inspects the guard at an Independence Day celebration, August 23, 1967. Mahatma Gandhi did much to encourage women's participation in public life during the years leading to Independence. Although many women are well-educated, overall the literary rate among females is only 38 percent (66 percent for males).

ministers, etc., with criminal records, rampant political corruption, sale and purchase of legislators to obtain majority and stay in power, mortgaging the interests of the nation and of future generations for self-interests in the business of power politics. (Kashyap, p. 474)

Parliamentary standards were in decline, but the press remained free, proud, and critical. The fastest-growing party, the BJP, emphasized Hindu nationalism rather than the secularism of the earlier Nehru period, but it is unclear how far the pendulum will swing in favor of emphasizing religion in politics.

GENDER ISSUES

With Mrs. Gandhi as prime minister, and such prominent women as Mrs. Vijayalakshmi Pandit as India's United Nations representative in the 1950s, Indian women have participated in public life at the

underground further consolidating Indira's reputation as a tough, determined leader.

Her Congress party was losing power in the states, however, and a judge found Indira guilty of (rather minor) infractions of election laws. In response, she abruptly declared the "Emergency" of 1975 with its jailing of the opposition, curtailment of free speech, and dictatorial rules to bring discipline to the country, including quotas of people to be rounded up for reproductive sterilization. Observers blamed the worst excesses of the Emergency on her younger son, Sanjay, whom Indira took as her most trusted adviser despite his arrogant thirst for power. When Indira lifted the Emergency in 1977 and called for general elections once again, she and her party were thrashed at the polls.

The Janata Party proved incapable of governing, however, and two years later the Congress (I) was re-elected. Indira, who had been jailed briefly for abuse of power, now returned as Prime Minister. Sanjay had crashed and died while flying a new stunt plane, so Indira, bereft, drafted her older son, Rajiv to join her as her principal adviser and colleague in the Congress.

Indira enjoyed balancing one faction of her party against another to keep power in her own hands, but in the northern state of Punjab, she lost the bal-

ance. One faction, demanding the creation of a separate Sikh nation, took up arms and turned the state into a battle ground and the Sikh Golden Temple into a fortress. After much delay, Indira ordered the army to capture and secure the Temple. Thousands died in the confrontation and sacred shrines were destroyed. Four months later, in 1984, two Sikh members of Indira's personal bodyguard took their revenge by assassinating her. Rajiv was immediately sworn in as Prime Minister, extending The Dynasty to a fourth generation.

Photograph of Indira Gandhi, 1970s.

New technology crosses gender lines. Power tillers provide a new technology more appropriate economically than either bullock drawn plows or tractors in some areas of India. They are available through collaboration with Japan (Mitsubishi). In entering her new occupation, the driver has received financial and technical assistance from SEWA, the Self Employed Women's Association in Ahmedabad.

highest political levels. The struggle for Independence recruited women and thus opened public life to increasing female participation, although after 1947 many returned to a less public life. In 1988, women held forty-six seats out of 537 in the lower house of Parliament, twenty-eight out of 245 in the upper, indicating a slowly increasing proportion. State government ratios are similar. With Independence, India instituted universal adult suffrage, and in each national election approximately 55 percent of women have voted, compared with about 60 percent of men. Constitutional amendments in 1992 reserved to women one-third of all elected positions in local government, and there is strong pressure to extend that reservation to state and central governments as well.

The 1955 Hindu Marriage Act assured Hindu women of the right to divorce and raised the age of marriage for Hindu women to fifteen (eighteen for males). The Hindu Succession Act of 1956 gave daughters equal rights with sons in inheriting their father's property. On the other hand, Parliament did not legislate new personal law for non-Hindus, so other religious communities continue under their traditional laws. The issue disturbs many feminists but they tread lightly here because many Muslims, even feminist Muslims, do not want the secular state to interfere in the religious law of their community.

Because family structures in India, especially north India, are both **patrilineal** and **patrilocal**, the birth of a female child is often regarded as a financial and even emotional burden. Years of childhood care and expense culminate in the girl's leaving home for marriage into another family, somewhat distant, with limited ties to the family of origin. The sex ratio in India, about 930 women to 1000 men, is one of the lowest in the world, and it suggests the

systematic neglect of females, especially young girls. Suicide rates for Indian women are high, and isolated cases of *sati* (suttee), in which a widow immolates herself on her husband's funeral pyre, continue. As amniocentesis becomes more widely available, allowing parents to know the sex of unborn children, abortion of females may result. The literacy rate (1997) among females is 38 percent as compared with 66 percent for males; but this is up from 8 percent and 25 percent, respectively, in 1951. South India's treatment of women is widely regarded as more egalitarian, perhaps because of different local traditions, including some influence of matrilineal systems.

Disconcerting results from Syracuse University anthropologist Susan Wadley's 1984 re-study of Karimpur village, about 100 miles (160 kilometers) from Delhi, suggest that the position of poor, rural women may actually deteriorate as a result of increasing general prosperity in the new economic system and of increasing urbanization.

There were several factors affecting women's work, all producing a marked decline in employment opportunities of women. First, with the relative decline of male employment in agriculture and the shift of landless men to urban-based jobs, women who had worked in agriculture alongside their male kin were displaced. Second, women traditionally employed in caste-based occupations as servants through *jajmani* [family patronage systems] were no longer so employed. Third, mechanization had replaced female labor in a variety of arenas. Finally, changes in cropping patterns had made female help in the fields less necessary. These factors all contributed to the marginalization of poor women, giving them less voice in their families and ultimately devaluing them. (p. 287)

An encouraging contrary development is the organization of working women into effective unions which provide both economic opportunity and political representation. In cities such as Bombay, Madras, and Ahmedabad, voluntary organizations of tens of thousands of working women have begun to gain access to capital for working-class women who carry on their own small businesses; to form cooperatives, which help them secure raw materials and market finished products; to lobby government for workers' safety, health, insurance, maternity, and job protection in non-unionized, small-scale shops; to develop new educational models for job training; and to create new systems of health delivery, especially for women. One of the most important of these organizations is the Self-Employed Women's Association (SEWA) in Ahmedabad, a daughter organization of the Textile Labour Union, which had been founded with the help of Mahatma Gandhi.

ECONOMIC, SOCIAL, AND TECHNOLOGICAL CHANGE SINCE INDEPENDENCE

Economically and technologically, India has accomplished the once seemingly impossible feat of producing enough food to feed its growing population. At Independence, India had 361 million people; by 2000 it had a billion. Mass-starvation during droughts in 1964–6 was averted only by the importation of 12 million tons of food grains each year, primarily from the United States. Then, in the late 1960s, the "green revolution" took root in India. New strains of wheat, developed in Mexico under the auspices of the Rockefeller Foundation, were introduced. They increased India's productivity even faster than her population. India, almost miraculously, proved able to feed itself, raising annual grain production by 2000 to about 200 million tons, compared with about 50 million tons at Independence. Further breakthroughs were sought in rice production, the country's other major crop.

Meanwhile, a "white revolution" in dairy production and distribution was also taking place.

Dairy cooperatives were formed throughout India, enabling village farmers to pool and ship their highly perishable products to urban markets—as fresh milk in refrigerated train cars, and as processed cheese and dairy products in conventional shipping—thus providing incentives for increasing production.

The revolutions in agriculture were not without their problems. First, ecologically, questions were raised about relying so exclusively on so few new strains of "miracle wheat." Were too many seeds coming from too few genetic baskets? Would the massive new quantities of chemical fertilizers needed to support the new seeds ultimately ruin the ecology? Second, economic growth increased disparities and tensions between haves and have-nots and between those who worked more entrepreneurially and those who did not. The new productivity benefited most those who already had the economic resources to afford the new seeds, fertilizers, and pesticides, and requisite irrigation water. The rich were getting richer and social tensions increased. Similarly, disparities between rich and poor states grew. The Punjab, in particular, progressed dramatically in transforming both its agriculture and small industries. The small northern state became the richest in India, the country's breadbasket.

Control of land and its redistribution is a matter for each state in India, and different states have enacted different policies. In general, redistribution has been accompanied by compensation paid by new owners to old, and the process has been peaceful but slow. Government implementation of family planning, rejected overwhelmingly in the wake of Indira Gandhi's program of forced sterilization in 1975–7, has been soft-pedalled ever since, yet birth rates have fallen to about twenty-six per thousand (1997), down from about forty-four per thousand at Independence. Life expectancy at birth has risen from about thirty years at Independence in 1947 to sixty-two years for men and sixty-three years for women in 1996. On the other hand, the World Bank reported 66 percent of India's children under age five as malnourished, 1990–96 (*World Development Report 1998/99*, p. 192).

Industrial productivity increased, but the structure of the workforce did not change—exactly the process Gandhi had feared. New machinery produced more goods more efficiently, but did not provide more jobs. The business and industrial sectors contributed only 5 percent to the nation's income in 1947; slightly more than 30 percent by the mid-

1980s (Hardgrave, p. 20). Industrial production multiplied almost five times between 1951 and 1980 (Hardgrave, p. 325). In the 1980s it was increasing almost 8 percent a year, achieving "a new growth trajectory" (Adams, pp. 77–100). Urbanization increased to 27 percent, up from 17 percent at Independence. On the other hand, the percentage of workers in industry essentially stagnated: about 10 percent in 1951; about 13 percent in 1991. Unemployment stayed steady at 8 percent.

Until the 1980s, industrial policy derived from Gandhi's and Nehru's philosophies. Gandhi had urged austere consumption levels, handicraft production, and national self-sufficiency through import substitution. Nehru implemented socialism, central planning, government control and development of the "commanding heights" of the economy—energy, steel, petroleum, banking—and regulation of the large-scale capitalist sector. Both Gandhi and Nehru stressed internal self-sufficiency in production. These policies were increasingly challenged by a new international political-economic wisdom in the 1980s based on the economic successes of the East Asian countries and the political successes of President Reagan in the USA and Prime Minister Thatcher in Britain. Increased consumption has spurred increased productivity, and a consumer society has begun to appear in India. Readers wishing to sense this development, as well as others in present-day India, might browse through the advertising as well as the news reports in *India Today*, a weekly news magazine published in India as well as in foreign editions.

High-tech innovation for both home and foreign markets increased productivity, and India began to manufacture submarines, computer software (of which it had become a world center) and hardware, machine tools, and even prepared to export nuclear power plants adapted to Third World conditions.

> There is widespread appreciation that India now has an impressive scientific and technological establishment and the capacity to assimilate the newest technological advances occurring elsewhere in the world. Securing access to world-class technologies has been the most important element of India's foreign economic policy in recent years. (Adams, p. 85)

The political scientist Myron Weiner has pointed out the extraordinary imbalance in India's educational expenditures, which strongly favors higher education while starving the primary schools.

These policies, rooted in traditional hierarchical attitudes and interests, have produced a skewed society, in which the highly educated elites compare with the best anywhere in the world, but overall literacy is only 52 percent. Again, Mahatma Gandhi's fears were coming true.

A new economic world, based on greater international trade, wider scope for domestic capitalist competition, and more efficient and competitive administration of government enterprises, was beckoning by 2000. Mahatma Gandhi's concern for the basic needs of the poor was de-emphasized, and Nehru's policies of a commanding government were criticized for placing bureaucratic obstructions in the way of economic growth. Foreign investors continued to complain of India's foot-dragging in opening markets, but the country was, in part, unwilling to jettison too quickly its concern for *swaraj*, internal self-sufficiency, which had motivated its struggle for independence. Internally, Indian businessmen also chafed, but India was moving decisively, although slowly, into active participation in the world economy.

INTERNATIONAL RELATIONS SINCE 1947

Finally, India's international stature has both grown and diminished from the time Nehru provided leadership to the third world movement as leader of the first "new nation" just after Independence. In its own region, especially after the division of Pakistan into two separate countries, India has become an unchallenged, sometimes resented, superpower. From 1974 until 1998, only India had tested nuclear "devices." Then in May 1998, India and Pakistan, one after the other, tested new nuclear weapons, announcing their arrival in the world "club" of nuclear powers, and the escalation of their competition. Almost immediately following the nuclear tests, skirmishing between the two countries along their military border in Kashmir resurfaced, sending chills throughout both now-nuclear states. India's military expenditures have risen from US$ 1.7 billion in 1960 to US$ 9.8 billion in 1987, where it has remained about level (in constant dollars).

In the larger world arena, India was the first major colony to win independence after World War II, and it served as a leader to other newly emerging countries. Nehru, in particular, provided articulate, innovative direction. At the turn of the century, with abundant human and institutional resources in absolute terms, India remains a model of democratic political stability and gradual economic growth in a nation of unparalleled heterogeneity. But its leadership role may have peaked. India's border war with, and defeat by, China in 1962 crippled its claim to third world harmony and leadership, and, in any case, political colonialism is no longer a major global issue. Economically, attention is flowing toward more open, more liberalized, and more expansive economies than India's, and India's persistent poverty and illiteracy make it a questionable model for others.

India today is occupied primarily in cultivating its own garden; coping with the tensions of religious, regional, linguistic, and caste diversity; struggling with a heritage of hierarchical practices difficult to overcome; dominating its region; and searching at both the grass-roots and large-scale levels for new technologies appropriate to its degree of economic development, pressures of population, and the need to create full employment. Eclectically, democratically, and reasonably successfully, India muddles through.

CHINA AND INDIA: HOW DO THEY COMPARE?

Both China and India won freedom from colonial control in the mid-twentieth century through movements led by a powerful, charismatic leader emphasizing the interests of the rural poor. After independence both countries diverted sharply from many of the programs of these leaders, India almost immediately, China some twenty-five years later. Both continued to emphasize agriculture, but they also built up industry. Indian democracy has become more deeply rooted, but also more corrupt. It has been indecisive about its commitment to the global economy and has, until now, attracted comparatively little international investment. The Chinese Communist Party, on the other hand, continued its tight control over the politics of the country, but encouraged the private market internally, and participation in the global market internationally. It has become a magnet for international investment, despite its dismal record in human rights.

In comparison with China, India has fallen behind in economic development as well as in indices of human welfare like education, nutrition, and life expectancy (sixty-three years in India, seventy years in China). Chinese policies of land redistribution and universal provision of health services and educational facilities have been far more thorough than India's. The dictatorship of China, with its strong statement of Chinese unified identity, has allowed it to implement new technological, economic, and social policies decisively, even as it has suppressed political freedom. By contrast, India's somewhat chaotic democracy, with its encouragement of multiple identities, has made such policy decisions difficult to resolve. The two huge countries that once spoke of friendship, now see each other as peaceful but wary rivals that have chosen different paths of development.

BIBLIOGRAPHY

Adams, John, "Breaking Away: India's Economy Vaults into the 1990s," in Bouton and Oldenburg, eds. *India Briefing, 1990*, 77–100.

Andors, Phyllis. *The Unfinished Liberation of Chinese Women 1949–1980* (Bloomington: University of Indiana Press, 1983).

Andrea, Alfred and James Overfield, eds. *The Human Record* (Boston: Houghton, Mifflin, 1990).

Blunden, Caroline and Mark Elvin. *Cultural Atlas of China* (New York: Facts on File, 1983).

Bouton, Marshall M. and Philip Oldenburg, eds. *India Briefing, 1990* (Boulder, CO: Westview Press, 1990).

—, *India Briefing: A Transformative Fifty Years* (Armonk, NY: M.E. Sharpe, 1999)

Brass, Paul. *The Politics of India since Independence* (Cambridge: Cambridge University Press, 2nd ed. 1994).

Brown, Judith M. *Modern India: The Origins of an Asian Democracy* (New York: Oxford University Press, 1984).

de Bary, W. Theodore *et al.*, *Sources of Chinese Tradition, Vol. 2* (New York: Columbia University Press, 1999).

Desai, Meghnad, "Economic Reform: Stalled by Politics?" in Oldenburg, ed., *India Briefing: Staying the Course*, 75–95.

Drèze, Jean and Amartya Sen. *India's Economic Development and Social Opportunity* (Delhi: Oxford University Press, 1998).

Ebrey, Patricia Buckley, ed. *Chinese Civilization: A Sourcebook* (New York: The Free Press, 1993).

Fairbank, John King. *The Great Chinese Revolution: 1800–1985* (New York: Harper & Row, 1986).

Fitzgerald, C.P. *The Birth of Communist China* (Baltimore: Penguin Books, 1964).

Goldman, Merle and Roderick MacFarquhar, eds. *The Paradox of China's Post-Mao Reforms* (Cambridge: Harvard University Press, 1999).

Hardgrave, Robert L. and Stanley Kochanek. *India: Government and Politics in a Developing Nation* (San Diego: Harcourt Brace Jovanovich, 4th ed., 1986).

Hart, Henry, ed. *Indira Gandhi's India* (Boulder, CO: Westview Press, 1976).

Hay, Stephen, ed. *Sources of Indian Tradition*, Vol. 2 (New York: Columbia University Press, 2nd ed., 1988).

India Today (news magazine).

Jack, Homer, ed. *The Gandhi Reader*, no. 1 (New York: Grove Press, 1956).

Jayakar, Pupul. *Indira Gandhi* (New York: Viking, 1992).

Karlekar, Hiranmay, ed., *Independent India: The First Fifty Years* (Delhi: Oxford University Press and the Indian Council for Cultural Relations, 1998).

Kashyap, Subhash C., "Fifty Years of Indian Parliament," in *Manorama Yearbook 1999* (Kotlayam, Kerala: Malayala Manorama, 1999), pp. 467–75.

Kennedy, Paul. *The Rise and Fall of the Great Powers* (New York: Random House, 1987).

Liang, Heng and Judith Shapiro. *Son of the Revolution* (New York: Vintage Books, 1983).

Meisner, Maurice. *Mao's China and After* (New York: The Free Press, 1986).

Naqvi, Hameeda Khatoon. *Urban Centers and Industries in Upper India 1556-1803* (New York: Asia Publishing House, 1968).

Nehru, Jawaharlal. *The Discovery of India* (Bombay: Asia Publishing House, 1960).

Oldenburg, Philip, ed. *India Briefing, 1991* (Boulder, CO: Westview Press, 1991).

—, ed. *India Briefing: Staying the Course* (Armonk, NY: M.E. Sharpe, 1995)

Pa Chin. *Family* (Garden City, N.Y.: Doubleday & Company, 1972).

Postel, Sandra. *Pillar of Sand: Can the Irrigation Miracle Last* (New York: W.W. Norton, 1999).

Raychaudhuri, Tapan and Irfan Habib, eds. *The Cambridge Economic History of India, Vol 1 c. 1200–c. 1700* (Cambridge: Cambridge University Press, 1982).

Rosenberg, Rosalind, "The 'Woman Question,'" in Richard W. Bulliet, ed. *The Columbia History of the 20th Century* (New York: Columbia University Press, 1998).

Rudolph, Lloyd I. and Susanne Hoeber Rudolph. *In Pursuit of Lakshmi* (Chicago: University of Chicago Press, 1987).

Schell, Orville. *The China Reader: The Reform Era* (New York: Vintage Books, 1999).

—, *Mandate of Heaven* (New York: Simon and Schuster, 1994).

Sievers, Sharon L., "Women in China, Japan, and Korea," in *Restoring Women to History: Asia* (Bloomington, IN: Organization of American Historians, 1988).

Snow, Edgar. *Red Star over China* (London: Victor Gollancz, 1968).

Spence, Jonathan D. *The Search for Modern China* (New York: W.W. Norton & Company, 1990).

Wadley, Susan, "The Village in 1984," in William H. Wiser and Charlotte Viall Wiser, *Behind Mud Walls 1930–1960* (Berkeley: University of California Press, 1989).

Weiner, Myron. *The Child and the State in India* (Princeton: Princeton University Press, 1991).

Wolf, Eric R. *Peasant Wars of the Twentieth Century* (New York: Harper & Row, 1969).

Wolpert, Stanley. *A New History of India* (New York: Oxford University Press, 6th ed., 1999).

Wu, Harry. *Bitter Winds* (New York: John Wiley, 1994)

THE MIDDLE EAST AND NORTH AFRICA

CHAPTER 21

1880s–2000

> *"The High Aswan Dam … has become a symbol of the will and determination of the people to fashion their lives."*
>
> GAMAL ABDEL NASSER

NATIONALISM, CULTURE, AND TECHNOLOGY

THE STUDY OF GEOGRAPHICAL REGIONS

From the comparative study of the huge countries of China and India, we turn in the next three chapters to three different regions of the world—the Middle East, sub-Saharan Africa, and Latin America. Each region has common internal cultural features and often seeks to act collectively in regard to common problems, but each is composed of numerous separate countries that are quite different in resource bases, ecology, language, history, culture, and religious beliefs and practices. As a result, these countries do not always agree on common policies; sometimes they fight one another in warfare. This makes an integrated account of each region difficult. Nevertheless, we shall consider the key issues in each of the three regions sequentially. All three regions have faced the challenge of colonialism and neo-colonialism, and of integrating policies for

national and cultural identity with policies for new technologies.

THE MIDDLE EAST AND NORTH AFRICA

The Middle East and North Africa include the entire Arab world; Iran, which is not an Arab country, but has its own engagement with Islam; Turkey, also not an Arab country, but historically also a cultural and political center of Islam; and Israel, with its 6 million citizens, four-fifths Jewish and one-fifth Arab, plus an additional 2.7 million Arabs under its general political control in Gaza and the West Bank. The geographical sweep of the region is vast, stretching some 3500 miles from Morocco to Iran. (The names "Middle East," and sometimes "Near East," refer to the region's geographical relationship to Western Europe. As a less Eurocentric designation, it is sometimes called "West Asia.") The outstanding issues on which we focus in the Middle East and North Africa in the twentieth century include:

- nationalist struggles against colonialism and neo-colonialism;

- the impact of abundant oil resources on income distribution, urbanization, education, internal and international migration, and technology;

- struggles over the maintenance of government stability;

- the place of religion in the cultural and political life of the state;

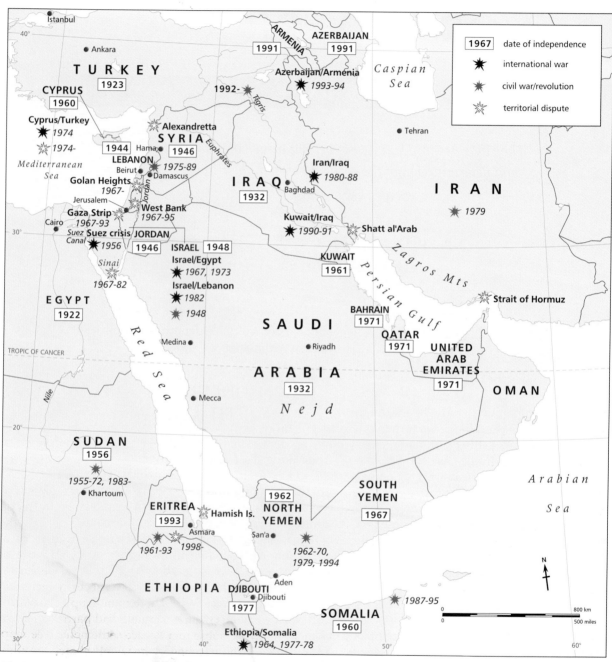

The Middle East since 1945 The presence of extensive oil and gas reserves, disputes over religious and political programs, the establishment of a Jewish homeland state of Israel in Palestine (1948), and the intervention of outside states have dominated the politics of the region. In addition to Arab–Israeli confrontations, an eight-year conflict between Iran and Iraq, a war over Iraq's invasion of Kuwait, and a multitude of civil wars and revolutions have kept the region in turmoil.

KEY VARIABLES IN THE MIDDLE EAST/NORTH AFRICA

	Turkey	Egypt	Iraq	Iran	Saudi Arabia	Algeria	Israel
Population (thousands)							
1960	27,509	25,922	6,847	20,301	4,075	10,800	2,114
1999	66,000	67,273	22,427	65,180	21,505	31,133	5,750
Per capita income, based on Gross Domestic Product (GDP) (US$) in constant 1987 US$							
1960	753	237	3,420	2,083	2,685	1,988	3,537
1995	1,865	726	2,000 (est.)	2,902	5,008	2,389	10,551
Urban dwellers (percentage)							
1965	32	41	51	37	39	38	81
1995	69	45	75	59	80	56	91
Female literacy (percentage)							
1970	35	20	18	17	2	11	–
1995	72	39	45	59	50	49	93
Oil reserves (billion barrels)							
	0.1	4	100	92	255	4.8	0.7
Military expenditure (US$million)							
1960	828	375	1,346	1,916	619	397	212
1997	8,110	2,743	1,250	4,695	18,151	2,134	11,143

Sources: World Bank, World Development Report, 1987 for percent urban 1965; UNICEF, *State of the World's Children*, 1984 for female literacy, 1970, reprinted in Richards and Waterbury, p. 88. *New York Times 2000 Atlas* for 1999 population, military expenditure; *Human Development Report 1998* for per capita income, urban percentage, female literacy.

- differing philosophies and methods of regional development and the difficult search for regional cooperation.

A series of case studies will reveal similarities and differences among several of the major states, and analyze their recent history of cooperation and conflict. The cases are drawn from Turkey, Egypt, Iraq, Iran, Saudi Arabia, Algeria, and Israel.

THE END OF THE OTTOMAN EMPIRE

Until the end of World War I, much of the Middle East was included in the Ottoman Empire. The *strength* of that empire meant that in many areas local political organizations based on national identity had not developed. This was true of Iraq, for example, among the countries we are studying. In other areas, especially Turkey and Egypt, national identities and organizations had formed, often in opposition to Ottoman control and regulation. The *weakness* of the Ottomans, on the other hand, had allowed European political, religious, and business interests to penetrate throughout the empire, along with some European technologies. Exposure to the West left the people of the Middle East wary of Western power and conscious of their own economic, technological, and organizational weaknesses. Feelings of resentment and insecurity increased with the defeat of the Ottoman Empire in World War I and its dismemberment and partial colonization in the subsequent peace settlements (see map, p. 716). These feelings were widely shared throughout the former Empire, but the new initiatives undertaken after the War were different in each country. The inheritor of the core of the former empire was Turkey. We turn to its responses first.

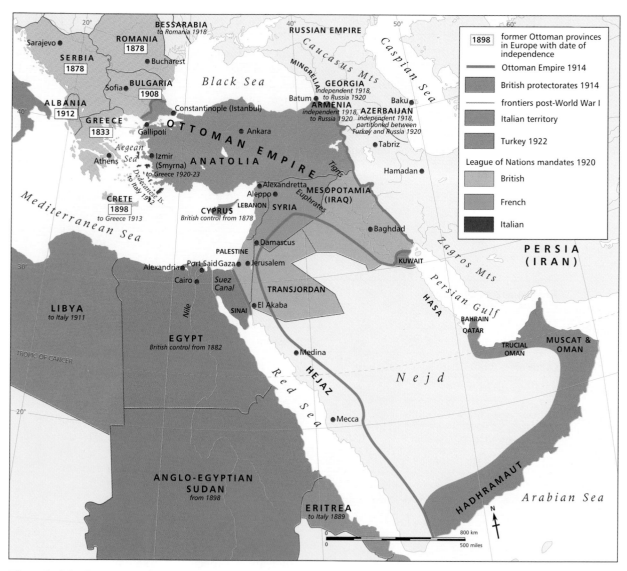

The end of the Ottoman Empire The last decades of the nineteenth century saw the Ottoman presence in Europe decline as Austria–Hungary, Russia, and several aspiring new nations challenged its power. Arab revolt and internal dissent, combined with the Turkish defeat in World War I, brought to an end 600 years of Ottoman domination. Turkey was the core residual state, while several other regions were mandated to British and French control.

TURKEY

Turkey faces in many directions. Its dominant population of Turkish peoples and its eastern Anatolian geography recall its ancient, central Asian ethnic origins. Its dominant religion, Islam, and the long history of the Ottoman Empire orient it to the Arab world. Its northern border with Russia ties it to eastern Europe. Its toe-hold in Thrace through Istanbul, its modernizing heritage through President Atatürk, its secularism, and its current political alignments with NATO and the Organization for Economic Cooperation and Development

turn it toward Europe. Turkey was born as a nation-state from the victory of the French and British in World War I that finally destroyed the sprawling, faltering, 500-year-old Ottoman Empire. The 1920 Peace Treaty of Sèvres carved Turkey into spheres of control and influence parceled out among France, Italy, and, most provocatively, Greece, the centuries-old Christian enemy of the Muslim Turks. An independent Armenian state was to be established in eastern Turkey on the shores of the Black Sea, and an independent Kurdistan just to the south of it.

Turkish General Mustafa Kemal (1881–1938) led a rebellion against the terms of the treaty, driving out the foreign troops stationed in Turkey. In eastern Anatolia, age-old hatreds inflamed further fighting, and thousands of Armenians were butchered. These murders followed previous massacres of Armenians by the Ottomans in 1894, and the genocidal murder of hundreds of thousands of Armenians—estimates run as high as 1.8 million—in 1915. The proposed Armenian state died in the carnage. (An Armenian state did emerge briefly to the northeast when the Russian empire collapsed in 1918, but it was recaptured and turned into a Soviet republic in 1920. In 1991, at the collapse of the USSR, Armenia again became an independent country.) Kemal also forced the proposed Kurdistan off the map of diplomatic negotiations. In 1922, Kemal forced the last sultan of the Ottoman Empire to abdicate, leaving Turkey as a constitutional republic. The 1923 Treaty of Lausanne recognized full Turkish sovereignty over virtually all of the new Turkish national state.

RISE OF SECULAR NATIONALISM 1923–1990s

As a military officer, Kemal understood Western technology and believed that Turkey should adopt Western ways because they were valuable and because otherwise Turkey would be crushed by the Western powers, just as the Ottoman Empire had been. In his years as president, from 1923 until his death in 1938, Mustafa Kemal curbed the power of religion in his overwhelmingly Muslim state. Declaring "Religion is like a heavy blanket that keeps the people of Turkey asleep," he abolished the office of caliph, the chief Muslim religious authority of the state, and abandoned all of Turkey's claims to leadership of the Muslim world. He abolished both Islamic law and polygamy. He introduced the Western calendar, adopted the metric system, granted universal adult suffrage (although he himself ruled as a dictator), replaced Arabic script with the Roman alphabet, established schooling which raised literacy dramatically, banned the fez hat and encouraged Turks to wear Western clothes, a plan that succeeded more among men than among women, many of whom continued to wear veils. He ordered official Turkish placenames, such as Istanbul and Ankara, to replace older forms such as Constantinople and Angora. He abolished Arabic personal titles and demanded that each Turk take a surname, Western style. Mustafa Kemal himself became Atatürk, Father of the Turks.

Atatürk promoted the armed forces as a pillar of the state. In 1931 he proclaimed:

> The Turkish nation has … always looked to the military … as the leader of movements to achieve lofty national ideals … when speaking of the army, I am speaking of the intelligentsia of the Turkish nation who are the true owners of this country. … The Turkish nation … considers its army the guardian of its ideals. (cited in Richards and Waterbury, p. 369)

For Atatürk, modernity was synonymous with technological modernization and cultural innovation. Economically, he began by relying on the

President Mustafa Kemal Pasha (later, Atatürk) inspects troops at the Officers' Training School in Constantinople (Istanbul). Behind him are the prime minister and the minister of war. Because of widespread support by the elite (comprising in the main officers and top civil servants), the Republican People's Party, formed by Mustafa Kemal, was able to implement policies unpopular with the masses.

THE MIDDLE EAST, NORTH AFRICA, AND ISRAEL

DATE	TURKEY	EGYPT	ALGERIA	ISRAEL
1910	• Up to 1.8 million Armenians massacred in eastern Anatolia (1915)			• British issue Balfour Declaration, supporting homeland for the Jews in Palestine (1917)
1920	• Peace Treaty of Sèvres carves Turkey into spheres of control (1920) • Treaty of Lausanne recognizes full Turkish sovereignty (1923)	• Wafd party wins limited national independence from the British (1922)		
1930	• President Mustafa Kemal Atatürk gets loan of $8 million from USSR (1932) • Atatürk institutes first five-year plan (1934)	• Formation of the militant Muslim Brotherhood organization		
1940	• After remaining neutral, Turkey sides with the Allies in 1945	• Wafd creates League of Arab States (1945)		• State of Israel created (1948)
1950	• Islam begins to play stronger role in social and poltical life • Joins NATO (1952)	• Banishment of King Faroud cuts many ties with the British (1952) • Gamal Abdel Nasser nationalizes Suez Canal, prompting Britain, France, and Israel to attack (1956)	• Revolution, led by National Liberation Front (FLN), meets French repression	

private sector and agricultural growth rather than a government-led economy and heavy industrialization. But in 1931, in the midst of the world depression, he moved to have "the Government ensure the welfare of the nation and the prosperity of the state." In 1932 he negotiated a loan of $8 million from the Soviet Union, which may well have been the first loan of its kind to a developing country, and used it to buy Soviet equipment for sugar refineries and a textile mill. In 1934, Atatürk instituted Turkey's first five-year plan, which included nationalizing banks and extending electricity to remote areas. With financing provided by the nationalized banks, the government promoted new industries: textiles, basic chemicals, cement, iron, paper and cellulose, synthetic fabrics, and hemp. A second five-year plan, adopted in 1938, just before

Atatürk's death, included programs for power generation, engineering, marine transport, and a heavy industrial center based on coal, steel, and cement at a new port on the Black Sea.

Turkey became a model for some of the larger, more secular new states emerging from the Ottoman Empire. An Iraqi army officer wrote: "I saw signs of progress which amazed me ... a social revolution in education and economics, and in cultural and spiritual affairs. I saw the pride of the Turks in their fatherland, pride in their nationalism, their self-reliance and their independence" (cited in Richards and Waterbury, pp. 187–8).

Turkey remained neutral for most of World War II, siding with the Allies in 1945. The war temporarily interrupted the modernization plans, but also ensured that Turkey would continue to build

THE MIDDLE EAST, NORTH AFRICA, AND ISRAEL

DATE	TURKEY	EGYPT	ALGERIA	ISRAEL
1960		• Nasser decrees socialist state (1961) • Six-Day War with Israel (1967)	• President Charles de Gaulle grants independence (1962)	• Israel occupies West Bank after Six-Day War (1967)
1970		• High Aswan Dam opened by President Anwar Sadat (1970) • Camp David peace talks result in treaty between Israel and Egypt (1979)		• Arab terrorists attack Israeli athletes at Munich Olympics (1972)
1980	• After military coup (1980), democratic rule returns (1983)	• Sadat assassinated (1981)	• Promise of multiple party system and free elections (1989) repeatedly broken by military governments	• Palestinians begin *intifadah* against Israeli control (1987)
1990	• Joins with Allies in expellling Iraqi forces from Kuwait (1991) • Tansu Cillar, country's first woman prime minister, is elected (1993)			• Jordan signs peace treaty with Israel (1995) • Assassination of President Yitzhak Rabin cripples peace process (1995)

up its industries. The emphasis on industrialization continued through the Cold War to the present.

Atatürk's secular nationalism drew the censure of more religious nationalists. Muhammad Iqbal (1877–1938), the poet of Pakistani nationalism, lamented: "The country is the darling of their hearts. ... Politics dethroned religion." After Atatürk's death religion re-negotiated a more flexible balance with secularism in Turkey's official life. Especially during the decade 1950–60, under the Democrat Party, state radio began to broadcast on religious themes; thousands of mosques were built; all Muslim children had compulsory instruction in religion; schools were established to train *ulama* once again.

The government of Turkey has alternated between democratic elections and military dictator-ships. Through the years, the armed forces have intervened periodically in politics when they judged the elected government too chaotic, religious, or incompetent. Sometimes they took over direct rule as in 1960 and 1980. Under military rule, the government again became more secular, but with significant recognition of Islam in politics and public life. Democratic rule was regained in 1983 after the military coup in 1980.

Turkey is now in the middle ranks of economic development with an average life expectancy of seventy-three years; per capita income of $6,100; literacy 82 percent; urbanization 71 percent; but only 14 percent of the workforce in industry and commerce. With a huge foot in western Asia and a toe in eastern Europe, Turkey has been actively courted economically and militarily by Western European

Kurdish refugees near the Turkish border with Iraq. Despite the promises of the Allies, and the preliminary treaties following World War I, an independent state for the Kurds never materialized, primarily because of Ataturk's opposition. In recent years these 15 million people, Muslims, with a language and a history of their own, have frequently been attacked and displaced by their host countries, especially Turkey and Iraq, who fear their potential nationalism.

powers and the United States. Sharing their fear of Russian expansion, especially through the Black Sea and the Dardenelles, Turkey joined the North Atlantic Treaty Organization (NATO) in 1952.

In 1991 it joined with Allied forces under the United States in expelling Iraqi forces from Kuwait (see p. 727). In the aftermath of this Persian Gulf war, millions of Kurdish people fled as refugees from northern Iraq into Turkey, intensifying their long-standing demands for the creation of a Kurdish state, a demand militantly opposed by Turkey. In 1993 Turkey elected Tansu Cillar, its first woman prime minister. In 1996 Turks elected a more religiously oriented Islamic prime minister, but he was forced from office by military pressure. Since 1997 a coalition government has been ruling as Turkey continues to balance many, sometimes conflicting identities.

EGYPT

Egypt has roughly the same population as Turkey, about 67 million, but it is less developed economically and industrially. While Turkey charts a course for itself alone, Egypt is the largest of the Arab countries and is usually considered the most culturally sophisticated, because of both its long experience with modern politics, and the range and depth of its cultural institutions.

BRITISH RULE 1882–1952

Despite nominal rule by the Ottomans, the military governor Muhammad Ali (1805–48) won effective

autonomy for Egypt, but from the time the British first intervened militarily in 1882 until 1956, Egypt fell under British hegemony. Britain expanded its economic interests in Egyptian cotton exports, lucrative interest on loans, and, most importantly, the Suez Canal, which opened in 1869 and facilitated intercontinental trade by shortening the route between Europe and Asia. "British based civil law ... increasingly displaced Shariah or Muslim religious law, and secular education competed with the religiously oriented mosque schools. All in all, Egypt was being transformed into a Western country infected with the many social problems one found in Europe" (Davidson, pp. 19– 21). When nationalists began to threaten the formal ruler, the *khedive*, Britain entered Egypt militarily at his request, propping up his government, securing their own investments, and becoming the unofficial power behind the throne.

Until 1952, attempts to free Egypt of British rule were stalled not only by British military power but also by deep and fundamental internal divisions. Egypt's first mass-nationalist party, the Wafd, for example, won limited national independence in 1922 and the withdrawal of British forces, except from the Suez Canal, in 1936. But Wafd policies of constitutional government, secularism, elective democracy, and public education antagonized the traditional religious *ulama*. The *ulama* preferred to maintain their religious protection under British rule rather than take their chances with the secular Wafd. The still more conservative and militant Muslim Brotherhood organization opposed both the Wafd and the *ulama*. Formed in the 1930s and 1940s and continuing as a powerful influence even today, the Brotherhood proposed a **theocratic** Islamic government, to be established by violence if necessary. Its founder, Hasan al-Banna, rallied the membership thus:

Dismantling of the blockade of the Suez Canal, set up during the Suez Crisis, 1956. The Egyptian frigate *Abukir*, loaded with explosives to form part of an effective blockade of the Suez Canal, is raised between two German salvage ships, the *Energie* and the *Ausdauer*. The *Abukir* was the last of a series of obstructions in the canal, and once it was raised and disposed of, the waterway could be reopened to navigation.

When asked what it is for which you call, reply that it is Islam, the message of Muhammad, the religion that contains within it government, and has as one of its obligations freedom. If you are told that you are political, answer that Islam admits no such distinction. If you are accused of being revolutionaries, say, "We are voices for right and for peace … If you rise against us or stand in the path of our message, then we are permitted by God to defend ourselves against your injustice."
(cited in Hourani, p. 348)

Less extreme nationalists and less militant Muslims, alarmed by these hardline policies, preferred the modernizing British alliance as a lesser obstacle to their programs.

During World War II, the British put the government in the hands of the Wafd as the most effective political force in the country. The new government used the increasingly sophisticated communication and transportation networks generated by warfare to convene and create the League of Arab States in 1945, consolidating Egypt's own role at the center of the Arab world. After the war, an army coup in 1952 drove King Farouk out of Egypt and cut many ties with the British.

The leader who finally emerged from the coup, Gamal Abdel Nasser (1918–70), played both sides in the developing Cold War to increase Egypt's leverage. In 1955 he joined with Tito of Yugoslavia and Nehru of India to convene in Bandung, Indonesia, the first major meeting of non-aligned states. In 1956 he nationalized the Suez Canal. When Britain, France, and Israel launched a concerted military attack to reclaim it, the United States supported Nasser and forced its own allies to withdraw. Nasser's bold program of anti-imperialism, unfettered independence, non-alignment, Arab unity, Arab socialism, and a strong reliance on a modernizing military establishment brought him enormous acclaim. He was achieving his goal of moving Egypt to a position of leadership in three circles: "the First Circle—the Arab Circle … the Second Circle—the African Continent Circle … the Third Circle—the circle encompassing continents and oceans—the Circle of our Brethren in Islam" (cited in Sigmund, pp. 154–5).

TECHNOLOGICAL INNOVATION 1956–2000

Nasser recognized the importance of technological innovation both to break colonial dependency and to cope with Egypt's massive population growth: from 26 million in 1960 to 68 million in 2000. His greatest showcase project, the building of a massive high dam on the upper Nile at Aswan, promised to multiply Egypt's hydroelectric power seven times; to store up to a year's water of the Nile, ensuring a reliable, constant supply for irrigation; and, most of all, to irrigate new land which could be distributed to the masses. While Nasser wanted the state to control large-scale, major industry, he wanted small farmers to have their own private lands. He declared:

The revolutionary solution to the land problem in Egypt is to in ease the number of land owners. This was the aim the land reform laws of 1952 and 1961.

It was o—in addition to the aim of raising productic —one of the reasons for the great irrigation projects, the powerful symbol of which is the High Aswan Dam. (Sigmund, p. 164)

PROFILE

Umm Kulthum

THE "VOICE OF EGYPT"

During her lifetime, singer Umm Kulthum Ibrahim al-Sayyid al-Baltaji was hailed as the "voice of Egypt" throughout the Arab world. News of her death on February 3, 1975 shocked her audiences from Morocco to Pakistan. The processional route of her funeral was thronged as "millions of Egyptian mourners took the body from the shoulders of its official bearers and bore it themselves by turns, carrying it for three hours through the streets of Cairo" (p. 193). The response to Umm Kulthum's death illustrated her importance to twentieth-century Egyptian cultural life. As ethnomusicologist Virginia Danielson has argued, the evolution of her repertoire paralleled the evolving political sophistication of her nation.

Umm Kulthum was born around 1904 to a poor family in the Nile Delta region. Her father was an *imam* who often sang at local religious festivals. Impressed by his daughter's powerful voice, al-Shaykh Ibrahim taught her how to sing. Her vocal technique—her inflection, pitch, pronunciation, and tone—was perfected during this adolescent training in Koranic recitation. She began her career performing alongside her father at weddings, respectfully dressed as a young boy. Her early lyrics derived from classical Arabic poetry, reflecting Islamic values while beginning to emphasize Egyptian nationalism.

In the early 1920s, her reputation spread to Cairo, where she soon relocated. There she was welcomed into Egypt's new film industry, starring in several motion pictures. From 1937 her live concerts were broadcast by Egyptian radio, and over the next thirty-six years her voice reached beyond Cairo's elite, concert-going public, resonating throughout the Middle East.

Photograph of Umm Kulthum, 1950s.

Umm Kulthum consistently defined herself as a religious woman in touch with the values of rural Egyptians. In her populism she had much in common with Gamal Abdel Nasser and Umm Kulthum quickly became associated with Nasser's regime, a personal friend of the President. She began to record patriotic songs for Egypt and other Arab countries, articulating in her lyrics positions on both domestic and foreign policies. Often "texts originally conceived as love lyrics acquired political meanings in the late 1960s: the sense of love lost extended to loss of land, national status, and international dignity" (Danielson, p.199). She was an outspoken supporter of Nasser even during the disastrous Six-Day War with Israel in 1967. In the wake of Egypt's defeat she toured the Middle East, donating to the Egyptian government the proceeds of her concerts, over $2,500,000. "Her trips took on the characteristics of state visits," making Umm Kulthum the cultural ambassador of her people (Danielson, p. 186). In gratitude, the state-owned Egyptian Radio network ensured that her music received substantial airtime. She also served as president of Egypt's Musicians Union.

An unconventional woman, Umm Kulthum achieved fame, fortune, and respectability despite her defiance of "popular conceptions of Arab women as submissive, sheltered, silent, and veiled" (Danielson, p. 20). Her connections to Cairo's wealthy classes, and to Nasser, brought strident criticism from many Egyptians who considered her a voice of conservatism rather than of socialist progress. Yet, Umm Kulthum's music celebrated Egyptian nationalism and Islam, inspiring millions of Arabs around the world and winning for her a place in their hearts.

The Camp David peace accords. In Maryland, September 1978, Israeli prime minister Menachem Begin, President Jimmy Carter, and Egyptian president Anwar el-Sadat relax during the historic Camp David peace talks that resulted in the 1979 treaty between Israel and Egypt. The Camp David Accords, documents signed by the leaders of Israel and Egypt, were a preliminary to the signing of the formal peace treaty between the two nations. The treaty returned the Sinai to Egypt.

The USA first promised to fund the Aswan Dam project but then withdrew in oppostion to state-ownership of the dam and to Nasser's international non-alignment. Nasser secured the support of the USSR in 1958 and went ahead. The project has had the difficulties of many similar gigantic dams, especially the problems of relocating people (and historic monuments) displaced by the dam and its new Lake Nasser; of inadequate drainage downriver; and of not releasing the vital silt of the Nile that fertilized Egypt's fields. Yet, on balance, thus far the project has helped satisfy many of Egypt's immediate food needs.

In 1957 Nasser launched a five-year plan for industry, and in 1960 a five-year plan for the entire economy. With a decree of socialism in 1961, the state took over most large-scale industry, all banking, foreign trade, utilities, marine transport, airlines, and new desert reclamation projects (Sigmund, p. 195). It had already undertaken a gigantic fertilizer plant at Aswan and an iron and steel complex at Helwan, 40 miles (65 kilometers) south of Cairo.

Many of the industrial gains were counter-balanced, however, by the catastrophic loss of the 1967 Six Day War to Israel. Nasser had challenged the Jewish state by ordering the United Nations peace-keeping forces to leave their buffer positions in the Sinai and then blockading Israeli shipping through the Strait of Tiran. When diplomacy failed,

Israel responded with a pre-emptive air strike, which destroyed the entire Egyptian airforce, and then proceeded to capture the Sinai, with its medium-sized oil fields; the Suez Canal, with its revenues; and, after Jordan and Syria joined Egypt, the West Bank of the Jordan River, including Jerusalem, and the Golan Heights. In six days Israel scored a massive victory; Egypt and her allies suffered a humiliating defeat.

Nasser lived on for three years, but he had lost most of his charismatic appeal. The decision by his successor, Anwar el-Sadat (1918–81), to negotiate peace with Israel, following another war in 1973 in which Egypt attacked and held its own against Israel, was undertaken largely because Egypt could no longer afford the costs of military confrontation. Sadat, boldly, flew to Jerusalem in 1977 personally to negotiate peace with the Israelis. When finally achieved through the mediation of US President Jimmy Carter, the peace agreement of 1979 returned to Egypt the Sinai peninsula with its oil wells and the Suez Canal, and gained US assistance of more than US$1 billion a year.

Sadat, Carter, and Israeli Prime Minister Menachem Begin were collectively awarded the Nobel Peace Prize. Other Arab nations, and many Egyptians, nevertheless viewed the accords as a betrayal, especially of Palestinian claims against the Israelis (see p. 737), and ejected Egypt from the Arab League. Internally, Sadat's crackdown on dissident

THE PERSIAN GULF STATES

DATE	IRAN	IRAQ	SAUDI ARABIA
1920	• Reza Khan seizes power (1921) and declares himself shah (1926)	• British establish Faisal I as king (r. 1922–33) • Oil discovered (1927)	• Wahabi sect, acting for Ibn Saud, captures Mecca (1924) and Medina (1925) • Ibn Saud consolidates rule in Battle of Sabila (1929)
1930	• Women ordered not to wear veils (1936)	• Anglo-Iraq Treaty grants Iraq formal independence (1930) • Accepted into the League of Nations (1932)	• Oil discovered (1938)
1940	• Muhammad Reza Pahlavi is designated shah by the British (1941)	• Ba'ath Party—pan-Arab socialist party—founded (1940)	• Ibn Saud meets with President Franklin Roosevelt to discuss regional threats to peace (1945)
1950	• Oilfields nationalized (1951) by prime minister Muhammad Mussadeq, who is deposed by shah with US backing (1953)	• In Baghdad Pact, Iraq joins Pakistan, Iran, and Britain to counter Soviet military threat (1955) • Internal revolt sees assassinations of King Faisal and Prince Abdul Ilah; declared a republic (1958)	• Saud II (r. 1953–64)
1960	• Ayatollah Khomeini leads abortive uprising against the shah (1963)	• Six-Day War against Israel (1967) • Ahmad Hasan al-Bakr establishes military government (1968) • Ba'ath government nationalizes all banks and 32 major companies	• Saud II forced to abdicate; replaced by his brother Faisal (r. 1964–75) • Joins with Jordan and Iraq against Israel in Six-Day War (1967)
1970	• 150,000 foreigners administering hi-tech industries • Shah flees and the exiled Khomeini returns from Paris to create Islamic state (1979) • Revolutionaries hold US hostages at embassy, leading to US trade embargo (1979)	• Saddam Hussein succeeds al-Bakr (1979)	• Oil embargo imposed on West (1973); later moderation • Faisal assassinated and succeeded by half-brother, Khalid (1975) • Muslim militants inspired by Iran seize Grand Mosque in Mecca (1979)
1980	• Iran–Iraq war (1980–8) • *Fatwa* (death sentence) proclaimed against British writer Salman Rushdie (1989)	• Iran–Iraq war (1980–8) • Chemical warfare against Kurdish rebels	
1990	• Election of Muhammad Khatami encourages trend toward moderate reform (1997)	• Saddam invades Kuwait, triggering Gulf War (1990) • Saddam refuses to allow West to inspect arms-production sites; limited UN sanctions continue	• Saudi Arabia supports USA in Gulf War against Iraq (1990) • Explosions at US military installations in Saudi show resentment of internal opposition forces

students, politicians, and religious leaders, and his inability to cope with continuing economic difficulties loosened his grip on the country. In October 1981 he was assassinated by a splinter group of the Muslim Brotherhood. His successor, Hosni Mubarak (b. 1928), however, maintained Sadat's general policies and became one of the Middle East's most adroit negotiators. Islamic militants continue to challenge his authority, and Mubarak has responded with a balance of some concessions and considerable official suppression. In 1991 Egypt was restored to its position as principal member of the Arab League.

Technologically and economically, three elements mark Egypt since Sadat. First, with female literacy at only about 39 percent, attempts to reduce the rate of population growth are hampered. Second, job opportunities in the oil-rich Persian Gulf states have attracted from 1 to 3 million (estimates vary) temporary emigrants from Egypt. The remittances they send back to Egypt are a substantial part of the nation's imports. Third, a new policy of "economic opening," *infitah*, began to reduce the government role in the economy and give greater encouragement to private business, part of a worldwide trend.

A mosque in Hasan Fathy's mud brick village of New Gourna near Luxor, Egypt, completed in 1948. Although meticulously planned in every detail by Fathy, the project was totally rejected by the people it was intended to house, and they twice flooded the new village to prevent their forced relocation there. The project was not a complete failure, however, as Fathy used the example to explain his principles and methods of architectural theory, the most important aspect being the need for modern architectural planning and implementation of policy for social housing.

THE PERSIAN GULF

With the overthrow of the Ottoman Empire that had ruled them, the Arabic-speaking nations of the Persian Gulf region, especially the large countries of Iraq and Saudi Arabia, looked forward to becoming independent, as had Turkey and Egypt. They also found that they would have to struggle against new imperial powers.

POLITICAL AND ECONOMIC BACKGROUND 1914–39

In 1916 the Sharif Husayn, of the Hashemite family that ruled Mecca, joined with the British in defeating the Ottomans in World War I. When Arab and British forces captured Damascus in 1918, the Sharif's son Faisal established a new, independent Arab government there. Albert Hourani, a leading historian of the Arab world, wrote: "The political structure within which most Arabs had lived for four centuries had disintegrated ... for the first time the claim that those who spoke Arabic constituted a nation and should have a state had been to some extent accepted by a great power" (pp. 316–17).

The British and French, however, had other plans. In the Sykes–Picot agreement of 1916, they agreed to divide up between themselves the area that today includes Iraq, Syria, Lebanon, Jordan, and Israel. League of Nations' mandates in 1922 generally confirmed the agreement. The French, therefore, deposed Faisal and divided his territory into two states, Syria and Lebanon, which they ruled more or less directly. The British acted more circumspectly. They established Faisal as the king of Iraq, where he reigned as Faisal I from 1922 until 1933. The Anglo-Iraqi Treaty of 1930 granted Iraq formal independence; Iraq remained under British surveillance. In Jordan, the British established Abdullah, another of the Sharif's sons, as ruler but controlled his government.

Iran, an Islamic but not an Arabic-speaking nation nor a part of the Ottoman Empire, asserted greater independence vis-à-vis Britain, and greater secularism vis-à-vis the *ulama*. A colonel, Reza Khan seized power in 1921 and declared himself shah in 1926, bringing both central authority and Western-style modernization, under army tutelage, to Iran. Following the example of Atatürk, the shah implemented secular education and law; curtailed the power of the *ulama*; ordered the men, except the *ulama*, to wear Western dress; and, after 1936, had women go without veils. Police were ordered to rip off veils from any women who defied the order. However, when the shah announced his neutrality in World War II, the British, with Soviet agreement, forced his abdication in favor of his son.

In its desert isolation, Saudi Arabia established greater independence, and held more tenaciously to Islamic law. King Ibn Saud (1880–1953) conquered Riyadh in 1902 and dispatched *ulama* of the Wahabi sect, the Ikhwan, or brotherhood, to establish some 200 ascetic communities at oases throughout the central part of the peninsula. In 1924 they captured Mecca, taking Medina and its surroundings in 1925. But as the king began to introduce such modern innovations as automobiles and telephones, the Ikhwan turned against him. In the decisive battle of Sabila in 1929, most of the Ikhwan were killed, as Ibn Saud consolidated his rule.

DISCOVERY OF OIL

The discovery of oil pushed the entire Persian Gulf region to the center of world struggles for power and wealth. The first commercially valuable strike was drilled at Masjid-i-Suleiman in Iran in 1908. Subsequently, oil was discovered in Iraq in 1927 and in Kuwait and Saudi Arabia in 1938. Exploration and discovery have continued unabated ever since.

Oil increased profoundly the international significance of the Persian Gulf region, on the one hand making it a focus for international rivalry and control, but, on the other, providing a resource with which the region could fight to assert its own independence and chart its own destiny. Oil brought the state enormous wealth and power. It provided the potential for the complete restructuring of national economic, social, and political life. It financed record military expenditures. Oil drilling and refining created much wealth but few jobs, and no clear direction for distribution or investment of profits. Policies for using the new wealth varied from country to country and ruler to ruler.

IRAQ

Iraq's politics have been tumultuous and brutal. During World War II, Iraq joined the Axis powers. The British defeated the Iraqi army and turned it against the Axis. After the war, however, the weakened European powers began to extricate themselves from Middle Eastern politics, and America began to play a more central role. In the Baghdad Pact of 1955, Iraq joined Pakistan, Iran, and Britain

in military opposition to Russian threats. Meanwhile, internal revolts overthrew successive Iraqi governments in 1948, 1952, and 1958. The last revolt, led by army officers, inspired in part by Nasser's Egyptian revolution, killed King Faisal, declared Iraq a republic, and terminated the military alliances with the West. Internal coups among army officers and leaders of the Ba'ath Party—an Arab socialist party founded in 1940 with pan-Arab nationalist aims—continued until Ahmad Hasan al-Bakr won out in 1968 and established a military government advocating secular "Arab socialism." Al-Bakr ruled until he was succeeded by his second-in-command, Saddam Hussein, in 1979.

Under the Ba'ath leaders, the state consolidated its economic and technological powers. Iraq's population more than tripled from 7 million in 1960 to 22 million in 2000. Iraqis streamed from the villages to the cities, raising the percentage of the urban population from 43 in 1960 to 75 in 1995. Baghdad, the capital, grew to 4 million, almost one-fifth of Iraq's population. In 1969 the Ba'ath government nationalized all banks and some thirty-two major industrial and commercial firms. In the early 1970s it nationalized the oil fields. The state came to control 75 percent of Iraq's gross domestic product and employed almost a quarter of all the workers in Iraq.

War with Iran and the West

Political consolidation was also a challenge. Many Middle Eastern borders are artificial creations of European colonizers. Most states include minority ethnic groups which have been feared and often persecuted by the majority.

In light of these political/demographic realities, Saddam Hussein sought first to eliminate challenges to Iraq and to himself, and then to extend the powers and the boundaries of the state. He regarded the Kurds, about 15 percent of Iraq's population, and largely resident in its northern, oil-rich regions, as potential rebels seeking their own separate state. He has repeatedly attacked them on the ground and from the air, sometimes with chemical weapons. Almost all the population of Iraq are Muslims, but they are divided by sect: 60 percent are Shi'ite, especially in the south, while Saddam is a Sunni (see pp. 341–2). He has often attacked the Shi'ites, perhaps fearing a potential alliance with the Shi'ites of Iran. In coming to power, Saddam systematically murdered potential opponents within the government and the military.

Gulf War aftermath. As Iraqi forces left Kuwait in 1991 they set on fire the oil wells in this country of oil wells. The economic and ecological damage was colossal and it took months for fire fighters, most of them from the United States, to bring the fires under control.

Saddam's rival, Hafez al-Assad (1930–2000) of neighboring Syria, acted with similar brutality in murdering between 10,000 and 25,000 Sunni Muslims in Hama, Syria, in 1982. Thomas Friedman, the *New York Times* Middle East correspondent, characterizes the political methods of both Saddam and Hafez:

> The real genius of Hafez Assad and Saddam Hussein is their remarkable ability to move back and forth among all three political traditions of their region, effortlessly switching from tribal chief to brutal autocrat to modernizing President with the blink of an eye. (p. 103)

In 1980, fearful of the appeal of religiously militant Shi'ite Iran to Iraq's Shi'ite majority and jealous of his neighbor's oil wealth, Saddam invaded Iran. An eight-year war ensued. Iran is not an Arab nation, and most Arab nations supported Iraq with weapons or money. (Syria, because of its own disputes with Iraq, sided with Iran.) The United Nations ceasefire, arranged in 1988, left the nations about where they had begun in terms of territory, but some 900,000 Iranians and 300,000 Iraqis had been killed. During the war, Iraq's military expenditure reached one-third of its entire gross national product, the highest of any country in the world.

In 1990, Saddam invaded Kuwait, a tiny neighboring country in the Persian Gulf with vast oil resources. A massive United Nations response, orchestrated by the United States, drove the Iraqis from Kuwait and destroyed much of their huge store of armaments, including chemical weapons and materials for nuclear weapons manufacture. In a war fought mostly through aerial bombardment followed by land sweeps, the allied forces lost relatively few forces while Iraq lost perhaps 100,000 soldiers and suffered enormous civilian damage and death as the technological infrastructure of urban life was destroyed. The long-term political effects of the war are not clear, but in the short term, the United States gained recognition in the Arab world as an active, significant power once again; the Kuwaiti royal family was restored to rule; Iraq had been humbled, but Saddam Hussein remained in power despite some US efforts to topple him; the military alliance of Saudi Arabia and Syria with the USA against Iraq over-rode long standing enmities and enabled peace talks to begin between Israel and her Arab neighbors, as well as with Palestinians. Subsequently Iraq began to rebuild its arsenals of conventional and biological weapons. Challenged by the United States and the United Nations, Saddam refused to allow full inspection of the sites of alleged weapons production. Despite a UN embargo against the sale of Iraq's oil in international markets, and despite America's intermittent bombing and its stated wish to see Saddam overthrown, he remained in power as a symbol of Arab resistance to Western hegemony.

IRAN 1970–2000

Iran's transformation during the twentieth century has oscillated dramatically. Periodic change within the government, especially revolutionary change in

1979, frequently reordered the priorities of the nation and often appeared to threaten the stability of the entire Persian Gulf region. The reformist administration of Shah Reza Khan after 1921 and his forced abdication in favor of his pro-British son, Muhammad Reza Pahlavi, in 1941, during World War II, together with the increased exploitation of Iran's oil resources at about this time had begun to bring new wealth to the kingdom. In 1951, prime minister Muhammad Mussadeq nationalized the Iranian oil industry against the shah's wishes. In response, Britain and the US conspired with the Iranian army in a coup that supported the shah and overthrew Mussadeq.

Deeply indebted to the West, the shah joined the American-inspired Baghdad Pact, invited additional Western oil investment, and proceeded to use Iran's oil wealth to fund deep and massive—but convulsive, erratic, and uneven—Westernization of the country. By the mid-1970s, about 150,000 foreigners had come to the country to run the new high-technology industries and to live a luxurious lifestyle in secluded "colonies." Opponents of the shah's system of forced modernization, including much of the student community, were pursued, jailed, and often tortured, by SAVAK, the shah's secret police.

Anthony Parsons, who was the British ambassador to Tehran at the time, describes the dislocations of the middle and later 1970s, when

serious inflation and a fall in the real value of the oil revenues necessitated a policy of economic retrenchment. ... [T]he alarming dislocations and disruptions of the boom were clear. The ports and railways were choked; skilled manpower had proved grossly inadequate and huge numbers of foreigners had been brought in to meet this deficiency; there had been a massive influx of the rural population into the capital, creating grim problems of inadequate housing and social deprivation. The distribution system was overstrained and local shortages of foodstuffs and other supplies were commonplace. The scale of corruption in the Court and the government, and in the entrepreneurial class and bureaucracy, had become a scandal even to the tolerant Iranians. (cited in Netton, p. 117)

THE RISE OF AYATOLLAH KHOMEINI

Opposition to the shah's forced modernization included *ulama* on the right who lamented the suppression of traditional religion; students and intellectuals on the left who were deprived of freedoms of expression; and farmers, new urban migrants, and many urban residents who were squeezed by inflation, recession, unemployment, and a loosening of what they felt to be the moral foundations of the society. In 1963 a religious

Iranian students dressed in the traditional black chador. Following the Islamic revolution in Iran in 1979, the status of women has been affected in diverse ways. Educational and health standards have risen sharply. At the same time Islamic rules regarding dress codes, marriage, divorce, child custody, and the right to work have been rigidly enforced. Many women have accepted regulations that might seem restrictive as statements of cultural pride in defiance of Western pressures. The chador covering became their "uniform" for participation in public life.

leader, the Ayatollah Khomeini (1902–89), led an abortive uprising against the shah. The army killed 15,000 rebels and exiled Khomeini. But from Paris the Ayatollah kept in contact with dissidents in Iran via tape recordings and telephone, and in 1979 he returned to lead popular demonstrations of as many as 5 million people. Now the shah was forced into exile. Islamic law, the **shari'a**, became the law of the land and Islamic government was introduced. Women were ordered to return to draping themselves in the *chador* as Iran became a theocracy. Khomeini explained:

> Islamic government is a government of divine law. The difference between Islamic government and constitutional government—whether monarchical or republican—lies in the fact that, in the latter system, it is the representatives of the people or those of the king who legislate and make laws. Whereas the actual authority belongs exclusively to God. No others, no matter who they may be, have the right to legislate, nor has any person the right to govern on any basis other than the authority that has been conferred by God. … It is the religious expert and no one else who should occupy himself with the affairs of the government. (Robinson, p. 171)

The religious fervor of the revolution astonished many Western observers.

Strategically located, rich in oil, religiously militant, and internally secure, Khomeini's revolutionary government terrified its neighbors and wreaked havoc on many others more distant. In its first two years, it executed 8000 people and exiled thousands. When America offered refuge to the exiled shah, who was suffering from cancer, Khomeini seized the American embassy in Tehran and held fifty-two of its staff hostage. President Carter failed to secure their release through negotiations. He then launched a guerrilla air rescue, which was aborted in humiliating failure. Carter's defeat in the 1980 election was due in part to these failures to cope with Iran.

Khomeini's militancy inspired Saudi religious dissidents in Saudi Arabia to attempt to trigger a revolt against their government by attacking the Great Mosque in Mecca during the *hajj* period in 1979. Three hundred were killed, and the Saudi government drew closer to the Americans. In Egypt, in 1981, Islamic militants, linked to Iran, assassinated President Anwar el-Sadat. In 1989, following the publication of the novel *The Satanic Verses*, Iranian clerics proclaimed the Indian-born British author, Salman Rushdie, a heretic and marked him for execution. A bounty of $5 million was placed on his head, and he was forced into hiding under the protection of the British government. In Beirut and other Middle Eastern centers, Western hostages were seized. Iraq's attack on Iran was inspired in part by fear that its Shi'a religious revolution would spill across the border. With Khomeini's death in 1989, more moderate leaders have come to power in Iran, seeking greater interchange with the rest of the world and limited political liberalization at home. The election of Mohammed Khatami, a moderate reformer, as president in 1997 continued that movement, and his party, newly formed, won major victories in local elections throughout Iran in 1999, including all the seats in Tehran, the capital.

Legal restrictions on women based on interpretations of religious principles continued, calling for Islamic dress codes and Islamic legal authority over marriage, divorce, child custody, and the right to work. Many reports from Iran indicated that women generally accepted these restrictions as a stand against Western culture and imperialism. Women's literacy rose to 59 percent, with 95 percent of girls of primary school age attending classes. Birth rates dropped from forty-nine per thousand under the shah to thirty-nine per thousand under Khomeini, and to thirty-four by 1996. The percentage of families using contraception rose from 3 to 23 in 1987 to 65 in 1994 (*World Resources*, 1987, p. 257; Sivard, 1996, p. 51). Feminism, nationalism, and religion in Iran were intertwined in a unique configuration that did not fit any stereotype.

SAUDI ARABIA

Until oil was discovered in 1938, Saudi Arabia could remain isolated from global currents of technological change. Thereafter, as guardian of the holy cities of Mecca and Medina, King Ibn Saud—the nation is named for his family—began to employ his newfound resources for the propagation of Islam and for his family. He helped to create such pan-Islamic groups as the World Muslim League, headquartered in Mecca, to spread Islam, adjudicate on Islamic issues, and support pan-Islamic causes; the Islamic Conference, to finance Islamic projects and economic development around the world; and the Arab League, established in 1945 to represent Arab political positions in international forums.

SPOTLIGHT
The Mosque
NEW DESIGNS FOR NEW SETTINGS

The mosque has provided a sense of identity and place throughout Islamic history. We have noted numerous examples: the Dome of the Rock in Jerusalem (see p. 342); the Great Mosque at Samarra, Iraq (see p. 358); the Great Mosque at Cordoba, Spain (see p. 357); the Hagia Sophia church, converted by the Ottomans into a mosque, partly through the addition of minarets (see p. 192).

The second half of the twentieth century once again saw dramatic changes in the Islamic world: the creation of new states; the flow of new wealth based on oil; the shift of population from village to city; and the growth of Muslim communities in Europe and the Americas. New mosque architecture reflected these changes while preserving tradition.

Pakistan became a new, independent state in 1947, established a new capital at Islamabad, and constructed the grand King Faisal Mosque (named for the king of Saudi Arabia who financed the project) as a symbol of new aspirations (**figure 1**). The mosque, completed in 1986, was constructed on open land slightly to the north of its city, echoing its setting in the foothills of the

Figure 1 King Faisal Mosque, Islamabad.

Hindu Kush. Turkish architect Vedat Dalokay designed a tent-like structure, built of concrete, flanked by four tall, slender minarets. Most traditional mosques are set at the center of their urban fabric. This one was set apart, representing not its city, but its nation.

At a completely different scale is the Corniche Mosque (**figure 2**) in Jeddah, Saudi Arabia. Jeddah was developing its sea front as a place of recreation outside the old walled city and incorporated a series of mosques into the design. Three of them were designed by the London-based Egyptian architect Abdel Wahed El-Wakil. His gem-like Corniche Mosque (1986) is the smallest. El-Wakil employed traditional forms in new arrangements, comparing the architect to the poet, "whose mere juxtaposition of common words expands the heart without seeking new words or changing the grammar" (Holod and Khan, p. 138).

In New York City, the architectural challenge was to create a pan-Islamic symbol to Muslims from around the world and to the overwhelmingly non-Muslim population of this world-city. The Islamic Cultural Center (**figure 3**), was completed in 1991, sponsored by the Islamic countries represented at the United Nations headquarters, with Kuwait supplying more than half the funds. The architectural

Figure 2 Corniche Mosque, Jeddah, Saudi Arabia.

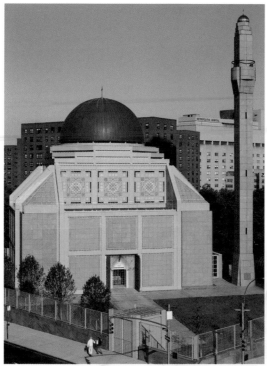

Figure 3 Islamic Cultural Center, New York City.

firm of Skidmore, Owings, and Merrill set the mosque on a raised platform, slightly back from the street, and at an angle conforming with the direction of Mecca. This setting, combined with the steel and copper clad dome and the 130 foot (40 meter) high minaret, assured the mosque a strong, identifiable presence even in its crowded upper East Side neighborhood. The etched glass border connecting the base with the dome provided the geometric designs characteristic of Islamic art and flooded the entire internal prayer area with breath-taking light.

Saudi Arabia has also counseled moderation in international politics. As early as 1945, King Ibn Saud had met with President Franklin Roosevelt of the United States to discuss threats to the peace in the Gulf area. Historians are just now uncovering agreements reached after World War II for US military protection in exchange for Saudi moderation in Middle Eastern affairs, especially in opposition to Israel; US access to military bases in Arabia; and guaranteed access to oil.

The oil revenues elevated Ibn Saud's family to unparalleled power among the desert rulers of Arabia. Ibn Saud's son, Faisal, who ruled from 1964 until his assassination by a nephew in 1975, forged from oil an international weapon for Arab political and economic as well as religious causes. In 1973, during the war with Israel, he and his oil minister, Shaikh Ahmed Yamani, instituted an embargo on all shipments of oil to the United States, and the other Arab states followed suit. (Libya acted one day ahead of Saudi Arabia.) With the end of the war, the embargo also ended, but Saudi Arabia transformed the Organization of Petroleum Exporting Countries (OPEC) into a cartel, raising prices and lowering production to increase profits. The price of oil leaped from $1.80 a barrel in 1970 to $11.65 in December 1973. The combined earnings of the petroleum exporters rose from $23 billion in 1972 to $140 billion by 1977.

The ruling family used this fortune for new development projects, creating an industrial infrastructure and expanding many cities. Foreign workers streamed in from Yemen, Oman, Egypt, and Pakistan. Assistance to poorer countries rose to $5.6 billion, almost 8 percent of its gross national product, and military expenditure reached $20.6 billion, over one-fifth of the gross national product.

With the influx of foreign workers, the population of Saudi Arabia began to shift in location and composition. In 1960, about 30 percent of the country was urban, but by 1997 the figure was about 84 percent. An estimated 43 percent of the population in 1975 were foreign workers. There was also a revolution in education with approximately one million children attending schools by 1980. Literacy rose from 2 percent in 1960 to 61 percent in 1995. Increasingly Saudis were being trained for technical work in the petroleum industry, agriculture, commerce, communications, finance, and the military.

Following the 1973 oil price and availability shocks, Saudi Arabia counseled moderation in OPEC's international market policies and lowered its prices, increasing its immense production to

THE OIL CRISES
1960–2000

1960 Organization of Petroleum Exporting Countries (OPEC) is formed by major oil exporters (excluding Canada and the USSR) to control development, output, and prices, to regulate Western oil companies, and to improve position of third-world countries by forcing Western countries to open their markets

1967–8 Middle East and North African oil-producing countries formed Organization of Arab Petroleum Exporting Countries (OAPEC) and imposed an embargo on the US, Britain, and West Germany for supporting Israel in the 1967 war, with grave results for European economies

1973 Yom Kippur War (Egypt and Syria attack Israel) is followed by OPEC's concerted action in restricting oil supplies, which led to worldwide recession; this has unlooked-for effect of reducing demand and thereby lessening power of OPEC

1980 Price of oil has risen to $30 a barrel from $3 in 1973, encouraging search for alternative fuels and non-OPEC suppliers

1986 Price of oil falls within the year from $28 to $10 a barrel, reflecting increased availability of alternative sources, including Norway, Britain, and Mexico

1991 OPEC members are Algeria, Ecuador, Gabon, Indonesia, Iran, Iraq, Kuwait, Libya, Nigeria, Qatar, Saudi Arabia, the United Arab Emirates, and Venezuela

2000 Negotiations between major OPEC producers and oil consumers demonstrate greater ability to find mutual compromises

ensure the lower levels. There were several reasons. A worldwide recession among industrialized countries in the 1970s demonstrated that excessive oil price rises could destroy the world economy. If that happened, the oil producers would suffer as well. Not only would they lose markets, but, ironically, the profitability of their international investments would decline. The profits from oil had become so overwhelming that some of the oil-rich countries, notably Saudi Arabia and, even more, the tiny kingdoms like Kuwait, could not invest it all internally. Their populations were too small—Saudi Arabia had only about 15 million people, Kuwait only about 2 million—and their economies were so undeveloped that they could not absorb all the oil income. Therefore, they invested their profits heavily in developed countries, and they did not want to see these investments founder. By the 1980s, Kuwait was earning more from its overseas investments than from its oil.

By the 1980s, the discovery of additional oil supplies in the North Sea, Alaska, Mexico, Venezuela, the USSR, and China, and the inability of the cartel to hold its internal line on production, sales, and price did bring a sharp slump in OPEC oil revenues. The reductions forced Saudi Arabia, as well as almost all the oil-producing states, to cut back on programs of economic modernization.

In the late 1970s the modernizing, secularizing, and socialist policies spreading in Egypt, Syria, and Iraq frightened the conservative Saudis. Jobs in the oil fields attracted 1,500,000 immigrant workers from the Arab world alone to the heretofore isolated kingdom, as they did throughout the Gulf region, and with them at least a taste of different, sometimes threatening ways of life. After 1979, the Iranian revolution presented a threat from the other side, from radical religious militants. Saudi Arabia also felt threatened by Iraq's 1990 invasion of Kuwait. So Saudi Arabia, a small nation, rapidly emerging from centuries of pastoral nomadism, conservative and committed to *shari'a* law and government, under an absolute monarchy, and possessed of one-fourth of the world's reserves of petroleum, sought further commercial and political accommodation with the United States and the West in international relations. They asked for, and hosted, American military assistance in driving Iraq out of Kuwait, further splitting the Arab world. Explosions at United States military installations in Saudi Arabia in 1995 and 1996 demonstrated, however, that internal opposition forces continued to be resentful of the Saudi-American accords.

NORTH AFRICA: ALGERIA

In the Maghreb, "the West" in Arabic, the countries of Morocco, Algeria, and Tunisia had experienced settler colonialization largely from France. Independence for Morocco and Tunisia came relatively easily and peacefully in 1956, but for Algeria only through violence and civil war (see Source, p. 735).

Algeria had the largest European settler community, and these settlers had become prosperous and comfortable. For them, Algeria was home. By the early 1950s, 80 percent of them had been born in Algeria and they were not eager to leave. The French in Algeria numbered one million, about 12 percent of the population, and they held one-third of the cultivable land. Officially Algeria was not a colony, but an integral part of France with constitutional representation in the French National Assembly.

THE MOVEMENT TOWARD INDEPENDENCE

The Algerians themselves moved only slowly toward seeing themselves as separate and independent from France. In the 1930s, the leader of the French-educated elite, Farhat Abbas, maintained, "I have questioned history; I have questioned the living and the dead; I have visited the cemeteries. The empires of the Arabs and Islam are in the past; our future is decisively linked to that of France" (cited in Lapidus, p. 687). But reformists were moving to create a more powerful Arab-Islamic nationalism, fostering social unity, distinct national consciousness and sense of destiny, and solidarity with other Arabs against foreign rule. The reform leader, Ben Badis, replied as follows to Farhat Abbas, "This Muslim nation is not France, it is not possible for it to be France. It does not want to become France, and even if it wanted to, it could not" (cited in Lapidus, p. 690).

THE ALGERIAN REVOLUTION

The Algerian revolution led by the National Liberation Front (FLN) in the mid-1950s was met by French repression. The two sides became increasingly entrenched. The violence ratcheted upward and spread not only throughout Algeria but to France as well. The governmental system of France, the Fourth Republic, was weak, and it fell as civil war seemed to threaten. The hero and leader of the

French resistance in World War II, Charles de Gaulle, was called into power under a new, more powerful constitution. Despite an apparent mandate to continue the war, de Gaulle chose to negotiate a settlement and finally granted independence in 1962, but only after 300,000 Algerians and 20,000 Frenchmen had been killed.

Virtually all the one million European residents left Algeria. Of the Algerians, only 7000 were in secondary school, and as of 1954, only seventy living native Algerians had had a university education. The leaders of the new state, hardened by their years of guerrilla warfare, and ideologically committed to centralized control, took over the tasks of development. They instituted a four-year plan in 1969, and nationalized the petroleum and natural gas resources that had been discovered only in 1956. They encouraged industrialization through one of the world's highest rates of investment, one-third of the national income. Oil revenues formed the base of this income, bringing in 30 percent of Algeria's GNP after the oil price rises of 1973. The government built good roads and basic metal and machine industries. As much as 27 percent of the workforce was employed in industry. Education also received attention, expenditure rising from 2.2 percent of GNP in 1960 to 10 percent in 1987. Literacy rose to 52 percent; with female literacy climbing rapidly from 11 percent in 1970, to 24 percent in 1980, to 49 percent in 1999. Agriculture, however, was neglected, and Algeria imports two-thirds of its food; rural migrants have streamed toward the cities, which now hold 57 percent of the population. Hundreds of thousands have migrated to France. The birth rate and population growth rate remain extremely high. Algeria had 11 million citizens in 1960; 31 million in 2000.

The new government and its successors were largely secular and dominated by professional army officers, but in Algeria, too, Islamic religious forces persist beneath the surface. As the new government did not seem to do enough to redistribute land, to end absentee landlordism, to redistribute income, and to increase the productivity of the economy, opposition arose, rallying around Islam, which again served as the voice of the poor. In 1989, a multiple party system and free elections were promised, but as Islamic militants seemed likely to

Charles de Gaulle visits Algiers in June, 1958. Algeria had been agitating for independence since 1954, and in 1956 Ben Bella, one of the main Algerian leaders, was arrested. Two years later a political crisis in France, precipitated by continuing Algerian frustration and pressure for independence, put de Gaulle into office as the new president of the Republic. De Gaulle maintained French rule in Algeria as long as possible, while he prepared the French people for the inevitable shift in power. Finally, in 1962, Algerians achieved independence and the French withdrew.

SOURCE
Conflicting Views of Colonialism

In the late 1930s and during World War II, the independence movement began to form. The French, and especially the colonists living in Algeria, prepared to fight politically and militarily to maintain control. They dominated the coastal cities of Algiers and Oran. Frantz Fanon (1926–61), a psychiatrist practising in Algeria, wrote a trenchant and bitter description of the urban situation. *The Wretched of the Earth* became a classic account of the segregation and cruelty of urban colonialism:

> The settlers' town is a strongly built town, all made of stone and steel. It is a brightly lit town; the streets are covered with asphalt, and the garbage cans swallow all the leavings, unseen, unknown and hardly thought about. The settler's feet are never visible, except perhaps in the sea; but there you're never close enough to see them. His feet are protected by strong shoes although the streets of his town are clean and even, with no holes or stones. The settler's town is a well-fed town, an easygoing town; its belly is always full of good things. The settler's town is a town of white people, of foreigners.
>
> The town belonging to the colonized people, at least the native town, the Negro village, the medina, the reservation, is a place of ill fame, peopled by men of evil repute. They are born there, it matters little where or how; they die there, it matters not where, nor how. It is a world without spaciousness; men live there on top of each other, and their huts are built one on top of the other. The native town is a hungry town, starved of bread, of meat, of shoes, of coal, of light. The native town is a crouching village, a town on its knees, a town wallowing in the mire. (Fanon, p. 39)

At the same time, hundreds of thousands of North Africans worked as laborers in Europe, a sign of the lack of opportunity at home. A touching poem by a Moroccan woman lamenting the departure of her husband tells the human as well as political dimensions of the emigration for employment:

> Germany, Belgium, France
> and Netherlands
> Where are you situated?
> Where are you?
> Where can I find you?
> I have never seen your countries, I do not
> speak your language.
> I have heard it said that you are beautiful,
> I have heard it said that you are clean.
> I am afraid, afraid that my love forgets
> me in your paradise.
> I ask you to save him for me.
> One day after our wedding he left,
> with his suitcase in his hand, his eyes looking
> ahead.
> You must not say that he is bad or aggressive;
> I have seen his tears, deep in his heart, when he
> went away.
> He looked at me with the eyes of a child;
> He gave me his small empty hand and asked me:
> "What should I do?"
> I could not utter a word; my heart bled for him.
>
> Germany, Belgium, France
> and Holland:
> I ask you to save him for me, so I can see him
> once a year.
> I knew him in his strength which could break
> stones
> I am afraid, jealousy is eating my heart.
> With you he stays one year, with me just one
> month
> to you he gives his health and his sweat,
> to me he only comes to recuperate.
> Then he leaves again to work for you, to beautify
> you as a bride, each day anew.
> And I, I wait; I am like a flower that
> withers more each day.
>
> He gives you his health and his power,
> with you he stays one year,
> with me only one month.
> I am afraid that he forgets me.
>
> I ask you: give him back to me.
> (Johnson and Bernstein, pp. 173–4.)

win, the military government frequently postponed or rigged them. Finally, regardless of who was elected, the ruling military council remained in power, with Islamic militants in violent opposition. Civil war continues in Algeria, with the death toll to date estimated at 50,000.

ISRAEL

Of all issues in the modern Middle East, Israeli–Arab relations have been the most discussed by historians. In Chapter 17 we have seen the emergence of Zionism—the Jewish quest for a homeland—as one of the many nationalist movements of nineteenth century Europe. The British government recognized this movement by issuing the Balfour Declaration in 1917, proposing their support for the establishment of a national homeland for the Jews in Palestine. In 1920, however, there were only about 60,000 Jews and ten times that number of Arabs living in the area. Jewish settlement increased between the two world wars, but with it came increasing conflict. Nazi persecution of Jews throughout World War II and the atrocities of the Holocaust (see p. 612) demonstrated a desperate need for a political state and refuge for the Jewish people which no nation had provided. Following the war, in 1947, a United Nations resolution agreed to the (re)establishment of an independent Jewish state in Palestine on land currently occupied by Arabs. The state of Israel was created in 1948.

ISRAEL AND THE ARAB WORLD: WHAT DO WE KNOW? HOW DO WE ASSESS ITS SIGNIFICANCE?

The relationships between Israeli and Arab combine and confront so many compelling issues and tell so many intertwined stories that collectively they have touched the imagination of much of the world. Historians recognize that the narrations through which they tell their stories—the plots, as historian Hayden White calls them—present the underlying structure of their understanding of the past. Each plot frames the historical story in a fundamentally different way. In considering Arab–Israeli relations, let us consider the variety of separate stories, "emplotments," that have been narrated and that need to be brought together in order for the "whole story" to begin to emerge.

Readers may begin to make their own choices as to which plot, or mix of plots, most accurately captures the complexity, drama, and passion of this historical relationship.

A Contest of Religions

The first emplotment, and perhaps the one told most frequently, sees Israeli–Arab relationships as a conflict between two historically competitive religious groups. Ever since 135 C.E., when the Jews were exiled by the Romans from Judaea (Israel), a land promised to them by God in the Bible, they sought to return. A few managed to remain throughout the ensuing 2000 years. All Jews, everywhere, were to recite in formal prayers morning, afternoon, and night, and after all meals, a reminder to God of his promise. The recreation of a modern Israel seemed to many Jews a partial fulfillment of those prayers.

When they arrived in the late nineteenth century, however, they found the land already occupied. The hundreds of thousands of Arabs resident in Palestine understood the return of Jews to Israel as a challenge to the religious supremacy they had themselves established throughout the Middle East since the time of Muhammad. The Muslims chanted Quranic verses telling of the Jews' rejection of Muhammad as God's special prophet, and they resented and opposed the Jewish resurgence on land that Muslims now occupied. This religiously based narrative told of a religious conflict dating back at least 1300 years.

A Clash of Nationalisms

The second emplotment tells of two secular nationalisms on a collision course. Nineteenth-century European nationalism inspired Jews in Europe to seek a homeland of their own once again. At first, the goal was expressed in cultural terms: to restore Hebrew as a living language of everyday national life; to work the land again after centuries of urban ghettoization; to live as a "normal" people with a land and culture of its own. Then, as **pogroms** against Jews resumed with unprecedented ferocity under Russian Czar Alexander III after 1881, the movement of Jewish nationalism became far more urgent and far more political.

Assimilated Jews, living more contentedly in the USA and Western European countries, at first discounted this argument. Even the Jews fleeing Russian pogroms headed mostly to the USA; only a

Mexican revolutionaries. General Francisco "Pancho" Villa and Emiliano Zapata (right), sporting his flamboyant moustache, sit together with their Mexican revolutionary army, men who had come from many different occupations and walks of life to join the ranks. The radical leaders hailed from different parts of the country, Zapata from south of Mexico City and Villa from the northern border, but they shared common goals.

imposing restrictions on foreign economic control. It protected Mexican workers by passing a labor code including minimum salaries and maximum hours, accident insurance, pensions, social benefits, and the right to unionize and strike. It placed severe restrictions on the church and clergy, denying them the rights to own property and to provide primary education. (Most of the revolutionaries were anti-clerical. Zapata was an exception in this, as the peasantry who followed him were extremely devoted to the church.) The constitution also decreed that no foreigner could be a minister or priest, vote, hold office, or criticize the government.

Enacting the new laws was easier than implementing them, but having the new constitution in place set a standard of accountability for government and served as a beacon for the continuing revolution. On the material level, not much changed at first. In 1920 Obregón deposed Carranza and became president. He distributed 3 million acres (1.2 million hectares) of land to peasants, 10 percent of whom benefited. This redistribution helped to establish the principles of the revolution, demonstrating good faith on the part of the state and putting new land into production, although the state did not provide the technical assistance needed to improve productivity. Politically, Obregón began to include new constituencies in his government, including the labor movement, represented by a Labor Party, and the peasants, represented by a National Agrarian Party. The institutionalization of their presence in government promised new stability through wider representation. The repre-

sentation, everyone recognized, was not only by social class but also by ethnicity and culture. *Mestizos* and even indigenous Indians achieved a place in government.

Obregón provided patronage for new artists, in particular a school of mural painters—Diego Rivera (1886–1957), David Alfaro Siqueiros (1894–1974), and José Clemente Orozco (1883–1949)—whose bold and powerful murals brought a new, unifying, national image to Mexico and achieved recognition throughout the world. Their huge murals, painted in some of Mexico's most honored public spaces, gave prominence to the Indians and working classes of Mexico in a new visual history of the country (see Spotlight, pp. 782–3). Mexico's struggle against the threefold problems of racial discrimination against Indians, economic discrimination against the poor, and the denial of both problems behind a façade of political rhetoric was an inspiration throughout Latin America.

Warfare continued, however, partly in the form of factional struggles among the various leaders, partly between the government and the church. Obregón was assassinated in 1924, and Plutarco Elías Calles (1877–1945) became president. The new ruling *caudillos* viewed the church as a rival for power, and as the government began to extend and enforce its anti-clerical policies in the mid-1920s, many of the clergy went on strike, refusing to perform services. The peasantry supported the clergy, and as many as 50,000 armed peasants confronted the government in the War of the Cristeros. Calles backed down, allowing the anti-clerical

SPOTLIGHT
Diego Rivera:
MURALIST PAINTER OF MEXICO'S HISTORY

The early, conventional artistic training which Diego Rivera (1886–1957) received in Mexico and in France gave no indication that he would create an entirely new way of understanding and representing the history of his people. But by the time he returned to Mexico in 1921 his country had passed through a decade of revolution and civil war that had seen more than a million people killed, a new system of government installed, and a new cultural policy proclaimed to celebrate the history of Mexico's *mestizo* peasants and workers. Three great muralists accepted this challenge: Rivera, Jose Clemente Orozco (1883–1949), and David Alfaro Siqueiros (1894–1974). Each filled vast public spaces with their murals, telling the history of Mexico in presentations which could be understood even by illiterate peasants, and yet win the recognition of

sophisticated critics as an important new art form.

Rivera, the most acclaimed of the three, was assigned the most prominent spaces, first the Ministry of Education and later

Figure 1 Diego Rivera, *The Conquest of Mexico* (detail), 1929–30.

the National Palace, both in the heart of Mexico City. Here he first painted a set of enormous murals depicting the history of Mexico from the arrival of Hernán Cortés and the *conquistadores* through the revolution of Rivera's own time, on to a proposed future of industrialization under a Marxist philosophy. At about the same time, 1929 to 1930, he painted a similar history of the conquest at the Cortés Palace in Cuernavaca. **Figure 1** is a detail from Cuernavaca focussing on *The Conquest of Mexico*. Rivera is unsparing in his representation of Spanish brutality and greed. Although soldiers do the dirtiest work, noblemen supervise and participate while priests look on greedily and make records of the spoils.

Figure 2 was painted in 1945 in a corridor of the National Palace. In this mural of *The Great City of Tenochtitlán*, Rivera reconstructs the life of the

Figure 2 Diego Rivera, *The Great City of Tenochtitlán* (detail), 1945.

Native Americans before the arrival of the Spanish. The background cityscape reminds the viewer of the majesty, power, and order of this earlier urban civilization, while the foreground represents the everyday lives of its inhabitants, from the ruler on his throne to the laborers who constructed the buildings. Rivera captures the pulse of life: women selling food in the marketplace, parents inspecting a child's teeth, merchants negotiating prices, artisans creating and selling their handicrafts, peasants bearing their agricultural products to the city, and, in the right foreground, a young woman seducing older men, with apparent success. He does not, however, touch on Aztec imperialism nor its human sacrifice of captured subjects.

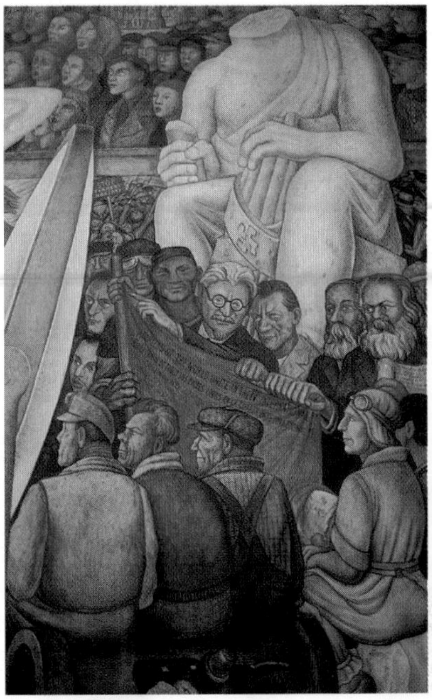

Figure 3 Diego Rivera, *Man at the Crossroads* (detail), 1934.

Rivera was invited to the United States to paint murals of workers' lives and struggles in the San Francisco Stock Exchange, the Detroit Institute of Arts, and New York's Rockefeller Center, although the last was canceled when Rivera insisted on painting Lenin into the mural. **Figure 3**, a detail from *Man at the Crossroads*, was to be part of the Rockefeller Center mural. John D. Rockefeller himself stopped the painting and had it destroyed, but Rivera copied it at the Palace of Fine Arts in Mexico City. This segment of the mural shows the communist leader Leon Trotsky unfurling a banner with the motto "Workers of the World Unite" in the midst of an assembly of workers. Engels and Marx look on.

legislation to lapse, and beginning a more sensitive accommodation between church and state, which has remained and deepened to the present. The government also entered into an alliance with the largest national labor confederation, the Confederación Regional Obrera Mexicana (CROM).

In 1928 Calles institutionalized a new, more comprehensive party, the National Revolutionary Party, which was the forerunner of today's Party of Institutionalized Revolution (PRI). The broad internal representation of the PRI elevated the party above the individual, solved the problem of succession in leadership, and brought an institutional stability to Mexico that has endured until today. Rule by *caudillos* was largely ended. No other Latin American country experienced such a fundamental program of radical revolution and agrarian reform until the 1950s.

Under Lázaro Cárdenas (1895–1970), president from 1934 to 1940, the PRI pushed the reforms still further. Cárdenas redistributed 45 million acres (18.2 million hectares) of land, starting a process by which 253 million acres (102.4 million hectares) would be redistributed by 1984. (Nevertheless, a rapidly expanding population has left several million peasants still landless—in absolute terms more than at the time of the revolution.) Cárdenas also stood up to foreign control of Mexico's economy by nationalizing Mexico's oil industry in 1938. Seventeen foreign oil companies had refused to accept a pro-union ruling of an arbitration council upheld by Mexico's Supreme Court. Cárdenas defied the foreign owners, deriding their arrogance and disregard for the Mexican workers:

Who is not aware of the irritating discrimination governing construction of the company camps? Comfort for the foreign personnel; misery, drabness, and insalubrity for the Mexicans. Refrigeration and protection against tropical insects for the former; indifference and neglect, medical services and supplies always grudgingly provided, for the latter; lower wages and harder, more exhausting labor for our people. (Andrea and Overfield, p. 453)

Cárdenas offered compensation to the companies and foreign governments, especially the United States where President Franklin Roosevelt was pursuing a "Good Neighbor Policy," did not intervene. Cárdenas established a new level of national pride in Mexico. His decision to retire from presidential politics at the end of his term in 1940 helped stabilize the structure of the modern Mexican state.

The PRI envisioned a one-party state which would include all the major interest groups and the contest for political power would take place within the party. The party, it argued, could institutionalize the revolution. Most analysts have been skeptical of both claims, however, arguing that a single party cannot balance all major factions indefinitely and that political revolutions cannot be institutionalized.

POST-REVOLUTIONARY MEXICO

The Cárdenas presidency was the last to attempt fundamental reforms on a nationwide scale. With the election of Miguel Aleman as president in 1946, political leadership passed into the hands of large-

Mexican women revolutionaries in fighting form. A group of rebel women and young girls, wearing traditional dress, practice their shooting skills during the Mexican Revolution in 1911. Those people opposed to the government in power were drawn from many different factions, but all fought together for a common cause.

scale business and agricultural interest groups, where it has remained ever since. The PRI won every presidential election through the end of the century, although it was frequently accused of cheating, its margins grew thinner, and in 1997 it lost majority control of the national legislature. The electorate doubled in 1958 when women were enfranchised.

Through the 1950s, 1960s, and 1970s Mexico's economy grew at the rate of 5 to 6 percent per year, with especial success after new oil reserves were discovered in Tabasco and Chiapas states. In the 1980s and 1990s, however, Mexico had to turn twice to an international consortium of lenders, led by the United States and the International Monetary Fund, for loans to bail out the economy—first when the international price of oil plummeted in the 1980s, leaving Mexico unable to pay its enormous international debts; second when the peso collapsed in 1994 after the establishment of the North American Free Trade Association (NAFTA), which linked the United States, Canada, and Mexico in an agreement to end all tariffs and trade barriers among them. By opening the markets of Mexico and the United States to competition NAFTA challenged Mexico to compete against the greater productivity of United States industrial technology and challenged the United States to compete against the lower wages of Mexican labor. Both sides feared a loss of jobs and markets. The value of the Mexican peso dropped sharply. The international consortium of lenders that intervened to shore up Mexico's economy imposed austerity measures that compromised Mexico's financial independence in the short run and brought cries of protest against the World Bank and the International Monetary Fund.

The Mexican economy has subsequently recovered. Much of its most recent growth has located along its northern border with the United States. Here *maquiladoras*, assembly plants, fuel the growth. United States industries ship component parts to the *maquiladoras* where they are assembled by relatively low-paid Mexican labor and shipped back into the United States tariff-free. Advocates of the *maquiladora* system see them as offering new job opportunities within the Mexican economy and cite their rapid growth as a success of NAFTA. Critics cite their low pay and poor working conditions compared to the United States.

Critics also point to evidence of some fundamental weaknesses in the Mexican economy: the steady stream of emigration to the United States of about 150,000 Mexicans arriving legally each year, and about an equal number illegally, and by the rapid rise of illegal drug cartels. Mexico began by serving as a transit point for drugs coming to the United States from Colombia; by 1965 an estimated two-thirds of all the marijuana and cocaine entering the United States came via Mexico. Mexican drug gangs were estimated in 1995 to be netting some $30 billion annually and to be exercising a profound effect on Mexican politics, by rewarding their friends and assassinating their enemies. Corruption was widespread and difficult to uproot.

ETHNIC CULTURE AND POWER IN THE REVOLUTION

On January 1, 1994, the very day NAFTA took effect, Maya Indians in the economically backward Chiapas state rose in armed confrontation against the policies of the central government, leaving forty-five dead. The incident called into question the cultural accomplishments of the Mexican revolution in uniting the people. Academic and journalistic analyses of the Chiapas uprising begin with the intense poverty of this most southern state of Mexico. The state is rich in oil, coffee plantations, and sugar, but in the mountainous regions, where most of Chiapas' Maya Indians live, the soil is poor and quickly exhausted by its meager corn crop. Second, although a minority of the population of the state, the Maya dominate the mountain regions and had historically resisted the Spanish takeover of the land. As remote, mountain Indians, they were scorned and persecuted both by the Spanish and by their mestizo successors. The Dominican Friar Bartolomé de Las Casas (p. 412) who protested the violence and slavery of the Spanish treatment of Indians in the sixteenth century, was a resident of this area and gathered much of his evidence here.

Much more recently, in 1960, Samuel Ruiz was appointed Bishop in San Cristobal, Las Casas' parish, and while he began as a conservative, the scenes he witnessed turned Ruiz into an advocate of liberation theology (see p. 802–3), boldly speaking out against oppression of the Indian population. In 1974 he organized the first Indian Congress assembly to raise political consciousness among the Indians. A total of 1250 came from 327 villages, and the protest movement of Chiapas Maya was born. Meanwhile, a clandestine revolutionary movement, the Forces of National Liberation (FLN) began to establish a local cell soon to be led by a young

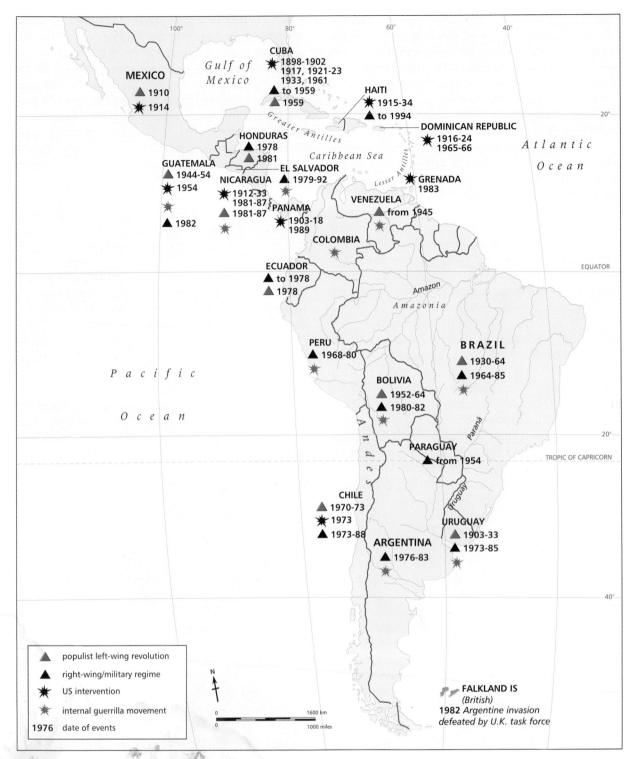

MEXICO
▲ 1910
✳ 1914

CUBA
✳ 1898-1902
1917, 1921-23
1933, 1961
▲ to 1959
▲ 1959

HAITI
✳ 1915-34
▲ to 1994

DOMINICAN REPUBLIC
✳ 1916-24
1965-66

HONDURAS
▲ 1978
▲ 1981

GUATEMALA
▲ 1944-54
✳ 1954
✳
▲ 1982

EL SALVADOR
▲ 1979-92

NICARAGUA
✳ 1912-33
1981-87
✳ 1981-87

PANAMA
✳ 1903-18
1989

GRENADA
1983

VENEZUELA
▲ from 1945

COLOMBIA

ECUADOR
▲ to 1978
▲ 1978

PERU
▲ 1968-80

BRAZIL
▲ 1930-64
▲ 1964-85

BOLIVIA
▲ 1952-64
▲ 1980-82

PARAGUAY
▲ from 1954

CHILE
▲ 1970-73
✳ 1973
▲ 1973-88

ARGENTINA
▲ 1976-83

URUGUAY
▲ 1903-33
▲ 1973-85

Gulf of Mexico

Greater Antilles

Caribbean Sea

Lesser Antilles

Atlantic Ocean

Pacific Ocean

Amazon

Amazonia

Andes

Paraná

Uruguay

EQUATOR

TROPIC OF CAPRICORN

100° 80° 60° 40°

20°

20°

40°

Legend:
▲ populist left-wing revolution
▲ right-wing/military regime
✳ US intervention
✳ internal guerrilla movement
1976 date of events

N

0   1600 km
0   1000 miles

FALKLAND IS
(British)
1982 *Argentine invasion
defeated by U.K. task force*

Latin American politics in the twentieth century Latin America has been beset by a bewildering range of revolutions, coups, insurrections, and foreign interventions by the United States. The map cannot do justice to the variety of revolutions, from communist in Cuba, to right-wing military in Chile and Argentina. It does, however, present a picture of a continent with vibrant, often unstable, politics.

guerrilla fighter known as *subcomandante* Marcos. Marcos became the chief spokesperson of the Chiapas revolt. These were the historical, ethnic, cultural, religious, political, organizational, and personal backgrounds to the revolt in Chiapas that captured the world's headlines.

The revolt of the Maya in Chiapas, calling themselves Zapatistas in honor of Emiliano Zapata, is still unresolved. Veteran researcher Enrique Krauze adds that fighting pits not only Maya against the government, but also Maya against Maya; more revolutionary groups against those eager to find a negotiated solution; Catholics against Protestants; and rival families against one another seeking vengeance in their ongoing feuds. The complexity of the fighting makes resolution more difficult. The breach between mestizos and Indians, however, continues to fester, even in Mexico.

MARKETS, THE MILITARY, AND EMERGING DEMOCRACY

In the 1920s, the foreign exchange earnings of most Latin American countries were based on the export of raw materials. In many countries, just one or two products were the key: coffee from Colombia, Brazil, and Costa Rica; bananas from Central America and Ecuador; tin from Bolivia; copper from Chile and Peru; sugar from Cuba. Through the 1920s, demand for many of these products began to wane, and during the Great Depression, the market declined by as much as 80 percent. Latin American economists led by Raul Prebísch (1901–85) of Argentina, argued for a new economic and technological policy, later called import substituting industrialization (ISI). Latin American countries must diversify their productivity and they must become internally more self-sufficient, thus reducing their dependence on international markets. They should build a buffer against the kind of catastrophe they had experienced when those markets collapsed.

Latin American countries began to industrialize further during World War II, when world markets could not provide their necessities. The trend continued after the war, with industrial growth exceeding agricultural. In Brazil, between 1945 and 1960, industry grew at an average of 9.4 percent per year and agriculture at 4 percent. In Venezuela, where oil was becoming a major export, industry grew at 8.5 percent, agriculture at 4.7 percent. But two elements of the policy were not working: Latin America was not becoming self-sufficient. The development of new industries actually required, at

Coffee remains a principal export of Latin American countries. In this 1933 photograph, two Colombian workers proudly disp   y the tools of their trade, including cultivating spades, heavy machetes, pruning spears, and an unusual step-cut bamboo ladder. I   the background are the fermentation tanks in which the outer pulp of the twin coffee beans is loosened before removal. To the ri   it is one of the many washing canals in which clear water from mountain streams washes the coffee before it is marketed.

least in the early years, more imports of machines and technology than the new industries exported in the form of finished products. Second, the profits of the new industries went predominantly to the urban middle classes. They did not reach the rural workers. Class and cultural tensions intensified. Workers and peasants protested, and governments repressed the protests, often employing violence.

Frequently, the military, a powerful force in most countries, intervened to restore order. By social background and occupational training, the military often favored technological modernization combined with social order. These policies continued in practice into the mid-1960s. In effect, public policy and the state itself were fractured. The interest groups that sought technological modernization did not take to heart the needs of the workers and peasants; at the same time, the workers and peasants did not appreciate the economic costs of their demands. Frequently split along cultural lines, neither side had much sympathy for the other. To understand more fully this split between opposing sides, it is instructive to study two other countries in more detail—Brazil and Argentina.

BRAZIL

Getúlio Vargas (1883–1954) came to power through a military revolution in 1930 and for the next fifteen years was president of Brazil. The economy, which was dependent on coffee, had been deeply wounded by the market crash, and Vargas moved to strengthen Brazil's central government at the expense of the states. He put down revolts, especially that of the São Paulo militia, and crushed attempted coups by communists in 1935 and fascists in 1937. In 1937, he proclaimed a new constitution, declaring an *Estado Novo*, or "new state." He committed the state to an active role in developing mining, oil, steel, electricity, chemicals, motor vehicles, and light aircraft, soliciting investment from both the United States and Germany, at a time when those two nations saw each other as enemies.

Brazil's industrialists, entrepreneurs, and military supported him. At the same time, Vargas understood that he had to gain the support of urban labor, so he created a Ministry of Labor, charging it with establishing new unions under governmental supervision. In bringing these disparate groups together, Vargas was following the German and Italian models of the corporate state (see pp. 578–80). He organized the Brazilian Labor Party, and his government passed wide-ranging social legislation, introducing a minimum wage, a 48-hour work week, annual vacations, maternity benefits and child care, retirement and pension plans—but it did not allow strikes. The reforms did not touch the peasantry.

The army, fearing, on the one hand, the growing power of the urban workers and, on the other, Vargas's strong-arm methods of stifling opposition, deposed him in 1945. A spectrum of three new parties emerged, a new constitution was enacted, and free elections were held every five years from 1945 through 1960. A literacy test was required for voting, and as literacy improved, the percentage of adults, male and female (female suffrage was enacted in 1932), registered to vote rose from 15 percent in 1945 to 25 percent in 1962. In 1950 Vargas was re-elected with the support of many conflicting interest groups of Brazil, but he could not satisfy them all. He could not invest Brazil's resources in industrialization while at the same time meeting the demands of the working classes for higher pay and more benefits. In his relationships with the United States, Brazil's largest external source of investment capital, he could not simultaneously satisfy those Brazilians who approved of foreign investment and those who criticized it as antinational.

In the end, pulled in conflicting directions, implicated in corruption charges leveled against his government, and under attack for the assassination of an opponent by a member of his own bodyguard, Vargas committed suicide in 1954. His successors continued his administration of limited democracy, a policy consistent with most other countries in Latin America. In 1961 Vargas's former Minister of Labor, João Goulart, became president. He was also unable to balance the conflicting interest groups, and in 1964 he moved decisively to the left, nationalizing the oil industry, expropriating large estates, granting the right to vote to enlisted soldiers, and legalizing the Communist Party. In response, the army deposed him and remained in power for the next twenty years.

Brazil's fall to military rule was consistent with events elsewhere. In 1959, only four Latin American states were ruled by the military. Between 1962 and 1964, however, the same fate befell eight additional countries in the region. In Brazil the military interpreted the national motto *ordem e progresso*, order and progress, aggressively. When confronted with guerrilla opposition in the cities, the generals used torture and death squads to suppress it.

Brazil's revolutionary president. Dr Getúlio Vargas, surrounded by Brazilian admirals and generals, assumes office at the Cattete Palace (the Brazilian equivalent of the White House) in Rio de Janeiro. After seizing power by revolution, he was sworn in as the provisional president of Brazil on November 19, 1930. As president, Vargas was able to play off the different political factions against each other, enabling his own rise to great power.

By 1968 Brazil's "economic miracle" was underway. The Brazilian economic rate of growth between 1968 and 1974 averaged 10–11 percent per year. Even after the oil shocks of 1973 (see p. 732), it remained at 4–7 percent per year. But income distribution was one of the least equitable in the world. The richest 10 percent saw their share of the nation's income rise from 40 percent in 1960 to 50 percent in 1980. The poorest 50 percent, however, received only 13 percent. In addition, to sustain its investments, Brazil borrowed on a large scale externally and printed money at home. Debt and inflation skyrocketed.

In 1985, the military stepped aside and José Sarney became Brazil's first civilian president in two decades. Civilian rule in the next ten years did not substantially improve the Brazilian economy. Moreover, accusations of theft or misappropriation of $20 million drove President Fernando Collor de Mello from office in 1992, and charges of corruption against the government of his successor in 1994 further undercut the legitimacy of government. Elected president in 1994, Fernando Henrique Cardoso adopted the globalization policies of open markets and privatization, brought down inflation and unemployment, supported land reform for the peasantry, and restored some confidence in government, earning reelection in 1998. But in 1999, the Brazilian currency was devalued once again, the International Monetary Fund continued to assert its own austerity demands over the Brazilian econ-

omy. Brazil still had not demonstrated the ability to produce sustainable economic growth. Some 50 million people, many of the Native Americans in remote areas, remained outside the market economy. The inequitable distribution of wealth in the country continued, leaving Brazil, in the words of President Cardoso, not so much underdeveloped as unjust.

ARGENTINA

In the early years of the twentieth century Argentina prospered and immigrants streamed into the country. By 1914 60 percent of Buenos Aires' population was foreign-born and 30 percent of them Italian. The wheat and beef of the *pampas* dominated Argentina's export economy while industrial production was small but growing, providing some 10 percent of the national income. Industrial workers, many of them immigrants, were demanding rights. In 1919, a metalworkers' strike developed into a general strike of all workers. The police responded by seeking out anarchists and radicals and by shooting demonstrators, and sometimes innocent passers-by, on the streets.

In 1929 the economy crashed. Because of the vulnerability of its food exports, Argentina suffered perhaps more than any other country in Latin America. Already the nation's politics had been split between the industrial interests in the cities and the rich landlords of the *estancias*, the estates of the *pampas*. Argentina had no better policies for reconciling these diverse interests than had Brazil.

In 1930 a military coup ousted President Yrigoyen and took power. The new government instituted import substituting industrialization (ISI) policies in the 1930s and saw the industrial sector grow to almost 20 percent of the national product by 1940. It expanded still further during World War II, when foreign supplies and markets were cut off. Because Argentina remained neutral during the war (until March 1945), the United States refused to supply the country with weapons, so the state began to manufacture its own armaments. Each increase in industrialization increased the tensions among industrialists, workers, and landlords of the estates.

In 1943 the army staged another coup and soon Colonel Juan D. Perón (1895–1974) emerged as its leader, basing his power on the urban laboring classes that he had organized and rewarded with benefits when he had been Minister of Labor from 1943 to 1945. Trade unions quadrupled in size. When military leaders jailed Perón, workers from the whole country converged on Buenos Aires in mass demonstrations, forcing his release. In the election of 1946, Perón, campaigning with and for the *descamisados*, "shirtless" workers, was elected president with 56 percent of the vote. But could he, or anyone, rule this politically fractured country? Identfying himself with the common people of Argentina, Perón promoted populism and nationalism, calling for sacrifices on behalf of the nation, and calling on the nation to serve the workers. He nationalized foreign-owned

Eva Duarte left the provincial Argentinian town in which she had been born in 1919 to seek her fortune in Buenos Aires as an actress. In 1943 she met Juan Perón, military officer in the junta that had recently seized power, and became his mistress and later his wife. Universally known as Evita, she campaigned strenuously among the working classes for her husband in his successful bid for the presidency in 1946. She led the women's division of his party; spearheaded the drive for women's suffrage, which was granted in 1947; established the Eva Perón Foundation that controlled social welfare services in Argentina; and often mediated between government and the labor unions.

In 1951, age thirty-two, at the height of her public powers but suffering from terminal cancer, Eva Perón published her autobiography, *My Mission in Life*, which was divided into three parts: "The Causes of My Mission," "The Workers and My Mission," and "Women and My Mission." Devotees and critics divided sharply on their evaluations of her presentation.

I was not, nor am I, anything more than a humble woman ... a sparrow in an immense flock of sparrows ... but Perón was and is a gigantic condor that flies high and sure among the summits and near to God. ... That is why neither my life nor my heart belongs to me, and nothing of all that I am or have is mine. All that I am, all that I have, all that I think and all that I feel, belongs to Perón.

Despite her own public career and power, Evita argued that the home was the most important place

Eva Perón in Buenos Aires, Argentina, April 8, 1952.

(British) railways, telephone companies, and oil resources. He paid off the foreign debt. He granted higher pay, better conditions, vacations, and other benefits to urban workers and kept them in state-sponsored unions. He crushed independent labor unions that challenged him, especially when the economy experienced a downturn after about 1949.

Perón was controversial and his wife, María Eva Duarte Perón (1919–52; see Profile, below), was even more so. A beautiful actress, born out of wedlock to an impoverished mother, she was accused of sleeping her way to the top of Argentina's power structure. Even more than Perón, however, Evita, as she chose to be called, identified closely with the masses. She implemented her own programs through a Social Aid Foundation, and she led the Peronist Women's Party, which won equal rights for women, including the vote, in 1947. Her presence, and her radio broadcasts on behalf of her husband and herself, encouraged popular support for Perón's government. Her death from cancer in 1952 at the age of thirty-three seriously reduced Perón's power and effectiveness.

Economic problems multiplied, interest groups clashed, and Perón could not solve the intractable conflicts. He clamped down decisively and violently, outlawing alternative unions on both the right and left, closing newspapers, jailing his opposition, and taking control of radio broadcasting. In 1955 anti-Peronist military officials drove him from office and into exile. Perón's popularity remained so strong among the masses, however, that he was recalled to Argentina in 1973 and won election as president, with his new wife Isabel as vice-president. Perón died the next year, and

---

for a woman, and that she should be paid by society for her work there.

> The mother of a family is left out of all security measures. She is the only worker in the world without a salary, or a guarantee, or limited working hours, or free Sundays, or holidays, or any rest, or indemnity for dismissal, or strikes of any kind. All that, we learned as girls, belongs to the sphere of love ... but the trouble is that after marriage, love often flies out of the window, and then everything becomes "forced labor" ... obligations without any rights! Free service in exchange for pain and sacrifice!
>
> I think one should commence by fixing a small monthly allowance for every woman who gets married, from the day of her marriage. A salary paid to the mothers by all the nation and which comes out of all the earnings of all the workers in the country, including the women. ...

She had hospitals and clinics, with first-rate equipment and medical personnel, built for poor people. Each day she herself spent hours in public audience with poor people. A young Catholic poet, José Maria Castineira de Dios, reported in admiration:

> There were human beings in that room with dirty clothes and they smelt very bad. Evita would place her fingers into their suppurating wounds for she was able to see the pain of all these people and feel it herself. She could touch the most terrible things with a Christian attitude that amazed me, kissing and letting herself be kissed.

On the other hand, Argentina's most distinguished man of letters, Jorge Luis Borges (1899–1986) publicly referred to Evita as a "whore," and he was not alone. Perón dismissed Borges from his government job in a library and shifted him to inspecting chickens in a public market (Winn, p. 148). Many in the upper classes and in the military feared in her the potential for revolution. British journalist Richard Bourne reported in 1967:

> As a crusade Eva's feminism was logically entwined with an attack on the oligarchy and a drive for industrialization and labour benefits: for the countryside, to the traditional eye of the rural landowners, was a man's world, and increasing industrialization must call on female labour which must itself get near to equal rights if male labour was not to suffer. The virulent dislike of Eva among wealthy women, though it focused on superficialities like her opulent jewellery and her décolleté dresses, testified, along with the latent hostility to her in the officer class, to the revolutionary nature of her role. (all quotations cited in Hanke and Rausch)

Eva Perón remains a charismatic figure beyond the boundaries of South America.

Isabel took over the presidency until ousted by a military coup in 1976.

The military government, supported by the United States, came to power with a Cold War view of world politics. It saw itself at war with the forces of communism, led within Latin America by Fidel Castro of Cuba (see below). It treated its domestic critics as enemies, carrying out a "dirty war" of terror against them. In seven years of military rule, some 10,000 (estimates run as high as 30,000) people "disappeared," vanished without a trace. In the midst of pervasive fear, hundreds of mothers of the *desaparecidos* (the disappeared) gathered each Thursday on the Plaza de Mayo, opposite the Presidential palace, silently brandishing pictures of their vanished children and demanding to know what had happened to them. (In Chile, where disappearances were a similar feature of the military government under General Augusto Pinochet, similar groups of women also gathered and demonstrated.) Las Madres de Plaza de Mayo became the conscience of Argentina. US President Jimmy Carter (1977–81), upholding the principles of human rights, ended American military aid to Argentina and the disappearances slackened temporarily, but President Reagan resumed American support and the kidnappings and murders increased once again.

The military regime fell in 1983. Its terrorism had alienated the people of Argentina; the economy had collapsed in 1981, leading to mass public protests, especially by the labor unions; and the military had been humiliated when the British defeated their attempt to capture the Malvinas (Falkland) Islands off the coast. Since 1983 governments have followed austerity plans that have controlled inflation and increased unemployment, leading to violent protests in the streets in 1997. After sixteen years, Peronist candidates lost the Chamber of Deputies in 1997 and the presidency in 1999 as a more left-wing government attempted to cope with a faltering economy.

UNITED STATES POLICIES IN LATIN AMERICA

As Latin Americans were creating new political, economic, social, and cultural strategies, they usually had to keep in mind, to some degree, the policies of the United States in the region. The Monroe Doctrine, issued in 1823 just after Latin America's revolutions against Spain and Portugal, declared the Americas out-of-bounds for European military intervention or colonization. The American declaration had the approval and support of the more powerful British government. However, as we have seen, the United States itself intervened frequently in Latin America. It encouraged Texas' war of independence from Mexico in 1836 and annexed Texas in 1845. In the Mexican–American war of 1846–8, the United States seized territory from Mexico, and in 1898 won Puerto Rico and Cuba in the Spanish–American War, annexing Puerto Rico and, through the Platt Amendment of 1898, establishing a kind of protectorate over Cuba. In 1903, the United States encouraged Panama to secede from Colombia, recognized its independence immediately, and negotiated for the right to build the Panama Canal.

The United States became the principal trade partner and source of investment capital for many Latin American countries. In the mid-1910s, it bought 75 percent of Mexico's exports, and 67 percent of Central America's. In exchange, the United States sold Mexico 50 percent of its imports, and Central America 75 percent of its. "Dollar diplomacy" was the order of the day. By 1929, 40 percent—$3.5 billion—of all United States foreign investment was in Latin America.

President William Howard Taft (1908–12) declared that he stood ready for "active intervention to secure our merchandise and our capitalists' opportunity for profitable investment" (Burns, p. 174). Between 1898 and 1934 the United States sent troops into Latin American countries more than thirty times, including Cuba, the Dominican Republic, Guatemala, Haiti, Honduras, Mexico, Nicaragua, and Panama. In 1904 President Theodore Roosevelt proclaimed a United States "police power" in the internal affairs of Latin American governments to redress "chronic wrongdoing." This "Roosevelt Corollary" was invoked most frequently to justify military intervention for the collection of debts owed to the American government or to American or European investors. The nations of Central America, in particular, were sometimes referred to, negatively, as "banana republics," connoting not only their reliance on single tropical fruits as the basis of their economies, but also their domination by the United States and their lack of effective control over their own politics.

In 1933 President Franklin Roosevelt inaugurated the "Good Neighbor Policy," to limit United States intervention. During the administration of Lázaro Cárdenas in Mexico, Roosevelt refused to act militarily when Cárdenas nationalized United States oil companies in 1938 and redistributed millions of acres of land in promoting "Mexican social-ism." Cárdenas ultimately compensated the oil companies and resolved to improve church–state relations. United States–Latin American relations gradually improved. Following World War II, the United States sought Latin American backing in the Cold War and in 1948 took the lead in establishing the Organization of American States (OAS) to address hemispheric issues.

Nicaragua

To overthrow a Nicaraguan government which had begun to grant economic concessions to govern-ments other than itself, the United States encour-aged a revolt in 1909 and dispatched marines to

An anti-American poster from the time of the Sandinista revolution, Nicaragua, 1979. Note the various drawings on the figure: military helicopters on the hat; a peace sign ("paz") among the little egghead representations of people massed together demonstrating; an ironic dollar bill with "In God we trust" on the leg. The final touch is the cowboy boot resting firmly on Uncle Sam's hat to keep him in check. Uncle Sam is even a sickly gray color in contrast with the brightly colored cowboy.

support it. They remained, with very few breaks, until 1933, training a Nicaraguan National Guard to join them in defense of United States interests. One Nicaraguan army officer, Augusto Cesar Sandino (1893–1934) rejected American hegemony and for seven years fought a guerrilla war against the US marines and the Nicaraguan National Guard until he was deceived during peace negotiations, arrest-ed, and murdered by officers of the National Guard under Anastasio Somoza Garcia (1896–1956). Somoza subsequently seized control of the nation-al government and, with the support of the United States, turned the presidency into a family dynasty for his two sons after him.

Disgusted with the wretched conditions of the common people at a time when Somoza and his allies were prospering, the editor of *La Prensa* turned his newspaper against the regime in the 1950s, and in the 1960s a movement largely com-posed of students, and naming itself the Sandinista Front for National Liberation in memory of Sandino, initiated an armed guerrilla revolt. As the Somoza government became more rapacious the resistance expanded and intensified, finally driving the government into exile. By the time the Sandinistas came to power in 1979, some 50,000 people had been killed in guerrilla warfare.

United States President Jimmy Carter attempt-ed an accommodation with the new Sandinista government, but his successor, Ronald Reagan, pursued a policy of de-stabilization with almost fanatic zeal. He froze loans which Carter had nego-tiated. He authorized the creation of a paramili-tary force—generally referred to as *Somocistas* or, more commonly, *contras*—to be based in neighbor-ing Honduras for raids across the border into Nicaragua. The United States Central Intelligence Agency (CIA) trained and supplied the contras, instructed them in terrorism, and also mined Nicaraguan harbors. These activities violated United States laws and treaties, and were con-demned by the World Court, which ordered the United States to end its military and paramilitary actions against Nicaragua. The Reagan administra-tion rejected the authority of the Court. When the Congress would not sanction further funding for this clandestine war, the administration arranged for some of the profits of a secret arms sale to Iran to be secretly diverted to financing it. The scandal rocked the Reagan administration and provided a window of opportunity for several Central American governments to negotiate a settlement of the civil war in Nicaragua, including an end to foreign military involvement and a call for honest elections. For his initiative in this effort, Costa Rican President Oscar Arias was awarded the Nobel Prize for Peace. The nine years of warfare, 1981 to 1990, had cost approximately 60,000 deaths and another 28,000 casualties. Since 1990, Nicaragua has been ruled by democratically elected governments and relationships with the United States have normalized.

Guatemala

Latin American critics of United States economic power were branded communists, and the United States often condemned as communist Latin American attempts to make their societies more egalitarian. In Guatemala, the world's second largest producer of bananas, Colonel Jacobo Arbenz (1913–71) won election as president in an open, free election in 1951. Arbenz proceeded to seize some 400,000 acres (161,880 hectares) of fallow land held by the United Fruit Company, a private company owned mostly by United States citizens. He offered compensation according to the value of the land declared for tax purposes by the company, but the company found this insufficient. Arbenz also wanted to build a highway from his capital to the Atlantic Ocean, which would have broken the company's transportation monopoly, and he proposed building a hydroelectric power plant which would free Guatemala from its dependence on a foreign supply. Finally, fearing an attack by exiles training in neighboring countries, Arbenz sought to buy arms from the United States. When the USA turned him down, he bought from Poland, which was then a communist country. Almost immediately a small Guatemalan army-in-exile of some 150 soldiers, equipped by the United States, attacked from Honduras. The Arbenz government fell, virtually without defenders. Arbenz's successor, Carlos Castillo Armas (1914–57) returned the lands taken from the United Fruit Company, abolished several political parties, disenfranchised all illiterates, about half the adult population, and had those who opposed him jailed, tortured, exiled, or executed. Castillo Armas was assassinated in mid-1957, and soon Guatemala plunged into a civil war in which 100,000 people died before a negotiated resolution was achieved in the 1990s. In 1999 President Bill Clinton, speaking in Guatemala, "apologized for US support of right-wing governments that killed tens of thousands of rebels and Mayan Indians in a thirty-six year civil war" (*New York Times Almanac* p. 16).

Chile

From 1964 to 1970, Eduardo Frei (1911–81) led a Christian Democratic government in Chile that began a program of agrarian reform and nationalized, with compensation, copper mines owned by United States private companies. Considered moderate, Frei had good relations with the United States government. In 1970, seeking more radical reform, the voters in Chile elected the socialist Salvador Allende (1908–73). The United States government and major transnational corporations opposed his election. Once in office, President Allende confirmed their fears. He increased agrarian reform, purchased control of most banks, and continued the nationalization of the foreign-owned copper industry, which produced three-fourths of Chile's exports. Allende increased the salaries of government workers and expanded medical and housing programs. The usual conflict arose between the desire to improve economic and social benefits, on the one hand, and the problem of finding resources to pay, on the other. Shortages and inflation resulted. The United States' government sharply reduced loans and aid to Allende's government, and international banks also cut loans. The United States Central Intelligence Agency, with a mandate to overthrow Allende, covertly financed strikes and opposition parties. Finally, the middle class, and especially women, who found the economic situation intolerable, persuaded the military to act. In September 1973 they attacked and bombed the presidential palace and Allende was killed.

General Augusto Pinochet (b. 1915), who headed the new government, immediately killed or detained thousands of Allende supporters, men and women. He ruled until 1988, feared and hated for his violence toward the opposition, but effective in restoring the economy, with the aid of advisers from the United States. In a plebiscite in 1988, Pinochet was rejected by Chile's voters, and the government passed to the opposition. Chile had returned to democracy.

Pinochet remained as head of the armed forces until his retirement in 1998. While in England for medical treatment, he was arrested in October 1998. Spain sought his extradition for the murder of Spanish citizens and some 3000 others during the period of his rule. On appeal, Britain's highest court set a new international precedent by ruling that Pinochet had no immunity as a former head of state and should be extradited for trial in Spain. Opinion conti_ ~d to be divided on the rights of one country to in. ~e in the policies of another until, in early 2000, the British government declared the eighty-four-year-old Pinochet unable to stand trial and returned him to Chile.

Panama

In 1878 a French company, with the permission of the government of Colombia, began to build a canal across Panama, then the most northern region of that nation. The project failed and was put up for sale. The US Congress agreed to pay $40 million for the rights, but the Colombian Congress refused to ratify the new agreement. In 1903, President Theodore Roosevelt encouraged the revolt of a small Panamanian independence movement and ordered American warships to block the arrival of Colombian troops. Three days after the revolt began, he recognized Panama as an independent country. Twelve days later the USA had its treaty, including powerful rights of interference in Panama's affairs for the protection of the canal and a ten-kilometer-(six-mile)-wide buffer zone along its sides. Panama began its national life as a protectorate of the United States.

In 1989 Panama's General Manuel Noriega suspended a presidential election which threatened to overthrow him and was also indicted in the United States on charges of drug trafficking. US troops stationed in the Canal Zone invaded Panama, kidnapped Noriega, and brought him to the United States for trial. The military operation succeeded but only after four days of fighting in which several hundred people were killed and 2 billion dollars worth of property was destroyed.

On the other hand, in 1977 Panama's military government had reached an agreement with US President Jimmy Carter for the return of the Canal Zone to full Panamanian control in 2000 and the transfer took place calmly, peacefully, and punctually on 31 December 1999.

CUBA

The greatest confrontation between any Latin American country and the United States followed the Cuban revolution of 1959. Fidel Castro (b. 1926), received his law degree in 1950 and, two years later, sued in Cuba's Constitutional Court to have the government of Cuban dictator Fulgencio Batista (1901–73) ruled unconstitutional. Batista had ruled Cuba from 1934 to 1944, and had returned as president, seizing power in 1952. Castro's suit was unsuccessful, and he took to the mountains to organize a guerrilla movement (see box, p. 798).

On July 26, 1953 (celebrated in Cuba as the origin of the revolution), Castro, with a few allies, attacked the Moncada military barracks in Santiago de Cuba. The attack failed. Castro was captured and sentenced to fifteen years in prison. At his sentencing, Castro declared "History will absolve me," and laid out his own six-point plan for Cuba:

- extensive land redistribution and collectivization, with common use of expensive equipment;

- limits on foreign investment and mobilization of Cuba's own capital through the national bank for investment in industrialization;

- housing policies that would enable each Cuban family to own its own home;

- full employment;

- full literacy in an educational system appropriate to an agrarian society;

- health care facilities for all.

He further claimed that adequate funding was already available within Cuba and could be mobilized by ending graft and scaling back military expenditures.

Released from jail in the general amnesty of 1955, Castro fled initially to the United States and Mexico, returning to Cuba and resuming guerrilla warfare in 1956. On January 1, 1959, he captured Havana, the capital, and declared a new government for Cuba. Contrary to his promises, Castro did not hold elections, declaring that "the intimate union and identification of the government with the people," made elections unnecessary. Although Castro denied that he was a communist and did, for a time, try to negotiate military and economic agreements with the United States, he soon established close military and economic ties with the Soviet bloc. In the Cold War environment of the time, the United States viewed Castro as a communist. When three multinational oil refineries refused to process oil brought to Cuba from the USSR, Castro expropriated the refineries. In response, the United States ended the special quota of sugar purchases it had guaranteed to Cuba since the 1930s. In December 1961, Castro announced his allegiance to Marxism-Leninism. From that time, Cuba became dependent upon the Soviet Union, replacing Batista's earlier dependence on the United States with this new alignment.

Castro then proceeded to carry out his announced program. He expropriated foreign assets, including $1 billion in North American property and investments. He collectivized farms, and centralized control of the economy in the hands of the government. He took human development issues seriously, and devoted money and energies to health, education, and cultural activities. Education and all medical services were free. Between 1958, the year before the revolution, and 1983, a quarter

Castro, victorious, en route to Havana. Fidel Castro embraces a child amongst a crowd of well-wishers shortly after taking power. In January 1959 Cuban dictator Fulgencio Batista was ousted by Castro and his popular revolutionary army. The revolutionaries had been hiding in the mountains since December 1956, fighting against Batista's regime. Their fight to overthrow the dictator was called the "26th July Movement," after the date of their first insurrection against Batista.

of a century later, life expectancy rose from fifty-eight years to over seventy-three years. The number of doctors rose from 6250 to 17,000; nurses from 400 to 32,000; and medical technicians from 500 to 29,000. Medical facilities began to reach the countryside. Both male and female literacy rates reached about 95 percent. The publication of books rose from 100 titles per year in 1958 to 800 titles in 1973, with the actual numbers of books increasing from 900,000 to 28 million. The living standards of most Cubans improved sharply. Most of the elites fled, however, with the acquiescence of the government, which was pleased to have them gone. These exiles were received with open arms in the United States, where they formed a new large community, centered in Miami, and lobbied heavily for the United States to take action against Castro.

Two confrontations between Cuba and the United States followed. The American government agreed to arm and support a group of Cuban exiles who wanted to invade the island on the assumption that Cuba's people would welcome the opportunity to overthrow Castro. When the exiles did invade, on April 17, 1961, at the Bay of Pigs, they were immediately defeated by Cuban armed forces. In the next year, Cuba was the focus of the most direct confrontation of the Cold War between the United States and the Soviet Union. The Soviet Union had positioned nuclear missiles in Cuba. They denied the existence of these missiles, but American reconnaissance aircraft obtained photographic evidence. President Kennedy demanded that they be withdrawn, even threatening nuclear warfare over the issue. As the world watched, terrified, the Soviet Union backed down and removed the missiles. In return the United States agreed not to invade Cuba and to remove US missiles from Turkey. Cuba sent 11,000 troops to Ethiopia in 1978 to fight against Somalia, and 50,000 troops to Angola to combat South African invading forces and the rebels they and the United States sponsored. The Cuban troops remained in Angola until agreement was reached to end the fighting in 1988.

These events of the early revolution caught the attention and imagination of the world. They tested the ability of a new revolutionary administration to establish a communist government just 90 miles (145 kilometers) off the mainland of the United States, spread the revolution, establish an independent foreign policy, and carry out a radical restructuring of the politics, economics, culture, and social life of the country. The achievements were mixed. Castro's government did not allow free and open

CUBA SINCE THE REVOLUTION—KEY EVENTS

1933	Fulgencio Batista (1901–73) seizes power
1944	Batista retires
1952	Batista seizes power again and begins repressive regime
1959	After two unsuccessful coups, Castro overthrows Batista and replaces 1940 constitution with a "Fundamental Law," making himself prime minister, his brother Raúl his deputy, and Che Guevara (1928–67) his number three
1960	All US businesses appropriated without compensation; US breaks off diplomatic relations; US embargo
1961	US sponsors unsuccessful invasion at Bay of Pigs; Castro announces creation of communist state with Marxist-Leninist program
1962	Cuba expelled from Organization of American States; Soviet nuclear missiles installed but subsequently removed on US threat of war
1965	Sole political party renamed Cuban Communist Party (PCC) as country, with Soviet help, makes significant economic and social progress
1972	Cuba becomes full member of the Moscow-based Council for Mutual Economic Assistance
1976	Castro elected president and new socialist constitution approved
1976–81	Cuba involved in international commitments, especially in Africa, where Cuban troops supported Luanda government of Angola against South African-backed rebels
1982	Cuba supports Argentina during Falkland War against Britain
1984	Castro seeks to improve relations with US
1988	Agreement reached with South Africa to withdraw forces from Angola
1989	Overseas military activity scaled back as Soviet support diminishes
1991	Withdrawal of Soviet troops and economic support; Cuban economy in depression

FOCUS
Che Guevara and Guerrilla Warfare

With the success of Mao's communist, agrarian revolution in China (see p. 687) and Castro's in Cuba, and continuing peasant uprisings around the world, including Vietnam, the 1960s were especially alive with rural guerrilla warfare. Usually led by young, vigorous, brave, and single-minded revolutionaries, the guerrilla movements had a powerful mystique, and a number of successes. Technologically, they demonstrated the potential of very simple technologies in conflict against the most sophisticated modern weapons. One of the most charismatic of the guerrilla warriors was Ernesto "Che" Guevara, who was born in Argentina in 1928, and was captured and killed while organizing a guerrilla movement in Bolivia in 1967. He participated in Castro's revolution in Cuba and was later appointed head of the national bank. But Guevara chose life as a full-time revolutionary, helping to establish guerrilla *focos*, revolutionary outposts, in many locations.

> Nuclei of relatively few persons choose places favorable for guerrilla warfare, sometimes with the intention of launching a counterattack or to weather a storm, and there they begin to take action. But the following must be made clear: At the beginning, the relative weakness of the guerrilla fighters is such that they should endeavor to pay attention only to the terrain, in order to become acquainted with the surroundings, establish connections with the population, and fortify the places that eventually will be converted into bases. The guerrilla unit can survive only if it starts by basing its development on the three following conditions: constant mobility, constant vigilance, constant wariness. ...
>
> We must carry the war into every corner the enemy happens to carry it—to his home, to his centers of entertainment: a total war. It is necessary to prevent him from having a moment of peace, a quiet moment outside his barracks or even inside; we must attack him wherever he may move. ...
>
> Our every action is a battle cry against imperialism, and a battle hymn to the people's unity against the great enemy of mankind: the United States of America. Wherever death may surprise us, let it be welcome, provided that this, our battle cry, may have reached some receptive ear and another hand may be extended to wield our weapons and other men be ready to intone the funeral dirge with the staccato singing of the machine gun and new battle cries of war and victory.

(Sigmund, pp. 370, 381)

(see guerrilla warfare in China, p. 687).

Ernesto "Che" Guevara, photographed in 1963 with his ever-present cigar during his tenure as Minister of Industry. He was born in Argentina, but joined Fidel Castro's revolutionary troops in Cuba. Together they launched the Cuban Revolution, from 1956 to 1959. Castro then appointed Che Minister of Industry, a post he held until 1965. That year Che left Cuba to organize revolutionary warfare elsewhere in Latin America. It was at Waucakwazu in the Bolivian jungle, on October 8, 1967, that he and a group of rebel troops were tracked down by Bolivian government troops and shot.

nationwide elections, but it did permit and even encourage its enemies to leave the island. Almost one million people departed, mostly for the United States. Cuba's health and welfare measures were models for the entire developing world. In the face of a US trade embargo, however, Cuba could not succeed in industrializing and diversifying the economy. The island has remained dependent on sugar as its principal export crop. The end of the Cold War presented new problems. Castro had exchanged dependence upon the United States for dependence upon the Soviet Union. With the collapse of the USSR, the Cuban economy lost billions of dollars in aid and trade. Its total production plummeted by one-third between 1989 and 1993. It recovered slightly but at the end of the century, its economy was in tatters. Confrontation with the United States continued, an apparent left-over relic of the Cold War, counterproductive to both sides.

CURRENT ISSUES AND TRENDS

RETURN TO CIVILIAN RULE 1980–2000

In the 1980s, many of the military administrations returned to civilian rule: Peru in 1980; Argentina in 1983; Brazil in 1989. Chile ended Pinochet's dictatorship and returned to democracy in 1990. By 2000 all of Latin America's largest countries were governed through formal democracies. Mexico, a one-party democracy since the revolution, found new parties arising and contesting for power. In the 1990s, these parties began to win local and state elections and built popular support for continuing challenges at the national level.

ECONOMICS AND TECHNOLOGY

To what degree will Latin American countries adjust their economic policies toward "development"—that is, increasing living standards for all their peoples—rather than just "growth"—that is, increasing national productivity with most of the benefits going only to a small elite? This question has occupied Latin America's thinking for two centuries and it remains unresolved.

Development possibilities had appeared robust in the 1970s, especially with the success of oil pro-

duction in Mexico, and international creditors extended huge loans. Pay-back time came in the 1980s, however, and the burdens were too great. The World Bank offered assistance in rescheduling the debts, but the Bank required rigorous schedules of repayment, and it required nations to restructure their economies to achieve these repayments. The World Bank remedies required cut-backs in subsidies of food to the poor, in social programs, and in state employment. As governments attempted to implement these policies, they were often met by rioting in the streets. World Bank policies might be economically sound, but they were politically and socially destabilizing. The historic conflict between economic necessity and social wishes resurfaced. Nevertheless, in the 1990s, the Bank and various national governments attempted to reach compromises acceptable to both.

A dramatic shift in international economic relations occurred in 1994, as Mexico joined the United States and Canada in the North American Free Trade Agreement (NAFTA) and in the "southern cone," Argentina, Brazil, Paraguay, and Uruguay established in 1995 a similar free-trade agreement among their 200 million people and almost $500 million economies, creating a single free-trade zone called MERCOSUR (Mercado Común del Cono Sur).

Borders were not, however, supposed to be open for trade in drugs. Nevertheless, billions of dollars in illegal drugs were being grown and processed in Latin American countries, notably Colombia, and shipped to Europe and the United States, often via Mexico. The trade brought enormous wealth to those who controlled it, corrupting governments by purchasing their complicity and by murdering leaders who opposed the traffic. Colombia suffered years of internal warfare, partly over the control of the drug trade. In the late 1990s, the murders of government officials and of drug traffickers showed that Mexico, too, was deeply involved in the trade. The trade flourished on the demand of consumers in the developed world and on the need for an economic cash crop among the peasantry in Latin America. Actions to control the trade within Latin America have had some limited effect, but the industry will continue until demand is reduced, and this problem is centered in the United States and Europe.

Another problem of the economic growth since the 1970s was its impact on ecology. Mexico City, Santiago, and São Paulo are among the most polluted cities in the world, with a constant blanket

Latin American drug trade. Processing coca leaves in Colombia, the first step to manufacturing the illegal drug cocaine. The farmers who grow the crop see but a fraction of the money gained from their labors. Drugs bound for consumers in the USA and Europe remain a lucrative business for the criminal barons of Latin America, and it is unlikely that manufacture will be forcibly stopped in the near future, despite increasing pressure from Western governments.

of smog lying over them. Dangerous pesticides—banned in the United States—are in widespread use. International attention has focussed especially on the destruction of two-thirds of Latin America's tropical rainforests, and the loss of thousands of plant and animal species. In the Amazon rainforest Brazil targeted massive projects of economic development, including oil and mineral exploration, and of settlement for its rapidly multiplying population. The regional capital of Manaus teemed with oil refineries, metal works, lumber mills—and pollution.

In the 1970s, the Trans-Amazon highway opened the rainforest to new settlement, and millions of peasants migrated in search of free land. They were followed by ranches and big business corporations. The soil itself proved to be unsuitable for agriculture and was soon eroded and abandoned, although many immigrants stayed on in the new cities. Indigenous populations of the Amazon, unable to defend themselves in the face of these commercially driven invasions, were pushed off ancestral lands and reduced to jobs at low wages in difficult conditions. Many contracted new diseases, or, like the Yanomami Indians of the Amazon, were poisoned by the mercury poured into the Amazon by gold miners and by the waste products of the new industries. Conflict between conservation activists and displaced Indians on the one hand and the pressures for agro-industrial development on the other often erupted into violence and in 1988 the environmental activist Chico Mendes was murdered.

Heavily criticized by the United States and others for destroying the rainforests, Latin American countries, especially Brazil, have replied with cries of hypocrisy. North America, too, was once covered with forests that were long ago cut down in the interests of "development." Latin Americans argue that they are being criticized only for coming to the process late. Moreover, they argue, they "develop" the Amazon basin because they need its wealth. If outsiders were serious in their criticisms, they would help to create alternative schemes that would allow economic development without ecological harm.

AMERINDIANS—OPPRESSION AND RESPONSE

From the earliest contact between Europeans and Native Americans, conflicts over issues of race, ethnicity, and culture have been at the center of Latin American history. We have seen the massive destruction of the Native American population in the sixteenth century (p. 457); the confrontation among Indians, *mestizos*, and Europeans throughout Mexico in the early twentieth-century revolution (pp. 780–4) and in Chiapas in the 1990s (see pp. 785–7); and, most recently, the struggles surrounding the development of the Amazon rainforest.

In the mountainous regions of the Andes, which run from Central America to Chile, the Amerindians have also been extremely ill-treated. Rigoberta Menchu, a Quiche Indian woman, spoke for the millions who suffered in her autobiography, *I, Rigoberta Menchu: An Indian Woman in Guatemala*, which was published in 1983, when she was twenty-three years old. This international bestseller served to focus attention on the brutal repression of Guatemala's indigenous communities that was carried out by the Guatemalan state during the civil war of the 1980s. In 1992, Menchu was awarded the Nobel Prize for Peace for her efforts at negotiating a settlement to this conflict, a process that continues.

Rigoberta Menchu. Menchu, a Guatemalan Indian, won the Nobel Peace Prize in 1992 for her efforts to reach a settlement in Guatemala's civil war. Her book, *I, Rigoberta Menchu: An Indian Woman in Guatemala*, was published in 1983 and became a bestseller. Although later challenged as exaggerated and "borrowed," the central truths of this autobiography are an accurate account of Indian oppression and suffering.

Her autobiography is anything but peaceful as Menchu describes the living and working conditions on the agricultural estates, **fincas**, of Guatemala where Indian workers die early deaths from the burden of the work and the lack of food and medical attention. Her younger brother died, as a child, from such fundamental poverty. When the Indian workers do not submit to the will of the **ladinos**, *mestizos* who own and run the *fincas*, they are beaten and tortured, and the women are raped. Those who protest the conditions on the *fincas* are murdered, often after brutal torture. Menchu writes of witnessing the torture and murder of her brother, and of viewing the raped and disfigured body of her dead mother. Rigoberta's father was a leading organizer against these conditions. In January 1981 he led a group which seized and occupied the Spanish embassy in Guatemala City to protest the militarization of the highlands. When Guatemalan security forces stormed the embassy, he and his twenty-six companions were burned to death. The publication of her autobiography, and her Nobel award, made Rigoberta one of the most prominent spokespersons of the Indian guerrilla movement and by the end of the century she had become perhaps the most well-known woman in Guatemala.

HOW DO WE KNOW?

American anthropologist David Stoll challenged the truthfulness of Rigoberta's accounts in his 1998 publication *Rigoberta Menchu and the Story of All Poor Guatemalans*. The book came as a bombshell. Stoll was doing research in a nearby region of Guatemala and, in the course of interviewing locals, he found that many of Rigoberta's accounts were exaggerated. Some which she reported as eyewitness accounts had actually been borrowed. Stoll argued that she heightened the drama of her stories to create more powerful propaganda for the guerrilla Indians whom she had now joined. She omitted the internal battles among different Indian groups and their difficulties in building a united movement.

The basic truth of the stories, however, held. An older rather than a younger brother had died of malnutrition; another brother had not been tortured and burned to death in front of her eyes, but had been executed by Guatemalan soldiers from ambush; Rigoberta herself was not uneducated but had finished seven years of convent education; she had not worked as a domestic servant for a rich family nor in abusive conditions on a coastal plantation, but she had served as a maid within the convent. She certainly wrote from within a civil war between the army and right-wing death squads on the one hand and anti-government guerrilla groups on the other, in which more than 100,000 civilians were killed, hundreds of thousands more were tortured, and thousands more "disappeared." The chief sponsor of an investigation into the violence, Bishop Juan Gerardi Conedera, was murdered in April 1998, two days after its report was made public. Stoll concluded that while Rigoberta's stories may not be entirely true as personal accounts, they properly represent the reality of her people, and she has, with their approval, become their voice.

RELIGION AND THE POOR

The social and economic changes of the twentieth century have transformed religious belief and practice. Spanish and Portuguese colonialism introduced Catholicism as Latin America's principal religious faith. In the nineteenth century, however, a schism occurred between conservatives who favored the maintenance of the traditional privileges of the Catholic church, and liberals who were often deeply critical. In the twentieth century, the influence of the church has been further challenged by urbanization, migration, and the spread of evangelical Protestantism. In some places the church has responded with new initiatives more in touch with the problems of the poor and the dispossessed.

In March 1980, Archbishop Oscar Romero of El Salvador was assassinated as he was officiating at the mass in a San Salvador chapel. The right-wing assassin had opposed the archbishop's message: "When all peaceful means have been exhausted, the church considers insurrection moral and justified" (Keen, p. 595). Romero had also advised soldiers that it was morally just to refuse to follow unjust orders. Romero was only one of about 850 church leaders who had been assassinated since the assassination of Camilo Torres, a priest and sociologist in Colombia. An outstanding scholar and teacher, Torres gave up on peaceful reform and joined Colombia's communist-led guerrillas. He was killed in a battle with government forces in February 1966. In December 1980, three American nuns and a lay missionary who had gone to work with poor refugees in El Salvador were also murdered by security officers of the state.

The church's identification with the poor was part of an international reassessment addressed by the Second Vatican Council (1962–5) in Rome that

Mexican painter Frida Kahlo's *Marxism Will Give Health to the Sick*, **1954.** Kahlo, who was married to Diego Rivera, the famous revolutionary muralist, mainly produced self-portraits that focussed on the physical pain, caused by an accident, which was a chronic feature of her life.

called for much greater concern with issues of material welfare and the maldistribution of wealth throughout the world. At the 1968 second conference of Latin American bishops at Medellín, Colombia, the bishops further supported this reorientation, and they reaffirmed it in 1979 at their meeting in Mexico.

In the late 1960s and 1970s a new school of thought, called **liberation theology**, took shape. Identifying with Jesus' ministry to the poor, it began to establish grass-roots organizations in poor neighborhoods of cities and in rural pockets of poverty. These *comunidades de base* combined study, prayer, and active efforts to identify, define, and solve the problems of their localities by directly confronting them and they challenged local leaders to effect change. Dom Helder Câmara, Archbishop of Recife, Brazil, stated the central perspective of liberation theology:

Come, Lord, do not smile and say you are already with us. Millions do not know You and to us who do, what is the difference? What is the point of Your presence if our lives do not alter? (Lernoux, p. 449)

As this movement threatened the state and the wealthy, it confronted powerful opposition and was willing to engage in violence if necessary.

The pope since 1978, John Paul II, also advocated for the poor:

> The voice of the Church, echoing the voice of human conscience … deserves and needs to be heard in our time when the growing wealth of a few parallels the growing poverty of the masses. (Lernoux, p. 409)

But he backed away from endorsing liberation theology. Its advocates claim to combine Christian ethics with Marxist politics, and the pope, who was raised in communist Poland, rejected the confrontational, Marxist orientation toward class struggle. As new posts opened, he appointed mostly conservative clergy, and as a result the clergy in Latin America have been deeply split. About 20 percent, especially in Brazil, have aligned themselves with liberation theology but the overwhelming majority have rejected this level of activism.

The most rapidly growing religious movement in Latin America, however, has been evangelical Protestantism. Its popularity has increased for several reasons: long-term missionary efforts from the United States; identification of the Catholic church with the powerful elites; and the movement's emotional appeals to the newly urbanizing and industrializing masses. Evangelical Protestantism claims between 30 and 50 million adherents throughout Latin America, perhaps 10 percent of the population. As new converts, they take their commitments seriously. Its missionaries work among the poor, especially the immigrants to the cities. Most eschew violence and condemn communism, promising salvation in the next lifetime rather than here and now. Some, however, also work actively for agrarian reform and social change.

THE "UNORGANIZED" SECTOR

Finally, the enormous cities of Latin America, exploding with the growth of new immigrants, demonstrate new ways in which citizens cope with poverty and urbanization. Academic researchers have found in the new urban immigrant communities far more hope than previously expected. They have come to distinguish "slums of hope" from "slums of despair."

As immigrants entered the cities, many of them found, or seized, their own parcels of land for housing. Frequently they acted together as communities, finding strength in numbers. Sometimes governments intervened and bulldozed their dwellings. Often, however, in deference to the numbers of people involved, they left the squatter settlers alone. As immigrants from rural areas, the settlers were accustomed to building and improving their own housing with whatever materials they found

Radical religion. A priest holds hands with members of the Base Christian Community in Panama. Proponents of liberation theology, which originated in Latin America in the 1960s, typically aligned themselves with left-wing, revolutionary movements, such as the Sandinistas in Nicaragua. When influential priests and bishops espoused a Marxist view of society and argued that the church's role was to assist the oppressed, they came into conflict with established Catholic authorities as well as political leaders.

available. Over the years, squatter settlements have often transformed themselves into middle-class housing colonies. The squatters gained reputations as upwardly mobile citizens, working to build a place for themselves in the face of enormous difficulties. Their slums were slums of hope.

Finding, and creating, jobs also became a do-it-yourself project. Governments offered little if any help in finding work, and existing large-scale enterprises preferred to hire more established workers. So the immigrants began to develop enterprises in the "unorganized" sector; they became self-employed. They took on jobs in local construction, sold goods door-to-door, pushed carts, created and peddled handicrafts. The ingenuity and creativity of these common people created a different kind of hope for the poor than the political confrontation of liberation theology. Hernando de Soto's study of this movement, *The Other Path*, emphasizes the initiative and dynamism of Peru's underground economy. Although many observers saw the political and the entrepreneurial routes to change as opposing one another, they might, in fact, well provide complementary approaches to improving the position of Latin America's people. We have seen in Latin America a deep, continuing disjuncture between political wishes and economic realities. These grass-roots movements so characteristic of Latin America at the turn of the twenty-first century, promised a way of combining both.

BIBLIOGRAPHY

Andrea, Alfred J. and James H. Overfield, eds. *The Human Record* (Boston: Houghton Mifflin, 3rd ed., 1998).

Azuela, Mariano. *The Underdogs*, trans. by E. Munguia, Jr. (New York: Signet Classic, 1963).

Berryman, Phillip. *Liberation Theology* (Philadelphia: Temple University Press, 1987).

Borges, Jorge Luis. *Borges: A Reader*, ed. by Emir Rodriguez Monegal and Alastair Reid (New York: E.P. Dutton, 1981).

Burns, E. Bradford. *Latin America: A Concise Interpretive History* (Englewood Cliffs, NJ: Prentice Hall, 5th ed., 1990).

Canby, Peter, "The Truth about Rigoberta Menchu," *New York Review of Books* XLVI, No. 6 (April 8, 1999), 28–33.

Cunha, Euclides da. *Rebellion in the Backlands (Os Sertoes)* trans. by Samuel Putnam (Chicago: University of Chicago Press, 1944).

Freire, Paulo. *Pedagogy of the Oppressed* (New York: Seabury Press, 1968).

Fuentes, Carlos. *The Death and Life of Artemio Cruz* (New York: Farrar, Straus and Giroux, 1964).

Gárcia Márquez, Gabriel. *One Hundred Years of Solitude*, trans. by Gregory Rabasa (New York: Harper and Row, 1970).

Gilbert, Alan and Joséf Gugler. *Cities, Poverty and Development: Urbanization in the Third World* (Oxford: Oxford University Press, 2nd ed., 1992).

Hanke, Lewis and Jane M. Rausch, eds. *People and Issues in Latin American History* (New York: Markus Wiener, 1990).

Keen, Benjamin. *A History of Latin America* (Boston: Houghton Mifflin, 6th ed., 2000).

Krauze, Enrique, "Chiapas: The Indians' Prophet," *New York Review of Books* XLVI, No. 20 (December 16, 1999), 65–77.

Lernoux, Penny. *Cry of the People* (New York: Penguin, 1982).

Mallon, Florencia E. *Peasant and Nation* (Berkeley: University of California Press, 1995).

—. "The Promise and Dilemma of Subaltern Studies: Perspectives from Latin American History," *American Historical Review*, XCIX No. 5 (December 1994), 491–515.

Menchu, Rigoberta. *I, Rigoberta Menchu: An Indian Woman in Guatemala*, trans. by Elisabeth Burgos Debray (London: Verso, 1984).

New York Times Almanac 2000. (New York: Penguin Reference Books, 1999).

Sigmund, Paul, ed. *The Ideologies of the Developing World* (New York: Praeger, 2nd ed. revised, 1972).

Sivard, Ruth Leger. *World Military and Social Expenditures 1996* (Washington: World Priorities Inc., 16th ed., 1996).

Soto, Hernando de. *The Other Path* (New York: Harper and Row, 1989).

Stoll, David. *Rigoberta Menchu and the Story of All Poor Guatemalans* (Boulder, CO: Westview, 1998).

Winn, Peter. *Americas: The Changing Face of Latin America and the Caribbean* (Berkeley: University of California Press, 1992).

Womack, John Jr. *Rebellion in Chiapas: An Historical Reader* (New York: New Press, 1999).

AFTERWORD

"Society also expects an interpretation of the past which is relevant to the present and a basis for formulating decisions about the future."

JOHN TOSH

SO WHAT?
MAKING SENSE OF IT ALL

SITUATING ONESELF IN HISTORY

Historians claim that history is more than just interesting. They claim it provides a necessary preparation for life by enriching human understanding and thus providing a basis for action. In the quotation introducing this afterword historian John Tosh writes that society expects historians to provide guidance in understanding the present and planning the future. P.B. and J.S. Medawar reinforce this expectation from their point of view as biologists:

> Human behavior can be genuinely purposive because only human beings guide their behavior by a knowledge of what happened before they were born and a preconception of what may happen after they are dead; thus only human beings find their way by a light that illumines more than the patch of ground they stand on. (cited in Boorstin, p. 557)

History provides this guidance. As Tosh points out: "History trains the mind, enlarges the sympathies, and provides a much needed historical perspective on some of the most pressing problems of our times" (p. 24). It teaches "practical lessons in public affairs." But the lessons are not simple, nor are they the same for all students. Each of us interprets the "lessons of history" according to an individual system of values. Tosh continues: "Different conceptions of the social order produce rival histories … History is a political battle ground" (p. 8). Our closing section addresses these diverse calls to action, making suggestions for practical, local engagement with today's global issues.

UNDERSTANDING THE WORLD THROUGH HISTORY

Throughout *The World's History* we have stressed history as a disciplined method of understanding the processes of change in human life, an understanding that helps in forming contemporary policy. The discipline begins by asking questions, posing problems, and addressing themes. For world history these are big questions, global problems, and universal themes.

By touching on virtually every region of the world and providing readers with a wide sampling of peoples and the societies they have built, this text has emphasized global coverage. Constant comparison and contrast among these societies have prepared readers to ask important questions: How have various societies coped with similar problems? What can be learned from their experience? By following a chronology of events and examining institutions and processes of global importance readers can understand more clearly how people work within their past heritage to create a new future. Studies of the interactions of individuals and societies in the past also provide examples for understanding these relationships today. The exploration of domestic life and gender and class relations in earlier societies enables readers to consider alternate possibilities for the future.

These explorations have employed all the social science disciplines as tools of understanding: anthropology, economics, geography, political science, and sociology. They have relied on the humanities—art and literature—to uncover the feelings and attitudes of people. Fundamental skills in reading and analyzing texts and artifacts underlie all these studies.

From beginning to end *The World's History* has emphasized multiple perspectives. What is important and consequential to one person may be less so to someone else. What appears beneficial to one may seem less so, or even harmful, to another. The historical characters have their differing perspectives; historians studying them have their own perspectives; and the study of these layers of perspectives helps readers to develop their own value systems.

The study of history can also encourage change. In so far as we find the present imperfect and seek to change it, we may find in the past some guidance to alternate institutions and practices, and to methods employed in achieving them. In demonstrating that human arrangements have not always been as they are today, nor need they be the same in the future, history may even be subversive. In all cases, the study of history beckons us to consider the kind of future we might like, and to make personal commitments to bringing it into existence.

UNDERSTANDING THROUGH CONTENT AND INFORMATION

The study and the teaching of history do carry with them civic responsibilities, although each person will interpret them in his or her own way. Some readers may find a place in science or technology, others in the military, some in economics and business, others in education or social work, still others in the creative and applied arts, some raising families in the home, others in the workplace earning a livelihood. Most of us will engage in several of these activities. The study of history encourages us to see our work in broader per-

spective—to see ourselves as part of the global, millennia-old pattern of human life.

A brief review of the contents of *The World's History* enables us to understand this global perspective and gives an opportunity to consider some possible world futures and possible commitments to encouraging those futures.

An understanding of early hominid life, for example, provides insight into contemporary human behavior (Part 1). Human evolution points to a need to sustain human roots in nature, and therefore a concern for the ecology of the globe. The establishment of small, kin-based bands indicates a need to nourish small-group relations, and to achieve satisfying inter-group relationships.

The earliest settlements demonstrate the need for leadership, government, and protection (Part 2). Composed 5000 years ago, *The Epic of Gilgamesh* points out the suffering of citizens under tyranny, and their need to curb excessive, arbitrary power. Hammurabi's *Code* demonstrates the critical importance of law to society. Large-scale armed battles, and the need for defense, had begun. Literature and the arts flourished, suggesting the importance of self-expression as a basic human characteristic. Jewelry, sometimes dazzling in its beauty, marked an early concern for personal adornment. Intense concern with the afterlife exhibited the human quest for transcendent meaning and a sense of purpose in life beyond everyday existence.

An examination of empires shows that from earliest times observers believed the desire for conquest was natural—as was the desire to be free (Part 3). Conquest and resistance coexisted. Empires rose and fell. Valuable lessons from these early experiences include: an understanding of the impermanence of conquest, a distrust of imperial power, a deeper sense of humility and compassion, and a recognition of people's ultimately unquenchable desire to be free from rule by others. Nevertheless, political/military/economic power is real, and we must decide when and how to build it, resist it, compromise with it, attempt to negotiate its benevolent application. Some readers will look forward to some form of global political structure which might bring greater order and stability to these relationships.

An exploration of five religious belief systems dating back thousands of years reveals these faiths to be still very much alive, although in modified forms, in today's world (Part 4). These systems have inspired some of the most noble artistic creations and humane teachings—as well as some of the most cruel persecutions. They again remind us that it is a part of being human to seek some understanding of one's place in the cosmos; that people create and join organizations locally and globally to find guidance and companionship in that quest; and that each person's search is unique and deserving of respect. People resist the imposition of unwelcome spiritual authority just as they resist political and military authorities that are imposed against their will. In every age some people have modified older religious systems and created new ones. Some have rejected supernatural teachings in favor of more humanistic perspectives.

By studying the beginnings of world trade and the emergence of a capitalist system (Part 5) we can gain greater insight into the principal economic system of the modern world—one in which business communities have achieved great power, asserting the belief that private gain is beneficial and will ultimately serve the public good. Alternate systems that vested power in other groups in society, especially religious, political, and military authorities, were also examined. These systems, typically, were unwilling to put their trust in the benevolence of entrepreneurs. Readers who are pleased with the capitalist system as it exists today will applaud and attempt to conserve it. Skeptics may advocate the return of earlier systems or the creation of new ones. All will recognize that the size and power of modern business enterprise modify the structure of the economy and require constant monitoring, although they will differ on the significance of the results.

Historians may not be able to study individual life stories of everyday people who did not leave personal records, but we may be able to understand a great deal from the study of mass movements (Part 6). Waves of migration, for example, affect masses of population in both the sending and the receiving areas, just as they transform the individual migrants themselves. Readers might give greater attention to large scale movements in our own day, including the tragic uprooting of tens of millions of refugees, and the displacement of indigenous peoples as "civilization" encroaches on their homelands. They may also consider the world's enormous population growth, which has restructured life everywhere on the planet and left virtually no empty frontiers for new settlements.

A consideration of the stated goals of revolutions and a comparison of them with actual results

demonstrates that humans have only limited control of the spin of events (Part 7). It also shows the need for skepticism in assessing revolutionary claims. In our examination of the industrial revolution (Chapter 16) we stressed the need to consider the consequences of technological change, and to evaluate the social and ecological consequences of technology as well as its productive potential. We also explored personal and group identities based on urbanization, nationalism, and gender—identities which remain central today. Most people today understand their place in the world, to an important degree, through their neighborhood and civic participation, their citizenship in a specific nation, and their gender. These identities are so ingrained that they are often taken for granted. But this afterword asks that we evaluate the kinds of cities and neighborhoods in which we wish to live and the kind of nation we wish to inhabit.

Our survey of how the major geographical/cultural regions of the world have used technology in the twentieth century (Part 8) invites readers to consider mechanisms by which immensely diverse peoples of the world can live together creatively. The survey raises many questions which are important to us as we enter a new millennium. What is an appropriate technology? Are some technologies so dangerous that they should be banned? What is the role and purpose of science in society? How can technology best serve human needs? What is an equitable balance between wealth and poverty among nations and individuals? How can individuals and groups best plan for the long-term future rather than just for the immediate present? Should nations begin to attempt to construct a new "social contract" which binds them into an international system just as citizens of individual countries are bound by national laws?

MAKING COMMITMENTS BASED ON VALUES

Understanding of the present and the past, in preparation for the future, is unified through the value system of the interpreter. On which story from the past shall we focus? Who shall we choose to highlight as our heroes and who as our villains? The choice depends in part on our agenda for the future. Are we most interested in ecology? Gender, class, or national identity? Our neighborhood, university, work, or religious community? Success in international business and politics? Current interests will help determine which pieces of the past we choose to engage with and studies of the past will guide us toward issues in the present.

In our era it may be difficult to make commitments. We live in an age of relativism. Events all around the globe are interrelated, but formulating a value system which provides global coherence, stability, creativity, and justice seems a far-distant goal.

The certainties of an age of triumphant empire are not ours. We seem to be in a world of constant international competition, although cooperation is also evident and abundant. Old truths are constantly challenged. Some philosophers of history, such as Michel Foucault and Jacques Derrida, argue that historical change cannot be guided at all; power is so diffused throughout society that no levers for effecting change are there to be grasped.

Yet we do choose and we do make commitments, for intuitively we know that we wish at least some small space on this planet to be "home," to reflect values and ways of life with which we feel comfortable, a place where people who share our values are our companions, and where people who endanger them are kept at some safe distance. This does not mean that we seek a boring uniformity; quite the contrary, we recognize that diversity fosters creativity, and we seek diversity and even disagreement, but without unnecessary antagonism. Changing the entire world may be beyond us, but we can work in our own space. We may, as the phrase goes, "Think globally; act locally." By transforming our immediate environment we set an example which others might follow, if they choose.

WHAT TO DO?

In concluding this course of study in world history, we hope that students will be prepared to pay increased attention to activities from places around the globe, and from other times in history—to listen to diverse forms of music, read world literature, travel, visit archaeological digs, follow international politics and markets. The internet puts the world at our fingertips.

Beyond a general concern for broadening your horizons, you may wish to become involved with specific organizations and individuals active in those world affairs you find most interesting. An abundance of opportunities awaits you. For example, most religious denominations have some overseas involvement; Oxfam, a secular organization, supports and promotes development projects among poor people around the world; ecological groups with international concerns include the Wildlife Fund for Nature and Greenpeace; and Amnesty International campaigns actively on behalf of prisoners of conscience around the world, putting pressure on dictatorial governments by exposing their activities. These organizations and many more keep their members and volunteers informed of international developments in their area of service, so the more you do the more you learn. One of them will address your own concerns. Try to accomplish as much as you can. As Rabbi Tarfon stated in the Talmud 2000 years ago, "It is not your duty to complete the task, but neither may you exempt yourself from undertaking it" (Aboth, II:21).

BIBLIOGRAPHY

Bennington, Geoffrey and Jacques Derrida. *Jacques Derrida*, trans. by Geoffrey Bennington (Chicago: University of Chicago Press, 1993).

Bloch, Marc. *The Historian's Craft*, trans. by Peter Putnam (New York: Vintage Books, 1964).

Boorstin, Daniel. *The Discoverers* (New Random House, 1983).

Bradley Commission on History in the Schools. *Building a History Curriculum* (Washington: Educational Excellence Network, 1988).

Carr, E.H. *What is History?* (Harmondsworth, Middlesex: Penguin Books, 1964).

"Aboth: Sayings of the Fathers," in Joseph H. Hertz, ed. Daily Prayer Book, rev. ed., pp. 610–721 (New York: Bloch Publishing, 1954).

Foucault, Michel. *The Archaeology of Knowledge*, trans. by A.M. Sheridan Smith (London: Tavistock, 1974).

Laqueur, Walter and Barry Rubin. *The Human Rights Reader* (New York: New American Library, 1989).

McNeill, William H. *Mythistory and Other Essays* (Chicago: University of Chicago, 1986).

Tosh, John. *The Pursuit of History*, 2nd ed. (New York: Longman, 1991).

White, Hayden. *Metahistory* (Baltimore, MD: Johns Hopkins University Press, 1973).

GLOSSARY

Pronunciation guides for selected terms are enclosed in parentheses, with the stressed syllable appearing in capital letters.

Abhidhamma (UB-ih-DUM-eh) One of the three principal divisions of the Buddhist scriptures, or Tripitaka, the others being the **Sutta** and the **Vinaya**. It comprises a logical analysis of the Buddha's teachings, arranged systematically, and is more impersonal and abstract than the Sutta. Its aim is meditational, and an important element involves an examination of states of consciousness.

agora (AG-o-rah) A central feature of ancient Greek town planning. Its chief function, like the Roman forum, was as a town market, but it also became the main social and political meeting place. Together with the acropolis, it normally housed the most important buildings of the town.

animist One who believes that the world is permeated by spiritual beings who have an interest in human affairs and may intervene in them. Animism is characteristic of most tribal peoples.

anthropology The scientific study of human beings in their social and physical aspects. Physical anthropologists study fossil remains to explain the origins and biological evolution of humans and the distinctive features of different races. Cultural anthropologists are concerned with the evolution of human society and cultures, especially through language. Social anthropologists have typically confined their work to "primitive" societies; they seek to analyze social norms, customs, belief, and ritual.

apartheid (a-PAHRT-hate) An Afrikaans word meaning "apartness," referring to racial segregation and implying white supremacy. The policy was officially implemented in South Africa in 1948, when increasingly restrictive laws against blacks were introduced. The establishment of the Bantu "homelands" effectively disenfranchised blacks from the South African body politic. Internal opposition and international censure, particularly the sanctions imposed by Britain and the United States in 1985, led to shifts in policy and enfranchisement, culminating in the election of a coalition government with a black majority in 1994.

asiento (a-SEE-en-toe) A contract between the Spanish crown and a private individual or sovereign power, by which the latter was granted exclusive rights to import a stipulated number of slaves into the Spanish American colonies in exchange for a fee. The British South Sea Company was granted a monopoly at the Treaty of Utrecht of 1713, a privilege that was relinquished for a lump sum in 1750.

assimilation The process by which different ethnic groups lose their distinctive cultural identity through contact with the dominant culture of a society, and gradually become absorbed and integrated into it.

balance of power In international relations, a policy that aims to secure peace by preventing any one state or alignment of states from becoming too dominant. Alliances are formed in order to build up a force equal or superior to that of the potential enemy. Such a policy was practiced in the ancient world, for example by the Greek city-states.

Balkanization The process by which a large political or geographical unit is broken into smaller ones, with the implication that hostilities may ensue. The term was coined to describe the fragmentation of the Ottoman Empire in the nineteenth and early twentieth centuries; it has also been applied to the emergence of independent states in post-colonial Africa and to the break-up of the former Soviet Union.

bas relief (bah reh-LEEF) In sculpture, relief is a term for any work in which the forms stand out from the background, whether a plane or a curved surface. In bas (or low) relief, the design projects only slightly from the background and the outlines are not undercut.

Bible From the Greek *biblia*, books. The Jewish bible, written in Hebrew, comprises the thirty-nine books of the Old Testament (a Christian designation), the canon of which was probably established by 100 C.E. Regarded as divinely inspired, these scriptures are made up of three parts: the Torah (Law), the first five books—Genesis to Deuteronomy—whose authorship is attributed to Moses; the Prophets; and the Writings (the Psalms, etc.). The Christian Church incorporated these books, together with the Apocrypha (supplementary books written in Greek) and the **New Testament** writings, into its bible, the form of which was fixed by the end of the fourth century C.E.

bourgeoisie (boor-ZHWA-zee) A French word that originally applied to the inhabitants of walled towns, who occupied a socio-economic position between the rural peasantry and the feudal aristocracy. With the development of industry, it became identified more with employers, as well as with other members of the "middle class," including professionals, artisans, and shopkeepers. (In Marxist theory, the word refers to those who own the tools of production and do not live by the sale of their labor, as opposed to the proletariat.)

cadre A nucleus of key personnel. Cadre was originally a French military term denoting the officers of a regiment; it is also applied to an organized group of political activists.

caliph (KAY-lif) The spiritual head and temporal ruler of the Muslim community. As successor to the prophet Muhammad, the caliph is invested with absolute civil and religious authority, providing that he rules in conformity with the law of the Quran and the **hadith**.

capitalism An economic system characterized by private or corporate ownership of the means of production and by private control over decisions on prices, production, and distribution of goods in a free, competitive market of **supply and demand**.

caravanserai (KAR-uh-VAN-suh-ree) In Middle Eastern countries, a public building for the use of travelers and caravans, usually situated outside the walls of a town. It comprises an arcaded two-storied courtyard with storerooms, stabling, and areas for food preparation on the ground floor and lodgings above. Massive walls with small, high windows and a single barred gateway provide protection at night.

cartel An association of independent producers or businessmen whose aim is to control the supply of a particular commodity or group of commodities in order to regulate or push up prices.

caste (KAST) An element in a hierarchical social system in which the ranks are strictly defined, usually according to descent, marriage, and occupation. In more rigorous caste systems, such as that of Hinduism in India, mobility from one caste (Sanskrit: *varna*) to another is prohibited, and traditions and ritual dictate rules for social intercourse as well as such matters as education, diet, and occupation.

caudillismo (kou-DEE-iz-moh) In Spanish America, a system of rule through *caudillos* (leaders), men with a strong personal following who wield almost absolute authority. It emerged during the nineteenth-century wars of independence, at a time when there was little social or political stability.

centuries The smallest units of the Roman army, each composed of some 100 foot-soldiers and commanded by a centurion. A legion was made up of 60 centuries. Centuries also formed political divisions of Roman citizens; they met in assembly to elect the chief magistrates and had some judicial powers.

chasidic (HAS-I-dic) A pietistic strand of orthodox Judaism that stresses the indwelling of God in all creation. Founded in Poland in the eighteenth century, it spread throughout eastern Europe; huge numbers of chasidic Jews perished under the Nazis during World War II. There are now communities in Israel, the United States, and Britain.

Cheka (CHECK-a) The secret police of early Soviet Russia, established by the Bolsheviks after the Revolution of 1917 to defend the regime against dissidents. Criticized for its severe brutality, the agency was reorganized in 1922.

Christmas The Christian feast celebrating the birth of Jesus Christ. The day of his actual birth is unknown, but the early Church probably chose this date because it coincided with pagan festivals of sun worship associated with the winter solstice. Pagan cults seem to have been the source of some popular customs connected with Christmas.

client state A state that is economically, politically, or militarily dependent on another state. During the Cold War, states such as Cuba and Guatemala supported the policies of the USSR and the USA, respectively, while receiving extensive assistance from them.

collectivization A policy that aims to transfer land from private to state or communal ownership. It was adopted by the Soviet government in the 1920s and implemented with increasing brutality; by 1936 almost all the peasants had joined the *kolkhozy* (large collective farms), although many resisted violently. The integration of agriculture into the state-controlled economy helped to supply the capital required for industrialization.

comprador (kahm-prah-DOOR) (Portuguese: "buyer") A Chinese merchant hired by Western traders to assist with their dealings in China. The comprador provided interpreters, workers, guards, and help over currency exchange.

Concordat (kahn-KOR-dat) A public agreement, subject to international law, between the Pope as head of the Roman Catholic church and a temporal ruler regulating the status, rights, and liberties of the church within the country concerned.

consul (KON-sul) Under the Roman Republic, one of the two magistrates holding supreme civil and military authority. Nominated by the Senate and elected by citizens in the Comita Centuriata (popular assembly), the consuls held office for one year and each had power of veto over the other. Their power was much restricted after the collapse of the Republic in 27 B.C.E., when the office fell under the control of the emperors.

contract labor Labor provided by workers under binding, legally enforceable contract, usually for a lengthy period, sometimes years, sometimes in organized gangs of laborers, and often for projects in distant locations. Compare **indentured labor**.

counterurbanization A shift in population from metropolitan areas to the country or smaller towns, a phenomenon of advanced industrial nations first identified in the 1970s. Since it tends to be the more affluent citizens who migrate, the process creates poor and decaying inner-city areas.

creole (KREE-ol) In the sixteenth to eighteenth centuries, a white person born in Spanish America of Spanish parents. Excluded from the highest offices under the Spanish colonial administration, the creoles became the leaders of revolution, and then the ruling class of the new independent nations. The term creole is also used more loosely, with a wide range of applications.

cuneiform (kyoo-NEE-uh-form) A writing system in use in the ancient Near East from around the end of the fourth millennium to the first century B.C.E. It was used for a number of languages in the area, but the earliest examples, on clay tablets, are in Sumerian. The name derives from the wedge-shaped marks (Latin: *cuneus*, a wedge) made by pressing the slanted edge of a stylus into soft clay. The signs were abstract versions of the earlier **pictograms**, and represented whole words or the sounds of syllables.

daimyo (DIH-my-oh) The feudal lords of Japan, who by the sixteenth century controlled almost the entire country. Their constant warfare was finally ended in 1603 under the Tokugawa **shogunate**; they subsequently served as local rulers, joined to the **shogun** by oath. In 1868, when imperial rule was restored, their domains or **han** were surrendered to the emperor; in 1871 they were given titles and pensioned off.

Daoism (Taoism) (DAO-iz-um) A religio-philosophical system of ancient China, which emerged in the sixth century B.C.E. Daoism rejected the activism of Confucianism, the other great Chinese philosophical tradition. It emphasized spontaneity and individual freedom, a *laissez-faire* attitude to life and government, simplicity, and the importance of mystical experience. True happiness could be attained only by surrendering to the Way or principle (Chinese: *dao*) of Nature. The principle texts of Daoism are the *Laozi* or *Classic of the Way and Its Power*, traditionally attributed to the philosopher Laozi, and the *Zhuangzi* of Zhuang Zou.

dar al-Islam (DAHR ahl-is-LAHM) The literal meaning of the Arabic words is "the abode of peace." The term refers to the land of Islam, or the territories in which Islam and its religious laws (**shari'a**) may be freely practiced.

deme (DEEM) A rural district or village in ancient Greece, or its members or inhabitants. The demes were a constituent part of the **polis** but had their own corporations with police powers, and their own cults, officials, and property. Membership of the deme was open only to adult males, and was hereditary; it also guaranteed membership of the polis itself.

depression A severe, long-term decline in the economic activities of production, consumption, employment, profits, and wages.

descamisados (des-cah-me-SAH-doze) The "shirtless ones," the urban poor of Argentina, who supported Juan Perón (1895–1974) and his wife Eva. They organized mass protests at his arrest in 1945; Perón had gained popular support through his wage and welfare measures while a minister in the government of 1943–5.

developed world Those countries that enjoy considerable wealth, derived largely from sophisticated industrialization, and characterized by high standards of living, healthcare, and literacy, advanced technological development, democratic constitutions, and world influence, as well as high labor costs and energy consumption. They comprise most of Europe, the United States, Canada, Japan, Australia, and New Zealand, the first areas to be industrialized.

developing world Those countries lacking advanced industrial development and money for investment, and with a low *per capita* income. Their economies are largely agrarian, often relying on one crop, with low yields. Labor is plentiful, cheap, and unskilled; levels of literacy are low; poverty, disease, and famine have not been eliminated. They include most Asian countries, as well as Africa and Latin America. (*See* **third world**.)

development of underdevelopment A theory developed by Latin American social scientists in the mid-1960s; also known as dependency theory. It argues that, despite the end of colonialism, wealthy nations such as the United States and members of the European Community continue to exercise great political control over **third world** countries through their domination of the global economy.

dhimmi (dim-MEE) A person who belongs to the class of "protected people" in the Islamic state, who could not be forcibly converted to Islam. They originally comprised the followers of the monotheistic religions cited in the Quran, the "People of the Book" (e.g., Jews and Christians), to whom scriptures had been revealed, and the principle has in some instances been extended to followers of other religions.

diaspora (die-AS-pur-uh) A dispersion of peoples. Most commonly used to refer to the dispersion of Jews among the Gentiles, which began with the Babylonian captivity of the sixth century B.C.E.; the Hebrew term for diaspora is *Galut*, "exile." Because of the special relationship between the Jews and the land of Israel, the term refers not only to their physical dispersion but also has religious, philosophical, and political connotations. The African diaspora refers to the settlement of people of African origin to new locations around the world. "Trade diaspora" has been used to refer to centers of trade in which traders from many different countries live and work.

diffusion The spread of ideas, objects, or traits from one culture to another. Diffusionism is an anthropological theory that cultural similarities among different groups can be explained by diffusion rather than **innovation**, and, in its most radical form, that they derive from a common source.

divine right of kings A political doctrine influential in the sixteenth and seventeenth centuries. It held that the monarch derived his or her authority from God and was therefore not accountable to earthly authority. James I of England (1603–25) was a foremost exponent.

dominance The imposition of alien government through force, as opposed to **hegemony**.

duma (DOO-ma) The Russian parliament established by Nicholas II in response to the Revolution of 1905. Its powers were largely restricted to the judicial and administrative areas; the czar retained control over the franchise. The first two dumas (1906, 1907) were radical and soon dissolved; the third (1907–12) was conservative; the fourth (1912–17) became a focus of opposition to the czarist regime, particularly over its conduct of World War I, and enforced Nicholas's abdication in 1917.

dyarchy A system of provincial government in British India introduced under the Government of India Act (1919). Crown-appointed councillors retained control of law and order, justice, and revenue, but Indian ministers, chosen by the governor from elected legislators, took over local government and such matters as education, health, public works, and agriculture. Dyarchy was superseded by full provincial autonomy in 1935.

Easter The principal feast of the Christian calendar celebrating the resurrection of Christ. It is preceded by the penitential season of Lent, which culminates in the solemnities of Holy Week and Good Friday, commemorating Jesus' crucifixion. The date varies, and can fall on any Sunday between March 22 and April 25. The feast was associated by the early Christians with the Jewish Passover, and in some Churches a vigil is held on the night of Holy Saturday.

econometrics The use of statistical techniques and mathematical models to analyze economic relationships. Econometrics may be applied by a government or private business to test the validity of an economic theory or to forecast future trends.

ecumene (EK-yoo-MEEN) A Greek word referring to the inhabited world and designating a distinct cultural-historical community.

empiricism (em-PEER-eh-cism) The theory that all knowledge originates in experience; the practice of relying on direct observation of events and experience for determining reality. Often contrasted with rationalism on the one hand and with mysticism on the other.

encomienda (en-co-me-EN-da) A concession from the Spanish crown to a Spanish American colonist, giving him permission to exact tribute – in gold, in kind, or in labor – from a specified number of Indians living in a certain area; in return he was to care for their welfare and instruct them in the Catholic faith. The system was designed to supply labor for the mines, but it was severely abused and later abolished.

enlightened despotism A benevolent form of absolutism, a system of government in which the ruler has absolute rights over his or her subjects. It implies that the ruler acts for the good of the people, not in self-interest.

epigraphy (eh-PIG-reh-fee) Inscriptions, usually on stone or metal, or the science of interpreting them.

Eucharist (YOO-kah-rist) From the Greek *eucharistia*, thanksgiving. The central **sacrament** and act of worship of the Christian Church, commemorating the Last Supper of Christ with his disciples, his sacrifice on the cross, and the redemption of mankind, and culminating in Holy Communion, when his Body and Blood in the form of water and wine are conveyed to the believer.

Eurocentricity A concentration on the history and culture of Europe, often disregarding other areas and influences.

existentialism A philosophical and literary movement that came to prominence after World War II, particularly associated with French intellectuals, notably Jean-Paul Sartre. It rejects metaphysics and epistemology, and is concerned with being rather than knowing; it stresses the uniqueness of each individual, and the need to find one's own authenticity.

exogamy (adj. exogamous) The practice by which a person is compelled to choose a marital partner from outside his or her own group or clan, the opposite of endogamy, the choice of partner from within the group. Sometimes the outside group from which the partner is to be chosen is specified.

extraterritoriality In international law, the immunities enjoyed by the official representatives of a sovereign state or international organization within a host country; they are in effect "foreign islands," and thus exempt from prosecution, interference, or constraint.

fascism (FASH-ism) A political philosophy, movement, or government that exalts the nation over the individual, the antithesis of liberal democracy. It advocates a centralized, autocratic government led by a disciplined party and headed by a dictatorial, charismatic leader. The term fascism was first introduced by Benito Mussolini in Italy in 1919 and takes its name from the Latin word *fasces*, the ancient symbol of state authority, a bundle of rods bound around an ax.

feminism The theory of the political, social, and economic equality of the sexes, and organized activity to bring about that condition by ending gender biases.

feudal (FEW-dull) Refers to both a social, military, and political system organized on the basis of land tenure and the manorial system of production. Property (the fief) was granted to a tenant (vassal) by a lord in exchange for an oath of allegiance and a promise to fulfill certain obligations, including military service, aid, and advice; in return, the lord offered protection and justice. Originally bestowed by investiture, the fief later became hereditary. Within the system, each person was bound to the others by a web of mutual responsibilities, from the king or emperor down to the **serfs**. Feudalism is particularly associated with medieval Europe, and with China and Japan. (*See* **manorial economy**.)

finca (FEEN-ca) A Spanish farm, country estate, or coffee plantation.

first world The advanced capitalist nations of the **developed world**, as opposed to the second world (countries with socialist state systems, particularly the former Soviet bloc) and the **third world**.

free market economy An economic system in which the means of production are largely privately owned and there is little or no government control over the markets, which operate according to **supply and demand**. The primary aim is to maximize profits, which are distributed to private individuals who have invested capital in an enterprise. The system is also known as a free enterprise economy or capitalism.

front-line A state that is bordered by a country engaged in armed conflict, and often drawn into the conflict.

garden city A planned town combining work, residential, agricultural, and recreational facilities, and surrounded by a rural belt. This influential idea was the British planner Ebenezer Howard's solution to rural depopulation and the urban overcrowding of the industrial age. Letchworth (1903) in southeast England was the first example.

gaucho (GAH-oocho) A nomadic cattle-herder, of any race, in the grasslands of South America, noted for his fearless riding and distinctive dress. Heroic figures in the colonial wars of independence, the gauchos became employees of the ranchers when the pampas were enclosed in the nineteenth century.

gazi (GAH-zee) A warrior or war leader in Islam, sometimes used as a military title among the Turks.

geo-politics The analysis of the effect of geographic environment on national policy and on the power relationships between nations. The theory that geography determines a nation's area of

struggle was particularly influential on Germany in the 1920s, and on the Nazis.

Girondins (juh-RAHN-dins) A French revolutionary group formed largely from the middle classes, many of them originally from the Gironde region. They were prominent in the Legislative Assembly (1791), urged war against Austria (1792), opposed the more radical **Montagnards**, and were overthrown in 1793.

glasnost (GLAZ-nohst) A Russian word meaning "openness," adopted as a political slogan by the Soviet leader Mikhail Gorbachev in 1986. It encouraged greater freedom of expression and genuine debate in social, political, and cultural affairs; with **perestroika**, it heralded greater democracy and improved relations with the West.

guild (GILD) A sworn association of people who gather for some common purpose. In the towns of medieval Europe, guilds of craftsmen or merchants were formed in order to protect and further the members' professional interests and for mutual aid. Merchant guilds organized trade in their locality and had important influence on local government. Craft guilds were confined to specific crafts or trades; they set and maintained standards of quality, regulated production and controlled recruitment through the apprenticeship system; they also had important social and religious functions. In India the guilds were associations of businessmen and producers who regulated weights and measures and prices and enforced quality control.

gulag (GOO-lahg) The acronym of Glavnoye, Upravleniye Ispravitelno Trudovykh Lagerey, the "Chief Administration of Corrective Labor Camps," a department of the Soviet secret police founded in 1934 under Stalin. It ran a vast network of forced labor camps throughout the USSR to which millions of citizens accused of "crimes against the state" were sent for punishment. The system was exposed by Alexandr Solzhenitsyn in *The Gulag Archipelago* (1973).

hacienda (ah-thee-EN-da) A large rural estate in Spanish America, originating with Spanish colonialization in the sixteenth century. The laborers, usually Indians, were in theory free wage earners, but in practice many became bound to the land through indebtedness to the owner. The owners (*haciendados*) controlled local and sometimes national government.

hadith (huh-DETH) Traditional records of the deeds and utterances of the prophet Muhammad, and the basis, after the

Quran, for Islamic theology and law. The hadith provide commentaries on the Quran and give guidance for social and religious life and everyday conduct.

han In Japan, the territory or feudal estate controlled by a **daimyo** under the Tokugawa **shogunate** (1603–1868). Although legally subject to the central government, each *han* formed an autonomous and self-sufficient economic unit, with its own military forces. They were abolished in 1871.

harijan (har-YAH-jahn) A Hindu term meaning children of God, applied by Mahatma Gandhi to the poorest classes of Indian society, including the **untouchables**.

hegemony (hih-JEM-o-nee) The predominance of one unit over the others in a group, for example one state in a confederation. It can also apply to the rule of an empire over its subject peoples, when the foreign government is exercised with their substantial consent. Hegemony usually implies exploitation but, more positively, it may connote leadership (*see* **dominance**).

heliocentric A system in which the sun is assumed to be at the center of the solar system—or of the universe—while Earth and the planets move around it. Ptolemy of Alexandria's geocentric or Earth-centered system dominated scientific thought in the Western world from the second century C.E. until the publication of Copernicus's *De revolutionibus orbium coelestium* in 1543. There was much religious and scientific controversy before his thesis was shown to be essentially correct.

hieroglyphs (HIGH-ur-o-glifs) The characters in a writing system based on the use of **pictograms** or **ideograms**. In ancient Egypt, hieroglyphics were largely used for monumental inscriptions. The symbols depict people, animals, and objects, which represent words, syllables, or sounds.

hijra (HIJ-reh) The "migration" or flight of Muhammad from Mecca, where his life was in danger, to Medina (then called Yathrib) in 622 C.E. The Islamic era (A.H.: After Hijra) is calculated from this date, which coincides with the establishment of the first Islamic state.

historiography The writing of history, or the theory and history of historical writing.

hoplite A heavily armed foot soldier of ancient Greece, whose function was to fight in close formation, usually in ranks of eight men. Hoplites were citizens with sufficient property to equip themselves with full personal armor, which consisted of a helmet with nasal and cheek pieces, a breastplate and greaves of bronze. Each soldier carried a heavy bronze shield, a short iron sword, and a long spear for thrusting.

humanism A term applied to the intellectual movement initiated in Western Europe in the fourteenth century by such men as Petrarch and Boccaccio and deriving from the rediscovery and study of Classical, particularly Latin, literary texts. The humanist program of studies included rhetoric, grammar, history, poetry, and moral philosophy (the humanities); the humanist scholar aimed to emulate Classical literary achievements. The examination of Classical civilization formed the inspiration for the **Renaissance**. Although humanism attached prime importance to human qualities and values, unlike its twentieth-century counterpart it in no way involved the rejection of Christianity.

icon (I-kon) A representation of Christ, the Virgin Mary, or other sacred personage or saint, usually a painted image on wood but also wrought in mosaic, ivory, and other materials. The term is usually applied to the sacred images of Eastern, particularly Byzantine and Orthodox, Christianity, where they are regarded as channels of grace. (*See also* **iconoclast, iconodule.**)

iconoclast (I-kon-o-klast) An image-breaker, or a person who rejects the veneration of **icons**, on the grounds that the practice is idolatrous. Strong disagreements over the cult of images in the Byzantine Empire led to attacks on the images themselves, and the use of icons was forbidden during the Iconoclastic Controversy (726–843 C.E.), when many were destroyed.

iconodule (I-kon-o-duel) A person who venerates **icons**. Iconodules defended the liturgical use of icons during the Iconoclastic Controversy (726–843 C.E.) in the Byzantine Empire. They argued that since God had assumed material form in the person of Jesus Christ, it was legitimate to represent him in visible images; moreover, the faithful could be stimulated to devotion through painted representations of God or the saints. They won their point by a Decree of the Second Council of Nicaea in 787, which was finally brought into practice in 843.

ideogram (ID-ee-o-gram) (alternative: ideograph) A character or figure in a writing system in which the idea of a thing is represented rather than its name. Languages such as Chinese use ideograms, but they cannot easily represent new or foreign words and huge numbers of symbols may be required to convey even basic information.

imam (ih-MAHM) In Islam, a title for a person whose leadership or example is to be followed, with several levels of meaning. In a general sense, it can refer to a leader of prayer in a mosque, or the head of a community or group. Among Shi'a Muslims, the title has special significance as applying to the successors of Muhammad, who were regarded as infallible and exercised absolute authority in both temporal and spiritual spheres (*see* **caliph**).

indentured labor Labor performed under signed indenture, or contract, which binds the laborer to work for a specific employer, for a specified time, usually years, often in a distant place, in exchange for transportation and maintenance. The indenture is usually very restrictive and its conditions harsh. After the abolition of slavery in the nineteenth century, in many regions like the Caribbean, imported, indentured labor (from Asia) was employed extensively. Compare **contract labor.**

Indo-Aryan (in-DOH-AIR-ee-un) A sub-group of the Indo-Iranian branch of the Indo-European group of languages, also called Indic and spoken in India, Sri Lanka, Bangladesh, and Pakistan. The Indo-Aryan languages descend from Sanskrit, the sacred language of Hinduism; they include Hindi, a literary language, the more colloquial Hindustani, and the widely spoken Sindhi, Bengali, Gujarati, Punabi, and Sinhalese.

Indo-European The largest family of languages, believed to be descended from a single unrecorded language spoken more than 5000 years ago in the steppe regions around the Black Sea, which later split into a number of dialects. The languages were carried into Europe and Asia by migrating peoples, who also transmitted their cultural heritage. The family includes the following sub-groups: Anatolian (the earliest recorded language, now extinct), Indo-Iranian, Armenian, Greek, Albanian, Tocharian, Celtic, Italic, Germanic, Baltic, and Slavic.

indulgences In the Roman Catholic church, the remission from the temporal penalty of an absolved sin, obtainable through good works or special prayers and granted by the church through the merits of Christ and the saints. The financial value often attached to indulgences in the late medieval church led to widespread abuse.

infitah An Arabic term meaning liberality and receptiveness to new ideas and arguments. In commerce, it implies expansion and freedom from restrictive rules and regulations.

innovation The explanation that similar cultural traits, techniques, or objects found among different groups of people were invented independently rather than spreading from one group to another, as in **diffusion**.

interregnum An interval between reigns (Latin: "between reigns"). The term may refer to the period of time between the death of a monarch and the accession of his successor, to a suspension of the usual government, or to the period of rule of an usurper.

irredentist An individual or group that seeks to restore territory to the state that once owned it.

Jacobins (jak-uh-bins) A French revolutionary party founded in 1789; the word derives from the popular name for the former Dominican convent in Paris, where meetings were held. It later became the most radical party of the Revolution, responsible, under Robespierre, for implementing the Reign of Terror and the execution of the king (1793).

janapada (juh-nah-pah-dah) A Sanskrit word that occurs in ancient texts with reference to a large political district.

janissary (JAN-ah-ser-ee) A member of the elite corps of Ottoman footsoldiers. Originally, in the late fourteenth century, they were Christian conscripts from the conquered Balkans who were forcibly converted to Islam and subjected to strict rules, including celibacy. Highly trained, they later became very powerful, frequently engineering palace coups; they were massacred after their insurrection in 1826.

jihad (jee-HAHD) An Arabic word meaning "striving," "effort," or "struggle," established in both the Quran and the **hadith** as an incumbent religious duty. It has been interpreted both as a spiritual battle to overcome evil and as a physical one against unbelievers.

keiretsu (kay-re-tsoo) Alliances of independent Japanese firms, either between large corporations in different industries or between a large corporation and sub-contractors. They are successors of the pre-war **zaibatsu**.

khedive (kah-DEEV) The title granted by the Ottoman sultan Abdulaziz to the hereditary pasha (viceroy) of Egypt in 1867. In 1904, when Egypt became a British protectorate, the title was replaced by that of Sultan.

kibbutz (kih-BOOTZ) An Israeli settlement, usually agricultural but sometimes industrial, in which wealth and property are held in common, profits are reinvested in the enterprise and decisions are made democratically. Work and meals are organized collectively and children housed away from their parents.

kulak (koo-LAK) A prosperous peasant in late czarist and early Soviet Russia. The leaders of local agricultural communities, kulaks owned sizeable farms and could afford to hire labor. They vigorously opposed Stalin's **collectivization** policy and were regarded as class enemies; large numbers were deported or executed, and their property confiscated.

ladino (lah-DEE-no) A Spanish-speaking inhabitant of Central America of predominantly Spanish descent, distinguished by their Western dress and habits. They are often engaged in small-scale commerce and agriculture, where they tend to use more modern farming methods than the Indians, and to concentrate more on cash crops.

laissez-faire (les-ay-FAIR) An economic policy of non-interference by government in the working of the market and the economic affairs of individuals. Proponents of the theory, which was developed in the eighteenth century, argued that an unregulated economy would work "naturally" at maximum efficiency and that the pursuit of self-interest would ultimately benefit society as a whole.

lateen (lah-TEEN) A triangular sail affixed to a long yard or crossbar at an angle of about 45 degrees to the mast, with the free corner secured near the stern. The sail was capable of taking the wind on either side. The rig, which was developed by the Arabs, revolutionized navigation because it enabled vessels to tack into the wind and thus to sail in almost any direction; with a square sail, ships could only sail with the wind behind them.

Legalism A school of Chinese philosophy that came into prominence during the period of the Warring States (481–422 B.C.E.) and had great influence on the policies of the Qin dynasty (221–207 B.C.E.). Legalists took a pessimistic view of human nature and believed that social harmony could only be attained through strong government control and the imposition of strict laws, enforced absolutely. The brutal application of this political theory under the Qin led to the fall of the dynasty, and Legalist philosophy was permanently discredited in Confucian philosophy.

leviathan A huge mythical and Biblical sea monster. Thomas Hobbes named his book *Leviathan* (1651) in describing the enormous size and power that he felt the state ought to have. The designation, often with negative connotations, continues to be applied to institutions, especially governments, of enormous size and power.

liberation theology A movement in the Roman Catholic church in Latin America that stresses the importance of translating religious faith into active political involvement in order to redress social wrongs. It views the church as belonging especially to the poor, and has been responsible for the establishment of local Christian groups or *communidades de base* to serve members' spiritual and physical needs.

madrasa (mah-DRASS-ah) A traditional Islamic school of higher education, principally of theology and law, literally a "place of study." The madrasa usually comprised a central courtyard surrounded by rooms in which the students resided and with a prayer room or mosque, where instruction took place. Tuition, board, and lodging were free. Studies could last for several years and primarily consisted of memorizing textbooks and lectures.

mahdi (MAH-dee) An Arabic word meaning "the right-guided one." According to Islamic tradition, a messianic leader will appear to restore justice, truth, and religion for a brief period before the Day of Judgment. Some Shi'a Muslims believe that the twelfth **imam** (ninth century C.E.) will reappear as the Mahdi. Several impostors have claimed the title.

maidan (MY-dahn) An open space or square in an Iranian town or city.

mandala (MUN-dull-eh) A symbolic circular diagram of complex geometric design used as an instrument of meditation or in the performance of sacred rites in Hinduism and Buddhism. Mandalas can be drawn, painted, wrought in metal, or traced on the ground. Buddhist examples are usually characterized by a series of concentric circles, representing universal harmony and containing religious figures, with the Buddha in the center.

mandate The authority given to a member power from the League of Nations—the organization set up in 1919 to settle international disputes through arbitration—to govern the former colonies of the German and Ottoman empires. Mandate also referred to the area of jurisdiction itself. In 1946 the system was replaced by the United Nations trusteeship system.

mangonel (MANG-geh-nell) An upright armed catapult worked by torsion. Mangonels of various types were used in China and the ancient world, as well as by the Mongols and in medieval Europe.

manorial economy An economic system based on the manor, or the lord's landed estate, the most common unit of agrarian organization in medieval Europe. The manor comprised the lord's own farm (the demesne) and the land farmed by peasant tenants or **serfs** who were legally dependent on the lord and owed him or her **feudal** service on the demesne. The manor was not completely self-contained but it aimed more at self-sufficiency than at the market and supported a steady increase in population up to the fourteenth century.

mantra (MUN-tra) A formula of utterances of words and sounds that are believed to possess spiritual power, a practice of both Hinduism and Buddhism. The efficacy of the mantra largely depends on the exacting mental discipline involved in uttering it correctly. Repetition or meditation on a particular mantra can induce a trancelike state, leading to a higher level of spiritual consciousness.

maroonage A situation of slaves in the West Indian islands in the early eighteenth century. They organized their escape and sometimes lived in communities in inaccessible mountainous regions or forests.

mazombo A direct descendant of Portuguese settlers in the Americas.

medieval A term coined in fifteenth-century Italy to describe the "middle ages," the period between antiquity and the contemporary Renaissance. It originally had negative connotations, for the Middle Ages were regarded as a period of artistic and cultural decline as compared to the lost glories of ancient Rome and the Renaissance attempts to emulate and surpass those achievements.

Meiji restoration The reforms effected in Japan in the name of the emperor Mutsuhito (r. 1867–1912), who was known as the Meiji emperor. During his reign constitutional changes restored the emperor to full power, displacing the militarily powerful **shogun**, and Japan adopted many western innovations as it became a modern industrial state.

mercantilism An economic policy pursued by many European nations between the sixteenth and eighteenth centuries. It aimed to strengthen an individual nation's economic power at the expense of its rivals by stockpiling reserves of bullion, which involved government regulation of trade. Measures included tariffs on imports, the passing of sumptuary laws to keep demand for imported goods low, the promotion of thrift, and the search for new colonies, both as a source for raw materials and as a market for the export of finished goods.

mestizo (mis-TEE-zo) A person of mixed race. In Central and South America it usually denotes a person of combined Indian and European descent.

mfecane A period of strife (1818–28) among the Bantu peoples of southern Africa, initiated by Zulu expansion under the warrior king Shaka and leading to the displacement of other tribes. It facilitated white colonial expansion in the area.

mihrab An arch or niche in the prayer hall of a mosque indicating the direction of Mecca. It is usually ornamented.

mir (MEER) A self-governing community of peasants in pre-revolutionary Russia having control over local forests, fisheries, and hunting grounds; arable land was allocated to each family according to size, in return for a fixed sum. The communes had elected officials and were responsible for the payment of taxes.

mita (MEE-tah) A system of forced labor in Peru, begun under Inca rule and continued by the Spanish colonists, by which Indian communities were required to contribute a set number of laborers for public works for a given period. Conditions were appalling, particularly in the mines, and many Indians perished. The system was abolished in 1821. (*See* **repartimiento**.)

monoculture A farming system devoted to the cultivation of a single crop, often a cash crop. Although monoculture can be more efficient, it is susceptible to the spread of disease and price fluctuations.

monopoly The exclusive control over the production or supply of a particular commodity or service for which there is no substitute. Because there is no competition, the supplier can fix the price of the product and maximize profits.

monotheism (MON-eh-thee-iz-um) The doctrine of the existence of only one God, or of the oneness of God, as opposed to polytheism, the belief in the existence of many gods, or atheism, the denial of the existence of God. The great monotheistic religions are Judaism, Christianity, and Islam, all of which believe in God as creator and as the source of the highest good.

Monophysites (moh-NOF-ih-sites) The supporters of a doctrine in the early Christian Church that held that the incarnate Christ possessed a single, wholly divine nature. They opposed the orthodox view that Christ had a double nature, one divine and one human, and emphasized his divinity at the expense of his capacity to experience real human suffering. The doctrine survived in the Coptic and some other Eastern Churches.

Montagnards (MAHN-ton-yards) Members of a radical French revolutionary party, closely associated with the **Jacobins** and supported by the artisans, shopkeepers, and **sansculottes**. They opposed the more moderate **Girondins** and controlled the Legislative Assembly and National Convention during the climax of the Revolution in 1793–4.

mulatto (mah-LAHT-oh) In the Americas, a person of mixed race, usually with parents of European and African origin.

nabob (NAY-bahb) A British employee of the East India Company who made a huge fortune in India, often through corruption, in the eighteenth century.

Negritude A mid-twentieth-century literary movement originating among French-speaking writers from Africa and the Caribbean in protest against French colonial rule and its policy of assimilation, which they felt assumed European cultural superiority. They emphasized the special qualities of African traditions and peoples, and hoped to inspire readers with a desire for independence.

neo-colonialism The control exercised by a state or group of states of the **developed world** over the economies and societies of the **developing world**. Although the latter countries may be legally independent, investment and economic control are often accompanied by political manipulation.

Neolithic (NEE-o-lith-ick) "New Stone Age"—the last division of the Stone Age, immediately preceding the development of metallurgy and corresponding to the ninth–fifth millennia B.C.E. It was characterized by the increasing domestication of animals and cultivation of crops, established agricultural communities, and the appearance of such crafts as pottery and weaving. Although tools and weapons were still made of stone, technological improvements enabled these to be ground and polished rather than flaked and chipped.

Neoplatonic (nee-o-PLAH-ton-ick) A philosophical system founded by Plotinus (205–270 C.E.) and influenced by Plato's theory of ideas. It emphasizes the transcendent, impersonal, and indefinable "One" as the ground of all existence and the source of an eternal world of goodness, beauty, and order, of which material existence is but a feeble copy. By cultivating the intellect and rejecting the material world, humans may become mystically united with the One. Neoplatonism, the last school of Greek philosophy, influenced both Christian theology and Islamic philosophy.

New Testament The second part of the Christian bible, written in Greek and containing the writings attributed to the first followers of Jesus. The twenty-seven books fall into four parts: the four Gospels, dealing with life of Christ; the Acts of the Apostles, concerning the early life of the Church; the Epistles (or letters), written mainly by St Paul; and the Book of Revelation. The canon was established by the end of the fourth century C.E.; the title indicates the Christian belief that Christ's life, death, and resurrection fulfilled prophecies in the Hebrew scriptures, the Old Testament.

oppida (OP-ee-dah) Large permanent settlements of the Celtic or Iron Age peoples of northwestern Europe. Fortified and usually on a raised site, they were often densely populated and housed specialist craftsmen, such as smiths and glassmakers. In the Roman world *oppidum* was a term of administrative law for a town to which no territory was juridically attached; it also applied to a provincial community of Roman citizens.

ordo (OR-doe) A military camp of considerable importance among the central Asian steppe peoples.

pacifism The belief that war can never be justified, and that arbitration should be used in place of force. It has a long history in the Buddhist, Jain, and Christian traditions, though the word itself was coined in the twentieth century. In recent centuries it has been held most notably by the Society of Friends (Quakers), the Plymouth Brethren, and Mahatma Gandhi and his followers.

Paleolithic (PAY-lee-o-lith-ick) "Old Stone Age"—the first division of the Stone Age (the earliest phase in a system devised in the nineteenth century to classify human technological development). The Paleolithic (c. 1.5 million B.C.E.–10,000 B.C.E.) extends to the end of the last Ice Age and is associated with the emergence of humans, the use of rudimentary tools of chipped stone or bone, and the practice of hunting and gathering. Evidence of painting and sculpture survives from the later, or Upper Paleolithic, period.

paterfamilias (pay-ter-fuh-MILL-ee-us) The head of a family or household in Roman law—always a male—and the only member to have full legal rights. The *paterfamilias* had absolute power over his family, which extended to life and death. The family included not only direct descendants of the *paterfamilias* through the male line, unless emancipated by him, but also adopted members and, in certain cases, wives. On his death, each son would become a *paterfamilias* in his own right.

patriarchy (PAY-tree-ar-kee) A social system in which the father or an elderly male has absolute authority over the family group. It is also applied to a society characterized by male-created and male-dominated institutions.

patrician (puh-TRISH-un) A member of the elite class of ancient Roman citizens. In the early days of the Republic, patricians held a monopoly of state and religious offices, but this privileged position was gradually eroded with the admission of other social classes to office (see **plebeian**).

patrilineal The tracing of ancestry and kinship through the male line only.

patrilocal Residence by a couple in or near the home of the male's family or group.

Pax Americana Literally "American peace," a Latin phrase derived by analogy from Pax Romana (the peace enforced within the boundaries of the Roman empire by Roman rule) to designate the relative tranquility established within the American sphere of influence after World War II.

Pax Romana (PAKS roh-MAHN-uh) The "Roman Peace," that is, the state of comparative concord prevailing within the boundaries of the Roman Empire from the reign of Augustus (27 B.C.E.–14 C.E.) to that of Marcus Aurelius (161–180 C.E.), enforced by Roman rule and military control.

Pentecost The Greek name for a Jewish festival that falls on the fiftieth day after Passover. The name was adopted by the Christian Church to commemorate the descent of the Holy Spirit on the Apostles of Christ and the beginning of their preaching mission on the fiftieth day after the resurrection of Christ at **Easter**.

perestroika (pair-es-TROY-ka) A Russian word meaning "restructuring," used, like **glasnost**, to describe the reforms introduced by the Soviet leader Mikhail Gorbachev after 1985. It marked the development of a more flexible socio-economic system, distinguished by a move to a market-oriented economy, increased private ownership, and decentralization.

phallocracy A feminist term applied to a society ruled by men, in which women are totally marginalized.

philology The study of languages, or comparative linguistics. Philologists identify common characteristics in languages, study their relationships and trace their origins.

philosophes (fee-luh-ZAWFS) A group of eighteenth-century French writers and philosophers who emphasized the supremacy of human reason and advocated freedom of expression and social, economic, and political reform. They included Voltaire, Montesquieu, Rousseau, and Diderot, editor of the *Encyclopédie* (1751–72), which manifested their ideas. The *philosophes* influenced

the ideals of the French Revolution and the American Declaration of Independence.

pictogram (alternative: pictograph) A pictorial symbol or sign representing an object or concept. Prehistoric examples have been found all over the world. Because of the difficulty of representing words other than concrete nouns, writing systems using pictograms generally evolved into those using **ideograms**.

plebeian (plih-BEE-un) A citizen of ancient Rome who was not a member of the privileged patrician class. Plebeians were originally excluded from state and religious offices and forbidden to marry patricians, but from the early fifth century B.C.E. they gradually achieved political equality, gaining admission to all Roman offices. From the later Republican period, the term **plebeian** implied low social class.

plebiscite A direct vote by the people of a district or country on a specific issue. The term usually refers to a choice of nationality, but it may also concern a matter of national policy or a selection of ruler or government.

pogrom (PO-grum) (Russian: "devastation") A violent attack on a minority group. The term is usually applied to attacks on Jews and Jewish property, particularly those that took place in the Russian Empire after the assassination of Alexander II in 1881 as a result of the government's anti-Semitic policy. There were further pogroms in eastern Europe, forcing many Jews to emigrate, and in Nazi Germany.

polis (POE-lis) The city-state of ancient Greece. It comprised not only the town, which was usually walled with a citadel (acropolis) and a market place (**agora**), but also the surrounding countryside. Ideally, the *polis* comprised the citizens, who could reside in either town or country; they participated in the government of the state and its religious affairs, contributed to its defense and economic welfare, and obeyed its laws.

praetor (PREE-tor) In ancient Rome, the name was originally applied to the consul as leader of an army. In 366 B.C.E. a further praetor was elected with special responsibility for the administration of justice in Rome, with the right of military command. Around 242 B.C.E. another praetor was created to deal with lawsuits involving foreigners. Further praetors were subsequently appointed to administer the increasing number of provinces. Under the Empire, the position eventually became an honorary appointment.

pre-history The period of time before written records began, which varied from place to place. In this period the study of human development is dependent on the evidence of material remains, such as stone tools or pottery.

primary source Original evidence for an event or fact, as opposed to reported evidence (*see* **secondary source**).

proletariat In Marxist theory, those who live solely by the sale of their labor, as opposed to the **bourgeoisie**. The term is usually applied to the wage workers engaged in industrial production.

proxy war A war waged between dependent, **client states** of larger, more powerful states that do not become directly involved in the fighting; for example the wars among Ethiopia, Somalia, and Eritrea, backed at different times in the 1970s and 1980s by the USSR and the USA. Civil wars between armed factions within a country, each backed by a different foreign power, as in the Congo in the 1960s, are also referred to as proxy wars.

Puranas (poo-RAH-nuz) A collection of poetic tales in Sanskrit, relating the myths and legends of Hinduism. The Puranas expound such topics as the destruction and creation of the world, the genealogy of the gods and patriarchs, the reigns and times of the heroes, and the history of royal dynasties.

quaestor (KWESS-ter) A junior official in ancient Rome. There were originally two, elected annually, but more were appointed as the empire expanded. Most were financial officials. The minimum age was twenty-five, and on completion of the tenure membership of the Senate was automatically conveyed.

Quran (koo-RAHN) The holy book of Islam, believed to contain the direct and authentic word of God as communicated to his prophet Muhammad in a series of revelations by the angel Gabriel. According to tradition, these were collected in the Quran under the caliph Uthman (d. 656) after Muhammad's death. Written in classical Arabic, the Quran is regarded as infallible and is the principal source of Islamic doctrine and law.

radiocarbon dating A method of estimating the age of organic matter, also known as Carbon-14 dating. Carbon dioxide contains a small proportion of the radioactive isotope carbon-14, which is produced in the upper atmosphere by cosmic rays. It is absorbed by green plants, and passes to animals via the food chain. When the organism dies, the amount of carbon-14 in its tissues steadily decreases, at a known rate. The date of death can thus be estimated by measuring the level of radioactivity. The method is mostly used for dating wood, peat, seeds, hair, textiles, skin, and leather.

raja (rah-SHA) An Indian king or princely ruler.

realpolitik (ray-AHL-poe-lee-teek) A German term meaning practical politics, that is, a policy determined by expediency rather than by ethical or ideological considerations.

Renaissance (REN-ay-sahnz) Literally "rebirth," a French term applied to the cultural and intellectual movement that spread throughout Europe from the fourteenth century. It was characterized by a new interest in Classical civilization, stimulated by the Italian poet Petrarch, and a response to the challenge of its models, which led to pride in contemporary achievement and renewed vigor in the arts and sciences. The new concept of human dignity found its inspiration in **humanism**.

reparations Payments due from defeated powers to the victors of war in compensation for their losses, also known as war indemnities.

repartimiento (ray-par-tee-mee-EN-toh) A system by which the Spanish crown allowed Spanish American colonists to employ Indians for forced labor, whether in agriculture or the mines. This had to be for the production of essential food or goods, and was for limited periods, but there was much abuse. (*See* **mita**.)

republic A state that is not ruled by a hereditary leader (a monarchy) but by a person or persons appointed under the constitution. The head of state may be elected and may or may not play a political role.

res publica (RAYS POO-bli-kah) The Latin term for a state in which all the citizens participate in government

sacrament In Christian theology, a rite or ritual that is an outward sign of a spiritual grace conveyed on the believer by Christ through the ministry of the Church. In the Orthodox and Roman Catholic Churches seven sacraments are recognized: baptism, confirmation, penance, the Eucharist, marriage, ordination, and anointing of the sick. The two most important of these, baptism and the **Eucharist**, are the only sacraments recognized by most Protestant Churches.

sahel (sah-HAYL) "Shore"—the northern and southern edges of the Sahara Desert. A semi-arid region of Africa, extending from Senegal eastwards to the Sudan and forming a transitional zone between the Sahara desert to the north and the belt

of **savanna** to the south. The area is dry for most of the year, with a short and unreliable rainy season, and is subject to long periods of drought. Low-growing grasses provide pasture for camels, pack oxen, cattle and sheep.

samizdat (SAHM-is-DAHT) From the Russian *sam-*, "self-", and *izdatel'stvo*, "publishing house." Literature printed (often in typescript) and circulated secretly to evade official suppression and punishment by the government; also this illegal, underground system of private publication.

samurai A member of the warrior class of feudal Japan, who became vassals of the **daimyo**. Characterized by their military skills and stoical pride, they valued personal loyalty, bravery, and honor more than life. During the peaceful years of the Tokugawa **shogunate** (1603–1867) they became scholars, bureaucrats, and merchants. The class was officially abolished in 1871.

sansculottes (sanz-koo-LAHT) (French: "without knee-breeches") In the French Revolution, members of the militant, generally poorer classes of Paris, so-called because they wore trousers rather than the knee-breeches of affluent society. The dress was also adopted by political activists. The name was proscribed after the fall of Robespierre in 1794.

sati (suttee) (sah-TEE) An ancient Hindu custom that requires widows to be burned on the funeral pyre of their husbands, or soon afterwards. The practice of self-immolation was officially abolished in British India in 1829.

satrapy (SAY-truh-pee) A province or colony in the Achaemenid or Persian Empire ruled by a satrap or governor. Darius I completed the division of the Empire into provinces, and established 20 satrapies with their annual tributes. The term satrapy can also refer to the period of rule of a satrap.

satyagraha (sut-yah-grah-hah) A Hindi expression meaning "truth force," applied to Gandhi's policy of non-violent opposition to British rule in India.

savanna (sah-VAN-ah) The grassland areas of the tropics and sub-tropics adjacent to the equatorial rain forests in each hemisphere and bordered by arid regions of desert. Savannas cover extensive parts of Africa, South America, and northern Australia. The natural vegetation is mainly grass with scattered shrubs and trees, the latter low and often flat-topped. The land is particularly suitable for cattle rearing.

scorched earth A strategy of defensive warfare, in which everything that might be of use to an invading army is destroyed

by the defending army as it retreats. Practiced by Russia in its retreat before the armies of Napoleon and, later, of Nazi Germany; also practiced by the Chinese in the face of Japanese invasion in the 1930s and 1940s.

secondary source Reported evidence for an event or fact, as opposed to original evidence (*see* **primary source**).

serf An agricultural worker or peasant bound to the land and legally dependent on the lord, characteristic of the **manorial economy** and the **feudal** system. Serfs had their own homes, plots, and livestock but they owed the lord labor, dues, and services. These services could be commuted to rent, but serfs remained chattels of the lord unless they were emancipated by him or her, or escaped. Serfdom declined in western Europe in the late medieval period, but persisted in parts of eastern Europe until the nineteenth century.

shaman (SHAH-men) In the religious beliefs of some Asian and American tribal societies, a person capable of entering into trances and believed to be endowed with supernatural powers, with the ability to cure the sick, find lost or stolen property, predict the future, and protect the community from evil spirits. A shaman may act as judge or ruler, and as a priest a shaman directs communal sacrifices and escorts the souls of the dead to the next world.

shari'a (sha-REE-ah) The "road" or sacred revealed law of Islam, based on the Quran and the traditional teachings of Muhammad. Since Islam does not distinguish between the religious and the secular spheres, Islamic law applies to every aspect of life. It covers such matters as marriage, divorce, inheritance, diet, and civil and criminal law.

shogun (SHOW-gun) The military dictator of Japan, a hereditary title held by three families between 1192 and 1867. Although they were legally subservient to the emperor, their military power gave them effective control of the country, and they also took on judicial and administrative functions. The Tokugawa Shogunate (1603–1867) established a powerful centralized government at Edo (Tokyo). Imperial rule was restored in 1868.

shogunate The government of the **shogun**.

signares (SEEN-yahr-es) African concubines of French traders in the Senegambia.

sinicization (sigh-ne-sigh-ZAY-shen) The adoption and absorption by foreign peoples of Chinese language, customs and culture.

social contract A mythical, underwritten agreement made at an early stage of human development among citizens in creating a government, or between citizens and a ruler, which defines the rights and obligations of each party to the contract. The citizens accept the authority of the state; and the state agrees to act only with the consent of the governed. The idea goes back to Plato and became influential in seventeenth- and eighteenth-century western Europe through the writings of Hobbes, Locke, and Rousseau.

sophist (SOF-ist) An itinerant professor of higher education in ancient Greece, who gave instruction for a fee. The subjects taught, which included oratory, grammar, ethics, mathematics, and literature, had the practical aim of equipping pupils for successful careers. The sophists were criticized for their ability to argue for any point of view regardless of its truth and for their emphasis on material success. They were prominent in the fifth and early fourth centuries B.C.E.

soviet A council, the primary unit of government in the Soviet Union at local, regional, and national levels, also adopted by other Communist regimes. Committees of workers' elected deputies first appeared in 1905 to coordinate revolutionary activities; they sprang up throughout the Russian Empire and were a crucial agent in the Revolution of 1917, forming the basis of Soviet administration thereafter.

statism The concentration of economic controls and planning in the hands of a highly centralized government; and the political philosophy advocating this system.

stela or **stele** (sing.); **stelae** (pl.) A freestanding upright slab, often bearing inscriptions or carved ornamentation. They are usually associated with temples and palaces and are carved with hieroglyphic inscriptions recording the exploits and genealogies of rulers.

Sufi (SOO-fee) In Islam, a member of one of the orders practicing mystical forms of worship that first arose in the eighth and ninth centuries C.E. Sufis interpret the words of Muhammad in a spiritual rather than a literal sense. Their goal is direct personal experience of God, achieved by fervent worship (*see* **tariqa**).

supply and demand In economics, the relationship between the amount of a commodity that producers are able and willing to sell (supply), and the quantity that consumers can afford and wish to buy (demand). The price fluctuates according to a product's availability and its desirability. Supply and demand thus controls a **free market economy**. In practice it is usually subject to some degree of regulation.

Sutta (SOOT-eh) The second section of the Buddhist scriptures or **Tripitaka**, the others being the **Abhidhamma** and the **Vinaya**. It contains the basic teachings of Buddhism, attributed to the Buddha himself, and expounded in a series of discourses in a lively and engaging style, employing allegories and parables. It also includes birth stories of the Buddha and other material.

swadeshi (svah-day-shee) "Of one's own country," a Hindi word used as a slogan in the Indian boycott of foreign goods, part of the protest against Britain's partition of Bengal in 1905. The Indian people were urged to use indigenous goods and to wear garments of *khadi*, homemade cloth.

swaraj (svah-raj) A Hindi word meaning "self-government" or "home rule," used as a slogan by Indian nationalists in their campaign for independence from British rule.

syncretism (SING-kri-tiz-ehm) The attempt to combine or harmonize doctrines and practices from different philosophical schools or religious traditions, or the absorption of foreign elements into one particular religion.

syllabary (SIL-eh-ber-ee) A writing system in which each symbol represents the syllable of a word (cf. ideogram). The system appears to have been used for some ancient Near Eastern languages, but Japanese is the only modern-day language to use a syllabary.

TaNaKh (tah-NAKH) A Hebrew term for the books of the Bible that are written in Hebrew. The word is composed of the initial letters of the words Torah (first five books of the Bible, traditionally attributed to Moses), Nevi'im (the books of the Prophets) and the Ketuvim (additional historical, poetic, and philosophic writings). This threefold division of the Bible is commonly found in the Talmud.

tariqa (tah-REE-cah) In Islam a generic term meaning "path," referring to the doctrines and methods of mysticism and esoterism. The word also refers to schools or brotherhoods of mystics, which were often situated at a mosque or the tomb of a Muslim saint.

technopolis A town or geographical area devoted to technological research and development.

teleology (tay-lee-OHL-o-gee) From the Greek word *telos*, "end," the philosophical study of final causes or purposes. A "final cause" is an event in the future for the sake of which an occurrence takes place. Teleology refers especially to any system that interprets nature or the universe as having design or purpose. It has been used to provide evidence for the existence of God.

themes A theme was originally a military unit stationed in one of the provinces of the Byzantine empire, but it later applied to the large military districts that formed buffer zones in the areas most vulnerable to Muslim invasion. By the ninth century the system was extended throughout the empire. Soldiers were given farms in the themes in exchange for military service, but they were later able to commute this for tax, which led to the decline of the system.

theocracy A system of government administered by priests or other religious body, in which God is regarded as the immediate ruler.

thermoluminescence A dating technique used for pottery or other fired material. Electrons produced by radiation will be trapped in the flaws of a crystal lattice, but will be liberated in the form of light when heated. The light emissions occur at a constant rate and can be measured when the substance is reheated, and correlated to the duration of exposure to radiation. The period of time that has elapsed since the crystal was last heated can then be estimated.

third world The countries outside the **first world** and the second world (countries with socialist state systems); more loosely, the **developing world**, which contains more than 70 percent of world population. The twenty-five least developed countries are sometimes characterized as "fourth world."

transhumance (trans-YOO-menz) A form of pastoralism or nomadism organized around the seasonal migration of livestock, practiced in areas that are too cold or wet for winter grazing. The animals are moved to mountain pastures in warm seasons and to lowland ones in winter, or between lower and upper latitudes, or between wet- and dry-season grazing areas.

trebuchet (TRAY-boo-shay) A military engine for hurling heavy missiles, operated by counterpoise, on the principle of the seesaw. Developed in China, the trebuchet first appeared in Europe in the twelfth century.

tribals The aboriginal peoples of the Indian sub-continent, who are outside the **caste** system and live quite separately from the rest of society, generally in remote places. They are thought to have migrated to India in pre-historic times, probably before the emergence of Hinduism.

tribune (TRIB-yoon) In ancient Rome, a **plebeian** officer elected by the plebeians and charged to protect their lives and properties, with a right of veto against legislative proposals of the Senate. The office was instituted during the fifth century B.C.E. and had great political influence under the Republic, but it lost its independence and most practical functions in the time of Augustus (27 B.C.E.–14 C.E.). Military tribunes were senior officers of the legions, elected by the people.

Tripitaka (try-PIT-eh-keh) The Sanskrit term for the Buddhist scriptures, the Pali Tipitaka or "threefold collection." It comprises the *Vinaya-pitaka*, which concerns the history, regulations, and discipline of Buddhism; the *Sutta-pitaka*, the fundamental teaching of Buddhism, attributed to the Buddha himself; and the *Abhidhamma-pitaka*, which are metaphysical speculations aimed at dissolving any mental resistance or rigidity that might stand in the way of authentic spiritual insight.

triumvirate (try-UM-vihr-ate) In ancient Rome a board of three men appointed for special administrative duties. An unofficial coalition between Julius Caesar, Pompey, and Crassus was formed in 60 B.C.E. After Caesar's murder in 44 B.C.E., a triumvirate that included his heir Octavian (later Augustus), Mark Antony, and Marcus Lepidus was appointed to maintain public order; it held almost absolute powers and lasted until 36 B.C.E.

ulama (OO-leh-ma) The theologians and legal experts of Islam. The *ulama* form a body of scholars who are competent to decide on religious matters. They include the imams of important mosques, teachers in religious faculties in universities, and judges.

umma (UM-ma) The community of believers in Islam, which transcends ethnic and political boundaries.

untouchables Members of the lowest castes of traditional Indian society or those outside the caste system; the "untouchable" groups were those engaged in "polluting" activities.

Vedas (VAY-duz) Sacred Hindu hymns or verses composed in Sanskrit around 1500–1000 B.C.E. Many Vedas were recited or chanted during rituals; they are largely concerned with the sacrificial worship of gods representing natural and cosmic forces. The foremost collection is the *Rigveda*, followed by the *Samaveda*, *Yajurveda*, and *Atharvaveda*; the *Brahmanas*, *Aranyakas*, and *Upanishads* are later commentaries but are also considered canonical.

Vinaya (VIN-eh-yeh) The first part of the Buddhist scriptures, or **Tripitaka**. It concerns the early history, regulations, and discipline of Buddhism, focusing in particular on rules for monks and nuns and on such practical subjects as ordination, holy days, dress, food, and medicine.

vodoun The popular religious cult of Haiti, as well as other areas of the Caribbean. It combines ritual elements from Roman Catholicism with theological and magical elements of West African origin. Vodoun ritual centers on animal sacrifice, drumming, and dance, and contact with a populous spirit world through trance.

warlord A local Chinese despot with a private army. The warlords attempted to seize power after the death of Yuan Shihkai, first president of Republican China, in 1916; their civil war was ended when Chiang Kai-shek unified the country in 1928. They continued to exert power until the Communist government took over in 1949.

web browser A software program that enables a user to find and retrieve information from the networked information services on the World Wide Web. The most common examples are Netscape Navigator and Microsoft Internet Explorer.

Yurt (YOORT) A portable dwelling used by the nomadic people of Central Asia, consisting of a tentlike structure of skin, felt or hand-woven textiles arranged over wooden poles, simply furnished with brightly colored rugs.

zaibatsu (zai-ba-tsoo) (Japanese: "wealthy clique") A large Japanese business corporation, usually under the control of a single family. A *zaibatsu* was a form of **cartel**, engaging in all important areas of economic activity and funded by its own bank. They emerged under the modernizing Meiji government (1867–1912) and were dissolved by the Allies in 1946 after World War II.

zemstvo (ZEMPST-voh) A rural council in the Russian Empire, established by Czar Alexander II in 1864 and abolished in 1917. The assemblies, which operated at both district and provincial level, comprised the representatives of individual landed proprietors and village communes (**mir**). They were concerned with such matters as primary education, road building, agricultural development, and public health.

ziggurat (ZIG-gu-rat) A temple tower of ancient Mesopotamia, constructed of square or rectangular terraces of diminishing size, usually with a shrine on top built of blue enamel bricks, the color of the sky. They were constructed of mud brick, often with a baked brick covering, and ascended by flights of steps or a spiral ramp. The sloping sides and terraces were sometimes planted with shrubs and trees. There were ziggurats in every important Sumerian, Babylonian, and Assyrian center.

zimbabwes (zim-BAHB-ways) Stone-walled enclosures or buildings built during the African Iron Age in the region of modern Zimbabwe and Mozambique. The structures were the courts of local rulers. They have been associated with foreign trade, integrated farming and animal husbandry, and gold production. The Great Zimbabwe is the ruins of the former capital of the Monomatapa Empire, situated in Zimbabwe and occupied from around the thirteenth to the sixteenth century C.E.

INDEX

Bold page numbers refer to picture
captions and to maps

American Declaration of Independence 489, **492**

American Federation of Labor 536

American Railway Union 536

American Revolution (War of American Independence) 426, **459**, 479, 480, 491-2, 493-4, 515

Americas, the: agriculture 40, 95, 102, 376; European discovery I-12, 373, 407; Pre-Columbian 378; *see also* Amerindians; Latin America; North America; United States

Amerindians/Native Americans I-12, 102, **102**, 410, 414, 456, 458, 459-60, 494, 509, 577, **801**, 800-2; classic cultures **96**, Aztecs; Inca civilization; Maya Indians *etc*

Amin, Idi 744, 759, 772

Amitabha (Amida) Buddha 278, 279, 287, 290

Ammianus Marcellinus 187, 321

Amnesty International 808

Amon (Egyptian deity) 73

Amon-Re (Egyptian deity) 73

Amorites, the 60, 124

Amos, Prophet 303

Amritsar massacre 694-5

Amsterdam 414, 422-3

An Lushan revolt 197, 222, 224, 229, 283

Analects, The (Confucius) 196, 205, 206-7

Anasazi people 102

Anatolia 34, 40, 46, **128**, **129**, 134, 138, 151, 152, 181, 185, 193, 339, 343, 348, 373, 406, 446, 452, 605

Andean civilizations 44, 51, 95, **96**, 105, 376; *see also* Chavín; Chimu, Huari; Inca civilization; Moche; Nazcas; Tiwanaku

Andors, Phyllis 686

Andrew, King of Hungary 361

Angkor Wat 234, 251, **251**, 271, 273

Angles **187**

Anglican Church 260, **415**, 417, 482

Angola 420, 551, 552, 553, 581, 623, 627, 744, 751, 754, 768, 797

animal domestication 21, 25, 34, 40, **41**, 89, 457

Animal Farm (Orwell) I-11

animal paintings, prehistoric 32, **32, 33**

Ankara 350

Annam 224

Anselm, St. 403

anti-Semitism *see* Jews, ghettoization and persecution

Antigone (Sophocles) 146

Antioch 322

Antiochus III, of Syria 163

Antoninus Pius, Emperor 166, 169, 316

Antwerp 399, 409, 414, 419

Anubis (Egyptian deity) 73

Anyang 88, 89, 91, **92**, 93

apartheid 744, 754-5, **755**, 758, 769

Appian Way **168**

Apuleius 160

aqueducts, Roman **167**, 169

Aquinas, St. Thomas 401

Arab League 729

Arabs: and British colonization 605; conquests 63, 192, 193, **218**, 222, 330, 339-40, 342, 448, 470; inventions 405; and Islam 332, 334, 343, 350; Israeli-Arab conflicts 580-1, 736, 737-40; oil producers *see* OPEC; scholars 403; traders **346, 347**; women 338-9, 360; *see also* Bedouins; Berbers; Saudi Arabia

Aramaic 54, 132

Arameans 129

Arbenz, Jacobo 778, 794

Archaean period 12

arches, triumphal **168, 306**

architecture/building: Bauhaus 608; Byzantine 192, **192**; Chinese 226; Egyptian 62, 65; Gothic 330; Greek 144-5, **144, 145**; Hindu **270**; Indus Valley 80; Islamic 356, 359, **359**, 363, *see also* mosques; Japanese **226**, 286, **286, 287**; Mughal **471**, 471-2; Neolithic Chinese 42-3, **43**; Roman **167**, 175, **181**; Teotihuacán 98, **99**; US **561**, 564; zimbabwes 112

Ardipithecus ramidus 15, 17, **18**, 22, 23, 24

Argentina 509, **510**, 511, 513, 776-7, 789-92; agriculture 596; economy 778-9, 780, 789-90, 791, 799

Arianism 321

Arias, Oscar 794

Arikamedu 249

Aristophanes 121, 146

Aristotle 38, 60, 120, 121, 136, 145, 146, 149, 152, 156-7, 355, 375, 403

Arius/Arianism 321

Arjun **236**, 266

Arkwright, Richard 519

Armas, Carlos Castillo 778, 794

Armenia/Armenians 188, 343, 542, 657, 716, 717; Church 326

armies 44; Arab 339-40, 360; Chinese 200, **200**, 210, **210**, 214, 229, 394; French 424, 425, 426; Greek 140, **140**; Japanese 588; Roman 161, 163, 172, 177, 182, 188, 190, 229

armor, first 202

Arnolfini Wedding Portrait, The (van Eyck) 404, **404**

Aro, the 469

Arrian Flavius Arrianus 154

Arses, of Persia 133

Artaxerxes I, of Persia 133

Artaxerxes II, of Persia 133

Artaxerxes III, of Persia 133

Artha-sastra (Kautilya) 231, 232, 235, 247, 261, 262, 263

Artsuko Tsujioka 620

Aryans 78, 83-5, 133, 232, 235, 247, 261, 262, 263

Asante, the 554, 581, 741

Ashikaga Shoguns 374

Ashok *see* Asoka Maurya, Emperor

Ashurbanipal, King of Akkad 5, 39, 57, 129

Asiha 338, 339

Asoka Maurya, Emperor 1-9, 231, **232**, 233-4, 235, 238, **238**, 240-1, **241**, 242, 248, 252, **276**, 278, 285

Assyrians 39, 45, 66, 124, 129, **129**, 130, 294, 296, 306; writing **52**

Astadhyayi (Panini) 246

astrolabes 405

astrology 363

astronomy 49, 334, 355, 356, **485**, 485-6, 487

Aswan Dam 702, 721, 723

Atahualpa, Emperor 412, **412**

Atatürk (General Mustafa Kemal) 716-19, **717**

Aten (Egyptian deity) 70, 71, 73

Atharva Veda 235

atheism 260

Athena (Greek deity) **144**, 145

Athena Nike, temple of (Athens) **145**

Athena Parthenos **145**

Athens 121, 136, 138, 139, 140, 143-6, **145**, 149, 150, 151, 154; Academy 146; Delian League 121, 150; Peloponnesian Wars 121, 143, 146, 148; Persian Wars 131, 138-43; slaves 149; *see also* Acropolis

Athos, Mount 323

atomic bombs **593**, 619, **619**, 622, 705, 710; *see also* Hiroshima, bombing of

Attalus I, of Pergamum **156**

Attila the Hun 188, 190, 246

Augustine, St., Bishop of Hippo 160, 169, 295, 319, **319**, 320, 322, 396, 401

Augustus, Emperor 159, 165-6, **165**, 169, 172-3, 174, 175, 177, 178, 182, 183, 186, 249

Aurangzeb, Emperor 436, 448, 472

Aurelian, Emperor 188, 189

Aurignacian period 5, **24**, 26, 29, **29**

Auschwitz concentration camp 617, 620

Australia 444, 456; agriculture 596; British settlement 460, **460**, 461, 462, 463; cave art 30-1; urbanization 560

Australopithecus 5, **9**, 14; *A. afarensis* 15, **15**, **16**, **18**, 23, 24; *A. africanus* 13, **19**; *A. boisei* **19**, 23; *A. robustus* 23

Austria 165, 185, 329, 490, 534, 578, 580, 609; *see also* Austro-Hungarian Empire

Austro-Hungarian Empire 602, 605

Avalokiteshvara 279

Averroes *see* Ibn Rushd

Avicenna *see* Ibn Sina

Awka, the 469

Ayuthia 271

Azikiwe, Nnamdi 743, 747

Azilian tools 29

Aztecs **I-13**, 94, **96**, 100, 105, 374, 376-7, **378**, 456

Ba'ath Party 726

Babur **447**, 448, 449

Babylon/Babylonians 39, 45, 52, 66, 82, 118, 124, 128, 129, **129**, 130, 131, 152, 154, 255, 304-5, 306

Bacchus (Roman deity) 183, 184

Bactra 180

Bactria 211, 246

Badis, Ben 733

Baghdad 307-8, 322, 329, 333, 334, 335, 343, 344, 348, 349, 351, 354, 355, 356, 373, 383, 384, 627; Pact (1955) 726, 728

Baha'is 260

Indra (Indian deity) 83, 263
Indus Valley civilization 44, 62, 77-85, **79**, **81**, **82**, **83**, **84**, 116, 152, 232, 235, 247, 261
Industrial Revolution/industrialization 432, 456, 476-7, 484, 517-24, **521**; and ecology 629; factory production 528-9; and gender relationships 569-71, 574; and imperialism 554-5; and population shifts 530; and social changes 530-2; and urbanization 558, 559, 560; and warfare 529; see also specific countries
Innocent III, Pope 322, 363
Inquisition: Roman 487; Spanish I-12, 363, 419
internal combustion engine 525
international corporations 634-5, 637
International Ladies Garment Workers' Union 536
International Monetary Fund 674, 789
international organizations 630; see also League of Nations; United Nations
Internet 599, 600, 636
Intrigues of the Warring States 196
inventions 405, 518-19, 524, 525, 528, 529
Ionian Revolt 121
Iqbal, Muhammad 719
Iran 133, 152, 180, 348, 355, 452, 713, 715, 724, 725, 727-9, 793; women 725-6, **728**, 729; see also Persia
Iraq 605, 715, 724, 725, 726-7, 733
Ireland 186
Ireton, General Henry 483
iron and iron industry 78, 82, 112, 113, 200, 520, **521**
irrigation systems 44, 56; Chimu 107; China 90, 200; Egypt 63, 69, 77; Moche 106-7; Muslim 356; Sumerian 46, 49; see also dams
Isaac 300
Isabella, of Castile see Ferdinand and Isabella
Isaiah, Prophet 302-3, 313
Isfahan 356, **359**, 452, 472
Ishmael 300
Isis (Egyptian deity) 72, 73
Islam/Muslims 192, 256, 260, 291, 325, **326**, 327, 332, **341**, **346**, 366-7, **415**, 446, 549, 633, 726-7, 728-9; in Africa **347**, 347-8, 350, 758, 760; agriculture 356; architecture 356, 359, **359**, 363, see also mosques; caliphate 339-44; and Christianity 321, 323, 327, 336, 338, 339, 360-3, 366-7; *dhimmi* status 346, 361; in Egypt 63; Five Pillars 336, 338; in India 262, 281, 342, 344-6, 373, 694, 699, 704, see also Mughal Empire; and Jews and Judaism 293-4, 336, 338, 339; mausolea 359; philosophers 333, 355, 363; *shari'a* (law) 338, 350, 358; Shi'as/Shi'ites and Sunnis 341, 342, 343, 344, **345**, 351, 452, 726, 727; in Spain 327, 329, 342, 347, 356, **357**, 358, 363-6, 403, see also *reconquista*; and trade 115, 222, 358, 382, 383; in Turkey 717, 719; and women 334-5, 338-9, 360; see also Ismailis; Muhammad, Prophet; Quran; Sufis
Islamabad: King Faisal Mosque 730, **730**

Ismaelis 341, 342, 344, 356
Isma'il, Shah 452
Israel 293, 294, 296, 301, 302, 303, 304, 305; Arab-Israeli conflict 580-1, 736, 737-40; Six Day War 723; State of 627, 669, 713, 715, 718, 719, 736, 737, **739**; see also Jews; Judaism
Israelites 124
Issus, battle of 151, **153**, 171
Istanbul **192**, 358, 472-3, 542, 605, 730, see also Constantinople
Italy: colonies **550**, 553, 554, **576**, **746**; invasion of Ethiopia 553-4, 606, 609, 610, 745-6; medieval 374, 397-8, 399, **400**; Renaissance 402-6; unification 578, **579**, 579-80; World War II 609; see also Etruscans; Florence; Milan; Roman Republic; Venice
Ivan III ("the Great"), Czar 432
Ivory Coast see Côte d'Ivoire
Iwakura Tonomi, Prince 584

Jackson, President Andrew 494
Jackson, Frederick 493
Jacobins 499, 566
jade 377, 386; burial suit **196**
Jahaanke, the 469
Jainism 233, 238, 260, 279, **279**
Jakarta 423, 557
Jamaica 456
James I, of England 481
James II, of England 482
janapadas 232, 239
Japan 373, 642-3, **576**, 582, **587**; agriculture 40, 585, 667; and China 195, 205, 217, **225**, 225-6, **226**, 228, 285, 286, **286**, 437-8, 548, 581, 582, 588-9, 606, 609, 663, 665, 687; Christianity 418, 438-9; comics **660**; economy 668-9, 670-1, 673, 675, 693; education 588, 668; energy resources 601; "guest workers" 672; Heian period 286; historical revisionism 668; industrialization and industry 557, 585-6, 661-2, 663, **671**, 672; interwar militarism 662-3; Jomon people 34, 41, 226; *kamis* 283, 285; and Korea see Korea; labor unions 667-8; life expectancy 596; literature 290; Meiji regime 583-5, 587-8, 659; and Mongols 384; pirates 437; pollution 669-70, **670**; population 586, 672; railroad 669; religions see Buddhism, Shinto; Russo-Japanese war 589, 644; samurai 582, 583, 588, 662, **662**; shogunates 374, 439, 582-3, 586, 588; Taiko reforms 227; trade 423, 438, 439, 582, 588; urbanization 586-7; US Occupation 666-8; women 672-3; work ethic 668, 672; World War I 602, 605, 659, 661; World War II 609-10, 611, 613-14, **614**, 619, 620, **663**, **664**, 665-6, **666**, 668; writing 226, 287; *zaibatsu* 661-2, 667
Jarrige, Jean-François 78-9
Java, Indonesia 42?, 468, 540, 542, 543; Borobudur 234, **250**, 2?1
Java Man 12-13
Jayavarman II, of Khmer 251
Jayavarman VII, of Khmer 251, 273

Jeddah: Corniche Mosque 730, **731**
Jefferson, Thomas 492
Jehangir 448
Jehovah 300
Jemaa, Nigeria: head **113**
Jenne 112, **381**
Jenne-jeno 44, 112, 113-16, **114**, 117
Jeremiah, Prophet 303
Jericho 46, **46**
Jerome, Saint 259
Jerusalem **300**, 302, 313, 322, 356, **738**; al-Aqsa 342; and Crusades 361-3; Dome of the Rock 255, **342**, 362; Muslim conquest 323, 334, 339, 361, 373; Roman conquest 164, 177, 305; Temples 131, 160, 177, 294, 298, 305, **305**, 307
Jesuits (Society of Jesus) 418, 438, 449
Jesus 184, 257, 261, 279, 294, 308-13, 336; disciples 308, 309, 313; miracles 313; Sermon on the Mount 310
jewelry 49, 94, 108, 109, **139**
Jewish Revolt 160, 177, **307**
Jews 131, 169, 260, 294, 301-2, 304-6, 322, 344; diaspora 306-8, **307**, 382; in France 498, 501; ghettoization and persecution 374, 401, 472, see also Holocaust; Holocaust I-12, 608, 611, 612-13, **613**, 736; in India 382; in Spain 363, 374, 407; traders **382**, 382-3, 401; see also Israel; Judaism; Zionism
Jiang Qing 690, 692
jihad 336
Jin dynasty 197, 215, 224
Jinan: Hill of the Thousand Buddhas **216**
Jingdi, Emperor **196**, 198
Jinnah, Muhammad ali 697, 699, 704
Job 301
Johannisberg **749**
Johanson, Donald 15, 23
John the Baptist, St. 310
John, St. **312**; Gospel 309
John, St., of Damascus 324
John, King of Jerusalem 361
John II, of Portugal **420**
John (João) VI, Dom, of Portugal 511
John Paul II, Pope 487, 656, **656**, 657, 803
Johnson, President Lyndon B. 633
joint-stock companies 424, 436; see also East India Company
Jomon people, Japan 34, 41, 226
Jordan 725, **739**
Jordan River valley 40
Joseph. St. 309
Josep?. ?, Emperor of Austria 490
Josephus 169
Josiah 296
Judaea 131, 177, 294, 304, 308, **308**, 309
Judah 296, 302, 303
Judaism 256, 257, 291, 293; and Christianity 293-4, 308, 366-7; festivals 298, 303; and Islam 293-4, 336, 338, 339; and scriptures 294-7, 300-4; and women 304; see also Torah
Jurassic period 12
Justinian I, Emperor 160, 178, 191-2, **323**
Jutes 187

comparative handful chose the more difficult, nationalistic route to Palestine. But then anti-Semitism resurfaced strongly in the 1890s in France. Assimilated Jews of Western Europe were shocked. The Austrian-Jewish journalist Theodor Herzl founded the modern political Zionist movement— "Zion" is a Biblical designation for Jerusalem—to restore to Jews a political homeland in their ancestral land of Palestine (see p. 580). At this time, with the Ottoman Empire still in place, and the period of the mandates far in the future, Arab nationalism had not yet surfaced. But, as we have seen above, by the 1920s, conditions had changed. The two nascent nationalisms, Arab and Zionist, grew up together, and were soon fighting for control of the same land.

The Struggle against Neo-colonialism

According to a third emplotment, Jews and Arabs were both incidental players in a story of European colonialism. In 1917, the British government issued the Balfour Declaration, redistributing parts of the conquered Ottoman Empire:

> His Majesty's Government view with favour the establishment in Palestine of a national home for the Jewish people, and will use their best endeavours to facilitate the achievement of this objective, it being clearly understood that nothing shall be done which may prejudice the civil and religious rights of existing non-Jewish communities in Palestine.

Through this declaration Britain inserted a foreign, Western-oriented political entity into the middle of the Middle East, fostering a politics of divide-and-rule. Zionists reading the declaration have emphasized "the establishment … of a national home for the Jewish people," while Arabs have stressed "nothing shall be done which may prejudice the civil and religious rights of existing non-Jewish communities." In this version of the story, Britain wrote the script; Arabs and Jews simply followed through, playing their assigned, antagonistic roles.

The nature of early Zionist settlement in the early twentieth century reinforced this colonial reading in Arab eyes. The Jewish immigrants, "pioneers" as they called themselves, came mostly from cities and small towns in eastern and central Europe. They had European educations, philosophies, technologies, and attitudes, and they usually viewed the Arabs among whom they settled as educationally backward and technologically primitive nomadic and farming peoples. Many of the Jewish settlers built egalitarian collective farms, **kibbutzim**, to maximize agricultural efficiency, achieve a social vision, and provide for their common defense. By contrast, they saw the local agricultural arrangements between *effendi* (landlords) and *fellahin* (tenants) as exploitative. The Zionists argued, with a kind of colonial paternalism, that they could help reform and modernize the land and the people. To some degree, with new medicine, farming, education, and industrial technology they were correct, but they took little account of the displacement of local society caused by their arrival and the anger it evoked. Armed Arab uprisings attempted unsuccessfully to halt and drive out Jewish immigration from the 1920s onward.

THE CREATION OF ISRAEL 1948

All three "stories," established by 1920, also influenced subsequent interpretations. For example, a central factor in the creation of Israel in 1948 was the Holocaust. For Jews, that catastrophe reaffirmed the desperate need for a political state and refuge, and they redoubled their efforts to achieve it. They tended to (mis)interpret the efforts of Arabs to block the creation of Israel, not as a struggle over control of land, but as a new Nazism, intent on root-and-branch destruction. This portrayal increased Jewish fear of, and opposition to, Arab concerns, and an Arab rhetoric of violence reinforced their apprehension. Arabs asked pointedly: Why should Christian guilt over a Holocaust in Europe be expiated by assigning to Jews lands held by Muslims in the eastern Mediterranean? Surely this was European colonialism parading as humanitarianism at Arab expense.

ARAB–ISRAELI CONFLICT

Another ironic reconstitution of the core stories grew out of the displacement of Palestinians from their homes in Israel. With the establishment of the State of Israel in 1948, and later with Israeli occupation of the West Bank of the Jordan River after the 1967 war, many Palestinians left, becoming the "wandering Jews" of the Middle East. Palestinians generally argue that they were forced out by armed intimidation; Jews claim that Palestinians followed their leaders' advice that they leave temporarily in order to return later in armed triumph. A great outpouring of revisionist historical writing by Israeli authors such as Benny Morris has provided documentary evidence on both sides. Whatever the immediate cause, some 600,000 Palestinians fled the borders of Israel at the time of the establishment of the State and the 1948 war. During and after the 1967 war still more left. Over the decades their numbers have multiplied to several millions.

Israelis apparently believed that the neighboring Arab states would absorb these exiles, as Israel absorbed more than a million Jews who immigrated from Arab states after 1948, either pulled by the attraction of a Jewish homeland or pushed by fear of future reprisals by Arabs. But the Arab states chose to leave the Palestinians in refugee status, living in refugee camps, or seeking employment in the oil fields, or leaving the area. The result has been a bitter irridentism, a desire to reclaim their homeland, represented among Palestinians primarily by the Palestine Liberation Organization (after 1996 the Palestine National Authority); militant hostility towards Israel; and unsettled refugee groups that threaten the stablility of neighboring states.

Israel's 1967 conquest of the West Bank and Gaza strip inflamed the tensions by placing one and a half million Palestinians under direct Israeli military occupation. The Palestinians wanted to establish a state of their own in this land. Fearing these territorial ambitions for a Palestinian state, the Israelis refused to end the occupation. In effect, the Israeli–Arab conflict now had two inter-related dimensions. The first was the internal struggle between two nations—Israel and a Palestine-striving-to-be-born—inhabiting a single geographical land. The second was the international strife between Israel and the surrounding Arab states. Through the 1970s and early 1980s, attacks within Israeli borders and terrorist attacks against international travellers, especially in airports and airplanes, and against the Israeli participants in the 1972 Munich Olympics, expressed Palestinian anger; Israeli bombings of refugee camps were a common response. In 1987 Palestinians in the West Bank and Gaza regions began the *intifada* (uprising), employing both civil disobedience and low-intensity violence in a pattern of continuous demonstrations to disrupt Israeli control. Israel cracked down and hardened its positions.

A major breakthrough in the external warfare came with the Egyptian peace treaty of 1979 (see p. 723). Further possibilities opened in the early 1990s as the Soviet Union dissolved, ending the superpower rivalries that had helped militarize the Middle East, and as wars against Iraq led to divisions and re-alignments among Arab states, perhaps allowing new openings toward Israel, too.

A breakthrough in the internal Israeli–Palestinian conflict came in 1993, when the government of Israel and the Palestine Liberation Organization signed an agreement to recognize each other, to cease fighting, and to extend at least limited self-rule to the Palestinians in Gaza and the West Bank. The assassination of Israeli Prime Minister Yitzhak Rabin by a Jewish extremist in 1995, followed by Arab militant attacks on Israeli buses later in the year, crippled the movement toward peace and indicated just how fragmented were the forces on both sides. The election of Benjamin Netanyahu as Israel's prime minister in 1996 slowed the "peace process." The election of his successor Ehud Barak in 1999 moved it forward. Dialogues are continuing.

Arabs fighting behind the walls of Jerusalem Old City, March 1948. The UN resolution that created the state of Israel in 1948 declared Jerusalem an international city. On the ground, however, Arabs and Jews fought bitterly over the city, partitioning it with walls and barbed wire into separate sections.

The peace agreements between Israel and the Palestinians opened the way for other Arab nations to normalize their relations with Israel. Jordan, under King Hussein, signed a peace treaty in 1994, and discussions were underway with Syria in 2000.

Israel itself had many internal problems: continuing social tensions among the amazingly diverse immigrant groups which have come to the country since 1948, especially between the Ashkenazic half from Europe and the Sephardic half from the Arab states themselves; assimilation of the hundreds of thousands of eastern European Jews seeking refuge after the USSR and its allies opened their gates to emigration in the 1980s; continuing religious antag-onism between the small minority of orthodox Jews and the vast majority who are secular; and wary apprehension between the 82 percent of Israel's population who are Jews and the 18 percent who are Arabs.

Israel had accomplished much of its nationalist, Zionist agenda, providing a home to 4.7 million Jews (as well as 1 million Arabs), almost all of them immigrants or the immediate descendants of immigrants who had arrived within the last century. Culturally they had taken the ancient Hebrew language and recreated it as a vehicle for everyday life, and for modern literature as well. They had done all this within a generally democratic framework,

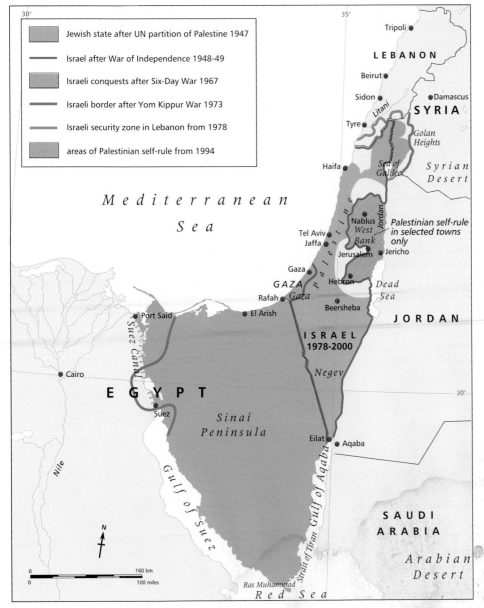

Legend:
- Jewish state after UN partition of Palestine 1947
- Israel after War of Independence 1948-49
- Israeli conquests after Six-Day War 1967
- Israeli border after Yom Kippur War 1973
- Israeli security zone in Lebanon from 1978
- areas of Palestinian self-rule from 1994

Israel and its neighbors. The creation, with Western support, of a Jewish homeland in Palestine in 1947 occurred at a time of increasing Arab nationalism. Israel's birth in 1948 was attended by war and more followed in 1956, 1967, 1973, and 1982. Peace treaties exist only with Egypt, which regained the Sinai peninsula, and Jordan (1994). Beginning in 1987, an *intifada* (uprising) by Palestinians has forced more attention on Israeli–Palestinian relations—an extremely vexed issue. In 1993, the Palestinian Liberation Organization and Israel began negotiations that would return land to Palestinian control and perhaps lead to a Palestinian state, while recognizing Israel's right to exist.

although Arab citizens received second-class treatment in terms of education, public services, and access to land, water, and jobs.

To make the land a liveable home they had introduced state-of-the-art farming technology, including methods of arid land agriculture which were a model for others. They had created light industries, notably the processing of industrial diamonds and, more recently, the production of computer software. Continuously at war, they had developed an arms industry, with the Uzi—one of the hand weapons—known throughout the world. The armed forces had become critical in the nation's life. Conscription was and remains universal: three years for men, two for women, with reserve service continuing for men to age 55. Israel's army had become the most powerful in the region and one of the most powerful in the world.

Although not acknowledged officially, the state almost certainly had developed nuclear weapons. Fearful of terrorism within the country, soldiers were on constant deployment. The annual expenditure on the armed forces was a staggering $1624 per capita in 1996, partly defrayed by substantial assistance from the United States.

All of these developments in technology, culture, economics, and politics tended to reinforce Israel's identity as more European than Middle Eastern. Its many ties to Western nations, and especially to the United States, further affirmed that identity. These contrasts between Israel and its Arab neighbors, in addition to the religious differences, and the bitter struggle of hostile nationalisms each claiming the same land, create a situation filled with tension, in a part of the world already beset by national and international tensions.

BIBLIOGRAPHY

American Historical Review XCVI No. 5 (December 1991), 1363–1496. Special Issue on the Historiography of the Modern Middle East.

Avishai, Bernard. *The Tragedy of Zionism* (New York: Farrar Straus Giroux: New York, 1985).

Danielson, Virginia. *The Voice of Egypt: Umm Kulthum, Arabic Song, and Egyptian Society in the Twentieth Century* (Chicago: University of Chicago Press, 1977).

Davidson, Lawrence. *Islamic Fundamentalism* (Westport, CN: Greenwood Press, 1998).

Fanon, Frantz. *The Wretched of the Earth*, trans. by Constance Farrington (New York: Grove Press, 1963).

Friedman, Thomas L. *From Beirut to Jerusalem* (New York: Farrar, Straus and Giroux, 1989).

Holod, Renata and Hasan-Uddin Khan, with Kimberly Mims. *The Contemporary Mosque: Architects, Clients, and Designs Since the 1950s* (New York: Rizzoli, 1997).

Hourani, Albert. *A History of the Arab Peoples* (Cambridge, MA: Belknap Press, Harvard University, 1991).

International Institute for Environment and Development and the World Resources Institute. *World Resources 1987* (New York: Basic Books, 1987).

Johnson, Hazel and Henry Bernstein, eds. *Third World Lives of Struggle* (London: Heinemann Educational Books Ltd., 1982).

Lapidus, Ira M. *A History of Islamic Societies* (Cambridge: Cambridge University Press, 1988).

Laqueur, Walter and Barry Rubin, eds. *The Israeli–Arab Reader* (New York City: Penguin, 5th ed., 1995).

Morris, Benny. *The Birth of the Palestinian Refugee Problem 1947–1949* (Cambridge: Cambridge University Press, 1988).

Morris, Benny. *Righteous Victims: A History of the Zionist-Arab Conflict, 1881–1999* (New York: Knopf, 1999).

Netton, Ian Richard, ed. *Arabia and the Gulf: From Traditional Society to Modern States* (London: Croom Helm, 1986).

New York Times 2000 Almanac (New York: Penguin, 1999).

Richards, Alan and John Waterbury. *A Political Economy of the Middle East* (Boulder, CO: Westview Press, 1990).

Robinson, Francis. *Atlas of the Islamic World since 1500* (New York: Facts on File, 1982).

Sachar, Howard M. *A History of Israel* (New York: Alfred A. Knopf, 1985).

Serageldin, Ismaïl with James Steele. *Architecture of the Contemporary Mosque* (London: Academy Editions, 1996).

Sigmund, Paul E., ed. *The Ideologies of the Developing Nations* (New York, Praeger, 2nd rev. ed., 1972).

Sivard, Ruth Leger. *World Military and Social Expenditures 1991* (Washington, DC: World Priorities, 14th ed., 1991, 16th ed., 1996).

Toubia, Nahid, ed. *Women of the Arab World* (London: Zed Books, 1988).

United Nations Development Program. *Human Development Report 1998* (New York: Oxford University Press, 1998).

Yergin, Daniel. *The Prize* (New York: Simon and Schuster, 1991).

SUB-SAHARAN AFRICA

CHAPTER

22

"What other countries have taken three hundred years to achieve, a once dependent territory must try to accomplish in a generation if it is to survive."

KWAME NKRUMAH

COLONIALISM, INDEPENDENCE, AND THEIR AFTERMATH

In 1914, most of sub-Saharan Africa was governed by Europeans, who ruled through the power of their technology, especially steamboats and machine guns, and military and administrative organization. Forty-three years later, in 1957, Ghana became the first black African colony to gain its independence. By the mid-1970s European direct political control of Africa was ended. Independence arrived with high hopes and aspirations for Africa's ability to establish effective democratic governments and prosperous economies. By 2000, however, neither the political nor the economic developments in the continenthad met these expectations. How was independence won? After independence, what political, economic, and social systems did African peoples implement to rule themselves, develop their economies, and formulate the appropriate technologies which they advocated? How were these systems working—or not working and why? This chapter looks at the period of colonial rule, anti-colonial revolt, and events since independence. Although most of its focus is on government, economics, and technology, it also considers cultural life, creativity, and the efforts to form new national and regional identities. A segment

of the chapter examines the **apartheid** system of South Africa, which was finally overthrown in the early 1990s.

TO WORLD WAR I: COLONIALISM ESTABLISHED

As we have seen in Chapter 16, after the slave trade was outlawed in the early 1800s Europeans searched for alternative sources of profit from Africa. Some wished to transfer plantation economies to Africa while others sought to cultivate and export tropical products such as tea, coffee, and palm oil. Still others wanted to explore for yet unknown potential mineral riches. (See pp. 549–54.)

Many states had flourished prior to the European arrival—the Asante and Oyo in West Africa, the Luba in Central Africa, and the Ganda and Bunyoro in the east—but only Ethiopia was still independent in 1914. (Liberia held nominal independence, but the indigenous peoples were actually subordinate to the control of an immigrant American-Liberian elite.)

By 1914, the European powers had "partitioned" Africa, carved it up among themselves, "pacified" the continent, implanted limited doses of European technologies, and introduced a light veneer of Western education, often in the form of missionary schools.

ECONOMIC INVESTMENT

Economically, the Europeans invested in the extension of cash cropping in the lands they seized, cultivating especially palm oil, peanuts, cotton, tea, coffee, and cocoa. They instituted patterns of continuous **monoculture** (the growing of a single commercial crop for sale) that were different from both of the more traditional patterns of mixed cropping and slash-and-burn agriculture primarily for food. Ultimately, the extension of monoculture, in peanuts for example, especially onto the fringes of the

Sahara desert, depleted and eroded the soil. The local Tuareg and Fulani residents then migrated northward into increasingly precarious desert enclaves, where they were tragically vulnerable to killing droughts (Franke and Chasin). European strategies for exploiting the natural environment pushed the limits of Africa's resources for human life, and for animal life as well. For example, the hunt for ivory, which was popular in Europe and Asia for billiard balls and piano keys as well as for ornaments and jewelry, depleted the elephant population.

As commercially valuable deposits of metals and minerals, including gold and diamonds, were discovered, Europeans initiated mining enterprises, especially in South Africa, Southern Rhodesia, the Gold Coast, and the Congo. During the years of the slave trade, the Europeans had remained mostly

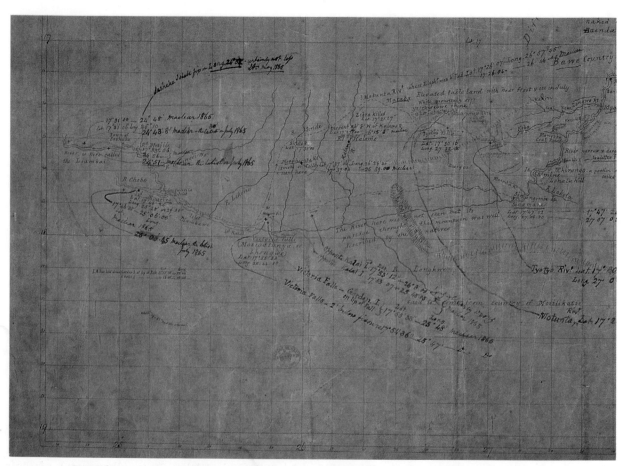

Chart of the Zambezi River, drawn by the explorer Dr David Livingstone, c.1865. As the first European into the heart of the African interior, Livingstone's explorations had a major impact on cartographers of the day. Already hailed in Britain for his discoveries of the Zambezi River and the Victoria Falls, by 1866 he was intent on finding the sources of the Nile, that most intriguing of problems for nineteenth-century explorers. In the event, it was the Congo River, not the Nile, that he found and explored. When Livingstone died, the Africans buried his heart beneath a favorite tree before sending the body for burial in Westminster Abbey, London. (*British Library, London*)

SUB-SAHARAN AFRICA

DATE	EAST & CENTRAL AFRICA	SOUTHERN AFRICA	WEST AFRICA
1900	• Belgian government takes over running of the Congo from King Leopold II (1908)	• South Africa: End of Boer War (1902)	
1910		• Boers and South Africans of British descent form Union of South Africa (1910) • South Africa: Native Lands Act (1913) • South Africa: African National Congress (ANC) formed (1913)	
1920			• The overtly political National Congress of British West Africa is founded (1920) • Sierra Leone Railway Workers Union strikes (1920, 1926) • Nigeria: 60 women killed while protesting against market taxes and licences (1929)
1930	• Italy invades Ethiopia (1935)	• Zambia copper belt affected by strikes (1935)	• Sierra Leone: strikes in the diamond mines (1936) • Nigerian Nnamdi Azikiwe founds *West African Pilot*, introducing revolutionary journalism to Africa (1937) • Senegal: Negritude movement led by poet and statesman Léopold Sédar Senghor
1940			• Workers strike on the Dakar–Niger railway (1947–8)
1950	• Kenya: Mau-Mau armed revolt against British rule (1952–7) • Belgium decides suddenly to pull out of the Congo, plunging the country into civil war (1959)		• France turns over local self-government to colonies in West and Equatorial Africa (1956) • Gold Coast (renamed Ghana) is first Black African country to win independence (1957) • Nigeria: Chinua Achebe, *Things Fall Apart* (1959)

along the coast. Now, to oversee, harvest, mine, and bring to market their new investments they steamed upriver in boats, laid new railway track—8000 miles (12,800 kilometers) in British Africa by 1946; 2600 miles (4100 kilometers) in French West and Equatorial Africa (Fieldhouse, p. 35)—and constructed feeder roads.

Africans had the worst jobs. Import-export activ- ities, banking, and administration and

ership were kept entirely in European hands. Finding difficulties in attracting African workers, and fearing that they would strike, Europeans invited foreign labor from other parts of their empires to immigrate under indenture contracts. By the beginning of World War I, communities of Indian immigrants had established themselves in East and South Africa. Although blocked from the "commanding heights" of the economy, the Indian

SUB-SAHARAN AFRICA

DATE	EAST & CENTRAL AFRICA	SOUTHERN AFRICA	WEST AFRICA
1960	• Sudan: Guerrilla warfare in the south grows into civil war (1961–72); continues intermittently • Eritrea is absorbed by Ethiopia (1962) • Rwanda and Burundi are made independent nations, created from single territory (1962) • Independence and civil war in Congo (Zaire) (1960) • Mobuto Sese Seko seizes power with US backing (1965)	• South Africa: Political protest at Sharpeville results in murder of 69 (1960) • Nelson Mandela and other African National Congress leaders jailed for life (1964)	• Ghana's Nkrumah deposed (1966) • Nigeria: Biafran War (1967–70) • Senegal: Senghor President (1960–80)
1970	• Uganda: Under Idi Amin's regime, 300,000 killed in ethnic war; Asians expelled from the country (1971–9) • Rwanda: tensions between rival Tutsi and Hutu tribes erupt in repeated warfare and massacres (from 1972) • Central African Republic: Emperor Bokassa I deposed (1979)	• Portugal's dictatorship overthrown; Mozambique and Angola (1974) • South Africa: Protest in Soweto against apartheid education policies lead to nationwide riots (1976)	• Jerry Rawlings to power in Ghana (1978)
1980	• Tanzania's Julius Nyerere retires (1985)	• South Africa only white-ruled country south of the Sahara (after 1980) • Commonwealth and US sanctions (1986)	• Nigeria: Wole Soyinka wins Nobel Prize for Literature (1986)
1990	• Somalia dissolves into severe civil warfare (1991) • Eritrea achieves independence from Ethiopia (1993), but war breaks out again in 1998 • Zaire (renamed Republic of Congo): Laurent Kabila seizes power, ending Mobuto's corrupt regime (1997); civil warfare continues, with neighboring contries also involved	• South Africa: President F.W. de Klerk lifts ban against ANC; Mandela freed (1990) • ANC wins 62 percent of vote in first free elections (1994) • National Truth Commission investigating abuses under apartheid (1995)	

immigrants gradually moved into significant positions in local trade and commerce. Africans, provided with little opportunity for formal education, generally did not enter into careers in business, and the resulting economic imbalance between immigrants and natives sowed a bitter harvest of dispossession and jealousy.

ADMINISTRATION

To administer their lands and investments, the British and French placed in each of their new colonies a governor, a council of advisers, law courts, police forces, army installations, and hospitals. Cities were built to house the administrative

Building the Uganda Railway, from Mombasa, Kenya, into the interior. The workers are laying track at the base of the Kikuyu Escarpment at Mile 363, c. 1900. The very steep sides of the escarpment, which form the walls of the Rift Valley, presented builders with the most difficult section of the route. Some 32,000 indentured laborers immigrated from India to build the railway, which helped Britain to maintain a presence in Uganda by its direct link with the port of Mombasa.

centers, introducing a pattern of favoring the city over the countryside that has persisted until today. To keep costs low, the colonizers coopted Africans into the administration, following two distinctly different patterns. In some regions they coopted local chiefs—or men whom they designated as chiefs—to serve as their administrative officials. This pattern of indirect rule, associated most strongly with Lord Lugard (1858–1945), who adapted it from British methods in India and introduced it into Nigeria in the early 1900s, was designed to keep Africans loyal to the colonizers by making the local rulers dependent upon the British, and by supporting these local rulers against any popular resistance. The alternative system was to educate in European fashion a **cadre** of less conservative leaders who would share European outlooks, values, and urban residence, and in some regions, especially in urbanized areas, this plan was also implemented. The response to new educational and administrative opportunities was not uniform. Some groups, especially the Fulbe in Nigeria, the Swahili in Tanganyika, and the Ganda in Uganda, showed considerable interest. These groups tended to ally themselves with the new administrative and economic innovations of the colonizers.

In some areas of Africa, particularly western Africa, Europeans did not come as settlers, but as administrators and business agents on temporary postings. But in other regions, notably southern and eastern Africa, Europeans came in greater numbers and took possession of the best lands for themselves, sometimes through dubious contracts, more often by force. As we saw on pp. 551–2, the European colonizers coerced the Africans to work on their plantations through levying taxes and restricting land ownership. The harsh employment policies of the Europeans created a part-time, uncommitted labor force reluctantly engaged in mines, plantations, administration, and urban occupations. Whenever they could, the Africans returned to working their own lands, mostly in subsistence farming.

All the European powers ruled their African colonies for profits, for prestige, and, as they saw it, to civilize the Africans. They differed in the degree of force they used to achieve these goals, with the British generally considered the least physically coercive. King Leopold II of Belgium, who had personal control of the Congo, was so brutal toward the Congolese, treating them little better than domesticated animals, that in 1908 the Belgian government took over authority from him.

COLONIALISM CHALLENGED 1914–57

WHAT DO WE KNOW?

WHAT DIFFERENCE DOES IT MAKE?

The Ghanaian historian Adu Boahen believes the turning point in colonial authority in Africa came with the Italian invasion of Ethiopia in 1935. Mussolini sought to avenge the humiliating defeat the Italians had suffered at the Battle of Adowa in

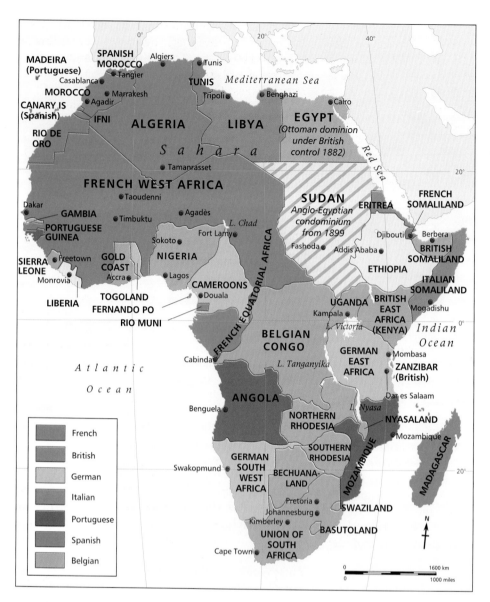

Africa in 1914 By the end of the nineteenth century, Africa presented European imperialists with their last chance to claim a "place in the sun." In a scramble for territory, Belgium, Germany, and Italy joined Spain, Portugal, Britain, and France in carving up the continent, riding roughshod over native concerns with brutal insensitivity. Conflict between the colonists was common, the Boer War between the British and Dutch in South Africa being the most bloody.

1896 and to start restoration of the Roman Empire. His conquest of this last remaining independent African state shocked public opinion not only in Africa but even in Europe and the United States—though not enough to prevent it (Boahen, pp. 90–91). It was no longer considered proper for European countries to establish new colonies.

By the end of World War II, the apparent inevitability and the moral sanction of European colonialism had been undermined. The South Asian countries of India, Pakistan, Sri Lanka, and Burma won their independence between 1947 and 1948. China's communist revolution expelled foreign interests in 1949. Military power and political leadership passed from the European colonizing powers to the United States and, to a lesser extent, the Soviet Union. Both took strong public stands against overseas colonialism, although Russia was itself seizing control of the countries of eastern Europe, and America's wealth and military strength commanded enormous power around the globe.

THE ORIGINS OF THE INDEPENDENCE MOVEMENTS

The African quest for independence was led by men newly educated in European ideals, including nationalism and democracy, and no longer willing to suffer in silence the arrogance of European domination. This educated elite was a tiny majority. In 1960 only about 16 percent of adults in Africa were literate, and the average enrollment in secondary schools was only 3 percent of the age group. So few universities had been established in Africa that students were far more likely to study abroad than at home. In 1960, 396 Kenyans were studying at Makerere University College in neighboring Uganda, the closest African university, while 1655 studied at universities abroad. Training in industrial and managerial skills was practically non-existent. The educated elites had disproportionate influence as they attempted to supplant the leadership of the traditional chiefs and assert their right to represent their nations.

Newspapers became important in mobilizing literate opinion as early as 1890. In 1935, the Nigerian Nnamdi Azikiwe (b. 1904) first edited the Accra *African Morning Post*, and in 1937 he founded in Lagos the *West African Pilot*, thereby introducing populist, revolutionary journalism to Africa. Azikiwe learned his journalism in the United States, where he also experienced at first hand American racism and the efforts of radical journalists to combat it. Returning to Africa, he helped to launch political movements and parties through his newspapers (July, p. 434).

Military service in two world wars provided another significant training ground in new values and skills. In World War I, the British recruited 26,000 Africans to serve under arms, and the French 180,000 (July, pp. 361–2); in World War II, 80,000 African soldiers fought inside France until the country was conquered by Germany in 1940; the British recruited 280,000 soldiers from East Africa and 167,000 from West Africa (Davidson, pp. 57–8). These soldiers travelled far from home and learned new ways of life. They learned the advantages of new technologies of organization and machinery, and they also saw the murder of whites by whites, and indeed were ordered by white Europeans to kill other white Europeans. They came to understand the underside of European treatment of other Europeans. At army bases they mingled with white women. Racial myths tumbled. After each war, soldiers returned home expecting and demanding political rewards for their military service. Frustrated at the end of World War I, they were received more respectfully following World War II.

SEEDS OF DISCONTENT

Labor organization in the mines, plantations, railroads, and docks also introduced new perspectives. Although the percentage of Africans at work in these European-controlled installations was small

—1 percent of the population of French West Africa, for example—the sheer numbers were substantial—167,000 in this case. Seasonal and migrant laborers as well as full-time workers carried back to their villages stories of industrial life.

Strikes further helped to consolidate African resentment against European economic control and racial supremacy. The Sierra Leone Railway Workers Union struck in 1920 and again in 1926. In 1925–6, the year of the "great strikes," mechanics, dock workers, and railway workers in West Africa went on strike. In 1935, the Zambian copper belt was affected, and in 1938–9, there were strikes in the diamond mines in Sierra Leone. From October 10, 1947 to March 19, 1948 workers struck the Dakar–Niger railway line and docks, a confrontation commemorated in Sembène Ousmane's novel *God's Bits of Wood* (see Source, p. 748). In 1947, 15,000 workers struck in Mombasa, Kenya. The mines of South Africa and the Belgian Congo, where conditions were especially severe, endured more numerous strikes. In order to secure higher wages for themselves and to discourage the employment of black strikebreakers, white workers formed separate unions. Striking blacks were on their own from the first organized strike of 9000 miners in 1913.

Other new organizations also found their activities spilling over into politics. African churches provided safe spaces in which politics could be discussed free from European censorship. Independent churches—called Ethiopian, Zionist, and Watchtower Churches—filled this need, and frequently opposed the missionary activities of white European churches. The black churches often supported the labor union activities of their members.

Gender also played a role. In 1929, at Aba in Nigeria, some 10,000 women gathered, with another 6000 assembling at Owerrinta, to protest new market taxes and market license requirements. These women felt more vulnerable than men since they had fewer alternatives to their market jobs. Some relief was offered, but only after sixty women were killed in confrontation with colonial authorities. Women had gathered before at Aba in 1925 to preserve their religion, which they felt to be under attack by Christians. Elsewhere and at other times women seem to have played a strong role in support of other protest movements.

Social clubs, literary circles, welfare associations, youth movements, and ethnic associations multiplied throughout Africa, becoming vehicles for political expression and protest. Some were

Our Only Hope for a New Life Lies in the Machine

Sembène's novel, *God's Bits of Wood*, tells of the workers' strike on the Dakar–Niger railway in West Africa from October 1947 to March 1948. Sembène describes the workers' realization that they have developed a commitment to their new industrial jobs. They have become new men:

> Like rejected lovers returning to a trysting place, they kept coming back to the areas surrounding the stations. Then they would just stand there, motionless, their eyes fixed on the horizon, scarcely speaking to each other. Sometimes a little block of five or six men would detach itself from the larger mass and drift off in the direction of the tracks. For a few minutes they would wander along the rails and then, suddenly, as though seized with panic, they would hasten back to the safety of the group they had left. Then again they would just stand there, or squat down in the shade of a sand hill, their eyes fixed on the two endless parallels, following them out until they joined and lost themselves in the brush. Something was being born inside them, as if the past and the future were coupling to breed a new kind of man, and it seemed to them that the wind was whispering a phrase they had often heard from Bakayoko: "The kind of man we were is dead, and our only hope for a new life lies in the machine, which knows neither a language nor a race." They said nothing, though, and only their eyes betrayed an inner torment brought on by the mounting terror of famine and inconsolable loneliness for the machine. (p. 76)

from the outset overtly political, most notably the National Congress of British West Africa, which was founded in 1920. Like almost all the others, it wanted a voice in colonial policies, an end to racial discrimination in government hiring, an expansion of educational opportunities, and greater opportunities for Africans in the economy. But most members still saw themselves as loyal subjects of the British crown, ending their resolutions with affirmations of "their attachment to the British connection and their unfeigned loyalty and devotion to the throne and person of His Majesty the King Emperor" (Boahen, p. 83).

PAN-AFRICANISM 1918–45

Bringing together these diverse groups from throughout the continent was a long-held dream that began to find its realization in five pan-African meetings between the end of World War I and the end of World War II. The Eurocentric transportation and communication systems available at the time required that all five congresses meet in Europe, or the United States; not until 1958 did an All-African People's Conference convene in Africa. (The first meeting of representatives of the African diaspora had been held in London in 1900, but its participants came mostly from the West Indies and the USA.) Racial justice was the unifying concern.

The 1919 congress was convened by W.E.B. Du Bois (1868–1963), the great American scholar and publicist, to coincide with the Paris peace conference (see p. 605). Participants called on the assembled powers to attend to the racial, economic, and political concerns of Africa. They also asked that Germany's African colonies be turned over to an international body, a kind of precursor of mandatory power. The request was not accepted. A second conference, convened in 1921, met sequentially in London, Brussels, and Paris. Its final manifesto called for an end to racism and inequality:

> The absolute equality of races—physical, political, and social—is the founding stone of world peace and human advancement. ... It is the shame of the world that today the relation between the main

groups of mankind and their mutual estimate and respect is determined chiefly by the degree to which one can subject the other to its service, enslaving labor, making ignorance compulsory, uprooting ruthlessly religion and customs, and destroying government, so that the favored Few may luxuriate in the toil of the tortured Many. (Andrea and Overfield, pp. 430–1)

African-Americans formed the majority at the first four Congresses. Some Africans, led by Blaise Diagne of Senegal, rejected American intervention:

We Frenchmen of Africa wish to remain French. ... None of us aspires to see French Africa delivered exclusively to the Africans as is demanded, though without any authority, by the American Negroes. (July, p. 378)

But many representatives felt that Diagne had sold out his earlier militancy to consolidate his own position in France. The third Congress, convened by Du Bois in London and Lisbon in 1923, and the fourth, in New York in 1927, continued the debate on Africa's proper relationship to Europe.

The Fifth Congress convened in Manchester, England, in 1945 under different conditions, with European empires about to crumble and African leadership more self-confident and militant. A new generation of African leaders, notably Kwame

South African miners' strike. Huge crowds of white miners demonstrate over pay and conditions in Bree Street, Johannesburg, during a strike in 1913. One striker was killed by police during these demonstrations. White and black workers had different unions to represent them, because the whites wanted to ensure they were on different pay scales and firmly separated from the blacks. Diamonds and gold were the mainstays of South Africa's economic development, so miners' strikes presented an unwelcome threat to the wealth and smooth running of the colony.

Nkrumah of Ghana and Jomo Kenyatta of Kenya, joined together in Manchester and demanded independence for Africa.

The British and French were prepared to be responsive, investing greater financial and development resources in Africa than ever before. Perhaps the new investments would encourage the colonies to remain within the imperial structures, or at least to accept post-independence cooperation with the former colonizers. Britain already had

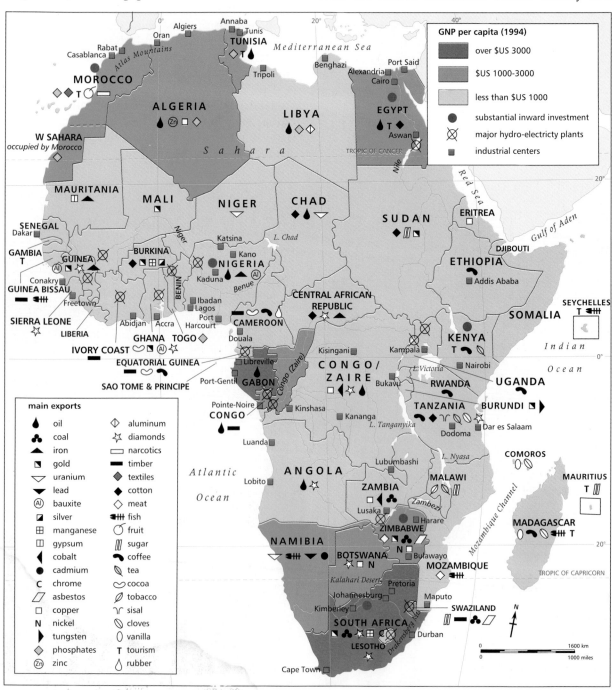

The economic development of Africa The legacy of European colonialism has determined Africa's economic development, with a persistent reliance upon primary products, mainly mineral wealth and cash crops. Both are widely exploited by multinational franchises, bringing little real economic benefit to local economies. Political instability, corruption, and natural disaster combine with low investment in education and health to create a general condition of underdevelopment. The northern tier of Arab states and South Africa stand out with greater wealth compared with the central part of the continent.

adopted these policies in 1940 by establishing the Colonial Development and Welfare Act, and in 1945 it added further legislation that channeled funds for development. France provided its colonies with similar, and slightly larger, funding known as FIDES.

Investment patterns suggested the importance ascribed to technology both in the development of Africa and in establishing the balance between Europe and Africa. Major hydroelectric schemes were introduced on the Nile at Jinja in Uganda, at Kariba on the Zambesi, between the Rhodesias, in the Gold Coast on the Volta River at Akasombo, and in Guinea at the Fria and Kimbo Rivers. Construction of the Inga dam on the lower Congo was interrupted by warfare. Agricultural, veterinary, and fishing technology were extended. Transportation networks were expanded and improved. Educational facilities were increased; teacher training schools were established; between 1945 and 1949 four university colleges were established by the British. (French higher education was still available only in France.) Local self-government was made more representative through election.

Even so, the African economies were weak, educational systems minuscule, and participation in electoral politics virtually non-existent, even in the British and French colonies. In the Belgian Congo and the Portuguese colonies of Angola and Mozambique, Africans were generally even more impoverished, less powerful, and treated with even less dignity. A brief overview of the winning of independence in a few of the major colonies indicates some of the differences, both in the policies of the colonizers and the resources and mobilization of the colonized.

WINNING INDEPENDENCE 1945–75

THE BRITISH COLONIES

The Gold Coast was the first black African country to win independence and, like several others, immediately chose a new name—Ghana—symbolically linking itself with historical traditions of earlier African empires. Ghana specialized in growing cash crops, like coffee, cocoa, and peanuts. It had mineral resources, generally untapped, in bauxite, gold, and manganese. It had few European settlers. In 1947, the United Gold Coast Convention organized to represent the political opinions of educated Ghanaians. It invited Kwame Nkrumah (1909– 72), recently returned from college in the United States, to serve as secretary. Nkrumah, more radical than most of the delegates, began by instigating riots, splintering the organization by founding the more militant Convention People's Party in 1949, and organizing a general strike in 1950. Jailed, Nkrumah was released when he won elected office in 1951. He negotiated with the British until independence was won in 1957. Always a pan-Africanist, Nkrumah in 1958 convened the All-African People's Conference at Accra, transferring the geographical locus of the movement to Africa, and inspiring national leaders throughout the continent.

Ghana's independence. Prime minister (later president) Kwame Nkrumah waves to a celebrating crowd as the Gold Coast colony becomes the newly independent country of Ghana on March 6, 1957. Nkrumah formed a one-party state in 1964, and his regime was ended by a military coup in 1966 during his absence on a trip to China.

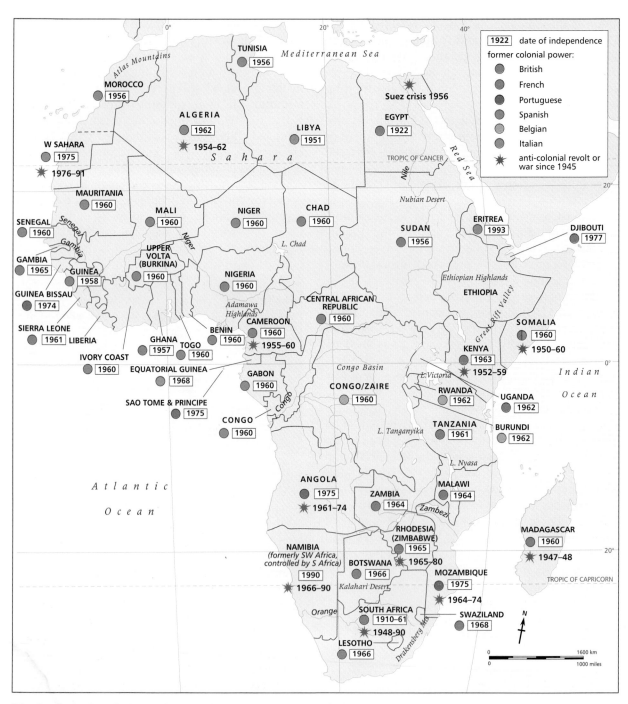

The decolonization of Africa Ethiopia had been colonized only briefly by Italy, Liberia had been established as an independent state, and Egypt had nominal independence from 1922, but most African states gained their independence after World War II, first those in North Africa, and then, following Ghana in 1957, those of sub-Saharan Africa. Each colonial power had its own pattern for granting independence. The British and French hoped to establish amicable relations, generally, while the Portuguese and Belgians left more bitterly.

In terms of education, resources, and political mobilization, Nigeria was as prepared for independence as Ghana; with 42 million people in 1960, it was the most populous country in Africa, seven times Ghana's size. Its borders, like those of most

African nations, had been drawn arbitrarily by its colonizers, yoking together unrelated, and often hostile, groups within the same country and separating related and often congenial groups by new international boundaries. Nigeria was composed of three distinct regions: the Hausa majority in the more desertlike north; the Yoruba-controlled southwest; and the Ibo-dominated southeast. The north was mostly Muslim; the south Christian. Creating a federal constitution that could harness these regions into a single nation delayed Nigeria's independence from Britain to 1960. (The new structure was imperfect and civil war broke out in 1967.)

Despite the relatively high educational levels of the leading Kikuyu and Luo ethnic groups, and their relatively high levels of politicization, Kenya's road to independence was blocked by a sizeable European settler community that continued militantly to claim its privileges, especially its land holdings in the rich highlands area. Six years of armed revolt led to the deaths of thirty-two European civilians, fifty-three European soldiers, and 11,503 Africans until independence from Great Britain was finally achieved in 1963.

THE FRENCH COLONIES

In contrast to the British, who had always thought of their African subjects as "other," different from themselves (compare Spotlight, pp. 428–9), the French proposed to assimilate Africans into the culture and politics of France. In 1956, France turned over local self-government to its colonies in West and Equatorial Africa, but kept external affairs in its own hands. In 1958, it offered each of its colonies the choice between complete independence, with neither ties to nor assistance from France, and more limited internal autonomy in a French-controlled federation. At first, only Guinea opted for independence, but by 1960, all but French Somaliland (Djibouti) made that choice.

Strong ties still continue between France and many of its former African colonies. The French reserve some rights of military intervention, and the former colonies seem to feel free to invoke such intervention as in Chad, where the French maintain a military presence, and in the Central African Republic, where French assistance was requested for overthrowing an unpopular dictator. Many African currencies are tied to the French franc through agreements that give France power over African central banks and financial policies. The number of French expatriates in high-ranking African governmental positions remains significant. In 1986, Côte d'Ivoire (the Ivory Coast) contained three times more French nationals than it had at the height of the colonial era. France's former colonies receive preferential trading rights within the European Union. Some critics see these relationships as neo-colonial.

THE BELGIAN COLONIES

Independence for the Belgian Congo (renamed Zaire 1971–97, and then the Democratic Republic of the Congo), was not planned. As neighboring countries moved toward independence, Congolese nationalists began to agitate as well. Rioting broke out. Belgium, which had done little to prepare for independence, envisioning it at least thirty years away, suddenly decided in 1959 to depart in a year, leaving the country in chaos that soon descended into civil war. The Congo had virtually no graduates of institutes of higher education and no administrative cadres trained to run a modern nation. The Belgian government had been one of the most cruel and exploitative, and at the independence ceremony transferring power from Belgium to the Congo, June 30, 1960, the new prime minister, Patrice Lumumba (1925–61), revealed the extent of Congolese bitterness:

> We are no longer your monkeys. … We have known the back-breaking works exacted from us in exchange for salaries which permit us neither to eat enough to satisfy our hunger, nor to dress and lodge ourselves decently, nor to raise our children as the beloved creatures they are.
>
> We have known the mockery, the insults, the blows submitted to morning, noon, and night because we were *nègres* [blacks]. We have known that our lands were despoiled in the name of supposedly legal text which in reality recognized only the right of the stronger. … And, finally, who will forget the hangings or the firing squads where so many of our brothers perished, or the cells into which were brutally thrown those who escaped the soldiers' bullets—the soldier whom the colonialists made the instruments of their domination?
> (Andrea and Overfield, 1st ed., pp. 507–8)

The two present-day countries of Rwanda and Burundi were also administered as the single territory of Ruanda-Urundi by Belgium under a League of Nations Mandate and then under United Nations Trusteeship. During Belgian rule, Ruanda-Urundi was dominated by the ethnic Tutsi minority (about 15 percent of the population). By favoring the Tutsi with administrative positions, the Belgians widened the gap between them and the 85 percent Hutu majority, and increased the

Aerial view of rioting in Leopoldville, Belgian Congo, January 6, 1959. The shot shows Congolese streaming through the streets, pillaging and burning the Belgian shops in the village. Riots raged for two days in the Congo capital, leaving thirty-five dead.

feelings of bitterness. After independence in 1962, and separate statehood for each country, rivalries and tensions between Tutsi and Hutu peoples became more intense and broke out in repeated massacres and warfare from 1972 to the present.

THE PORTUGUESE COLONIES

The Belgians finally left of their own accord. Portugal, ruled at home by a dictator, was not about to give up control of its large overseas colonies of Angola and Mozambique where many Portuguese had settled. It governed harshly, with repressive labor policies that forced some 65,000 to 100,000 Mozambiquans to travel each year to work in the mines of South Africa's Rand. Each person had to keep an identification passbook at all times. The press was rigidly censored. The police were ruthless. Most of all, Portugal, alone among the European colonizers, believed that its own future greatness depended on its continuing control over African colonies. Supported by South Africa, Portugal fought fiercely against guerrilla freedom fighters. The USSR and Cuba dispatched troops to aid the guerrillas, and the struggle became thoroughly internationalized. In 1974, however, a domestic revolution overthrew Portugal's dictatorship, and a year later Portugal freed its colonies.

SOUTH AFRICA

After 1980, South Africa remained the only white-ruled country south of the Sahara. South Africa's whites—some 8 million out of a total population of almost 40 million in 1990—had come to view themselves as Africans. The first major group, settlers from the Netherlands called Afrikaners or Boers, were pushed by later immigrants from Britain into a "great trek" north of the Orange River. The South Africans of British descent defeated the Boers in three years of warfare, 1899–1902, but the two groups finally came together to form the Union of South Africa in 1910, and they adopted the Afrikaners' harsher policies toward the black majority. Wages and conditions in the European mines were so abysmal that Africans would not work them. Chinese contract laborers were imported. The 1913 Native Land Acts restricted African residence and purchase of land to only 13 percent of the surface of the country, effectively forcing black Africans into service as landless laborers in white-controlled farming and industry. The labor market had two impermeable tiers, the top with better conditions and pay for whites, the bottom for blacks. Nonwhites had no political rights.

Still more restrictive laws after 1948 established apartheid (segregation of the races). Blacks working in the cities could not legally establish residence, but had to commute long distances each day from black residential areas or stay in dormitory settings, leaving their families behind in the village areas.

Black African frustration, resentment, and anger at first expressed itself principally through independent Ethiopian Churches as early as the 1870s and 1880s. The African National Congress (ANC) formed in 1913 and grew steadily over several decades as a constitutional party of protest. As other African nations began to win independence, Europeans urged South Africa to liberalize its racial policies.

But the government of South Africa stubbornly resisted. It confronted unarmed political protest in March 1960 at Sharpeville with a massacre in which sixty-nine were killed and many were wounded. The African National Congress now shifted to strikes and armed protest, but renounced attacks on people, limiting itself to sabotage of property. The South African government continued to crack down, maintaining its apartheid policies and sentencing ANC leader Nelson Mandela (b. 1918), a forty-six-year-old lawyer, to life imprisonment (see Source, p. 756).

The ANC and the general movement for racial justice were crippled but not killed off by this action. As Zambia and Zimbabwe, Angola and Mozambique won independence and majority rule, world attention focussed on South Africa as the last remaining center of white, minority rule. In addition, the newly independent, **front-line** nations sheltered members of the ANC and other movements for majority rule, including some dedicated to guerrilla warfare. Through the United Nations as well as through unilateral actions, many nations adopted sanctions against South Africa, restricting or stopping trade; "disinvesting" or withdrawing economic investments; and ending diplomatic, cultural, and sports exchanges. South Africa was to be treated as a pariah nation, cut off from intercourse with much of the rest of the world until it moved toward racial equality.

Enforcing the sanctions proved difficult. South Africa was a regional economic powerhouse, with rich resources: 85 percent of the world's known platinum; two-thirds of its chromium; half its gold;

Seaside segregation. South African apartheid manifests itself on a beach in Durban, in 1985. The sign, written in English and Afrikaans, proclaims that the beach "is reserved for the sole use of the members of the white race group." Apartheid (Afrikaans for "apartness"), the policy of separate development and segregation of the races of South Africa, was supported and encouraged by the Nationalist Party when it came to power in 1948. With the African National Congress in power in South Africa, the country is emerging from the constraints of its racial policies and bu'' a more united nation.

Nelson Mandela's Speech to the Court at His Trial, 1964

The African people were not part of the Government and did not make the laws by which they were governed. We believed in the words of the Universal Declaration of Human Rights, that "the will of the people shall be the basis of authority of the Government". ... The ANC refused to dissolve but instead went underground. ... All lawful modes of expressing opposition ... had been closed by legislation, and we were placed in a position in which we had either to accept a permanent state of inferiority or to defy the Government. ...

The Whites enjoy what may well be the highest standard of living in the world, whilst Africans live in poverty and misery. Forty percent of the Africans live in hopelessly overcrowded and, in some cases, drought-stricken Reserves, where soil erosion and the overworking of the soil makes it impossible for them to live properly off the land. Thirty percent are laborers, labor tenants, and squatters on white farms and work and live under conditions similar to those of the serfs of the Middle Ages. The other 30 percent live in towns where they have developed economic and social habits which bring them closer in many respects to White standards. Yet most Africans, even in this group, are impoverished by low incomes and high cost of living ... the laws which are made by the Whites are designed to preserve this situation. ...

I have fought against white domination. I have cherished the ideal of a democratic and free society in which all persons live together in harmony and with equal opportunities. It is an ideal which I hope to live for and to achieve. But if needs be, it is an ideal for which I am prepared to die. (Andrea and Overfield, 3rd ed., pp. 486–8)

half its manganese; and substantial proportions of its gem-quality diamonds. Its GNP, which had been 30 percent of all of sub-Saharan Africa's in 1960, increased to 35 percent by 1987. Geo-politically, 90 percent of Europe's oil passes by its waters. Many large and powerful nations saw sanctions as self-destructive and did not fully comply. The front-line states had tens of thousands of workers who subsisted only through jobs in the South African mines and industries; these states continued surreptitious trade and diplomatic relationships. In addition, to withstand guerrilla threats, South Africa increased its military personnel from 24,000 in 1960 to 97,000 in 1987, and its military expenditures from US$243 million to US$3292 million, equal to about 50 percent of the military expenditures of all of black Africa combined (Sivard, p. 53). Nevertheless, the sanctions did gradually exact their toll; isolation was painful, culturally and diplomatically as well as economically. The contin-

uing expansion of independence among the African states brought black rule ever closer to South Africa's borders, and unrest within the country continued. In 1976 protests against government educational policies began in Soweto, a black township outside Pretoria, and led to nationwide riots in which 600 people were killed. Some liberalization was granted: black labor unions were legalized, the prohibition of interracial sex was abolished, segregation in public transportation ended. Finally in 1990, the new government of President F.W. de Klerk (b. 1936) lifted its ban against the ANC and freed Nelson Mandela after twenty-seven years in prison. It repealed apartheid laws and began wary and difficult negotiations with the ANC for transition to majority rule. In 1993, de Klerk's National Party and the ANC under Mandela's leadership agreed on the principle of a new constitution.

In 1994 elections, open equally to all races on the principle of one person-one vote, the ANC won 62

A new and democratic dawn for South Africa. South African president Nelson Mandela and second deputy president F.W. de Klerk address a huge crowd in front of the Union Building in Pretoria, after the inauguration ceremony on May 10, 1994. Only a few years earlier it would have been inconceivable that the imprisoned Nelson Mandela could ever attain high office in a country so firmly wedded to the policies of apartheid.

First-time voters, South Africa, 1994. Residents of the Western Transvaal queue to vote for the first time in South Africa's multiracial elections in 1994. After years of apartheid and oppression, black South Africans showed a respect and devotion to their new democracy that inspired citizens of democracies around the world who often took for granted their own right to vote and to participate in governance.

percent of the vote. Since 1995 a national Truth Commission has been investigating abuses under apartheid in the past in an effort to clear the air for further interracial cooperation in the future.

EVALUATING THE LEGACY OF COLONIALISM

Colonialism brought ambiguous, paradoxical configurations to Africa. On the one hand it brought Africa into the world economy, opening markets, building infrastructure, and tapping mineral and industrial wealth. On the other hand it geared Africa's economy not to the needs of Africans, but rather to the wishes of the economic and political leaders of the outside world, leaving much of Africa with an ecologically and economically vulnerable monoculture, and with mines, industry, and plantations in the hands of foreigners. African economies were, for example, oriented to European demands, while the commercial and transportation links within Africa itself were neglected. Cities grew on the basis of government's administrative needs, drew rural people away from their roots and culture, and developed a "colonial mentality" that valued European urban forms over African patterns of settlement. Meanwhile most of the population continued in a subsistence economy of simple technology. A large number remained pastoralists.

Devaluing local religions, the colonizers introduced and facilitated the spread of Christian missionaries and educators. (The improved transportation and communication systems facilitated the spread of Islam as well.) Many Africans joined the newly growing Ethiopian Church movement, which espoused Christianity without its European bias.

Political borders were drawn in colonial offices, artificially bringing together ethnic groups that were unrelated to one another. In Nigeria, for example, Hausa, Yoruba, and Ibo peoples each constituted about 20 percent of the population, with other smaller groups making up the rest. In Kenya, the Kikuyu were about 20 percent of the population; Luo, Luhya, Kelenjin, and Kamba each 10–15 percent, with an admixture of Asians, Arabs, and Europeans completing the demographic picture. Uganda included such diverse groups as the Ganda, Langi, Acholi, and Lugbara ethnic groups of the south and west, with Nilotic ethnic groups stronger in the north, and a substantial community of South Asians, mostly in the cities. In the Congo, the main groups were the Kongo, the Luba, the Mongo, and the Rwanda. In Senegal it was the Wolof, Serer, Peuhl, Diola, Toucouleur, and Malinke; in Côte d'Ivoire, the Baule, Bete, Senufo, and Malinke. Even if these groups had not begun as rivals, they often became so as they competed for positions in the new administrative apparatus.

Language, too, divided people. In most of the forty-seven countries of sub-Saharan Africa "no one language is spoken as the first language, or mother tongue, by a majority of the people" (Sklar, pp. 100–1). The official languages of administration and public life were European even though most people could not speak, read, or write them. Africans were torn between earlier, local ethnic identities and the new identities of language, religion, culture, and administrative systems that were being imprinted upon them arbitrarily. Nigerian Nobel laureate Chinua Achebe (b. 1930) captured the internal rift in the spirit of many African intellectuals and political leaders in a series of novels beginning with *Things Fall Apart* (1959).

INDEPENDENCE AND AFTER

Among many of the elites, however, colonialism sowed the seeds of anti-colonialism, nationalism, and pan-Africanism. Kwame Nkrumah had told the people of Ghana and of all Africa, "Seek first the political kingdom and everything else shall be added to you" (Salvatore, p. 56). Expectations at independence were high. But within a few years many of the expectations were dashed. Some observers blamed the problems on neo-colonialism. The colonial rulers had granted formal independence, but they continued to maintain economic, cultural, and even political influence, or hegemony. The international market place frequently forced Africans to sell their primary products at low prices, while they had to pay top dollar for expensive imported manufactures. In such situations, foreign economic assistance brought foreign influence. In the midst of the Cold War, America and Russia frequently intervened, each supporting its own favored local leader with money and often with arms. African states shook under the strain.

INTERNAL POLITICS

After independence, almost all of the African states maintained their national unity, but often unity

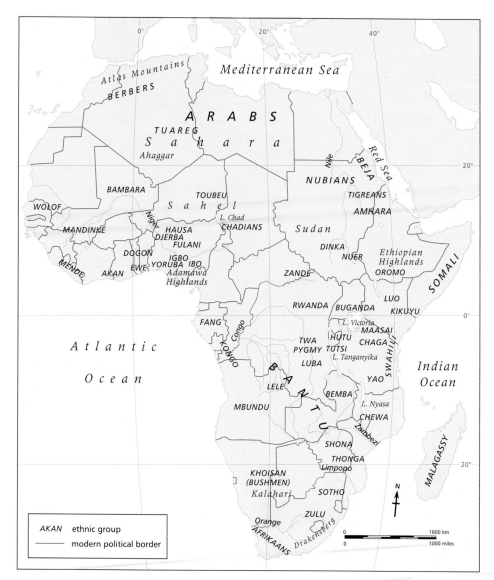

Ethnic groups in Africa
The insensitivity to local conditions of many European colonial administrators created a template of territorial boundaries which failed to match the underlying cultural map of Africa and its peoples. The results of this were seen in post-independence internecine conflicts between ethnic groups hemmed into artificial national territories: Congo (Zaire), Nigeria, Uganda, Angola, Zimbabwe, Sudan, and, more recently, Rwanda and Burundi are among those that have reaped this bitter harvest.

was preserved only by the use of military force in civil wars. The revolt and secession of the Ibo peoples in the Biafra region of Nigeria, Africa's largest country demographically, precipitated 1 million deaths between 1967 and 1970 in one of the first, and worst, of these civil wars. Yet, in the long run, the decision to re-align Nigeria into twelve states conforming more closely to ethnic borders, and the relatively compassionate terms of the peace settlement, ultimately helped to foster national unity.

In the sprawling Sudan, the largest country in Africa geographically, ethnic, regional, and religious conflicts between the more Arabic, Islamic north, and the more Nilotic, Christian and **animist** south were, again, built into the fabric of the artificially created nation. The south began guerrilla warfare in 1961, and this continued and grew

into a civil war that lasted until 1972. Armed conflict resumed in 1982 and continues until today. Neighboring Chad had similar ethnic, religious, and linguistic divisions, but here the southern, black, Christian and animist factions have proved more powerful than the northern, more Islamic groups. External forces entered the combat, with Libya backing the northerners and France entering on the side of the south. The potential for further conflict in this arid, resource-poor, agricultural country remains.

In Uganda, the dominant Ganda and their king, the Kabaka, were attacked by coalitions of other ethnic groups in 1966. Continued fighting in Uganda, especially after General Idi Amin came to power (1971–9), saw up to 300,000 people killed, and the entire community of Asian origin, mostly

Indians, driven out of the country. In all these cases, however, national borders remained intact.

EXCEPTIONS: ALTERING BORDERS

In the Horn of Africa, the constituent units of Ethiopia—Eritrea, Tigre, and Ogaden—and neighboring Somalia fought for years. Here, a new state and new borders were created. Eritrea, which had been absorbed by Ethiopia in 1962, fought for its independence continuously, until achieving it in 1993. In 1998 war broke out again between Eritrea and Ethiopia, partly over claims concerning ambiguous borders from colonial days, partly over trade and economics. Some 50,000 people died before a tentative peace agreement was reached in August 1999.

Somalia fought against Ethiopia primarily for control of the Ogaden region. Intervention by Americans, Russians, Cubans, and others exacerbated the warfare throughout the 1970s and 1980s, which ended with the end of the Cold War. In 1988, a peace agreement was reached between Somalia and Ethiopia, but in 1991, Somalia dissolved into civil warfare so severe that the United Nations declared it to be a country without a government. Continuing fighting has spread as far as the Congo.

Both of the tiny, contiguous states of Rwanda and Burundi (see p. 753) have been wracked by conflict between the formerly dominant Tutsi people, and their former underlings, the Hutu. In both countries the Hutu have now become dominant, but only after three decades of brutal ethnic warfare left some 750,000 people dead. Hundreds of thousands of refugees, fleeing to the neighboring Congo internationalized the conflict. Uganda, to the north, also entered the factional and ethnic fighting. This situation is still in flux. Hutu–Tutsi warfare is not yet over.

FOCUS

Traditional Institutions and National Governments

In many countries, the state incorporated traditional ethnic and religious leaders into the administration in order to encourage their loyalty to the new institution. The participation of tribal chieftains, at least informally, was often critical. In the areas near the Sahara, where Islam is a very powerful religious presence, the support of the organizations of pious men, *sufis*, became important to the cohesion of the state, in patterns we have explored for earlier times and other places in Chapter 11. The political scientist Conor Cruise O'Brien describes the importance of a *sufi* lodge in Senegal both to the welfare of its inhabitants and to governmental stability:

The lodge is sited at the tomb of a revered saint, and apart from pious pilgrimage, it exists for the task of sacred instruction. But the social purposes of the *zawiya* are wonderfully varied, a true func-tion-alist's utopia; an inn to accommodate the pious traveller, a school to instruct the faithful, a court to arbitrate differences sacred or profane, a market place and farm to provide for the material sustenance of the believers, a miniature welfare state for the distribution of alms, as well as a church and a final resting place for the bones of the devout. The conventional label of lodge seems inadequate to cover such a social range which, if anything, brings to mind the glories of the medieval Christian monastery. In political terms the *zawiya* can accommodate to hard times, to a surrounding anarchy or civil war, by a self-encapsulating autarchy; all the tasks of government are after all already included within its purposes. Under a secure state authority the *zawiya* can develop an intermediary political role and convert the faithful into a negotiable clientele. The sacredly sanctioned hierarchy of the sufi *zawiya* then becomes a parallel hierarchy of government, valuable to state authority as resting on a true popular devotion. In multiparty situations one can even see the *zawiya* converted to the political purposes of a party cell. (cited in Sklar, pp. 92–3)

REFUGEES

Ethnic, religious, and regional strife, combined with poverty and dictatorship, and inflamed by foreign intervention, has encouraged persecution and flight in many regions of Africa. In 1979 Africa held 2 million refugees; in 1989, 4 million; in 1996, 5 million, with Congo (Zaire) alone holding more than a million, and Guinea and Tanzania sheltering more than a half million each. (See Spotlight, pp. 764–5.)

ECONOMIC ISSUES

Africa's economic record since independence has been as discouraging as its politics, to which it is related. The per capita income in sub-Saharan Africa dropped from a high of $671 in 1980 to $520 in 1995 (figured in constant 1987 dollars). Total exports decreased by 7 percent from 1980 to 1996, although imports rose by 16 percent. Population was up between 1980 and 1995 by 62 percent, but food production rose by only 43 percent.

Some 42 percent of adults, including 52 percent of adult females, are illiterate. Some 48 percent of the population is without access to safe drinking water; 48 percent are without access to health services, 55 percent without access to sanitation. Of all children under age five, 30 percent are underweight. Life expectancy is 51 years, at least ten years lower than any other region of the world. Almost a third of the population (31 percent) is not expected to live to age forty.

Around 70 percent of the world's incidence of HIV-positive infection and AIDS occurs in sub-Saharan Africa, about 25 million cases (see picture, p. 766). With little public health information and few facilities, people lack the resources to prevent the spread of the disease. In 2000, the Security Council of the United Nations began to discuss the AIDS epidemic in Africa as a security issue, "because that problem could decimate the economic, political, and military establishments in many countries" (*New York Times*, January 11, 2000).

Consumption of electricity per person decreased by about 2 percent between 1980 and 1995. In 1995, sub-Saharan Africa had the lowest ratio of daily newspapers, television sets, and telephone main lines of any region of the world. (All data from *World Development Report, 1998/99*.) "There are more telephone lines in Manhattan or in Tokyo than in the whole of sub-Saharan Africa. ... Africa remains, by and large, the switched-off region of the world"

(Castells, pp. 92–3). At the dawning of an information age, sub-Saharan Africa is ill-equipped to participate. It lacks not only the technology, but also the personnel to operate it and the centers for training them. Why?

ROOTS OF THE ECONOMIC PROBLEMS: AN ECONOMIC AND HISTORIOGRAPHIC DEBATE

Lack of a Capitalist Class and Ethic

Many observers found the roots of Africa's economic problems in its colonial legacy. Giampaolo Calchi-Novati, of the University of Pisa, blamed the lack of a capitalist class on the patterns of European capitalist colonialism, which had stunted the growth of African entrepreneurship:

> The ancient self-sufficiency of African society was lost forever. As the continent was opened up and transport improved, European products were able to penetrate into Africa, also at the expense of the newly born African industry. At the same time it spelled the end of any proto-capitalistic class already existing in the various African states since no local organization had the capacity to stand up to competition from the colonial power and from the companies. (cited in Salvatore, p. 57)

Few Africans had been educated in modern business, technology, and organization. Again, this was a product of the lack of educational systems introduced under colonial rule.

Moreover, in the first years after independence, capitalism was widely condemned for its association with the colonial rulers and as a philosophy of greed rather than community welfare (compare Chapters 13 and 16 for similar views elsewhere and earlier). A variety of socialist alternatives were favored, including: local, collective ownership; large-scale collectivization; state ownership; and state planning. President Julius Nyerere of Tanzania (see Profile, p. 763) chose the first two, linking them to African conditions, and called for the reconstruction of *ujamaa*, the village community:

> In the old days, the African had never aspired to the possession of personal wealth for the purpose of dominating any of his fellows. He had never had laborers or factory hands to do his work for him. But then came the foreign capitalists. ... Our first

step, therefore, must be to re-educate ourselves; to regain our former attitude of mind. ... And in rejecting the capitalist attitude of mind which colonization brought into Africa, we must reject also the capitalist methods which go with it. One of these is individual ownership of land. (cited in Sigmund, rev. ed., p. 291)

Kwame Nkrumah of Ghana, in language reminiscent of Trotsky, stressed the need for state control to achieve

a total mobilization of brain and manpower resources. What other countries have taken three hundred years to achieve, a once dependent territory must try to accomplish in a generation if it is to survive. Unless it is, as it were, "jet-propelled," it will lag behind and thus risk everything for which it has fought. (cited in Sigmund, 1st ed., p. 186)

Such policies, no matter how congenial with the African past or promising for the future, did not lead to growth.

International Debts

For a time the most successful economy seemed to be that of Côte d'Ivoire, a country that vigorously promoted individual enterprise and participation in the global economy, especially through the production and sale of coffee and cocoa, and through links with French expertise. From 1965 to 1980 Côte d'Ivoire experienced a 6.8 percent annual growth rate. Then, in the 1980s, prices for coffee and cocoa plunged. In the decade 1980–90, Côte d'Ivoire's per capita income dropped by one-third (*World Development Report 1998*, p. 142). Dependence on the volatile international market crippled the economy.

Many African countries concentrated on producing just one or two major exports, almost always raw materials from agriculture or mining, which rendered them similarly vulnerable. In 1986, the total manufactured exports from all of sub-Saharan Africa were only $3.2 billion. The rapid jump in oil prices, the oil shocks of the 1970s which triggered a world economic slump, added to the difficulties.

International debts multiplied. By the end of 1988 for sub-Saharan Africa these had reached nearly $135 billion, eighteen times the 1980 figure and equal to the region's total gross domestic product. By the early 1990s they had reached $180

billion and by 1995, $224 billion. Foreign investors were frightened off. Private international investment had been $6 billion in 1980; in 1985 it registered a disinvestment of $1 billion; by 1995, investment had resumed at $2.2 billion. The combination of unstable international market prices, growing international debt, and disinvestment demonstrated Africa's economic dependency and vulnerability.

When the World Bank offered desperately needed investment capital, it demanded that borrowers adopt more market-oriented policies (as in Latin America, see p. 787). Such policies included a reduction or ending of subsidies in the domestic prices of basic commodities, the devaluation of inflated currencies, and the enforced schedules for repayment of debt. Greater domestic economic efficiency was also demanded, which often meant firing the excess workers who padded government employment roles. The World Bank wanted to end **statism**, government policies that siphoned off capital for the state and its own officials. The Bank's policies made sense on the yearly economic balance sheet, but they created great pain. Government employees lost their jobs; the price of subsidized food went up. Riots often followed these reforms, testing the political will of leaders, who, naturally enough, questioned the wisdom of the World Bank. Was the Bank simply a new form of colonial control, a new mechanism for telling Africans how to conduct their business so that Western businessmen could make greater profits? African governments and intellectuals debated this question.

By 2000 most of Africa, like most of the developing world, sought increasing participation in the world economy. At the same time, the World Bank was becoming less strict in the belt-tightening conditions it imposed, recognizing the need for governments to continue to provide certain fundamental services, such as education, medical assistance, and sometimes food subsidies, to their people.

Dictatorship and Corruption

D.K. Fieldhouse of Cambridge University argues: "African governments have never, despite their protestations, been primarily concerned with economic growth but rather with maintenance of political power and the distribution of wealth to themselves and their supporters" (p. 94).

Throughout Africa the search for appropriate governments, and leaders, has been tortuous.

PROFILE
Julius Nyerere
TANZANIA'S "TEACHER"

Although Julius Kambarage Nyerere served as the first President of the United Republic of Tanzania for over twenty years, he shunned the titles typically bestowed upon heads of state. Instead of *Mtukufu* (His Majesty) or *Mheshimiwa* (Honorable), Nyerere preferred the appellations of *Mwalimu* (Teacher) and *Ndugu* (Comrade). Nyerere refused to live in a palatial residence subsidized by his government, preferring his own small house for himself and his family. He identified himself with the masses of impoverished Africans and his lifestyle mirrored the radically egalitarian social philosophy he articulated at the start of his long political career.

Nyerere was born in 1922 in colonial Tanganyika. He attended Makerere College in Uganda and the University of Edinburgh in Scotland, studying history and economics. He taught at several Roman Catholic schools in Africa before he became president of the Tanganyika African National Union (TANU) in 1954. In 1955, Nyerere traveled to United Nations headquarters in New York City on behalf of TANU, agitating for the independence of Tanganyika, then part of the British Empire. Tanganyika gained its independence in 1961, merging with the island of Zanzibar three years later to become the United Republic of Tanzania with Nyerere as President. Nyerere insisted that colonialism was at the root of Tanzania's severe economic and social problems. The Europeans "created a system of 'haves' and 'have-nots'" in what had been a "traditional African society of equals who knew no class" divisions. In 1967, Nyerere issued his famous Arusha Declaration, outlining his socialist prescription for Tanzania.

Photograph of President Julius Nyerere, 1970s.

Western critics accused Nyerere of supporting Communism because he pursued a policy of non-alignment throughout the Cold War. While he advocated both Pan-Africanism and Third World unity, Nyerere insisted that Tanzanian socialism was not synonymous with Marxism-Leninism. Rather, it was centered upon the African concept of *ujamaa*, the Swahili word for "family-hood." Nyerere sought to eliminate the gap between rich and poor by organizing the countryside into self-sufficient agricultural cooperatives. These new communities were designed to restore an egalitarian social order that encouraged both individual initiative and national economic growth. Yet, by the mid-1970s, it was clear that this program, characterized by forced resettlement and the occasional "use of extralegal, coercive authority," was not working. In 1985, Nyerere retired from office, leaving Tanzania a one-party state and one of the poorest countries in the world.

Even though Nyerere did not bring wealth to his country, he focused on improving the quality of life for the masses. Tanzania's infant mortality rate plummeted, life expectancy increased, and literacy rates rose substantially for both men and women. When Nyerere died in October 1999 Tanzanians recalled his legacy with pride. His administration marked a long period of internal stability within the new nation and his decision to relinquish his power peacefully established a constitutional precedent for the presidential succession process in Tanzania. *Mwalimu* Nyerere had upheld the importance of human as well as economic development.

SPOTLIGHT
Refugees and Exiles

The wars and political instability of the twentieth century have forced millions of people to flee their homes as refugees. Earlier in the century, World Wars I and II triggered mass exoduses as people were driven from their homes by invading troops, or chose to flee battlefields. At the end of World War II, the United Nations established international and regional commissions to help settle the millions of displaced persons of the war. The Partition of India and Pakistan in 1947 created an estimated 12 million refugees, about half of them Muslims fleeing India, half Hindus and Sikhs fleeing West and East Pakistan (later Bangladesh) for India (see picture, p. 705). In 1948 and after, warfare between Israelis and Arabs created several hundred thousand Palestinian refugees, a number swollen to millions by 2000. In the last decades of the century, the largest numbers of refugees, millions of them, have been Africans.

Figure 1 shows one section of the 250,000 refugees from civil war in Rwanda crossing the border into Tanzania in 1994. They travel by foot and by bicycle, taking with them whatever personal possessions they can carry. In part, Africa's refugee problems remain so intractable because the political situation has not stabilized. Ethnic groups, such as the Hutu and Tutsi, continue to fight, and national governments attempt to consolidate their own borders and to encroach on others. The borders between Rwanda, Burundi, Congo, Kenya, and Tanzania continue to witness streams of refugees at the end

Figure 1 Rwandan refugees at Rusomo, Tanzania, May 1, 1994.

Figure 2 Eritrean refugee in Bethnal Green, London, 1995.

Figure 3 Wole Soyinka at UNESCO, Paris, October 16, 1986.

of the twentieth century. The United Nations, individual nations, churches, and numerous voluntary associations such as Oxfam and Médecins sans Frontières (Doctors without Borders—which was awarded the Nobel Prize for Peace in 1999), have provided food, makeshift shelter, and medical treatment for these refugees, as they did earlier with others. The numbers and the suffering are, however, overwhelming.

Refugees move not only *en masse*, but also as individuals. Often an initial mass flight is followed by individuals seeking homes for themselves. **Figure 2** shows a woman from Eritrea now living in Bethnal Green, London. From the picture alone we cannot tell whether she thinks of herself as a refugee far from home, radically disoriented, and eager to return, or as a new immigrant beginning to make her way in a new setting, or as some mixed combination of both.

Figure 3 of Nigerian playwright Wole Soyinka celebrating his Nobel Prize for Literature in 1986 presents a very different face of refugee status. Soyinka had fallen foul of the Nigerian government in 1967 and had been held in political detention for two years. In 1995 he was exiled from Nigeria and its highly corrupt military administration, in part for speaking out on behalf of writer and political critic Ken Saro-Wiwa, who was hanged by the government. Soyinka is now a refugee living in the United States. Like many other refugees of conscience, and very much unlike the streams of refugees in figure 1, Soyinka's economic and social conditions may be excellent, but he, too, cannot go "home."

A giant AIDS poster in Lusaka, Zambia, where the disease is rife. AIDS has been a severe problem in many African countries, with rates of infection up to 25 percent of the adult population. It is an enormous task to educate people about the dangers of unprotected sex.

Consider Ghana. Kwame Nkrumah, the leader of Ghana's independence struggle and its first prime minister in 1957 and first President in 1960, declared Ghana a one-party state in 1964. By 1966, Nkrumah was considered so dictatorial that the Ghanaian military overthrew him in a coup while he was out of the country.

Following the example of Ghana, one-party states, and coups launched to displace them, began to characterize African politics. By about 1980, some forty African states were ruled by military or quasi-military administrations. In the Central African Republic, Jean-Bédel Bokassa (1921–96) spent $22 million, one quarter of his nation's annu-

al revenues, in a ceremony installing himself as emperor. When he was deposed in 1979, Bokassa was convicted of numerous murders of soldiers, civilians, and students.

Sociologist and planner, Manuel Castells also places blame on the "predatory state," and gives further examples from sub-Saharan Africa's two largest states, the Congo with 47 million people and Nigeria with 114 million. For thirty-two years, the Congo was dominated by Mobutu Sese Seko. Mobutu had been a sergeant in Belgium's colonial army. He seized power with US and Western backing in 1965, ending a five-year civil war between pro-communist and anti-communist factions. He renamed the country Zaire and for three decades he placed it at the disposal of the CIA and other Western agencies that used it as a staging base for activities throughout the continent. In exchange he ruled with a free hand, looting some ten billion dollars from the Congo's mineral income and depositing it in personal bank accounts in Europe, while leaving most Congolese in poverty (Castells, pp. 99–100).

Mobutu played ethnic groups against one another, while he controlled his nation's enterprises in cobalt, industrial diamonds, and copper. He gained personal control over foreign aid and investment, but spent little on social services and infrastructure. He and his army became so corrupt that his regime collapsed before a guerrilla invasion in 1997, leaving behind a devastated economy and polity. Laurent Kabila, who led the forces overthrowing Mobutu, inflamed new opposition, and within a year the Congo was plunged into continuing civil war.

Nigeria holds one-fifth of the entire population of sub-Saharan Africa. It is rich in oil, and oil revenues bring the government 80 percent of its income. When even these revenues seemed inadequate for the nation's rulers, they turned also "to a whole array of illicit deals, including international drug trafficking, money laundering, and smuggling" (Castells, p. 103). Nigeria's politics have been tumultuous, and the country has suffered secession and civil war among its major provinces. For twenty-six of its forty years of independence Nigeria has been ruled by military officials although elections were restored in 1999. Because of the warfare and the predatory nature of the rulers, the Nigerian people were at virtually the same economic level in 1995 as at independence.

Manipulation of Ethnic Identity

Castells extends his argument: The failure of the economy was primarily a failure of the state, and the failure of the state resulted from a misplaced sense of ethnic identity. The process of this perverse development began in colonial times and continued into independence. To rule effectively, colonial governments believed that they would have to base their administration on local social and political organizations. They believed that indigenous "tribes" were these organizations and therefore they gave the "tribes" and their leaders more power than they had previously commanded. "Belonging to a certain tribe was the only acknowledged channel to access resources" (Castells, p. 107). To be powerful was to build up one's own tribe, to compete with others, and to win. People's identity and loyalty was vested not in the state but in the tribe. The state therefore lacked the legitimacy and the capacity to mobilize the entire nation in pursuit of collective economic development. Initiated in colonial times, the same disastrous system lives on today.

CULTURAL LIFE

In cultural terms, Africa did not forget its own heritage in music, art, and architecture. Even during the high tide of colonialism, African forms remained potent, even influencing the colonizing countries, as the art of Picasso, Matisse, Brancusi, and others testifies (see p. 618). But indigenous traditions were deeply threatened and in large part destroyed by Western formal education administered through foreign governments and churches, and by the foreign cultural values that reigned supreme, especially in the newly constructed urban centers of trade and rule. Nigerian geographer Akin Mabogunje argues in *Urbanization in Nigeria* that the physical forms of these cities and the European-designed plantations and industrial and mining centers, with their European architecture, gridiron street plans, and barracks structures for African workers, destroyed the traditional housing and family patterns of Africans who came to live and work there.

In part, the traditional forms endured because they were so deeply a part of Africa: the legends and history of the *griot*; the music of the stringed *mbira* and the various forms of drumming; the dances of Africa; the grace and function of the residential compound and its several huts for different family members. These forms endured more strongly in the countryside than in the city. But in the 1930s these traditions began to assert themselves among the Western-educated elites as well. The movement for **Negritude** was born among Africans resident in Europe itself. Negritude was defined by Léopold Sédar Senghor (b. 1906), one of its principal exponents, as "the whole complex of civilized values—cultural, economic, social, and political—which characterize the black peoples, or, more precisely, the Negro-African world" (cited in Sigmund, rev. ed., p. 249).

The movement was strongest in French-speaking Africa, where cultural assimilation was taken more seriously than in the more politically oriented British areas. Wole Soyinka (b. 1934), Nobel Prize winning playwright from Nigeria (see Spotlight, pp. 764–5), described Negritude as "a revolt against the successful assimilative strategy of French and Portuguese colonialism. . . . [It] held undisputed sway in the formulation of creative sensibilities for the next two decades" even in Anglophone Africa (cited in Boahen, p. 564). The leading exponents of the worldwide movement, Léopold Sédar Senghor of Senegal, Aimé Cesaire (b. 1913) of Martinique in the French-speaking West Indies, and Léon Damas of French Guiana, asserted the link between cultural and political nationalism. Senghor, author and editor of several volumes of poetry (see Source, p. 771), was also the leader of the independence movement in Senegal and later (1960–80) its first president.

Some African critics complained that Negritude glossed over class struggle and formal politics, but the movement raised African consciousness in other, perhaps equally fundamental ways.

African art and music have emphasized continuity of tradition rather than innovation, and vernacular products of the group rather than new creativity of the individual artist. Artists worked within received canons and African art tends to recreate the wooden, bronze, and terracotta sculpture and reliefs; the baskets and woven containers; the decorated calabashes and gourds; and the ivory, stone, and beaded jewellery of tradition. Paradoxically, leading Western artists, like Picasso, considered African traditional art "modern."

Some innovation, nevertheless, linked past and present, as in the Oshogbo artists of Nigeria, who introduced new techniques and materials, including aluminum, to carry out traditional themes. Technology enabled instruments and styles to spread throughout Africa rapidly. Gerhard Kubik, of the University of Vienna, traces the spread of the *likembe*, now one of Africa's most popular and widely used instruments. Invented in the Congo, it was carried upriver by porters and colonial servants in the late nineteenth century to non-Bantu areas. By the beginning of the twentieth century it had been adopted in Uganda. By the 1950s it had also spread even to the !Kung of southeastern Angola. Towards the end of the century Jonah Sithole transposed the music of the Shona *mbira* (likembe) to guitar as he accompanied dreadlocked Thomas Mapfumo in his songs of Zimbabwe and patriotism.

Jimoh Buraimo, *Obatala and the Devil*, 1970s. Jimoh Buraimo was one of the leading artists in the Mbari Mbayo Club in Oshogbo, Nigeria. Founded in the 1960s by Duro Ladipo, a Yoruba playwright, with the help of visiting European artists, the club promoted artistic expression that drew on Yoruba traditions to create new, fresh forms in art, music, and drama. (*University of Bremen*)

African music and dance had spread with slavery to the western hemisphere, especially to Latin America, where the group life of the slaves remained more intact than in the United States, partly because slavery and the slave trade continued so much longer there. Interaction between African music and dance and that of the diaspora continue actively today. The music of the Congo, for example, influences, especially, the music of the West Indies and Brazil, and vice versa, and it has become popular in Europe and the United States as well. New beats, syncopations, and even musical instruments flow freely throughout Africa and the diaspora. Reggae flourishes everywhere as a medium of political protest as well as popular dance and artistic creativity, from Bob Marley in the West Indies to Alpha Blondy in West Africa. Ballets Africains, the national dance troup of Guinea, performs throughout the world.

When Paul Simon, the American pop singer, traveled to South Africa in 1985 to work and perform with black musicians there, some criticized his going into that country while apartheid was still in effect. Simon argued, however, that infusing more mainstream American popular music with that of such groups as Tao Ea Matsekha, General M.D. Shirinda and the Gaza Sisters, the Boyoyo Boys Band, Ladysmith Black Mambazo and the Soweto Rhythm Section, and such individual artists as Youssou N'dour, Joseph Shabala, and Chikapa "Ray" Phiri, would help all the musicians and would invigorate all international popular music. Simon's *Graceland* album, 1986, demonstrated the wisdom of his choice, and his 1990 *Rhythm of the Saints*, which added Brazilian diaspora influences, pushed the fusion further. Modern technology transports the sounds, the sights, and the performers themselves back and forth across the oceans.

CINEMA

Cinema production began in Africa as part of the colonial enterprise. In 1935 Britain established in Tanganyika (later Tanzania) the Bantu Educational Cinema Experiment, which later grew into the Colonial Film Unit, to spread British conceptions of appropriate colonial life to their African subjects. The Belgians established a Film and Photo Bureau in the Congo in 1947, and Catholic missions established their own film production centers for propagating religious doctrines. Almost all these activities shut down after independence.

More recently, however, France established a Consortium Audio-visuel International in the 1960s to help its former colonies develop their own films, and they have been a great success. The distinguished Senegalese social-realist novelist Ousmane Sembène (b. 1923) helped lead the way. For more than a quarter century he has told stories of mod-ern Africa through a series of films from *La Noire de …* (1966) to *Guelowaar* (1993). The film festival in Ouagadougou, Burkina Faso, has become one of the most important annual cultural events of today's Africa. Of special interest to historians, Dani Kouyate of Burkina Faso has produced *Keita: the Heritage of a Griot*, which depicts an urban schoolboy suddenly confronted by the arrival from the countryside of a distant relative, a *griot* or traditional custodian of folk history. Through his stories, the *griot* shows the young boy that historical knowledge has more dimensions and interpretations than are taught in school. The movie theaters of Africa continue to screen more films from the United States and India than indigenous productions, bringing many charges of cultural imperialism, an issue in itself, but the African film industry continues to grow and to make its own significant contribution to local, and international, culture.

LITERATURE

African literature has also flourished in poetry, essays, plays, and novels. Frequently, this creativity blends traditional African rhythms in word and song mixed with a profound sexuality, confusion over the loss of an old identity and the search for a new, and despair over the bitter politics of both colonial and post-colonial life. Consider this poem of Negritude from Senghor's student days in Paris. He tells of his homesickness for Africa, evoked by the vision of a beautiful black woman:

Relentlessly She Drives Me

[For two balafongs]
Relentlessly she drives me through the thickets of Time.
My black blood hounds me through the crowd to the clearing where white night sleeps.
Sometimes I turn round in the street and see again the palm tree smiling under the breeze.
Her voice brushes me like the soft lisping sweep of a wing and I say
"Yes it is Signare!" I have seen the sun set in the blue eyes of a fair negress.
At Sèvres-Babylon or Balangar, amber and gongo, her scent was near and spoke to me.

Yesterday in church at the Angelus, her eyes shone
  like candles burnishing
Her skin with bronze. My God, my God, why do
  you tear my pagan senses shrieking out of me?
I cannot sing your plain chant that has no swing to
  it, I cannot dance it.
Sometimes a cloud, a butterfly, raindrops on my
  boredom's window pane.
Relentlessly she drives me across the great spaces of
  Time.
My black blood hounds me, to the solitary heart of
  the night.

(cited in Okpewho, p. 52)

For John Pepper Clark of Nigeria, dance and the dancer evoke the magic and power of traditional Africa, from which he, as an intellectual trained in European ways, a "lead-tether'd scribe," may be irrevocably cut off:

Agbor Dancer

See her caught in the throb of a drum
Tippling from hide-brimmed stem
Down lineal veins to ancestral core
Opening out in her supple tan
Limbs like fresh foliage in the sun.

See how entangled in the magic
Maze of music
In trance she treads the intricate
Pattern rippling crest after crest
To meet the green clouds of the forest.

Tremulous beats wake trenchant
In her heart a descant
Tingling quick to her finger tips
And toes virginal habits long
Too atrophied for pen or tongue.

Could I, early sequester'd from my tribe,
Free a lead-tether'd scribe
I should answer her communal call
Lose myself in her warm caress
Intervolving earth, sky and flesh.

(cited in Okpewho, p. 66)

Finally Dennis Brutus, of South Africa, condemns the masters of apartheid in his country. He reflects that all people may be capable of wishing "arbitrary exercise of power," but not on the obscene scale enforced by the masters of apartheid:

Their Behaviour

Their guilt
is not so different from ours:
—who has not joyed in the arbitrary exercise of
  power
or grasped for himself what might have been
  another's
and who has not used superior force in the moment
  when he could,
(and who of us has not been tempted to these
  things?)—
so, in their guilt,
the bared ferocity of teeth,
chest-thumping challenge and defiance,
the deafening clamour of their prayers
to a deity made in the image of their prejudice
which drowns the voice of conscience,
is mirrored our predicament
but on a social, massive, organised scale
which magnifies enormously
as the private déshabillé of love
becomes obscene in orgies.

(Okpewho, p. 63)

Africa's best-known novelist is probably Chinua Achebe (b. 1930) of Nigeria. In a series of novels, from *Things Fall Apart* through *No Longer at Ease* and *A Man of the People*, to *Anthills of the Savannah*, Achebe depicts and laments the cultural uprooting of his people under colonialism and finds that independence brings new problems. The indigenous rulers are as greedy and ruthless for power in their own way as were the foreigners.

Wole Soyinka, also a novelist, poet, essayist, and translator, and also of Nigeria, brings into his work not only the political and cultural issues of the day, but also the ancestors, gods, and spirits of the past and present who act upon them. He has written the autobiography of his childhood, *Ake*, alive with humor and fantasy, and the play *The Lion and the Jewel*, filled with what he calls a "total artwork" of spectacle, music, and choreography in celebration of the vitality of traditional culture. In more somber plays, such as *Kongi's Harvest* and *The Road*, Soyinka confronts death, both physiological and cultural. A political activist for democratic values, Soyinka was imprisoned in 1967–9, and in 1995 was exiled by Nigeria's military dictatorship in part because of his outspoken defense of political critic Ken Saro-Wiwa, who was hanged. In 1986 Soyinka was awarded the Nobel Prize for Literature, suggesting that regardless of Africa's political, economic, and

SOURCE
"Prayer to Masks"

Senghor's poem "Prayer to Masks," written after World War II, and looking forward to independence, addresses the masks that represent his, and Africa's, ancestors, and prays that their ancient wisdom and rhythms may be able to repair the destruction the world has suffered. War-devastated Europe is in need of the wisdom and the rhythm of Africa.

Prayer to Masks

Masks! Masks!
Black mask red mask, you white-and-black
  masks
Masks of the four points from which the Spirit
  blows
In silence I salute you!
Nor you the least, the Lion-headed Ancestor
You guard this place forbidden to all laughter of
  women, to all smiles that fade
You distil this air of eternity in which I breathe
  the air of my Fathers.
Masks of unmasked faces, stripped of the marks
  of illness and the lines of age

You who have fashioned this portrait, this my
  face bent over the altar of white paper
In your own image, hear me!
The Africa of the empires is dying, see, the agony
  of a pitiful princess
And Europe too where we are joined by the
  navel.
Fix your unchanging eyes upon your children,
  who are given orders
Who give away their lives like the poor their last
  clothes.
Let us report present at the rebirth of the World
Like the yeast which white flour needs.
For who would teach rhythm to a dead world of
  machines and guns?
Who would give the cry of joy to wake the dead
  and the bereaved at dawn?
Say, who would give back the memory of life to
  the man whose hopes are smashed?
They call us men of coffee cotton oil
They call us men of death.
We are the men of the dance, whose feet draw
  new strength pounding the hardened earth.

(cited in Okpewho, p. 134)

---

technological difficulties, its artistry succeeded in capturing the twentieth-century world.

AFRICAN HISTORY: HOW DO WE KNOW?

In another cultural dimension, the formal study, preservation, and transmission of history took on new vigor and new directions. Africans argued that their history, from ancient times to the present, had been hidden from view by European colonials. With independence it would be recovered. Significant examples of this evolution are the eight-volume *Cambridge History of Africa* and the parallel eight-volume *UNESCO General History of Africa*, edited by African historians. In volume I of the UNESCO series, Philip Curtin explained the significance of the new history:

A recovery of African history has been an important part of African development over recent decades, not an expensive frill that could be set aside until more pressing aspects of development were well in hand. … The fact that African history was seriously neglected until the 1950s is only one symptom of a large phenomenon in historical studies. The colonial period in Africa left an intellectual legacy to be overcome, just as it had in other parts of the world. … African history had been more neglected than that of other non-European regions and … African history had been even more distorted by racist myths. … It takes a long time to uproot prejudice. ("Recent Trends," pp. 54–71)

New paths in the study of African history opened. The recording and analysis of oral history, a crucial approach in a region where written records were very limited, opened a fruitful new method. Cheikh

Anta Diop of Senegal, who argued for the prominence of Africa, especially Egypt, in the early history of Greece and Mediterranean Europe, helped popularize revisionist anti-Eurocentric perspectives. And the construction and expansion of new historical and anthropological museums in many cities across Africa encourages the formation of a new local, national, and pan-African consciousness.

WHAT DIFFERENCE DOES IT MAKE?

Ending foreign colonial rule throughout sub-Saharan Africa, and internal racist, white rule in southern Africa was one of the great political achievements of the twentieth century. Independence promised to be the light at the end of the tunnel. But then other tunnels followed, many of them products of Africa's recent history. Colonial rule had pulled people out of old identities without allowing for the natural formation of new ones. "Tribal" groups that previously had more flexible boundaries were made more rigid. Chieftains, who once drew their power from the authority of their people, turned instead to colonial administrators for validation. After independence they often continued to draw personal political and economic support from the former colonial powers, or from the new leaders of the Cold War blocs, the USA and the USSR, while neglecting the welfare of their own citizens. Often they favored their own ethnic group in competition over others, winning victories but engendering deep animosities. There are many examples; the butchery between the Tutsi and Hutu in Rwanda and Burundi has been especially horrifying. Fragmented identities in Africa have sharply limited the ability to move forward at improving economies, finding appropriate technologies, stabilizing humane political systems, and improving the quality of life.

Colonial rule did not provide adequate formal education for administering a modern country, and post-colonial networks often encouraged those few with such training to turn, like the tribal leaders under colonialism, less to the needs of their nation and more to the personal benefits to be gained through their international connections. Of course, not all were self-seeking: Nelson Mandela won universal acclaim for governing inclusively on behalf of the best interests of all his fellow citizens. But others such as Amin and Mobutu stood out for their ruthlessness, greed, and ethnic favoritism. Citizens did speak out, but in many states this brought exile or even execution.

The outside world encouraged African nations to choose sides, arm themselves, and fight in Cold War battles that, intrinsically, had little to do with them. The global economy, with the sharp ups and downs of the international market place, repeatedly encouraged mini-booms in African economies, only to squelch them as the price of Africa's raw materials—agricultural and mineral—suddenly plummeted, and the prices of imports rose steadily. Assistance from the World Bank and other agencies frequently imposed conditions of great hardship. Scared off by Africa's troubled politics and weak economies, international investors have mostly looked elsewhere. The transition to newer information technologies that is currently transforming the world has hardly touched sub-Saharan Africa.

Optimists argue that the turn of the twenty-first century may once again be witness to some light at the end of the tunnel. South Africa's multi-racial government is functioning, although with some, expected, frictions. Nigeria, the largest of several nations moving in this direction, returned to a democratically elected government in 1999. Investment is returning, albeit in small quantities. Some small-scale technologies are bringing local improvements to life: oil presses, windmills, solar energy, more efficient cook stoves, sheet metal water tanks, and agro-forestry that integrates forest products in the overhead canopy with ground crops below. These programs bring step-by-step incremental change, introducing local people and resources into the process of sustainable development. Pessimists cite the poverty, the deficiencies in human services and education, the many deadly civil wars, the haunting shadow of military dictatorship perpetually in the background, the stalking HIV virus, the relentless competition of the international market place. They doubt whether small-scale technologies will be adequate to transform countries whose national treasuries are so often being looted on a large scale. Historians watch, attemping to keep their eyes wide open.

BIBLIOGRAPHY

Accelerated Development in Sub-Saharan Africa (Washington: The World Bank, 1981).

Achebe, Chinua. *Things Fall Apart* (New York: Anchor Books, ed. 1994).

Amin, Samir. *Unequal Development* (Delhi: Oxford University Press, 1979).

Andrea, Alfred and James H. Overfield, eds. *The Human Record: Sources of Global History,* 2 vols. (Boston: Houghton Mifflin, 1st ed., 1990; 3rd ed., 1998).

Ayittey, George B. *Africa in Chaos* (New York: St. Martin's Griffin, 1998).

Bates, Robert H., V.Y. Mudimbe, and Jean O'Barr, eds. *Africa and the Disciplines* (Chicago: University of Chicago Press, 1993).

Berry, Sara, "Economic Change in Contemporary Africa," in Martin and O'Meara, eds. *Africa,* 359–74.

Boahen, A. Adu, ed. *Africa under Colonial Domination 1880–1935: [UNESCO] General History of Africa,* VII (Berkeley: University of California Press, 1985).

Cambridge History of Africa (New York: Cambridge University Press, 6 vols., 1975–86).

Castells, Manuel. *The Information Age: Economy, Society and Culture. Vol. III: End of Millennium* (Malden, MA: Blackwell, 1998).

Coquery-Vidrovitch, Catherine. *Africa: Endurance and Change South of the Sahara,* trans. by David Maisel (Berkeley: University of California Press, 1988).

Curtin, Philip, Steven Feierman, Leonard Thompson, and Jan Vansina. *African History from Earliest Times to Independence* (New York: Longman, 2nd ed., 1995).

Curtin, Philip D. "Recent Trends in African Historiography and Their Contribution to History in General," in *[UNESCO] General History of Africa,* Vol. 1, 54–71.

Davidson, Basil. *Modern Africa* (London: Longman, 1983).

Diawara, Manthia. *African Cinema* (Bloomington: University of Indiana Press, 1992).

Fieldhouse, D.K. *Black Africa 1945–1980* (London: Allen and Unwin, 1986).

Frank, Andre Gunder. *Dependent Accumulation and Underdevelopment* (New York: Monthly Review Press, 1979).

Franke, Richard W. and Barbara H. Chasin. *Seeds of Famine* (Totowa, NJ: Rowman and Allanheld Publishers, 1980).

Gulhati, Ravi. *The Making of Economic Policy in Africa* (Washington: The World Bank, 1990).

Harden, Blaine. *Africa: Dispatches from a Fragile Continent* (Boston: Houghton Mifflin, 1990).

Harrison, Paul. *The Greening of Africa* (London: Palladin, 1987).

Jegede, Dele, "Popular Culture in Urban Africa," in Martin and O'Meara, eds. *Africa,* 273–94.

July, Robert W. *A History of the African People* (Prospect Heights, IL: Waveland Press, 4th ed. 1992).

Mabogunje, Akin L. *Urbanization in Nigeria* (New York: Africana Publishing Corporation, 1968).

Martin, Phyllis M., and Patrick O'Meara, eds. *Africa* (Bloomington: University of Indiana Press, 1995).

New York Times 2000 Almanac (New York: Penguin Books, 1999).

Okpewho, Isidore, ed. *The Heritage of African Poetry* (Harlow, Essex: Longman Group, 1985).

Oliver, Roland and Anthony Atmore. *Africa since 1800* (Cambridge: Cambridge University Press, 3rd ed., 1981).

Pacey, Arnold. *Technology in World Civilization: A Thousand Year History* (Oxford: Basil Blackwell, 1990).

Ravenhill, John, ed. *Africa in Economic Crisis* (London: Macmillan Press, 1986).

Rodney, Walter. *How Europe Underdeveloped Africa* (Washington: Howard University Press, 1982).

Salvatore, Dominick, ed. *African Development Prospects: A Policy Modelling Approach* (New York: Taylor and Francis, 1989).

Sembène. *God's Bits of Wood,* trans. by Francis Price (London: Heinemann, 1970).

Sigmund, Paul E. *The Ideologies of the Developing Nations* (New York: Praeger Publishers, 1st ed., 1963; rev. ed., 1967; second rev. ed., 1972).

Sivard, Ruth Leger. *World Military and Social Expenditures 1996* (Washington: World Priorities, 16th ed., 1996).

Sklar, Richard L. "The African Frontier for Political Science," in Bates, *et al., Africa and the Disciplines,* 83–110.

Smillie, Ian. *Mastering the Machine: Poverty, Aid, and Technology* (Boulder, CO: Westview Press, 1991).

Stryker, Richard and Stephen N. Ndegwa, "The African Development Crisis," in Martin and O'Meara, eds. *Africa,* 375–95.

United Nations Development Program. *Human Development Report 1998* (New York: Oxford University Press, 1998).

[UNESCO] General History of Africa (Berkeley: University of California Press, 8 vols., 1981–92).

Winchester, N. Brian, "African Politics since Independence," in Martin and O'Meara, eds. *Africa,* 347–88.

World Almanac and Book of Facts 2000 (Mahwah, NJ: World Almanac Books, 1999).

World Bank. *World Development Report, 1998/99* (New York: Oxford University Press, 1998).

CHAPTER
23 LATIN AMERICA

"Poor Mexico: So far from God, so close to the United States."

PORFIRIO DÍAZ

THE SEARCH FOR AN INTERNATIONAL POLICY ON ECONOMICS AND TECHNOLOGY AND A DOMESTIC POLICY ON ETHNICITY AND CULTURE

The countries of Latin America are different from one another, and yet they have much in common with each other and with many newly independent countries of the world. They have been struggling with colonial and postcolonial legacies and the complex problems of economic development and technological change since the 1820s. Revolutions and counter-revolutions have continually restructured internal relationships between the elites, the masses, and the military. In this chapter we first examine these issues in broad terms and then consider in more detail the experiences of four countries: Brazil and Mexico, the two largest; Argentina, the most European; and Cuba, the most radical.

LATIN AMERICAN DIVERSITY TODAY

Including the independent island states of the Caribbean, Latin America consists of thirty-three independent countries with a total population of just under a half billion people, a total that has risen, astonishingly, from about 38 million in 1900 and 166 million in 1950. About one out of every three Latin Americans is Brazilian (165 million people) and one out of five is Mexican (about 100 million people). The next largest countries, Colombia and Argentina, have approximately 35 million people each.

Most Latin Americans—about 300 million people—speak Spanish, but most of Brazil's population speaks Portuguese. In addition, about 100 million people speak indigenous Indian languages as their mother tongue, although most of them also speak Spanish or Portuguese. A few small groups in the Caribbean and in the eastern Brazilian state of Bahia continue to speak Yoruba, thereby sustaining a link with cultures in Africa, from where their ancestors had been brought as slaves. In the islands of the Caribbean French, English, and Dutch are spoken, reflecting the languages of the former colonizers, and in a few places Hindustani, reflecting the south Asian origins of some of the immigrants. Most Latin

GNP per capita (1995)

over $US 3000

$US 2000-3000

less than $US 2000

● substantial inward investment

■ industrial centers

main exports

● oil		◇ beef	
♣ coal		◆ wool	
▲ iron		▧ wheat	
Ⓐⓛ bauxite		◯ fruit	
◣ gold		◌ tobacco	
◪ silver		▭ narcotics	
Ⓩⓝ zinc		◗ coffee	
N nickel		▮▮ sugar	
◯ lead		◗ bananas	
□ copper		● nutmeg	
△ tin		◝ soya	
✦ emeralds		◌ rice	
✧ diamonds		◀╫╫ fish/shellfish	
◠ fertilizers		T tourism	
▬ timber		◎ financial services	
◆ cotton			

The economic development of Latin America Following the Great Depression and World War II, ' nations of Latin America sought to move beyond their dependence upon the export of primary goods—minerals, timber, and food. Investment from North America and Europe allowed some industrial development in Chile, Argentina, Brazil, and Mexico, but was often undermined by political instability. Development throughout the region is diverse as are economic policies.

LATIN AMERICA

DATE	MEXICO	BRAZIL	ARGENTINA
1910	• Revolution begins (1910) in response to exploitation by foreign companies, political elites, and thirst for land reform • Under President Carranza, new reforming constitution (1917)	• During World War I, USA buying about a third of Brazil's exports	• Receives $10 billion in foreign investments between 1870 and 1920 • Metalworkers' strike develops into general strike (1919)
1920	• Álvaro Obregón forces Carranza to flee capital and becomes president (1920); assassinated (1924) • Militant Catholic priests lead peasants in the War of the Cristeros (1926–9) • Plutarco Calles forms National Revolutionary Party (later renamed PRI) (1929), which retains power today		• Economy crashes badly, intensified by vulnerability of food exports (1929)
1930	• Under Lázaro Cárdenas (1934–40), PRI continues reforms, redistributing land and nationalizing oil industry	• After military revolution, Getúlio Vargas sweeps to power (1930); sets up totalitarian state, Estado Novo • Female suffrage enacted (1932)	• Army coup ousts President Yrigoyen from power (1930)
1940	• After election of Miguel Aleman, political control passes to large-scale business interests (1946)	• Army deposes Vargas (1945)	• Colonel Juan D. Perón comes to power in another army coup (1943) • "Evita" Perón campaigns for equal rights for women, including the vote, granted in 1947

Americans, reflecting their colonial heritage, are Catholic (about 90 percent), but the percentage is declining as more people turn to evangelical Protestantism.

Latin Americans are on the move. In the late nineteenth and early twentieth centuries, labor-hungry Latin America countries welcomed more immigrants—particularly from Europe—in proportion to their populations than any other region of the world, including the United States. Today, the movement is more internal. People are moving, especially out of villages, "pulled" by the attraction of greater opportunities elsewhere. Cities seem to promise job possibilites, "bright lights," and necessities, such as schools and doctors. Other people are "pushed" out of their current locations because

of the scarcity of opportunities. The enormous population growth over the last forty years has filled up the countryside. Moreover, as farming is mechanized, agricultural work diminishes, creating a "push" factor. In 1900, perhaps 20 percent of Latin America's people lived in cities. By 1950, four out of every ten people lived in cities, and at the end of the century about three out of four people did so. The two largest cities, Mexico City and São Paulo (Brazil), have between 15 and 20 million inhabitants each—as many as all the cities of the continent held in 1900. Nevertheless, because of the immense population growth, the rural population has remained steady at 100 million throughout the second half of the twentieth century.

LATIN AMERICA

DATE	MEXICO	BRAZIL	ARGENTINA
1950	• Electorate doubled, as women get the vote (1958)	• Vargas re-elected (1951–4) but US opposes his program, including minimum wage, and he is deposed in right-wing military-backed coup	• Evita dies from cancer (1952) • Perón driven from power by military officials (1955)
1960	• An estimated two-thirds of cocaine and marijuana enters USA via Mexico	• "Economic miracle" underway (1968), with growth rates averaging 10 percent for next six years, but serious inequality in distribution of wealth	
1970	• Steady economic growth, 1950s–1980s, based largely on oil		• Perón, with wife Isabel as vice-president, re-elected (1973) • Military coup (1976) leads to "dirty war" and at least 10,000 "disappeared"; demonstrations by Las Madres de Plaza de Mayo
1980	• Collapse of oil price forces Mexico to turn to IMF and other international lenders		• Argentina invades the Malvinas (Falkland Islands); defeated by Britain (1982)
1990	• North American Free Trade Association (NAFTA) (1994) • Peso collapses • 145 Maya Indians killed in riots in Chiapas state (1994)	• President Fernando Collor de Mello driven from power on corruption charges (1992) • International Monetary Fund loans give the IMF influence over Brazilian policy • MERCOSUR, free-trade zone (1995)	• Single free-trade zone, MERCOSUR, established between Argentina, Brazil, Paraguay, and Uruguay (1995)

Governments also offered new land to settlers. Brazil, in particular, has attempted to satisfy the land hunger of its population by opening vast tracts in the Amazon River basin and inviting millions of immigrants into these virgin lands. These new invasions solved some problems but created new ones as well (see p. 800). Many Spanish-speaking peoples have also emigrated to the United States in sizeable numbers, and today, between 25 and 30 million Hispanic-Americans live in the continental United States.

A few figures on living standards help to fill out the picture of the overall conditions and of the diversity within the continent today. The average life expectancy at birth is sixty-nine years (compared with seventy-seven years in the USA), but it varies from a high of seventy-seven years in Costa Rica to fifty-six years in Haiti. In the two largest countries, Brazil and Mexico, it is sixty-seven and seventy-two years, respectively. Female literacy is 85 percent overall (99 percent in the USA), ranging from 98 percent in Guyana and Uruguay, to 42 percent in Haiti, with Brazil at 83 percent and Mexico at 87 percent. The gross national product per capita averages $3,940 (that of the USA is $29,080), with a range from $8,950 in Argentina to $380 in Haiti. Brazil is at about $4,790; Mexico at $3,700. In world terms, Latin American countries lie about the middle range, not nearly as rich as the developed countries of Europe and North America, but not nearly as poor as most regions of sub-Saharan Africa or South Asia. They are at about the same standard as Eastern Europe.

TECHNOLOGY, INDUSTRIALIZATION, AND LATIN AMERICAN ELITES 1870–1916

Through the late nineteenth and early twentieth centuries, Latin America began to industrialize, largely with investments from overseas. At first, Britain was the principal investor, but after World War I the United States assumed that role. Between 1870 and 1919, Argentina alone received $10 billion in foreign investments, about half of which came from Britain. At the time of the Great Depression in the 1930s, United States private investments in Latin America had reached $3.5 billion, 40 percent of all the investments in the region, and these investments paid for new railway lines, mining, agricul-

DATE	GUATEMALA	CHILE	CUBA
	LATIN AMERICA		
1950	• Jacobo Arbenz president (1954); continues program of reform, including nationalizing United Fruit Company's land, leading to US-backed coup • Carlos Castillo Armas president (1954); land reforms halted • Civil war, lasting almost 40 years, begins (1958)		• Castro attacks Moncada military barracks in Santiago de Cuba (1953); Castro captured and sentenced to 15 years in prison • Castro released in general amnesty (1955); resumes guerrilla struggle (1956) • Castro captures Havana and declares new government (1959) • Cuban–US relations soar
1960		• Eduardo Frei (1964–70) leads Christian Democratic government with program of agrarian reform and moderate nationalization	• In the Bay of Pigs incident, exiles invasion defeated by Cuban armed forces (1961) • Cuban missile crisis; President Kennedy demands Soviet nuclear missiles be removed from Cuban soil (1962)
1970		• Relations with USA sour as socialist Salvador Allende is elected (1970) • CIA covertly finances strikes and opposition parties (1970–3) • Military bomb presidential palace; Allende killed (1973) • General Augusto Pinochet heads new government (1973)	• Cuba sends tens of thousands of troops to fight in Ethiopia and Angola, in support of left-wing governments
1980		• Pinochet voted out, after 15 years of violence toward the opposition (1988)	• End of Cold War ends economic support from USSR (1989)
1990	• Negotiated resolution to civil war, in which over 100,000 killed (1993) • Bill Clinton apologizes for US support of brutal right-wing governments (1999)	• Pinochet arrested in Britain, after Spain seeks his extradition; landmark ruling gives no automatic immunity to former heads of state (1998)	• Total production plummets by one-third between 1989 and 1993

Steaming into the Americas.
The Central Railway, Peru, was constructed with great feats of engineering, during the 1870s and 1890s. Here, the train *San Francisco* waits at the official opening of the Verrugas Bridge on the Transandine Railway (the early name of the Central Railway). Flags were raised in honor of the American construction and British ownership of the railroad. In the Andes, a railroad was needed to transport the copper from Cerro de Pasco, but there were few links between coastal towns. Today most railroads are nationalized.

ture, and ocean shipping, including the refrigerated compartments that enabled Argentinians to ship their beef profitably to Europe. This, in turn, made it possible to fence off the *pampas*, the great Argentinian plains, and turn them into ranches. The **gauchos**, the emblem of Argentina, were reduced in status from free-ranging cowboys to employees of the ranches (as happened in the United States about fifty years earlier).

For the most part, these economic and technological innovations were initiated by foreigners in search of profits. Most of the investments were concentrated in primary production—that is, farming and mining—rather than in industrial manufacturing. At the time of World War I, for example, the United States was buying about one-third of Brazil's exports, mostly coffee, rubber, and cocoa. (Half of Brazil's export was coffee.) Members of the creole elites, who saw that they too could share in the new earnings and win some acceptability among Europeans, joined in the new commerce. But for the most part the initiatives came from outside.

Most of the creole elites were content to treat their nations as private estates. Control and patronage mattered—money and profits were means to an end, not the end in itself. In an essay, *Ariel*, written in 1898, the Uruguayan philosopher José Enrique Rodó (1872–1917) analyzed Latin America's move in the direction of an industrial democracy, on the United States model, and rejected it. He saw that path as barbaric and inconsistent with the more leisurely, elitist, civilized world of the creole rulers of Latin America. In the absence of democratic systems, most governments in Latin America were still in the hands of *caudillos*, strongmen who governed on their own authority.

Not everyone was content with a system of control by *hacendado* and *caudillo* elites. Businessmen who were participating in the new commerce and industry began to think of new goals: more education, more industrialization, more independence from foreign investors and more consistent government, with a larger, formal voice in politics for themselves. Toward the end of the nineteenth century, a huge influx of immigrants from Europe, especially Italy, brought with it ideas of industrial development and union representation, and by the early twentieth century, important labor unions were in place in the larger nations of Latin America. Another group advocating reform and national pride was the army, especially its junior officers. Often drawn from middle-class urban families and aware of modern technology through their knowledge of weaponry, army officers were more used to the importance of education, industrialization, business, and stable government.

In some countries these groups worked together and achieved their goals, but even the most progressive states like Argentinia and Uruguay failed to undertake perhaps the most influential reform of all. They did not restructure the land-holding patterns that left wealthy landlords in charge of impoverished peasants. The reformers were urban people, and they were frequently related to the landlords; they had little practical sympathy for the agricultural laborers and no intention of sharing power with them. As early as 1896, a revolt among the peasants in Canudos, northeast Brazil, raised the fundamental issue: Could the economic and industrial changes that were beginning to affect Latin American cities and commercial agriculture also reach the peasantry? The Canudos revolt—commemorated in Euclides da Cunha's classic novel *Os Sertões* (*The Backlands*)—failed, but its echoes still reverberate today.

THE MEXICAN REVOLUTION 1910–20

In 1910, in Mexico, urban and rural leaders rose up against the dictatorship of Porfirio Díaz (1830–1915), who had been ruling the country since 1876. At the age of eighty, Díaz seemed poised to retire from the presidency. Under his leadership Mexico had seen the development of mining, oil drilling, and railways, in addition to increasing exports of raw agricultural products, especially henequen fibers used in making rope. The middle-class urban creole elite had prospered, but the salaries of the urban workers had declined, and rural peasants had fared even worse. Ninety-five percent of the rural peasantry owned no land, while fewer than 200 Mexican families owned 25 percent of the land, and foreign investors owned another 20–25 percent. One single hacienda spread over 13 million acres (5.3 million hectares) and another over 11 million acres (4.5 million hectares). Huge tracts of land lay fallow and unused while peasants went hungry. Finally, on a political level, no system of orderly succession had been worked out for Mexico. The reins of power rested in the hands of Díaz and his allies alone.

Democratic voting existed for a limited electorate, but when Díaz changed his mind and ran again for president he imprisoned his principal challenger, Francisco Madero (1873–1913). Díaz won, but rebellions against his continuing rule broke out across Mexico and he soon resigned and went into exile in Paris. Regional leaders then asserted their influence as Mexico sank into civil war. The warfare was both personal and factional. It concerned differences in policy among the factions and the appropriate division of power between the central government and the states.

Many of the leaders who contested for power were *mestizos*, people of mixed race and culture (see Chapter 15), who demanded a dramatic break with the past control by the creole elite. The two most radical, Francisco "Pancho" Villa (1877–1923) from the northern border region and Emiliano Zapata (1879–1919) from the state of Morelos, just south of Mexico City, advocated significant land reform, and implemented it in the areas they captured during the civil war. They attracted mixed groups of followers, including farm workers, agricultural colonists, former soldiers, unemployed laborers, cowboys, and delinquents. In November 1911 Zapata declared the revolutionary Plan of Ayala, which called for the return of land to Indian *pueblos* (villages). Tens of thousands of impoverished peasants followed him, heeding his cry of "Tierra y Libertad"—"Land and Liberty" and accepting his view that it was "Better to die on one's feet than to live on one's knees." Zapata's supporters seized large sugar estates, haciendas with which they had been in conflict for years. By including previously scorned groups and attending to their agendas, the revolution became more radical and agrarian.

With Díaz in exile, Madero became president, but he was removed by a coup and then assassinated in 1913. General Víctoriano Huerta (1854–1916) attempted to take over and to re-establish a repressive government like that of Díaz. Opposed by all the other major leaders—Venustiano Carranza, Álvaro Obregón, Plutarco Elías Calles, Villa, and Zapata—and also by President Woodrow Wilson of the United States, who sent American troops into Veracruz to express his displeasure with Huerta, the general was forced from power in March 1914. Obregón (1880–1928), another general, who made free use of the machine gun, won out militarily, but he agreed to serve under Carranza (1859–1920), who had himself installed as provisional president.

The civil war continued and control of Mexico City changed hands several times, but ultimately the more conservative leaders, Carranza and Obregón, forced out Villa and Zapata. Carranza became president in 1916 and convened a constituent assembly which produced the Mexican Constitution of 1917, promising land reform and